# THE COMPLETE ENCYCLOPEDIA OF HOCKEY

# THE COMPLETE ENCYCLOPEDIA OF HOCKEY

## Edited by
## Zander Hollander and Hal Bock

AN ASSOCIATED FEATURES BOOK

NAL BOOKS
NEW AMERICAN LIBRARY
TIMES MIRROR
NEW YORK AND SCARBOROUGH, ONTARIO

## PHOTO CREDITS

Hockey Hall of Fame: 2, 3, 4, 5, 7, 9, 10 (right and left), 11, 12, 13, 14, 16, 19, 20, 21, 22, 23, 25, 26, 28, 31, 32, 33 (right and left), 34, 36, 37, 38, 41, 43, 44, 47, 48, 49, 50, 52, 56, 58, 59, 60, 61, 62, 63, 65, 66, 67 (top), 68, 69, 70, 72, 80, 83, 85, 88, 89, 157, 159, 163, 164, 166, 176, 181, 187, 190, 192, 193, 194 (right and left), 204, 209, 238, 239, 240, 241, 244, 246, 247, 249, 251, 252, 257, 260, 279; UPI: 30, 39, 40, 45, 64, 71, 74, 77, 78, 81, 90, 97, 100, 108, 110, 113, 119, 120, 122, 130, 141, 145, 152, 185, 195, 196, 197, 210, 214, 216, 218, 284, 288, 289, 291, 292, 294, 295, 298, 426; Bruce Bennett: Facing title page, 137, 138, 243, 266; Paul Bereswill: 115, 286; David Bier: 253; Clifton Boutelle: 169, 254, 259; Nancy Hogue: 128; Scotty Kilpatrick: 87, 101, 160, 168, 175, 186, 236; Madison Square Garden: 95, 162; Larry Morris: 103; NHL: vi, 131, 270, 271, 272, 273 (bottom), 274 (top and bottom), 275, 276, 277 (top and bottom), 278 (top and bottom); New York Daily News/Charles Hoff: 91; New York Rangers: 54, 65, 195, 273 (top); Rich Pilling: 125, 129, 132, 133, 140, 143, 144, 149, 151, 171, 172, 182; Public Archives of Canada: Facing page 1; Dick Raphael: 111; Ken Regan: 93, 102, 146, 156; Robert Shaver: 117, 123, 124, 127, 134, 142, 179, 198, 215, 303, 425, 430; Barton Silverman: 98, 104, 106, 154, 184, 198, 242; Toronto Maple Leafs: 258; Wide World: 46, 51, 65, 73, 94, 165, 178, 199, 208, 248, 296, 299, 300, 301.

## JACKET PHOTO CREDITS

Front Cover: Mummery/Strong. Back Cover: Rich Pilling.

## COLOR INSERT CREDITS

Dan Baliotti: Bobby Orr
Harold Barkley: Bobby Hull, Maurice Richard
Bruce Bennett: Mike Bossy, Tony Esposito, New York Islanders, Larry Robinson
Rich Pilling: Ken Dryden, Guy Lafleur
Dick Raphael: Bobby Clarke
Barton Silverman: Gordie Howe
George Tiedemann: Wayne Gretzky

Originally published as *The Complete Encyclopedia of Ice Hockey*
Copyright © Associated Features Inc., 1970, 1974

Copyright © 1983 by Associated Features Inc.
All Rights Reserved
An Associated Features Book
NAL Books/The New American Library, Inc.

 NAL BOOKS TRADEMARK REG. U.S. PAT. OFF. AND FOREIGN COUNTRIES
REGISTERED TRADEMARK—MARCA REGISTRADA
HECHO EN HARRISONBURG, VIRGINIA, U.S.A.

SIGNET, SIGNET CLASSICS, MENTOR, PLUME, MERIDIAN and NAL
BOOKS are published *in the United States* by
The New American Library, Inc., 1633 Broadway, New York,
New York 10019, *in Canada* by The New American Library of Canada
Limited, 81 Mack Avenue, Scarborough, Ontario M1L 1M8

Library of Congress Catalog Number 83-62080
ISBN: 0-453-00449-0
Designed by SOHO Studios
First Printing, November, 1983
1 2 3 4 5 6 7 8 9
Printed in the United States of America

*To the pioneers,
the peewees and the pros*

Clarence S. Campbell (left) reigned as president of the National Hockey League for 30 years before John A. Ziegler, Jr. took the helm in 1977.

# FOREWORD

My predecessor, Clarence S. Campbell, wrote a foreword for the first edition of *The Complete Encyclopedia of Hockey*. So much of what he had to say is appropriate to this revised edition that I have taken the liberty of excerpting parts of it:

"This is a truly remarkable combination of accurate historical information about the NHL from its inception assembled in chronological order; bibliographical data about many stars of the game both past and present, as well as leading officials; interesting incidents and anecdotes about the Stanley Cup; selections of memorable moments which produced intense thrills, and the current official individual and team records of the league.

"The writing is superb, which, by the generous use of direct quotes, makes the events and the personalities both lively and exciting. The book is extensively illustrated with about two hundred photographs which add to its interest and authenticity."

This new edition brings us forward with the same scholarship and readability. From great moments to great players to great teams, *The Complete Encyclopedia of Hockey* is a comprehensive documentation of all the ingredients that make our game the most exciting sport in the world. The encyclopedia is quite obviously the result of prodigious research. It will be a valuable and welcome addition to the reference library of any hockey collector, fan or journalist.

*John A. Ziegler, Jr.*
President
National Hockey League

# ACKNOWLEDGMENTS

The research, writing and editing of *The Complete Encyclopedia of Hockey* was not a two-man job. It could never have been done without the aid of a number of talented hockey specialists and believers who deserve recognition for helping achieve the goal.

The editors thank Tim Moriarty of *Newsday,* for the writing of the chapters on The Greatest Players and The Officials, Larry Fox of the New York *Daily News* and Moriarty, for Hockey's Memorable Moments; Reyn Davis of the Winnipeg *Free Press,* for the World Hockey Association; Ben Olan of The Associated Press, for The All-Star Game and The Hall of Fame, and Pat Calabria of *Newsday,* for the season's roundups starting with 1974-75.

We acknowledge Eric Compton of the New York *Daily News* for his enormous all-around contributions and we salute the statisticians—the late Jerry Ahrens, who compiled The All-Time NHL Player Register for the first edition in 1970; Art Friedman, for the update in 1974, and Jeff Shermack, for this third edition.

Others who have helped make the encyclopedia a reality include Clarence S. Campbell and John A. Ziegler, Jr., respectively former and present presidents of the NHL; Maurice (Lefty) Reid, curator and secretary of the Hockey Hall of Fame; Bill Chadwick, announcer, former referee and member of the Hockey Hall of Fame; Rodger Gottlieb, Frank Kelly, Bill Himmelman, David Rosen, Richard Sherwin, Lee Stowbridge, Benny Ercolani, Ron Andrews, Frank Polnaszek, John and Janet Halligan and the other team publicity directors of the NHL.

A special note of thanks to Gerry Burstein and the SOHO Studio, for creative design; to George Monette and the Twin Company, for conscientious typesetting; to Richard Rossiter of New American Library, for design of the cover; to Jerry Ozer, for on-the-deadline indexing, and to Phyllis Hollander, for playing goal and driving the Zamboni.

# CONTENTS

# INTRODUCTION

In the more than three decades since the founding of the National Hockey League, hockey has grown from a simple game on the frozen lakes and ponds of Canada to one played on artificial ice in huge indoor arenas across the whole of North America. Today 21 NHL teams perform for stadium crowds that reach almost 20,000 and before additional millions on television. And there are avid followers of the minor leagues as well.

On the amateur level, the sport is a major attraction in the Winter Olympics, has its own world championships, and is played by increasing numbers of colleges, secondary schools and junior and peewee teams.

As the slap shots of the shooters got faster, the reflexes of the defensemen and goalies quicker, and the response of the fans more ardent, it was obvious that the sport lacked a single, comprehensive work providing all the information a hockey devotee would want to know.

Thus was born *The Complete Encyclopedia of Hockey*—with the goal of including not only the vital facts and figures but the drama, the history and the heroics that have made the game so special to its growing army of fans.

In this third edition, the encyclopedia covers every NHL season, including the climactic Stanley Cup playoffs and the All-Star Games, plus the late World Hockey Association. We have profiled the sport's outstanding forwards, greatest defensemen and best goalies. These selections may provoke argument, but controversy, after all, is the lifeblood of any sport. We have tried to capture the excitement and significance of 11 of hockey's most memorable moments. And we have cited the members of the Hockey Hall of Fame.

For those who seek voluminous statistics, we have compiled all-time hockey records. These include not only the well-known feats of the superstars, but the season and career records of every man who has ever worn the jersey of an NHL team—more than 3,000 players.

Since there is more to the complete picture of hockey than the NHL and the other major leagues of the past, we have included material on the Olympic Games, world championships and collegiate championships—all another part of the ice.

*Zander Hollander*
and
*Hal Bock*

*Hockey in the Yukon, circa 1900.*

# HOW IT ALL BEGAN
# 1917-1924

The family tree of the National Hockey League has its roots in the years around the turn of the century with branches spreading from the eastern provinces of Quebec and Ontario clear across the vast prairie land of Canada to the west and British Columbia.

It is rich with legendary hockey names—Frank and Lester Patrick, Edouard (Newsy) Lalonde, Fred (Cyclone) Taylor, Frank Nighbor, Joe Malone—men who built the game from pastime to profession and nurtured it from the frozen ponds in small mining towns to packed big-city arenas.

Hockey began as a seven-man game with upright posts embedded in the ice for goals. There were no nets, no blue lines, no red lines and no face-off circles on the ice. But by the time the pioneers got through with it, the game closely resembled the sport we know today.

The Amateur Hockey Association of Canada and the Ontario Hockey Association were among the first organized hockey leagues in Canada. Players and teams freely shifted from league to league in those early years.

Finally, in 1910, there were two major leagues operating in competition with each other. The Canadian Hockey Association listed Ottawa, Quebec and three Montreal teams—the Shamrocks, the Nationals and All-Montreal. The National Hockey Association had teams in Cobalt, Haileybury and Renfrew and two in Montreal—the Wanderers and the Canadiens.

The bidding war for players was spirited. The Patrick brothers signed with Renfrew for $3,000 each and the same club lured Cyclone Taylor away from Ottawa and offered an Edmonton player $1,000 to come east for a single game.

Aware that the war would ruin them, the two leagues came to an understanding and merged into the single National Hockey Association, a seven-team league composed of Renfrew, Cobalt, Haileybury, Ottawa and three Montreal teams—the Shamrocks, the Wanderers and the Canadiens.

The Patrick brothers went west that year and organized their own league—the Pacific Coast Hockey Association, with franchises in Vancouver, Victoria and New Westminster. The Patricks were veterans of the teamhopping in the East and started player raids of their own to lure established stars to their new league. Many, including Taylor, Lalonde and Nighbor, went west.

With top talent migrating to it, the Pacific Coast Hockey Association gained stature and eventually a series was started, pitting the PCHA and NHA champions against each other in a playoff for the Stanley Cup.

In 1912, the NHA introduced six-man hockey and added numbers to players' jerseys. A year before, hockey's traditional two 30-minute periods had been switched to three periods of 20 minutes each. Slowly but surely, the sport was changing.

In 1913, the PCHA introduced blue lines, dividing the ice into three sections. It was the same year that, for the first time, assists as well as goals were credited to a player's scoring totals.

A year later, the NHA followed suit, crediting assists as well as goals. The Eastern circuit also allowed referees to start dropping the puck on face-offs instead of placing it between the two sticks, thus saving a lot of bruised knuckles.

And in the West, a referee named Mickey Ion, destined to become one of the greatest officials in the history of the game, began picking an All-Star team—a custom which added considerable interest to the game.

In 1914, Canada went to war and with the conflict came problems for hockey. Many players were called up to serve in the Army and some were given deferments conditional upon their not playing hockey.

Train schedules were disrupted, causing cancellation of some games. The NHA clubs turned over the entire proceeds of their exhibition games to patriotic causes and a portion of the regular-season income to the Red Cross.

By 1917, the NHA had evolved into a six-team circuit composed of the Montreal Wanderers, Montreal Canadiens, Ottawa, Toronto, Quebec and the Northern Fusiliers—an Army team representing the 228th Battalion of the Canadian Army.

When the 228th was ordered overseas, it was forced to withdraw from the league, leaving five teams and an unbalanced schedule. After considerable bickering, it was decided that Eddie Livingstone's Toronto team would also be dropped and its players redistributed.

There is some evidence that Livingstone was not the most popular man among his fellow owners and it was their desire to rid themselves of him that led to the creation of a new league—the National Hockey League.

## 1917–18

Tired of intra-league squabbling, much of which had centered around the Toronto franchise and its com-

Vancouver's Fred (Cyclone) Taylor was the Pacific Coast Hockey League's scoring champion in 1917-18.

bative owner, Eddie Livingstone, NHA owners met in Montreal's Windsor Hotel on November 22, 1917, to settle their problems once and for all.

Their solution was a simple one. They simply created their own league and left Livingstone in the NHA all by himself. The new circuit would be called the National Hockey League, with franchises going to Ottawa, the Montreal Wanderers, Montreal Canadiens and Toronto, provided Livingstone was not included in that team's operation. Quebec was also granted a franchise, but chose not to play that first year and its players were divided among the other four teams in what turned out to be the NHL's first intra-league draft.

Major Frank Robinson, president of the NHA, bowed out and Frank Calder, secretary-treasurer of the NHA, was elected president of the new league. A 22-game schedule, running from December 19 through March 10, was adopted.

Joe Malone, Quebec's best player, wound up with the Canadiens and on opening night he scored five goals as Montreal whipped Ottawa, 7–4. Malone, playing in only 20 games, won the first NHL scoring crown with 44 goals—a pace that has never been matched.

The Wanderers opened at home with a 10–9 victory over Toronto in a game that attracted only 700 fans. That was the only victory the Wanderers ever managed in the NHL. They dropped five straight games and then, on January 2, 1918, a $150,000 fire burned Westmount Arena to the ground, leaving them without a home rink.

The Canadiens, who had shared the Arena with the Wanderers, moved into the 3,250-seat Jubilee rink for the remainder of the season but the Wanderers dropped out of the league with owner Sam Lichtenhein apparently happy to be out of what had been a losing venture.

A major rule change was adopted during the NHL's first season that was to affect the art of goaltending forever. Until then, goalies had been forced to stand up to defend their nets and in 1914 a rule was added by the NHA imposing $2 fines on goalies who sprawled on the ice to make a save. Now the rule was changed and goalies were permitted to assume any position they wished.

If the rule helped, the statistics don't show it. The legendary Georges Vezina of the Canadiens led the league with 84 goals allowed in 21 games—a 4.0 average that is not very good by today's standards.

*Frank Calder was appointed president of the newly-formed National Hockey League in 1917.*

In addition to Malone, the top shooters were Ottawa's Cy Denneny with 36 goals in 22 games, Reg Noble of Toronto with 28 in 20 and Newsy Lalonde of the Canadiens, who had 23 goals in 14 games.

The Canadiens, first-half champions, and Toronto, winners of the second half, played off for the NHL title with Toronto taking the two-game, total-goals playoff, 10–7.

In the West, the PCHA, cut back to three teams by the departure of Spokane, had a tight race almost all season. But Seattle finally finished two games in front of Vancouver and four up on Portland.

Vancouver's Cyclone Taylor led the league with 32 goals, including one game-winner against Seattle scored with his back to the goal. It was a routine

*The Canadiens' Joe Malone was the first NHL scoring champion, with 44 goals in 20 games in 1917-18.*

play for Taylor, who boasted that he once scored a goal in the NHA by skating backwards through the whole Ottawa team.

In the two-game total-goals playoff between the top two teams, Vancouver defeated Seattle, three goals to two. The Millionaires traveled east to face Toronto for the Stanley Cup and split the first four games. Then the Arenas captured the deciding fifth game and the Cup, 2–1, as Corbett Denneny scored the winning goal.

## 1917–18

### FINAL STANDINGS

#### First Half

| | W | L | T | PTS | GF | GA |
|---|---|---|---|---|---|---|
| Montreal C. | 10 | 4 | 0 | 20 | 81 | 47 |
| Toronto | 8 | 6 | 0 | 16 | 71 | 75 |
| Ottawa | 5 | 9 | 0 | 10 | 67 | 79 |
| Montreal W. | 1 | 5 | 0 | 2 | 17 | 35 |

Montreal Wanderers forced to withdraw from league after home rink burned down on January 2, 1918.

#### Second Half

| | W | L | T | PTS | GF | GA |
|---|---|---|---|---|---|---|
| Toronto | 5 | 3 | 0 | 10 | 37 | 34 |
| Ottawa | 4 | 4 | 0 | 8 | 35 | 35 |
| Montreal C. | 3 | 5 | 0 | 6 | 34 | 37 |

Toronto defeated Montreal Canadiens in playoffs and won regular-season championship.

### LEADING SCORERS

| | G |
|---|---|
| Malone, Montreal C. | 44 |
| Denneny, Ottawa | 36 |
| Noble, Toronto | 28 |
| Lalonde, Montreal C. | 23 |
| Denneny, Toronto | 20 |
| Pitre, Montreal C. | 17 |
| Cameron, Toronto | 17 |
| Darragh, Ottawa | 14 |
| Hyland, Montreal, W.-Ottawa | 14 |
| Gerard, Ottawa | 13 |
| Skinner, Toronto | 13 |

No records of assists were compiled.

## 1918–19

The demise of the Wanderers the year before had left the NHL with just three teams—the Montreal Canadiens, Toronto Arenas and Ottawa Senators. There was, though, a possibility that Quebec, which had not operated in 1917–18, might join the league for its second season.

President Frank Calder, reelected for a five-year term, drew up two schedules for the new season—one for a three-team league, one for a four-team league.

When Quebec's ownership failed to meet an NHL

*Joe Hall starred on defense for the Canadiens before dying of influenza in the spring of 1919.*

deadline for declaring its intentions, the league suspended the franchise and went with the three-team schedule. With the end of World War I, it was expected that many players would be returning from the Army. But few were discharged in time and when the season started, the teams had much the same personnel as the year before.

The NHL adopted several important rule changes including the adoption of the PCHA's blue-line idea. This divided the ice surface into three zones with forward passing permitted in the 40-foot-wide center area. Kicking the puck was also allowed and assists were added to regular-season statistics. Penalty rules were reshuffled. A minor penalty would leave a team shorthanded for three minutes, a major penalty would cost five minutes and for a match penalty, no substitute would be allowed for the penalized player.

The 18-game regular season started on December 21 with Ottawa beating Montreal, 5–2. The Canadiens bounced back to lose only two more games and captured the first-half championship. Ottawa, a so-so 5–5 in the first half, won seven of eight games and took the second-half title.

Toronto, heavily favored after winning the Stanley Cup the year before, started in reverse, dropping six of its first seven games. The Arenas never righted themselves and finished in last place in both halves.

Newsy Lalonde, the Canadiens' fiery player-manager, won the scoring title with 21 goals and Ottawa's Clint Benedict was the top goalie with two shutouts and a 3.0 average in 18 games.

In the playoff between the Canadiens and Ottawa, Montreal dominated. Lalonde's team won the first three games, dropped the fourth and then wrapped up the series in the fifth game. The format had been changed from total goals in two games to a best-of-seven series.

In the PCHA, Portland's franchise was transferred to Victoria with Lester Patrick set as the team's player-manager. Lester's younger brother, Frank, was serving his sixth term as president of the league.

Seattle beat Vancouver in the opening game and held onto the league lead for six weeks before the defending champion Vancouver Millionaires took over. Vancouver won the regular-season title by one game and Cyclone Taylor again was the scoring champ with 23 goals—one more than Seattle's Bernie Morris.

There was a celebrated fight between Cully Wilson of Seattle and Vancouver's mild-mannered Mickey MacKay in which Wilson's cross-check broke MacKay's jaw. The incident cost Wilson a $50 fine, match penalty and eventual suspension from the league.

In the two-game, total-goals playoff, Seattle defeated Vancouver, 7–5, scoring six goals in the first game. That set up the Stanley Cup series against Montreal.

The NHL champion Canadiens dropped two of the first three games, played a scoreless tie in the fourth and then tied the series by winning the fifth. But the deciding sixth game was never played. The Canadiens' ranks had been shredded by the great influenza epidemic which covered the continent. Bad Joe Hall, a defenseman, was hospitalized, and four others, including Newsy Lalonde, were confined to their hotel by the disease. The series was ended with no Cup winner—the only time in history that has happened. Hall never recovered. He died in a Seattle hospital.

# 1918–19

## FINAL STANDINGS

### First Half

| | W | L | T | PTS | GF | GA |
|---|---|---|---|---|---|---|
| Montreal | 7 | 3 | 0 | 14 | 57 | 50 |
| Ottawa | 5 | 5 | 0 | 10 | 39 | 40 |
| Toronto | 3 | 7 | 0 | 6 | 43 | 49 |

### Second Half

| | W | L | T | PTS | GF | GA |
|---|---|---|---|---|---|---|
| Ottawa | 7 | 1 | 0 | 14 | 32 | 14 |
| Montreal | 3 | 5 | 0 | 6 | 31 | 28 |
| Toronto | 2 | 6 | 0 | 4 | 22 | 43 |

Montreal defeated Ottawa in playoffs and won regular-season championship.

## LEADING SCORERS

| | G | A | PTS |
|---|---|---|---|
| Lalonde, Montreal C. | 23 | 9 | 32 |
| Cleghorn, Montreal C. | 23 | 6 | 29 |
| Nighbor, Ottawa | 18 | 4 | 22 |
| Denneny, Ottawa | 18 | 4 | 22 |
| Pitre, Montreal C. | 14 | 4 | 18 |
| Skinner, Toronto | 12 | 3 | 15 |
| Noble, Toronto | 11 | 3 | 14 |
| Cameron, Toronto-Ottawa | 11 | 3 | 14 |
| Darragh, Ottawa | 12 | 1 | 13 |
| Randall, Ottawa | 7 | 6 | 13 |

# 1919–20

The player shuttle created between East and West when the Patrick brothers organized the Pacific Coast Hockey Association was in full swing.

Moving west from the NHL was a youngster used sparingly the year before by Toronto. But Jack Adams would one day be back and make his mark as a player, coach and executive in the National League.

Alf Skinner and Rusty Crawford also jumped to the PCHA while Cully Wilson, a rough, tough right wing, who was banned from the coast league for his overly aggressive play, showed up in the NHL with Toronto. His style stayed the same and he was the most penalized player in the league that season, spending 79 minutes sitting out infractions.

Toronto's management, disturbed over the team's disappointing performance the year before, undertook a rebuilding job. The first step was to change the club's nickname from the Arenas to the St. Patricks, perhaps in an attempt to attract the luck of the Irish.

The Quebec Bulldogs operated their franchise and reclaimed players who had been assigned to other teams for the NHL's first two seasons. The most dominant was Joe Malone, who had won the scoring title in the league's first year of operation and now returned to Quebec from the Montreal Canadiens.

Malone was the standout on what was a dismal Quebec team. On January 31 he went on a tear of seven goals in a single game against Toronto, setting an NHL record that still stands. He almost matched that performance a little more than one month later when he scored six times against Ottawa in the final game of the season.

Malone finished the season with 39 goals and nine assists for 48 points and his second scoring title in three years. But despite his brilliance, Quebec won only four games all year and finished last. Newsy Lalonde of the Canadiens gave Malone a run for the scoring title with 37 goals and six assists for 43 points.

Ottawa's Clint Benedict was the top goalie, posting a 2.7 goals-against average and five shutouts for the 24-game season. No other netminder in the league recorded a single shutout that year.

With World War I over, Canadians began paying more attention to hockey and crowds began growing in size. On February 21, Ottawa's game at Toronto attracted 8,500—a record.

Ottawa won both halves of the NHL's split schedule, eliminating the need for the playoffs. The Senators would represent the NHL in the battle for the

*Seattle's Frank Foyston won the PCHA scoring title in 1919-20.*

Stanley Cup against either Seattle, the PCHA champion, or second-place Vancouver. Frank Foyston of Seattle had won the PCHA scoring crown and he led a 6–0 romp in the second game that gave Seattle the two-game, total-goals playoff over the Millionaires, 7–3.

Seattle traveled east to play Ottawa for the Cup but when it arrived, there was a problem. Seattle's red, white and green uniforms closely resembled Ottawa's red, white and black. The conflict was resolved when the Senators agreed to change to white sweaters.

Ottawa took the Cup in five games—the last two played on Toronto's artificial ice after hot weather turned Ottawa's natural surface to slush.

# 1919–20

## FINAL STANDINGS

### First Half

|  | W | L | T | PTS | GF | GA |
|---|---|---|---|---|---|---|
| Ottawa | 9 | 3 | 0 | 18 | 59 | 23 |
| Montreal | 8 | 4 | 0 | 16 | 62 | 51 |
| Toronto | 5 | 7 | 0 | 10 | 52 | 62 |
| Quebec | 2 | 10 | 0 | 4 | 44 | 81 |

### Second Half

|  | W | L | T | PTS | GF | GA |
|---|---|---|---|---|---|---|
| Ottawa | 10 | 2 | 0 | 20 | 62 | 41 |
| Toronto | 7 | 5 | 0 | 14 | 67 | 44 |
| Montreal | 5 | 7 | 0 | 10 | 67 | 62 |
| Quebec | 2 | 10 | 0 | 4 | 47 | 96 |

## LEADING SCORERS

|  | G | A | PTS |
|---|---|---|---|
| Malone, Quebec | 39 | 9 | 48 |
| Lalonde, Montreal C. | 36 | 6 | 42 |
| Denneny, Toronto | 23 | 12 | 35 |
| Nighbor, Ottawa | 26 | 7 | 33 |
| Noble, Toronto | 24 | 7 | 31 |
| Darragh, Ottawa | 22 | 5 | 27 |
| Arbour, Montreal C. | 22 | 4 | 26 |
| Wilson, Toronto | 21 | 5 | 26 |
| Broadbent, Ottawa | 19 | 4 | 23 |
| Cleghorn, Montreal C. | 19 | 3 | 22 |
| Pitre, Montreal C. | 15 | 7 | 22 |

# 1920–21

Quebec's dismal showing the season before left the team's owners disenchanted and the Bulldogs faded from the NHL picture for the second and final time.

Percy Thompson of Hamilton, Ontario, purchased the franchise for $5,000, moved the club to Hamilton and changed the nickname to the Tigers. It was obvious that the same players who had failed in Quebec would not do much better in Hamilton and an SOS was sent out to the other teams in the league, asking for player help.

The last time that had happened was in 1917, the NHL's first season, when the undermanned Montreal Wanderers appealed for help. The other clubs refused then and the result was Montreal's eventual dropout from the league. It was perhaps with this in mind that the NHL responded favorably to Hamilton's plight.

Toronto contributed Goldie Prodgers, Joe Matte and Cecil (Babe) Dye, Montreal ticketed Bill Couture to the Tigers and Joe Malone led the leftovers from Quebec which included Eddie Carpenter, George Carey and Tom McCarthy.

The makeshift team stung the Canadiens with a 5–0 shutout in its home opener on December 22. Dye scored two goals and Toronto promptly reclaimed him from Hamilton and shipped Mickey Roach to take his place with the Tigers.

The move turned out to be a smart one because Dye scored more goals than anyone in the league, finishing with 35. He had 37 total points, four less than Newsy Lalonde of the Canadiens, whose 33 goals and eight assists for 41 points led the league. It was Lalonde's second scoring title and both times he won because his assists gave him more total points than the leading goal-scorer.

After the opening victory, Hamilton slipped badly and finished in the cellar for both halves of the season, managing only six victories in 24 games. Ottawa won the first-half title with an 8–2 record, three games better than Toronto's 5–5. But the Senators, saddled by a seven-game losing streak, slipped to third in the second half, behind both Toronto and the Canadiens.

Despite the second-half slump, Ottawa's Clint Benedict finished as the top goalie with a 3.1 goals-against average and two shutouts. In the NHL playoffs against second-half champ Toronto, Benedict and the Senators regained their touch. Ottawa shut out the St. Pats, 5–0, in the opener and came back with a 2–0 whitewashing to sweep the series.

Vancouver won the PCHA title by one-half game over Seattle—the difference being a 4–4 tie which Seattle played at Victoria on March 4, Moose Johnson night. Johnson, a veteran defenseman, was honored before the game and then the teams played through three overtimes before agreeing to let the game end as a tie.

In the two-game playoff, Vancouver romped, outscoring Seattle, 13–2. The Millionaires then met Ottawa for the Stanley Cup. The opening game at-

*Victoria's Ernie (Moose) Johnson was known as the man with the longest reach in hockey.*

tracted a record 11,000 fans. The teams split the first four games and then Ottawa won the fifth, 2–1, for the Cup.

## 1920–21

### FINAL STANDINGS

#### First Half

| | W | L | T | PTS | GF | GA |
|---|---|---|---|---|---|---|
| Ottawa | 8 | 2 | 0 | 16 | 49 | 23 |
| Toronto | 5 | 5 | 0 | 10 | 39 | 47 |
| Montreal | 4 | 6 | 0 | 8 | 37 | 51 |
| Hamilton | 3 | 7 | 0 | 6 | 34 | 38 |

#### Second Half

| | W | L | T | PTS | GF | GA |
|---|---|---|---|---|---|---|
| Toronto | 10 | 4 | 0 | 20 | 66 | 53 |
| Montreal | 9 | 5 | 0 | 18 | 75 | 48 |
| Ottawa | 6 | 8 | 0 | 12 | 48 | 52 |
| Hamilton | 3 | 11 | 0 | 6 | 58 | 94 |

Ottawa defeated Toronto in playoffs and won regular-season championship.

### LEADING SCORERS

| | G | A | PTS |
|---|---|---|---|
| Lalonde, Montreal C. | 33 | 8 | 41 |
| Denneny, Ottawa | 34 | 5 | 39 |
| Dye, Toronto | 35 | 2 | 37 |
| Malone, Hamilton | 30 | 4 | 34 |
| Cameron, Toronto | 18 | 9 | 27 |
| Noble, Toronto | 20 | 6 | 26 |
| Prodgers, Hamilton | 18 | 8 | 26 |
| Denneny, Toronto | 17 | 6 | 23 |
| Nighbor, Ottawa | 18 | 3 | 21 |
| Berlinquette, Montreal C. | 12 | 9 | 21 |

## 1921–22

This was a year of major changes for hockey in both the East and the West. The NHL dropped the split schedule and its first- and second-half champions, substituting instead a single schedule with playoffs between the top two teams. The PCHA introduced the penalty shot which was awarded to a player who was interfered with after breaking in alone on the goalie. There was a new league in the West and some new owners in the East.

George Kennedy, one of the founders of the NHL and owner of the Montreal club, died in 1921 and his widow sold the club to Joe Cattarinich and Leo Dandurand for $11,000. Cattarinich and Dandurand were anxious to get Sprague Cleghorn, a defenseman who had starred for the Wanderers, back to Montreal and they accomplished this in a roundabout fashion.

The NHL, still trying to help the Hamilton club, devised the plan which eventually brought Cleghorn to the Canadiens. Players with the Wanderers when the club dissolved in 1918, said the NHL, became the property of the league. Cleghorn was one of these players and the NHL simply claimed him from

Ottawa and assigned him to Hamilton. Provided with this windfall, the Tigers promptly offered Cleghorn to the Canadiens, who, they knew, were anxious to get him.

A neat package was arranged with Billy Couture and Cleghorn going to Montreal in exchange for Harry Mummery, Amos Arbour and Cully Wilson. It was the first major, multiple-player trade in the NHL.

The trade reunited Sprague Cleghorn with his brother, Odie, and the two ran wild one week in January. Each scored four goals on January 14 against Hamilton and they combined for six goals against Ottawa a few days later. Interestingly, this spree came shortly after Newsy Lalonde walked out on the team, claiming he couldn't get along with his new bosses. Frank Calder, president of the league, mediated the dispute and after missing four games, Lalonde returned. But his days in Montreal were numbered.

On February 1, Sprague Cleghorn almost wiped out the Ottawa team singlehandedly. He cut Eddie Gerard and Cy Denneny and charged Frank Nighbor. All three Ottawa players missed two games because of injuries and Cleghorn drew a match foul plus a $15 fine. Ottawa police tried to arrest him for assault in the wake of his one-man war.

Despite Cleghorn's rambunctious play, Montreal finished third behind Ottawa and Toronto. Harry (Punch) Broadbent of Ottawa established a record with at least one goal in 16 consecutive games and

*Odie Cleghorn (right) was a star forward on the Canadiens and his older brother, Sprague, played defense on the same team.*

a total of 25 during the streak. He finished as the leading scorer with 32 goals and 46 points.

Toronto defeated Ottawa, 5–4, in the first game of the total goals playoff and then battled the Senators to a scoreless tie in the second to clinch the Stanley Cup berth.

In the West, Jack Adams, playing center for Vancouver, led the PCHA in scoring with 25 goals. But Seattle, with Frank Foyston and Jim Riley scoring 16 goals each, finished in first place.

In Victoria, a combative goalie named Norm Fowler was thrown out of two games within 10 days for fighting and the team's manager, Lester Patrick, made his debut as a goalie.

Vancouver won the playoff with goalie Hugh Lehman turning in a pair of 1–0 shutouts over Seattle.

A new league, the Western Canada Hockey League, with clubs in Calgary, Edmonton, Saskatoon and Regina, had been formed and its players included Red Dutton, Bill Cook and Dick Irvin. Regina finished second but knocked off pennant winner Edmonton in the playoff and challenged Vancouver for the right to represent the West in the Stanley Cup series against Toronto. Regina took the first game, 2–1, but Vancouver recovered with a 4–0 victory in the second game to clinch the playoff.

In the Stanley Cup series, Vancouver and Toronto split the first four games and then Babe Dye fired four goals, pacing a 5–1 St. Pats' victory that clinched the series and the Cup in the fifth contest.

# 1921–22

### FINAL STANDINGS

|          | W  | L  | T | PTS | GF  | GA  |
|----------|----|----|---|-----|-----|-----|
| Ottawa   | 14 | 8  | 2 | 30  | 106 | 84  |
| Toronto  | 13 | 10 | 1 | 27  | 98  | 97  |
| Montreal | 12 | 11 | 1 | 25  | 88  | 94  |
| Hamilton | 7  | 17 | 0 | 14  | 88  | 105 |

Toronto defeated Ottawa in playoffs and won regular-season championship.

### LEADING SCORERS

|                          | G  | A  | PTS |
|--------------------------|----|----|-----|
| Broadbent, Ottawa        | 32 | 14 | 46  |
| Denneny, Ottawa          | 27 | 12 | 39  |
| Dye, Toronto             | 30 | 7  | 37  |
| Malone, Hamilton         | 25 | 7  | 32  |
| Cameron, Toronto         | 19 | 8  | 27  |
| Denneny, Toronto         | 19 | 7  | 26  |
| Noble, Toronto           | 17 | 8  | 25  |
| S. Cleghorn, Montreal C. | 21 | 3  | 24  |
| O. Cleghorn, Montreal C. | 17 | 7  | 24  |
| Reise, Hamilton          | 9  | 14 | 23  |

*Toronto's Babe Dye had a five-goal game en route to the 1922-23 scoring title.*

# 1922–23

The split between Newsy Lalonde and Leo Dandurand could not be mended and eventually Montreal dealt its great star to Saskatoon of the new Western League. In return, the Canadiens received the rights to an amateur named Aurel Joliat, a slightly built left wing who belonged to Saskatoon but was playing with Iroquois Falls.

Joliat weighed about 140 pounds and was hardly an imposing athlete. The thought that Montreal had traded one of hockey's early greats for this little guy

*Little Aurel Joliat came to the Canadiens in a big trade in 1922-23.*

placed an extra burden on Joliat. But he was equal to it and was to develop into an outstanding NHL player.

In another trade, Montreal sent Bert Corbeau and Edmond Bouchard to Hamilton for Joe Malone, then in the twilight of his career. Vancouver swapped Jack Adams to Toronto for Corbett Denneny.

Joliat scored two goals in his first game for Montreal but Babe Dye had five for Toronto and the St. Pats beat the Canadiens, 7–2. It was the start of a fine season for Dye, who was to win the scoring title with 26 goals and 11 assists for 37 points.

Ottawa won the regular-season title, edging Montreal with Toronto finishing third. Clint Benedict again led the goalies with a 2.3 average and four shutouts in 24 games. It was the fifth straight year that he was the top goaltender.

Perhaps the most significant event of the season took place in Toronto's Mutual Street Arena in March 1923. That was when a young man named Foster Hewitt, sitting in an airless glass booth erected in three seat spaces and talking into an upright telephone, broadcast radio's first hockey game.

It was the start of a new era for the sport.

In the playoffs, Ottawa blanked the Canadiens, 2–0, in the first game and won the Cup berth on the basis of total goals although it lost the second game, 2–1. Billy Couture and Sprague Cleghorn played viciously in the opener, injuring several Ottawa players with their sticks and elbows. Owner Leo Dandurand was so disturbed at the display that he suspended both of them for the second game, without waiting for the league to act.

Lalonde flourished in the dual role of player-manager with Saskatoon and led the Western League in scoring with 29 goals in 26 games. But his team finished last, with Edmonton taking the regular-season title as well as the two-game, total-goals playoff over Regina.

The PCHA eliminated the position of rover and adopted six-man hockey which had been played in the East for some time. Victoria's Frank Fredrickson led the scorers with 41 goals in 30 games but Vancouver finished first and beat Victoria in the playoffs.

Ottawa, its ranks thinned by injuries, went west for the Stanley Cut playoffs and eliminated Vancouver in four games and then took Edmonton in two straight to clinch it. After watching the gritty show put on by the undermanned Senators, Frank Patrick,

president of the PCHA, called them the greatest team he had ever seen.

## 1922–23

### FINAL STANDINGS

|  | W | L | T | PTS | GF | GA |
|---|---|---|---|---|---|---|
| Ottawa | 14 | 9 | 1 | 29 | 77 | 54 |
| Montreal C. | 13 | 9 | 2 | 28 | 73 | 61 |
| Toronto | 13 | 10 | 1 | 27 | 82 | 88 |
| Hamilton | 6 | 18 | 0 | 12 | 81 | 110 |

Ottawa defeated Montreal Canadiens in playoffs and won regular-season championship.

### LEADING SCORERS

|  | G | A | PTS |
|---|---|---|---|
| Dye, Toronto | 26 | 11 | 37 |
| Denneny, Ottawa | 21 | 10 | 31 |
| Adams, Toronto | 19 | 9 | 28 |
| B. Boucher, Montreal C. | 23 | 4 | 27 |
| O. Cleghorn, Montreal C. | 19 | 7 | 26 |
| Roach, Hamilton | 17 | 8 | 25 |
| G. Boucher, Ottawa | 15 | 9 | 24 |
| Joliat, Montreal C. | 13 | 9 | 22 |
| Noble, Toronto | 12 | 10 | 22 |
| Wilson, Hamilton | 16 | 3 | 19 |

## 1923–24

Until this year, hockey players had no individual trophy for which to compete. There was the scoring championship, of course, and the satisfaction of playing for the Stanley Cup winner for some, but no single award that a player could go after and call his own.

This all changed in 1924 when Dr. David Hart, father of Cecil Hart, a manager-coach of the Montreal Canadiens, contributed a trophy to the league. The Hart Trophy was to be awarded to the Most Valuable Player in the league and the first one went to Frank Nighbor, Ottawa's smooth-skating center.

Nighbor, whose poke check repeatedly relieved opponents of the puck, won the award by a single vote over Sprague Cleghorn, the Canadiens' boisterous defenseman.

It was ironic that Nighbor and Cleghorn were the top contestants for the first Hart Trophy. Their styles were a study in contrasts. Nighbor was a gentlemanly sort who rarely was involved in trouble on the ice while Cleghorn seemed to cause a ruckus wherever he went.

In fact, Sprague's rough play caused an NHL meeting at midseason to consider his suspension. The Ottawa club claimed Cleghorn was trying to injure opponents deliberately, citing a spearing in-

*Cy Denneny of Ottawa fell down a well but climbed out and won the 1923-24 scoring crown.*

cident against Cy Denneny. The charges were rejected by the league and in Montreal's next game against Ottawa, Cleghorn charged Lionel Hitchman into the boards and earned a one-game suspension.

Ottawa's Denneny won the scoring crown with 22 goals despite a bizarre experience near the end of the season. The Ottawa club was on its way to Montreal for a game when the team train became snowbound. The Senators were stuck all night and Denneny, scrounging about for some food, somehow fell down a well. Luckily he emerged without injury. The game, of course, had to be postponed.

Georges Vezina of Montreal led the goalies with a 2.0 average and three shutouts, barely edging Clint Benedict. Ottawa took the regular-season title but Montreal beat the Senators in the total-goals playoff, 5–2, with a newcomer, Howie Morenz, starring.

In the PCHA, Seattle dropped eight straight games but came out of the slump and managed to win the regular-season crown. Mickey MacKay of Vancouver led the scorers with 23 goals and teammate Hugh Lehman was the top goalie with a 2.7 average for the 30-game season.

Calgary took the Western title and Bill Cook of Saskatoon was the scoring champ with 26 goals. Regina's Red McCusker had a 2.2 average, best among the goaltenders.

Vancouver eliminated Seattle in the PCHA playoff and Calgary ousted Regina in the Western series. Then Calgary earned a bye into the Stanley Cup finals by beating Vancouver in the three-game series before both teams came east to face Montreal.

The Canadiens whipped Vancouver, 3–2 and 2–1, in the semifinals and then defeated Calgary for the Cup, winning 6–1 and 3–0.

# 1923–24

## FINAL STANDINGS

| | W | L | T | PTS | GF | GA |
|---|---|---|---|---|---|---|
| Ottawa | 16 | 8 | 0 | 32 | 74 | 54 |
| Montreal C. | 13 | 11 | 0 | 26 | 59 | 48 |
| Toronto | 10 | 14 | 0 | 20 | 59 | 85 |
| Hamilton | 9 | 15 | 0 | 18 | 63 | 68 |

Montreal defeated Ottawa in playoffs and won regular-season championship.

| LEADING SCORERS | G | A | PTS |
|---|---|---|---|
| Denneny, Ottawa | 22 | 1 | 23 |
| B. Boucher, Montreal C. | 16 | 6 | 22 |
| Joliat, Montreal C. | 15 | 5 | 20 |
| Dye, Toronto | 17 | 2 | 19 |
| G. Boucher, Ottawa | 14 | 5 | 19 |
| Burch, Hamilton | 16 | 2 | 18 |
| Clancy, Ottawa | 9 | 8 | 17 |
| Morenz, Montreal C. | 13 | 3 | 16 |
| Adams, Toronto | 13 | 3 | 16 |
| Noble, Toronto | 12 | 3 | 15 |

◄ *Frank Nighbor of Ottawa won the NHL's first Hart Trophy as the Most Valuable Player in 1923-24.*

# 2

# THE YANKS ARE COMING
# 1924-1929

By 1924, the four-team National Hockey League had taken hold and fans were attracted to games in ever larger numbers. Hockey's popularity had grown to the point where NHL brass was seriously considering expansion into the United States. The Pacific Coast Hockey Association had been successfully operating American franchises at Seattle and Portland and there was reason to believe that a team in the eastern U.S. would enjoy similar success.

There was no problem in finding a market for expanding the prospering league. Bids for franchises came from New York, Boston, Philadelphia and Pittsburgh. And Montreal interests were seeking a second team for that city. The league decided to move slowly on expansion, a policy that would continue for many years.

The groundwork for adding new teams was laid in 1924 when Thomas J. Duggan was granted options to operate two United States franchises. Duggan interested Boston sportsman Charles Adams and on October 12, 1924, final plans were made at Montreal's Windsor Hotel.

◀ *Reg Noble had to trade in his Toronto St. Pats' jersey for a Montreal Maroons' model.*

Adams would operate the Boston team with Art Ross, an NHL referee, chosen to manage the club. Donat Raymond and Thomas Strachan were granted a second Montreal franchise and New York would get a team for the 1926 season. The price for a new franchise was $15,000.

The league was clearly moving forward and the best proof of that was to look at the stars. Men like Newsy Lalonde and Joe Malone, who had come to the NHL as established players, were gone and in their place was a new breed—players like Aurel Joliat and Howie Morenz, who started their professional careers in the NHL and established themselves as first-line players in that league.

But with expansion came problems for the National Hockey League and its struggle to survive was to undergo a severe test in its very first year of international operation.

## 1924–25

With the addition of the new Boston team called the Bruins and the Montreal Maroons, the NHL also expanded its schedule, upping the total from 24 to

30 games. And this change was to cause a minor rebellion and a player strike late in the season.

Hamilton's Red Green, one of three players who scored five goals in a single game this season, was at the center of the squabble. The Tigers had won the regular-season race and under a new playoff plan, the first-place finishers were to meet the winners of a series between the second- and third-place teams.

But Green, acting as a spokesman for the Hamilton players, pointed out that he had signed a two-year contract the season before which called for a 24-game schedule and that now he had already played 30 and was being asked to play even more for the same salary. Green and his teammates wanted $200 each to play against the winner of the semifinal series between Toronto and the Montreal Canadiens.

Frank Calder, the NHL president, refused to yield to the strikers and declared that the semifinal winner would represent the league in the Stanley Cup playoffs. On April 17, the NHL suspended the Hamilton players and fined them $200 each for their action.

The Maroons and Bruins assembled teams composed mostly of amateurs and old pros. Montreal came up with Clint Benedict and Harry Broadbent from Ottawa, Louis Berlinquette from Saskatoon and Reg Noble from Toronto, among others. Alf Skinner, Bernie Morris and Norm Fowler, all lured from the West, turned up with Boston.

The Bruins opened at home with a victory over the Maroons but then dropped 11 straight games. The Maroons inaugurated their new home, the Montreal Forum, by losing to their crosstown rivals, the Canadiens.

Toronto's Babe Dye won the scoring title with 38 goals and 44 points and Georges Vezina of the Canadiens was the top goalie with a 1.9 average and five shutouts. Billy Burch of Hamilton won the Hart Trophy as the league's MVP and a new award donated by Lady Byng, the wife of Canada's governor general, went to Frank Nighbor, the Hart winner the year before. The Lady Byng Trophy was awarded the player who best combined sportsmanship with effective play.

The Canadiens beat Toronto, 3–2 and 2–0, in the playoffs and because of Hamilton's stand, Montreal advanced to the Stanley Cup finals against Victoria, which had joined the WCHL with Vancouver when

Seattle bowed out of the PCHA, leaving that league with just two teams.

Victoria finished third behind Saskatoon and Calgary and knocked both clubs off in the WCHL playoffs, with Jack Walker starring. Victoria defeated Montreal in the first two playoff games as Walker scored four goals. The Canadiens won the third game and then Walker set up two goals by Frank Fredrickson that gave the Westerners the fourth game and the Cup.

## 1924–25

### FINAL STANDINGS

|  | W | L | T | PTS | GF | GA |
|---|---|---|---|---|---|---|
| Hamilton | 19 | 10 | 1 | 39 | 90 | 60 |
| Toronto | 19 | 11 | 0 | 38 | 90 | 84 |
| Montreal C. | 17 | 11 | 2 | 36 | 93 | 56 |
| Ottawa | 17 | 12 | 1 | 35 | 83 | 66 |
| Montreal M. | 9 | 19 | 2 | 20 | 45 | 65 |
| Boston | 6 | 24 | 0 | 12 | 49 | 119 |

Montreal Canadiens defeated Toronto and Hamilton in playoffs and won the regular-season title.

| LEADING SCORERS | G | A | PTS |
|---|---|---|---|
| Dye, Toronto | 38 | 6 | 44 |
| Denneny, Ottawa | 27 | 15 | 42 |
| Joliat, Montreal C. | 29 | 11 | 40 |
| Morenz, Montreal C. | 27 | 7 | 34 |
| B. Boucher, Montreal C. | 18 | 13 | 31 |
| Adams, Toronto | 21 | 8 | 29 |
| Burch, Hamilton | 20 | 4 | 24 |
| R. Green, Hamilton | 19 | 4 | 23 |
| Day, Toronto | 10 | 12 | 22 |
| Herberts, Boston | 17 | 5 | 22 |

## 1925–26

The Hamilton club was sold to a New York group which paid $75,000 for the franchise. The team was renamed the Americans and rented a new sports palace, Madison Square Garden, for its home ice.

The Amerks drew 17,000 fans on opening night in the Garden and big-league hockey became an instant success in New York.

A seventh team was added to the circuit with Odie Cleghorn, the long-time Canadiens' star, named to the NHL Board of Governors to represent the new team, the Pittsburgh Pirates.

Cleghorn would also serve as playing-manager of the Pirates. The team, made up essentially of

*Albert (Battleship) Leduc, a Canadiens' defenseman, scored against the New York Americans on the opening night of a new Madison Square Garden in 1925.*

players from the United States Amateur League, fared remarkably well, with Cleghorn's rapid line changes always keeping fresh legs on the ice.

Pittsburgh spoiled the home opener of the Canadiens with a 1–0 victory and Montreal lost more than just a hockey game in that one. Midway through the game, the Canadiens' great goalie, Georges Vezina, collapsed on the ice from a high fever. Vezina, who had never missed a game in 15 years with the Canadiens, was suffering from tuberculosis and died four months later.

There were new stars around the league. Ottawa's Alex Connell had an amazing 15 shutouts and 1.2 goals-against average in 36 games and the Maroons introduced Nels Stewart, who played both center and defense, and won the scoring title with 34 goals in his rookie season. Stewart also captured the Hart Trophy and Frank Nighbor took the Lady Byng Trophy for the second consecutive year.

Ottawa won the regular-season title with two of the league's newest teams, the Maroons and the Pirates, finishing second and third. Boston was fourth and the New York Americans fifth, leaving the bottom two spots to Toronto and the Canadiens.

The Maroons eliminated Pittsburgh in the two-game, total-goals playoff, 6–4, and then whipped champion Ottawa as Clint Benedict shut out his former teammates, 1–0, in the final game.

In the West, the troubles of the old PCHA seemed to spread to the WCHL. Regina's franchise was shifted to Portland and the name Canada was dropped from the league's title, making it the Western Hockey League.

Bill Cook of Saskatoon and Dick Irvin of Portland tied for the scoring lead with 31 goals apiece and a youngster named Eddie Shore made quite a name for himself on defense with Edmonton, which edged Saskatoon for the regular-season title. Third-place Victoria eliminated Saskatoon and Edmonton in the playoffs and advanced to the Stanley Cup finals against the Montreal Maroons.

Nels Stewart and Clint Benedict dominated the final series as the Maroons captured the Cup. Stewart scored six goals in four games and Benedict shut out the Westerners three times.

The 1926 series was to mark the last time any league other than the NHL competed for the Stanley Cup. The floundering WHL folded its tent. Its players drifted east to the still-expanding National League,

*Rookie Nels Stewart of the Montreal Maroons won the scoring championship and MVP trophy in 1925-26.*

which was getting ready to add three more American teams.

## 1925–26

### FINAL STANDINGS

|            | W  | L  | T | PTS | GF | GA  |
|------------|----|----|---|-----|----|-----|
| Ottawa     | 24 | 8  | 4 | 52  | 77 | 42  |
| Montreal M.| 20 | 11 | 5 | 45  | 91 | 73  |
| Pittsburgh | 19 | 16 | 1 | 39  | 82 | 70  |
| Boston     | 17 | 15 | 4 | 38  | 92 | 85  |
| New York A.| 12 | 20 | 4 | 28  | 68 | 89  |
| Toronto    | 12 | 21 | 3 | 27  | 92 | 114 |
| Montreal C.| 11 | 24 | 1 | 23  | 79 | 108 |

### LEADING SCORERS

|                      | G  | A  | PTS |
|----------------------|----|----|-----|
| Stewart, Montreal M. | 34 | 8  | 42  |
| Denneny, Ottawa      | 24 | 12 | 36  |
| Herberts, Boston     | 26 | 5  | 31  |
| Cooper, Boston       | 28 | 3  | 31  |
| Morenz, Montreal C.  | 23 | 3  | 26  |
| Joliat, Montreal C.  | 17 | 9  | 26  |
| Adams, Toronto       | 21 | 5  | 26  |
| Burch, New York A.   | 22 | 3  | 25  |
| Smith, Ottawa        | 16 | 9  | 25  |
| Nighbor, Ottawa      | 12 | 13 | 25  |

## 1926–27

Writers called this era the Golden Age of Sports, and the NHL was about to make itself a solid part of the scene which included baseball's Babe Ruth, tennis' Bill Tilden, football's Red Grange, boxing's Jack Dempsey and golf's Bobby Jones.

The success of the New York Americans at Madison Square Garden inspired the Garden owners to seek a franchise of their own, and they were awarded one. The team, called the Rangers, was one of three new clubs added to the NHL, the others being the Detroit Cougars and the Chicago Black Hawks. With the Western and Pacific Coast Leagues now defunct, there were plenty of players available.

The 10-team league was split into two divisions, the American and the Canadian. The four Canadian teams—Ottawa, Toronto, the Montreal Maroons and Montreal Canadiens—and New York's Americans comprised the Canadian Division. The American Division listed the three new teams—the Rangers, Detroit and Chicago—along with Pittsburgh and Boston.

The players came from professional as well as amateur ranks. A package deal was arranged with

the Western loop in which whole rosters of players became available for a total of $25,000 per club.

Bill Cook and his brother Bun both wound up in New York, where Conn Smythe was assembling the Rangers. Eddie Shore went to Boston, where he would become perhaps the greatest defenseman in NHL history. Detroit came up with Frank Foyston and Frank Fredrickson while Dick Irvin and Mickey MacKay landed in Chicago.

Smythe had a falling out with the Garden management and was dismissed before the Rangers ever played a game. Lester Patrick was brought in from the West to run the New York team. Smythe went home to his native Toronto, determined to get even with the New York brass. The last-place St. Pats were in trouble and up for sale and Smythe raised $160,000 and made the deal. The club's name was changed to the Maple Leafs and flourished under Smythe's shrewd control.

In Montreal, the owners of the Canadiens donated a trophy to the league in the memory of Georges Vezina to be awarded annually to the goaltender on the team which was the least-scored-upon club in the league. George Hainsworth, Vezina's successor with the Canadiens, won the first one.

Howie Morenz took the Canadian Division scoring title with 32 points, including 25 goals. Bill Cook of the Rangers scored 33 goals and won the American Division scoring race with 37 points. Herb Gardiner of the Canadiens was named the MVP and Hart Trophy winner while Billy Burch of the New York Americans got the Lady Byng.

Ottawa won the Canadian Division and the Rangers took the American Division regular-season titles. Six teams qualified for the Stanley Cup playoffs with Ottawa and Boston reaching the finals and the Senators winning in four games.

## 1926–27

### FINAL STANDINGS

#### Canadian Division

|  | W | L | T | PTS | GF | GA |
|---|---|---|---|---|---|---|
| Ottawa | 30 | 10 | 4 | 64 | 86 | 69 |
| Montreal C. | 28 | 14 | 2 | 58 | 99 | 67 |
| Montreal M. | 20 | 20 | 4 | 44 | 71 | 68 |
| New York A. | 17 | 25 | 2 | 36 | 82 | 91 |
| Toronto | 15 | 24 | 5 | 35 | 79 | 94 |

#### American Division

|  | W | L | T | PTS | GF | GA |
|---|---|---|---|---|---|---|
| New York R. | 25 | 13 | 6 | 56 | 95 | 72 |
| Boston | 21 | 20 | 3 | 45 | 97 | 89 |
| Chicago | 19 | 22 | 3 | 41 | 115 | 116 |
| Pittsburgh | 15 | 26 | 3 | 33 | 79 | 108 |
| Detroit | 12 | 28 | 4 | 28 | 76 | 105 |

Duncan (Mickey) MacKay came from Vancouver to join the Chicago Black Hawks in 1926-27.

| LEADING SCORERS | G | A | PTS |
|---|---|---|---|
| Bill Cook, New York R. | 33 | 4 | 37 |
| Irvin, Chicago | 18 | 18 | 36 |
| Morenz, Montreal C. | 25 | 7 | 32 |
| Frederickson, Detroit-Boston | 18 | 13 | 31 |
| Dye, Chicago | 25 | 5 | 30 |
| Bailey, Toronto | 15 | 13 | 28 |
| Boucher, New York R. | 13 | 15 | 28 |
| Burch, New York A. | 19 | 8 | 27 |
| Oliver, Boston | 18 | 6 | 24 |
| Keats, Boston-Detroit | 16 | 8 | 24 |

# 1927–28

There have been many hexes in sports history but none so mysterious as the eerie Curse of Muldoon which shackled the Chicago Black Hawks for 40 years. It was in 1927 that Pete Muldoon administered it.

Muldoon had been brought in to coach the new Chicago team when the NHL added three franchises in 1926. The team had done moderately well, winning 19 games in a 44-game season and finishing third to qualify for the playoffs. They were the highest-scoring team in the league with 115 goals but also allowed more goals than anyone else, 116.

So Muldoon was understandably distressed when Hawks' owner Fred McLaughlin dismissed him at the start of the 1927–28 season. In fact, Muldoon was said to be so distressed, he placed his curse on McLaughin and the Hawks. As comeuppance for his unjust dismissal, Muldoon told McLaughlin, Chicago would never win an NHL title.

Sour grapes one might say, but it's a fact that for 40 years the Hawks never did win the regular-season championship and only when they finally did make it was the curse wiped out.

Muldoon's successors didn't do nearly as well with the Hawks as he had done in their first season. Barney Stanley and Hugh Lehman split the job and Chicago managed only seven victories all season, finishing a dismal last in the American Division race won by Boston. The Canadiens finished first in the Canadian Division.

The individual stars were Hart Trophy winner Howie Morenz, the scoring champ with 33 goals and

*The great Ranger line: (left to right) Bill Cook, Frank Boucher and Bun Cook.*

*Ottawa goalie Alex Connell set an NHL record by registering six consecutive shutouts in 1927-28.*

51 total points, and Frank Boucher of the Rangers, who led the American Division with 35 points and won the Lady Byng Trophy.

George Hainsworth again won the goalie's Vezina Trophy but the most outstanding goaltending job was turned in by Alex Connell of Ottawa, who set a record with six straight shutouts and 446 minutes, nine seconds of scoreless hockey. Connell became the center of contention the night Lester Patrick went in to play goal.

The Rangers had advanced to the Stanley Cup final by eliminating Pittsburgh and Boston while the Montreal Maroons knocked off Ottawa and the Canadiens. The Maroons won the first game of the finals, 2–0.

Early in the second period of the next game, Nels Stewart fired a shot that caught Ranger goalie Lorne Chabot in the eye. Chabot could not continue and Patrick asked Eddie Gerard, manager of the Maroons, for permission to use Ottawa's Connell, who was in the stands watching the game, as a replacement.

Gerard refused and when Patrick asked permission to use a minor leaguer who was in the stands,

Gerard again refused. Patrick, seething, returned to the Ranger dressing room to tell his club what had happened.

"What do we do now?" he asked.

"How about you playing goal?" suggested Frank Boucher, half-kidding, half-serious.

Patrick, 44, had retired as a player several years earlier. But he mulled over Boucher's suggestion and said, "Okay, I'll do it."

The Rangers protected Lester like a piece of fine china. Patrick made 18 saves, allowed one goal and New York won the game in overtime.

After losing the next game, New York came back to win the final two games and the Stanley Cup.

# 1927–28

## FINAL STANDINGS

### Canadian Division

|  | W | L | T | PTS | GF | GA |
|---|---|---|---|---|---|---|
| Montreal C. | 26 | 11 | 7 | 59 | 116 | 48 |
| Montreal M. | 24 | 14 | 6 | 54 | 96 | 77 |
| Ottawa | 20 | 14 | 10 | 50 | 78 | 57 |
| Toronto | 18 | 18 | 8 | 44 | 89 | 88 |
| New York A. | 11 | 27 | 6 | 28 | 63 | 128 |

### American Division

|  | W | L | T | PTS | GF | GA |
|---|---|---|---|---|---|---|
| Boston | 20 | 13 | 11 | 51 | 77 | 70 |
| New York R. | 19 | 16 | 9 | 47 | 97 | 79 |
| Pittsburgh | 19 | 17 | 8 | 46 | 67 | 76 |
| Detroit | 19 | 19 | 6 | 44 | 88 | 79 |
| Chicago | 7 | 34 | 3 | 17 | 68 | 134 |

## LEADING SCORERS

|  | G | A | PTS |
|---|---|---|---|
| Morenz, Montreal C. | 33 | 18 | 51 |
| Joliat, Montreal C. | 28 | 11 | 39 |
| Boucher, New York R. | 23 | 12 | 35 |
| Hay, Detroit | 22 | 13 | 35 |
| Stewart, Montreal M. | 27 | 7 | 34 |
| Gagne, Montreal C. | 20 | 10 | 30 |
| Bun Cook, New York R. | 14 | 14 | 28 |
| Carson, Toronto | 20 | 6 | 26 |
| Finnigan, Ottawa | 20 | 5 | 25 |
| Bill Cook, New York R. | 18 | 6 | 24 |
| Keats, Chicago-Detroit | 14 | 10 | 24 |

# 1928–29

A rule designed to hype hockey offenses was introduced in 1928, but instead it became the year of the goalie around the NHL. The new rule allowed forward passing in all three zones on the ice—that is, the defensive zone, the area between blue lines, and the offensive zone. There was still no red line in the game and the ice was divided by only the two blue lines.

Previously, forward passing was allowed only in a team's defensive zone or center ice, but never in the offensive area. Eventually, the rule change would affect the game and open play up, but not this season.

In Montreal, little George Hainsworth almost obliterated the memory of the great Georges Vezina. In 44 games, goaltender Hainsworth recorded an incredible 22 shutouts.

Hainsworth allowed 43 goals all year—an average of less than one per game. The highest scoring team in the league was Boston, winner of the American Division race. The Bruins scored a total of 89 goals—a shade over two per game.

One of Hainsworth's shutouts came against Ottawa on December 22, 1928, a special date for Montreal and for hockey. It marked the first NHL broadcast of a Montreal game and started an era that brought hockey into the home regularly. Arthur Dupont, founder of radio station CJAD, handled the French broadcast and columnist Elmer Ferguson did the English.

"The hockey people looked upon radio with a great deal of suspicion," noted Dupont. "They feared that if stories of the games came into the home without cost, it would ruin the attendance. So we were limited to a brief description of the third period and afterwards a summary of the entire game."

As it developed, of course, broadcasts increased hockey interest and now the radio-television industry plays a major role in the sport.

With the goalies dominating play, Toronto's Ace Bailey captured the scoring crown with 32 points—22 of them on goals. Carson Cooper of Detroit was the top scorer in the American Division with 18 goals and 27 points.

Hainsworth easily won the Vezina Trophy, but another goalie, Roy Worters of the New York Americans, took the Hart as MVP. The Rangers' Frank Boucher won the Lady Byng.

A new playoff arrangement matched the first-place, second-place and third-place teams in each division against each other. The winners of the series between second-place teams and the series between the third-place finishers clashed in the semifinal with that winner advancing to the Stanley

# BOSTON BRUINS
## WORLD CHAMPIONS
### Stanley Cup Winners
#### AMERICAN DIVISION CHAMPIONS · PRINCE OF WALES TROPHY WINNERS
#### SEASON 1928-29

"DUTCH" KLEIN   "BILL" CARSON   GEO. OWEN   HARRY OLIVER   WIN GREEN, *trainer*   MYLES LANE   NORMAN "DUTCH" GAINOR   AUBREY "DIT" CLAPPER
PERCY GALBRAITH   EDDIE SHORE   "MICKEY" McKAY   ART ROSS, *mgr.*   FRED HITCHMAN   CY DENNENY   RALPH "COONEY" WEILAND
"TINY" THOMPSON

### ★ FINAL STANDING N.H.L., 1928-29
#### AMERICAN DIVISION

|  | P | W | L | D | Pts. | Goals For | Agst. |
|---|---|---|---|---|---|---|---|
| BOSTON | 44 | 26 | 13 | 5 | 57 | 89 | 52 |
| N.Y. RANGERS | 44 | 21 | 13 | 10 | 52 | 72 | 65 |
| DETROIT | 44 | 19 | 16 | 9 | 47 | 72 | 63 |
| PITTSBURGH | 44 | 9 | 27 | 8 | 26 | 46 | 80 |
| CHICAGO | 44 | 7 | 29 | 8 | 22 | 33 | 85 |

### *Playoffs*.
#### — N.H.L. CHAMPIONSHIP —
##### SERIES "A"
MARCH 19 .. BOSTON 1, CANADIENS 0
MARCH 21 .. BOSTON 1, CANADIENS 0
MARCH 23 .. BOSTON 3, CANADIENS 2
##### SERIES "B" (2 GAMES - TOTAL GOALS)
MARCH 19 .. N.Y. RANGERS 0, N.Y. AMERICANS 0
MARCH 21 .. N.Y. RANGERS 1, N.Y. AMERICANS 0
##### SERIES "C" (2 GAMES - TOTAL GOALS)
MARCH 19 .. TORONTO 3, DETROIT 1
MARCH 21 .. TORONTO 4, DETROIT 1
##### SERIES "D" (2 OUT OF 3 GAMES)
MARCH 24 .. N.Y. RANGERS 1, TORONTO 0
MARCH 26 .. N.Y. RANGERS 2, TORONTO 1
##### STANLEY CUP (FINAL - 2 OUT OF 3 GAMES)
##### SERIES "E"
MARCH 28 .. BOSTON 2, N.Y. RANGERS 0
MARCH 29 .. BOSTON 2, N.Y. RANGERS 1

### FINAL STANDING N.H.L., 1928-29 ★
#### CANADIAN DIVISION

|  | P | W | L | D | Pts. | Goals For | Agst. |
|---|---|---|---|---|---|---|---|
| CANADIENS | 44 | 22 | 7 | 15 | 59 | 71 | 43 |
| N.Y. AMERICANS | 44 | 19 | 13 | 12 | 50 | 53 | 53 |
| TORONTO | 44 | 21 | 18 | 5 | 47 | 85 | 69 |
| OTTAWA | 44 | 14 | 17 | 13 | 41 | 54 | 67 |
| MONTREAL | 44 | 15 | 20 | 9 | 39 | 67 | 65 |

*Charles F. Adams*, PRESIDENT

*Arthur H. Ross*, VICE PRES. & GEN. MGR.

*Ralph F. Burkard*, TREASURER

*Frank Ryan*, PUBLICITY DIRECTOR

Cup finals against the winner of the series between the two first-place clubs.

Toronto eliminated Detroit in two straight games and the Rangers knocked off the Americans in two straight. Then New York beat Toronto to advance to the finals against Boston, which had eliminated the Canadiens. The Bruins won the Cup in two games as rookie goalie Tiny Thompson turned in his third playoff shutout in five games. Thompson allowed three goals in the five games, a playoff goals-against average of 0.60.

## 1928–29

### FINAL STANDINGS

#### Canadian Division

| | W | L | T | PTS | GF | GA |
|---|---|---|---|---|---|---|
| Montreal C. | 22 | 7 | 15 | 59 | 71 | 43 |
| New York A. | 19 | 13 | 12 | 50 | 53 | 53 |
| Toronto | 21 | 18 | 5 | 47 | 85 | 69 |
| Ottawa | 14 | 17 | 13 | 41 | 54 | 67 |
| Montreal M. | 15 | 20 | 9 | 39 | 67 | 65 |

#### American Division

| | W | L | T | PTS | GF | GA |
|---|---|---|---|---|---|---|
| Boston | 26 | 13 | 5 | 57 | 89 | 52 |
| New York R. | 21 | 13 | 10 | 52 | 72 | 65 |
| Detroit | 19 | 16 | 9 | 47 | 72 | 63 |
| Pittsburgh | 9 | 27 | 8 | 26 | 46 | 80 |
| Chicago | 7 | 29 | 8 | 22 | 33 | 85 |

### LEADING SCORERS

| | G | A | PTS |
|---|---|---|---|
| Bailey, Toronto | 22 | 10 | 32 |
| Stewart, Montreal M. | 21 | 8 | 29 |
| Cooper, Detroit | 18 | 9 | 27 |
| Morenz, Montreal C. | 17 | 10 | 27 |
| Blair, Toronto | 12 | 15 | 27 |
| Boucher, New York R. | 10 | 16 | 26 |
| Oliver, Boston | 17 | 6 | 23 |
| Bill Cook, New York R. | 15 | 8 | 23 |
| Ward, Montreal M. | 14 | 8 | 22 |
| Finnigan, Ottawa | 15 | 4 | 19 |

◄ *Ace Bailey of Toronto took scoring honors in 1928-29.*

# A NEW WORLD OF OFFENSE 1929-1942

The NHL had taken a firm hold in the 1920s, expanding from four teams to 10 and emerging as the sport's universally recognized major league. But in the '30s, problems would arise. There was the American Depression and the shock waves traveled right through the Canadian sport which had franchises in five United States cities. And there was the complaint that hockey was too defensive a game . . . that the offenses were stymied.

Lester Patrick, boss of the New York Rangers, agreed with the detractors to some extent.

"I believe in keeping the game wide open," said Patrick at the height of the debate over whether to remove all restrictions on forward passing. "Our followers are entitled to action . . . not for a few brief moments, but for three full 20-minute periods of a game.

"The open style of play calls for better stickhandling and speedier skating. What better system could the coaches and managers adopt to preserve and further popularize the fastest game in the world."

The NHL eventually went along with Patrick's

◄ *The Montreal Maroons' Clint Benedict: Hockey's first masked goalie.*

ideas and, predictably, the game opened up considerably. The economic problems, however, caused several club shifts and a couple of franchise casualties.

But stickhandling and speed, the two qualities Patrick talked about, combined to give hockey a loyal core of fans that grew and grew, despite the Depression. The sport had its rough moments, it is true, but the game's brass, from NHL President Frank Calder on down, pulled it through the periods of crisis.

## 1929-30

It would take more than a Depression to stop Conn Smythe, who was determined to build the Toronto Maple Leafs into an NHL power, if for no other reason than to prove to Madison Square Garden's owners just how valuable a man they had lost when they fired him three years before.

Smythe needed a bigger arena for his club but raising the money to build one was a problem. So Smythe solved the financial question by turning to the trade unions and builders for help. As partial payment of wages, the workmen would receive stock in Maple Leaf Gardens.

*Chicago's Johnny Gottselig chases puck behind net in 1929 match vs. Montreal Maroons.*

The solution worked out beautifully for all parties. Smythe got his new arena and his shareholders had a part in what would become a highly successful sports and entertainment center.

But the Maple Leafs spent their next-to-last season in the old Arena Gardens and it was less than a total success. They finished fourth in the Canadian Division even though they introduced a good-looking rookie named Charlie Conacher, who was destined for NHL stardom.

The new rules allowing passing in all three zones added scoring punch throughout the league and Boston's Cooney Weiland was the leading point-maker with 73, including 43 goals. The Bruins, with Weiland setting the pace, were the highest scoring team in the league and their goalie, Tiny Thompson, allowed the fewest goals. The combination gave Boston a fantastic 38 victories in 44 games, including one record stretch of 14 straight victories. Naturally, the Bruins won the American Division title.

Hec Kilrea of Ottawa was the leading scorer in the Canadian Division with 58 points, three more

than Nels Stewart of the Montreal Maroons, who won the Hart Trophy as MVP. Tiny Thompson broke George Hainsworth's three-year hold on the Vezina Trophy and Frank Boucher took the Lady Byng again.

While the Bruins won their division crown by 30 points, Ottawa and the two Montreal teams staged a three-way battle for Canadian Division honors. The Maroons and Canadiens both finished with 51 points and Ottawa had 50. The Maroons were recognized as the first-place team because they had more victories (23) than the Canadiens (21).

That was a break for the Canadiens because it meant the Maroons would have to face Boston's powerhouse in the opening Stanley Cup series. Sure enough, the Bruins eliminated the Maroons in four games while the Canadiens got past Chicago in the two-game, total-goals playoff. The Rangers eliminated Ottawa but then the Canadiens took the Rangers and stunned the Bruins, winning the Cup finale in two straight games.

Clint Benedict, the Maroons' great goalie, made hockey history by using the first face mask ever that season. It happened after Howie Morenz of the Canadiens had broken Benedict's nose with a shot. Benedict didn't stay with the protection, however, and it would be almost three decades before a goalie would try a mask again.

## 1929–30

### FINAL STANDINGS

#### Canadian Division

| | W | L | T | PTS | GF | GA |
|---|---|---|---|---|---|---|
| Montreal M. | 23 | 16 | 5 | 51 | 141 | 114 |
| Montreal C. | 21 | 14 | 9 | 51 | 142 | 114 |
| Ottawa | 21 | 15 | 8 | 50 | 138 | 118 |
| Toronto | 17 | 21 | 6 | 40 | 116 | 124 |
| New York A. | 14 | 25 | 5 | 33 | 113 | 161 |

#### American Division

| | W | L | T | PTS | GF | GA |
|---|---|---|---|---|---|---|
| Boston | 38 | 5 | 1 | 77 | 179 | 98 |
| Chicago | 21 | 18 | 5 | 47 | 117 | 111 |
| New York R. | 17 | 17 | 10 | 44 | 136 | 143 |
| Detroit | 14 | 24 | 6 | 34 | 117 | 133 |
| Pittsburgh | 5 | 36 | 3 | 13 | 102 | 185 |

### LEADING SCORERS

| | G | A | PTS |
|---|---|---|---|
| Weiland, Boston | 43 | 30 | 73 |
| Boucher, New York R. | 26 | 36 | 62 |
| Clapper, Boston | 41 | 20 | 61 |
| Bill Cook, New York R. | 29 | 30 | 59 |
| Kilrea, Ottawa | 36 | 22 | 58 |
| Stewart, Montreal M. | 39 | 16 | 55 |
| Morenz, Montreal C. | 40 | 10 | 50 |
| Himes, New York A. | 28 | 22 | 50 |
| Lamb, Ottawa | 29 | 20 | 49 |
| Gainor, Boston | 18 | 31 | 49 |

*The 1929-30 scoring title went to Ralph (Cooney) Weiland of Boston.*

## 1930–31

The saga of how he financed Maple Leaf Gardens proved how determined Conn Smythe could be. In 1930, he decided that one of the things his Maple Leafs needed for improvement was a player of King Clancy's ability.

*Roy Worters of the Amerks was the 1930-31 Vezina Trophy winner.*

Smythe asked how much it would take to get Clancy away from Ottawa. A couple of players and cash . . . say about $35,000 . . . he was told.

The players Smythe had. The cash was another story. He had most of his assets tied up in the construction of the Leafs' new home. But if $35,000 was what he needed to get Clancy, Smythe decided he'd come up with it.

He raised some capital from friends, giving himself a little room to maneuver. Then he bet the bundle on a longshot horse—his own Rare Jewel. Naturally, the horse won and Smythe had the price for Clancy.

Smythe's wheeling and dealing was typical of the problems of Depression-burdened owners. The Pittsburgh club was forced to move to Philadelphia because of poor attendance. The Pirates changed their name to the Quakers but were doomed anyway. They lasted just that season in Philadelphia.

In Detroit, the club changed its nickname from the Cougars to the Falcons in an effort to lift sagging interest. But with money in short supply, especially in the automobile capital, there was little left over to spend on watching hockey games.

Another step to inject interest around the league was the introduction of an All-Star team. The first squad selected was a study in immortals. The forward line included Howie Morenz of the Canadiens

The Detroit Falcons' Ebbie Goodfellow led the
American Division with 48 points in 1930-31.

Herb Drury was a center for the Quakers, who
lasted just the 1930-31 season in Philadelphia.

at center, his linemate Aurel Joliat at left wing and Bill Cook of the New York Rangers at right wing. The defensemen were Boston's Eddie Shore and King Clancy of Toronto. Charlie Gardiner of Chicago was picked as the goalie.

Morenz led the league in scoring with 28 goals and 51 points and won the Hart Trophy as the MVP. Frank Boucher took his fourth straight Lady Byng and Roy Worters of the New York Americans edged out Gardiner for the Vezina Trophy. Detroit's Ebbie Goodfellow led the American Division scorers with 48 points.

In the playoffs, division champs Boston and the Montreal Canadiens went five games before the Canadiens won. Three of the games went into overtime. Chicago eliminated Toronto and then whipped the Rangers, who had knocked off the Maroons.

In the final round, the Canadiens won their second straight Cup, coming from behind to beat the Black Hawks in the five-game playoffs.

Just as the Pittsburgh-Philadelphia franchise was in trouble in the American Division, the Canadian Division's Ottawa team had fallen on lean days. The Senators won just 10 games, finished in last place and requested and were granted a one-year leave of absence from the league.

## 1930–31

### FINAL STANDINGS

#### Canadian Division

| | W | L | T | PTS | GF | GA |
|---|---|---|---|---|---|---|
| Montreal C. | 26 | 10 | 8 | 60 | 129 | 89 |
| Toronto | 22 | 13 | 9 | 53 | 118 | 99 |
| Montreal M. | 20 | 18 | 6 | 46 | 105 | 106 |
| New York A. | 18 | 16 | 10 | 46 | 76 | 74 |
| Ottawa | 10 | 30 | 4 | 24 | 91 | 142 |

#### American Division

| | W | L | T | PTS | GF | GA |
|---|---|---|---|---|---|---|
| Boston | 28 | 10 | 6 | 62 | 143 | 90 |
| Chicago | 24 | 17 | 3 | 51 | 108 | 78 |
| New York R. | 19 | 16 | 9 | 47 | 106 | 87 |
| Detroit | 16 | 21 | 7 | 39 | 102 | 105 |
| Philadelphia | 4 | 36 | 4 | 12 | 76 | 184 |

### LEADING SCORERS

| | G | A | PTS |
|---|---|---|---|
| Morenz, Montreal C. | 28 | 23 | 51 |
| Goodfellow, Detroit | 25 | 23 | 48 |
| Conacher, Toronto | 31 | 12 | 43 |
| Bill Cook, New York R. | 30 | 12 | 42 |
| Bailey, Toronto | 23 | 19 | 42 |
| Primeau, Toronto | 9 | 32 | 41 |
| Stewart, Montreal M. | 25 | 14 | 39 |
| Boucher, New York R. | 12 | 27 | 39 |
| Weiland, Boston | 25 | 13 | 38 |
| Bun Cook, New York R. | 18 | 17 | 35 |
| Joliat, Montreal C. | 13 | 22 | 35 |

## 1931–32

The departure of Ottawa and Philadelphia left the NHL with eight clubs, four in each division. The schedule was increased to 48 games per club, possibly in an effort to increase team income during the dreary Depression days.

It was a gala night in Toronto on November 12 when Conn Smythe proudly unveiled his new Maple Leaf Gardens. A crowd of 13,542 packed the arena for the game between Toronto and Chicago. But the Black Hawks, who had never won a game in Toronto before, spoiled the party by upsetting the Leafs, 3–1.

*Toronto's Joe Primeau ended Frank Boucher's hold on the Lady Byng Trophy in 1931-32.*

The anger that burned within Smythe against New York and the Ranger organization could not be extinguished until he built the Leafs into a powerhouse. This was to be the year for him to get even, although it didn't start out that way. Toronto slumped into last place after one month and Smythe hired Dick Irvin to replace Art Duncan as coach. Irvin had been fired by Chicago the year before but when he took over the Leafs, they acted like a brand-new club.

Toronto soared from last to first place with Charlie Conacher, Harvey Jackson and Joe Primeau providing the fire-power. Jackson won the Canadian Division scoring title with 53 points, three more than Primeau. Conacher finished fourth with 48 and only Howie Morenz managed to squeeze his way between the Toronto trio with 49 points.

Morenz won his second straight Hart Trophy as the MVP while Primeau ended Frank Boucher's four-year domination of the Lady Byng award. Charlie Gardiner of Chicago won the Vezina again and was named the All-Star goalie for the second time.

Jackson, a left wing, and Morenz, a center, both made the All-Star team along with right wing Bill Cook of the New York Rangers, whose 34 goals and 48 points led American Division scorers. The defensemen selected were Boston's Eddie Shore and bald-headed Ching Johnson of the Rangers, who delighted in breaking up the rushes of Montreal's Aurel Joliat by sweeping the little guy's cap off his head.

Toronto finished second behind the Canadiens in the Canadian Division while the Rangers won the American Division crown. Now, if only the playoffs worked out properly, Smythe thought, he'd finally have a chance at his revenge.

After Chicago's Charlie Gardiner shut out Toronto in the first game, the Leafs exploded for a 6–1 victory to eliminate the Black Hawks on total goals. The Maroons beat Detroit in the other quarterfinal while, happily for Smythe, the Rangers advanced to the finals by eliminating the Canadiens.

Toronto got past the Maroons in the two-game, total-goals semifinal and now it was the Leafs and the Rangers for the Stanley Cup. Conacher, Primeau, Hap Day and the other Leafs ran wild, beating the Rangers in three straight games and scoring six goals in each of them. The Stanley Cup was the ultimate ornament to adorn Smythe's new Maple Leaf Gardens. Conn's revenge was served!

# 1931–32

## FINAL STANDINGS

### Canadian Division

| | W | L | T | PTS | GF | GA |
|---|---|---|---|---|---|---|
| Montreal C. | 25 | 16 | 7 | 57 | 128 | 111 |
| Toronto | 23 | 18 | 7 | 53 | 155 | 127 |
| Montreal | 19 | 22 | 7 | 45 | 142 | 139 |
| New York A. | 16 | 24 | 8 | 40 | 95 | 142 |

### American Division

| | W | L | T | PTS | GF | GA |
|---|---|---|---|---|---|---|
| New York R. | 23 | 17 | 8 | 54 | 134 | 112 |
| Chicago | 18 | 19 | 11 | 47 | 86 | 101 |
| Detroit | 18 | 20 | 10 | 46 | 95 | 108 |
| Boston | 15 | 21 | 12 | 42 | 122 | 117 |

## LEADING SCORERS

| | G | A | PTS |
|---|---|---|---|
| Jackson, Toronto | 28 | 25 | 53 |
| Primeau, Toronto | 13 | 37 | 50 |
| Morenz, Montreal C. | 24 | 25 | 49 |
| Bill Cook, New York R. | 34 | 14 | 48 |
| Conacher, Toronto | 34 | 14 | 48 |
| Trottier, Montreal M. | 26 | 18 | 44 |
| Smith, Montreal M. | 11 | 33 | 44 |
| Siebert, Montreal M. | 21 | 18 | 39 |
| Clapper, Boston | 17 | 22 | 39 |
| Joliat, Montreal C. | 15 | 24 | 39 |

# 1932–33

In an effort to tighten belts during the height of the Depression, NHL owners decided to put a ceiling of $70,000 on club payrolls with no single player to be paid more than $7,500. That represented a 10 percent slice for most teams and the players staged a small revolution over the move.

There were big-name holdouts all over the league, including Frank Boucher of the Rangers, Reg Noble and Hap Emms of Detroit, the Canadiens' Aurel Joliat, Lorne Chabot of Toronto and Hooley Smith of the Montreal Maroons. President Frank Calder was given permission to suspend the dissidents but eventually all of the holdouts fell into line.

Seat prices were slashed, too. The top price was $3 and fans could get into most arenas for as little as 50 cents.

Ottawa returned to the league after a one-year hiatus with Cy Denneny as its coach. Other great former players also turned up as coaches: Newsy Lalonde with the Canadiens and Jack Adams in Detroit, where the team was about to adopt its third name, the Red Wings. In New York, Colonel John Hammond, who was instrumental in bringing hockey to Madison Square Garden, first with the Americans and then with the Rangers, resigned. As a result,

*A former Canadiens' star, Newsy Lalonde returned to coach his old team in 1932-33.*

coach Lester Patrick took on the added titles of general manager and vice president of the Rangers.

Before the season started, the Rangers sold goalie John Ross Roach to Detroit for $11,000. It was a worthwhile investment for the Cougars-Falcons-Red Wings. Roach was named the All-Star goalie on a team that included Bill Cook and Frank Boucher of the Rangers, and Baldy Northcott of the Montreal Maroons up front, and a defense of Boston's Eddie Shore and the Rangers' Ching Johnson.

Cook took the scoring title with 50 points, 28 of them goals, Boucher reclaimed the Lady Byng and Shore became the first fulltime defenseman to win the Hart Trophy. Boston's Tiny Thompson took the Vezina.

The Bruins and Detroit ended with identical records of 25–15–8 in the American Division with Boston recognized as the champion because the Bruins had scored more goals (124) than the Red Wings (111). Toronto won the Canadian Division race.

In the playoffs, the Maple Leafs eliminated the Bruins in five games. It was one of the most memorable playoff series as four of the games went into overtime and the final one lasted six extra periods.

Detroit eliminated the Montreal Maroons and the Rangers ousted the Canadiens in the quarterfinals. Then New York finished Detroit off and went up against the bone-weary Leafs in the final series.

With Toronto softened up by the prolonged series against Boston, the Rangers had an easy time, winning in four games. The heroes were the Cook brothers, Bill and Bun, and their center, Frank Boucher, all of whom had been signed for New York by Toronto's boss, Conn Smythe.

## 1932–33

### FINAL STANDINGS

| Canadian Division | W | L | T | PTS | GF | GA |
|---|---|---|---|---|---|---|
| Toronto | 24 | 18 | 6 | 54 | 119 | 111 |
| Montreal M. | 22 | 20 | 6 | 50 | 135 | 119 |
| Montreal C. | 18 | 25 | 5 | 41 | 92 | 115 |
| New York A. | 15 | 22 | 11 | 41 | 91 | 118 |
| Ottawa | 11 | 27 | 10 | 32 | 88 | 131 |

| American Division | W | L | T | PTS | GF | GA |
|---|---|---|---|---|---|---|
| Boston | 25 | 15 | 8 | 58 | 124 | 88 |
| Detroit | 25 | 15 | 8 | 58 | 111 | 93 |
| New York R. | 23 | 17 | 8 | 54 | 135 | 107 |
| Chicago | 16 | 20 | 12 | 44 | 88 | 101 |

| LEADING SCORERS | G | A | PTS |
|---|---|---|---|
| Bill Cook, New York R. ................................. | 28 | 22 | 50 |
| Jackson, Toronto ...................................... | 27 | 17 | 44 |
| Northcott, Montreal M. ................................ | 22 | 21 | 43 |
| Smith, Montreal M. .................................... | 20 | 21 | 41 |
| Haynes, Montreal M. .................................. | 16 | 25 | 41 |
| Joliat, Montreal C. ..................................... | 18 | 21 | 39 |
| Barry, Boston .......................................... | 24 | 13 | 37 |
| Bun Cook, New York R. ............................... | 22 | 15 | 37 |
| Stewart, Boston ....................................... | 18 | 18 | 36 |
| Morenz, Montreal C. .................................. | 14 | 21 | 35 |

## 1933–34

Eddie Shore was the epitome of a hockey bad man. He was a no-nonsense guy who was the scourge of the Bruins' blue line—the most feared defenseman in hockey. And in December 1933, Shore was part of one of the most dramatic incidents in the game's history.

The Bruins were at home against Toronto, with the Maple Leafs leading, 1–0, when a pair of quick penalties left Toronto two men short. Dick Irvin sent defensemen King Clancy and Red Horner and forward Ace Bailey out to kill the time.

Bailey, a former scoring champ, was an excellent puckcarrier and stickhandler—just what the Leafs needed with the Bruins enjoying a two-man edge. He won a face-off and dodged Boston skaters, protecting the puck for a full minute before another face-off was called because Ace was not advancing the puck.

Bailey won the second face-off as well, again stickhandled for awhile and finally shot the puck into the Bruins' end, forcing Boston to retreat. Shore picked the rubber up and started up ice. Clancy met him and dumped him, regaining the puck for Toronto. As Shore slowly got up, he saw Bailey, still winded from his earlier one-man show, in front of him.

Eddie set sail for the Leaf star, caught him from behind and flipped him with his shoulder. Bailey hit the ice with a dull thud and lay motionless, seriously injured. When Shore grinned at Horner, skating to Bailey's aid, Red decked the Bruin defenseman with an uppercut.

Bailey hovered between life and death for several days with a severe head injury. He finally pulled through but never played hockey again. In February, Maple Leaf Gardens hosted a benefit game for Bailey between Toronto and a team of NHL All-Stars. The meeting at center ice between Bailey and Shore

*Toronto fans stepped out to honor their King Clancy.*

was shrouded in silence until the two embraced. That hug brought a thunderous roar from the crowd and eased the tension that had been building before the meeting.

"I know it was an accident," said Bailey, exonerating Shore.

Toronto's Kid Line—Harvey (Busher) Jackson, Joe Primeau, and Charlie Conacher—was challenging the Cooks and Frank Boucher of the Rangers as the top scoring line in the league. The Toronto unit finished 1–2–3 in scoring in the Canadian Division with Conacher leading the league with 52 points including 32 goals, Primeau scoring 46 points and Jackson 38. Boucher's 44 points led American Division scorers.

Conacher, Primeau and Boucher were named to the NHL All-Star team along with defensemen King Clancy of Toronto and Lionel Conacher, Charlie's brother, of Chicago, and Black Hawk goalie Charlie Gardiner. Aurel Joliat of the Canadiens was the MVP and Boucher, as usual, won the Lady Byng. The Vezina went to Chicago's Gardiner, who starred in the playoffs and led the Hawks to the Stanley Cup.

Toronto finished first in the Canadian Division but lost in the playoffs to Detroit, the American Division pennant winners. Chicago eliminated the Canadiens and then the Montreal Maroons, who had finished off the Rangers.

Chicago took the Stanley Cup from Detroit in four games. Two of them went into double overtime with Gardiner shutting out the Red Wings in the last one.

In the celebration that followed the victory, Chicago's Roger Jenkins wheeled Gardiner through the city's Loop section in a wheelbarrow, never dreaming his buddy would be dead from a brain hemorrhage a scant eight weeks later.

## 1933–34

### FINAL STANDINGS

#### Canadian Division

|  | W | L | T | PTS | GF | GA |
|---|---|---|---|---|---|---|
| Toronto | 26 | 13 | 9 | 61 | 174 | 119 |
| Montreal C. | 22 | 20 | 6 | 50 | 99 | 101 |
| Montreal M. | 19 | 18 | 11 | 49 | 117 | 122 |
| New York A. | 15 | 23 | 10 | 40 | 104 | 132 |
| Ottawa | 13 | 29 | 6 | 32 | 115 | 143 |

#### American Division

|  | W | L | T | PTS | GF | GA |
|---|---|---|---|---|---|---|
| Detroit | 24 | 14 | 10 | 58 | 113 | 98 |
| Chicago | 20 | 17 | 11 | 51 | 88 | 83 |
| New York R. | 21 | 19 | 8 | 50 | 120 | 113 |
| Boston | 18 | 25 | 5 | 41 | 111 | 130 |

### LEADING SCORERS

|  | G | A | PTS |
|---|---|---|---|
| Conacher, Toronto | 32 | 20 | 52 |
| Primeau, Toronto | 14 | 32 | 46 |
| Boucher, New York R. | 14 | 30 | 44 |
| Barry, Boston | 27 | 12 | 39 |
| Dillon, New York R. | 13 | 26 | 39 |
| Stewart, Boston | 21 | 17 | 38 |
| Jackson, Toronto | 20 | 18 | 38 |
| Joliat, Montreal C. | 22 | 15 | 37 |
| Smith, Montreal M. | 18 | 19 | 37 |
| Thompson, Chicago | 20 | 16 | 36 |

## 1934–35

The Ottawa franchise, still floundering after two more last-place finishes, was shifted to St. Louis,

where the team was christened the Eagles. In a shift almost as momentous, the legendary Howie Morenz was dealt to Chicago.

Morenz and Montreal had been synonymous and the great center never acclimated himself to his new team. He finished the season with a mere eight goals, far down in the American Division scoring list. Syd Howe, who split the season between Detroit and St. Louis, led the American Division scorers with 47 points while Charlie Conacher of Toronto and his linemate, Busher Jackson, were 1–2 in Canadian Division scoring. Conacher won the title with 57 points and Jackson finished second with 44.

The penalty shot, long a popular feature of Western League hockey, was introduced in the NHL, which now had several Western figures in its coaching ranks. There was Lester Patrick in New York, Dick Irvin in Toronto, Jack Adams in Detroit and Lester's brother, Frank Patrick, in Boston.

Scotty Bowman, purchased by Detroit along with Howe for $50,000 from St. Louis in midseason, was the first player ever to score on a penalty shot in the NHL. It came against Alex Connell, the Montreal Maroons' great goalie.

A couple of new names made their first appearances on the All-Star team. They were goalie Lorne Chabot, acquired by Chicago from Toronto to replace the deceased Gardiner, and defenseman Earl Seibert of the New York Rangers. Also chosen were Boston's Eddie Shore on defense and a forward line of Charlie Conacher and Busher Jackson from Toronto and Frank Boucher of the Rangers.

Chabot won the Vezina Trophy and Shore took the Hart Trophy. Frank Boucher won the Lady Byng for the seventh time in eight years and was awarded permanent possession of the trophy, which would be replaced by a new one.

Toronto, with the Conacher-Jackson-Joe Primeau "Kid Line" dominating the league, easily won the Canadian Division title while Boston squeezed past Chicago by one point to take the American Division.

In the playoffs, the Maple Leafs dropped the opener to Boston and then beat the Bruins three straight to advance to the Stanley Cup finals. Meanwhile, the Montreal Maroons eliminated Chicago on

*Charlie Conacher of Toronto won the scoring crown in 1934-35 and led the Maple Leafs to the top of the Canadian Division.*

consecutive shutouts by Alex Connell and then knocked off the Rangers, who had topped the Canadiens.

In the final round, it was a matchup of two hot goalies—Connell of the Maroons and George Hainsworth of Toronto, who had allowed Boston just two goals in four games in the opening round. Connell proved to be hotter, giving up only four goals as the Maroons captured the Stanley Cup with three straight victories.

◄ *Ranger Frank Boucher took permanent possession of the original Lady Byng Trophy in 1934-35.*

## 1934–35

### FINAL STANDINGS

*Canadian Division*

| | W | L | T | PTS | GF | GA |
|---|---|---|---|---|---|---|
| Toronto | 30 | 14 | 4 | 64 | 157 | 111 |
| Montreal M. | 24 | 19 | 5 | 53 | 123 | 92 |
| Montreal C. | 19 | 23 | 6 | 44 | 110 | 145 |
| New York A. | 12 | 27 | 9 | 33 | 100 | 142 |
| St. Louis | 11 | 31 | 6 | 28 | 86 | 144 |

*American Division*

| | W | L | T | PTS | GF | GA |
|---|---|---|---|---|---|---|
| Boston | 26 | 16 | 6 | 58 | 129 | 112 |
| Chicago | 26 | 17 | 5 | 57 | 118 | 88 |
| New York R. | 22 | 20 | 6 | 50 | 137 | 139 |
| Detroit | 19 | 22 | 7 | 45 | 127 | 114 |

### LEADING SCORERS

| | G | A | PTS |
|---|---|---|---|
| Conacher, Toronto | 36 | 21 | 57 |
| Howe, Detroit-St. Louis | 22 | 25 | 47 |
| Aurie, Detroit | 17 | 29 | 46 |
| Boucher, New York R. | 13 | 32 | 45 |
| Jackson, Toronto | 22 | 22 | 44 |
| Lewis, Detroit | 16 | 27 | 43 |
| Chapman, New York A. | 9 | 34 | 43 |
| Barry, Boston | 20 | 20 | 40 |
| Schriner, New York A. | 18 | 22 | 40 |
| Stewart, Boston | 21 | 18 | 39 |
| Thompson, Chicago | 16 | 23 | 39 |

## 1935–36

The St. Louis franchise was dissolved only one year after being moved from Ottawa. This reduced the NHL to eight teams, four in each division. The Ea-

gles' players were distributed to other clubs around the league and there were some good ones available. Boston probably came up with the best in Bill Cowley, who developed into a star.

Carl Voss, who had started in the league with the New York Rangers three seasons earlier, continued to move from club to club. Voss had already played with the New York Rangers, Detroit, Ottawa and St. Louis and that season moved on to the New York Americans after the Eagles folded. He would also play for the Montreal Maroons and Chicago Black Hawks before ending his career after six years in the NHL.

The Americans boasted the league's top scorer, second-year man Dave (Sweeney) Schriner, a left wing, who had 45 points, including 19 goals. The leading scorer in the American Division was Detroit's Marty Barry, with 21 goals and a total of 40 points.

Schriner was named to the All-Star team along with Toronto's Charlie Conacher and Hooley Smith of the Montreal Maroons, Boston defensemen Eddie Shore and Babe Siebert and Tiny Thompson, the Bruins' goalie.

Thompson also won the Vezina Trophy and wrote his name in the record book as the first goalie to assist on a scoring play. It happened on a goal by defenseman Siebert, who scored after taking a pass from the goalie.

Eddie Shore won the Hart Trophy, his third MVP

*Defenseman Eddie Shore of the Bruins was MVP in 1935-36.*

◄ *Boston's Tiny Thompson recorded an historic assist in 1935-36.*

award in four years, while Chicago's Doc Romnes took the Lady Byng. The Black Hawks also had the league's hottest rookie, an American-born goalie named Mike Karakas, who stepped in when Lorne Chabot was injured and played so well that the Hawks sold Chabot to the Maroons. Chicago also dealt Howie Morenz to the Rangers, a move that still left the great center homesick for Montreal.

The Montreal Maroons won the Canadian Division race by two points over Toronto while Detroit had an easier time, taking the American Division by six points over Boston. The opening game of the Stanley Cup playoffs between the Maroons and Red Wings was a memorable one.

The goalies, Detroit's Norm Smith and Lorne Chabot of the Maroons, played shutout hockey through the 60-minute regulation game and the scoreless tie lasted through five periods of overtime. Finally, with 3½ minutes remaining in the sixth extra period, Modere (Mud) Bruneteau put a shot past Chabot. The Arena clock read 2:25 A.M. and the goal ended 176 minutes, 30 seconds of futility. It remains the longest game ever played.

The Red Wings went on to win the next two games, eliminating the Maroons. Toronto ousted Boston and then downed the Americans, who had beaten Chicago. Then Detroit took the Maple Leafs in the four-game finale to capture the Stanley Cup.

## 1935–36

### FINAL STANDINGS

#### Canadian Division

| | W | L | T | PTS | GF | GA |
|---|---|---|---|---|---|---|
| Montreal M. | 22 | 16 | 10 | 54 | 114 | 106 |
| Toronto | 23 | 19 | 6 | 52 | 126 | 106 |
| New York A. | 16 | 25 | 7 | 39 | 109 | 122 |
| Montreal C. | 11 | 26 | 11 | 33 | 82 | 123 |

#### American Division

| | W | L | T | PTS | GF | GA |
|---|---|---|---|---|---|---|
| Detroit | 24 | 16 | 8 | 56 | 124 | 103 |
| Boston | 22 | 20 | 6 | 50 | 92 | 83 |
| Chicago | 21 | 19 | 8 | 50 | 93 | 92 |
| New York R. | 19 | 17 | 12 | 50 | 91 | 96 |

### LEADING SCORERS

| | G | A | PTS |
|---|---|---|---|
| Schriner, New York A. | 19 | 26 | 45 |
| Barry, Detroit | 21 | 19 | 40 |
| Thompson, Chicago | 17 | 23 | 40 |
| Thoms, Toronto | 23 | 15 | 38 |
| Conacher, Toronto | 23 | 15 | 38 |
| Smith, Montreal M. | 19 | 19 | 38 |
| Romnes, Chicago | 13 | 25 | 38 |
| Chapman, New York A. | 10 | 28 | 38 |
| Lewis, Detroit | 14 | 23 | 37 |
| Northcott, Montreal M. | 15 | 21 | 36 |

# 1936–37

It was a year for the great lines. Two immortal ones broke up and another one was reunited, but with a tragic outcome.

In New York, the famous Bill Cook-Frank Boucher-Bun Cook unit was finished when the Rangers sold Bun Cook to Boston. The trio had scored more than 1,000 points playing together for the Rangers ever since the team came into the league a decade earlier. In Toronto, Joe Primeau announced his retirement, breaking up the Kid Line he had comprised along with Charlie Conacher and Busher Jackson.

In Montreal, the Canadiens brought Howie Morenz back from his two years of exile in Chicago and New York and no one was happier about the move than the veteran center.

Reunited with his old linemates, Aurel Joliat and Johnny Gagnon, Morenz played inspired hockey. He had scored 20 points at midseason when tragedy struck. Going into a corner after the puck, Morenz got his skates caught in a rut in the ice and snapped a bone in his leg.

The accident and his ability to overcome it weighed heavily on Morenz' mind as he lay in a Montreal hospital. Two months later, on March 8, his heart gave out and he died.

The funeral services were held at center ice in the Montreal Forum and 25,000 fans, many of them in tears, filed past his bier to pay their last respects to one of hockey's truly great stars.

The New York Americans, with owner Bill Dwyer in deep financial trouble, had their franchise taken over by the league. NHL President Frank Calder was to act as advisor to the club.

President Calder also introduced a trophy to be awarded annually to the league's top rookie. The first one went to Toronto's Syl Apps, a pole vaulter at the 1936 Berlin Olympics who turned pro with the Leafs after returning from the Games. Apps finished second in the Canadian Division scoring race with 45 points, one less than Sweeney Schriner of the New York Americans, who captured his second straight scoring crown. Detroit's Marty Barry led American Division scorers with 44 points.

The Red Wings dominated the All-Star team,

*The Hart Trophy was awarded to the Canadiens' Babe Siebert in 1936-37.*

gaining four of the six spots. Detroit's Larry Aurie was named at right wing, Marty Barry at center, Ebbie Goodfellow at one defense post and Norm Smith at goal. Toronto's Busher Jackson at left wing and defenseman Babe Siebert of the Montreal Canadiens were the only non-Red Wings named. Siebert won the Hart Trophy, Barry the Lady Byng and Smith the Vezina.

The Canadiens edged the Montreal Maroons for the Canadian Division title while Detroit won the American Division race. In the playoffs, the Red Wings beat the Canadiens in the first two games, then dropped two straight before winning the decisive fifth game.

The New York Rangers first eliminated Toronto and then the Maroons, who had beaten Boston. In the Stanley Cup finals, Marty Barry and substitute goalie Earl Robertson helped the Red Wings come from behind with two straight victories to capture the five-game series.

## 1936–37

### FINAL STANDINGS

#### Canadian Division

| | W | L | T | PTS | GF | GA |
|---|---|---|---|---|---|---|
| Montreal C. | 24 | 18 | 6 | 54 | 115 | 111 |
| Montreal M. | 22 | 17 | 9 | 53 | 126 | 110 |
| Toronto | 22 | 21 | 5 | 49 | 119 | 115 |
| New York A. | 15 | 29 | 4 | 34 | 122 | 161 |

#### American Division

| | W | L | T | PTS | GF | GA |
|---|---|---|---|---|---|---|
| Detroit | 25 | 14 | 9 | 59 | 128 | 102 |
| Boston | 23 | 18 | 7 | 53 | 120 | 110 |
| New York R. | 19 | 20 | 9 | 47 | 117 | 106 |
| Chicago | 14 | 27 | 7 | 35 | 99 | 131 |

### LEADING SCORERS

| | G | A | PTS |
|---|---|---|---|
| Schriner, New York A. | 21 | 25 | 46 |
| Apps, Toronto | 16 | 29 | 45 |
| Barry, Detroit | 17 | 27 | 44 |
| Aurie, Detroit | 23 | 20 | 43 |
| Jackson, Toronto | 21 | 19 | 40 |
| Gagnon, Montreal C. | 20 | 16 | 36 |
| Gracie, Montreal M. | 11 | 25 | 36 |
| Stewart, Boston-New York A. | 23 | 12 | 35 |
| Thompson, Chicago | 17 | 18 | 35 |
| Cowley, Boston | 13 | 22 | 35 |

## 1937–38

Clem Loughlin had set a longevity record by lasting three seasons in the revolving door for coaches op-

*Toronto's Syl Apps, a former Olympic pole vaulter, was the 1936-37 Rookie of the Year.*

*The Rangers' Cecil Dillon shared an All-Star berth with Toronto's Gordie Drillon in 1937-38.*

erated by Chicago's boss, Major Fred McLaughlin. In 10 years, McLaughlin had employed an even dozen coaches—11 of them over the first seven seasons. When Loughlin was shown to the exit door in 1937, he was replaced by a baseball umpire and hockey referee named Bill Stewart, who would pilot Chicago to its first Stanley Cup.

A baseball umpire? Well, McLaughlin was like that, often depending for advice in running his hockey club on distinctly un-hockey types. Stewart, at least, did have some refereeing in his background.

In Boston, the Bruins assembled a new line destined for a long run of glory. Milt Schmidt was the center and his wingmen were Bobby Bauer and Woody Dumart—The Kraut Line.

Lester Patrick, coach of the New York Rangers, brought up his son, Muzz, to join his brother, Lynn, and give the Rangers three Patricks. New York also added a rookie named Bryan Hextall who was to star during the war years and later see both his sons play in the NHL.

Toronto's Gordie Drillon won the scoring title with 52 points, 26 of them goals. Drillon was part of considerable confusion caused by the similarity in name with another fine right wing, Cecil Dillon of the Rangers. In fact, both were selected to the All-Star team—the only time in history that two players were chosen for the same position on the first team.

The other All-Stars were left wing Paul Thompson of Chicago, who led American Division scorers with 44 points, Boston's Bill Cowley at center, defensemen Eddie Shore of the Bruins and Babe Siebert of the Montreal Canadiens and Boston's Tiny Thompson, Paul's brother, in goal.

Shore recaptured the MVP Hart Trophy—his fourth in six years—Drillon was the Lady Byng winner and Tiny Thompson took the Vezina for the fourth time. Chicago's Cully Dahlstrom won the Calder Trophy as the top rookie.

Toronto and Boston won the division championships and the Maple Leafs whipped the Bruins in three straight games to advance to the final round of the Stanley Cup playoffs. Meanwhile, in an intracity showdown, the New York Americans eliminated the Rangers and reached the semifinals against Chicago, which had come from behind to beat the Montreal Canadiens. The Black Hawks ousted the Americans and found themselves up against Toronto's powerhouse for the Stanley Cup.

Against Toronto, the Hawks were simply in over their heads. They had won just 14 of 48 games during the regular season and made the playoffs by only two points. Toronto, on the other hand, had won or tied 33 of their 48 games and had easily won the Canadian Division.

What was worse, Mike Karakas, Chicago's goalie, came up with an injured toe before the opening game. Coach Bill Stewart was not about to repeat Lester Patrick's feat of playing goal. Instead, he asked permission of the Leafs to use Dave Kerr, the Rangers' goalie. Conn Smythe refused and the Hawks wound up with Alfie Moore, a minor leaguer, in the nets, but not before Stewart and Smythe en-

gaged in a brief jostling match outside the dressing room.

The Hawks won the opener, 3–1, and Moore thumbed his nose at the Leafs' bench. In the second game, with Moore ruled ineligible by NHL President Frank Calder, the Hawks came up with Paul Goodman, another minor leaguer who was fished out of a movie theater just two hours before the game began. He was beaten by the Leafs, 5–1, to even the series.

In the third game, Karakas returned and the Hawks won, 2–1, on Doc Romnes' goal with 4:05 left in the game. The Leafs argued that the shot had hit the post but were overruled by referee Clarence

*Lorne Carr of the N.Y. Americans gets congratulations from coach Red Dutton after winning goal against Chicago in 1938 playoffs.*

Campbell, a man who would play a different role in the NHL in later years.

The Hawks won the fourth game and the Cup, making Stewart the toast of Chicago—for about nine months.

## 1937–38

### FINAL STANDINGS

| | W | L | T | PTS | GF | GA |
|---|---|---|---|---|---|---|
| *Canadian Division* | | | | | | |
| Toronto | 24 | 15 | 9 | 57 | 151 | 127 |
| New York A. | 19 | 18 | 11 | 49 | 110 | 111 |
| Montreal C. | 18 | 17 | 13 | 49 | 123 | 128 |
| Montreal M. | 12 | 30 | 6 | 30 | 101 | 149 |
| *American Division* | | | | | | |
| Boston | 30 | 11 | 7 | 67 | 142 | 89 |
| New York R. | 27 | 15 | 6 | 60 | 149 | 96 |
| Chicago | 14 | 25 | 9 | 37 | 97 | 139 |
| Detroit | 12 | 25 | 11 | 35 | 99 | 133 |

### LEADING SCORERS

| | G | A | PTS |
|---|---|---|---|
| Drillon, Toronto | 26 | 26 | 52 |
| Apps, Toronto | 21 | 29 | 50 |
| Thompson, Chicago | 22 | 22 | 44 |
| Mantha, Montreal C. | 23 | 19 | 42 |
| Dillon, New York R. | 21 | 18 | 39 |
| Cowley, Boston | 17 | 22 | 39 |
| Schriner, New York A. | 21 | 17 | 38 |
| Thoms, Toronto | 14 | 24 | 38 |
| Smith, New York R. | 14 | 23 | 37 |
| Stewart, New York A. | 19 | 17 | 36 |
| N. Colville, New York R. | 17 | 19 | 36 |

## 1938–39

For years the Maroons were fighting a losing battle attracting fan support while the Canadiens enjoyed far more popularity in Montreal. Finally, the Maroons asked permission to shift to St. Louis. The league refused but did grant the franchise a one-year leave of absence to regroup its forces. But when they sold most of their players to other clubs, it became apparent that the Maroons were through for good.

The demise of the Maroons left seven teams still operating and they were grouped in a single division with six clubs qualifying for the rather crowded playoffs. Only Chicago, whose Bill Stewart was dismissed in midseason and replaced by Paul Thompson, missed.

In Boston, manager Art Ross took a dramatic step. He sold goalie Tiny Thompson, a Bruins' favorite for a decade, to Detroit. The reason was Ross' conviction that a youngster from Eveleth, Minnesota, was ready for the NHL. And Frank Brimsek really was ready.

Brimsek had played the Bruins' first two games while Thompson recovered from an eye ailment. Then Tiny returned and Brimsek was farmed out to Providence. But Thompson was 33 and Ross was

*Rookie Frank Brimsek of the Bruins totalled 10 shutouts in 1938-39.*

anxious to create a spot for the good-looking rookie who had succeeded Chicago's Mike Karakas at Eveleth High School. On November 28, the deal was made, with the Bruins receiving $15,000 from the Red Wings. Brimsek returned two days later.

The Canadiens beat him, 2–0, in his first game and then Brimsek produced three straight shutouts. His shutout streak extended to 231 minutes, 54 seconds, breaking Thompson's modern mark of 224:47.

After Brimsek's sensational streak was broken, he started another one. Three more shutouts—one against Thompson and the Red Wings—gave him six in seven games and another unbelievable streak of 220 minutes, 24 seconds of scoreless hockey.

The Boston fans, never easy to please, were unhappy to lose Thompson but Brimsek's fantastic debut made him an instant hero. He turned in 10 shutouts in 41 games, earning the Vezina Trophy as top goalie, the Calder Trophy as top rookie, a spot on the All-Star team and the nickname "Mr. Zero."

The other All-Stars were defensemen Eddie Shore and Dit Clapper of Boston, Toronto's center, Syl Apps, right wing Gordie Drillon of the Maple Leafs and left wing Hector (Toe) Blake of the Montreal Canadiens. Blake was the scoring champion with 47 points, including 24 goals, and captured the Hart Trophy while Clint Smith of the New York Rangers won the Lady Byng.

The Bruins won the regular-season title by 16 points over the Rangers and then the two clubs staged one of the most memorable playoff battles in history. Boston took the first three games—two of them on overtime goals by Mel Hill, an obscure 10-goal scorer during the regular season. Then the Rangers roared back to win three straight and tie the series. In the seventh game, Hill struck again, beating the Rangers eight minutes into the third overtime period and earning forever the nickname of "Sudden Death" Hill.

Toronto ripped through the New York Americans and Detroit, which had eliminated the Canadiens. In the finals, the Bruins whipped the Leafs in five games to claim their first Stanley Cup in a decade.

*Hector (Toe) Blake of the Canadiens won scoring and MVP honors in 1938-39.*

## 1938–39

### FINAL STANDINGS

|  | W | L | T | PTS | GF | GA |
|---|---|---|---|---|---|---|
| Boston | 36 | 10 | 2 | 74 | 156 | 76 |
| New York R. | 26 | 16 | 6 | 58 | 149 | 105 |
| Toronto | 19 | 20 | 9 | 47 | 114 | 107 |
| New York A. | 17 | 21 | 10 | 44 | 119 | 157 |
| Detroit | 18 | 24 | 6 | 42 | 107 | 128 |
| Montreal | 15 | 24 | 9 | 39 | 115 | 146 |
| Chicago | 12 | 28 | 8 | 32 | 91 | 132 |

### LEADING SCORERS

|  | G | A | PTS |
|---|---|---|---|
| Blake, Montreal | 24 | 23 | 47 |
| Schriner, New York A. | 13 | 31 | 44 |
| Cowley, Boston | 8 | 34 | 42 |
| Smith, New York R. | 21 | 20 | 41 |
| Barry, Detroit | 13 | 28 | 41 |
| Apps, Toronto | 15 | 25 | 40 |
| Anderson, New York A. | 13 | 27 | 40 |
| Gottselig, Chicago | 16 | 23 | 39 |
| Haynes, Montreal | 5 | 33 | 38 |
| Conacher, Boston | 26 | 11 | 37 |
| Carr, New York A. | 19 | 18 | 37 |
| N. Colville, New York R. | 18 | 19 | 37 |
| Watson, New York R. | 15 | 22 | 37 |

## 1939–40

The guns of Europe began firing before the 1939 hockey season got underway and before long the NHL would feel the manpower squeeze of world conflict. But, for the time being at least, the league's operations were not affected by the events overseas.

Ironically, the hottest line in the league was Boston's Milt Schmidt, Woody Dumart and Bobby Bauer, tabbed the "Kraut Line" because of their Germanic extractions. But the name proved a bit unpopular at this sensitive time so the "Kraut Line" was re-christened the "Kitchener Kids" because the trio all hailed from Kitchener, Ontario.

Schmidt, the center, led the league in scoring with 52 points, 22 of them on goals. Dumart and Bauer tied for second with 43 points apiece.

The All-Star team had Schmidt at center, Bryan Hextall of the Rangers at right wing and Montreal's Toe Blake at left wing. The defensemen were Aubrey (Dit) Clapper of the Bruins and Detroit's Ebbie Goodfellow. Davey Kerr of the Rangers was the goalie.

Goodfellow won the Hart Trophy and Bobby Bauer the Lady Byng. Kerr won the Vezina and a 28-year-old Ranger rookie, Kilby MacDonald, took the Calder.

For the first time since they came into the league,

*Woody Dumart played left wing on the Bruins' high-scoring Kraut Line.*

the Bruins had to get along without the great Eddie Shore patrolling their blue line. Shore had become owner and manager of the minor league Springfield Indians and was available only for Boston's home games. The Bruins quickly tired of this arrangement and sold Eddie to the New York Americans. Shore finished the season with the Amerks and then retired to build the Springfield club into a rewarding financial operation.

Even without Shore, the Bruins finished first in the regular-season race, again beating out the Rangers. But New York got revenge for the heartbreaking playoff loss of the year before by eliminating Boston in the Stanley Cup series, four games to two.

Toronto got by Chicago and Detroit eliminated the New York Americans in other playoff matchups. When the Maple Leafs and Red Wings met in the semifinals it turned into a little war. A 15-minute brawl marred the final game with every player on the ice and 17 who left the opposing benches joining in.

"The Wings are a bunch of hoodlums," declared

*Davey Kerr of the Rangers won the Vezina Trophy and led the Stanley Cup champions in 1939-40.*

the Toronto management. To which Jack Adams, manager of the Red Wings, replied, "We're just sorry we can't play the Leafs seven nights in a row."

In the Stanley Cup finale, the Rangers beat Toronto in six games, three of the New York victories coming in overtime. That wiped out the bad overtime memories Boston's "Sudden Death" Hill had left the year before.

## 1939–40

### FINAL STANDINGS

| | W | L | T | PTS | GF | GA |
|---|---|---|---|---|---|---|
| Boston | 31 | 12 | 5 | 67 | 170 | 98 |
| New York R. | 27 | 11 | 10 | 64 | 136 | 77 |
| Toronto | 25 | 17 | 6 | 56 | 134 | 110 |
| Chicago | 23 | 19 | 6 | 52 | 112 | 120 |
| Detroit | 16 | 26 | 6 | 38 | 90 | 126 |
| New York A. | 15 | 29 | 4 | 34 | 106 | 140 |
| Montreal | 10 | 33 | 5 | 25 | 90 | 167 |

### LEADING SCORERS

| | G | A | PTS |
|---|---|---|---|
| Schmidt, Boston | 22 | 30 | 52 |
| Dumart, Boston | 22 | 21 | 43 |
| Bauer, Boston | 17 | 26 | 43 |
| Drillon, Toronto | 21 | 19 | 40 |
| Cowley, Boston | 13 | 27 | 40 |
| Hextall, New York R. | 24 | 15 | 39 |
| N. Colville, New York R. | 19 | 19 | 38 |
| Howe, Detroit | 14 | 23 | 37 |
| Blake, Montreal | 17 | 19 | 36 |
| Armstrong, New York A. | 16 | 20 | 36 |

## 1940–41

Dick Irvin left Toronto and moved into the coaching job at Montreal, hoping to rebuild the Canadiens, who had fallen on lean times. Irvin would do such a successful job that his teams of the early 1940s were hockey's most dynamic squads. And the rea-

*The Rangers celebrate their Stanley Cup triumph in 1940.*

son for much of his success was a scouting job he did for the Canadiens shortly before becoming the club's coach. It was on that trip that he discovered a junior hockey player named Maurice Richard, who was destined to become one of the greatest scorers in hockey history.

Before the season started, Irvin predicted a fourth-place finish for Montreal—three notches higher than they had finished the year before. Asked his thoughts about the league's top rookie, he placed the name of his own Johnny Quilty in a sealed envelope.

Quilty made it but the Canadiens didn't. Montreal finished sixth but Quilty captured the Calder Trophy as the league's best rookie. Boston's Bill Cowley won the scoring title with 62 points—only 17 of them goals. Cowley also was the MVP and Bobby Bauer of the Bruins won his second straight Lady Byng. Turk Broda of Toronto won the Vezina, edging out Detroit's Johnny Mowers on the final night of the season. It marked the first time a Maple Leaf had been the NHL's top goaltender.

The All-Star team had Broda in goal, Boston's Dit Clapper and Toronto's Wally Stanowski on defense, Cowley at center, Bryan Hextall of the Rangers and Sweeney Schriner, now with Toronto, on the wings.

The Bruins were the class of the league again and captured their fourth straight regular-season title. They set two records, going 15 games without a loss on the road over one stretch and 23 without a setback over another.

Boston finished five points in front of Toronto and knocked off the Maple Leafs in the opening round of the Stanley Cup playoffs. Detroit eliminated the Rangers and then Chicago, which had disposed of Montreal in the opening round.

In the Cup finals, the Bruins swept past the Red Wings in four straight games with Milt Schmidt and Eddie Wiseman, the player they had obtained from the Americans in the Eddie Shore deal the year before, starring.

War clouds had convinced players and executives around the league that it would not be long before the events in Europe and the Pacific would affect the NHL. Conn Smythe, owner of the Maple Leafs, advised all of his players to volunteer for military training and most of the club joined the Toronto

Scottish Reserve. Other players around the league followed suit and before long many of them were trading shoulder pads and hockey sticks for field packs and rifles.

## 1940–41

### FINAL STANDINGS

|            | W  | L  | T  | PTS | GF  | GA  |
|------------|----|----|----|-----|-----|-----|
| Boston     | 27 | 8  | 13 | 67  | 168 | 102 |
| Toronto    | 28 | 14 | 6  | 62  | 145 | 99  |
| Detroit    | 21 | 16 | 11 | 53  | 112 | 102 |
| New York R.| 21 | 19 | 8  | 50  | 143 | 125 |
| Chicago    | 16 | 25 | 7  | 39  | 112 | 139 |
| Montreal   | 16 | 26 | 6  | 38  | 121 | 147 |
| New York A.| 8  | 29 | 11 | 27  | 99  | 186 |

### LEADING SCORERS

|                          | G  | A  | PTS |
|--------------------------|----|----|-----|
| Cowley, Boston           | 17 | 45 | 62  |
| Hextall, New York R.     | 26 | 18 | 44  |
| Drillon, Toronto         | 23 | 21 | 44  |
| Apps, Toronto            | 20 | 24 | 44  |
| L. Patrick, New York R.  | 20 | 24 | 44  |
| Howe, Detroit            | 20 | 24 | 44  |
| N. Colville, New York R. | 14 | 28 | 42  |
| Wiseman, Boston          | 16 | 24 | 40  |
| Bauer, Boston            | 17 | 22 | 39  |
| Schriner, Toronto        | 24 | 14 | 38  |
| R. Conacher, Boston      | 24 | 14 | 38  |
| Schmidt, Boston          | 13 | 25 | 38  |

## 1941–42

The National Hockey League season was less than one month old in December 1941, when suddenly, hockey didn't seem very important anymore. It was on the morning of December 7 that Japanese bombs poured down on United States ships anchored in Pearl Harbor and plunged the U.S. into World War II.

On the night of December 7, the New York Rangers defeated Boston, 5–4, Chicago nipped the Americans, who had changed the designation of their franchise from New York to Brooklyn, 5–4, and Detroit edged Montreal, 3–2. But nobody cared about the results that night.

The next morning, many of the same fans who had packed hockey arenas the night before lined up at recruiting stations as America went to war. Hockey players, too, did their part.

Of the 14 players listed in the Ranger lineup the night of December 7, 10 eventually wound up in uniform. It was the same throughout the league as the service rolls swelled with top NHL talent. The

*Ranger Bryan Hextall skated off with the scoring title in 1941-42.*

names included Muzz and Lynn Patrick, Sid Abel, Boston's "Kraut Line" of Milt Schmidt, Woody Dumart and Bobby Bauer, Terry and Ken Reardon, Howie Meeker, Black Jack Stewart, goalies Jim Henry and Chuck Rayner and scores of others.

But, as it had 25 years before when confronted by another world conflict, the NHL continued through World War II without a single interruption in its schedule.

On the day that Japan attacked Pearl Harbor, Bryan Hextall of the Rangers and Toronto's Gordie Drillon shared the NHL scoring lead. Hextall went on to capture the championship with 56 points, two

points more than his teammate Lynn Patrick. Both Rangers made the All-Star team along with Toronto center Syl Apps, defensemen Tommy Anderson of the Brooklyn Americans and Earl Seibert of Chicago and goalie Frankie Brimsek of Boston.

Anderson won the Hart Trophy as MVP, Apps took the Lady Byng, Brimsek captured the Vezina Trophy and Grant Warwick of the Rangers was the Calder Trophy winner.

Red Dutton's troubled Americans weathered one of the longest holdouts in hockey history when Busher Jackson could not reach terms with the club. Finally, in desperation, Dutton shipped Jackson to

Boston for $7,500 in January. Dutton also traded Lorne Carr to Toronto for four players. But nothing worked right for the Amerks. When they finished last and their cross-town rivals, the Rangers, won the regular-season title, it marked the end of the Americans. They dropped out of the league at the conclusion of the season.

Toronto eliminated the first-place Rangers in the opening round of the playoffs while Detroit eliminated the Canadiens and then the Bruins, who had knocked out Chicago. That set up a final round meeting between the Red Wings and Maple Leafs—one of the most amazing series in Stanley Cup history.

Detroit stunned the favored Leafs by winning the first three games—two of them at Toronto. Billy Taylor of the Leafs kidded newsmen before the next game, saying, "Don't worry about us, we'll beat them four straight."

Few observers, except perhaps Taylor, were prepared for what followed. The Leafs shook up their lineup and with seldom-used Don Metz and Ernie Dickens supplying the spark, won the next four games and the Stanley Cup. It was Taylor who set up Sweeney Schriner's second goal of the game and the final one of the series in Toronto's 3–1 victory in the seventh game.

## 1941–42

### FINAL STANDINGS

|  | W | L | T | PTS | GF | GA |
|---|---|---|---|---|---|---|
| New York | 29 | 17 | 2 | 60 | 177 | 143 |
| Toronto | 27 | 18 | 3 | 57 | 158 | 136 |
| Boston | 25 | 17 | 6 | 56 | 160 | 118 |
| Chicago | 22 | 23 | 3 | 47 | 145 | 155 |
| Detroit | 19 | 25 | 4 | 42 | 140 | 147 |
| Montreal | 18 | 27 | 3 | 39 | 134 | 173 |
| Brooklyn | 16 | 29 | 3 | 35 | 133 | 175 |

### LEADING SCORERS

|  | G | A | PTS |
|---|---|---|---|
| Hextall, New York | 24 | 32 | 56 |
| L. Patrick, New York | 32 | 22 | 54 |
| Grosso, Detroit | 23 | 30 | 53 |
| Watson, New York | 15 | 37 | 52 |
| Abel, Detroit | 18 | 31 | 49 |
| Blake, Montreal | 17 | 28 | 45 |
| Thoms, Chicago | 15 | 30 | 45 |
| Drillon, Toronto | 23 | 18 | 41 |
| Apps, Toronto | 18 | 23 | 41 |
| Anderson, Brooklyn | 12 | 29 | 41 |

# A SOLID SIX
# 1942-1967

With the exit of the Americans, the NHL was down to six teams—Detroit, Chicago, Montreal, New York, Boston and Toronto. This solid foundation would remain intact until the ambitious expansion program of the NHL's second half-century.

The war years would bring important changes to the NHL. Before the conflict was over, Frank Boucher, the creative center of the Rangers, who now coached the New York club, was to suggest the adoption of a red line at center ice to speed up the game. Overtime periods would be done away with in the interest of maintaining tight wartime travel schedules.

And Montreal's Maurice Richard emerged as the game's first truly superscorer. The Rocket, as Richard became known, was to be the key man on one of the most devastating teams in hockey history—the Canadiens of the mid-1950s. They were so proficient that they forced a rule change to keep them from utterly dominating the sport.

In Detroit, a young man named Gordie Howe arrived on the scene with little advance notice and established himself as hockey's greatest scorer and its longevity king. It was Howe and Richard who

◄ *Bloodied Jimmy Orlando of Detroit looks to referee King Clancy for help after a fight with Toronto's Gaye Stewart in 1943.*

ruled the game in the fifties along with the Canadiens and the Red Wings.

And then came the 1960s and Bobby Hull, the dynamic blond bomber of the Chicago Black Hawks, who epitomized hockey's next era of bigger, stronger, faster players.

The period would see the shifting of the league's administration from President Frank Calder, who had been head man since the NHL's inception in 1917, to Red Dutton and then to Clarence Campbell, the ex-referee, who would be at the helm when big-league hockey swung into its most successful era.

## 1942–43

Numerous NHL players and executives were in the service by the time the 1942 season began and early in the season a major rule change was enacted. Because of the tight train schedules during the war, NHL teams had to be precise about the length of games. Thus, they eliminated overtime.

Until then, when a game was tied at the end of three regulation periods, the teams played a 10-minute overtime period in an attempt to break the deadlock. Unlike Stanley Cup overtimes, the extra periods were not sudden death but lasted a full 10

*Rookie-of-the-Year honors in 1942-43 went to Toronto's Gaye Stewart.*

Calder suffered a heart attack. Two weeks later, the man who had been at the head of the league since its inception in 1917 was dead. The Governors chose Dutton as president pro tem with the understanding that Clarence Campbell, the man Calder had chosen as his successor, would eventually take over.

Chicago's Bentley brothers, Doug and Max, battled Bill Cowley of Boston for the scoring title. Doug Bentley finally won the crown with 73 points, including 33 goals. Cowley had 72 points and Max Bentley 70.

Cowley and Doug Bentley made the All-Star team along with Toronto's Lorne Carr, Black Jack Stewart of Detroit and Earl Seibert of Chicago on defense, and Johnny Mowers of Detroit in goal. Cowley also won the Hart Trophy while Mowers took the Vezina. The Lady Byng went to Max Bentley and Gaye Stewart of Toronto won the Calder.

In Montreal, the Canadiens introduced Maurice Richard, a young right winger, who scored five goals in 16 games before a broken ankle put him out of action.

Detroit won the regular-season title by four points over Boston while Toronto finished third and the Canadiens made it to fourth place—their highest finish in five seasons—and the final playoff spot in the six-team league. The Red Wings eliminated the Maple Leafs and Boston dropped the Canadiens in the Stanley Cup semifinals. Then, with Carl Liscombe and Sid Abel starring, Detroit flashed past the Bruins in four straight games to capture the Cup.

## 1942–43

### FINAL STANDINGS

| | W | L | T | PTS | GF | GA |
|---|---|---|---|---|---|---|
| Detroit | 25 | 14 | 11 | 61 | 169 | 124 |
| Boston | 24 | 17 | 9 | 57 | 195 | 176 |
| Toronto | 22 | 19 | 9 | 53 | 198 | 159 |
| Montreal | 19 | 19 | 12 | 50 | 181 | 191 |
| Chicago | 17 | 18 | 15 | 49 | 179 | 180 |
| New York | 11 | 31 | 8 | 30 | 161 | 253 |

### LEADING SCORERS

| | G | A | PTS |
|---|---|---|---|
| D. Bentley, Chicago | 33 | 40 | 73 |
| Cowley, Boston | 27 | 45 | 72 |
| M. Bentley, Chicago | 26 | 44 | 70 |
| L. Patrick, New York | 22 | 39 | 61 |
| Carr, Toronto | 27 | 33 | 60 |
| Taylor, Toronto | 18 | 42 | 60 |
| Hextall, New York | 27 | 32 | 59 |
| Blake, Montreal | 23 | 36 | 59 |
| Lach, Montreal | 18 | 40 | 58 |
| O'Connor, Montreal | 15 | 43 | 58 |

minutes. Therefore, it was possible to have goals scored during overtime but for the game to still end in a tie.

Referee Bill Chadwick, a leading NHL official of the 1940s, felt the elimination of the extra period was a good thing for hockey. "Overtimes benefitted the stronger teams," he said. "It gave them 10 more minutes to wear down weaker competition. If a weak club held a stronger one to a tie for 60 minutes, it ought to be worth something."

With the Americans out of the league, the schedule was increased from 48 to 50 games. Red Dutton, the Amerks' head man, was disconsolate at the demise of his club but he was to be back in hockey much faster than he expected.

On his way to a meeting of the league's Board of Governors in Toronto in January, President Frank

*Black Hawk Doug Bentley beat out his brother Max and Boston's Bill Cowley for the scoring championship in 1942-43.*

## 1943–44

The war had ravaged NHL rosters, leaving only youngsters, service rejects or over-age veterans. The situation was so desperate that in New York, coach Frank Boucher of the Rangers attempted a comeback at the age of 42. Boucher's return at center ice lasted 15 games and he averaged almost a point per game for hapless New York.

It was Boucher and Art Ross, Boston's manager, who pushed for, and eventually got, legislation introducing the center red line. The mid-ice divider was introduced at the start of the 1943 season in an effort to speed up the game. Boucher explained the reasoning behind it.

"My thought was that hockey had become a see-saw affair," said Boucher. "Defending teams were jammed in their own end for minutes because they

*Detroit's Syd Howe set NHL record with six goals against the Rangers on February 3, 1944.*

couldn't pass their way out against the new five-man attack."

Before the red line was introduced, players could not pass the puck out of their defensive zone but had to carry it out themselves. This was difficult with five opposing skaters to weave through and Boucher suggested a solution.

"Why not allow teams to pass their way out of trouble, say up to mid-ice," he reasoned. "Use a red line to divide the ice. It would open the dam for the defending team and restore end-to-end play."

The idea was adopted and speeded up the game considerably.

Boston's Herbie Cain won the scoring race with 36 goals and 82 points but missed the first All-Star team. Chicago's Doug Bentley, Lorne Carr of Toronto and Bill Cowley of Boston were named to the All-Star forward line, with Toronto's Babe Pratt and Earl Seibert of Chicago on defense and Montreal's Bill Durnan in goal. Pratt was the Hart Trophy winner, Clint Smith of Chicago took the Lady Byng, Durnan won the Vezina and Toronto's Gus Bodnar captured the Calder.

And in Montreal, coach Dick Irvin assembled a new line. He used Elmer Lach, who spoke only English, at center; Toe Blake, fluent in French and English, on left wing, and young Maurice Richard, the darling of the French-Canadian fans, on the right side. The unit was tagged the Punch Line and produced 82 goals—32 of them by the fiery Richard.

*The league's MVP in 1943-44 was Toronto's Babe Pratt.*

With Durnan doing an outstanding job in goal and the Punch Line racing through the league, Montreal dropped just five games and won the regular-season championship by 15 points over Detroit. It was the start of a dynasty.

There were two notable goal-scoring feats. Detroit's Syd Howe blasted six goals in a 12–2 romp over the Rangers, setting a modern mark for most goals in a single game. And Toronto's Gus Bodnar, a rookie, set a record for the fastest goal by a first-year man when he scored just 15 seconds after hitting the ice in his debut, also against the Rangers.

In the Stanley Cup playoffs, Richard really took off. The Rocket scored all five goals in the Canadiens' second-game victory and Montreal finished off Toronto in the opening round before sweeping past Chicago in four straight games for the Cup. Richard set a Cup record with 12 goals in the nine playoff games.

## 1943–44

### FINAL STANDINGS

| | W | L | T | PTS | GF | GA |
|---|---|---|---|---|---|---|
| Montreal | 38 | 5 | 7 | 83 | 234 | 109 |
| Detroit | 26 | 18 | 6 | 58 | 214 | 177 |
| Toronto | 23 | 23 | 4 | 50 | 214 | 174 |
| Chicago | 22 | 23 | 5 | 49 | 178 | 187 |
| Boston | 19 | 26 | 5 | 43 | 223 | 268 |
| New York | 6 | 39 | 5 | 17 | 162 | 310 |

### LEADING SCORERS

| | G | A | PTS |
|---|---|---|---|
| Cain, Boston | 36 | 46 | 82 |
| D. Bentley, Chicago | 38 | 39 | 77 |
| Carr, Toronto | 36 | 38 | 74 |
| Liscombe, Detroit | 36 | 37 | 73 |
| Lach, Montreal | 24 | 48 | 72 |
| Smith, Chicago | 23 | 49 | 72 |
| Cowley, Boston | 30 | 41 | 71 |
| Mosienko, Chicago | 32 | 38 | 70 |
| Jackson, Boston | 28 | 41 | 69 |
| Bodnar, Toronto | 22 | 40 | 62 |

## 1944–45

Maurice Richard's playoff explosion the year before set the stage for the Montreal star's greatest season. The Rocket zoomed through the NHL's 50-game schedule at an incredible goal-per-game pace, scoring a record 50 times. He had 15 goals in one nine-game stretch, including five goals in one game. Ten

*Rugged Ted Lindsay broke in with the Red Wings in 1944-45.*

times during the season he scored two or more goals in a single game.

Richard was the first to score 50 goals in a season and the only one ever to do it in a 50-game season. His accomplishment is often compared to the record he erased—Joe Malone's 44 goals in a 22-game season in 1917–18, the NHL's first year of operation. Malone's record was established in the era before forward passing; Richard's came in the modern era. Critics often pointed out that Richard's feat came against watered-down teams weakened by the war but the fact remains that the Rocket was the first man to hit the magic 50.

Richard's linemates also flourished from his record spree and the Punch Line finished 1–2–3 in scoring. Center Elmer Lach led all scorers with 80 points, Richard finished second with 73 points and left wing Toe Blake was third with 67.

The Canadiens dominated the league, winning the title again, this time by 13 points. Five Montreal players—Richard, Lach, Blake, defenseman Butch Bouchard and goalie Bill Durnan made the All-Star team with only Detroit defenseman Flash Hollett breaking the Canadiens' monopoly. Lach was the MVP, Chicago's Bill Mosienko won the Lady Byng Trophy, Durnan took the Vezina and Toronto's Frank McCool captured the Calder.

The Canadiens had lost only eight regular-season games in 1944–45 and a total of just 14 games (one in the playoffs) in two seasons while winning two straight league titles and the Stanley Cup. They were, quite naturally, favored to take the Cup again.

But Toronto stung Montreal with two quick victories in the opening round of the playoffs and eliminated the Canadiens in six games. Detroit wiped out a two-game Boston edge and whipped the Bruins in their semifinal series. That set up a final round between the Maple Leafs and Red Wings.

Detroit almost erased the memory of the embarrassing Cup loss to the Leafs three years earlier, when they had blown a three-game lead. This time, it was Toronto which won the first three games—all of them shutouts by rookie goalie Frank McCool.

Suddenly the Red Wings bounced back, just as the Leafs had done in 1942. Detroit won three straight games and it looked like history was about

*Montreal's Emil (Butch) Bouchard was an All-Star ▶ defenseman in 1944-45.*

to repeat. But Toronto finally halted the storybook comeback by winning the seventh game on defenseman Babe Pratt's goal.

## 1944–45

### FINAL STANDINGS

|  | W | L | T | PTS | GF | GA |
|---|---|---|---|---|---|---|
| Montreal | 38 | 8 | 4 | 80 | 228 | 121 |
| Detroit | 31 | 14 | 5 | 67 | 218 | 161 |
| Toronto | 24 | 22 | 4 | 52 | 183 | 161 |
| Boston | 16 | 30 | 4 | 36 | 179 | 219 |
| Chicago | 13 | 30 | 7 | 33 | 141 | 194 |
| New York | 11 | 29 | 10 | 32 | 154 | 247 |

### LEADING SCORERS

|  | G | A | PTS |
|---|---|---|---|
| Lach, Montreal | 26 | 54 | 80 |
| Richard, Montreal | 50 | 23 | 73 |
| Blake, Montreal | 29 | 38 | 67 |
| Cowley, Boston | 25 | 40 | 65 |
| Kennedy, Toronto | 29 | 25 | 54 |
| Mosienko, Chicago | 28 | 26 | 54 |
| Carveth, Detroit | 26 | 28 | 54 |
| DeMarco, New York | 24 | 30 | 54 |
| Smith, Chicago | 23 | 31 | 54 |
| S. Howe, Detroit | 17 | 36 | 53 |

## 1945–46

With World War II drawing to a close, hockey players began returning to the sport. Players came back throughout the season, causing a constant shuffle of rosters throughout the NHL.

Many had lost the best hockey years of their lives while in service and found it difficult to make moves that once were second nature to them. Four years of war had robbed many of that vital extra measure of speed that separated the average players from the stars.

Some clubs, the Rangers among them, felt a sense of responsibility to the returnees and stuck with them until it became all too apparent that they just weren't able to keep up with the NHL pace anymore.

Chicago's Max Bentley got back in time to start the season with the Black Hawks and proved that his service years had not affected his hockey ability.

Kraut Liners Milt Schmidt (left) and Woody Dumart (14) backcheck against Rangers in 1945-46 game.

*All-Star backliner John Crawford of Boston wore this helmet to protect his bald head.*

Bentley won the scoring title with 31 goals and 61 points and earned the Hart Trophy as the league's MVP.

Bentley was picked as the All-Star center on a team that included Montreal's Maurice Richard at right wing, Gaye Stewart of Toronto at left wing, Montreal's Butch Bouchard and Boston's Jack Crawford on defense and Montreal goalie Bill Durnan, who won his third straight Vezina Trophy. The Lady Byng went to Montreal's Toe Blake and Edgar Laprade of the Rangers won the Calder Trophy as the NHL's best rookie.

Richard did not come close to the record goal-scoring pace he had maintained the year before, and finished with 27—less than three other players, including his linemate, Toe Blake.

Despite the Rocket's reduced output, the Cana-

diens won their third straight regular-season title, this time by five points over Boston. But they at least looked mortal, losing 17 games—just one less than they had dropped in combined regular-season and Stanley Cup play for the previous two years.

The NHL had a new look for the service returnees. In addition to the powerful Canadiens, who had been little more than also-rans when the war started, there was the red line and a new system of three officials—two linesmen as well as a referee—for every game. Goal lights were made mandatory.

In the playoffs, the Punch Line carried the Canadiens to their second Stanley Cup in three years. Blake and Richard had seven goals each and Elmer Lach added five and 12 assists as Montreal shredded Chicago in four games and Boston in five to clinch the Cup.

## 1945–46

### FINAL STANDINGS

|  | W | L | T | PTS | GF | GA |
|---|---|---|---|---|---|---|
| Montreal | 28 | 17 | 5 | 61 | 172 | 134 |
| Boston | 24 | 18 | 8 | 56 | 167 | 156 |
| Chicago | 23 | 20 | 7 | 53 | 200 | 178 |
| Detroit | 20 | 20 | 10 | 50 | 146 | 159 |
| Toronto | 19 | 24 | 7 | 45 | 174 | 185 |
| New York | 13 | 28 | 9 | 35 | 144 | 191 |

### LEADING SCORERS

|  | G | A | PTS |
|---|---|---|---|
| M. Bentley, Chicago | 31 | 30 | 61 |
| Stewart, Toronto | 37 | 15 | 52 |
| Blake, Montreal | 29 | 21 | 50 |
| Smith, Chicago | 26 | 24 | 50 |
| Richard, Montreal | 27 | 21 | 48 |
| Mosienko, Chicago | 18 | 30 | 48 |
| DeMarco, New York | 20 | 27 | 47 |
| Lach, Montreal | 13 | 34 | 47 |
| Kaleta, Chicago | 19 | 27 | 46 |
| Taylor, Toronto | 23 | 18 | 41 |
| Horeck, Chicago | 20 | 21 | 41 |

## 1946–47

Red Dutton had successfully steered the NHL through the war years and before the 1946–47 season he announced his retirement. The new NHL president was Clarence Campbell, a former referee, a Rhodes scholar, a lieutenant colonel in the Canadian Army and on the legal staff at the Nuremberg Trials. All this was experience that would serve Campbell well at one time or another in the ensuing years.

In Montreal, Tommy Gorman announced his re-

*Goalie Turk Broda of Toronto stops bid for a goal by Boston's Bep Guidolin in 1946-47 action.*

tirement as general manager of the Canadiens and his replacement was Frank Selke, who for many years had played a key role in Conn Smythe's Toronto operation. Selke's move to Montreal reunited him with another ex-Smythe employee, Canadiens' coach Dick Irvin.

Detroit introduced a slope-shouldered, rawboned right wing who would one day become hockey's top star. But Gordie Howe was just another rookie and his seven-goal season hardly portended greatness.

The league increased its schedule from 50 to 60 games and introduced a system of bonuses for All-Star selection and individual trophy winners. From then on, in addition to the honor of being selected,

each player would get a $1,000 bonus from the league. In addition, the NHL boosted to $127,000 the regular-season and Stanley Cup playoff pools, making it more profitable than ever before for individuals and teams to do well.

Montreal's power-laden Canadiens reaped most of the benefits from the NHL's new affluence. They won their fourth straight regular-season title and gained four of the six first team All-Star berths. Goalie Bill Durnan, defensemen Butch Bouchard and Kenny Reardon and right winger Maurice Richard were the Canadiens' All-Star selections. Milt Schmidt of Boston at center and Doug Bentley of Chicago at left wing completed the team.

*Former referee Clarence S. Campbell took over the presidency of the NHL in the fall of 1946.*

Durnan won his fourth Vezina Trophy in a row—the first goalie to turn that trick. Richard took the Hart Trophy and Boston's Bobby Bauer was the Lady Byng winner. The Calder Trophy went to Toronto's Howie Meeker, who had been so badly wounded during the war that he was told he would never be able to play hockey again.

Chicago's Max Bentley won his second straight scoring title with 72 points—one more than Richard, who fired 45 goals. Interestingly, Richard earned the MVP designation in a season when he scored five goals less than his record 50. The year he scored 50, the Rocket's linemate, Elmer Lach, was the MVP.

The Canadiens breezed past Boston in the five-game opening series of the Stanley Cup playoffs and then faced Toronto, which had knocked off Detroit in five games. The Canadiens won the opener of the final series, 6–0, prompting goalie Bill Durnan to scoff at the Leafs. "How did these guys get in the playoffs anyway?" needled Durnan. He soon found out.

*Defenseman Ken Reardon of Montreal was voted to the All-Star team in 1946-47.*

*The Toronto Maple Leafs: Stanley Cup champions in 1946-47.*

Toronto bounced back with three straight victories that left Montreal on the brink of elimination. The Canadiens won the fifth game but the Leafs took game No. 6 and the Stanley Cup. It was in the midst of the final series that a high-sticking episode cost Richard a $250 fine and a one-game suspension by Campbell—the first of several scrapes involving the fiery Canadiens' star and the placid president of the league.

## 1946–47

### FINAL STANDINGS

|          | W  | L  | T  | PTS | GF  | GA  |
|----------|----|----|----|-----|-----|-----|
| Montreal | 34 | 16 | 10 | 78  | 189 | 138 |
| Toronto  | 31 | 19 | 10 | 72  | 209 | 172 |
| Boston   | 26 | 23 | 11 | 63  | 190 | 175 |
| Detroit  | 22 | 27 | 11 | 55  | 190 | 193 |
| New York | 22 | 32 | 6  | 50  | 167 | 186 |
| Chicago  | 19 | 37 | 4  | 42  | 193 | 274 |

### LEADING SCORERS

|                      | G  | A  | PTS |
|----------------------|----|----|-----|
| M. Bentley, Chicago  | 29 | 43 | 72  |
| Richard, Montreal    | 45 | 26 | 71  |
| Taylor, Detroit      | 17 | 46 | 63  |
| Schmidt, Boston      | 27 | 35 | 62  |
| Kennedy, Toronto     | 28 | 32 | 60  |
| D. Bentley, Chicago  | 21 | 34 | 55  |
| Bauer, Boston        | 30 | 24 | 54  |
| R. Conacher, Detroit | 30 | 24 | 54  |
| Mosienko, Chicago    | 25 | 27 | 52  |
| Dumart, Boston       | 24 | 28 | 52  |

## 1947–48

The NHL pension plan was born in 1947, with contributions by both the players and the league. In an effort to build pension revenue, an annual All-Star game was initiated, pitting the previous season's All-Star squad against the winners of the Stanley Cup.

The game was to be played just before the beginning of the regular season.

Toronto's Maple Leaf Gardens hosted the first All-Star affair and a crowd of 14,169 paid $25,865 to watch the All-Stars defeat Toronto, 4–3. Financially, the game was off to a good start. But the opening classic was marred when Bill Mosienko of Chicago fractured his left ankle.

The Maple Leafs were anxious to retain the Stanley Cup they had won the previous spring and Conn Smythe decided the best way to achieve that was to get Max Bentley into a Toronto uniform. That would not be easy since Bentley had won two straight scoring championships and, along with his brother Doug, provided Chicago with a very healthy gate attraction.

But the Black Hawks' farm system had not produced much in the way of NHL talent and Chicago was short of bodies. That gave Smythe the opening he needed. The Maple Leaf boss assembled an attractive package of Gus Bodnar, Gaye Stewart, Bob Goldham, Bud Poile and Ernie Dickens which the Hawks could not turn down. Bentley and Cy Thomas went to the Leafs in the seven-player swap.

Smythe's bold move paid off. The Leafs soared to the top of the league and won the regular-season title as Bentley contributed 54 points, including 26 goals. The scoring title, however, went to Montreal's Elmer Lach, who had 31 goals and 61 points. The season marked the breakup of the Canadiens' potent Punch Line, on which Lach was the center. Toe Blake, the left wing, suffered a broken ankle in January, which ended his playing career.

A combination of circumstances, not the least of them injuries to Blake and others, dropped the Canadiens to fifth place and out of the playoffs.

Buddy O'Connor, traded by Montreal to New York before the season, won both the Hart and Lady Byng trophies—the first player to capture both in the same season. Toronto's Turk Broda took the Vezina and Detroit's Jimmy McFadden was the Calder winner.

In Detroit, the Red Wings assembled a line of Sid Abel at center, Ted Lindsay on left wing and Gordie Howe on the right side and tabbed it the Production Line. And it produced handsomely with 63 goals—33 of them by Lindsay.

The league was rocked late in the season by a gambling scandal which led to lifetime suspensions of two players—Billy Taylor of the Rangers and Don Gallinger of Boston. President Clarence Campbell emphasized that no games had been fixed and that Gallinger and Taylor were punished for betting on games. A similar charge had resulted in a midseason suspension for Babe Pratt two seasons earlier but Pratt was reinstated after missing nine games.

Detroit dominated the All-Star team with Ted Lindsay at left wing and Bill Quackenbush and Jack Stewart on defense. The other choices were goalie Turk Broda of Toronto and linemates Elmer Lach and Maurice Richard of Montreal.

*Montreal's Elmer Lach was the 1947-48 scoring champion.*

While the Wings led in All-Star picks, it was the Maple Leafs who dominated the Stanley Cup play-offs. Toronto whipped Boston in five games and then clinched its second straight Cup by beating Detroit in four straight. In the final series, the Leafs held the Red Wings' vaunted Production Line to a single goal.

## 1947–48

### FINAL STANDINGS

| | W | L | T | PTS | GF | GA |
|---|---|---|---|---|---|---|
| Toronto | 32 | 15 | 13 | 77 | 182 | 143 |
| Detroit | 30 | 18 | 12 | 72 | 187 | 148 |
| Boston | 23 | 24 | 13 | 59 | 167 | 168 |
| New York | 21 | 26 | 13 | 55 | 176 | 201 |
| Montreal | 20 | 29 | 11 | 51 | 147 | 169 |
| Chicago | 20 | 34 | 6 | 46 | 195 | 225 |

### LEADING SCORERS

| | G | A | PTS |
|---|---|---|---|
| Lach, Montreal | 30 | 31 | 61 |
| O'Connor, New York | 24 | 36 | 60 |
| D. Bentley, Chicago | 20 | 37 | 57 |
| Stewart, Toronto-Chicago | 27 | 29 | 56 |
| M. Bentley, Chicago-Toronto | 26 | 28 | 54 |
| Poile, Toronto-Chicago | 25 | 29 | 54 |
| Richard, Montreal | 28 | 25 | 53 |
| Apps, Toronto | 26 | 27 | 53 |
| Lindsay, Detroit | 33 | 19 | 52 |
| R. Conacher, Chicago | 22 | 27 | 49 |

## 1948–49

When he first saw Sid Abel, Ted Lindsay and Gordie Howe on a line together, Jack Adams knew the Detroit trio would be something special. And he was right. Starting in 1948, the Production Line led the Red Wings to one of the most successful eras in NHL history—seven straight league titles.

Abel, Lindsay and Howe meshed together like precision gears and Adams, the genial Detroit general manager, marveled at the trio's uncanny anticipation. "They could score goals in their sleep," Adams once remarked. "They always seem to know where the play will develop."

Abel, the center, was the playmaker. Lindsay, at left wing, was a fierce checker and competitor who was deadly in the corners. And right winger Howe had a marvelous shot and could control the puck for what seemed like minutes on end.

Howe, only 21, was Adams' pet. The Detroit boss had almost lost the shy youngster in his first training camp when someone forgot to furnish him with a Red Wing jacket which Adams had promised. When made aware of the problem, Adams produced the

*Two great goalies: Montreal's Bill Durnan (left) and Toronto's Turk Broda.*

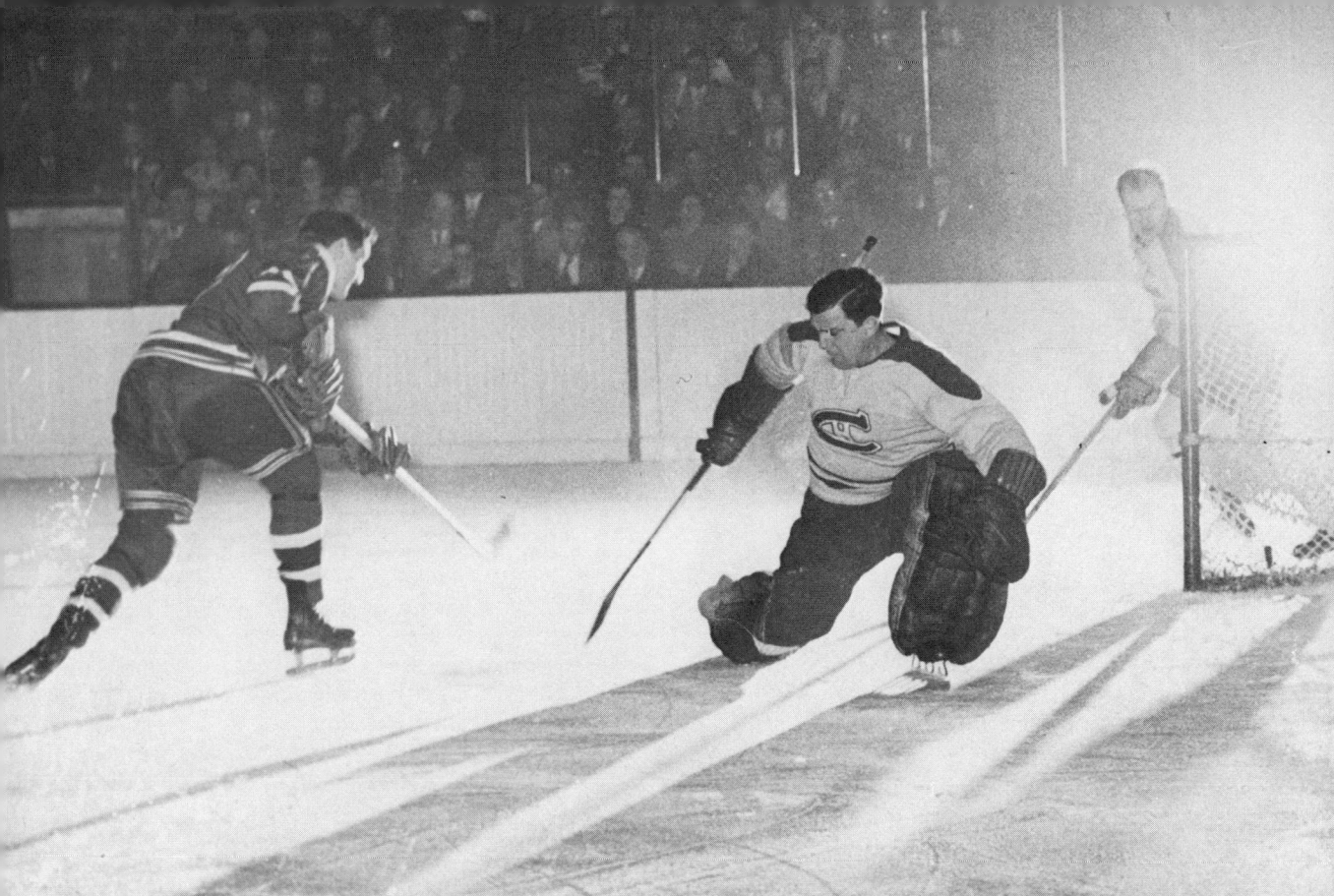

*Ranger Don Raleigh gets one by Vezina Trophy winner Bill Durnan of Montreal in 1948-49 matchup.*

jacket in record time and Howe stayed with the Wings.

Injuries limited Howe to 40 games in 1948–49 and he scored just 12 goals. But Abel and Lindsay kept the Production Line output healthy with 54 goals between them. Goalie Harry Lumley had a 2.42 goals-against average and six shutouts as the Red Wings won the regular-season title by nine points over Boston. But the best goaltending job was turned in by Montreal's Bill Durnan, who won his fifth Vezina Trophy in six years with a 2.10 average and 10 shutouts. Durnan had four shutouts in a row over one stretch and established a modern record by not allowing a goal for 309 minutes, 21 seconds.

Roy Conacher of Chicago and teammate Doug Bentley staged an exciting battle for the scoring title, with Conacher finally winning it. He finished with 68 points, two more than Bentley.

Conacher was chosen as the left wing on the All-Star team with Maurice Richard of Montreal at right wing and Sid Abel of Detroit at center. Two Detroit defensemen, Jack Stewart and Bill Quackenbush, and Montreal's goalie, Durnan, completed the team. Despite his limited output, Gordie Howe made the second All-Star squad.

Abel won the Hart Trophy and Quackenbush became the first defenseman to take the Lady Byng. Penti Lund of the Rangers won the Calder Trophy.

In the playoffs, the Production Line riddled Montreal, scoring 12 of Detroit's 17 goals, eight of them by Howe. That put the Red Wings in the Stanley Cup finals against Toronto, which had beaten Boston in five games.

Turk Broda, the Leafs' great goalie, was more than a match for the Production Line. Broda allowed just five goals in four games and Sid Smith's hat trick in the second game set the tone as Toronto won the Cup in four straight.

*Chicago's Roy Conacher, upholding family tradition, was an All-Star in 1948-49.*

The victory, marking the Leafs' second four-game sweep in two seasons, made them the first NHL team to take three straight Stanley Cups.

## 1948–49

### FINAL STANDINGS

|  | W | L | T | PTS | GF | GA |
|---|---|---|---|---|---|---|
| Detroit | 34 | 19 | 7 | 75 | 195 | 145 |
| Boston | 29 | 23 | 8 | 66 | 178 | 163 |
| Montreal | 28 | 23 | 9 | 65 | 152 | 126 |
| Toronto | 22 | 25 | 13 | 57 | 147 | 161 |
| Chicago | 21 | 31 | 8 | 50 | 173 | 211 |
| New York | 18 | 31 | 11 | 47 | 133 | 172 |

### LEADING SCORERS

|  | G | A | PTS |
|---|---|---|---|
| R. Conacher, Chicago | 26 | 42 | 68 |
| D. Bentley, Chicago | 23 | 43 | 66 |
| Abel, Detroit | 28 | 26 | 54 |
| Lindsay, Detroit | 26 | 28 | 54 |
| J. Conacher, Detroit-Chicago | 26 | 23 | 49 |
| Ronty, Boston | 20 | 29 | 49 |
| Watson, Toronto | 26 | 19 | 45 |
| Reay, Montreal | 22 | 23 | 45 |
| Bodnar, Chicago | 19 | 26 | 45 |
| Peirson, Boston | 22 | 21 | 43 |

## 1949–50

Detroit's Production Line, with a healthy Gordie Howe rejoining Sid Abel and Ted Lindsay, tore through the league and finished 1-2-3 in the scoring race, matching the feat which Boston's Kraut Line, Montreal's Punch Line and Toronto's Kid Line had previously performed.

Lindsay won the scoring title with 78 points, Abel finished with 69 and Howe had 68. The trio combined for an amazing 215 points, including 92 goals—35 of them by Howe.

Despite Howe's brilliant season, he had to settle for a second-team All-Star berth. For the second straight year the right wing spot on the first team went to Montreal's Maurice Richard, who scored 43 goals, the most in the league. The intense rivalry would continue through the early 1950s with the two men occupying the two All-Star berths eight times over a nine-year period.

Throughout the league, fans argued the relative merits of the two right wingers and the extended debate created quite a feud between the Canadiens and Red Wings. Once, in a ruckus on the ice, Howe knocked Richard down. When the Rocket got up, Abel rubbed salt in the wound with a taunt. Richard

wheeled and teed off on Abel, breaking his nose with a punch.

The other All-Stars in 1950 were Lindsay and Abel, defensemen Kenny Reardon of Montreal and Gus Mortson of Toronto and goaltender Bill Durnan of Montreal.

It was Durnan's sixth All-Star selection in seven seasons and he also captured his sixth Vezina Trophy. They were also his last, for he stunned Montreal by quitting in the midst of the Stanley Cup playoffs, saying that the pressure of big-league goaltending had simply become too much.

Two other goalies won individual awards that season Chuck Rayner of the Rangers was the Hart winner and Jack Gelineau, a rookie who beat Frank Brimsek out of the Boston netminding job, took the Calder Trophy. The Lady Byng winner was Edgar Laprade of the Rangers.

Detroit finished first in the regular-season race and met Toronto in one Stanley Cup semifinal while the Rangers tangled with the Canadiens in the other. Going into the series, the Red Wings had dropped 11 straight playoff games to the Leafs and been eliminated three straight years by Toronto.

In the opening game of the series, a devastating injury almost cost Gordie Howe his life. Ted Kennedy sidestepped a Howe check and Gordie plunged face-first into the boards. He suffered a concussion, a broken nose, a fractured right cheekbone and a scratched eyeball.

The Wings, beaten by 5–0 in that opener and deprived of their top scorer, gallantly bounced back and defeated the Maple Leafs in seven games. The Rangers hung three straight defeats on the Canadiens and then Bill Durnan went to Dick Irvin before the fourth game and asked that the Montreal coach use rookie Gerry McNeil in his place. McNeil won the fourth game but New York finished Montreal off in the fifth.

In the Stanley Cup finals, the Rangers led three

*Frank Brimsek, playing his last year in the NHL as a Black Hawk, stops the Bruins' Red Sullivan in 1949-50.*

games to two and were leading, 4–3, in the third period of the sixth game. But goals by Ted Lindsay and Sid Abel gave the Red Wings the game and tied the series. In the seventh game, Pete Babando's overtime goal sank New York and delivered the Stanley Cup to Detroit.

## 1949–50

### FINAL STANDINGS

|  | W | L | T | PTS | GF | GA |
|---|---|---|---|---|---|---|
| Detroit | 37 | 19 | 14 | 88 | 229 | 164 |
| Montreal | 29 | 22 | 19 | 77 | 172 | 150 |
| Toronto | 31 | 27 | 12 | 74 | 176 | 173 |
| New York | 28 | 31 | 11 | 67 | 170 | 189 |
| Boston | 22 | 32 | 16 | 60 | 198 | 228 |
| Chicago | 22 | 38 | 10 | 54 | 203 | 244 |

### LEADING SCORERS

|  | G | A | PTS |
|---|---|---|---|
| Lindsay, Detroit | 23 | 55 | 78 |
| Abel, Detroit | 34 | 35 | 69 |
| Howe, Detroit | 35 | 33 | 68 |
| M. Richard, Montreal | 43 | 22 | 65 |
| Ronty, Boston | 23 | 36 | 59 |
| R. Conacher, Chicago | 25 | 31 | 56 |
| D. Bentley, Chicago | 20 | 33 | 53 |
| Peirson, Boston | 27 | 25 | 52 |
| Prystai, Chicago | 29 | 22 | 51 |
| Guidolin, Chicago | 17 | 34 | 51 |

## 1950–51

Jack Adams was never a stand-pat general manager and although Detroit had won two straight titles, the Red Wings' boss shook them up before the 1950–51 season. He engineered a mammoth nine-player trade with Chicago—the biggest deal in NHL history.

Shuttled off to Chicago were forwards Al Dewsbury, Don Morrison and Pete Babando, defenseman Jack Stewart and goalie Harry Lumley. Babando's overtime goal had won the Stanley Cup for the Wings the season before, Stewart had made the first All-Star team three times and Lumley had turned in a 2.35 goals-against average the season before.

In return, Adams got defenseman Bob Goldham, forwards Gaye Stewart and Metro Prystai and goalie Jim Henry. Perhaps the main reason for making the trade was to give Terry Sawchuk a clear shot at the Red Wings' goalie job.

Sawchuk was not yet 21 when he became the Red Wings' regular goalie. The youngster did a spectacular job in his rookie season, with a 1.98

*Maple Leafs (left to right) Sid Smith, Max Bentley and Bill Barilko celebrate playoff success en route to 1950-51 Stanley Cup championship.*

goals-against average and a league-leading 11 shutouts. He was the easy winner of the Calder Trophy and was named to the first All-Star team.

The other All-Stars included Detroit's Gordie Howe, who won the scoring championship with 88 points and scored 43 goals—one more than his right wing rival, Montreal's Maurice Richard. The other forwards were Howe's linemate, Ted Lindsay on left wing, and Boston's Milt Schmidt at center. Red Kelly of Detroit and Bill Quackenbush of Boston were picked as the defensemen.

Schmidt won the Hart Trophy and Kelly took the Lady Byng, becoming the second Red Wing defenseman in three years to win the trophy for gentlemanly play. In spite of Sawchuk's incredible first-year statistics, he was not the Vezina Trophy winner. That honor went to Al Rollins, who split Toronto's netminding with veteran Turk Broda. Rollins played 40 games compared to Sawchuk's 70 and had a 1.75 goals-against average.

The Red Wings finished first with 44 victories and 13 ties, accumulating a record 101 points. But they were only six points up on Toronto, which won 41 games. It was a busy season for President Clarence Campbell. He slapped three-game suspensions and $300 fines each on Ted Lindsay of Detroit and Bill Ezinicki of Boston for a midseason brawl. Gus Mortson of Toronto used his stick on Chicago's Adam Brown in March and it cost him a two-game suspension and $200 fine. Maurice Richard, still steaming over a game misconduct penalty he had drawn from referee Hugh McLean the night before, grabbed McLean in New York's Picadilly Hotel and as a result of the confrontation, Campbell fined the Rocket $500.

In the Stanley Cup opening round, the Canadiens were decided underdogs to the Red Wings. But Montreal won the first two games—both of them on overtime goals by Maurice Richard. Detroit squared the series by taking the next two but Montreal came right back and eliminated the Red Wings by winning the fifth and sixth games.

Toronto took Boston in five games and advanced to the finals against Montreal. The Maple Leafs and Canadiens set a record of sorts as all five games of their series went into overtime.

In the fifth game, Toronto was trailing, 2–1, In the final period when coach Joe Primeau yanked goalie Turk Broda to make room for an extra attacker. The maneuver paid off with Tod Sloan's game-tying goal with just 32 seconds remaining.

Less than three minutes into overtime, defenseman Bill Barilko won the game and the Cup for the Leafs with a goal. It was the last one he ever scored. Two months later, he was killed in a plane crash.

## 1950–51

### FINAL STANDINGS

|          | W  | L  | T  | PTS | GF  | GA  |
|----------|----|----|----|-----|-----|-----|
| Detroit  | 44 | 13 | 13 | 101 | 236 | 139 |
| Toronto  | 41 | 16 | 13 | 95  | 212 | 138 |
| Montreal | 25 | 30 | 15 | 65  | 173 | 184 |
| Boston   | 22 | 30 | 18 | 62  | 178 | 197 |
| New York | 20 | 29 | 21 | 61  | 169 | 201 |
| Chicago  | 13 | 47 | 10 | 36  | 171 | 280 |

### LEADING SCORERS

|                       | G  | A  | PTS |
|-----------------------|----|----|-----|
| Howe, Detroit         | 43 | 43 | 86  |
| M. Richard, Montreal  | 42 | 24 | 66  |
| M. Bentley, Toronto   | 21 | 41 | 62  |
| Abel, Detroit         | 23 | 38 | 61  |
| Schmidt, Boston       | 22 | 39 | 61  |
| Kennedy, Toronto      | 18 | 43 | 61  |
| Lindsay, Detroit      | 24 | 35 | 59  |
| Sloan, Toronto        | 31 | 25 | 56  |
| Kelly, Detroit        | 17 | 37 | 54  |
| Smith, Toronto        | 30 | 21 | 51  |
| Gardner, Toronto      | 23 | 28 | 51  |

## 1951–52

Detroit won its fourth straight regular-season championship, but the most exciting moments of the season came on March 23 in a meaningless game between New York and Chicago. That was the night Bill Mosienko made hockey history.

The Rangers and Black Hawks were out of the race for a playoff berth when they met that night at Madison Square Garden. New York was fifth and Chicago last. The Rangers, who had used Chuck Rayner and Emile Francis in goal during most of the season went with Lorne Anderson in this particular game.

Mosienko, one of Chicago's top scorers, was playing on a line with Gus Bodnar and George Gee. At 6:09 of the third period, Bodnar fed the puck to Mosienko and the right wing fired a goal. The puck was brought back for a face-off and at 6:20 the combination clicked again. Then another face-off and at 6:30 another goal by Mosienko. Three goals in 21 seconds earned him a spot in the record book for the quickest hat trick in NHL history.

*Bruins' Jim Henry congratulates Montreal's Maurice Richard after Canadiens eliminated Boston from 1952 playoffs.*

In Detroit, the Red Wings were dreaming about the Stanley Cup. And it was no idle dream, either. The Wings had ripped through the regular season, rolling up 100 points—just one point under the record they had established the season before. They finished 22 points ahead of second-place Montreal.

Gordie Howe won his second straight scoring title with 86 points, the same number he had posted the year before. He scored 47 goals, making a serious run at Maurice Richard's record of 50. Howe was chosen MVP and named to the right wing spot on the All-Star team. The other All-Stars were Detroit's Ted Lindsay at left wing, Montreal's Elmer Lach at center, Red Kelly of Detroit and Doug Harvey of Montreal on defense and Detroit's Terry Sawchuk in goal.

Sawchuk took the Vezina Trophy with a 1.94 goals-against average and a league-leading 12 shutouts. Toronto's Sid Smith won the Lady Byng and Montreal's Bernie Geoffrion, nicknamed Boom

Boom for his jet-powered slap shots, took the Calder Trophy as the top rookie.

Montreal battled through seven games before eliminating Boston in the Stanley Cup semifinals. The Canadiens took the deciding game when Maurice Richard skated through four Bruins and then fought off Bill Quackenbush, the last defender, before beating Jim Henry for the tie-breaking goal with four minutes to play. The significant thing about the goal is that Richard remembers very little about it. He had spent the second period of the game in the clinic at the Montreal Forum having six stitches put in his head after being pelted by Leo Labine.

"I was dizzy and a few times when I got the puck I didn't know whether I was skating toward our goal or their goal," Richard said.

Richard's heroics got the Canadiens into the final round but the Rocket couldn't help against the Red Wing juggernaut. Howe and Ted Lindsay scored five goals between them and Sawchuk turned in his third and fourth shutouts of the playoffs as Detroit swept to the Stanley Cup in four straight games. In eight playoff games Sawchuk allowed only five goals—an incredible 0.62 goals-against average.

## 1951–52

### FINAL STANDINGS

|  | W | L | T | PTS | GF | GA |
| --- | --- | --- | --- | --- | --- | --- |
| Detroit | 44 | 14 | 12 | 100 | 215 | 133 |
| Montreal | 34 | 26 | 10 | 78 | 195 | 164 |
| Toronto | 29 | 25 | 16 | 74 | 168 | 157 |
| Boston | 25 | 29 | 16 | 66 | 162 | 176 |
| New York | 23 | 34 | 13 | 59 | 192 | 219 |
| Chicago | 17 | 44 | 9 | 43 | 158 | 241 |

*Montreal's Doug Harvey, an All-Star, starts up ice in 1951-52 action against the Bruins.*

## LEADING SCORERS

| | G | A | PTS |
|---|---|---|---|
| Howe, Detroit | 47 | 39 | 86 |
| Lindsay, Detroit | 30 | 39 | 69 |
| Lach, Montreal | 15 | 50 | 65 |
| Raleigh, New York | 19 | 42 | 61 |
| Smith, Toronto | 27 | 30 | 57 |
| Geoffrion, Montreal | 30 | 24 | 54 |
| Mosienko, Chicago | 31 | 22 | 53 |
| Abel, Detroit | 17 | 36 | 53 |
| Kennedy, Toronto | 19 | 33 | 52 |
| Schmidt, Boston | 21 | 29 | 50 |
| Peirson, Boston | 20 | 30 | 50 |

# 1952–53

Detroit's Production Line was broken up before the 1952–53 season when Sid Abel asked to be traded to Chicago. The Black Hawks wanted Abel as coach and Jack Adams, the Detroit general manager, did not stand in the way of his veteran center man.

Abel's replacement was Alex Delvecchio, who flourished playing between Gordie Howe and Ted Lindsay. He scored 59 points, including 43 assists. The switch in centers made little difference to right winger Howe and left winger Lindsay. They finished 1-2 in scoring for the second straight year with Gordie accumulating 95 points and making his most serious run at Maurice Richard's 50-goal record, finishing with 49. Lindsay had 71 points, including 32 goals.

The departure of Abel didn't seem to hurt the Red Wings, who won their fifth straight regular-season title, but it had a major effect on Chicago, the club Abel took over. Doubling as a player-coach, Abel piloted the Black Hawks to a third-place tie with Boston for Chicago's first playoff berth in seven years.

The scoring crown was Howe's third straight and he became the first man in NHL history to put three together. Similarly, the Red Wings made NHL his-

Detroit goalie Terry Sawchuk gets help from teammate Marcel Pronovost in holding off Boston's Milt Schmidt in 1953.

tory with their fifth straight league title. Boston twice and Montreal once had strung four regular-season titles together, but no team had ever managed five.

Howe and Lindsay were named right wing and left wing on the first All-Star team for the third straight year. The other All-Stars were Boston center Fleming Mackell, defensemen Red Kelly of Detroit and Doug Harvey of Montreal and goalie Terry Sawchuk of Detroit.

Howe won his second consecutive Hart Trophy as MVP, Kelly was the Lady Byng winner and Sawchuk, with a 1.90 average, won the Vezina. The Calder Trophy went to New York goalie Lorne (Gump) Worsley—the third goalie in four years to be honored as the NHL's top rookie.

Early in the season, Maurice Richard scored his 324th career goal, tying the NHL record held by another Montreal great, Nels Stewart. On November 8, he scored No. 325 to set the new standard. On the same night, Richard's center, Elmer Lach, scored the 200th goal of his career.

In the playoffs, the powerful Red Wings, who had breezed to the Stanley Cup in eight straight games the year before, ruled as heavy favorites. They battered Boston, 7–0, in the opening game and looked like a sure thing to repeat as champions. But some clutch scoring by Ed Sandford and heroic goaltending by Sugar Jim Henry gave the Bruins a six-game first-round victory over Detroit.

Chicago held a three-to-two edge in games against Montreal in the other semifinal when Gerry McNeil went to coach Dick Irvin of the Canadiens and suggested that he use Jacques Plante, a rookie, in goal. It was a repeat of Bill Durnan's action during the playoffs in 1950 when he had gone to Irvin and asked to be replaced by McNeil. Plante allowed the Black Hawks one goal in two games and the Canadiens advanced to the final round against Boston.

With Plante and McNeil dividing the netminding, Montreal whipped the Bruins in five games to capture the Stanley Cup.

## 1952–53

### FINAL STANDINGS

|  | W | L | T | PTS | GF | GA |
|---|---|---|---|---|---|---|
| Detroit | 36 | 16 | 18 | 90 | 222 | 133 |
| Montreal | 28 | 23 | 19 | 75 | 155 | 148 |
| Boston | 28 | 29 | 13 | 69 | 152 | 172 |
| Chicago | 27 | 28 | 15 | 69 | 169 | 175 |
| Toronto | 27 | 30 | 13 | 67 | 156 | 167 |
| New York | 17 | 37 | 16 | 50 | 152 | 211 |

| LEADING SCORERS | G | A | PTS |
|---|---|---|---|
| Howe, Detroit | 49 | 46 | 95 |
| Lindsay, Detroit | 32 | 39 | 71 |
| M. Richard, Montreal | 28 | 33 | 61 |
| Hergesheimer, New York | 30 | 29 | 59 |
| Delvecchio, Detroit | 16 | 43 | 59 |
| Ronty, New York | 16 | 38 | 54 |
| Prystai, Detroit | 16 | 34 | 50 |
| Kelly, Detroit | 19 | 27 | 46 |
| Olmstead, Montreal | 17 | 28 | 45 |
| Mackell, Boston | 27 | 17 | 44 |
| McFadden, Chicago | 23 | 21 | 44 |

## 1953–54

The Chicago Black Hawks slipped back into the NHL's cellar after their one-season move into the playoffs and established a record for futility in 1953–54. They managed only 12 victories and lost 51 times. Both are NHL records for 70-game seasons.

Ironically, the Black Hawks did achieve one important honor that season. Goalie Al Rollins was named the Most Valuable Player in the league. The award might very well have been for heroism in the face of a season-long barrage of enemy shots. Four of the 12 Chicago victories were shutouts by Rollins and the 242 goals allowed by the Black Hawks were the most in the league.

Even more ironic is the fact that Harry Lumley, whom Chicago had traded to Toronto for Rollins and three other players the year before, won the Vezina Trophy, a spot on the All-Star team and a line in the NHL record book with 13 shutouts, the most ever. But the MVP was Rollins.

Gordie Howe and the Detroit Red Wings again ruled the league. Howe won an unprecedented fourth straight scoring title with 81 points and the Red Wings captured an unprecedented sixth consecutive regular-season championship.

Howe and his Detroit linemate, Ted Lindsay, made the first All-Star team for the fourth straight year. Montreal center Ken Mosdell, defensemen Doug Harvey of Montreal and Red Kelly of Detroit and Lumley, Toronto's goalie, completed the team. It was the third straight All-Star berth for Kelly and Harvey.

Kelly also won his third Lady Byng Trophy in four years and also captured a new award, the James Norris Trophy, as the league's top defenseman. The trophy was presented by the four children of the late former owner-president of the Detroit Red Wings. Camille Henry of New York took the Calder Trophy.

*Toronto's Harry Lumley blanked 13 opponents and won the Vezina Trophy in 1953-54.*

Detroit needed just five games to eliminate Toronto, and Montreal took Boston in four straight in the opening rounds of the Stanley Cup playoffs.

Then the Canadiens and Red Wings went at each other in the final round in a memorable series that stretched over seven games. The Red Wings, with Gordie Howe, Ted Lindsay and Alex Delvecchio starring, won three of the first four contests. Then Canadiens' coach Dick Irvin changed goalies, recalling 31-year-old Gerry McNeil from the minors to replace Jacques Plante.

McNeil shut out the Red Wings in the fifth game, which Montreal won on an overtime goal by Ken Mosdell. Then he beat them, 4–1, to even the series at three games apiece.

The seventh game went into overtime tied at 1–1. With 4½ minutes gone in the extra period, Detroit's Tony Leswick lofted a shot toward McNeil. Doug Harvey, the Canadiens' superlative defenseman, lifted his glove to flick the puck away. Instead, it glanced off Harvey's glove, over McNeil's shoulder and into the Montreal net, giving Detroit the Stanley Cup.

The Canadiens stormed off the ice instead of congratulating the Red Wings as custom dictated. "If I had shaken hands," stormed coach Dick Irvin, "I wouldn't have meant it. I refuse to be a hypocrite."

## 1953–54

### FINAL STANDINGS

|  | W | L | T | PTS | GF | GA |
|---|---|---|---|---|---|---|
| Detroit | 37 | 19 | 14 | 88 | 191 | 132 |
| Montreal | 35 | 24 | 11 | 81 | 195 | 141 |
| Toronto | 32 | 24 | 14 | 78 | 152 | 131 |
| Boston | 32 | 28 | 10 | 74 | 177 | 181 |
| New York | 29 | 31 | 10 | 68 | 161 | 182 |
| Chicago | 12 | 51 | 7 | 31 | 133 | 242 |

| LEADING SCORERS | G | A | PTS |
|---|---|---|---|
| Howe, Detroit | 33 | 48 | 81 |
| M. Richard, Montreal | 37 | 30 | 67 |
| Lindsay, Detroit | 26 | 36 | 62 |
| Geoffrion, Montreal | 29 | 25 | 54 |
| Olmstead, Montreal | 15 | 37 | 52 |
| Kelly, Detroit | 16 | 33 | 49 |
| Reibel, Detroit | 15 | 33 | 48 |
| Sanford, Boston | 16 | 31 | 47 |
| Mackell, Boston | 15 | 32 | 47 |
| Mosdell, Montreal | 22 | 24 | 46 |
| Ronty, New York | 13 | 33 | 46 |

# 1954–55

Montreal was piecing together a powerful young team to make a run at Detroit's domination of the NHL. There was tall Jean Beliveau, the slick center from Quebec whom the Canadiens wanted so badly they purchased the rights to an entire amateur league to get him. There was flamboyant Boom Boom Geoffrion, a hard-shooting right winger. There was cool Doug Harvey, perhaps the finest defenseman in the league since Eddie Shore. There was colorful Jacques Plante in goal. And there was the Rocket—Maurice Richard.

The Rocket was always No. 1 with the Canadiens' fans. He was the heart of the club. The fiery Frenchman with the Gallic glare was long on talent and short on temper. It was the latter that got him in trouble, costing him the scoring title and leading to the riot of Ste. Catherine Street which rocked the hockey world in March 1955.

Richard, Geoffrion and Beliveau were racing for the scoring title when the Rocket's temper sabotaged him. It was March 13 in Boston when Richard lost his poise, attacked Hal Laycoe of the Bruins

*Montreal goalie Jacques Plante and teammate Butch Bouchard are down but not out as they block scoring attempt by Rangers' Don Raleigh in 1955.*

with his stick and took a punch at linesman Cliff Thompson.

Clarence Campbell, the league president, was outraged by Richard's behavior and suspended the star for the final three games of the regular season as well as the entire playoffs. Campbell showed up at the Montreal Forum on March 17 to watch the Canadiens play Detroit in a battle for first place. When the president took his seat, he was greeted with some hooting as well as a shower of peanuts and programs. Then a tear gas bomb was thrown on the ice at about the same moment that a fan approached Campbell's box with hand extended as if to shake, and then whacked the president.

Outside the building, more trouble was brewing. As fans poured out of the besieged Forum, they turned into a mob, rumbling down Ste. Catherine Street, Montreal's main avenue, and looting stores.

The next day, Richard went on the radio to plead in French for calm. "I will take my punishment," he said, "and come back next year to help the club and the younger players to win the Stanley Cup."

The suspension left Richard with 74 points and Geoffrion edged past him with 75 to win the scoring crown. Beliveau finished third with 73. Richard was named to the All-Star team along with Beliveau at center and Sid Smith of Toronto at left wing. The defensemen, again, were Doug Harvey of Montreal and Red Kelly of Detroit with Toronto's Harry Lumley in goal.

Smith won the Lady Byng Trophy while Terry Sawchuk of Detroit took the Vezina with a league-leading 12 shutouts and a 1.94 average. It was the fifth straight season in which his goals-against average was less than two per game. The Norris Trophy went to Harvey, the Hart Trophy to Toronto's Ted Kennedy and the Calder to Ed Litzenberger of Chicago.

Detroit edged Montreal for the regular-season title, winning its seventh straight crown by just two points. In the Stanley Cup semifinals, the Red Wings whipped Toronto in four straight and the Canadiens needed five games to eliminate Boston.

In an effort to beat the Red Wings, Montreal coach Dick Irvin alternated his goalies, Jacques Plante and Charlie Hodge. But the Wings, winning all their games at home and none in Montreal, took the series and the Cup, four games to three, as Alex Delvecchio scored twice in the seventh game.

General manager Jack Adams guided Detroit to its seventh Stanley Cup in 1954-55.

# 1954–55

### FINAL STANDINGS

|  | W | L | T | PTS | GF | GA |
|---|---|---|---|---|---|---|
| Detroit | 42 | 17 | 11 | 95 | 204 | 134 |
| Montreal | 41 | 18 | 11 | 93 | 228 | 157 |
| Toronto | 24 | 24 | 22 | 70 | 147 | 135 |
| Boston | 23 | 26 | 21 | 67 | 169 | 188 |
| New York | 17 | 35 | 18 | 52 | 150 | 210 |
| Chicago | 13 | 40 | 17 | 43 | 161 | 235 |

### LEADING SCORERS

|  | G | A | PTS |
|---|---|---|---|
| Geoffrion, Montreal | 38 | 37 | 75 |
| M. Richard, Montreal | 38 | 36 | 74 |
| Beliveau, Montreal | 37 | 36 | 73 |
| Reibel, Detroit | 25 | 41 | 66 |
| Howe, Detroit | 29 | 33 | 62 |
| Sullivan, Chicago | 19 | 42 | 61 |
| Olmstead, Montreal | 10 | 48 | 58 |
| Smith, Toronto | 33 | 21 | 54 |
| Mosdell, Montreal | 22 | 32 | 54 |
| Lewicki, New York | 29 | 24 | 53 |

# 1955–56

There were important personnel changes around the league in 1955–56—both on the players' benches and behind them. After 14 seasons as coach of the Canadiens, Dick Irvin left Montreal and moved on

*Montreal goalie Jacques Plante hurdles a fallen Maple Leaf in 1955-56
action. Plante's 1.86 goals-against average netted him the Vezina
Trophy.*

to Chicago, where the challenge of rebuilding the Black Hawks seemed enormous. Irvin's replacement was Toe Blake, left wing on the old Punch Line. In New York, Phil Watson, always a firebrand, took over as coach, replacing Muzz Patrick, who in turn took over from Frank Boucher as the Rangers' general manager.

Detroit shook up its Stanley Cup champions and a series of trades left the Red Wings with only nine players from the squad that had captured the Cup the previous spring. In the biggest trade, Jack Adams swapped four players, including goalie Terry Sawchuk, to Boston for five Bruins. The Sawchuk deal was made because the Red Wing management felt that Terry's nerves were getting the best of him and also because Adams had a ready-made replacement in young Glenn Hall.

Adams also consummated an eight-player trade with Chicago as the Black Hawks feverishly tried to move out of the league's lower echelon. They didn't make it, but the Rangers did. New scoring punch from a group of recently-graduated junior players including Andy Bathgate, Dean Prentice and Ron Murphy, as well as a stiffened defense supplied by Bill Gadsby, Harry Howell and the fans' favorite, Louie Fontinato, vaulted New York to third place—its highest finish in 14 years.

Fontinato, a rookie, accumulated 202 minutes in penalties—spending the equivalent of more than 10 periods sitting out infractions. The New York fans loved his brawling and nicknamed him Louie the Leaper.

In Montreal, Blake added three rookies—Henri Richard, the younger brother of Maurice, defenseman Jean Guy Talbot, and forward Claude Provost. The Canadiens were clearly the class of the league and finished with 100 points, losing only 15 of their 70 games. Three of the top four scorers were Canadiens, including the champion, Jean Beliveau, who had 47 goals among his 88 points.

Beliveau was named to the All-Star team along with teammates Maurice Richard, Doug Harvey and Jacques Plante. Beliveau and Richard were joined on the forward line by Detroit's Ted Lindsay while Bill Gadsby of New York won the other defense spot alongside Harvey and in front of goaltender Plante.

Plante won the Vezina Trophy with a 1.86 goals-against average, Harvey took the Norris Trophy and Beliveau was named MVP. Detroit's Earl (Dutch) Reibel won the Lady Byng while Glenn Hall, Sawchuk's replacement at Detroit, was the Calder Trophy winner.

Montreal finished off New York in five games and Detroit eliminated Toronto, also in five, in the opening rounds of the Stanley Cup playoffs. Then, with Beliveau, Bernie Geoffrion, Rocket Richard and Bert Olmstead supplying the firepower, Montreal beat Detroit in five games to win its first Stanley Cup in a decade.

# 1955–56

## FINAL STANDINGS

| | W | L | T | PTS | GF | GA |
|---|---|---|---|---|---|---|
| Montreal | 45 | 15 | 10 | 100 | 222 | 131 |
| Detroit | 30 | 24 | 16 | 76 | 183 | 148 |
| New York | 32 | 28 | 10 | 74 | 204 | 203 |
| Toronto | 24 | 33 | 13 | 61 | 153 | 181 |
| Boston | 23 | 34 | 13 | 59 | 147 | 185 |
| Chicago | 19 | 39 | 12 | 50 | 155 | 216 |

## LEADING SCORERS

| | G | A | PTS |
|---|---|---|---|
| Beliveau, Montreal | 47 | 41 | 88 |
| Howe, Detroit | 38 | 41 | 79 |
| M. Richard, Montreal | 38 | 33 | 71 |
| Olmstead, Montreal | 14 | 56 | 70 |
| Sloan, Toronto | 37 | 29 | 66 |
| Bathgate, New York | 19 | 47 | 66 |
| Geoffrion, Montreal | 29 | 33 | 62 |
| Reibel, Detroit | 17 | 39 | 56 |
| Delvecchio, Detroit | 25 | 26 | 51 |
| Creighton, New York | 20 | 31 | 51 |
| Gadsby, New York | 9 | 42 | 51 |

# 1956–57

Montreal's powerhouse Canadiens became the scourge of the league with a collection of the finest shooters ever to occupy a single team's roster at the same time. Maurice Richard, Jean Beliveau, Boom Boom Geoffrion, Bert Olmstead, Dickie Moore and the others were all expert marksmen. And when coach Toe Blake assembled a power play to take advantage of an enemy penalty, the Canadiens' shooters could turn a game around.

Blake used Geoffrion and Doug Harvey at the points on power plays because of their hard, accurate shots. Up front he would employ Richard at

*The Canadiens' Henri Richard splits Ranger ▶ defensemen Lou Fontinato (on ice) and Harry Howell in 1956-57 encounter.*

right wing, Beliveau at center and Moore or Olmstead at left wing. The effect was devastating. The Canadiens often would score two or three goals on a single penalty because at the time the rules required a penalized player to spend his full two minutes in the penalty box, regardless of how often the team with the manpower edge scored.

But the Canadiens made a travesty of the rule and eventually it had to be changed, specifically because of Montreal's proficiency. Starting in 1956–57, as soon as the team with the manpower edge scored, the penalized player was allowed to return to the ice and restore his team to full strength.

Detroit's assessment of Terry Sawchuk's nerves proved accurate when the ex-Red Wing goalie walked out on the Bruins in midseason, saying he was ill. The Bruins put in a hurry-up call to Springfield of the American League and came up with Don Simmons to replace Sawchuk. Ironically, on the day he left Boston, Sawchuk was named to the All-Star team for the first half of the season. With Terry sitting out the second half, Glenn Hall, his replacement at Detroit, captured the final All-Star designation.

The other All-Stars were Detroit's Red Kelly and Montreal's Doug Harvey on defense, Jean Beliveau of Montreal at center and Detroit's Ted Lindsay and Gordie Howe on the wings.

Howe won his fifth scoring championship with 89 points, including 44 goals and also captured the Hart Trophy as MVP. The Lady Byng went to New York's Andy Hebenton, while Montreal's Jacques Plante took the Vezina, Larry Regan of Boston won the Calder and Harvey captured the Norris.

Detroit won its eighth regular-season crown in nine years, beating out the Canadiens by six points. But the Red Wings were upset by Boston's determined Bruins in the Stanley Cup semifinal series. Detroit bowed when Boston rallied for three goals in the third period to win the deciding seventh contest.

Montreal eliminated New York in five games with Boom Boom Geoffrion exploding for three goals in the third engagement. The Canadiens faced the Bruins for the Stanley Cup and Maurice Richard set the tone by exploding for four goals in the 5–1 opening-game victory. The Rocket scored three times in the second period and Don Simmons, the victim of the assault, said simply, "It was humiliating." It took the Canadiens just five games to clinch the Cup.

# 1956–57

## FINAL STANDINGS

|  | W | L | T | PTS | GF | GA |
|---|---|---|---|---|---|---|
| Detroit | 38 | 20 | 12 | 88 | 198 | 157 |
| Montreal | 35 | 23 | 12 | 82 | 210 | 155 |
| Boston | 34 | 24 | 12 | 80 | 195 | 174 |
| New York | 26 | 30 | 14 | 66 | 184 | 227 |
| Toronto | 21 | 34 | 15 | 57 | 174 | 192 |
| Chicago | 16 | 39 | 15 | 47 | 169 | 225 |

## LEADING SCORERS

|  | G | A | PTS |
|---|---|---|---|
| Howe, Detroit | 44 | 45 | 89 |
| Lindsay, Detroit | 30 | 55 | 85 |
| Beliveau, Montreal | 33 | 51 | 84 |
| Bathgate, New York | 27 | 50 | 77 |
| Litzenberger, Chicago | 32 | 32 | 64 |
| M. Richard, Montreal | 33 | 29 | 62 |
| McKenney, Boston | 21 | 39 | 60 |
| Moore, Montreal | 29 | 29 | 58 |
| H. Richard, Montreal | 18 | 36 | 54 |
| Ullman, Detroit | 16 | 36 | 52 |

# 1957–58

Two marvelously talented rookie left wings broke into the NHL in 1957–58. Toronto's Frank Mahovlich won the Calder Trophy as the top rookie, but it was Chicago's Bobby Hull who was to emerge as one of the game's most dynamic stars.

In Detroit, Jolly Jack Adams was again active in the player market. He took Terry Sawchuk back from the Bruins in exchange for Johnny Bucyk and made room for his returning goaltender by swapping Glenn Hall and Ted Lindsay to Chicago for four players. It was rumored that part of the reason Adams unloaded Lindsay was the veteran left wing's active participation in the formation of an NHL Players' Association.

It was the best of times and it was the worst of times for Montreal's Maurice Richard. On October 19, he scored his 500th regular-season goal, but less than one month later he collided with Toronto's Marc Reaume and his Achilles tendon was almost completely severed. For a time, it was feared that the 36-year-old Rocket's career might be over.

In February, the Canadiens again were jolted by an injury. This time it was Boom Boom Geoffrion, leading the league in goals at the time. The Boomer ran into teammate Andre Pronovost during a workout and ruptured a bowel. He was given the last rites of the Roman Catholic Church before major stomach surgery saved his life.

*The Black Hawks unveiled dynamic Bobby Hull in 1957-58.*

Despite the injuries, the Canadiens carried on and finished first, 19 points ahead of the surprising Rangers, who had uncovered a new scoring star in Andy Bathgate. Part of the reason for the Canadiens' success was left winger Dickie Moore, who played the last five weeks of the season with a cast on his right wrist but still won the scoring championship with 84 points as well as an All-Star berth.

Despite the Rocket's injury, there was a Richard on the All-Star team. Brother Henri, the Pocket Rocket, who finished second to Moore in scoring with 80 points, was picked as the center. Gordie

*Toronto's Frank Mahovlich won the Calder Trophy in 1957-58 and became known as "The Big M."*

Howe of Detroit was on right wing, with Bill Gadsby of New York and Doug Harvey of Montreal as the defensemen and Chicago's Glenn Hall in goal.

Howe won Most Valuable Player honors and Harvey took the Norris Trophy as the top defenseman for the fourth straight year. Camille Henry of the Rangers won the Lady Byng, Montreal's Jacques Plante, who had started using a mask in practice, was the Vezina winner and Toronto's Frank Mahovlich took the Calder. Mahovlich had 20 goals and 16 assists compared to Bobby Hull's 13 goals and 34 assists.

Maurice Richard, who had missed 42 regular-season games after his injury and had scored only 15 goals all year, was the spark that drove the Canadiens to their third straight Stanley Cup. Montreal swept Detroit in four games with Richard's hat trick in the final contest leading a last-period comeback that erased a two-goal deficit and gave the Canadiens a 4–3 victory.

Boston, which had eliminated New York in six

games, was tied at two games apiece with Montreal when the Rocket's overtime goal in the fifth game put the Canadiens in the driver's seat. Montreal finished off Boston in the sixth game as Richard completed the 10 playoff games with 11 goals.

## 1957–58

### FINAL STANDINGS

| | W | L | T | PTS | GF | GA |
|---|---|---|---|---|---|---|
| Montreal | 43 | 17 | 10 | 96 | 250 | 158 |
| New York | 32 | 25 | 13 | 77 | 195 | 188 |
| Detroit | 29 | 29 | 12 | 70 | 176 | 207 |
| Boston | 27 | 28 | 15 | 69 | 199 | 194 |
| Chicago | 24 | 39 | 7 | 55 | 163 | 202 |
| Toronto | 21 | 38 | 11 | 53 | 192 | 226 |

### LEADING SCORERS

| | G | A | PTS |
|---|---|---|---|
| Moore, Montreal | 36 | 48 | 84 |
| H. Richard, Montreal | 28 | 52 | 80 |
| Bathgate, New York | 30 | 48 | 78 |
| Howe, Detroit | 33 | 44 | 77 |
| Horvath, Boston | 30 | 36 | 66 |
| Litzenberger, Chicago | 32 | 30 | 62 |
| Mackell, Boston | 20 | 40 | 60 |
| Beliveau, Montreal | 27 | 32 | 59 |
| Delvecchio, Detroit | 21 | 38 | 59 |
| McKenney, Boston | 28 | 30 | 58 |

## 1958–59

Conn Smythe never was a very good loser and when his Toronto Maple Leafs slipped into the NHL cellar, he decided it was time for action. Smythe sought out George (Punch) Imlach, director of player personnel for Boston, and offered him a front office spot with the Leafs. Imlach accepted, provided that the position was that of general manager. The Leafs had no one doing that particular job, so Smythe agreed.

A week after he was named general manager, Imlach decided that Billy Reay, Toronto's coach, wasn't doing a good enough job. Imlach went on a talent hunt and lured the best man available—Punch Imlach.

The Maple Leafs had several new faces besides Imlach's. They had swapped Jim Morrison to Boston for defenseman Allan Stanley and signed another new defenseman in 21-year-old Carl Brewer. Bert Olmstead was acquired from Montreal and Imlach picked up a 33-year-old journeyman goalie, Johnny Bower, from Cleveland of the American League.

They all played a role in Toronto's helter-skelter stretch run to a playoff spot. With 20 games left to

play, the Maple Leafs were in the cellar. On the final night of the regular season they won their fifth straight game while New York was losing its sixth in the last seven. As a result, Toronto sneaked into the fourth and final playoff spot, one point ahead of the embarrassed Rangers, who had to refund thousands of dollars worth of useless playoff tickets.

Montreal easily captured the regular-season title, beating Boston by 18 points. Detroit, meanwhile, had fallen on lean times and dipped all the way into the league basement despite a 32-goal season by Gordie Howe.

Dickie Moore of Montreal won his second straight scoring title with a record 96 points and earned the left wing spot on the All-Star team. Three other Canadiens also made the All-Stars, with Jacques Plante in goal, Jean Beliveau at center and Tom Johnson on defense. Johnson beat out teammate Doug Harvey, who missed the first team after seven straight selections. Right winger Andy Bathgate and defenseman Bill Gadsby of the Rangers completed the squad.

Bathgate won the Hart Trophy, Plante took his fourth straight Vezina and Johnson ended Harvey's four-year monopoly of the Norris Trophy. Montreal's Ralph Backstrom captured the Calder Trophy and Alex Delvecchio of Detroit was the Lady Byng winner.

*Montreal's Jean Beliveau breaks into a grin as his shot beats Toronto's Johnny Bower.*

Maurice Richard of Montreal missed 28 games with a fractured ankle and was virtually useless to the Canadiens in the playoffs. But his loss made little difference to the Montreal powerhouse. The Canadiens eliminated Chicago in six games and ousted Toronto, which had eliminated Boston, in five games for an unprecedented fourth consecutive Stanley Cup.

## 1958–59

### FINAL STANDINGS

|          | W  | L  | T  | PTS | GF  | GA  |
|----------|----|----|----|-----|-----|-----|
| Montreal | 39 | 18 | 13 | 91  | 258 | 158 |
| Boston   | 32 | 29 | 9  | 73  | 205 | 215 |
| Chicago  | 28 | 29 | 13 | 69  | 197 | 208 |
| Toronto  | 27 | 32 | 11 | 65  | 189 | 201 |
| New York | 26 | 32 | 12 | 64  | 201 | 217 |
| Detroit  | 25 | 37 | 8  | 58  | 167 | 218 |

| LEADING SCORERS | G | A | PTS |
|-----------------|----|----|----|
| Moore, Montreal | 41 | 55 | 96 |
| Believeau, Montreal | 45 | 46 | 91 |
| Bathgate, New York | 40 | 48 | 88 |
| Howe, Detroit | 32 | 46 | 78 |
| Litzenberger, Chicago | 33 | 44 | 77 |
| Geoffrion, Montreal | 22 | 44 | 66 |
| Sullivan, New York | 21 | 42 | 63 |
| Hebenton, New York | 33 | 29 | 62 |
| McKenney, Boston | 32 | 30 | 62 |
| Sloan, Chicago | 27 | 35 | 62 |

## 1959–60

The pressures of modern hockey had taken their toll on goaltenders. There was Montreal's Bill Durnan, who retired prematurely because of nerves; Montreal's Gerry McNeil, another early retiree, and Terry Sawchuk, who left Boston in midseason when he

*The Rocket, Maurice Richard of the Canadiens, battles Chicago's Elmer (Moose) Vasko for the puck in 1959-60.*

*Chicago's Stan Mikita was a high-flying rookie in 1959-60.*

began seeing too much rubber. Montreal's Jacques Plante was determined not to let that happen to him.

Plante had been using a mask in practice for two years after fracturing first one and then the other cheekbone during workouts. Jacques had approached coach Toe Blake about wearing the mask during a game but Blake would not allow it.

Then, on November 1, 1959, a shot by New York's Andy Bathgate crunched into Plante's profile, inflicting a gash that took seven stitches.

When Plante subsequently emerged from the dressing room wearing a mask, he looked like a creature from outer space. How could he follow the puck through the mask's tiny eye slits? The answer was that Plante somehow saw it. That night, he beat the Rangers, 3–1, for Montreal's eighth straight game without a loss. The Canadiens tacked 10 more on to that streak as fans around the league flocked to see the masked marvel at work.

Plante captured his fifth consecutive Vezina Tro-

phy, but the All-Star goalie berth went to Chicago's Glenn Hall. Chicago's Bobby Hull won the scoring race in an exciting battle with Boston's Bronco Horvath. Hull finished with 39 goals and 81 points—one point more than Horvath—and was the left wing on the All-Star team.

Gordie Howe of Detroit was the All-Star right wing with Montreal's Jean Beliveau at center. The defensemen were Marcel Pronovost of Detroit and Doug Harvey of Montreal. Howe won the Hart Trophy as MVP, Don McKenney of Boston was the Lady Byng winner, Harvey took the Norris and Chicago's Bill Hay, who centered for Hull, won the Calder.

The Canadiens won their third straight regular-season title, beating Toronto by 13 points. Then Montreal eliminated Chicago in four games in the opening round of the playoffs, with Plante turning in shutouts in the last two.

The Maple Leafs, perhaps inspired by a pile of 1,250 dollar bills that coach Punch Imlach placed in the middle of the dressing room floor as a reminder of the difference between winning and losing, eliminated Detroit in six games.

But Montreal swept past Toronto in the finals in four straight games, to win the Stanley Cup in the minimum of eight games.

# 1959–60

## FINAL STANDINGS

| | W | L | T | PTS | GF | GA |
|---|---|---|---|---|---|---|
| Montreal | 40 | 18 | 12 | 92 | 255 | 178 |
| Toronto | 35 | 26 | 9 | 79 | 199 | 195 |
| Chicago | 28 | 29 | 13 | 69 | 191 | 180 |
| Detroit | 26 | 29 | 15 | 67 | 186 | 197 |
| Boston | 28 | 34 | 8 | 64 | 220 | 241 |
| New York | 17 | 38 | 15 | 49 | 187 | 247 |

## LEADING SCORERS

| | G | A | PTS |
|---|---|---|---|
| Hull, Chicago | 39 | 42 | 81 |
| Horvath, Boston | 39 | 41 | 80 |
| Beliveau, Montreal | 34 | 40 | 74 |
| Bathgate, New York | 26 | 48 | 74 |
| H. Richard, Montreal | 30 | 43 | 73 |
| Howe, Detroit | 28 | 45 | 73 |
| Geoffrion, Montreal | 30 | 41 | 71 |
| McKenney, Boston | 20 | 49 | 69 |
| Stasiuk, Boston | 29 | 39 | 68 |
| Prentice, New York | 32 | 34 | 66 |

# 1960–61

An era came to an end in 1960 when Montreal's Maurice Richard retired. After 18 professional sea-

sons and 544 goals, the Rocket was off the ice. But that didn't keep his name out of the hockey headlines.

That was because for the first time since 1953, when Gordie Howe scored 49 times, there was a genuine threat to the Rocket's record of 50 goals in a season. It would be more correct to say there were two threats, but Frank Mahovlich's early-season pace obscured Bernie Geoffrion's run at the Rocket's mark.

By midseason, Mahovlich, Toronto's hard-skating left wing, had 37 goals and seemed a cinch to top 50. Geoffrion, on the other hand, missed six games with injuries and had only 29 goals going into the final six weeks of the season. And 14 of those had come over one 11-game stretch.

The defenses keyed on Mahovlich over those final weeks and Toronto's Big M finished with 48 goals. Geoffrion, a streaky player, hit another hot spell, exploding for 18 goals in 13 games and scoring his 50th of the season in the Canadiens' 68th game—ironically against Mahovlich's team, the Maple Leafs.

Geoffrion did not score in either of the last two games of the regular season, but won the scoring title with his 50 goals and 45 assists for 95 points. He was the All-Star right wing with Toronto's Mahovlich at left wing and Jean Beliveau of Montreal at center. The defensemen were Doug Harvey of Montreal and Marcel Pronovost of Detroit with Toronto's Johnny Bower in goal.

Bower ended Jacques Plante's five-year hold on the Vezina Trophy while Geoffrion earned the Hart Trophy and Harvey won the Norris for the sixth time. Dave Keon of Toronto was the Calder winner and Red Kelly, switched from defense to center after being traded to Toronto, won his fourth Lady Byng.

The Canadiens captured their fourth straight regular-season championship, beating out Toronto by two points. And Montreal was favored to continue its string of five consecutive Stanley Cups when it opened the playoffs against third-place Chicago.

But the Black Hawks intimidated the Canadiens with some tough body work and got consecutive shutouts from goalie Glenn Hall in the fifth and sixth games to beat Montreal, four games to two. The

*The 1960-61 Rookie of the Year was Dave Keon ▶ of Toronto.*

turning point may have come in the third game, won in triple overtime by Chicago on Murray Balfour's goal. Montreal coach Toe Blake was so incensed at the officiating of Dalton McArthur that he rushed on the ice and took a swing at the referee. That sortie cost Toe $2,000.

Detroit knocked out Toronto in five games, setting up the final for the Stanley Cup between the third-place Black Hawks and fourth-place Red Wings. Unflattering remarks about the officiating cost coach Rudy Pilous and general manager Tommy Ivan of the Black Hawks $500 between them but the fines didn't hurt too much because Chicago took the Cup in six games.

## 1960–61

### FINAL STANDINGS

| | W | L | T | PTS | GF | GA |
|---|---|---|---|---|---|---|
| Montreal | 41 | 19 | 10 | 92 | 254 | 188 |
| Toronto | 39 | 19 | 12 | 90 | 234 | 176 |
| Chicago | 29 | 24 | 17 | 75 | 198 | 180 |
| Detroit | 25 | 29 | 16 | 66 | 195 | 215 |
| New York | 22 | 38 | 10 | 54 | 204 | 248 |
| Boston | 15 | 42 | 13 | 43 | 176 | 254 |

### LEADING SCORERS

| | G | A | PTS |
|---|---|---|---|
| Geoffrion, Montreal | 50 | 45 | 95 |
| Beliveau, Montreal | 32 | 58 | 90 |
| Mahovlich, Toronto | 48 | 36 | 84 |
| Bathgate, New York | 29 | 48 | 77 |
| Howe, Detroit | 23 | 49 | 72 |
| Ullman, Detroit | 28 | 42 | 70 |
| Kelly, Toronto | 20 | 50 | 70 |
| Moore, Montreal | 35 | 34 | 69 |
| H. Richard, Montreal | 24 | 44 | 68 |
| Delvecchio, Detroit | 27 | 35 | 62 |

## 1961–62

In August, the Hockey Hall of Fame erected on the Canadian National Exhibition grounds at Toronto, was officially opened. Built at a cost of $500,000, the hockey shrine honored 89 players, executives and referees from hockey's past.

But it was a player very much of the present who created the excitement, Chicago's blond bombshell, Bobby Hull. A scoring champion two years earlier at the age of 21, Hull boasted a slap shot clocked at better than 100 miles per hour.

Hull started his record run slowly and had only 16 goals after 40 games. But then, like Geoffrion had done the year before, when he tied Maurice Richard's record of 50 goals, Bobby went on a tear.

*Gordie Howe of Detroit displays the puck with which he scored his 500th regular-season goal on March 14, 1962.*

Fourteen goals in nine games, including four in one night, left him 20 goals away from the record with 20 games to play. He needed an average of one goal per game and he got them. He was blanked in only four of the Hawks' final 20 games but made up for those scoreless nights with four two-goal games. He scored his 50th on the final night of the season in New York.

His 84 points gave Hull a tie for the scoring championship with New York's Andy Bathgate. Both received $1,000 from the league but Hull took the Art Ross Trophy emblematic of the scoring title because he had 22 more goals.

New York, led by Bathgate and player-coach Doug Harvey, acquired from Montreal in a trade for defenseman Lou Fontinato, made it to the playoffs for the first time in four seasons, barely beating out Detroit. A goal on a penalty shot by Bathgate against the Red Wings in New York virtually clinched the spot for New York. In the same game, Gordie Howe, killing a Detroit penalty, scored the 500th regular-season goal of his NHL career.

Bathgate was chosen at right wing on the All-Star

team and Hull at left wing. The center was slender Stan Mikita of Chicago, who finished the season with 77 points, tied for third with Howe behind Hull and Bathgate. Jean Guy Talbot of Montreal and Harvey of New York were picked on defense and Montreal's Jacques Plante in goal. It was the 10th time in 11 years that Harvey had been selected as a first-team All-Star defenseman. In the other year he made the second team.

Harvey took his seventh Norris Trophy while Plante captured the Hart Trophy as well as his sixth Vezina. The Calder Trophy went to Montreal's Bobby Rousseau and Toronto's Dave Keon took the Lady Byng.

Montreal captured its fifth straight regular-season title, but again the Canadiens went up against the rambunctious Black Hawks in the playoffs. Montreal, playing at home, won the first two games, but Chicago rebounded to take four straight games with Mikita and Hull the key men.

Toronto eliminated New York in six games, winning the pivotal fifth one in double overtime on Red Kelly's goal despite a superb performance by New York goalie Gump Worsley, who stopped 56 shots.

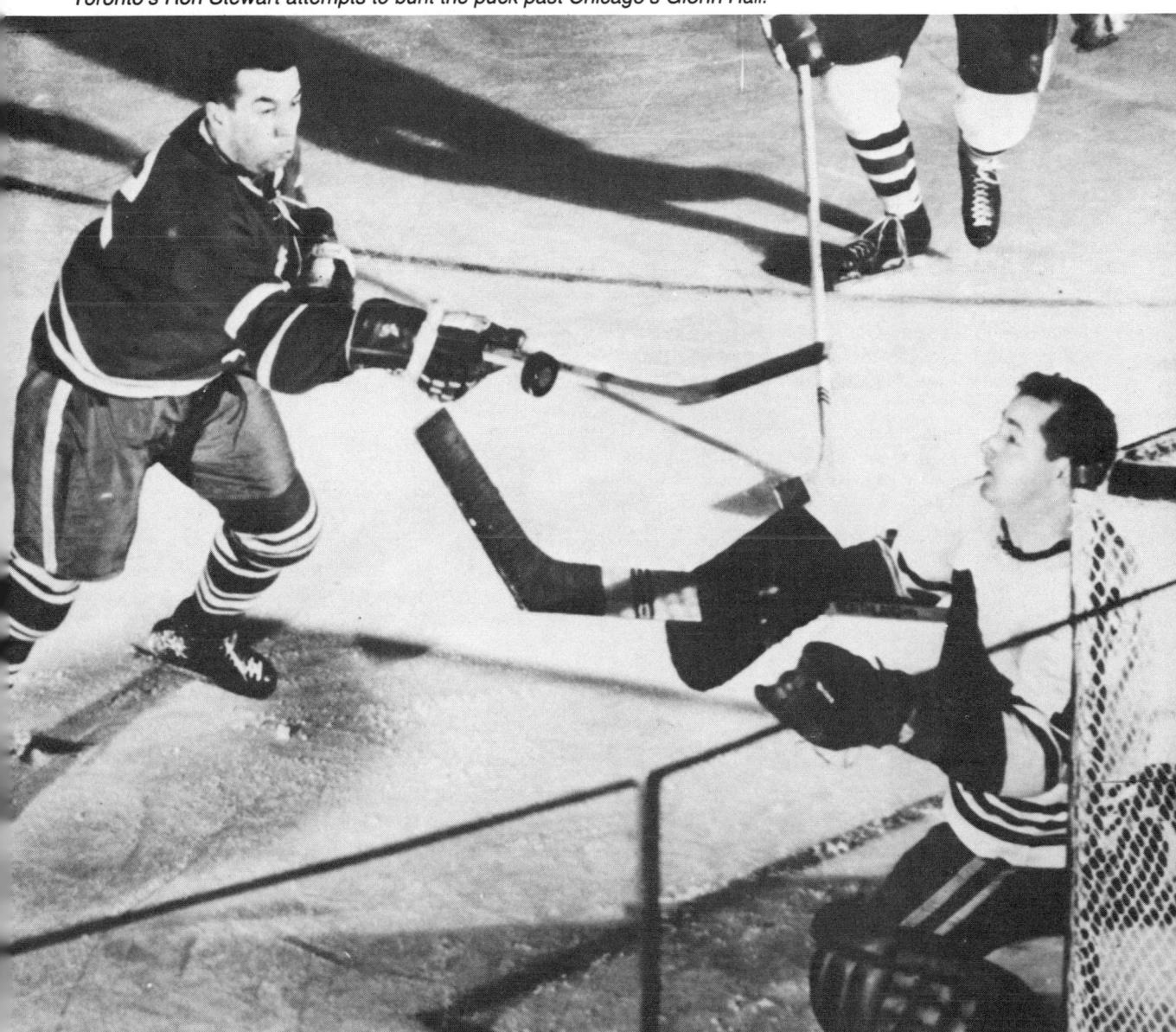

*Toronto's Ron Stewart attempts to bunt the puck past Chicago's Glenn Hall.*

The Leafs went on to win the Stanley Cup in six games against Chicago, the series turning on an 8–4 romp in the fifth game in which Toronto's Bob Pulford scored three goals.

## 1961–62

### FINAL STANDINGS

|  | W | L | T | PTS | GF | GA |
|---|---|---|---|---|---|---|
| Montreal | 42 | 14 | 14 | 98 | 259 | 166 |
| Toronto | 37 | 22 | 11 | 85 | 232 | 180 |
| Chicago | 31 | 26 | 13 | 75 | 217 | 186 |
| New York | 26 | 32 | 12 | 64 | 195 | 207 |
| Detroit | 23 | 33 | 14 | 60 | 184 | 219 |
| Boston | 15 | 47 | 8 | 38 | 177 | 306 |

### LEADING SCORERS

|  | G | A | PTS |
|---|---|---|---|
| Hull, Chicago | 50 | 34 | 84 |
| Bathgate, New York | 28 | 56 | 84 |
| Howe, Detroit | 33 | 44 | 77 |
| Mikita, Chicago | 25 | 52 | 77 |
| Mahovlich, Toronto | 33 | 38 | 71 |
| Delvecchio, Detroit | 26 | 43 | 69 |
| Backstrom, Montreal | 27 | 38 | 65 |
| Ullman, Detroit | 26 | 38 | 64 |
| Hay, Chicago | 11 | 52 | 63 |
| Provost, Montreal | 33 | 29 | 62 |

## 1962–63

Punch Imlach, coach of the Toronto Maple Leafs, was tired of playing bridesmaid to Montreal's bride. For three straight seasons Imlach had finished second behind the Canadiens. It wasn't Imlach's idea of success.

Punch realized he had to strengthen his defense and he decided the man who could do it was a youngster named Kent Douglas, who was playing at Springfield in the American League. Owner Eddie Shore, himself a former defenseman of some repute, demanded a high price. It cost Imlach five players to get Douglas in a Leaf uniform but the move paid off. Douglas became the first defenseman to win the Calder Trophy as the outstanding rookie. And the Maple Leafs put on a late surge to catch Chicago and win the regular-season title. Toronto finished one point ahead of the Black Hawks in the NHL's closest race in years. Only five points separated the Leafs in first place and Detroit in fourth.

Gordie Howe of Detroit won his sixth scoring championship with 38 goals and 86 points. Howe was also the MVP and right wing on the All-Star team. The other All-Stars were Toronto's Frank Mahovlich on left wing, Chicago's Stan Mikita at center, Pierre Pilote of Chicago and Carl Brewer of Toronto on defense and Glenn Hall of Chicago in goal.

Hall won the Vezina Trophy but had his iron-man streak of consecutive regular-season games ended at 502 when a back ailment forced him out of a game in early November. It was the first game Hall had missed since coming into the league in 1954.

In Detroit, Jack Adams ended 35 years of association with the Red Wings to become president of the Central Hockey League, where the NHL clubs had some of their most promising players developing.

But Adams' absence didn't bother Detroit fans. They were too fascinated by Howe's scoring heroics and the antics of defenseman Howie Young, who accumulated an unbelievable record 273 minutes in penalties—the equivalent of more than 4½ games.

The Red Wings kept their rooters happy in the opening round of the playoffs, eliminating Chicago in six games. Even the individual heroics of Bobby Hull, who scored eight goals despite a lame shoulder, a broken nose and a 10-stitch cut on his face, couldn't save the Black Hawks.

Montreal, weakened by late-season injuries to defensemen Lou Fontinato and Tom Johnson, bowed to Toronto in five games. Then the Maple Leafs took Detroit in five to win the Stanley Cup for the second straight year.

## 1962–63

### FINAL STANDINGS

|  | W | L | T | PTS | GF | GA |
|---|---|---|---|---|---|---|
| Toronto | 35 | 23 | 12 | 82 | 221 | 180 |
| Chicago | 32 | 21 | 17 | 81 | 194 | 178 |
| Montreal | 28 | 19 | 23 | 79 | 225 | 183 |
| Detroit | 32 | 25 | 13 | 77 | 200 | 194 |
| New York | 22 | 36 | 12 | 56 | 211 | 233 |
| Boston | 14 | 39 | 17 | 45 | 198 | 281 |

### LEADING SCORERS

|  | G | A | PTS |
|---|---|---|---|
| Howe, Detroit | 38 | 48 | 86 |
| Bathgate, New York | 35 | 46 | 81 |
| Mikita, Chicago | 31 | 45 | 76 |
| Mahovlich, Toronto | 36 | 37 | 73 |
| Richard, Montreal | 23 | 50 | 73 |
| Beliveau, Montreal | 18 | 49 | 67 |
| Bucyk, Boston | 27 | 39 | 66 |
| Delvecchio, Detroit | 20 | 44 | 64 |
| B. Hull, Chicago | 31 | 31 | 62 |
| Oliver, Boston | 22 | 40 | 62 |

*Montreal's Jacques Plante, turning away a shot by Detroit's Parker McDonald, wound up the 1961-62 season with his sixth Vezina Trophy.*

## 1963–64

Detroit's Gordie Howe entered his 19th National Hockey League season with 540 goals—just four away from the career record held by his great rival, Montreal's Maurice Richard. Howe and the other Red Wings were affected by the record as his teammates continually sought to set him up, often ignoring their own scoring chances.

On October 27, playing in Detroit's Olympia Stadium against Richard's old team, the Canadiens, Howe tied the record at 544. The goal came despite tenacious checking by Montreal's Gilles Tremblay,

who held Howe to two shots on goal all night. Defenseman Bill Gadsby earned his 400th NHL assist on Howe's historic goal.

Now, with his 544th in the books, Howe went for the record-breaker. Again the tension gripped both him and his teammates every time he took the ice. Finally, after two weeks of frustration, the break came. On November 10 at Detroit, Howe was killing a penalty against Montreal when he and Bill McNeill broke into Canadiens' ice. Gadsby flashed up the left side to make it a three-man rush and Howe fired the record-breaker.

"I knew he would get it," conceded Maurice Rich-

*Concentration is the key for Montreal's Jean Beliveau as he faces off against the Rangers' Lou Angotti in 1963-64.*

ard after Howe had shattered his record. "He's a great player. How about that, scoring both goals (his 544th and 545th) against my old team."

Like his record of 50 goals in 50 games, however, Richard could point out that it took him 978 games to reach 544, while Howe needed 1,132 games to achieve 545.

Chicago teammates Bobby Hull and Stan Mikita staged an exciting battle in the scoring race. Hull's booming shot produced a league-leading 43 goals, four more than Mikita. But the slick Chicago center had 50 assists and 89 points to win the scoring championship.

For the second straight year the Black Hawks finished one point away from first place, this time behind Montreal. Many Chicago observers thought back to 1927 and the curse Pete Muldoon was alleged to have put on Chicago when he was fired as coach.

The Hawks dominated the All-Star balloting with Mikita, Hull and Ken Wharram named up front along with teammates Pierre Pilote on defense and Glenn Hall in goal. It was only the second time in history that one team had placed five men on the first All-Star squad. The only non-Black Hawk chosen was defenseman Tim Horton of Toronto.

Montreal's Jean Beliveau won the Hart Trophy, Ken Wharram of Chicago took the Lady Byng, Pierre Pilote of Chicago won the Norris, Jacques Laperriere of Montreal captured the Calder and Charlie Hodge of Montreal, who took over when Jacques Plante was traded to New York, won the Vezina.

In February, Punch Imlach pulled off another major trade, dealing five players to New York for Andy Bathgate and Don McKenney. Eventually, the trade worked out in the Rangers' favor but its immediate effect was to help the Maple Leafs to their third straight Stanley Cup.

Bathgate and McKenney combined for nine goals and 12 assists between them as the Leafs eliminated Montreal in seven games and won the Cup in seven against Detroit.

## 1963–64

### FINAL STANDINGS

|           | W  | L  | T  | PTS | GF  | GA  |
|-----------|----|----|----|-----|-----|-----|
| Montreal  | 36 | 21 | 13 | 85  | 209 | 167 |
| Chicago   | 36 | 22 | 12 | 84  | 218 | 169 |
| Toronto   | 33 | 25 | 12 | 78  | 192 | 172 |
| Detroit   | 30 | 29 | 11 | 71  | 191 | 204 |
| New York  | 22 | 38 | 10 | 54  | 186 | 242 |
| Boston    | 18 | 40 | 12 | 48  | 170 | 212 |

### LEADING SCORERS

| LEADING SCORERS | G | A | PTS |
|---|---|---|---|
| Mikita, Chicago | 39 | 50 | 89 |
| B. Hull, Chicago | 43 | 44 | 87 |
| Beliveau, Montreal | 28 | 50 | 78 |
| Bathgate, New York-Toronto | 19 | 58 | 77 |
| Howe, Detroit | 26 | 47 | 73 |
| Wharram, Chicago | 39 | 32 | 71 |
| Oliver, Boston | 24 | 44 | 68 |
| Goyette, New York | 24 | 41 | 65 |
| Gilbert, New York | 24 | 40 | 64 |
| Keon, Toronto | 23 | 37 | 60 |

# 1964–65

NHL teams made two important front-office changes in 1964–65. First, in Montreal, Frank Selke retired as managing director of the Canadiens and was succeeded by Sammy Pollock, an organization man who had worked his way up through the Canadiens' vast network of farm teams. And in New York, Emile Francis succeeded Muzz Patrick as general manager of the Rangers. Francis, a journeyman goaltender in his playing days, had spent five years tutoring the top Ranger junior prospects at the club's Guelph, Ontario, farm. Included among his students were Rod Gilbert and Jean Ratelle, two developing Ranger stars.

Detroit, fed up with the penalty-drawing antics of Howie Young, had traded the defenseman to Chicago for a minor-league goalie named Roger Crozier. The Red Wings, anxious to protect the young prospect, exposed veteran Terry Sawchuk to the draft, thinking his age, 34, would deter any claim. But Punch Imlach, who had remarkable success with elderly players at Toronto, most notably goalie Johnny Bower, claimed Sawchuk. That made Crozier the Red Wings' regular goalie and he didn't disappoint.

A shrimp at 5-foot-8 and 160 pounds, Crozier displayed remarkable reflexes. He sprung at shots as though his life depended on them. It may have been a carryover from his childhood. He was one of 14 children and that can cause plenty of scrambling.

Crozier's 2.42 goals-against average earned him the Calder Trophy and a berth on the All-Star team. And, combined with the goal-scoring of Norm Ullman, Alex Delvecchio and Gordie Howe, Crozier's performance led Detroit to its first regular-season title since 1957. Ullman scored 42 goals and finished second in the scoring race behind Chicago's Stan Mikita, who had 87 points. Howe had 29 goals and

Detroit's Terry Sawchuk blocks shot as Toronto's George Armstrong waits for rebound in 1965.

76 points—third in the scoring race—and Delvecchio posted 25 goals and 67 points.

Ullman was the All-Star center, beating out Mikita. Chicago's Bobby Hull was picked at left wing and Claude Provost of Montreal at right wing. The defensemen were Pierre Pilote of Chicago and Jacques Laperriere of Montreal, with Crozier in goal.

Toronto's goaltending was split down the middle with Johnny Bower playing 34 games and Terry Sawchuk 36. When the Maple Leafs finished with the fewest goals scored against them, the goalies refused to accept the Vezina Trophy unless both their names were inscribed on it and unless both received an equal cash award. The league agreed and the two-goalie system became a permanent part of the Vezina award.

Chicago's Hull won both the Lady Byng and the Hart Trophy—the first man to take the two awards in the same year since the Rangers' Buddy O'Connor in 1947–48. Pierre Pilote was the Norris winner for the third straight season.

Hull, who had 37 goals in his first 35 games, fell victim to injuries and the worst slump of his career and finished with 39 goals for the season. But Bobby exploded during the playoffs, scoring eight goals in the seven-game semifinal victory over Detroit. The Hawks won the sixth and seventh games to take the series.

But the Canadiens, who had survived a brutal warlike series to eliminate Toronto in the semifinals, silenced Hull in the finals. Hull scored only two goals as Montreal whipped Chicago in seven games to

win the Stanley Cup. Gump Worsley's seventh-game shutout clinched it.

A new award, the Conn Smythe Trophy, honoring the outstanding player of the playoffs, went to Montreal captain Jean Beliveau, who scored eight goals in 13 playoff games.

## 1964–65

### FINAL STANDINGS

| | W | L | T | PTS | GF | GA |
|---|---|---|---|---|---|---|
| Detroit | 40 | 23 | 7 | 87 | 224 | 175 |
| Montreal | 36 | 23 | 11 | 83 | 211 | 185 |
| Chicago | 34 | 28 | 8 | 76 | 224 | 176 |
| Toronto | 30 | 26 | 14 | 74 | 204 | 173 |
| New York | 20 | 38 | 12 | 52 | 179 | 246 |
| Boston | 21 | 43 | 6 | 48 | 166 | 253 |

### LEADING SCORERS

| | G | A | PTS |
|---|---|---|---|
| Mikita, Chicago | 28 | 59 | 87 |
| Ullman, Detroit | 42 | 41 | 83 |
| Howe, Detroit | 29 | 47 | 76 |
| B. Hull, Chicago | 39 | 32 | 71 |
| Delvecchio, Detroit | 25 | 42 | 67 |
| Provost, Montreal | 27 | 37 | 64 |
| Gilbert, New York | 25 | 36 | 61 |
| Pilote, Chicato | 14 | 45 | 59 |
| Bucyk, Boston | 26 | 29 | 55 |
| Backstrom, Montreal | 25 | 30 | 55 |
| Esposito, Chicago | 23 | 32 | 55 |

## 1965–66

In response to considerable pressure to expand the size of the league, the NHL decided in October, 1965, to add six new teams by 1967. Four months later, franchises were awarded to Los Angeles, Oakland, Minneapolis-St. Paul, Pittsburgh and Philadelphia. A sixth franchise was granted to St. Louis in April. The cost of joining the league would be $2 million per team.

On the ice, Bobby Hull of the Black Hawks made the big noise again. For years Hull had threatened the 50-goal mark he shared with Maurice Richard and Bernie Geoffrion. But something always stalled his drive. This time, nothing happened.

Hull opened the season with two hat tricks in the first week and had 15 goals in 11 games. A pair of four-goal games and three straight two-goal nights kept him on target. Hull had 44 goals in 45 games—a fantastic goal-per-game average. He hit the magic 50 mark in Chicago's 57th game. Then, he and the Hawks, feeling the record pressure, went scoreless for three games. Finally, on March 12 in Chicago, Hull scored No. 51 against New York goalie Cesare

*Ted Lindsay of Detroit scores final goal of his career, No. 379, against Boston's Jack Norris, in the spring of 1965.*

◄ *Chicago's Bobby Hull strikes back at one of his defensive shadows, Boston's Ed Westfall.*

Maniago, setting off a 7½ minute demonstration by ecstatic Chicago fans. Ironically, Maniago, then playing for Toronto, had been the victim of Bernie Geoffrion's record-tying 50th goal in 1961.

Hull finished with 54 goals and a record 97 points, winning the Hart Trophy and the left wing spot on the All-Star team for the fifth time. Detroit's Gordie Howe was picked at right wing for the ninth time and Chicago's Stan Mikita made it at center for the fourth time. Jacques Laperriere of Montreal and Pierre Pilote of Chicago were the defensemen, Pilote for the fourth straight year. Chicago's "Mr. Goalie," Glenn Hall, made the team for the sixth time.

Detroit's Alex Delvecchio won the Lady Byng Trophy, Brit Selby of Toronto took the Calder and Laperriere broke Pilote's three-year grip on the Norris. The Vezina went to Montreal goalies Gump Worsley and Charlie Hodge.

The Black Hawks, led by Hull, made another run at the top but again fell short, finishing eight points behind Montreal. Toronto was third and Detroit, pennant winners the year before, slipped to fourth.

Montreal and Toronto seemed to declare war on each other in the opening round of the playoffs. Twenty-six penalties were doled out in the second game and that was topped by record totals of 35 penalties and 154 minutes in the next game. The fights were a standoff but the Canadiens won the hockey games, sweeping four straight.

Detroit eliminated the Black Hawks, four games to two, and when the Red Wings stung the Canadiens by winning the first two games of the final series in Montreal, it appeared that Red Wing defenseman Bill Gadsby, playing in his 20th and final season, might finally drink champagne from the Stanley Cup. But it was not to be. The Canadiens roared back with four straight victories to win their second consecutive Cup. Roger Crozier, Detroit's heroic goalie, was awarded the Conn Smythe Trophy as the outstanding player of the playoffs.

*Rangers climb over glass to aid general manager Emile Francis, who was involved in a fracas in the stands in 1965 game against Detroit.*

## 1965–66

### FINAL STANDINGS

|  | W | L | T | PTS | GF | GA |
|---|---|---|---|---|---|---|
| Montreal | 41 | 21 | 8 | 90 | 239 | 173 |
| Chicago | 37 | 25 | 8 | 82 | 240 | 187 |
| Toronto | 34 | 25 | 11 | 79 | 208 | 187 |
| Detroit | 31 | 27 | 12 | 74 | 221 | 194 |
| Boston | 21 | 43 | 6 | 48 | 174 | 275 |
| New York | 18 | 41 | 11 | 47 | 195 | 261 |

### LEADING SCORERS

|  | G | A | PTS |
|---|---|---|---|
| B. Hull, Chicago | 54 | 43 | 97 |
| Mikita, Chicago | 30 | 48 | 78 |
| Rousseau, Montreal | 30 | 48 | 78 |
| Beliveau, Montreal | 29 | 48 | 77 |
| Howe, Detroit | 29 | 46 | 75 |
| Ullman, Detroit | 31 | 41 | 72 |
| Delvecchio, Detroit | 31 | 38 | 69 |
| Nevin, New York | 29 | 33 | 62 |
| Richard, Montreal | 22 | 39 | 61 |
| Oliver, Boston | 18 | 42 | 60 |

## 1966–67

The National Hockey League celebrated its 50th anniversary season by signing a $3.5 million television contract with the Columbia Broadcasting System providing for Game-of-the-Week coverage.

After laboring for 40 years under the Curse of Muldoon, which had been cast by their first coach after he felt he was unjustly fired, the Chicago Black Hawks finally broke the spell and won their first NHL regular-season title.

The Hawks won convincingly, beating Montreal by 17 points. Bobby Hull reached the 50-goal plateau for the third time in his fabulous career, finishing with 52. But the scoring crown went to teammate Stan Mikita, who set a record with 62 assists and tied Hull's mark of 97 points in a season.

The surprise team of the year was the Rangers, who flirted with first place and could have finished as high as second going into the final weekend of the season. The key men were Rod Gilbert, Phil Goyette, goalie Ed Giacomin, who had been acquired from the minors for four players two seasons earlier, and Bernie Geoffrion, lured out of retirement by general manager-coach Emile Francis. Gilbert had 28 goals, Goyette's 49 assists were second only to Mikita, Giacomin was the All-Star goalie and

Geoffrion contributed 17 goals on the ice and a winning spirit in the dressing room.

Joining Giacomin on the All-Star team were New York defenseman Harry Howell, a 15-year veteran enjoying his finest season, Chicago defenseman Pierre Pilote, picked for the fifth straight year, and three Black Hawk forwards—Hull, Mikita and Ken Wharram.

Mikita, the scoring champion, also won the Hart Trophy and the Lady Byng, becoming the first triple crown winner in NHL history. Chicago goalies Glenn Hall and Denis DeJordy shared the Vezina Trophy while Harry Howell won the Norris and 18-year-old Bobby Orr of Boston took the Calder.

The expansion teams were busily assembling front office staffs to scout the established teams and their farm systems for the upcoming stocking draft. Philadelphia hired Bud Poile as general manager and Keith Allen as coach. Pittsburgh came up with Jack Riley as general manager and Red Sullivan as coach. Minnesota gave both jobs to Wren Blair and St. Louis did the same with Lynn Patrick. Oakland would give both posts to Bert Olmstead and Los Angeles would name Larry Regan as general manager and Red Kelly as coach.

In the playoffs, Montreal staged a five-goal third-period rally to wipe out a Ranger lead in the first game and then burst by the demoralized New Yorkers in four straight games. Terry Sawchuk, who had achieved a landmark with his 100th career shutout during the season, led Toronto past Chicago in six games and the Maple Leafs faced the Canadiens for the Cup.

Again, it was Sawchuk's sparkling goaltending and some opportunistic scoring by Jim Pappin, Pete Stemkowski, Bob Pulford and Dave Keon that pulled the Maple Leafs through. Toronto won its 11th Stanley Cup in six games with the Smythe Trophy going to Keon.

# 1966–67

## FINAL STANDINGS

|  | W | L | T | PTS | GF | GA |
|---|---|---|---|---|---|---|
| Chicago | 41 | 17 | 12 | 94 | 264 | 170 |
| Montreal | 32 | 25 | 13 | 77 | 202 | 188 |
| Toronto | 32 | 27 | 11 | 75 | 204 | 211 |
| New York | 30 | 28 | 12 | 72 | 188 | 189 |
| Detroit | 27 | 39 | 4 | 58 | 212 | 241 |
| Boston | 17 | 43 | 10 | 44 | 182 | 253 |

## LEADING SCORERS

|  | G | A | PTS |
|---|---|---|---|
| Mikita, Chicago | 35 | 62 | 97 |
| B. Hull, Chicago | 52 | 28 | 80 |
| Ullman, Detroit | 26 | 44 | 70 |
| Wharram, Chicago | 31 | 34 | 65 |
| Howe, Detroit | 25 | 40 | 65 |
| Rousseau, Montreal | 19 | 44 | 63 |
| Esposito, Chicago | 21 | 40 | 61 |
| Goyette, New York | 12 | 49 | 61 |
| Mohns, Chicago | 25 | 35 | 60 |
| Richard, Montreal | 21 | 34 | 55 |
| Delvecchio, Detroit | 17 | 38 | 55 |

◄ *Boston's Bobby Orr was an obvious choice as Rookie of the Year in 1966-67.*

*Terry Sawchuk of Los Angeles halts scoring attempt by New York's Orland Kurtenbach in 1967-68.*

# COAST-TO-COAST
# 1967-1979

It was the most ambitious undertaking ever attempted by a major sport, and many predicted it wouldn't work. But the National Hockey League went ahead with its expansion program anyway, and in a span of 11 years grew from six to 17 teams.

The biggest increase came at the start of the 1967–68 season, when the league doubled in size to 12 franchises. For the first time, hockey became a coast-to-coast sport, as teams were placed in Los Angeles and Oakland. The four other new teams were also in the U.S.—Minnesota, Philadelphia, Pittsburgh and St. Louis.

The Montreal Canadiens continued their championship tradition in the first two seasons of expansion play, but then a young defenseman named Bobby Orr and a sharpshooting center named Phil Esposito brought the Boston Bruins into the limelight, winning the Stanley Cup in two out of the next three seasons.

Teams were added in 1970 (Buffalo and Vancouver), 1972 (New York Islanders and Atlanta) and 1974 (Kansas City and Washington), bringing the league total to 18 teams.

The Philadelphia Flyers made league history when they became the first expansion team to win the Cup in 1972–73, but after another year at the top, the Flyers gave way to a restoration of the Canadiens' dynasty as Montreal, led by super-scorer Guy Lafleur and goalie Ken Dryden, won the Cup four years in a row.

Along the way, competition from the rival World Hockey Association sent players' salaries soaring; Clarence Campbell stepped down as NHL president after serving for 31 years, replaced in 1977 by John A. Ziegler, Jr., and the league was pared to 17 teams when the franchises in Cleveland and Minnesota merged in 1978.

## 1967–68

On June 6, 1967, the most ambitious expansion program in sports history became a reality. The league doubled in size with six new teams stocked with 20 players each drafted from the established teams, and added as the NHL's West Division. The six older clubs became the East Division and a 74-game schedule was adopted.

Some good names were available and chosen by the six new clubs. Goalie Glenn Hall went to the St. Louis Blues and goalie Terry Sawchuk to the Los Angeles Kings. The Pittsburgh Penguins came up with high-scoring Andy Bathgate. The first player drafted was forward Dave Balon, chosen by the

Minnesota North Stars. Defensemen Bob Baun and Kent Douglas both were chosen by the San Francisco-Oakland entry, called the California Seals. The Philadelphia Flyers drafted goaltenders Doug Favell and Bernie Parent.

The first meeting between an established team and an expansion team came on opening night when the Montreal Canadiens nipped the Pittsburgh Penguins, 2–1, as Jean Beliveau scored the 400th goal of his career.

For the season, expansion clubs won 40 games, lost 86 and tied 18 against the established teams. Los Angeles, coached by Red Kelly, was 10-12-2 for the best West record against the East. Of the established teams, Toronto had the most trouble with the new division. The Maple Leafs were under .500 with a 10-11-3 record and that figured impor-

tantly in their tumble to fifth place—their first season out of the playoffs in a decade. New York enjoyed the best record against the West, 17-4-3, and this helped the Rangers to a second-place finish.

In midseason the California entry decided to shed its San Francisco image and was renamed the Oakland Seals. Of the six new teams, the Seals had the toughest time at the gate and there was repeated talk about a possible shift of the franchise to Vancouver, British Columbia. But the Seals remained in Oakland.

Both divisions produced exciting races. Montreal finished four points ahead of the charging Rangers. New York's attack was led by Rod Gilbert and Jean Ratelle, who had played hockey together since their childhood days in Montreal. Gilbert scored 29 goals and Ratelle 32. Gilbert had four goals in one night

at Montreal and set an NHL record with 16 shots on net in that game. Philadelphia edged Los Angeles by one point for the West crown but the big scorer in the division was Minnesota's Wayne Connelly, who had 35 goals.

Chicago's Stan Mikita captured his fourth scoring title in five seasons with 40 goals and 87 points and repeated as a triple trophy winner, adding the Hart and Lady Byng to his scoring championship. Gump Worsley and Rogatien Vachon of Montreal shared the Vezina Trophy while Boston's Bobby Orr took the Norris and teammate Derek Sanderson won the Calder.

Worsley was the All-Star goalie with Orr and Toronto's Tim Horton on defense and Stan Mikita and Bobby Hull of Chicago and Detroit's Gordie Howe up front. Howe celebrated his 40th birthday on the final night of the season and finished with 39 goals, his highest total in 12 seasons. Hull had 44, his lowest total in three seasons.

The new Stanley Cup playoff format provided for intra-division playoffs involving the first four teams and then a Cup final between the survivors. In the East, Montreal breezed through Boston in four straight and then took Chicago in five after the Black Hawks had rallied from a two-game deficit to eliminate the Rangers. In the West, Minnesota and St. Louis emerged victorious in a pair of exciting seven-game series against Los Angeles and Philadelphia. Then the Blues struggled through seven games to beat off the North Stars.

In the final, Montreal swept four straight games, winning the Cup. Twice the expansion Blues forced the Canadiens into overtime and each of the four games was decided by one goal. Glenn Hall, the St. Louis goalie, won the Smythe Trophy for his playoff performance.

"The expansion," NHL president Clarence Campbell said, "was successful beyond our fondest hopes."

It was a year of triumph and tragedy. The triumph was successful doubling in size of the league. The tragedy was the death in January of Bill Masterton, a Minnesota forward, who struck his head on the ice after a collision and never regained consciousness. It was the first game-related fatality in NHL history.

◄ *The efficient poke check, as demonstrated by Boston's Bobby Orr against the Rangers' Phil Goyette.*

# 1967–68

## FINAL STANDINGS

### East Division

| | W | L | T | PTS | GF | GA |
|---|---|---|---|---|---|---|
| Montreal | 42 | 22 | 10 | 94 | 236 | 167 |
| New York | 39 | 23 | 12 | 90 | 226 | 183 |
| Boston | 37 | 27 | 10 | 84 | 259 | 216 |
| Chicago | 32 | 26 | 16 | 80 | 212 | 222 |
| Toronto | 33 | 31 | 10 | 76 | 209 | 176 |
| Detroit | 27 | 35 | 12 | 66 | 245 | 257 |

### West Division

| | W | L | T | PTS | GF | GA |
|---|---|---|---|---|---|---|
| Philadelphia | 31 | 32 | 11 | 73 | 173 | 179 |
| Los Angeles | 31 | 33 | 10 | 72 | 200 | 224 |
| St. Louis | 27 | 31 | 16 | 70 | 177 | 191 |
| Minnesota | 27 | 32 | 15 | 69 | 191 | 226 |
| Pittsburgh | 27 | 34 | 13 | 67 | 195 | 216 |
| Oakland | 15 | 42 | 17 | 47 | 153 | 219 |

## LEADING SCORERS

| | G | A | PTS |
|---|---|---|---|
| Mikita, Chicago | 40 | 47 | 87 |
| Esposito, Boston | 35 | 49 | 84 |
| Howe, Detroit | 39 | 43 | 82 |
| Ratelle, New York | 32 | 46 | 78 |
| Gilbert, New York | 29 | 48 | 77 |
| B. Hull, Chicago | 44 | 31 | 75 |
| Ullman, Detroit-Toronto | 35 | 37 | 72 |
| Delvecchio, Detroit | 22 | 48 | 70 |
| Bucyk, Boston | 30 | 39 | 69 |
| Wharram, Chicago | 27 | 42 | 69 |

# 1968–69

In his 23rd NHL season at the age of 40, Gordie Howe scored more points than he ever had before. Detroit's wonder man finished the season with an incredible 103 points, eight more than his previous high.

It was good enough for third place in the scoring race. That's because 1968–69 went down in NHL history as the year of the scorer, with records falling all around the league.

Chicago's Bobby Hull shattered the 50-goal plateau for the fourth time and pushed his own single season mark to an almost unbelievable 58 goals. He finished with 107 scoring points. That was good enough for second place in the scoring race.

The man of the year was Phil Esposito, a tall, almost gangly center, who set Boston and the NHL on its collective ear. Esposito, who had centered for Hull when Bobby scored 54 goals, shattered all scoring records with an amazing 126 points including 49 goals.

Esposito, Hull and Howe all soared past the 100-point mark, easily smashing the NHL single-season point record of 97 shared by Hull and teammate

*Red Berenson of St. Louis scores the first of his modern-record six goals against the Philadelphia Flyers on November 7, 1968.*

Stan Mikita. In fact, Mikita scored 97 points this year and was considered a disappointment to the Black Hawks.

The record-making wasn't confined to the established East Division teams either. In November, Red Berenson, a castoff, scored six goals for St. Louis, tying the single-game record set a quarter of a century earlier by Syd Howe of Detroit.

The St. Louis club, led by Berenson, raced to the West Division championship, winning it by a whopping 19 points. Jacques Plante, drafted from New York and lured out of retirement by the Blues, joined Glenn Hall in goal and the two veterans shared the Vezina Trophy for fewest goals allowed.

In the East, Montreal and Boston battled down to the final weekend before the Canadiens clinched first place for rookie coach Claude Ruel, who took over when Toe Blake retired.

The Canadiens and Bruins swept past New York and Toronto in four straight games as the Stanley Cup playoffs got underway. Then Montreal beat Boston in six games—three of the victories coming on overtime goals—to qualify for the Cup finals.

St. Louis shattered Philadelphia in four games and repeated the sweep against Los Angeles which had ousted Oakland in seven. But in the finals, the Blues were no match for Montreal. The powerful Canadiens swept to their 16th Stanley Cup in the minimum of four games, repeating their 1967–68 sweep of St. Louis.

Esposito, who led all playoff scorers with 18 points, won the Hart Trophy as MVP and was named center on the All-Star team. The other All-Stars were Hull and Howe, Boston's Bobby Orr, who broke all scoring records for defensemen with 21 goals, Toronto's Tim Horton and St. Louis goalie Glenn Hall.

Orr won the Norris Trophy as the outstanding defenseman while Detroit's Alex Delvecchio took the Lady Byng and Danny Grant of the Minnesota North Stars won the Calder as Rookie of the Year.

## 1968–69

### FINAL STANDINGS

#### East Division

| | W | L | T | PTS | GF | GA |
|---|---|---|---|---|---|---|
| Montreal | 46 | 19 | 11 | 103 | 271 | 202 |
| Boston | 42 | 18 | 16 | 100 | 303 | 221 |
| New York | 41 | 26 | 9 | 91 | 231 | 196 |
| Toronto | 35 | 26 | 15 | 85 | 234 | 217 |
| Detroit | 33 | 31 | 12 | 78 | 239 | 221 |
| Chicago | 34 | 33 | 9 | 77 | 280 | 246 |

#### West Division

| | W | L | T | PTS | GF | GA |
|---|---|---|---|---|---|---|
| St. Louis | 37 | 25 | 14 | 88 | 204 | 157 |
| Oakland | 29 | 36 | 11 | 69 | 219 | 251 |
| Philadelphia | 20 | 35 | 21 | 61 | 174 | 225 |
| Los Angeles | 24 | 42 | 10 | 58 | 185 | 260 |
| Pittsburgh | 20 | 45 | 11 | 51 | 189 | 252 |
| Minnesota | 18 | 43 | 15 | 51 | 189 | 270 |

| LEADING SCORERS | G | A | PTS |
|---|---|---|---|
| Esposito, Boston | 49 | 77 | 126 |
| B. Hull, Chicago | 58 | 49 | 107 |
| Howe, Detroit | 44 | 59 | 103 |
| Mikita, Chicago | 30 | 67 | 97 |
| Hodge, Boston | 45 | 45 | 90 |
| Cournoyer, Montreal | 43 | 44 | 87 |
| Delvecchio, Detroit | 25 | 58 | 83 |
| Berenson, St. Louis | 35 | 47 | 82 |
| Beliveau, Montreal | 33 | 49 | 82 |
| Mahovlich, Detroit | 49 | 29 | 78 |

## 1969–70

It had been 29 long, frustrating years between champagne sips out of the Stanley Cup for the Boston Bruins. But with a super player like Bobby Orr in the lineup, it was only a matter of time before the Bruins returned to the top. This was the year.

Orr shattered all scoring records for defensemen,

*The Esposito brothers go head-to-head: Boston's Phil tries to score against Chicago's Tony in 1969-70.*

exploding for 33 goals, 87 assists and 120 points. He became the first defenseman in history to win the scoring title, only the fourth player ever to go over 100 points and fell just six short of the record of 126 established by his teammate, Phil Esposito, the year before.

Exposito finished with 99 points for second place in the scoring race. But the family pride was protected by Phil's younger brother, Chicago's Tony, who won the Calder Trophy as Rookie of the Year and the Vezina as the Black Hawks allowed fewer goals than any other team in the league.

Tony Esposito was drafted by Chicago from Montreal and took the league by storm. He turned in a record-breaking 15 shutouts and led the Hawks from a last-place finish in 1969 to first place in 1970. The East Division race was not decided until the final night of the season and then with some bizarre developments.

New York had led the East for 3½ months but wilted under an avalanche of injuries, dropping from the lead March 1. Boston and Chicago took over, battling head-to-head for the top spot. Meanwhile, New York, Detroit and Montreal battled it out for the other three playoff berths.

In the West, St. Louis clinched its second consecutive title early and watched with interest as Philadelphia tied its way out of the playoffs. The Flyers set a record with 24 deadlocks and, although tied with Oakland in points, lost the final playoff spot in the West because the Seals had more victories.

The same thing happened in the East where Boston and Chicago tied in points but the Black Hawks had more victories and were awarded first place. The Rangers beat out the Canadiens for fourth on the basis of more goals scored. The two teams finished with identical won-lost-tied marks and only a nine-goal binge on the final day allowed New York to make it.

Montreal's elimination ended a 22-year string of playoff appearances for that team and marked the first time in history that no Canadian team was in the playoffs.

Boston captured the Cup, beating New York, Chicago and St. Louis and winning the last 10 games in a row. St. Louis eliminated Minnesota and Pittsburgh before being swept out in the finals for the third straight year.

Orr became the first man in history to win four individual trophies in a single season, taking the

Ross as scoring champ, the Norris as best defenseman, the Hart as regular-season MVP and the Smythe as playoff MVP. Tony Esposito captured the Calder and Vezina and Phil Goyette of St. Louis won the Lady Byng.

The Esposito brothers—Chicago's goalie, Tony, and Boston's center, Phil—made the All-Star team along with Gordie Howe of Detroit, Bobby Hull of Chicago, and defensemen Brad Park of New York and the incredible Orr.

## 1969–70

### FINAL STANDINGS

#### East Division

| | W | L | T | PTS | GF | GA |
|---|---|---|---|---|---|---|
| Chicago | 45 | 22 | 9 | 99 | 250 | 170 |
| Boston | 40 | 17 | 19 | 99 | 277 | 216 |
| Detroit | 40 | 21 | 15 | 95 | 246 | 199 |
| New York | 38 | 22 | 16 | 92 | 246 | 189 |
| Montreal | 38 | 22 | 16 | 92 | 244 | 201 |
| Toronto | 29 | 34 | 13 | 71 | 222 | 242 |

#### West Division

| | W | L | T | PTS | GF | GA |
|---|---|---|---|---|---|---|
| St. Louis | 37 | 27 | 12 | 86 | 224 | 179 |
| Pittsburgh | 26 | 38 | 12 | 64 | 182 | 238 |
| Minnesota | 19 | 35 | 22 | 60 | 224 | 257 |
| Oakland | 22 | 40 | 14 | 58 | 169 | 243 |
| Philadelphia | 17 | 35 | 24 | 58 | 197 | 225 |
| Los Angeles | 14 | 52 | 10 | 38 | 168 | 290 |

### LEADING SCORERS

| | G | A | PTS |
|---|---|---|---|
| Orr, Boston | 33 | 87 | 120 |
| Esposito, Boston | 43 | 56 | 99 |
| Mikita, Chicago | 39 | 47 | 86 |
| Goyette, St. Louis | 29 | 49 | 78 |
| Tkaczuk, New York | 27 | 50 | 77 |
| Ratelle, New York | 32 | 42 | 74 |
| Berenson, St. Louis | 33 | 39 | 72 |
| Parise, Minnesota | 24 | 48 | 72 |
| Howe, Detroit | 31 | 40 | 71 |
| Mahovlich, Detroit | 38 | 32 | 70 |
| Balon, New York | 33 | 37 | 70 |
| McKenzie, Boston | 29 | 41 | 70 |

## 1970–71

Goaltending has always been a tough way to earn a living but it never was tougher than during the 1970–71 season when the Boston Bruins assembled what may have been the greatest scoring machine in the history of hockey.

The cast was headed by Phil Esposito, the bull of a center who had set a single-season scoring record two years earlier when he totaled 126 points. Espo attacked his record with a vengeance and shattered it with an avalanche of goals and assists. He finished with 152 points, an all-time record that was split exactly down the middle with 76 goals and

Ken Dryden had only appeared in six regular-season NHL games
when he led Montreal to the Stanley Cup in 1971.

76 assists. The 76 goals, a truly remarkable achievement, shattered Bobby Hull's old single-season record by 18.

Esposito thus became the fourth man in NHL history to soar past the 50-goal mark. Not long after he made it, teammate Johnny Bucyk also shot past 50, making the Bruins the first team ever to have two 50-goal scorers on the same team. Bucyk finished with 51 goals and 116 points but that total was only third in the NHL scoring race. Squeezed between scoring champion Esposito and Bucyk was Boston's fantastic defenseman, Bobby Orr, who totaled 139 points, 19 more than he had the year before when he won the scoring crown.

Fourth place in the scoring race belonged to another Bruin, Esposito's linemate, Ken Hodge, who also went over 100 points. Two more Boston players, Wayne Cashman and Johnny McKenzie, finished seventh and eighth, completing a remarkable Bruin domination of the league's top scorers.

Boston finished with a record 399 goals for the season, an average of better than five goals per game. With that kind of attack, it was no surprise that the Bruins zoomed to the East Division championship, losing only 14 games all season. The West crown went to the Chicago Black Hawks, shifted to the expansion division in a realignment of teams when two new teams, Buffalo and Vancouver, were added to the East.

In the playoffs, defending champion Boston and its awesome scoring machine ranked as heavy favorites. But the Bruins ran into a hot goalie, Montreal rookie Ken Dryden, and the Canadiens eliminated Boston in seven games—a stunning first-round upset. Montreal then knocked off Minnesota to advance to the final round. Chicago eased its way past Philadelphia and then struggled seven games, three of them stretching into overtime, before eliminating New York. That sent the Canadiens against the Black Hawks for the Cup and Montreal won it in a pulsating seven-game showdown.

Dryden, who had played only six regular-season games before the playoffs, emerged as the Canadiens' hero and won the Smythe Trophy as the Cup's

MVP. The regular-season MVP was Orr, who also won his fourth straight Norris Trophy as the best defenseman. The Calder Trophy for Rookie of the Year went to Buffalo center Gilbert Perreault and the Lady Byng for clean play was awarded to Boston's Bucyk. Goalies Ed Giacomin and Gilles Villemure of the defensive-minded Rangers shared the Vezina Trophy as New York allowed fewer goals than any other team.

Esposito, Hodge, Bucyk and Orr made the All-Star team along with Montreal defenseman J. C. Tremblay and Ranger goalie Giacomin.

The year was otherwise notable in that it was presumed to be the valedictory for two of the NHL's greatest stars, Detroit's Gordie Howe and Montreal's Jean Beliveau. Howe scored 23 goals for a 25-year career total of 786. Beliveau scored 25, finishing his 18-year career with 507.

## 1970–71

### FINAL STANDINGS

#### East Division

|  | W | L | T | PTS | GF | GA |
|---|---|---|---|---|---|---|
| Boston | 57 | 14 | 7 | 121 | 399 | 207 |
| New York | 49 | 18 | 11 | 109 | 259 | 177 |
| Montreal | 42 | 23 | 13 | 97 | 291 | 216 |
| Toronto | 37 | 33 | 8 | 82 | 248 | 211 |
| Buffalo | 24 | 39 | 15 | 63 | 217 | 291 |
| Vancouver | 24 | 46 | 8 | 56 | 229 | 296 |
| Detroit | 22 | 45 | 11 | 55 | 209 | 308 |

#### West Division

|  | W | L | T | PTS | GF | GA |
|---|---|---|---|---|---|---|
| Chicago | 49 | 20 | 9 | 107 | 277 | 184 |
| St. Louis | 34 | 25 | 19 | 87 | 223 | 208 |
| Philadelphia | 28 | 33 | 17 | 73 | 207 | 225 |
| Minnesota | 28 | 34 | 16 | 72 | 191 | 223 |
| Los Angeles | 25 | 40 | 13 | 63 | 239 | 303 |
| Pittsburgh | 21 | 37 | 20 | 62 | 221 | 240 |
| California | 20 | 53 | 5 | 45 | 199 | 320 |

### LEADING SCORERS

|  | G | A | PTS |
|---|---|---|---|
| Esposito, Boston | 76 | 76 | 152 |
| Orr, Boston | 37 | 102 | 139 |
| Bucyk, Boston | 51 | 65 | 116 |
| Hodge, Boston | 43 | 62 | 105 |
| B. Hull, Chicago | 44 | 52 | 96 |
| Ullman, Toronto | 34 | 51 | 85 |
| Cashman, Boston | 21 | 58 | 79 |
| McKenzie, Boston | 31 | 46 | 77 |
| Keon, Toronto | 38 | 38 | 76 |
| Beliveau, Montreal | 25 | 51 | 76 |
| Stanfield, Boston | 24 | 52 | 76 |

## 1971–72

There has always been considerable debate over whether there is more prestige for a team to win a

*Defensive play of young Brad Park, chasing Chicago's Dennis Hull here, helped Rangers reach the Stanley Cup finals in 1972.*

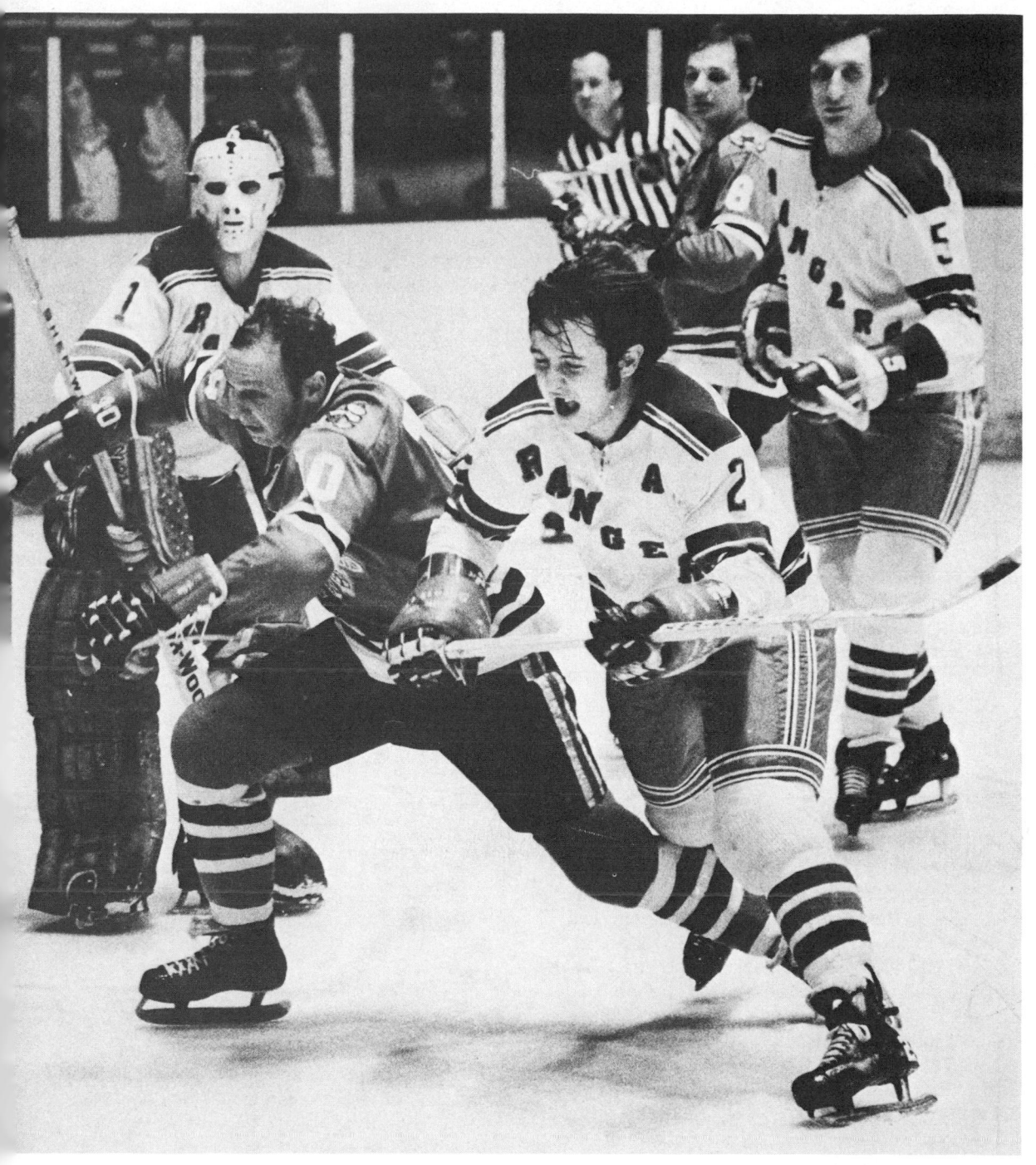

National Hockey League regular-season title or to capture the post-season Stanley Cup playoffs instead. Coming out on top of the six-month, 78-game regular-season grind is a test of staying power, but the tension and excitement of the playoffs for Lord Stanley's battered old mug have a way of stealing the thunder. People tend to remember the Stanley Cup champions longer.

The Boston Bruins solved this all very simply in 1971–72. They just won everything available to them. Led by the scoring tandem of center Phil Esposito and defenseman Bobby Orr, the Bruins zoomed to a first-place finish in the East Division, finishing 10 points ahead of the New York Rangers and losing just 13 games, a record for the 78-game season. It was the second straight regular-season crown for the boisterous Bruins. But the season before, they had been submarined in the first round of the playoffs by Montreal. This time there was no Stanley Cup slip. Boston zipped to the Cup, losing only three of 15 post-season games.

Esposito and Orr finished 1–2 in the scoring race for the third straight season. Esposito won the title with 133 points, including 66 goals. Orr finished second with 117 points, including 37 goals, matching his total of the year before. Both made the All-Star team along with Ranger defenseman Brad Park, right wing Rod Gilbert of the Rangers, left wing Bobby Hull of Chicago and Chicago goalie Tony Esposito (Phil's brother).

The scoring title was the third in four years for Esposito, but he couldn't break the stranglehold Orr was establishing on the Hart Trophy as Most Valuable Player. Bobby won the MVP award for the third straight year and also took his fifth consecutive Norris Trophy as the league's finest defenseman. The Lady Byng Trophy for clean and effective play went to Jean Ratelle of the New York Rangers, and Montreal's Ken Dryden, playoff hero a year earlier, took the Calder Trophy as Rookie of the Year. Dryden, despite his previous season's playoff heroics, was still eligible for the rookie award based on his limited regular-season duty the year before. Chicago's Tony Esposito and Gary Smith shared the Vezina Trophy as the Black Hawks achieved the league's best defensive record.

There was considerable talk around the hockey world about the establishment of another league to challenge the NHL. Most NHL officials shrugged off the talk as just that. But there was some scurrying

around by the league's expansion committee and a quite sudden decision was made to add two new franchises for 1972–73. One would go to Long Island and the other to Atlanta. The development of the World Hockey Association and the establishment of those two new NHL francises were linked. The key was a handsome new building on Long Island, the Nassau County Memorial Coliseum. The WHA was eying the arena to house its New York team. But the NHL moved faster and placed a franchise in the building first. It was the first of many skirmishes between the two leagues.

## 1971–72

### FINAL STANDINGS

#### East Division

| | W | L | T | PTS | GF | GA |
|---|---|---|---|---|---|---|
| Boston | 54 | 13 | 11 | 119 | 330 | 204 |
| New York | 48 | 17 | 13 | 109 | 317 | 192 |
| Montreal | 46 | 16 | 16 | 108 | 307 | 205 |
| Toronto | 33 | 31 | 14 | 80 | 209 | 208 |
| Detroit | 33 | 35 | 10 | 76 | 261 | 262 |
| Buffalo | 16 | 43 | 19 | 51 | 203 | 289 |
| Vancouver | 20 | 50 | 8 | 48 | 203 | 297 |

#### West Division

| | W | L | T | PTS | GF | GA |
|---|---|---|---|---|---|---|
| Chicago | 46 | 17 | 15 | 107 | 256 | 166 |
| Minnesota | 37 | 29 | 12 | 86 | 212 | 191 |
| St. Louis | 28 | 39 | 11 | 67 | 208 | 247 |
| Pittsburgh | 26 | 38 | 14 | 66 | 220 | 258 |
| Philadelphia | 26 | 38 | 14 | 66 | 200 | 236 |
| California | 21 | 39 | 18 | 60 | 216 | 288 |
| Los Angeles | 20 | 49 | 9 | 49 | 206 | 305 |

### LEADING SCORERS

| | G | A | PTS |
|---|---|---|---|
| Esposito, Boston | 66 | 67 | 133 |
| Orr, Boston | 37 | 80 | 117 |
| Ratelle, New York | 46 | 63 | 109 |
| Hadfield, New York | 50 | 56 | 106 |
| Gilbert, New York | 43 | 54 | 97 |
| F. Mahovlich, Montreal | 43 | 53 | 96 |
| B. Hull, Chicago | 50 | 43 | 93 |
| Cournoyer, Montreal | 47 | 36 | 83 |
| Bucyk, Boston | 32 | 51 | 83 |
| Clarke, Philadelphia | 35 | 46 | 81 |
| Lemaire, Montreal | 32 | 49 | 81 |

## 1972–73

The summer before the National Hockey League's 1972–73 season was unlike any the league had ever experienced. The off-season had always offered a serene time of recuperation for players and exec-

*Philadelphia center Bobby Clarke became the first ▶*
*player from the West Division to be named MVP*
*in 1972-73.*

utives. But this summer, there was frenzied activity at all levels.

First, there was the matter of the World Hockey Association. The new league asserted itself with 12 franchises and stocked rosters by signing players whose NHL contracts were expiring. The lure of large bonuses and new challenges drew about 70 former NHL performers. The most important was Chicago star Bobby Hull, who signed a 10-year contract for $2.75 million with the new Winnipeg Jets. Hull received $1 million up front, an unprecedented bonus put together by all the franchises in the league, who knew how important an established star like Bobby would be to the new league.

Stung by the defections, the NHL went to court and sued. The legal steps prevented Hull and some others from playing early in the season but injunctions later permitted them to perform in the WHA.

While the WHA was sniping at the NHL on one front, the older league took on an international series against Russia's world champions, a long awaited test of the best professionals against the best of the so-called amateurs. Many confident observers predicted an NHL sweep of the eight-game series as Team Canada (composed only of NHL players) began training in August. The first four games were to be played in early September in Canada starting in Montreal and then moving on to Toronto, Winnipeg and Vancouver. The last four would be played in Moscow later in the month.

The Russians stunned the Canadians, winning two and tying another of the four games in Canada. When the series moved to Moscow, Team Canada finally pulled itself together and managed to win three times, taking the World Series of hockey by the barest of margins. Paul Henderson's goal in the final minute of the final game produced the deciding victory.

WHA defections hurt many NHL teams. The newly-franchised New York Islanders, for example, lost seven of their 20 expansion draft choices to the new league and wound up setting an all-time futility record with 60 losses in their first season.

Montreal and Chicago won their division races and the Canadiens again captured the Stanley Cup, finishing off Chicago in six games. Boston's Phil Esposito captured his third straight scoring title and fourth in five years, leading the scorers with 130 points, including 55 goals.

Bobby Orr won the Norris Trophy as the NHL's

best defenseman for a record sixth straight year. The Hart Trophy as Most Valuable Player went to Philadelphia's Bobby Clarke, a remarkable young center who became the first West Division player to take that award. Gil Perreault of Buffalo won the Lady Byng Trophy for clean and effective play and the Calder Trophy as Rookie of the Year went to Steve Vickers of the New York Rangers.

Three Canadiens, goalie Ken Dryden, defenseman Guy Lapointe and left winger Frank Mahovlich, made the All-Star team along with Boston's Orr on defense, Esposito at center and Mickey Redmond of Detroit at right wing.

## 1972–73

### FINAL STANDINGS

#### East Division

| | W | L | T | PTS | GF | GA |
|---|---|---|---|---|---|---|
| Montreal | 52 | 10 | 16 | 120 | 329 | 184 |
| Boston | 51 | 22 | 5 | 107 | 330 | 235 |
| New York R. | 47 | 23 | 8 | 102 | 297 | 208 |
| Buffalo | 37 | 27 | 14 | 88 | 257 | 219 |
| Detroit | 37 | 29 | 12 | 86 | 265 | 243 |
| Toronto | 27 | 41 | 10 | 64 | 247 | 279 |
| Vancouver | 22 | 47 | 9 | 53 | 233 | 339 |
| New York I. | 12 | 60 | 6 | 30 | 170 | 347 |

#### West Division

| | W | L | T | PTS | GF | GA |
|---|---|---|---|---|---|---|
| Chicago | 42 | 27 | 9 | 93 | 284 | 225 |
| Philadelphia | 37 | 30 | 11 | 85 | 296 | 256 |
| Minnesota | 37 | 30 | 11 | 85 | 254 | 230 |
| St. Louis | 32 | 34 | 12 | 76 | 233 | 251 |
| Pittsburgh | 32 | 37 | 9 | 73 | 257 | 265 |
| Los Angeles | 31 | 36 | 11 | 73 | 232 | 245 |
| Atlanta | 25 | 38 | 15 | 65 | 191 | 239 |
| California | 16 | 46 | 16 | 48 | 213 | 323 |

### LEADING SCORERS

| | G | A | PTS |
|---|---|---|---|
| Esposito, Boston | 55 | 75 | 130 |
| Clarke, Philadelphia | 37 | 67 | 104 |
| Orr, Boston | 29 | 72 | 101 |
| MacLeish, Philadelphia | 50 | 50 | 100 |
| Lemaire, Montreal | 44 | 51 | 95 |
| Ratelle, New York | 41 | 53 | 94 |
| Redmond, Detroit | 52 | 41 | 93 |
| Bucyk, Boston | 40 | 53 | 93 |
| F. Mahovlich, Montreal | 38 | 55 | 93 |
| Pappin, Chicago | 41 | 51 | 92 |

## 1973–74

Ever since 1967, when the National Hockey League orchestrated its most ambitious expansion program by doubling in size from six to twelve teams, the magic word had been parity. The lords of the NHL lived for the day when the expansion infants could compete on an even keel with the established

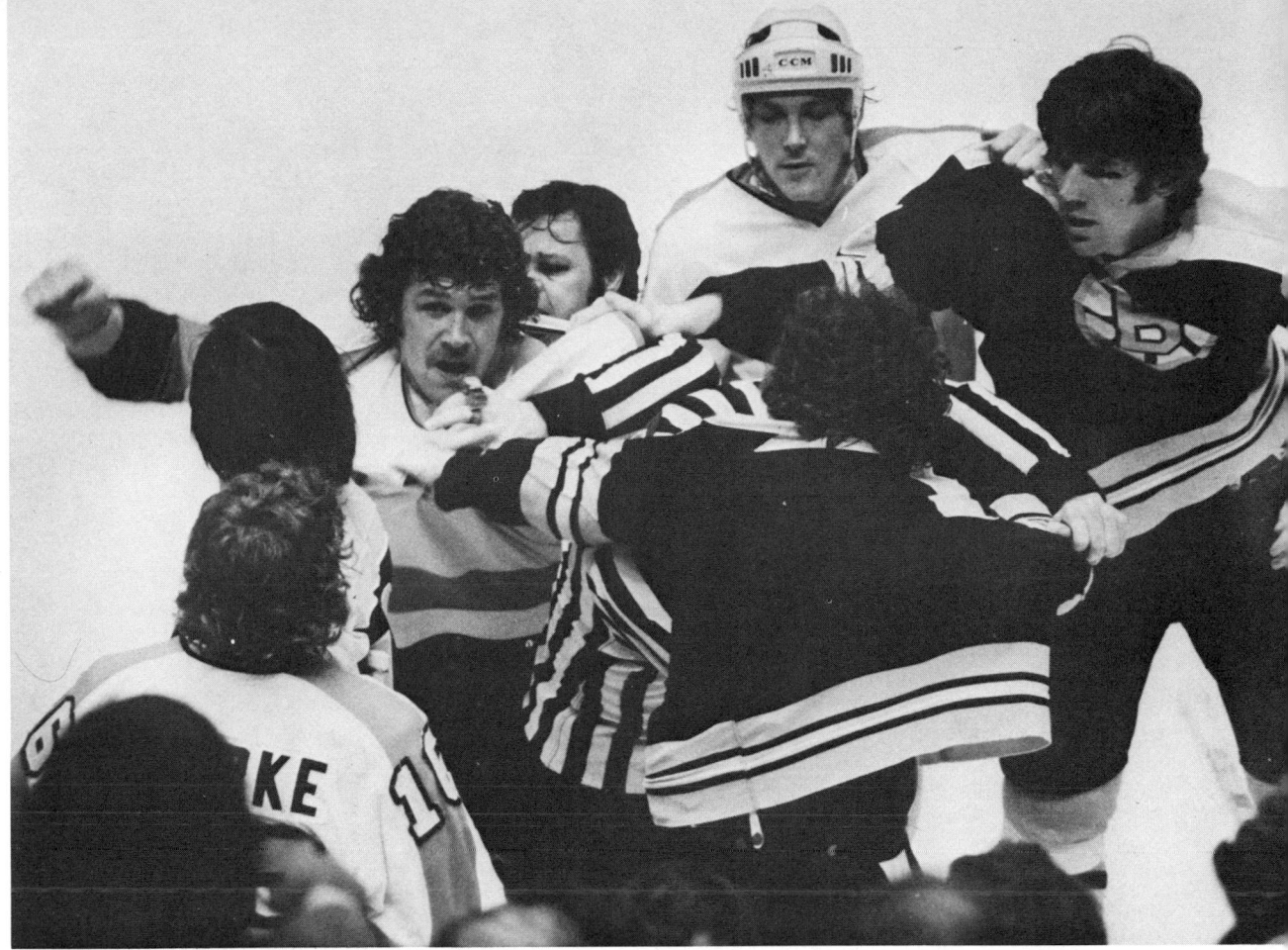

*The Flyers, led by Dave (The Hammer) Schultz, fought their way to the Stanley Cup in 1974.*

teams. They longed to be able to say that on any given night, any team could beat any other team.

For a long time, that just wasn't so. The expansion teams always seemed a stride or two behind the established clubs. And on those rare occasions when a new club rose up to kayo one of its big brothers, the loss was considered a total disaster. The expansion teams were whipping boys. Parity was a dream for the distant future.

Then, in 1973–74, along came the Broad Street Bullies, alias Philadelphia Flyers. The team of tough guys was led by Bobby Clarke, a diabetic center with a choir-boy expression, and goalie Bernie Parent, who was the first NHL player to jump to the World Hockey Association, and also one of the first to jump back.

The Flyers lived by the coaching creed of scholarly-looking Fred Shero, who often said, "If you can't

beat the other team in the alley you can't beat them on the ice." First Philadelphia would win the alley fight, then repeat on the ice. "We take the most direct route to the puck," philosophized Clarke, captain of the Bullies, "and we arrive in ill humor."

Most of the Flyers were acquired by general manager Keith Allen through clever trades. In one of his deals, Allen swapped goalie Parent to Toronto to bring a forward named Rick MacLeish to Philadelphia. Parent studied for two seasons under his goaltending idol, Jacques Plante, then fled to the WHA. MacLeish, meanwhile, developed into a 50-goal scorer for the talented young Flyers.

When Parent grew disenchanted with the WHA, he let it be known that he wanted to return to the older league. Allen immediately swung a deal for his rights with Toronto and then signed the goalie to a multiyear contract with Philadelphia.

*Bobby Clarke sipped from the Stanley Cup after the Flyers became the first expansion team to win the championship in 1974.*

Back with the Flyers, Parent found some old friends in veteran defensemen Joe Watson and Ed Van Impe, both leftovers from the original Philadelphia expansion team, and some new friends in tough Andre Dupont and Barry Ashbee, acquired through trades, and youngsters Jim Watson and Tom Bladon, draft choices. Together, the defensemen and Parent gave the Flyers the stingiest defense in the NHL. The goalie played in a backbreaking 73 games and compiled a sparkling 1.89 average with 12 shutouts—by far the best individual netminding numbers in the NHL.

The Flyers won the West Division crown by a comfortable seven points over Chicago—the first time the established Black Hawks had missed win-

ning the crown in four seasons in the expansionist West Division. In the East, Boston, led by scoring champion Phil Esposito, finished a fat 14 points ahead of runnerup Montreal. Esposito won his fourth straight scoring title and fifth in the last six years with 145 points.

En route to their division crown, the Flyers led the NHL with a staggering 1,750 penalty minutes, 600 minutes more than the next most penalized team. Of the total, a record 348 minutes belonged to the club's No. 1 hatchetman, Dave Schultz.

In the opening round of the playoffs, Philadelphia wiped out the surprising Atlanta Flames in four straight games and Boston did the same to Toronto. Chicago went five to eliminate Los Angeles while

the New York Rangers knocked off the defending Stanley Cup champion Montreal Canadiens in six games.

The semifinals were a struggle. The Bruins eliminated Chicago in six games and Philadelphia had to go seven to beat New York. That was a landmark victory. It marked the first time an expansion team had eliminated an established club in the playoffs. Parity, it seemed, was on its way. Two weeks later, it arrived.

Paced by Parent, the Flyers defeated the Bruins in the six-game championship round and brought the Stanley Cup to Philadelphia. The clincher was a 1–0 shutout spun by Parent with the only goal scored, ironically, by MacLeish, the man for whom the goalie once was traded.

Parent, whose airtight goaltending earned him the Conn Smythe Trophy as the Most Valuable Player of the playoffs, and Chicago's Tony Esposito were co-winners of the Vezina Trophy as the netminders with the lowest goals-against average during the regular season.

Boston's Phil Esposito won the Hart Trophy as the league's MVP, while teammate Bobby Orr was the winner of the Norris Trophy as the NHL's top defenseman for a record seventh consecutive season.

New York Islander defenseman Denis Potvin won the Calder as Rookie of the Year. Boston's John Bucyk got the Lady Byng for sportsmanship and ability.

## 1973–74

### FINAL STANDINGS

#### East Division

| | W | L | T | PTS | GF | GA |
|---|---|---|---|---|---|---|
| Boston | 52 | 17 | 9 | 113 | 349 | 221 |
| Montreal | 45 | 24 | 9 | 99 | 293 | 240 |
| New York R. | 40 | 24 | 14 | 94 | 300 | 251 |
| Toronto | 35 | 27 | 16 | 86 | 274 | 230 |
| Buffalo | 32 | 34 | 12 | 76 | 242 | 250 |
| Detroit | 20 | 39 | 10 | 68 | 255 | 319 |
| Vancouver | 24 | 43 | 11 | 59 | 224 | 296 |
| New York I. | 19 | 41 | 18 | 56 | 182 | 247 |

#### West Division

| | W | L | T | PTS | GF | GA |
|---|---|---|---|---|---|---|
| Philadelphia | 50 | 16 | 12 | 112 | 273 | 164 |
| Chicago | 41 | 14 | 23 | 105 | 272 | 164 |
| Los Angeles | 33 | 33 | 12 | 78 | 233 | 231 |
| Atlanta | 30 | 34 | 14 | 74 | 214 | 238 |
| Pittsburgh | 28 | 41 | 9 | 65 | 242 | 273 |
| St. Louis | 26 | 40 | 12 | 64 | 206 | 248 |
| Minnesota | 23 | 38 | 17 | 63 | 235 | 275 |
| California | 13 | 55 | 10 | 36 | 195 | 342 |

| LEADING SCORERS | G | A | PTS |
|---|---|---|---|
| Esposito, Boston | 68 | 77 | 145 |
| Orr, Boston | 32 | 90 | 122 |
| Hodge, Boston | 50 | 55 | 105 |
| Cashman, Boston | 30 | 59 | 89 |
| Clarke, Philadelphia | 35 | 52 | 87 |
| Martin, Buffalo | 52 | 34 | 86 |
| Apps, Pittsburgh | 24 | 61 | 85 |
| Sittler, Toronto | 38 | 46 | 84 |
| L. MacDonald, Pittsburgh | 43 | 39 | 82 |
| Park, New York R. | 25 | 57 | 82 |
| D. Hextall, Minnesota | 20 | 62 | 82 |

## 1974–75

The addition of two new franchises and realignment of the 18 teams into four divisions set the stage for a season in which the Philadelphia Flyers would be seeking a repeat of their stunning Stanley Cup success.

The new entries were the Kansas City Scouts and the Washington Capitals, and the divisions, named for hockey notables, were the James Norris and Jack Adams in the Prince of Wales Conference and the Lester Patrick and Conn Smythe in the Clarence Campbell Conference.

If the newest members of the league quickly became discouraged en route to last-place finishes in their divisions, at least they could take heart in the gallant strides made by the New York Islanders. An expansion team just three years earlier, the Islanders climbed into a second-place tie with the rival New York Rangers behind the Flyers in the Patrick Division and then found themselves matched against the Rangers in the best-of-three first-round playoff series.

The teams split the first two games and in an electrifying finish the Islanders won out when J. P. Parise scored a goal in just 11 seconds of overtime—a league record.

The Islanders lost the first three games of the quarterfinal round against Pittsburgh, but rallied to win the last four, becoming the first team in 33 years to win a series after losing the first three games. In the semifinal against the Flyers, the Islanders lost the decisive seventh game after again tying a series with three straight triumphs.

Philadelphia went on to defeat the Buffalo Sabres in six games in the finals, becoming the first team to win the Stanley Cup two years in a row since Montreal won in 1968 and 1969.

*Los Angeles defenseman Bob Murdoch drops his stick but not his hold on Atlanta's Eric Vail in 1974-75.*

Influenced by the success of the Flyers' roughhouse tactics, more players began to fight and violence in the game increased. Two players were charged with assault for their involvement in fighting incidents. Dave Forbes of the Boston Bruins was put on trial for punching Henry Boucha of the Minnesota North Stars, but the trial ended in a hung jury and the charges were dropped. And Detroit's Dan Maloney was charged with assaulting Brian Glennie of Toronto. But there were still victories scored by the most graceful players of the generation.

Boston defenseman Bobby Orr won his second scoring title with 135 points, ending the four-year stranglehold on the award by teammate Phil Es-

*Bernie Parent's play in the nets helped the Flyers ▶ knock off Buffalo in the Cup finals in 1975.*

posito. It was the sixth straight season either Orr or Esposito had won the scoring championship.

Philadelphia's Bobby Clarke, the feisty center, won the Hart Trophy as Most Valuable Player for the second time in three years while Orr won the Norris as best defenseman for the seventh straight time. The Lady Byng for gentlemanly play went to Los Angeles center Marcel Dionne. Atlanta Flames left wing Eric Vail won the Calder as Rookie of the Year and goalie Bernie Parent of the Flyers won the Vezina.

Parent also won the Conn Smythe as playoff MVP and was named to the All-Star team with teammate Clarke. Others on the team were defensemen Orr and Islander Denis Potvin and wingers Guy Lafleur of Montreal and Richard Martin of Buffalo.

## 1974–75

### FINAL STANDINGS

#### Prince of Wales Conference

##### Norris Division

| | W | L | T | PTS | GF | GA |
|---|---|---|---|---|---|---|
| Montreal | 47 | 14 | 19 | 113 | 374 | 225 |
| Los Angeles | 42 | 17 | 21 | 105 | 269 | 185 |
| Pittsburgh | 37 | 28 | 15 | 89 | 326 | 289 |
| Detroit | 23 | 45 | 12 | 58 | 259 | 335 |
| Washington | 8 | 67 | 5 | 21 | 181 | 446 |

##### Adams Division

| | | | | | | |
|---|---|---|---|---|---|---|
| Buffalo | 49 | 16 | 15 | 113 | 354 | 240 |
| Boston | 40 | 26 | 14 | 94 | 345 | 245 |
| Toronto | 31 | 33 | 16 | 78 | 280 | 309 |
| California | 19 | 48 | 13 | 51 | 212 | 316 |

#### Clarence Campbell Conference

##### Patrick Division

| | | | | | | |
|---|---|---|---|---|---|---|
| Philadelphia | 51 | 18 | 11 | 113 | 293 | 181 |
| New York R. | 37 | 29 | 14 | 88 | 319 | 276 |
| New York I. | 33 | 25 | 22 | 88 | 264 | 221 |
| Atlanta | 34 | 31 | 15 | 83 | 243 | 233 |

##### Smythe Division

| | | | | | | |
|---|---|---|---|---|---|---|
| Vancouver | 38 | 32 | 10 | 86 | 271 | 254 |
| St. Louis | 35 | 31 | 14 | 84 | 269 | 267 |
| Chicago | 37 | 35 | 8 | 82 | 268 | 241 |
| Minnesota | 23 | 50 | 7 | 53 | 221 | 341 |
| Kansas City | 15 | 54 | 11 | 41 | 184 | 328 |

### LEADING SCORERS

| | G | A | PTS |
|---|---|---|---|
| Orr, Boston | 46 | 89 | 135 |
| Esposito, Boston | 61 | 66 | 127 |
| Dionne, Detroit | 47 | 74 | 121 |
| Lafleur, Montreal | 53 | 66 | 119 |
| P. Mahovlich, Montreal | 35 | 82 | 117 |
| Clarke, Philadelphia | 27 | 89 | 116 |
| Robert, Buffalo | 40 | 60 | 100 |
| Gilbert, New York | 36 | 61 | 97 |
| Perreault, Buffalo | 39 | 57 | 96 |
| Martin, Buffalo | 52 | 43 | 95 |

*The Flower, Guy Lafleur, led the Canadiens to their 19th Stanley Cup in 1976.*

## 1975–76

For years, the argument had reigned: could swifter, more inventive players challenge the dominance of the stronger, more aggressive teams and the style that had been popularized by the Philadelphia Flyers? The answer, it seemed, was an emphatic yes.

The Flyers' string of successes was ended not by a more violent team, but by a faster one. The Montreal Canadiens did not have anyone as powerful as Dave Schultz, the Flyer who perennially led the league in penalty minutes. But Montreal did have Guy Lafleur, a slender, graceful right wing whose

name translated from French was, appropriately enough, "The Flower."

Lafleur led Montreal back into the championship ranks. After being dethroned by Philadelphia, the two-time winner, Montreal won the Stanley Cup for the 19th time. Like Lafleur, the Canadiens were simply overwhelming. They finished the season with 58 victories and 127 points—both records. They had only 11 defeats, just one more than the record they held for fewest losses in one season. They led the league in virtually ever offensive and defensive category and they did it with one of the lowest penalty-minute totals of any team—an average of 12.2 a game—half of what the Flyers averaged.

In the playoffs, they won 12 of 13 games, sweeping Philadelphia in four games in the finals. In all but three of those games, the Canadiens held their opponent to three goals or fewer. Lafleur, who won the scoring title with 125 points, had 17 points in the playoffs.

This was a season marked by the trade that brought Bruin Phil Esposito to the Rangers and Brad Park to Boston. It was also a year in which Boston's Bobby Orr, operated on again because of his ailing

*Toronto's Darryl Sittler had 100 points in 1975-76, including a 10-point night against the Bruins on February 7, 1976.*

left knee, played only 10 games. And Toronto's Darryl Sittler set a mark for most points in a game when he recorded six goals and four assists against Boston.

Philadelphia tied a league record by going unbeaten in 23 straight games (17-0-6) and the Kansas City Scouts, in their second season, set a record for futility by going 27 games without a victory (0-21-6).

Although Philadelphia was toppled as Stanley Cup champion, the Flyers did have Bobby Clarke, the winner of the Hart Trophy as Most Valuable Player. It was the third time in four years Clarke had won the award and he became only the second center, along with the legendary Howie Morenz, to win it a third time.

New York Islander center Bryan Trottier was the winner of the Calder as Rookie of the Year; Montreal goalie Ken Dryden won the Vezina and Jean Ratelle won the Lady Byng for gentlemanly play. Philadelphia's Reggie Leach, despite his team's defeat in the finals, was the Conn Smythe Trophy winner as playoff MVP after scoring a playoff record 19 goals.

Lafleur, Dryden, Clarke and Park made the All-Star team along with defenseman Denis Potvin of the New York Islanders and left wing Bill Barber of Philadelphia.

## 1975–76

### FINAL STANDINGS
### Prince of Wales Conference

#### Norris Division

|  | W | L | T | PTS | GF | GA |
|---|---|---|---|---|---|---|
| Montreal | 58 | 11 | 11 | 127 | 337 | 174 |
| Los Angeles | 38 | 33 | 9 | 85 | 263 | 265 |
| Pittsburgh | 35 | 33 | 12 | 82 | 339 | 303 |
| Detroit | 26 | 44 | 10 | 62 | 226 | 300 |
| Washington | 11 | 59 | 10 | 32 | 224 | 394 |

#### Adams Division

|  | W | L | T | PTS | GF | GA |
|---|---|---|---|---|---|---|
| Boston | 48 | 15 | 17 | 113 | 313 | 237 |
| Buffalo | 46 | 21 | 13 | 105 | 339 | 240 |
| Toronto | 34 | 31 | 15 | 83 | 294 | 276 |
| California | 27 | 42 | 11 | 65 | 250 | 278 |

### Clarence Campbell Conference

#### Patrick Division

|  | W | L | T | PTS | GF | GA |
|---|---|---|---|---|---|---|
| Philadelphia | 51 | 13 | 16 | 118 | 348 | 209 |
| New York I. | 42 | 21 | 17 | 101 | 297 | 190 |
| Atlanta | 35 | 33 | 12 | 82 | 262 | 237 |
| New York R. | 29 | 42 | 9 | 67 | 262 | 333 |

#### Smythe Division

|  | W | L | T | PTS | GF | GA |
|---|---|---|---|---|---|---|
| Chicago | 32 | 30 | 18 | 82 | 254 | 261 |
| Vancouver | 33 | 32 | 15 | 81 | 271 | 272 |
| St. Louis | 29 | 37 | 14 | 72 | 249 | 290 |
| Minnesota | 20 | 53 | 7 | 47 | 195 | 303 |
| Kansas City | 12 | 56 | 12 | 36 | 190 | 351 |

### LEADING SCORERS

|  | G | A | PTS |
|---|---|---|---|
| Lafleur, Montreal | 56 | 69 | 125 |
| Clarke, Philadelphia | 30 | 89 | 119 |
| Perreault, Buffalo | 44 | 69 | 113 |
| Barber, Philadelphia | 50 | 62 | 112 |
| Larouche, Pittsburgh | 53 | 58 | 111 |
| Ratelle, New York R.-Boston | 36 | 69 | 105 |
| P. Mahovlich, Montreal | 34 | 71 | 105 |
| Pronovost, Pittsburgh | 52 | 52 | 104 |
| Sittler, Toronto | 41 | 59 | 100 |
| Apps, Pittsburgh | 32 | 67 | 99 |

## 1976–77

If there was any doubt that the Montreal Canadiens had been restored to the National Hockey League's most privileged class, it was quickly dispelled in the 1976–77 season. Coming off their Stanley Cup success of the season before, it seemed there was little the Canadiens could do to improve upon their resounding record.

Guy Lafleur, who already had begun to establish himself as the most recognizable—and the most coveted—player of his generation was soon surrounded by invaluable helpmates. The Canadiens, in fact, were so rich in talent that they all but saved the All-Star selections for themselves.

In one of the most lopsided voting totals ever, the Canadiens placed four of their members on the first team—right wing Lafleur, defenseman Larry Robinson, goalie Ken Dryden and Lafleur's linemate, left wing Steve Shutt. The only players to interrupt the Montreal domination were Los Angeles center Marcel Dionne and Toronto defenseman Borje Salming. Not only that, but one more Canadien, defenseman Guy Lapointe, was named to the second team.

Who could argue with the choices? The Canadiens won a record 60 games, lost a mere eight, and set another record with the total of 132 points. The Philadelphia Flyers, the team with the second-best overall record, had 20 fewer points. And the Los Angeles Kings, second to Montreal in the Norris Division, were 49 points behind. Not since the league broke into four divisions had one team so easily commanded a season.

*The Canadiens' Larry Robinson, checking ▶ Buffalo's Gil Perreault, was the NHL's best defenseman in 1976-77.*

*The 1976-77 Lady Byng Trophy went to smooth-skating Marcel Dionne of Los Angeles.*

In their own palace, the Montreal Forum, the Canadiens lost only once in 40 games, tying the modern NHL record for fewest losses at home. But while the Canadiens were obviously delighted to be in their home, two other teams found new homes to start the season when the league approved a pair of franchise shifts.

The Kansas City Scouts, struggling both on the ice and in the accounting department, were sold to Denver oilman Jack Vickers, who moved the team to his home city and renamed the club the Colorado Rockies. Alas, the changes were merely cosmetic. The Rockies won only 20 games and finished with just 54 points, the second-worst total in the league.

The Cleveland Barons did not fare much better. Transplanted from Oakland, where they were known as the Seals in the NHL's six-team expansion of 1967, the Barons played in suburban Richfield in a cavernous arena that was located next to a sprawling farm. Encouraged by only a few fans willing to make the journey there, the Barons won only 25 games.

Montreal charged through the playoffs, losing only two games—both to the New York Islanders in a semifinal series—and swept the Boston Bruins in the finals when Jacques Lemaire scored an overtime goal at 4:32 in the fourth game. Montreal was once more led by Lafleur, who had finished the reg-

ular-season with a league-leading 136 points, 56 of them goals.

Not surprisingly, the Canadiens swept most of the NHL postseason awards. Lafleur, besides being the Art Ross winner as scoring champion, won the Hart Trophy as Most Valuable Player and the Conn Smythe as the playoff MVP. Robinson won the Norris as best defenseman, while Willi Plett of Atlanta won the Calder as Rookie of the Year. Dionne won the Lady Byng for good conduct for the second time in three years.

# 1976–77

## FINAL STANDINGS
### Prince of Wales Conference

#### Norris Division

|  | W | L | T | PTS | GF | GA |
|---|---|---|---|---|---|---|
| Montreal | 60 | 8 | 12 | 132 | 387 | 171 |
| Los Angeles | 34 | 31 | 15 | 83 | 271 | 241 |
| Pittsburgh | 34 | 33 | 13 | 81 | 240 | 252 |
| Washington | 24 | 42 | 14 | 62 | 221 | 307 |
| Detroit | 16 | 55 | 9 | 41 | 183 | 309 |

#### Adams Division

|  | W | L | T | PTS | GF | GA |
|---|---|---|---|---|---|---|
| Boston | 49 | 23 | 8 | 106 | 312 | 240 |
| Buffalo | 48 | 24 | 8 | 104 | 301 | 220 |
| Toronto | 33 | 32 | 15 | 81 | 301 | 285 |
| Cleveland | 25 | 42 | 13 | 63 | 240 | 292 |

### Clarence Campbell Conference

#### Patrick Division

|  | W | L | T | PTS | GF | GA |
|---|---|---|---|---|---|---|
| Philadelphia | 48 | 16 | 16 | 112 | 323 | 213 |
| New York I. | 47 | 21 | 12 | 106 | 288 | 193 |
| Atlanta | 34 | 34 | 12 | 80 | 264 | 265 |
| New York R. | 29 | 37 | 14 | 72 | 272 | 310 |

#### Smythe Division

|  | W | L | T | PTS | GF | GA |
|---|---|---|---|---|---|---|
| St. Louis | 32 | 39 | 9 | 73 | 239 | 276 |
| Minnesota | 23 | 39 | 18 | 64 | 240 | 310 |
| Chicago | 26 | 43 | 11 | 63 | 240 | 298 |
| Vancouver | 25 | 42 | 13 | 63 | 235 | 294 |
| Colorado | 20 | 46 | 14 | 54 | 226 | 307 |

## LEADING SCORERS

|  | G | A | PTS |
|---|---|---|---|
| Lafleur, Montreal | 56 | 80 | 136 |
| Dionne, Los Angeles | 53 | 69 | 122 |
| Shutt, Montreal | 60 | 45 | 105 |
| MacLeish, Philadelphia | 49 | 48 | 97 |
| Perreault, Buffalo | 39 | 56 | 95 |
| Young, Minnesota | 29 | 66 | 95 |
| Ratelle, Boston | 33 | 61 | 94 |
| McDonald, Toronto | 46 | 44 | 90 |
| Sittler, Toronto | 38 | 52 | 90 |
| Clarke, Philadelphia | 27 | 63 | 90 |

# 1977–78

While the Montreal Canadiens again were the dominant force in 1977–78, at least one team served

*Mike Bossy of the Islanders broke in with a bang in 1977-78 when he scored a rookie-record 53 goals.*

notice that it was on its way to the top. In fact, the team, the New York Islanders, turned out to be the only one that had been able to win a playoff game from the Canadiens the previous two years—and it won three of them.

The rise of the Islanders really was no surprise. It had been coming for some time. The Islanders had been known for their defense, but finally were able to add a gifted scorer, Mike Bossy, to give them the goal-getting punch they needed. It happened that the young man was born and raised in Montreal and had played outstanding junior hockey on the city's outskirts in Laval.

Yet, for some reason, Bossy had gone untouched in the first round of the amateur draft until the Islanders made him the 15th player chosen. Six other right wings already had been taken, but Bossy was confident he could help the Islanders. And when contract negotiations with his new club temporarily collapsed, Bossy boldly told general manager Bill Torrey: "I'll score 50 goals for you."

Torrey laughed. No Islander had ever scored that many goals. No rookie had ever scored that many goals. But Bossy had the last laugh. By the time he ended his rookie year, he had 53 goals and was sixth in the scoring race with 91 points, the most ever by a first-year right wing. The Islanders, with center Bryan Trottier and defenseman Denis Potvin, had three of the first six scorers in the league.

The Islanders won their first Patrick Division title, dethroning Philadelphia, and clearly were one of the most imposing threats to end Montreal's Stanley Cup reign. But the Islanders were not the only team to make a vast improvement during the season. Detroit vaulted from the league's worst record to a second-place finish behind Montreal in the Norris Division.

Still, the Canadiens again led the league during

*The Bruins' John Wensink won this battle, but his teammates lost the war when they were eliminated by Montreal in the 1978 finals.*

*John A. Ziegler, Jr., became the fourth president of the NHL in 1977, succeeding Clarence Campbell, who had served 31 years.*

A major factor was the play of goaltender Ken Dryden, who shared the Vezina Trophy as the league's outstanding goalie with Michel Larocque. Another reason for the Canadiens' success was Larry Robinson, the defenseman who was the Conn Smythe Trophy winner as the Most Valuable Player in the playoffs.

But while Dryden was named to the All-Star team, Robinson was supplanted by Denis Potvin of the Islanders and Brad Park of the Bruins. Trottier, a center; teammate Clark Gillies, a left wing, and Lafleur were the other selections. Bossy won the Calder Trophy as Rookie of the Year, Lafleur won the Hart as MVP for the second straight season, Potvin regained the Norris as best defenseman and Los Angeles' Butch Goring won the Lady Byng for gentlemanly play.

Off the ice, John A. Ziegler, Jr., became the fourth president in the 61-year history of the NHL, succeeding Clarence Campbell, who had been president since 1946. A Michigan-born lawyer, Ziegler played amateur hockey and was a quarterback in football and a shortstop in baseball as a Detroit schoolboy. His bachelor and law degrees were achieved at the University of Michigan.

the season with 129 points, and with 59 victories failed by one to equal their own league record of 60 set the year before. The Boston Bruins, the other threat to the Canadiens, had 113 points, two more than the Islanders.

But in a stunning playoff upset, the Islanders were eliminated by the Toronto Maple Leafs when Lanny McDonald scored at 4:13 of overtime in the seventh game.

After sweeping the upstart Toronto team in the semifinals, the Canadiens faced the Bruins for the second year in a row in the final round. Boston had failed to win even a single game in the championship series the year before. This time they managed to win two as the Canadiens captured the Cup for the third consecutive year. While Montreal still had the dependable scoring of Guy Lafleur, who during the season won his third straight scoring title with 132 points, it also had a mighty defense. The Canadiens allowed only 12 goals in the final series against Boston.

## 1977–78

### FINAL STANDINGS

#### Prince of Wales Conference

##### Norris Division

|  | W | L | T | PTS | GF | GA |
|---|---|---|---|---|---|---|
| Montreal | 59 | 10 | 11 | 129 | 359 | 183 |
| Detroit | 32 | 34 | 14 | 78 | 252 | 266 |
| Los Angeles | 31 | 34 | 15 | 77 | 243 | 245 |
| Pittsburgh | 25 | 37 | 18 | 68 | 254 | 321 |
| Washington | 17 | 49 | 14 | 48 | 195 | 321 |

##### Adams Division

|  | W | L | T | PTS | GF | GA |
|---|---|---|---|---|---|---|
| Boston | 51 | 18 | 11 | 113 | 333 | 218 |
| Buffalo | 44 | 19 | 17 | 105 | 288 | 215 |
| Toronto | 41 | 29 | 10 | 92 | 271 | 237 |
| Cleveland | 22 | 45 | 13 | 57 | 230 | 325 |

#### Clarence Campbell Conference

##### Patrick Division

|  | W | L | T | PTS | GF | GA |
|---|---|---|---|---|---|---|
| New York I. | 48 | 17 | 15 | 111 | 334 | 210 |
| Philadelphia | 45 | 20 | 15 | 105 | 296 | 200 |
| Atlanta | 34 | 27 | 19 | 87 | 274 | 252 |
| New York R. | 30 | 37 | 13 | 73 | 279 | 280 |

##### Smythe Division

|  | W | L | T | PTS | GF | GA |
|---|---|---|---|---|---|---|
| Chicago | 32 | 29 | 19 | 83 | 230 | 220 |
| Colorado | 19 | 40 | 21 | 59 | 257 | 305 |
| Vancouver | 20 | 43 | 17 | 57 | 239 | 320 |
| St. Louis | 20 | 47 | 13 | 53 | 195 | 304 |
| Minnesota | 18 | 53 | 9 | 45 | 218 | 325 |

*Things were looking up for the Rangers and Pat Hickey after they stunned the regular-season champion Islanders in the 1979 playoffs.*

| LEADING SCORERS | G | A | PTS |
|---|---|---|---|
| Lafleur, Montreal | 60 | 72 | 132 |
| Trottier, New York I. | 46 | 77 | 123 |
| Sittler, Toronto | 45 | 72 | 117 |
| Lemaire, Montreal | 36 | 61 | 97 |
| D. Potvin, New York I. | 30 | 64 | 94 |
| Bossy, New York I. | 53 | 38 | 91 |
| O'Reilly, Boston | 29 | 61 | 90 |
| Perreault, Buffalo | 41 | 48 | 89 |
| Clarke, Philadelphia | 21 | 68 | 89 |
| McDonald, Toronto | 47 | 40 | 87 |
| Paiement, Colorado | 31 | 56 | 87 |

## 1978–79

New York is a city of extremes and its fans are no different. They can be fiercely loyal and terribly impatient. They can jeer with witless vengeance and cheer with boundless passion. And for the honor of doing any of those, they will pay handsomely for their tickets.

Some even paid as much as $500 a ticket when the Rangers galvanized the city in a glorious march to the Stanley Cup finals, a march orchestrated by coach Fred Shero in his first year at the helm. "Freddie the Fog" had been hired away from the Philadelphia Flyers and almost immediately transformed the downtrodden Rangers into a success.

With the help of Swedish stars Ulf Nilsson and Anders Hedberg, who signed contracts for $600,000 a year apiece after defecting from the World Hockey Association, Shero confirmed his reputation as a genius. Although the Rangers finished in third place in the Patrick Division, they finished only four points behind second-place Philadelphia.

Not only did the Rangers then knock off Shero's old team in the quarterfinals, but they faced the rival

New York Islanders in the semifinals, an electrifying series that was a scalper's delight.

The Islanders had become the first expansion team ever to lead the league in points. They had Bryan Trottier, who led the league in scoring with 134 points and Mike Bossy, who scored 69 goals, the second-highest total ever, including goals in 10 straight games to equal the modern NHL record. The Rangers had spirit.

Seeking their first Stanley Cup since 1940, the Rangers upset the Islanders in six games and went on to meet the defending champion Montreal Canadiens. Finally, the magic vanished. After winning the opening game, the Rangers failed to win another and Montreal won its fourth straight title.

The Rangers had to console themselves with a magnificent ticker-tape parade down Broadway while the stunned Islanders could take heart only in a spate of postseason awards. Trottier won the Hart Trophy as Most Valuable Player and teammate Denis Potvin was given the Norris as best defenseman. Minnesota center Bobby Smith won the Calder as Rookie of the Year, Atlanta's Bob MacMillan won the Lady Byng as the most gentlemanly player and Montreal left wing Bob Gainey was named winner of the Conn Smythe as playoff MVP.

Three Islanders—Trottier, Potvin and left wing Clark Gillies—were named to the All-Star team, along with right wing Guy Lafleur of Montreal and teammates Ken Dryden, a goalie, and Larry Robinson, a defenseman.

*Ken Dryden led the Canadiens to their fourth straight Cup in 1979 and then retired to pursue a career In law.*

# 1978–79

## FINAL STANDINGS
### Prince of Wales Conference

#### Norris Division

|  | W | L | T | PTS | GF | GA |
|---|---|---|---|---|---|---|
| Montreal | 52 | 17 | 11 | 115 | 337 | 204 |
| Pittsburgh | 36 | 31 | 13 | 85 | 281 | 279 |
| Los Angeles | 34 | 34 | 12 | 80 | 292 | 286 |
| Washington | 24 | 41 | 15 | 63 | 273 | 338 |
| Detroit | 23 | 41 | 16 | 62 | 252 | 295 |

#### Adams Division

|  | W | L | T | PTS | GF | GA |
|---|---|---|---|---|---|---|
| Boston | 43 | 23 | 14 | 100 | 316 | 270 |
| Buffalo | 36 | 28 | 16 | 88 | 280 | 263 |
| Toronto | 34 | 33 | 13 | 81 | 267 | 252 |
| Minnesota | 28 | 40 | 12 | 68 | 257 | 289 |

### Clarence Campbell Conference

#### Patrick Division

|  | W | L | T | PTS | GF | GA |
|---|---|---|---|---|---|---|
| New York I. | 51 | 15 | 14 | 116 | 358 | 214 |
| Philadelphia | 40 | 25 | 15 | 95 | 281 | 248 |
| New York R. | 40 | 29 | 11 | 91 | 316 | 292 |
| Atlanta | 41 | 31 | 8 | 90 | 327 | 280 |

#### Smythe Division

|  | W | L | T | PTS | GF | GA |
|---|---|---|---|---|---|---|
| Chicago | 29 | 36 | 15 | 73 | 244 | 277 |
| Vancouver | 25 | 42 | 13 | 63 | 217 | 291 |
| St. Louis | 18 | 50 | 12 | 48 | 249 | 348 |
| Colorado | 15 | 53 | 12 | 42 | 210 | 331 |

## LEADING SCORERS

|  | G | A | PTS |
|---|---|---|---|
| Trottier, New York I. | 47 | 87 | 134 |
| Dionne, Los Angeles | 59 | 71 | 130 |
| Lafleur, Montreal | 52 | 77 | 129 |
| Bossy, New York I. | 69 | 57 | 126 |
| MacMillan, Atlanta | 37 | 71 | 108 |
| Chouinard, Atlanta | 50 | 57 | 107 |
| D. Potvin, New York I. | 31 | 70 | 101 |
| Federko, St. Louis | 31 | 64 | 95 |
| Taylor, Los Angeles | 43 | 48 | 91 |
| Gillies, New York I. | 35 | 56 | 91 |

# 6

# MERGER 1979-1983

The costly war with the World Hockey Association finally came to an end in 1979, when the two professional leagues reached agreement on a merger. The NHL jumped from 17 to 21 franchises with the addition of four WHA clubs—the Quebec Nordiques, Edmonton Oilers, Winnipeg Jets and Hartford Whalers. The merger, along with the signings of several European stars, changed the game dramatically.

The days of the Flyers' overly-physical style were gone, as the games became free-skating and wide-open. As a result, scoring totals skyrocketed. Leading the surge was Edmonton's Wayne Gretzky, who in his first three years in the league set every scoring record imaginable and became the game's No. 1 attraction.

The Montreal Canadiens' domination came to an end in the first year of the merger as parity enabled the expansion teams of the 1970s to rise to the top. In the forefront were the New York Islanders, who ruled the game in the early 1980s. Led by all-around center Bryan Trottier and sniper Mike Bossy, the Islanders could play either style—physical or finesse—with equal ability.

◄ *The merger with the WHA brought superstar Wayne Gretzky to the NHL in 1979.*

More and more teams scouted Europe in search of talent. The Nordiques signed three Czechoslovakian brothers, the Stastnys, all of whom became stars, and other Europeans defected soon after. The league once almost exclusively made up on Canadians, took on an international flavor.

## 1979–80

Clearly, the 1979-80 season was an historic one for the National Hockey League. Armistice with the World Hockey Association was achieved when the NHL agreed to absorb four of the WHA teams and in return the WHA agreed to pay off its other teams and cease operation.

With the addition of the surviving Quebec Nordiques, Winnipeg Jets, Edmonton Oilers and Hartford Whalers, the 21-team league moved to a balanced 80-game schedule. Each team would play every other team four times, with the top 16 point-getters earning playoff spots.

Two of the new teams—Edmonton and Hartford—made the playoffs, but both were near the bottom of the league and it was obvious that by and large the talent was spread thin among the old WHA squads; indeed, the NHL had stripped the incoming

teams of many of their best players in a reentry draft, with each of the four WHA teams permitted to protect only two goalies and two skaters.

One notable exception was that of a thin, pimpled 19-year-old named Wayne Gretzky, the Edmonton Oiler who was the most exciting and productive player in all of hockey. Before the merger, the Oilers struck an agreement that called for Gretzky remaining their property. It was, to say the least, a wise move.

In his first NHL season, although he technically did not qualify as a rookie because of his WHA service, Gretzky scored 51 goals and tied for the league lead in points with 137 along with Los Angeles' Marcel Dionne. But Gretzky only managed to help the Oilers claim the 16th and final playoff spot.

The biggest success of the season was that of the New York Islanders. Upset in the playoffs a year earlier and having struggled through the 1979–80 season, finally finishing fifth in points, the Islanders became only the second expansion team, along with the Philadelphia Flyers, to win a Stanley Cup. It came eight years after the team's birth in the 1972 expansion draft.

To do it, the Islanders made one of the most pivotal trades in history, landing center Butch Goring from Los Angeles right at the March trading deadline. With Goring in the lineup, the Islanders finished the season unbeaten in their last 12 games. They went on to defeat Goring's old team in the first round, Boston in the quarterfinals and Buffalo in the semifinals.

That earned the Islanders their first berth ever in

*Islander goalie Billy Smith chugs champagne from the Cup after defeating the Flyers in 1980.*

the finals against divisional rival Philadelphia. And the Islanders managed to win the opening game when Denis Potvin scored a rare power-play goal in overtime. The Islanders went on to win the series in six games on Bobby Nystrom's overtime goal.

Gretzky was the Hart Trophy winner as Most Valuable Player and winner of the Lady Byng for gentlemanly play. Montreal's Larry Robinson won the Norris as best defenseman, Boston defenseman Ray Bourque won the Calder as Rookie of the Year and Islander center Bryan Trottier won the Smythe as playoff MVP.

Robinson, Bourque and Dionne were named to the All-Star team, along with Montreal right wing Guy Lafleur and Los Angeles left wing Charlie Simmer.

## 1979–80

### FINAL STANDINGS

#### Prince of Wales Conference

##### Norris Division

| | W | L | T | PTS | GF | GA |
|---|---|---|---|---|---|---|
| Montreal | 47 | 20 | 13 | 107 | 328 | 240 |
| Los Angeles | 30 | 36 | 14 | 74 | 290 | 313 |
| Pittsburgh | 30 | 37 | 13 | 73 | 251 | 303 |
| Hartford | 27 | 34 | 19 | 73 | 303 | 312 |
| Detroit | 26 | 43 | 11 | 63 | 268 | 306 |

##### Adams Division

| | | | | | | |
|---|---|---|---|---|---|---|
| Buffalo | 47 | 17 | 16 | 110 | 318 | 201 |
| Boston | 46 | 21 | 13 | 105 | 310 | 234 |
| Minnesota | 36 | 28 | 16 | 88 | 311 | 253 |
| Toronto | 35 | 40 | 5 | 75 | 304 | 327 |
| Quebec | 25 | 44 | 11 | 61 | 248 | 313 |

#### Clarence Campbell Conference

##### Patrick Division

| | | | | | | |
|---|---|---|---|---|---|---|
| Philadelphia | 48 | 12 | 20 | 116 | 327 | 254 |
| New York I. | 39 | 28 | 13 | 91 | 281 | 247 |
| New York R. | 38 | 32 | 10 | 86 | 308 | 284 |
| Atlanta | 35 | 32 | 13 | 83 | 282 | 269 |
| Washington | 27 | 40 | 13 | 67 | 261 | 293 |

##### Smythe Division

| | | | | | | |
|---|---|---|---|---|---|---|
| Chicago | 34 | 27 | 19 | 87 | 241 | 250 |
| St. Louis | 34 | 34 | 12 | 80 | 266 | 278 |
| Vancouver | 27 | 37 | 16 | 70 | 256 | 281 |
| Edmonton | 28 | 39 | 13 | 69 | 301 | 322 |
| Winnipeg | 20 | 49 | 11 | 51 | 214 | 314 |
| Colorado | 19 | 48 | 13 | 51 | 234 | 308 |

### LEADING SCORERS

| | G | A | PTS |
|---|---|---|---|
| Dionne, Los Angeles | 53 | 84 | 137 |
| Gretzky, Edmonton | 51 | 86 | 137 |
| Lafleur, Montreal | 50 | 75 | 125 |
| Perreault, Buffalo | 40 | 66 | 106 |
| Rogers, Hartford | 44 | 61 | 105 |
| Trottier, New York I. | 42 | 62 | 104 |
| Simmer, Los Angeles | 56 | 45 | 101 |
| Stoughton, Hartford | 56 | 44 | 100 |
| Sittler, Toronto | 40 | 57 | 97 |
| MacDonald, Edmonton | 46 | 48 | 94 |
| Federko, St. Louis | 38 | 56 | 94 |

*Butch Goring led the Islanders to a second Cup and was named playoff MVP in 1981.*

## 1980–81

The New York Islanders began the 1980–81 season as Stanley Cup defenders, but there were skeptics who felt the championship was a fluke and their reign would be short-lived.

How wrong they were! Not even Edmonton's Wayne Gretzky could steal the Islanders' thunder, although he tried mightily. The Great Gretzky, proving his share of the scoring championship the season before in his first NHL campaign was no mistake, broke Phil Esposito's scoring record by recording an astonishing 164 points—29 more than his nearest rival—including 109 assists to break a record held by none other than Bobby Orr.

But the swift center could only lead his Edmonton team to a 15th-place finish overall in the regular-season standings. The Oilers did upset Montreal in the first round of the playoffs, but then fell in the quarterfinals to the Islanders, the team that would go on to win it all again.

There seemed to be nothing the Islanders lacked. While Gretzky piled up points, Islander Mike Bossy stockpiled goals. He scored 68 of them, one below his career high and the third-highest total in history. But Bossy's first 50 goals came in his first 50 games, tying the record set by Maurice (Rocket) Richard 38 years before and unequaled since.

Even the way Bossy, a sharp-shooting right wing, grabbed a piece of the record was dramatic. He had 48 in 49 games and appeared to be falling short when the final minutes in the 50th game against the Quebec Nordiques began to tick away. But Bossy scored twice in the last four minutes, the second time with under two minutes remaining, to earn another line in the record book.

*Pittsburgh's Randy Carlyle won the Norris Trophy as the league's top defenseman in 1980-81.*

Bossy still wasn't finished. He scored a playoff record 35 points and helped the Islanders sweep the rival New York Rangers in four games in the semifinals and dispatch the Minnesota North Stars in just five games in the finals, a convincing show that finally earned the Islanders respect. But the Conn Smythe Trophy as playoff MVP went to Butch Goring, who scored five goals in the finals, including three in one game.

For his record performance, Gretzky won the Hart Trophy as Most Valuable Player for the second straight season. Pittsburgh's Randy Carlyle won the Norris as best defenseman and teammate Rick Kehoe won the Lady Byng for sportsmanship. Peter Stastny, a native of Czechoslovakia and a member of the Quebec Nordiques, won the Calder as Rookie of the Year.

Bossy, Gretzky and Carlyle were named to the All-Star team along with Los Angeles left wing Charlie Simmer, St. Louis goalie Mike Liut and defenseman Denis Potvin of the New York Islanders.

Of any losers during the season, the Winnipeg Jets would have had to rate at the top—or the bottom. They went a record 30 games without winning a game. Overall, they were 9–57–14.

## 1980–81

### FINAL STANDINGS
### Prince of Wales Conference
#### Norris Division

|             | W  | L  | T  | PTS | GF  | GA  |
|-------------|----|----|----|-----|-----|-----|
| Montreal    | 45 | 22 | 13 | 103 | 332 | 232 |
| Los Angeles | 43 | 24 | 13 | 99  | 337 | 290 |
| Pittsburgh  | 30 | 37 | 13 | 73  | 302 | 345 |
| Hartford    | 21 | 41 | 18 | 60  | 292 | 372 |
| Detroit     | 19 | 43 | 18 | 56  | 252 | 339 |

#### Adams Division

|           | W  | L  | T  | PTS | GF  | GA  |
|-----------|----|----|----|-----|-----|-----|
| Buffalo   | 39 | 20 | 21 | 99  | 327 | 250 |
| Boston    | 37 | 30 | 13 | 87  | 316 | 272 |
| Minnesota | 35 | 28 | 17 | 87  | 291 | 263 |
| Quebec    | 30 | 32 | 18 | 78  | 314 | 318 |
| Toronto   | 28 | 37 | 15 | 71  | 322 | 367 |

### Clarence Campbell Conference
#### Patrick Division

|              | W  | L  | T  | PTS | GF  | GA  |
|--------------|----|----|----|-----|-----|-----|
| New York I.  | 48 | 18 | 14 | 110 | 355 | 260 |
| Philadelphia | 41 | 24 | 15 | 97  | 313 | 249 |
| Calgary      | 39 | 27 | 14 | 92  | 329 | 298 |
| New York R.  | 30 | 36 | 14 | 74  | 312 | 317 |
| Washington   | 26 | 36 | 18 | 70  | 286 | 317 |

#### Smythe Division

|            | W  | L  | T  | PTS | GF  | GA  |
|------------|----|----|----|-----|-----|-----|
| St. Louis  | 45 | 18 | 17 | 107 | 352 | 281 |
| Chicago    | 31 | 33 | 16 | 78  | 304 | 315 |
| Vancouver  | 28 | 32 | 20 | 76  | 289 | 301 |
| Edmonton   | 29 | 35 | 16 | 74  | 328 | 327 |
| Colorado   | 22 | 45 | 13 | 57  | 258 | 344 |
| Winnipeg   | 9  | 57 | 14 | 32  | 246 | 400 |

### LEADING SCORERS

|                        | G  | A   | PTS |
|------------------------|----|-----|-----|
| Gretzky, Edmonton      | 55 | 109 | 164 |
| Dionne, Los Angeles    | 58 | 77  | 135 |
| K. Nilsson, Calgary    | 49 | 82  | 131 |
| Bossy, New York I.     | 68 | 51  | 119 |
| Taylor, Los Angeles    | 47 | 65  | 112 |
| P. Stastny, Quebec     | 39 | 70  | 109 |
| Simmer, Los Angeles    | 56 | 49  | 105 |
| Rogers, Hartford       | 40 | 65  | 105 |
| Federko, St. Louis     | 31 | 73  | 104 |
| Richard, Quebec        | 52 | 51  | 103 |
| Middleton, Boston      | 44 | 59  | 103 |
| Trottier, New York I.  | 31 | 72  | 103 |

## 1981–82

He stood a lean and bony 165 pounds, barely reached 5-11 on his tiptoes and with his thin, innocent face looked more like a schoolboy than the greatest player of his generation—maybe the greatest of any generation. Edmonton's Wayne Gretzky was 21 years old and no one had ever done what he did in 1981–82.

Having already shattered the scoring record a year earlier, Gretzky went on to destroy it, amassing 212 points, an incredible 65 more than anyone else and 107 more than his closest teammate. Included in Gretzky's total was a record 92 goals, which broke Phil Esposito's record by 16, and a record 120 assists.

The New York Islanders won their third straight Stanley Cup and won a record 15 consecutive games in the process, but it was clearly the season of No. 99, known to his Edmonton fans as "The Kid."

Gretzky became the National Hockey League's first million-dollar-a-year performer, negotiating the record pact shortly after scoring 50 goals in his first 39 games, breaking the record set by Maurice (Rocket) Richard 30 years earlier and equaled by New York Islander Mike Bossy the year before.

Taking a cue from their slender center, the Oilers vaulted from 15th place in 1980–81 to a second-place finish overall in the point standings, behind only the champion Islanders. But the Oilers were upset in the first round of the playoffs by Los Angeles, the team with the worst record of any of the 16 playoff entrants.

Edmonton's ouster only served to make the Islanders' march to their third straight title that much easier. They became only the third franchise, joining Toronto and Montreal, to win as many as three consecutive Stanley Cups in a season.

Bossy, the quick right wing, led the Islanders in

*A snap of the wrist and Wayne Gretzky breaks the NHL record for goals. It was No. 77 and it came against Buffalo's Don Edwards on February 24, 1982.*

the playoffs, earning the Conn Smythe Trophy as playoff MVP after scoring 17 goals, seven of them in a four-game finals sweep of Vancouver, tying a 26-year-old record set by Jean Beliveau.

Bossy and Gretzky were named to the All-Star

◄ *Peter Stastny and brothers Anton (left) and Marian (middle) led Quebec into the semifinals in the 1982 playoffs.*

team with Edmonton left wing Mark Messier, Islander goalie Bill Smith and defensemen Ray Bourque of Boston and Doug Wilson of Chicago.

To no one's surprise, Gretzky was the first unanimous choice as Hart Trophy winner as the Most Valuable Player, joining Bobby Orr as the only player to win the award three straight seasons.

Wilson won the Norris as best defenseman, Boston right wing Rick Middleton won the Lady Byng

The Great Gretzky meets Goldie Hawn and Burt Reynolds after his record-setting goal.

for gentlemanly play and Winnipeg center Dale Hawerchuk won the Calder as Rookie of the Year.

## 1981–82

### FINAL STANDINGS

#### Prince of Wales Conference

##### Patrick Division

| | W | L | T | PTS | GF | GA |
|---|---|---|---|---|---|---|
| New York I. | 54 | 16 | 10 | 118 | 385 | 250 |
| New York R. | 39 | 27 | 14 | 92 | 316 | 306 |
| Philadelphia | 38 | 31 | 11 | 87 | 325 | 313 |
| Pittsburgh | 31 | 36 | 13 | 75 | 310 | 337 |
| Washington | 26 | 41 | 13 | 65 | 319 | 338 |

##### Adams Division

| | | | | | | |
|---|---|---|---|---|---|---|
| Montreal | 46 | 17 | 17 | 109 | 360 | 223 |
| Boston | 43 | 27 | 10 | 96 | 323 | 285 |
| Buffalo | 39 | 26 | 15 | 93 | 307 | 273 |
| Quebec | 33 | 31 | 16 | 82 | 356 | 345 |
| Hartford | 21 | 41 | 18 | 60 | 264 | 351 |

#### Clarence Campbell Conference

##### Norris Division

| | | | | | | |
|---|---|---|---|---|---|---|
| Minnesota | 37 | 23 | 20 | 94 | 346 | 288 |
| Winnipeg | 33 | 33 | 14 | 80 | 319 | 332 |
| St. Louis | 32 | 40 | 8 | 72 | 315 | 349 |
| Chicago | 30 | 38 | 12 | 72 | 332 | 363 |
| Toronto | 20 | 44 | 16 | 56 | 298 | 380 |
| Detroit | 21 | 47 | 12 | 54 | 270 | 351 |

##### Smythe Division

| | | | | | | |
|---|---|---|---|---|---|---|
| Edmonton | 48 | 17 | 15 | 111 | 417 | 295 |
| Vancouver | 30 | 33 | 17 | 77 | 290 | 286 |
| Calgary | 29 | 34 | 17 | 75 | 334 | 345 |
| Los Angeles | 24 | 41 | 15 | 63 | 314 | 369 |
| Colorado | 18 | 49 | 13 | 49 | 241 | 362 |

| LEADING SCORERS | G | A | PTS |
|---|---|---|---|
| Gretzky, Edmonton | 92 | 120 | 212 |
| Bossy, New York I. | 64 | 83 | 147 |
| P. Stastny, Quebec | 46 | 93 | 139 |
| Maruk, Washington | 60 | 76 | 136 |
| Trottier, New York I. | 50 | 79 | 129 |
| D. Savard, Chicago | 32 | 87 | 119 |
| Dionne, Los Angeles | 50 | 67 | 117 |
| Smith, Minnesota | 43 | 71 | 114 |
| Ciccarelli, Minnesota | 55 | 52 | 107 |
| Taylor, Los Angeles | 39 | 67 | 106 |

## 1982–83

As the teams went deeper into the 1982–83 season, the question seemed to be not whether the New York Islanders could win another Stanley Cup championship, but rather which team would succeed them. The Islanders slumped and suffered during the season, but when the playoffs ended, the Islanders possessed their fourth straight title, earning themselves a slice of immortality.

They became only the second franchise to win that many consecutive championships, joining the five-time winners from Montreal (1956–60) and the Canadiens' four-time winners (1976–79). While there were record-setting performances by individuals on other teams, they seemed to pale in com-

parison to the Islanders' fourth championship in just their 11th season of existence.

Not even Wayne Gretzky, who again led the league in scoring with 196 points, could stop the Islanders' charge to the Cup. Gretzky was held without a goal and with just four assists as the Islanders swept the Edmonton Oilers in four games in the final series. The Islanders were led by goalie Billy Smith, who won the Conn Smythe Trophy as playoff MVP, and Mike Bossy, who set an NHL playoff record with five game-winning goals in one season.

Bossy also tied Guy Lafleur's regular-season record of six straight 50-goal seasons and became the first player to score 60 goals three straight years. Marcel Dionne of Los Angeles became the first player to score 100 points in seven consecutive seasons, breaking the mark held by Lafleur and Bobby Orr. Boston goalie Pete Peeters went 31 games without a loss, one shy of the record held by his coach, Gerry Cheevers, and the Oilers set a record by scoring 424 goals.

Still, the biggest accomplishment belonged to the Islanders. They finished a disappointing sixth in points during the season, the worst finish ever for a Cup winner, but defeated Washington in the preliminary round of the playoffs and the New York Rangers in the Patrick Division finals. After disposing of the Rangers, the Islanders met Boston, the team that led the league during the season with 110 points.

Following a six-game elimination of the Bruins in the Prince of Wales Conference final, the Islanders finished off the Oilers for their second straight finals sweep, adding it to the one the previous year against Vancouver. Smith was the hero. He shut out the Oilers in the opening game, 2-0, the first goalie to blank them since he did it two years earlier. He held the high-scoring Oilers to just six goals in the series while running his career playoff record to 73-24.

That represented vindication for both Smith and the Islanders. Smith failed to win a game for two months during the regular season and the Islanders went through a stretch when they could not assemble back-to-back victories for two months. The four

*His first season as a Bruin, goalie Pete Peeters posted a streak of 31 games without a defeat and won the Vezina Trophy.*

*Islander goalie Billy Smith, MVP of the Stanley Cup playoffs, frustrated Wayne Gretzky (99) and his Edmonton teammates.*

Stanley Cups put the Islanders fifth among all NHL teams and with his 97th career playoff victory, Islander coach Al Arbour moved right behind Scotty Bowman (111) and Dick Irvin (100), who lead the all-time list.

But not all the records set were glowing ones. Islander Billy Carroll, a center, set an all-time record for forwards by playing in 69 straight games without scoring a goal. And the Canadiens suffered their third straight preliminary-round elimination, which hadn't happened in the long and regal history of the franchise.

Besides winning the Ross Trophy for leading the league in scoring, Gretzky also was awarded his fourth straight MVP award, the most times anyone has ever won the trophy consecutively. Peeters got the Vezina Trophy for best regular-season goaltender, Washington's Rod Langway captured the Norris Trophy for top defenseman and Bossy took the Lady Byng Trophy for sportsmanship and high standard of playing ability. Philadelphia's Bobby Clarke won the Selke Trophy as best defensive forward and Chicago's Steve Larmer was Rookie of the Year.

The Oilers placed two players, Gretzky and Mark

Messier, on the All-Star team. Joining them were Bossy, Peeters, Langway and Philadelphia's Mark Howe.

## 1982–83

### FINAL STANDINGS
#### Prince of Wales Conference

##### Adams Division

| | W | L | T | PTS | GF | GA |
|---|---|---|---|---|---|---|
| Boston | 50 | 20 | 10 | 110 | 327 | 228 |
| Montreal | 42 | 24 | 14 | 98 | 350 | 286 |
| Buffalo | 38 | 29 | 13 | 89 | 318 | 285 |
| Quebec | 34 | 34 | 12 | 80 | 343 | 336 |
| Hartford | 19 | 54 | 7 | 45 | 261 | 403 |

##### Patrick Division

| | W | L | T | PTS | GF | GA |
|---|---|---|---|---|---|---|
| Philadelphia | 49 | 23 | 8 | 106 | 326 | 240 |
| New York I. | 42 | 26 | 12 | 96 | 302 | 226 |
| Washington | 39 | 25 | 16 | 94 | 306 | 283 |
| New York R. | 35 | 35 | 10 | 80 | 306 | 287 |
| New Jersey | 17 | 49 | 14 | 48 | 230 | 338 |
| Pittsburgh | 18 | 53 | 9 | 45 | 257 | 394 |

#### Clarence Campbell Conference

##### Norris Division

| | | | | | | |
|---|---|---|---|---|---|---|
| Chicago | 47 | 23 | 10 | 104 | 338 | 268 |
| Minnesota | 40 | 24 | 16 | 96 | 321 | 290 |
| Toronto | 28 | 40 | 12 | 68 | 293 | 330 |
| St. Louis | 25 | 40 | 15 | 65 | 285 | 316 |
| Detroit | 21 | 44 | 15 | 57 | 263 | 344 |

##### Smythe Division

| | | | | | | |
|---|---|---|---|---|---|---|
| Edmonton | 47 | 21 | 12 | 106 | 424 | 315 |
| Calgary | 32 | 34 | 14 | 78 | 321 | 317 |
| Vancouver | 30 | 35 | 15 | 75 | 303 | 309 |
| Winnipeg | 33 | 39 | 8 | 74 | 311 | 333 |
| Los Angeles | 27 | 41 | 12 | 66 | 308 | 365 |

### LEADING SCORERS

| | G | A | PTS |
|---|---|---|---|
| Gretzky, Edmonton | 71 | 125 | 196 |
| P. Stastny, Quebec | 47 | 77 | 124 |
| Savard, Chicago | 35 | 85 | 120 |
| Bossy, New York I. | 60 | 58 | 118 |
| Dionne, Los Angeles | 56 | 51 | 107 |
| Pederson, Boston | 46 | 61 | 107 |
| Messier, Edmonton | 48 | 58 | 106 |
| Goulet, Quebec | 57 | 48 | 105 |
| Anderson, Edmonton | 48 | 56 | 104 |
| Nilsson, Calgary | 46 | 58 | 104 |
| Kurri, Edmonton | 45 | 59 | 104 |

*Held scoreless in the Islanders' sweep to their fourth consecutive Stanley Cup, a dejected Wayne Gretzky accepts the reality of defeat in the third period of the final game.*

# THE GREATEST PLAYERS

Selection of hockey's all-time greatest players is sure to spark lively debates among fans everywhere. The editors realized this when they sought the ten best forwards, ten best defensemen and ten best goalies. Opinions were obtained from former and current players, club officials and hockey writers and broadcasters who have spanned the NHL almost from its beginnings.

In the end it was the editors who made the selections of the players whose profiles appear in this chapter.

## THE FORWARDS
## They Make the Headlines

### JEAN BELIVEAU

The Montreal Canadiens purchased an entire hockey league in order to make Jean Beliveau a member of their team. It happened in 1953 while Beliveau was completing his third season for the Quebec Aces of the Quebec Senior League. The league was classified as "amateur," although its players received modest salaries. Modest, that is, except for Jean Beliveau. His annual salary was $20,000.

Beliveau, like many amateur tennis players in those days, claimed he couldn't afford to turn professional. It got to be extremely embarrassing for the Canadiens, who owned the negotiating rights to the young star. The fans were clamoring for big Jean in Montreal, but he wouldn't budge from Quebec City.

Then, in the most unusual measure ever taken

◀ Jean Beliveau

to obtain a player, the Canadiens purchased the entire Quebec Senior League and the pro rights to all its players. The new owners turned the league professional, leaving Beliveau with no choice but to join Montreal. He received a $20,000 bonus for signing and a five-year, $105,000 contract, a fantastic salary for a 23-year-old rookie.

Jean Beliveau, though, was worth every Canadian penny the Montreal club paid him. He went on to become the highest-scoring center in NHL history with 1,219 points. He finished with 507 goals when he retired in 1971 after 18 NHL seasons. That year, Beliveau had led the Canadiens to their 10th Stanley Cup since he joined the team.

To watch Beliveau in action was to marvel at the deceptive grace of this big bear on skates. A Gulliver in the icy world of comparative Lilliputians, he was 6-3 and weighed 210 pounds. He didn't appear to skate quickly, but few could keep up with him. He had all the right instincts and all the right shots.

Rival players were awed by Beliveau's size and strength when he broke into the NHL. Bill Ezinicki, a vicious body-checker in his glory days with Toronto and Boston, remembers the first time he lined up Beliveau for one of his patented hip checks. "It was like running into the side of a big oak tree," Ezinicki recalled. "I bounced right off the guy and landed on the seat of my pants."

In those days, Beliveau had only one flaw in his makeup. His disposition was better suited to the priesthood than the savage atmosphere of the hockey rink. He was cross-checked, hooked and belted in every NHL rink. He didn't hit back because, he said, "I want to play hockey." He maintained that attitude until his third season with the Canadiens when he decided to retaliate. He wound up among the league's penalty leaders, a fact he wasn't proud of, but he also won the league's scoring title.

No longer did rival ruffians pick on Jean Beliveau. He had arrived—as a player and as a man—in the NHL. Other honors followed. In his 18 years with the Canadiens he was named to the All-Star team ten times and twice won the Hart Trophy as the league's Most Valuable Player.

Toe Blake, Beliveau's coach for 13 years, summed up big Jean's value to the Canadiens this way: "In all the time he's been in hockey I've never heard anybody say a bad word against him. As a hockey player and a gentleman, Jean Beliveau is pretty hard to beat."

# MIKE BOSSY

The scenario rarely changes. Mike Bossy of the New York Islanders has the puck. Mike Bossy carries it into the right face-off circle or into the slot or into No Man's Land in front of the net. Mike Bossy shoots. Quicker than a wink. Poof! The puck is in the net.

In Bossy's first six seasons in the National Hockey League he totaled 365 goals and 693 points—an average of 61 goals and 116 points a season. He established a league record for right wings during the 1981–82 season when he accounted for 147 points on 64 goals and 83 assists. Under normal circumstances, those numbers would have earned Bossy his first NHL scoring championship, but that was the season Wayne Gretzky rewrote the record book with 92 goals and 212 points.

Bossy gained considerable satisfaction in 1982 when he sparked the Islanders to their third straight Stanley Cup championship and was named winner of the Conn Smythe Trophy as MVP of the playoffs. He also outpolled the great Gretzky in the balloting for the NHL All-Star team that year.

The following year, Bossy notched 60 goals for the third straight year and became the first player to do so. In 1983, Bossy's 17 goals in the playoffs led the Islanders to a fourth consecutive Stanley Cup. His career playoff goal total soared to 69, third-highest in history behind Jean Beliveau and Maurice Richard.

It seems inconceivable now that 13 NHL teams passed up the chance to pick Bossy in the first round of the 1977 amateur draft, allowing general manager Bill Torrey to grab him for the Islanders. At the time Bossy was considered a one-dimensional sharp-shooter. He has since developed into an exquisite passer and playmaker. And nobody, not even Gretzky, can match Bossy's quick release when he takes aim at rival goaltenders.

Most players wait until the puck has settled on their stick before they shoot. Not Mike Bossy. When he sees the pass coming, he times his shot so the reception of the pass and the shot itself become one motion. The advantage of that shooting style is that goalies seldom have time to react.

"I feel the quicker I get the shot away, the better chance I have of scoring," Bossy said. "I try to pick a spot, high or low, but other than that I don't think about it. I just shoot."

He has been shooting that way since he tied on

*Mike Bossy*

his first pair of skates. He even scored 21 goals in a single game while playing youth hockey in the Montreal suburb of Laval.

Bossy was a sad-eyed, homesick 20-year-old when he joined the Islanders at their training camp in 1977. He had married his teenage sweetheart, Lucie, that summer and had to leave home without her. "A lot of nights I had tears in my eyes," he recalled. His bride eventually joined him on Long Island and Bossy went on to set a league record for rookies by scoring 53 goals in 73 games. He also won the Calder (Rookie of the Year) Trophy.

When hockey violence became an issue, Bossy took a stand. Although he is a solid 185 pounds and six feet tall, Bossy proclaimed, "I won't fight," meaning he refused to scuffle with antagonists. One exception: Bossy lost the caps on three teeth during a rare high-sticking exchange with Dean Hopkins of the Los Angeles Kings in 1981. "I was teed off because Hopkins cross-checked me from behind," Bossy explained later. "I was about to tell him what an ass he was when he cross-checked me in the mouth. I guess you can't talk to guys like that."

Tiger Williams of the Vancouver Canucks shadowed Bossy during the final round of the 1982 Stanley Cup playoffs and attempted to provoke Bossy. He failed. The frustrated Williams admitted: "He'd be a fool to rough it or fight."

Early in the 1981-82 season, Bossy signed a new long-term contract with the Islanders. Estimates of his salary ranged from $500,000 to $600,000 a year—more than any other player in the league with the exception of Wayne Gretzky.

Clearly, Mike Bossy is worth every penny.


# PHIL ESPOSITO

On the night of January 9, 1981, Phil Esposito faced one of the toughest assignments of his life—his farewell address as a player. He was about to play his final game for the New York Rangers against the Buffalo Sabres at Madison Square Garden. A center-ice ceremony before the game was meant to be brief, but the crowd of 17,501 gave Esposito a lengthy standing ovation and chanted "ESPO! ESPO!"

As the applause rumbled down from the mezzanine, Esposito nodded and smiled, then raised his hands. "Please," he said. "I've been preparing for this for 10 years." The crowd roared and Esposito continued. "My world seemed to shatter when I was traded here from Boston. But after the initial shock, which took a long time, I fell in love with New York."

That was it. After 1,282 games covering 18 National Hockey League seasons, Phil Esposito was retiring as the second highest scorer in history. He failed to score a goal that night, but he did pick up an assist. It raised his career total to 1,590 points based on 717 goals and 873 assists. Only Gordie Howe had more goals (801) and more points (1,850).

Howe was at the Garden that night as the keynote speaker and presented Esposito with a number "77" sweater.

Esposito was a month shy of his 39th birthday at the time of his retirement. "I couldn't handle the pressure any more," he told friends. "It really affected me . . . For my whole life as a hockey player, I told myself if I wasn't satisfied, I should do something else. This year I wasn't satisfied . . . I gave it all I had, but I had nothing left to give."

Born in Sault Ste. Marie, Ontario, Esposito grew up shooting pucks at his kid brother, Tony. "He was younger," explained Phil, "so he had to be the goalie." They would play the same roles years later in the NHL.

The Black Hawks sponsored the minor hockey program in Sault Ste. Marie, and in those days that was enough for an NHL club to gain the rights to the local hockey playing talent. That's how Phil filtered into the Chicago Black Hawks' system. He spent two years in the minors before being called up to Chicago midway through the 1963–64 season.

Three goals in 27 NHL games gave no clue to the kind of scoring that Esposito would one day produce. A bit clumsy on his skates, Phil's major asset was his strength, and the Hawks used him to center superstar Bobby Hull. In the next three seasons, he scored 71 goals, many of them on rebounds of Hull bombs.

In 1967, the Hawks went shopping for a tough defenseman and asked Boston about Gilles Marotte. The talks expanded and finally on May 15, the deal was completed. Marotte, center Pit Martin and minor-league goalie Jack Norris went to Chicago, with Esposito and two other forwards, Ken Hodge and Fred Stanfield, moving to the Bruins.

In 8½ seasons with Boston, Espo won five scoring

*Phil Esposito*

championships and finished second twice. He was the first man to go over 100 points in a single season and he passed the 50-goal plateau five times. He enjoyed his greatest season in 1970–71 when he established records for most goals (76) and most points (152). Both records later were erased by Wayne Gretzky.

It is no coincidence that the Bruins ended a 29-year wait and won two Stanley Cups following the arrival of Esposito. The first Cup came in 1970 and, en route to it, Boston eliminated Chicago in four games. The scoring star for Boston was Esposito and it was accomplished at the expense of his goal-tending brother, Tony, who had wound up with the Hawks after graduating from Michigan Tech.

Fans in Boston and New York were shocked when the Bruins traded Esposito to the Rangers in a five-player deal early in the 1975–76 season. The 6–1, 212-pound center was shocked, too. He displayed only flashes of his old form with the Rangers—notably in the 1979 Stanley Cup playoffs when he sparked New York into the finals against the Montreal Canadiens. The Canadiens won the series in five games.

Following his retirement, Esposito became an analyst on telecasts of Ranger games.

# WAYNE GRETZKY

He looks too thin, too fragile to be playing professional hockey. Five feet, 11 inches and 165 pounds,

*Wayne Gretzky*

maybe. He could wear a fur coat on Halloween and go out disguised as a pipe cleaner. When he joins his teammates for those stress and strength tests at training camp, he invariably finishes near the bottom of the class.

But don't let Wayne Gretzky's looks deceive you. When it comes to scoring goals and setting up goals, he is at the top of the class.

Jean Beliveau and Phil Esposito were bigger. Rocket Richard, Gordie Howe and Bobby Hull were stronger. However, none of these former superstars ever enjoyed the type of season Gretzky had in 1981–82. The Edmonton Oilers' center scored 50 goals in his first 39 games that season, smashing a record first set by Richard and later matched by Mike Bossy of the New York Islanders.

Gretzky went on from there to wipe out Esposito's single-season, goal-scoring record. Esposito scored 76 in 78 games in 1970–71. Gretzky eclipsed that mark in his 64th game and finished the season with an amazing 92 goals, 120 assists and 212 points.

Gretzky won the Hart Trophy as the league's Most Valuable Player for the third straight year and the Ross Trophy as scoring champion for the second

consecutive year. He also was named to the All-Star team for the third time.

The 22-year-old center continued to dominate the game in 1982–83. He again won the Hart and the Ross and led the Oilers to the Stanley Cup finals.

"He's a natural goal scorer, just like I was," Rocket Richard said. "He's moving all the time and it seems the players trying to check him can't catch him."

"Ever try to catch a feather?" said Dennis Sobchuk, a former Gretzky teammate. "That's what Wayne is like."

Bruce MacGregor, the Oilers' assistant general manager, likened Gretzky to a man who was MacGregor's teammate on the Detroit Red Wings in the sixties. "I see a lot of similarities between Wayne and Gordie Howe," MacGregor said. "When you walked through a hotel lobby with Gordie, people buzzed. It's the same with Wayne."

People have been buzzing about Wayne Gretzky since his early days in his hometown of Brantford, Ontario. When he was 10, he scored 378 goals in 85 games. "It seems that Wayne was always in the spotlight," said his father, Walter.

Wayne Gretzky was only 17 when he signed his first pro contract for $1.7 million and joined the Indianapolis Racers of the old World Hockey Association at the start of the 1978–79 season. When the Racers ran out of money after only eight games, he was sold to the Oilers and signed another contract—for 21 years and more than $5 million. They also gave the kid a No. 99 jersey, which is symbolic, because that signature meant he would be under contract until 1999.

Gretzky totaled 46 goals and 110 points in his first pro season. The WHA folded in 1979 and the Oilers were granted an NHL franchise. Gretzky recalls his NHL baptism with a wry smile. "Everywhere I went they thought I would get killed because of my size," he said. "I heard a lot of talk then that I'd never get 110 points like I did in the WHA." He did better than that, totaling 137 points on 51 goals and 86 assists.

There was no stopping Gretzky. In his second NHL season he established NHL records for most points (164) and most assists (109) and became the first NHL player to average two points a game.

In 1982, a week before he turned 21, Gretzky renegotiated his contract with the Oilers and became the highest-paid player in NHL history at more than $1 million a year. Peter Pocklington, the owner of the Oilers, said the new contract also included

"a large piece of real estate," which he later identified as a shopping center in western Canada.

Wayne Gretzky, considered too thin for pro hockey, was now its fattest wage-earner.

# GORDIE HOWE

Gordie Howe, looking a little uncomfortable in a tuxedo, was grinning as he approached the speaker's rostrum in the Canadian Room of the Royal York Hotel in Toronto. The occasion was the 1982 Hockey Hall of Fame dinner, and Howe was there to receive the initial presentation of the Milestone Award, instituted by the National Hockey League to honor players and coaches who have achieved milestones during their careers.

Howe glanced about the room, packed with almost 900 diners, and was still grinning as he began his acceptance speech. He recalled how he had dreamed during his youth of playing in the NHL. "I would have been happy to play just one season," he said. Now the audience was laughing—not at Howe but with him.

Gordie Howe was the most durable player in the history of pro hockey. He played not one season but 32—26 in the NHL and six in the World Hockey Association.

The dictionary defines durability as "the ability to withstand decay or wear." It is the word that best describes Howe and his fabulous career. The six-foot, 205-pound right wing from the wheat fields of Saskatchewan started his career with the Detroit Red Wings at the age of 18 in 1946. He finished it with the Hartford Whalers at the age of 52 in 1980.

Howe's statistics for his pro career are astounding. Including playoff games, he totaled 2,421 games, 1,071 goals, 1,518 assists, 2,589 points and 2,418 penalty minutes.

He was hailed throughout the hockey world as a seemingly indestructible man of steel. Howe's career—and his life—were almost snuffed out in his third season with the Red Wings. He collided with Toronto's Ted Kennedy during a 1950 Stanley Cup playoff game, crashed head on into the sideboards and suffered a severe brain injury. He hovered between life and death while surgeons operated to relieve pressure on his brain.

The injury left him with a slight facial tic; there are times when his dark eyes blink uncontrollably. His

*Gordie Howe*

teammates called him "Blinky," and it was a mark of Howe's class that he never resented the nickname. He frequently startled newsmen with remarks like "Old Blinky was flying tonight" or "Did you see old Blinky miss that goal in the second period?"

Even in the twilight of his career, Howe remained an amazing athlete—the complete hockey player. He was big and tough and sometimes a little rough. He could still shoot with the best NHL marksmen; he could set up plays; he acted as the triggerman on power plays; he killed penalties.

Jean Beliveau of the Montreal Canadiens claimed "Gordie Howe is the best hockey player I have ever seen." It is an interesting assessment from a man who once was a teammate of Maurice (Rocket) Richard. But even Richard admits, "Howe was a better all-around player than I was."

Blessed with a powerful body, Howe would have made an ideal heavyweight boxer. He had the sloping shoulders of a fighter, his neck thick and his muscular arms dangling loosely like the limbs of an oak tree. He had his share of fights on the ice, the most memorable taking place in 1959 when he tangled with Lou Fontinato of the New York Rangers. Fontinato's nose was broken, and his whole face needed considerable repairs.

Howe, though, was no troublemaker. He just kept rolling along, content to score goals and accumulate records and honors. He was named to the NHL's All-Star team 21 times. He won the league's scoring title six times and was a six-time winner of the Hart Trophy as the league's MVP.

He ended his 25-year career with the Red Wings in 1971, sat out two years, then made an historic return in 1973 in order to play with sons Marty and Mark in the WHA.

Gordie Howe was with the Hartford Whalers when they joined three other WHA teams in the NHL in 1979. He played in all 80 games in the Whalers' first season in the NHL, then retired for the second time and became the team's director of player development.

# BOBBY HULL

It started from the instant he cradled the puck on the curved blade of his stick. One . . . two strides . . . and he was in full flight, skating and slamming his way across the neutral zone and into enemy territory. By this time a chorus of sound enveloped the rink, rising into a long, drawn-out OOOHH! as this whirlwind on skates fired one of his patented slap shots.

The puck, traveling at more than 100 miles per hour, invariably wound up high in the net and Bobby Hull had scored another goal.

This scene was enacted and reenacted on an average of 40 times a season from the time of Hull's arrival in the NHL in 1957. In the 23 years that followed, nobody scored nearly as many goals or caused nearly as much excitement as this ruggedly handsome, blond-haired muscleman from the little Ontario town of Point Anne.

Hull was only 18 years old when he quit the junior ranks to turn pro with the Chicago Black Hawks. His great magnetism and goal-scoring ability turned a franchise which was losing money into the richest in the NHL. And as the Hawks grew in wealth, so did Bobby Hull. He became the league's first $100,000-a-year player when he signed a four-year, $400,000 contract at the start of the 1968–69 season. Other income from endorsements, several purebred cattle farms he owned and league awards and playoff money swelled his earnings that season to approximately $200,000.

In 1972, he accepted a $1,000,000 offer from the World Hockey Association to play for the Winnipeg Jets. Despite missing 15 games because of court suits initiated by the NHL aimed at blocking his move to the new league, Hull reached the 50-goal plateau for the sixth time in his career.

Hull enjoyed his greatest season in 1974–75 when he scored a record 77 goals in 78 games and totaled 142 points for Winnipeg. He was playing then on a line with two Swedish imports, center Ulf Nilsson and right wing Anders Hedberg. "They make the game fun for me," Hull said. "They're also my legs."

Hull's strong legs started to weaken in 1979, the year the Jets were admitted into the NHL. He also was experiencing shoulder problems. He ended his eight-year stay in Winnipeg late in the 1979–80 season when the Jets traded him to the Hartford Whalers. Gordie Howe also was winding up his career with the Whalers, and the two greats played on the same line in a handful of games.

Hull was the highest-scoring left wing in hockey history with 1,018 goals and 2,017 points when he

*Bobby Hull*

retired in 1980. He was 41. He joined the New York Rangers at their training camp in 1981, attempting a comeback. But he was released before the start of the regular season and he returned to his farm in Ontario.

What made Bobby Hull so great? He combined some of the talents of his most famed predecessors—the speed of Howie Morenz, the goal-scoring instincts of Maurice Richard, the strength and control of Gordie Howe—into a blend of the perfect hockey player.

He was the fastest skater in hockey (28.3 miles per hour with the puck, 29.7 m.p.h. without it). He had the fastest shot: his slap shot was clocked at 118.3 m.p.h., nearly 35 m.p.h. above the league average. And then there were the Hull muscles. He didn't have an ounce of excess baggage on his 5–10, 195-pound frame.

Hull totaled only 31 goals in his first two seasons with the Black Hawks, then developed the slap shot that was the bane of all goalies. He scored 50 goals in the 1961–62 season to equal a league record and progressively increased the mark to 58 in 1968–69. In his first 15 NHL seasons, he totaled 604 goals, won the league scoring championship three times and played left wing on the NHL All-Star team 10 times.

The supreme compliment came from Stan Mikita,

the former Black Hawks' center. "To say that Bobby was a great hockey player is to labor the point," Mikita said. "He was all of that, of course. But the thing I admired about him was the way he handled people. He always enjoyed signing autographs for fans and was a genuine nice guy."

# TED LINDSAY

No man on skates was ever too big or too tough for Ted Lindsay to challenge. He was small (5–8 and 160 pounds), but he always carried a big stick. And he used that stick—and his fists—to cut down some

*Ted Lindsay*

of the biggest, meanest men in the National Hockey League.

His tormentors called him "Scarface" or "Terrible Ted." Lindsay didn't mind. The scar tissue on his thin but rugged face represented his badge of courage. He stopped counting the stitches when they reached 400. And the nickname "Terrible" only applied to his reputation for getting into trouble, because as a player he was magnificent.

Lindsay broke into the NHL in 1944, making the big jump from the junior ranks to the Detroit Red Wings at the age of 19. Playing left wing on Detroit's memorable Production Line with Gordie Howe and Sid Abel, Lindsay helped the Red Wings win eight league titles (including seven in a row) and four Stanley Cup championships in the late 1940s and early '50s.

A member of nine All-Star teams and the league's leading scorer in 1949–50, Lindsay retired in 1960 after 16 years of service, 13 with the Red Wings and the last three with the Chicago Black Hawks. He totaled 365 goals and 458 assists, a league high for left wings until Bobby Hull passed the goals figure in 1968.

Lindsay had established a partnership with another former Detroit player, Marty Pavelich, in a plastics firm late in his playing career. Now he was able to devote all his time to this prosperous business. But he missed the excitement of the brawling world of hockey.

After four years of retirement, he returned to the Red Wings as a player. He was 39 years old. Asked why he would risk possible injury by attempting a comeback at that age, Lindsay said, "It's certainly not the money. I'm well off. I just had this desire to wind up my career with the Red Wings."

The Red Wings—and their fans—welcomed Lindsay back with open arms. He launched his comeback against the Toronto Maple Leafs in Detroit's opening game of the 1964–65 season. A crowd of 14,323, largest ever to see a Detroit home opener, greeted the old battler and he responded by dealing out several vicious bodychecks to assorted Maple Leafs. Ted Lindsay was back, and soon the whole league knew it.

In a game at Montreal he drew a $25 fine for spearing Ted Harris, a rugged defenseman who towered seven inches over Lindsay and outweighed him by 40 pounds. Claude Larose, a Montreal youngster with a reputation for being reasonably talented with his fists, tried to even matters. Lindsay gripped his stick with both hands and slashed Larose across the legs. Larose, 17 years Lindsay's junior, hobbled away in pain.

Lindsay's comeback lasted only one season, but it was a season in which the Red Wings won their first league championship in eight years. They wouldn't have done it without old man Lindsay, who scored 14 goals and, coincidentally, was among the league leaders in penalties. Clarence Campbell, the president of the National Hockey League who had earlier scoffed at Lindsay's return, called it one of the most amazing comebacks in professional sports.

A year later, Ted Lindsay was inducted into the Hockey Hall of Fame.

# HOWIE MORENZ

Babe Ruth and Bobby Jones, Bill Tilden and Jack Dempsey—these were the men who dominated America's Golden Era of Sport in the Roaring Twenties. During that same period of bathtub gin and flappers and ragtime jazz, Canada had its own hero. He was Howie Morenz of the Montreal Canadiens, the greatest hockey player of his generation.

To the French-speaking fans of the Province of Quebec, Howie Morenz was *L'homme-eclair*. In English he was the same thing: the top man.

Morenz was a center for the Canadiens for 12 years and near the end of his career played with the Chicago Black Hawks and the New York Rangers. Once, in a 44-game season, he scored 40 goals—a remarkable achievement. He totaled 270 goals during his National Hockey League career and was among the first group of players admitted to the Hockey Hall of Fame in 1945.

A happy-go-lucky man with large, smiling eyes, a receding hairline and a heavy beard, Morenz was a typical sports hero of the 1920s. He was colorful and glamorous, hockey's fastest man on skates and a fiery competitor. Toe Blake, the most successful coach in the history of the Canadiens, was a rookie player with Montreal when Morenz was approaching the end of the line. He remembers Morenz: "He was an inspiration for all of us . . . a man with remarkable skills who laughed hard and played hard."

Dazzling speed and guile were Morenz's trademarks. A contemporary of his, Ott Heller of the Rangers, once remarked: "When Howie skates full

*Howie Morenz*

speed, everyone else on the ice seems to be skating backward." Morenz's shot was equally impressive. Once he broke a goalie's nose with one of his bullet-like drives. Another time his shot caught a netminder square in the forehead, flipping him over on his back.

Although he never played at more than 165 pounds, Morenz body-checked with the ferocity of a giant. He was so swift, so skillful and so fearless that the wildly nationalistic French-Canadians of Montreal were undisturbed when they discovered his secret sin: Howie Morenz was of German ancestry.

He was born in the Ontario village of Mitchell in 1902, moving with his family to Stratford, Ontario, at the age of 14. He attracted the attention of the Canadiens when he scored nine goals in an amateur game in Montreal in 1922. The following year he turned pro with the Canadiens for a $1,000 bonus and quickly earned the nickname of "The Stratford Streak."

Off the ice, Morenz's pace was just as fast. He sang and played the ukulele. He was a clothes horse; he changed his suits twice and sometimes three times a day. He wore spats. He was a charming and cosmopolitan young man living swiftly in the charming, cosmopolitan city of Montreal.

Then, suddenly, he was no longer quite so young. After 11 seasons with the Canadiens he was traded, first to Chicago in 1934 and then to the New York Americans the following year. In 1936, he was repurchased by the Canadiens. On the night of January 28, 1937, in the midst of a fine comeback, Morenz broke four bones in his left leg and ankle in a game against Chicago. Five weeks later, the bones were knitting well when he fell to the cold floor of a Montreal hospital. An embolism had stopped his heart.

Howie Morenz was dead at the age of 34. The funeral service was held at center ice in the Montreal Forum, where thousands of fans wept openly for "Le Grand Morenz."

## MAURICE (ROCKET) RICHARD

Long after Maurice Richard retired in 1960, there were National Hockey League goalies who would sit around in locker rooms or coffee shops and recall what it was like to face the old Rocket from Montreal.

*Maurice Richard*

Glenn Hall, who was an All-Star netminder with Detroit and Chicago before winding up with the St. Louis Blues, had a rather unique memory of Richard. "What I remember most about the Rocket were his eyes," Hall says. "When he came flying toward you with the puck on his stick, his eyes were all lit up, flashing and gleaming like a pinball machine. It was terrifying."

Richard terrified goalies like Hall for 18 seasons, all with the Montreal Canadiens. He totaled 544 regular-season goals, a record until Gordie Howe wiped it out in 1963. He was the first to score 50 goals in one season (1944–45), and he is the only one to have reached that figure in a 50-game schedule.

There was nothing quite so dramatic as a Richard goal. He would run, not glide, down the ice, cut in from right wing as he neared the cage and then use either a forehand or backhand shot to fool rival goalies. That was another of Richard's great, unmatched talents. He was ambidextrous, a right wing with an unorthodox left-hand shot.

"The Rocket did everything by instinct and with brute strength," said Frank Selke Sr., who was the Canadiens' general manager during Richard's record-breaking years. "He was the greatest opportunist the game has ever known."

Bill Chadwick, a former referee and a member of hockey's Hall of Fame, was another Richard admirer. "He was the greatest scorer I ever saw from the blue line in," Chadwick said. "And his strength was amazing. I saw him carry defensemen on his back right up to the goal mouth and score."

Richard learned the rudiments of the game as a teenager in Montreal's Lafontaine Park in the years preceding World War II. He was a prolific scorer in the city's Park League, but appeared too injury-prone to become a real star. He broke an ankle while playing amateur hockey, then fractured a wrist. He was finally promoted to the Canadiens in 1942, but was sidelined early by another broken ankle. "It looks as if we have a brittle-boned player on our hands," sighed Tommy Gorman, then the Canadiens' manager.

Gorman even considered releasing Richard, but the Rocket became stronger as he reached manhood, shook off his injuries and developed into a small bull on skates. He stood a shade under six feet and weighed 190 pounds at the height of his career. Many teams used two players to "shadow"

the Rocket. He considered it a compliment. And when they got in his way, he would simply bowl them over and then glare at them with dark, menacing eyes.

He had a mean temper which got him into frequent scrapes with players and officials. His suspension by NHL president Clarence Campbell in 1955 for carving up a Boston player with his stick and punching a linesman precipitated a riot in the Montreal Forum.

All of Richard's transgressions, though, were forgotten when he was rushed into the Hockey Hall of Fame in 1961. This honor normally isn't bestowed on a player until at least the third year of his retirement. Maurice Richard had only been retired for nine months!

# MILT SCHMIDT

He would glide behind the Boston net to pick up the puck and then start up ice. As he reached center ice he was under a full head of steam, his cowlick flying, his neck outthrust, his prominent nose sticking out like the prow of a ship. And he never had to look down at the puck, which he was shifting back and forth, left to right, right to left, on the end of his stick.

When he crossed the blue line and entered enemy territory he would skate around or barge through rival defensemen until he was close enough to the net to release his famed wrist shot. Then, bingo! The puck was in the cage and all Boston went wild.

This was Milt Schmidt in action, the kid from Kitchener, the center of the much-feared Kraut Line, who in 16 years as a player for the Bruins scored 229 goals and ranked among the most fiery competitors in the history of the National Hockey League.

One of his greatest admirers was Art Ross, who coached and managed the Bruins during Schmidt's big years. "Schmidt was the fastest playmaker of all time," Ross said. "By that I mean no player ever skated at full tilt the way he did and was still able to make the play."

It was Ross who scouted Schmidt and signed him to a Bruins' contract in 1935. Milt played one season of minor-league hockey at Providence, then moved up to the Bruins and was reunited with two of his

old school pals, Bobby Bauer and Woody Dumart. That was the beginning of the Kraut Line, so named because all three came from the Kitchener-Waterloo area of Ontario, which was predominantly German in origin.

With Schmidt as their center and leader, the Krauts led the Bruins to four straight regular-season NHL championships beginning in 1938. Boston also won two Stanley Cup titles during that same period.

Injuries frequently slowed Schmidt but never stopped him from playing. "That's the only trouble with Milt," Ross once said. "If he would not put so much of his heart and soul into his play, he wouldn't be injured so much."

In one Stanley Cup playoff series against Toronto, when both his knees were so banged up from repeated injuries that he couldn't bend them, he had his legs taped from the ankle to the thigh and then had himself lifted off the table and onto his skates.

Referees, normally impartial, were frequently amazed at Schmidt's courage. "Milt had more guts than any player I ever saw," said Bill Chadwick. Red Storey, another retired referee, said, "I'd take five Milt Schmidts, put my grandmother in the nets and we'd beat any team."

Schmidt was named to the NHL All-Star team four times and won the league's Most Valuable Player award in 1951 at the age of 33. He served as the Bruins' coach following his retirement as a player in 1955, then became the club's general manager.

He claimed he received his greatest thrill in 1952 when he scored the 250th goal of his career. It was Milt Schmidt Night at Boston Garden and Bauer came out of retirement for that one game to play alongside his old Kraut linemates. "That was a great night," Schmidt said. "The goal and the ovation we got from the fans . . . I'll never forget it."

Hockey fans—in Boston and everywhere—will never forget Milt Schmidt either.

*Milt Schmidt*

# THE DEFENDERS
## Behind the Blue Line

## FRANK (KING) CLANCY

The setting was Toronto's Maple Leaf Gardens just before the outbreak of World War II. The hometown Maple Leafs were involved in a rough game with Montreal, and referee Frank (King) Clancy was finding it difficult controlling the tempers of the players and the fans. When one rinkside customer went so far as to compare Clancy with the less personable end of a horse, the referee, always quick with a quip, bellowed, "If it wasn't for a horse you wouldn't have had me playing in this joint for six years."

It was a classic stopper. And Clancy, of course, was right. A horse did figure in his trade from Ottawa to Toronto in 1930. It developed this way: Conn Smythe, the owner of the Maple Leafs, made a hefty bet on a horse named Rare Jewel at longshot odds that year and collected $14,000. He used his winnings as a down payment to acquire Clancy from Ottawa. The total price was $35,000 and two players—a record hockey transaction in those days.

Clancy was worth it, too, for he turned out to be a "rare jewel" for the Maple Leafs. He helped spark them to the Stanley Cup in his second year with the club and went on to lead them to two regular-season NHL titles before retiring as a player in 1936.

In his 16 years as one of the NHL's greatest rushing defensemen (he spent his first 10 seasons with Ottawa), Clancy totaled 136 goals and assisted on 145. He was named to four All-Star teams, starting with the first one in 1930. Those are impressive credentials for a man who once was considered too puny to play hockey.

Clancy, born in Ottawa in 1902, entered the NHL as a 150-pound teenager. Most rival defensemen outweighed him by at least 30 pounds. But Clancy made up for his lack of heft with great speed and agility. And he never backed away from a brawl, although he admits he won only one fight, against Boston's Eddie Shore, of all people. "I socked Eddie once as he was getting to his feet and skated like mad to the other end of the rink," he said.

Boston fans used to ride Clancy the most. He recalled one night when a Bostonian seated behind the Toronto bench needled him until he could stand it no longer. He turned to the fan and said, "You think you're pretty tough, buddy. Okay, stay around after the game and we'll see how tough you are."

*King Clancy*

Teammate Charlie Conacher overheard Clancy's challenge and grinned. "King, you'll be the next heavyweight champion of the world if you can handle that fan," Conacher said. "Didn't you recognize him? He's Jack Sharkey the heavyweight champion of the world."

Clancy didn't keep his appointment with the champ.

The colorful Irishman with the dented nose and bellowing voice served as a coach both before and after his 11-year service as an NHL referee. His last coaching job was a three-year tenure with his beloved Maple Leafs (1954–56). He later was named an assistant to general manager-coach Punch Imlach of the Leafs.

"I'm sort of a good-will ambassador," he explained.

Hockey never had a better one than King Clancy.

# VICTOR (DIT) CLAPPER

There are various yardsticks by which a player can be measured for greatness in professional hockey. One is the number of goals he scores. Another is longevity. In both areas, Dit Clapper had few peers.

An even-tempered, six-foot, 200-pounder from Hastings, Ontario, Clapper was the National Hockey League's first 20-year man. He played all those 20 years with the Boston Bruins, the first 10 as a right wing, the last 10 as a defenseman. He wound up his playing career in 1947 with 228 goals, a very respectable total for a man who drifted between two positions.

Clapper arrived in the NHL with the oddest nickname in hockey. His parents christened him Aubrey Victor and called him Vic. "I couldn't say Vic," Clapper once explained. "I lisped and the name came out Dit. It stuck, sort of."

It was a name to stick in the minds of selectors for hockey's Hall of Fame. In 1947, Dit Clapper became the first active player to be named to the Hall. He had earned it. The late Bobby Bauer, one of Clapper's teammates on those great Boston clubs in the years preceding World War II, once hailed Dit as "the athlete's type of athlete. He was a big guy, but he used his heft to stop fights."

Clapper was a top-notch lacrosse player as a

Dit Clapper

teenager, but he gave up that sport to play junior hockey in Toronto. He signed his first pro contract with the Bruins at the age of 19 in 1926, played half a season in the minors, then moved up to Boston in 1927.

Although a defenseman up to that time, Clapper was converted into a right wing by the Bruins and

eventually wound up on Boston's Dynamite Line with Cooney Weiland and Dutch Gainor. In his second full season with Boston, the Bruins won the NHL championship and the Stanley Cup. The next year the Bruins repeated as NHL champions and Clapper enjoyed his greatest season, totaling 41 goals and 20 assists.

In 1937, Clapper returned to his old position on defense. He sparked the Bruins to four more league titles and two more Stanley Cup championships. These were Boston's glory years in the NHL. The Bruins had Frank Brimsek, the original "Mr. Zero," in goal, the famed Kraut Line of Bauer, Milt Schmidt and Woody Dumart to lead the attack, and good old Dit Clapper on defense.

Clapper was named to the first All-Star team in three successive years (1939–40–41). In 1942, he suffered a severed Achilles tendon in a game at Toronto. It was thought he would never play again, but he made a remarkable recovery and two years later was named to the All-Star team for the sixth time.

Boston fans will never forget Clapper's retirement ceremony on February 12, 1947. He stood at center ice in Boston Garden, wearing his familiar No. 5 jersey and looking as handsome as ever. Then, while a capacity crowd of 14,000 looked on approvingly, he received $7,500 in gifts. It was only part payment for all the thrills Dit Clapper had given his devoted followers for 20 glorious years.

## DOUG HARVEY

Most hockey players are content to master only a few facets of the game. Doug Harvey literally controlled every part of it during his great years as a defenseman for the Montreal Canadiens.

Pacemaking is what set him apart from his contemporaries. He could slow down or speed up the tempo of most games with his extraordinary talents.

If the Canadiens wanted to kill time, Harvey would bring the puck up ice slowly, maneuvering his way past forechecking forwards until he reached the blue line. Then he would weave back and forth along the line, sliding soft passes to teammates and never becoming rattled.

If the Canadiens were trailing and attempting to beat the clock, it was Harvey who invariably led their fast-break up ice. And once the puck was in the enemy zone, he would station himself at the left point, waiting for a return pass and protecting against a possible breakaway by a rival player.

*Doug Harvey*

Harvey performed all these functions in a calm, almost lackadaisical fashion. He never seemed to fully extend himself, yet he was the unchallenged leader of the powerful Canadiens when they swept to an unprecedented five straight Stanley Cup championships from 1956 through 1960.

A native of Montreal, Harvey turned to hockey only after rejecting tempting offers from pro football and baseball scouts. It was the right choice—for him and for the Canadiens. During 13 seasons with Montreal he was named to the first NHL All-Star team nine times and once to the second team. He earned the Norris Trophy as the league's outstanding defenseman six times.

The only fault most experts found with Harvey was a minor one: he didn't shoot enough. (The most goals he scored in a season was nine.) He claimed he would rather finesse his way to within shooting range and set up a goal for a teammate than try one of his own slap shots. "I didn't have a bonus for goals," he once said, "so why not set up the guys who needed them?"

A hero to every youngster in Montreal, Harvey encountered trouble with the Canadiens' front office when he became involved with the organization of the NHL Players' Association. In 1961 he was traded to the New York Rangers and became their player-coach, leading the league's one-time patsies into the Stanley Cup playoffs for the first time in four years. During that same 1961–62 season he won his seventh Norris Trophy and once again was named to the All-Star team.

Harvey surrendered the coaching position after one season—he disliked the responsibility—but remained with the Rangers as a player for another 18 months. "When I was a coach, I couldn't be one of the boys," he said. "This way if I want a beer with them, I get a beer."

He then drifted to the minors, playing in Baltimore, St. Paul, Quebec City, Pittsburgh and Kansas City. He returned to the NHL with the St. Louis Blues during the 1968 Stanley Cup playoffs and, ironically, wound up playing against his old Montreal club in the final round.

Although he was then 45 years old, Harvey remained with St. Louis for the 1968–69 season as a defenseman and assistant coach. The next year he became defensive coach for Los Angeles before retiring.

# CHING JOHNSON

More than a decade after his retirement as a player, Ching Johnson was serving as a linesman in a game in Washington, D.C., between the New York Rovers and the Washington Lions of the Eastern Hockey League. The game was spirited and Johnson was kept busy trying to keep up with the flow of action.

Suddenly, a Washington player slithered into the open in the New York zone. Johnson, fat and fifty, forgot himself. For that split-second, he wasn't an official any longer. He was the defenseman he once was with the New York Rangers and his goal was in danger. He cut over in front of the onrushing Washington forward and crunched him to the ice with a solid body check.

Johnson, the linesman, later apologized. "You know, I just can't explain it," he said. "Here was that guy racing for the goal and I just had to stop him. Why? Instinct, I guess. The old habit was too deep within me. I forgot where I was and what I was doing."

Something like this could happen only to Ching Johnson, a star for 11 years with the Rangers. He was one of the New York club's pioneer players, joining the team when it was organized in 1926 and staying on until 1937. His fearlessness, his one-man sorties on the opposition's net, were something to behold.

Year after year, he handled his duties on the Ranger defense even when his large body (he was a 210-pound six-footer) was racked with pain. But he ignored the skate cuts, the welts and the bruises while he went about his business of protecting the New York goal. His rugged face was creased by a permanent pixielike grin. He smiled when he knocked people down and he smiled when he, himself, was sent sprawling to the ice.

The hockey "wars" Johnson engaged in were mild compared to his service with a Canadian Army trench mortar outfit in France in World War I. He was gassed at Passchandaelle, recovered and returned home to Winnipeg, where he launched his hockey career with a semipro team.

"I was a big, awkward kid then," he once recalled. "I couldn't skate very well. I looked like an elephant on skates. But after a while I started to get the hang of it."

Johnson moved from the semipros of Winnipeg to the old Central League. He was pushing 30 when he joined Bill and Bun Cook, Frank Boucher and Taffy Abel on that first Ranger team. "I told the Rangers I was 28 when I joined them," he said, "but I was almost two years older. That's why I demanded a three-year contract. I didn't think I could last any longer."

He lasted 12 years in New York, completing his NHL career by playing one season with the Americans in 1938. He bowed out with fine credentials—a member of two Stanley Cup championship teams and a four-time member of the league All-Stars. He was admitted into the Hockey Hall of Fame in 1958.

◄ *Ching Johnson*

# LEONARD PATRICK (RED) KELLY

The key lyrics in that old song, "Has Anybody Here Seen Kelly?" have always served to remind fans of the most versatile All-Star in the history of the National Hockey League. He is Leonard Patrick Kelly. And if he wasn't the Kelly mentioned in the song, he should have been, for "his hair is red and his eyes are blue and he is Irish through and through."

NHL fans first saw Red Kelly in 1947 when he joined the Detroit Red Wings as a pink-cheeked youth of 19, fresh from the junior ranks. A native of Toronto, he was ignored by the Maple Leafs when one of their scouts predicted he wasn't good enough to last 20 games in the NHL. It was a poor prediction. Kelly lasted 20 years.

Kelly spent the first 12½ years of his NHL career with Detroit. During that time the Red Wings won eight league championships and four Stanley Cup titles. Kelly was a defenseman then, the best rushing defenseman in the league. He was the first winner of the Norris Trophy, awarded annually to the league's outstanding defenseman, in 1954. He was named to the All-Star team six times and was a three-time winner of the Lady Byng (good sportsmanship) Trophy.

All these honors came Kelly's way while he was playing at Detroit. Then, late in the 1959–60 season, he returned home. The Maple Leafs, convinced that they had made a mistake in letting him get away the first time, talked the Red Wings into a trade after Kelly had balked at being peddled to the New York Rangers.

Kelly will never forget his first game in a Toronto uniform. "I was finally where I'd always wanted to be," he recalled. "When the people stood up and clapped and cheered me I felt so tight I nearly burst."

The Maple Leafs, aware of Kelly's great playmaking ability, converted him into a center. He turned out to be just as valuable at his new position. In his first full season with Toronto, he propelled the previously disorganized Maple Leafs into the Stanley Cup finals, where they were finally stopped by the Chicago Black Hawks.

Toronto coach Punch Imlach called Kelly "my ace in the hole." The flaming redhead's greatest contribution to the Maple Leafs was the remarkable change he brought about in Frank Mahovlich, a

brooding young man with a great talent who increased his goal output from 18 to 48 the first season he played on a line with Kelly.

Kelly's style was so economical it almost looked lazy. He was a worker, though. He served two terms in the Canadian Parliament while playing for Toronto, but the extra duties as a legislator didn't hamper his play. He scored 119 goals in 7½ seasons with the Maple Leafs, giving him a career total of 281, and he sipped champagne from the Stanley Cup four more times.

Following retirement as a player in 1967, Kelly became coach of the Los Angeles Kings. The Kings were picked by everybody to finish last, but Kelly—then the only pilot in the NHL without previous coaching experience—led his team to second place in the West. He moved to Pittsburgh for 1969–70 and the Penguins finished second.

Red stayed as coach of the Penguins for the next 2½ seasons, piloting them to one more playoff berth before moving on to Toronto for a four-year stay.

## BOBBY ORR

He was always looked upon as the boy next door, the one with the winning smile and the gracious manner. Square-jawed and thick-necked, there was never an ounce of fat on his five-foot, 11-inch body. And he was looked upon in many quarters as the best defenseman in hockey history.

Bobby Orr was something special. "All Bobby did was change the face of hockey all by himself," said a former teammate, Phil Esposito.

Orr revolutionized the role of the defenseman with his slick passing and playmaking and end-to-end dashes. He also was responsible in part for elevating the salary structure of National Hockey League players.

Orr signed a record bonus contract with the Boston Bruins at the age of 18 in 1966 and four years later he became the first defenseman in NHL history to win the scoring title when he led the Bruins to the Stanley Cup championship.

Appropriately enough, it was Orr's overtime goal that won the fourth and final game of the playoffs for the Bruins and brought them their first Stanley

*Bobby Orr*

Cup in 29 years. It was his ninth goal and 20th point of the playoffs, both records. During the regular season, Bobby had made history with record-cracking totals of 33 goals, 87 assists and 120 points to win the scoring title.

The Bruins discovered Orr in 1962 playing midget hockey in his home town of Parry Sound, Ontario. He was only 14 but he had everything even then. Boston moved him into junior hockey at Oshawa and in three years playing defense there, he averaged 33 goals per season, an amazing output at the time.

It cost Boston $75,000 for a two-year agreement to get young Bobby's name on an NHL contract, the best investment the team ever made.

Orr won the Calder Trophy as Rookie of the Year in 1967. "Bobby was a star from the moment they played the National Anthem in his first NHL game," said Harry Sinden, Orr's first coach in Boston. Veteran Harry Howell won the Norris Trophy as the best defenseman that year and was delighted. "I'm glad I won it now," said Howell, then 36, "because it's going to belong to Orr from now on."

Howell's prediction was fulfilled. Orr won the Norris Trophy eight straight years and in 1970 he became the first man in history to nail down four individual trophies in a single season. He took the Norris as top defenseman, the Art Ross Trophy for scoring, the Hart Trophy as the Most Valuable Player in the regular season and the Conn Smythe Trophy as MVP in the playoffs.

Orr repeated as playoff MVP in 1972 when he led the Bruins to the Stanley Cup championship again. He also won his third consecutive Hart Trophy as regular-season MVP, becoming the first man in NHL history to win it more than two straight times.

Orr scored a career-high 46 goals and won his second scoring title with 135 points in 1974-75. He also was named to the NHL first All-Star team for the eighth consecutive year. However, constant knee problems were slowing him down. He ended his 10-year association with the Bruins in 1976, became a free agent and signed a $3 million, five-year contract with the Chicago Black Hawks.

He sat out the 1977–78 season after undergoing his sixth knee operation, attempted a comeback the following year but was forced to quit after appearing in six games. His last game was on November 1, 1978, against the Vancouver Canucks in Chicago.

"My knees can't handle playing anymore," he said. He was 30 years old.

Orr held or shared 12 individual records at the time of his retirement. He totaled 270 goals and 915 points in 657 games—remarkable figures for a defenseman. He was voted into the Hockey Hall of Fame in 1979.

Orr received his greatest accolade, though, when the Boston Globe conducted a poll to determine the greatest athlete in the city's history. It was not Ted Williams or Carl Yastrzemski, Bob Cousy or Bill Russell. The winner was Bobby Orr.

# BRAD PARK

Misfortune and heartbreak walked hand in hand with Brad Park during most of his career. Yet he overcame all to become a standout defenseman in the National Hockey League. He played on knees that had no cartilage and on ankles weakened by fractures, and became a hero to fans in two cities.

His heart was broken on a November day in 1975 when the Rangers traded him and Jean Ratelle to the Boston Bruins for Phil Esposito and Carol Vadnais. Park, who had been the Rangers' captain and the darling of the gallery gods at Madison Square Garden, quickly shook off the shock of that trade and eventually became the darling of the gallery gods at Boston Garden.

Misfortune seized Park early in life. He was only 17 when he suffered torn cartilage in his left knee while playing in a Junior A game. The following season he required surgery for ligament damage in his right knee. He fractured his right ankle in his second season with the Rangers in 1969.

Park's knee problems followed him to Boston. In his first season with the Bruins, he caught his left skate in a hole on the ice against the Islanders in Nassau Coliseum and required surgery to remove torn cartilage. Park's fourth and last cartilage (two in each knee) was removed during the 1978-79 season, but his right-knee problems persisted.

He considered retiring in 1980, changed his mind and enjoyed an injury-free season in 1980–81. "Brad had a sensational season," said Harry Sinden, the Bruins' general manager. "There wasn't a better defenseman in the NHL."

*Brad Park*

On December 11, 1980, Park became only the second defenseman in NHL history to collect 500 assists. The first was Bobby Orr, who was Park's teammate for a brief period during the 1975–76 season. When they skated onto the ice for a Boston power play, taking up positions on opposite points, rivals shuddered.

Park always was a dangerous point man. During the 1981–82 and 1982–83 seasons, he scored 13 of his 24 goals on power plays and he completed 1982–83 with 600 career assists, fifth-highest among active playmakers in the NHL.

Park grew up in the Toronto Maple Leafs' junior system and was drafted by the Rangers in 1966 when the Leafs, through an oversight, left him unprotected in the amateur draft. King Clancy, a Toronto vice president, used to moan over that mistake. "I don't know how we ever let that boy get away," he said.

Park was barely 20 years old when he showed

up at the Rangers' training camp in 1968. He was the last player cut before the season started and was sent to the American League for more seasoning. But his minor-league career lasted just 17 games. The Rangers lost Harry Howell with an injury and Park was called up as his replacement. Park never saw the minors again.

Early in his rookie season, Park cracked the NHL record book when he assisted on four goals in a game against Pittsburgh. Later in the season, he scored his first NHL goal—the final one in a 9–0 romp over the Bruins. Delighted by the goal, he leaped high in the air and landed ingloriously on his backside. When he picked himself up and brushed himself off, Park grinned and said, "I'm okay. That first goal was worth it."

Park was named to the NHL's first All-Star team five times and twice to the second team. He appeared in the Stanley Cup playoffs for 15 consecutive years from 1969 through 1983.

# LARRY ROBINSON

Larry Robinson, who developed into a king among defensemen in the National Hockey League, did not have a regal background. He was a farm kid from eastern Ontario who remembers getting up at dawn and stumbling into the hen house to pick up eggs.

He was born in 1951 in the hamlet of Winchester, about 30 miles from Ottawa, but the family home was in Marvelville, a town of about 2,000. His dairy-farming family also worked the soil around another locale ignored by many mapmakers—Metcalf, Ontario.

But everybody wanted to know about Marvelville. "Marvelville's population is about . . ." Robinson liked to say with a pause. "Well, if a dog dies, everybody knows about it."

From those beginnings, Robinson became an All-Star with the Montreal Canadiens. He is considered the prototype defenseman of modern hockey. Big

*Larry Robinson*

(6–3 and 212 pounds), strong, tough, mobile. He skates and handles the puck well enough to be a forward, a spot he occasionally plays.

Robinson enjoyed his greatest season in 1976–77 when he totaled 19 goals and 85 assists and won the Norris Trophy as the league's outstanding defenseman. The following year, he won the Smythe Trophy as the MVP of the Stanley Cup playoffs. He sipped champagne from the Stanley Cup for the fourth straight year in 1979 and was named to the All-Star team for the third time in 1980.

Success did not spoil Larry Robinson. "When I think back to when I was a kid, I never dreamed of anything like this, like the things I have now," he admitted. "When I watched the NHL players on TV, I never thought of a hockey player as a person making a lot of money. You know what I got when I turned pro? Well, it was $7,100 a year."

He went on from there to earn $200,000 a year. However, there were times when it appeared he would never make it to the NHL. Most pro prospects are placed on a Junior A team when they are 15 or 16, but not Robinson. He spent two years playing Tier Two in Brockville, Ontario, before moving up to the Kitchener Rangers of the Ontario Hockey Association.

Those were rough times for Robinson, then 19 years old. "I got $60 a week for playing hockey," he told Toronto reporter Al Strachan. "But I was married and that wasn't enough to feed a family. I had a job during the day working for a beverage company. I'd get up at seven and deliver pop all day. I'd finish about four and we'd practice at 5:30. That job paid me $80 a week.

"Then there were the games at night. It was pretty hectic. We really scraped and scraped. In the summer, I worked on road construction. I was really worried. I didn't want to live like that all my life, but what would happen if I didn't make it in hockey? What was I going to do?"

Robinson's worries eased slightly when the Canadiens made him their fourth pick (20th overall) in the 1971 amateur draft. He spent his first two seasons as a pro with Nova Scotia of the American League. Midway though his third season at Nova Scotia, he was called up to Montreal as a replacement for the injured Pierre Bouchard. He never returned to the minors.

Larry Robinson started his 10th season with the Canadiens in 1982. "This is too tough a game and too tough a league to play in if the game doesn't have a little fun in it," he said. "Well, it still is fun for me."

# EDDIE SHORE

All the hockey greats—past and present—were gathered in a midtown New York restaurant for the annual Lester Patrick awards dinner in the spring of 1970. At a table near the rear of the dining room, the Patrick winner with the scarred features of a retired boxer was discussing hockey and how it had changed in recent years.

"The accent is on speed now," he said. "I guess it's better for the fans, but I liked it better in the old days. Then it was pretty much a 50–50 proposition. You socked the other guy and the other guy socked you."

The bald-headed man was Eddie Shore, who socked a lot of guys and caught a few socks in return during a brilliant 14-year career as the meanest defenseman in the National Hockey League.

Shore came out of Edmonton, Alberta, in 1929 to join the Boston Bruins. He infused them with a spirit and color which promptly lifted them from last place to second place in the NHL's American Division. Previously ignored by Bostonians, the Bruins also developed a loyal following—and all because of Shore. He was a drawing card wherever he went because of his free-swinging style, his cold and brutal attacks on rival players, and his brilliance on defense. He was the most applauded player of his time—and received the most boos, too.

Hammy Moore, who was the Boston trainer during Shore's heyday, once described Eddie's style of attack. "He was the only player I ever saw who had the whole arena standing every time he rushed down the ice," Moore said. "When Shore carried the puck you were always sure something would happen. He would either end up bashing somebody, get into a fight or score a goal."

Shore totaled 108 NHL goals, a mighty respectable number for a defenseman, before retiring in 1940. He was named the league's Most Valuable Player four times and was voted to the All-Star team seven times.

But there are even more impressive statistics. He accumulated the astounding total of 978 stitches on his rugged body. He had his nose broken 14 times,

*Eddie Shore*

his jaw shattered five times and he lost most of his teeth.

Shore's most celebrated fight occurred on December 12, 1933, in Toronto; it was one he always regretted. Red Horner of the Maple Leafs started it by slamming Shore into the boards. Shore picked himself up and went after Horner. He flew down the ice and, mistaking Ace Bailey for Horner, flattened Bailey with a vicious check.

Bailey's head struck the ice and he was taken to a hospital with a fractured skull. His life was saved by delicate brain surgery, but he was never able to play hockey again.

The memory of that near-tragedy haunted Shore for many years. But he went on to play great defense for the Bruins and then the New York Americans before finally hanging up his skates and becoming fulltime owner of the Springfield Indians of the American Hockey League.

As a club owner, Shore remained a fighter. He fought with his players at contract time and with other owners in the committee rooms. Eddie Shore won most of those fights, too.

He was elected to the Hockey Hall of Fame in 1947.

## JACK STEWART

Jack Stewart did more to perfect the art of the teeth-rattling body check than any defenseman in the history of the National Hockey League.

There were bigger men in the league when Stewart was patrolling the backline for the Detroit Red Wings in the 1930s and '40s, but none hit with the shattering force of this 5–11, 185-pound wheat farmer from Pilot Mound, Manitoba.

The late Jack Adams, who coached Stewart during most of his 10 years with Detroit, was always impressed by his star defenseman's strength. "He was one of the strongest guys I've ever seen in a hockey uniform," Adams remarked. "He worked hard on his farm all summer and that probably accounted for it."

Frank Boucher, the former coach and general manager of the New York Rangers, was another Stewart admirer. "Jack played defense a lot like Ching Johnson, my old teammate," Boucher said.

"He went all out in every game. And he was tough. Hockey was no tea party to Jack Stewart."

Stewart also was responsible for the development of other great Detroit defensemen both before and after World War II. Bill Quackenbush and Red Kelly attained stardom while paired with Stewart. "Jack did all the heavy work," said Lynn Patrick, the former coach of the Boston Bruins who claimed he received the hardest body checks of his career from Stewart. "He was always advising the other defensemen and if they made an error, Jack was there to back them up."

Hockey fans will always remember Stewart for his body-checking, but he was a good blocking defenseman as well. He could clear the puck out of his zone quickly and rarely made a bad pass. He could also skate faster than most spectators realized, but they came to see him hit.

It was this penchant for flattening rival skaters that eventually produced a series of injuries and forced Stewart's retirement. After 10 great seasons at Detroit, during which he was named to five All-Star teams and was a member of two Stanley Cup championship teams, Stewart was traded to the Chicago Black Hawks in 1950.

Shortly after joining the Hawks, Stewart was sidelined with a slipped disc in his back. Surgery followed and it appeared then that the man known as "Black Jack" had played his last game. But Stewart wasn't ready to quit. He spent long hours exercising, even while flat on his back in the hospital, and promised, "I'll be back, maybe next year."

He did come back the following season, but couldn't shake the injury jinx. In a game against the Rangers, Stewart suffered a fractured skull in a collision with teammate Clare Martin and New York's Edgar Laprade. That did it. Midway through the 1951–52 season, Black Jack Stewart retired.

Ebbie Goodfellow, the Black Hawks' coach, was saddened by Stewart's loss. "We're going to miss Jack," he said. "He was a great one." The selection committee of the Hockey Hall of Fame agreed when it voted Stewart into the Hall in 1964.

*Jack Stewart*

# THE GOALIES
## The Last Man

### FRANKIE BRIMSEK

No player ever made a more spectacular debut in the National Hockey League than Frankie Brimsek, the frozen-faced "Mr. Zero" of the Boston Bruins.

In his first eight games as Boston's regular netminder in December 1938, Brimsek turned in six shutouts, wiped out a league record for consecutive scoreless minutes, and helped the Boston citizenry forget the sadness that enveloped them when Tiny Thompson was sold to Detroit.

The Bruins elevated Brimsek from their Providence, Rhode Island, farm club after Thompson, a great favorite with Boston fans, had been peddled

to the Red Wings for $15,000. "I'll never forget my debut in Boston," Brimsek recalled. "Thompson was a popular guy and a great goalie. I could feel the coolness of the fans as soon as I joined the club. They were waiting for me to kick one."

Brimsek, though, turned that Boston coolness into hand-clapping warmth in less than a month. After losing to the Montreal Canadiens, 2–0, in his first game as Thompson's replacement, Brimsek posted three consecutive shutouts. He added three more shutouts in Boston's next four games to surpass Thompson's scoreless record with 231 minutes and 54 seconds of flawless netminding.

The Bruins' followers now were ready to run Brimsek against old Jim Curley for mayor of Boston. Another factor that contributed to Brimsek's popularity—at least with fans in the United States—was his birthplace. He was born and raised in Eveleth, Minn., and thereby became an oddity in pro hockey—an American-born All-Star.

From Boston's Back Bay to the fish wharves of San Francisco, Brimsek was hailed as hockey's "Mr. Zero." He climaxed his first year with the Bruins by sparking them to the NHL title and the Stanley Cup championship. He won the Vezina Trophy as the league's most proficient goalie, the Calder (Rookie of the Year) Trophy and a berth on the NHL's first All-Star team.

The Bruins won two more NHL championships and another Stanley Cup behind Brimsek's nifty goaltending in the next three years. He entered the U.S. Coast Guard in 1943 and served two years aboard a patrol craft in the South Pacific. He returned to the Bruins from his World War II duty in 1945 and found it difficult to regain his old form in goal.

Brimsek reasoned that his years aboard ship had "tied up" his legs. "I was a little shaky when I got back," he admitted. "My legs and my nerves were shot."

After putting in four postwar seasons with Boston, Brimsek asked the Bruins to trade him to Chicago, where he would be closer to his Minnesota home, his family and business interests. The Bruins complied and traded him to the Black Hawks in 1949. He played one season for Chicago and then retired.

In 1966, the selection committee of the Hockey Hall of Fame remembered "Mr. Zero" and made him a member of that exclusive club.

◀ *Frankie Brimsek*

# WALTER (TURK) BRODA

Professional hockey can thank an anonymous school principal for launching the career of one of the outstanding clutch goaltenders of all time.

It all began for Walter (Turk) Broda when he was a chubby youngster in Brandon, Manitoba, where he was born on May 15, 1914. One day the principal at his public school announced he was organizing a hockey team. Young Broda, called "Turkey Egg" because of the freckles on his face, tried out for a defense position. It was a bad choice.

"I'm sorry," his principal said, "we have all the defensemen we need." Broda started to leave the ice. "Wait a minute," the principal said. "We need a goaltender, Walter. Get into the goal."

Turk Broda was a goaltender from that day. He started his pro career in the Detroit organization and landed with Toronto through sheer luck. Conn Smythe, the Toronto club owner, was seeking a replacement for Hall of Famer George Hainsworth in 1936 when he scouted a minor-league playoff game between the Detroit Olympias and the Windsor (Ontario) Bulldogs.

Smythe had received glowing reports on the Windsor goalie, Earl Robertson. But when the Olympias trounced Windsor, 8–1, the Maple Leafs' boss forgot all about Robertson. "I like the fellow tending goal for the other team," Smythe said. The other goalie was Broda.

Smythe wasted no time purchasing Broda from Detroit for $8,000. Early in the 1936–37 season, Turk replaced Hainsworth as the Maple Leafs' regular goalie. He held the job for 14 seasons, during which he helped Toronto win five Stanley Cup championships. He twice won the Vezina Trophy as the National Hockey League's top netminder and earned berths on three All-Star teams.

Broda was always at his best when the pressure was greatest, especially in playoff games. He allowed only 211 goals (a record 2.08 average) in 101 playoff games, the most ever for a goalie. In the 1949 championship playoffs he gave up only four goals as the Maple Leafs swept Detroit in four straight games. In the 1951 playoffs he was again brilliant, allowing only nine goals in eight games.

A happy-go-lucky man of Polish extraction, Broda was inclined to be overweight, a condition which frequently aroused the ire of Smythe. Early in the 1949–50 season, when the Leafs failed to win in six games, Smythe called the chubby Broda into his

*Turk Broda*

office. "I'm not running a fat man's team," the owner said. "I'm taking you out of the nets and you're not coming back until you get down to 190 pounds." At the time Broda scaled almost 200.

The goalie knew Smythe wasn't kidding. He launched a crash diet. He turned his back on des-serts. He went to a gym and was steamed, boiled and pounded. It was a Herculean effort for Broda, but he regained his job after missing only one game.

After retiring as a player in 1952, Broda turned to coaching. He was elected to the Hockey Hall of Fame in 1967.

It was said of Maurice (Rocket) Richard: "When he came flying toward you with the puck on his stick, his eyes were all lit up, flashing and gleaming like a pinball machine. It was terrifying."

Ageless Gordie Howe played 26 seasons in the NHL and six in the WHA.

*Bobby Hull was the highest-scoring left wing in hockey history.*

*Bobby Orr revolutionized the defenseman's role and became the first at his position to win the NHL scoring title.*

*Ken Dryden was an octopus in goal, enabling the Canadiens to win six Stanley Cups, four in a row.*

One of the best right wings of all time, Guy (The Flower) Lafleur was the first player to score at least 50 goals in six consecutive seasons.

A fierce competitor, center Bobby Clarke three times won the Hart Trophy as the NHL's Most Valuable Player.

Workhorse Tony Esposito leads the active goalies with 75 career shutouts.

Larry Robinson anchored the defense for the Canadiens when they won four straight Stanley Cups in the 1970s.

*A dynamic pure-shooting threat from anywhere, Mike Bossy was a prime force in the Islanders' four consecutive Stanley Cup championships.*

*Record-smashing Wayne Gretzky is the most exciting—and highest-paid—player in the game today.*

# KEN DRYDEN

During a time-out, he would stand in front of the net, leaning forward slightly, and using his large goalie stick as a support post. He grasped the top of the stick with his catching glove and folded his blocker over it. When he was tired, he would lower his head so that his chin rested on his forearms.

That was Ken Dryden's at-ease stance. Once play resumed and the action moved into the Montreal Canadiens' end of the rink, Dryden was a crouched panther, waiting to repulse the next enemy attack. And because he was a big man at 6–4 and 205 pounds, he covered a lot of net. "He's a bleeping octopus," is the way Phil Esposito once described Dryden.

Ken Dryden also was a rarity among goalies—an articulate scholar-athlete. He worked his way through Cornell University on a partial hockey scholarship, then worked his way through law school with his earnings as an All-Star goalie with the Canadiens. He took a sabbatical from the Canadiens during the 1973–74 season to fulfill his law school requirements, working with a Toronto law firm, and was paid $137 a week.

Some members of the hockey establishment were surprised when Dryden retired in 1979 at the age of 31. He was then at the peak of his career and earning $200,000 a year. Why retire? "This was a decision I had to make some time in my life," Dryden said. "I'm certain that I would have enjoyed playing a couple of more years. But this seems the most appropriate time to move on to new challenges."

It was expected Dryden would enter law practice or politics following his retirement. Instead, he took his wife Lynda and two children to England, settled down in a brownstone house in Cambridge and wrote a book on his hockey experiences. He had much to write about. Consider some of his accomplishments:

*Ken Dryden*

• He made his debut with the Canadiens at the tail end of the 1970–71 season, allowed only nine goals in six games, then sparked the Canadiens to the Stanley Cup championship and won the Smythe Trophy as the MVP of the playoffs.

• He won the Calder (Rookie of the Year) Trophy at the end of the 1971–72 season.

• In seven-plus seasons with the Canadiens, he totaled 46 shutouts and had a 2.24 goals-allowed average. His average for 112 playoff games was 2.40.

• He played in every playoff game, helping the Canadiens win six Stanley Cups, four in succession.

• He was named to the NHL All-Star team five times, led the league in shutouts four times and won or shared the Vezina Trophy five times.

Scotty Bowman, who was Dryden's coach at Montreal, always used one word to describe Dryden—consistent. "Ken would lose one game, but he rarely lost two in a row," Bowman said. "Oh, he was so consistent."

It was Dryden's intellect, though, that set him apart from his teammates and rivals. His postgame analyses were masterpieces of logic, language and, often, self-deprecating humor.

Once, while being interviewed by Frank Orr of the Toronto Star, he commented on his love affair with hockey. "It's a beautiful thing with its rhythms and patterns, its esthetics, although I never felt I contributed much in that way. I never liked to watch myself in game films. Before I saw myself on TV, I always figured I was Nureyev on skates, dipping and darting across the goal crease. Then I saw myself on TV and realized I was a dump truck. I was an elephant on wheels."

Dump truck? Elephant? Hardly.

Ken Dryden was what Phil Esposito labelled him—a bleeping octopus.

# BILL DURNAN

Bill Durnan's career as a National Hockey League goaltender was short in terms of service and sweet in terms of personal satisfaction.

He broke into the NHL in 1943 as a 29-year-old rookie with the Montreal Canadiens and, after seven brilliant seasons, was forced to quit the club in the middle of the 1950 Stanley Cup playoffs because

of frayed nerves. But in that comparatively short time he established records which still stand.

During the 1948–49 season, Durnan set the league's modern record for the longest shutout sequence when he held the opposition scoreless for 309 minutes and 21 seconds. He was the first goalie to win the Vezina Trophy four consecutive years (1944 through 1947). Turk Broda of Toronto interrupted his string in 1948, but Durnan won the trophy for the next two years, giving him a record six in seven years.

Durnan's appearances on the league's All-Star first team matched his Vezina Trophy accomplishments. He made the squad as a rookie in 1944 and repeated each year except for 1948 when Broda again prevented him from fashioning a seven-year sweep.

Looking back on his career, Durnan once attributed his great success to the fact that he was ambidextrous.

"It was a tremendous asset and I owe that gift to Steve Faulkner, one of my coaches in a church league in Toronto when I was just a youngster," he said. "Steve showed me how to switch the stick from one hand to the other. It wasn't easy at first because I was so young and the stick seemed so heavy. But Steve kept after me and gradually the stick became lighter and I could switch it automatically."

This ability to use either hand to catch flying pucks or to bat them away with his stick was perfected by Durnan during a long career in the amateur ranks. By the time he finally turned pro with the Canadiens he was an accomplished netminder who rarely permitted a rebound in front of his cage.

In his rookie year with Montreal, Durnan gave up only 109 goals in 50 games. That was the same season (1943–44) that Maurice Richard scored his record 50 goals. Sparked by Durnan's netminding and Richard's scoring, the Canadiens lost only five of 50 games in winning the NHL pennant and then skated off with the Stanley Cup.

A big, friendly man who packed 200 pounds on his 6–2 frame, Durnan soon found that the pressures that eventually engulf every major-league goalie were ruining his health. "It got so bad that I couldn't sleep on the night before a game," he said. "I couldn't keep my meals down. I felt that nothing was worth that kind of agony."

Injuries—another occupational hazard of goalies—also bothered Durnan. Late in the 1949–50

*Bill Durnan*

season, he suffered a severely-gashed head from an opponent's skate. He recovered in time for the playoffs, but midway through a semifinal series against the New York Rangers he asked to be replaced in the nets.

Bill Durnan had played his last game. In a short span of seven years in the NHL he had accomplished great feats and won many awards. His most cherished came in 1964 when he was named to the Hockey Hall of Fame.

## TONY ESPOSITO

Tony Esposito becomes rueful when he recalls what it was like growing up in Sault Ste. Marie, Ontario, with his brother Phil. "It was always 'Phil did this' and 'Phil did that' and it used to make me feel awful inferior," the younger Esposito said.

That was back in the late 1950s when the Espositos were teenagers. Everybody was predicting hockey stardom for Phil Esposito, while Tony's future was slightly blurred. He even quit hockey for one year and concentrated on high school football.

Tony Esposito shrugged off that inferior feeling once he reached the National Hockey League. For while Phil was setting scoring records with the Boston Bruins, his brother developed into an All-Star goalie with the Chicago Black Hawks. In time, they became one of hockey's most famous brother combinations.

The road Tony Esposito followed to stardom took several twists—all of them fortuitous. When he graduated from high school, he turned down a football

scholarship to a major U.S. college ("I can't even remember the name of the school now") and accepted a hockey scholarship to Michigan Tech. He helped Michigan Tech win the NCAA championship in 1965, was named to the All-America team and was drafted by the Montreal Canadiens.

Esposito turned pro in 1967 and spent a season with the Vancouver team of the Western League. The following season, he was with Houston of the Central League when the Canadiens encountered a manpower shortage among their goalies. Gump Worsley was hospitalized and Rogie Vachon suffered a broken hand. Esposito was called up from Houston. He made his first NHL start against brother Phil and the Bruins at Boston Garden on December 5, 1968.

*Tony Esposito*

It was a classic confrontation—the first time the Espositos opposed each other since their street-hockey days in Sault Ste. Marie. "I think I was more nervous than Tony that night," Phil recalled. "In fact, it was probably the most frightful game of my entire career. I had been a pro since 1962 and was in my sixth season in the NHL. I was an established player, getting ready to shoot pucks at my own brother, who had been in the league only a week."

In the Montreal dressing room, coach Claude Ruel was advising Tony Esposito to relax. "But how could I relax?" Tony said. "I was about to face the Bruins and my own brother, who was then tearing the league apart. I wondered how I would react if Phil skated in on me and fired one of his wicked shots."

It didn't take Phil long to test his brother. He scored with eight minutes gone in the opening period, added a third-period goal, and the game ended in a 2–2 tie. Poetic justice.

Two months later, Tony Esposito was back in the minors—even though he had allowed only 32 goals in 13 appearances with the Canadiens. But during the NHL meetings in Montreal, on June 11, 1969, the Black Hawks plucked Tony off Montreal's un-protected list for the $30,000 draft price. It was one of the best investments the Black Hawks ever made.

Tony enjoyed a brilliant first season with Chicago. He won the Vezina Trophy with a 2.17 goals-allowed average, established a league record with 15 shut-outs, was named to the All-Star team and won the Calder (Rookie of the Year) Trophy.

He went on to earn a share of the Vezina on two other occasions, was named to the first or second All-Star team four more times, and helped the Black Hawks win four straight division titles (a total of nine through 1983).

Tony Esposito also earned a reputation as a work-horse (he averaged 60 games a season) and as a solid playoff performer (3.07 average in 99 games through 1983).

There never was anything inferior about Phil Es-posito's kid brother.

# GLENN HALL

Glenn Hall once offered a terse explanation of what it is like to be a major-league goaltender. "Playing goal is a winter of torture for me," he said. "I often look at those guys who can whistle and laugh before a game and shake my head. You'd think they didn't have a care in the world. Me? I'm plain miserable before every game."

Hall's main problem was a nervous stomach. Early in his career he used to become physically ill just sitting in the locker room waiting for a game to start. The attacks became less frequent as he grew older, but the butterflies were always there.

Despite these pregame seizures of anxiety, Hall once played 502 consecutive games in the National Hockey League. He launched the streak in his first full season in the league in 1955–56 when he played all 70 games with the Detroit Red Wings. He didn't miss a game with Detroit the following season, then moved on to Chicago, where he put in five additional 70-game campaigns before the string was finally snapped in November 1962.

Hall was born and raised in Humboldt, Saskatch-ewan, a railway center, where he learned to tend goal on outdoor rinks. He turned pro with the old Indianapolis team in the American Hockey League in 1951, then put in three seasons with Edmonton of the Western League before moving up to the Red Wings. He was an immediate success with Detroit, winning the Calder Trophy as the NHL's top rookie in 1956.

After two seasons with the Red Wings, he was sent to the Black Hawks in the same celebrated six-player trade that put Hall of Famer Ted Lindsay in a Chicago uniform. During 10 years with the Black Hawks, Hall won the Vezina Trophy as the league's outstanding goalie three times and was named to the All-Star first team five times.

He reached his peak in the spring of 1961 when the Black Hawks won the Stanley Cup champion-ship for the first time in 23 years. In the semifinals against Montreal he was at his acrobatic best, hold-ing the Canadiens scoreless for 135 minutes and 26 seconds at one stage of the series. And that Montreal team boasted such feared sharpshooters as Jean Belleveau, Bernie Geoffrion, Dickie Moore and Henri Richard.

At the end of each season, Hall would advise the Black Hawks that he was considering retiring, but the lure of a fatter contract would always prompt him to change his mind. Then, once the season had started, he would have further doubts. "Plenty of

*Glenn Hall*

times I'm tempted to climb into my car and head for home," he confessed.

When the St. Louis Blues plucked Hall from Chicago in hockey's first expansion draft in 1967, he was ready to quit again and become a gentleman farmer in Edmonton, Alberta. He was then 36 years old. However, the promise of the largest salary ever paid a goaltender—an estimated $45,000 — encouraged him to leave his 160-acre farm for St. Louis.

Hall's great goaltending led the expansion club into the finals of the 1968 Stanley Cup playoffs against Montreal. The Blues were defeated in four straight games, all of which were decided by one goal. But Hall won the Conn Smythe Trophy as the outstanding performer in the playoffs.

Then, in 1968–69 he teamed with Jacques Plante to win his third Vezina Trophy and earned his 11th All-Star team berth in 14 NHL seasons. He hung up his skates at the end of the 1970–71 season.

# JACQUES PLANTE

From a 50-cents-per-game goaltender with a factory team in Quebec to a $35,000-a-year All-Star in the National Hockey League was the road Jacques Plante traveled during a playing career that spanned more than two decades.

It all started back in Plante's home town of Shawinigan Falls, Quebec, when he was 15 years old. "I was playing goal for a factory team," he recalled. "We didn't get paid, so one day my father suggested that I ask the coach for some money. The coach agreed to give me 50 cents a game if I didn't tell any of the other players about it.

"Even 50 cents meant a lot to me in those days. I was the oldest of 11 children. We couldn't afford a radio . . . or luxuries of any kind. The only time we had soft drinks was at Christmas."

Plante went on from there to earn $85 a week as a netminder for Quebec City in a junior amateur

league and turned pro with the Montreal Royals in the old Quebec Senior League at the age of 22 in 1951. He made his NHL debut the following season with the Montreal Canadiens in a Stanley Cup play-off game at Chicago.

That first game with the Canadiens is still stamped in Plante's memory. "I was so nervous I couldn't tie my skates," he said. But he shut out the Black Hawks, 3–0. Jacques Plante was on his way to becoming one of the highest-salaried goalies in pro hockey.

He spent 10 glorious years with the Canadiens, helping them to five straight Stanley Cup championships (1956 through 1960). He won the Vezina Trophy as the league's top netminder a record-tying six times (five in a row) and was a member of the NHL All-Star team six times. In 1962, he became only the fourth goaltender in NHL history to win the Hart (Most Valuable Player) Trophy.

Plante's flair for the dramatic and his inventiveness also marked his career at Montreal. He became a roving goalie early in his career ("One of the amateur teams I played for was so bad I had to always chase the puck behind the cage"), and he perfected this art with the Canadiens.

He also will be remembered as the man who popularized the goalie mask in the NHL. It happened in a game against the New York Rangers on November 1, 1959. Struck in the face by an Andy Bathgate shot, he went to the dressing room, had the wound stitched, and then returned to the ice wearing a cream-colored plastic face mask. Before long, most pro goalies adopted the mask as part of their equipment.

Plante was traded to New York in 1963, spent a year and a half with the Rangers and then retired to become a salesman with a Canadian brewery. In 1968, the St. Louis Blues offered him $35,000 to

*Jacques Plante*

make a comeback. The lanky French-Canadian, approaching his 40th birthday, couldn't resist the offer. He packed his pads and his mask and moved to St. Louis, where he shared the goaltending with 37-year-old Glenn Hall. Together, they won the Vezina Trophy and led the Blues to two consecutive West titles.

Then he was sold to Toronto in 1970 and spent three seasons with the Maple Leafs. In March 1973, Boston, looking for playoff help, purchased the 44-year-old goalie from the Leafs. He ended his career with Edmonton in the WHA in 1974-75.

## TERRY SAWCHUK

Terry Sawchuk used to quote that old nursery rhyme which insisted "Sticks and stones may break my bones, but names will never harm me." Only in Sawchuk's case it was sticks and pucks which broke his bones. And the names that people called him did hurt.

In more than two decades of professional hockey, Sawchuk overcame the following injuries and ailments to earn his place among hockey's top 10 goalies: a broken right arm that didn't heal properly and wound up inches shorter than his left arm, severed hand tendons, a fractured instep, infectious mononucleosis, punctured lungs, ruptured discs, bone chips in his elbows that required three operations, a ruptured appendix and innumerable cuts on his face and body, one of which almost cost him the sight in his right eye.

But the injury that hurt the most involved his pride. It happened in 1956 when he left the Boston Bruins in midseason after his bout with mononucleosis. "Those Boston reporters called me everything in the book, including a quitter," he said. "It was so bad

*Terry Sawchuk*

I threatened to sue four newspapers for libel. I didn't go through with it, though. I guess those guys have to make a living, too."

He experienced his first pains of anguish when he was 10 years old back home in Winnipeg, Manitoba. His older brother, Mike, a goalie, developed a heart murmur and died. Terry inherited Mike's goalie pads and seven years later (1947) he broke into professional hockey as a fuzzy-cheeked netminder with Omaha of the United States Hockey League. He won the league's rookie award that season, spent the next two years in the American Hockey League and then joined Detroit in 1950.

Sawchuk's unorthodox, gorilla-like crouch in the nets immediately captured the imagination of Detroit fans. It also helped him capture many awards. He won the Vezina Trophy, awarded to the NHL's most proficient goaltender, three times and shared a fourth. His goals-against average was less than two per game in each of his first five seasons with Detroit.

The Red Wings traded Sawchuk to the Bruins in 1955, reacquired him two years later and then lost him to Toronto in the draft in 1964. He was picked up by Los Angeles in the 1967 expansion draft and a year later returned to Detroit, then went to New York for the 1969–70 season.

Hailed as the only NHL goalie to record more than 100 career shutouts, Sawchuk credited most of his success to his crouching style. "When I'm crouching low, I can keep better track of the puck through the players' legs on screen shots," he explained.

Ironically, this doughty figure who had survived many injuries on the ice died as a result of an off-the-ice incident in May 1970.

## GEORGES VEZINA

Goaltending, as Georges Vezina knew it in the first quarter of the century, was a different art than it is today. He played when a netminder was not permitted to sprawl on the ice to block shots. So Georges Vezina stood straight and tall in front of his net during a brilliant 15-year career with the Montreal Canadiens from 1910 to 1925.

*Georges Vezina*

Vezina was a product of the northlands of Quebec. He was born in 1887 in the lumber city of Chicoutimi on the Saguenay River. He was 23 years old and playing goal for an amateur team in Chicoutimi when he first came to the attention of the Canadiens.

It was in February 1910, when the Canadiens made an exhibition tour of the Province of Quebec. They were then kingpins of the National Association of Hockey, a forerunner of the National Hockey League. A game was arranged between Montreal's great pros and the Chicoutimi amateurs led by Vezina. However, the gangling, six-foot netminder didn't play like an amateur. He shut out the powerful Canadiens. In the fall of that same year, Vezina was playing for Montreal.

He went on to become one of Montreal's most valuable and loved players. With Vezina guarding the nets, the Canadiens won the NHA championship twice, the NHL championship three times and the Stanley Cup twice.

The most impressive part of Vezina's game was his coolness. In time, he became known throughout the NHL as the "Chicoutimi Cucumber." Even while the action swirled around him, he moved with a tireless, quiet dignity. In one historic game between Montreal and Ottawa, with the league championship awaiting the victor, the poker-faced Vezina turned back 78 of 79 shots.

He was also known as Montreal's "Silent Habitant," a man of few words who never complained. His whole life revolved around his large family (he was the father of 22 children), yet even those in his own household did not know he was fighting for his life when he played his last game on November 28, 1925.

The Canadiens' opponent in the old Mt. Royal Arena in Montreal that night was Pittsburgh. After a scoreless first period, Vezina left the ice bleeding from the mouth. He collapsed in the dressing room, returned for the start of the second period, then collapsed again and had to leave the game. Only then did his family and friends learn he had tuberculosis. Four months later, at the age of 39, he passed away.

The memory of Georges Vezina, the quiet man, is perpetuated in the trophy awarded each year to the NHL's outstanding goaltender. It is an impressive trophy—almost as impressive as the Hall of Famer it honors.

# LORNE (GUMP) WORSLEY

A friend once asked Gump Worsley why he never wore a mask while tending goal in the slap-shot world of the National Hockey League. The Gumper smiled impishly and answered, "My face is my mask."

Worsley was an enigma. He thought nothing of standing up barefaced against the booming shots NHL players fired his way. But try and get him in an airplane and Worsley would break out in a cold sweat. The Gumper had an abiding distrust of air travel.

An unlikely looking athlete, the crew-cut, pint-sized goalie brought a perfect temperament to his job. He was a cherubic happy-go-lucky soul who never let his nerve-wracking job get the best of him . . . until his team had to fly from one city to another.

Worsley's fear of flying dated back to his amateur hockey days when he was with the New York Rovers. On a return flight from Milwaukee, one of the plane's engines caught fire and forced an emergency landing. The players survived but Worsley's psyche didn't. After that experience, the Gump suffered terribly every time he stepped into a plane. He would sit on the aisle, clench the armrests as tightly as he could and hang on for dear life. "It's the one time I don't talk," said Worsley. "I'm too scared to say anything."

Worsley was born in Montreal and grew up in a tough end of town where his buddies decided he looked like comic-strip character Andy Gump and tagged him with that nickname. Gump was 20 when he turned pro and two years later he found himself guarding goal for the otherwise defenseless New York Rangers.

Night after distressing night, Worsley would skate out to meet 40-shot and 50-shot onslaughts from the opposition. Once a newsman asked the New York goalie which team gave him the most trouble. Worsley never broke stride, answering quickly, "The Rangers."

New York's coach in those days was fiery Phil Watson. After a bad performance by his club, Watson started blasting his players publicly. He accused Worsley, a plump little soul, of having "a beer belly." Gump bristled at that crack. "He should know better than that," snapped the goalie. "He knows I only drink Scotch."

*Gump Worsley*

Worsley's career took an odd twist in 1963 when, after a decade in the shooting gallery at New York, he was traded to Montreal's defense-oriented Canadiens. After his experiences with the Rangers, this was a piece of cake for the Gumper. He subsequently shared two Vezina Trophies and helped the Canadiens to four Stanley Cups.

Worsley was pushing 35 and had been playing pro hockey for 15 years when he sipped champagne from the Stanley Cup for the first time in 1965. He was not supposed to start in the final game for the Canadiens against the Black Hawks, but coach Toe Blake changed his mind at the last minute and inserted Worsley into the lineup. Gump responded by shutting out the Hawks, 4–0.

"Nothing has ever matched that thrill," Worsley said. "The first Cup victory is always the biggest moment in a hockey player's life. Many a thought raced through my mind that night as we shook hands at center ice. I remembered the old days with the Rangers and the trips back to the minors and I was glad I didn't quit before I got a chance to play with a championship team."

Early in the 1969–70 season, Worsley suffered a nervous breakdown and was idle for several months. Then Minnesota obtained the rights to negotiate with the 40-year-old goalie and he was lured back in February 1970. Playing with the enthusiasm of a rookie, Worsley helped the North Stars into the playoffs for three straight years.

He finally donned a mask during parts of the North Stars' 1973–74 season—his last as a player. His professional career spanned 24 seasons. He had a 2.91 goals-allowed average for 860 regular-season games in the NHL (43 shutouts) and was elected to the Hall of Fame in 1980.

# THE STANLEY CUP

Ever since 1893, when Lord Stanley of Preston, the Earl of Derby and Governor-General of Canada, invested 10 pounds—about $48.67—in a squat, punch-bowl-shaped trophy to symbolize amateur hockey supremacy, men have spent fortunes and lifetimes pursuing that elusive piece of silverware.

Its history is nearly as legendary and exciting as the game of hockey itself. At various times, Lord Stanley's Cup has been tossed in a graveyard, drop-kicked into a canal, dumped out of an automobile and stolen from its showcase. Each time, however, the Cup was rescued and it continues today as the oldest trophy in competition among athletes in North America.

Ironically, Lord Stanley never saw a Cup game. Shortly after one of his aides, Lord Kilcoursie, announced the Governor-General's intention of introducing a challenge cup symbolic of the amateur hockey championship of Canada, Lord Stanley returned to his native England. That's where he was on March 22, 1894, when the Ottawa Generals and Montreal Amateur Athletic Association met for the Cup. For the record, Montreal won, 3–1, and the distinction of scoring the first Stanley Cup goal belongs to one Chauncey Kirby of Ottawa.

There is evidence that Lord Kilcoursie had more than a passing role in Lord Stanley's decision to initiate the Cup. Kilcoursie played hockey with Lord Stanley's sons and his deep interest in the sport soon spread to his boss.

Lord Stanley's guidelines for presenting the Cup were simple enough. It was to go to the leading hockey club in Canada and the first recipient in 1893 was the Montreal A.A.A. When Lord Stanley left Canada to return to England, he designated two Ottawa sportsmen—Sheriff Sweetland and P. D. Ross—as trustees for the Cup, and they sifted through the various challenges from leagues all over Canada which wanted their chance to play for the trophy.

In those early days, hockey was an amateur sport played by seven-man teams on outdoor rinks built for curling. Two portable poles, embedded in the ice with no net between them, constituted the goals, and goal judges stood behind these makeshift targets with no padding to protect them. Conditions were truly primitive and it was an appropriate setting for the most fantastic Cup challenge in history—that of Dawson City in 1905.

The Ottawa Silver Seven were the Cup holders from 1903 through 1906, successfully defending it against nine challenges from all parts of Canada. But none of the challengers could match the 1905 Yukon team's effort.

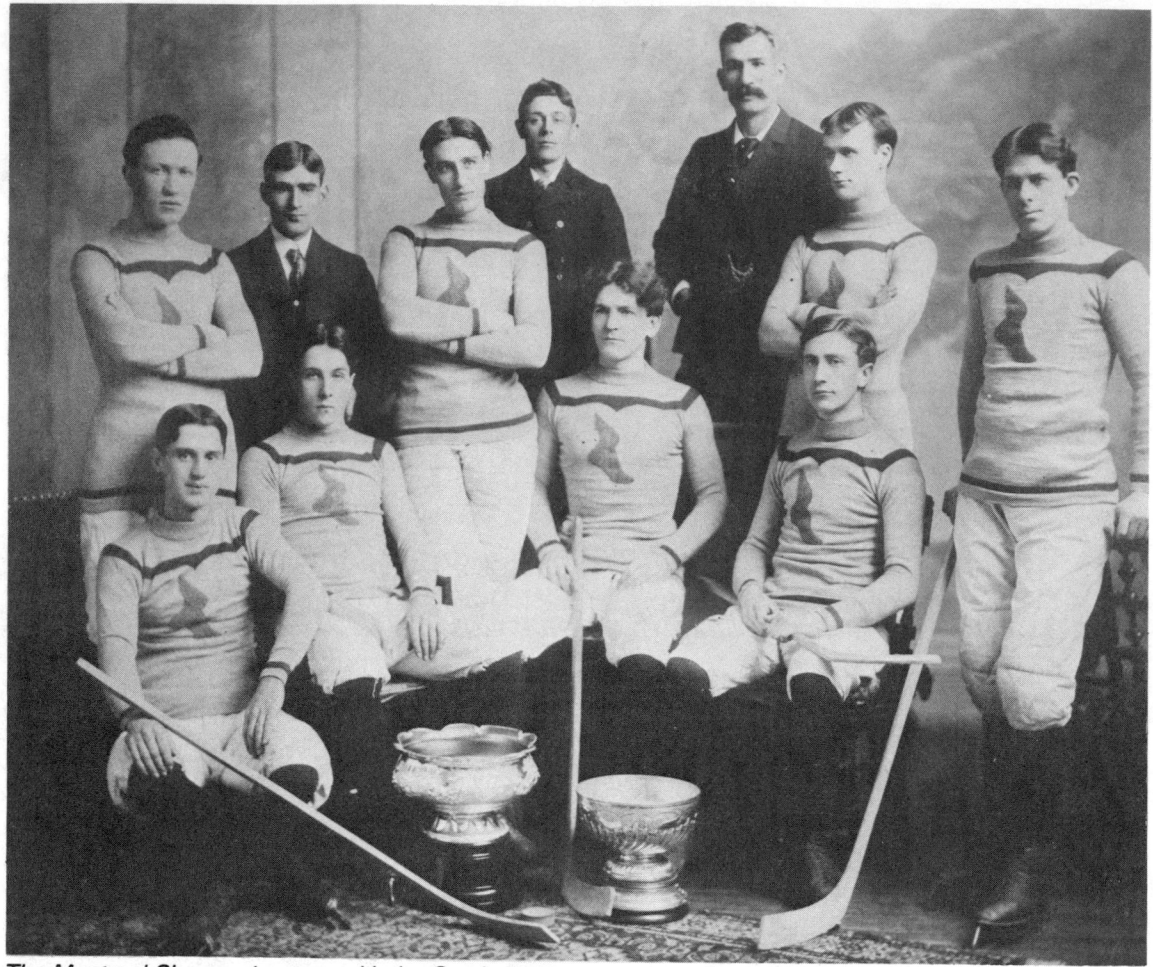

*The Montreal Shamrocks pose with the Cup in 1899.*

Colonel Joe Boyle, a wealthy Dawson City prospector, bankrolled the team's 23-day journey to Ottawa. The happy-go-lucky gold diggers traveled by dog sled, boat and train to cover the 4,400 miles. They made 46 miles by dogs the first day and 41 the second. Some of the players were forced to remove their boots because of blistered feet on the third day, with the temperature dropping to 20 below zero.

They missed a boat connection at Skagway by two hours and had to wait five days at the docks before catching another boat from Seattle to Vancouver. Then they took a train on to Ottawa. They arrived in Ottawa, January 12, 1905, a day before

the best-of-three series against the Silver Seven was to begin.

It was all for naught. The team that traveled the farthest to try for the Cup suffered the most lopsided elimination. The Klondikers lost the first game, 9–2, and the second and final game, 23–3. Frank McGee of Ottawa scored an unbelievable 14 goals in the second-game rout—eight of them in a span of eight minutes, twenty seconds. What makes it truly unbelievable is that McGee was blind in one eye.

The year before the Klondike challenge, Ottawa had beaten off the Brandon Wheat Kings and the only notable thing about that challenge was the fact that Brandon goalie Doug Morrison incurred a pen-

alty and was replaced in the nets by a teammate, Lester Patrick. A quarter of a century later, Patrick, then 44 and coach of the New York Rangers, would duplicate the feat and take over in goal during another Stanley Cup game.

The prestige of fielding a winning hockey team—possibly a Stanley Cup winner—was quite tantalizing to Canadian communities and the better players found themselves being offered fat contracts. Hockey's amateur posture was disappearing, and soon the Stanley Cup's would, too.

By 1907 the Eastern Canadian Amateur Hockey Association had deleted the "Amateur" from its name. And in 1910 when the National Hockey Association—forerunner of the National Hockey League—came into existence, the Stanley Cup became the goal of professional hockey teams.

When Lester Patrick and his brother Frank moved westward to organize the Pacific Coast Hockey League in 1913, a Stanley Cup series matching East and West was inaugurated. After the PCHL went out of business in 1927, the trophy became exclusively an NHL award.

Although there were no American teams in the NHL until 1924, it was seven years earlier that a U.S. team first captured the cherished Cup. In 1917, the Seattle Metropolitans, coached by Pete Muldoon, beat the Montreal Canadiens in the Cup series and transported the Cup below the border for the first time.

Through the years, the Cup has had varied adventures. It has been the most sought and at the same time most neglected trophy in sport.

Shortly after the turn of the century, following one of the Ottawa Silver Seven's several successful defenses, some members of the team were lugging the trophy back from a victory banquet. For kicks no doubt, it was suggested by one of the players that he could successfully boot the mug into Rideau Canal. And just to prove his point, he did.

The next day, when they realized what they had done, the Ottawa players rushed back to Rideau. Luckily the canal had been frozen over, and there, slightly the worse for wear but still intact, sat the Stanley Cup.

*Ottawa right wing Jack Darragh played on four Stanley Cup teams, beginning in 1911.*

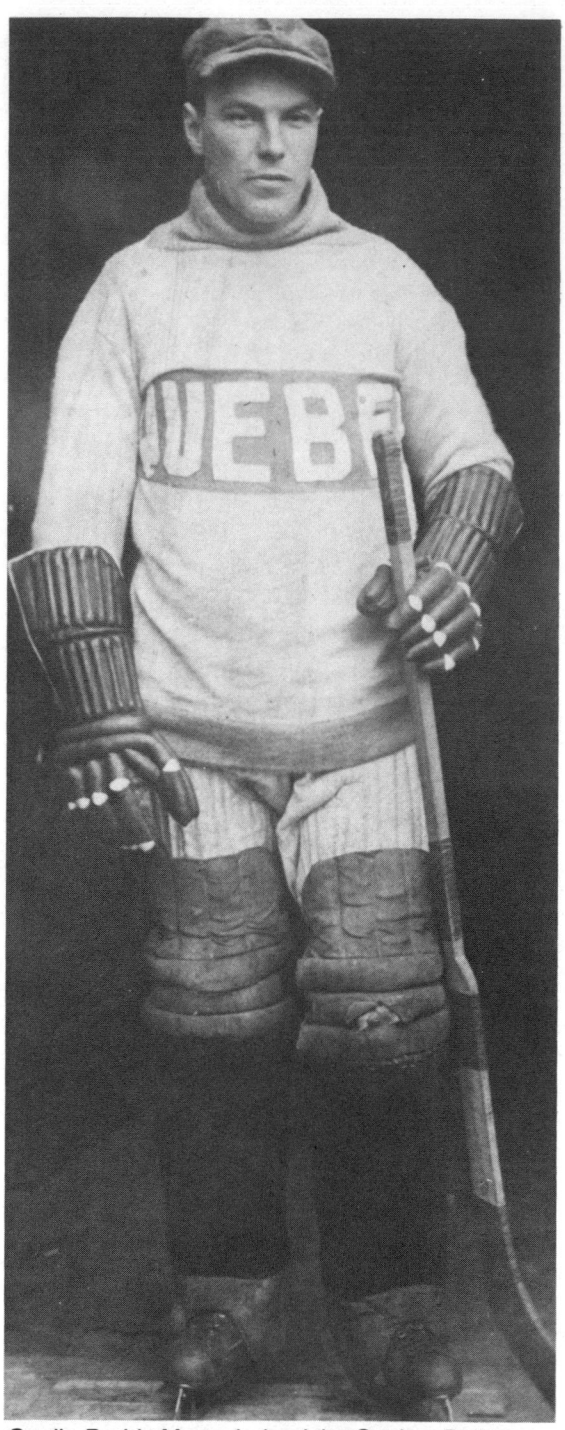

Goalie Paddy Moran helped the Quebec Bulldogs win back-to-back Cups in 1912 and 1913.

*Russell (Barney) Stanley wears a Calgary Tigers uniform here, but in 1915 he played for the Vancouver Millionaires, who won the Stanley Cup.*

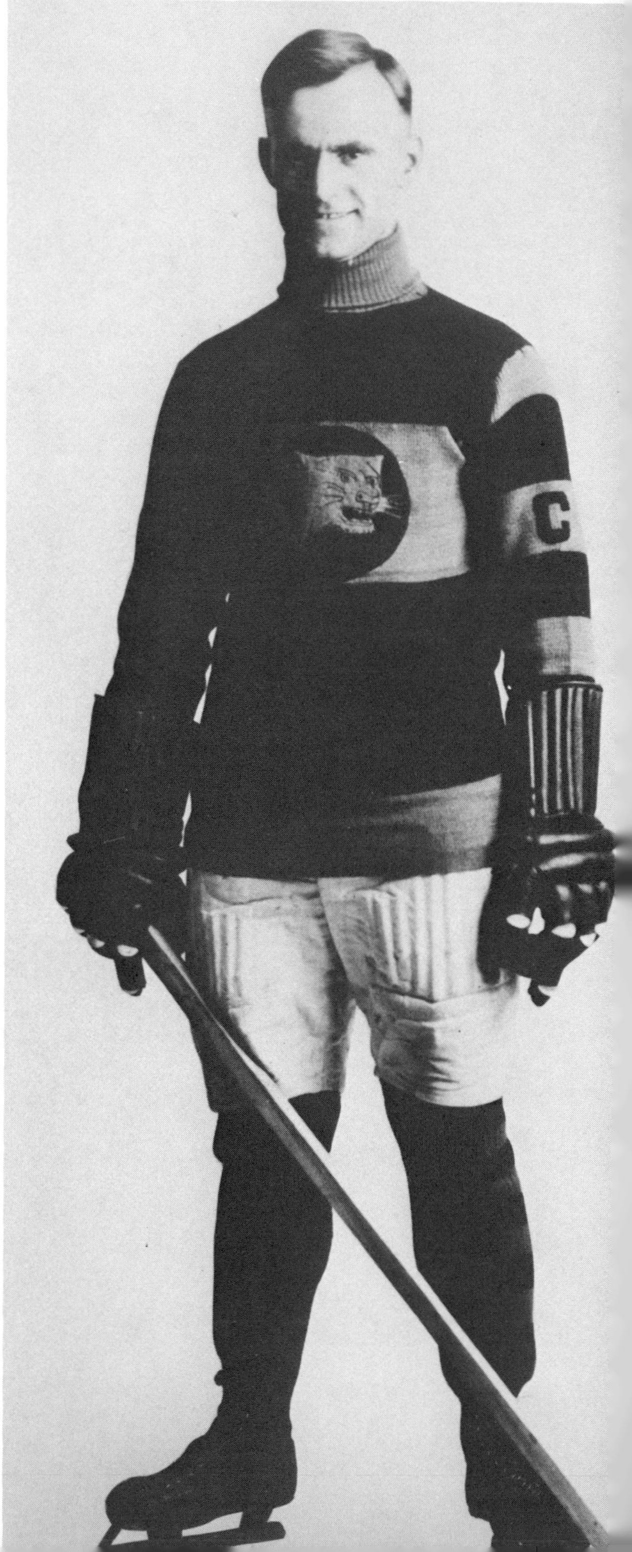

Shortly after that, the Cup did a brief turn as a flower pot. That happened when the Montreal team gathered around the silver mug for a picture in a local photographer's studio. When the posing was over, the players left the studio, and the Cup as well.

The photographer's mother found the deserted silverware and, not knowing its significance, filled it with earth and planted geraniums. Eventually, the photographer discovered it and rescued Lord Stanley's Cup.

In 1924, the Montreal Canadiens were celebrating their Cup victory at a downtown hotel when it was suggested that the celebration be moved to owner Leo Dandurand's home. A group of players, the Cup in tow, started out driving for Dandurand's home when a tire blew out. In the course of changing the tire, the Cup somehow was removed from the car and placed on the sidewalk. When the repairs were completed, the celebrants took off for Dandurand's again.

It wasn't until the Canadiens reached their destination that they missed the Cup. They scurried back to the spot and, sure enough, sitting there undisturbed, waiting for them, was the Cup.

Another time, an official of the Kenora Thistles stormed out of a meeting of hockey executives with the Cup under his arm. Angered over the refusal of his colleagues to authorize the use of two borrowed players during a Cup series, he was prepared to act drastically.

"Where are you going with the Cup?" he was asked. He replied quite simply: "I'm going to throw it in the Lake of Woods."

There are those who swear he would have, too, had compromise not been reached on the use of the two disputed players.

Once, during the Ottawa Silver Seven's Cup reign, one member of the team decided to cap off a celebration by taking the mug home with him to show to his mother. The idea wasn't terribly popular with his teammates and in the ensuing scuffle, the Cup was tossed over a cemetery fence.

In 1962, the Cup was on display in the lobby of the Chicago Stadium while the Black Hawks and Montreal Canadiens battled for it on the ice inside the arena. When Chicago took a commanding edge in the game, a Montreal fan left his seat. He went to the lobby, broke into the showcase, lifted out the

*Strong defense of Red Kelly (left) helped Detroit defeat Montreal and win the Stanley Cup in 1954.*

Cup and was on his way out the door before he was stopped. He, too, had a simple explanation.

"I was taking it back to Montreal, where it belongs," he said.

Stanley Cup play is hockey's World Series. Through the years it has been packed with individual and team heroics that live on and even tend to expand as the years go by. The stories include some of hockey's most cherished lore.

• There was the 1919 series, the only time no decision was reached. The Montreal Canadiens had traveled west to play Seattle for the Cup and the teams split the first five games (one tie). But the great flu epidemic had riddled the ranks of the Montreal team, leaving five players bedridden. The series was halted because of the wave of illness and no Cup champion was declared. Joe Hall, one of the Canadiens' stars, never recovered and died in a Seattle hospital.

• There was the 1922 series, when Lester Patrick,

*The Canadiens' goalie Gump Worsley and defenseman Jacques Laperriere (2) were standouts as Montreal swept Boston en route to 1968 Cup triumph.*

*Henri Richard grasps the Cup after Montreal downed Chicago in the 1973 finals.*

boss of the Vancouver team, allowed crippled Toronto to use defenseman Eddie Gerard as an emergency replacement. Gerard starred in two straight Toronto victories that cost Vancouver the Cup. Six years later, Patrick, the New York Ranger coach, went to Gerard, then general manager of the Montreal Maroons, and asked permission to use a borrowed goaltender when regular Lorne Chabot was injured. Gerard refused and Patrick, at age 44, went in to play goal, won the game and the inspired Rangers went on to take the Cup.

• There was the 1936 series, when the longest game in hockey history was played. Modere Bru-

neteau, a rookie who had scored only two goals during the regular season for Detroit, broke the scoreless tie against the Montreal Maroons with the only goal of the night at 16:30 of the sixth overtime period, ending 176 minutes, 30 seconds of scoreless hockey.

• There was the 1939 series, when Mel (Sudden Death) Hill of Boston personally slew the Rangers. Hill, a Ranger reject, scored the winning overtime goal in three of the Bruins' four victories over New York that year.

• There was the 1942 series, when the Detroit Red Wings beat Toronto in the first three games and with

*Captain Bobby Clarke leads triumphant parade of Flyers after Philadelphia ousted Buffalo to win the Cup in 1975.*

*It's all over: Bobby Nystrom has just beaten Philadelphia goalie Pete Peeters with the overtime goal that brought the Islanders their first Stanley Cup in 1980.*

their mouths watering for a taste of Stanley Cup champagne, went into an incredible collapse, losing four straight, the series and the Cup.

• There was the 1951 series, when Toronto beat Montreal in five games, all of them going into overtime. The winning goal in the final game was scored by defenseman Bill Barilko, who was in midair when his shot went in. It was the last goal he ever scored. A few months later, Barilko died in a plane wreck.

• There was the 1952 series, when Detroit swept through to the Stanley Cup in eight straight games and goalie Terry Sawchuk allowed a total of just five goals for an astounding 0.62 Stanley Cup average. Sawchuk's feat overshadowed Montreal's Maurice Richard, who emerged from a first-aid room with six stitches holding his forehead together to score the Canadiens' winning goal against Boston in the semifinals.

• There was the 1964 series, when Toronto defenseman Bob Baun was carried off the ice on a stretcher during the sixth game against Detroit when his right leg crumpled under him. Baun demanded that the doctors pump some pain-killer into the leg and he skated out to score the winning, sudden-death goal. Only after the Leafs took game No. 7 and the Cup, did the defenseman consent to have X-rays taken. That's when they found a broken bone in his ankle.

• And there was the 1980 series, when the Islanders' Bob Nystrom scored in overtime of the sixth game to defeat Philadelphia and bring the New York area its first Stanley Cup in four decades. The Islanders won six of seven overtime games in the march to their first Cup.

Lord Stanley's original investment of $48.67 has obviously brought rich and assorted dividends.

# STANLEY CUP WINNERS

| Season | Champions | Manager | Coach |
|---|---|---|---|
| 1892–93 | Montreal A.A.A. | ——— | |
| 1894–95 | Montreal Victorias | ——— | Mike Grant* |
| 1895–96 | Winnipeg Victorias | ——— | |
| 1896–97 | Montreal Victorias | ——— | Mike Grant* |
| 1897–98 | Montreal Victorias | ——— | F. Richardson |
| 1898–99 | Montreal Shamrocks | ——— | H. J. Trihey* |
| 1899–1900 | Montreal Shamrocks | ——— | H. J. Trihey* |
| 1900–01 | Winnipeg Victorias | ——— | |
| 1901–02 | Montreal A.A.A. | ——— | R. R. Boon* |
| 1902–03 | Ottawa Silver Seven | ——— | A. T. Smith |
| 1903–04 | Ottawa Silver Seven | ——— | A. T. Smith |
| 1904–05 | Ottawa Silver Seven | ——— | A. T. Smith |
| 1905–06 | Montreal Wanderers | ——— | ——— |
| #1906–07 | Kenora Thistles (January) | F. A. Hudson | Tommy Phillips* |
| #1906–07 | Montreal Wanderers (March) | R. R. Boon | Cecil Blachford |
| 1907–08 | Montreal Wanderers | R. R. Boon | Cecil Blachford |
| 1908–09 | Ottawa Senators | ——— | Bruce Stuart* |
| 1909–10 | Montreal Wanderers | R. R. Boon | Pud Glass* |
| 1910–11 | Ottawa Senators | ——— | Bruce Stuart* |
| 1911–12 | Quebec Bulldogs | M. J. Quinn | C. Nolan |
| **1912–13 | Quebec Bulldogs | M. J. Quinn | Joe Marlowe* |
| 1913–14 | Toronto Blue Shirts | Jack Marshall | Scotty Davidson* |
| 1914–15 | Vancouver Millionaires | Frank Patrick | Frank Patrick |
| 1915–16 | Montreal Canadiens | George Kennedy | George Kennedy |
| 1916–17 | Seattle Metropolitans | Pete Muldoon | Pete Muldoon |
| 1917–18 | Toronto Arenas | Charlie Querrie | Dick Carroll |
| ***1918–19 | No champion | | |
| 1919–20 | Ottawa Senators | Tommy Gorman | Pete Green |
| 1920–21 | Ottawa Senators | Tommy Gorman | Pete Green |
| 1921–22 | Toronto St. Pats | Charlie Querrie | Eddie Powers |
| 1922–23 | Ottawa Senators | Tommy Gorman | Pete Green |
| 1923–24 | Montreal Canadiens | Leo Dandurand | Leo Dandurand |
| 1924–25 | Victoria Cougars | Lester Patrick | Lester Patrick |
| 1925–26 | Montreal Maroons | Eddie Gerard | Eddie Gerard |
| 1926–27 | Ottawa Senators | Dave Gill | Dave Gill |
| 1927–28 | New York Rangers | Lester Patrick | Lester Patrick |
| 1928–29 | Boston Bruins | Art Ross | Cy Denneny |
| 1929–30 | Montreal Canadiens | Cecil Hart | Cecil Hart |
| 1930–31 | Montreal Canadiens | Cecil Hart | Cecil Hart |
| 1931–32 | Toronto Maple Leafs | Conn Smythe | Dick Irvin |
| 1932–33 | New York Rangers | Lester Patrick | Lester Patrick |
| 1933–34 | Chicago Black Hawks | Tommy Gorman | Tommy Gorman |
| 1934–35 | Montreal Maroons | Tommy Gorman | Tommy Gorman |
| 1935–36 | Detroit Red Wings | Jack Adams | Jack Adams |
| 1936–37 | Detroit Red Wings | Jack Adams | Jack Adams |
| 1937–38 | Chicago Black Hawks | Bill Stewart | Bill Stewart |
| 1938–39 | Boston Bruins | Art Ross | Art Ross |
| 1939–40 | New York Rangers | Lester Patrick | Frank Boucher |
| 1940–41 | Boston Bruins | Art Ross | Cooney Weiland |
| 1941–42 | Toronto Maple Leafs | Conn Smythe | Hap Day |
| 1942–43 | Detroit Red Wings | Jack Adams | Jack Adams |
| 1943–44 | Montreal Canadiens | Tommy Gorman | Dick Irvin |
| 1944–45 | Toronto Maple Leafs | Conn Smythe | Hap Day |
| 1945–46 | Montreal Canadiens | Tommy Gorman | Dick Irvin |
| 1946–47 | Toronto Maple Leafs | Conn Smythe | Hap Day |
| 1947–48 | Toronto Maple Leafs | Conn Smythe | Hap Day |
| 1948–49 | Toronto Maple Leafs | Conn Smythe | Hap Day |
| 1949–50 | Detroit Red Wings | Jack Adams | Tommy Ivan |
| 1950–51 | Toronto Maple Leafs | Conn Smythe | Joe Primeau |
| 1951–52 | Detroit Red Wings | Jack Adams | Tommy Ivan |
| 1952–53 | Montreal Canadiens | Frank Selke | Dick Irvin |
| 1953–54 | Detroit Red Wings | Jack Adams | Tommy Ivan |
| 1954–55 | Detroit Red Wings | Jack Adams | Jimmy Skinner |
| 1955–56 | Montreal Canadiens | Frank Selke | Toe Blake |
| 1956–57 | Montreal Canadiens | Frank Selke | Toe Blake |
| 1957–58 | Montreal Canadiens | Frank Selke | Toe Blake |
| 1958–59 | Montreal Canadiens | Frank Selke | Toe Blake |
| 1959–60 | Montreal Canadiens | Frank Selke | Toe Blake |
| 1960–61 | Chicago Black Hawks | Tommy Ivan | Rudy Pilous |
| 1961–62 | Toronto Maple Leafs | Punch Imlach | Punch Imlach |
| 1962–63 | Toronto Maple Leafs | Punch Imlach | Punch Imlach |
| 1963–64 | Toronto Maple Leafs | Punch Imlach | Punch Imlach |
| 1964–65 | Montreal Canadiens | Sam Pollock | Toe Blake |
| 1965–66 | Montreal Canadiens | Sam Pollock | Toe Blake |
| 1966–67 | Toronto Maple Leafs | Punch Imlach | Punch Imlach |
| 1967–68 | Montreal Canadiens | Sam Pollock | Toe Blake |
| 1968–69 | Montreal Canadiens | Sam Pollock | Claude Ruel |
| 1969–70 | Boston Bruins | Milt Schmidt | Harry Sinden |
| 1970–71 | Montreal Canadiens | Sam Pollock | Al MacNeil |
| 1971–72 | Boston Bruins | Milt Schmidt | Tom Johnson |
| 1972–73 | Montreal Canadiens | Sam Pollock | Scotty Bowman |
| 1973–74 | Philadelphia Flyers | Keith Allen | Fred Shero |
| 1974–75 | Philadelphia Flyers | Keith Allen | Fred Shero |
| 1975–76 | Montreal Canadiens | Sam Pollock | Scotty Bowman |
| 1976–77 | Montreal Canadiens | Sam Pollock | Scotty Bowman |
| 1977–78 | Montreal Canadiens | Sam Pollock | Scotty Bowman |
| 1978–79 | Montreal Canadiens | Irving Grundman | Scotty Bowman |
| 1979–80 | New York Islanders | Bill Torrey | Al Arbour |
| 1980–81 | New York Islanders | Bill Torrey | Al Arbour |
| 1981–82 | New York Islanders | Bill Torrey | Al Arbour |
| 1982–83 | New York Islanders | Bill Torrey | Al Arbour |

*Indicates captain. In the early years the teams were frequently run by the captain.

**Victoria defeated Quebec in challenge series. No official recognition.

***In the spring of 1919 the Montreal Canadiens traveled to Seattle to meet Seattle, PCHL champions. After five games had been played—teams were tied at two wins each and one tie—the series was called off by the local Department of Health because of the influenza epidemic that hospitalized a number of Montreal players, including Joe Hall, who died from it.

#Split season

# STANLEY CUP PLAYOFF RECORDS

(Editors' note: 1927 was the first year that the Stanley Cup was competed for exclusively by the National Hockey League. Until then, other leagues challenged for the Cup. The following records begin with that year.)

## TEAM

**Most Stanley Cup championships**—20, Montreal Canadiens

**Most final series appearances**—26, Montreal Canadiens.

**Most years in playoffs**—53, Montreal Canadiens.

**Most consecutive Stanley Cup championships**—5, Montreal (1956–60).

**Most consecutive final series appearances**—10, Montreal (1951–60).

**Most consecutive playoff appearances**—21, Montreal (1949–69).

**Most goals, both teams, four-game series**—36, Boston Bruins-St. Louis Blues, 1972 semifinal. Boston won best-of-seven series, 4–0, outscoring St. Louis, 28–8.

**Most goals, one team, four-game series**—28, Boston Bruins, 1972 semifinal, outscoring St. Louis, 28–8.

**Most goals, both teams, five-game series**—50, Los Angeles Kings-Edmonton Oilers, 1982 division semifinal. Los Angeles won best-of-five series, 3–2, outscoring Edmonton, 27–23.

**Most goals, one team, five-game series**—35, Edmonton Oilers, 1983 division final, outscoring Calgary, 35–13.

**Most goals, both teams, six-game series**—56, Montreal-Chicago Black Hawks, 1973 final. Montreal won best-of-seven series, 4–2, outscoring Chicago, 33–23.

**Most goals, one team, six-game series**—33, Montreal, 1973 final, outscoring Chicago, 33–23.

**Most goals, both teams, seven-game series**—56, Philadelphia Flyers-Toronto Maple Leafs, 1976 quarterfinal. Philadelphia won best-of-seven series, 4–3, outscoring Toronto, 33–23.

**Most goals, one team, seven-game series**—33, Philadelphia, 1976 quarterfinal, outscoring Toronto, 33–23.

**Fewest goals, both teams, four-game series**—9, Toronto-Boston, 1935 semifinal. Toronto won best-of-five series, 3–1, outscoring Boston, 7–2.

**Fewest goals, one team, four-game series**—2, Boston, 1935 semifinal, outscored by Toronto, 7–2; Montreal, 1952 final, outscored by Detroit, 11–2.

**Fewest goals, both teams, five-game series**—11, New York Rangers-Montreal Maroons, 1928 final. Rangers won best-of-five series, 3–2, although being outscored by Montreal, 6–5.

**Fewest goals, one team, five-game series**—5, New York Rangers, 1928 final, outscored by Montreal Maroons, 6–5.

**Fewest goals, both teams, six-game series**—22, Toronto-Boston, 1951 semifinal. Toronto defeated Boston, 4–1, with one tie in best-of-seven series, outscoring Boston, 17–5.

**Fewest goals, one team, six-game series**—5, Boston, 1951 semifinal, outscored by Toronto, 17–5.

**Fewest goals, both teams, seven-game series**—18, Toronto-Detroit Red Wings, 1945 final. Toronto defeated Detroit, 4–3, in series, each team scoring nine goals.

**Fewest goals, one team, seven-game series**—9, Toronto, 1945 final, against Detroit; Detroit, 1945 final, against Toronto.

**Most goals, both teams, one game**—18, Los Angeles-Edmonton, 1982 division semifinal. Los Angeles 10, Edmonton 8.

**Most goals, one team, one game**—11, Montreal, March 30, 1944. Canadiens 11, Toronto 0.

**Most goals, both teams, one period**—9, New York Rangers-Philadelphia, April 24, 1979, third period. Rangers scored six goals, Philadelphia three, as Rangers won, 8–3; Chicago-Montreal, May 8, 1973, second period. Chicago scored five goals, Montreal four as Chicago won, 8–7.

**Most goals, one team, one period**—7, Montreal, March 30, 1944, in third period against Toronto while winning, 11–0.

**Longest overtime**—116 minutes, 30 seconds. Detroit-Montreal Maroons at Montreal, March 24–25, 1936, Detroit 1, Maroons 0. Mud Bruneteau scored at 16:30 of sixth overtime period.

**Shortest overtime**—11 seconds. New York Islanders-New York Rangers, April 11, 1975. Islanders won, 4–3, on goal by J. P. Parise.

**Most overtime games, final series**—5, Toronto-Montreal, 1951. Toronto defeated Canadiens, 4–1, in best-of-seven series.

**Most overtime games, semifinal series**—4, Toronto-Boston, 1933. Toronto won best-of-five series, 3–2; Boston-New York Rangers, 1939, Boston won best-of-seven series, 4–3; St. Louis-Minnesota, 1968, St. Louis won best-of-seven series, 4–3.

**Most overtime games, one playoff year**—16, in 1982. Of 71 games played.

**Fewest overtime games, one playoff year**—0, in 1963. None of 16 games went to overtime, the only year since 1926 that no overtime was required.

**Most consecutive playoff game victories**—11, Montreal (three times). April 16, 1959 to March 23,

1961, April 28, 1968 to April 17, 1969, and May 6, 1976 to April 2, 1977; Boston Bruins, April 14, 1970 to April 8, 1971.

**Most consecutive victories, one playoff year**—10, Boston, 1970.

**Most shutouts, one playoff year, all teams**—8 (three times): 1937, when 17 games were played, 1975 (51 games) and 1980 (67 games).

**Fewest shutouts, one playoff year, all teams**—0, in 1959. In 18 games.

**Most shutouts, both teams, one series**—5, in 1945 and 1950. Toronto-Detroit both times, with Toronto getting three shutouts and Detroit two in each series.

**Most penalties, both teams, one series**—157, Philadelphia-Toronto, 1976 quarterfinal. Philadelphia drew 92 penalties and Toronto 65.

**Most penalty minutes, both teams, one series**—560, Vancouver-Chicago, 1982 conference final. Vancouver had 285 minutes, Chicago 275.

**Most penalties, one team, one series**—92, Philadelphia, vs. Toronto in 1976 quarterfinal.

**Most penalty minutes, one team, one series**—295, Philadelphia, 1976 quarterfinal vs. Toronto.

**Most penalties and penalty minutes, both teams, one game**—58 penalties, 267 minutes, New York Rangers-Los Angeles, April 9, 1981. Rangers had 30 penalties for 142 minutes, Kings 28 penalties for 125 minutes.

**Most penalties, one team, one game**—30. Philadelphia, at Toronto, April 15, 1976, and New York Rangers, at Los Angeles, April 9, 1981.

**Most penalty minutes, one team, one game**—142, New York Rangers, at Los Angeles, April 9, 1981.

**Most penalties, both teams, one period**—43, New York Rangers-Los Angeles, April 9, 1981, first period. Rangers had 24 penalties, Kings 19.

**Most penalty minutes, both teams, one period**—248, New York Islanders at Boston, April 17, 1980, first period. Each team had 124 minutes.

**Most penalties and most penalty minutes, one team, one period**—24 penalties, 125 minutes, New York Rangers, at Los Angeles, April 9, 1981, first period.

**Fewest penalties, both teams, one series**—19, Detroit-Toronto, 1945 final. Detroit received ten minors and Toronto nine minors.

**Fewest penalties, one team, one series**—9, Toronto, 1945 final.

**Fastest two goals, both teams**—5 seconds, Pittsburgh at Buffalo, April 14, 1979, first period. Gil Perreault scored for Buffalo at 12:59 and Jim Hamilton for Pittsburgh at 13:04.

**Fastest two goals, one team**—5 seconds, Detroit, vs. Chicago, April 11, 1965, second period. Norm Ullman scored at 17:35 and 17:40.

**Fastest three goals, both teams**—36 seconds, Los

Angeles at Edmonton, April 7, 1982, first period. Steve Bozek of Los Angeles scored at 6:00, Edmonton's Tom Roulston at 6:16 and Risto Siltanen of Edmonton at 6:36.

**Fastest three goals, one team**—23 seconds, Toronto, vs. Atlanta, April 12, 1979, first period. Darryl Sittler scored at 4:04 and 4:16 and Ron Ellis at 4:27.

**Fastest four goals, one team**—2 minutes, 35 seconds, Montreal, vs. Toronto, March 30, 1944, third period. Toe Blake scored at 7:58 and again at 8:37, Maurice Richard at 9:17 and Ray Getliffe at 10:33.

**Fastest five goals, one team**—3 minutes, 36 seconds, Montreal, vs. Toronto, March 30, 1944, third period. Toe Blake scored at 7:58 and 8:37, Maurice Richard at 9:17, Ray Getliffe at 10:33 and Buddy O'Connor at 11:34.

# INDIVIDUAL

**Most years in playoffs**—20, Gordie Howe, Detroit and Hartford.

**Most consecutive years in playoffs**—16, Jean Beliveau, Montreal (1954–69).

**Most playoff games**—180, Henri Richard, Montreal.

**Most points in playoffs**—176, Jean Beliveau, Montreal, 79 goals and 97 assists.

**Most goals in playoffs**—82, Maurice Richard, Montreal.

**Most assists in playoffs**—97, Jean Beliveau, Montreal.

**Most penalty minutes in playoffs**—412, Dave Schultz, Philadelphia, Los Angeles and Buffalo.

**Most shutouts in playoffs**—14, Jacques Plante, Montreal, New York Rangers and St. Louis.

**Most playoff games by a goaltender**—115, Glenn Hall, Detroit, Chicago and St. Louis.

**Most points, one playoff year**—38, Wayne Gretzky, Edmonton, 1983 (12 goals, 26 assists) vs. Winnipeg, Calgary, Chicago and New York Islanders.

**Most goals, one playoff year**—19, Reggie Leach, Philadelphia, 1976, vs. Toronto, Boston and Montreal.

**Most assists, one playoff year**—26, Wayne Gretzky, Edmonton Oilers, 1983, vs. Winnipeg, Calgary, Chicago and New York Islanders.

**Most points by a defenseman, one playoff year**—25, Denis Potvin, New York Islanders, 1981 (8 goals, 17 assists) vs. Toronto, Edmonton, New York Rangers and Minnesota.

**Most goals by a defenseman, one playoff year**—9, Bobby Orr, Boston, 1970, vs. New York Rangers, Chicago and St. Louis; Brad Park, Boston, 1978, vs. Chicago, Philadelphia and Montreal.

**Most assists by a defenseman, one playoff year**—19, Bobby Orr, Boston, 1972, vs. Toronto, St. Louis and New York Rangers.

**Most penalty minutes, one playoff year**—139, Dave

Schultz, Philadelphia, 1974, vs. Atlanta, New York Rangers and Boston.

**Most power-play goals, one playoff year**—9, Mike Bossy, New York Islanders, 1981, in 18 games.

**Most shorthanded goals, one playoff year**—3, Derek Sanderson, Boston, 1969; Bill Barber, Philadelphia, 1980, Lorne Henning, New York Islanders, 1980, and Wayne Gretzky, Edmonton, 1983.

**Most points in final series**—12, Gordie Howe, Detroit, 1955, in seven games vs. Montreal; Yvan Cournoyer, Montreal, 1973, in six games vs. Chicago, and Jacques Lemaire, Montreal, 1973, in six games vs. Chicago.

**Most goals in final series**—7, Jean Beliveau, Montreal, 1956, in five games vs. Detroit, and Mike Bossy, New York Islanders, 1982, in four games vs. Vancouver.

**Most assists in final series**—9, Jacques Lemaire, Montreal, 1973, in six games vs. Chicago.

**Most wins by a goaltender, one playoff year**—15, Billy Smith, New York Islanders, 1980, 1982.

**Most shutouts, one playoff year**—4, Clint Benedict, Montreal Maroons, 1928; Dave Kerr, New York Rangers, 1937; Frank McCool, Toronto, 1945; Terry Sawchuk, Detroit, 1952; Bernie Parent, Philadelphia, 1975, and Ken Dryden, Montreal, 1977.

**Most consecutive shutouts**—3, Frank McCool, Toronto, 1945. Shut out Detroit April 6, 1–0, April 8, 2–0, and April 12, 1–0.

**Longest shutout sequence**—248 minutes, 32 seconds. Norm Smith, Detroit, 1936.

**Most points, one game**—7, Wayne Gretzky, Edmonton, vs. Calgary, April 17, 1983 (four goals, three assists).

**Most goals, one game**—5, Maurice Richard, Montreal, vs. Toronto, March 23, 1944; Darryl Sittler, Toronto, vs. Philadelphia, April 22, 1976, and Reggie Leach, Philadelphia, vs. Boston, May 6, 1976.

**Most assists, one game**—6, Mikko Leinonen, New York Rangers, vs. Philadelphia, April 8, 1982.

**Most points by a defenseman, one game**—5, Eddie Bush, Detroit, at Toronto, April 9, 1942 (one goal, four assists); Bob Dailey, Philadelphia, vs. Minnesota, May 1, 1980 (one goal, four assists), and Denis Potvin, New York Islanders, vs. Edmonton, April 17, 1981 (three goals, two assists).

**Most penalties, one game**—8, Forbes Kennedy, Toronto, at Boston, April 2, 1969; Kim Clackson, Pittsburgh, at Boston, April 14, 1980.

**Most penalty minutes, one game**—42, Dave Schultz, Philadelphia, at Toronto, April 2, 1969 (two majors, one minor, three misconducts).

**Most points, one period**—4, Maurice Richard, Montreal, vs. Toronto, March 29, 1945; Dickie Moore, Montreal, vs. Boston, March 25, 1954; Barry Pederson, Boston, vs. Buffalo, April 8, 1982, and Peter McNab, Boston, at Buffalo, April 11, 1982.

**Most goals, one period**—3, held by 15 players, most recently Mike Bossy, New York Islanders, vs. Boston, May 7, 1983.

**Most assists, one period**—3, held by 27 players, most recently Wayne Gretzky, Edmonton, vs. Chicago, April 24, 1983.

**Fastest two goals**—5 seconds, Norm Ullman, Detroit, vs. Chicago, April 11, 1965.

**Fastest goal from start of game and period**—6 seconds, Don Kozak, Los Angeles, vs. Boston, April 17, 1977.

**Most game-winning goals, career**—18, Maurice Richard, Montreal.

**Most overtime goals, career**—6, Maurice Richard, Montreal.

**Most overtime goals, one season**—3, Mel Hill, Boston, 1939, Maurice Richard, Montreal, 1951.

**Most three-goals-or-more games**—7, Maurice Richard, Montreal.

**Most three-goal games, one playoff series**—2, Doug Bentley, Chicago, vs. Detroit, 1944; Norm Ullman, Detroit, vs. Chicago, 1964; Mark Messier, Edmonton, vs. Calgary, 1983, and Mike Bossy, New York Islanders, vs. Boston, 1983.

# OFFICIALS' PLAYOFF RECORDS

**Most games as referee**—105, Bill Chadwick, 1941–55.
**Most games as linesman**—220, Matt Pavelich, 1957–79.

*Lester Patrick, at age 44, donned the goalie's pads in a memorable
Stanley Cup game.*

# HOCKEY'S MEMORABLE MOMENTS

*In the more than half century of the National Hockey League, there have been many memorable moments—individual feats, team performances and rare games. The editors have chosen eleven of these unforgettable happenings on ice.*

## April 7, 1928
## MAROONS VS. RANGERS

The New York Rangers entered the finals of the 1928 Stanley Cup playoffs at a distinct disadvantage. Because of previous commitments, their own arena, Madison Square Garden, was unavailable and the entire series had to be played on the home ice of the Montreal Maroons. Montreal took advantage of the situation and won the first game of the best-of-five series, 2–0.

After a scoreless first period in the second game, the outlook appeared even more grim for the orphaned New Yorkers. A few minutes into the second session, Nels Stewart, the big Maroon center who was the greatest scorer of his time, skated in slowly on the New York goal and let loose a blistering shot that hit the goalie, Lorne Chabot, in the left eye.

Chabot fell unconscious, with blood dripping down his cheek. The crowd of 12,000 in Montreal's Forum sat silently as he was carried off on a stretcher.

There was no such thing as a substitute goalie in those days. Lester Patrick, a once-great defenseman who served as manager and coach of the Rangers, had only 10 minutes to find a replacement.

Alex Connell, a big-league goalie for Ottawa, was in the stands, but Eddie Gerard, the Maroons' manager, refused to let him play. "If I let you take Connell, it could cost me. Suckers were born yesterday and you're talking to the wrong man. I can't hear you," Gerard laughed.

So Patrick returned to his players and told them they would have to finish the game with a goalie from their own squad. It took Frank Boucher, the irrepressible center, to break the gloom. "How about you playing goal?" he asked.

Patrick, 44 years old and long since retired as a player, demurred. "I'm too old," he protested. But he and his players knew that he had had at least some goaltending experience. Back in hockey's dark ages, goaltenders when penalized had to serve time in the penalty box like any other player. And one of the other members of the team had to take over goal. On the rare occasions when this was necessary, Patrick drew the assignment. Surveying

the desperate situation this night of April 7, 1928, Patrick knew he would have to do it again.

Patrick was actually trembling as his players helped him into more elaborate goalie equipment than he had ever worn before, and, on shaky legs, he skated onto the ice to kick out a few of the easy test shots his players made sure he couldn't miss.

Then he announced he was ready and the Rangers went out to play the most inspired game of their lives. They flattened every Montreal player who dared skate near the nets guarded by their white-haired leader and, 30 seconds into the third period, took a 1–0 lead on a goal by Bill Cook. However, with six minutes to play, Montreal tied the game on a shot by Stewart and it went into overtime.

Frustrated at being stymied by an old man and with the crowd cheering the visitors, the enraged Maroons mounted attack after attack on the Ranger goal. But, after 7:05 of overtime, the clever Boucher stole the puck, broke in alone and scored the winner.

Patrick, in tears, was half-dragged and half-carried off the ice by his players to a tremendous ovation from the crowd.

He didn't attempt an encore. A rookie, Joe Miller, was in goal when the Rangers won two of the next three games to capture the Stanley Cup—the perfect ending for the series in which the gallant Lester Patrick had provided their finest hour.

# March 24–25, 1936
# RED WINGS VS. MAROONS

The clock in Montreal's Forum the night of March 24, 1936, showed 8:34 when the referee dropped the puck to start the first-round Stanley Cup playoff series between the Montreal Maroons, champion of the National Hockey League's Canadian Division, and the Detroit Red Wings, titlist in the American Division.

Playoff games, especially in the early going, usually are played close to the vest and nobody was surprised when the first period was scoreless and marked only by three minor penalties.

The second period was more of the same, the only excitement being a mild scuffle that drew two-minute penalties for Marty Barry of the Wings and Jimmy Ward of the Maroons. The third period also was scoreless and the fans were getting restless.

After a brief intermission, the teams went into a 20-minute sudden-death overtime session. No score. Then a second overtime period. No score. And a third. And a fourth. Near the end of the fifth overtime, Barry, the Detroit center set up left winger Herb Lewis with a perfect pass. Lewis appeared to have Maroon goalie Lorne Chabot beaten, but his shot hit the post and bounced out.

That flurry finished the action in the fifth overtime, which amounted to the eighth 20-minute period. After 4:46 of the sixth overtime, the Red Wings and Maroons owned the record for the longest Cup play-off game. They broke the mark of 144 minutes, 46 seconds set in 1933 when Toronto defeated Boston, 1–0.

In that game, after about 100 minutes of overtime, league president Frank Calder had refused a request that the game be resumed the following night. Calder, however, was willing to toss a coin to decide the winner, but his plan was vetoed by the Maple Leafs.

The Red Wings and Maroons knew they had to play to a decision. The break didn't come until 16:30 had elapsed in the sixth overtime, or just short of three regulation games. Detroit goalie Norm Smith repulsed a Maroon rush with his 90th save and Hec Kilrea headed up ice in a two-man dash with rookie Mud Bruneteau. Bruneteau, who had scored only two goals all season, managed to skate past the weary Maroon defense. As Lionel Conacher lost his footing on the rough ice, Mud took a pass from Kilrea, faked Chabot, who had stopped 66 shots, out of position and poked home the winner into an open net.

At 2:25 A.M. of March 25, five hours and 51 minutes after play had begun, hockey's longest game ended. The defeat seemed to take something out of the Maroons, who lost the next two games and were eliminated from the playoffs while the Red Wings went on to win the Stanley Cup.

# March 23, 1944
# CANADIENS VS.
# MAPLE LEAFS

Stanley Cup playoff games usually emphasize defense. The checking is tight and rough. In the short series with a lot at stake, errors can be fatal. The Montreal Canadiens had run away with the regular-season championship of 1943–44. They lost only

five games out of 50 on the schedule (with seven ties) and finished 25 points ahead of second-place Detroit.

The Stanley Cup series opened in Montreal with the Canadiens playing third-place Toronto. In a close-checking game, the Maple Leafs won the opener, 3–1. The two teams met again two nights later, March 23, 1944, in Montreal's Forum as the fans wondered how long the Leafs could hold off the powerful Canadiens, namely Maurice (Rocket) Richard.

Bob Davidson, a big, close-checking forward for the Leafs, always drew the assignment of guarding Richard. The Rocket, a 23-year-old French-Canadian, was only in his second season in the National Hockey League but already merited special attention. Davidson and the Leafs were successful through a scoreless first period. But in the second period the home team broke loose.

Taking passes from Toe Blake and defenseman Mike McMahon, Richard wheeled in and beat Leaf goalie Paul Bibeault for the first goal of the game at 1:48. Seventeen seconds later Richard scored again on assists from his famous linemates, Blake and Elmer Lach.

Now that Montreal had a two-goal lead, Toronto had to abandon its conservative checking game. The Leafs needed goals. They got one from Reg Hamilton after 8:50 of the second period, but Richard matched that with his third goal of the night on assists from Lach and Blake at 16:46. The fiery-tempered Richard achieved his hat trick in a single period even though he twice had been set down for two-minute penalties.

The crowd gave its idol an ovation as he left the ice after the second period, but there was more to come. The Canadiens were determined not to sit on their two-goal lead. The fabulous Flying Frenchmen came out flying for the final period. After only a minute of play, Richard again was set up by Lach and Blake on the famous Punch Line, and he scored his fourth goal. And, at 8:34 he scored a fifth. The final score of the game was Richard 5, Toronto 1.

After NHL games at the Forum, the three top stars of the contest are honored. This time the crowd of 12,500 was able to give a continuous ovation. Star No. 3, Star No. 2 and Star No. 1—all Maurice Richard! Richard's five goals—a Stanley Cup record that would not be equalled until 32 years later, by Darryl Sittler and Reggie Leach—demoralized the

Leafs, who lost the next three games as well, the final by an 11–0 score.

"I didn't know until after the game that the five goals set a record," Richard said. "I only had six or seven shots on net all game and each goal was scored in a different way. The funny thing is that when we beat the Leafs, 11–0, I only scored two goals.

"The Leafs always were a close-checking club and they used to put Bob Davidson out to check me every game. Sometimes he stayed so close to me that I got angry and that night, I guess, I took it out on him—and the puck."

# April 21, 1951
# MAPLE LEAFS VS. CANADIENS

Bill Barilko never really seemed destined for fame. Curly-haired and good-looking, he was a 190-pound defenseman for the Toronto Maple Leafs. Only 19 when the Leafs called him up from the minors at the end of the 1946–47 season, Barilko quickly established himself as a defensive defenseman, the kind who doesn't score goals, doesn't make All-Star teams and doesn't get his picture in the papers very often.

Only among rival players, whom he delighted in belting into the boards, did Barilko gain any real measure of fame and respect. He never scored more than seven goals in a season as a major leaguer and his most outstanding statistic was the 147 minutes in penalties he amassed in 1947–48, his first full year in the NHL. That penalty total led the NHL and for most of his short career he was up among the penalty leaders.

But, while he wasn't a star, Barilko was no slouch, either, and in each of his first three seasons he played an important role as the Maple Leafs won the Stanley Cup. The Leafs lost in the first round of the 1950 playoffs to Detroit, the eventual winner, and in 1951 Toronto found itself back in the finals against the Montreal Canadiens.

The Maple Leafs won the Cup, four games to one, but the series was not as one-sided as it appeared. Every game was decided in a sudden-death overtime.

Barilko was a key figure in the first game. Near

*Toronto's Bill Barilko scored the winning goal to clinch the Stanley Cup in 1951.*

the end of regulation time, Maurice Richard fired what seemed a sure goal at an open Toronto net, only to see Barilko dive full-length to block the shot and preserve the 2–2 tie. Sid Smith then scored the winner for Toronto after 5:51 of overtime. The second game went to Montreal, 3–2, after 2:55 of overtime on a goal by Maurice Richard.

The series moved to Montreal for the next two games and Toronto took both. Ted Kennedy won the first game, 2–1, after 4:47 of overtime and Harry Watson the second, 3–2, after 5:15.

The Leafs returned home to a joyous greeting at Maple Leaf Gardens as they prepared to clinch the Cup in the fifth game on April 21, 1951. For once it didn't look as if the game would go into overtime. With a minute to go, Montreal held a 2–1 lead. But Toronto coach Joe Primeau pulled his goalie and, with an extra skater on the ice, the Leafs got a goal from Tod Sloan with 32 seconds left to force the game into overtime.

After only 2:53, it was sudden death for the Canadiens. Barilko, who hadn't recorded a goal or an assist in the series, took a pass from Howie Meeker at mid-ice and in blind desperation fired a shot at the goal as he crossed the blue line. He actually flung himself in the air with the force of his effort and the puck skipped past Montreal goalie Gerry McNeil. The Stanley Cup returned to Toronto.

After the season, Barilko went home to Timmons, a mining town in northern Ontario. For the first time he was a national hero. He didn't get to enjoy it for long. That August, he and a friend, Dr. Henry Hudson, flew into northern Canada on a fishing trip in the doctor's private plane. They were never heard from again.

Some 15 years later, what was believed to be the wreckage of their plane was discovered, reviving briefly memories of the low-scoring but hard-hitting defenseman who once won a Stanley Cup for Toronto.

# March 23, 1952
# BLACK HAWKS VS.
# RANGERS

Bill Mosienko, a 30-year-old right winger for the Chicago Black Hawks, and Lorne Anderson, a 20-year-old goalie for the amateur New York Rovers, each had a hope as the 1952 hockey season went into its final days before the Stanley Cup playoffs. Mosienko, looking at the NHL record book with some friends, remarked, "Gee, it would be nice to have my name in there with some of the hockey greats." Anderson's wish was more simple, to play in the National Hockey League.

The dream came true for both, but for Anderson it was more like a nightmare.

The Rangers faced their final three games of the season already eliminated from the playoffs. Cincinnati, a minor-league team, had owned the rights to Ranger goalie Emile (Cat) Francis, so the NHL regular was shipped down to help that American Hockey League team in its playoff quest. As a result, the Rangers called up Anderson to finish the season.

The New Yorkers won Anderson's first game, 6–4, over Boston, but lost the second, 6–3, to Detroit. The final game of the 1952 season was played on March 23 with the Rangers and Black Hawks performing before a mere 3,254 fans in Madison Square Garden.

This was what is called a "brother-in-law" game. The final placings had long since been decided and nobody wanted to get hurt. With virtually no checking, referee George Gravel did not call a single penalty in the entire 60-minute game.

However, that's not to say there wasn't plenty of action. The Black Hawks' Gus Bodnar scored first with Mosienko getting an assist. Then the Rangers scored three times before the visitors tallied again—and it was still only the first period! The Rangers scored twice more for a 5–2 lead after two periods and expanded this margin to 6–2 in the opening minutes of the third as Ed Slowinski completed the three-goal hat trick.

But then, in a shocking explosion, Mosienko, the speedy 5–6 right winger, made hockey history.

In almost leisurely but precise fashion, the Hawks formed for the attack. Bodnar, the center, passed off to Mosienko and his little winger beat the defenseman to rap home a goal from in front of the net. The time was 6:09 of the third period.

After the goal, there was a face-off at center ice. Bodnar won the draw and hit the streaking Mosienko just as Bill was crossing the blue line. Mosienko took the pass, shot and scored, The time was 6:20 of the third period. Only 11 seconds had elapsed.

Again there was a face-off, again Bodnar controlled the puck, but this time he passed off to George Gee on the left wing. Gee carried over the Ranger blue line, spotted Mosienko breaking toward the net and laid a perfect pass on the right winger's stick. Mosienko fired it past Anderson and, as the red light flashed again, the clock showed 6:30 had elapsed. Mosienko had scored three goals in 21 seconds. No player—or team—had ever scored three times in such a short period of time. Mosienko's dream had come true. He landed in the record book, breaking the old mark by 43 seconds, as the Hawks scored twice more to win, 7–6.

*The pucks say it for Chicago's Bill Mosienko after his three-goal outburst against Rangers.*

Mosienko went on to play three more full seasons for the Black Hawks and retired at age 32 after the 1954–55 campaign with a career total of 258 goals.

As for the unfortunate Anderson, who had surrendered 17 goals in his brief trial, he never played in another big-league game.

## November 1, 1959
## CANADIENS VS. RANGERS

By 1959 Jacques Plante's reputation as one of the greatest hockey goaltenders of all time was firmly established. He had already won four Vezina Trophies, the award that annually goes to the top goalie in the National Hockey League. And his success as a roving goalie for the Montreal Canadiens had revolutionized the techniques of playing his position.

But, as he skated out on the ice against the Rangers in New York on November 1, 1959, he also had some other souvenirs of his dangerous profession:

the scars of 200 stitches in his face, a nose broken four times, a fractured skull and two broken cheekbones.

The fractured cheekbones had come in each of Plante's first two big-league seasons. Both times he was hurt in practice from a shot by a teammate. After the second injury he had a plastic mask designed and he wore it in workouts.

The mask was a bit awkward, but during the 1958–59 season, Plante learned that a mask had been developed that would fit snugly against his face. It was just what he wanted, for now the blind spots of the old mask were eliminated. Before the season, Plante asked coach Toe Blake if he could wear the mask during games.

It was not unprecedented, Clint Benedict of the Montreal Maroons had worn one briefly in 1929, but discarded it. Goalies were traditionally barefaced after that and Blake was a traditionalist. He turned down Plante.

However, in less than two months, tradition was

*Montreal's bloodied Jacques Plante dons the mask for the first time in a game against the Rangers on November 1, 1959.*

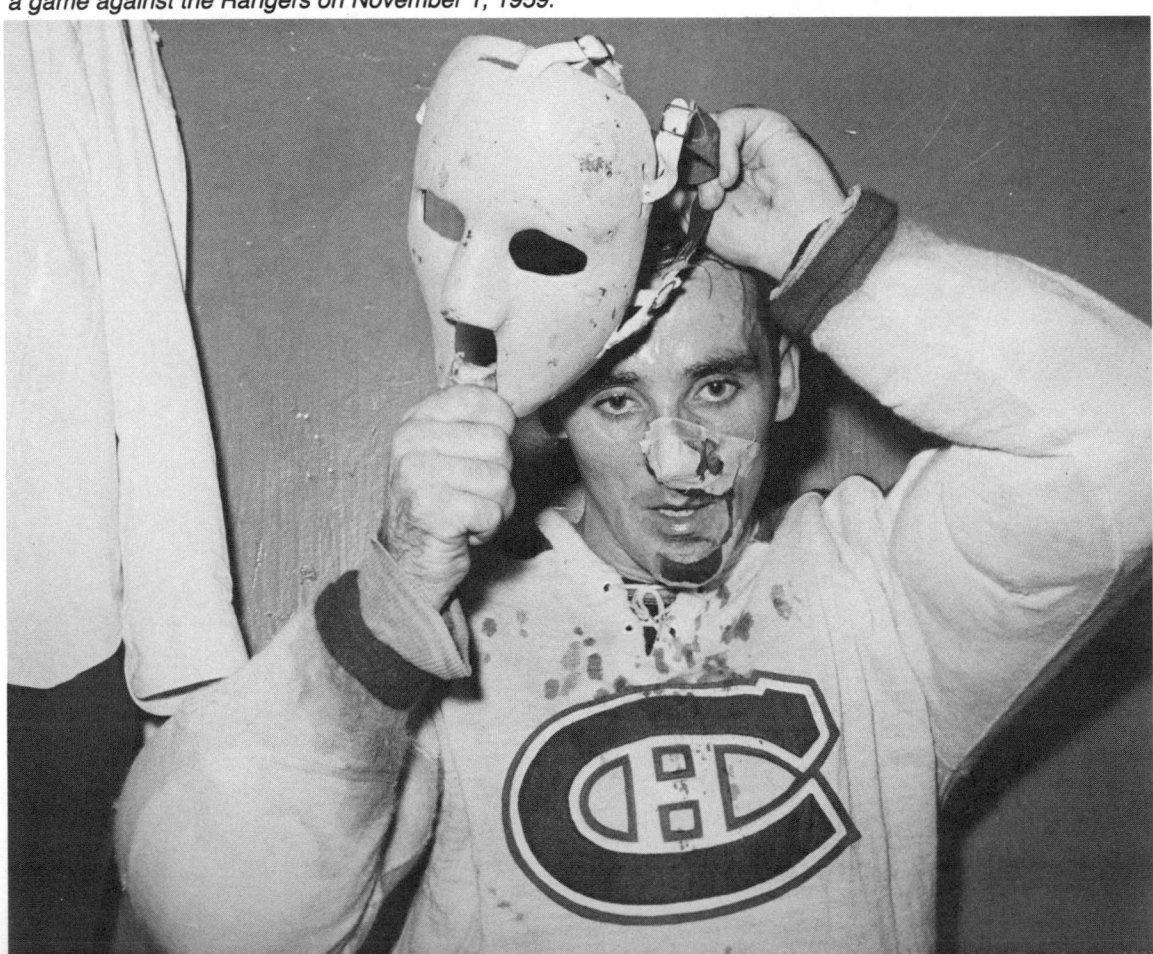

broken. It happened in this game against the Rangers, scoreless for eight minutes until Andy Bathgate, the New Yorkers' hardest shooter, let loose a 25-foot backhander from the left of the net.

Plante, screened by the mass of players, never saw the puck until it smashed into his face, ripping open his cheek and nose. He fell to the ice, blood staining his uniform and the Garden ice. But he recovered enough to walk unassisted to the dressing room with a towel held against his face. It took seven stitches to close the wound.

At that time NHL teams did not carry a spare goalie. It was up to the home club to have someone on hand who could fill in during an emergency. Some teams called on their assistant trainer; others, in Canada especially, would have available the teenage goalie from their junior team in the same city. The Rangers used a fortyish and pudgy weekend amateur named Joe Schaefer. When Schaefer had to play, it really was an emergency.

That was the situation as Plante sat up on the first-aid table. Twenty minutes had elapsed. The game had to resume. Plante looked at Blake, ' I won't go back on unless I can wear the mask," he said grimly. Blake, who had fought the new device so stubbornly, had to agree. And hockey history was made.

Fortunately, Plante played well with the mask. The Canadiens beat the Rangers, 3–1, with the losers' only goal coming in the final period. Montreal had arrived at the Garden with an unbeaten streak of seven. They made it eight against the Rangers and finally extended it to 18 before losing to Toronto, 1–0. In the last 11 games of the streak, or all the time he wore the mask, Plante gave up only 13 goals.

The Montreal management reluctantly went along with Plante. "I had to show good results to keep the mask," he later commented, and he did, winning three more Vezina Trophies. And masks for goalies eventually became commonplace.

# November 10, 1963
# RED WINGS VS. CANADIENS

It was like Babe Ruth's 714 home runs. When Maurice Richard retired from the National Hockey League in 1960 with 544 goals in regular-season play, no-body was even close. And nobody, Rocket's French-Canadian fans insisted, would ever approach his scoring record.

But when the 1963–64 campaign began, Gordie Howe, Detroit's durable right winger, was close. He started the season with 540 and it seemed only a matter of time until he passed the Rocket. Only an injury could stop the husky, slope-shouldered Howe from overtaking Richard.

On October 27, 1963, Howe and the Red Wings were playing host to the Canadiens. Gordie had 543 goals and the proud Habitants were determined that Howe would not join the Rocket in the record book at their expense. Toe Blake, coach of the Canadiens, made sure that a line centered by Richard's brother, Henri, was always on ice against Howe's line. It was more than a psychological ploy. When Henri was on the ice, he controlled the puck. And Howe couldn't score without it.

Then Blake assigned Gilles Tremblay, a Montreal winger, to forget about scoring himself and to concentrate on shadowing Howe.

The strategy almost worked. Howe was limited to only two shots all game. But the second was a goal. At 11:04 of the third period Howe got a step on Tremblay and deflected Bruce MacGregor's goal-mouth pass past Montreal netminder Gump Worsley. It wasn't a picture goal, but it counted and Jean Beliveau, captain of the Canadiens, gravely skated over to shake Howe's hand.

However, the battle was only half over for Howe, then 34 and in his 18th pro season. Now he had to break the record and, game after game, the pressure mounted. Detroit had lost to Montreal, 6–4, the night Howe tied Richard after failing to score in 10 previous games and the whole team suffered as the Red Wings tried to help their captain register No. 545.

But there was nothing coach Sid Abel could do. The Wings lost three of their next five games. Howe's nervous twitch became more pronounced, and newsmen and photographers ran out of clean shirts as they followed Howe from city to city in hope of recording the monumental goal.

Two weeks later, they found themselves back in Detroit's glistening Olympia Stadium. Another sell-out crowd of more than 15,000 jammed the building—and again Montreal provided the opposition. The only major change was that instead of Gump

Worsley, the Canadiens had little Charlie Hodge in goal.

Again the Canadiens were determined to protect the Rocket's record and again they concentrated solely on stopping Howe. The first period was scoreless but Detroit scored twice in 47 seconds to take a 2–0 lead after 5½ minutes of the second period. At the 13:57 mark, Alex Faulkner of the Wings was penalized five minutes for high-sticking and the redoubtable Howe came along with Billy McNeill to help kill the penalty.

The Canadiens mounted one of their fierce power assaults when McNeill dug out the puck from against the boards deep in the Detroit zone. Howe moved behind him and yelled, "Get going!" The little winger took off down the right wing and swung to the middle of the ice as he crossed into Montreal territory with Howe behind him to the right and defenseman Bill Gadsby on the left wing. As they approached the Canadien goal, McNeill slid the puck to Howe, who, with one motion, swiped a 15-foot shot just off the ice past Hodge and into the cage.

As the red light flashed with 15:06 gone in the period, Hodge slammed his stick against the top of the cage and skated to the sidelines. He knew there would be a prolonged ovation after what McNeill called a "perfect goal."

It was also perfect as Howe passed the Rocket by scoring when his team was short a man. And, unlike the night he tied the record, it came when his team was winning, 3–0, not losing. To Howe, that was as important as any record.

# March 12, 1966
# BLACK HAWKS VS. RANGERS

Maurice (Rocket) Richard of the Montreal Canadiens became the first player in National Hockey League history to score 50 goals during the 1944–45 season. Then, in 1960–61, Bernie (Boom-Boom) Geoffrion of the same team did it, too. And the following year Bobby Hull of the Chicago Black Hawks also turned the trick in the final game of the season.

Now it was the end of the 1965–66 campaign. Hull, the Golden Jet, had missed five games because of torn knee ligaments but he already had his 50 after 57 games of the 70-game schedule.

The sky seemed the limit for Hull, then 27 years old and a handsome, husky, muscular picture athlete. But game 58 passed, and Hull didn't score; then game 59 and game 60 and still the powerful left winger appeared anchored at 50 goals.

On the night of March 12, a Saturday, Hull skated out on the ice of massive Chicago Stadium as 21,000 fans—4,000 more than listed capacity—watched to see if he could make his 51st goal against the fifth-place New York Rangers.

The first period was scoreless and then the Rangers scored twice in the second 20 minutes to take a 2–0 lead as the rest of the Black Hawks seemed to be standing around waiting for Hull to get his record.

As the third period opened, Hull assisted on a goal by teammate Chico Maki and then, with 4:05 gone, Harry Howell of the Rangers was sent off with a two-minute penalty for slashing.

Back on the ice went Hull as perhaps hockey's most explosive point man on the power play. Howell had been in the penalty box almost a minute and a half when the Hawks gathered to start another rush against the under-manned Rangers. Bill Hay and Lou Angotti fed the puck up to Hull and then watched, almost as spectators, as the Golden Jet moved slowly to his left, stopped, crossed the New York blue line and then, as his teammates swooped toward the net, fired a deceptively swift wrist shot at Ranger goalie Cesare Maniago.

Eric Nesterenko, another Black Hawk forward, was near the goal-mouth at the time and he tipped Maniago's stick as the Ranger goalie, who had also given up Geoffrion's 50th goal, tried vainly to make a split save.

As the puck zipped past Maniago and the red light flashed to signify a score, the crowd erupted into what was to be a 7½-minute ovation. But Hull, for a moment, stood still, nerves tingling. If Nesterenko had tipped the puck on its way past Maniago, he, not Hull, would get the goal.

But the official scorer settled all doubts. Hull had his 51st goal after 5:34 of the third period. He skated over to the section where his wife was sitting and whispered to her through the protective glass, "Well, I did it." Then, as he skated around the ice to acknowledge the applause, Hull reached down and put on one of the dozens of hats that frenzied fans had skimmed onto the ice.

*Chicago's Bobby Hull netted his record-setting 51st goal against the Rangers on March 12, 1966.*

It was a glorious moment for Hull. A couple of weeks earlier, the normally placid star had exploded into a fistfight with a close-checking rival. He had considered quitting because of the pressure of the 51-goal quest. But now the tensions were past. The Hawks went on to win the game, 4–2, and Bobby went on to score three more goals during the rest of the season to put the record at 54. But, as Hull could testify, the 51st was the hardest.

## March 2, 1969
## BRUINS VS. PENGUINS

The National Hockey League was founded in 1917 and for more than 50 years no player had ever scored 100 points in a single season.

For awhile, the scoring mark belonged to Dickie Moore, a shifty left wing who totaled 96 points for Montreal in 1958–59. Then, in 1965–66 Chicago's Bobby Hull boosted the mark to 97 and a year later, another Black Hawk player, Stan Mikita, also reached 97.

Mikita's 97 points came in the last year that the NHL operated with just six teams. The next year, six new clubs were added and even though scoring predictably increased, it was spread around more. Mikita repeated as scoring champion but his total fell to 87 points, 10 below the standard he shared with Hull.

That same year, Chicago swapped a center named Phil Esposito to Boston. Espo had been Hull's center in Bobby's 97-point season and was considered a caddy for the great left wing. But he proved to be more than that. Much more.

Esposito gave Mikita a battle for the scoring crown that year, finishing with 84 points, only three less than the Chicago pivot. The next year, Espo exploded, scoring points at a record-setting pace. It became apparent in February that the NHL's 100-point plateau was going to be broken by the sad-eyed center who set up shop in front of goalies and refused to be moved out of there.

With linemates Ken Hodge on the right and Ron Murphy on the left, Esposito flourished. As the season turned into March, its final month, he had 97

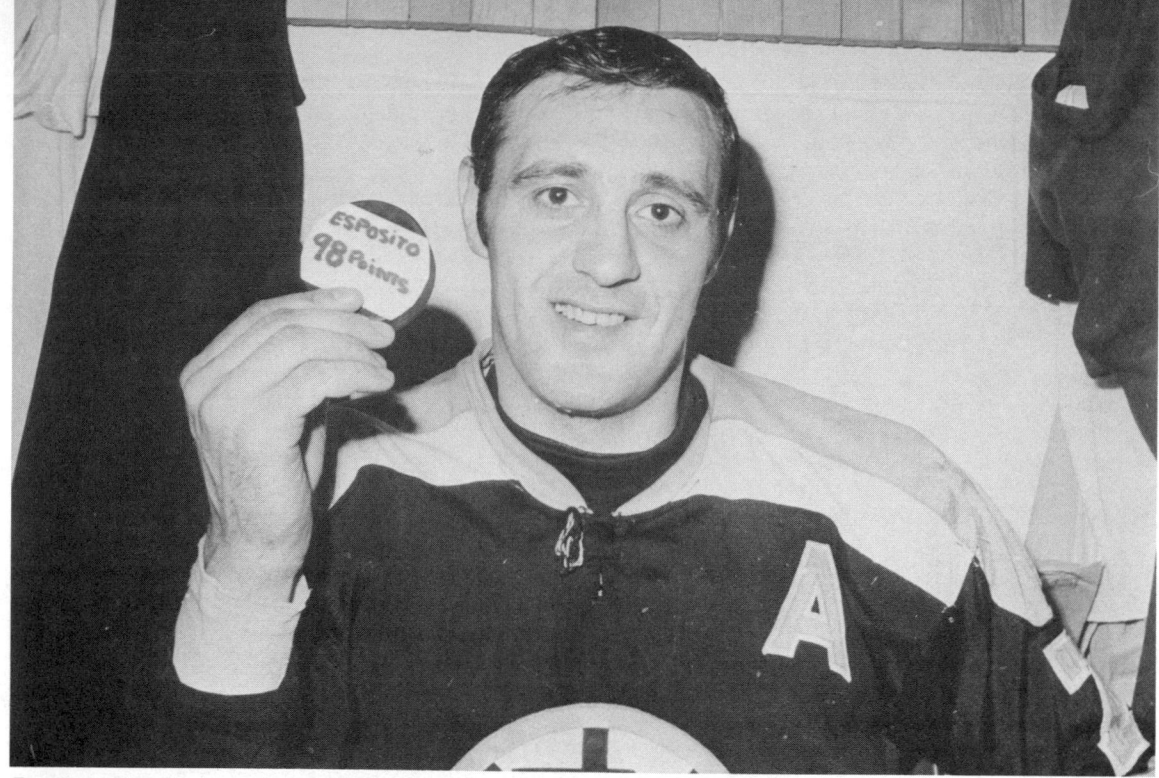

*Boston's Phil Esposito snapped Stan Mikita's one-season scoring mark on March 1, 1969. The next night, he became the first player to crack the 100-point barrier.*

points. On March 1, in a game against the New York Rangers, Esposito cracked the mark with point No. 98. He had been stopped on 10 shots in the first two periods by goalie Ed Giacomin before finally slipping a shorthanded goal past the New York netminder. Later, he assisted on a goal by Bobby Orr for his 99th point.

That set the stage for Pittsburgh's visit to Boston Garden the next night. The Penguins were determined to keep Espo off the scoreboard. He was going to get point No. 100 some place but Pittsburgh didn't want to be the victims.

"Joe Daley was the Pittsburgh goaltender and he did a good job over the first two periods," Esposito would recount. "I had two shots and no goals."

As the Bruins returned to the ice for the game's final 20 minutes, a youngster shouted to Esposito. "Please get that one-hundredth point, Phil. I want to be able to say I saw it."

Esposito obliged. With only 17 seconds gone in the period, passes from Ted Green and Hodge sprung Espo, cutting in from the left side. "Daley

moved to his right," recalled Esposito, "and hit the ice. I slipped it underneath him."

The fans showered Espo with all kinds of debris, including a football helmet, saluting the historic 100th point. Espo added 26 more points that year for the first of four scoring championships in five seasons. In each of those years, he scored more than 100 points and in 1970–71 he reached his high with 152 points, including 76 goals.

Both records would stand for a decade—until a young man named Wayne Gretzky surfaced as an unprecedented scoring machine.

## February 7, 1976
## MAPLE LEAFS VS. BRUINS

It did not figure to be an exciting game. In fact, it shaped up as a mismatch. The Boston Bruins came into Maple Leaf Gardens on the night of February 7, 1976, as the hottest team in the National Hockey

League. They were unbeaten in seven games and had lost only one of the previous 17 outings. And now they were about to face the Maple Leafs, who had won but one of their last seven games.

A day earlier, Harold Ballard, the Leafs' bombastic owner, claimed he was "determined to find a sensational center" to play between the team's top wingers, Lanny McDonald and Errol Thompson. "We'd set off a time bomb if we had a helluva center in there," Ballard said.

Coach Red Kelly had inserted Darryl Sittler into the spot earlier in the week—mainly because Sittler also had been in a slump with only five goals in his previous 17 games. It turned out to be a dynamite move.

Sittler, performing before a sellout crowd of 16,485, rewrote the NHL record book that night, scoring six goals (on 10 shots) and adding four assists in the Leafs' 11–4 thumping of the Bruins and a rookie goalie named Dave Reece.

Sittler's 10 points smashed the one-game NHL standard of eight, set by Maurice (Rocket) Richard of the Montreal Canadiens in 1944 (five goals, three assists), and equaled by teammate Bert Olmstead (four goals, four assists) 10 years later. Sittler's six goals tied the "modern era" record set by Syd Howe of Detroit in 1944 and matched by Red Berenson of St. Louis in 1968.

Joe Malone set the all-time one-game goal mark with seven while playing for the Quebec Bulldogs in 1920. However, an unofficial split exists in NHL history, created by the 1943 introduction of the cen-

*Toronto's Darryl Sittler exploded for a 10-point night against Boston.*

ter red line, which loosely divides the early and modern eras.

Sittler, 25 years old at the time of his epic performance, was numbed by it all. "It was a night when every time I had the puck, something seemed to happen," he said. "Sure, I got some bounces, and I don't think it was one of their goalie's greatest nights."

Oddly Sittler did not score a goal in the opening period, but he did pick up two assists. In the second period, he had three goals and two assists. He completed his big night with three more goals in the final period. It was the first time an NHL player scored hat tricks in consecutive periods.

Dave Reece, the sad rookie who served as Sittler's sieve, was never to be permitted to forget that memorable night. He appeared in 13 other games for the Bruins that season, then drifted back to the minor leagues.

# February 24, 1982
# SABRES VS. OILERS

Phil Esposito was shadowing Wayne Gretzky. Everywhere that Gretzky went, Esposito was sure to follow. The trail began in Edmonton, then it was on to Detroit and, finally, it was time to shuffle off to Buffalo.

The date was February 24, 1982, and the Edmonton Oilers, led by the Great Gretzky, were playing the Buffalo Sabres in Memorial Auditorium. Esposito was the most interested spectator in the capacity crowd of 16,433 that night. Eleven years earlier, he had scored a record 76 goals in 78 games while playing for the Boston Bruins.

Gretzky had equalled Espo's record against the Red Wings in Detroit at the start of the Oilers' road trip. Now it was three nights later and Esposito squirmed in his seat as the Oilers and the Sabres carried a 3–3 tie into the final 10 minutes. Gretzky had taken seven shots at Buffalo goalie Don Edwards without scoring. Would Wayne have to wait another night for the record-breaker?

Then, with less than seven minutes left to play, Gretzky stole the puck from Buffalo's Steve Patrick just inside the Sabres' blue line. As Gretzky skated into the slot, Buffalo defenseman Richie Dunn attempted to slow him down by hooking his stick across Gretzky's arms. Gretzky brushed the stick away and shot the puck low, from about 12 feet. It went between Edwards' legs, and the record was broken.

Esposito came onto the ice to congratulate the 21-year-old center. "Attaway, Wayne," Esposito said. "Now I can get back to New York."

A year earlier, Esposito had retired as a player and became a television commentator for Ranger games. He knew from the moment Gretzky arrived on the NHL scene that his record was in jeopardy. So did Patsy Esposito, Phil's father. The elder Esposito had seen Gretzky play amateur hockey in Sault Ste. Marie, Ontario, where Phil was born and raised, and predicted then that Gretzky would be a record-breaker.

Gretzky did not stop at goal No. 77 against the Sabres. He added two more in the final two minutes, giving him 79 in 64 games. He completed the season with an astounding 92 goals, 120 assists and 212 points.

Gretzky received a telegram of congratulations from Ronald Reagan, President of the United States. That impressed him. He was also impressed by the fact that Don Edwards, the man who surrendered the record goal, skated the length of the ice to shake his hand.

Gretzky predicted his record also would be broken eventually. "Maybe I'll break it," he said with a grin.

◄ His Edmonton teammates mob Wayne Gretzky after he broke Phil Esposito's goal-scoring record.

# THE ALL-STAR GAME

A new formula for the National Hockey League's All-Star game was introduced in Montreal on January 21, 1969, when players representing the circuit's East and West Divisions faced off at the start of the 22nd annual classic.

This change was prompted by the expansion of the league from six to 12 teams and from one to two divisions at the start of the 1967–68 season.

The game originated in 1947 when the defending champion Toronto Maple Leafs played a team comprised of the best players of the other five clubs as selected by hockey writers and broadcasters. The vote was based on performance during the 1946–47 campaign.

The Stanley Cup titleholder vs. All-Star team format remained until 1951 when members of the First Team All-Stars of the 1950–51 season opposed the Second Team. In 1953 the league reverted to the original system, which lasted through 1968. In that year the Montreal Canadiens, 1966–67 Cup titleholders, opposed the best players of the other 11 teams.

The 1967 game was the first played in midseason.

◀ *All-time All-Stars: Bobby Hull (left) and Gordie Howe.*

All the preceding 19 games were played before the start of the regular campaign.

In games against the Cup champions, the All-Stars won nine times, lost seven and tied three. The 1951 and 1952 games between the first and second team All-Stars ended in ties.

Starting with 1969, each member of the winning All-Star team received $500 and the losers $250. Prior to that time, there were no financial rewards for the competing players. In the 1980s, winning players received $1,000 each and the losers $750.

The first 12 players on each team are selected by a vote of members of the Professional Hockey Writers' Association—three from each city. The rest of the squad is picked by the All-Star coaches, but one requirement is that each NHL team have at least one representative.

### FIRST GAME
### October 13, 1947 at Toronto
### All-Stars 4, Toronto 3

Left wing Doug Bentley of the Chicago Black Hawks broke a 3–3 tie by drilling a shot past goalie Turk Broda in the second minute of the third period

to give the All-Stars a 4–3 victory over the Maple Leafs.

Maurice Richard of Montreal and Syl Apps of the Leafs also starred. Richard assisted on the game-winning goal and scored once himself while Apps collected a goal and an assist.

Bill Mosienko, Chicago right wing, suffered a fractured left ankle when he was checked into the boards early in the second period.

*All-Stars*: Goal-Durnan (Montreal), Brimsek (Boston). Defense-Bouchard (Montreal), Reardon (Montreal), Stewart (Detroit), Quackenbush (Detroit). Forwards-M. Bentley (Chicago), D. Bentley (Chicago), Mosienko (Chicago), Warwick (New York), M. Richard (Montreal), Laprade (New York), Lindsay (Detroit), Dumart (Boston), Schmidt (Boston), Bauer (Boston), Leswick (New York), Coach-Dick Irvin (Montreal).

*Toronto*: Goal-Broda. Defense-Goldham, Stanowski, Mortson, Thomson, Barilko. Forwards-Watson, N. Metz, Poile, Kennedy, Apps, Ezinicki, Lynn, Meeker, Stewart, Klukay, Mackell. Coach-Hap Day.

Referee-King Clancy. Linesmen-Ed Mepham, Jim Primeau.

First Period: 1. Toronto, Watson (Ezinicki) 12:29. Penalties-Mortson, Leswick, Ezinicki 2, Reardon.

Second Period: 2. Toronto, Ezinicki (Apps, Watson) 1:03. 3. All-Stars, M. Bentley (Reardon) 4:39. 4. Toronto, Apps (Watson, Mortson) 5:01. 5. All-Stars, Warwick (Laprade, Reardon) 17:35. Penalties-Lynn, Reardon 2.

Third Period: 6. All-Stars, M. Richard (unassisted) 0:28. 7. All-Stars, D. Bentley (Schmidt, M. Richard) 1:26. Penalties-Mortson 2, Bouchard, Ezinicki, Schmidt.

Attendance-14,138.


## SECOND GAME
### November 3, 1948 at Chicago
### All-Stars 3, Toronto 1

Goals by Gaye Stewart, Ted Lindsay and Woody Dumart enabled the All-Stars to defeat the Maple Leafs, 3–1. Dumart accounted for the most spectacular tally when he skated the length of the ice and put the puck past goalie Turk Broda at 3:06 of the second period.

Dumart's goal gave the All-Stars a 2–0 lead. Max Bentley scored for Toronto two minutes later. Stewart, however, added an insurance goal for the visitors with only 28 seconds remaining in the second period. Only eight penalties were handed out by referee Bill Chadwick.

*All-Stars*: Goal-Brimsek (Boston), Durnan (Montreal). Defense-Stewart (Detroit), Quackenbush (Detroit), N. Colville (New York), Reardon (Montreal), Bouchard (Montreal). Forwards-Lindsay (Detroit), D. Bentley (Chicago), M. Richard (Montreal), Laprade (New York), Howe (Detroit), Stewart (Chicago), Dumart (Boston), Schmidt (Boston), Lach (Montreal), Leswick (New York), Poile (Chicago). Coach-Tommy Ivan (Detroit).

*Toronto*: Goal-Broda. Defense-Thomson, Mortson, Boesch, Barilko, Mathers, Juzda. Forwards-H. Watson, M. Bentley, Klukay, Kennedy, Meeker, Ezinicki, Lynn, Costello, Mackell, Gardner. Coach-Hap Day.

Referee-Bill Chadwick. Linesmen-Sam Babcock, Mush March.

First Period: No scoring. Penalties-Ezinicki, Reardon.

Second Period: 1. All-Stars, Lindsay (M. Richard, Lach) 1:35. 2. All-Stars, Dumart (unassisted) 3:06. 3. Toronto, M. Bentley (Costello) 5:13. 4. All-Stars, Stewart (D. Bentley) 19:32. Penalties-Mortson, Howe (major), Stewart, Bouchard, Juzda.

Third Period: No scoring. Penalty-Bouchard.

Attendance-12,794.


## THIRD GAME
### October 10, 1949 at Toronto
### All-Stars 3, Toronto 1

Bob Goldham, a Chicago defenseman, registered the tying goal and assisted on the winner by Paul Ronty as the All-Stars defeated the Maple Leafs, 3–1, for their third straight victory over the Stanley Cup champions.

In the 15th minute of the second period, Goldham, after a rink-long dash, passed neatly to Boston's Ronty, who put the All-Stars ahead, 2–1. Goldham had tied the score with two minutes left in the opening period after Bill Barilko had found the nets for the Leafs three minutes earlier.

*All-Stars*: Goal-Durnan (Montreal), Rayner (New York). Defense-Stewart (Detroit), Goldham (Chicago), Egan (New York), Quackenbush (Boston), Harmon (Montreal), Reardon (Montreal). Forwards-O'Connor (New York), R. Conacher (Chicago), D. Bentley (Chicago), Mosienko (Chicago), M. Richard (Montreal), Laprade (New York), Abel (Detroit), Howe (Detroit), Lindsay (Detroit), Leswick (New York) Ronty (Boston). Coach-Tommy Ivan (Detroit).

*Toronto*: Goal-Broda. Defense-Thomson, Boesch, Juzda, Barilko. Forwards-Watson, M. Bentley, Klukay, Meeker, Lynn, Mackell, Kennedy, Gardner, Timgren, Dawes, Smith. Coach-Hap Day.

Referee-Bill Chadwick. Linesmen-Ed Mepham, Jim Primeau.

First Period: 1. Toronto, Barilko (Watson, Gardner) 15:22. 2. All-Stars, Goldham (Laprade) 18:03. Penalties-M. Richard, Meeker, Thomson, Howe.

Second Period: 3. All-Stars, Ronty (Goldham) 14:42. Penalties-Harmon, Thomson, Boesch, Egan, Smith.

Third Period: 4. All-Stars, D. Bentley (Quackenbush) 2:38. Penalties-None.

Attendance-13,541.

## FOURTH GAME
## October 8, 1950 at Detroit
## Detroit 7, All-Stars 1

Left wing Ted Lindsay scored three goals in leading the Red Wings to a 7–1 triumph over the All-Stars, snapping the Stars' three-year winning streak.

Lindsay beat goalie Chuck Rayner of the Rangers only 19 seconds after the opening face-off. He scored again with three minutes remaining in the first period and registered No. 3 with five minutes left in the game.

Terry Sawchuk, a rookie, also was a standout for the Red Wings. He made 25 saves in goal, several of them spectacular stops.

*All-Stars*: Goal-Rayner (New York), Broda (Toronto). Defense-Stewart (Chicago), Mortson (Toronto), Thomson (Toronto), Harmon (Montreal), Quackenbush (Boston), Bouchard (Montreal). Forwards-D. Bentley (Chicago), Mosienko (Chicago), M. Richard (Montreal), Laprade (New York), Kennedy (Toronto), Leswick (New York), Ronty (Boston), Smith (Toronto), Peirson (Boston). Coach-Lynn Patrick (Boston).

*Detroit*: Goal-Sawchuk. Defense-Goldham, Kelly, Reise, Fogolin, Pronovost. Forwards-Lindsay, Gee, Howe, Peters, Stewart, Abel, McFadden, Prystai, Pavelich, Carveth, Black, Couture. Coach-Tommy Ivan.

Referee-George Gravel. Linesmen-George Hayes, Doug Young.

First Period: 1. Detroit, Lindsay (Howe) 0:19. 2. Detroit, Lindsay (Abel) 17:12. Penalties-M. Richard, Leswick 2, Abel, Pronovost, D. Bentley.

Second Period: 3. Detroit, Howe (Lindsay, Kelly) 11:12. 4. Detroit, Peters (Prystai, Kelly) 18:36. 5. Detroit, Pavelich (Prystai, Peters) 19:44. Penalty-Couture.

Third Period: 6. Detroit, Prystai (Pavelich) 7:36. 7. Detroit, Lindsay (unassisted) 14.28. 8. All-Stars, Smith (Peirson) 18:27. Penalties-Peters, Stewart.

Attendance-9,166.

## FIFTH GAME
## October 9, 1951 at Toronto
## First Team All-Stars 2, Second Team All-Stars 2

Ken Mosdell's goal midway through the third period and two fistfights highlighted a 2–2 tie between the First and Second All-Star teams.

Mosdell, a Montreal forward, forged the deadlock for the Second Team when he converted passes from Tod Sloan and Gus Mortson at 9:25 of the final session.

The fisticuffs involved Detroit's Gordie Howe and Montreal's Maurice Richard in one match and Detroit's Ted Lindsay and Toronto's Ted Kennedy in the other.

*First Team*: Goal-Sawchuk (Detroit), Lumley (Chicago). Defense-Kelly (Detroit), Quackenbush (Boston), Eddolls (New York), Fogolin (Chicago), Dewsbury (Chicago). Forwards-Schmidt (Boston), Howe (Detroit), Lindsay (Detroit), Raleigh (New York), Peirson (Boston), Sandford (Boston), Sinclair (New York), D. Bentley (Chicago), Stewart (New York), Bodnar (Chicago). Coach-Joe Primeau, Toronto.

*Second Team*: Goal-Rayner (New York), McNeil (Montreal). Defense-Thomson (Toronto), Reise (Detroit), Bouchard (Montreal), Harvey (Montreal), Mortson (Toronto). Forwards-Kennedy (Toronto), Abel (Detroit), M. Richard (Montreal), Smith (Toronto), M. Bentley (Toronto), Sloan (Toronto), Watson (Toronto), Mosdell (Montreal), Meger (Montreal), Curry (Montreal). Coach-Dick Irvin (Montreal).

Referee-Bill Chadwick. Linesmen-Sam Babcock, Bill Morrison.

First Period: 1. First Team, Howe (Lindsay, Schmidt) 7:59. Penalties-Curry, Eddolls, Sloan.

Second Period: 2. Second Team, Sloan (Watson, M. Bentley) 2:26. 3. First Team, Peirson (Stewart, Raleigh) 16:49. Penalties-Raleigh, Lindsay.

Third Period: 4. Second Team, Mosdell (Sloan, Mortson) 9:25. Penalties-Lindsay, Howe.

Attendance-11,469.

## SIXTH GAME
## October 5, 1952 at Detroit
## First Team All-Stars 1, Second Team All-Stars 1

Maurice (Rocket) Richard, taking a pass from defenseman Hy Buller, scored at 1:36 of the third period to give the Second Team All-Stars a 1–1 tie with the First Team.

Marty Pavelich of Detroit had put the First Team in front at 9:57 of the second period after taking passes from Bill Mosienko and Dave Creighton.

After Richard, Montreal's great right wing, tied the score, each team had several scoring opportunities but no success against goalies Terry Sawchuk of Detroit and Gerry McNeil of Montreal.

*First Team*: Goal-Sawchuk (Detroit). Defense-Kelly (Detroit), Harvey (Montreal), Mortson (Chicago), Quackenbush (Boston), Reise (New York), Goldham (Detroit). Forwards-Lach (Montreal), Howe (Detroit), Lindsay (Detroit), Creighton (Boston), Sandford (Boston), Pavelich (Detroit), Mosienko (Chicago), Leswick (Detroit), Sinclair (Detroit). Coach-Tommy Ivan (Detroit).

*Second Team*: Goal-Henry (Boston), McNeil (Montreal). Defense-Thomson (Toronto), Buller (New York), Johnson (Montreal), Flaman (Toronto), Bouchard (Montreal). Forwards-Schmidt (Boston), M. Richard (Montreal), Smith (Toronto), Watson (Toronto), Geoffrion (Montreal), Sloan (Toronto), Curry (Montreal), Reay (Montreal), Mosdell (Montreal), Megar (Montreal), Coach-Dick Irvin (Montreal).

Referee-Bill Chadwick. Linesmen-Doug Young, George Hayes.

First Period: No scoring. Penalties-Buller, Thomson, M. Richard.

Second Period: 1. First Team, Pavelich (Mosienko, Creighton) 9:57. Penalties-Bouchard, Thomson 2.

Third Period: 2. Second Team, M. Richard (Buller) 1:36. Penalty-Lach.

Attendance-10,680.

## SEVENTH GAME
## October 3, 1953 at Montreal
## All-Stars 3, Montreal 1

Wally Hergesheimer of the New York Rangers scored two power-play goals in the opening period and paced the All-Stars to a 3–1 victory over the Canadiens.

Both of Hergesheimer's tallies came on plays originated by Detroit defenseman Red Kelly. Maurice Richard put Montreal on the scoreboard in the fifth minute of the third period. However, Detroit's Alex Delvecchio put the game out of reach with a goal into an empty net with 33 seconds left to play.

Kelly and Montreal's Bert Olmstead received major penalties for fighting in the third period.

*All-Stars*: Goal-Sawchuk (Detroit). Defense-Kelly (Detroit), Quackenbush (Boston), Gadsby (Chicago), Thom-

son (Toronto), Reise (New York), Mortson (Chicago). Forwards-Howe (Detroit), Lindsay (Detroit), Delvecchio (Detroit), Sandford (Boston), Smith (Toronto), Prystai (Detroit), Hergesheimer (New York), Mosienko (Chicago), Ronty (New York), Watson (Toronto). Coach-Lynn Patrick (Boston).

*Montreal*: Goal-McNeil. Defense-Harvey, St. Laurent, Bouchard, Johnson, MacPherson. Forwards-Moore, Curry, Olmstead, Beliveau, Geoffrion, Gamble, M. Richard, MacKay, Lach, McCormack, Mosdell, Meger, Davis, Mazur. Coach-Dick Irvin.

Referee-Red Storey. Linesmen-Sam Babcock, Doug Davies.

First Period: 1. All-Stars, Hergesheimer (Ronty, Kelly) 4:06. 2. All-Stars, Hergesheimer (Kelly) 5:25. Penalties-Meger, MacPherson, Lindsay.

Second Period-No scoring. Penalties-Mortson, St. Laurent, Howe, Richard.

Third Period: 3. Montreal, M. Richard (Harvey, Beliveau) 4:30. 4. All-Stars, Delvecchio (unassisted) 19:27. Penalties-Kelly, Olmstead, Smith.

Attendance-14,153.

## EIGHTH GAME
## October 2, 1954 at Detroit
## Detroit 2, All-Stars 2

Toronto's Gus Mortson and Boston's Doug Mohns fired second-period goals that enabled the All-Stars to gain a 2–2 deadlock with the Red Wings.

The game was featured by the stellar goaltending of Terry Sawchuk, who played all 60 minutes for the Wings, and Toronto's Harry Lumley and Chicago's Al Rollins, who split the netminding chores for the Stars.

Alex Delvecchio and Gordie Howe collected Detroit's goals, Delvecchio midway in the opening period and Howe 10 minutes later.

*All-Stars*: Goal-Lumley (Toronto), Rollins (Chicago). Defense-Harvey (Montreal), Mortson (Chicago), Horton (Toronto), Gadsby (Chicago), Howell (New York), Quackenbush (Boston). Forwards-Geoffrion (Montreal), Mackell (Boston), Smith (Toronto), M. Richard (Montreal), Kennedy (Toronto), Beliveau (Montreal), Sandford (Boston), Raleigh (New York), Mosdell (Montreal), Ronty (New York), Mohns (Boston). Coach-King Clancy (Toronto).

*Detroit*: Goal-Sawchuk. Defense-Goldham, Pronovost, Kelly, Woit, Allen. Forwards-Lindsay, Leswick, Howe, Prystai, Skov, Reibel, Delvecchio, Wilson, Dineen, Poile, Bonin. Coach-Jim Skinner.

Referee-Bill Chadwick. Linesmen-George Hayes, Bill Morrison.

First Period: 1. Detroit, Delvecchio (Lindsay, Reibel) 9:50. 2. Detroit, Howe (Reibel, Kelly) 19:55. Penalties-Mortson, Bonin 2, Mackell, Howell.

Second Period: 3. All-Stars, Mortson (Gadsby, Kennedy) 4:19. 4. All-Stars, Mohns (Beliveau) 13:10. Penalties-Dineen, Bonin, Howell, Sandford, Mohns.

Third Period: No scoring. Penalties-Lindsay, Mortson, Woit.

Attendance-10,689.

## NINTH GAME
## October 2, 1955 at Detroit
## Detroit 3, All-Stars 1

Earl (Dutch) Reibel scored twice as the Red Wings extended their unbeaten streak on home ice to 26 games by downing the All-Stars, 3-1.

The Wings, who finished the 1954-55 season with 19 victories and six ties at the Olympia, took the lead 57 seconds into the second period when Gordie Howe beat Toronto's Harry Lumley. Reibel made it 2-0 five minutes later. Doug Harvey of Montreal scored the Stars' only goal at 16:38 of the third period.

With a minute left in the game, All-Star coach Dick Irvin replaced goalie Terry Sawchuk with an extra forward and Reibel slid a long shot into the empty cage.

*All-Stars*: Goal-Lumley (Toronto), Sawchuk (Boston). Defense-Harvey (Montreal), Flaman (Boston), Morrison (Toronto), Stanley (Chicago), Martin (Chicago). Forwards-Beliveau (Montreal), M. Richard (Montreal), Smith (Toronto), Mosdell (Montreal), Geoffrion (Montreal), Lewicki (New York), Sullivan (Chicago), Litzenberger (Chicago), Stewart (Toronto), Labine (Boston), Watson (Chicago). Coach-Dick Irvin (Chicago).

*Detroit*: Goal-Hall. Defense-Goldham, Pronovost, Kelly, Godfrey, Hillman, Hollingworth. Forwards-Lindsay, Reibel, Howe, Delvecchio, Pavelich, Sandford, Chevrefils, Dineen, Toppazzini, Bucyk, Corcoran. Coach-Jim Skinner.

First Period: No scoring. Penalties-Flaman, Corcoran, Geoffrion, Stewart, Bucyk, Stanley, Morrison.

Second Period: 1. Detroit, Howe (Reibel, Delvecchio) 0:57. 2. Detroit, Reibel (Howe, Lindsay) 5:43. Penalties-Corcoran, Hollingworth.

Third Period. 3. All-Stars, Harvey (Beliveau, Smith) 16:38. 4. Detroit, Reibel (Goldham, Lindsay) 19:33. Penalties-Hollingworth, Harvey.

Attendance-10,111.

## TENTH GAME
## October 9, 1956 at Montreal
## Montreal 1, All-Stars 1

The Canadiens and All-Stars played to a 1-1 tie in a game that marked the introduction of the new power-play regulation.

Maurice Richard clicked on a power play for Montreal only 33 seconds after the Rangers' Red Sullivan had been penalized for holding in the 15th minute of the second period.

Sullivan came out of the penalty box immediately after Richard's tally. Before the rule change, a player serving a minor penalty had to spend the full two minutes in the penalty box even if his team was scored against while shorthanded.

Detroit's Ted Lindsay evened the score four minutes after Richard's tally.

*All-Stars*: Goal-Hall (Detroit), Sawchuk (Boston). Defense-Gadsby (New York), Kelly (Detroit), Flaman (Boston), Mortson (Chicago), Morrison (Toronto), Bolton (Toronto). Forwards-Lindsay (Detroit), Sloan (Toronto), Howe (Detroit), Delvecchio (Detroit), Labine (Boston), Duff (Toronto), Armstrong (Toronto), Mickoski (Chicago), Wilson (Chicago), Hergesheimer (Chicago), Creighton (New York), Sullivan (New York). Coach-Jim Skinner (Detroit).

*Montreal*: Goal-Plante. Defense-Harvey, St. Laurent, Johnson, Turner, Talbot. Forwards-Beliveau, Geoffrion, Olmstead, Curry, Leclair, M. Richard, Moore, H. Richard, Marshall, Provost. Coach-Toe Blake.

Referee-Red Storey. Linesmen-Doug Davies, Bill Roberts.

First Period: No scoring. Penalties-Flaman, Beliveau 2.

Second Period: 1. Montreal, M. Richard (Olmstead, Harvey) 14:58. 2. All-Stars, Lindsay (Mortson) 18:48. Penalties-Mortson, Sullivan.

Third Period: No scoring. Penalties-Labine, Mortson.

Attendance-13,095.

## ELEVENTH GAME
## October 5, 1957 at Montreal
## All-Stars 5, Montreal 3

Gordie Howe of the Detroit Red Wings and Dean Prentice of the New York Rangers each scored in the third period and gave the All-Stars a 5-3 triumph over the Canadiens.

Howe broke a 3-3 tie at 8:11 and Prentice registered an insurance marker with 3:10 left in the game.

The Canadiens had taken a 3–2 lead in the second period on goals by Bert Olmstead and Stan Smrke, but the Rangers' Andy Bathgate tied it for the Stars at 18:14 of the second period on assists from Prentice and Chicago's Ed Litzenberger.

*All-Stars*: Goal-Hall (Chicago). Defense-Kelly (Detroit), Flaman (Boston), Gadsby (New York), Morrison (Toronto), M. Pronovost (Detroit), Stanley (Boston). Forwards-Howe (Detroit), Lindsay (Chicago), Litzenberger (Chicago), Chevrefils (Boston), Bathgate (New York), Duff (Toronto), Delvecchio (Detroit), Prentice (New York), Migay (Toronto), Armstrong (Toronto), McKenney (Boston). Coach-Milt Schmidt (Boston).

*Montreal*: Goal-Plante. Defense-Harvey, St. Laurent, Johnson, Turner, Talbot. Forwards-Beliveau, M. Richard, Curry, Olmstead, Smrke, Moore, Provost, H. Richard, Bonin, Goyette, A. Pronovost, Marshall. Coach-Toe Blake.

Referee-Red Storey. Linesmen-Doug Davis, Bill Morrison.

First Period: 1. All-Stars, Kelly (unassisted) 1:06. 2. Montreal, M. Richard (H. Richard, Moore) 10:53. 3. All-Stars, Stanley (Prentice, Migay) 19:55. Penalties-Migay, Talbot, Howe 2, Harvey.

Second Period: 4. Montreal, Olmstead (Johnson) 0:33. 5. Montreal, Smrke (Bonin) 9:13. 6. All-Stars, Bathgate (Prentice, Litzenberger) 18:14. Penalties-Talbot, Chevrefils, Johnson.

Third Period: 7. All-Stars, Howe (Chevrefils, Morrison) 8:11. 8. All-Stars, Prentice (Bathgate, Litzenberger) 16:50. Penalties-Flaman 2, Olmstead.

Attendance-13,003.

## TWELFTH GAME
## October 4, 1958 at Montreal
## Montreal 6, All-Stars 3

Maurice Richard scored Montreal's first and final goals as the Canadiens defeated the All-Stars, 6–3, and ended a three-year non-winning streak for the Stanley Cup champions.

Referee Eddie Powers handed out six minor penalties and four led to goals. Andy Bathgate of the Rangers scored twice for the All-Stars while Bob Pulford of Toronto notched the visitors' other goal.

The Canadiens' Bernie (Boom Boom) Geoffrion suffered pulled neck and chest muscles from a body-check by Detroit's Red Kelly.

*All-Stars*: Goal-Hall (Chicago). Defense-Gadsby (New York), Flaman (Boston), M. Pronovost (Detroit), Mohns (Boston), Kelly (Detroit), St. Laurent (Chicago). Forwards-

Howe (Detroit), Bathgate (New York), Henry (New York), Sullivan (New York), Delvecchio (Detroit), Toppazzini (Boston), Harris (Toronto), Duff (Toronto), Litzenberger (Chicago), McKenney (Boston), Pulford (Toronto). Coach-Milt Schmidt (Boston).

*Montreal*: Goal-Plante. Defense-Harvey, Johnson, Turner, Talbot, Cushenan. Forwards-Beliveau, Geoffrion, Backstrom, M. Richard, Moore, Provost, McDonald, H. Richard, Bonin, Goyette, Marshall, A. Pronovost. Coach-Toe Blake.

Referee-Eddie Powers. Linesmen-George Hayes, Bill Morrison.

First Period: 1. Montreal, M. Richard (Harvey, Moore) 9:19. 2. Montreal, Geoffrion (H. Richard) 16:20. Penalties-Henry, Harvey.

Second Period: 3. Montreal, Marshall (Provost) 2:33. 4. Montreal, H. Richard (Talbot, Moore) 5:08. 5. All-Stars, Pulford (Toppazzini, Harris) 11:39. Penalty-Turner.

Third Period: 6. All-Stars, Bathgate (Litzenberger, Henry) 3:55. 7. Montreal, McDonald (Provost, Marshall) 7:43. 8. All-Stars, Bathgate (Pulford, Sullivan) 13:54. 9. Montreal, M. Richard (Moore, H. Richard) 16:04. Penalties-Mohns, Duff, Provost.

Attendance-13,989.

## THIRTEENTH GAME
## October 3, 1959 at Montreal
## Montreal 6, All-Stars 1

Big Jean Beliveau scored twice and defenseman Doug Harvey collected three assists as the Canadiens trounced the All-Stars, 6–1.

The Stars were considerably weakened by the absence of holdouts Bobby Hull, Tod Sloan and Pierre Pilote of Chicago and Bob Pulford, Dick Duff and Tim Horton of Toronto. They had not signed contracts for the season and therefore were ineligible to play.

Leading by 2–1 going into the third period, Montreal buried the Stars under a four-goal avalanche in the final 20 minutes. The marksmen were Beliveau, Dickie Moore, Henri Richard and Andre Pronovost.

*All-Stars*: Goal-Sawchuk (Detroit). Defense-M. Pronovost (Detroit), Gadsby (New York), Flaman (Boston), Brewer (Toronto), Mohns (Boston). Forwards-Bathgate (New York), Howe (Detroit), Delvecchio (Detroit), Sullivan (New York), Toppazzini (Boston), Mahovlich (Toronto), Olmstead (Toronto), Litzenberger (Chicago), McKenney (Boston), Armstrong (Toronto). Coach-Punch Imlach (Toronto).

*Montreal*: Goal-Plante. Defense-Johnson, Harvey, Turner,

Langlois, J. C. Tremblay. Forwards-Beliveau, Moore, H. Richard, Geoffrion, Backstrom, Hicke, M. Richard, Provost, McDonald, Bonin, Goyette, Marshall, A. Pronovost. Coach-Toe Blake.

Referee-Frank Udvari. Linesmen-George Hayes, Bob Frampton.

First Period: No scoring. Penalties-None.

Second Period: 1. Montreal, Beliveau (Hicke, Harvey) 4:25. 2. Montreal, McDonald (Backstrom, Geoffrion) 13:43. 3. All-Stars, McKenney (Litzenberger) 18:30. Penalties-None.

Third Period: 4. Montreal, Moore (H. Richard, Johnson) 7:44. 5. Montreal, H. Richard (Moore, Harvey) 9:31. 6. Montreal, Beliveau (Hicke, Bonin) 11:54. 7. Montreal, Pronovost (Harvey) 15:51. Penalties-Tremblay, Bathgate, Turner.

Attendance-13,818.


## FOURTEENTH GAME
## October 1, 1960 at Montreal
## All-Stars 2, Montreal 1

Andy Hebenton took a pass from his New York Ranger teammate, Red Sullivan, and beat goalie Jacques Plante at 15:51 of the second period to give the All-Stars a 2–1 victory over the Canadiens.

Frank Mahovlich of Toronto got the other Stars' goal in the opening minute of the second period and Claude Provost tied the score for the Canadiens 11 minutes later.

This was the first All-Star game in which Maurice Richard, the Canadiens' brilliant right wing, did not participate. He had announced his retirement as a player the previous month.

*All-Stars*: Goal-Hall (Chicago). Defense-M. Pronovost (Detroit), Stanley (Toronto), Pilote (Chicago), Gadsby (New York), Kelly (Toronto), Armstrong (Boston). Forwards-Howe (Detroit), Hull (Chicago), Horvath (Boston), Stasiuk (Boston), Ullman (Detroit), Bathgate (New York), Hay (Chicago), Hebenton (New York), Sullivan (New York), McKenney (Boston), Mahovlich (Toronto), Pulford (Toronto). Coach-Punch Imlach (Toronto).
*Montreal*: Goal-Plante. Defense-Harvey, Langlois, Johnson, Turner, Talbot. Forwards-Beliveau, Geoffrion, Bonin, Backstrom, Hicke, Moore, Provost, H. Richard, Marshall, A. Pronovost. Coach-Toe Blake.

Referee-Eddie Powers. Linesmen-George Hayes, Neil Armstrong.

First Period: No scoring. Penalty-Talbot.

Second Period: 1. All-Stars, Mahovlich (Pilote, Kelly) 0:40. 2. Montreal, Provost (Backstrom, A. Pronovost)

11:40. 3. All-Stars, Hebenton (Sullivan) 15:51. Penalties-Sullivan, Hull, Johnson.

Third Period: No scoring. Penalties-Hicke, Gadsby, Pilote, Harvey.

Attendance-13,949.


## FIFTEENTH GAME
## October 7, 1961 at Chicago
## All-Stars 3, Chicago 1

Teammates Gordie Howe and Alex Delvecchio of the Detroit Red Wings each scored one goal and assisted on another to lead the All-Stars to a 3–1 triumph over the Black Hawks.

Delvecchio opened the scoring in the 12th minute of the opening period and Howe closed it in the 12th minute of the second session. Norm Ullman, another Red Wing, assisted on both tallies.

Eric Nesterenko beat Toronto goalie Johnny Bower for Chicago's only tally at 6:26 of the second period.

*All-Stars*: Goal-Bower (Toronto), Worsley (New York). Defense-Harvey (New York), Pronovost (Detroit), Boivin (Boston), Stanley (Toronto), Brewer (Toronto), Mohns (Boston). Forwards-Richard (Montreal), McKenney (Boston), Ullman (Detroit), Bathgate (New York), Geoffrion (Montreal), Howe (Detroit), Provost (Montreal), Mahovlich (Toronto), Moore (Montreal), Delvecchio (Detroit), Goyette (Montreal). Coach-Sid Abel (Detroit).
*Chicago*: Goal-Hall. Defense-Turner, Pilote, Vasko, Evans, Fleming, St. Laurent. Forwards-Hall, Balfour, Horvath, Murphy, Hay, Melnyk, McDonald, Nesterenko, Hull, Wharram, Maki, Mikita. Coach-Rudy Pilous.

Referee-Frank Udvari. Linesmen-George Hayes, Neil Armstrong.

First Period: 1. All-Stars, Delvecchio (Ullman, Howe) 11:37. Penalties-Mahovlich, Hay, Vasko.

Second Period: 2. All-Stars, McKenney (Pronovost, Bathgate) 2:37. 3. Chicago, Nesterenko (Pilote, Hull) 6:26. 4. All-Stars, Howe (Delvecchio, Ullman) 11:38. Penalties-Goyette, Nesterenko 3, McKenney, Mahovlich 2.

Third Period: No scoring. Penalties-Pilote, Richard, Hull.

Attendance-14,534.


## SIXTEENTH GAME
## October 6, 1962 at Toronto
## Toronto 4, All-Stars 1

The Maple Leafs erupted for all their goals in the opening period against Montreal goalie Jacques

Plante and went on to defeat the All-Stars, 4–1, for their first victory in the annual classic.

Dick Duff, Bob Pulford, Frank Mahovlich and Eddie Shack beat Plante, who had captured the Vezina Trophy the previous season.

Detroit's Gordie Howe scored the only goal for the Stars. It was his seventh in the competition and enabled him to tie the record held by the retired Maurice Richard.

*All-Stars*: Goal-Plante (Montreal), Hall (Chicago), Worsley (New York). Defense-Harvey (New York), Talbot (Montreal), Pilote (Chicago), Mohns (Boston), Boivin (Boston). Forwards-McKenney (Boston), Howe (Detroit), Hull (Chicago), Geoffrion (Montreal), Bathgate (New York), Ullman (Detroit), Delvecchio (Detroit), Backstrom (Montreal), Prentice (New York). Coach-Rudy Pilous (Chicago).

*Toronto*: Goal-Bower. Defense-Brewer, Horton, Douglas, Baun, Hillman, Stanley. Forwards-Kelly, Mahovlich, Nevin, Duff, Armstrong, Stewart, Keon, Harris, Pulford, Shack, MacMillan, Litzenberger. Coach-Punch Imlach.

Referee-Eddie Powers. Linesmen-Matt Pavelich, Ron Wicks.

First Period: 1. Toronto, Duff (Armstrong, Douglas) 5:22. 2. All-Stars, Howe (Delvecchio, Pilote) 7:26. 3. Toronto, Pulford (Stewart) 10:45. 4. Toronto, Mahovlich (Stanley) 13:03. 5. Toronto, Shack (Keon) 19:32. Penalties-Mohns, Nevin, McKenney, Brewer, Shack, Howe.

Second Period: No scoring. Penalties-Kelly, Howe, Brewer.

Third Period: No scoring. Penalties-Baun, Boivin, Shack. Attendance-14,197.

## SEVENTEENTH GAME
## October 5, 1963 at Toronto
## Toronto 3, All-Stars 3

Frank Mahovlich, Toronto's big left wing, scored two goals and collected an assist as the Leafs played a 3–3 tie with the All-Stars.

The Leafs held the lead three times, but each time the Stars rallied for a deadlock. Mahovlich scored his team's first two goals and Ed Litzenberger's tally put Toronto in front, 3–2, at 2:56 of the third period. Just 27 seconds later, Detroit defenseman Marcel Pronovost drilled the puck home from the point.

*All-Stars*: Goal-Hall (Chicago), Sawchuk (Detroit). Defense-Pilote (Chicago), Vasko (Chicago), Howell (New York), Johnson (Boston), Pronovost (Detroit). Forwards-

Howe (Detroit), Richard (Montreal), Bathgate (New York), Hull (Chicago), Delvecchio (Detroit), Ullman (Detroit), Prentice (Boston), Oliver (Boston), Henry (New York), Bucyk (Boston), Geoffrion (Montreal), Provost (Montreal), Beliveau (Montreal). Coach-Sid Abel (Detroit).

*Toronto*: Goal-Bower, Simmons. Defense-Baun, Horton, Hillman, Douglas, Stanley. Forwards-Mahovlich, Shack, Kelly, Harris, Pulford, Nevin, Keon, Litzenberger, MacMillan, Stewart, Duff, Armstrong. Coach-Punch Imlach.

Referee-Frank Udvari. Linesmen-Matt Pavelich, Neil Armstrong.

First Period: 1. Toronto, Mahovlich (Armstrong, Baun) 2:22. 2. All-Stars, Richard (Henry, Howe) 4:08. 3. Toronto, Mahovlich (Keon, Litzenberger) 12:11. 4. All-Stars, Hull (Geoffrion) 19:27. Penalties-Stanley, Howell, Duff.

Second Period: No scoring. Penalties-Pronovost, Horton 2, Baun, Hull.

Third Period: 5. Toronto, Litzenberger (Mahovlich, Kelly) 2:56. 6. All-Stars, Pronovost (Bucyk, Oliver) 3:23. Penalty-Stanley.

Attendance-14,003.

## EIGHTEENTH GAME
## October 10, 1964 at Toronto
## All-Stars 3, Leafs 2

Montreal's Jean Beliveau scored the tie-breaking goal with six minutes remaining in the second period and led the All-Stars to a 3–2 victory over the Maple Leafs.

Beliveau's goal snapped a 1–1 deadlock. Gordie Howe of Detroit and Bobby Hull of Chicago assisted on the play.

Murray Oliver of Boston put the Stars in front, 3–1, in the seventh minute of the third period, offsetting a Leafs' goal by Jim Pappin later in the session.

*All-Stars*: Goal-Hall (Chicago), Hodge (Montreal). Defense-Vasko (Chicago), Pilote (Chicago), Laperriere (Montreal), Howell (New York), Boivin (Boston). Forwards-Beliveau (Montreal), Howe (Detroit), B. Hull (Chicago), Delvecchio (Detroit), Gilbert (New York), Oliver (Boston), Henry (New York), Mikita (Chicago), Bucyk (Boston), Provost (Montreal). Coach-Sid Abel (Detroit).

*Toronto*: Goal-Bower, Sawchuk. Defense-Horton, Douglas, Baun, Brewer, Hillman. Forwards-Pulford, Stewart, Shack, Keon, McKenney, Armstrong, Harris, Ehman, Pappin, Ellis, Bathgate, Mahovlich. Coach-Punch Imlach.

Referee-Frank Udvari. Linesmen-Ron Wicks, Neil Armstrong.

First Period: No scoring. Penalties-Bathgate, Howell, Baun, Douglas, Oliver.

Second Period: 1. All-Stars, Boivin (Laperriere, Oliver) 10:47. 2. Toronto, Douglas (Bathgate, Mahovlich) 11:45. 3. All-Stars, Beliveau (Hull, Howe) 13:51. Penalties-Laperriere, Mikita, Baun, Howell, Hodge (served by Gilbert).

Third Period: 4. All-Stars, Oliver (Bucyk, Howell) 6:11. 5. Toronto, Pappin (Ehman) 13:35. Penalties-Stewart, Pilote, Douglas, Provost.

Attendance-14,200.

## NINETEENTH GAME
## October 20, 1965 at Montreal
## All-Stars 5, Montreal 2

Gordie Howe of Detroit shattered the career All-Star game record for goals by scoring his eighth and ninth while leading the All-Stars to a 5–2 victory over the Canadiens.

The veteran right winger, who also assisted on two other scores, broke the mark of seven goals he shared with the Canadiens' Maurice Richard. Howe broke another All-Star record by lifting his career-point total to 16. He played on a line with Norm Ullman, also of Detroit, and Chicago's Bobby Hull.

*All-Stars*: Goal-Hall (Chicago), Crozier (Detroit), Johnston (Boston). Defense-Gadsby (Detroit), Pilote (Chicago), Howell (New York), Pronovost (Toronto), Green (Boston), Baun (Toronto). Forwards-Ullman (Detroit), Howe (Detroit), Hull (Chicago), Ellis (Toronto), Hadfield (New York), Gilbert (New York), Oliver (Boston), Bucyk (Boston), Mahovlich (Toronto), Nesterenko (Chicago), Delvecchio (Detroit), Mohns (Chicago). Coach-Billy Reay (Chicago).

*Montreal*: Goal-Hodge, Worsley. Defense-J. C. Tremblay, Harris, Laperriere, Talbot, Harper. Forwards-Beliveau, Rousseau, Duff, Backstrom, Larose, Provost, Richard, Balon, G. Tremblay, Ferguson, Berenson. Coach-Toe Blake.

Referee-Art Skov. Linesmen-Matt Pavelich, Neil Armstrong.

First Period: No scoring. Penalties-Harris 2, Gadsby, Beliveau, Larose, Pronovost.

Second Period: 1. Montreal, Beliveau (Duff, Rousseau) 6:48. 2. Montreal, Laperriere (Backstrom, Larose) 11:00. 3. All-Stars, Ullman (Hull, Howe) 12:40. 4. All-Stars, Hull (Howe, Oliver) 16:35. 5. All-Stars, Howe (Ullman, Baun) 19:19. Penalty-Balon.

Third Period: 6. All-Stars, Bucyk (Gadsby, Oliver) 10:01. 7. All-Stars, Howe (unassisted) 18:39. Penalties-Ellis, Ferguson, Howell 2.

Attendance-13,351.

## TWENTIETH GAME
## January 18, 1967 at Montreal
## Montreal 3, All-Stars 0

John Ferguson, Montreal's aggressive left wing, scored twice as the Canadiens blanked the All-Stars, 3–0, in a dull, listless contest, the first annual All-Star Game played in midseason.

Speedy Henri Richard put the Canadiens in front at 14:03 of the opening period when he converted passes from Bobby Rousseau and Terry Harper to beat Chicago's Glenn Hall, who was in the Stars' nets.

Ferguson scored less than two minutes later and again with only eight seconds remaining in the game.

*All-Stars*: Goal-Hall (Chicago), Giacomin (New York). Defense-Stanley (Toronto), Howell (New York), Stapleton (Chicago), Neilson (New York), Pilote (Chicago). Forwards-Ullman (Detroit), Mikita (Chicago), Keon (Toronto), Oliver (Boston), Howe (Detroit), Gilbert (New York), Nevin (New York), B. Hull (Chicago), Mahovlich (Toronto), Bucyk (Boston), Delvecchio (Detroit). Coach-Sid Abel (Detroit).

*Montreal*: Goal-Hodge, Bauman. Defense-Laperriere, Talbot, Harper, J. C. Tremblay, Harris, Roberts. Forwards-Richard, Beliveau, Backstrom, Balon, Provost, Larose, Cournoyer, Rousseau, Rochefort, Duff, G. Tremblay, Ferguson. Coach-Toe Blake.

Referee-Vern Buffey. Linesmen-Matt Pavelich, Neil Armstrong.

First Period: 1. Montreal, Richard (Rousseau, Harper) 14:03. 2. Montreal, Ferguson (Larose) 15:59. Penalties-None.

Second Period: No scoring. Penalties-Howell, Richard, Ferguson.

Third Period: 3. Montreal, Ferguson (Richard, Rousseau) 19:52. Penalties-None.

Attendance-14,284.

## TWENTY-FIRST GAME
## January 16, 1968 at Toronto
## Toronto 4, All-Stars 3

The Maple Leafs came from behind on second-period goals by Allan Stanley and Pete Stemkowski to defeat the All-Stars, 4–3, before a record All-Star crowd of 15,740.

The Stars took a 2–1 lead on Ken Wharram's goal

in the opening minute of the second period. But Stanley, on passes from Stemkowski and Wayne Carleton, tied the score seven minutes later and Stemkowski put the Leafs in front to stay at 16:36.

A moment of silence was observed before the start of the game in tribute to Bill Masterton, the Minnesota forward who died the previous day from a head injury received in a game three days earlier.

*All-Stars*: Goal-Giacomin (New York), Hall (St. Louis). Defense-Pilote (Chicago), Howell (New York), Orr (Boston), Laperriere (Montreal), Baun (Oakland), J. C. Tremblay (Montreal). Forwards-Mikita (Chicago), B. Hull (Chicago), Beliveau (Montreal), Ullman (Detroit), Howe (Detroit), Bucyk (Boston), Schinkel (Pittsburgh), Rochefort (Philadelphia), Balon (Minnesota), Marshall (New York). Coach-Toe Blake (Montreal).

*Toronto*: Goal-Gamble, A. Smith. Defense-Rupp, Horton, L. Hillman, Pronovost, Stanley. Forwards-Keon, Mahovlich, Ellis, Armstrong, Oliver, Stemkowski, Walton, Pappin, Pulford, Conacher, Carleton. Coach-Punch Imlach.

Referee-Bill Friday. Linesmen-Brent Castleman and Pat Shetler.

First Period: 1. Toronto, Oliver (Mahovlich, L. Hillman) 5:56. 2. All-Stars, Mikita (Hull, J. C. Tremblay) 19:53. Penalty-Stemkowski.

Second Period: 3. All-Stars, Wharram (Mikita) 0:35. 4. Toronto, Stanley (Stemkowski, Carleton) 7:56. 5. Toronto, Stemkowski (Carleton, Rupp) 16:36. Penalty-Howe.

Third Period: 6. All-Stars, Ellis (Mahovlich, L. Hillman) 3:31. 7. All-Stars, Ullman (Howe, Orr) 8:23. Penalties-Howe, Walton.

Attendance-15,740.

## TWENTY-SECOND GAME
## January 21, 1969 at Montreal
## East 3, West 3

For the first time, the All-Star Game pitted a squad from the new NHL West Division against one from the established East Division.

Claude Larose of Minnesota scored a goal with less than three minutes to play to give the underdog West a 3–3 standoff against the powerful East.

*East All-Stars*: Goal-Giacomin (New York), Cheevers (Boston). Defense-Orr (Boston), J. C. Tremblay (Montreal), Harris (Montreal), Green (Boston), Horton (Toronto), Stapleton (Chicago). Forwards-Beliveau (Montreal), Nevin (New York), Howe (Detroit), D. Hull (Chicago), Esposito (Boston), Ullman (Toronto), Rousseau (Montreal), R. Hull

(Chicago), Gilbert (New York), Mikita (Chicago), Mahovlich (Detroit). Coach-Toe Blake (Montreal).

*West All-Stars*: Goal-Hall (St. Louis), Parent (Philadelphia), Plante (St. Louis). Defense-Van Impe (Philadelphia), Arbour (St. Louis), Harvey (St. Louis), Vasko (Minnesota), Picard (St. Louis), Vadnais (Oakland), White (Los Angeles). Forwards-Berenson (St. Louis), O'Shea (Minnesota), Hicke (Oakland), Hampson (Oakland), Schinkel (Pittsburgh), Roberts (St. Louis), Larose (Minnesota), McDonald (St. Louis), Grant (Minnesota). Coach-Scotty Bowman (St. Louis).

Referee-John Ashley. Linesmen-Neil Armstrong, Matt Pavelich.

First Period: 1. West, Berenson (Harvey, Picard) 4:43. 2. East, Mahovlich (Rousseau, Stapleton) 17:32. Penalty-Vadnais.

Second Period: 3. West, Roberts (Berenson, Picard) 1:53. Penalties-Horton, White.

Third Period: 4. East, Mahovlich (Harris, Gilbert) 3:11. 5. East, Nevin (Ullman) 7:20. 6. West, Larose (Grant, O'Shea) 17:07. Penalties-White, Harvey.

Attendance-16,256.

## TWENTY-THIRD GAME
## January 20, 1970 at St. Louis
## East 4, West 1

Chicago's Bobby Hull scored one goal and set up another by Gordie Howe of Detroit as the East All-Stars completely dominated the play and whipped the West, 4–1.

The East set a record with 44 shots on goal, including 20 in the last period, all of which were stopped by Jacques Plante of St. Louis. All of the East goals came in the first 30 minutes against Philadelphia's Bernie Parent. The West had just 17 shots, a record low.

Each team scored in the first 37 seconds with Jacques Laperriere hitting for the East and Pittsburgh's Dean Prentice for the West. The two goals were the fastest in All-Star history.

*East All-Stars*: Goal-Giacomin (New York), T. Esposito (Chicago). Defense-Orr (Boston), Laperriere (Montreal), Neilson (New York), Park (New York), Savard (Montreal), Brewer (Detroit). Forwards-P. Esposito (Boston), Bucyk (Boston), Howe (Detroit), Ratelle (New York), Tkaczuk (New York), Ellis (Toronto), Keon (Toronto), Lemaire (Montreal), B. Hull (Chicago), Gilbert (New York), McKenzie (Boston), Mahovlich (Detroit). Coach-Claude Ruel (Montreal).

*West All-Stars*: Goal-Hall (St. Louis), Parent (Philadelphia), Plante (St. Louis). Defense-Arbour (St. Louis), White (Los Angeles), Woytowich (Pittsburgh), Howell (Oakland), B. Plager (St. Louis), Vadnais (Oakland). Forwards-Berenson (St. Louis), St. Marseille (St. Louis), Clarke (Philadelphia), Goyette (St. Louis), Parise (Minnesota), Prentice (Pittsburgh), Roberts (St. Louis), O'Shea (Minnesota), Larose (Minnesota), McDonald (St. Louis), Goldsworthy (Minnesota), Grant (Minnesota), Sabourin (St. Louis). Coach-Scotty Bowman (St. Louis).

Referee-Art Skov. Linesmen-Matt Pavelich, Claude Bechard.

First Period: 1. East, Laperriere (unassisted) 0:20. 2. West, Prentice (Berenson, Woytowich) 0:37. 3. East, Howe (B. Hull, Lemaire) 7:20. Penalties-Park, St. Marseille.

Second Period-4. East, B. Hull (Brewer) 3:26. 5. East, Tkaczuk (McKenzie, Bucyk) 9:37. Penalties-Woytowich.

Third Period-No scoring. Penalties-Woytowich.

Attendance-16,587.

## TWENTY-FOURTH GAME
### January 19, 1971 at Boston
### West 2, East 1

The Chicago Black Hawks had moved from the East to the West Division at the start of the 1970–71 season and the expansion division reaped an immediate benefit in the All-Star game.

Black Hawk teammates Bobby Hull and Chico Maki scored goals in the first 4½ minutes and that was enough for a 2–1 West victory over the East. Montreal's Yvan Cournoyer got one goal for the East at 6:19 of the first period but the game was scoreless after that.

A crowd of 14,790 paid a record $79,000 to watch the defense-dominated game.

*East All-Stars*: Goal-Giacomin (New York), Villemure (New York). Defense-Park (New York), Tremblay (Montreal), Orr (Boston), Tallon (Vancouver), Neilson (New York), Smith (Boston). Forwards-Bucyk (Boston), P. Esposito (Boston), Hodge (Boston), Howe (Detroit), Westfall (Boston), Perreault (Buffalo), Cournoyer (Montreal), Keon (Toronto), Balon (New York), Ratelle (New York), P. Mahovlich (Montreal), F. Mahovlich (Montreal). Coach-Harry Sinden (Boston).

*West All-Stars*: Goal-Wakely (St. Louis), T. Esposito (Chicago). Defense-White (Chicago), Magnuson (Chicago), Harris (Minnesota), Roberts (St. Louis), B. Plager (St. Louis), Stapleton (Chicago). Forwards-Martin (Chicago), Berenson (St. Louis), B. Hull (Chicago), D. Hull

(Chicago), Sabourin (St. Louis), Ecclestone (St. Louis), Clarke (Philadelphia), C. Maki (Chicago), Flett (Los Angeles), Grant (Minnesota), Mikita (Chicago), Polis (Pittsburgh). Coach-Scotty Bowman (St. Louis).

Referee-Bill Friday. Linesmen-Neil Armstrong, John D'Amico.

First period: 1. West, C. Maki (unassisted) 0:36. 2. West, R. Hull (Flett) 4:38. 3. East, Cournoyer (D. Smith, Balon) 6:19. Penalties-Harris, F. Mahovlich, R. Hull.

Second period: No scoring. Penalties-Bucyk.

Third period: No scoring. Penalties-Stapleton, Magnuson.

Attendance-14,790.

## TWENTY-FIFTH GAME
### January 25, 1972 at Minnesota
### East 3, West 2

Behind, 2–0, on West goals by Bobby Hull and Simon Nolet, the East Division All-Stars roared back to tie the score on second-period goals by Jean Ratelle and Johnny McKenzie. Then Phil Esposito's third-period score gave the East the victory in the silver anniversary game.

A crowd of 15,423 braved sub-zero Minnesota temperatures to watch the clash of the two divisions. Esposito scored the winning goal against Gump Worsley, goaltender for the host Minnesota North Stars.

*East All-Stars*: Goal-Dryden (Montreal), Villemure (New York). Defense-Park (New York), Tremblay (Montreal), Orr (Boston), Seiling (New York), Smith (Boston). Forwards-Berenson (Detroit), R. Martin (Buffalo), P. Esposito (Boston), Gilbert (New York), Tallon (Vancouver), Perreault (Buffalo), Hadfield (New York), Cournoyer (Montreal), Henderson (Toronto), McKenzie (Boston), Ratelle (New York), F. Mahovlich (Montreal). Coach-Al MacNeil (Montreal).

*West All-Stars*: Goal-Worsley (Minnesota), T. Esposito (Chicago). Defense-White (Chicago), Magnuson (Chicago), Harris (Minnesota), Vadnais (California), Mohns (Minnesota), Stapleton (Chicago). Forwards-Unger (St. Louis), Goldsworthy (Minnesota), R. Hull (Chicago), D. Hull (Chicago), Lonsberry (Los Angeles), P. Martin (Chicago), Clarke (Philadelphia), C. Maki (Chicago), Nolet (Philadelphia), Mikita (Chicago), Polis (Pittsburgh). Coach-Billy Reay (Chicago).

Referee-Bruce Hood. Linesmen-Matt Pavelich, Claude Bechard.

First period: 1. West, R. Hull (P. Martin, C. Maki) 17:01. Penalty-Hadfield.

Second period: 2. West, Nolet (D. Hull) 1:11. 3. East, Ratelle (Tremblay, Gilbert) 3:48. 4. East, McKenzie (Park, Seiling) 18:45. Penalty-White.

Third period: 5. East, P. Esposito (Smith, Orr) 1:09. Penalties-White, P. Esposito, Tremblay, Mohns.

Attendance-15,423.

## TWENTY-SIXTH GAME
## January 30, 1973 at New York
## East 5, West 4

Greg Polis, who arrived only hours before gametime following the birth of his first child in Pittsburgh, emerged as the star of the game, first ever at New York's Madison Square Garden.

Polis scored two goals for the West and drove off with the car awarded to the game's Most Valuable Player. The East, however, drove off with the victory with Bobby Schmautz scoring the decisive goal with only six minutes left to play.

A record All-Star crowd of 17,500 watched the game.

*East All-Stars*: Goal-Giacomin (New York R.), Villemure (New York R.). Defense- Savard (Montreal), Park (New York R.), G. Bergman (Detroit), Orr (Boston), Lapointe (Montreal), Smith (Boston). Forwards-R. Martin (Buffalo), P. Esposito (Boston), Hodge (Boston), Schmautz (Vancouver), Cournoyer (Montreal), Keon (Toronto), Robert (Buffalo), Westfall (New York I.), Ratelle (New York R.), Henderson (Toronto), Lemaire (Montreal), F. Mahovlich (Montreal). Coach-Tom Johnson (Boston).

*West All-Stars*: Goal-T. Esposito (Chicago), Vachon (Los Angeles). Defense-White (Chicago), Harper (Los Angeles), Marotte (Los Angeles), Gibbs (Minnesota), B. Plager (St. Louis), Manery (Atlanta). Forwards-P. Martin (Chicago), Pappin (Chicago), Unger (St. Louis), D. Hull (Chicago), Parise (Minnesota), Dornhoefer (Philadelphia), Clarke (Philadelphia), Berry (Los Angeles), Mikita (Chicago), Polis (Pittsburgh), J. Johnston (California), MacDonald (Pittsburgh).

Referee-Lloyd Gilmour. Linesmen-Neil Armstrong, John D'Amico.

First period: No scoring. Penalties-Orr, Bergman.

Second period: 1. West, Polis (Clarke, MacDonald) 0:55. 2. East, Robert (Park) 3:56. 3. East, F. Mahovlich (unassisted) 16:27. 4. East, Henderson (P. Esposito, Hodge) 19:12. 5. West, P. Martin (D. Hull, Pappin) 19:29. Penalty-Hodge.

Third period: 6. East, Lemaire (F. Mahovlich) 3:19. 7. West, Polis (unassisted) 4:27. 8. West, Harper (Mikita) 9:27. 9. East, Schmautz (Savard) 13:59. Penalty-White.

Attendance-17,500.

## TWENTY-SEVENTH GAME
## January 29, 1974 at Chicago
## West 6, East 4

Stan Mikita, with a goal and two assists, and Garry Unger, with a goal and assist, led the expansionist West to a come-from-behind 6–4 triumph over the East.

The East jumped to a 2–0 lead in the first period but the West roared back to score three unanswered goals in the second. Unger, voted the game's Most Valuable Player, scored what proved to be the winning goal at 7:54 of the final period. The 10 goals were the most scored in an All-Star contest.

A capacity crowd of 17,100 attended the game at Chicago Stadium.

## TWENTY-EIGHTH GAME
## January 21, 1975 at Montreal
## Wales Conference 7,
## Campbell Conference 1

NHL expansion turned the All-Star game into a battle of conferences: the Prince of Wales Conference against the Clarence Campbell Conference. In this first such pairing, Wales won easily, 7–1, at the Montreal Forum before a capacity crowd of 16,080.

Syl Apps Jr., son of a former NHL great, scored twice for Wales and was voted the game's MVP. Apps was the first son of an NHL All-Star to appear in an All-Star game.

*East All-Stars*: Goal-Gilbert (Boston), D. Dryden (Buffalo). Defense-Smith (Boston), Park (New York R.), D. Potvin (New York I.), Robinson (Montreal), McKenny (Toronto), Guevremont (Vancouver). Forwards-P. Esposito (Boston), Ullman (Toronto), Martin (Buffalo), Cashman (Boston), Westfall (New York I.), F. Mahovolich (Montreal), Hodge (Boston), Cournoyer (Montreal), Schmautz (Vancouver), Redmond (Detroit), Berenson (Detroit), Richard (Montreal). Coach-Scotty Bowman (Montreal).

*West All-Stars*: Goal-Parent (Philadelphia), T. Esposito (Chicago). Defense-White (Chicago), Burrows (Pittsburgh), Awrey (St. Louis), B. Plager (St. Louis), Van Impe (Philadelphia), Joe Watson (Philadelphia). Forwards-Clarke (Philadelphia), Hextall (Minnesota), Mikita (Chicago), Unger (St. Louis), D. Hull (Chicago), MacDonald (Pittsburgh), Johnston (California), Berry (Los Angeles), Goldsworthy (Minnesota), McDonough (Atlanta), Pappin (Chicago), Martin (Chicago). Coach-Billy Reay (Chicago).

First Period: 1. East, F. Mahovlich (Cournoyer, Ullman)

3:33. 2. East, Cournoyer (Ullman) 16:20. Penalty-Martin.

Second Period: 3. West, Berry (Mikita) 5:59. 4. West, McDonough (Clarke, MacDonald) 13:55. 5. West, MacDonald (B. Plager, Awrey) 19:07. Penalties-Hextall, Berenson.

Third Period: 6. West, Mikita (Unger, White) 2:25. 7. West, Unger (White, Mikita) 7:54. 8. East, D. Potvin (unassisted) 9:55. 9. East, M. Redmond (Berenson) 14:55. 10. West, P. Martin (Pappin) 19:13. Penalty-Plager.

Attendance-17,100.

*Campbell All-Stars*: Goal-Parent (Philadelphia), Smith (Vancouver). Defense-Park (New York R.), Van Impe (Philadelphia), Jarrett (Chicago), D. Potvin (New York I.), Pratt (Vancouver), Watson (Philadelphia). Forwards-Barber (Philadelphia), Unger (St. Louis), Pappin (Chicago), Vickers (New York R.), Gilbert (New York R.), Bennett (Atlanta), Lysiak (Atlanta), Clarke (Philadelphia), Nolet (Kansas City), Westfall (New York I.), Mikita (Chicago), Hextall (Minnesota). Coach-Fred Shero (Philadelphia).

*Wales All-Stars*: Goal-Vachon (Los Angeles), Dryden (Montreal). Defense-Harper (Los Angeles), Murdoch (Los Angeles), Orr (Boston), Korab (Buffalo), Lapointe (Montreal), Vadnais (Boston). Forwards-Luce (Buffalo), Esposito (Boston), Martin (Buffalo), Dionne (Detroit), Robert (Buffalo), Dupere (Washington), Pronovost (Pittsburgh), Lafleur (Montreal), Johnston (California), O'Reilly (Boston), Apps (Pittsburgh), Sittler (Toronto). Coach-Bep Guidolin (Boston-Kansas City).

Referee-Wally Harris. Linesmen-Leon Stickle, Claude Bechard.

First period: 1. Wales, Apps (Johnston, Vadnais) 9:38. 2. Wales, Luce (O'Reilly, Dupere) 12:02. 3. Wales, Sittler (Lafleur) 14:22. 4. Campbell, Potvin (Unger) 19:41. Penalties-None.

Second period: 5. Wales, Esposito (Lafleur, Murdoch) 19:16. Penalties-Vickers, Luce, Harper, Korab.

Third period: 6. Wales, Apps (Robert, Martin) 3:25. 7. Wales, O'Reilly (unassisted) 5:43. 8. Wales, Orr (Lafleur, Sittler) 7:19.

Penalties-Watson, Clarke.

Attendance-16,080.

# TWENTY-NINTH GAME
## January 20, 1976 at Philadelphia
## Wales Conference 7,
## Campbell Conference 5

Montreal's Pete Mahovlich scored a goal and three assists to pace Wales to a 7–5 victory over Campbell in the highest-scoring All-Star game ever played.

It was a close game until midway of the second period, when Campbell coach Fred Shero inserted Philadelphia's Wayne Stephenson in goal. The

Wales Stars scored on their first three shots against Stephenson to open a 6–1 lead. They coasted the rest of the way before a crowd of 16,436 at the Philadelphia Spectrum.

*Campbell All-Stars*: Goal-Resch (New York I.), Stephenson (Philadelphia). Defense-Vadnais (New York R.), Russell (Chicago), D. Potvin (New York I.), Dupont (Philadelphia), Marks (Chicago), Watson (Philadelphia). Forwards-Unger (St. Louis), Vickers (New York R.), Paiement (Kansas City), Ververgaert (Vancouver), Barber (Philadelphia), Goldsworthy (Minnesota), Harris (New York I.), Bennett (Atlanta), Lysiak (Atlanta), Trottier (New York I.), MacLeish (Philadelphia), Leach (Philadelphia). Coach-Fred Shero (Philadelphia).

*Wales All-Stars*: Goal-Thomas (Toronto), Dryden (Montreal). Defense-Park (Boston), Robinson (Montreal), Burrows (Pittsburgh), Lapointe (Montreal), Korab (Buffalo), Salming (Toronto). Forwards-Larouche (Pittsburgh), Clement (Washington), Martin (Buffalo), Pronovost (Pittsburgh), Lafleur (Montreal), Ramsay (Buffalo), MacAdam (California), Sheppard (Boston), Dionne (Los Angeles), Shutt (Montreal), Mahovlich (Montreal), Maloney (Detroit). Coach-Floyd Smith (Buffalo).

Referee-Lloyd Gilmour. Linesmen-John D'Amico, Neil Armstrong.

First period: 1. Wales, Martin (Mahovlich, Lafleur) 6:01. 2. Campbell, Bennett (Dupont) 16:59. 3. Wales, Mahovlich (Lapointe, Lafleur) 18:31. 4. Wales, Park (Mahovlich, Martin) 19:00. Penalties-None.

Second period: 5. Wales, MacAdam (Maloney) 9:34. 6. Wales, Lafleur (Mahovlich, Martin) 11:54. 7. Wales, Dionne (unassisted) 13:51. 8. Wales, Maloney (Larouche, MacAdam) 16:59. Penalty-Barber.

Third period: 9. Campbell, Ververgaert (Trottier, Harris) 4:33. 10. Campbell, Ververgaert (Trottier, Harris) 4:43. 11. Campbell, D. Potvin (unassisted) 14:17. 12. Campbell, Vickers (Unger, D. Potvin) 14:46. Penalty-Marks.

Attendance-16,436.

# THIRTIETH GAME
## January 25, 1977 at Vancouver
## Wales Conference 4,
## Campbell Conference 3

Rick Martin of Buffalo scored two third-period goals, including the game-winner with under two minutes to play, as Wales won their third straight over Campbell, 4–3, at the Pacific Coliseum in Vancouver.

Martin, voted MVP, scored at the four-minute mark to give the Wales a 3–2 lead. After Phil Esposito tied it with a goal at 12:23, Martin beat Chico

Resch from in close with 1:56 remaining for the winning score before a crowd of 15,613.

*Campbell All-Stars*: Goal-Parent (Philadelphia), Resch (New York I.). Defense-Snepsts (Vancouver), Bladon (Philadelphia), Russell (Chicago), D. Potvin (New York I.), Joe Watson (Philadelphia), Jim Watson (Philadelphia). Forwards-Gilbert (New York R.), Unger (St. Louis), Paiement (Colorado), Lysiak (Atlanta), Dornhoefer (Philadelphia), Murdoch (New York R.), Clarke (Philadelphia), Young (Minnesota), MacLeish (Philadelphia), Nystrom (New York I.), Vail (Atlanta), Esposito (New York R.). Coach-Fred Shero (Philadelphia).

*Wales All-Stars*: Goal-Dryden (Montreal), Desjardins (Buffalo). Defense-Turnbull (Toronto), Lapointe (Montreal), Schoenfeld (Buffalo), Savard (Montreal), Robinson (Montreal), Salming (Toronto), Park (Boston). Forwards-Martin (Buffalo), McNab (Boston), McDonald (Toronto), Lafleur (Montreal), Perreault (Buffalo), Pronovost (Pittsburgh), Libett (Detroit), Charron (Washington), MacAdam (Cleveland), Gainey (Montreal), Dionne (Los Angeles). Coach-Scotty Bowman (Montreal).

Referee-Ron Wicks. Linesmen-Matt Pavelich, Ron Finn.

First period: 1. Campbell, Vail (Potvin) 2:54. 2. Wales, McDonald (Gainey, McNab) 6:22. Penalties-Campbell bench, Dornhoefer, Lapointe.

Second period: 3. Campbell, MacLeish (Nystrom, Potvin) 11:56. 4. Wales, McDonald (Perreault, Robinson) 19:27. Penalties-Potvin, Lapointe, Paiement, Joe Watson.

Third period: 5. Wales, Martin (Dionne, Robinson) 4:00. 6. Campbell, Esposito (Gilbert, Dornhoefer) 12:23. 7. Wales, Martin (Dionne, Lafleur) 18:04. Penalties-Russell, Salming.

Attendance-15,607.


## THIRTY-FIRST GAME
### January 24, 1978 at Buffalo
### Wales Conference 3,
### Campbell Conference 2

Wales continued its domination of the All-Star classic, defeating Campbell, 3–2, for the fourth straight year.

Buffalo's Gil Perreault scored at 3:55 of sudden-death overtime for the winning score, but the MVP award went to New York Islander goalie Billy Smith, who stopped 16 shots in the first 30 minutes of action. A crowd of 16,433 attended the game at the Buffalo Auditorium.

*Campbell All-Stars*: Goal-Smith (New York I.), Stephenson (Philadelphia). Defense-Dailey (Philadelphia), Bladon

(Philadelphia), Vadnais (New York R.), D. Potvin (New York I.), Watson (Philadelphia), Beck (Colorado). Forwards-Barber (Philadelphia), Bossy (New York I.), Paiement (Colorado), Gillies (New York I.), Clement (Atlanta), Ververgaert (Vancouver), Unger (St. Louis), Boldirev (Chicago), Clarke (Philadelphia), Trottier (New York I.), Esposito (New York R.), Eriksson (Minnesota). Coach-Fred Shero (Philadelphia).

*Wales All-Stars*: Goal-Dryden (Montreal), Vachon (Los Angeles). Defense-Savard (Montreal), Robinson (Montreal), Salming (Toronto), Park (Boston), Larson (Detroit). Forwards-Pronovost (Pittsburgh), Shutt (Montreal), Martin (Buffalo), McDonald (Toronto), Lafleur (Montreal), Perreault (Buffalo), Sirois (Washington), Cournoyer (Montreal), Dionne (Los Angeles), Maruk (Cleveland), O'Reilly (Boston), Gainey (Montreal), Sittler (Toronto). Coach-Scotty Bowman (Montreal).

Referee-Bruce Hood. Linesmen-John D'Amico, Leon Stickle.

First period: 1. Campbell, Barber (unassisted) 1:25. 2. Campbell, Potvin (Clarke) 12:12. Penalties-Salming, Gillies.

Second period: 3. Wales, Sittler (Robinson, Park) 19:32. Penalties-Dailey, Smith, McDonald, Vadnais.

Third period: 4. Wales, Martin (Dionne, O'Reilly) 18:21. Penalties-None.

Overtime: 5. Wales, Perreault (Shutt, Salming) 3:55. Penalties-None.

Attendance-16,433.


## THIRTY-SECOND GAME
### February 5, 1980 at Detroit
### Wales Conference 6,
### Campbell Conference 3

After a year's absence due to the Challenge Cup series against the Soviet Union, the All-Star game was returned to its regular format. And, as usual, Wales won, this time by a 6–3 count before 21,002 fans at Joe Louis Arena in Detroit. It was the fifth straight triumph for Wales.

Reggie Leach, who scored a goal and assist for Campbell, was voted MVP, but it was 51-year-old Gordie Howe who stole the show. Howe, playing in his final All-Star game, had an assist on the Wales' final goal and earned a long ovation from the largest crowd ever to attend an NHL game.

*Campbell All-Stars*: Goal-Peeters (Philadelphia), Esposito (Chicago). Defense-Lindgren (Vancouver), McEwen (Colorado), Picard (Washington), Greschner (New

York R.), Watson (Philadelphia), Barnes (Philadelphia). Forwards-Barber (Philadelphia), Lukowich (Winnipeg), McDonald (Edmonton), Nilsson (Atlanta), MacLeish (Philadelphia), Bossy (New York I.), Trottier (New York I.), Federko (St. Louis), Propp (Philadelphia), Leach (Philadelphia), Esposito (New York R.), Gretzky (Edmonton). Coach-Al Arbour (New York I.).

*Wales All-Stars*: Goal-Edwards (Buffalo), Meloche (Minnesota). Defense-Stackhouse (Pittsburgh), Hartsburg (Minnesota), Schoenfeld (Buffalo), Robinson (Montreal), Burrows (Toronto), Larson (Detroit). Forwards-Ratelle (Boston), Cloutier (Quebec), Howe (Hartford), Lafleur (Montreal), Perreault (Buffalo), Murphy (Los Angeles), Goring (Los Angeles), Dionne (Los Angeles), Gainey (Montreal), Gare (Buffalo), Payne (Minnesota), Sittler (Toronto). Coach-Scotty Bowman (Montreal).

Referee-Dave Newell. Linesmen-John D'Amico, Ray Scapinello.

First period: 1. Wales, Robinson (unassisted) 3:58. 2. Wales, Payne (Murphy, Goring) 4:19. 3. Campbell, Leach (McEwen) 7:15. Penalty-Hartsburg.

Second period: 4. Campbell, Nilsson (Federko, MacLeish) 6:03. Penalties-None.

Third period: 5. Campbell, Propp (P. Esposito, Leach) 4:14. 6. Wales, Stackhouse (Sittler, Lafleur) 11:40. 7. Wales, Hartsburg (Cloutier, Ratelle) 12:40. 8. Wales, Larson (Payne, Perreault) 13:12. 9. Wales, Cloutier (Howe) 16:06. Penalties-None.

Attendance-21,002.


## THIRTY-THIRD GAME
### February 10, 1981 at Los Angeles
### Campbell Conference 4,
### Wales Conference 1

Campbell finally got into the win column as it posted a 4–1 victory over Wales. The triumph snapped the Wales' five-game victory streak.

Although outshot, 43–25, Campbell got outstanding goaltending from Mike Liut and Pete Peeters. Liut, voted MVP, stopped 18 shots in the first period and seven more in the middle period before Peeters relieved him.

A crowd of 16,005 watched the game played at the Los Angeles Forum.

*Campbell All-Stars*: Goal-Liut (St. Louis), Peeters (Philadelphia). Defense-Dailey (Philadelphia), Wilson (Philadelphia), Ramage (Colorado), Potvin (New York I.), Murray (Chicago), McCarthy (Vancouver). Forwards-Barber (Philadelphia), Babych (St. Louis), Gartner (Washington),

Bourne (New York I.), Lukowich (Winnipeg), Nilsson (Calgary), Holmgren (Philadelphia), Johnstone (New York R.), Williams (Vancouver), Bossy (New York I.), Federko (St. Louis), Gretzky (Edmonton). Coach-Pat Quinn (Philadelphia).

*Wales All-Stars*: Goal-Lessard (Los Angeles), Beaupre (Minnesota). Defense-Langway (Montreal), Picard (Toronto), Howe (Hartford), Bourque (Boston), Carlyle (Pittsburgh), Larson (Detroit). Forwards-Simmer (Los Angeles), Middleton (Boston), Kehoe (Pittsburgh), Smith (Minnesota), Dionne (Los Angeles), Rogers (Hartford), Taylor (Los Angeles), Ogrodnick (Detroit), Gare (Buffalo), Shutt (Montreal), Gainey (Montreal), P. Stastny (Quebec). Coach-Scotty Bowman (Buffalo).

Referee-Bryan Lewis. Linesmen-Jim Christison, Gerard Gauthier.

First period: 1. Campbell, Nilsson (Barber, Holmgren) :45. 2. Campbell, Barber (Johnstone) 8:02. Penalties-Bourne, Williams.

Second period: 3. Campbell, Babych (Johnstone, Federko) 16:12. Penalties-None.

Third period: 4. Wales, Ogrodnick (Howe, Kehoe) 6:13. 5. Campbell, Wilson (Bossy, Gretzky) 10:18. Penalties-None.

Attendance-16,005.


## THIRTY-FOURTH GAME
### February 9, 1982 at Landover, Md.
### Wales Conference 4,
### Campbell Conference 2

Mike Bossy scored late in the second period to snap a 2–2 tie and then added an insurance goal early in the third period to send Wales to a 4–2 decision over the Campbell Conference Stars at Landover, Maryland.

While MVP Bossy was providing the offense, goaltenders Michel Dion and Don Edwards combined to stop 29 shots and help Wales win for the sixth time in seven games. A capacity crowd of 18,130 was on hand.

*Campbell All-Stars*: Goal-Fuhr (Edmonton), Meloche (Minnesota). Defense-Hartsburg (Minnesota), Coffey (Edmonton), Wilson (Chicago), Manno (Toronto), Rautakallio (Calgary), Snepsts (Vancouver). Forwards-Gretzky (Edmonton), Savard (Chicago), Smith (Minnesota), Taylor (Los Angeles), Hawerchuk (Winnipeg), Ciccarelli (Minnesota), Lever (Colorado), Vaive (Toronto), Messier (Edmonton), Secord (Chicago), Sutter (St. Louis), Ogrodnick (Detroit). Coach-Glen Sonmor (Minnesota).

*A super sombrero is fitting for Wayne Gretzky after he scores four goals in the 1983 All-Star Game.*

*Wales All-Stars*: Goal-Dion (Pittsburgh), Edwards (Buffalo). Defense-Ramsey (Buffalo), Bourque (Boston), Robinson (Montreal), Carlyle (Pittsburgh), Beck (New York R.), Langway (Montreal). Forwards-Trottier (New York I.), P. Stastny (Quebec), Acton (Montreal), Maruk (Washington), Stoughton (Hartford), Bossy (New York I.), Propp (Philadelphia), Middleton (Boston), Duguay (New York R.), Barber (Philadelphia), Tardif (Quebec), Tonelli (New York I.). Coach-Al Arbour (New York I.).

Referee-Wally Harris. Linesmen-Ron Finn, Swede Knox.

First period: 1. Campbell, Vaive (Sutter) 2:32. 2. Wales, Bourque (Maruk, Carlyle) 12:03. 3. Wales, Tardif (Middleton, Stastny) 13:27. Penalties-Tardif, Hartsburg.

Second period: 4. Campbell, Gretzky (Coffey, Ciccarelli) 0:26. 5. Wales, Bossy (Beck, Tonelli) 17:10. Penalties-Hawerchuk, Tardif.

Third period: 6. Wales, Bossy (Robinson) 1:19. Penalty-Stoughton.

Attendance-18,130.

## THIRTY-FIFTH GAME
### February 8, 1983 at Uniondale, N.Y.
### Campbell Conference 9,
### Wales Conference 3

Wayne Gretzky scored four goals in the final period, shattering four All-Star Game records and helping the Campbell Conference post a 9–3 victory over the Wales Conference at Nassau Coliseum.

Gretzky's outburst helped the Campbells turn a close 3–2 game into a rout and hand the Wales Stars only their second loss in eight games. A capacity crowd of 15,230 witnessed Gretzky's feat.

*Campbell All-Stars:* Goal-Bannerman (Chicago), Garrett (Vancouver). Defense-Huber (Detroit), Hartsburg (Minnesota), Murray (Chicago), Coffey (Edmonton), Wilson (Chicago), Babych (Winnipeg). Forwards-Broten (Minne-

sota), McDonald (Calgary), B. Sutter (St. Louis), Kurri (Edmonton), Messier (Edmonton), McCarthy (Minnesota), Vaive (Toronto), Dionne (Los Angeles), Savard (Chicago), Ciccarelli (Minnesota), Secord (Chicago), Gretzky (Edmonton). Coach-Roger Neilson (Vancouver).

*Wales All-Stars:* Goal-Peeters (Boston), Lindbergh (Philadelphia). Defense-Potvin (New York I.), Bourque (Boston), Howe (Philadelphia), Langevin (New York I.), Ramsey (Buffalo), Langway (Washington). Forwards-Francis (Hartford), Pederson (Boston), Walter (Montreal), Maloney (New York R.), Goulet (Quebec), Kehoe (Pittsburgh), Trottier (New York I.), Bossy (New York I.), M. Stastny (Quebec), P. Stastny (Quebec), Marini (New Jersey), Sittler (Philadelphia). Coach-Al Arbour (New York I.).

Referee-Bob Myers. Linesmen-Ryan Bozak, Leon Stickle.

First period: 1. Wales, Goulet (P. Stastny) 3:41. 2. Campbell, Babych (McDonald, Sutter) 11:37. 3. Wales, Bourque (unassisted) 19:01. Penalties-Sutter, Langevin.

Second period: 4. Campbell, Ciccarelli (Broten, Secord) 3:01. 5. Campbell, McCarthy (Ciccarelli, Murray) 14:51. Penalties-None.

Third period: 6. Campbell, Gretzky (Kurri, Coffey) 6:20. 7. Campbell, McDonald (Sutter, Dionne) 7:29. 8. Campbell, Gretzky (Messier, Kurri) 10:31. 9. Wales, Maloney (Marini) 14:04. 10. Campbell, Gretzky (Wilson, Messier) 15:32. 11. Campbell, Vaive (unassisted) 17:15. 12. Campbell, Gretzky (Messier) 19:18. Penalties-Ramsey.

Attendance-15,230.

# ALL-STAR GAME RECORDS

## INDIVIDUAL

**Most games played**—23, Gordie Howe, Detroit and Hartford.

**Most goals, lifetime**—10, Gordie Howe, Detroit and Hartford.

**Most goals, one game**—4, Wayne Gretzky, Campbell Conference, 1983.

**Most Goals, one period**—4, Wayne Gretzky, Campbell Conference, third period, 1983.

**Most assists, lifetime**—9, Gordie Howe, Detroit and Hartford.

**Most assists, one game**—3, Doug Harvey, Montreal, 1959; Dickie Moore, Montreal, 1958; Guy Lafleur, Wales Conference, 1975; Pete Mahovlich, Wales Conference, 1976; Mark Messier, Campbell Conference, 1983.

**Most assists, one period**—3, Mark Messier, Campbell Conference, third period, 1983.

**Most points, lifetime**—19, Gordie Howe, Detroit and Hartford.

**Most points, one game**—4, Ted Lindsay, Detroit, 1950; Gordie Howe, NHL All-Stars, 1965; Pete Mahovlich, Wales Conference, 1976; Wayne Gretzky, Campbell Conference, 1983.

**Most points, one period**—4, Wayne Gretzky, Campbell Conference, third period, 1983.

**Most penalties, lifetime**—12, Gordie Howe, Detroit and Hartford.

**Most penalty minutes, lifetime**—27, Gordie Howe, Detroit and Hartford.

**Fastest goal at start of game and period**—19 seconds, Ted Lindsay, Detroit, 1950.

**Most games played by a goalie**—13, Glenn Hall, Detroit, Chicago, St. Louis.

**Most goals against, one game**—7, Pelle Lindbergh, Wales Conference, 1983.

**Most goals against, one period**—6, Pelle Lindbergh, Wales Conference, third period, 1983.

**Most goals, both teams, one game**—12, Wales Conference 7, Campbell Conference 5, 1976; Campbell Conference 9, Campbell Conference 3, 1983.

**Most goals, one team, one game**—9, Campbell Conference, 1983.

**Most goals, one team, one period**—6, Campbell Conference, third period, 1983.

**Most goals, both teams, one period**—7, Campbell Conference (6), Wales Conference (1), third period, 1983.

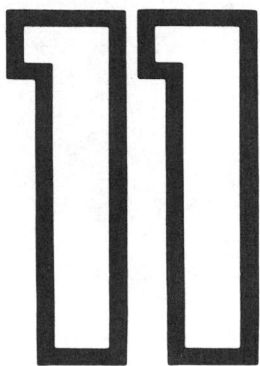

# THE OFFICIALS

It is safe to assume that Sir William Gilbert of the operatic composing team of Gilbert and Sullivan never met an ice hockey referee. He was born in Victorian London in 1836 and died in 1911, long before hockey was introduced to his country. If he were living today, he presumably would show the same compassion for referees that he did for policemen.

The lot of the hockey referee isn't a happy one either. His constabulary duties consist of bringing discipline and control to 60 minutes of speed and confusion on ice. Players skim along the frozen surface at 20 to 30 miles an hour; there are violent collisions at great speed; sticks are swung like clubs, and pucks whiz over the ice and through the air at upwards of 100 mph.

This is the referee's work day:

◄ *A referee's life can be dangerous, as Frank Udvari discovers. He holds on for dear life as Gordie Howe crashes an opponent into the boards in a mid-1950s' game.*

He skates between 15 and 20 miles in an average game. He must match the fastest player stride for stride and be on top of every play. The players' bench disgorges fresh skaters as though they were traveling through a revolving door but the harried referee gets no rest, except between periods.

And then there are the hazards of the job. While he is trying to control the game and the players, the referee may be tripped, jammed into the corners, boarded, draped over the protective glass, slashed by a skate, hit by a flying puck or pelted with programs, fruit, vegetables, eggs, overshoes—or squid.

Squid? "You better believe it," said Bill Chadwick, the only American-born referee to be named to the Hockey Hall of Fame. "I was working a Stanley Cup playoff game in Detroit in 1952 when a fan tossed something at me which missed and landed on the ice. I went over to pick it up, but after one look I spun around and skated off in a hurry. I thought at first it was a baby octopus. I found out later it was a squid. But octopus or squid, it sure scared hell out of me."

Chadwick's admission of fear was not uncommon. Fear grips most referees—as it does the policeman on the beat. Referees of yore like Bill Chadwick, who later became a New York Ranger radio and television announcer; Red Storey, Cooper Smeaton,

*Mickey Ion (left) and Cooper Smeaton, both members of the Hall of Fame, spell out who's in charge.*

Mickey Ion, King Clancy and Mike Rodden were—as many are today—threatened with physical violence while serving in the National Hockey League.

They learned to live with this fear and eventually wound up in hockey's Hall of Fame because they had courage—courage to render a decision and make it stick in the face of taunts from players, coaches and hostile fans.

Clancy earned his berth in the Hall of Fame as a fighting defenseman. But he is also remembered as a fighting referee, a 150-pound bantam rooster of a man who never allowed himself to be intimidated by a player or coach, a club owner or a fan.

Asked once to explain how he managed to make the shift from player to referee, Clancy said, "I always gave the players a second chance. Maybe that's because I was a player myself. When they skated up to me and said, 'Why you little so-and-so, you couldn't referee a girls' basketball game,' I always gave 'em the same answer. I'd shout right back, 'What did you say?' Hell, they'd never repeat it and the whole thing would end right there."

Clancy never permitted the crowd to sway his decisions. "Hockey fans are the same everywhere," he said. "They all want to see the home team win, and the referee is never right. But I figured a guy paying his way into the rink had a right to boo me. I didn't mind. It just rolled off my thick Irish skin."

In Clancy's mind, Mickey Ion was hockey's most outstanding referee. "When Mickey refereed a game, he was in complete charge," he said. "There's never been anyone to equal him. One night in Boston, Mickey was knocked over the boards and landed in a fan's lap. Boston scored while he was scrambling back over the boards, but Mickey didn't allow it. He wasn't on the ice and he said nobody was allowed to score unless he was there to see it."

Clancy, who served as a referee for 11 years following his retirement as a player in 1936, will never forget the instructions Ion gave him and Rabbit McVeigh before they worked their first Stanley Cup playoff game in 1938.

"Mickey came into the officials' room and started lecturing us," Clancy said. "He said, 'Crack down

on those players right from the start. Don't take anything from anybody. And remember this: There are 15,000 idiots out there, including the players. You two guys are the only sane ones in the building.' And, you know, there were times when I think Mickey was right."

In the early days of pro hockey, referees were picked haphazardly. Retired and active players assisted in the officiating and were not paid. The first referees of the Stanley Cup playoffs were chosen from among the executives of the competing leagues.

Smeaton and Ion got their starts as referees before the first World War. They were paid—sometimes.

"When I was working, we got paid by the game," Smeaton recalled. "But if one of the bosses didn't like your work just once, you didn't come back. And you didn't get paid either."

The referee was the sole official in Smeaton's day. "There were no linesmen to help out," he said. "I had to call the offsides, the penalties, break up the fights and do the arguing. And what fights we had.

"One night in Toronto, Art Ross and Minnie McGiffen were actually arrested for assaulting each

*Referee Bill Chadwick, disciplining the Canadiens' Murph Chamberlain, worked 16 years in the NHL.*

other in a game. After the game I was sitting in the referee's room when a fan knocked on the door. He accused me of holding McGiffen while Ross hit him.

"I got peeved and invited the guy into the room. When I got finished with him he didn't feel too good. They had to carry him out. I had to sneak out of the rink by the back door because the crowd and the police were coming after me."

Mike Rodden, one of Smeaton's contemporaries, found this common invasion of the referee's room too much for him one night in Chicago. He had just finished refereeing a game when the Black Hawks' owner, Major Frederic McLaughlin, bolted into the room.

Normally cold and aloof, McLaughlin launched a sarcastic tirade at Rodden which he punctuated with threats of physical harm. It lasted until the referee took off his skates. Then Rodden pointed to the exit and told the astounded McLaughlin if he didn't get out he would toss him through the door.

Chadwick had similar experiences.

"When I first started refereeing [in 1941], you were more or less at the mercy of the club owners," he said. "You'd have a waiting line outside your door after every period. The owners would be there and the coaches, too. You couldn't keep 'em out. They'd walk in, give you hell and then walk out.

"The referees had nobody to turn to for support. There was no referee-in-chief. All we had was the league president and he was only an intermediary. Then Clarence Campbell took over as president [in 1947] and he backed us up because he knew our problems. He had been a referee."

It was during Red Dutton's reign as NHL president that Chadwick endured his most trying experience with mob violence. He was working a playoff game between the Canadiens and the Black Hawks in Chicago Stadium in 1943. One of his calls infuriated the Chicago fans, who went on a wild rampage, littering the ice with debris while crying for Chadwick's scalp.

The harassed referee ducked for cover, then dispatched a courier to Dutton in his front-row box, asking what he should do. Dutton's answer was starkly brief: "You got yourself into this, now get yourself out."

"I needed a police escort to get out of the building

*Mike Rodden wore the whistle for 1,187 NHL games.*

that night," Chadwick recalled. "The next game I worked there I was picked up at my hotel by detectives, who escorted me to the stadium and then back to the hotel following the game. Those Chicago fans really gave me a hard time."

The Hawks' rooters didn't exactly love King Clancy, either. One female customer used to enjoy sticking a hat pin into his derriere. "Oh, she was a lovely lady," Clancy said. "She occupied a seat close to the ice and every time I would jump onto the sideboards to get out of the way she'd come running and jab me with the hat pin."

Why so much abuse? "In no other sport are referees charged so much with the responsibility of who wins and loses," said Frank Udvari, an NHL referee for 16 years. "That's why we're such a focal point for criticism."

The NHL even encourages referee identification. Although it has long been said the best-officiated games are the ones in which the referees go unnoticed, the NHL in 1977 began putting the names of the officials on the back of their jerseys. Officials in other sports are usually identified by numbers.

So hockey fans are more conscious of the whistle blowers and their respective reputations. Indeed, "Who's the ref?" is one of the first questions asked at any NHL game.

Many referees, past and present, readily admit that the job has one other serious drawback. It deals with non-fraternizing. The loneliness of the long-distance runner is minor compared to the life of a referee, who is prohibited from mingling with players, club officials or fans.

"Sometimes it gets so lonely you almost go out of your mind," said Bill Friday, a top referee in the 1960s and '70s. "I remember one Christmas Eve I had to spend on the road. I walked the streets for several hours, thinking of my wife and children back home in Hamilton [Ontario].

"Know what I finally did? I stopped in a men's wear store and bought myself a shirt. I had it gift-wrapped, took it to my hotel room and slipped it under the bed. The next morning, I reached under the bed and took it out and read the card: 'Merry Christmas, Bill,' and then opened the package. I just wanted to be able to open something."

Chadwick claimed it was even tougher when he

*Red Storey refereed from 1951 through 1959.*

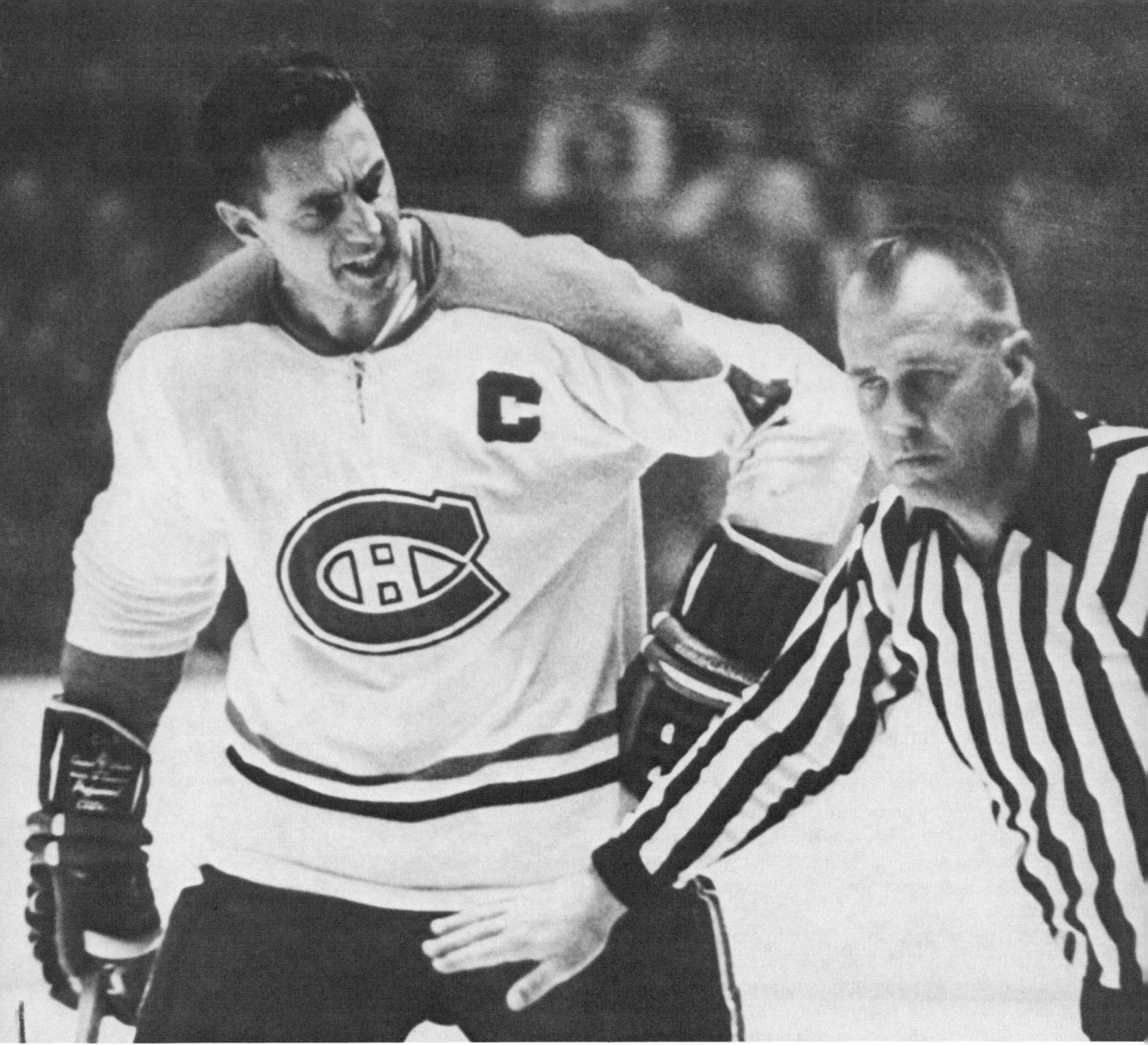

*Referee Art Skov wants no part of complaining Canadien Jean Beliveau.*

was officiating. "The referees now have some companionship," he said. "They travel with the linesmen or arrange to meet them in the various cities. In my day the referee traveled alone and lived alone. I spent half my time in hotel lobbies or movies.

"You couldn't associate with the players, but I always talked to them. I figured if they talked to me off the ice I had a better chance of dealing with them in tight situations on the ice. The big thing is to get the respect of the players."

Chadwick refereed 1,200 regular-season games and 125 playoff games (both records) during his 16 years of service in the NHL. He said he never would have established these longevity records if he hadn't cultivated the respect of the players.

"I never had any real trouble, even with the so-called tough guys," he noted. "My secret was to be consistent but not over-officious. If a referee called everything by the book you'd have nobody on the ice and less people in the stands. You have to use

common sense, set a standard and hold it through the entire game.

"The only problem I've noticed among the current referees is a tendency to fluctuate. Some call every infraction at the start of a game and then loosen up or vice versa. A good referee has to be consistent."

Even consistency has its drawbacks. Andy van Hellemond, widely regarded as one of the best of the active referees in the 1980s, was hit twice by players in two separate incidents in the 1981–82 season. As a result, the NHL passed a rule that went into effect in 1982–83 calling for an automatic 20-game suspension for any player who intentionally strikes an official.

When Chadwick, a native New Yorker, broke into the NHL he was paid $75 a game. He was the league's highest-paid official when he retired in 1955, earning approximately $13,000 a year. In 1983, the pay scale for referees ranged from $30,000 to $70,000.

According to Scotty Morrison, the NHL's chief of officiating since 1964, career longevity in hockey differs from other sports in which officials are still active when they are 55 years old. "In hockey the demands are so strenuous that our referees are retiring at 45 or 46. Beyond that, they just can't keep up with the play," he said.

"It's a good job," said Vern Buffey, who was referee-in-chief of the WHA. "Sure, the traveling is tough and we took a lot of abuse. But you got used to it."

Or to paraphrase the words of Sir William Gilbert, the referee's lot still is not a happy one. But at least the pay is good.

*Andy van Hellemond is recognized as one of the NHL's best modern referees.*

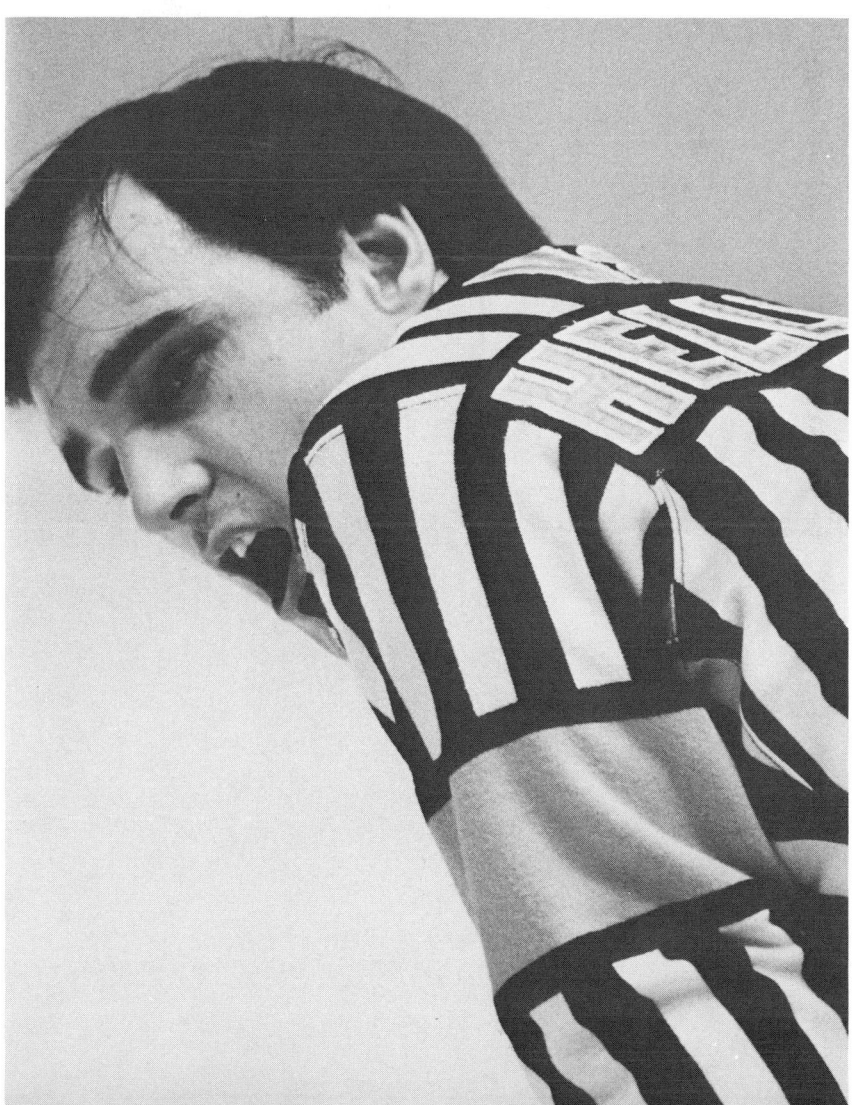

*The Hockey Hall of Fame in Toronto.*

# 12

# THE HALL OF FAME

On Saturday, August 26, 1961, John F. Diefenbaker, Prime Minister of Canada, stood on a platform in front of a newly-erected building on the grounds of the Canadian National Exhibition in Toronto.

He was flanked by members of the Hockey Hall of Fame Governing Committee, including Clarence S. Campbell, president of the National Hockey League.

Diefenbaker walked to the microphone and said, "I now officially proclaim the opening of the Hockey Hall of Fame Building."

The development climaxed several years of frustration and negotiation. Kingston, Ontario, had originally been selected as the site of the shrine at which the NHL officials would perpetuate the memories of the sport's founders, distinguished club executives, players and referees.

However, the proposed Kingston project ran into difficulties and, in 1960, an agreement was reached by the National Hockey League, the Canadian National Exhibition and the city of Toronto. The contract stipulated that the NHL would pay for the erection of the Hockey Hall of Fame Building over a period of six to eight years.

It normally takes five years after retirement for a player or a referee to be eligible for membership in the Hockey Hall of Fame. However, the Hall's eligibility requirements stipulate that "in exceptional cases, this period may be shortened by the Hockey Hall of Fame Committee."

Members are divided into three categories: players, referees and builders. The builders' group comprises league and club executives of the NHL and other professional and amateur leagues, and includes those who have helped with the development and promotion of the sport.

Clarence Campbell, former president of the NHL, is chairman of the Hall of Fame governing committee which elects builders and referees. Players are elected by the Selection Committee, whose chairman is Tom Fitzgerald, who was a longtime hockey writer on the Boston *Globe*. Maurice (Lofty) Reid is director and curator.

## PLAYERS

**Sidney Gerald (Sid) Abel**: Starred on Red Wings' Production Line (with Gordie Howe and Ted Lindsay) in the 1940s. Later coached Wings to seven playoff berths in 10 seasons behind the bench.

**John James (Jack) Adams**: Star forward for the Toronto Arenas, Toronto St. Pats and Ottawa Senators. Later coached and served as general manager of the Detroit Red Wings.

**Sylvanus (Syl) Apps**: A center who was the first

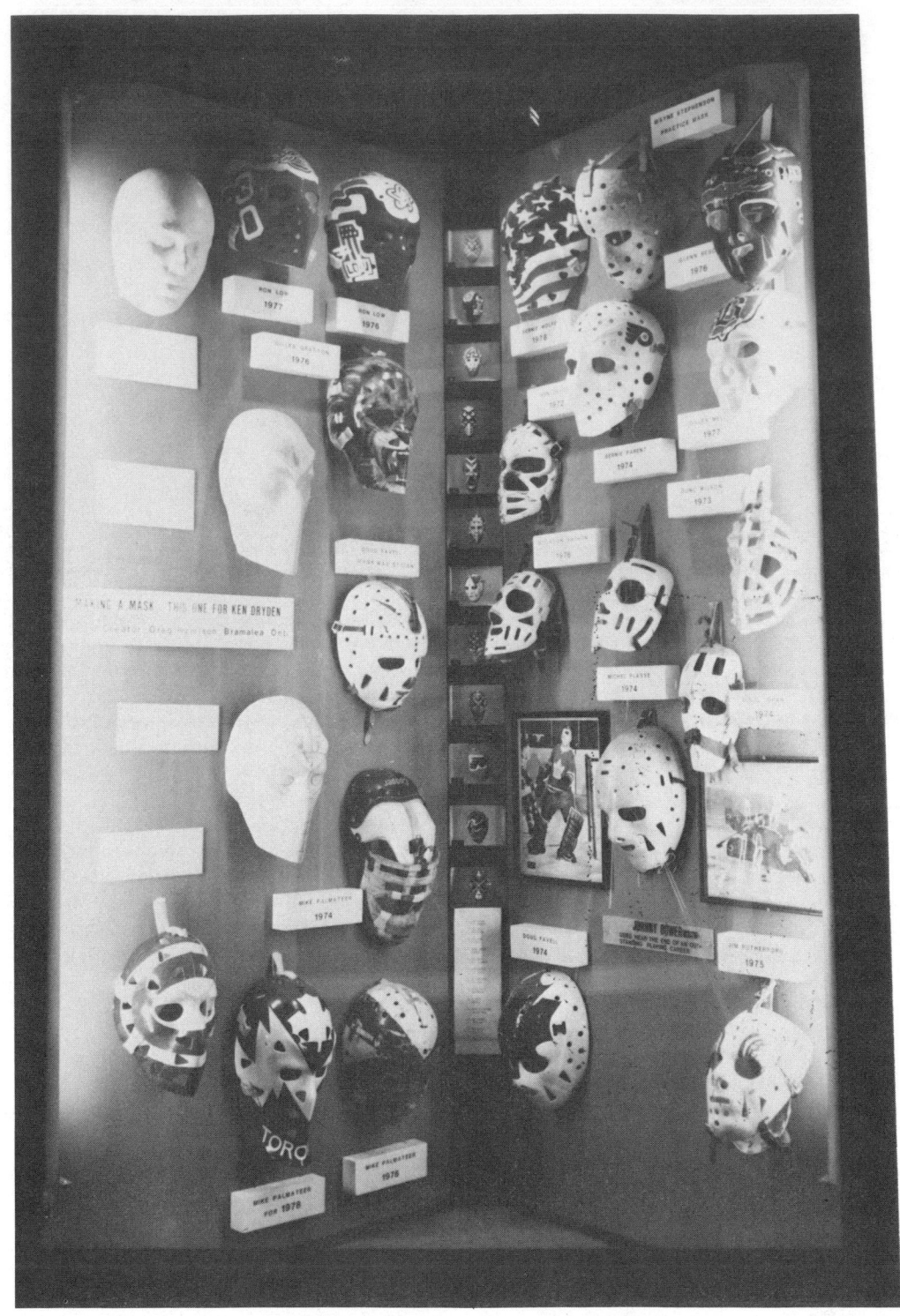

◄ *One exhibit shows the evolution of goalies' masks.*

winner of the Calder Trophy as the Rookie of the Year for 1936–37. Played entire big-league career with Toronto Maple Leafs.

**George Armstrong**: One of the greatest clutch players in Toronto history. When the Leafs won four Stanley Cups in the 1960s, George had 20 goals and 20 assists in the 45 playoff games the team played.

**Irwin W. (Ace) Bailey**: Played only 7½ years in NHL due to fractured skull that ended career. Led league with 22 goals in 44 games in 1928–29 and was one of league's top penalty-killers.

**Donald Bain**: Never played professional hockey. Was a standout center for the Winnipeg Victorias, an outstanding amateur team, in the late 1890s and early 1900s.

**Hobart (Hobey) Baker**: Born in Wissahickon, Pa., he captained Princeton's team to two intercollegiate championships. Later played for St. Nicholas amateur team. Also starred in football.

**Martin A. (Marty) Barry**: A center on the productive Detroit Red Wing line of the mid-1930s which included Larry Aurie and Herbie Lewis. Also played for New York Americans and Boston Bruins.

**Andrew James (Andy) Bathgate**: Averaged nearly a point a game in 17-year career despite playing with badly damaged knee. Starred for New York Rangers in 1950s and 1960s. Was league MVP in 1958–59, when he had 88 points.

**Jean Beliveau**: Scored 507 goals in 18 seasons with Montreal Canadiens as one of the most respected players in hockey history. Played on 10 Stanley Cup championship teams.

**Clint Benedict**: A goalie on five winning Stanley Cup teams, four with Ottawa and one with the Montreal Maroons. Allowed only three goals in a four-game Cup series while with Maroons in 1926–27.

**Douglas Wagner (Doug) Bentley**: Left wing on crack Chicago Black Hawk line with brother Max Bentley and Bill Mosienko. Played for Hawks from 1939 to 1951.

**Maxwell (Max) Bentley**: A clever center and a fine stickhandler for the Chicago Black Hawks and

*Hobey Baker never played pro hockey but made the Hall of Fame due to a brilliant career at Princeton.*

Toronto Maple Leafs. Was voted the NHL's Most Valuable Player in 1945–46.

**Hector (Toe) Blake**: A left wing for the Montreal Maroons and Montreal Canadiens. Was member of great Canadiens' line that included Maurice Richard and Elmer Lach. Later coached Canadiens to eight Stanley Cup crowns.

**Richard (Dickie) Boon**: Played for amateur teams in the Montreal area in the late 1890s and for the Montreal Wanderers in 1904 and 1905.

**Emile (Butch) Bouchard**: A Montreal Canadiens' defenseman for 14 years starting in 1941–42. Named to NHL's first All-Star team three times.

**Frank Boucher**: A center on the famous New York Ranger line that also included the Cook brothers, Bill and Bun. Winner of record seven Lady Byng Trophies. Also was a Ranger coach and general manager.

**George (Buck) Boucher**: An older brother of Frank Boucher, he was a leading defenseman for

*Turk Broda was a champ in the nets and at the dinner table.*

the Ottawa Senators and Montreal Maroons from 1917 to 1929.

**John W. Bower**: Didn't make his mark on a fulltime basis until he was 34, when he became the workhorse goalie as Maple Leafs won four Stanley Cups in the 1960s. Had 37 career shutouts.

**Russell Bowie**: Was a rover for the Montreal Victorias for 10 years in the early 1900s. Had career total of 234 goals.

◄ *Andy Bathgate starred for 17 years in the NHL and averaged nearly a point a game.*

**Frank Brimsek**: A native of Eveleth, Minn., he was nicknamed "Mr. Zero" because he twice had three consecutive shutouts as a goalie for the Boston Bruins. Starred in the late 1930s and early 1940s.

**Harry L. (Punch) Broadbent**: As a forward he played for four Stanley Cup-winning teams, three as a member of the Ottawa Senators and one with the Montreal Maroons.

**Walter (Turk) Broda**: Played goal 16 seasons for the Toronto Maple Leafs. Had reputation for excellence in important games.

**John P. Bucyk**: Played for 23 years in NHL, 21

*Johnny Bucyk played 21 years with the Boston Bruins and helped them win two Stanley Cups.*

of them with the Boston Bruins. Scored 556 goals and helped Bruins win two Stanley Cups (1970, 1972). Two-time Lady Byng winner.

**William (Billy) Burch**: Born in Yonkers, N.Y., in 1900, he became star of New York Americans in the 1920s. Led his team in scoring five times.

**Harold (Hugh) Harry Cameron**: Was famous for rushes up ice while playing defense for the Toronto Arenas and Toronto St. Pats.

**Francis (King) Clancy**: Was outstanding scoring defenseman for the Ottawa Senators and Toronto Maple Leafs. Also was an NHL referee and a coach for the Leafs and Montreal Maroons.

**Aubry (Dit) Clapper**: Played right wing and right defense for the Boston Bruins. Spent 20 years as a player in the NHL and also coached the Bruins for two seasons.

**Sprague Cleghorn**: A defenseman, he played for

Ottawa, Toronto, the Montreal Canadiens and Boston Bruins. Played 18 years as a professional and retired in 1928.

**Neil Colville**: Center on New York Rangers' standout line of late 1930s and 1940s that included brother Mac Colville and Alex Shibicky. Later played as a defenseman for the Rangers.

**William (Bill) Cook**: A big, strong sharpshooter from the right wing position, he played for 12 years with the New York Rangers. One of original Rangers, who came into NHL in 1926.

**Art Coulter**: Prototype defensive defenseman with Black Hawks and Rangers in the 1930s. Scored only 30 goals in 11 NHL seasons but was on three Cup winners.

**Charlie (Chuck) Conacher**: A husky, hard-shooting right wing, he played for 10 years for the Toronto Maple Leafs. Was member of standout line of Conacher-Joe Primeau-Harvey Jackson. Also played for Detroit and New York Americans.

**Alex Connell**: As a goalie for the Ottawa Senators, he once posted a record 446 minutes, six seconds without being scored on. The streak included six consecutive shutouts.

**Yvan Cournoyer**: Blazing speed gave him nickname "The Roadrunner" during 15-year career with Canadiens. Played on ten Stanley Cup winners and scored 25 or more goals 12 straight seasons.

**Bill Cowley**: A clever center, he starred for the Boston Bruins in the late 1930s and early 1940s. Scored 195 goals in 13 NHL seasons.

**Samuel Russell (Rusty) Crawford**: A fast-skating forward, he played amateur and professional hockey from 1906 through 1929. Ottawa Senators and Toronto Arenas were among his teams.

**John Proctor (Jack) Darragh**: A clever stickhandler and a speedy skater from the right wing position, he was also noted for possessing an effective backhand shot. Played mostly for the Ottawa Senators.

**Allan (Scotty) Davidson**: A rugged, powerful defenseman, he starred for Kingston and Toronto before the formation of the NHL. Was shifted to forward toward the end of his career.

**Clarence (Happy) Day**: A sound, steady de-

*Toronto's Happy Day coached the Leafs to five Stanley Cups after his playing days were over.*

fenseman for 10 years with the Toronto Maple Leafs and later with the New York Americans. Was also an NHL referee, coach and general manager of the Maple Leafs.

**Alex Delvecchio**: Red Wings' iron man who missed just 43 games in 22 seasons with club. Scored 456 goals in 1,549 games and won Lady Byng Trophy for clean play three times.

**Cyril (Cy) Denneny**: A relatively slow-skating left wing, but he possessed one of the most accurate shots among players of his era. Played 11 years with Ottawa, starting in 1917, and had one season at Boston.

**Gordon Drillon**: Averaged 22 goals a season when 20-goal scorers were rare. Played six years with Maple Leafs in the 1930s and led team in scoring three straight seasons.

**Charles Graham Drinkwater**: Starred as an amateur player late in the 19th century. Played on championship teams at McGill University in Montreal and for the Montreal Victorias.

**Ken Dryden:** Backbone of six Stanley Cup champions with Montreal in the 1970s. Won Smythe, Calder and Vezina Trophies and recorded miniscule 2.24 goals-against average in 397 NHL games.

**Thomas Dunderdale**: First Australian-born player to achieve Hall of Fame status. Played 12 years in the PCHA and scored more goals than any player in the league.

**William Ronald (Bill) Durnan**: Captured the Vezina Trophy six times, including four in succession, while playing for the Montreal Canadiens. Named five times as NHL's first All-Star team goalie.

**Mervyn (Red) Dutton**: Starred as defenseman for Calgary of the Western Canadian League, then for Montreal Maroons and New York Americans of NHL. Was also coach of Americans and served as league president from 1943 to 1945.

**Cecil (Babe) Dye**: Greatest goal scorer of the 1920s. Playing for the Toronto St. Pats, he scored 163 goals in 149 games over six seasons. Finished career with 200 goals in 255 games.

**Arthur Farrell**: A stylish player, he was with the Montreal Shamrocks when they won the Stanley Cup in 1898–99 and the championship of the Canadian Amateur League.

*Red Dutton, player and coach, served as second president of the NHL.*

**Frank Foyston**: Standout in Western Canadian League from 1916 to 1926 while with Seattle and Victoria, compiling 186 goals. Later, played two years for the Detroit Cougars.

**Frank Fredrickson**: An outstanding amateur player and a star in the Pacific Coast, Western Canadian and National Hockey Leagues. As a center, he played in the NHL for Detroit, Boston and Pittsburgh, also coaching and managing Pittsburgh in 1930–31.

**Bill Gadsby**: Overcame polio to become one of NHL's best defensemen for 20 seasons. Played for Black Hawks, Rangers and Red Wings and was named first-team All-Star three times.

**Charles (Chuck) Gardiner**: A brilliant goalie for the Chicago Black Hawks for seven consecutive seasons starting in 1928. Twice winner of the Vezina Trophy. Also made first All-Star team twice.

**Herbert Martin (Herb) Gardiner**: Turned pro at 31 years of age with Calgary of the Western Canadian League. He joined the Montreal Canadiens four years later and was named the league's Most Valuable Player.

**James Henry (Jimmy) Gardner**: Played for the Montreal Shamrocks, Montreal Wanderers and Montreal Canadiens. Also coached the Hamilton, Ont., team of the NHL in 1924–25.

**Bernie Geoffrion**: Nicknamed "Boom Boom" for the sound his slap shot made as it crashed against the boards. Produced 393 goals in 16 seasons with New York Rangers and Montreal. Coached Rangers for half a season, later coached Atlanta and did short stint at Montreal.

**Eddie Gerard**: As a defenseman and captain, he led the Ottawa Senators to three Stanley Cup titles. Coached the Montreal Maroons in 1926 and was manager of the New York Americans in 1931.

**Rod Gilbert**: Set or equalled 20 team scoring records during brilliant 16-year career with New York Rangers. Totaled 1,021 points in 1,065 games despite playing with a bad back.

**Hamilton Livingstone (Billy) Gilmour**: Played for the Ottawa Silver Seven, winners of three straight Stanley Cup crowns starting in 1902–03.

**Frank (Moose) Goheen**: A defenseman born in White Bear, Minn., he played for St. Paul in the U.S.

*Bernie Geoffrion was nicknamed "Boom Boom" for his hard slap shot.*

*The Rangers' record book is dominated by Rod Gilbert.*

Amateur Association and was a member of the 1920 American Olympic team.

**Ebenezer R. (Ebbie) Goodfellow**: Started out as a center, but was moved to defense by the Detroit Red Wings. Was named the NHL's Most Valuable Player in 1939–40.

**Michael (Mike) Grant**: Joined the Montreal Victorias in 1894 when they won the Stanley Cup. Later organized exhibition games in the United States.

**Wilfred (Shorty) Green**: Was player in senior league in northern Ontario until he turned pro with the Hamilton Tigers of the NHL in 1923. Later played for the New York Americans.

**Silas (Si) Griffis**: A defenseman known for his speed, he turned pro with the Kenora Thistles in 1907 when they defeated the Montreal Wanderers for the Stanley Cup. He was also a defenseman and captain for the Vancouver Millionaires, who won the Stanley Cup in 1915.

**George Hainsworth**: Recorded 22 shutouts dur-ing 44-game NHL schedule while with the Montreal Canadiens in 1928–29. Won Vezina Trophy three straight years and later was traded to Toronto.

**Glenn Hall**: An All-Star goalie for 11 of his 18 years in the NHL. Holds record for most consecutive games by a goaltender (502) and ended career with excellent 2.51 goals-against average.

**Joseph Henry (Joe) Hall**: Noted as a slam-bang defenseman. Played for Kenora Thistles, Montreal Shamrocks, Quebec Bulldogs and Montreal Canadiens, through 1918–19.

**Douglas Norman (Doug) Harvey**: Seven-time winner of the James Norris Trophy as NHL's leading defenseman. Named to All-Star team 11 times in 17 seasons. Played the point on Montreal's awesome power play during the 1950s.

**George Hay**: Was forward in western Canada with Winnipeg, Regina and Portland until he joined the Chicago Black Hawks in 1926. Later played for Detroit Cougars and Red Wings.

**William Milton (Riley) Hern**: Mostly a goalie, but played some as a forward. Starred for the Montreal Wanderers when they won the Stanley Cup in 1907, 1908 and 1910.

**Bryan Hextall**: Scored 20 or more goals in seven of 12 seasons with the Rangers in the 1930s and 1940s. Three-time All-Star who led NHL in scoring in 1941–42 with 56 points.

**Harry (Hap) Holmes**: Starred in five professional leagues over a 15-year goaltending career. Played on four Stanley Cup champions. Memory is perpetuated by trophy carrying his name awarded to leading goalie in American Hockey League each season.

**Charles Thomas (Tom) Hooper**: Played as forward for Kenora Thistles starting in 1901. Was on Kenora team which won Stanley Cup by defeating the Montreal Wanderers in 1907.

**G. Reginald (Red) Horner**: A 6–2, 202-pound defenseman, he was rough and tough, and accumulated 1,254 penalty minutes during 12 years with the Toronto Maple Leafs starting in 1928.

**Miles Gilbert (Tim) Horton**: Inspirational leader of great Maple Leaf teams of the 1960s. Strong defenseman who played 18 years before tragic auto accident claimed his life in 1974.

**Gordie Howe**: Holds all-time records for goals, assists and points. Played for 25 years with Detroit Red Wings and was named to the All-Star team in 21 of those years. Six-time scoring champion and six-time winner of the Hart Trophy as MVP. Made remarkable comeback, playing six more seasons in the WHA, then one more in the NHL before he retired at the age of 52.

**Sydney Harris (Syd) Howe**: A forward, he shares the modern record of six goals in a game made with the Detroit Red Wings in 1944. Spent 16 seasons in the NHL.

**Harry Howell**: Appeared in more games (1,581) than any defenseman in the history of major-league hockey. Had 24-year career in NHL and WHA and was Norris Trophy winner in 1966–67 while with Rangers.

**Robert Marvin (Bobby) Hull**: Left wing who scored over 900 goals in brilliant 23-year career in NHL and WHA. Most dominant scorer of the 1960s, cracking 50-goal barrier five times with Chicago. Career total of 610 NHL goals is third on all-time list.

*Dick Irvin played briefly for Chicago before becoming a successful coach in the NHL.*

**John Bower (Bouse) Hutton**: Goalie for the Ottawa Silver Seven Cup champions of 1903 and 1904. Also was star goalie in lacrosse.

**Harry Hyland**: A right winger, he turned pro with the Montreal Shamrocks in 1908–09. Joined the Montreal Wanderers the next year and remained with them until 1918 when he became member of Ottawa Senators.

**James Dickenson (Dick) Irvin**: Played for Regina and Portland of Western Canadian League and for Chicago Black Hawks of NHL as a forward. Also coached Black Hawks, Toronto and Montreal Canadiens, winning four Stanley Cup titles.

**Harvey (Busher) Jackson**: Gained fame on Toronto's "Kid Line" with Charlie Conacher and Joe Primeau in 1930s. Led Leafs to three NHL titles. Named to five All-Star teams and won scoring title in 1932–33. Finished career with New York Americans and Boston Bruins.

**Ivan (Ching) Johnson**: Was one of the original New York Rangers in 1926–27. A defenseman who relished delivering hard bodychecks, he played in the NHL for 12 years, the last with the New York Americans.

**Ernie (Moose) Johnson**: Played for Montreal Wanderers until 1910 when moved to New Westminster of Pacific Coast League. Was defenseman throughout most of career, but also played forward.

**Thomas Christian Johnson**: Played on six Stanley Cup winners during 15-year career as defenseman for Montreal and Boston in the 1950s and 1960s. Norris Trophy winner in 1958–59.

**Aurel Joliat**: A 140-pound left wing, he played on a line with the great Howie Morenz for the Montreal Canadiens. Was exceptionally fast and clever. Started 16-year career with Canadiens in 1922.

**Gordon (Duke) Keats**: A forward, he was a longtime star in the Western Canadian League, mostly with Edmonton. Later played for Boston, Detroit and Chicago of NHL.

**Leonard (Red) Kelly**: Broke into NHL in 1947 and played 20 seasons as top defenseman for Detroit and center for Toronto. Won Lady Byng Trophy four times and played on eight Stanley Cup winners.

**Theodore (Ted) Kennedy**: As a center, he sparked the Toronto Maple Leafs to five Stanley Cup championships. Was team captain from 1948 until retirement in 1955.

**Elmer James Lach**: Was center on line with Maurice Richard in 1944–45 when the Rocket scored a record 50 goals in 50 games. Played for Montreal Canadiens for 14 years, three times being voted to league's first All-Star team.

**Edouard (Newsy) Lalonde**: Started pro career with Cornwall in 1905 and was one of finest scorers and roughest players of his era. Played with Montreal Canadiens of NHL and with other teams in the National Hockey Association and Pacific Coast Hockey Association.

**Jean Baptiste (Jack) Laviolette**: Played both as a forward and a defenseman for the Montreal Canadiens from 1909 to 1918. He had outstanding speed. Played on a line with Newsy Lalonde.

**Hughie Lehman**: A professional goalie for 19 years. Standout in Pacific Coast Hockey Association for New Westminster and Vancouver. Played for Chicago Black Hawks in 1926–27, their first season in NHL.

**Percy LeSueur**: Goalie for the Ottawa Senators from 1906 to 1913. Played for Toronto in 1914 and later coached Hamilton team of the NHL.

**R. B. Theodore (Ted) Lindsay**: Aggressive, combative, productive left wing for Detroit Red Wings. One of the highest career scorers at his position. Emerged from four-year retirement as player in 1964–65 and helped Wings win league title.

**Harry Lumley**: Signed by Detroit when he was only 16, he became one of NHL's greatest goaltenders in 16-year career. Recorded 71 shutouts in regular season and seven more in playoffs.

**Duncan (Mickey) MacKay**: Played forward for the Vancouver Millionaires from 1914 to 1926. He joined the Chicago Black Hawks in 1926–27 and later played for Pittsburgh and Boston of the NHL.

**Frank Mahovlich**: A star from first season, 1958, when he was Rookie of Year. Played on six Stanley Cup winners with Montreal and Toronto and finished career with 533 goals and 1,103 points.

**Joe Malone**: Scored 44 goals during 22-game schedule in 1917–18, his first NHL season with the Montreal Canadiens. Holds NHL record of seven goals in a Stanley Cup game.

**Sylvio Mantha**: Played defense for the Montreal Canadiens for 13 years, starting in 1923–24. Team finished in first place nine times during that period. Was player-coach for Boston Bruins in 1936.

**Jack Marshall**: Played for the Montreal Wanderers when they won the Stanley Cup in 1906, 1908

and 1910. Was captain of Toronto team which won Cup in 1914.

**Fred G. (Steamer) Maxwell**: A star amateur who never became a professional, his position was that of rover when each team consisted of seven players. Played senior hockey in Winnipeg, starting in 1909. Later became a coach of amateur and professional teams.

**Frank McGee**: A forward for the Ottawa Silver Seven. In a Stanley Cup game against Dawson City in 1905, he scored 14 goals, including eight in succession during a span of eight minutes and 20 seconds.

**William George (Billy) McGimsie**: Was a center for 10 years for the Kenora Thistles. Played in several Stanley Cup series against the Montreal Wanderers and Ottawa Silver Seven, the first in 1903.

**George McNamara**: Helped the Toronto team win the Stanley Cup in 1914 while playing defense. Before that he was with the Montreal Wanderers and with Waterloo of the Trolley League.

**Stanley (Stan) Mikita**: One of the greatest play-making centers in NHL history, he chalked up 926 assists in 22 years with the Chicago Black Hawks. Led league in scoring four times and twice won Hart and Lady Byng Trophies.

**Dickie Moore**: Twice led NHL in scoring despite assortment of serious injuries. Left wing helped Canadiens win six Stanley Cups in his 12 years there, starting in 1951. Scored 608 points in 719 NHL games.

**Patrick Joseph (Paddy) Moran**: A stand-up goalie who used his stick to good advantage, he turned pro with the Quebec Bulldogs in 1902. Played for Haileybury in 1911, but returned to Quebec and helped the Bulldogs win the Stanley Cup in 1912 and 1913.

**Howie Morenz**: A flashy, dynamic center, he starred for 14 years in the NHL, mostly with the Montreal Canadiens. Montreal traded him to Chicago in 1934 and he moved to the New York Rangers in 1935 before returning to the Canadiens for the 1936–37 campaign.

**William (Bill) Mosienko**: Best remembered for scoring three goals in record 21 seconds while playing for Chicago against the New York Rangers on March 23, 1952. Was right wing on line with Bentley brothers, Max and Doug.

**Frank Nighbor**: A center, he played pro hockey

*Boston's Harry Oliver, a 155-pound forward, played 11 seasons in the NHL.*

*Marcel Pronovost patrolled NHL blue lines for 20 years and played on five Stanley Cup winners.*

in leagues in Eastern and Western Canada from 1915 to 1929. Starred for Vancouver Millionaires and Ottawa Senators. Scored 41 goals in 20 games in 1916–17.

**Reginald (Reg) Noble**: Primarily a left wing, but played some defense for Toronto Arenas, Toronto St. Pats, Montreal Maroons and Detroit Cougars. Helped Maroons win Stanley Cup in 1925–26.

**Harold (Harry) Oliver**: Played as a forward for 11 NHL seasons for the Boston Bruins and New York Americans. Weighed only 155 pounds and rarely was penalized. Helped Bruins win two Stanley Cup crowns.

**Bobby Orr**: Six knee operations cut brilliant NHL career to nine years with Boston and Chicago. The only defenseman ever to win a scoring championship (he did it twice), Orr scored 915 points in 657 games. Won Norris Trophy as best defenseman eight consecutive years through 1974–75 season.

**Lester Patrick**: Patriarch of famous hockey family, he was an outstanding player for the Montreal Wanderers and Renfrew Millionaires. He helped form the Pacific Coast Hockey Association and, in 1926, came east to coach and manage the New York Rangers in their first NHL season. Remained with Rangers until 1946.

**Lynn Patrick**: Fearing charges of nepotism, his father, Lester, wouldn't put Lynn on the New York Rangers until another club threatened to claim him. In his decade with the team, Lynn led Rangers in scoring twice and scored 335 points in 455 games.

**Tommy Phillips**: Was a hard-shooting, slick stickhandling forward for the Kenora Thistles. In 1906, he scored seven goals in a two-game Stanley Cup series against the Montreal Wanderers.

**Pierre Pilote**: Defenseman broke in with Chicago in 1956 and did not miss a game his first five seasons. Three-time Norris Trophy winner had 498 points in 890 regular-season games.

**Didier (Pit) Pitre**: Joined the Montreal Canadiens in 1909 and was noted for his blistering shot. A 200-pound forward, he played for the Canadiens until 1923 when he retired.

**Jacques Plante**: The first goalie to popularize the mask, Plante had an outstanding 2.34 goals-against average in 837 games and recorded 82 shutouts. Played on six of Montreal's Stanley Cup champions.

**Walter (Babe) Pratt**: A defenseman, he began pro career with New York Rangers in January 1936,

and was traded to Toronto in November 1942. A standout offensive player for a rearguard.

**A. Joseph (Joe) Primeau**: Center for famous Kid Line that included Charlie Conacher and Harvey Jackson. A clever stickhandler and playmaker and an excellent penalty-killer for the Toronto Maple Leafs.

**Marcel Pronovost**: Twenty-year veteran of NHL play who played integral role on five Stanley Cup winners. Broke in with Detroit in 1950 and played there 15 years before trade to Toronto. Solid defender scored 345 points in 1,206 games.

**Harvey Pulfrod**: Played defense for the Ottawa Silver Seven from 1893 to 1908. Was one of the most effective bodycheckers of his era and had reputation for being a clean player.

**Bill Quackenbush**: The cleanest defenseman in NHL history, he collected only 95 minutes of penalties in 13 seasons. A five-time All-Star with Detroit and Boston, he was Lady Byng winner in 1949.

**Frank Rankin**: Played rover position when each team played with seven men. Starred for teams in Stratford, Ont., and Toronto beginning in 1906–07 season.

**Claude Earl (Chuck) Rayner**: Played 10 seasons in the NHL, all of them in New York. Had 25 career shutouts and was named to All-Star team three times. Named winner of the Hart Trophy as Most Valuable Player in 1949–50, the second goalie to win that award.

**Kenneth (Ken) Reardon**: A rugged, fearless defenseman for the Montreal Canadiens, starting in 1940–41. Voted to the NHL All-Star team four times. Later, was a front-office executive for the Canadiens.

**J. Henri Richard**: Younger brother of Rocket Richard played on 11 Stanley Cup champions in Montreal. Twice led the league in assists and finished with 1,046 points in 1,256 games.

**Maurice (Rocket) Richard**: The famed Montreal

*Henri Richard (left) and Alex Delvecchio were rewarded for brilliant careers with their election to the Hall of Fame.*

Canadiens' right wing, whose 544 career goals stood as the record until broken by Detroit's Gordie Howe. Played 18 NHL seasons before retiring after the 1959–60 campaign. Voted into the Hall of Fame only nine months after retirement in September 1960.

**George Richardson**: Never a professional, but an outstanding amateur from Kingston, Ont. Was with Queen's University team which won the Allan Cup in 1909.

**Gordon Roberts**: Played for Montreal Wanderers while attending McGill University and studying medicine. When he graduated, he moved west to practice but continued playing hockey. Set an all-time scoring record in Pacific Coast Hockey Association with 43 goals in 23 games.

**Arthur Howey (Art) Ross**: Turned pro with the Kenora Thistles in 1906. Also played for Haileybury and the Montreal Wanderers. Later was coach and general manager of the Boston Bruins.

**Blair Russell**: A left-wing amateur star for the Montreal Victorias in the early 1900s. On February 23, 1905, he scored six goals in one game.

**Ernie Russell**: Top scorer for the Montreal Wanderers, for whom he scored 32 goals during a 12-game regular-season schedule in 1910.

**J. D. (Jack) Ruttan**: A leading amateur player starting in 1905–06 with the Armstrong's Point team of Winnipeg. Also played in the Manitoba University League and the Winnipeg Senior League.

**Terry Sawchuk**: Considered one of greatest goalies in history. Played more seasons, more games and had more shutouts than any other netminder. Finished career with 103 shutouts, only goalie ever to reach the century mark.

**Fred Scanlan**: A forward for the Montreal Shamrocks, winners of the Stanley Cup in 1898–99 and 1899–1900. Known for his clever play and accurate shot.

**Milton Conrad (Milt) Schmidt**: A strong skater, smart stickhandler and prolific scorer, he centered Boston's famous Kraut Line that also included Bobby Bauer and Woody Dumart.

**David (Sweeney) Schriner**: A left winger, he starred for the New York Americans and Toronto Maple Leafs. Twice won the NHL's scoring title, in 1935–36 and 1936–37.

**Earl Walter Seibert**: Was noted for his ability as a rushing defenseman for the New York Rangers,

Chicago Black Hawks and Detroit Red Wings. Voted to circuit's first All-Star team four times.

**Oliver Levi Seibert**: Earl Seibert's father. Was member of the Berlin Rangers, winners of the Western Ontario Association title from 1900 to 1906. Was a forward during most of his career.

**Edward (Eddie) Shore**: Generally regarded as the greatest defenseman of all time. Played for the Boston Bruins for 13½ years, then was traded to

*Bullet Joe Simpson was a New York Americans' defenseman and general manager.*

the New York Americans, for whom he played a half season.

**Albert (Babe) Siebert**: Was outstanding left wing for Montreal Maroons. Switched to defense in the mid-1930s and continued to star with the New York Rangers, Boston Bruins and Montreal Canadiens.

**Harold (Bullet Joe) Simpson**: A fast-skating defenseman, he played for teams in Winnipeg and Edmonton before joining the New York Americans in 1925. Was general manager of the Americans from 1932 to 1935.

**Alfred E. (Alf) Smith**: Was captain of the Ottawa Silver Seven in 1903, 1904 and 1905. Also captained the Pittsburgh Athletic Club in 1909, his final year as a player.

**Reginald (Hooley) Smith**: Combined with Nels Stewart and Babe Siebert to form Montreal Maroons' great "S" line in the 1930s. Scored 200 goals in 17 seasons as right wing and part-time defenseman.

**Thomas Smith**: An early star, he played for three Stanley Cup champion teams before formation of National Hockey League. Won three scoring titles and twice scored nine goals in a single game. Also had an eight-goal game, a six-goal game and five times scored five goals in a game.

**Allan Stanley**: Durable defenseman played in 1,244 games over 21-year NHL career. Helped Toronto win four Stanley Cups in early 1960s and played in eight All-Star games.

**Russell (Barney) Stanley**: A forward for the Stanley Cup winning Vancouver Millionaires in the 1914–15 season. Was named general manager-coach of the Chicago Black Hawks in 1927.

**John (Black Jack) Stewart**: A defensive star for the Detroit Red Wings for 10 years starting in 1938–39. Named to the league's first All-Star team three times.

**Nelson (Nels) Stewart**: A forward, he held the career scoring record of 324 goals until it was broken by Maurice Richard. Starred for the Montreal Maroons, Boston Bruins and New York Americans.

**Bruce Stuart**: A center, he played for the Portage Lakes team of Houghton, Mich., in the early 1900s. Later played for the Montreal Wanderers and the Ottawa Silver Seven.

**Hod Stuart**: A brother of Bruce Stuart, he also played in Houghton, Mich., and for the Montreal Wanderers. Was a defenseman.

**Fred (Cyclone) Taylor**: A high-scoring forward for teams in Houghton, Mich., Ottawa, Renfrew and Vancouver. He was a whirlwind on the ice and is reported to have scored a goal once while skating backwards.

**Cecil (Tiny) Thompson**: Was a goalie in the NHL for 12 seasons, 10 for the Boston Bruins and two for the Detroit Red Wings. Twice was voted to the league's first All-Star team.

**Harry Trihey**: Starred for McGill University and as a captain for the Montreal Shamrocks when the latter won two Stanley Cup titles.

**Norm Ullman**: Scored 20 or more goals in 16 of his 20 seasons in NHL. Centering for Detroit and Toronto, he scored a total of 1,229 points. He led the NHL with 42 goals in 1964–65.

**Georges Vezina**: Turned pro as a goalie with the Montreal Canadiens in 1910 and played with them until November 1925. Died of tuberculosis the following year. Trophy for the goalies is awarded annually in his memory.

**John Phillip (Jack) Walker**: Credited with having originated the hook check. Starred mostly on the West Coast for teams in Seattle and Victoria. Also played for Detroit in 1926–27 and 1927–28.

**Martin (Marty) Walsh**: Played for Ottawa in the Eastern Canada Amateur Association, starting in 1908. Was leading scorer of the National Hockey Association for three seasons.

**Harry Watson**: Played all three forward positions on crack amateur teams, including the Toronto Granites. Was with the Granites in 1924 when they represented Canada and won the Olympic title.

**Ralph (Cooney) Weiland**: Played 11 seasons in NHL. Twice a member of Stanley Cup champions, he coached Boston to the Cup in 1940–41. After leaving pros, he launched a successful coaching career at Harvard University.

**Harry Westwick**: Was a rover for the Ottawa Silver Seven when they won three consecutive Stanley Cup titles in the early 1900s.

**Fred Whitcroft**: A prolific scorer, he played for the Kenora Thistles and Peterborough Colts. Later played for Edmonton where he scored 49 goals in 1908.

**Gordon Allan (Phat) Wilson**: Ranked among the all-time great amateur players. Was one of the stars of teams in Port Arthur, Ont., from 1918 to 1933.

**Lorne (Gump) Worsley**: A two-time Vezina Tro-

phy winner and member of four Stanley Cup winners, Worsley had 43 shutouts and a 2.93 goals-against average in 24 seasons. Played for three NHL teams and had greatest success at Montreal in the late 1960s.

**Roy Worters**: Only 5–2 and 130 pounds, Worters starred in the NHL for 12 seasons, mostly with the New York Americans. Compiled fine 2.36 goals-against average in 488 games and won both the Hart and Vezina trophies.

# REFEREES

**John Ashley**: Worked 605 games over 12 NHL seasons and was regarded as league's best when he retired in 1972.

**William L. (Bill) Chadwick**: A native New Yorker, he officiated NHL games for 16 years. Introduced hand signals to explain penalties such as holding and tripping.

**Chaucer Elliott**: Started refereeing in 1903 and worked in the Ontario Hockey Association for 10 seasons.

**Robert W. (Bobby) Hewitson**: An NHL referee for almost 10 years until 1934. Later he became secretary and curator of the Hockey Hall of Fame.

**Fred J. (Mickey) Ion**: Was a leading official in amateur leagues and in the Pacific Coast and National Hockey Leagues until 1943.

**Michael J. (Mike) Rodden**: Refereed 1,187 NHL games and 1,677 in other leagues.

**J. Cooper Smeaton**: Was referee-in-chief of the NHL until 1937. Also officiated in amateur leagues and in the National Hockey Association.

**Roy A. (Red) Storey**: An NHL referee from 1951 until he resigned on April 11, 1959. Worked more than 2,000 games in various circuits.

**Frank Udvari**: Was the eighth referee elected to the Hall of Fame and the first in nine years when he was named in 1973. Officiated through 1966 and has been a supervisor of officials for league ever since.

# BUILDERS

**Charles F. Adams**: Organizer of the Boston Bruins in 1924, first American team in the National Hockey League. Also negotiated for the erection of the Boston Garden.

**Weston W. Adams, Sr.**: Longtime president and chairman of the board of both the Boston Bruins and Boston Garden. Was a goalie at Harvard when his father, Charles F. Adams, was awarded Boston franchise, first NHL franchise in United States.

**Frank Ahearn**: A director, president and owner of the Ottawa Senators. Became president in 1922 and held that position until 1934 when the franchise was transferred to St. Louis.

**J. F. (Bunny) Ahearne**: Served as president of the International Ice Hockey Federation from 1957 through 1975, organizing European, Olympic and other international hockey events.

**Sir Montagu Allan**: A Montreal financier and sportsman, he presented the Allan Cup for competition in 1908. The trophy is emblematic of the Senior Amateur Championship of Canada.

**Harold E. Ballard**: Has spent much of his life building amateur and professional hockey in his native Toronto. Has been principal owner of Maple Leafs since 1962–63 and a respected league figure.

**J. P. Bickell**: First president, and then chairman of the board, of Maple Leaf Gardens. Award named after him is given to outstanding Toronto player each season.

**George V. Brown**: A pioneer of hockey in the United States. Organized the Boston Athletic Association hockey team and was the manager of the Boston Arena and Boston Garden.

**Walter A. Brown**: Was president of the Boston Bruins and general manager of Boston Garden. Also coached the Boston Olympics to five U.S. national titles between 1930 and 1940.

**Frank Buckland**: Coached and organized junior hockey around Toronto for 40 years and served the Ontario Hockey Association as both president and treasurer.

**J. A. (Jack) Butterfield**: Largely credited with keeping minor-league hockey alive when the NHL expanded in 1967. Served as president of the American Hockey League, starting in 1966.

**Frank Calder**: First president of the National Hockey League. Served from 1917 until his death in February 1943. Trophy in his memory is awarded annually to outstanding rookie player.

**Angus Daniel Campbell**: Played an important part in the development of amateur hockey in Cobalt, Ont., area. Was the first president of the Northern Ontario Association, which was formed in 1919.

**Clarence S. Campbell**: President of the National Hockey League from September 1946 through 1976–77. Earlier was an NHL referee.

**Joseph Cattarinich**: One of the original owners of the Canadiens in 1921, he was partly responsible for Montreal's proud NHL heritage.

**Joseph (Leo) Dandurand**: Was among three persons who purchased the Montreal Canadiens in November 1921. He later coached the Canadiens. Was a delegate to the organizing meeting in 1914 of the Canadian Amateur Hockey Association.

**Frank Dilio**: A president and secretary of the Junior Amateur Hockey Association. Later served as registrar and secretary of the Quebec Amateur Hockey Association until 1962.

**George Dudley**: Was president of the Canadian Amateur Hockey Association, the Ontario Hockey Association and the International Ice Hockey Federation. Headed the hockey section of the 1960 Olympic Games.

**Jimmie Dunn**: A leading administrator and executive of junior teams and leagues in Western Canada.

**Emile Francis**: Staunch supporter of amateur hockey in the United States since the 1960s. A former NHL goalie, he turned around sagging franchises in New York and St. Louis as a coach and top executive.

**J. L. (Jack) Gibson**: Organizer of the first hockey league in the world—the International League in 1904–05.

**Thomas Patrick Gorman**: Among the founders of the National Hockey League. Coached or managed seven Stanley Cup-winning teams while with the Montreal Canadiens and Maroons, Ottawa Senators and Chicago Black Hawks.

**Charles Hay**: Oil company executive coordinated negotiations for 1972 series between Canada and Soviet Union. Organized Team Canada that participated in historic eight-game series.

**Jim Hendy**: President of the United States League and later general manager of the Cleveland Barons of the American League. Published the "Hockey Guide," a leading statistical compendium in the early 1930s.

**William Archibald Hewitt**: A secretary of the Ontario Hockey Association and a secretary and registrar for the Canadian Amateur Association. Was a sports editor of the Toronto Star.

**Foster William Hewitt**: A hockey broadcaster for 50 years. Renowned for his exciting descriptions of games involving the Toronto Maple Leafs.

**Fred J. Hume**: A leading amateur hockey executive in Western Canada. Later, helped develop the New Westminster professional team and the Western Hockey League.

**Tommy Ivan**: Coached Red Wings to three Stanley Cup crowns in early 1950s and then moved on to rebuild struggling Chicago franchise. One of game's greatest coaches and executives.

**W. M. (Bill) Jennings**: One of the principal architects of NHL expansion in 1967. Served as president of the New York Rangers and a governor of the league for nearly 20 years.

**Gordon Juckes**: Served the Canadian Amateur Hockey Association in executive positions from 1960 through 1978.

**General John Reed Kilpatrick**: President of the New York Rangers and Madison Square Garden for 22 years. Also served on the Board of Governors of the NHL.

**G. A. (Al) Leader**: President of the Western Hockey League for 25 years until his retirement in 1969.

**Robert LeBel**: Former president of three amateur hockey groups and a life member of both the Quebec and Canadian Amateur Hockey Associations.

**Thomas F. Lockhart**: Organizer and president of the Amateur Hockey Association of the United States and the Eastern Hockey League. Was also a business manager of the New York Rangers.

**Paul Loicq**: A native of Belgium, he was a president of the International Ice Hockey Federation. Credited with having helped influence the Winter Olympic Games Committee to include hockey on the program.

**Major Frederic McLaughlin**: Pioneered professional hockey in Chicago. Was an owner and the first president of the Black Hawks and nicknamed the team in honor of the Black Hawk division he commanded during World War I.

**Sen. Hartland de Montarville Molson**: Former owner of the Montreal Canadiens.

**Francis Nelson**: A vice-president of the Ontario Hockey Association and an OHA Governor to the Amateur Athletic Union of Canada.

**Bruce A. Norris**: Became one of youngest owners in pro sport in 1955 when he took over Detroit Red Wings at age 31. Ran the Detroit franchise until 1982.

**James Norris**: He purchased Detroit's NHL fran-

chise in 1933 and changed the name of the team from the Falcons to the Red Wings. He was also an owner of the Detroit Olympia and Chicago Stadium.

**James D. Norris**: Became a co-owner of the Chicago Black Hawks in 1946 after helping his father, James Norris, with the administrative duties of the Detroit Red Wings.

**William M. Northey**: President of the Montreal Amateur Athletic Association and a managing director of the Montreal Forum. Was the first trustee of the Allan Cup when it was presented for amateur competition.

**John Ambrose O'Brien**: Helped with the formation of the National Hockey Association in December 1909, a five-team league which included the Montreal Canadiens and the Montreal Wanderers.

**Frank Patrick**: With his brother, Lester Patrick, he played for the famed Renfrew Millionaires. The two later organized the Pacific Coast Hockey Association. Frank also coached the Boston Bruins and was a general manager of the Montreal Canadiens.

**Allan W. Pickard**: An executive for several teams and leagues in Western Canada. He was a president of the Saskatchewan Amateur Association and the Canadian Amateur Association.

**Sam Pollock**: Director of personnel for the Canadiens from 1950 through 1964, during which time the team won six Stanley Cups. Assembled Team Canada '76, winners of the Canada Cup.

**Lord Stanley of Preston**: As Governor General of Canada in 1893, he donated the Stanley Cup to the championship hockey club of the Dominion.

**Senator Donat Raymond**: A president of the Montreal Maroons and Montreal Canadiens, he headed the Canadian Arena Company which financed the construction of the Montreal Forum in 1924.

**John Ross Robertson**: A member of the Canadian Parliament, he donated trophies to the winners of the senior, intermediate and junior divisions of the Ontario Hockey Association.

**Claude C. Robinson**: Was the first secretary of the Canadian Amateur Association and managed the Canadian team in the 1932 Olympic Games.

**Philip D. Ross**: Named by Lord Stanley one of the trustees of the Stanley Cup in 1893 and served in that role for 56 years.

**Frank J. Selke**: Worked as coach, manager and front-office executive for almost 60 years. Was with the Toronto Maple Leafs in various capacities before becoming managing director of the Montreal Canadiens in 1946.

**Harry Sinden:** Never played in NHL, but made mark as coach and general manager of Boston Bruins. Coached team to first championship in 29 years in 1970 and was GM of Bruins' Cup-winning team two years later.

**Frank D. Smith**: A founder in 1911 and later secretary-treasurer of the Beaches Hockey League, which became the Toronto Hockey League.

**Conn Smythe**: Long-time, fiery president of the Toronto Maple Leafs. Was instrumental in the building of Maple Leaf Gardens, which was opened in November 1931.

**Captain James T. Sutherland**: An organizer of teams and leagues in the Kingston, Ont., area, he coached the Kingston Junior team and served as president of the Ontario Hockey Association and the Canadian Amateur Hockey Association.

**Anatoli V. Tarasov**: Generally regarded as the architect of hockey in the Soviet Union. Coached Soviets to nine amateur titles and three Olympic gold medals before retiring in 1972.

**Lloyd Turner**: Helped organize the Western Canadian League in 1918. Coached and managed the Fort William, Ont., team and was a founder of teams and leagues in Calgary, Alta.

**W. Thayer Tutt**: Instrumental in the progress of amateur hockey in the United States. Helped start NCAA tournament and later served as International Ice Hockey Federation president.

**Carl P. Voss**: Named first referee-in-chief of NHL in 1950 and made enormous contributions in the scouting of referees and linesmen.

**Fred Waghorne**: A native of England, he was among the founders of the Toronto Hockey League. As a referee, he was responsible for introducing a whistle for stopping play during a game. A bell had been used previously.

**Arthur M. Wirtz**: Got into the hockey business in 1931 when, in partnership with James Norris, he bought Detroit Red Wings. Switched holdings to native Chicago in 1954, where he rebuilt Black Hawks into one of NHL's most prosperous franchises.

**William Wirtz**: Joined Chicago Black Hawks in 1952 and served two terms as chairman of the NHL Board of Governors. Helped formulate expansion plans and was largely responsible for their success.

# THE UNITED STATES
# HOCKEY HALL OF FAME

The United States Hockey Hall of Fame is located in Eveleth, Minnesota, which bills itself as "The Hockey Capital of the U.S.A." This midwestern mining community has sent more than a dozen players to the National Hockey League and one of its natives, Mark Pavelich, starred on the 1980 U.S. gold-medal Olympic hockey team.

The Hall, whose director is Roger Godin, has been open to the public since 1973. It honors notable American players and their feats, and it tributes the sport's innovators. Its "Evolution of Hockey Time Tunnel" traces the evolution of hockey and the exhibits reflect every level of hockey—youth, college, international, professional.

A nine-man committee selects the new enshrinees each year.

The members:

## PLAYERS

*Abel, Clarence (Taffy)
*Baker, Hobart (Hobey)
Bartholome, Earl
Bessone, Peter
Brimsek, Frank (Mr. Zero)
Chaisson, Ray
Chase, John P.
Cleary, William (Bill)
Cleary, Robert (Bob)
*Conroy, Anthony
Dahlstrom, Carl (Cully)
DesJardins, Victor
Dill, Bob
Everett, Doug

Garrison, John B.
Goheen, Frank (Moose)
Harding, Austin
Inglehart, Stewart
Johnson, Virgil
Karakas, Mike
Lane, Myles J.
Linder, Joseph
LoPresti, Sam
Mariucci, John
Mayasich, John
Moe, William
Moseley, Fred
Nelson, Hubert (Hub)
Olsen, Eddie
Owen, George Jr.
*Palmer, Winthrop (Ding)
Purpur, Clifford (Fido)
Riley, William (Bill)
Romnes, Elwin (Doc)
Williams, Tommy
*Winters, Frank (Caddy)

## COACHES

*Gordon, Malcolm
Heylinger, Victor
*Jeremiah, Edward J.
Kelly, John (Snooks)
Riley, Jack
*Stewart, Bill
*Thompson, Clifford
*Winsor, Alfred (Ralph)

## REFEREE

Chadwick, William (Bill)

## ADMINISTRATORS

*Brown, George V.
*Brown, Walter A.
Bush, Walter Jr.
Clark, Donald M.
*Gibson, J. C. (Doc)
*Jennings, William
Kahler, F. W. (Nick)
Lockhart, Thomas F.
Marvin, Calvin
Ridder, Robert
Tutt, WilliamT.
*Wright, Lyle Z.

*Deceased

# NHL RECORDS

## INDIVIDUAL

**Most seasons played**—26, Gordie Howe, Detroit, 1946–47 through 1970–71; Hartford, 1979–80.

**Most games played**—1,767, Gordie Howe, Detroit, Hartford.

**Most goals**—801, Gordie Howe, Detroit, Hartford.

**Most assists**—1,049, Gordie Howe, Detroit, Hartford.

**Most points**—1,850, Gordie Howe, Detroit, Hartford.

**Most penalty minutes**—2,700, Dave Williams, Toronto, Vancouver, 1974–75 to 1982–83.

**Most consecutive games played**—914, Garry Unger, Toronto, Detroit, St. Louis, Atlanta, from Feb. 24, 1968, through Dec. 21, 1979.

**Most consecutive games played, goalie**—502, Glenn Hall, Detroit, Chicago, start of 1955–56 season through first 12 games of 1962–63.

**Most career shutouts, goalie**—103, Terry Sawchuk, Detroit, Boston, Toronto, Los Angeles, New York, 1949–50 through 1969–70.

**Most times scoring three or more goals, game**—32, Phil Esposito, Chicago, Boston, N.Y. Rangers, 1963–64 through 1980–81. (27 three-goal games, 5 four-goal games).

**Most goals, season**—92, Wayne Gretzky, Edmonton, 1981–82.

◀ *Peter Stastny set a record with 109 points in his rookie season.*

**Most assists, season**—125, Wayne Gretzky, Edmonton, 1982–83.

**Most points, season**—212, Wayne Gretzky, Edmonton, 1981–82.

**Most goals, season, by a defenseman**—46, Bobby Orr, Boston, 1974–75.

**Most assists, season, by a defenseman**—102, Bobby Orr, Boston, 1970–71.

**Most points, season, by a defenseman**—139, Bobby Orr, Boston, 1970–71.

**Most power-play goals, season**—28, Phil Esposito, 1971–72 and Mike Bossy, N.Y. Islanders, 1980–81.

**Most shorthanded goals, season**—10, Marcel Dionne, Detroit, 1974–75.

**Most goals, season, rookie**—53, Mike Bossy, New York Islanders, 1977–78.

**Most assists, season, rookie**—70, Peter Stastny, Quebec, 1980–81.

**Most points, season, rookie**—109, Peter Stastny, Quebec, 1980–81.

**Most penalty minutes, season**—472, Dave Schultz, Philadelphia, 1974–75.

**Most shutouts, season, goalie**—22, George Hainsworth, Montreal, 1928–29; modern record: 15, Tony Esposito, Chicago, 1969–70.

**Longest consecutive shutout streak, minutes, by goalie**—461 minutes, 29 seconds, Alex Connell, Ottawa, 1927–28; modern record: 309 minutes, 21 seconds, Bill Durnan, Montreal, 1948–49.

**Longest consecutive goal-scoring streak**—16 games,

Punch Broadbent, Ottawa, 1921–22; modern record: 13, Charlie Simmer, Los Angeles, 1979–80.

**Most goals, game**—7, Joe Malone, Quebec, Jan. 31, 1920; modern record: 6, Syd Howe, Detroit, Feb. 3, 1944; Red Berenson, St. Louis, Nov. 7, 1968; Darryl Sittler, Toronto, Feb. 7, 1976.

**Most assists, game**—7, Billy Taylor, Detroit, March 16, 1947; Wayne Gretzky, Edmonton, Feb. 15, 1980.

**Most points, game**—10, Darryl Sittler, Toronto, Feb. 7, 1976.

**Most penalties, game**—9, Jim Dorey, Toronto, Oct. 16, 1968; Dave Schultz, Pittsburgh, Apr. 6, 1978; Randy Holt, Los Angeles, March 11, 1979; Russ Anderson, Pittsburgh, Jan. 19, 1980; Kim Clackson, Quebec, Mar. 8, 1981.

**Most penalty minutes, game**—67, Randy Holt, Los Angeles, March 11, 1979 (1 minor, 3 majors, 2 misconducts, 3 game misconducts).

**Most goals, game, defenseman**—5, Ian Turnbull, Toronto, Feb. 2, 1977.

**Most assists, game, defenseman**—6, Babe Pratt, Toronto, Jan. 8, 1944; Pat Stapleton, Chicago, March 30, 1969; Bobby Orr, Boston, Jan. 1, 1973; Ron Stackhouse, Pittsburgh, March 8, 1975.

**Most points, game, defenseman**—8, Tom Bladon, Philadelphia, Dec. 11, 1977.

**Most goals, period**—4, seven players, most recently Bryan Trottier, N.Y. Islanders, Feb. 13, 1982.

**Most assists, period**—4, twenty players, most recently Wayne Gretzky, Edmonton, Feb. 4, 1983.

**Most points, period**—6, Bryan Trottier, New York Islanders, Dec. 23, 1978.

**Fastest goal, first NHL game**—15 seconds, Gus Bodnar, Toronto, Oct. 30, 1943.

**Fastest goal, start of game**—5 seconds, Doug Smail, Winnipeg, Dec. 20, 1981.

**Fastest two goals**—4 seconds, Nels Stewart, Montreal Maroons, Jan. 3, 1931.

**Fastest three goals**—21 seconds, Bill Mosienko, Chicago, March 23, 1952.

# TEAM

**Most points, season**—132, Montreal Canadiens, 1976–77.

**Fewest points, season**—12, Philadelphia Quakers, 1930–31; modern: 21, Washington Capitals, 1974–75.

**Most victories, season**—60, Montreal Canadiens, 1976–77.

**Fewest victories, season**—4, Philadelphia Quakers, 1930–31; modern: 8, Washington Capitals, 1974–75.

**Most losses, season**—67, Washington Capitals, 1974–75.

**Most ties, season**—24, Philadelphia Flyers, 1969–70.

**Longest winning streak**—15 games, New York Islanders, Jan. 21, 1982 through Feb. 20, 1982.

**Longest unbeaten streak**—35 games, Philadelphia Flyers, Oct. 14, 1979, through Jan. 6, 1980 (25 wins, 10 ties).

**Longest consecutive-game winning streak, home**—20 games, Boston Bruins, Dec. 3, 1929 through March 18, 1930; Philadelphia Flyers, Jan. 4, 1976 through April 3, 1976.

**Longest unbeaten streak, home**—34 games, Montreal Canadiens, Nov. 1, 1976 through Apr. 2, 1977.

**Longest unbeaten streak, road**—23 games, Montreal Canadiens, Nov. 27, 1974 through March 12, 1975.

**Longest losing streak**—17 games, Washington Capitals, Feb. 18, 1975 through March 26, 1975.

**Longest consecutive-game winless streak**—30 games, Winnipeg Jets, Oct. 19, 1980 through Dec. 28, 1980.

**Longest non-shutout streak**—230 games, Quebec Nordiques, Feb. 9, 1980 through Jan. 12, 1983.

**Most consecutive shutout losses**—8, Chicago Black Hawks, 1928–29.

**Most shutouts, season**—22, Montreal Canadiens, 1928–29; modern: 15, Chicago Black Hawks, 1969–70.

**Most goals, season**—424, Edmonton Oilers, 1982–83.

**Fewest goals, season**—33, Chicago Black Hawks, 1928–29; modern: 133, Chicago Black Hawks, 1953–54.

**Most goals against, season**—446, Washington Capitals, 1974–75.

**Fewest goals against, season**—42, Ottawa Senators, 1925–26; modern: 131, Toronto Maple Leafs, 1953–54 and Montreal Canadiens, 1955–56.

**Most assists, season**—706, Edmonton Oilers, 1981–82.

**Most scoring points, one season**—1,123, Edmonton Oilers, 1981–82.

**Fewest assists, season**—45, New York Rangers, 1926–27; modern: 206, Chicago Black Hawks, 1953–54.

**Most power-play goals, season**—99, Pittsburgh Penguins, 1981–82.

**Most shorthanded goals, season**—25, Boston Bruins, 1970–71.

**Most power-play goals against, season**—110, Pittsburgh Penguins, 1982–83.

**Most shorthanded goals against, season**—20, Minnesota North Stars, 1982–83.

**Most penalty minutes, season**—2,621, Philadelphia Flyers, 1980–81.

**Most goals, one team, game**—16, Montreal Canadiens, March 3, 1920.

**Most goals, two teams, game**—21, Montreal Canadiens 14, Toronto St. Pats 7, Jan. 10, 1920; modern: 19, Boston Bruins 10, New York Rangers 9, March 4, 1944 and Detroit Red Wings 10, Boston Bruins 9, March 16, 1944.

**Most consecutive goals, one team, game**—15, Detroit Red Wings, Jan. 23, 1944, vs. N.Y. Rangers.

**Most points, one team, game**—40, Buffalo Sabres, Dec. 21, 1975, vs. Washington Capitals.

**Most points, both teams, game**—53, Quebec Nordiques 33, Washington Capitals 20, Feb. 22, 1981.

**Most shots on goal, one team, game**—83, Boston Bruins, March 4, 1941, vs. Chicago Black Hawks (Sam LoPresti, goalie).

**Most shots on goal, both teams, game**—141, New York Americans 73, Pittsburgh Pirates 68, Dec. 26, 1925.

**Most penalties and penalty minutes, both teams, game**—84 penalties, 406 minutes, Minnesota North Stars at Boston Bruins, Feb. 26, 1981.

**Most goals, one team, period**—9, Buffalo Sabres, March 19, 1981, vs. Toronto Maple Leafs.

**Most points, one team, period**—23, New York Rangers, Nov. 21, 1971, vs. California Seals; Buffalo Sabres, Dec. 21, 1975, vs. Washington Capitals; Buffalo Sabres, March 19, 1981, vs. Toronto Maple Leafs.

**Most shots on goal, one team, period**—37, Boston Bruins, March 4, 1941, vs. Chicago Black Hawks.

**Most penalties, both teams, period**—67, Minnesota North Stars (34) at Boston Bruins (33), Feb. 26, 1981.

**Most penalty minutes, both teams, period**—372, Los Angeles Kings (184) at Philadelphia Flyers (188), March 11, 1979.

**Most penalty minutes, one team, period**—188, Philadelphia Flyers, March 11, 1979, vs. Los Angeles Kings.

**Fastest scoring, both teams**—8 goals; 4 minutes and 52 seconds, March 19, 1938, Toronto 5 goals, New York Americans 3.

**Fastest five goals, one team**—2 minutes and 7 seconds, Pittsburgh Penguins, Nov. 22, 1972.

**Fastest four goals, one team**—1 minute and 20 seconds, Boston Bruins, Jan. 21, 1945.

**Fastest three goals, one team**—20 seconds, Boston Bruins, Feb. 5, 1971.

**Fastest two goals, one team**—4 seconds, Montreal Maroons, Jan. 3, 1931; Buffalo Sabres, Oct. 17, 1974.

# THE TROPHIES

## HART MEMORIAL TROPHY

Awarded to the league's Most Valuable Player. Se-
lected in a vote of hockey writers and broadcasters.
The award was presented by the National Hockey
League in 1960 after the original Hart Trophy was
retired to the Hockey Hall of Fame. The original Hart
Trophy was donated in 1923 by Dr. David A. Hart,
father of Cecil Hart, former manager-coach of the
Montreal Canadiens.

| | |
|---|---|
| 1923–24 | Frank Nighbor, Ottawa |
| 1924–25 | Billy Burch, Hamilton |
| 1925–26 | Nels Stewart, Montreal M. |
| 1926–27 | Herb Gardiner, Montreal C. |
| 1927–28 | Howie Morenz, Montreal C. |
| 1928–29 | Roy Worters, New York A. |
| 1929–30 | Nels Stewart, Montreal M. |
| 1930–31 | Howie Morenz, Montreal C. |
| 1931–32 | Howie Morenz, Montreal C. |
| 1932–33 | Eddie Shore, Boston |
| 1933–34 | Aurel Joliat, Montreal C. |
| 1934–35 | Eddie Shore, Boston |
| 1935–36 | Eddie Shore, Boston |
| 1936–37 | Babe Siebert, Montreal C. |
| 1937–38 | Eddie Shore, Boston |
| 1938–39 | Toe Blake, Montreal C. |
| 1939–40 | Ebbie Goodfellow, Detroit |
| 1940–41 | Bill Cowley, Boston |
| 1941–42 | Tommy Anderson, New York A. |
| 1942–43 | Bill Cowley, Boston |
| 1943–44 | Babe Pratt, Toronto |
| 1944–45 | Elmer Lach, Montreal C. |
| 1945–46 | Max Bentley, Chicago |
| 1946–47 | Maurice Richard, Montreal |
| 1947–48 | Buddy O'Connor, New York |
| 1948–49 | Sid Abel, Detroit |
| 1949–50 | Charlie Rayner, New York |
| 1950–51 | Milt Schmidt, Boston |
| 1951–52 | Gordie Howe, Detroit |
| 1952–53 | Gordie Howe, Detroit |
| 1953–54 | Al Rollins, Chicago |
| 1954–55 | Ted Kennedy, Toronto |
| 1955–56 | Jean Beliveau, Montreal |
| 1956–57 | Gordie Howe, Detroit |
| 1957–58 | Gordie Howe, Detroit |
| 1958–59 | Andy Bathgate, New York |
| 1959–60 | Gordie Howe, Detroit |
| 1960–61 | Bernie Geoffrion, Montreal |
| 1961–62 | Jacques Plante, Montreal |
| 1962–63 | Gordie Howe, Detroit |
| 1963–64 | Jean Beliveau, Montreal |
| 1964–65 | Bobby Hull, Chicago |
| 1965–66 | Bobby Hull, Chicago |
| 1966–67 | Stan Mikita, Chicago |
| 1967–68 | Stan Mikita, Chicago |
| 1968–69 | Phil Esposito, Boston |
| 1969–70 | Bobby Orr, Boston |
| 1970–71 | Bobby Orr, Boston |
| 1971–72 | Bobby Orr, Boston |
| 1972–73 | Bobby Clarke, Philadelphia |
| 1973–74 | Phil Esposito, Boston |
| 1974–75 | Bobby Clarke, Philadelphia |
| 1975–76 | Bobby Clarke, Philadelphia |
| 1976–77 | Guy Lafleur, Montreal |
| 1977–78 | Guy Lafleur, Montreal |
| 1978–79 | Bryan Trottier, New York I. |
| 1979–80 | Wayne Gretzky, Edmonton |
| 1980–81 | Wayne Gretzky, Edmonton |
| 1981–82 | Wayne Gretzky, Edmonton |
| 1982–83 | Wayne Gretzky, Edmonton |

# ART ROSS TROPHY

Awarded to the player who compiles the highest number of scoring points during the regular season.

If players are tied for the lead, the trophy is awarded to the one with the most goals. If still tied, it is given to the player with the fewer number of games played. If these do not break the deadlock, the trophy is presented to the player who scored his first goal of the season at the earliest date.

The trophy was presented by Art Ross, the former manager-coach of the Boston Bruins, to the NHL in 1947.

| Season | Player and Clubs | Games Played | Goals | Assists | Points |
|---|---|---|---|---|---|
| 1917–18 | Joe Malone, Mtl. Canadiens | 20 | 44 | — | 44 |
| 1918–19 | Newsy Lalonde, Mtl. Canadiens | 17 | 23 | 9 | 32 |
| 1919–20 | Joe Malone, Quebec | 24 | 39 | 9 | 48 |
| 1920–21 | Newsy Lalonde, Mtl. Canadiens | 24 | 33 | 8 | 41 |
| 1921–22 | Punch Broadbent, Ottawa | 24 | 32 | 14 | 46 |
| 1922–23 | Babe Dye, Toronto | 22 | 26 | 11 | 37 |
| 1923–24 | Cy Denneny, Ottawa | 21 | 22 | 1 | 23 |
| 1924–25 | Babe Dye, Toronto | 29 | 38 | 6 | 44 |
| 1925–26 | Nels Stewart, Montreal | 36 | 34 | 8 | 42 |
| 1926–27 | Bill Cook, N.Y. Rangers | 44 | 33 | 4 | 37 |
| 1927–28 | Howie Morenz, Mtl. Canadiens | 43 | 33 | 18 | 51 |
| 1928–29 | Ace Bailey, Toronto | 44 | 22 | 10 | 32 |
| 1929–30 | Cooney Weiland, Boston | 44 | 43 | 30 | 73 |
| 1930–31 | Howie Morenz, Mtl. Canadiens | 39 | 28 | 23 | 51 |
| 1931–32 | Harvey Jackson, Toronto | 48 | 28 | 25 | 53 |
| 1932–33 | Bill Cook, N.Y. Rangers | 48 | 28 | 22 | 50 |
| 1933–34 | Charlie Conacher, Toronto | 42 | 32 | 20 | 52 |
| 1934–35 | Charlie Conacher, Toronto | 48 | 36 | 21 | 57 |
| 1935–36 | Dave Schriner, N.Y. Americans | 48 | 19 | 26 | 45 |
| 1936–37 | Dave Schriner, N.Y. Americans | 48 | 21 | 25 | 46 |
| 1937–38 | Gordie Drillon, Toronto | 48 | 26 | 26 | 52 |
| 1938–39 | Toe Blake, Mtl. Canadiens | 48 | 24 | 23 | 47 |
| 1939–40 | Milt Schmidt, Boston | 48 | 22 | 30 | 52 |
| 1940–41 | Bill Cowley, Boston | 46 | 17 | 45 | 62 |
| 1941–42 | Bryan Hextall, N.Y. Rangers | 48 | 24 | 32 | 56 |
| 1942–43 | Doug Bentley, Chicago | 50 | 33 | 40 | 73 |
| 1943–44 | Herbie Cain, Boston | 48 | 36 | 46 | 82 |
| 1944–45 | Elmer Lach, Montreal | 50 | 26 | 54 | 80 |
| 1945–46 | Max Bentley, Chicago | 47 | 31 | 30 | 61 |
| 1946–47 | Max Bentley, Chicago | 60 | 29 | 43 | 72 |
| 1947–48 | Elmer Lach, Montreal | 60 | 30 | 31 | 61 |
| 1948–49 | Roy Conacher, Chicago | 60 | 26 | 42 | 68 |
| 1949–50 | Ted Lindsay, Detroit | 69 | 23 | 55 | 78 |
| 1950–51 | Gordie Howe, Detroit | 70 | 43 | 43 | 86 |
| 1951–52 | Gordie Howe, Detroit | 70 | 47 | 39 | 86 |
| 1952–53 | Gordie Howe, Detroit | 70 | 49 | 46 | 95 |
| 1953–54 | Gordie Howe, Detroit | 70 | 33 | 48 | 81 |
| 1954–55 | Bernie Geoffrion, Montreal | 70 | 38 | 37 | 75 |
| 1955–56 | Jean Beliveau, Montreal | 70 | 47 | 41 | 88 |
| 1956–57 | Gordie Howe, Detroit | 70 | 44 | 45 | 89 |
| 1957–58 | Dickie Moore, Montreal | 70 | 36 | 48 | 84 |
| 1958–59 | Dickie Moore, Montreal | 70 | 41 | 55 | 96 |
| 1959–60 | Bobby Hull, Chicago | 70 | 39 | 42 | 81 |
| 1960–61 | Bernie Geoffrion, Montreal | 64 | 50 | 45 | 95 |
| 1961–62 | Bobby Hull, Chicago | 70 | 50 | 34 | 84 |
| 1962–63 | Gordie Howe, Detroit | 70 | 38 | 48 | 86 |
| 1963–64 | Stan Mikita, Chicago | 70 | 39 | 50 | 89 |
| 1964–65 | Stan Mikita, Chicago | 70 | 28 | 59 | 87 |
| 1965–66 | Bobby Hull, Chicago | 65 | 54 | 43 | 97 |
| 1966–67 | Stan Mikita, Chicago | 70 | 35 | 62 | 97 |
| 1967–68 | Stan Mikita, Chicago | 72 | 40 | 47 | 87 |
| 1968–69 | Phil Esposito, Boston | 74 | 49 | 77 | 126 |
| 1969–70 | Bobby Orr, Boston | 76 | 33 | 87 | 120 |
| 1970–71 | Phil Esposito, Boston | 78 | 76 | 76 | 152 |
| 1971–72 | Phil Esposito, Boston | 76 | 66 | 67 | 133 |
| 1972–73 | Phil Esposito, Boston | 78 | 55 | 75 | 130 |
| 1973–74 | Phil Esposito, Boston | 78 | 68 | 77 | 145 |
| 1974–75 | Bobby Orr, Boston | 80 | 46 | 89 | 135 |
| 1975–76 | Guy Lafleur, Montreal | 80 | 56 | 69 | 125 |
| 1976–77 | Guy Lafleur, Montreal | 80 | 56 | 80 | 136 |
| 1977–78 | Guy Lafleur, Montreal | 78 | 60 | 72 | 132 |
| 1978–79 | Bryan Trottier, New York I. | 76 | 47 | 87 | 134 |
| 1979–80 | Marcel Dionne, Los Angeles | 80 | 53 | 84 | 137 |
| 1980–81 | Wayne Gretzky, Edmonton | 80 | 55 | 109 | 164 |
| 1981–82 | Wayne Gretzky, Edmonton | 80 | 92 | 120 | 212 |
| 1982–83 | Wayne Gretzky, Edmonton | 80 | 71 | 125 | 196 |

# VEZINA TROPHY

Awarded to the goalie voted most valuable by the hockey writers and broadcasters. Up until the 1981–82 season, the trophy was awarded to the goalie or goalies for the team which gives up the fewest goals during the regular season.

The trophy was presented to the NHL in 1926–27 by the owners of the Montreal Canadiens in memory of Georges Vezina, former Canadien goalie.

| | |
|---|---|
| 1926–27 | George Hainsworth, Montreal C. |
| 1927–28 | George Hainsworth, Montreal C. |
| 1928–29 | George Hainsworth, Montreal C. |
| 1929–30 | Tiny Thompson, Boston |
| 1930–31 | Roy Worters, New York A. |
| 1931–32 | Charlie Gardiner, Chicago |
| 1932–33 | Tiny Thompson, Boston |

| | |
|---|---|
| 1933–34 | Charlie Gardiner, Chicago |
| 1934–35 | Lorne Chabot, Chicago |
| 1935–36 | Tiny Thompson, Boston |
| 1936–37 | Normie Smith, Detroit |
| 1937–38 | Tiny Thompson, Boston |
| 1938–39 | Frank Brimsek, Boston |
| 1939–40 | Davey Kerr, New York |
| 1940–41 | Turk Broda, Toronto |
| 1941–42 | Frank Brimsek, Boston |
| 1942–43 | Johnny Mowers, Detroit |
| 1943–44 | Bill Durnan, Montreal |
| 1944–45 | Bill Durnan, Montreal |
| 1945–46 | Bill Durnan, Montreal |
| 1946–47 | Bill Durnan, Montreal |
| 1947–48 | Turk Broda, Toronto |
| 1948–49 | Bill Durnan, Montreal |
| 1949–50 | Bill Durnan, Montreal |
| 1950–51 | Al Rollins, Toronto |
| 1951–52 | Terry Sawchuk, Detroit |
| 1952–53 | Terry Sawchuk, Detroit |
| 1953–54 | Harry Lumley, Toronto |
| 1954–55 | Terry Sawchuk, Detroit |
| 1955–56 | Jacques Plante, Montreal |
| 1956–57 | Jacques Plante, Montreal |
| 1957–58 | Jacques Plante, Montreal |
| 1958–59 | Jacques Plante, Montreal |
| 1959–60 | Jacques Plante, Montreal |
| 1960–61 | Johnny Bower, Toronto |
| 1961–62 | Jacques Plante, Montreal |
| 1962–63 | Glenn Hall, Chicago |
| 1963–64 | Charlie Hodge, Montreal |
| 1964–65 | Terry Sawchuk, Toronto |
| | Johnny Bower, Toronto |
| 1965–66 | Lorne Worsley, Montreal |
| | Charlie Hodge, Montreal |
| 1966–67 | Glenn Hall, Chicago |
| | Denis DeJordy, Chicago |
| 1967–68 | Lorne Worsley, Montreal |
| | Rogatien Vachon, Montreal |
| 1968–69 | Glenn Hall, St. Louis |
| | Jacques Plante, St. Louis |
| 1969–70 | Tony Esposito, Chicago |
| 1970–71 | Ed Giacomin, New York |
| | Gilles Villemure, New York |
| 1971–72 | Tony Esposito, Chicago |
| | Gary Smith, Chicago |
| 1972–73 | Ken Dryden, Montreal |
| 1973–74 | Bernie Parent, Philadelphia |
| | Tony Esposito, Chicago |
| 1974–75 | Bernie Parent, Philadelphia |
| 1975–76 | Ken Dryden, Montreal |
| 1976–77 | Ken Dryden, Montreal |
| | Michel Larocque, Montreal |
| 1977–78 | Ken Dryden, Montreal |
| | Michel Larocque, Montreal |
| 1978–79 | Ken Dryden, Montreal |
| | Michel Larocque, Montreal |
| 1979–80 | Bob Sauve, Buffalo |
| | Don Edwards, Buffalo |
| 1980–81 | Richard Sevigny, Montreal |
| | Denis Herron, Montreal |
| | Michel Larocque, Montreal |
| 1981–82 | Bill Smith, New York I. |
| 1982–83 | Pete Peeters, Boston |

# WILLIAM M. JENNINGS AWARD

Awarded to the goalie or goalies on the team which gives up the fewest goals during the regular season. To be eligible, a goalie must play at least 25 games.

The trophy was presented to the NHL in 1982 in memory of William M. Jennings, an architect of the league's expansion from six teams to the present 21.

| 1981–82 | Denis Herron, Montreal |
| | Rick Wamsley, Montreal |
| 1982–83 | Billy Smith, New York I. |
| | Roland Melanson, New York I. |

# FRANK J. SELKE TROPHY

Awarded to the forward "who best excels in the defensive aspects of the game." Selection is by the hockey writers and broadcasters.

The trophy was presented to the NHL in 1977 in honor of Frank J. Selke, who spent more than 60 years in the game as coach, manager and front-office executive.

| 1977–78 | Bob Gainey, Montreal |
| 1978–79 | Bob Gainey, Montreal |
| 1979–80 | Bob Gainey, Montreal |
| 1980–81 | Bob Gainey, Montreal |
| 1981–82 | Steve Kasper, Boston |
| 1982–83 | Bobby Clarke, Philadelphia |

# JAMES NORRIS MEMORIAL TROPHY

Awarded to the league's best defenseman. Selected by a vote of hockey writers and broadcasters.

It was presented in 1953 by the four children of the late James Norris Sr., in memory of the former owner-president of the Detroit Red Wings.

| | |
|---|---|
| 1953–54 | Red Kelly, Detroit |
| 1954–55 | Doug Harvey, Montreal |
| 1955–56 | Doug Harvey, Montreal |
| 1956–57 | Doug Harvey, Montreal |
| 1957–58 | Doug Harvey, Montreal |
| 1958–59 | Tom Johnson, Montreal |
| 1959–60 | Doug Harvey, Montreal |
| 1960–61 | Doug Harvey, Montreal |
| 1961–62 | Doug Harvey, New York |
| 1962–63 | Pierre Pilote, Chicago |
| 1963–64 | Pierre Pilote, Chicago |
| 1964–65 | Pierre Pilote, Chicago |
| 1965–66 | Jacques Laperriere, Montreal |
| 1966–67 | Harry Howell, New York R. |
| 1967–68 | Bobby Orr, Boston |
| 1968–69 | Bobby Orr, Boston |
| 1969–70 | Bobby Orr, Boston |
| 1970–71 | Bobby Orr, Boston |
| 1971–72 | Bobby Orr, Boston |
| 1972–73 | Bobby Orr, Boston |
| 1973–74 | Bobby Orr, Boston |
| 1974–75 | Bobby Orr, Boston |
| 1975–76 | Denis Potvin, New York I. |
| 1976–77 | Larry Robinson, Montreal |
| 1977–78 | Denis Potvin, New York I. |
| 1978–79 | Denis Potvin, New York I. |
| 1979–80 | Larry Robinson, Montreal |
| 1980–81 | Randy Carlyle, Pittsburgh |
| 1981–82 | Doug Wilson, Chicago |
| 1982–83 | Rod Langway, Washington |

# CALDER MEMORIAL TROPHY

Awarded to the league's outstanding rookie. Selected by a vote of hockey writers and broadcasters. It was originated in 1937 by Frank Calder, first president of the NHL. After his death in 1943, the league presented the Calder Memorial Trophy in his memory.

To be eligible to receive the trophy, a player cannot have participated in more than 20 games in any preceding season or in six or more games in each of any two preceding seasons.

From 1932–33 to 1936–37 the top rookies were named but no trophy was presented.

| | |
|---|---|
| 1932–33 | Carl Voss, Detroit |
| 1933–34 | Russ Blinco, Montreal M. |
| 1934–35 | Dave Schriner, New York A. |
| 1935–36 | Mike Karakas, Chicago |
| 1936–37 | Syl Apps, Toronto |
| 1937–38 | Cully Dahlstrom, Chicago |
| 1938–39 | Frank Brimsek, Boston |
| 1939–40 | Kilby MacDonald, New York R. |
| 1940–41 | Johnny Quilty, Montreal C. |
| 1941–42 | Grant Warwick, New York R. |
| 1942–43 | Gaye Stewart, Toronto |
| 1943–44 | Gus Bodnar, Toronto |
| 1944–45 | Frank McCool, Toronto |
| 1945–46 | Edgar Laprade, New York R. |
| 1946–47 | Howie Meeker, Toronto |
| 1947–48 | Jim McFadden, Detroit |
| 1948–49 | Pentti Lund, New York R. |
| 1949–50 | Jack Gelineau, Boston |
| 1950–51 | Terry Sawchuk, Detroit |
| 1951–52 | Bernie Geoffrion, Montreal |
| 1952–53 | Lorne Worsley, New York R. |
| 1953–54 | Camille Henry, New York R. |
| 1954–55 | Ed Litzenberger, Chicago |
| 1955–56 | Glenn Hall, Detroit |
| 1956–57 | Larry Regan, Boston |
| 1957–58 | Frank Mahovlich, Toronto |
| 1958–59 | Ralph Backstrom, Montreal |
| 1959–60 | Bill Hay, Chicago |
| 1960–61 | Dave Keon, Toronto |
| 1961–62 | Bobby Rousseau, Montreal |
| 1962–63 | Kent Douglas, Toronto |
| 1963–64 | Jacques Laperriere, Montreal |
| 1964–65 | Roger Crozier, Detroit |
| 1965–66 | Brit Selby, Toronto |
| 1966–67 | Bobby Orr, Boston |
| 1967–68 | Derek Sanderson, Boston |
| 1968–69 | Danny Grant, Minnesota |
| 1969–70 | Tony Esposito, Chicago |
| 1970–71 | Gil Perreault, Buffalo |
| 1971–72 | Ken Dryden, Montreal |
| 1972–73 | Steve Vickers, New York R. |
| 1973–74 | Denis Potvin, New York I. |
| 1974–75 | Eric Vail, Atlanta |
| 1975–76 | Bryan Trottier, New York I. |
| 1976–77 | Willi Plett, Atlanta |
| 1977–78 | Mike Bossy, New York I. |
| 1978–79 | Bobby Smith, Minnesota |
| 1979–80 | Ray Bourque, Boston |
| 1980–81 | Peter Stastny, Quebec |
| 1981–82 | Dale Hawerchuk, Winnipeg |
| 1982–83 | Steve Larmer, Chicago |

# CONN SMYTHE TROPHY

Awarded to the Most Valuable Player in the Stanley Cup Playoffs. Selected in a vote of the NHL Governors.

The trophy was presented by Maple Leaf Gardens Ltd. in 1964 to honor the former coach, manager, president and owner of the Toronto Maple Leafs.

| | |
|---|---|
| 1964–65 | Jean Beliveau, Montreal |
| 1965–66 | Roger Crozier, Detroit |
| 1966–67 | Dave Keon, Toronto |
| 1967–68 | Glenn Hall, St. Louis |
| 1968–69 | Serge Savard, Montreal |
| 1969–70 | Bobby Orr, Boston |
| 1970–71 | Ken Dryden, Montreal |
| 1971–72 | Bobby Orr, Boston |
| 1972–73 | Yvan Cournoyer, Montreal |
| 1973–74 | Bernie Parent, Philadelphia |
| 1974–75 | Bernie Parent, Philadelphia |
| 1975–76 | Reggie Leach, Philadelphia |
| 1976–77 | Guy Lafleur, Montreal |
| 1977–78 | Larry Robinson, Montreal |
| 1978–79 | Bob Gainey, Montreal |
| 1979–80 | Bryan Trottier, New York I. |
| 1980–81 | Butch Goring, New York I. |
| 1981–82 | Mike Bossy, New York I. |
| 1982–83 | Billy Smith, New York I. |

# LADY BYNG TROPHY

Awarded to the player combining the highest type of sportsmanship and gentlemanly conduct plus a high standard of playing ability. Selected by a vote of hockey writers and broadcasters.

Lady Byng, the wife of the Governor-General of Canada in 1925, presented the trophy to the NHL during that year.

| | |
|---|---|
| 1924–25 | Frank Nighbor, Ottawa |
| 1925–26 | Frank Nighbor, Ottawa |
| 1926–27 | Billy Burch, New York A. |
| 1927–28 | Frank Boucher, New York R. |
| 1928–29 | Frank Boucher, New York R. |
| 1929–30 | Frank Boucher, New York R. |
| 1930–31 | Frank Boucher, New York R. |
| 1931–32 | Joe Primeau, Toronto |
| 1932–33 | Frank Boucher, New York R. |
| 1933–34 | Frank Boucher, New York R. |
| 1934–35 | Frank Boucher, New York R. |
| 1935–36 | Doc Romnes, Chicago |
| 1936–37 | Marty Barry, Detroit |
| 1937–38 | Gordie Drillon, Toronto |
| 1938–39 | Clint Smith, New York R. |
| 1939–40 | Bobby Bauer, Boston |
| 1940–41 | Bobby Bauer, Boston |
| 1941–42 | Syl Apps, Toronto |
| 1942–43 | Max Bentley, Chicago |
| 1943–44 | Clint Smith, Chicago |
| 1944–45 | Bill Mosienko, Chicago |
| 1945–46 | Toe Blake, Montreal |
| 1946–47 | Bobby Bauer, Boston |
| 1947–48 | Buddy O'Connor, New York R. |
| 1948–49 | Bill Quackenbush, Detroit |
| 1949–50 | Edgar Laprade, New York R. |
| 1950–51 | Red Kelly, Detroit |
| 1951–52 | Sid Smith, Toronto |
| 1952–53 | Red Kelly, Detroit |
| 1953–54 | Red Kelly, Detroit |
| 1954–55 | Sid Smith, Toronto |
| 1955–56 | Earl Reibel, Detroit |
| 1956–57 | Andy Hebenton, New York R. |
| 1957–58 | Camille Henry, New York R. |
| 1958–59 | Alex Delvecchio, Detroit |
| 1959–60 | Don McKenney, Boston |
| 1960–61 | Red Kelly, Toronto |
| 1961–62 | Dave Keon, Toronto |
| 1962–63 | Dave Keon, Toronto |
| 1963–64 | Ken Wharram, Chicago |
| 1964–65 | Bobby Hull, Chicago |
| 1965–66 | Alex Delvecchio, Detroit |
| 1966–67 | Stan Mikita, Chicago |
| 1967–68 | Stan Mikita, Chicago |
| 1968–69 | Alex Delvecchio, Detroit |
| 1969–70 | Phil Goyette, St. Louis |
| 1970–71 | Johnny Bucyk, Boston |
| 1971–72 | Jean Ratelle, New York R. |
| 1972–73 | Gil Perreault, Buffalo |
| 1973–74 | John Bucyk, Boston |
| 1974–75 | Marcel Dionne, Detroit |
| 1975–76 | Jean Ratelle, NYR-Boston |
| 1976–77 | Marcel Dionne, Los Angeles |
| 1977–78 | Butch Goring, Los Angeles |
| 1978–79 | Bob MacMillan, Atlanta |
| 1979–80 | Wayne Gretzky, Edmonton |
| 1980–81 | Rick Kehoe, Pittsburgh |
| 1981–82 | Rick Middleton, Boston |
| 1982–83 | Mike Bossy, New York I. |

# BILL MASTERTON TROPHY

Awarded by the Professional Hockey Writers' Association to "the NHL player who exemplifies the qualities of perseverance, sportsmanship and dedication to hockey." Named for the late Minnesota North Star player.

| | |
|---|---|
| 1967–68 | Claude Provost, Montreal |
| 1968–69 | Ted Hampson, Oakland |
| 1969–70 | Pit Martin, Chicago |
| 1970–71 | Jean Ratelle, New York R. |
| 1971–72 | Bobby Clarke, Philadelphia |
| 1972–73 | Lowell MacDonald, Pittsburgh |
| 1973–74 | Henri Richard, Montreal |
| 1974–75 | Don Luce, Buffalo |
| 1975–76 | Rod Gilbert, New York R. |
| 1976–77 | Ed Westfall, New York I. |
| 1977–78 | Butch Goring, Los Angeles |
| 1978–79 | Serge Savard, Montreal |
| 1979–80 | Al MacAdam, Minnesota |
| 1980–81 | Blake Dunlop, St. Louis |
| 1981–82 | Glenn Resch, Colorado |
| 1982–83 | Lanny McDonald, Calgary |

# JACK ADAMS AWARD

Awarded by the National Hockey League Broadcasters' Association to the "NHL coach adjudged to have contributed the most to his team's success." It is presented in memory of the late Jack Adams, longtime coach and general manager of the Detroit Red Wings.

| | |
|---|---|
| 1973–74 | Fred Shero, Philadelphia |
| 1974–75 | Bob Pulford, Los Angeles |
| 1975–76 | Don Cherry, Boston |
| 1976–77 | Scotty Bowman, Montreal |
| 1977–78 | Bobby Kromm, Detroit |
| 1978–79 | Al Arbour, New York I. |
| 1979–80 | Pat Quinn, Philadelphia |
| 1980–81 | Red Berenson, St. Louis |
| 1981–82 | Tom Watt, Winnipeg |
| 1982–83 | Orval Tessier, Chicago |

# PRINCE OF WALES TROPHY

The Prince of Wales donated the trophy to the NHL in 1924. From 1927–28 to 1937–38, it was presented to the team finishing first in the American Division of the NHL. From 1938–39 through 1966–67, it was given to the first-place team in the one-division league. It was subsequently awarded to the first-place finisher in the East Division. Beginning with 1981–82, the trophy has gone to the team advancing to the Stanley Cup finals as the winner of the Wales Conference.

| | | | |
|---|---|---|---|
| 1924–25 | Montreal C. | 1954–55 | Detroit |
| 1925–26 | Montreal M. | 1955–56 | Montreal |
| 1926–27 | Ottawa | 1956–57 | Detroit |
| 1927–28 | Boston | 1957–58 | Montreal |
| 1928–29 | Boston | 1958–59 | Montreal |
| 1929–30 | Boston | 1959–60 | Montreal |
| 1930–31 | Boston | 1960–61 | Montreal |
| 1931–32 | New York R. | 1961–62 | Montreal |
| 1932–33 | Boston | 1962–63 | Montreal |
| 1933–34 | Detroit | 1963–64 | Montreal |
| 1934–35 | Boston | 1964–65 | Detroit |
| 1935–36 | Detroit | 1965–66 | Montreal |
| 1936–37 | Detroit | 1966–67 | Chicago |
| 1937–38 | Boston | 1967–68 | Montreal |
| 1938–39 | Boston | 1968–69 | Montreal |
| 1939–40 | Boston | 1969–70 | Chicago |
| 1940–41 | Boston | 1970–71 | Boston |
| 1941–42 | New York R. | 1971–72 | Boston |
| 1942–43 | Detroit | 1972–73 | Montreal |
| 1943–44 | Montreal | 1973–74 | Boston |
| 1944–45 | Montreal | 1974–75 | Buffalo |
| 1945–46 | Montreal | 1975–76 | Montreal |
| 1946–47 | Montreal | 1976–77 | Montreal |
| 1947–48 | Toronto | 1977–78 | Montreal |
| 1948–49 | Detroit | 1978–79 | Montreal |
| 1949–50 | Detroit | 1979–80 | Buffalo |
| 1950–51 | Detroit | 1980–81 | Montreal |
| 1951–52 | Detroit | 1981–82 | New York I. |
| 1952–53 | Detroit | 1982–83 | New York I. |
| 1953–54 | Detroit | | |

# CLARENCE S. CAMPBELL BOWL

Named for the former president of the NHL, the award originally was given to the champions of the West Division. Since 1981–82, it has gone to the team advancing to the Stanley Cup finals as the winner of the Campbell Conference.

| | | | |
|---|---|---|---|
| 1967–68 | Philadelphia | 1975–76 | Philadelphia |
| 1968–69 | St. Louis | 1976–77 | Philadelphia |
| 1969–70 | St. Louis | 1977–78 | New York I. |
| 1970–71 | Chicago | 1978–79 | New York I. |
| 1971–72 | Chicago | 1979–80 | Philadelphia |
| 1972–73 | Chicago | 1980–81 | New York I. |
| 1973–74 | Philadelphia | 1981–82 | Vancouver |
| 1974–75 | Philadelphia | 1982–83 | Edmonton |

# LESTER PATRICK TROPHY

Awarded for outstanding service to hockey in the United States. Eligible recipients are players, officials, coaches, executives and referees.

Selected by a six-man committee consisting of the President of the NHL, an NHL Governor, a hockey writer for a U.S. national news service, a nationally syndicated sports columnist, an ex-player in the Hockey Hall of Fame and a sports director of a U.S. national radio-television network.

Presented by the New York Rangers in 1966 to honor the memory of the long-time general manager and coach of the New York Rangers.

| | | | |
|---|---|---|---|
| 1965–66 | Jack Adams | 1975–76 | Stan Mikita |
| 1966–67 | Gordie Howe | | George Leader |
| | Charles Adams | | Bruce Norris |
| | James Norris, Sr. | 1976–77 | John Bucyk |
| 1967–68 | Tom Lockhart | | Murray Armstrong |
| | Walter Brown | | John Mariucci |
| | John R. Kilpatrick | 1977–78 | Phil Esposito |
| 1968–69 | Bobby Hull | | Tom Fitzgerald |
| | Edward Jeremiah | | Bill Tutt |
| 1969–70 | Eddie Shore | | William Wirtz |
| | Jim Hendy | 1978–79 | Bobby Orr |
| 1970–71 | Bill Jennings | 1979–80 | Robert Clarke |
| | John Sollenberger | | Edward Snider |
| | Terry Sawchuk | | Fred Shero |
| 1971–72 | Clarence Campbell | | U.S. Olympic |
| | John Kelly | | hockey team |
| | Cooney Weiland | 1980–81 | Charles Schulz |
| | James D. Norris | 1981–82 | Emile Francis |
| 1972–73 | Walter Bush, Jr. | 1982–83 | Bill Torrey |
| 1973–74 | Alex Delvecchio | | |
| | Murray Murdoch | | |
| 1974–75 | Donald Clark | | |
| | Bill Chadwick | | |
| | Tommy Ivan | | |

# THE ALL-STAR TEAMS

Selected by a vote of hockey writers and broadcasters in the 21 NHL cities at the end of each season. The balloting originated with the 1930–31 campaign.

## 1930–31

| First | | Second |
|---|---|---|
| Gardiner, Chicago | Goal | Thompson, Boston |
| Shore, Boston | Defense | Mantha, Montreal C. |
| Clancy, Toronto | Defense | Johnson, New York R. |
| Morenz, Montreal C. | Center | Boucher, New York R. |
| Bill Cook, New York R. | Right Wing | Clapper, Boston |
| Joliat, Montreal C. | Left Wing | Bun Cook, New York R. |

## 1931–32

| | | |
|---|---|---|
| Gardiner, Chicago | Goal | Worters, New York A. |
| Shore, Boston | Defense | Mantha, Montreal C. |
| Johnson, New York R. | Defense | Clancy, Toronto |
| Morenz, Montreal C. | Center | Smith, Montreal M. |
| Bill Cook, New York R. | Right Wing | C. Conacher, Toronto |
| Jackson, Toronto | Left Wing | Joliat, Montreal C. |

## 1932–33

| | | |
|---|---|---|
| Roach, Detroit | Goal | Gardiner, Chicago |
| Shore, Boston | Defense | Clancy, Toronto |
| Johnson, New York R. | Defense | L. Conacher, Montreal M. |
| Boucher, New York R. | Center | Morenz, Montreal C. |
| Bill Cook, New York R. | Right Wing | C. Conacher, Toronto |
| Northcott, Montreal M. | Left Wing | Jackson, Toronto |

## 1933–34

| | | |
|---|---|---|
| Gardiner, Chicago | Goal | Worters, New York A. |
| Clancy, Toronto | Defense | Shore, Boston |
| L. Conacher, Chicago | Defense | Johnson, New York R. |
| Boucher, New York R. | Center | Primeau, Toronto |
| C. Conacher, Toronto | Right Wing | Bill Cook, New York R. |
| Jackson, Toronto | Left Wing | Joliat, Montreal C. |

## 1934–35

| | | |
|---|---|---|
| Chabot, Chicago | Goal | Thompson, Boston |
| Shore, Boston | Defense | Wentworth, Montreal M. |
| Seibert, New York R. | Defense | Coulter, Chicago |
| Boucher, New York R. | Center | Weiland, Detroit |
| C. Conacher, Toronto | Right Wing | Clapper, Boston |
| Jackson, Toronto | Left Wing | Joliat, Montreal C. |

## 1935–36

| | | |
|---|---|---|
| Thompson, Boston | Goal | Cude, Montreal C. |
| Shore, Boston | Defense | Seibert, Chicago |
| Seibert, Boston | Defense | Goodfellow, Detroit |
| Smith, Montreal M. | Center | Thoms, Toronto |
| C. Conacher, Toronto | Right Wing | Dillon, New York R. |
| Schriner, New York A. | Left Wing | Thompson, Chicago |

## 1936–37

| | | |
|---|---|---|
| Smith, Detroit | Goal | Cude, Montreal C. |
| Siebert, Montreal C. | Defense | Seibert, Chicago |
| Goodfellow, Detroit | Defense | C. Conacher, Montreal M. |
| Barry, Detroit | Center | Chapman, New York A. |
| Aurie, Detroit | Right Wing | Dillon, New York R. |
| Jackson, Toronto | Left Wing | Schriner, New York A. |

## 1937–38

| | | |
|---|---|---|
| Thompson, Boston | Goal | Kerr, New York R. |
| Shore, Boston | Defense | Coulter, New York R. |
| Siebert, Montreal C. | Defense | Seibert, Chicago |
| Cowley, Boston | Center | Apps, Toronto |
| *Dillon, New York R. | Right Wing | *Drillon, Toronto |
| Thompson, Chicago | Left Wing | Blake, Montreal C. |

## 1938–39

| | | |
|---|---|---|
| Brimsek, Boston | Goal | Robertson, New York A. |
| Shore, Boston | Defense | Seibert, Chicago |
| Clapper, Boston | Defense | Coulter, New York R. |
| Apps, Toronto | Center | N. Colville, New York R. |
| Drillon, Toronto | Right Wing | Bauer, Boston |
| Blake, Montreal C. | Left Wing | Gottselig, Chicago |

## 1939–40

| | | |
|---|---|---|
| Kerr, New York R. | Goal | Brimsek, Boston |
| Clapper, Boston | Defense | Coulter, New York R. |
| Goodfellow, Detroit | Defense | Seibert, Chicago |
| Schmidt, Boston | Center | N. Colville, New York R. |
| Hextall, New York R. | Right Wing | Bauer, Boston |
| Blake, Montreal C. | Left Wing | Dumart, Boston |

## 1940–41

| | | |
|---|---|---|
| Broda, Toronto | Goal | Brimsek, Boston |
| Clapper, Boston | Defense | Seibert, Chicago |
| Stanowski, Toronto | Defense | Heller, New York R. |
| Cowley, Boston | Center | Apps, Toronto |
| Hextall, New York R. | Right Wing | Bauer, Boston |
| Schriner, Toronto | Left Wing | Dumart, Boston |

## 1941–42

| | | |
|---|---|---|
| Brimsek, Boston | Goal | Broda, Toronto |
| Seibert, Chicago | Defense | Egan, New York A. |
| Anderson, New York A. | Defense | McDonald, Toronto |
| Apps, Toronto | Center | Watson, New York R. |
| Hextall, New York R. | Right Wing | Drillon, Toronto |
| L. Patrick, New York R. | Left Wing | Abel, Detroit |

## 1942–43

| | | |
|---|---|---|
| Mowers, Detroit | Goal | Brimsek, Boston |
| Seibert, Chicago | Defense | Crawford, Boston |
| Stewart, Detroit | Defense | Hollett, Boston |
| Cowley, Boston | Center | Apps, Toronto |
| Carr, Toronto | Right Wing | Hextall, New York R. |
| D. Bentley, Chicago | Left Wing | L. Patrick, New York R. |

## 1943–44

| | | |
|---|---|---|
| Durnan, Montreal | Goal | Bibeault, Toronto |
| Seibert, Chicago | Defense | Bouchard, Montreal |
| Pratt, Toronto | Defense | Clapper, Boston |
| Cowley, Boston | Center | Lach, Montreal |
| Carr, Toronto | Right Wing | Richard, Montreal |
| D. Bentley, Chicago | Left Wing | Cain, Boston |

*Dillon and Drillon tied for first place in the voting and shared positions on the first and second teams.

## 1944–45

| First Team | Position | Second Team |
|---|---|---|
| Durnan, Montreal | Goal | Karakas, Chicago |
| Bouchard, Montreal | Defense | Harmon, Montreal |
| Hollett, Detroit | Defense | Pratt, Toronto |
| Lach, Montreal | Center | Cowley, Boston |
| Richard, Montreal | Right Wing | Mosienko, Chicago |
| Blake, Montreal | Left Wing | S. Howe, Detroit |

## 1945–46

| First Team | Position | Second Team |
|---|---|---|
| Durnan, Montreal | Goal | Brimsek, Boston |
| Crawford, Boston | Defense | Reardon, Montreal |
| Bouchard, Montreal | Defense | Stewart, Detroit |
| M. Bentley, Chicago | Center | Lach, Montreal |
| Richard, Montreal | Right Wing | Mosienko, Chicago |
| Stewart, Toronto | Left Wing | Blake, Montreal |

## 1946–47

| First Team | Position | Second Team |
|---|---|---|
| Durnan, Montreal | Goal | Brimsek, Boston |
| Reardon, Montreal | Defense | Stewart, Detroit |
| Bouchard, Montreal | Defense | Quackenbush, Detroit |
| Schmidt, Boston | Center | M. Bentley, Chicago |
| Richard, Montreal | Right Wing | Bauer, Boston |
| D. Bentley, Chicago | Left Wing | Dumart, Boston |

## 1947–48

| First Team | Position | Second Team |
|---|---|---|
| Broda, Toronto | Goal | Brimsek, Boston |
| Quackenbush, Detroit | Defense | Reardon, Montreal |
| Stewart, Detroit | Defense | N. Colville, New York |
| Lach, Montreal | Center | O'Connor, New York |
| Richard, Montreal | Right Wing | Poile, Chicago |
| Lindsay, Detroit | Left Wing | Stewart, Chicago |

## 1948–49

| First Team | Position | Second Team |
|---|---|---|
| Durnan, Montreal | Goal | Rayner, New York |
| Quackenbush, Detroit | Defense | Harmon, Montreal |
| Stewart, Detroit | Defense | Reardon, Montreal |
| Abel, Detroit | Center | D. Bentley, Chicago |
| Richard, Montreal | Right Wing | Howe, Detroit |
| Conacher, Chicago | Left Wing | Lindsay, Detroit |

## 1949–50

| First Team | Position | Second Team |
|---|---|---|
| Durnan, Montreal | Goal | Rayner, New York |
| Mortson, Toronto | Defense | Reise, Detroit |
| Reardon, Montreal | Defense | Kelly, Detroit |
| Abel, Detroit | Center | Kennedy, Toronto |
| Richard, Montreal | Right Wing | Howe, Detroit |
| Lindsay, Detroit | Left Wing | Leswick, New York |

## 1950–51

| First Team | Position | Second Team |
|---|---|---|
| Sawchuk, Detroit | Goal | Rayner, New York |
| Kelly, Detroit | Defense | Thomson, Toronto |
| Quackenbush, Boston | Defense | Reise, Detroit |
| Schmidt, Boston | Center | Abel, Detroit |
| | | Kennedy, Toronto |
| Howe, Detroit | Right Wing | Richard, Montreal |
| Lindsay, Detroit | Left Wing | Smith, Toronto |

## 1951–52

| First Team | Position | Second Team |
|---|---|---|
| Sawchuk, Detroit | Goal | Henry, Boston |
| Kelly, Detroit | Defense | Buller, New York |
| Harvey, Montreal | Defense | Thomson, Toronto |
| Lach, Montreal | Center | Schmidt, Boston |
| Howe, Detroit | Right Wing | Richard, Montreal |
| Lindsay, Detroit | Left Wing | Smith, Toronto |

## 1952–53

| First Team | Position | Second Team |
|---|---|---|
| Sawchuk, Detroit | Goal | McNeil, Montreal |
| Kelly, Detroit | Defense | Quackenbush, Boston |
| Harvey, Montreal | Defense | Gadsby, Chicago |
| Mackell, Boston | Center | Delvecchio, Detroit |
| Howe, Detroit | Right Wing | Richard, Montreal |
| Lindsay, Detroit | Left Wing | Olmstead, Montreal |

## 1953–54

| First Team | Position | Second Team |
|---|---|---|
| Lumley, Toronto | Goal | Sawchuk, Detroit |
| Kelly, Detroit | Defense | Gadsby, Chicago |
| Harvey, Montreal | Defense | Horton, Toronto |
| Mosdell, Montreal | Center | Kennedy, Toronto |
| Howe, Detroit | Right Wing | Richard, Montreal |
| Lindsay, Detroit | Left Wing | Sandford, Boston |

## 1954–55

| First Team | Position | Second Team |
|---|---|---|
| Lumley, Toronto | Goal | Sawchuk, Detroit |
| Harvey, Montreal | Defense | Goldham, Detroit |
| Kelly, Detroit | Defense | Flaman, Boston |
| Beliveau, Montreal | Center | Mosdell, Montreal |
| Richard, Montreal | Right Wing | Geoffrion, Montreal |
| Smith, Toronto | Left Wing | Lewicki, New York |

## 1955–56

| First Team | Position | Second Team |
|---|---|---|
| Plante, Montreal | Goal | Hall, Detroit |
| Harvey, Montreal | Defense | Kelly, Detroit |
| Gadsby, New York | Defense | Johnson, Montreal |
| Beliveau, Montreal | Center | Sloan, Toronto |
| M. Richard, Montreal | Right Wing | Howe, Detroit |
| Lindsay, Detroit | Left Wing | Olmstead, Montreal |

## 1956–57

| First Team | Position | Second Team |
|---|---|---|
| Hall, Detroit | Goal | Plante, Montreal |
| Harvey, Montreal | Defense | Flaman, Boston |
| Kelly, Detroit | Defense | Gadsby, New York |
| Beliveau, Montreal | Center | Litzenberger, Chicago |
| Howe, Detroit | Right Wing | M. Richard, Montreal |
| Lindsay, Detroit | Left Wing | Chevrefils, Boston |

## 1957–58

| First Team | Position | Second Team |
|---|---|---|
| Hall, Chicago | Goal | Plante, Montreal |
| Harvey, Montreal | Defense | Flaman, Boston |
| Gadsby, New York | Defense | Pronovost, Detroit |
| H. Richard, Montreal | Center | Beliveau, Montreal |
| Howe, Detroit | Right Wing | Bathgate, New York |
| Moore, Montreal | Left Wing | Henry, New York |

## 1958–59

| First Team | Position | Second Team |
|---|---|---|
| Plante, Montreal | Goal | Sawchuk, Detroit |
| Johnson, Montreal | Defense | Pronovost, Detroit |
| Gadsby, New York | Defense | Harvey, Montreal |
| Beliveau, Montreal | Center | H. Richard, Montreal |
| Bathgate, New York | Right Wing | Howe, Detroit |
| Moore, Montreal | Left Wing | Delvecchio, Detroit |

## 1959–60

| First Team | Position | Second Team |
|---|---|---|
| Hall, Chicago | Goal | Plante, Montreal |
| Harvey, Montreal | Defense | Stanley, Toronto |
| Pronovost, Detroit | Defense | Pilote, Chicago |
| Beliveau, Montreal | Center | Horvath, Boston |
| Howe, Detroit | Right Wing | Geoffrion, Montreal |
| Hull, Chicago | Left Wing | Prentice, New York |

### 1960–61

| | | |
|---|---|---|
| Bower, Toronto | Goal | Hall, Chicago |
| Harvey, Montreal | Defense | Stanley, Toronto |
| Pronovost, Detroit | Defense | Pilote, Chicago |
| Beliveau, Montreal | Center | H. Richard, Montreal |
| Geoffrion, Montreal | Right Wing | Howe, Detroit |
| Mahovlich, Toronto | Left Wing | Moore, Montreal |

### 1961–62

| | | |
|---|---|---|
| Plante, Montreal | Goal | Hall, Chicago |
| Harvey, New York | Defense | Brewer, Toronto |
| Talbot, Montreal | Defense | Pilote, Chicago |
| Mikita, Chicago | Center | Keon, Toronto |
| Bathgate, New York | Right Wing | Howe, Detroit |
| Hull, Chicago | Left Wing | Mahovlich, Toronto |

### 1962–63

| | | |
|---|---|---|
| Hall Chicago | Goal | Sawchuk, Detroit |
| Pilote, Chicago | Defense | Horton, Toronto |
| Brewer, Toronto | Defense | Vasko, Chicago |
| Mikita, Chicago | Center | Richard, Montreal |
| Howe, Detroit | Right Wing | Bathgate, New York |
| Mahovlich, Toronto | Left Wing | Hull, Chicago |

### 1963–64

| | | |
|---|---|---|
| Hall, Chicago | Goal | Hodge, Montreal |
| Pilote, Chicago | Defense | Vasko, Chicago |
| Horton, Toronto | Defense | Laperriere, Montreal |
| Mikita, Chicago | Center | Beliveau, Montreal |
| Wharram, Chicago | Right Wing | Howe, Detroit |
| Hull, Chicago | Left Wing | Mahovlich, Toronto |

### 1964–65

| | | |
|---|---|---|
| Crozier, Detroit | Goal | Hodge, Montreal |
| Pilote, Chicago | Defense | Gadsby, Detroit |
| Laperriere, Montreal | Defense | Brewer, Toronto |
| Ullman, Detroit | Center | Mikita, Chicago |
| Provost, Montreal | Right Wing | Howe, Detroit |
| B. Hull, Chicago | Left Wing | Mahovlich, Toronto |

### 1965–66

| | | |
|---|---|---|
| Hall, Chicago | Goal | Worsley, Montreal |
| Laperriere, Montreal | Defense | Stanley, Toronto |
| Pilote, Chicago | Defense | Stapleton, Chicago |
| Mikita, Chicago | Center | Beliveau, Montreal |
| Howe, Detroit | Right Wing | Rousseau, Montreal |
| B. Hull, Chicago | Left Wing | Mahovlich, Toronto |

### 1966–67

| | | |
|---|---|---|
| Giacomin, New York | Goal | Hall, Chicago |
| Pilote, Chicago | Defense | Horton, Toronto |
| Howell, New York | Defense | Orr, Boston |
| Mikita, Chicago | Center | Ullman, Detroit |
| Wharram, Chicago | Right Wing | Howe, Detroit |
| B. Hull, Chicago | Left Wing | Marshall, New York |

### 1967–68

| | | |
|---|---|---|
| Worsley, Montreal | Goal | Giacomin, New York |
| Orr, Boston | Defense | J. C. Tremblay, Montreal |
| Horton, Toronto | Defense | Neilson, New York |
| Mikita, Chicago | Center | Esposito, Boston |
| Howe, Detroit | Right Wing | Gilbert, New York |
| B. Hull, Chicago | Left Wing | Bucyk, Boston |

### 1968–69

| | | |
|---|---|---|
| Hall, St. Louis | Goal | Giacomin, New York |
| Orr, Boston | Defense | Green, Boston |
| Horton, Toronto | Defense | Harris, Montreal |
| Esposito, Boston | Center | Beliveau, Montreal |
| Howe, Detroit | Right Wing | Cournoyer, Montreal |
| B. Hull, Chicago | Left Wing | F. Mahovlich, Detroit |

### 1969–70

| | | |
|---|---|---|
| Esposito, Chicago | Goal | Giacomin, New York |
| Orr, Boston | Defense | Brewer, Detroit |
| Park, New York | Defense | Laperriere, Montreal |
| Esposito, Boston | Center | Mikita, Chicago |
| Howe, Detroit | Right Wing | McKenzie, Boston |
| B. Hull, Chicago | Left Wing | F. Mahovlich, Detroit |

### 1970–71

| | | |
|---|---|---|
| Giacomin, New York | Goal | Plante, Toronto |
| Orr, Boston | Defense | Park, New York |
| Tremblay, Montreal | Defense | Stapleton, Chicago |
| Esposito, Boston | Center | Keon, Toronto |
| Hodge, Boston | Right Wing | Cournoyer, Montreal |
| Bucyk, Boston | Left Wing | B. Hull, Chicago |

### 1971–72

| | | |
|---|---|---|
| Esposito, Chicago | Goal | Dryden, Montreal |
| Orr, Boston | Defense | White, Chicago |
| Park, New York | Defense | Stapleton, Chicago |
| Esposito, Boston | Center | Ratelle, New York |
| Gilbert, New York | Right Wing | Cournoyer, Montreal |
| B. Hull, Chicago | Left Wing | Hadfield, New York |

### 1972–73

| | | |
|---|---|---|
| Dryden, Montreal | Goal | Esposito, Chicago |
| Orr, Boston | Defense | Park, New York R. |
| Lapointe, Montreal | Defense | White, Chicago |
| Esposito, Boston | Center | Clarke, Philadelphia |
| Redmond, Detroit | Right Wing | Cournoyer, Montreal |
| F. Mahovlich, Montreal | Left Wing | D. Hull, Chicago |

### 1973–74

| | | |
|---|---|---|
| Parent, Philadelphia | Goal | Esposito, Chicago |
| Orr, Boston | Defense | White, Chicago |
| Park, New York R. | Defense | Ashbee, Philadelphia |
| Esposito, Boston | Center | Clarke, Philadelphia |
| Hodge, Boston | Right Wing | Redmond, Detroit |
| Martin, Buffalo | Left Wing | Cashman, Boston |

### 1974–75

| | | |
|---|---|---|
| Parent, Philadelphia | Goal | Vachon, Los Angeles |
| Orr, Boston | Defense | Lapointe, Montreal |
| D. Potvin, New York I. | Defense | Salming, Toronto |
| Clarke, Philadelphia | Center | Esposito, Boston |
| Lafleur, Montreal | Right Wing | Robert, Buffalo |
| Martin, Buffalo | Left Wing | Vickers, New York R. |

### 1975–76

| | | |
|---|---|---|
| Dryden, Montreal | Goal | Resch, New York I. |
| D. Potvin, New York I. | Defense | Salming, Toronto |
| Park, Boston | Defense | Lapointe, Montreal |
| Clarke, Philadelphia | Center | Perreault, Buffalo |
| Lafleur, Montreal | Right Wing | Leach, Philadelphia |
| Barber, Philadelphia | Left Wing | Martin, Buffalo |

## 1976–77

| | | | |
|---|---|---|---|
| Dryden, Montreal | Goal | Vachon, Los Angeles | |
| Robinson, Montreal | Defense | D. Potvin, New York I. | |
| Salming, Toronto | Defense | Lapointe, Montreal | |
| Dionne, Los Angeles | Center | Perreault, Buffalo | |
| Lafleur, Montreal | Right Wing | McDonald, Toronto | |
| Shutt, Montreal | Left Wing | Martin, Buffalo | |

## 1977–78

| | | | |
|---|---|---|---|
| Dryden, Montreal | Goal | Edwards, Buffalo | |
| D. Potvin, New York I. | Defense | Robinson, Montreal | |
| Park, Boston | Defense | Salming, Toronto | |
| Trottier, New York I. | Center | Sittler, Toronto | |
| Lafleur, Montreal | Right Wing | Bossy, New York I. | |
| Gillies, New York I. | Left Wing | Shutt, Montreal | |

## 1978–79

| | | | |
|---|---|---|---|
| Dryden, Montreal | Goal | Resch, New York I. | |
| D. Potvin, New York I. | Defense | Salming, Toronto | |
| Robinson, Montreal | Defense | Savard, Montreal | |
| Trottier, New York I. | Center | Dionne, Los Angeles | |
| Lafleur, Montreal | Right Wing | Bossy, New York I. | |
| Gillies, New York I. | Left Wing | Barber, Philadelphia | |

## 1979–80

| | | | |
|---|---|---|---|
| Esposito, Chicago | Goal | Edwards, Buffalo | |
| Robinson, Montreal | Defense | Salming, Toronto | |
| Bourque, Boston | Defense | Schoenfeld, Buffalo | |
| Dionne, Los Angeles | Center | Gretzky, Edmonton | |
| Lafleur, Montreal | Right Wing | Gare, Buffalo | |
| Simmer, Los Angeles | Left Wing | Shutt, Montreal | |

## 1980–81

| | | | |
|---|---|---|---|
| Liut, St. Louis | Goal | Lessard, Los Angeles | |
| Potvin, New York I. | Defense | Robinson, Montreal | |
| Carlyle, Pittsburgh | Defense | Bourque, Boston | |
| Gretzky, Edmonton | Center | Dionne, Los Angeles | |
| Bossy, New York I. | Right Wing | Taylor, Los Angeles | |
| Simmer, Los Angeles | Left Wing | Barber, Philadelphia | |

## 1981–82

| | | | |
|---|---|---|---|
| Smith, New York I. | Goal | Fuhr, Edmonton | |
| Wilson, Chicago | Defense | Coffey, Edmonton | |
| Bourque, Boston | Defense | Engblom, Montreal | |
| Gretzky, Edmonton | Center | Trottier, New York I. | |
| Bossy, New York I. | Right Wing | Middleton, Boston | |
| Messier, Edmonton | Left Wing | Tonelli, New York I. | |

## 1982–83

| | | | |
|---|---|---|---|
| Peeters, Boston | Goal | Melanson, New York I. | |
| Howe, Philadelphia | Defense | Bourque, Boston | |
| Langway, Washington | Defense | Coffey, Edmonton | |
| Gretzky, Edmonton | Center | Savard, Chicago | |
| Bossy, New York I. | Right Wing | McDonald, Calgary | |
| Messier, Edmonton | Left Wing | Goulet, Quebec | |

# WORLD HOCKEY ASSOCIATION

The World Hockey Association was an enigma. Loved by some but hated by others, the WHA led a turbulent seven years (1972–79) of existence that rocked hockey institutions.

Many would say the WHA was nothing more than a carpet-bagging league, constantly on the prowl searching for gullible owners in new cities populated by naive fans.

But others would argue long into the night, extolling the merits of the league, not the least of which was bargaining power for players and the emergence of major-league hockey in areas that would have been forever overlooked by the National Hockey League.

At one time or another, the league embraced 32 teams in 24 cities, 20 of which were eventually abandoned.

Reliable estimates say the owners of those 32 teams lost $50 million while the 803 players who performed in the WHA earned $120 million. The agents—virtually unheard of until the new league came along—collected 10 percent of their bounty.

◀ *Bobby Hull and wife said "Thanks a million" after Hull jumped to the WHA in 1972.*

Almost every player in professional hockey benefited in some way from the WHA. Owners of NHL teams scrambled to keep their organizations intact, even if it meant doubling or tripling the salaries of minor leaguers.

Born of enterprising Californians, buoyed by the creation of the American Basketball Association, their original brainchild, the WHA was founded by Gary Davidson and Dennis Murphy.

Not steeped in hockey, both would be gone before the league would reach its third anniversary.

Two players, each a legend in his time, made the WHA go. Bobby Hull, a personable, 33-year-old superstar with the Chicago Black Hawks, left the NHL and its followers aghast when he signed a $2.75-million contract to coach and play for the Winnipeg Jets.

Possessed of a pioneer spirit and the notion that he was improving the lot of all players, Hull joined the league on June 27, 1972. Enticing him, too, was $1 million up front.

Other established players followed him to the new league. Among them were Gerry Cheevers, Dave Keon, Johnny McKenzie, Frank Mahovlich and J.C. Tremblay.

But no signing had the impact Gordie Howe's did.

In a historic event, the 46-year-old NHL immortal and his teenage sons, Mark and Marty, joined the Houston Aeros in June 1973.

It was more than a publicity stunt. Not only did he play 419 games, collecting 508 points, but he was a two-time All-Star on right wing and won MVP honors once.

Fittingly, the league championship trophy was sponsored by a finance company, Avco.

The Avco Cup was won by Winnipeg on three occasions as the Jets blended Europeans and Canadians into a championship team. Perhaps the finest line in professional hockey at the time was the combination of Hull and two young Swedes, Ulf Nilsson and Anders Hedberg.

Houston, led by the Howes, won the Avco Cup twice while the Quebec Nordiques and New England Whalers were champions once.

Although the league died in June 1979, it left a legacy. Four of its original teams—the Edmonton Oilers, Hartford (New England) Whalers, Quebec Nordiques and Winnipeg Jets—were admitted to the NHL. They had proven themselves.

## 1972–73

The WHA thought big. Twelve teams drafted 1,081 persons, not all of them players. One would-be general manager, Scotty Munro of the Calgary Broncos, picked Soviet Premier Alexei Kosygin.

Unable to post $100,000 performance bonds, two

*A rare photo of Derek Sanderson in WHA garb. Sanderson only played eight games in the league before going back to the NHL.*

franchises—Miami and Calgary—pulled out before the season began. Cleveland and Chicago took their places.

The first player signed was left winger Steve Sutherland, swiped off the Port Huron Wings International League roster by the Los Angeles Sharks.

By August, most than 300 players were under contract. Among them was a center, Derek Sanderson, who signed a 10-year pact with the Philadelphia Blazers for a reported $2.325 million. He played only eight games and was bought out for $1 million.

An Alberta right winger, Ron Anderson, scored the WHA's first goal on October 11 in Ottawa. The Oilers won, 7–4.

The New England Whalers did the best job of recruiting and reaped their just reward—winning the first WHA championship.

Based in Boston, where they divided their time between the Arena and the Garden, the Whalers were led by a stout defense manned by such stalwarts as Rick Ley and Brad Selwood, plucked off the roster of the Toronto Maple Leafs; Jim Dorey, from the New York Rangers, and Ted Green, the former Bruin who would show he could bounce back from a serious head injury. Their coach was Jack Kelley, a respected tactician from Boston University.

New England (46–30–2) won the Eastern Division while the Western was won by Winnipeg (43–31–4). They met in a best-of-seven league final, with the Whalers winning in five games.

Center Andre Lacroix of Philadelphia won the first scoring championship with 50 goals and 74 assists.

## 1972–73

### FINAL STANDINGS

#### Eastern Division

|  | W | L | T | PTS | GF | GA |
|---|---|---|---|---|---|---|
| New England | 46 | 30 | 2 | 94 | 318 | 263 |
| Cleveland | 43 | 32 | 3 | 89 | 287 | 239 |
| Philadelphia | 38 | 40 | 0 | 76 | 288 | 305 |
| Ottawa | 35 | 39 | 4 | 74 | 279 | 301 |
| Quebec | 33 | 40 | 5 | 71 | 276 | 313 |
| New York | 33 | 43 | 2 | 68 | 303 | 334 |

#### Western Division

|  | W | L | T | PTS | GF | GA |
|---|---|---|---|---|---|---|
| Winnipeg | 43 | 31 | 4 | 90 | 285 | 249 |
| Houston | 39 | 35 | 4 | 82 | 284 | 269 |
| Los Angeles | 37 | 35 | 6 | 80 | 259 | 250 |
| Alberta | 38 | 37 | 3 | 79 | 269 | 256 |
| Minnesota | 38 | 37 | 3 | 79 | 250 | 269 |
| Chicago | 26 | 50 | 2 | 54 | 245 | 295 |

| LEADING SCORERS | G | A | PTS |
|---|---|---|---|
| Lacroix, Philadelphia | 50 | 74 | 124 |
| Ward, New York | 51 | 67 | 118 |
| Lawson, Philadelphia | 61 | 45 | 106 |
| Webster, New England | 53 | 50 | 103 |
| Hull, Winnipeg | 51 | 52 | 103 |
| Beaudin, Winnipeg | 38 | 65 | 103 |
| Bordeleau, Winnipeg | 47 | 54 | 101 |
| Caffery, New England | 39 | 61 | 100 |
| Labossiere, Houston | 36 | 60 | 93 |
| Carleton, Ottawa | 42 | 49 | 91 |

## 1973–74

The Houston Aeros were older than most teams. Many of their players had been stars in the old Western Hockey League.

However, their coach, Bill Dineen, had his eye on two youngsters. Mark and Marty Howe were showing signs of becoming excellent hockey players with a junior team, the Toronto Marlies.

Bill Dineen knew he couldn't sign any Canadian youngsters before their 19th birthday. But the Howe boys were Americans.

Not one to take advantage of his friends or his friends' children, Dineen thought he should call Gordie to seek his permission. Howe, idle and disgruntled in his self-described role as vice-president in charge of paper clips for the Detroit Red Wings, asked Dineen if he would like to make it a threesome—Gordie to return to active play, joined by his sons.

The caper was pulled off and the Aeros finished in first place (48–25–5) in the Western Division, then roared through the playoffs, sweeping the Chicago Cougars in four straight games for the championship.

It was a season in which the Ottawa Nationals became the Toronto Toros, Philadelphia moved to Vancouver and the New York Raiders became the Golden Blades and then the Jersey Knights when bill collectors chased them out of New York to Cherry Hill, New Jersey, a suburb of Philadelphia.

Mike (Shakey) Walton of the Minnesota Fighting Saints won the league scoring championship with 57 goals and 60 assists. But the league's Most Valuable Player was none other than Gordie Howe, a 47-year-old phenomenon.

*The Howe family, father Gordie and sons Marty and Mark, take the ice for their first WHA game together on September 25, 1973.*

## 1973–74

### FINAL STANDINGS

#### Eastern Division

| | W | L | T | PTS | GF | GA |
|---|---|---|---|---|---|---|
| New England | 43 | 31 | 4 | 90 | 291 | 260 |
| Toronto | 41 | 33 | 4 | 86 | 304 | 272 |
| Cleveland | 37 | 32 | 9 | 83 | 266 | 264 |
| Chicago | 38 | 35 | 5 | 81 | 271 | 273 |
| Quebec | 38 | 36 | 4 | 80 | 306 | 280 |
| New Jersey | 32 | 42 | 4 | 68 | 268 | 313 |

#### Western Division

| | W | L | T | PTS | GF | GA |
|---|---|---|---|---|---|---|
| Houston | 48 | 25 | 5 | 101 | 318 | 219 |
| Minnesota | 44 | 32 | 2 | 90 | 332 | 275 |
| Edmonton | 38 | 37 | 3 | 79 | 268 | 269 |
| Winnipeg | 34 | 39 | 5 | 73 | 264 | 296 |
| Vancouver | 27 | 50 | 1 | 55 | 278 | 345 |
| Los Angeles | 25 | 53 | 0 | 50 | 239 | 339 |

### LEADING SCORERS

| | G | A | PTS |
|---|---|---|---|
| Walton, Minnesota | 57 | 60 | 117 |
| Lacroix, New Jersey | 31 | 80 | 111 |
| G. Howe, Houston | 31 | 69 | 100 |
| Hull, Winnipeg | 53 | 42 | 95 |
| Connelly, Minnesota | 42 | 53 | 95 |
| Carleton, Toronto | 37 | 55 | 92 |
| Lawson, Vancouver | 50 | 38 | 88 |
| Campbell, Vancouver | 27 | 61 | 88 |
| Bernier, Quebec | 37 | 49 | 86 |
| Lund, Houston | 33 | 53 | 86 |

## 1974–75

Interest in the WHA was at an all-time high. An All-Star team represented Canada in an eight-game series with the Soviet National team. Although it was

able to win only one game, the WHA did receive considerable publicity for itself and its players.

The Indianapolis Racers and Phoenix Roadrunners were accepted as expansion franchises. The New Jersey Knights finally found a home, moving to San Diego, where they became the Mariners, and the New England Whalers, lured by a new convention center, left Boston for Hartford, Connecticut.

The Los Angeles Sharks were on the move, too. They headed for Detroit and became the Michigan Stags, then the Baltimore Blades. Slowly, they were going down the tubes.

The 14-team league was divided into three divisions—the Canadian, Western and Eastern. The head office was moved from Newport Beach, California, to Toronto. And the league bank was located

*San Diego's Andre Lacroix led the WHA with 147 points in 1974-75.*

in Winnipeg, where Ben Hatskin sat as chairman of the board.

League attendance jumped from 2.7 million to 4.1 with the Howes and Houston leading the way.

Bobby Hull was creating a stir, too, frolicking beside his new Swedish linemates, Anders Hedberg and Ulf Nilsson, in Winnipeg.

Hull scored 77 goals in 78 games. But the scoring championship went to Andre Lacroix of San Diego with 41 goals and 106 assists on a line with Wayne Rivers and Rick Sentes. Rivers had 54 goals.

Sparked by Ron Grahame's three shutouts and Mark Howe's 22 points, Houston breezed through the playoffs, suffering only one loss. The Quebec Nordiques were no match for the Aeros in the final as Houston won in four straight games.

# 1974–75

## FINAL STANDINGS

### Canadian Division

| | W | L | T | PTS | GF | GA |
|---|---|---|---|---|---|---|
| Quebec | 46 | 32 | 0 | 92 | 331 | 299 |
| Toronto | 43 | 33 | 2 | 88 | 349 | 304 |
| Winnipeg | 38 | 35 | 5 | 81 | 322 | 293 |
| Vancouver | 37 | 39 | 2 | 76 | 256 | 270 |
| Edmonton | 36 | 38 | 4 | 76 | 279 | 279 |

### Eastern Division

| | W | L | T | PTS | GF | GA |
|---|---|---|---|---|---|---|
| New England | 43 | 30 | 5 | 91 | 274 | 279 |
| Cleveland | 35 | 40 | 3 | 73 | 236 | 258 |
| Chicago | 30 | 47 | 1 | 61 | 261 | 312 |
| Indianapolis | 18 | 57 | 3 | 39 | 216 | 338 |

### Western Division

| | W | L | T | PTS | GF | GA |
|---|---|---|---|---|---|---|
| Houston | 53 | 25 | 0 | 106 | 369 | 247 |
| San Diego | 43 | 31 | 4 | 90 | 326 | 268 |
| Minnesota | 42 | 33 | 3 | 87 | 308 | 279 |
| Phoenix | 39 | 31 | 8 | 86 | 300 | 265 |
| Baltimore | 21 | 53 | 4 | 46 | 205 | 341 |

## LEADING SCORERS

| | G | A | PTS |
|---|---|---|---|
| Lacroix, San Diego | 41 | 106 | 147 |
| Hull, Winnipeg | 77 | 65 | 142 |
| Bernier, Quebec | 54 | 68 | 122 |
| Nilsson, Winnipeg | 26 | 94 | 120 |
| Lund, Houston | 33 | 75 | 108 |
| Rivers, San Diego | 54 | 53 | 107 |
| Hedberg, Winnipeg | 53 | 47 | 100 |
| G. Howe, Houston | 34 | 65 | 99 |
| Dillon, Toronto | 29 | 66 | 95 |
| Walton, Minnesota | 48 | 45 | 93 |

# 1975–76

The Winnipeg Jets were a unique hockey club. They were owned by no one. More than 5,000 citizens had put up amounts ranging from $25 to $25,000

to keep the team viable. Shares were non-redeemable.

Some donors actually put their shares in the name of their pets. But the Jets weren't going to the dogs.

Their lineup included nine Europeans—two Finns and seven Swedes. They trained in Finland and Sweden and even stopped off in Prague, Czechoslovakia, for two exhibition games against the National team.

Returning the favor, the Czechs flew the Jets home to Canada free of charge.

Then, at Christmas, they traveled to Moscow for the Izvestia Cup. They became a better hockey club, perfecting a whirling style of play that frustrated their professional opponents.

Fourteen teams started the season but only 12 finished. The Minnesota Fighting Saints and Denver Spurs went by the wayside. The Spurs, a new entry owned by Ivan Mullenix of St. Louis, lasted only 41 games. The Vancouver Blazers moved to Calgary, where they became the Cowboys. The Cincinnati Stingers joined up and the Chicago Cougars dropped out.

The Indianapolis Racers (35–39–6), Houston Aeros (35–27–0) and Winnipeg (52–27–2) won divisional titles, and the Jets emerged as league champions. They swept the defending champions from Houston in the Avco Cup final.

The Quebec Nordiques gained some consolation when left winger Marc Tardif won the scoring championship with 71 goals and 77 assists for 148 points, a league record.

# 1975–76

## FINAL STANDINGS

### Canadian Division

| | W | L | T | PTS | GF | GA |
|---|---|---|---|---|---|---|
| Winnipeg | 52 | 27 | 2 | 106 | 345 | 254 |
| Quebec | 50 | 27 | 4 | 104 | 371 | 316 |
| Calgary | 41 | 35 | 4 | 86 | 307 | 282 |
| Edmonton | 27 | 49 | 5 | 59 | 268 | 345 |
| Toronto | 24 | 52 | 5 | 53 | 335 | 398 |

### Eastern Division

| | W | L | T | PTS | GF | GA |
|---|---|---|---|---|---|---|
| Indianapolis | 35 | 39 | 6 | 76 | 245 | 247 |
| Cleveland | 35 | 40 | 5 | 75 | 273 | 279 |
| New England | 33 | 40 | 7 | 73 | 255 | 290 |
| Cincinnati | 35 | 44 | 1 | 71 | 285 | 340 |

### Western Division

| | W | L | T | PTS | GF | GA |
|---|---|---|---|---|---|---|
| Houston | 53 | 27 | 0 | 106 | 341 | 263 |
| Phoenix | 39 | 35 | 6 | 84 | 302 | 287 |
| San Diego | 36 | 38 | 6 | 78 | 303 | 290 |
| Minnesota | 30 | 25 | 4 | 64 | 211 | 212 |
| Ottawa | 14 | 26 | 1 | 29 | 134 | 172 |

*Mike Walton soared, but the Minnesota Fighting Saints fell by the wayside in 1975-76.*

## LEADING SCORERS

| | G | A | PTS |
|---|---|---|---|
| Tardif, Quebec | 71 | 77 | 148 |
| Hull, Winnipeg | 53 | 70 | 123 |
| Cloutier, Quebec | 60 | 54 | 114 |
| Nilsson, Winnipeg | 38 | 76 | 114 |
| Ftorek, Phoenix | 41 | 72 | 113 |
| Bordeleau, Quebec | 37 | 72 | 109 |
| Hedberg, Winnipeg | 50 | 55 | 105 |
| Houle, Quebec | 51 | 52 | 103 |
| Bernier, Quebec | 34 | 68 | 102 |
| G. Howe, Houston | 32 | 70 | 102 |

# 1976–77

The WHA, upon completing its fourth season, had survived longer than anyone had thought. Its teams had gradually grown stronger, and challenges were sought.

Even the warlords of the NHL had begun to mellow. Passively, they agreed to a 21-game exhibition series in September. The benefits would be twofold. The games would not only serve as preseason conditioners, but the competition between leagues would serve as a built-in rivalry.

When the series was over, the WHA teams had won 13 games, tied two others and lost six.

"Game in and game out, our teams can play with their teams," said Howard Baldwin, the WHA president. "We proved it indisputably."

Political points, to be sure.

Internally, the new league continued to lose teams and gain cities. A second edition of the Minnesota Fighting Saints lasted only 42 games. The Toronto Toros moved to Birmingham, Alabama, and became the Bulls.

But the big newsmakers were the Quebec Nordiques, Robbie Ftorek, the Howes and Anders Hedberg, the Swedish Express of the Winnipeg Jets.

Suffering from a case of "Bolinitis"—a malady named after the difficult Houston Aero owner, George Bolin—the Howes left Texas for New England. Ftorek, a small but dynamic center with the lowly Phoenix Roadrunners, became the first Amer-

*Quebec's Real Cloutier captured the WHA's 1976-77 scoring title.*

ican-born athlete to win MVP honors in major professional hockey.

Hedberg, a 25-year-old right winger, broke one of hockey's most prestigious records, scoring 51 goals in 49 games, breaking the "50 in 50" mark previously set in the NHL by Maurice (The Rocket) Richard.

The Nordiques won their first Avco Cup by beating Winnipeg in a final series that went the full seven games. Veteran center Serge Bernier was a terror in the playoffs, collecting 14 goals and 22 assists in 17 games. The scoring champion was his teammate, Real (Buddy) Cloutier, with 66 goals, 75 assists for 141 points.

# 1976–77

## FINAL STANDINGS

### Eastern Division

| | W | L | T | PTS | GF | GA |
|---|---|---|---|---|---|---|
| Quebec | 47 | 31 | 3 | 97 | 353 | 295 |
| Cincinnati | 39 | 37 | 5 | 83 | 354 | 303 |
| Indianapolis | 36 | 37 | 8 | 80 | 276 | 305 |
| New England | 35 | 40 | 6 | 76 | 275 | 290 |
| Birmingham | 31 | 46 | 4 | 66 | 289 | 309 |
| Minnesota | 19 | 18 | 5 | 43 | 136 | 129 |

### Western Division

| | W | L | T | PTS | GF | GA |
|---|---|---|---|---|---|---|
| Houston | 50 | 24 | 6 | 106 | 320 | 241 |
| Winnipeg | 46 | 32 | 2 | 94 | 366 | 291 |
| San Diego | 40 | 37 | 4 | 84 | 284 | 283 |
| Edmonton | 34 | 43 | 4 | 72 | 243 | 304 |
| Calgary | 31 | 43 | 7 | 69 | 252 | 296 |
| Phoenix | 28 | 48 | 4 | 60 | 281 | 383 |

## LEADING SCORERS

| | G | A | PTS |
|---|---|---|---|
| Cloutier, Quebec | 66 | 75 | 141 |
| Hedberg, Winnipeg | 70 | 61 | 131 |
| Nilsson, Winnipeg | 39 | 85 | 124 |
| Ftorek, Phoenix | 46 | 71 | 117 |
| Lacroix, San Diego | 32 | 82 | 114 |
| Tardif, Quebec | 49 | 60 | 109 |
| Leduc, Cincinnati | 52 | 55 | 107 |
| Bordeleau, Quebec | 32 | 75 | 107 |
| Stoughton, Cincinnati | 52 | 52 | 104 |
| Napier, Birmingham | 60 | 36 | 96 |
| Sobchuk, Cincinnati | 44 | 52 | 96 |
| Bernier, Quebec | 43 | 53 | 96 |

# 1977–78

Howard Baldwin was in tears as he stood in the lobby of the Auberge des Gouverneurs in Quebec City the morning after the WHA's sixth All-Star game. His bags were packed and he was on his way home to Hartford to inspect the damage. At 4 A.M., he had received a call informing him that the roof of the Hartford Civic Center had collapsed under the weight of snow.

Baldwin, the Whalers' trustee and president of the WHA, could barely speak. The hopes and dreams of his franchise hinged on the building that injected new life into downtown Hartford. However, nearby Springfield, in Massachusetts, came to the rescue by making the arena available to the Whalers.

It was the second piece of bad news the WHA had received. The other haymaker landed earlier in the boardrooms where men representing the Winnipeg Jets announced details of an offer two of their top players had received from the New York Rangers. Anders Hedberg and Ulf Nilsson would eventually go for $2.4 million.

Now, the National Hockey League was raiding the WHA.

Only eight teams surfaced for the sixth season. Ray Kroc (McDonald's hamburger king) decided he had wasted enough money on the San Diego Mariners. The Phoenix Roadrunners lost their backers, too, and so did the Calgary Cowboys.

The survivors were lumped into one division. As a novelty, All-Star teams from the Soviet Union and Czechoslovakia played eight-game schedules in the WHA.

Scoring champ and MVP was Marc Tardif, the Quebec left winger who shattered his own record with 65 goals and 89 assists for 154 points.

The Birmingham Bulls, coached by Glen Sonmor, were the rogues of the league. Before each game a Baptist minister would read the invocation. Then the brawling would start. After the games, Sonmor would lead the fans in song at The Bar Across The Street.

The Jets, however, were the class of the league. Reeling off 50 wins in the regular season, they gathered momentum in the playoffs to eliminate Birmingham in five and New England in four to win their second Avco Cup.

# 1977–78

## FINAL STANDINGS

| | W | L | T | PTS | GF | GA |
|---|---|---|---|---|---|---|
| Winnipeg | 50 | 28 | 2 | 102 | 381 | 270 |
| New England | 44 | 31 | 5 | 93 | 335 | 269 |
| Houston | 42 | 34 | 4 | 88 | 296 | 302 |
| Quebec | 40 | 37 | 3 | 83 | 349 | 347 |
| Edmonton | 38 | 39 | 3 | 79 | 309 | 307 |
| Birmingham | 36 | 41 | 3 | 75 | 287 | 314 |
| Cincinnati | 35 | 42 | 3 | 73 | 298 | 332 |
| Indianapolis | 24 | 51 | 5 | 53 | 267 | 353 |
| Soviet All-Stars | 3 | 4 | 1 | 7 | 27 | 36 |
| Czechoslovakia | 1 | 6 | 1 | 3 | 21 | 40 |

*Anders Hedberg and Ulf Nilsson helped Winnipeg win the Avco Cup in 1978, then skated off to the NHL.*

## LEADING SCORERS

| | G | A | PTS |
|---|---|---|---|
| Tardif, Quebec | 65 | 89 | 154 |
| Cloutier, Quebec | 56 | 73 | 129 |
| U. Nilsson, Winnipeg | 37 | 89 | 126 |
| Hedberg, Winnipeg | 63 | 59 | 122 |
| Hull, Winnipeg | 46 | 71 | 117 |
| Lacroix, Houston | 36 | 77 | 113 |
| Ftorek, Cincinnati | 59 | 50 | 109 |
| K. Nilsson, Winnipeg | 42 | 65 | 107 |
| G. Howe, New England | 34 | 62 | 96 |
| M. Howe, New England | 30 | 61 | 91 |

# 1978–79

No one really believed the WHA's seventh season would be its last. Hopes had been built up before.

As early as April 1973, the WHA and NHL had met to discuss a possible merger.

Gradually, the number of teams was dwindling. What had once been a 14-team league was now reduced to six. The league was running out of cities. But there was a movement afoot to incorporate a division in Europe.

The WHA was alive and kicking as evidenced by two shrewd moves. Nelson Skalbania, the flamboyant Vancouver businessman, had robbed the cradle of Canadian hockey. Acting on behalf of his team, the Indianapolis Racers, Skalbania signed Wayne Gretzky, a 17-year-old sensation, to a personal services contract.

Indianapolis fans, who had never heard of him before, showed only a casual interest in the skinny, blond kid. With only a few season tickets sold, Skalbania started looking for a buyer. He found two prospects in Winnipeg's Michael Gobuty and Edmonton's Peter Pocklington.

Boarding a plane in Indianapolis, Gretzky didn't know where it would land. Pocklington sweetened his offer. The pilot was instructed to proceed to Edmonton. Days later, the Racers folded.

The Jets had already spent a bundle, buying 12 contracts from the folding Houston Aeros.

Real (Buddy) Cloutier of Quebec won his second scoring championship with 75 goals, 54 assists for a total of 129 points.

Edmonton, led by Gretzky's 110 points, finished on top with a 48–30–2 record. But the Oilers couldn't capture their first and the last Avco Cup.

Sparked by the Houston acquisitions, most notably Terry Ruskowski, Rich Preston and Morris Lu-

kowich, the Jets whipped Edmonton in five games in the league final.

The last Avco Cup was theirs. And still is.

## 1978–79

### FINAL STANDINGS

|  | W | L | T | PTS | GF | GA |
|---|---|---|---|---|---|---|
| Edmonton | 48 | 30 | 2 | 98 | 340 | 266 |
| Quebec | 41 | 34 | 5 | 87 | 288 | 271 |
| Winnipeg | 39 | 35 | 6 | 84 | 307 | 306 |
| New England | 37 | 34 | 9 | 83 | 298 | 287 |
| Cincinnati | 33 | 41 | 6 | 72 | 274 | 284 |
| Birmingham | 32 | 42 | 6 | 70 | 286 | 311 |

### LEADING SCORERS

|  | G | A | PTS |
|---|---|---|---|
| Cloutier, Quebec | 75 | 54 | 129 |
| Ftorek, Cincinnati | 39 | 77 | 116 |
| Gretzky, Edmonton | 46 | 64 | 110 |
| M. Howe, New England | 42 | 65 | 107 |
| K. Nilsson, Winnipeg | 39 | 68 | 107 |
| Lukowich, Winnipeg | 65 | 34 | 99 |
| Tardif, Quebec | 41 | 55 | 96 |
| Lacroix, New England | 32 | 56 | 88 |
| Sullivan, Winnipeg | 46 | 40 | 86 |
| Ruskowski, Winnipeg | 20 | 66 | 86 |

*Wayne Gretzky makes sure he'll be an Edmonton Oiler for some time as he signs a 20-year contract in 1979.*

# 15

# ANOTHER PART OF THE ICE

The world of hockey is by no means limited to the National Hockey League. It has an extensive minor league network which includes the American, International, Central and Atlantic Coast Leagues as well as flourishing amateur and collegiate programs in both the United States and Canada.

And as the years go by, more and more players graduate from the Olympic and collegiate ranks into the National Hockey League. Red Berenson, the first superstar of the NHL's expansion West Division in the late 1960s, graduated from Michigan and led all collegiate scorers in 1961–62. Tony Esposito, the standout goalie of the Chicago Black Hawks, was an All-American at Michigan Tech.

Tommy Williams, who played for years with the Boston Bruins in the '60s, was a member of the United States' championship Olympic squad of 1960. The 1980 gold-medal U.S. team contributed several men to the ranks of the NHL, including Ken Morrow of the New York Islanders, Mike Ramsey of the Buffalo Sabres, Neil Broten of the Minnesota North Stars and Dave Christian of the Winnipeg Jets.

◄ *Members of victorious U.S. Olympic hockey team sing national anthem at the awards ceremony in Lake Placid in 1980.*

The National Collegiate Athletic Association started an annual hockey tournament in 1948 and Michigan has dominated the competition, winning the national title seven times. Olympic competition at the Winter Olympics began in 1920 and a separate World Championship tournament began in 1924. In recent years, with rare exceptions, the Soviet Union has dominated both competitions.

## COLLEGE HOCKEY

From somewhat modest beginnings, collegiate hockey in the United States has grown tremendously in recent years. There are highly successful Christmas tournaments as well as the climactic NCAA tournament in March.

U.S. colleges recruit players from Canada and the program has become almost as extensive as the one the schools follow in tracking down talented football players. Most collegiate rosters are stacked with Canadian imports, but in recent years more and more American-born youths are playing hockey in college. The U.S. triumph in the 1980 Olympic Games has provided incentive for home-grown talent to pursue the sport.

A number of collegiate players have successfully

*Brad Shelstad of the University of Minnesota stops Michigan Tech's George Lyle in 1974 NCAA championship game won by Minnesota.*

moved into professional hockey. The number seems to be increasing as more youngsters recognize the value of a college education before trying pro hockey.

A list of collegiate champions and runners-up follows:

**1948**
1. Michigan
2. Dartmouth

**1949**
1. Boston College
2. Dartmouth

**1950**
1. Colorado College
2. Boston University

**1951**
1. Michigan
2. Brown

**1952**
1. Michigan
2. Colorado College

**1953**
1. Michigan
2. Minnesota

**1954**
1. R.P.I.
2. Minnesota

**1955**
1. Michigan
2. Colorado College

**1956**
1. Michigan
2. Michigan Tech

**1957**
1. Colorado College
2. Michigan

**1958**
1. Denver University
2. North Dakota

**1959**
1. North Dakota
2. Michigan State

**1960**
1. Denver University
2. Michigan Tech

**1961**
1. Denver University
2. St. Lawrence

**1962**
1. Michigan Tech
2. Clarkson

**1963**
1. North Dakota
2. Denver University

**1964**
1. Michigan
2. Denver University

**1965**
1. Michigan Tech
2. Boston College

**1966**
1. Michigan State
2. Clarkson

**1967**
1. Cornell
2. Boston University

**1968**
1. Denver University
2. North Dakota

**1969**
1. Denver University
2. Cornell

**1970**
1. Cornell
2. Clarkson

**1971**
1. Boston University
2. Minnesota

**1972**
1. Boston University
2. Cornell

**1973**
1. Wisconsin
2. Denver University

**1974**
1. Minnesota
2. Michigan Tech

**1975**
1. Michigan Tech
2. Minnesota

**1976**
1. Minnesota
2. Michigan Tech

**1977**
1. Wisconsin
2. Michigan

**1978**
1. Boston University
2. Boston College

**1979**
1. Minnesota
2. North Dakota

**1980**
1. North Dakota
2. Northern Michigan

**1981**
1. Wisconsin
2. Minnesota

**1982**
1. North Dakota
2. Wisconsin

**1983**
1. Wisconsin
2. Harvard

## OLYMPIC GAMES

When the Winter Olympics began in 1924, hockey was one of the sports on the schedule. It had been added to the Olympic program in 1920, when there was a single competition instead of separate winter and summer Games. Canada dominated at first, winning the championship in each of the first four Olympic competitions. The Canadians won two more titles following World War II before the Soviet Union started a domination which led to five championships in the next seven Games. The two times the Russians missed were in 1960 and 1980, and in both cases it was the United States that pulled major upsets.

The Americans were given little chance to win in 1960, but were determined to score an upset. "We knew with a couple of breaks we could upset the odds," recalled goaltender Jack McCartan. The U.S. team had one thing going for them: the Games were held at Squaw Valley, California.

After winning four games in the preliminaries, the Americans passed a big test by edging Canada, 2-1, as McCartan made 39 saves. The U.S. squad then rallied to stun the Russians, 3-2, setting up the championship game against Czechoslovakia. Again the Americans rallied, scoring six times in the final period to win, 9-4, and take the gold.

Twenty years later, another group of young Americans gave their country an even bigger thrill as they

*Action at the 1932 Winter Olympics in Lake Placid, as Germany (dark uniforms) defends against Canada.*

came from nowhere to skate off with the Olympic gold.

The 1980 Games were again held in the United States—at Lake Placid, New York—and once more the U.S. team was a heavy underdog. Just a few days before the Games began, the Americans lost, 11–3, to the Russians in an exhibition game. U.S. coach Herb Brooks was hoping his team could get a silver or bronze medal.

They didn't; they came home with the gold. After tying Sweden with a last-minute goal in their opening game, the Americans raced to four straight wins to advance to the semifinals. Awaiting them there were the vaunted Soviets. Before the game, Brooks told his players, "You were born to be hockey players. You were meant to be here. This moment is yours."

And the game was theirs, too, as Mike Eruzione snapped a tie with ten minutes left and the U.S. held on for a stunning 4–3 victory. That sent the Americans into the finals against Finland in a game that would settle it all.

The U.S. squad, which averaged just 20 years of age, spotted the Finns a 2–1 lead going into the last period but then roared back for three goals. When the game ended, thousands of fans started singing "God Bless America" and waving American flags. The Soviet streak of four consecutive Olympic gold

medals had been stopped. The U.S. had its gold and the Russians had to settle for silver.

The list of Olympic medal winners follows:

**1920**
1. Canada
2. USA
3. Czechoslovakia

**1924**
1. Canada
2. USA
3. Great Britain

**1928**
1. Canada
2. Sweden
3. Switzerland

**1932**
1. Canada
2. USA
3. Germany

**1936**
1. Great Britain
2. Canada
3. USA
No Olympics in 1940 or 1944

**1948**
1. Canada
2. Czechoslovakia
3. Switzerland

**1952**
1. Canada
2. USA
3. Sweden

**1956**
1. Soviet Union
2. USA
3. Canada

**1960**
1. USA
2. Canada
3. Soviet Union

**1964**
1. Soviet Union
2. Sweden
3. Czechoslovakia

**1968**
1. Soviet Union
2. Czechoslovakia
3. Canada

**1972**
1. Soviet Union
2. USA
3. Czechoslovakia

**1976**
1. Soviet Union
2. Czechoslovakia
3. West Germany

**1980**
1. USA
2. Soviet Union
3. Sweden

*Paul Johnson (far right) has just scored the winning goal for the U.S. in its 2-1 decision over Canada in the 1960 Olympic semifinals at Squaw Valley, California.*

Rob McClanahan beats
Finnish goalie Jorma
Valtonen to break tie and
clinch gold medal for U.S.
at the 1980 Winter
Olympics.

# WORLD CHAMPIONSHIPS

Except for Olympic years, hockey stages a yearly world championship tournament. The Soviet Union has monopolized the competition, winning the crown nine straight years from 1963 through 1971 and 17 of the 21 years through 1983.

The Russians are acknowledged as the best amateur players in the world and it is especially remarkable when one considers that they didn't even take up hockey until the late 1940s.

But the Russian team plays as a unit virtually year-round and it shows in the world tournaments, when they are frequently playing teams, such as the U.S., that get together for a relatively short period before the competition.

The list of world championship results follows:

**1924**
1. Canada
2. USA
3. Great Britain

**1928**
1. Canada
2. Sweden
3. Switzerland

**1930**
1. Canada
2. Germany
3. Switzerland

**1931**
1. Canada
2. USA
3. Austria

**1932**
1. Canada
2. USA
3. Germany

**1933**
1. USA
2. Canada
3. Czechoslovakia

**1934**
1. Canada
2. USA
3. Germany

**1935**
1. Canada
2. Switzerland
3. Great Britain

**1936**
1. Great Britain
2. Canada
3. USA

**1937**
1. Canada
2. Great Britain
3. Switzerland

**1938**
1. Canada
2. Great Britain
3. Czechoslovakia

**1939**
1. Canada
2. USA
3. Switzerland

**1947**
1. Czechoslovakia
2. Sweden
3. Austria

**1948**
1. Canada
2. Czechoslovakia
3. Switzerland

**1949**
1. Czechoslovakia
2. Canada
3. USA

**1950**
1. Canada
2. USA
3. Switzerland

**1951**
1. Canada
2. Sweden
3. Switzerland

**1952**
1. Canada
2. USA
3. Sweden

**1953**
1. Sweden
2. German Federal Republic
3. Switzerland

**1954**
1. Soviet Union
2. Canada
3. Sweden

**1955**
1. Canada
2. Soviet Union
3. Czechoslovakia

**1956**
1. Soviet Union
2. USA
3. Canada

**1957**
1. Sweden
2. Soviet Union
3. Czechoslovakia

**1958**
1. Canada
2. Soviet Union
3. Sweden

**1959**
1. Canada
2. Soviet Union
3. Czechoslovakia

**1960**
1. USA
2. Canada
3. Soviet Union

**1961**
1. Canada
2. Czechoslovakia
3. Soviet Union

**1962**
1. Sweden
2. Canada
3. USA

**1963**
1. Soviet Union
2. Sweden
3. Czechoslovakia

**1964**
1. Soviet Union
2. Sweden
3. Czechoslovakia

**1965**
1. Soviet Union
2. Czechoslovakia
3. Sweden

**1966**
1. Soviet Union
2. Czechoslovakia
3. Canada

**1967**
1. Soviet Union
2. Sweden
3. Canada

**1968**
1. Soviet Union
2. Czechoslovakia
3. Canada

**1969**
1. Soviet Union
2. Sweden
3. Czechoslovakia

**1970**
1. Soviet Union
2. Sweden
3. Czechoslovakia

**1971**
1. Soviet Union
2. Czechoslovakia
3. Sweden

**1972**
1. Czechoslovakia
2. Soviet Union
3. Sweden

**1973**
1. Soviet Union
2. Sweden
3. Czechoslovakia

**1974**
1. Soviet Union
2. Czechoslovakia
3. Sweden

**1975**
1. Soviet Union
2. Czechoslovakia
3. Sweden

**1976**
1. Czechoslovakia
2. Soviet Union
3. Sweden

**1977**
1. Czechoslovakia
2. Sweden
3. Soviet Union

**1978**
1. Soviet Union
2. Czechoslovakia
3. Canada

**1979**
1. Soviet Union
2. Czechoslovakia
3. Sweden

**1980**
1. USA
2. Soviet Union
3. Sweden

**1981**
1. Soviet Union
2. Sweden
3. Czechoslovakia

**1982**
1. Soviet Union
2. Czechoslovakia
3. Canada

**1983**
1. Soviet Union
2. Czechoslovakia
3. Canada

# INTERNATIONAL CHALLENGES

The Soviet Union's dominance of the Olympic and world championship tournaments led to an inevitable argument over who was better: the Russians or the National Hockey League professionals. The question was answered on the ice in the 1970s.

The first confrontation came in 1972, when the NHL All-Stars played the Russians in an eight-game series. The NHL team won, but just barely, when Paul Henderson scored in the last minute of the final game, to give his squad a 4–3–1 edge in games.

In 1974, the World Hockey Association sent an All-Star team to Russia to play the Soviets in an eight-game series, and this time the Russians won four and tied three of the games.

In 1976, the NHL stars of Team Canada defeated Czechoslovakia on an overtime goal by Darryl Sittler that enabled Canada to capture the Canada Cup tournament.

The NHL All-Stars met the Soviets in a three-game Challenge Cup series at New York's Madison Square Garden in February, 1979 and the Russians rallied after dropping the first game to take the set, two games to one. The USSR continued its winning ways in the 1981 Canada Cup. The Soviets walloped the Canadians, 8–1, in the final game to take home the Cup.

*Team Canada and the Soviet national team tangle in front of the net in an historic eight-game series in 1972.*

# 16

# ALL-TIME NHL PLAYER REGISTER

The following sections (the first covering all but goalies; the second for goalies) include the record of every player who has ever appeared in an NHL regular-season game. In addition, NHL players who performed in the World Hockey Association also have their WHA records listed.

During the middle 1920s and until the late 1930s, the category listing games played was not recorded in official league records. Therefore, in a number of instances, they do not appear here.

Where information is missing, it was unavailable.

The following are the abbreviations used for the various teams:

| | |
|---|---|
| Alb (WHA) | Alberta Oilers |
| Atl | Atlanta Flames |
| Balt (WHA) | Baltimore Blades |
| Birm (WHA) | Birmingham Bulls |
| Bos | Boston Bruins |
| Brk | Brooklyn Americans |
| Buf | Buffalo Sabres |
| Cal | California Seals |
| Calg | Calgary Flames |
| Calg (WHA) | Calgary Cowboys |
| Chi | Chicago Black Hawks |
| Chi (WHA) | Chicago Cougars |
| Cin (WHA) | Cincinnati Stingers |
| Clev | Cleveland Barons |
| Clev (WHA) | Cleveland Crusaders |
| Col | Colorado Rockies |
| Den (WHA) | Denver Spurs |
| Det | Detroit Cougars, Falcons, Red Wings |
| Edm or Edm (WHA) | Edmonton Oilers |
| Ham | Hamilton Tigers |
| Hart or Hart (WHA) | Hartford Whalers |
| Hou (WHA) | Houston Aeros |
| Ind (WHA) | Indianapolis Racers |
| KC | Kansas City Scouts |
| LA | Los Angeles Kings |
| LA (WHA) | Los Angeles Sharks |
| Mich (WHA) | Michigan Stags |
| Minn | Minnesota North Stars |
| Minn (WHA) | Minnesota Fighting Saints |

| | |
|---|---|
| Mont | Montreal Canadiens |
| MontM | Montreal Maroons |
| MontW | Montreal Wanderers |
| NE (WHA) | New England Whalers |
| NJ | New Jersey Devils |
| NJ (WHA) | New Jersey Knights |
| NYA | New York Americans |
| NYI | New York Islanders |
| NYR | New York Rangers |
| NY (WHA) | New York Golden Blades, Raiders |
| Oak | Oakland Seals |
| Ott | Ottawa Senators |
| Ott (WHA) | Ottawa Nationals |
| Phil | Philadelphia Flyers |
| PhilQ | Philadelphia Quakers |
| Phil (WHA) | Philadelphia Blazers |
| Phoe (WHA) | Phoenix Roadrunners |
| Pitt | Pittsburgh Penguins |
| PittPi | Pittsburgh Pirates |
| Que | Quebec Bulldogs, Nordiques |
| Que (WHA) | Quebec Nordiques |
| SD (WHA) | San Diego Mariners |
| StL | St. Louis Blues |
| StLE | St. Louis Eagles |
| Tor | Toronto Arenas, Maple Leafs, St. Pats |
| Tor (WHA) | Toronto Toros |
| Van | Vancouver Canucks |
| Van (WHA) | Vancouver Blazers |
| Wash | Washington Capitals |

| | |
|---|---|
| Winn or Winn (WHA) | Winnipeg Jets |

**CANADIAN PROVINCES**

| | |
|---|---|
| Alta. | Alberta |
| B.C. | British Columbia |
| Man. | Manitoba |
| N.B. | New Brunswick |
| Nfld. | Newfoundland |
| N.S. | Nova Scotia |
| Ont. | Ontario |
| P.E.I. | Prince Edward Island |
| Que. | Quebec |
| Sask. | Saskachewan |
| Yuk. | The Yukon |
| N.W.T. | Northwest Territory |

**EXPLANATION OF ABBREVIATIONS**

| | |
|---|---|
| **A** | Assists |
| **AVE** | Average goals-against per game |
| **AGP** | Average goals-against per period |
| **G** | Goals scored |
| **GA** | Goals against |
| **GP** | Games played |
| **NHL** | National Hockey League |
| **Pts** | Points scored |
| **Sho** | Shutouts |
| **Per** | Periods |
| **WHA** | World Hockey Association |

# FORWARDS and DEFENSEMEN

| Season | Club | GP | G | A | Pts. |
|---|---|---|---|---|---|
| **ABBOT, Reginald** *Forward* | | | | | |
| b. Winnipeg, Man., Feb. 4, 1930 | | | | | |
| 1952-53 | Montreal | 3 | 0 | 0 | 0 |
| **ABEL, Clarence John (Taffy)** *Defenseman* | | | | | |
| b. Sault Ste. Marie, Mich., May 28, 1900 | | | | | |
| 1926-27 | New York R | 44 | 8 | 4 | 12 |
| 1927-28 | New York R | 22 | 0 | 1 | 1 |
| 1928-29 | New York R | 33 | 2 | 1 | 3 |
| 1929-30 | Chicago | 38 | 3 | 3 | 6 |
| 1930-31 | Chicago | 43 | 0 | 1 | 1 |
| 1931-32 | Chicago | 48 | 3 | 3 | 6 |
| 1932-33 | Chicago | 47 | 0 | 4 | 4 |
| 1933-34 | Chicago | 46 | 2 | 1 | 3 |
| | **Totals** | 321 | 18 | 18 | 36 |
| **ABEL, Gerald Scott (Gerry)** *Forward* | | | | | |
| b. Detroit, Mich., Dec. 25, 1944 | | | | | |
| 1966-67 | Detroit | 1 | 0 | 0 | 0 |
| **ABEL, Sidney Gerald** *Forward* | | | | | |
| b. Melville, Sask., Feb. 22, 1918 | | | | | |
| 1938-39 | Detroit | 15 | 1 | 1 | 2 |
| 1939-40 | Detroit | 24 | 1 | 5 | 6 |
| 1940-41 | Detroit | 47 | 11 | 22 | 37 |
| 1941-42 | Detroit | 48 | 18 | 31 | 49 |
| 1942-43 | Detroit | 49 | 18 | 24 | 42 |
| 1945-46 | Detroit | 7 | 0 | 2 | 2 |
| 1946-47 | Detroit | 60 | 19 | 29 | 48 |
| 1947-48 | Detroit | 60 | 14 | 30 | 44 |
| 1948-49 | Detroit | 60 | 28 | 26 | 54 |
| 1949-50 | Detroit | 70 | 34 | 35 | 69 |
| 1950-51 | Detroit | 69 | 23 | 38 | 61 |
| 1951-52 | Detroit | 62 | 17 | 36 | 53 |
| 1952-53 | Chicago | 39 | 5 | 4 | 9 |
| | **Totals** | 610 | 189 | 283 | 472 |
| **ABGRALL, Dennis Harvey** *Forward* | | | | | |
| b. Mooseomin, Sask., Apr. 24, 1953 | | | | | |
| 1975-76 | Los Angeles | 13 | 0 | 2 | 2 |
| 1976-77 | Cincinnati (WHA) | 80 | 23 | 39 | 62 |
| 1977-78 | Cincinnati (WHA) | 65 | 13 | 11 | 24 |
| | **NHL Totals** | 13 | 0 | 2 | 2 |
| | **WHA Totals** | 145 | 36 | 50 | 86 |
| **ABRAHAMSSON, Thommy** *Defenseman* | | | | | |
| b. Umea, Sweden, Apr. 12, 1947 | | | | | |
| 1974-75 | New England (WHA) | 76 | 8 | 22 | 30 |
| 1975-76 | New England (WHA) | 63 | 14 | 21 | 35 |
| 1976-77 | New England (WHA) | 64 | 6 | 24 | 30 |
| 1980-81 | Hartford | 32 | 6 | 11 | 17 |
| | **NHL Totals** | 32 | 6 | 11 | 17 |
| | **WHA Totals** | 203 | 28 | 67 | 95 |
| **ACHTYMICHUK, Eugene Edward (Gene)** | | | | | |
| *Forward* | | | | | |
| b. Lamont, Alta., Sept. 7, 1932 | | | | | |
| 1956-57 | Montreal | 3 | 0 | 0 | 0 |
| 1957-58 | Montreal | 16 | 3 | 5 | 8 |
| 1958-59 | Detroit | 12 | 0 | 0 | 0 |
| | **Totals** | 31 | 3 | 5 | 8 |
| **ACOMB, Douglas Raymond** *Forward* | | | | | |
| b. Toronto, Ont., May 15, 1949 | | | | | |
| 1969-70 | Toronto | 2 | 0 | 1 | 1 |

| Season | Club | GP | G | A | Pts. |
|---|---|---|---|---|---|
| **ACTON, Keith Edward** *Forward* | | | | | |
| b. Newmarket, Ont., Apr. 15, 1958 | | | | | |
| 1979-80 | Montreal | 2 | 0 | 1 | 1 |
| 1980-81 | Montreal | 61 | 15 | 24 | 39 |
| 1981-82 | Montreal | 78 | 36 | 52 | 88 |
| 1982-83 | Montreal | 78 | 24 | 26 | 50 |
| | **Totals** | 219 | 75 | 103 | 178 |
| **ADAM, Douglas Patrick** *Forward* | | | | | |
| b. Toronto, Ont., Sept. 7, 1923 | | | | | |
| 1949-50 | New York R | 4 | 0 | 1 | 1 |
| **ADAM, Russ** *Forward* | | | | | |
| b. Windsor, Ont., May 5, 1961 | | | | | |
| 1982-83 | Toronto | 8 | 1 | 2 | 3 |
| **ADAMS, Greg** *Forward* | | | | | |
| b. Duncan, B.C., May 31, 1960 | | | | | |
| 1980-81 | Philadelphia | 6 | 3 | 0 | 3 |
| 1981-82 | Philadelphia | 33 | 4 | 15 | 19 |
| 1982-83 | Hartford | 79 | 10 | 13 | 23 |
| | **Totals** | 118 | 17 | 28 | 45 |
| **ADAMS, John E. (Jack)** *Forward* | | | | | |
| b. Calgary, Alta., May 5, 1920 | | | | | |
| 1940-41 | Montreal | 42 | 6 | 12 | 18 |
| **ADAMS, John J. (Jack)** *Forward* | | | | | |
| b. Ft. William, Ont., June 14, 1895 | | | | | |
| 1917-18 | Toronto | 8 | 0 | 0 | 0 |
| 1918-19 | Toronto | 17 | 3 | 3 | 6 |
| 1922-23 | Toronto | 23 | 19 | 9 | 28 |
| 1923-24 | Toronto | 22 | 13 | 3 | 16 |
| 1924-25 | Toronto | 27 | 21 | 8 | 29 |
| 1925-26 | Toronto | 36 | 21 | 5 | 26 |
| 1926-27 | Ottawa | 40 | 5 | 1 | 6 |
| | **Totals** | 173 | 82 | 29 | 111 |
| **ADAMS, Stewart** *Forward* | | | | | |
| b. 1904 | | | | | |
| 1929-30 | Chicago | 26 | 4 | 6 | 10 |
| 1930-31 | Chicago | 36 | 5 | 13 | 18 |
| 1931-32 | Chicago | 26 | 0 | 5 | 5 |
| 1932-33 | Toronto | 9 | 0 | 2 | 2 |
| | **Totals** | 97 | 9 | 26 | 35 |
| **ADDUONO, Rick** *Forward* | | | | | |
| b. Thunder Bay, Ont., Jan. 25, 1955 | | | | | |
| 1975-76 | Boston | 1 | 0 | 0 | 0 |
| 1978-79 | Birmingham (WHA) | 80 | 20 | 33 | 53 |
| 1979-80 | Atlanta | 3 | 0 | 0 | 0 |
| | **NHL Totals** | 4 | 0 | 0 | 0 |
| | **WHA Totals** | 80 | 20 | 33 | 53 |
| **AFFLECK, Robert Bruce** *Defenseman* | | | | | |
| b. Salmon Arm, B.C., May 5, 1954 | | | | | |
| 1974-75 | St Louis | 13 | 0 | 2 | 2 |
| 1975-76 | St Louis | 80 | 4 | 26 | 30 |
| 1976-77 | St Louis | 80 | 5 | 20 | 25 |
| 1977-78 | St Louis | 75 | 4 | 14 | 18 |
| 1978-79 | St Louis | 26 | 1 | 3 | 4 |
| 1979-80 | Vancouver | 5 | 0 | 1 | 1 |
| | **Totals** | 279 | 14 | 66 | 80 |

| Season | Club | GP | G | A | Pts. |
|---|---|---|---|---|---|
| **AHERN, Fredrick Vincent Jr.** *Forward* | | | | | |
| b. Boston, Mass., Feb. 12, 1952 | | | | | |
| 1974-75 | California | 3 | 2 | 1 | 3 |
| 1975-76 | California | 44 | 17 | 8 | 25 |
| 1976-77 | Cleveland | 25 | 4 | 4 | 8 |
| 1977-78 | Clev-Col | 74 | 8 | 17 | 25 |
| | **Totals** | 146 | 31 | 30 | 61 |
| **AHRENS, Chris** *Defenseman* | | | | | |
| b. San Bernardino, Calif., July 31, 1952 | | | | | |
| 1973-74 | Minnesota | 3 | 0 | 1 | 1 |
| 1974-75 | Minnesota | 44 | 0 | 2 | 2 |
| 1975-76 | Minnesota | 2 | 0 | 0 | 0 |
| 1976-77 | Minnesota | 2 | 0 | 0 | 0 |
| 1977-78 | Minnesota | 1 | 0 | 0 | 0 |
| 1977-78 | Edmonton (WHA) | 4 | 0 | 0 | 0 |
| | **NHL Totals** | 52 | 0 | 3 | 3 |
| | **WHA Totals** | 4 | 0 | 0 | 0 |
| **AILSBY, Lloyd** *Defenseman* | | | | | |
| b. Lac Pelletier, Sask., May 11, 1917 | | | | | |
| 1951-52 | New York R | 3 | 0 | 0 | 0 |
| **ALBRIGHT, Clinton Howard** *Forward* | | | | | |
| b. Winnipeg, Man., Feb. 28, 1926 | | | | | |
| 1948-49 | New York R | 59 | 14 | 5 | 19 |
| **ALDCORN, Gary William** *Forward* | | | | | |
| b. Shaunavon, Sask., Mar. 7, 1935 | | | | | |
| 1956-57 | Toronto | 22 | 5 | 1 | 6 |
| 1957-58 | Toronto | 59 | 10 | 14 | 24 |
| 1958-59 | Toronto | 5 | 0 | 3 | 3 |
| 1959-60 | Detroit | 70 | 22 | 29 | 51 |
| 1960-61 | Det-Bos | 70 | 4 | 9 | 13 |
| | **Totals** | 226 | 41 | 53 | 94 |
| **ALEXANDER, Arthur Claire** *Defenseman* | | | | | |
| b. Collingwood, Ont., June 16, 1945 | | | | | |
| 1974-75 | Toronto | 42 | 7 | 11 | 18 |
| 1975-76 | Toronto | 33 | 2 | 6 | 8 |
| 1976-77 | Toronto | 48 | 1 | 12 | 13 |
| 1977-78 | Vancouver | 32 | 8 | 18 | 26 |
| 1978-79 | Edmonton (WHA) | 54 | 8 | 23 | 31 |
| | **NHL Totals** | 155 | 18 | 47 | 65 |
| | **WHA Totals** | 54 | 8 | 23 | 31 |
| **ALEXANDRE, Arthur** *Forward* | | | | | |
| 1931-32 | Montreal | 10 | 0 | 2 | 2 |
| 1932-33 | Montreal | 1 | 0 | 0 | 0 |
| | **Totals** | 11 | 0 | 2 | 2 |
| **ALLAN, Jeff** *Defenseman* | | | | | |
| b. Hull, Que., May 17, 1957 | | | | | |
| 1977-78 | Cincinnati (WHA) | 2 | 0 | 0 | 0 |
| 1977-78 | Cleveland | 4 | 0 | 0 | 0 |
| | **NHL Totals** | 4 | 0 | 0 | 0 |
| | **WHA Totals** | 2 | 0 | 0 | 0 |
| **ALLEN, Courtney Keith (Bingo)** *Defenseman* | | | | | |
| b. Saskatoon, Sask., Aug. 21, 1923 | | | | | |
| 1953-54 | Detroit | 10 | 0 | 4 | 4 |
| 1954-55 | Detroit | 18 | 0 | 0 | 0 |
| | **Totals** | 28 | 0 | 4 | 4 |

**ALLEN, George Trenholme** *Defenseman*
b. Bayfield, N.B., July 27, 1914

| Season | Club | GP | G | A | Pts. |
|---|---|---|---|---|---|
| 1938-39 | New York R | 19 | 6 | 6 | 12 |
| 1939-40 | Chicago | 47 | 10 | 12 | 22 |
| 1940-41 | Chicago | 44 | 14 | 17 | 31 |
| 1941-42 | Chicago | 43 | 7 | 13 | 20 |
| 1942-43 | Chicago | 47 | 10 | 14 | 24 |
| 1943-44 | Chicago | 45 | 17 | 24 | 41 |
| 1945-46 | Chicago | 44 | 11 | 15 | 26 |
| 1946-47 | Montreal | 49 | 7 | 14 | 21 |
| | **Totals** | 338 | 82 | 115 | 197 |

**ALLEN, Vivan Mariner (Squee)** *Forward*
b. Bayfield, N.B., Sept. 9, 1916

| Season | Club | GP | G | A | Pts. |
|---|---|---|---|---|---|
| 1940-41 | New York A | — | 0 | 1 | 1 |

**ALLEY, Steve** *Forward*
b. Anoka, Minn., Dec. 29, 1953

| Season | Club | GP | G | A | Pts. |
|---|---|---|---|---|---|
| 1977-78 | Birmingham (WHA) | 27 | 8 | 12 | 20 |
| 1978-79 | Birmingham (WHA) | 78 | 17 | 24 | 41 |
| 1979-80 | Hartford | 7 | 1 | 1 | 2 |
| 1980-81 | Hartford | 8 | 2 | 2 | 4 |
| | **NHL Totals** | 15 | 3 | 3 | 6 |
| | **WHA Totals** | 105 | 25 | 36 | 61 |

**ALLISON, Michael Earnest** *Forward*
b. Fort Francis, Ont., Mar. 28, 1961

| Season | Club | GP | G | A | Pts. |
|---|---|---|---|---|---|
| 1980-81 | New York R | 75 | 26 | 38 | 64 |
| 1981-82 | New York R | 48 | 7 | 15 | 22 |
| 1982-83 | New York R | 39 | 11 | 9 | 20 |
| | **Totals** | 162 | 44 | 62 | 106 |

**ALLISON, Raymond Peter** *Forward*
b. Cranbrook, B.C., Mar. 4, 1959

| Season | Club | GP | G | A | Pts. |
|---|---|---|---|---|---|
| 1979-80 | Hartford | 64 | 16 | 12 | 28 |
| 1980-81 | Hartford | 6 | 1 | 0 | 1 |
| 1981-82 | Philadelphia | 51 | 17 | 37 | 54 |
| 1982-83 | Philadelphia | 67 | 21 | 30 | 51 |
| | **Totals** | 188 | 55 | 79 | 134 |

**ALLUM, William** *Defenseman*
b. Winnipeg, Man., Oct. 9, 1916

| Season | Club | GP | G | A | Pts. |
|---|---|---|---|---|---|
| 1939-40 | Chicago | 1 | 0 | 0 | 0 |
| 1940-41 | New York R | 1 | 0 | 1 | 1 |
| | **Totals** | 2 | 0 | 1 | 1 |

**AMADIO, David** *Defenseman*
b. Glace Bay, N.S., Apr. 23, 1939

| Season | Club | GP | G | A | Pts. |
|---|---|---|---|---|---|
| 1957-58 | Detroit | 2 | 0 | 0 | 0 |
| 1967-68 | Los Angeles | 58 | 4 | 6 | 10 |
| 1968-69 | Los Angeles | 65 | 1 | 5 | 6 |
| | **Totals** | 125 | 5 | 11 | 16 |

**AMODEO, Michael** *Defenseman*
b. Toronto, Ont., June 22, 1952

| Season | Club | GP | G | A | Pts. |
|---|---|---|---|---|---|
| 1972-73 | Ottawa (WHA) | 61 | 1 | 14 | 15 |
| 1973-74 | Toronto (WHA) | 77 | 0 | 11 | 11 |
| 1974-75 | Toronto (WHA) | 64 | 1 | 13 | 14 |
| 1975-76 | Toronto (WHA) | 31 | 4 | 8 | 12 |
| 1977-78 | Winnipeg (WHA) | 3 | 1 | 1 | 2 |
| 1978-79 | Winnipeg (WHA) | 64 | 4 | 18 | 22 |
| 1979-80 | Winnipeg | 19 | 0 | 0 | 0 |
| | **NHL Totals** | 19 | 0 | 0 | 0 |
| | **WHA Totals** | 300 | 11 | 65 | 76 |

**ANDERSON, Dale Norman** *Defenseman*
b. Regina, Sask., Mar. 5, 1932

| Season | Club | GP | G | A | Pts. |
|---|---|---|---|---|---|
| 1956-57 | Detroit | 13 | 0 | 0 | 0 |

**ANDERSON, Earl** *Forward*
b. Roseau, Minn., Feb. 24, 1951

| Season | Club | GP | G | A | Pts. |
|---|---|---|---|---|---|
| 1974-75 | Detroit | 45 | 7 | 3 | 10 |
| 1975-76 | Boston | 5 | 0 | 1 | 1 |
| 1976-77 | Boston | 40 | 10 | 11 | 21 |
| | **Totals** | 90 | 17 | 15 | 32 |


**ANDERSON, Glenn Chris** *Forward*
b. Vancouver, B.C., Oct. 2, 1960

| Season | Club | GP | G | A | Pts. |
|---|---|---|---|---|---|
| 1980-81 | Edmonton | 58 | 30 | 23 | 53 |
| 1981-82 | Edmonton | 80 | 38 | 67 | 105 |
| 1982-83 | Edmonton | 72 | 48 | 56 | 104 |
| | **Totals** | 210 | 116 | 146 | 262 |

**ANDERSON, James William** *Forward*
b. Pembroke, Ont., Dec. 1, 1930

| Season | Club | GP | G | A | Pts. |
|---|---|---|---|---|---|
| 1967-68 | Los Angeles | 7 | 1 | 2 | 3 |

**ANDERSON, John Murray** *Forward*
b. Toronto, Ont., Mar. 28, 1957

| Season | Club | GP | G | A | Pts. |
|---|---|---|---|---|---|
| 1977-78 | Toronto | 17 | 1 | 2 | 3 |
| 1978-79 | Toronto | 71 | 15 | 11 | 26 |
| 1979-80 | Toronto | 74 | 25 | 28 | 53 |
| 1980-81 | Toronto | 75 | 17 | 26 | 43 |
| 1981-82 | Toronto | 69 | 31 | 26 | 57 |
| 1982-83 | Toronto | 80 | 31 | 49 | 80 |
| | **Totals** | 386 | 120 | 142 | 262 |

**ANDERSON, Murray Craig** *Defenseman*
b. Dauphin, Man., Aug. 28, 1949

| Season | Club | GP | G | A | Pts. |
|---|---|---|---|---|---|
| 1974-75 | Washington | 38 | 0 | 1 | 1 |

**ANDERSON, Perry** *Forward*
b. Barrie, Ont., Oct. 14, 1961

| Season | Club | GP | G | A | Pts. |
|---|---|---|---|---|---|
| 1981-82 | St. Louis | 5 | 1 | 2 | 3 |
| 1982-83 | St. Louis | 18 | 5 | 2 | 7 |
| | **Totals** | 23 | 6 | 4 | 10 |

**ANDERSON, Ronald** *Forward*
b. Moncton, N.B., Jan. 21, 1950

| Season | Club | GP | G | A | Pts. |
|---|---|---|---|---|---|
| 1974-75 | Washington | 28 | 9 | 7 | 16 |

**ANDERSON, Ronald Chester (Goings)**
*Forward*
b. Red Deer, Alta., July 29, 1945

| Season | Club | GP | G | A | Pts. |
|---|---|---|---|---|---|
| 1967-68 | Detroit | 18 | 2 | 0 | 2 |
| 1968-69 | Det-LA | 63 | 3 | 5 | 8 |
| 1969-70 | St Louis | 59 | 9 | 9 | 18 |
| 1970-71 | Buffalo | 74 | 14 | 12 | 26 |
| 1971-72 | Buffalo | 37 | 0 | 4 | 4 |
| 1972-73 | Alberta (WHA) | 73 | 14 | 15 | 29 |
| 1973-74 | Edmonton (WHA) | 19 | 5 | 2 | 7 |
| | **NHL Totals** | 251 | 28 | 30 | 58 |
| | **WHA Totals** | 92 | 19 | 17 | 36 |

**ANDERSON, Russell Vincent** *Defenseman*
b. Minneapolis, Minn., Feb. 12, 1955

| Season | Club | GP | G | A | Pts. |
|---|---|---|---|---|---|
| 1976-77 | Pittsburgh | 66 | 2 | 11 | 13 |
| 1977-78 | Pittsburgh | 74 | 2 | 16 | 18 |
| 1978-79 | Pittsburgh | 72 | 3 | 13 | 16 |
| 1979-80 | Pittsburgh | 76 | 5 | 22 | 27 |
| 1980-81 | Pittsburgh | 34 | 3 | 14 | 17 |
| 1981-82 | Pitt-Hart | 56 | 1 | 4 | 5 |
| 1982-83 | Hartford | 57 | 0 | 6 | 6 |
| | **Totals** | 435 | 16 | 86 | 102 |

**ANDERSON, Thomas Linton (Cowboy)**
*Defenseman*
b. Edinburgh, Scotland, July 9, 1911

| Season | Club | GP | G | A | Pts. |
|---|---|---|---|---|---|
| 1934-35 | Detroit | 26 | 5 | 2 | 7 |
| 1935-36 | New York A | 22 | 3 | 2 | 5 |
| 1936-37 | New York A | 41 | 10 | 15 | 25 |
| 1937-38 | New York A | 46 | 4 | 21 | 25 |
| 1938-39 | New York A | 48 | 13 | 27 | 40 |
| 1939-40 | New York A | 48 | 12 | 19 | 31 |
| 1940-41 | New York A | 35 | 3 | 12 | 15 |
| 1941-42 | New York A | 48 | 12 | 29 | 41 |
| | **Totals** | 314 | 62 | 127 | 189 |

**ANDERSSON, Kent-Erik** *Forward*
b. Orebro, Sweden, May 24, 1951

| Season | Club | GP | G | A | Pts. |
|---|---|---|---|---|---|
| 1977-78 | Minnesota | 73 | 15 | 18 | 33 |
| 1978-79 | Minnesota | 41 | 9 | 4 | 13 |
| 1979-80 | Minnesota | 61 | 9 | 10 | 19 |
| 1980-81 | Minnesota | 77 | 17 | 24 | 41 |
| 1981-82 | Minnesota | 70 | 9 | 12 | 21 |
| 1982-83 | New York R | 71 | 8 | 20 | 28 |
| | **Totals** | 393 | 67 | 88 | 155 |


**ANDREA, Paul Lawrence** *Forward*
b. North Sydney, N.S., July 31, 1941

| Season | Club | GP | G | A | Pts. |
|---|---|---|---|---|---|
| 1965-66 | New York R | 4 | 1 | 1 | 2 |
| 1967-68 | Pittsburgh | 65 | 11 | 21 | 32 |
| 1968-69 | Pittsburgh | 25 | 7 | 6 | 13 |
| 1970-71 | Cal-Buf | 56 | 12 | 21 | 33 |
| 1972-73 | Clev (WHA) | 66 | 21 | 30 | 51 |
| 1973-74 | Clev (WHA) | 69 | 15 | 18 | 33 |
| | **NHL Totals** | 150 | 31 | 49 | 80 |
| | **WHA Totals** | 135 | 36 | 48 | 84 |

**ANDREWS, Lloyd** *Forward*

| Season | Club | GP | G | A | Pts. |
|---|---|---|---|---|---|
| 1921-22 | Toronto | 11 | 0 | 0 | 0 |
| 1922-23 | Toronto | 23 | 5 | 4 | 9 |
| 1923-24 | Toronto | 12 | 2 | 1 | 3 |
| 1924-25 | Toronto | 7 | 1 | 0 | 1 |
| | **Totals** | 53 | 8 | 5 | 13 |

**ANDREYCHUK, Dave** *Forward*
b. Hamilton, Ont., Sept. 29, 1963

| Season | Club | GP | G | A | Pts. |
|---|---|---|---|---|---|
| 1982-83 | Buffalo | 43 | 14 | 23 | 37 |

**ANDRUFF, Ronald Nicholas** *Forward*
b. Chemainus, B.C., July 10, 1953

| Season | Club | GP | G | A | Pts. |
|---|---|---|---|---|---|
| 1974-75 | Montreal | 5 | 0 | 0 | 0 |
| 1975-76 | Montreal | 1 | 0 | 0 | 0 |
| 1976-77 | Colorado | 66 | 4 | 18 | 22 |
| 1977-78 | Colorado | 78 | 15 | 18 | 33 |
| 1978-79 | Colorado | 3 | 0 | 0 | 0 |
| | **Totals** | 153 | 19 | 36 | 55 |

**ANGOTTI, Louis Frederick** *Forward*
b. Toronto, Ont., Jan. 16, 1938

| Season | Club | GP | G | A | Pts. |
|---|---|---|---|---|---|
| 1964-65 | New York R | 70 | 9 | 8 | 17 |
| 1965-66 | NYR-Chi | 51 | 6 | 12 | 18 |
| 1966-67 | Chicago | 63 | 6 | 12 | 18 |
| 1967-68 | Philadelphia | 70 | 12 | 37 | 49 |
| 1968-69 | Pittsburgh | 71 | 17 | 20 | 37 |
| 1969-70 | Chicago | 70 | 12 | 26 | 38 |
| 1970-71 | Chicago | 65 | 9 | 16 | 25 |
| 1971-72 | Chicago | 65 | 5 | 10 | 15 |
| 1972-73 | Chicago | 77 | 15 | 22 | 37 |
| 1973-74 | St Louis | 51 | 12 | 23 | 35 |
| 1974-75 | Chicago (WHA) | 26 | 2 | 5 | 7 |
| | **NHL Totals** | 664 | 103 | 186 | 289 |
| | **WHA Totals** | 26 | 2 | 5 | 7 |

**ANSLOW, Hubert Wallace (Hub)** *Forward*
b. Pembroke, Ont., Mar. 23, 1926

| Season | Club | GP | G | A | Pts. |
|---|---|---|---|---|---|
| 1947-48 | New York R | 2 | 0 | 0 | 0 |

**ANTONOVICH, Michael J.** *Forward*
b. Calumet, Minn., Oct. 18, 1951

| Season | Club | GP | G | A | Pts. |
|---|---|---|---|---|---|
| 1972-73 | Minnesota (WHA) | 75 | 20 | 19 | 39 |
| 1973-74 | Minnesota (WHA) | 68 | 21 | 29 | 50 |
| 1974-75 | Minnesota (WHA) | 67 | 24 | 26 | 50 |
| 1975-76 | Minnesota (WHA) | 57 | 25 | 21 | 46 |
| 1975-76 | Minnesota | 12 | 0 | 2 | 2 |
| 1976-77 | Minn-Ed-NE (WHA) | 75 | 40 | 31 | 71 |
| 1977-78 | New England (WHA) | 75 | 32 | 35 | 67 |
| 1978-79 | New England (WHA) | 69 | 20 | 27 | 47 |
| 1979-80 | Hartford | 5 | 0 | 1 | 1 |
| 1981-82 | Minnesota | 2 | 0 | 0 | 0 |
| 1982-83 | New Jersey | 30 | 7 | 7 | 14 |
| | **NHL Totals** | 49 | 7 | 10 | 17 |
| | **WHA Totals** | 486 | 182 | 188 | 370 |

**APPS, Joseph Sylvanus (Syl)** *Forward*
b. Paris, Ont., Jan. 18, 1915

| Season | Club | GP | G | A | Pts. |
|---|---|---|---|---|---|
| 1936-37 | Toronto | 48 | 16 | 29 | 45 |
| 1937-38 | Toronto | 47 | 21 | 29 | 50 |
| 1938-39 | Toronto | 44 | 15 | 25 | 40 |
| 1939-40 | Toronto | 27 | 13 | 17 | 30 |
| 1940-41 | Toronto | 41 | 20 | 24 | 44 |
| 1941-42 | Toronto | 38 | 18 | 23 | 41 |
| 1942-43 | Toronto | 29 | 23 | 17 | 40 |
| 1945-46 | Toronto | 40 | 24 | 16 | 40 |
| 1946-47 | Toronto | 54 | 25 | 24 | 49 |
| 1947-48 | Toronto | 55 | 26 | 27 | 53 |
| | **Totals** | 423 | 201 | 231 | 432 |

| Season | Club | GP | G | A | Pts. |
|---|---|---|---|---|---|
| **APPS, Sylvanus Marshall (Syl) Jr.** *Forward* b. Toronto, Ont., Aug. 1, 1947 | | | | | |
| 1970-71 | NYR-Pitt | 62 | 10 | 18 | 28 |
| 1971-72 | Pittsburgh | 72 | 15 | 44 | 59 |
| 1972-73 | Pittsburgh | 77 | 29 | 56 | 85 |
| 1973-74 | Pittsburgh | 75 | 24 | 61 | 85 |
| 1974-75 | Pittsburgh | 79 | 24 | 55 | 79 |
| 1976-76 | Pittsburgh | 80 | 32 | 67 | 99 |
| 1976-77 | Pittsburgh | 72 | 18 | 43 | 61 |
| 1977-78 | Pitt-LA | 79 | 19 | 33 | 52 |
| 1978-79 | Los Angeles | 80 | 7 | 30 | 37 |
| 1979-80 | Los Angeles | 51 | 5 | 16 | 21 |
| | **Totals** | 747 | 183 | 443 | 616 |
| **ARBOUR, Alger (Al)** *Defenseman* b. Sudbury, Ont., Nov. 1, 1932 | | | | | |
| 1953-54 | Detroit | 36 | 0 | 1 | 1 |
| 1956-57 | Detroit | 44 | 1 | 6 | 7 |
| 1957-58 | Detroit | 69 | 1 | 6 | 7 |
| 1958-59 | Chicago | 70 | 2 | 10 | 12 |
| 1959-60 | Chicago | 57 | 1 | 5 | 6 |
| 1960-61 | Chicago | 53 | 3 | 2 | 5 |
| 1961-62 | Toronto | 52 | 1 | 5 | 6 |
| 1962-63 | Toronto | 4 | 1 | 0 | 1 |
| 1963-64 | Toronto | 6 | 0 | 1 | 1 |
| 1965-66 | Toronto | 4 | 1 | 1 | 1 |
| 1967-68 | St Louis | 74 | 1 | 10 | 11 |
| 1968-69 | St Louis | 67 | 1 | 6 | 7 |
| 1969-70 | St Louis | 68 | 0 | 3 | 3 |
| 1970-71 | St Louis | 22 | 0 | 2 | 2 |
| | **Totals** | 626 | 12 | 58 | 70 |
| **ARBOUR, Amos** *Forward* | | | | | |
| 1918-19 | Montreal | 1 | 0 | 0 | 0 |
| 1919-20 | Montreal | 20 | 22 | 4 | 26 |
| 1920-21 | Montreal | 22 | 14 | 3 | 17 |
| 1921-22 | Hamilton | 23 | 8 | 3 | 11 |
| 1922-23 | Hamilton | 23 | 6 | 1 | 7 |
| 1923-24 | Toronto | 20 | 1 | 2 | 3 |
| | **Totals** | 109 | 51 | 13 | 64 |
| **ARBOUR, Ernest (Ty)** *Forward* | | | | | |
| 1926-27 | Pittsburgh Pi | 41 | 7 | 8 | 15 |
| 1927-28 | Chicago | 39 | 5 | 5 | 10 |
| 1928-29 | Chicago | 44 | 3 | 4 | 7 |
| 1929-30 | Chicago | 42 | 10 | 8 | 18 |
| 1930-31 | Chicago | 41 | 3 | 3 | 6 |
| | **Totals** | 207 | 28 | 28 | 56 |
| **ARBOUR, Jack** *Forward* | | | | | |
| 1926-27 | Detroit | 39 | 4 | 1 | 5 |
| 1928-29 | Toronto | 10 | 1 | 0 | 1 |
| | **Totals** | 49 | 5 | 1 | 6 |
| **ARBOUR, John Gilbert (Jack)** *Defenseman* b. Niagara Falls, Ont., Sept. 28, 1945 | | | | | |
| 1965-66 | Boston | 2 | 0 | 0 | 0 |
| 1967-68 | Boston | 4 | 0 | 1 | 1 |
| 1968-69 | Pittsburgh | 17 | 0 | 2 | 2 |
| 1970-71 | Van-StL | 66 | 1 | 6 | 7 |
| 1971-72 | St Louis | 17 | 0 | 0 | 0 |
| 1972-73 | Minnesota (WHA) | 76 | 6 | 27 | 33 |
| 1973-74 | Minnesota (WHA) | 77 | 6 | 43 | 49 |
| 1974-75 | Minnesota (WHA) | 70 | 11 | 45 | 54 |
| 1975-76 | Den-Minn (WHA) | 42 | 2 | 17 | 19 |
| 1976-77 | Minn-Calg (WHA) | 70 | 4 | 34 | 38 |
| | **NHL Totals** | 106 | 1 | 9 | 10 |
| | **WHA Totals** | 335 | 29 | 164 | 193 |
| **ARCHAMBAULT, Michel** *Forward* b. St. Hyacinthe, Que., Sept. 27, 1950 | | | | | |
| 1972-73 | Quebec (WHA) | 57 | 12 | 25 | 37 |
| 1976-77 | Chicago | 3 | 0 | 0 | 0 |
| | **NHL Totals** | 3 | 0 | 0 | 0 |
| | **WHA Totals** | 57 | 12 | 25 | 37 |
| **ARMSTRONG, George Edward (Chief)** *Forward* b. Skead, Ont., July 6, 1930 | | | | | |
| 1949-50 | Toronto | 2 | 0 | 0 | 0 |
| 1951-52 | Toronto | 20 | 3 | 3 | 6 |
| 1952-53 | Toronto | 52 | 14 | 11 | 25 |
| 1953-54 | Toronto | 63 | 17 | 15 | 32 |
| 1954-55 | Toronto | 66 | 10 | 18 | 28 |
| 1955-56 | Toronto | 67 | 16 | 32 | 48 |
| 1956-57 | Toronto | 54 | 18 | 26 | 44 |
| 1957-58 | Toronto | 59 | 17 | 25 | 42 |
| 1958-59 | Toronto | 59 | 20 | 16 | 36 |
| 1959-60 | Toronto | 70 | 23 | 28 | 51 |
| 1960-61 | Toronto | 47 | 14 | 19 | 33 |
| 1961-62 | Toronto | 70 | 21 | 32 | 53 |
| 1962-63 | Toronto | 70 | 19 | 24 | 43 |
| 1963-64 | Toronto | 66 | 20 | 17 | 37 |
| 1964-65 | Toronto | 59 | 15 | 22 | 37 |
| 1965-66 | Toronto | 70 | 16 | 35 | 51 |
| 1966-67 | Toronto | 70 | 9 | 24 | 33 |
| 1967-68 | Toronto | 62 | 13 | 21 | 34 |
| 1968-69 | Toronto | 53 | 11 | 16 | 27 |
| 1969-70 | Toronto | 49 | 13 | 15 | 28 |
| 1970-71 | Toronto | 59 | 7 | 18 | 25 |
| | **Totals** | 1187 | 296 | 417 | 713 |
| **ARMSTRONG, Murray Alexander** *Forward* b. Manor, Sask., Jan. 1, 1916 | | | | | |
| 1937-38 | Toronto | 9 | 0 | 0 | 0 |
| 1938-39 | Toronto | 3 | 0 | 1 | 1 |
| 1939-40 | New York A | 48 | 16 | 20 | 36 |
| 1940-41 | New York A | 47 | 10 | 14 | 24 |
| 1941-42 | New York A | 45 | 6 | 22 | 28 |
| 1943-44 | Detroit | 28 | 12 | 22 | 34 |
| 1944-45 | Detroit | 50 | 15 | 24 | 39 |
| 1945-46 | Detroit | 40 | 8 | 18 | 26 |
| | **Totals** | 270 | 67 | 121 | 188 |
| **ARMSTRONG, Norman Gerrard (Red)** *Defenseman* b. Owen Sound, Ont., Oct. 17, 1938 | | | | | |
| 1962-63 | Toronto | 7 | 1 | 1 | 2 |
| **ARMSTRONG, Robert Richard** *Defenseman* b. Toronto, Ont., Apr. 7, 1931 | | | | | |
| 1950-51 | Boston | 2 | 0 | 0 | 0 |
| 1952-53 | Boston | 55 | 0 | 8 | 8 |
| 1953-54 | Boston | 64 | 2 | 10 | 12 |
| 1954-55 | Boston | 57 | 1 | 3 | 4 |
| 1955-56 | Boston | 68 | 0 | 12 | 12 |
| 1956-57 | Boston | 57 | 1 | 15 | 16 |
| 1957-58 | Boston | 47 | 1 | 4 | 5 |
| 1958-59 | Boston | 60 | 1 | 9 | 10 |
| 1959-60 | Boston | 69 | 5 | 14 | 19 |
| 1960-61 | Boston | 54 | 0 | 10 | 10 |
| 1961-62 | Boston | 9 | 2 | 1 | 3 |
| | **Totals** | 542 | 13 | 86 | 99 |
| **ARNASON, Charles (Chuck)** *Forward* b. Dauphin, Man., July 15, 1951 | | | | | |
| 1971-72 | Montreal | 17 | 3 | 0 | 3 |
| 1972-73 | Montreal | 19 | 1 | 1 | 2 |
| 1973-74 | Atl-Pitt | 74 | 20 | 11 | 31 |
| 1974-75 | Pittsburgh | 78 | 26 | 32 | 58 |
| 1975-76 | Pitt-KC | 69 | 21 | 13 | 34 |
| 1976-77 | Colorado | 61 | 13 | 10 | 23 |
| 1977-78 | Col-Clev | 69 | 25 | 21 | 46 |
| 1978-79 | Minn-Wash | 14 | 0 | 2 | 2 |
| | **Totals** | 411 | 109 | 90 | 199 |
| **ARNIEL, Scott** *Forward* b. Cornwall, Ont., Sept. 17, 1962 | | | | | |
| 1981-82 | Winnipeg | 17 | 1 | 8 | 9 |
| 1982-83 | Winnipeg | 75 | 13 | 5 | 18 |
| | **Totals** | 92 | 14 | 13 | 27 |
| **ARSHENKOFF, Ronald** *Forward* b. Grand Forks, B.C., June 13, 1957 | | | | | |
| 1979-80 | Edmonton | 4 | 0 | 0 | 0 |
| **ARTHUR, Frederick Edward** *Defenseman* b. Toronto, Ont., Mar. 6, 1961 | | | | | |
| 1980-81 | Hartford | 3 | 0 | 0 | 0 |
| 1981-82 | Philadelphia | 74 | 1 | 7 | 8 |
| | **Totals** | 77 | 1 | 7 | 8 |
| **ARUNDEL, John O'Gorman** *Defenseman* b. Winnipeg, Man., Nov. 4, 1927 | | | | | |
| 1949-50 | Toronto | 3 | 0 | 0 | 0 |
| **ASHBEE, William Barry** *Defenseman* b. Weston, Ont., July 28, 1939 | | | | | |
| 1965-66 | Boston | 14 | 0 | 3 | 3 |
| 1970-71 | Philadelphia | 64 | 4 | 23 | 27 |
| 1971-72 | Philadelphia | 73 | 6 | 14 | 20 |
| 1972-73 | Philadelphia | 64 | 1 | 17 | 18 |
| 1973-74 | Philadelphia | 69 | 4 | 13 | 17 |
| | **Totals** | 274 | 15 | 70 | 85 |
| **ASHBY, Donald Alan** *Forward* b. Kamloops, B.C., Mar. 8, 1955 | | | | | |
| 1975-76 | Toronto | 50 | 6 | 15 | 21 |
| 1976-77 | Toronto | 76 | 19 | 23 | 42 |
| 1977-78 | Toronto | 12 | 1 | 2 | 3 |
| 1978-79 | Tor-Col | 15 | 2 | 3 | 5 |
| 1979-80 | Col-Edm | 29 | 10 | 10 | 20 |
| 1980-81 | Colorado | 6 | 2 | 3 | 5 |
| | **Totals** | 188 | 40 | 56 | 96 |
| **ASHTON, Brent Kenneth** *Forward* b. Saskatoon, Sask., May 18, 1960 | | | | | |
| 1979-80 | Vancouver | 47 | 5 | 14 | 19 |
| 1980-81 | Vancouver | 77 | 18 | 11 | 29 |
| 1981-82 | Colorado | 80 | 24 | 36 | 60 |
| 1982-83 | New Jersey | 76 | 14 | 19 | 33 |
| | **Totals** | 280 | 61 | 80 | 141 |
| **ASHWORTH, Frank** *Forward* b. Moose Jaw, Sask., Oct. 16, 1927 | | | | | |
| 1946-47 | Chicago | 18 | 5 | 4 | 9 |
| **ASMUNDSON, Oscar** *Forward* b. Red Deer, Alta., Nov. 17, 1908 | | | | | |
| 1932-33 | New York R | 48 | 5 | 10 | 15 |
| 1933-34 | New York R | 46 | 2 | 6 | 8 |
| 1934-35 | St Louis E | 14 | 4 | 7 | 11 |
| 1936-37 | New York A | 1 | 0 | 0 | 0 |
| 1937-38 | Montreal | 2 | 0 | 0 | 0 |
| | **Totals** | 111 | 11 | 23 | 34 |
| **ATANAS, Walter (Ants)** *Forward* b. Hamilton, Ont., Dec. 22, 1922 | | | | | |
| 1944-45 | New York R | 49 | 13 | 8 | 21 |
| **ATKINSON, Steven John (Steve)** *Forward* b. Toronto, Ont., Oct. 16, 1948 | | | | | |
| 1968-69 | Boston | 1 | 0 | 0 | 0 |
| 1970-71 | Buffalo | 57 | 20 | 18 | 38 |
| 1971-72 | Buffalo | 67 | 14 | 10 | 24 |
| 1972-73 | Buffalo | 61 | 9 | 9 | 18 |
| 1973-74 | Buffalo | 70 | 6 | 10 | 16 |
| 1974-75 | Washington | 46 | 11 | 4 | 15 |
| 1975-76 | Toronto (WHA) | 52 | 2 | 6 | 8 |
| | **NHL Totals** | 302 | 60 | 51 | 111 |
| | **WHA Totals** | 52 | 2 | 6 | 8 |
| **ATTWELL, Robert Allan** *Forward* b. Spokane, Wash., Dec. 26, 1959 | | | | | |
| 1979-80 | Colorado | 7 | 1 | 1 | 2 |
| 1980-81 | Colorado | 15 | 0 | 4 | 4 |
| | **Totals** | 22 | 1 | 5 | 6 |
| **ATTWELL, Ronald** *Forward* b. Humber Summit, Ont., Feb. 9, 1935 | | | | | |
| 1967-68 | NYR-StL | 22 | 1 | 7 | 8 |
| **AUBIN, Normand** *Forward* b. St. Leonard, Que., July 26, 1960 | | | | | |
| 1981-82 | Toronto | 43 | 14 | 12 | 26 |
| 1982-83 | Toronto | 26 | 4 | 1 | 5 |
| | **Totals** | 69 | 18 | 13 | 31 |

**AUBRY, Pierre** *Forward*
b. Cap de la Madeleine, Que., April 15, 1960

| Season | Club | GP | G | A | Pts. |
|---|---|---|---|---|---|
| 1980-81 | Quebec | 1 | 0 | 0 | 0 |
| 1981-82 | Quebec | 62 | 10 | 13 | 23 |
| 1982-83 | Quebec | 77 | 7 | 9 | 16 |
| | **Totals** | 140 | 17 | 22 | 39 |

**AUBUCHON, Oscar** *Forward*
b. St. Hyacinthe, Que., Jan. 1, 1917

| Season | Club | GP | G | A | Pts. |
|---|---|---|---|---|---|
| 1942-43 | Boston | 3 | 3 | 0 | 3 |
| 1943-44 | Bos-NYR | 47 | 16 | 12 | 28 |
| | **Totals** | 50 | 19 | 12 | 31 |

**AUGE, Les** *Defenseman*
b. St. Paul, Minn., May 16, 1953

| Season | Club | GP | G | A | Pts. |
|---|---|---|---|---|---|
| 1980-81 | Colorado | 6 | 0 | 3 | 3 |

**AURIE, Harry Lawrence (Larry)** *Forward*
b. Sudbury, Ont., Feb. 8, 1905

| Season | Club | GP | G | A | Pts. |
|---|---|---|---|---|---|
| 1927-28 | Detroit | 44 | 13 | 3 | 16 |
| 1928-29 | Detroit | 35 | 1 | 1 | 2 |
| 1929-30 | Detroit | 43 | 14 | 5 | 19 |
| 1930-31 | Detroit | 41 | 12 | 6 | 18 |
| 1931-32 | Detroit | 48 | 12 | 8 | 20 |
| 1932-33 | Detroit | 45 | 12 | 11 | 23 |
| 1933-34 | Detroit | 48 | 16 | 19 | 35 |
| 1934-35 | Detroit | 48 | 17 | 29 | 46 |
| 1935-36 | Detroit | 44 | 16 | 18 | 34 |
| 1936-37 | Detroit | 45 | 23 | 20 | 43 |
| 1937-38 | Detroit | 47 | 10 | 9 | 19 |
| 1938-39 | Detroit | 1 | 1 | 0 | 1 |
| | **Totals** | 489 | 150 | 129 | 279 |

**AWREY, Donald William** *Defenseman*
b. Kitchener, Ont., July 18, 1943

| Season | Club | GP | G | A | Pts. |
|---|---|---|---|---|---|
| 1963-64 | Boston | 16 | 1 | 0 | 1 |
| 1964-65 | Boston | 47 | 2 | 3 | 5 |
| 1965-66 | Boston | 70 | 4 | 3 | 7 |
| 1966-67 | Boston | 4 | 1 | 0 | 1 |
| 1967-68 | Boston | 74 | 3 | 12 | 15 |
| 1968-69 | Boston | 73 | 0 | 13 | 13 |
| 1969-70 | Boston | 73 | 3 | 10 | 13 |
| 1970-71 | Boston | 74 | 4 | 21 | 25 |
| 1971-72 | Boston | 34 | 1 | 8 | 9 |
| 1972-73 | Boston | 78 | 2 | 17 | 19 |
| 1973-74 | St Louis | 75 | 5 | 16 | 21 |
| 1974-75 | StL-Mont | 76 | 1 | 19 | 20 |
| 1975-76 | Montreal | 72 | 0 | 12 | 12 |
| 1976-77 | Pittsburgh | 74 | 1 | 12 | 13 |
| 1977-78 | New York R | 78 | 2 | 8 | 10 |
| 1978-79 | Colorado | 56 | 1 | 4 | 5 |
| | **Totals** | 974 | 31 | 158 | 189 |

**AYERS, Thomas Vernon** *Defenseman*
b. Toronto, Ont., Apr. 27, 1909

| Season | Club | GP | G | A | Pts. |
|---|---|---|---|---|---|
| 1930-31 | New York A | 20 | 2 | 1 | *3 |
| 1931-32 | New York A | 43 | 2 | 4 | 6 |
| 1932-33 | New York A | 48 | 0 | 3 | 3 |
| 1933-34 | Montreal M | 17 | 0 | 0 | 0 |
| 1934-35 | St Louis E | 48 | 2 | 2 | 4 |
| 1935-36 | New York R | 28 | 0 | 4 | 4 |
| | **Totals** | 210 | 6 | 14 | 20 |

**BABANDO, Peter Joseph** *Forward*
b. Braeburn, Pa., May 10, 1925

| Season | Club | GP | G | A | Pts. |
|---|---|---|---|---|---|
| 1947-48 | Boston | 60 | 23 | 11 | 34 |
| 1948-49 | Boston | 58 | 19 | 14 | 33 |
| 1949-50 | Detroit | 55 | 6 | 6 | 12 |
| 1950-51 | Chicago | 70 | 18 | 19 | 37 |
| 1951-52 | Chicago | 49 | 11 | 14 | 25 |
| 1952-53 | Chi-NYR | 58 | 9 | 9 | 18 |
| | **Totals** | 350 | 86 | 73 | 159 |

**BABIN, Mitch** *Forward*
b. Kapuskasing, Ont., Dec. 1, 1954

| Season | Club | GP | G | A | Pts. |
|---|---|---|---|---|---|
| 1975-76 | St. Louis | 8 | 0 | 0 | 0 |

**BABY, John George** *Defenseman*
b. Sudbury, Ont., May 18, 1957

| Season | Club | GP | G | A | Pts. |
|---|---|---|---|---|---|
| 1977-78 | Cleveland | 24 | 2 | 7 | 9 |
| 1978-79 | Minnesota | 2 | 0 | 1 | 1 |
| | **Totals** | 26 | 2 | 8 | 10 |

**BABYCH, David Michael** *Defenseman*
b. Edmonton, Alta., May 23, 1961

| Season | Club | GP | G | A | Pts. |
|---|---|---|---|---|---|
| 1980-81 | Winnipeg | 69 | 6 | 38 | 44 |
| 1981-82 | Winnipeg | 79 | 19 | 49 | 68 |
| 1982-83 | Winnipeg | 79 | 13 | 61 | 74 |
| | **Totals** | 227 | 38 | 148 | 186 |

**BABYCH, Wayne Joseph** *Forward*
b. Edmonton, Alta., June 6, 1958

| Season | Club | GP | G | A | Pts. |
|---|---|---|---|---|---|
| 1978-79 | St Louis | 67 | 27 | 36 | 63 |
| 1979-80 | St Louis | 59 | 26 | 35 | 61 |
| 1980-81 | St Louis | 78 | 54 | 42 | 96 |
| 1981-82 | St Louis | 51 | 19 | 25 | 44 |
| 1982-83 | St Louis | 71 | 16 | 23 | 39 |
| | **Totals** | 326 | 142 | 161 | 303 |

**BACKMAN, Michael Charles** *Forward*
b. Halifax, N.S., Jan. 2, 1955

| Season | Club | GP | G | A | Pts. |
|---|---|---|---|---|---|
| 1981-82 | New York R | 3 | 0 | 2 | 2 |
| 1982-83 | New York R | 7 | 1 | 3 | 4 |
| | **Totals** | 10 | 1 | 5 | 6 |

**BACKOR, Peter** *Defenseman*
b. Ft. William, Ont., Apr. 29, 1919

| Season | Club | GP | G | A | Pts. |
|---|---|---|---|---|---|
| 1944-45 | Toronto | 36 | 4 | 5 | 9 |

**BACKSTROM, Ralph Gerald** *Forward*
b. Kirkland Lake, Ont., Sept. 18, 1937

| Season | Club | GP | G | A | Pts. |
|---|---|---|---|---|---|
| 1956-57 | Montreal | 3 | 0 | 0 | 0 |
| 1957-58 | Montreal | 2 | 0 | 1 | 1 |
| 1958-59 | Montreal | 64 | 18 | 22 | 40 |
| 1959-60 | Montreal | 64 | 13 | 15 | 28 |
| 1960-61 | Montreal | 69 | 12 | 20 | 32 |
| 1961-62 | Montreal | 66 | 27 | 38 | 65 |
| 1962-63 | Montreal | 70 | 23 | 12 | 35 |
| 1963-64 | Montreal | 70 | 8 | 21 | 29 |
| 1964-65 | Montreal | 70 | 25 | 30 | 55 |
| 1965-66 | Montreal | 67 | 22 | 20 | 42 |
| 1966-67 | Montreal | 69 | 14 | 27 | 41 |
| 1967-68 | Montreal | 70 | 20 | 25 | 45 |
| 1968-69 | Montreal | 72 | 13 | 28 | 41 |
| 1969-70 | Montreal | 72 | 19 | 24 | 43 |
| 1970-71 | Mont-LA | 49 | 15 | 17 | 32 |
| 1971-72 | Los Angeles | 76 | 23 | 29 | 52 |
| 1972-73 | LA-Chi | 79 | 26 | 32 | 58 |
| 1973-74 | Chicago (WHA) | 78 | 33 | 50 | 83 |
| 1974-75 | Chicago (WHA) | 70 | 15 | 24 | 39 |
| 1975-76 | Ott-NE (WHA) | 79 | 35 | 48 | 83 |
| | **NHL Totals** | 1157 | 316 | 407 | 723 |
| | **WHA Totals** | 227 | 83 | 122 | 205 |

**BAILEY, Garnet Edward (Ace)** *Forward*
b. Lloydminster, Sask., June 13, 1948

| Season | Club | GP | G | A | Pts. |
|---|---|---|---|---|---|
| 1968-69 | Boston | 8 | 3 | 3 | 6 |
| 1969-70 | Boston | 58 | 11 | 11 | 22 |
| 1970-71 | Boston | 36 | 0 | 6 | 6 |
| 1971-72 | Boston | 73 | 9 | 13 | 22 |
| 1972-73 | Bos-Det | 70 | 10 | 24 | 34 |
| 1973-74 | Det-StL | 67 | 16 | 17 | 33 |
| 1974-75 | StL-Wash | 71 | 19 | 39 | 58 |
| 1975-76 | Washington | 67 | 13 | 19 | 32 |
| 1976-77 | Washington | 78 | 19 | 27 | 46 |
| 1977-78 | Washington | 40 | 7 | 12 | 19 |
| 1978-79 | Edmonton (WHA) | 38 | 5 | 4 | 9 |
| | **NHL Totals** | 568 | 107 | 171 | 278 |
| | **WHA Totals** | 38 | 5 | 4 | 9 |

**BAILEY, Irvine Wallace (Ace)** *Forward*
b. Bracebridge, Ont., July 3, 1903

| Season | Club | GP | G | A | Pts. |
|---|---|---|---|---|---|
| 1926-27 | Toronto | 42 | 15 | 13 | 28 |
| 1927-28 | Toronto | 43 | 9 | 3 | 12 |
| 1928-29 | Toronto | 44 | 22 | 10 | 32 |
| 1929-30 | Toronto | 43 | 22 | 21 | 43 |
| 1930-31 | Toronto | 40 | 23 | 19 | 42 |
| 1931-32 | Toronto | 41 | 8 | 5 | 13 |
| 1932-33 | Toronto | 47 | 10 | 8 | 18 |
| 1933-34 | Toronto | 13 | 2 | 3 | 5 |
| | **Totals** | 313 | 111 | 82 | 193 |

**BAILEY, Reid** *Defenseman*
b. Toronto, Ont., May 28, 1956

| Season | Club | GP | G | A | Pts. |
|---|---|---|---|---|---|
| 1980-81 | Philadelphia | 17 | 1 | 3 | 4 |
| 1981-82 | Philadelphia | 10 | 0 | 0 | 0 |
| 1982-83 | Toronto | 1 | 0 | 0 | 0 |
| | **Totals** | 28 | 1 | 3 | 4 |

**BAILEY, Robert Allen** *Forward*
b. Kenora, Ont., May 29, 1931

| Season | Club | GP | G | A | Pts. |
|---|---|---|---|---|---|
| 1953-54 | Toronto | 48 | 2 | 7 | 9 |
| 1954-55 | Toronto | 32 | 4 | 2 | 6 |
| 1955-56 | Toronto | 6 | 0 | 0 | 0 |
| 1957-58 | Chi-Det | 64 | 9 | 12 | 21 |
| | **Totals** | 150 | 15 | 21 | 36 |

**BAIRD, Kenneth Stewart (Ken)** *Defenseman*
b. Flin Flon, Man., Feb. 1, 1951

| Season | Club | GP | G | A | Pts. |
|---|---|---|---|---|---|
| 1971-72 | California | 10 | 0 | 2 | 2 |
| 1972-73 | Alberta (WHA) | 75 | 14 | 15 | 29 |
| 1973-74 | Edmonton (WHA) | 68 | 17 | 19 | 36 |
| 1974-75 | Edmonton (WHA) | 77 | 30 | 28 | 58 |
| 1975-76 | Edmonton (WHA) | 48 | 13 | 24 | 37 |
| 1976-77 | Edm-Calg (WHA) | 9 | 1 | 2 | 3 |
| 1977-78 | Edmonton (WHA) | 6 | 2 | 4 | 6 |
| | **NHL Totals** | 10 | 0 | 2 | 2 |
| | **WHA Totals** | 283 | 77 | 92 | 169 |

**BAKER, William Robert** *Defenseman*
b. Grand Rapids, Minn., Nov. 29, 1956

| Season | Club | GP | G | A | Pts. |
|---|---|---|---|---|---|
| 1980-81 | Mont-Col | 31 | 5 | 15 | 20 |
| 1981-82 | Col-StL | 49 | 3 | 8 | 11 |
| 1982-83 | New York R | 70 | 4 | 14 | 18 |
| | **Totals** | 150 | 12 | 37 | 49 |

**BALDWIN, Douglas** *Defenseman*
b. Winnipeg, Man., Nov. 2, 1922

| Season | Club | GP | G | A | Pts. |
|---|---|---|---|---|---|
| 1945-46 | Toronto | 15 | 0 | 1 | 1 |
| 1946-47 | Detroit | 4 | 0 | 0 | 0 |
| 1947-48 | Chicago | 5 | 0 | 0 | 0 |
| | **Totals** | 24 | 0 | 1 | 1 |

**BALFOUR, Earl Frederick** *Forward*
b. Toronto, Ont., Jan. 4, 1933

| Season | Club | GP | G | A | Pts. |
|---|---|---|---|---|---|
| 1951-52 | Toronto | 3 | 0 | 0 | 0 |
| 1953-54 | Toronto | 17 | 0 | 1 | 1 |
| 1955-56 | Toronto | 59 | 14 | 5 | 19 |
| 1957-58 | Toronto | 1 | 0 | 0 | 0 |
| 1958-59 | Chicago | 70 | 10 | 8 | 18 |
| 1959-60 | Chicago | 70 | 3 | 5 | 8 |
| 1960-61 | Chicago | 68 | 3 | 3 | 6 |
| | **Totals** | 288 | 30 | 22 | 52 |

**BALFOUR, Murray** *Forward*
b. Regina, Sask., Aug. 24, 1936

| Season | Club | GP | G | A | Pts. |
|---|---|---|---|---|---|
| 1956-57 | Montreal | 2 | 0 | 0 | 0 |
| 1957-58 | Montreal | 3 | 1 | 1 | 2 |
| 1959-60 | Chicago | 61 | 18 | 12 | 30 |
| 1960-61 | Chicago | 70 | 21 | 27 | 48 |
| 1961-62 | Chicago | 49 | 15 | 15 | 30 |
| 1962-63 | Chicago | 65 | 10 | 23 | 33 |
| 1963-64 | Chicago | 41 | 2 | 10 | 12 |
| 1964-65 | Boston | 15 | 0 | 2 | 2 |
| | **Totals** | 306 | 67 | 90 | 157 |

**BALL, Terry James** *Defenseman*
b. Selkirk, Man., Nov. 29, 1944

| Season | Club | GP | G | A | Pts. |
|---|---|---|---|---|---|
| 1967-68 | Philadelphia | 1 | 0 | 0 | 0 |
| 1969-70 | Philadelphia | 61 | 7 | 18 | 25 |
| 1970-71 | Buffalo | 2 | 0 | 0 | 0 |
| 1971-72 | Buffalo | 10 | 0 | 1 | 1 |
| 1972-73 | Minnesota (WHA) | 78 | 6 | 34 | 40 |
| 1973-74 | Minnesota (WHA) | 71 | 8 | 28 | 36 |
| 1974-75 | Minnesota (WHA) | 76 | 8 | 37 | 45 |
| 1975-76 | Clev-Cin (WHA) | 61 | 5 | 29 | 34 |
| 1976-77 | Birmingham (WHA) | 23 | 1 | 6 | 7 |
| | **NHL Totals** | 74 | 7 | 19 | 26 |
| | **WHA Totals** | 309 | 28 | 134 | 162 |

| Season | Club | GP | G | A | Pts. |
|---|---|---|---|---|---|

**BALON, David Alexander (Dave)** *Forward*
b. Wakaw, Sask., Aug. 2, 1937

| Season | Club | GP | G | A | Pts. |
|---|---|---|---|---|---|
| 1959-60 | New York R | 3 | 0 | 0 | 0 |
| 1960-61 | New York R | 13 | 1 | 2 | 3 |
| 1961-62 | New York R | 30 | 4 | 11 | 15 |
| 1962-63 | New York R | 70 | 11 | 13 | 24 |
| 1963-64 | Montreal | 70 | 24 | 18 | 42 |
| 1964-65 | Montreal | 63 | 18 | 23 | 41 |
| 1965-66 | Montreal | 45 | 3 | 7 | 10 |
| 1966-67 | Montreal | 48 | 11 | 8 | 19 |
| 1967-68 | Minnesota | 73 | 15 | 32 | 47 |
| 1968-69 | New York R | 75 | 10 | 21 | 31 |
| 1969-70 | New York R | 76 | 33 | 37 | 70 |
| 1970-71 | New York R | 78 | 36 | 24 | 60 |
| 1971-72 | NYR-Van | 75 | 23 | 24 | 47 |
| 1972-73 | Vancouver | 57 | 3 | 2 | 5 |
| 1973-74 | Quebec (WHA) | 9 | 0 | 0 | 0 |
| | **NHL Totals** | 776 | 192 | 222 | 414 |
| | **WHA Totals** | 9 | 0 | 0 | 0 |

**BALTIMORE, Bryon Don** *Defenseman*
b. Whitehorse, Yuk., Aug. 26, 1952

| Season | Club | GP | G | A | Pts. |
|---|---|---|---|---|---|
| 1974-75 | Chicago (WHA) | 77 | 8 | 12 | 20 |
| 1975-76 | Ott-Ind (WHA) | 78 | 2 | 18 | 20 |
| 1976-77 | Indianapolis (WHA) | 55 | 0 | 15 | 15 |
| 1977-78 | Ind-Cin (WHA) | 50 | 3 | 16 | 19 |
| 1978-79 | Ind-Cin (WHA) | 71 | 5 | 11 | 16 |
| 1979-80 | Edmonton | 2 | 0 | 0 | 0 |
| | **NHL Totals** | 2 | 0 | 0 | 0 |
| | **WHA Totals** | 331 | 18 | 72 | 90 |

**BALUIK, Stanley** *Forward*
b. Port Arthur, Ont., Oct. 5, 1935

| Season | Club | GP | G | A | Pts. |
|---|---|---|---|---|---|
| 1959-60 | Boston | 7 | 0 | 0 | 0 |

**BANDURA, Jeff Mitchell Joseph** *Defenseman*
b. White Rock, B.C., Apr. 4, 1957

| Season | Club | GP | G | A | Pts. |
|---|---|---|---|---|---|
| 1980-81 | New York R | 2 | 0 | 1 | 1 |

**BARBE, Andre Joseph** *Forward*
b. Coniston, Ont., July 27, 1923

| Season | Club | GP | G | A | Pts. |
|---|---|---|---|---|---|
| 1950-51 | Toronto | 1 | 0 | 0 | 0 |

**BARBER, William (Bill)** *Forward*
b. Callander, Ont., July 11, 1952

| Season | Club | GP | G | A | Pts. |
|---|---|---|---|---|---|
| 1972-73 | Philadelphia | 69 | 30 | 34 | 64 |
| 1973-74 | Philadelphia | 75 | 34 | 35 | 69 |
| 1974-75 | Philadelphia | 79 | 34 | 37 | 71 |
| 1975-76 | Philadelphia | 80 | 50 | 62 | 112 |
| 1976-77 | Philadelphia | 73 | 20 | 35 | 55 |
| 1977-78 | Philadelphia | 80 | 41 | 31 | 72 |
| 1978-79 | Philadelphia | 79 | 34 | 46 | 80 |
| 1979-80 | Philadelphia | 79 | 40 | 32 | 72 |
| 1980-81 | Philadelphia | 80 | 43 | 42 | 85 |
| 1981-82 | Philadelphia | 80 | 45 | 44 | 89 |
| 1982-83 | Philadelphia | 66 | 27 | 33 | 60 |
| | **Totals** | 840 | 398 | 431 | 829 |

**BARILKO, William** *Defenseman*
b. Timmins, Ont., Mar. 25, 1927

| Season | Club | GP | G | A | Pts. |
|---|---|---|---|---|---|
| 1946-47 | Toronto | 18 | 3 | 7 | 10 |
| 1947-48 | Toronto | 57 | 5 | 9 | 14 |
| 1948-49 | Toronto | 60 | 5 | 4 | 9 |
| 1949-50 | Toronto | 59 | 7 | 10 | 17 |
| 1950-51 | Toronto | 58 | 6 | 6 | 12 |
| | **Totals** | 252 | 26 | 36 | 62 |

**BARKLEY, Douglas** *Defenseman*
b. Lethbridge, Alta., Jan 6, 1937

| Season | Club | GP | G | A | Pts. |
|---|---|---|---|---|---|
| 1957-58 | Chicago | 3 | 0 | 0 | 0 |
| 1959-60 | Chicago | 3 | 0 | 0 | 0 |
| 1962-63 | Detroit | 70 | 3 | 24 | 27 |
| 1963-64 | Detroit | 67 | 11 | 21 | 32 |
| 1964-65 | Detroit | 67 | 5 | 20 | 25 |
| 1965-66 | Detroit | 43 | 5 | 15 | 20 |
| | **Totals** | 253 | 24 | 80 | 104 |

**BARLOW, Robert George (Bob)** *Forward*
b. Hamilton, Ont., June 17, 1935

| Season | Club | GP | G | A | Pts. |
|---|---|---|---|---|---|
| 1969-70 | Minnesota | 70 | 16 | 17 | 33 |
| 1970-71 | Minnesota | 7 | 0 | 0 | 0 |
| 1974-75 | Phoenix (WHA) | 51 | 6 | 20 | 26 |
| | **NHL Totals** | 77 | 16 | 17 | 33 |
| | **WHA Totals** | 51 | 6 | 20 | 26 |

**BARNES, Blair** *Forward*
b. Ithaca, N.Y., Sept. 21, 1960

| Season | Club | GP | G | A | Pts. |
|---|---|---|---|---|---|
| 1982-83 | Los Angeles | 1 | 0 | 0 | 0 |

**BARNES, Norman Leonard Charles**
*Defenseman*
b. Toronto, Ont., Aug. 24, 1953

| Season | Club | GP | G | A | Pts. |
|---|---|---|---|---|---|
| 1976-77 | Philadelphia | 1 | 0 | 0 | 0 |
| 1979-80 | Philadelphia | 59 | 4 | 21 | 25 |
| 1980-81 | Phil-Hart | 76 | 1 | 13 | 14 |
| 1981-82 | Hartford | 20 | 1 | 4 | 5 |
| | **Totals** | 156 | 6 | 38 | 44 |

**BARR, Dave** *Forward*
b. Toronto, Ont., Nov. 30, 1960

| Season | Club | GP | G | A | Pts. |
|---|---|---|---|---|---|
| 1981-82 | Boston | 2 | 0 | 0 | 0 |
| 1982-83 | Boston | 10 | 1 | 1 | 2 |
| | **Totals** | 12 | 1 | 1 | 12 |

**BARRETT, Frederick William (Fred)**
*Defenseman*
b. Ottawa, Ont., Jan. 26, 1950

| Season | Club | GP | G | A | Pts. |
|---|---|---|---|---|---|
| 1970-71 | Minnesota | 57 | 0 | 13 | 13 |
| 1972-73 | Minnesota | 46 | 2 | 4 | 6 |
| 1973-74 | Minnesota | 40 | 0 | 7 | 7 |
| 1974-75 | Minnesota | 62 | 3 | 18 | 21 |
| 1975-76 | Minnesota | 79 | 2 | 9 | 11 |
| 1976-77 | Minnesota | 60 | 1 | 8 | 9 |
| 1977-78 | Minnesota | 79 | 0 | 15 | 15 |
| 1978-79 | Minnesota | 45 | 1 | 9 | 10 |
| 1979-80 | Minnesota | 80 | 8 | 14 | 22 |
| 1980-81 | Minnesota | 62 | 4 | 8 | 12 |
| 1981-82 | Minnesota | 69 | 1 | 15 | 16 |
| 1982-83 | Minnesota | 51 | 1 | 3 | 4 |
| | **Totals** | 730 | 23 | 123 | 146 |

**BARRETT, John David** *Defenseman*
b. Ottawa, Ont., July 1, 1958

| Season | Club | GP | G | A | Pts. |
|---|---|---|---|---|---|
| 1980-81 | Detroit | 56 | 3 | 10 | 13 |
| 1981-82 | Detroit | 69 | 1 | 12 | 13 |
| 1982-83 | Detroit | 79 | 4 | 10 | 14 |
| | **Totals** | 204 | 8 | 32 | 40 |

**BARRIE, Douglas Robert (Doug)**
*Defenseman*
b. Edmonton, Alta., Oct. 2, 1946

| Season | Club | GP | G | A | Pts. |
|---|---|---|---|---|---|
| 1968-69 | Pittsburgh | 8 | 1 | 1 | 2 |
| 1970-71 | Buffalo | 75 | 4 | 23 | 27 |
| 1971-72 | Buf-LA | 75 | 5 | 18 | 23 |
| 1972-73 | Alberta (WHA) | 54 | 9 | 22 | 31 |
| 1973-74 | Edmonton (WHA) | 69 | 4 | 27 | 31 |
| 1974-75 | Edmonton (WHA) | 78 | 12 | 33 | 45 |
| 1975-76 | Edmonton (WHA) | 79 | 4 | 21 | 25 |
| 1976-77 | Edmonton (WHA) | 70 | 8 | 19 | 27 |
| | **NHL Totals** | 158 | 10 | 42 | 52 |
| | **WHA Totals** | 350 | 37 | 122 | 159 |

**BARRY, Edward** *Forward*
b. Wellesley, Mass., Oct. 9, 1919

| Season | Club | GP | G | A | Pts. |
|---|---|---|---|---|---|
| 1946-47 | Boston | 19 | 1 | 3 | 4 |

**BARRY, Martin J.** *Forward*
b. Quebec City, Que., Dec. 8, 1905

| Season | Club | GP | G | A | Pts. |
|---|---|---|---|---|---|
| 1927-28 | New York A | 7 | 1 | 0 | 1 |
| 1929-30 | Boston | 44 | 18 | 15 | 33 |
| 1930-31 | Boston | 44 | 20 | 11 | 31 |
| 1931-32 | Boston | 48 | 21 | 17 | 38 |
| 1932-33 | Boston | 48 | 24 | 13 | 37 |
| 1933-34 | Boston | 48 | 27 | 12 | 39 |
| 1934-35 | Boston | 48 | 20 | 20 | 40 |
| 1935-36 | Detroit | 48 | 21 | 19 | 40 |
| 1936-37 | Detroit | 48 | 17 | 27 | 44 |
| 1937-38 | Detroit | 48 | 9 | 20 | 29 |
| 1938-39 | Detroit | 48 | 13 | 28 | 41 |
| 1939-40 | Montreal | 30 | 4 | 10 | 14 |
| | **Totals** | 509 | 195 | 192 | 387 |

**BARRY, William Raymond (Ray)** *Forward*
b. Boston, Mass., Oct. 4, 1928

| Season | Club | GP | G | A | Pts. |
|---|---|---|---|---|---|
| 1951-52 | Boston | 18 | 1 | 2 | 3 |

**BARTLETT, James Baker (Rocky)** *Forward*
b. Verdun, Que., May 27, 1932

| Season | Club | GP | G | A | Pts. |
|---|---|---|---|---|---|
| 1954-55 | Montreal | 2 | 0 | 0 | 0 |
| 1955-56 | New York R | 12 | 0 | 1 | 1 |
| 1958-59 | New York R | 70 | 11 | 9 | 20 |
| 1959-60 | New York R | 44 | 8 | 4 | 12 |
| 1960-61 | Boston | 63 | 15 | 9 | 24 |
| | **Totals** | 191 | 34 | 23 | 57 |

**BARTON, Clifford J.** *Forward*
b. Sault Ste. Marie, Mich., Sept. 3, 1907

| Season | Club | GP | G | A | Pts. |
|---|---|---|---|---|---|
| 1929-30 | Pittsburgh Pi. | 41 | 4 | 2 | 6 |
| 1930-31 | Philadelphia Q | 44 | 6 | 7 | 13 |
| 1939-40 | New York R | 3 | 0 | 0 | 0 |
| | **Totals** | 88 | 10 | 9 | 19 |

**BATHE, Francis Lenard** *Defenseman*
b. Oshawa, Ont., Sept. 27, 1954

| Season | Club | GP | G | A | Pts. |
|---|---|---|---|---|---|
| 1974-75 | Detroit | 19 | 0 | 3 | 3 |
| 1975-76 | Detroit | 7 | 0 | 1 | 1 |
| 1977-78 | Philadelphia | 1 | 0 | 0 | 0 |
| 1978-79 | Philadelphia | 21 | 1 | 3 | 4 |
| 1979-80 | Philadelphia | 47 | 0 | 7 | 7 |
| 1980-81 | Philadelphia | 44 | 0 | 3 | 3 |
| 1981-82 | Philadelphia | 28 | 1 | 3 | 4 |
| 1982-83 | Philadelphia | 57 | 1 | 8 | 9 |
| | **Totals** | 224 | 3 | 28 | 31 |

**BATHGATE, Andrew James (Andy)** *Forward*
b. Winnipeg, Man., Aug. 28, 1932

| Season | Club | GP | G | A | Pts. |
|---|---|---|---|---|---|
| 1952-53 | New York R | 18 | 0 | 1 | 1 |
| 1953-54 | New York R | 20 | 2 | 2 | 4 |
| 1954-55 | New York R | 70 | 20 | 20 | 40 |
| 1955-56 | New York R | 70 | 19 | 47 | 66 |
| 1956-57 | New York R | 70 | 27 | 50 | 77 |
| 1957-58 | New York R | 65 | 30 | 48 | 78 |
| 1958-59 | New York R | 70 | 40 | 48 | 88 |
| 1959-60 | New York R | 70 | 26 | 48 | 74 |
| 1960-61 | New York R | 70 | 29 | 48 | 77 |
| 1961-62 | New York R | 70 | 28 | 56 | 84 |
| 1962-63 | New York R | 70 | 35 | 46 | 81 |
| 1963-64 | NYR-Tor | 71 | 19 | 58 | 77 |
| 1964-65 | Toronto | 55 | 16 | 29 | 45 |
| 1965-66 | Detroit | 70 | 15 | 32 | 47 |
| 1966-67 | Detroit | 60 | 8 | 23 | 31 |
| 1967-68 | Pittsburgh | 74 | 20 | 39 | 59 |
| 1970-71 | Pittsburgh | 76 | 15 | 29 | 44 |
| | **Totals** | 1069 | 349 | 624 | 973 |

**BATHGATE, Frank Douglas** *Forward*
b. Winnipeg, Man., Feb. 14, 1930

| Season | Club | GP | G | A | Pts. |
|---|---|---|---|---|---|
| 1952-53 | New York R | 2 | 0 | 0 | 0 |

**BAUER, Robert Theordore** *Forward*
b. Waterloo, Ont., Feb. 16, 1915

| Season | Club | GP | G | A | Pts. |
|---|---|---|---|---|---|
| 1936-37 | Boston | 1 | 1 | 0 | 1 |
| 1937-38 | Boston | 48 | 20 | 14 | 34 |
| 1938-39 | Boston | 48 | 13 | 18 | 31 |
| 1939-40 | Boston | 48 | 17 | 26 | 43 |
| 1940-41 | Boston | 48 | 17 | 22 | 39 |
| 1941-42 | Boston | 36 | 13 | 22 | 35 |
| 1945-46 | Boston | 39 | 11 | 10 | 21 |
| 1946-47 | Boston | 58 | 30 | 24 | 54 |
| 1951-52 | Boston | 1 | 1 | 1 | 2 |
| | **Totals** | 327 | 123 | 137 | 260 |

**BAUMGARTNER, Michael Edward**
*Defenseman*
b. Roseau, Minn., Jan. 30, 1949

| Season | Club | GP | G | A | Pts. |
|---|---|---|---|---|---|
| 1974-75 | Kansas City | 17 | 0 | 0 | 0 |

| Season | Club | GP | G | A | Pts. |
|---|---|---|---|---|---|

**BAUN, Robert Neil (Bob)** *Defenseman*
b. Lanigan, Sask., Sept. 9, 1936

| Season | Club | GP | G | A | Pts. |
|---|---|---|---|---|---|
| 1956-57 | Toronto | 20 | 0 | 5 | 5 |
| 1957-58 | Toronto | 67 | 1 | 9 | 10 |
| 1958-59 | Toronto | 51 | 1 | 8 | 9 |
| 1959-60 | Toronto | 61 | 8 | 9 | 17 |
| 1960-61 | Toronto | 70 | 1 | 14 | 15 |
| 1961-62 | Toronto | 65 | 4 | 11 | 15 |
| 1962-63 | Toronto | 48 | 4 | 8 | 12 |
| 1963-64 | Toronto | 52 | 4 | 14 | 18 |
| 1964-65 | Toronto | 70 | 0 | 18 | 18 |
| 1965-66 | Toronto | 44 | 0 | 6 | 6 |
| 1966-67 | Toronto | 54 | 2 | 8 | 10 |
| 1967-68 | Oakland | 67 | 3 | 10 | 13 |
| 1968-69 | Detroit | 76 | 4 | 16 | 20 |
| 1969-70 | Detroit | 71 | 1 | 18 | 19 |
| 1970-71 | Det-Tor | 69 | 1 | 20 | 21 |
| 1971-72 | Toronto | 74 | 2 | 12 | 14 |
| 1972-73 | Toronto | 5 | 1 | 1 | 2 |
| | **Totals** | 964 | 37 | 187 | 224 |

**BAXTER, Paul Gordon** *Defenseman*
b. Winnipeg, Man., Oct. 25, 1955

| Season | Club | GP | G | A | Pts. |
|---|---|---|---|---|---|
| 1974-75 | Cleveland (WHA) | 5 | 0 | 0 | 0 |
| 1975-76 | Cleveland (WHA) | 67 | 3 | 7 | 10 |
| 1976-77 | Quebec (WHA) | 66 | 6 | 17 | 23 |
| 1977-78 | Quebec (WHA) | 76 | 6 | 29 | 35 |
| 1978-79 | Quebec (WHA) | 76 | 10 | 36 | 46 |
| 1979-80 | Quebec | 61 | 7 | 13 | 20 |
| 1980-81 | Pittsburgh | 51 | 5 | 14 | 19 |
| 1981-82 | Pittsburgh | 76 | 9 | 34 | 43 |
| 1982-83 | Pittsburgh | 75 | 11 | 21 | 32 |
| | **NHL Totals** | 263 | 32 | 82 | 114 |
| | **WHA Totals** | 290 | 25 | 89 | 114 |

**BEATON, Alexander Francis** *Forward*
b. Antigonish, N.S., Apr. 28, 1953

| Season | Club | GP | G | A | Pts. |
|---|---|---|---|---|---|
| 1975-76 | Cincinnati (WHA) | 29 | 2 | 3 | 5 |
| 1976-77 | Edmonton (WHA) | 68 | 4 | 9 | 13 |
| 1977-78 | Birmingham (WHA) | 67 | 6 | 9 | 15 |
| 1978-79 | New York R | 2 | 0 | 0 | 0 |
| 1979-80 | New York R | 23 | 1 | 1 | 2 |
| | **NHL Totals** | 25 | 1 | 1 | 2 |
| | **WHA Totals** | 153 | 12 | 21 | 33 |

**BEATTIE, John (Red)** *Forward*
b. Ibstock, England, 1907

| Season | Club | GP | G | A | Pts. |
|---|---|---|---|---|---|
| 1930-31 | Boston | 32 | 10 | 11 | 21 |
| 1931-32 | Boston | 1 | 0 | 0 | 0 |
| 1932-33 | Boston | 48 | 8 | 12 | 20 |
| 1933-34 | Boston | 48 | 9 | 13 | 22 |
| 1934-35 | Boston | 48 | 9 | 18 | 27 |
| 1935-36 | Boston | 48 | 14 | 18 | 32 |
| 1936-37 | Boston | 48 | 8 | 7 | 15 |
| 1937-38 | Det-NYA | 31 | 4 | 6 | 10 |
| 1938-39 | New York A | 12 | 0 | 0 | 0 |
| | **Totals** | 316 | 62 | 85 | 147 |

**BEAUDIN, Norman Joseph Andrew (Norm)**
*Forward*
b. Montmartre, Sask., Nov. 28, 1941

| Season | Club | GP | G | A | Pts. |
|---|---|---|---|---|---|
| 1967-68 | St Louis | 13 | 1 | 1 | 2 |
| 1970-71 | Minnesota | 12 | 0 | 1 | 1 |
| 1972-73 | Winnipeg (WHA) | 78 | 38 | 65 | 103 |
| 1973-74 | Winnipeg (WHA) | 74 | 27 | 28 | 55 |
| 1974-75 | Winnipeg (WHA) | 77 | 16 | 31 | 47 |
| | **NHL Totals** | 25 | 1 | 2 | 3 |
| | **WHA Totals** | 229 | 81 | 124 | 205 |

**BEAUDOIN, Serge** *Defenseman*
b. Montreal, Que., Nov. 30, 1952

| Season | Club | GP | G | A | Pts. |
|---|---|---|---|---|---|
| 1973-74 | Vancouver (WHA) | 26 | 1 | 11 | 12 |
| 1974-75 | Vancouver (WHA) | 4 | 0 | 0 | 0 |
| 1975-76 | Phoenix (WHA) | 76 | 0 | 21 | 21 |
| 1976-77 | Phoenix (WHA) | 77 | 6 | 24 | 30 |
| 1977-78 | Cin-Birm (WHA) | 77 | 8 | 26 | 34 |
| 1978-79 | Birmingham (WHA) | 72 | 5 | 21 | 26 |
| 1979-80 | Atlanta | 3 | 0 | 0 | 0 |
| | **NHL Totals** | 3 | 0 | 0 | 0 |
| | **WHA Totals** | 332 | 20 | 103 | 123 |

**BECK, Barry David** *Defenseman*
b. Vancouver, B.C., June 3, 1957

| Season | Club | GP | G | A | Pts. |
|---|---|---|---|---|---|
| 1977-78 | Colorado | 75 | 22 | 38 | 60 |
| 1978-79 | Colorado | 63 | 14 | 28 | 42 |
| 1979-80 | Col-NYR | 71 | 15 | 50 | 65 |
| 1980-81 | New York R | 75 | 11 | 23 | 34 |
| 1981-82 | New York R | 60 | 9 | 29 | 38 |
| 1982-83 | New York R | 66 | 12 | 22 | 34 |
| | **Totals** | 410 | 83 | 190 | 273 |

**BECKETT, Robert Owen** *Forward*
b. Unionville, Ont., Apr. 8, 1936

| Season | Club | GP | G | A | Pts. |
|---|---|---|---|---|---|
| 1956-57 | Boston | 18 | 0 | 3 | 3 |
| 1957-58 | Boston | 9 | 0 | 0 | 0 |
| 1961-62 | Boston | 34 | 7 | 2 | 9 |
| 1963-64 | Boston | 7 | 0 | 1 | 1 |
| | **Totals** | 68 | 7 | 6 | 13 |

**BEDARD, James Leo** *Defenseman*
b. Admiral, Sask., Nov. 19, 1927

| Season | Club | GP | G | A | Pts. |
|---|---|---|---|---|---|
| 1949-50 | Chicago | 6 | 0 | 0 | 0 |
| 1950-51 | Chicago | 17 | 1 | 1 | 2 |
| | **Totals** | 23 | 1 | 1 | 2 |

**BEDNARSKI, John Severn** *Defenseman*
b. Thunder Bay, Ont., July 4, 1952

| Season | Club | GP | G | A | Pts. |
|---|---|---|---|---|---|
| 1974-75 | New York R | 35 | 1 | 10 | 11 |
| 1975-76 | New York R | 59 | 1 | 8 | 9 |
| 1976-77 | New York R | 5 | 0 | 0 | 0 |
| 1979-80 | Edmonton | 1 | 0 | 0 | 0 |
| | **Totals** | 100 | 2 | 18 | 20 |

**BEERS, Ed** *Forward*
b. Netherlands, Oct. 12, 1959

| Season | Club | GP | G | A | Pts. |
|---|---|---|---|---|---|
| 1981-82 | Calgary | 5 | 1 | 1 | 2 |
| 1982-83 | Calgary | 41 | 11 | 15 | 26 |
| | **Totals** | 46 | 12 | 16 | 28 |

**BEHLING, Clarence Roy** *Defenseman*
b. Kitchener, Ont., Mar. 16, 1916

| Season | Club | GP | G | A | Pts. |
|---|---|---|---|---|---|
| 1942-43 | Detroit | 2 | 1 | 0 | 1 |

**BEHLING, Richard** *Defenseman*
b.

| Season | Club | GP | G | A | Pts. |
|---|---|---|---|---|---|
| 1940-41 | Detroit | 2 | 0 | 0 | 0 |

**BELANGER, Alain** *Forward*
b. St. Janvier, Que., Jan. 18, 1956

| Season | Club | GP | G | A | Pts. |
|---|---|---|---|---|---|
| 1977-78 | Toronto | 9 | 0 | 1 | 1 |

**BELISLE, Daniel George** *Forward*
b. South Porcupine, Ont., May 9, 1937

| Season | Club | GP | G | A | Pts. |
|---|---|---|---|---|---|
| 1960-61 | New York R | 4 | 2 | 0 | 2 |

**BELIVEAU, Jean Arthur** *Forward*
b. Trois-Rivieres, Que., Aug. 31, 1931

| Season | Club | GP | G | A | Pts. |
|---|---|---|---|---|---|
| 1950-51 | Montreal | 2 | 1 | 1 | 2 |
| 1952-53 | Montreal | 3 | 5 | 0 | 5 |
| 1953-54 | Montreal | 44 | 13 | 21 | 34 |
| 1954-55 | Montreal | 70 | 37 | 36 | 73 |
| 1955-56 | Montreal | 70 | 47 | 41 | 88 |
| 1956-57 | Montreal | 69 | 33 | 51 | 84 |
| 1957-58 | Montreal | 55 | 27 | 32 | 59 |
| 1958-59 | Montreal | 64 | 45 | 46 | 91 |
| 1959-60 | Montreal | 60 | 34 | 40 | 74 |
| 1960-61 | Montreal | 69 | 32 | 58 | 90 |
| 1961-62 | Montreal | 43 | 18 | 23 | 41 |
| 1962-63 | Montreal | 69 | 18 | 49 | 67 |
| 1963-64 | Montreal | 68 | 28 | 50 | 78 |
| 1964-65 | Montreal | 58 | 20 | 23 | 43 |
| 1965-66 | Montreal | 67 | 29 | 48 | 77 |
| 1966-67 | Montreal | 53 | 12 | 26 | 38 |
| 1967-68 | Montreal | 59 | 31 | 37 | 68 |
| 1968-69 | Montreal | 69 | 33 | 49 | 82 |
| 1969-70 | Montreal | 63 | 19 | 30 | 49 |
| 1970-71 | Montreal | 70 | 25 | 51 | 76 |
| | **Totals** | 1125 | 507 | 712 | 1219 |

**BELL, Harry** *Defenseman*
b. Regina, Sask., Oct. 31, 1925

| Season | Club | GP | G | A | Pts. |
|---|---|---|---|---|---|
| 1946-47 | New York R | 1 | 0 | 1 | 1 |

**BELL, Joseph Alexander** *Forward*
b. Portage la Prairie, Man., Nov. 27, 1923

| Season | Club | GP | G | A | Pts. |
|---|---|---|---|---|---|
| 1942-43 | New York R | 15 | 2 | 5 | 7 |
| 1946-47 | New York R | 47 | 6 | 4 | 10 |
| | **Totals** | 62 | 8 | 9 | 17 |

**BELL, William** *Defenseman-Forward*
b. Lachine, Que., June 10, 1891

| Season | Club | GP | G | A | Pts. |
|---|---|---|---|---|---|
| 1917-18 | Mont W&C | 8 | 1 | 0 | 1 |
| 1918-19 | Montreal | 1 | 0 | 0 | 0 |
| 1920-21 | Montreal | 4 | 0 | 0 | 0 |
| 1921-22 | Mont-Ott | 23 | 2 | 1 | 3 |
| 1922-23 | Montreal | 15 | 0 | 0 | 0 |
| 1923-24 | Montreal | 10 | 0 | 0 | 0 |
| | **Totals** | 61 | 3 | 1 | 4 |

**BELLAND, Neil** *Defenseman*
b. Parry Sound, Ont., Apr. 3, 1961

| Season | Club | GP | G | A | Pts. |
|---|---|---|---|---|---|
| 1981-82 | Vancouver | 28 | 3 | 6 | 9 |
| 1982-83 | Vancouver | 14 | 2 | 4 | 6 |
| | **Totals** | 42 | 5 | 10 | 15 |

**BELLEFEUILLE, Peter** *Forward*

| Season | Club | GP | G | A | Pts. |
|---|---|---|---|---|---|
| 1925-26 | Toronto | 36 | 14 | 2 | 16 |
| 1926-27 | Tor-Det | 31 | 6 | 0 | 6 |
| 1928-29 | Detroit | 1 | 1 | 0 | 1 |
| 1929-30 | Detroit | 24 | 5 | 2 | 7 |
| | **Totals** | 92 | 26 | 4 | 30 |

**BELLEMER, Andrew** *Defenseman*
b. Penetang, Ont., July 3, 1904

| Season | Club | GP | G | A | Pts. |
|---|---|---|---|---|---|
| 1932-33 | Montreal M | 16 | 0 | 0 | 0 |

**BELLOWS, Brian** *Forward*
b. St. Catharines, Ont., Sept. 1, 1964

| Season | Club | GP | G | A | Pts. |
|---|---|---|---|---|---|
| 1982-83 | Minnesota | 78 | 35 | 30 | 65 |

**BEND, John Linthwaite** *Forward*
b. Poplar Point, Man., Dec. 20, 1922

| Season | Club | GP | G | A | Pts. |
|---|---|---|---|---|---|
| 1942-43 | New York R | 8 | 3 | 1 | 4 |

**BENNETT, Curt Alexander** *Forward*
b. Regina, Sask., Mar. 27, 1948

| Season | Club | GP | G | A | Pts. |
|---|---|---|---|---|---|
| 1970-71 | St Louis | 4 | 2 | 0 | 2 |
| 1971-72 | St Louis | 31 | 3 | 5 | 8 |
| 1972-73 | NYR-Atl | 68 | 18 | 18 | 36 |
| 1973-74 | Atlanta | 71 | 17 | 24 | 41 |
| 1974-75 | Atlanta | 80 | 31 | 33 | 64 |
| 1975-76 | Atlanta | 80 | 34 | 31 | 65 |
| 1976-77 | Atlanta | 76 | 22 | 25 | 47 |
| 1977-78 | Atl-StL | 75 | 10 | 24 | 34 |
| 1978-79 | St Louis | 74 | 14 | 19 | 33 |
| 1979-80 | Atlanta | 21 | 1 | 3 | 4 |
| | **Totals** | 580 | 152 | 182 | 334 |

**BENNETT, Frank** *Forward*
b. Toronto, Ont.

| Season | Club | GP | G | A | Pts. |
|---|---|---|---|---|---|
| 1943-44 | Detroit | 7 | 0 | 1 | 1 |

**BENNETT, Harvey A.** *Forward*
b. Cranston, R.I., Aug. 9, 1952

| Season | Club | GP | G | A | Pts. |
|---|---|---|---|---|---|
| 1974-75 | Pittsburgh | 7 | 0 | 0 | 0 |
| 1975-76 | Pitt-Wash | 74 | 15 | 13 | 28 |
| 1976-77 | Wash-Phil | 69 | 14 | 14 | 28 |
| 1977-78 | Phil-Minn | 66 | 12 | 10 | 22 |
| 1978-79 | St Louis | 52 | 3 | 9 | 12 |
| | **Totals** | 268 | 44 | 46 | 90 |

**BENNETT, Max** *Forward*
b. Cobalt, Ont., Nov. 4, 1912

| Season | Club | GP | G | A | Pts. |
|---|---|---|---|---|---|
| 1935-36 | Montreal | — | 0 | 0 | 0 |

**BENNETT, William** *Forward*
b. Warwich, R.I., May 31, 1953

| Season | Club | GP | G | A | Pts. |
|---|---|---|---|---|---|
| 1978-79 | Boston | 7 | 1 | 4 | 5 |
| 1979-80 | Hartford | 24 | 3 | 3 | 6 |
| | **Totals** | 31 | 4 | 7 | 11 |

| Season | Club | GP | G | A | Pts. |
|--------|------|----|----|----|------|

**BENNING, Jim** *Defenseman*
b. Edmonton, Alta., Apr. 29, 1963

| Season | Club | GP | G | A | Pts. |
|--------|------|----|----|----|------|
| 1981-82 | Toronto | 74 | 7 | 24 | 31 |
| 1982-83 | Toronto | 74 | 5 | 17 | 22 |
| | **Totals** | **148** | **12** | **41** | **53** |

**BENOIT, Joseph** *Forward*
b. St. Albert, Alta., Feb. 27, 1916

| 1940-41 | Montreal | 45 | 16 | 16 | 32 |
|---------|----------|----|----|----|----|
| 1941-42 | Montreal | 46 | 20 | 16 | 36 |
| 1942-43 | Montreal | 49 | 30 | 27 | 57 |
| 1945-46 | Montreal | 39 | 9 | 10 | 19 |
| 1946-47 | Montreal | 6 | 0 | 0 | 0 |
| | **Totals** | **185** | **75** | **69** | **144** |

**BENSON, Robert** *Defenseman*
b. Buffalo, N.Y.

| 1924-25 | Boston | 8 | 0 | 1 | 1 |
|---------|--------|----|----|----|----|

**BENSON, William Lloyd** *Forward*
b. Winnipeg, Man., July 29, 1920

| 1940-41 | New York A | 24 | 3 | 4 | 7 |
|---------|-----------|----|----|----|----|
| 1941-42 | New York A | 45 | 8 | 21 | 29 |
| | **Totals** | **69** | **11** | **25** | **36** |

**BENTLEY, Douglas Wagner** *Forward*
b. Delisle, Sask., Sept. 3, 1916

| 1939-40 | Chicago | 39 | 12 | 7 | 19 |
|---------|---------|----|----|----|----|
| 1940-41 | Chicago | 46 | 8 | 20 | 28 |
| 1941-42 | Chicago | 38 | 12 | 14 | 26 |
| 1942-43 | Chicago | 50 | 33 | 40 | 73 |
| 1943-44 | Chicago | 50 | 38 | 39 | 77 |
| 1945-46 | Chicago | 36 | 19 | 21 | 40 |
| 1946-47 | Chicago | 52 | 21 | 34 | 55 |
| 1947-48 | Chicago | 60 | 20 | 37 | 57 |
| 1948-49 | Chicago | 58 | 23 | 43 | 66 |
| 1949-50 | Chicago | 64 | 20 | 33 | 53 |
| 1950-51 | Chicago | 44 | 9 | 23 | 32 |
| 1951-52 | Chicago | 8 | 2 | 3 | 5 |
| 1953-54 | New York R | 20 | 2 | 10 | 12 |
| | **Totals** | **565** | **219** | **324** | **543** |

**BENTLEY, Maxwell Herbert Lloyd** *Forward*
b. Delisle, Sask., Mar. 1, 1920

| 1940-41 | Chicago | 36 | 7 | 10 | 17 |
|---------|---------|----|----|----|----|
| 1941-42 | Chicago | 39 | 13 | 17 | 30 |
| 1942-43 | Chicago | 47 | 26 | 44 | 70 |
| 1945-46 | Chicago | 47 | 31 | 30 | 61 |
| 1946-47 | Chicago | 60 | 29 | 43 | 72 |
| 1947-48 | Chi-Tor | 59 | 26 | 28 | 54 |
| 1948-49 | Toronto | 60 | 19 | 22 | 41 |
| 1949-50 | Toronto | 69 | 23 | 18 | 41 |
| 1950-51 | Toronto | 67 | 21 | 41 | 62 |
| 1951-52 | Toronto | 69 | 24 | 17 | 41 |
| 1952-53 | Toronto | 36 | 12 | 11 | 23 |
| 1953-54 | New York R | 57 | 14 | 18 | 32 |
| | **Totals** | **646** | **245** | **299** | **544** |

**BENTLEY, Reginald** *Forward*
b. Delisle, Sask., May 3, 1914

| 1942-43 | Chicago | 11 | 1 | 2 | 3 |
|---------|---------|----|----|----|----|

**BERENSON, Gordon Arthur (Red)** *Forward*
b. Regina, Sask., Dec. 8, 1939

| 1961-62 | Montreal | 4 | 1 | 2 | 3 |
|---------|----------|----|----|----|----|
| 1962-63 | Montreal | 37 | 2 | 6 | 8 |
| 1963-64 | Montreal | 69 | 7 | 9 | 16 |
| 1964-65 | Montreal | 3 | 1 | 2 | 3 |
| 1965-66 | Montreal | 23 | 3 | 4 | 7 |
| 1966-67 | New York R | 30 | 0 | 5 | 5 |
| 1967-68 | NYR-StL | 74 | 24 | 30 | 54 |
| 1968-69 | St Louis | 76 | 35 | 47 | 82 |
| 1969-70 | St Louis | 67 | 33 | 39 | 72 |
| 1970-71 | StL-Det | 69 | 21 | 38 | 59 |
| 1971-72 | Detroit | 78 | 28 | 41 | 69 |
| 1972-73 | Detroit | 78 | 13 | 30 | 43 |
| 1973-74 | Detroit | 76 | 24 | 42 | 66 |
| 1974-75 | Det-StL | 71 | 15 | 22 | 37 |
| 1975-76 | St Louis | 72 | 20 | 27 | 47 |
| 1976-77 | St Louis | 80 | 21 | 28 | 49 |
| 1977-78 | St Louis | 80 | 13 | 25 | 38 |
| | **Totals** | **987** | **261** | **397** | **658** |

**BERGDINON** *Forward*

| 1925-26 | Boston | 2 | 0 | 0 | 0 |
|---------|--------|----|----|----|----|

**BERGERON, Michel** *Forward*
b. Chicoutimi, Que., Nov. 11, 1954

| 1974-75 | Detroit | 25 | 10 | 7 | 17 |
|---------|---------|----|----|----|----|
| 1975-76 | Detroit | 72 | 32 | 27 | 59 |
| 1976-77 | Detroit | 74 | 21 | 12 | 33 |
| 1977-78 | Det-NYI | 28 | 10 | 6 | 16 |
| 1978-79 | Washington | 30 | 7 | 6 | 13 |
| | **Totals** | **229** | **80** | **58** | **138** |

**BERGERON, Yves** *Forward*
b. Malartic, Que., Jan. 11, 1952

| 1972-73 | Quebec (WHA) | 65 | 14 | 19 | 33 |
|---------|--------------|----|----|----|----|
| 1974-75 | Pittsburgh | 2 | 0 | 0 | 0 |
| 1975-76 | Pittsburgh | 1 | 0 | 0 | 0 |
| | **NHL Totals** | **3** | **0** | **0** | **0** |
| | **WHA Totals** | **65** | **14** | **19** | **33** |

**BERGLOFF, Bob** *Defenseman*
b. Dickinson, N.D., July 26, 1958

| 1982-83 | Minnesota | 2 | 0 | 0 | 0 |
|---------|-----------|----|----|----|----|

**BERGMAN, Gary Gunnar** *Defenseman*
b. Kenora, Ont., Oct. 7, 1938

| 1964-65 | Detroit | 58 | 4 | 7 | 11 |
|---------|---------|----|----|----|----|
| 1965-66 | Detroit | 61 | 3 | 16 | 19 |
| 1966-67 | Detroit | 70 | 5 | 30 | 35 |
| 1967-68 | Detroit | 74 | 13 | 28 | 41 |
| 1968-69 | Detroit | 76 | 7 | 30 | 37 |
| 1969-70 | Detroit | 69 | 6 | 17 | 23 |
| 1970-71 | Detroit | 68 | 8 | 25 | 33 |
| 1971-72 | Detroit | 75 | 6 | 31 | 37 |
| 1972-73 | Detroit | 68 | 3 | 28 | 31 |
| 1973-74 | Det-Minn | 68 | 3 | 29 | 32 |
| 1974-75 | Detroit | 76 | 5 | 25 | 30 |
| 1975-76 | Kansas City | 75 | 5 | 33 | 38 |
| | **Totals** | **838** | **68** | **299** | **367** |

**BERGMAN, Thommie Lars Rudolf**
*Defenseman*
b. Munkfors, Sweden, Dec. 10, 1947

| 1972-73 | Detroit | 75 | 9 | 12 | 21 |
|---------|---------|----|----|----|----|
| 1973-74 | Detroit | 43 | 0 | 3 | 3 |
| 1974-75 | Detroit | 18 | 0 | 1 | 1 |
| 1974-75 | Winnipeg (WHA) | 49 | 4 | 15 | 19 |
| 1975-76 | Winnipeg (WHA) | 81 | 11 | 30 | 41 |
| 1976-77 | Winnipeg (WHA) | 42 | 2 | 24 | 26 |
| 1977-78 | Winnipeg (WHA) | 62 | 5 | 28 | 33 |
| 1977-78 | Detroit | 14 | 1 | 6 | 7 |
| 1978-79 | Detroit | 68 | 10 | 17 | 27 |
| 1979-80 | Detroit | 28 | 1 | 5 | 6 |
| | **NHL Totals** | **246** | **21** | **44** | **65** |
| | **WHA Totals** | **234** | **22** | **97** | **119** |

**BERLINQUETTE, Louis** *Forward*

| 1917-18 | Montreal | 20 | 2 | 0 | 2 |
|---------|----------|----|----|----|----|
| 1918-19 | Montreal | 18 | 5 | 3 | 8 |
| 1919-20 | Montreal | 24 | 7 | 7 | 14 |
| 1920-21 | Montreal | 24 | 12 | 9 | 21 |
| 1921-22 | Montreal | 24 | 12 | 5 | 17 |
| 1922-23 | Montreal | 24 | 2 | 3 | 5 |
| 1924-25 | Montreal M | 29 | 4 | 2 | 6 |
| 1925-26 | Pittsburgh Pi | 30 | 0 | 0 | 0 |
| | **Totals** | **193** | **44** | **29** | **73** |

**BERNIER, Serge Joseph** *Forward*
b. Padoue, Que., Apr. 29, 1947

| 1968-69 | Philadelphia | 1 | 0 | 0 | 0 |
|---------|--------------|----|----|----|----|
| 1969-70 | Philadelphia | 1 | 0 | 1 | 1 |
| 1970-71 | Philadelphia | 77 | 23 | 28 | 51 |
| 1971-72 | Phil-LA | 70 | 23 | 22 | 45 |
| 1972-73 | Los Angeles | 75 | 22 | 46 | 68 |
| 1973-74 | Quebec (WHA) | 74 | 37 | 49 | 86 |
| 1974-75 | Quebec (WHA) | 76 | 54 | 68 | 122 |
| 1975-76 | Quebec (WHA) | 70 | 34 | 68 | 102 |
| 1976-77 | Quebec (WHA) | 74 | 43 | 53 | 96 |
| 1977-78 | Quebec (WHA) | 58 | 26 | 52 | 78 |
| 1978-79 | Quebec (WHA) | 65 | 36 | 46 | 82 |
| 1979-80 | Quebec | 32 | 8 | 14 | 22 |
| | **NHL Totals** | **256** | **76** | **111** | **187** |
| | **WHA Totals** | **417** | **230** | **336** | **566** |

**BERRY, Douglas Alan** *Forward*
b. New Westminster, B.C., June 3, 1957

| 1979-80 | Colorado | 75 | 7 | 23 | 30 |
|---------|----------|----|----|----|----|
| 1980-81 | Colorado | 46 | 3 | 10 | 13 |
| | **Totals** | **121** | **10** | **33** | **43** |

**BERRY, Fred** *Forward*
b. Stoney Plains, Alta., Mar. 26, 1956

| 1976-77 | Detroit | 3 | 0 | 0 | 0 |
|---------|---------|----|----|----|----|

**BERRY, Ken** *Forward*
b. Vancouver, B.C., June 21, 1960

| 1981-82 | Edmonton | 15 | 2 | 3 | 5 |
|---------|----------|----|----|----|----|

**BERRY, Robert Victor** *Forward*
b. Montreal, Que., Nov. 29, 1943

| 1968-69 | Montreal | 2 | 0 | 0 | 0 |
|---------|----------|----|----|----|----|
| 1970-71 | Los Angeles | 77 | 25 | 38 | 63 |
| 1971-72 | Los Angeles | 78 | 17 | 22 | 39 |
| 1972-73 | Los Angeles | 78 | 36 | 28 | 64 |
| 1973-74 | Los Angeles | 77 | 23 | 33 | 56 |
| 1974-75 | Los Angeles | 80 | 25 | 23 | 48 |
| 1975-76 | Los Angeles | 80 | 20 | 22 | 42 |
| 1976-77 | Los Angeles | 69 | 13 | 25 | 38 |
| | **Totals** | **541** | **159** | **191** | **350** |

**BESLER, Phillip Rudolph**
*Defenseman-Forward*
b. Melville, Sask., Dec. 9, 1913

| 1935-36 | Boston | 9 | 0 | 0 | 0 |
|---------|--------|----|----|----|----|
| 1936-37 | New York A | 1 | 0 | 0 | 0 |
| 1938-39 | Chi-Det | 23 | 1 | 4 | 5 |
| 1939-40 | New York A | 1 | 0 | 0 | 0 |
| | **Totals** | **34** | **1** | **4** | **5** |

**BESSONE, Peter** *Defenseman*
b. New Bedford, Mass., Jan. 13, 1913

| 1937-38 | Detroit | 6 | 0 | 1 | 1 |
|---------|---------|----|----|----|----|

**BETHEL, John Charles** *Forward*
b. Montreal, Que., Apr. 15, 1957

| 1979-80 | Winnipeg | 17 | 0 | 2 | 2 |
|---------|----------|----|----|----|----|

**BETTIO, Silvio Angelo** *Forward*
b. Copper Cliff, Ont., Dec. 1, 1928

| 1949-50 | Boston | 44 | 9 | 12 | 21 |
|---------|--------|----|----|----|----|

**BEVERLEY, Nicholas Gerald (Nick)**
*Defenseman*
b. Toronto, Ont., Apr. 21, 1947

| 1969-70 | Boston | 2 | 0 | 0 | 0 |
|---------|--------|----|----|----|----|
| 1971-72 | Boston | 1 | 0 | 0 | 0 |
| 1972-73 | Boston | 75 | 1 | 10 | 11 |
| 1973-74 | Bos-Pitt | 68 | 2 | 14 | 16 |
| 1974-75 | New York R | 57 | 3 | 15 | 18 |
| 1975-76 | New York R | 63 | 1 | 8 | 9 |
| 1976-77 | NYR-Minn | 61 | 2 | 17 | 19 |
| 1977-78 | Minnesota | 57 | 7 | 14 | 21 |
| 1978-79 | LA-Col | 59 | 2 | 7 | 9 |
| 1979-80 | Colorado | 46 | 0 | 9 | 9 |
| | **Totals** | **489** | **18** | **94** | **112** |

**BIALOWAS, Dwight Joseph** *Defenseman*
b. Regina, Sask., Sept. 8, 1952

| 1973-74 | Atlanta | 11 | 0 | 0 | 0 |
|---------|---------|----|----|----|----|
| 1974-75 | Atl-Minn | 77 | 5 | 19 | 24 |
| 1975-76 | Minnesota | 58 | 5 | 18 | 23 |
| 1976-77 | Minnesota | 18 | 1 | 9 | 10 |
| | **Totals** | **164** | **11** | **46** | **57** |

**BIANCHIN, Wayne Richard** *Forward*
b. Nanaimo, B.C., Sept. 6, 1953

| 1973-74 | Pittsburgh | 69 | 12 | 13 | 25 |
|---------|-----------|----|----|----|----|
| 1974-75 | Pittsburgh | 2 | 0 | 0 | 0 |
| 1975-76 | Pittsburgh | 14 | 1 | 5 | 6 |
| 1976-77 | Pittsburgh | 79 | 28 | 6 | 34 |
| 1977-78 | Pittsburgh | 61 | 20 | 13 | 33 |
| 1978-79 | Pittsburgh | 40 | 7 | 4 | 11 |
| 1979-80 | Edmonton | 11 | 0 | 0 | 0 |
| | **Totals** | **276** | **68** | **41** | **109** |

| Season | Club | GP | G | A | Pts. |
|---|---|---|---|---|---|
| **BIDNER, Richard** *Forward* | | | | | |
| b. Petrolia, Ont., July 4, 1961 | | | | | |
| 1981-82 | Washington | 12 | 2 | 1 | 3 |
| **BIGNELL, Larry Irvin** *Defenseman* | | | | | |
| b. Edmonton, Alta., Jan. 7, 1950 | | | | | |
| 1973-74 | Pittsburgh | 20 | 0 | 3 | 3 |
| 1975-76 | Ottawa (WHA) | 41 | 5 | 5 | 10 |
| | **NHL Totals** | 20 | 0 | 3 | 3 |
| | **WHA Totals** | 41 | 5 | 5 | 10 |
| **BILODEAU, Gilles** *Forward* | | | | | |
| b. St. Prime, Que., July 31, 1955 | | | | | |
| 1975-76 | Toronto (WHA) | 14 | 0 | 1 | 1 |
| 1976-77 | Birmingham (WHA) | 34 | 2 | 6 | 8 |
| 1977-78 | Birmingham (WHA) | 59 | 2 | 2 | 4 |
| 1978-79 | Quebec (WHA) | 36 | 3 | 6 | 9 |
| 1979-80 | Quebec | 9 | 0 | 1 | 1 |
| | **NHL Totals** | 9 | 0 | 1 | 1 |
| | **WHA Totals** | 143 | 7 | 15 | 22 |
| **BIONDA, Jack Arthur** *Defenseman* | | | | | |
| b. Huntsville, Ont., Sept. 18, 1933 | | | | | |
| 1955-56 | Toronto | 13 | 0 | 1 | 1 |
| 1956-57 | Boston | 35 | 2 | 3 | 5 |
| 1957-58 | Boston | 42 | 1 | 4 | 5 |
| 1958-59 | Boston | 3 | 0 | 1 | 1 |
| | **Totals** | 93 | 3 | 9 | 12 |
| **BLACK, Stephen** *Forward* | | | | | |
| b. Ft. William, Ont., Mar. 31, 1927 | | | | | |
| 1949-50 | Detroit | 69 | 7 | 14 | 21 |
| 1950-51 | Det-Chi | 44 | 4 | 6 | 10 |
| | **Totals** | 113 | 11 | 20 | 31 |
| **BLACKBURN, John Donald (Don)** *Forward* | | | | | |
| b. Kirkland Lake, Ont., May 14, 1938 | | | | | |
| 1962-63 | Boston | 6 | 0 | 5 | 5 |
| 1967-68 | Philadelphia | 67 | 9 | 20 | 29 |
| 1968-69 | Philadelphia | 48 | 7 | 9 | 16 |
| 1969-70 | New York R | 3 | 0 | 0 | 0 |
| 1970-71 | New York R | 1 | 0 | 0 | 0 |
| 1972-73 | NYI-Minn | 60 | 7 | 10 | 17 |
| 1973-74 | New England (WHA) | 75 | 20 | 39 | 59 |
| 1974-75 | New England (WHA) | 50 | 18 | 32 | 50 |
| | **NHL Totals** | 185 | 23 | 44 | 67 |
| | **WHA Totals** | 125 | 38 | 71 | 109 |
| **BLACKBURN, Robert John (Bob)** | | | | | |
| *Defenseman* | | | | | |
| b. Rouyn, Que., Feb. 1, 1938 | | | | | |
| 1968-69 | New York R | 11 | 0 | 0 | 0 |
| 1969-70 | Pittsburgh | 60 | 4 | 7 | 11 |
| 1970-71 | Pittsburgh | 64 | 4 | 5 | 9 |
| | **Totals** | 135 | 8 | 12 | 20 |
| **BLADE, Henry Gordon** *Forward* | | | | | |
| b. Peterborough, Ont., Apr. 28, 1921 | | | | | |
| 1946-47 | Chicago | 18 | 1 | 3 | 4 |
| 1947-48 | Chicago | 6 | 1 | 0 | 1 |
| | **Totals** | 24 | 2 | 3 | 5 |
| **BLADON, Tom** *Defenseman* | | | | | |
| b. Edmonton, Alta., Dec. 29, 1952 | | | | | |
| 1972-73 | Philadelphia | 78 | 11 | 31 | 42 |
| 1973-74 | Philadelphia | 70 | 12 | 22 | 34 |
| 1974-75 | Philadelphia | 76 | 9 | 20 | 29 |
| 1975-76 | Philadelphia | 80 | 14 | 23 | 37 |
| 1976-77 | Philadelphia | 80 | 10 | 43 | 53 |
| 1977-78 | Philadelphia | 79 | 11 | 24 | 35 |
| 1078 70 | Pittsburgh | 78 | 4 | 23 | 27 |
| 1979-80 | Pittsburgh | 57 | 2 | 6 | 8 |
| 1980-81 | Edm-Winn-Det | 12 | 0 | 5 | 5 |
| | **Totals** | 610 | 73 | 197 | 270 |
| **BLAINE, Gary James** *Forward* | | | | | |
| b. St. Boniface, Man., Apr. 19, 1933 | | | | | |
| 1954-55 | Montreal | 1 | 0 | 0 | 0 |

| Season | Club | GP | G | A | Pts. |
|---|---|---|---|---|---|
| **BLAIR, Andrew Dryden** *Forward* | | | | | |
| b. Winnipeg, Man., Feb. 27, 1908 | | | | | |
| 1928-29 | Toronto | 44 | 12 | 15 | 27 |
| 1929-30 | Toronto | 42 | 11 | 10 | 21 |
| 1930-31 | Toronto | 44 | 11 | 8 | 19 |
| 1931-32 | Toronto | 48 | 9 | 14 | 23 |
| 1932-33 | Toronto | 43 | 6 | 9 | 15 |
| 1933-34 | Toronto | 47 | 14 | 9 | 23 |
| 1934-35 | Toronto | 45 | 6 | 14 | 20 |
| 1935-36 | Toronto | 48 | 5 | 4 | 9 |
| 1936-37 | Chicago | 43 | 0 | 3 | 3 |
| | **Totals** | 404 | 74 | 86 | 160 |
| **BLAIR, Charles** *Forward* | | | | | |
| b. Scotland, July, 23, 1928 | | | | | |
| 1948-49 | Toronto | 1 | 0 | 0 | 0 |
| **BLAIR, George (Dusty)** *Forward* | | | | | |
| b. South Porcupine, Ont., Sept. 15, 1929 | | | | | |
| 1950-51 | Toronto | 2 | 0 | 0 | 0 |
| **BLAISDELL, Michael Walter** *Forward* | | | | | |
| b. Moose Jaw, Sask., Jan 18, 1960 | | | | | |
| 1980-81 | Detroit | 32 | 3 | 6 | 9 |
| 1981-82 | Detroit | 80 | 23 | 32 | 55 |
| 1982-83 | Detroit | 80 | 18 | 23 | 41 |
| | **Totals** | 192 | 44 | 61 | 105 |
| **BLAKE, Francis J. (Mickey)** *Defenseman* | | | | | |
| b. Barriefield, Ont., Oct. 31, 1912 | | | | | |
| 1934-35 | St Louis E | 7 | 1 | 1 | 2 |
| 1935-36 | Toronto | 8 | 0 | 0 | 0 |
| | **Totals** | 15 | 1 | 1 | 2 |
| **BLAKE, Hector (Toe)** *Forward* | | | | | |
| b. Victoria Mines, Ont., Aug. 21, 1912 | | | | | |
| 1934-35 | Montreal M | 3 | 0 | 0 | 0 |
| 1935-36 | Montreal | 13 | 1 | 2 | 3 |
| 1936-37 | Montreal | 43 | 10 | 12 | 22 |
| 1937-38 | Montreal | 43 | 17 | 16 | 33 |
| 1938-39 | Montreal | 48 | 24 | 23 | 47 |
| 1939-40 | Montreal | 48 | 17 | 19 | 36 |
| 1940-41 | Montreal | 48 | 12 | 20 | 32 |
| 1941-42 | Montreal | 48 | 17 | 28 | 45 |
| 1942-43 | Montreal | 48 | 23 | 36 | 59 |
| 1943-44 | Montreal | 41 | 26 | 33 | 59 |
| 1944-45 | Montreal | 49 | 29 | 38 | 67 |
| 1945-46 | Montreal | 50 | 29 | 21 | 50 |
| 1946-47 | Montreal | 60 | 21 | 29 | 50 |
| 1947-48 | Montreal | 32 | 9 | 15 | 24 |
| | **Totals** | 574 | 235 | 292 | 527 |
| **BLIGHT, Richard Derek** *Forward* | | | | | |
| b. Portage la Prairie, Man., Oct. 17, 1955 | | | | | |
| 1975-76 | Vancouver | 74 | 25 | 31 | 56 |
| 1976-77 | Vancouver | 78 | 28 | 40 | 68 |
| 1977-78 | Vancouver | 80 | 25 | 38 | 63 |
| 1978-79 | Vancouver | 56 | 5 | 10 | 15 |
| 1979-80 | Vancouver | 33 | 12 | 6 | 18 |
| 1980-81 | Vancouver | 3 | 1 | 0 | 1 |
| 1982-83 | Los Angeles | 2 | 0 | 0 | 0 |
| | **Totals** | 326 | 96 | 125 | 221 |
| **BLINCO, Russell Percival (Beaver)** *Forward* | | | | | |
| b. Grand Mere, Que., Mar. 12, 1908 | | | | | |
| 1933-34 | Montreal M | 31 | 14 | 9 | 23 |
| 1934-35 | Montreal M | 48 | 13 | 14 | 27 |
| 1935-36 | Montreal M | 46 | 13 | 10 | 23 |
| 1936-37 | Montreal M | 44 | 6 | 12 | 18 |
| 1937-38 | Montreal M | 47 | 10 | 9 | 21 |
| 1938-39 | Chicago | 47 | 3 | 12 | 15 |
| | **Totals** | 263 | 59 | 66 | 125 |
| **BLOCK, Kenneth Ritchard** *Defenseman* | | | | | |
| b. Grunthal, Man., Mar. 18, 1944 | | | | | |
| 1970-71 | Vancouver | 1 | 0 | 0 | 0 |
| 1972-73 | New York (WHA) | 78 | 5 | 53 | 58 |
| 1973-74 | Jersey (WHA) | 74 | 3 | 43 | 46 |
| 1974-75 | SD-Ind (WHA) | 73 | 1 | 28 | 29 |
| 1975-76 | Indianapolis (WHA) | 79 | 1 | 25 | 26 |
| 1976-77 | Indianapolis (WHA) | 52 | 3 | 10 | 13 |

| Season | Club | GP | G | A | Pts. |
|---|---|---|---|---|---|
| 1977-78 | Indianapolis (WHA) | 77 | 1 | 25 | 26 |
| 1978-79 | Indianapolis (WHA) | 22 | 2 | 3 | 5 |
| | **NHL Totals** | 1 | 0 | 0 | 0 |
| | **WHA Totals** | 455 | 16 | 187 | 203 |
| **BLOOM, Michael Carroll** *Forward* | | | | | |
| b. Ottawa, Ont., Apr. 12, 1952 | | | | | |
| 1973-74 | San Diego (WHA) | 76 | 25 | 44 | 69 |
| 1974-75 | Wash-Det | 80 | 11 | 27 | 38 |
| 1975-76 | Detroit | 76 | 13 | 17 | 30 |
| 1976-77 | Detroit | 45 | 6 | 3 | 9 |
| | **Totals** | 277 | 55 | 91 | 146 |
| **BLOMQVIST, Timo** *Defenseman* | | | | | |
| b. Helsinki, Finland, Jan. 23, 1961 | | | | | |
| 1981-82 | Washington | 44 | 1 | 11 | 12 |
| 1982-83 | Washington | 61 | 1 | 17 | 18 |
| | **Totals** | 105 | 2 | 28 | 30 |
| **BLUM, John** *Defenseman* | | | | | |
| b. Detroit, Mich., Oct. 8, 1959 | | | | | |
| 1982-83 | Edmonton | 5 | 0 | 3 | 3 |
| **BODDY, Greg Allen** *Defenseman* | | | | | |
| b. Ponoka, Alta., Mar. 19, 1949 | | | | | |
| 1971-72 | Vancouver | 40 | 2 | 5 | 7 |
| 1972-73 | Vancouver | 74 | 3 | 11 | 14 |
| 1973-74 | Vancouver | 53 | 2 | 10 | 12 |
| 1974-75 | Vancouver | 72 | 11 | 12 | 23 |
| 1975-76 | Vancouver | 34 | 5 | 6 | 11 |
| 1976-77 | SD-Edm (WHA) | 64 | 2 | 19 | 21 |
| | **NHL Totals** | 273 | 23 | 44 | 67 |
| | **WHA Totals** | 64 | 2 | 19 | 21 |
| **BODNAR, August (Gus)** *Forward* | | | | | |
| b. Ft. William, Ont., Aug. 24, 1925 | | | | | |
| 1943-44 | Toronto | 50 | 22 | 40 | 62 |
| 1944-45 | Toronto | 49 | 8 | 36 | 44 |
| 1945-46 | Toronto | 49 | 14 | 23 | 37 |
| 1946-47 | Toronto | 39 | 4 | 6 | 10 |
| 1947-48 | Chicago | 46 | 13 | 22 | 35 |
| 1948-49 | Chicago | 59 | 19 | 26 | 45 |
| 1949-50 | Chicago | 70 | 11 | 28 | 39 |
| 1950-51 | Chicago | 44 | 8 | 12 | 20 |
| 1951-52 | Chicago | 69 | 14 | 26 | 40 |
| 1952-53 | Chicago | 66 | 16 | 13 | 29 |
| 1953-54 | Chi-Bos | 59 | 9 | 18 | 27 |
| 1954-55 | Boston | 67 | 4 | 4 | 8 |
| | **Totals** | 667 | 142 | 254 | 396 |
| **BOEHM, Ronald John** *Forward* | | | | | |
| b. Allan, Sask., Aug. 14, 1943 | | | | | |
| 1967-68 | Oakland | 16 | 2 | 1 | 3 |
| **BOESCH, Garth Vernon** *Defenseman* | | | | | |
| b. Millestone, Sask., Oct. 7, 1920 | | | | | |
| 1946-47 | Toronto | 35 | 4 | 5 | 9 |
| 1947-48 | Toronto | 45 | 2 | 7 | 9 |
| 1948-49 | Toronto | 59 | 1 | 10 | 11 |
| | **Totals** | 139 | 7 | 22 | 29 |
| **BOILEAU, Marc Claude** *Forward* | | | | | |
| b. Pointe Claire, Que., Sept. 3, 1932 | | | | | |
| 1961-62 | Detroit | 54 | 5 | 6 | 11 |
| **BOILEAU, Rene** *Forward* | | | | | |
| 1925-26 | New York A | 7 | 0 | 0 | 0 |
| **BOIMISTRUCK, Fred** *Defenseman* | | | | | |
| b. Sudbury, Ont., Jan. 14, 1962 | | | | | |
| 1981-82 | Toronto | 57 | 2 | 11 | 13 |
| 1982-83 | Toronto | 26 | 2 | 3 | 5 |
| | **Totals** | 83 | 4 | 14 | 18 |
| **BOISVERT, Serge** *Forward* | | | | | |
| b. Drummondville, Ont., June 1, 1959 | | | | | |
| 1982-83 | Toronto | 17 | 0 | 2 | 2 |

| Season | Club | GP | G | A | Pts. |
|---|---|---|---|---|---|
| **BOIVIN, Leo Joseph** *Defenseman* | | | | | |
| b. Prescott, Ont., Aug. 2, 1932 | | | | | |
| 1951-52 | Toronto | 2 | 0 | 1 | 1 |
| 1952-53 | Toronto | 70 | 2 | 13 | 15 |
| 1953-54 | Toronto | 58 | 1 | 6 | 7 |
| 1954-55 | Tor-Bos | 66 | 6 | 11 | 17 |
| 1955-56 | Boston | 68 | 4 | 16 | 20 |
| 1956-57 | Boston | 55 | 2 | 8 | 10 |
| 1957-58 | Boston | 33 | 0 | 4 | 4 |
| 1958-59 | Boston | 70 | 5 | 16 | 21 |
| 1959-60 | Boston | 70 | 4 | 21 | 25 |
| 1960-61 | Boston | 57 | 6 | 17 | 23 |
| 1961-62 | Boston | 65 | 5 | 18 | 23 |
| 1962-63 | Boston | 62 | 2 | 24 | 26 |
| 1963-64 | Boston | 65 | 10 | 14 | 24 |
| 1964-65 | Boston | 67 | 3 | 10 | 13 |
| 1965-66 | Bos-Det | 62 | 0 | 10 | 10 |
| 1966-67 | Detroit | 69 | 4 | 17 | 21 |
| 1967-68 | Pittsburgh | 73 | 9 | 13 | 22 |
| 1968-69 | Pitt-Minn | 69 | 6 | 19 | 25 |
| 1969-70 | Minnesota | 69 | 3 | 13 | 16 |
| | **Totals** | 1150 | 72 | 251 | 323 |
| **BOLAND, Michael John** *Defenseman* | | | | | |
| b. London, Ont., Oct. 29, 1954 | | | | | |
| 1974-75 | Kansas City | 1 | 0 | 0 | 0 |
| 1978-79 | Buffalo | 22 | 1 | 2 | 3 |
| | **Totals** | 23 | 1 | 2 | 3 |
| **BOLDIREV, Ivan** *Forward* | | | | | |
| b. Zranjanin, Yugoslavia, Aug. 15, 1949 | | | | | |
| 1970-71 | Boston | 2 | 0 | 0 | 0 |
| 1971-72 | Bos-Cal | 68 | 16 | 25 | 41 |
| 1972-73 | California | 56 | 11 | 23 | 34 |
| 1973-74 | California | 78 | 25 | 31 | 56 |
| 1974-75 | Chicago | 80 | 24 | 43 | 67 |
| 1975-76 | Chicago | 78 | 28 | 34 | 62 |
| 1976-77 | Chicago | 80 | 24 | 38 | 62 |
| 1977-78 | Chicago | 80 | 35 | 45 | 80 |
| 1978-79 | Chi-Atl | 79 | 35 | 43 | 78 |
| 1979-80 | Atl-Van | 79 | 32 | 35 | 67 |
| 1980-81 | Vancouver | 72 | 26 | 33 | 59 |
| 1981-82 | Vancouver | 78 | 33 | 40 | 73 |
| 1982-83 | Van-Det | 72 | 18 | 37 | 55 |
| | **Totals** | 902 | 307 | 427 | 734 |
| **BOLDUC, Daniel George** *Forward* | | | | | |
| b. Waterville, Maine, Apr. 6, 1953 | | | | | |
| 1975-76 | New England (WHA) | 14 | 2 | 5 | 7 |
| 1976-77 | New England (WHA) | 33 | 8 | 3 | 11 |
| 1977-78 | New England (WHA) | 41 | 5 | 5 | 10 |
| 1978-79 | Detroit | 56 | 16 | 13 | 29 |
| 1979-80 | Detroit | 44 | 6 | 5 | 11 |
| | **NHL Totals** | 100 | 22 | 18 | 40 |
| | **WHA Totals** | 88 | 15 | 13 | 28 |
| **BOLDUC, Michel** *Defenseman* | | | | | |
| b. Ange-Gardien, Que., Mar. 13, 1961 | | | | | |
| 1981-82 | Quebec | 3 | 0 | 0 | 0 |
| 1982-83 | Quebec | 7 | 0 | 0 | 0 |
| | **Totals** | 10 | 0 | 0 | 0 |
| **BOLL, Frank Thurman (Buzz)** *Forward* | | | | | |
| b. Fillmore, Sask., Mar. 6, 1911 | | | | | |
| 1933-34 | Toronto | 42 | 12 | 8 | 20 |
| 1934-35 | Toronto | 47 | 14 | 4 | 18 |
| 1935-36 | Toronto | 44 | 15 | 13 | 28 |
| 1936-37 | Toronto | 25 | 6 | 3 | 9 |
| 1937-38 | Toronto | 44 | 14 | 11 | 25 |
| 1938-39 | Toronto | 11 | 0 | 0 | 0 |
| 1939-40 | New York A | 47 | 5 | 10 | 15 |
| 1940-41 | New York A | 47 | 12 | 14 | 26 |
| 1941-42 | New York A | 48 | 11 | 15 | 26 |
| 1942-43 | Boston | 43 | 25 | 27 | 52 |
| 1943-44 | Boston | 39 | 19 | 25 | 44 |
| | **Totals** | 437 | 133 | 130 | 263 |
| **BOLONCHUK, Larry** *Defenseman* | | | | | |
| b. Winnipeg, Man., Feb. 26, 1952 | | | | | |
| 1972-73 | Vancouver | 15 | 0 | 0 | 0 |
| 1975-76 | Washington | 1 | 0 | 1 | 1 |

| Season | Club | GP | G | A | Pts. |
|---|---|---|---|---|---|
| 1976-77 | Washington | 9 | 0 | 0 | 0 |
| 1977-78 | Washington | 49 | 3 | 8 | 11 |
| | **Totals** | 74 | 3 | 9 | 12 |
| **BOLTON, Hugh Edward** *Defenseman* | | | | | |
| b. Toronto, Ont., Apr. 15, 1929 | | | | | |
| 1949-50 | Toronto | 2 | 0 | 0 | 0 |
| 1950-51 | Toronto | 13 | 1 | 3 | 4 |
| 1951-52 | Toronto | 60 | 3 | 13 | 16 |
| 1952-53 | Toronto | 9 | 0 | 0 | 0 |
| 1953-54 | Toronto | 9 | 0 | 0 | 0 |
| 1954-55 | Toronto | 69 | 2 | 19 | 21 |
| 1955-56 | Toronto | 67 | 4 | 16 | 20 |
| 1956-57 | Toronto | 6 | 0 | 0 | 0 |
| | **Totals** | 235 | 10 | 51 | 61 |
| **BONAR, Daniel** *Forward* | | | | | |
| b. Brandon, Man., Sept. 23, 1956 | | | | | |
| 1980-81 | Los Angeles | 71 | 11 | 15 | 26 |
| 1981-82 | Los Angeles | 79 | 13 | 23 | 36 |
| 1982-83 | Los Angeles | 20 | 1 | 1 | 2 |
| | **Totals** | 170 | 25 | 39 | 64 |
| **BONIN, Marcel** *Forward* | | | | | |
| b. Montreal, Que., Sept. 12, 1932 | | | | | |
| 1952-53 | Detroit | 37 | 4 | 9 | 13 |
| 1953-54 | Detroit | 1 | 0 | 0 | 0 |
| 1954-55 | Detroit | 69 | 16 | 20 | 36 |
| 1955-56 | Boston | 67 | 9 | 9 | 18 |
| 1957-58 | Montreal | 66 | 15 | 24 | 39 |
| 1958-59 | Montreal | 57 | 13 | 30 | 43 |
| 1959-60 | Montreal | 59 | 17 | 34 | 51 |
| 1960-61 | Montreal | 65 | 16 | 35 | 51 |
| 1961-62 | Montreal | 33 | 7 | 14 | 21 |
| | **Totals** | 454 | 97 | 175 | 272 |
| **BOO, James McQuaid** *Defenseman* | | | | | |
| b. Rolla, Mo., Nov. 12, 1954 | | | | | |
| 1977-78 | Minnesota | 6 | 0 | 0 | 0 |
| **BOONE, Carl George (Buddy)** *Forward* | | | | | |
| b. Kirkland Lake, Ont., Sept. 11, 1932 | | | | | |
| 1957-58 | Boston | 34 | 5 | 3 | 8 |
| **BOOTHMAN, George Edward** *Forward* | | | | | |
| b. Calgary, Alta., Sept. 25, 1916 | | | | | |
| 1942-43 | Toronto | 9 | 1 | 1 | 2 |
| 1943-44 | Toronto | 49 | 16 | 18 | 34 |
| | **Totals** | 58 | 17 | 19 | 36 |
| **BORDELEAU, Christian Gerard** *Forward* | | | | | |
| b. Noranda, Que., Sept. 23, 1947 | | | | | |
| 1968-69 | Montreal | 13 | 1 | 3 | 4 |
| 1969-70 | Montreal | 48 | 2 | 13 | 15 |
| 1970-71 | St Louis | 78 | 21 | 32 | 53 |
| 1971-72 | StL-Chi | 66 | 14 | 17 | 31 |
| 1972-73 | Winnipeg (WHA) | 78 | 47 | 54 | 101 |
| 1973-74 | Winnipeg (WHA) | 75 | 26 | 49 | 75 |
| 1974-75 | Winn-Que (WHA) | 71 | 23 | 41 | 64 |
| 1975-76 | Quebec (WHA) | 74 | 37 | 72 | 109 |
| 1976-77 | Quebec (WHA) | 72 | 32 | 75 | 107 |
| 1977-78 | Quebec (WHA) | 26 | 9 | 22 | 31 |
| 1978-79 | Quebec (WHA) | 16 | 5 | 12 | 17 |
| | **NHL Totals** | 205 | 38 | 65 | 103 |
| | **WHA Totals** | 412 | 179 | 325 | 504 |
| **BORDELEAU, Jean-Pierre** *Forward* | | | | | |
| b. Noranda, Que., June 13, 1949 | | | | | |
| 1971-72 | Chicago | 3 | 0 | 2 | 2 |
| 1972-73 | Chicago | 73 | 15 | 15 | 30 |
| 1973-74 | Chicago | 64 | 11 | 9 | 20 |
| 1974-75 | Chicago | 59 | 7 | 8 | 15 |
| 1975-76 | Chicago | 76 | 12 | 18 | 30 |
| 1976-77 | Chicago | 60 | 15 | 14 | 29 |
| 1977-78 | Chicago | 76 | 15 | 25 | 40 |
| 1978-79 | Chicago | 63 | 15 | 21 | 36 |
| 1979-80 | Chicago | 45 | 7 | 14 | 21 |
| | **Totals** | 519 | 97 | 126 | 223 |

| Season | Club | GP | G | A | Pts. |
|---|---|---|---|---|---|
| **BORDELEAU, Paulin Joseph** *Forward* | | | | | |
| b. Noranda, Que., Jan. 29, 1953 | | | | | |
| 1973-74 | Vancouver | 68 | 11 | 13 | 24 |
| 1974-75 | Vancouver | 67 | 17 | 31 | 48 |
| 1975-76 | Vancouver | 48 | 5 | 12 | 17 |
| 1976-77 | Quebec (WHA) | 80 | 42 | 41 | 83 |
| 1977-78 | Quebec (WHA) | 77 | 42 | 23 | 65 |
| 1978-79 | Quebec (WHA) | 77 | 17 | 12 | 29 |
| | **NHL Totals** | 183 | 33 | 56 | 89 |
| | **WHA Totals** | 234 | 101 | 76 | 177 |
| **BOROTSIK, John Nicholas** *Forward* | | | | | |
| b. Brandon, Man., Nov. 26, 1949 | | | | | |
| 1974-75 | St Louis | 1 | 0 | 0 | 0 |
| **BOSCHMAN, Laurie Joseph** *Forward* | | | | | |
| b. Major, Sask., June 4, 1960 | | | | | |
| 1979-80 | Toronto | 80 | 16 | 32 | 48 |
| 1980-81 | Toronto | 53 | 14 | 19 | 33 |
| 1981-82 | Tor-Edm | 65 | 11 | 22 | 33 |
| 1982-83 | Edm-Winn | 74 | 11 | 17 | 28 |
| | **Totals** | 272 | 52 | 90 | 142 |
| **BOSSY, Michael** *Forward* | | | | | |
| b. Montreal, Que., Jan. 22, 1957 | | | | | |
| 1977-78 | New York I | 73 | 53 | 38 | 91 |
| 1978-79 | New York I | 80 | 69 | 57 | 126 |
| 1979-80 | New York I | 75 | 51 | 41 | 92 |
| 1980-81 | New York I | 79 | 68 | 51 | 119 |
| 1981-82 | New York I | 80 | 64 | 83 | 147 |
| 1982-83 | New York I | 79 | 60 | 58 | 118 |
| | **Totals** | 466 | 365 | 328 | 693 |
| **BOSTROM, Helge** *Defenseman* | | | | | |
| b. Winnipeg, Man., Jan. 9, 1894 | | | | | |
| 1929-30 | Chicago | 21 | 0 | 1 | 1 |
| 1930-31 | Chicago | 38 | 2 | 2 | 4 |
| 1931-32 | Chicago | 13 | 0 | 0 | 0 |
| 1932-33 | Chicago | 18 | 1 | 0 | 1 |
| | **Totals** | 90 | 3 | 3 | 6 |
| **BOTELL, Mark** *Defenseman* | | | | | |
| b. Scarborough, Ont., Aug. 27, 1961 | | | | | |
| 1981-82 | Philadelphia | 32 | 4 | 10 | 14 |
| **BOTHWELL, Timothy** *Defenseman* | | | | | |
| b. Vancouver, B.C., May 6, 1955 | | | | | |
| 1978-79 | New York R | 1 | 0 | 0 | 0 |
| 1979-80 | New York R | 45 | 4 | 6 | 10 |
| 1980-81 | New York R | 3 | 0 | 1 | 1 |
| 1981-82 | New York R | 13 | 0 | 3 | 3 |
| 1982-83 | St Louis | 61 | 4 | 11 | 15 |
| | **Totals** | 123 | 8 | 21 | 29 |
| **BOTTING, Cameron Allen** *Forward* | | | | | |
| b. Kingston, Ont., Mar. 10, 1954 | | | | | |
| 1975-76 | Atlanta | 2 | 0 | 1 | 1 |
| **BOUCHA, Henry Charles** *Forward* | | | | | |
| b. Warroad, Minn., June 1, 1951 | | | | | |
| 1971-72 | Detroit | 16 | 1 | 0 | 1 |
| 1972-73 | Detroit | 73 | 14 | 14 | 28 |
| 1973-74 | Detroit | 70 | 19 | 12 | 31 |
| 1974-75 | Minnesota | 51 | 15 | 14 | 29 |
| 1975-76 | Kansas City | 28 | 4 | 7 | 11 |
| 1975-76 | Minnesota (WHA) | 36 | 15 | 20 | 35 |
| 1976-77 | Colorado | 9 | 0 | 2 | 2 |
| | **NHL Totals** | 247 | 53 | 49 | 102 |
| | **WHA Totals** | 36 | 15 | 20 | 35 |
| **BOUCHARD, Edmond** *Forward* | | | | | |
| b. Trois-Rivieres, Que. | | | | | |
| 1921-22 | Montreal | 18 | 1 | 4 | 5 |
| 1922-23 | Hamilton | 24 | 5 | 12 | 17 |
| 1923-24 | Ham-Mont | 24 | 5 | 0 | 5 |
| 1924-25 | Hamilton | 29 | 2 | 2 | 4 |
| 1925-26 | New York A | 34 | 3 | 1 | 4 |
| 1926-27 | New York A | 38 | 2 | 1 | 3 |
| 1927-28 | New York A | 43 | 1 | 0 | 1 |
| 1928-29 | NYA-Pitt | 17 | 0 | 0 | 0 |
| | **Totals** | 227 | 19 | 20 | 39 |

| Season | Club | GP | G | A | Pts. |
|---|---|---|---|---|---|
| **BOUCHARD, Emile Joseph (Butch)** | | | | | |
| *Defenseman* | | | | | |
| b. Montreal, Que., Sept. 11, 1920 | | | | | |
| 1941-42 | Montreal | 44 | 0 | 6 | 6 |
| 1942-43 | Montreal | 45 | 2 | 16 | 18 |
| 1943-44 | Montreal | 39 | 5 | 14 | 19 |
| 1944-45 | Montreal | 50 | 11 | 23 | 34 |
| 1945-46 | Montreal | 45 | 7 | 10 | 17 |
| 1946-47 | Montreal | 60 | 5 | 7 | 12 |
| 1947-48 | Montreal | 60 | 4 | 6 | 10 |
| 1948-49 | Montreal | 27 | 3 | 3 | 6 |
| 1949-50 | Montreal | 69 | 1 | 7 | 8 |
| 1950-51 | Montreal | 52 | 3 | 10 | 13 |
| 1951-52 | Montreal | 60 | 3 | 9 | 12 |
| 1952-53 | Montreal | 58 | 2 | 8 | 10 |
| 1953-54 | Montreal | 70 | 1 | 10 | 11 |
| 1954-55 | Montreal | 70 | 2 | 15 | 17 |
| 1955-56 | Montreal | 36 | 0 | 0 | 0 |
| **Totals** | | 785 | 49 | 144 | 193 |
| **BOUCHARD, Pierre** *Defenseman* | | | | | |
| b. Longueuil, Que., Feb. 20, 1948 | | | | | |
| 1970-71 | Montreal | 51 | 0 | 3 | 3 |
| 1971-72 | Montreal | 60 | 3 | 5 | 8 |
| 1972-73 | Montreal | 41 | 0 | 7 | 7 |
| 1973-74 | Montreal | 60 | 1 | 14 | 15 |
| 1974-75 | Montreal | 79 | 3 | 9 | 12 |
| 1975-76 | Montreal | 66 | 1 | 11 | 12 |
| 1976-77 | Montreal | 73 | 4 | 11 | 15 |
| 1977-78 | Montreal | 59 | 4 | 6 | 10 |
| 1978-79 | Washington | 1 | 0 | 0 | 0 |
| 1979-80 | Washington | 54 | 5 | 9 | 14 |
| 1980-81 | Washington | 50 | 3 | 7 | 10 |
| 1981-82 | Washington | 1 | 0 | 0 | 0 |
| **Totals** | | 595 | 24 | 82 | 106 |
| **BOUCHARD, Richard Joseph** *Forward* | | | | | |
| b. Lettelier, Man., Dec. 2, 1934 | | | | | |
| 1954-55 | New York R | 1 | 0 | 0 | 0 |
| **BOUCHER, Clarence** *Defenseman* | | | | | |
| b. Sudbury, Ont. | | | | | |
| 1926-27 | New York A | 10 | 0 | 1 | 1 |
| 1927-28 | New York A | 37 | 2 | 1 | 3 |
| **Totals** | | 47 | 2 | 2 | 4 |
| **BOUCHER, Francois X. (Frank) (Raffles)** | | | | | |
| *Forward* | | | | | |
| b. Ottawa, Ont., Oct. 7, 1901 | | | | | |
| 1921-22 | Ottawa | 24 | 9 | 1 | 10 |
| 1926-27 | New York R | 44 | 13 | 15 | 28 |
| 1927-28 | New York R | 44 | 23 | 12 | 35 |
| 1928-29 | New York R | 44 | 10 | 16 | 26 |
| 1929-30 | New York R | 42 | 26 | 36 | 62 |
| 1930-31 | New York R | 44 | 12 | 27 | 39 |
| 1931-32 | New York R | 48 | 12 | 23 | 35 |
| 1932-33 | New York R | 46 | 7 | 28 | 35 |
| 1933-34 | New York R | 48 | 14 | 30 | 44 |
| 1934-35 | New York R | 48 | 13 | 32 | 45 |
| 1935-36 | New York R | 48 | 11 | 18 | 29 |
| 1936-37 | New York R | 44 | 7 | 13 | 20 |
| 1937-38 | New York R | 18 | 0 | 1 | 1 |
| 1943-44 | New York R | 15 | 4 | 10 | 14 |
| **Totals** | | 557 | 161 | 262 | 423 |
| **BOUCHER, George (Buck)** *Defenseman* | | | | | |
| b. Ottawa, Ont., 1896 | | | | | |
| 1917-18 | Ottawa | 22 | 9 | 0 | 9 |
| 1918-19 | Ottawa | 17 | 5 | 2 | 7 |
| 1919-20 | Ottawa | 22 | 10 | 4 | 14 |
| 1920-21 | Ottawa | 23 | 12 | 5 | 17 |
| 1921-22 | Ottawa | 23 | 12 | 8 | 20 |
| 1922-23 | Ottawa | 23 | 15 | 9 | 24 |
| 1923-24 | Ottawa | 21 | 14 | 5 | 19 |
| 1924-25 | Ottawa | 28 | 15 | 4 | 19 |
| 1925-26 | Ottawa | 36 | 8 | 4 | 12 |
| 1926-27 | Ottawa | 44 | 8 | 3 | 11 |
| 1927-28 | Ottawa | 44 | 7 | 5 | 12 |
| 1928-29 | Ott-Mont M | 41 | 4 | 2 | 6 |
| 1929-30 | Montreal M | 39 | 2 | 6 | 8 |
| 1930-31 | Montreal M | 31 | 0 | 0 | 0 |
| 1931-32 | Chicago | 43 | 1 | 5 | 6 |
| **Totals** | | 457 | 122 | 62 | 184 |
| **BOUCHER, Robert** *Forward* | | | | | |
| b. Ottawa, Ont. | | | | | |
| 1923-24 | Montreal | 12 | 0 | 0 | 0 |
| **BOUCHER, William** *Forward* | | | | | |
| b. Ottawa, Ont. | | | | | |
| 1921-22 | Montreal | 24 | 17 | 5 | 22 |
| 1922-23 | Montreal | 24 | 23 | 4 | 27 |
| 1923-24 | Montreal | 23 | 16 | 6 | 22 |
| 1924-25 | Montreal | 30 | 18 | 13 | 31 |
| 1925-26 | Montreal | 34 | 8 | 5 | 13 |
| 1926-27 | Mont-Bos | 35 | 6 | 0 | 6 |
| 1927-28 | New York A | 43 | 5 | 2 | 7 |
| **Totals** | | 213 | 93 | 35 | 128 |
| **BOUDREAU, Bruce Allan** *Forward* | | | | | |
| b. Toronto, Ont., Jan. 9, 1955 | | | | | |
| 1975-76 | Minnesota (WHA) | 30 | 3 | 6 | 9 |
| 1976-77 | Toronto | 15 | 2 | 5 | 7 |
| 1977-78 | Toronto | 40 | 11 | 18 | 29 |
| 1978-79 | Toronto | 26 | 4 | 3 | 7 |
| 1979-80 | Toronto | 2 | 0 | 0 | 0 |
| 1980-81 | Toronto | 39 | 10 | 14 | 24 |
| 1981-82 | Toronto | 12 | 0 | 2 | 2 |
| **NHL Totals** | | 134 | 27 | 42 | 69 |
| **WHA Totals** | | 30 | 3 | 6 | 9 |
| **BOUDRIAS, Andre** *Forward* | | | | | |
| b. Montreal, Que., Sept. 19, 1943 | | | | | |
| 1963-64 | Montreal | 4 | 1 | 4 | 5 |
| 1964-65 | Montreal | 1 | 0 | 0 | 0 |
| 1966-67 | Montreal | 2 | 0 | 1 | 1 |
| 1967-68 | Minnesota | 74 | 18 | 35 | 53 |
| 1968-69 | Minn-Chi | 73 | 8 | 19 | 27 |
| 1969-70 | St Louis | 50 | 3 | 14 | 17 |
| 1970-71 | Vancouver | 77 | 25 | 41 | 66 |
| 1971-72 | Vancouver | 78 | 27 | 34 | 61 |
| 1972-73 | Vancouver | 77 | 30 | 40 | 70 |
| 1973-74 | Vancouver | 78 | 16 | 59 | 75 |
| 1974-75 | Vancouver | 77 | 16 | 62 | 78 |
| 1975-76 | Vancouver | 71 | 7 | 31 | 38 |
| 1976-77 | Quebec (WHA) | 74 | 12 | 31 | 43 |
| 1977-78 | Quebec (WHA) | 66 | 10 | 17 | 27 |
| **NHL Totals** | | 662 | 151 | 340 | 491 |
| **WHA Totals** | | 140 | 22 | 48 | 70 |
| **BOUGHNER, Barry Michael** *Forward* | | | | | |
| b. Delhi, Ont., Jan. 29, 1948 | | | | | |
| 1969-70 | Oakland | 4 | 0 | 0 | 0 |
| 1970-71 | California | 16 | 0 | 0 | 0 |
| **Totals** | | 20 | 0 | 0 | 0 |
| **BOURBONNAIS, Dan** *Forward* | | | | | |
| b. Winnipeg, Man., Mar. 6, 1962 | | | | | |
| 1981-82 | Hartford | 24 | 3 | 9 | 12 |
| **BOURBONNAIS, Rick** *Forward* | | | | | |
| b. Toronto, Ont., Apr. 20, 1955 | | | | | |
| 1975-76 | St Louis | 7 | 0 | 0 | 0 |
| 1976-77 | St Louis | 33 | 6 | 8 | 14 |
| 1977-78 | St Louis | 31 | 3 | 7 | 10 |
| **Totals** | | 71 | 9 | 15 | 24 |
| **BOURCIER, Conrad** *Forward* | | | | | |
| b. Montreal, Que., May 28, 1916 | | | | | |
| 1935-36 | Montreal | — | 0 | 0 | 0 |
| **BOURCIER, Jean Louis** *Forward* | | | | | |
| b. Montreal, Que., Jan. 3, 1912 | | | | | |
| 1935-36 | Montreal | — | 0 | 1 | 1 |
| **BOURGAULT, Leo A.** *Defenseman* | | | | | |
| b. Sturgeon Falls, Ont., Jan. 17, 1903 | | | | | |
| 1926-27 | Tor-NYR | 42 | 2 | 1 | 3 |
| 1927-28 | New York R | 37 | 7 | 0 | 7 |
| 1928-29 | New York R | 44 | 2 | 3 | 5 |
| 1929-30 | New York R | 44 | 7 | 6 | 13 |
| 1930-31 | NYR-Ott | 38 | 0 | 5 | 5 |
| 1932-33 | Mont-Chi | 50 | 2 | 2 | 4 |
| 1933-34 | Montreal | 48 | 4 | 3 | 7 |
| 1934-35 | Montreal | 4 | 0 | 0 | 0 |
| **Totals** | | 307 | 24 | 20 | 44 |
| **BOURGEOIS, Charles** *Defenseman* | | | | | |
| b. Moncton, N.B., Nov. 11, 1959 | | | | | |
| 1982-83 | Calgary | 15 | 2 | 3 | 5 |
| **BOURNE, Robert Glen** *Forward* | | | | | |
| b. Kindersley, Sask., June 21, 1954 | | | | | |
| 1974-75 | New York I | 77 | 16 | 23 | 39 |
| 1975-76 | New York I | 14 | 2 | 3 | 5 |
| 1976-77 | New York I | 75 | 16 | 19 | 35 |
| 1977-78 | New York I | 80 | 30 | 33 | 63 |
| 1978-79 | New York I | 80 | 30 | 31 | 61 |
| 1979-80 | New York I | 73 | 15 | 25 | 40 |
| 1980-81 | New York I | 78 | 35 | 41 | 76 |
| 1981-82 | New York I | 76 | 27 | 26 | 53 |
| 1982-83 | New York I | 77 | 20 | 42 | 62 |
| **Totals** | | 630 | 191 | 243 | 434 |
| **BOURQUE, Raymond Jean** *Defenseman* | | | | | |
| b. Montreal Que., Dec. 18, 1960 | | | | | |
| 1979-80 | Boston | 80 | 17 | 48 | 65 |
| 1980-81 | Boston | 67 | 27 | 29 | 56 |
| 1981-81 | Boston | 65 | 17 | 49 | 66 |
| 1982-83 | Boston | 65 | 22 | 51 | 73 |
| **Totals** | | 277 | 83 | 177 | 260 |
| **BOUTETTE, Patrick Michael** *Forward* | | | | | |
| b. Windsor, Ont., Mar. 1, 1952 | | | | | |
| 1975-76 | Toronto | 77 | 10 | 22 | 32 |
| 1976-77 | Toronto | 80 | 18 | 18 | 36 |
| 1977-78 | Toronto | 80 | 17 | 19 | 36 |
| 1978-79 | Toronto | 80 | 14 | 19 | 33 |
| 1979-80 | Tor-Hart | 79 | 13 | 35 | 48 |
| 1980-81 | Hartford | 80 | 28 | 52 | 80 |
| 1981-82 | Pittsburgh | 80 | 23 | 51 | 74 |
| 1982-83 | Pittsburgh | 80 | 27 | 29 | 56 |
| **Totals** | | 646 | 150 | 245 | 395 |
| **BOUTILIER, Paul Andre** *Defenseman* | | | | | |
| b. Sydney, N.S., May 3, 1963 | | | | | |
| 1981-82 | New York I | 1 | 0 | 0 | 0 |
| 1982-83 | New York I | 29 | 4 | 5 | 9 |
| **Totals** | | 30 | 4 | 5 | 9 |
| **BOWMAN, Ralph (Scotty)** *Defenseman* | | | | | |
| b. Winnipeg, Man., Jan. 20, 1911 | | | | | |
| 1933-34 | Ottawa | 46 | 0 | 2 | 2 |
| 1934-35 | StLE-Det | 43 | 3 | 5 | 8 |
| 1935-36 | Detroit | 48 | 3 | 2 | 5 |
| 1936-37 | Detroit | 43 | 0 | 1 | 1 |
| 1937-38 | Detroit | 46 | 0 | 2 | 2 |
| 1938-39 | Detroit | 43 | 2 | 3 | 5 |
| 1939-40 | Detroit | 11 | 0 | 2 | 2 |
| **Totals** | | 280 | 8 | 17 | 25 |
| **BOWMAN, Robert Kirk** *Forward* | | | | | |
| b. Leamington, Ont., Sept. 30, 1952 | | | | | |
| 1973-74 | Los Angeles (WHA) | 10 | 0 | 2 | 2 |
| 1976-77 | Chicago | 55 | 10 | 13 | 23 |
| 1977-78 | Chicago | 33 | 1 | 4 | 5 |
| **NHL Totals** | | 88 | 11 | 17 | 28 |
| **WHA Totals** | | 10 | 0 | 2 | 2 |
| **BOWNASS, John (Jack)** *Defenseman* | | | | | |
| b. Winnipeg, Man., July 27, 1930 | | | | | |
| 1957-58 | Montreal | 4 | 0 | 1 | 1 |
| 1958-59 | New York R | 35 | 1 | 2 | 3 |
| 1959-60 | New York R | 37 | 2 | 5 | 7 |
| 1961-62 | New York R | 4 | 0 | 0 | 0 |
| **Totals** | | 80 | 3 | 8 | 11 |
| **BOWNESS, Richard Gary** *Forward* | | | | | |
| b. Moncton, N.B., Jan. 25, 1955 | | | | | |
| 1975-76 | Atlanta | 5 | 0 | 0 | 0 |
| 1976-77 | Atlanta | 28 | 0 | 4 | 4 |
| 1977-78 | Detroit | 61 | 8 | 11 | 19 |
| 1978-79 | St Louis | 24 | 1 | 3 | 4 |
| 1979-80 | St Louis | 10 | 1 | 2 | 3 |
| 1980-81 | Winnipeg | 45 | 8 | 17 | 25 |
| **Totals** | | 173 | 18 | 37 | 55 |

| Season | Club | GP | G | A | Pts. |
|---|---|---|---|---|---|

**BOYD, Irvin (Yank)** *Forward*
b. Ardmore, Pa., Nov. 13, 1908

| Season | Club | GP | G | A | Pts. |
|---|---|---|---|---|---|
| 1931-32 | Boston | 29 | 2 | 1 | 3 |
| 1942-43 | Boston | 20 | 6 | 5 | 11 |
| 1943-44 | Boston | 5 | 0 | 1 | 1 |
| | **Totals** | 54 | 8 | 7 | 15 |

**BOYD, Randy** *Defenseman*
b. Coniston, Ont., Jan. 23, 1962

| 1981-82 | Pittsburgh | 23 | 0 | 2 | 2 |
|---|---|---|---|---|---|
| 1982-83 | Pittsburgh | 56 | 4 | 14 | 18 |
| | **Totals** | 79 | 4 | 16 | 20 |

**BOYD, William C.** *Forward*
b. Belleville, Ont., May 15, 1898

| 1926-27 | New York R | 41 | 4 | 1 | 5 |
|---|---|---|---|---|---|
| 1927-28 | New York R | 43 | 4 | 0 | 4 |
| 1928-29 | New York R | 11 | 0 | 0 | 0 |
| 1929-30 | New York A | 44 | 7 | 6 | 13 |
| 1934 | Detroit | 40 | 2 | 3 | 5 |
| | **Totals** | 179 | 17 | 10 | 27 |

**BOYER, Walter (Wally)** *Forward*
b. Cowan, Man., Sept. 27, 1937

| 1965-66 | Toronto | 46 | 4 | 17 | 21 |
|---|---|---|---|---|---|
| 1966-67 | Chicago | 42 | 5 | 6 | 11 |
| 1967-68 | Oakland | 74 | 13 | 20 | 33 |
| 1968-69 | Pittsburgh | 62 | 10 | 19 | 29 |
| 1969-70 | Pittsburgh | 72 | 11 | 12 | 23 |
| 1970-71 | Pittsburgh | 68 | 11 | 30 | 41 |
| 1971-72 | Pittsburgh | 1 | 0 | 1 | 1 |
| 1972-73 | Winnipeg (WHA) | 70 | 6 | 28 | 34 |
| | **NHL Totals** | 365 | 54 | 105 | 159 |
| | **WHA Totals** | 70 | 6 | 28 | 34 |

**BOZEK, Steve** *Forward*
b. Castlegar, B.C., Nov. 26, 1960

| 1981-82 | Los Angeles | 71 | 33 | 23 | 56 |
|---|---|---|---|---|---|
| 1982-83 | Los Angeles | 53 | 13 | 13 | 26 |
| | **Totals** | 124 | 46 | 36 | 82 |

**BRACKENBOROUGH, John** *Forward*

| 1925-26 | Boston | 7 | 0 | 0 | 0 |
|---|---|---|---|---|---|

**BRACKENBURY, John Curtis** *Forward*
b. Kapuskasing, Ont., Jan. 31, 1952

| 1973-74 | Chicago (WHA) | 4 | 0 | 1 | 1 |
|---|---|---|---|---|---|
| 1974-75 | Minnesota (WHA) | 7 | 0 | 0 | 0 |
| 1975-76 | Minn-Que (WHA) | 74 | 8 | 14 | 22 |
| 1976-77 | Quebec (WHA) | 77 | 16 | 13 | 29 |
| 1977-78 | Quebec (WHA) | 33 | 4 | 9 | 13 |
| 1978-79 | Quebec (WHA) | 70 | 13 | 13 | 26 |
| 1979-80 | Quebec | 63 | 6 | 8 | 14 |
| 1980-81 | Edmonton | 58 | 2 | 7 | 9 |
| 1981-82 | Edmonton | 14 | 0 | 2 | 2 |
| 1982-83 | St. Louis | 6 | 1 | 0 | 1 |
| | **NHL Totals** | 141 | 9 | 17 | 26 |
| | **WHA Totals** | 265 | 41 | 50 | 91 |

**BRADLEY, Barton William** *Forward*
b. Ft. William, Ont., July 29, 1930

| 1949-50 | Boston | 1 | 0 | 0 | 0 |
|---|---|---|---|---|---|

**BRADLEY, Walter Lyle** *Forward*
b. Lloydminster, Sask., July 31, 1943

| 1973-74 | California | 4 | 1 | 0 | 1 |
|---|---|---|---|---|---|
| 1976-77 | Cleveland | 2 | 0 | 0 | 0 |
| | **Totals** | 6 | 1 | 0 | 1 |

**BRAGNALO, Richard James** *Forward*
b. Thunder Bay, Ont., Dec. 1, 1951

| 1975-76 | Washington | 19 | 2 | 10 | 12 |
|---|---|---|---|---|---|
| 1976-77 | Washington | 80 | 11 | 12 | 23 |
| 1977-78 | Washington | 44 | 2 | 13 | 15 |
| 1978-79 | Washington | 2 | 0 | 0 | 0 |
| | **Totals** | 145 | 15 | 35 | 50 |

**BRANIGAN, Andrew John** *Defenseman*
b. Winnipeg, Man., Apr. 11, 1922

| 1940-41 | New York A | 6 | 1 | 0 | 1 |
|---|---|---|---|---|---|
| 1941-42 | New York A | 21 | 0 | 2 | 2 |
| | **Totals** | 27 | 1 | 2 | 3 |

**BRASAR, Per-Olov** *Forward*
b. Falun, Sweden, Sept. 30, 1950

| 1977-78 | Minnesota | 77 | 20 | 37 | 57 |
|---|---|---|---|---|---|
| 1978-79 | Minnesota | 68 | 6 | 28 | 34 |
| 1979-80 | Minn-Van | 70 | 10 | 24 | 34 |
| 1980-81 | Vancouver | 80 | 22 | 41 | 63 |
| 1981-82 | Vancouver | 53 | 6 | 12 | 18 |
| | **Totals** | 348 | 64 | 142 | 206 |

**BRAYSHAW, Russell Ambrose** *Forward*
b. Saskatoon, Sask., Jan. 17, 1918

| 1944-45 | Chicago | 43 | 5 | 9 | 14 |
|---|---|---|---|---|---|

**BREITENBACH, Ken** *Defenseman*
b. Welland, Ont., Jan. 9, 1955

| 1975-76 | Buffalo | 7 | 0 | 0 | 0 |
|---|---|---|---|---|---|
| 1976-77 | Buffalo | 31 | 0 | 5 | 5 |
| 1978-79 | Buffalo | 30 | 1 | 8 | 9 |
| | **Totals** | 68 | 1 | 13 | 14 |

**BRENNAN, Douglas R** *Defenseman*
b. Peterborough, Ont., Jan. 10, 1905

| 1931-32 | New York R | 38 | 4 | 3 | 7 |
|---|---|---|---|---|---|
| 1932-33 | New York R | 48 | 5 | 4 | 9 |
| 1933-34 | New York R | 37 | 0 | 0 | 0 |
| | **Totals** | 123 | 9 | 7 | 16 |

**BRENNAN, Thomas** *Forward*
b. Philadelphia, Pa., Jan. 2, 1921

| 1943-44 | Boston | 11 | 2 | 1 | 3 |
|---|---|---|---|---|---|
| 1944-45 | Boston | 1 | 0 | 1 | 1 |
| | **Totals** | 12 | 2 | 2 | 4 |

**BRENNEMAN, John** *Forward*
b. Fort Erie, Ont., Jan. 5, 1943

| 1964-65 | Chi-NYR | 39 | 4 | 3 | 7 |
|---|---|---|---|---|---|
| 1965-66 | New York R | 11 | 0 | 0 | 0 |
| 1966-67 | Toronto | 41 | 6 | 4 | 10 |
| 1967-68 | Det-Oak | 40 | 10 | 10 | 20 |
| 1968-69 | Oakland | 21 | 1 | 2 | 3 |
| | **Totals** | 152 | 21 | 19 | 40 |

**BRETTIO, Joseph** *Defenseman*
b. Hibbling, Minn., Nov. 29, 1913

| 1944-45 | Chicago | 3 | 0 | 0 | 0 |
|---|---|---|---|---|---|

**BREWER, Carl Thomas** *Defenseman*
b. Toronto, Ont., Oct. 21, 1938

| 1957-58 | Toronto | 2 | 0 | 0 | 0 |
|---|---|---|---|---|---|
| 1958-59 | Toronto | 69 | 3 | 21 | 24 |
| 1959-60 | Toronto | 67 | 4 | 19 | 23 |
| 1960-61 | Toronto | 51 | 1 | 14 | 15 |
| 1961-62 | Toronto | 67 | 1 | 22 | 23 |
| 1962-63 | Toronto | 70 | 2 | 23 | 25 |
| 1963-64 | Toronto | 57 | 4 | 9 | 13 |
| 1964-65 | Toronto | 70 | 4 | 23 | 27 |
| 1969-70 | Detroit | 70 | 2 | 37 | 39 |
| 1970-71 | St Louis | 19 | 2 | 9 | 11 |
| 1971-72 | St Louis | 42 | 2 | 16 | 18 |
| 1979-80 | Toronto | 20 | 0 | 5 | 5 |
| | **Totals** | 604 | 25 | 198 | 223 |

**BRICKLEY, Andy** *Forward*
b. Melrose, Mass., Oct. 9, 1961

| 1982-83 | Philadelphia | 3 | 1 | 1 | 2 |
|---|---|---|---|---|---|

**BRIDEN, Archie** *Forward*

| 1926-27 | Bos-Det | 42 | 5 | 2 | 7 |
|---|---|---|---|---|---|
| 1929-30 | Pittsburgh Pi | 29 | 4 | 3 | 7 |
| | **Totals** | 71 | 9 | 5 | 14 |

**BRIDGMAN, Melvin John** *Forward*
b. Trenton, Ont., Apr. 28, 1956

| 1975-76 | Philadelphia | 80 | 23 | 27 | 50 |
|---|---|---|---|---|---|
| 1976-77 | Philadelphia | 70 | 19 | 38 | 57 |
| 1977-78 | Philadelphia | 76 | 16 | 32 | 48 |
| 1978-79 | Philadelphia | 76 | 24 | 35 | 59 |
| 1979-80 | Philadelphia | 74 | 16 | 31 | 47 |
| 1980-81 | Philadelphia | 77 | 14 | 37 | 51 |
| 1981-82 | Phil-Calg | 72 | 33 | 54 | 87 |
| 1982-83 | Calgary | 79 | 19 | 31 | 50 |
| | **Totals** | 604 | 164 | 285 | 449 |

**BRIERE, Michel** *Forward*
b. Shawinigan Falls, Que., Oct. 21, 1949

| 1969-70 | Pittsburgh | 76 | 12 | 32 | 44 |
|---|---|---|---|---|---|

**BRINDLEY, Douglas Allen** *Forward*
b. Walkerton, Ont., June 8, 1949

| 1970-71 | Toronto | 3 | 0 | 0 | 0 |
|---|---|---|---|---|---|
| 1972-73 | Cleveland (WHA) | 73 | 15 | 11 | 26 |
| 1973-74 | Cleveland (WHA) | 30 | 13 | 9 | 22 |
| | **NHL Totals** | 3 | 0 | 0 | 0 |
| | **WHA Totals** | 103 | 28 | 20 | 48 |

**BRINK, Milton** *Forward*

| 1936-37 | Chicago | 5 | 0 | 0 | 0 |
|---|---|---|---|---|---|

**BRISSON, Gerald** *Forward*
b. St. Boniface, Man., Sept. 3, 1937

| 1962-63 | Montreal | 4 | 0 | 2 | 2 |
|---|---|---|---|---|---|

**BROADBENT, Harry L. (Punch)** *Forward*
b. Ottawa, Ont., July 13, 1892

| 1918-19 | Ottawa | 8 | 4 | 2 | 6 |
|---|---|---|---|---|---|
| 1919-20 | Ottawa | 20 | 19 | 4 | 23 |
| 1920-21 | Ottawa | 9 | 4 | 1 | 5 |
| 1921-22 | Ottawa | 24 | 32 | 14 | 46 |
| 1922-23 | Ottawa | 24 | 14 | 0 | 14 |
| 1923-24 | Ottawa | 22 | 9 | 4 | 13 |
| 1924-25 | Montreal M | 30 | 15 | 4 | 19 |
| 1925-26 | Montreal M | 36 | 12 | 5 | 17 |
| 1926-27 | Montreal M | 42 | 9 | 5 | 14 |
| 1927-28 | Ottawa | 43 | 3 | 2 | 5 |
| 1928-29 | New York A | 44 | 1 | 4 | 5 |
| | **Totals** | 302 | 122 | 45 | 167 |

**BRODEN, Connell** *Forward*
b. Montreal, Que., Apr. 6, 1932

| 1955-56 | Montreal | 3 | 0 | 0 | 0 |
|---|---|---|---|---|---|
| 1957-58 | Montreal | 3 | 2 | 1 | 3 |
| | **Totals** | 6 | 2 | 1 | 3 |

**BROOKS, Gordon John (Gord)** *Forward*
b. Cobourg, Ont., Sept. 11, 1950

| 1971-72 | St Louis | 2 | 0 | 0 | 0 |
|---|---|---|---|---|---|
| 1973-74 | St Louis | 30 | 6 | 8 | 14 |
| 1974-75 | Washington | 38 | 1 | 10 | 11 |
| | **Totals** | 70 | 7 | 18 | 25 |

**BROPHY, Bernard** *Forward*
b. Collingwood, Ont.

| 1925-26 | Montreal | 10 | 0 | 0 | 0 |
|---|---|---|---|---|---|
| 1928-29 | Detroit | 37 | 2 | 4 | 6 |
| 1929-30 | Detroit | 15 | 2 | 0 | 2 |
| | **Totals** | 62 | 4 | 4 | 8 |

**BROSSART, William (Bill)** *Defenseman*
b. Allan, Sask., May 29, 1949

| 1970-71 | Philadelphia | 1 | 0 | 0 | 0 |
|---|---|---|---|---|---|
| 1971-72 | Philadelphia | 42 | 0 | 4 | 4 |
| 1972-73 | Philadelphia | 4 | 0 | 1 | 1 |
| 1973-74 | Toronto | 17 | 0 | 1 | 1 |
| 1974-75 | Tor-Wash | 16 | 1 | 0 | 1 |
| 1975-76 | Washington | 49 | 0 | 8 | 8 |
| | **Totals** | 129 | 1 | 14 | 15 |

| Season | Club | | GP | G | A | Pts. |
|---|---|---|---|---|---|---|

**BROTEN, Aaron** *Forward*
b. Roseau, Minn., Nov. 14, 1960

| Season | Club | GP | G | A | Pts. |
|---|---|---|---|---|---|
| 1981-82 | Colorado | 58 | 15 | 24 | 39 |
| 1982-83 | New Jersey | 73 | 16 | 39 | 55 |
| | **Totals** | 131 | 31 | 63 | 94 |

**BROTEN, Neal Lamoy** *Forward*
b. Roseau, Minn., Nov. 29, 1959

| Season | Club | GP | G | A | Pts. |
|---|---|---|---|---|---|
| 1980-81 | Minnesota | 3 | 2 | 0 | 2 |
| 1981-82 | Minnesota | 73 | 38 | 59 | 97 |
| 1982-83 | Minnesota | 79 | 32 | 45 | 77 |
| | **Totals** | 159 | 72 | 104 | 176 |

**BROWN, Adam** *Forward*
b. Johnstone, Scotland, Feb. 4, 1920

| Season | Club | GP | G | A | Pts. |
|---|---|---|---|---|---|
| 1941-42 | Detroit | 28 | 6 | 9 | 15 |
| 1943-44 | Detroit | 50 | 24 | 18 | 42 |
| 1945-46 | Detroit | 48 | 20 | 11 | 31 |
| 1946-47 | Det-Chi | 64 | 19 | 30 | 49 |
| 1947-48 | Chicago | 32 | 7 | 10 | 17 |
| 1948-49 | Chicago | 58 | 8 | 12 | 20 |
| 1949-50 | Chicago | 25 | 2 | 2 | 4 |
| 1950-51 | Chicago | 53 | 10 | 12 | 22 |
| 1951-52 | Boston | 33 | 8 | 9 | 17 |
| | **Totals** | 391 | 104 | 113 | 217 |

**BROWN, Dave** *Forward*
b. Saskatoon, Sask., Oct. 12, 1962

| Season | Club | GP | G | A | Pts. |
|---|---|---|---|---|---|
| 1982-83 | Philadelphia | 2 | 0 | 0 | 0 |

**BROWN, Fred** *Forward*
b. Kingston, Ont.

| Season | Club | GP | G | A | Pts. |
|---|---|---|---|---|---|
| 1927-28 | Montreal M | 13 | 1 | 0 | 1 |

**BROWN, George** *Defenseman-Forward*
b. Winnipeg, Man., May 17, 1912

| Season | Club | GP | G | A | Pts. |
|---|---|---|---|---|---|
| 1936-37 | Montreal | 27 | 4 | 6 | 10 |
| 1937-38 | Montreal | 34 | 1 | 7 | 8 |
| 1938-39 | Montreal | 18 | 1 | 9 | 10 |
| | **Totals** | 79 | 6 | 22 | 28 |

**BROWN, Gerald William Joseph** *Forward*
b. Edmonton, Alta., July 7, 1917

| Season | Club | GP | G | A | Pts. |
|---|---|---|---|---|---|
| 1941-42 | Detroit | 13 | 4 | 4 | 8 |
| 1945-46 | Detroit | 10 | 0 | 1 | 1 |
| | **Totals** | 23 | 4 | 5 | 9 |

**BROWN, Jim** *Defenseman*
b. Canton, N.Y., Mar. 1, 1960

| Season | Club | GP | G | A | Pts. |
|---|---|---|---|---|---|
| 1982-83 | Los Angeles | 3 | 0 | 1 | 1 |

**BROWN, Keith Jeffrey** *Defenseman*
b. Corner Brook, Nfld., May 6, 1960

| Season | Club | GP | G | A | Pts. |
|---|---|---|---|---|---|
| 1979-80 | Chicago | 76 | 2 | 18 | 20 |
| 1980-81 | Chicago | 80 | 9 | 34 | 43 |
| 1981-82 | Chicago | 33 | 4 | 20 | 24 |
| 1982-83 | Chicago | 50 | 4 | 27 | 31 |
| | **Totals** | 239 | 19 | 99 | 118 |

**BROWN, Larry Wayne** *Defenseman*
b. Brandon, Man., Apr. 14, 1947

| Season | Club | GP | G | A | Pts. |
|---|---|---|---|---|---|
| 1969-70 | New York R | 15 | 0 | 3 | 3 |
| 1970-71 | Det-NYR | 64 | 2 | 5 | 7 |
| 1971-72 | Philadelphia | 12 | 0 | 0 | 0 |
| 1972-73 | Los Angeles | 55 | 0 | 7 | 7 |
| 1973-74 | Los Angeles | 45 | 0 | 4 | 4 |
| 1974-75 | Los Angeles | 78 | 1 | 15 | 16 |
| 1975-76 | Los Angeles | 74 | 2 | 5 | 7 |
| 1976-77 | Los Angeles | 55 | 1 | 6 | 7 |
| 1977-78 | Los Angeles | 57 | 1 | 8 | 9 |
| | **Totals** | 455 | 7 | 53 | 60 |

**BROWN, Patrick Cornelius (Conny)** *Forward*
b. Van Kleek Hill, Ont., Jan. 11, 1917

| Season | Club | GP | G | A | Pts. |
|---|---|---|---|---|---|
| 1938-39 | Detroit | 2 | 1 | 0 | 1 |
| 1939-40 | Detroit | 36 | 8 | 3 | 11 |
| 1940-41 | Detroit | 3 | 1 | 2 | 3 |

---

| Season | Club | GP | G | A | Pts. |
|---|---|---|---|---|---|
| 1941-42 | Detroit | 9 | 0 | 3 | 3 |
| 1942-43 | Detroit | 23 | 5 | 16 | 21 |
| | **Totals** | 73 | 15 | 24 | 39 |

**BROWN, Stanley** *Forward*
b. North Bay, Ont., May 9, 1898

| Season | Club | GP | G | A | Pts. |
|---|---|---|---|---|---|
| 1926-27 | New York R | 24 | 6 | 2 | 8 |
| 1927-28 | Detroit | 24 | 2 | 0 | 2 |
| | **Totals** | 48 | 8 | 2 | 10 |

**BROWN, Stewart Arnold (Arnie)** *Defenseman*
b. Apsley, Ont., Jan. 28, 1942

| Season | Club | GP | G | A | Pts. |
|---|---|---|---|---|---|
| 1961-62 | Toronto | 2 | 0 | 0 | 0 |
| 1963-64 | Toronto | 4 | 0 | 0 | 0 |
| 1964-65 | New York R | 58 | 1 | 11 | 12 |
| 1965-66 | New York R | 64 | 1 | 7 | 8 |
| 1966-67 | New York R | 69 | 2 | 10 | 12 |
| 1967-68 | New York R | 74 | 1 | 25 | 26 |
| 1968-69 | New York R | 74 | 10 | 12 | 22 |
| 1969-70 | New York R | 73 | 15 | 21 | 36 |
| 1970-71 | NYR-Det | 75 | 5 | 18 | 23 |
| 1971-72 | Detroit | 77 | 2 | 23 | 25 |
| 1972-73 | NYI-Atl | 63 | 5 | 8 | 13 |
| 1973-74 | Atlanta | 48 | 2 | 6 | 8 |
| 1974-75 | Mich-Van (WHA) | 60 | 3 | 5 | 8 |
| | **NHL Totals** | 681 | 44 | 141 | 185 |
| | **WHA Totals** | 60 | 3 | 5 | 8 |

**BROWNE, Cecil** *Forward*

| Season | Club | GP | G | A | Pts. |
|---|---|---|---|---|---|
| 1927-28 | Chicago | 12 | 2 | 0 | 2 |

**BROWNSCHIDLE, Jeff** *Defenseman*
b. Buffalo, N.Y., Mar. 1, 1959

| Season | Club | GP | G | A | Pts. |
|---|---|---|---|---|---|
| 1981-82 | Hartford | 3 | 0 | 1 | 1 |
| 1982-83 | Hartford | 4 | 0 | 0 | 0 |
| | **Totals** | 7 | 0 | 1 | 1 |

**BROWNSCHIDLE, John J. Jr.** *Defenseman*
b. Buffalo, N.Y., Oct. 2, 1955

| Season | Club | GP | G | A | Pts. |
|---|---|---|---|---|---|
| 1977-78 | St Louis | 40 | 2 | 15 | 17 |
| 1978-79 | St Louis | 64 | 10 | 24 | 34 |
| 1979-80 | St Louis | 77 | 12 | 32 | 44 |
| 1980-81 | St Louis | 71 | 5 | 23 | 28 |
| 1981-82 | St Louis | 80 | 5 | 33 | 38 |
| 1982-83 | St Louis | 72 | 1 | 22 | 23 |
| | **Totals** | 404 | 35 | 149 | 184 |

**BRUBAKER, Jeffrey J.** *Forward*
b. Frederick, Md., Feb. 24, 1958

| Season | Club | GP | G | A | Pts. |
|---|---|---|---|---|---|
| 1978-79 | New England (WHA) | 12 | 0 | 0 | 0 |
| 1979-80 | Hartford | 3 | 0 | 1 | 1 |
| 1980-81 | Hartford | 43 | 5 | 3 | 8 |
| 1981-82 | Montreal | 3 | 0 | 1 | 1 |
| | **NHL Totals** | 49 | 5 | 5 | 10 |
| | **WHA Totals** | 12 | 0 | 0 | 0 |

**BRUCE, Arthur Gordon** *Forward*
b. Ottawa, Ont., May 9, 1919

| Season | Club | GP | G | A | Pts. |
|---|---|---|---|---|---|
| 1940-41 | Boston | 7 | 0 | 1 | 1 |
| 1941-42 | Boston | 15 | 4 | 8 | 12 |
| 1945-46 | Boston | 5 | 0 | 0 | 0 |
| | **Totals** | 27 | 4 | 9 | 13 |

**BRUCE, Morley** *Defenseman*

| Season | Club | GP | G | A | Pts. |
|---|---|---|---|---|---|
| 1917-18 | Ottawa | 7 | 0 | 0 | 0 |
| 1919-20 | Ottawa | 21 | 1 | 0 | 1 |
| 1920-21 | Ottawa | 21 | 3 | 1 | 4 |
| 1921-22 | Ottawa | 23 | 4 | 0 | 4 |
| | **Totals** | 72 | 8 | 1 | 9 |

**BRUMWELL, James Murray** *Defenseman*
b. Calgary, Alta., Mar. 31, 1960

| Season | Club | GP | G | A | Pts. |
|---|---|---|---|---|---|
| 1980-81 | Minnesota | 1 | 0 | 0 | 0 |
| 1981-82 | Minnesota | 21 | 0 | 3 | 3 |
| 1982-83 | New Jersey | 59 | 5 | 14 | 19 |
| | **Totals** | 81 | 5 | 17 | 22 |

---

**BRUNETEAU, Edward Ernest Henry** *Forward*
b. St. Boniface, Man., Aug. 1, 1919

| Season | Club | GP | G | A | Pts. |
|---|---|---|---|---|---|
| 1940-41 | Detroit | 12 | 1 | 1 | 2 |
| 1943-44 | Detroit | 2 | 0 | 1 | 1 |
| 1944-45 | Detroit | 42 | 12 | 13 | 25 |
| 1945-46 | Detroit | 46 | 17 | 12 | 29 |
| 1946-47 | Detroit | 60 | 9 | 14 | 23 |
| 1947-48 | Detroit | 18 | 1 | 1 | 2 |
| 1948-49 | Detroit | 1 | 0 | 0 | 0 |
| | **Totals** | 181 | 40 | 42 | 82 |

**BRUNETEAU, Modere (Mud)** *Forward*
b. St. Boniface, Man., Nov. 28, 1914

| Season | Club | GP | G | A | Pts. |
|---|---|---|---|---|---|
| 1935-36 | Detroit | 23 | 2 | 0 | 2 |
| 1936-37 | Detroit | 45 | 9 | 7 | 16 |
| 1937-38 | Detroit | 23 | 3 | 6 | 9 |
| 1938-39 | Detroit | 19 | 3 | 7 | 10 |
| 1939-40 | Detroit | 46 | 10 | 14 | 24 |
| 1940-41 | Detroit | 44 | 11 | 17 | 28 |
| 1941-42 | Detroit | 48 | 14 | 19 | 33 |
| 1942-43 | Detroit | 50 | 23 | 22 | 45 |
| 1943-44 | Detroit | 39 | 35 | 18 | 53 |
| 1944-45 | Detroit | 43 | 23 | 24 | 47 |
| 1945-46 | Detroit | 28 | 6 | 4 | 10 |
| | **Totals** | 408 | 139 | 138 | 277 |

**BRYDGE, William** *Defenseman*
b. Renfrew, Ont., 1901

| Season | Club | GP | G | A | Pts. |
|---|---|---|---|---|---|
| 1926-27 | Toronto | 41 | 6 | 3 | 9 |
| 1928-29 | Detroit | 31 | 2 | 2 | 4 |
| 1929-30 | New York A | 39 | 2 | 6 | 8 |
| 1930-31 | New York A | 44 | 2 | 5 | 7 |
| 1931-32 | New York A | 48 | 2 | 8 | 10 |
| 1932-33 | New York A | 48 | 4 | 15 | 19 |
| 1933-34 | New York A | 48 | 6 | 7 | 13 |
| 1934-35 | New York A | 46 | 2 | 6 | 8 |
| 1935-36 | New York A | 22 | 0 | 0 | 0 |
| | **Totals** | 367 | 26 | 52 | 78 |

**BRYDSON, Glenn** *Forward*
b. Swansea, Ont., Nov. 7, 1910

| Season | Club | GP | G | A | Pts. |
|---|---|---|---|---|---|
| 1930-31 | Montreal M | 12 | 0 | 0 | 0 |
| 1931-32 | Montreal M | 46 | 12 | 13 | 25 |
| 1932-33 | Montreal M | 48 | 11 | 17 | 28 |
| 1933-34 | Montreal M | 42 | 4 | 5 | 9 |
| 1934-35 | St Louis E | 48 | 11 | 18 | 29 |
| 1935-36 | NYR-Chi | 51 | 10 | 16 | 26 |
| 1936-37 | Chicago | 30 | 7 | 7 | 14 |
| 1937-38 | Chicago | 19 | 1 | 3 | 4 |
| | **Totals** | 296 | 56 | 79 | 135 |

**BRYDSON, Gordon** *Forward*
b. Toronto, Ont.

| Season | Club | GP | G | A | Pts. |
|---|---|---|---|---|---|
| 1929-30 | Toronto | 8 | 2 | 0 | 2 |

**BUBLA, Jiri** *Defenseman*
b. Usti nad Labem, Czechoslovakia,
Jan. 27, 1950

| Season | Club | GP | G | A | Pts. |
|---|---|---|---|---|---|
| 1981-82 | Vancouver | 23 | 1 | 1 | 2 |
| 1982-83 | Vancouver | 72 | 2 | 28 | 30 |
| | **Totals** | 95 | 3 | 29 | 32 |

**BUCHANAN, Allaster William** *Forward*
b. Winnipeg, Man., May 17, 1927

| Season | Club | GP | G | A | Pts. |
|---|---|---|---|---|---|
| 1948-49 | Toronto | 3 | 0 | 1 | 1 |
| 1949-50 | Toronto | 1 | 0 | 0 | 0 |
| | **Totals** | 4 | 0 | 1 | 1 |

**BUCHANAN, Michael** *Defenseman*
b. Sault Ste. Marie, Ont., Mar. 1, 1932

| Season | Club | GP | G | A | Pts. |
|---|---|---|---|---|---|
| 1951-52 | Chicago | 1 | 0 | 0 | 0 |

**BUCHANAN, Ralph L. (Bucky)** *Forward*
b. Bout de l'isle, Que., Dec. 28, 1922

| Season | Club | GP | G | A | Pts. |
|---|---|---|---|---|---|
| 1948-49 | New York R | 2 | 0 | 0 | 0 |

| Season | Club | GP | G | A | Pts. |
|---|---|---|---|---|---|

**BUCHANAN, Ronald Leonard** *Forward*
b. Montreal, Que., Nov. 15, 1944

| Season | Club | GP | G | A | Pts. |
|---|---|---|---|---|---|
| 1966-67 | Boston | 3 | 0 | 0 | 0 |
| 1969-70 | St Louis | 2 | 0 | 0 | 0 |
| 1972-73 | Clev (WHA) | 75 | 37 | 44 | 81 |
| 1973-74 | Clev (WHA) | 49 | 18 | 27 | 45 |
| 1974-75 | Clev-Edm-Ind (WHA) | 58 | 24 | 24 | 48 |
| | **NHL Totals** | 5 | 0 | 0 | 0 |
| | **WHA Totals** | 182 | 79 | 95 | 174 |

**BUCYK, John Paul** *Forward*
b. Edmonton, Alta., May 12, 1935

| Season | Club | GP | G | A | Pts. |
|---|---|---|---|---|---|
| 1955-56 | Detroit | 38 | 1 | 8 | 9 |
| 1956-57 | Detroit | 66 | 10 | 11 | 21 |
| 1957-58 | Boston | 68 | 21 | 31 | 52 |
| 1958-59 | Boston | 69 | 24 | 36 | 60 |
| 1959-60 | Boston | 56 | 16 | 36 | 52 |
| 1960-61 | Boston | 70 | 19 | 20 | 39 |
| 1961-62 | Boston | 67 | 20 | 40 | 60 |
| 1962-63 | Boston | 69 | 27 | 39 | 66 |
| 1963-64 | Boston | 62 | 18 | 36 | 54 |
| 1964-65 | Boston | 68 | 26 | 29 | 55 |
| 1965-66 | Boston | 63 | 27 | 30 | 57 |
| 1966-67 | Boston | 59 | 18 | 30 | 48 |
| 1967-68 | Boston | 72 | 30 | 39 | 69 |
| 1968-69 | Boston | 70 | 24 | 42 | 66 |
| 1969-70 | Boston | 76 | 31 | 38 | 69 |
| 1970-71 | Boston | 78 | 51 | 65 | 116 |
| 1971-72 | Boston | 78 | 32 | 51 | 83 |
| 1972-73 | Boston | 78 | 40 | 53 | 93 |
| 1973-74 | Boston | 76 | 31 | 44 | 75 |
| 1974-75 | Boston | 78 | 29 | 52 | 81 |
| 1975-76 | Boston | 77 | 36 | 47 | 83 |
| 1976-77 | Boston | 49 | 20 | 23 | 43 |
| 1977-78 | Boston | 53 | 5 | 13 | 18 |
| | **Totals** | 1540 | 556 | 813 | 1369 |

**BUHR, Douglas Leonard** *Forward*
b. Vancouver, B.C., June 29, 1949

| Season | Club | GP | G | A | Pts. |
|---|---|---|---|---|---|
| 1974-75 | Kansas City | 6 | 0 | 2 | 2 |

**BUKOVICH, Anthony John** *Forward*
b. Painesdale, Mich., Aug. 30, 1917

| Season | Club | GP | G | A | Pts. |
|---|---|---|---|---|---|
| 1943-44 | Detroit | 3 | 0 | 1 | 1 |
| 1944-45 | Detroit | 14 | 7 | 2 | 9 |
| | **Totals** | 17 | 7 | 3 | 10 |

**BULLARD, Michael Brian** *Forward*
b. Ottawa, Ont., Mar. 10, 1961

| Season | Club | GP | G | A | Pts. |
|---|---|---|---|---|---|
| 1980-81 | Pittsburgh | 15 | 1 | 2 | 3 |
| 1981-82 | Pittsburgh | 75 | 37 | 27 | 64 |
| 1982-83 | Pittsburgh | 57 | 22 | 22 | 44 |
| | **Totals** | 147 | 60 | 51 | 111 |

**BULLER, Hyman** *Defenseman*
b. Montreal, Que., Mar. 15, 1926

| Season | Club | GP | G | A | Pts. |
|---|---|---|---|---|---|
| 1943-44 | Detroit | 7 | 0 | 3 | 3 |
| 1944-45 | Detroit | 2 | 0 | 0 | 0 |
| 1951-52 | New York R | 68 | 12 | 23 | 35 |
| 1952-53 | New York R | 70 | 7 | 18 | 25 |
| 1953-54 | New York R | 41 | 3 | 14 | 17 |
| | **Totals** | 188 | 22 | 58 | 80 |

**BULLEY, Edward H.** *Forward*
b. Windsor, Ont., Mar. 25, 1955

| Season | Club | GP | G | A | Pts. |
|---|---|---|---|---|---|
| 1976-77 | Chicago | 2 | 0 | 0 | 0 |
| 1977-78 | Chicago | 79 | 23 | 28 | 51 |
| 1978-79 | Chicago | 75 | 27 | 23 | 50 |
| 1979-80 | Chicago | 66 | 14 | 17 | 31 |
| 1980-81 | Chicago | 68 | 18 | 16 | 34 |
| 1981-82 | Chicago | 59 | 12 | 18 | 30 |
| 1982-83 | Washington | 39 | 4 | 9 | 13 |
| | **Totals** | 388 | 98 | 111 | 209 |

**BURCH, William (Billy)** *Defenseman-Forward*
b. Yonkers, N.Y., Nov. 20, 1900

| Season | Club | GP | G | A | Pts. |
|---|---|---|---|---|---|
| 1922-23 | Hamilton | 10 | 6 | 2 | 8 |
| 1923-24 | Hamilton | 24 | 16 | 2 | 18 |
| 1924-25 | Hamilton | 27 | 20 | 4 | 24 |
| 1925-26 | New York A | 36 | 22 | 3 | 25 |
| 1926-27 | New York A | 43 | 19 | 8 | 27 |
| 1927-28 | New York A | 32 | 10 | 2 | 12 |
| 1928-29 | New York A | 44 | 11 | 5 | 16 |
| 1929-30 | New York A | 35 | 7 | 3 | 10 |
| 1930-31 | New York A | 44 | 14 | 8 | 22 |
| 1931-32 | New York A | 48 | 7 | 15 | 22 |
| 1932-33 | Bos-Chi | 47 | 5 | 1 | 6 |
| | **Totals** | 390 | 133 | 53 | 186 |

**BURCHELL, Frederick (Skippy)** *Forward*
b. Montreal, Que., Jan. 9, 1931

| Season | Club | GP | G | A | Pts. |
|---|---|---|---|---|---|
| 1950-51 | Montreal | 2 | 0 | 0 | 0 |
| 1953-54 | Montreal | 2 | 0 | 0 | 0 |
| | **Totals** | 4 | 0 | 0 | 0 |

**BURDON, Glen** *Forward*
b. Regina, Sask., Aug. 4, 1954

| Season | Club | GP | G | A | Pts. |
|---|---|---|---|---|---|
| 1974-75 | Kansas City | 11 | 0 | 2 | 2 |

**BUREGA, William** *Defenseman*
b. Winnipeg, Man., Mar. 13, 1932

| Season | Club | GP | G | A | Pts. |
|---|---|---|---|---|---|
| 1955-56 | Toronto | 4 | 0 | 1 | 1 |

**BURKE, Edward** *Forward*
b. Toronto, Ont., June 3, 1907

| Season | Club | GP | G | A | Pts. |
|---|---|---|---|---|---|
| 1931-32 | Boston | 16 | 3 | 0 | 3 |
| 1932-33 | New York A | 15 | 2 | 0 | 2 |
| 1933-34 | New York A | 46 | 20 | 10 | 30 |
| 1934-35 | New York A | 29 | 4 | 10 | 14 |
| | **Totals** | 106 | 29 | 20 | 49 |

**BURKE, Martin Alphonsos** *Defenseman*
b. Toronto, Ont., Jan. 28, 1903

| Season | Club | GP | G | A | Pts. |
|---|---|---|---|---|---|
| 1927-28 | PittPi-Mont | 46 | 2 | 1 | 3 |
| 1928-29 | Montreal | 44 | 4 | 2 | 6 |
| 1929-30 | Montreal | 44 | 2 | 11 | 13 |
| 1930-31 | Montreal | 44 | 2 | 5 | 7 |
| 1931-32 | Montreal | 48 | 3 | 6 | 9 |
| 1932-33 | Ott-Mont | 45 | 2 | 5 | 7 |
| 1933-34 | Montreal | 45 | 1 | 4 | 5 |
| 1934-35 | Chicago | 48 | 2 | 2 | 4 |
| 1935-36 | Chicago | 48 | 0 | 3 | 3 |
| 1936-37 | Chicago | 42 | 1 | 3 | 4 |
| 1937-38 | Montreal | 50 | 0 | 5 | 5 |
| | **Totals** | 504 | 19 | 47 | 66 |

**BURMISTER, Roy** *Forward*
b. Collingwood, Ont., 1909

| Season | Club | GP | G | A | Pts. |
|---|---|---|---|---|---|
| 1929-30 | New York A | 39 | 1 | 1 | 2 |
| 1930-31 | New York A | 11 | 0 | 0 | 0 |
| 1931-32 | New York A | 16 | 3 | 2 | 5 |
| | **Totals** | 66 | 4 | 3 | 7 |

**BURNETT, James Kelvin (Kelly)** *Forward*
b. Lachine, Que., June 16, 1926

| Season | Club | GP | G | A | Pts. |
|---|---|---|---|---|---|
| 1952-53 | New York R | 3 | 1 | 0 | 1 |

**BURNS, Charles Frederick** *Forward*
b. Detroit, Mich., Feb. 14, 1936

| Season | Club | GP | G | A | Pts. |
|---|---|---|---|---|---|
| 1958-59 | Detroit | 70 | 9 | 11 | 20 |
| 1959-60 | Boston | 62 | 10 | 17 | 27 |
| 1960-61 | Boston | 62 | 15 | 26 | 41 |
| 1961-62 | Boston | 70 | 11 | 17 | 28 |
| 1962-63 | Boston | 68 | 12 | 10 | 22 |
| 1967-68 | Oakland | 73 | 9 | 26 | 35 |
| 1968-69 | Pittsburgh | 76 | 13 | 38 | 51 |
| 1969-70 | Minnesota | 50 | 3 | 13 | 16 |
| 1970-71 | Minnesota | 76 | 9 | 19 | 28 |
| 1971-72 | Minnesota | 77 | 11 | 14 | 25 |
| 1972-73 | Minnesota | 65 | 4 | 7 | 11 |
| | **Totals** | 749 | 106 | 198 | 304 |

**BURNS, Gary** *Forward*
b. Cambridge, Mass., Jan. 16, 1955

| Season | Club | GP | G | A | Pts. |
|---|---|---|---|---|---|
| 1980-81 | New York R | 11 | 2 | 2 | 4 |

**BURNS, Norman** *Forward*
b. Youngstown, Alta., Feb. 20, 1918

| Season | Club | GP | G | A | Pts. |
|---|---|---|---|---|---|
| 1941-42 | New York R | 11 | 0 | 4 | 4 |

**BURNS, Robert** *Forward*
b. Gore Bay, Ont., Apr. 4, 1905

| Season | Club | GP | G | A | Pts. |
|---|---|---|---|---|---|
| 1928-29 | Chicago | 6 | 0 | 0 | 0 |
| 1929-30 | Chicago | 11 | 1 | 0 | 1 |
| | **Totals** | 17 | 1 | 0 | 1 |

**BURNS, Robert Arthur (Robin)** *Forward*
b. Montreal, Que., Aug. 27, 1946

| Season | Club | GP | G | A | Pts. |
|---|---|---|---|---|---|
| 1970-71 | Pittsburgh | 10 | 0 | 3 | 3 |
| 1971-72 | Pittsburgh | 5 | 0 | 0 | 0 |
| 1972-73 | Pittsburgh | 26 | 0 | 2 | 2 |
| 1974-75 | Kansas City | 71 | 18 | 15 | 33 |
| 1975-76 | Kansas City | 78 | 13 | 18 | 31 |
| | **Totals** | 190 | 31 | 38 | 69 |

**BURROWS, David James (Dave)** *Defenseman*
b. Toronto, Ont., Jan. 11, 1949

| Season | Club | GP | G | A | Pts. |
|---|---|---|---|---|---|
| 1971-72 | Pittsburgh | 77 | 2 | 10 | 12 |
| 1972-73 | Pittsburgh | 78 | 3 | 24 | 27 |
| 1973-74 | Pittsburgh | 71 | 3 | 14 | 17 |
| 1974-75 | Pittsburgh | 78 | 2 | 15 | 17 |
| 1975-76 | Pittsburgh | 80 | 7 | 22 | 29 |
| 1976-77 | Pittsburgh | 69 | 3 | 6 | 9 |
| 1977-78 | Pittsburgh | 67 | 4 | 15 | 19 |
| 1978-79 | Toronto | 65 | 2 | 11 | 13 |
| 1979-80 | Toronto | 80 | 3 | 16 | 19 |
| 1980-81 | Tor-Pitt | 59 | 0 | 2 | 2 |
| | **Totals** | 724 | 29 | 135 | 164 |

**BURTON, Cumming Scott** *Forward*
b. Sudbury, Ont., May 12, 1936

| Season | Club | GP | G | A | Pts. |
|---|---|---|---|---|---|
| 1955-56 | Detroit | 3 | 0 | 0 | 0 |
| 1957-58 | Detroit | 20 | 0 | 1 | 1 |
| 1958-59 | Detroit | 14 | 0 | 1 | 1 |
| | **Totals** | 37 | 0 | 2 | 2 |

**BURTON, Nelson Keith** *Forward*
b. Sydney, N.S., Nov. 6, 1957

| Season | Club | GP | G | A | Pts. |
|---|---|---|---|---|---|
| 1977-78 | Washington | 5 | 1 | 0 | 1 |
| 1978-79 | Washington | 3 | 0 | 0 | 0 |
| | **Totals** | 8 | 1 | 0 | 1 |

**BUSH, Edward Webster** *Defenseman*
b. Collingwood, Ont., July 11, 1918

| Season | Club | GP | G | A | Pts. |
|---|---|---|---|---|---|
| 1938-39 | Detroit | 8 | 0 | 0 | 0 |
| 1941-42 | Detroit | 18 | 4 | 6 | 10 |
| | **Totals** | 26 | 4 | 6 | 10 |

**BUSKAS, Rod** *Defenseman*
b. Wetaskiwin, Alta., Jan. 7, 1961

| Season | Club | GP | G | A | Pts. |
|---|---|---|---|---|---|
| 1982-83 | Pittsburgh | 41 | 2 | 2 | 4 |

**BUSNIUK, Michael** *Defenseman*
b. Thunder Bay, Ont., Dec. 31, 1951

| Season | Club | GP | G | A | Pts. |
|---|---|---|---|---|---|
| 1979-80 | Philadelphia | 71 | 2 | 18 | 20 |
| 1980-81 | Philadelphia | 72 | 1 | 5 | 6 |
| | **Totals** | 143 | 3 | 23 | 26 |

**BUSNIUK, Ronald Edward (Ron)** *Forward*
b. Ft. William, Ont., Aug. 13, 1948

| Season | Club | GP | G | A | Pts. |
|---|---|---|---|---|---|
| 1972-73 | Buffalo | 1 | 0 | 0 | 0 |
| 1973-74 | Buffalo | 5 | 0 | 3 | 3 |
| 1974-75 | Minnesota (WHA) | 73 | 2 | 21 | 23 |
| 1975-76 | Minn-NE (WHA) | 70 | 2 | 14 | 16 |
| 1976-77 | NE-Edm (WHA) | 84 | 3 | 11 | 14 |
| 1977-78 | Edmonton (WHA) | 59 | 2 | 18 | 20 |
| | **NHL Totals** | 6 | 0 | 3 | 3 |
| | **WHA Totals** | 286 | 9 | 64 | 73 |

| Season | Club | GP | G | A | Pts. |
|---|---|---|---|---|---|
| **BUSWELL, Walter Gerald** *Defenseman* | | | | | |
| b. Montreal, Que., Nov. 6, 1907 | | | | | |
| 1932-33 | Detroit | — | 2 | 4 | 6 |
| 1933-34 | Detroit | — | 1 | 2 | 3 |
| 1934-35 | Detroit | — | 1 | 3 | 4 |
| 1935-36 | Montreal | — | 0 | 2 | 2 |
| 1936-37 | Montreal | — | 0 | 4 | 4 |
| 1937-38 | Montreal | — | 2 | 15 | 17 |
| 1938-39 | Montreal | — | 3 | 7 | 10 |
| 1939-40 | Montreal | — | 1 | 3 | 4 |
| | **Totals** | — | 10 | 40 | 50 |

| Season | Club | GP | G | A | Pts. |
|---|---|---|---|---|---|
| **BUTCHER, Garth** *Defenseman* | | | | | |
| b. Regina, Sask., Jan. 8, 1963 | | | | | |
| 1981-82 | Vancouver | 5 | 0 | 0 | 0 |
| 1982-83 | Vancouver | 55 | 1 | 13 | 14 |
| | **Totals** | 60 | 1 | 13 | 14 |

| Season | Club | GP | G | A | Pts. |
|---|---|---|---|---|---|
| **BUTLER, Jerome Patrick (Jerry)** *Forward* | | | | | |
| b. Sarnia, Ont., Feb. 27, 1951 | | | | | |
| 1972-73 | New York R | 8 | 1 | 0 | 1 |
| 1973-74 | New York R | 26 | 6 | 10 | 16 |
| 1974-75 | New York R | 78 | 17 | 16 | 33 |
| 1975-76 | St Louis | 66 | 17 | 24 | 41 |
| 1976-77 | St Louis | 80 | 12 | 20 | 32 |
| 1977-78 | StL-Tor | 82 | 9 | 9 | 18 |
| 1978-79 | Toronto | 76 | 8 | 7 | 15 |
| 1979-80 | Tor-Van | 78 | 11 | 12 | 23 |
| 1980-81 | Vancouver | 80 | 12 | 15 | 27 |
| 1981-82 | Vancouver | 25 | 3 | 1 | 4 |
| | **Totals** | 599 | 96 | 114 | 210 |

| Season | Club | GP | G | A | Pts. |
|---|---|---|---|---|---|
| **BUTLER, John Richard (Dick)** *Forward* | | | | | |
| b. Delisle, Sask., June 2, 1926 | | | | | |
| 1947-48 | Chicago | 7 | 2 | 0 | 2 |

| Season | Club | GP | G | A | Pts. |
|---|---|---|---|---|---|
| **BUTTERS, William Joseph** *Defenseman* | | | | | |
| b. St. Paul, Minn., Jan 10, 1951 | | | | | |
| 1974-75 | Minnesota (WHA) | 24 | 2 | 2 | 4 |
| 1975-76 | Minn-Hou (WHA) | 73 | 0 | 19 | 19 |
| 1976-77 | Minn-Edm-NE (WHA) | 75 | 1 | 17 | 18 |
| 1977-78 | New England (WHA) | 45 | 1 | 13 | 14 |
| 1977-78 | Minnesota | 23 | 1 | 0 | 1 |
| 1978-79 | Minnesota | 49 | 0 | 4 | 4 |
| | **NHL Totals** | 72 | 1 | 4 | 5 |
| | **WHA Totals** | 217 | 4 | 51 | 55 |

| Season | Club | GP | G | A | Pts. |
|---|---|---|---|---|---|
| **BUTTREY, Gordon** *Forward* | | | | | |
| b. Regina, Sask., Mar. 17, 1926 | | | | | |
| 1943-44 | Chicago | 10 | 0 | 0 | 0 |

| Season | Club | GP | G | A | Pts. |
|---|---|---|---|---|---|
| **BUYNAK, Gordon** *Defenseman* | | | | | |
| b. Detroit, Mich., Mar. 19, 1954 | | | | | |
| 1974-75 | St. Louis | 4 | 0 | 0 | 0 |

| Season | Club | GP | G | A | Pts. |
|---|---|---|---|---|---|
| **BYERS, Gordon Charles** *Defenseman* | | | | | |
| b. Eganville, Ont., Mar. 11, 1930 | | | | | |
| 1949-50 | Boston | 1 | 0 | 1 | 1 |

| Season | Club | GP | G | A | Pts. |
|---|---|---|---|---|---|
| **BYERS, Jerry** *Forward* | | | | | |
| b. Kentville, N.S., Mar. 29, 1952 | | | | | |
| 1972-73 | Minnesota | 14 | 0 | 2 | 2 |
| 1973-74 | Minnesota | 10 | 0 | 0 | 0 |
| 1974-75 | Atlanta | 12 | 1 | 1 | 2 |
| 1977-78 | New York R | 7 | 1 | 2 | 3 |
| | **Totals** | 43 | 2 | 5 | 7 |

| Season | Club | GP | G | A | Pts. |
|---|---|---|---|---|---|
| **BYERS, Michael Arthur** *Forward* | | | | | |
| b. Toronto, Ont., Sept. 11, 1946 | | | | | |
| 1967-68 | Toronto | 10 | 2 | 2 | 4 |
| 1968-69 | Tor-Phil | 10 | 0 | 2 | 2 |
| 1970-71 | Los Angeles | 72 | 27 | 18 | 45 |
| 1971-72 | LA-Buf | 74 | 13 | 12 | 25 |
| 1972-73 | LA-NE (WHA) | 75 | 25 | 21 | 46 |
| 1973-74 | New England (WHA) | 78 | 29 | 21 | 50 |

| Season | Club | GP | G | A | Pts. |
|---|---|---|---|---|---|
| 1974-75 | New England (WHA) | 72 | 22 | 26 | 48 |
| 1975-76 | NE-Cin (WHA) | 41 | 7 | 6 | 13 |
| | **NHL Totals** | 166 | 42 | 34 | 76 |
| | **WHA Totals** | 266 | 83 | 74 | 157 |

| Season | Club | GP | G | A | Pts. |
|---|---|---|---|---|---|
| **CAFFERY, John** *Forward* | | | | | |
| b. Kingston, Ont., June 30, 1934 | | | | | |
| 1954-55 | Toronto | 3 | 0 | 0 | 0 |
| 1956-57 | Boston | 47 | 2 | 2 | 4 |
| 1957-58 | Boston | 7 | 1 | 0 | 1 |
| | **Totals** | 57 | 3 | 2 | 5 |

| Season | Club | GP | G | A | Pts. |
|---|---|---|---|---|---|
| **CAFFERY, Terrance Michael** *Forward* | | | | | |
| b. Toronto, Ont., Apr. 1, 1949 | | | | | |
| 1969-70 | Chicago | 6 | 0 | 0 | 0 |
| 1970-71 | Minnesota | 8 | 0 | 0 | 0 |
| 1972-73 | New England (WHA) | 74 | 39 | 61 | 100 |
| 1973-74 | New England (WHA) | 67 | 15 | 37 | 52 |
| | **NHL Totals** | 14 | 0 | 0 | 0 |
| | **WHA Totals** | 141 | 54 | 98 | 152 |

| Season | Club | GP | G | A | Pts. |
|---|---|---|---|---|---|
| **CAHAN, Lawrence Louis (Larry)** *Defenseman* | | | | | |
| b. Ft. William, Ont., Dec. 25, 1933 | | | | | |
| 1954-55 | Toronto | 58 | 0 | 6 | 6 |
| 1955-56 | Toronto | 21 | 0 | 2 | 2 |
| 1956-57 | New York R | 61 | 5 | 4 | 9 |
| 1957-58 | New York R | 34 | 1 | 1 | 2 |
| 1958-59 | New York R | 16 | 1 | 0 | 1 |
| 1961-62 | New York R | 57 | 2 | 7 | 9 |
| 1962-63 | New York R | 56 | 6 | 14 | 20 |
| 1963-64 | New York R | 53 | 4 | 8 | 12 |
| 1964-65 | New York R | 26 | 0 | 5 | 5 |
| 1967-68 | Oakland | 74 | 9 | 15 | 24 |
| 1968-69 | Los Angeles | 72 | 3 | 11 | 14 |
| 1969-70 | Los Angeles | 70 | 4 | 8 | 12 |
| 1970-71 | Los Angeles | 67 | 3 | 11 | 14 |
| 1972-73 | Chicago (WHA) | 76 | 1 | 10 | 11 |
| | **NHL Totals** | 665 | 38 | 92 | 130 |
| | **WHA Totals** | 76 | 1 | 10 | 11 |

| Season | Club | GP | G | A | Pts. |
|---|---|---|---|---|---|
| **CAHILL, Charles** *Forward* | | | | | |
| 1925-26 | Boston | 31 | 0 | 1 | 1 |

| Season | Club | GP | G | A | Pts. |
|---|---|---|---|---|---|
| **CAIN, Herbert** *Forward* | | | | | |
| b. Newmarket, Ont., Dec. 24, 1913 | | | | | |
| 1933-34 | Montreal M | 30 | 4 | 5 | 9 |
| 1934-35 | Montreal M | 44 | 20 | 7 | 27 |
| 1935-36 | Montreal M | 48 | 5 | 13 | 18 |
| 1936-37 | Montreal M | 42 | 13 | 17 | 30 |
| 1937-38 | Montreal M | 47 | 11 | 19 | 30 |
| 1938-39 | Montreal | 45 | 13 | 14 | 27 |
| 1939-40 | Boston | 48 | 21 | 10 | 31 |
| 1940-41 | Boston | 41 | 8 | 10 | 18 |
| 1941-42 | Boston | 35 | 8 | 10 | 18 |
| 1942-43 | Boston | 45 | 18 | 18 | 36 |
| 1943-44 | Boston | 48 | 36 | 46 | 82 |
| 1944-45 | Boston | 50 | 32 | 13 | 45 |
| 1945-46 | Boston | 48 | 17 | 12 | 29 |
| | **Totals** | 571 | 206 | 194 | 400 |

| Season | Club | GP | G | A | Pts. |
|---|---|---|---|---|---|
| **CAIN, James F. (Dutch)** *Defenseman* | | | | | |
| b. Newmarket, Ont. | | | | | |
| 1924-25 | Montreal M | 28 | 4 | 0 | 4 |
| 1925-26 | Toronto | 33 | 0 | 0 | 0 |
| | **Totals** | 61 | 4 | 0 | 4 |

| Season | Club | GP | G | A | Pts. |
|---|---|---|---|---|---|
| **CAIRNS, Donald** *Forward* | | | | | |
| b. Calgary, Alta., Oct. 8, 1955 | | | | | |
| 1975-76 | Kansas City | 7 | 0 | 0 | 0 |
| 1976-77 | Colorado | 2 | 0 | 1 | 1 |
| | **Totals** | 9 | 0 | 1 | 1 |

| Season | Club | GP | G | A | Pts. |
|---|---|---|---|---|---|
| **CALDER, Eric** *Defenseman* | | | | | |
| b. Kitchener, Ont., July 26, 1963 | | | | | |
| 1981-82 | Washington | 1 | 0 | 0 | 0 |
| 1982-83 | Washington | 1 | 0 | 0 | 0 |
| | **Totals** | 2 | 0 | 0 | 0 |

| Season | Club | GP | G | A | Pts. |
|---|---|---|---|---|---|
| **CALLADINE, Norman** *Forward* | | | | | |
| b. Peterborough, Ont., 1916 | | | | | |
| 1942-43 | Boston | 3 | 0 | 1 | 1 |
| 1943-44 | Boston | 49 | 16 | 27 | 43 |
| 1944-45 | Boston | 11 | 3 | 1 | 4 |
| | **Totals** | 63 | 19 | 29 | 48 |

| Season | Club | GP | G | A | Pts. |
|---|---|---|---|---|---|
| **CALLANDER, Leonard Drew** *Forward* | | | | | |
| b. Regina, Sask., Aug. 17, 1956 | | | | | |
| 1976-77 | Philadelphia | 2 | 1 | 0 | 1 |
| 1977-78 | Philadelphia | 1 | 0 | 0 | 0 |
| 1978-79 | Phil-Van | 32 | 4 | 1 | 5 |
| 1979-80 | Vancouver | 4 | 1 | 1 | 2 |
| | **Totals** | 39 | 6 | 2 | 8 |

| Season | Club | GP | G | A | Pts. |
|---|---|---|---|---|---|
| **CALLIGHEN, Brett** *Forward* | | | | | |
| b. Toronto, Ont., May 15, 1953 | | | | | |
| 1976-77 | NE-Edm (WHA) | 62 | 15 | 26 | 41 |
| 1977-78 | Edmonton (WHA) | 80 | 20 | 30 | 50 |
| 1978-79 | Edmonton | 71 | 31 | 39 | 70 |
| 1979-80 | Edmonton | 59 | 23 | 35 | 58 |
| 1980-81 | Edmonton | 55 | 25 | 35 | 60 |
| 1981-82 | Edmonton | 46 | 8 | 19 | 27 |
| | **NHL Totals** | 231 | 87 | 138 | 215 |
| | **WHA Totals** | 142 | 35 | 56 | 91 |

| Season | Club | GP | G | A | Pts. |
|---|---|---|---|---|---|
| **CALLIGHEN, Francis Charles Winslow (Patsy)** *Defenseman* | | | | | |
| b. Toronto, Ont., Feb. 13, 1906 | | | | | |
| 1927-28 | New York R | 36 | 0 | 0 | 0 |

| Season | Club | GP | G | A | Pts. |
|---|---|---|---|---|---|
| **CAMAZZOLA, Anthony Bert** *Defenseman* | | | | | |
| b. Vancouver, B.C., Sept. 11, 1962 | | | | | |
| 1981-82 | Washington | 3 | 0 | 0 | 0 |

| Season | Club | GP | G | A | Pts. |
|---|---|---|---|---|---|
| **CAMERON, Alan Richard** *Defenseman* | | | | | |
| b. Edmonton, Alta., Oct. 21, 1955 | | | | | |
| 1975-76 | Detroit | 38 | 2 | 8 | 10 |
| 1976-77 | Detroit | 80 | 3 | 13 | 16 |
| 1977-78 | Detroit | 63 | 2 | 7 | 9 |
| 1978-79 | Detroit | 9 | 0 | 3 | 3 |
| 1979-80 | Winnipeg | 63 | 3 | 11 | 14 |
| 1980-81 | Winnipeg | 29 | 1 | 2 | 3 |
| | **Totals** | 282 | 11 | 44 | 55 |

| Season | Club | GP | G | A | Pts. |
|---|---|---|---|---|---|
| **CAMERON, Angus (Scotty)** *Forward* | | | | | |
| b. Prince Albert, Sask., Nov. 5, 1921 | | | | | |
| 1942-43 | New York R | 35 | 8 | 11 | 19 |

| Season | Club | GP | G | A | Pts. |
|---|---|---|---|---|---|
| **CAMERON, Craig Lauder** *Forward* | | | | | |
| b. Edmonton, Alta., July 19, 1945 | | | | | |
| 1966-67 | Detroit | 1 | 0 | 0 | 0 |
| 1967-68 | St Louis | 32 | 7 | 2 | 9 |
| 1968-69 | St Louis | 72 | 11 | 5 | 16 |
| 1970-71 | St Louis | 78 | 14 | 6 | 20 |
| 1971-72 | Minnesota | 64 | 2 | 1 | 3 |
| 1972-73 | New York I | 72 | 19 | 14 | 33 |
| 1973-74 | New York I | 78 | 15 | 14 | 29 |
| 1974-75 | NYI-Minn | 77 | 11 | 13 | 24 |
| 1975-76 | Minnesota | 78 | 8 | 10 | 18 |
| | **Totals** | 552 | 87 | 65 | 152 |

| Season | Club | GP | G | A | Pts. |
|---|---|---|---|---|---|
| **CAMERON, David William** *Forward* | | | | | |
| b. Charlottetown, P.E.I., July 29, 1958 | | | | | |
| 1981-82 | Colorado | 66 | 11 | 12 | 23 |
| 1982-83 | New Jersey | 35 | 5 | 4 | 9 |
| | **Totals** | 101 | 16 | 16 | 32 |

| Season | Club | GP | G | A | Pts. |
|---|---|---|---|---|---|
| **CAMERON, Harold Hugh (Harry)** *Defenseman* | | | | | |
| b. Pembroke, Ont., Feb. 6, 1890 | | | | | |
| 1917-18 | Toronto | 20 | 17 | 0 | 17 |
| 1918-19 | Tor-Ott | 14 | 11 | 3 | 14 |
| 1919-20 | Tor-Mont | 23 | 16 | 1 | 17 |
| 1920-21 | Toronto | 24 | 18 | 9 | 27 |
| 1921-22 | Toronto | 24 | 19 | 8 | 27 |
| 1922-23 | Toronto | 22 | 9 | 6 | 15 |
| | **Totals** | 127 | 90 | 27 | 117 |

**CAMERON, William** *Forward*
b. Timmins, Ont., 1904

| Season | Club | GP | G | A | Pts. |
|---|---|---|---|---|---|
| 1923-24 | Montreal | 18 | 0 | 0 | 0 |
| 1925-26 | New York A | 21 | 0 | 0 | 0 |
| | **Totals** | **39** | **0** | **0** | **0** |

**CAMPBELL, Bryan Albert** *Forward*
b. Sudbury, Ont., Mar. 27, 1944

| Season | Club | GP | G | A | Pts. |
|---|---|---|---|---|---|
| 1967-68 | Los Angeles | 44 | 6 | 15 | 21 |
| 1968-69 | Los Angeles | 18 | 2 | 1 | 3 |
| 1969-70 | LA-Chi | 45 | 5 | 5 | 10 |
| 1970-71 | Chicago | 78 | 17 | 37 | 54 |
| 1971-72 | Chicago | 75 | 5 | 13 | 18 |
| 1972-73 | Philadelphia (WHA) | 75 | 25 | 48 | 73 |
| 1973-74 | Vancouver (WHA) | 76 | 27 | 62 | 89 |
| 1974-75 | Vancouver (WHA) | 78 | 29 | 34 | 63 |
| 1975-76 | Cincinnati (WHA) | 77 | 22 | 50 | 72 |
| 1976-77 | Ind-Edm (WHA) | 74 | 13 | 46 | 59 |
| 1977-78 | Edmonton (WHA) | 53 | 7 | 13 | 20 |
| | **NHL Totals** | **260** | **35** | **71** | **106** |
| | **WHA Totals** | **433** | **123** | **253** | **376** |

**CAMPBELL, Colin John** *Defenseman*
b. London, Ont., Jan. 28, 1953

| Season | Club | GP | G | A | Pts. |
|---|---|---|---|---|---|
| 1973-74 | Vancouver (WHA) | 78 | 3 | 20 | 23 |
| 1974-75 | Pittsburgh | 59 | 4 | 15 | 19 |
| 1975-76 | Pittsburgh | 64 | 7 | 10 | 17 |
| 1976-77 | Colorado | 54 | 3 | 8 | 11 |
| 1977-78 | Pittsburgh | 55 | 1 | 9 | 10 |
| 1978-79 | Pittsburgh | 65 | 2 | 18 | 20 |
| 1979-80 | Edmonton | 72 | 2 | 11 | 13 |
| 1980-81 | Vancouver | 42 | 1 | 8 | 9 |
| 1981-82 | Vancouver | 47 | 0 | 8 | 8 |
| 1982-83 | Detroit | 53 | 1 | 7 | 8 |
| | **NHL Totals** | **511** | **21** | **94** | **115** |
| | **WHA Totals** | **78** | **3** | **20** | **23** |

**CAMPBELL, David** *Defenseman*
b. Lachute, Que., Apr. 27, 1896

| Season | Club | GP | G | A | Pts. |
|---|---|---|---|---|---|
| 1920-21 | Montreal | 3 | 0 | 0 | 0 |

**CAMPBELL, Donald** *Forward*
b. Drumheller, Alta., July 12, 1925

| Season | Club | GP | G | A | Pts. |
|---|---|---|---|---|---|
| 1943-44 | Chicago | 17 | 1 | 3 | 4 |

**CAMPBELL, Earl (Spiff)** *Defenseman*

| Season | Club | GP | G | A | Pts. |
|---|---|---|---|---|---|
| 1923-24 | Ottawa | 18 | 4 | 1 | 5 |
| 1924-25 | Ottawa | 30 | 0 | 0 | 0 |
| 1925-26 | New York A | 29 | 1 | 0 | 1 |
| | **Totals** | **77** | **5** | **1** | **6** |

**CAMPBELL, Scott** *Defenseman*
b. Toronto, Ont., June 22, 1957

| Season | Club | GP | G | A | Pts. |
|---|---|---|---|---|---|
| 1977-78 | Houston (WHA) | 75 | 8 | 29 | 37 |
| 1978-79 | Winnipeg (WHA) | 74 | 3 | 15 | 18 |
| 1979-80 | Winnipeg | 63 | 3 | 17 | 20 |
| 1980-81 | Winnipeg | 14 | 1 | 4 | 5 |
| 1981-82 | St Louis | 3 | 0 | 0 | 0 |
| | **NHL Totals** | **80** | **4** | **21** | **25** |
| | **WHA Totals** | **149** | **11** | **44** | **55** |

**CAMPBELL, Wade** *Defenseman*
b. Peace River, Alta., Feb. 1, 1961

| Season | Club | GP | G | A | Pts. |
|---|---|---|---|---|---|
| 1982-83 | Winnipeg | | | | |

**CAMPEAU, Jean Claude (Tod)** *Forward*
b. St. Jerome, Que., June 4, 1923

| Season | Club | GP | G | A | Pts. |
|---|---|---|---|---|---|
| 1943-44 | Montreal | 2 | 0 | 0 | 0 |
| 1947-48 | Montreal | 14 | 2 | 2 | 4 |
| 1948-49 | Montreal | 26 | 3 | 7 | 10 |
| | **Totals** | **42** | **5** | **9** | **14** |

**CARBOL, Leo** *Defenseman*
b. Ottawa, Ont., June 5, 1912

| Season | Club | GP | G | A | Pts. |
|---|---|---|---|---|---|
| 1942-43 | Chicago | 6 | 0 | 1 | 1 |


**CARBONNEAU, Guy** *Forward*
b. Sept Iles, Que., Mar. 18, 1960

| Season | Club | GP | G | A | Pts. |
|---|---|---|---|---|---|
| 1980-81 | Montreal | 2 | 0 | 1 | 1 |
| 1982-83 | Montreal | 77 | 18 | 29 | 47 |
| | **Totals** | **79** | **18** | **30** | **48** |

**CARDIN, Claude** *Forward*
b. Sorel, Que., May 28, 1943

| Season | Club | GP | G | A | Pts. |
|---|---|---|---|---|---|
| 1967-68 | St Louis | 1 | 0 | 0 | 0 |

**CARDWELL, Stephen Michael (Steve)**
*Forward*
b. Toronto, Ont., Aug. 13, 1950

| Season | Club | GP | G | A | Pts. |
|---|---|---|---|---|---|
| 1970-71 | Pittsburgh | 5 | 0 | 1 | 1 |
| 1971-72 | Pittsburgh | 28 | 7 | 8 | 15 |
| 1972-73 | Pittsburgh | 20 | 2 | 2 | 4 |
| 1973-74 | Minnesota (WHA) | 77 | 23 | 23 | 46 |
| 1974-75 | Cleveland (WHA) | 75 | 9 | 13 | 22 |
| | **NHL Totals** | **53** | **9** | **11** | **20** |
| | **WHA Totals** | **152** | **32** | **36** | **68** |

**CAREY, George** *Forward*

| Season | Club | GP | G | A | Pts. |
|---|---|---|---|---|---|
| 1919-20 | Quebec | 20 | 11 | 5 | 16 |
| 1920-21 | Hamilton | 20 | 7 | 1 | 8 |
| 1921-22 | Hamilton | 23 | 3 | 2 | 5 |
| 1922-23 | Hamilton | 5 | 1 | 0 | 1 |
| 1923-24 | Toronto | 4 | 0 | 0 | 0 |
| | **Totals** | **72** | **22** | **8** | **30** |

**CARLETON, Kenneth Wayne** *Forward*
b. Sudbury, Ont., Aug. 4, 1946

| Season | Club | GP | G | A | Pts. |
|---|---|---|---|---|---|
| 1965-66 | Toronto | 2 | 0 | 1 | 1 |
| 1966-67 | Toronto | 5 | 1 | 0 | 1 |
| 1967-68 | Toronto | 65 | 8 | 11 | 19 |
| 1968-69 | Toronto | 12 | 1 | 3 | 4 |
| 1969-70 | Tor-Bos | 49 | 6 | 20 | 26 |
| 1970-71 | Boston | 69 | 22 | 24 | 46 |
| 1971-72 | California | 76 | 17 | 14 | 31 |
| 1972-73 | Ottawa (WHA) | 76 | 42 | 49 | 91 |
| 1973-74 | Toronto (WHA) | 78 | 37 | 55 | 92 |
| 1974-75 | New England (WHA) | 73 | 35 | 39 | 74 |
| 1975-76 | NE-Edm (WHA) | 60 | 17 | 37 | 54 |
| | **NHL Totals** | **278** | **55** | **73** | **128** |
| | **WHA Totals** | **287** | **131** | **180** | **311** |

**CARLIN, Brian John** *Forward*
b. Calgary, Alta., June 13, 1950

| Season | Club | GP | G | A | Pts. |
|---|---|---|---|---|---|
| 1971-72 | Los Angeles | 5 | 1 | 0 | 1 |
| 1972-73 | Alberta (WHA) | 64 | 12 | 22 | 34 |
| | **NHL Totals** | **5** | **1** | **0** | **1** |
| | **WHA Totals** | **64** | **12** | **22** | **34** |

**CARLSON, Jack Anthony** *Forward*
b. Virginia, Minn., Aug. 23, 1954

| Season | Club | GP | G | A | Pts. |
|---|---|---|---|---|---|
| 1974-75 | Minnesota (WHA) | 32 | 5 | 5 | 10 |
| 1975-76 | Minn-Edm (WHA) | 68 | 9 | 11 | 20 |
| 1976-77 | Minn-NE (WHA) | 71 | 11 | 8 | 19 |
| 1977-78 | New England (WHA) | 67 | 9 | 20 | 29 |
| 1978-79 | New England (WHA) | 34 | 2 | 7 | 9 |
| 1978-79 | Minnesota | 16 | 3 | 0 | 3 |
| 1980-81 | Minnesota | 43 | 7 | 2 | 9 |
| 1982-83 | St Louis | 54 | 6 | 1 | 7 |
| | **NHL Totals** | **113** | **16** | **3** | **19** |
| | **WHA Totals** | **272** | **36** | **51** | **87** |

**CARLSON, Steve Edward** *Forward*
b. Virginia, Minn., Aug. 26, 1955

| Season | Club | GP | G | A | Pts. |
|---|---|---|---|---|---|
| 1975-76 | Minnesota (WHA) | 10 | 0 | 1 | 1 |
| 1976-77 | Minn-NE (WHA) | 52 | 9 | 17 | 26 |
| 1977-78 | New England (WHA) | 38 | 6 | 7 | 13 |
| 1979-80 | Los Angeles | 52 | 9 | 12 | 21 |
| | **NHL Totals** | **52** | **9** | **12** | **21** |
| | **WHA Totals** | **100** | **15** | **25** | **40** |


**CARLYLE, Randy Robert** *Defenseman*
b. Sudbury, Ont., Apr. 19, 1956

| Season | Club | GP | G | A | Pts. |
|---|---|---|---|---|---|
| 1976-77 | Toronto | 45 | 0 | 5 | 5 |
| 1977-78 | Toronto | 49 | 2 | 11 | 13 |
| 1978-79 | Pittsburgh | 70 | 13 | 34 | 47 |
| 1979-80 | Pittsburgh | 67 | 8 | 28 | 36 |
| 1980-81 | Pittsburgh | 76 | 16 | 67 | 83 |
| 1981-82 | Pittsburgh | 73 | 11 | 64 | 75 |
| 1982-83 | Pittsburgh | 61 | 15 | 41 | 56 |
| | **Totals** | **451** | **65** | **250** | **315** |

**CARON, Alain Luc (Boom-Boom)** *Forward*
b. Dolbeau, Que., Apr. 27, 1938

| Season | Club | GP | G | A | Pts. |
|---|---|---|---|---|---|
| 1967-68 | Oakland | 58 | 9 | 13 | 22 |
| 1968-69 | Montreal | 2 | 0 | 0 | 0 |
| 1972-73 | Quebec (WHA) | 68 | 36 | 27 | 63 |
| 1973-74 | Quebec (WHA) | 59 | 31 | 15 | 46 |
| 1974-75 | Que-Balt (WHA) | 68 | 15 | 8 | 23 |
| | **NHL Totals** | **60** | **9** | **13** | **22** |
| | **WHA Totals** | **195** | **82** | **50** | **132** |

**CARPENTER, Everar Lorne (Eddie)**
*Defenseman*
b. Hartford, Mich.

| Season | Club | GP | G | A | Pts. |
|---|---|---|---|---|---|
| 1919-20 | Quebec | 24 | 8 | 3 | 11 |
| 1920-21 | Hamilton | 20 | 2 | 1 | 3 |
| | **Totals** | **44** | **10** | **4** | **14** |

**CARPENTER, Robert** *Forward*
b. Beverly, Mass., July 13, 1963

| Season | Club | GP | G | A | Pts. |
|---|---|---|---|---|---|
| 1981-82 | Washington | 80 | 32 | 35 | 67 |
| 1982-83 | Washington | 80 | 32 | 37 | 69 |
| | **Totals** | **160** | **64** | **72** | **136** |

**CARR, Alfred (Red)** *Forward*
b. Winnipeg, Man.

| Season | Club | GP | G | A | Pts. |
|---|---|---|---|---|---|
| 1943-44 | Toronto | 5 | 0 | 1 | 1 |

**CARR, Eugene William (Gene)** *Forward*
b. Nanaimo, B.C., Sept. 17, 1951

| Season | Club | GP | G | A | Pts. |
|---|---|---|---|---|---|
| 1971-72 | StL-NYR | 74 | 11 | 10 | 21 |
| 1972-73 | New York R | 50 | 9 | 10 | 19 |
| 1973-74 | NYR-LA | 50 | 7 | 16 | 23 |
| 1974-75 | Los Angeles | 80 | 7 | 32 | 39 |
| 1975-76 | Los Angeles | 38 | 8 | 11 | 19 |
| 1976-77 | Los Angeles | 68 | 15 | 12 | 27 |
| 1977-78 | LA-Pitt | 75 | 19 | 37 | 56 |
| 1978-79 | Atlanta | 30 | 3 | 8 | 11 |
| | **Totals** | **465** | **79** | **136** | **215** |

**CARR, Lorne Bell** *Forward*
b. Stoughton, Sask., July 2, 1910

| Season | Club | GP | G | A | Pts. |
|---|---|---|---|---|---|
| 1933-34 | New York R | 14 | 0 | 0 | 0 |
| 1934-35 | New York A | 48 | 17 | 14 | 31 |
| 1935-36 | New York A | 44 | 8 | 10 | 18 |
| 1936-37 | New York A | 48 | 18 | 16 | 34 |
| 1937-38 | New York A | 48 | 16 | 7 | 23 |
| 1938-39 | New York A | 46 | 19 | 18 | 37 |
| 1939-40 | New York A | 48 | 8 | 17 | 25 |
| 1940-41 | New York A | 48 | 13 | 19 | 32 |
| 1941-42 | Toronto | 47 | 16 | 17 | 33 |
| 1942-43 | Toronto | 50 | 27 | 33 | 60 |
| 1943-44 | Toronto | 50 | 36 | 38 | 74 |
| 1944-45 | Toronto | 47 | 21 | 25 | 46 |
| 1945-46 | Toronto | 42 | 5 | 8 | 13 |
| | **Totals** | **580** | **204** | **222** | **426** |

**CARRIERE, Larry** *Defenseman*
b. Montreal, Que., Jan. 30, 1952

| Season | Club | GP | G | A | Pts. |
|---|---|---|---|---|---|
| 1972-73 | Buffalo | 40 | 2 | 8 | 10 |
| 1973-74 | Buffalo | 78 | 6 | 24 | 30 |
| 1974-75 | Buffalo | 80 | 1 | 11 | 12 |
| 1975-76 | Atlanta | 75 | 4 | 15 | 19 |
| 1976-77 | Atlanta | 25 | 2 | 3 | 5 |
| 1977-78 | Van-LA-Buf | 18 | 0 | 3 | 3 |
| 1979-80 | Toronto | 2 | 0 | 1 | 1 |
| | **Totals** | **318** | **15** | **65** | **80** |

| Season | Club | GP | G | A | Pts. |
|---|---|---|---|---|---|

**CARRIGAN, Eugene** *Forward*
b. Edmonton, Alta., July 5, 1906

| Season | Club | GP | G | A | Pts. |
|---|---|---|---|---|---|
| 1930-31 | New York R | 33 | 2 | 0 | 2 |
| 1934-35 | St Louis E | — | 0 | 1 | 1 |
| | **Totals** | — | 2 | 1 | 3 |

**CARROLL, George** *Defenseman*

| 1924-25 | Mont-Bos | 15 | 0 | 0 | 0 |
|---|---|---|---|---|---|

**CARROLL, Gregory John** *Forward*
b. Gimli, Man., Nov. 10, 1956

| 1976-77 | Cincinnati (WHA) | 77 | 15 | 39 | 54 |
|---|---|---|---|---|---|
| 1977-78 | Cin-NE (WHA) | 74 | 15 | 27 | 42 |
| 1978-79 | Wash-Det | 60 | 7 | 15 | 22 |
| 1979-80 | Hartford | 71 | 13 | 19 | 32 |
| | **NHL Totals** | 131 | 20 | 34 | 54 |
| | **WHA Totals** | 151 | 30 | 66 | 96 |

**CARROLL, William Allan** *Forward*
b. Toronto, Ont., Jan. 19, 1959

| 1980-81 | New York I | 18 | 4 | 4 | 8 |
|---|---|---|---|---|---|
| 1981-82 | New York I | 72 | 9 | 20 | 29 |
| 1982-83 | New York I | 71 | 1 | 11 | 12 |
| | **Totals** | 161 | 14 | 35 | 49 |

**CARRUTHERS, Dwight** *Defenseman*
b. Lashburn, Sask., Nov. 7, 1944

| 1965-66 | Detroit | 1 | 0 | 0 | 0 |
|---|---|---|---|---|---|
| 1967-68 | Philadelphia | 1 | 0 | 0 | 0 |
| | **Totals** | 2 | 0 | 0 | 0 |

**CARSE, Robert Allison** *Forward*
b. Edmonton, Alta., July 19, 1919

| 1939-40 | Chicago | 22 | 3 | 5 | 8 |
|---|---|---|---|---|---|
| 1940-41 | Chicago | 42 | 9 | 9 | 18 |
| 1941-42 | Chicago | 33 | 7 | 16 | 23 |
| 1942-43 | Chicago | 47 | 10 | 22 | 32 |
| 1947-48 | Montreal | 22 | 3 | 3 | 6 |
| | **Totals** | 166 | 32 | 55 | 87 |

**CARSE, William Alexander** *Forward*
b. Edmonton, Alta., May 29, 1914

| 1938-39 | New York R | 1 | 0 | 1 | 1 |
|---|---|---|---|---|---|
| 1939-40 | Chicago | — | 10 | 13 | 23 |
| 1940-41 | Chicago | — | 5 | 15 | 20 |
| 1941-42 | Chicago | 43 | 13 | 14 | 27 |
| | **Totals** | — | 28 | 43 | 71 |

**CARSON, Frank** *Forward*
b. Parry Sound, Ont., Jan. 12, 1902

| 1925-26 | Montreal M | 16 | 2 | 1 | 3 |
|---|---|---|---|---|---|
| 1926-27 | Montreal M | 44 | 2 | 3 | 5 |
| 1927-28 | Montreal M | 21 | 0 | 1 | 1 |
| 1930-31 | New York A | 44 | 6 | 7 | 13 |
| 1931-32 | Detroit | 31 | 10 | 14 | 24 |
| 1932-33 | Detroit | 45 | 12 | 13 | 25 |
| 1933-34 | Detroit | 47 | 10 | 9 | 19 |
| | **Totals** | 248 | 42 | 48 | 90 |

**CARSON, Gerald (Stub)** *Defenseman*
b. Parry Sound, Ont., Oct. 10, 1905

| 1928-29 | Mont-NYR | 40 | 0 | 0 | 0 |
|---|---|---|---|---|---|
| 1929-30 | Montreal | 35 | 1 | 0 | 1 |
| 1932-33 | Montreal | 48 | 5 | 2 | 7 |
| 1933-34 | Montreal | 48 | 5 | 1 | 6 |
| 1934-35 | Montreal | 48 | 0 | 5 | 5 |
| 1936-37 | Montreal M | 41 | 1 | 3 | 4 |
| | **Totals** | 260 | 12 | 11 | 23 |

**CARSON, Lindsay Warren** *Forward*
b. Oxbow, Sask., Nov. 21, 1960

| 1981-82 | Philadelphia | 18 | 0 | 1 | 1 |
|---|---|---|---|---|---|
| 1982-83 | Philadelphia | 78 | 18 | 19 | 37 |
| | **Totals** | 96 | 18 | 20 | 38 |

**CARSON, William Joseph** *Forward*
b. Bracebridge, Ont., Nov. 25, 1900

| 1926-27 | Toronto | 40 | 16 | 6 | 22 |
|---|---|---|---|---|---|
| 1927-28 | Toronto | 32 | 20 | 6 | 26 |
| 1928-29 | Tor-Bos | 43 | 11 | 8 | 19 |
| 1929-30 | Boston | 44 | 7 | 4 | 11 |
| | **Totals** | 159 | 54 | 24 | 78 |

**CARTER, Ronald** *Forward*
b. Montreal, Que., Mar. 14, 1958

| 1979-80 | Edmonton | 2 | 0 | 0 | 0 |
|---|---|---|---|---|---|

**CARTER, William** *Forward*
b. Cornwall, Ont., Dec. 2, 1937

| 1957-58 | Montreal | 1 | 0 | 0 | 0 |
|---|---|---|---|---|---|
| 1960-61 | Boston | 8 | 0 | 0 | 0 |
| 1961-62 | Montreal | 7 | 0 | 0 | 0 |
| | **Totals** | 16 | 0 | 0 | 0 |

**CARVETH, Joseph Gordon** *Forward*
b. Regina, Sask., Mar. 21, 1918

| 1940-41 | Detroit | 19 | 2 | 1 | 3 |
|---|---|---|---|---|---|
| 1941-42 | Detroit | 29 | 6 | 11 | 17 |
| 1942-43 | Detroit | 43 | 18 | 18 | 36 |
| 1943-44 | Detroit | 46 | 21 | 35 | 56 |
| 1944-45 | Detroit | 50 | 26 | 28 | 54 |
| 1945-46 | Detroit | 48 | 17 | 18 | 35 |
| 1946-47 | Boston | 51 | 21 | 15 | 36 |
| 1947-48 | Bos-Mont | 57 | 9 | 19 | 28 |
| 1948-49 | Montreal | 60 | 15 | 22 | 37 |
| 1949-50 | Mont-Det | 71 | 14 | 18 | 32 |
| 1950-51 | Detroit | 30 | 1 | 4 | 5 |
| | **Totals** | 504 | 150 | 189 | 339 |

**CASHMAN, Wayne John** *Forward*
b. Kingston, Ont., June 24, 1945

| 1964-65 | Boston | 1 | 0 | 0 | 0 |
|---|---|---|---|---|---|
| 1967-68 | Boston | 12 | 0 | 4 | 4 |
| 1968-69 | Boston | 51 | 8 | 23 | 31 |
| 1969-70 | Boston | 70 | 9 | 26 | 35 |
| 1970-71 | Boston | 77 | 21 | 58 | 79 |
| 1971-72 | Boston | 74 | 23 | 29 | 52 |
| 1972-73 | Boston | 76 | 29 | 39 | 68 |
| 1973-74 | Boston | 78 | 30 | 59 | 89 |
| 1974-75 | Boston | 42 | 11 | 22 | 33 |
| 1975-76 | Boston | 80 | 28 | 43 | 71 |
| 1976-77 | Boston | 65 | 15 | 37 | 52 |
| 1977-78 | Boston | 76 | 24 | 38 | 62 |
| 1978-79 | Boston | 75 | 27 | 40 | 67 |
| 1979-80 | Boston | 44 | 11 | 21 | 32 |
| 1980-81 | Boston | 77 | 25 | 35 | 60 |
| 1981-82 | Boston | 64 | 12 | 31 | 43 |
| 1982-83 | Boston | 65 | 4 | 11 | 15 |
| | **Totals** | 1027 | 277 | 516 | 793 |

**CASSIDY, Thomas** *Forward*
b. Blind River, Ont., Mar. 15, 1952

| 1977-78 | Pittsburgh | 26 | 3 | 4 | 7 |
|---|---|---|---|---|---|

**CASSOLATO, Anthony Gerry** *Forward*
b. Guelph, Ont., May 7, 1956

| 1976-77 | San Diego (WHA) | 43 | 13 | 12 | 25 |
|---|---|---|---|---|---|
| 1977-78 | Birmingham (WHA) | 77 | 18 | 25 | 43 |
| 1978-79 | Birmingham (WHA) | 64 | 13 | 7 | 20 |
| 1979-80 | Washington | 9 | 0 | 2 | 2 |
| 1980-81 | Washington | 2 | 0 | 0 | 0 |
| 1981-82 | Washington | 12 | 1 | 4 | 5 |
| | **NHL Totals** | 23 | 1 | 6 | 7 |
| | **WHA Totals** | 184 | 44 | 44 | 88 |

**CERESINO, Raymond** *Forward*
b. Port Arthur, Ont., Apr. 24, 1929

| 1948-49 | Toronto | 12 | 1 | 1 | 2 |
|---|---|---|---|---|---|

**CHAD, John** *Forward*
b. Provost, Alta., Sept. 16, 1919

| 1939-40 | Chicago | 22 | 8 | 3 | 11 |
|---|---|---|---|---|---|
| 1940-41 | Chicago | 44 | 7 | 18 | 25 |
| 1945-46 | Chicago | 13 | 0 | 1 | 1 |
| | **Totals** | 79 | 15 | 22 | 37 |

**CHALMERS, William (Chick)** *Forward*
b. Stratford, Ont., Jan 24, 1934

| 1953-54 | New York R | 1 | 0 | 0 | 0 |
|---|---|---|---|---|---|

**CHAMBERLAIN, Erwin Groves (Murph)**
*Forward*
b. Shawville, Que., Feb. 14, 1915

| 1937-38 | Toronto | 43 | 4 | 12 | 16 |
|---|---|---|---|---|---|
| 1938-39 | Toronto | 48 | 10 | 16 | 26 |
| 1939-40 | Toronto | 40 | 5 | 17 | 22 |
| 1940-41 | Montreal | 45 | 10 | 15 | 25 |
| 1941-42 | Mont-NYA | 36 | 12 | 12 | 24 |
| 1942-43 | Boston | 45 | 9 | 24 | 33 |
| 1943-44 | Montreal | 47 | 15 | 32 | 47 |
| 1944-45 | Montreal | 32 | 2 | 12 | 14 |
| 1945-46 | Montreal | 40 | 12 | 14 | 26 |
| 1946-47 | Montreal | 49 | 10 | 10 | 20 |
| 1947-48 | Montreal | 30 | 6 | 3 | 9 |
| 1948-49 | Montreal | 54 | 5 | 8 | 13 |
| | **Totals** | 509 | 100 | 175 | 275 |

**CHAMPAGNE, Andre Joseph Orius** *Forward*
b. Eastview, Ont., Sept. 19, 1943

| 1962-63 | Toronto | 2 | 0 | 0 | 0 |
|---|---|---|---|---|---|

**CHAPMAN, Arthur V.** *Forward*
b. Winnipeg, Man., May 29, 1907

| 1930-31 | Boston | 44 | 7 | 7 | 14 |
|---|---|---|---|---|---|
| 1931-32 | Boston | 48 | 11 | 14 | 25 |
| 1932-33 | Boston | 46 | 3 | 6 | 9 |
| 1933-34 | Bos-NYA | 47 | 5 | 12 | 17 |
| 2934-35 | New York A | 47 | 9 | 34 | 43 |
| 1935-36 | New York A | 47 | 10 | 28 | 38 |
| 1936-37 | New York A | 39 | 8 | 23 | 31 |
| 1937-38 | New York A | 44 | 2 | 27 | 29 |
| 1938-39 | New York A | 43 | 3 | 19 | 22 |
| 1930-40 | New York A | 25 | 4 | 6 | 10 |
| | **Totals** | 430 | 62 | 176 | 238 |

**CHAPMAN, Blair Douglas** *Forward*
b. Lloydminster, Sask., June 13, 1956

| 1976-77 | Pittsburgh | 80 | 14 | 23 | 37 |
|---|---|---|---|---|---|
| 1977-78 | Pittsburgh | 75 | 24 | 20 | 44 |
| 1978-79 | Pittsburgh | 71 | 10 | 8 | 18 |
| 1979-80 | Pitt-StL | 64 | 25 | 26 | 51 |
| 1980-81 | St Louis | 55 | 20 | 26 | 46 |
| 1981-82 | St Louis | 18 | 6 | 11 | 17 |
| 1982-83 | St Louis | 39 | 7 | 11 | 18 |
| | **Totals** | 402 | 106 | 125 | 231 |

**CHARLEBOIS, Robert Richard (Chuck)**
*Forward*
b. Cornwall, Ont., May 27, 1944

| 1967-68 | Minnesota | 7 | 1 | 0 | 1 |
|---|---|---|---|---|---|
| 1972-73 | Ottawa (WHA) | 78 | 24 | 39 | 63 |
| 1973-74 | New England (WHA) | 74 | 4 | 7 | 11 |
| 1974-75 | New England (WHA) | 8 | 1 | 0 | 1 |
| 1975-76 | New England (WHA) | 28 | 3 | 3 | 6 |
| | **NHL Totals** | 7 | 1 | 0 | 1 |
| | **WHA Totals** | 188 | 32 | 49 | 81 |

**CHARRON, Guy Joseph Jean** *Forward*
b. Verdun, Que., Jan. 24, 1949

| 1969-70 | Montreal | 5 | 0 | 0 | 0 |
|---|---|---|---|---|---|
| 1970-71 | Mont-Det | 39 | 10 | 6 | 16 |
| 1971-72 | Detroit | 64 | 9 | 16 | 25 |
| 1972-73 | Detroit | 75 | 18 | 18 | 36 |
| 1973-74 | Detroit | 76 | 25 | 30 | 55 |
| 1974-75 | Det-KC | 77 | 14 | 39 | 53 |
| 1975-76 | Kansas City | 78 | 27 | 44 | 71 |
| 1976-77 | Washington | 80 | 36 | 46 | 82 |
| 1977-78 | Washington | 80 | 38 | 35 | 73 |
| 1978-79 | Washington | 80 | 28 | 42 | 70 |
| 1979-80 | Washington | 33 | 11 | 20 | 31 |
| 1980-81 | Washington | 47 | 5 | 13 | 18 |
| | **Totals** | 734 | 221 | 309 | 530 |

| Season | Club | GP | G | A | Pts. |
|---|---|---|---|---|---|

**CHARTRAW, Raymond Richard** *Forward-Defenseman*
b. Caracas, Venezuela, July 13, 1954

| Season | Club | GP | G | A | Pts. |
|---|---|---|---|---|---|
| 1974-75 | Montreal | 12 | 0 | 0 | 0 |
| 1975-76 | Montreal | 16 | 1 | 3 | 4 |
| 1976-77 | Montreal | 43 | 3 | 4 | 7 |
| 1977-78 | Montreal | 68 | 4 | 12 | 16 |
| 1978-79 | Montreal | 62 | 5 | 11 | 16 |
| 1979-80 | Montreal | 66 | 5 | 7 | 12 |
| 1980-81 | Mont-LA | 35 | 1 | 7 | 8 |
| 1981-82 | Los Angeles | 33 | 2 | 8 | 10 |
| 1982-83 | LA-NYR | 57 | 5 | 7 | 12 |
| | **Totals** | 392 | 26 | 59 | 85 |

**CHECK, Lude** *Forward*
b. Brandon, Man., May 22, 1919

| Season | Club | GP | G | A | Pts. |
|---|---|---|---|---|---|
| 1943-44 | Detroit | 1 | 0 | 0 | 0 |
| 1944-45 | Chicago | 26 | 6 | 2 | 8 |
| | **Totals** | 27 | 6 | 2 | 8 |

**CHERNOFF, Michael Terrance** *Forward*
b. Yorkton, Sask., May 13, 1946

| Season | Club | GP | G | A | Pts. |
|---|---|---|---|---|---|
| 1968-69 | Minnesota | 1 | 0 | 0 | 0 |
| 1973-74 | Vancouver (WHA) | 36 | 11 | 10 | 21 |
| 1974-75 | Vancouver (WHA) | 3 | 0 | 0 | 0 |
| | **NHL Totals** | 1 | 0 | 0 | 0 |
| | **WHA Totals** | 39 | 11 | 10 | 21 |

**CHERNOMAZ, Richard** *Forward*
b. Selkirk, Man., Sept. 1, 1963

| Season | Club | GP | G | A | Pts. |
|---|---|---|---|---|---|
| 1981-82 | Colorado | 2 | 0 | 0 | 0 |

**CHERRY, Richard** *Defenseman*
b. Kingston, Ont., Mar. 18, 1937

| Season | Club | GP | G | A | Pts. |
|---|---|---|---|---|---|
| 1956-57 | Boston | 6 | 0 | 0 | 0 |
| 1968-69 | Philadelphia | 71 | 9 | 6 | 15 |
| 1969-70 | Philadelphia | 68 | 3 | 4 | 7 |
| | **Totals** | 145 | 12 | 10 | 22 |

**CHEVREFILS, Real** *Forward*
b. Timmins, Ont., May 2, 1932

| Season | Club | GP | G | A | Pts. |
|---|---|---|---|---|---|
| 1951-52 | Boston | 33 | 8 | 17 | 25 |
| 1952-53 | Boston | 69 | 19 | 14 | 33 |
| 1953-54 | Boston | 14 | 4 | 1 | 5 |
| 1954-55 | Boston | 64 | 18 | 22 | 40 |
| 1955-56 | Bos-Det | 63 | 14 | 12 | 26 |
| 1956-57 | Boston | 70 | 31 | 17 | 48 |
| 1957-58 | Boston | 44 | 9 | 9 | 18 |
| 1958-59 | Boston | 30 | 1 | 5 | 6 |
| | **Totals** | 387 | 104 | 97 | 201 |

**CHICOINE, Daniel** *Forward*
b. Sherbrooke, Que., Nov. 30, 1957

| Season | Club | GP | G | A | Pts. |
|---|---|---|---|---|---|
| 1977-78 | Cleveland | 6 | 0 | 0 | 0 |
| 1978-79 | Minnesota | 1 | 0 | 0 | 0 |
| 1979-80 | Minnesota | 24 | 1 | 2 | 3 |
| | **Totals** | 31 | 1 | 2 | 3 |

**CHINNICK, Richard Vaughn** *Forward*
b. Chatham, Ont., Aug. 15, 1953

| Season | Club | GP | G | A | Pts. |
|---|---|---|---|---|---|
| 1973-74 | Minnesota | 1 | 0 | 1 | 1 |
| 1974-75 | Minnesota | 3 | 0 | 1 | 1 |
| | **Totals** | 4 | 0 | 2 | 2 |

**CHIPPERFIELD, Ronald James** *Forward*
b. Brandon, Man., Mar. 28, 1954

| Season | Club | GP | G | A | Pts. |
|---|---|---|---|---|---|
| 1974-75 | Vancouver (WHA) | 78 | 19 | 20 | 39 |
| 1975-76 | Calgary (WHA) | 75 | 42 | 41 | 83 |
| 1976-77 | Calgary (WHA) | 81 | 27 | 27 | 54 |
| 1977-78 | Edmonton (WHA) | 80 | 33 | 52 | 85 |
| 1978-79 | Edmonton (WHA) | 55 | 32 | 37 | 69 |
| 1979-80 | Edm-Que | 79 | 22 | 23 | 45 |
| 1980-81 | Quebec | 4 | 0 | 1 | 1 |
| | **NHL Totals** | 83 | 22 | 24 | 46 |
| | **WHA Totals** | 369 | 153 | 177 | 330 |

**CHISHOLM, Alexander (Lex)** *Forward*
b. Galt, Ont., Apr. 1, 1915

| Season | Club | GP | G | A | Pts. |
|---|---|---|---|---|---|
| 1939-40 | Toronto | 31 | 6 | 8 | 14 |
| 1940-41 | Toronto | 31 | 4 | 0 | 4 |
| | **Totals** | 62 | 10 | 8 | 18 |

**CHISHOLM, Arthur** *Forward*

| Season | Club | GP | G | A | Pts. |
|---|---|---|---|---|---|
| 1960-61 | Boston | 3 | 0 | 0 | 0 |

**CHORNEY, Marc** *Defenseman*
b. Sudbury, Ont., Nov. 8, 1957

| Season | Club | GP | G | A | Pts. |
|---|---|---|---|---|---|
| 1980-81 | Pittsburgh | 8 | 1 | 6 | 7 |
| 1981-82 | Pittsburgh | 60 | 1 | 6 | 7 |
| 1982-83 | Pittsburgh | 67 | 3 | 5 | 8 |
| | **Totals** | 135 | 5 | 17 | 22 |

**CHOUINARD, Guy Camil** *Forward*
b. Quebec City, Que., Oct. 20, 1956

| Season | Club | GP | G | A | Pts. |
|---|---|---|---|---|---|
| 1974-75 | Atlanta | 5 | 0 | 0 | 0 |
| 1975-76 | Atlanta | 4 | 0 | 2 | 2 |
| 1976-77 | Atlanta | 80 | 17 | 33 | 50 |
| 1977-78 | Atlanta | 73 | 28 | 30 | 58 |
| 1978-79 | Atlanta | 80 | 50 | 57 | 107 |
| 1979-80 | Atlanta | 76 | 31 | 46 | 77 |
| 1980-81 | Calgary | 52 | 31 | 52 | 83 |
| 1981-82 | Calgary | 64 | 23 | 57 | 80 |
| 1982-83 | Calgary | 80 | 13 | 59 | 72 |
| | **Totals** | 514 | 193 | 336 | 529 |

**CHRISTIAN, David** *Forward*
b. Warrood, Minn., May 12, 1959

| Season | Club | GP | G | A | Pts. |
|---|---|---|---|---|---|
| 1979-80 | Winnipeg | 15 | 8 | 10 | 18 |
| 1980-81 | Winnipeg | 80 | 28 | 43 | 71 |
| 1981-82 | Winnipeg | 80 | 25 | 51 | 76 |
| 1982-83 | Winnipeg | 55 | 18 | 26 | 44 |
| | **Totals** | 230 | 79 | 130 | 209 |

**CHRISTIE, Michael Hunt** *Defenseman*
b. Big Spring, Tex., Dec. 20, 1949

| Season | Club | GP | G | A | Pts. |
|---|---|---|---|---|---|
| 1974-75 | California | 34 | 0 | 14 | 14 |
| 1975-76 | California | 78 | 3 | 18 | 21 |
| 1976-77 | Cleveland | 79 | 6 | 27 | 33 |
| 1977-78 | Clev-Col | 69 | 3 | 14 | 17 |
| 1978-79 | Colorado | 68 | 1 | 10 | 11 |
| 1979-80 | Colorado | 74 | 1 | 17 | 18 |
| 1980-81 | Col-Van | 10 | 1 | 1 | 2 |
| | **Totals** | 412 | 15 | 101 | 116 |

**CHRISTOFF, Steve** *Forward*
b. Richfield, Minn., Jan. 23, 1958

| Season | Club | GP | G | A | Pts. |
|---|---|---|---|---|---|
| 1979-80 | Minnesota | 20 | 8 | 7 | 15 |
| 1980-81 | Minnesota | 56 | 26 | 13 | 39 |
| 1981-82 | Minnesota | 69 | 26 | 30 | 56 |
| 1982-83 | Calgary | 45 | 9 | 8 | 17 |
| | **Totals** | 190 | 69 | 58 | 127 |

**CHRYSTAL, Robert Harry** *Defenseman*
b. Winnipeg, Man., Apr. 30, 1930

| Season | Club | GP | G | A | Pts. |
|---|---|---|---|---|---|
| 1953-54 | New York R | 64 | 5 | 5 | 10 |
| 1954-55 | New York R | 68 | 6 | 9 | 15 |
| | **Totals** | 132 | 11 | 14 | 25 |

**CHURCH, John** *Defenseman*
b. Kamsack, Sask., May 24, 1915

| Season | Club | GP | G | A | Pts. |
|---|---|---|---|---|---|
| 1938-39 | Toronto | 5 | 0 | 2 | 2 |
| 1939-40 | Toronto | 39 | 1 | 4 | 5 |
| 1940-41 | Toronto | 15 | 0 | 1 | 1 |
| 1941-42 | Tor-NYA | 42 | 1 | 6 | 7 |
| 1945-46 | Boston | 43 | 2 | 6 | 8 |
| | **Totals** | 144 | 4 | 19 | 23 |

**CICCARELLI, Dino** *Forward*
b. Sarnia, Ont., Aug. 2, 1960

| Season | Club | GP | G | A | Pts. |
|---|---|---|---|---|---|
| 1980-81 | Minnesota | 32 | 18 | 12 | 30 |
| 1981-82 | Minnesota | 76 | 55 | 52 | 107 |
| 1982-83 | Minnesota | 77 | 37 | 38 | 75 |
| | **Totals** | 185 | 110 | 102 | 212 |

**CIESLA, Henry Edward (Hank)** *Forward*
b. St. Catharines, Ont., Oct. 15, 1934

| Season | Club | GP | G | A | Pts. |
|---|---|---|---|---|---|
| 1955-56 | Chicago | 70 | 8 | 23 | 31 |
| 1956-57 | Chicago | 70 | 10 | 8 | 18 |
| 1957-58 | New York R | 60 | 2 | 6 | 8 |
| 1958-59 | New York R | 69 | 9 | 14 | 23 |
| | **Totals** | 269 | 26 | 51 | 77 |

**CIRELLA, Joe** *Defenseman*
b. Hamilton, Ont., May 9, 1963

| Season | Club | GP | G | A | Pts. |
|---|---|---|---|---|---|
| 1981-82 | Colorado | 65 | 7 | 12 | 19 |
| 1982-83 | New Jersey | 2 | 0 | 1 | 1 |
| | **Totals** | 67 | 7 | 13 | 20 |

**CLACKSON, Kimbel Gerald** *Defenseman*
b. Saskatoon, Sask., Feb. 13, 1955

| Season | Club | GP | G | A | Pts. |
|---|---|---|---|---|---|
| 1975-76 | Indianapolis (WHA) | 77 | 1 | 12 | 13 |
| 1976-77 | Indianapolis (WHA) | 71 | 3 | 8 | 11 |
| 1977-78 | Winnipeg (WHA) | 52 | 2 | 7 | 9 |
| 1978-79 | Winnipeg (WHA) | 71 | 0 | 12 | 12 |
| 1979-80 | Pittsburgh | 45 | 0 | 3 | 3 |
| 1980-81 | Quebec | 61 | 0 | 5 | 5 |
| | **NHL Totals** | 106 | 0 | 8 | 8 |
| | **WHA Totals** | 271 | 6 | 39 | 45 |

**CLANCY, Francis Michael (King)** *Defenseman*
b. Ottawa, Ont., Feb. 25, 1903

| Season | Club | GP | G | A | Pts. |
|---|---|---|---|---|---|
| 1921-22 | Ottawa | 24 | 4 | 5 | 9 |
| 1922-23 | Ottawa | 24 | 3 | 1 | 4 |
| 1923-24 | Ottawa | 24 | 9 | 8 | 17 |
| 1924-25 | Ottawa | 29 | 14 | 5 | 19 |
| 1925-26 | Ottawa | 35 | 8 | 4 | 12 |
| 1926-27 | Ottawa | 43 | 9 | 10 | 19 |
| 1927-28 | Ottawa | 39 | 8 | 7 | 15 |
| 1928-29 | Ottawa | 44 | 13 | 2 | 15 |
| 1929-30 | Ottawa | 44 | 17 | 23 | 40 |
| 1930-31 | Toronto | 44 | 7 | 14 | 21 |
| 1931-32 | Toronto | 48 | 10 | 9 | 19 |
| 1932-33 | Toronto | 48 | 13 | 12 | 25 |
| 1933-34 | Toronto | 46 | 11 | 17 | 28 |
| 1934-35 | Toronto | 47 | 5 | 16 | 21 |
| 1935-36 | Toronto | 47 | 5 | 10 | 15 |
| 1936-37 | Toronto | 6 | 1 | 0 | 1 |
| | **Totals** | 592 | 137 | 143 | 280 |

**CLANCY, Terrance John** *Forward*
b. Ottawa, Ont., Apr. 2, 1943

| Season | Club | GP | G | A | Pts. |
|---|---|---|---|---|---|
| 1967-68 | Oakland | 7 | 0 | 0 | 0 |
| 1968-69 | Toronto | 2 | 0 | 0 | 0 |
| 1969-70 | Toronto | 52 | 6 | 5 | 11 |
| 1972-73 | Toronto | 32 | 0 | 1 | 1 |
| | **Totals** | 93 | 6 | 6 | 12 |

**CLAPPER, Aubrey Victor (Dit)** *Defenseman-Forward*
b. Newmarket, Ont., Feb. 9, 1907

| Season | Club | GP | G | A | Pts. |
|---|---|---|---|---|---|
| 1927-28 | Boston | 40 | 4 | 1 | 5 |
| 1928-29 | Boston | 40 | 9 | 2 | 11 |
| 1929-30 | Boston | 44 | 41 | 20 | 61 |
| 1930-31 | Boston | 43 | 22 | 8 | 30 |
| 1931-32 | Boston | 48 | 17 | 22 | 39 |
| 1932-33 | Boston | 48 | 14 | 14 | 28 |
| 1933-34 | Boston | 48 | 10 | 12 | 22 |
| 1934-35 | Boston | 48 | 21 | 16 | 37 |
| 1935-36 | Boston | 44 | 12 | 13 | 25 |
| 1936-37 | Boston | 48 | 17 | 8 | 25 |
| 1937-38 | Boston | 46 | 6 | 9 | 15 |
| 1938-39 | Boston | 42 | 13 | 13 | 26 |
| 1939-40 | Boston | 44 | 10 | 18 | 28 |
| 1940-41 | Boston | 48 | 8 | 18 | 26 |
| 1941-42 | Boston | 32 | 3 | 12 | 15 |
| 1942-43 | Boston | 38 | 5 | 18 | 23 |
| 1943-44 | Boston | 50 | 6 | 25 | 31 |
| 1944-45 | Boston | 46 | 8 | 14 | 22 |
| 1945-46 | Boston | 30 | 2 | 3 | 5 |
| 1946-47 | Boston | 6 | 0 | 0 | 0 |
| | **Totals** | 833 | 228 | 248 | 476 |

**CLARK, Dan** *Defenseman*
b. Toronto, Ont., Nov. 3, 1957

| Season | Club | GP | G | A | Pts. |
|---|---|---|---|---|---|
| 1978-79 | New York R | 4 | 0 | 1 | 1 |

| Season | Club | GP | G | A | Pts. |
|---|---|---|---|---|---|

**CLARK, Gordon Corson** *Forward*
b. Glasgow, Scotland, May 31, 1952

| Season | Club | GP | G | A | Pts. |
|---|---|---|---|---|---|
| 1974-75 | Boston | 1 | 0 | 0 | 0 |
| 1975-76 | Boston | 7 | 0 | 1 | 1 |
| 1978-79 | Cincinnati (WHA) | 21 | 3 | 3 | 6 |
| | **NHL Totals** | 8 | 0 | 1 | 1 |
| | **WHA Totals** | 21 | 3 | 3 | 6 |

**CLARKE, Robert Earle (Bobby)** *Forward*
b. Flin Flon, Man., Aug. 13, 1949

| 1969-70 | Philadelphia | 76 | 15 | 31 | 46 |
|---|---|---|---|---|---|
| 1970-71 | Philadelphia | 77 | 27 | 36 | 63 |
| 1971-72 | Philadelphia | 78 | 35 | 46 | 81 |
| 1972-73 | Philadelphia | 78 | 37 | 67 | 104 |
| 1973-74 | Philadelphia | 77 | 35 | 52 | 87 |
| 1974-75 | Philadelphia | 80 | 27 | 89 | 116 |
| 1975-76 | Philadelphia | 76 | 30 | 89 | 119 |
| 1976-77 | Philadelphia | 80 | 27 | 63 | 90 |
| 1977-78 | Philadelphia | 71 | 21 | 68 | 89 |
| 1978-79 | Philadelphia | 80 | 16 | 57 | 73 |
| 1979-80 | Philadelphia | 76 | 12 | 57 | 69 |
| 1980-81 | Philadelphia | 80 | 19 | 46 | 65 |
| 1981-82 | Philadelphia | 62 | 17 | 46 | 63 |
| 1982-83 | Philadelphia | 80 | 23 | 62 | 85 |
| | **Totals** | 1071 | 341 | 809 | 1150 |

**CLEGHORN, Ogilvie (Odie)** *Forward*
b. Montreal, Que., 1891

| 1918-19 | Montreal | 17 | 23 | 6 | 29 |
|---|---|---|---|---|---|
| 1919-20 | Montreal | 21 | 19 | 3 | 22 |
| 1920-21 | Montreal | 21 | 5 | 4 | 9 |
| 1921-22 | Montreal | 23 | 21 | 3 | 24 |
| 1922-23 | Montreal | 24 | 19 | 7 | 26 |
| 1923-24 | Montreal | 22 | 3 | 3 | 6 |
| 1924-25 | Montreal | 30 | 3 | 2 | 5 |
| 1925-26 | Pittsburgh Pi | 17 | 3 | 1 | 4 |
| 1926-27 | Pittsburgh Pi | 3 | 0 | 0 | 0 |
| 1927-28 | Pittsburgh Pi | 2 | 0 | 0 | 0 |
| | **Totals** | 180 | 96 | 29 | 125 |

**CLEGHORN, Sprague** *Defenseman*
b. Montreal, Que., 1890

| 1918-19 | Ottawa | 18 | 6 | 6 | 12 |
|---|---|---|---|---|---|
| 1919-20 | Ottawa | 21 | 16 | 5 | 21 |
| 1920-21 | Ott-Tor | 16 | 5 | 5 | 10 |
| 1921-22 | Montreal | 24 | 17 | 7 | 24 |
| 1922-23 | Montreal | 24 | 9 | 4 | 13 |
| 1923-24 | Montreal | 23 | 8 | 3 | 11 |
| 1924-25 | Montreal | 27 | 8 | 1 | 9 |
| 1925-26 | Boston | 28 | 6 | 5 | 11 |
| 1926-27 | Boston | 42 | 7 | 1 | 8 |
| 1927-28 | Boston | 33 | 2 | 2 | 4 |
| | **Totals** | 256 | 84 | 39 | 123 |

**CLEMENT, William H. (Bill)** *Forward*
b. Buckingham, Que., Dec. 20, 1950

| 1971-72 | Philadelphia | 49 | 9 | 14 | 23 |
|---|---|---|---|---|---|
| 1972-73 | Philadelphia | 73 | 14 | 14 | 28 |
| 1973-74 | Philadelphia | 39 | 9 | 8 | 17 |
| 1974-75 | Philadelphia | 68 | 21 | 16 | 37 |
| 1975-76 | Wash-Atl | 77 | 23 | 31 | 54 |
| 1976-77 | Atlanta | 67 | 17 | 26 | 43 |
| 1977-78 | Atlanta | 70 | 20 | 30 | 50 |
| 1978-79 | Atlanta | 65 | 12 | 23 | 35 |
| 1979-80 | Atlanta | 64 | 7 | 14 | 21 |
| 1980-81 | Calgary | 78 | 12 | 20 | 32 |
| 1981-82 | Calgary | 69 | 4 | 12 | 16 |
| | **Totals** | 719 | 148 | 208 | 356 |

**CLINE, Bruce** *Forward*
b. Massawippi, Que., Nov. 14, 1931

| 1956-57 | New York R | 30 | 2 | 3 | 5 |
|---|---|---|---|---|---|

**CLIPPINGDALE, Steve** *Forward*
b. Vancouver, B.C., Apr. 29, 1956

| 1976-77 | Los Angeles | 16 | 1 | 2 | 3 |
|---|---|---|---|---|---|
| 1979-80 | Washington | 3 | 0 | 0 | 0 |
| | **Totals** | 19 | 1 | 2 | 3 |

**CLOUTIER, Real** *Forward*
b. St. Emile, Que., July 30, 1956

| 1974-75 | Quebec (WHA) | 63 | 26 | 27 | 53 |
|---|---|---|---|---|---|
| 1975-76 | Quebec (WHA) | 80 | 60 | 54 | 114 |
| 1976-77 | Quebec (WHA) | 76 | 66 | 75 | 141 |
| 1977-78 | Quebec (WHA) | 73 | 56 | 73 | 129 |
| 1978-79 | Quebec (WHA) | 77 | 75 | 54 | 129 |
| 1979-80 | Quebec | 67 | 42 | 47 | 89 |
| 1980-81 | Quebec | 34 | 15 | 16 | 31 |
| 1981-82 | Quebec | 67 | 37 | 60 | 97 |
| 1982-83 | Quebec | 68 | 28 | 39 | 67 |
| | **NHL Totals** | 236 | 122 | 162 | 284 |
| | **WHA Totals** | 369 | 283 | 283 | 566 |

**CLOUTIER, Rejean** *Defenseman*
b. Windsor, Ont., Feb. 15, 1960

| 1979-80 | Detroit | 3 | 0 | 1 | 1 |
|---|---|---|---|---|---|
| 1981-82 | Detroit | 2 | 0 | 1 | 1 |
| | **Totals** | 5 | 0 | 2 | 2 |

**CLOUTIER, Roland** *Forward*
b. Rouyn-Noranda, Que., Oct. 6, 1957

| 1977-78 | Detroit | 1 | 0 | 0 | 0 |
|---|---|---|---|---|---|
| 1978-79 | Detroit | 19 | 6 | 6 | 12 |
| 1979-80 | Quebec | 14 | 2 | 3 | 5 |
| | **Totals** | 34 | 8 | 9 | 17 |

**CLUNE, Walter James** *Defenseman*
b. Toronto, Ont., Feb. 29, 1930

| 1955-56 | Montreal | 5 | 0 | 0 | 0 |
|---|---|---|---|---|---|

**COALTER, Gary Merritt Charles** *Forward*
b. Toronto, Ont., July 8, 1950

| 1973-74 | California | 4 | 0 | 0 | 0 |
|---|---|---|---|---|---|
| 1974-75 | Kansas City | 30 | 2 | 4 | 6 |
| | **Totals** | 34 | 2 | 4 | 6 |

**COATES, Stephen John** *Forward*
b. Toronto, Ont., July 2, 1950

| 1976-77 | Detroit | 5 | 1 | 0 | 1 |
|---|---|---|---|---|---|

**COCHRANE, Glen Macleod** *Defenseman*
b. Cranbrook, B.C., Jan. 29, 1958

| 1978-79 | Philadelphia | 1 | 0 | 0 | 0 |
|---|---|---|---|---|---|
| 1979-80 | Philadelphia | 31 | 1 | 8 | 9 |
| 1981-82 | Philadelphia | 63 | 6 | 12 | 18 |
| 1982-83 | Philadelphia | 77 | 2 | 22 | 24 |
| | **Totals** | 172 | 9 | 42 | 51 |

**COFFEY, Paul Douglas** *Defenseman*
b. Weston, Ont., June 1, 1961

| 1980-81 | Edmonton | 74 | 9 | 23 | 32 |
|---|---|---|---|---|---|
| 1981-82 | Edmonton | 80 | 29 | 60 | 89 |
| 1982-83 | Edmonton | 80 | 29 | 67 | 96 |
| | **Totals** | 234 | 67 | 150 | 217 |

**COFLIN, Hugh Alexander** *Defenseman*
b. Blaine Lake, Sask., Dec. 15, 1928

| 1950-51 | Chicago | 31 | 0 | 3 | 3 |
|---|---|---|---|---|---|

**COLLEY, Thomas** *Forward*
b. Toronto, Ont., Aug. 21, 1953

| 1974-75 | Minnesota | 1 | 0 | 0 | 0 |
|---|---|---|---|---|---|

**COLLINGS, Norman (Dodger)** *Forward*
b. Bradford, Ont.

| 1934-35 | Montreal | — | 0 | 1 | 1 |
|---|---|---|---|---|---|

**COLLINS, William Earl (Bill)** *Forward*
b. Ottawa, Ont., July 13, 1943

| 1967-68 | Minnesota | 71 | 9 | 11 | 20 |
|---|---|---|---|---|---|
| 1968-69 | Minnesota | 75 | 9 | 10 | 19 |
| 1969-70 | Minnesota | 74 | 29 | 9 | 38 |
| 1970-71 | Mont-Det | 76 | 11 | 18 | 29 |
| 1971-72 | Detroit | 71 | 15 | 25 | 40 |
| 1972-73 | Detroit | 78 | 21 | 21 | 42 |
| 1973-74 | Det-StL | 66 | 15 | 17 | 32 |
| 1974-75 | St Louis | 70 | 22 | 15 | 37 |

**CLOUTIER, Real** (continued above)

| 1975-76 | New York R | 50 | 4 | 4 | 8 |
|---|---|---|---|---|---|
| 1976-77 | Phil-Wash | 63 | 12 | 15 | 27 |
| 1977-78 | Washington | 74 | 10 | 9 | 19 |
| | **Totals** | 768 | 157 | 154 | 311 |

**COLLYARD, Robert Leander** *Forward*
b. Hibbing, Minn., Oct. 16, 1949

| 1973-74 | St Louis | 10 | 1 | 3 | 4 |
|---|---|---|---|---|---|

**COLVILLE, Mathew Lamont (Mac)** *Forward*
b. Edmonton, Alta., Jan. 8, 1916

| 1935-36 | New York R | 18 | 1 | 4 | 5 |
|---|---|---|---|---|---|
| 1936-37 | New York R | 46 | 7 | 12 | 19 |
| 1937-38 | New York R | 48 | 14 | 14 | 28 |
| 1938-39 | New York R | 48 | 7 | 21 | 28 |
| 1939-40 | New York R | 47 | 7 | 14 | 21 |
| 1940-41 | New York R | 47 | 14 | 17 | 31 |
| 1941-42 | New York R | 46 | 14 | 16 | 30 |
| 1945-46 | New York R | 39 | 7 | 6 | 13 |
| 1946-47 | New York R | 14 | 0 | 0 | 0 |
| | **Totals** | 353 | 71 | 104 | 175 |

**COLVILLE, Neil Macneil**
*Defenseman-Forward*
b. Edmonton, Alta., Aug. 4, 1914

| 1935-36 | New York R | 1 | 0 | 0 | 0 |
|---|---|---|---|---|---|
| 1936-37 | New York R | 45 | 10 | 18 | 28 |
| 1937-38 | New York R | 45 | 17 | 19 | 36 |
| 1938-39 | New York R | 47 | 18 | 19 | 37 |
| 1939-40 | New York R | 48 | 19 | 19 | 38 |
| 1940-41 | New York R | 48 | 14 | 28 | 42 |
| 1941-42 | New York R | 48 | 8 | 25 | 33 |
| 1944-45 | New York R | 4 | 0 | 1 | 1 |
| 1945-46 | New York R | 49 | 5 | 4 | 9 |
| 1946-47 | New York R | 60 | 4 | 16 | 20 |
| 1947-48 | New York R | 55 | 4 | 12 | 16 |
| 1948-49 | New York R | 14 | 0 | 5 | 5 |
| | **Totals** | 464 | 99 | 166 | 265 |

**COLWILL, Leslie John** *Forward*
b. Devide, Sask., Jan. 1, 1935

| 1958-59 | New York R | 69 | 7 | 6 | 13 |
|---|---|---|---|---|---|

**COMEAU, Reynald** *Forward*
b. Montreal, Que., Oct. 25, 1948

| 1971-72 | Montreal | 4 | 0 | 0 | 0 |
|---|---|---|---|---|---|
| 1972-73 | Atlanta | 77 | 21 | 21 | 42 |
| 1973-74 | Atlanta | 78 | 11 | 23 | 34 |
| 1974-75 | Atlanta | 75 | 14 | 20 | 34 |
| 1975-76 | Atlanta | 79 | 17 | 22 | 39 |
| 1976-77 | Atlanta | 80 | 15 | 18 | 33 |
| 1977-78 | Atlanta | 79 | 10 | 22 | 32 |
| 1978-79 | Colorado | 70 | 8 | 10 | 18 |
| 1979-80 | Colorado | 22 | 2 | 5 | 7 |
| | **Totals** | 564 | 98 | 141 | 239 |

**COMIER, Roger** *Forward*

| 1925-26 | Montreal | — | 0 | 0 | 0 |
|---|---|---|---|---|---|

**CONACHER, Brian Kennedy** *Forward*
b. Toronto, Ont., Aug. 31, 1941

| 1961-62 | Toronto | 1 | 0 | 0 | 0 |
|---|---|---|---|---|---|
| 1965-66 | Toronto | 2 | 0 | 0 | 0 |
| 1966-67 | Toronto | 66 | 14 | 13 | 27 |
| 1967-68 | Toronto | 64 | 11 | 14 | 25 |
| 1971-72 | Detroit | 22 | 3 | 1 | 4 |
| 1972-73 | Ottawa (WHA) | 69 | 8 | 19 | 27 |
| | **NHL Totals** | 155 | 28 | 28 | 56 |
| | **WHA Totals** | 69 | 8 | 19 | 27 |

**CONACHER, Charles William (Pete) Jr.**
*Forward*
b. Toronto, Ont., July 29, 1932

| 1951-52 | Chicago | 2 | 0 | 1 | 1 |
|---|---|---|---|---|---|
| 1952-53 | Chicago | 41 | 5 | 6 | 11 |
| 1953-54 | Chicago | 70 | 19 | 9 | 28 |
| 1954-55 | Chi-NYR | 70 | 12 | 11 | 23 |
| 1955-56 | New York R | 41 | 11 | 11 | 22 |
| 1957-58 | Toronto | 5 | 0 | 1 | 1 |
| | **Totals** | 229 | 47 | 39 | 86 |

**CONACHER, Charles William (Chuck) Sr.**
*Forward*
b. Toronto, Ont., Dec. 10, 1909

| Season | Club | GP | G | A | Pts. |
|---|---|---|---|---|---|
| 1929-30 | Toronto | 38 | 20 | 9 | 29 |
| 1930-31 | Toronto | 37 | 31 | 12 | 43 |
| 1931-32 | Toronto | 44 | 34 | 14 | 48 |
| 1932-33 | Toronto | 40 | 14 | 19 | 33 |
| 1933-34 | Toronto | 42 | 32 | 20 | 52 |
| 1934-35 | Toronto | 47 | 36 | 21 | 57 |
| 1935-36 | Toronto | 44 | 23 | 15 | 38 |
| 1936-37 | Toronto | 15 | 3 | 5 | 8 |
| 1937-38 | Toronto | 19 | 7 | 9 | 16 |
| 1938-39 | Detroit | 40 | 8 | 15 | 23 |
| 1939-40 | New York A | 47 | 10 | 18 | 28 |
| 1940-41 | New York A | 46 | 7 | 16 | 23 |
| | **Totals** | 459 | 225 | 173 | 398 |

**CONACHER, James** *Forward*
b. Motherwell, Scotland, May 5, 1921

| Season | Club | GP | G | A | Pts. |
|---|---|---|---|---|---|
| 1945-46 | Detroit | 20 | 1 | 5 | 6 |
| 1946-47 | Detroit | 33 | 16 | 13 | 29 |
| 1947-48 | Detroit | 60 | 17 | 23 | 40 |
| 1948-49 | Det-Chi | 59 | 26 | 23 | 49 |
| 1949-50 | Chicago | 66 | 13 | 20 | 33 |
| 1950-51 | Chicago | 52 | 10 | 27 | 37 |
| 1951-52 | Chi-NYR | 21 | 1 | 2 | 3 |
| 1952-53 | New York R | 17 | 1 | 4 | 5 |
| | **Totals** | 338 | 85 | 117 | 202 |

**CONACHER, Lionel (The Big Train)**
*Defenseman*
b. Toronto, Ont., May 24, 1901

| Season | Club | GP | G | A | Pts. |
|---|---|---|---|---|---|
| 1925-26 | Pittsburgh Pi | 33 | 9 | 4 | 13 |
| 1926-27 | PittPi-NYA | 40 | 8 | 9 | 17 |
| 1927-28 | New York A | 36 | 11 | 6 | 17 |
| 1928-29 | New York A | 44 | 5 | 2 | 7 |
| 1929-30 | New York A | 39 | 4 | 6 | 10 |
| 1930-31 | Montreal M | 35 | 4 | 3 | 7 |
| 1931-32 | Montreal M | 46 | 7 | 9 | 16 |
| 1932-33 | Montreal M | 47 | 7 | 21 | 28 |
| 1933-34 | Chicago | 48 | 10 | 13 | 23 |
| 1934-35 | Montreal M | 40 | 2 | 6 | 8 |
| 1935-36 | Montreal M | 47 | 7 | 7 | 14 |
| 1936-37 | Montreal M | 45 | 6 | 19 | 25 |
| | **Totals** | 500 | 80 | 105 | 185 |

**CONACHER, Patrick John** *Forward*
b. Edmonton, Alta., May 1, 1959

| Season | Club | GP | G | A | Pts. |
|---|---|---|---|---|---|
| 1979-80 | New York R | 17 | 0 | 5 | 5 |
| 1982-83 | New York R | 5 | 0 | 1 | 1 |
| | **Totals** | 22 | 0 | 6 | 6 |

**CONACHER, Roy Gordon** *Forward*
b. Toronto, Ont., Oct. 5, 1916

| Season | Club | GP | G | A | Pts. |
|---|---|---|---|---|---|
| 1938-39 | Boston | 47 | 26 | 11 | 37 |
| 1939-40 | Boston | 31 | 18 | 12 | 30 |
| 1940-41 | Boston | 41 | 24 | 14 | 38 |
| 1941-42 | Boston | 43 | 24 | 13 | 37 |
| 1945-46 | Boston | 4 | 2 | 1 | 3 |
| 1946-47 | Detroit | 60 | 30 | 24 | 54 |
| 1947-48 | Chicago | 52 | 22 | 27 | 49 |
| 1948-49 | Chicago | 60 | 26 | 42 | 68 |
| 1949-50 | Chicago | 70 | 25 | 31 | 56 |
| 1950-51 | Chicago | 70 | 26 | 24 | 50 |
| 1951-52 | Chicago | 12 | 3 | 1 | 4 |
| | **Totals** | 490 | 226 | 200 | 426 |

**CONN, Maitland (Red)** *Forward*
b. Hartley, Man., Oct. 25, 1908

| Season | Club | GP | G | A | Pts. |
|---|---|---|---|---|---|
| 1933-34 | New York A | 48 | 4 | 17 | 21 |
| 1934-35 | New York A | 45 | 5 | 11 | 16 |
| | **Totals** | 93 | 9 | 28 | 37 |

**CONNELLY, Wayne Francis** *Forward*
b. Rouyn, Que., Dec. 16, 1939

| Season | Club | GP | G | A | Pts. |
|---|---|---|---|---|---|
| 1960-61 | Montreal | 3 | 0 | 0 | 0 |
| 1961-62 | Boston | 61 | 8 | 12 | 20 |
| 1962-63 | Boston | 18 | 2 | 6 | 8 |
| 1963-64 | Boston | 26 | 2 | 3 | 5 |
| 1966-67 | Boston | 64 | 13 | 17 | 30 |
| 1967-68 | Minnesota | 74 | 35 | 21 | 56 |


| Season | Club | GP | G | A | Pts. |
|---|---|---|---|---|---|
| 1968-69 | Minn-Det | 74 | 18 | 25 | 43 |
| 1969-70 | Detroit | 76 | 23 | 36 | 59 |
| 1970-71 | Det-StL | 79 | 13 | 29 | 42 |
| 1971-72 | StL-Vanc | 68 | 19 | 25 | 44 |
| 1972-73 | Minnesota (WHA) | 78 | 40 | 30 | 70 |
| 1973-74 | Minnesota (WHA) | 78 | 42 | 53 | 95 |
| 1974-75 | Minnesota (WHA) | 76 | 38 | 33 | 71 |
| 1975-76 | Minn-Clev (WHA) | 71 | 29 | 25 | 54 |
| 1976-77 | Calg-Edm (WHA) | 63 | 18 | 21 | 39 |
| | **NHL Totals** | 543 | 133 | 174 | 307 |
| | **WHA Totals** | 366 | 167 | 162 | 329 |

**CONNOLLY, Albert Patrick (Bert)** *Forward*
b. Montreal, Que., Apr. 22, 1909

| Season | Club | GP | G | A | Pts. |
|---|---|---|---|---|---|
| 1934-35 | New York R | 47 | 10 | 11 | 21 |
| 1935-36 | New York R | 25 | 2 | 2 | 4 |
| 1937-38 | Chicago | — | 1 | 2 | 3 |
| | **Totals** | — | 13 | 15 | 28 |

**CONNOR, Cameron Duncan** *Forward*
b. Winnipeg, Man., Aug. 10, 1954

| Season | Club | GP | G | A | Pts. |
|---|---|---|---|---|---|
| 1974-75 | Phoenix (WHA) | 57 | 9 | 19 | 28 |
| 1975-76 | Phoenix (WHA) | 73 | 18 | 21 | 39 |
| 1976-77 | Houston (WHA) | 76 | 35 | 32 | 67 |
| 1977-78 | Houston (WHA) | 68 | 21 | 16 | 37 |
| 1978-79 | Montreal | 23 | 1 | 3 | 4 |
| 1979-80 | Edm-NYR | 49 | 7 | 16 | 23 |
| 1980-81 | New York R | 15 | 1 | 3 | 4 |
| 1982-83 | New York R | 1 | 0 | 0 | 0 |
| | **NHL Totals** | 88 | 9 | 22 | 31 |
| | **WHA Totals** | 274 | 83 | 88 | 171 |

**CONNORS, Harry** *Forward*
b. Ottawa, Ont.

| Season | Club | GP | G | A | Pts. |
|---|---|---|---|---|---|
| 1927-28 | Boston | 42 | 9 | 1 | 10 |
| 1928-29 | New York A | 44 | 6 | 2 | 8 |
| 1929-30 | Bos-Ott | 37 | 1 | 2 | 3 |
| 1930-31 | Ottawa | 9 | 0 | 0 | 0 |
| | **Totals** | 132 | 16 | 5 | 21 |

**CONNORS, Robert** *Defenseman*

| Season | Club | GP | G | A | Pts. |
|---|---|---|---|---|---|
| 1926-27 | New York A | 5 | 1 | 0 | 1 |
| 1928-29 | Detroit | 40 | 13 | 3 | 16 |
| 1929-30 | Detroit | 32 | 3 | 7 | 10 |
| | **Totals** | 77 | 17 | 10 | 27 |

**CONTINI, Joseph Mario** *Forward*
b. Galt, Ont., Jan. 29, 1957

| Season | Club | GP | G | A | Pts. |
|---|---|---|---|---|---|
| 1977-78 | Colorado | 37 | 12 | 9 | 21 |
| 1978-79 | Colorado | 30 | 5 | 12 | 17 |
| 1980-81 | Minnesota | 1 | 0 | 0 | 0 |
| | **Totals** | 68 | 17 | 21 | 38 |

**CONVEY, Edward** *Forward*
b. Toronto, Ont.

| Season | Club | GP | G | A | Pts. |
|---|---|---|---|---|---|
| 1930-31 | New York A | 2 | 0 | 0 | 0 |
| 1931-32 | New York A | 21 | 1 | 0 | 1 |
| 1932-33 | New York A | 13 | 0 | 0 | 0 |
| | **Totals** | 36 | 1 | 0 | 1 |

**COOK, Alex (Bud)** *Forward*
b. Kingston, Ont., Nov. 15, 1907

| Season | Club | GP | G | A | Pts. |
|---|---|---|---|---|---|
| 1931-32 | Boston | 28 | 4 | 4 | 8 |
| 1933-34 | Ottawa | 18 | 1 | 0 | 1 |
| 1934-35 | St Louis E | 4 | 0 | 0 | 0 |
| | **Totals** | 50 | 5 | 4 | 9 |

**COOK, Frederick Joseph (Bun)** *Forward*
b. Kingston, Ont., Sept. 18, 1903

| Season | Club | GP | G | A | Pts. |
|---|---|---|---|---|---|
| 1926-27 | New York R | 44 | 14 | 9 | 23 |
| 1927-28 | New York R | 44 | 14 | 14 | 28 |
| 1928-29 | New York R | 43 | 13 | 5 | 18 |
| 1929-30 | New York R | 43 | 24 | 18 | 42 |
| 1930-31 | New York R | 44 | 18 | 17 | 35 |
| 1931-32 | New York R | 45 | 14 | 20 | 34 |
| 1932-33 | New York R | 48 | 22 | 15 | 37 |
| 1933-34 | New York R | 48 | 18 | 15 | 33 |


| Season | Club | GP | G | A | Pts. |
|---|---|---|---|---|---|
| 1934-35 | New York R | 48 | 13 | 21 | 34 |
| 1935-36 | New York R | 26 | 4 | 5 | 9 |
| 1936-37 | Boston | 44 | 4 | 5 | 9 |
| | **Totals** | 477 | 158 | 144 | 302 |

**COOK, Lloyd** *Defenseman*

| Season | Club | GP | G | A | Pts. |
|---|---|---|---|---|---|
| 1924-25 | Boston | 4 | 1 | 0 | 1 |

**COOK, Robert Arthur** *Forward*
b. Sudbury, Ont., Jan. 6, 1946

| Season | Club | GP | G | A | Pts. |
|---|---|---|---|---|---|
| 1970-71 | Vancouver | 2 | 0 | 0 | 0 |
| 1972-73 | Det-NYI | 46 | 11 | 7 | 18 |
| 1973-74 | New York I | 22 | 2 | 1 | 3 |
| 1974-75 | Minnesota | 2 | 0 | 1 | 1 |
| | **Totals** | 72 | 13 | 9 | 22 |

**COOK, Thomas John** *Forward*
b. Ft. William, Ont., May 17, 1903

| Season | Club | GP | G | A | Pts. |
|---|---|---|---|---|---|
| 1929-30 | Chicago | 41 | 14 | 16 | 30 |
| 1930-31 | Chicago | 44 | 15 | 14 | 29 |
| 1931-32 | Chicago | 48 | 12 | 13 | 25 |
| 1932-33 | Chicago | 48 | 12 | 14 | 26 |
| 1933-34 | Chicago | 37 | 5 | 9 | 14 |
| 1934-35 | Chicago | 48 | 13 | 18 | 31 |
| 1935-36 | Chicago | 47 | 4 | 8 | 12 |
| 1936-37 | Chicago | 15 | 0 | 2 | 2 |
| 1937-38 | Montreal M | 21 | 2 | 4 | 6 |
| | **Totals** | 349 | 77 | 98 | 175 |

**COOK, William Osser** *Forward*
b. Brantford, Ont., Oct. 9, 1896

| Season | Club | GP | G | A | Pts. |
|---|---|---|---|---|---|
| 1926-27 | New York R | 44 | 33 | 4 | 37 |
| 1927-28 | New York R | 43 | 18 | 6 | 24 |
| 1928-29 | New York R | 43 | 15 | 8 | 23 |
| 1929-30 | New York R | 44 | 29 | 30 | 59 |
| 1930-31 | New York R | 44 | 30 | 12 | 42 |
| 1931-32 | New York R | 48 | 34 | 14 | 48 |
| 1932-33 | New York R | 48 | 28 | 22 | 50 |
| 1933-34 | New York R | 48 | 13 | 13 | 26 |
| 1934-35 | New York R | 48 | 21 | 15 | 36 |
| 1935-36 | New York R | 44 | 7 | 10 | 17 |
| 1936-37 | New York R | 21 | 1 | 4 | 5 |
| | **Totals** | 475 | 229 | 138 | 367 |

**COOPER, Carson** *Forward*
b. Cornwall, Ont.

| Season | Club | GP | G | A | Pts. |
|---|---|---|---|---|---|
| 1924-25 | Boston | 12 | 5 | 3 | 8 |
| 1925-26 | Boston | 36 | 28 | 3 | 31 |
| 1926-27 | Bos-Mont | 24 | 9 | 3 | 12 |
| 1927-28 | Detroit | 43 | 15 | 2 | 17 |
| 1928-29 | Detroit | 43 | 18 | 9 | 27 |
| 1929-30 | Detroit | 44 | 18 | 18 | 36 |
| 1930-31 | Detroit | 44 | 14 | 14 | 28 |
| 1931-32 | Detroit | 48 | 3 | 5 | 8 |
| | **Totals** | 294 | 110 | 57 | 167 |

**COOPER, Edward William** *Forward*
b. Loon Lake, Sask., Aug. 28, 1960

| Season | Club | GP | G | A | Pts. |
|---|---|---|---|---|---|
| 1980-81 | Colorado | 47 | 7 | 7 | 14 |
| 1981-82 | Colorado | 2 | 1 | 0 | 1 |
| | **Totals** | 49 | 8 | 7 | 15 |

**COOPER, Harold (Hal)** *Forward*
b. New Liskeard, Ont., Aug. 29, 1915

| Season | Club | GP | G | A | Pts. |
|---|---|---|---|---|---|
| 1944-45 | New York R | 8 | 0 | 0 | 0 |

**COOPER, Joseph** *Defenseman*
b. Winnipeg, Man., Dec. 14, 1914

| Season | Club | GP | G | A | Pts. |
|---|---|---|---|---|---|
| 1935-36 | New York R | 1 | 0 | 0 | 0 |
| 1936-37 | New York R | 48 | 0 | 3 | 3 |
| 1937-38 | New York R | 46 | 3 | 2 | 5 |
| 1938-39 | Chicago | 17 | 3 | 3 | 6 |
| 1939-40 | Chicago | 44 | 4 | 7 | 11 |
| 1940-41 | Chicago | 40 | 5 | 5 | 10 |
| 1941-42 | Chicago | 47 | 6 | 14 | 20 |
| 1943-44 | Chicago | 13 | 1 | 0 | 1 |
| 1944-45 | Chicago | 50 | 4 | 17 | 21 |
| 1945-46 | Chicago | 50 | 2 | 7 | 9 |
| 1946-47 | New York R | 59 | 2 | 8 | 10 |
| | **Totals** | 415 | 30 | 66 | 96 |

| Season | Club | GP | G | A | Pts. |
|---|---|---|---|---|---|

**COPP, Robert Alonzo** *Defenseman*
b. Port Elgin, N.B., Nov. 15, 1918

| Season | Club | GP | G | A | Pts. |
|---|---|---|---|---|---|
| 1942-43 | Toronto | 28 | 3 | 9 | 12 |
| 1950-51 | Toronto | 2 | 0 | 0 | 0 |
| | **Totals** | 30 | 3 | 9 | 12 |

**CORBEAU, Bert** *Defenseman*

| Season | Club | GP | G | A | Pts. |
|---|---|---|---|---|---|
| 1917-18 | Montreal | 20 | 8 | 0 | 8 |
| 1918-19 | Montreal | 16 | 2 | 1 | 3 |
| 1919-20 | Montreal | 23 | 11 | 5 | 16 |
| 1920-21 | Montreal | 24 | 12 | 1 | 13 |
| 1921-22 | Montreal | 22 | 4 | 7 | 11 |
| 1922-23 | Hamilton | 21 | 10 | 3 | 13 |
| 1923-24 | Toronto | 24 | 8 | 6 | 14 |
| 1924-25 | Toronto | 30 | 4 | 3 | 7 |
| 1925-26 | Toronto | 36 | 5 | 5 | 10 |
| 1926-27 | Toronto | 41 | 1 | 2 | 3 |
| | **Totals** | 257 | 65 | 33 | 98 |

**CORCORAN, Norman** *Forward*
b. Toronto, Ont., Aug. 15, 1931

| Season | Club | GP | G | A | Pts. |
|---|---|---|---|---|---|
| 1949-50 | Boston | 1 | 0 | 0 | 0 |
| 1952-53 | Boston | 1 | 0 | 0 | 0 |
| 1954-55 | Boston | 2 | 0 | 0 | 0 |
| 1955-56 | Det-Chi | 25 | 1 | 3 | 4 |
| | **Totals** | 29 | 1 | 3 | 4 |

**CORRIGAN, Charles Hubert Patrick (Chuck)**
*Defenseman*
b. Moosomin, Sask., May 22, 1916

| Season | Club | GP | G | A | Pts. |
|---|---|---|---|---|---|
| 1940-41 | New York A | 15 | 2 | 2 | 4 |

**CORRIGAN, Michael Douglas** *Forward*
b. Ottawa, Ont., Jan. 11, 1946

| Season | Club | GP | G | A | Pts. |
|---|---|---|---|---|---|
| 1967-68 | Los Angeles | 5 | 0 | 0 | 0 |
| 1969-70 | Los Angeles | 36 | 6 | 4 | 10 |
| 1970-71 | Vancouver | 76 | 21 | 28 | 49 |
| 1971-72 | Van-LA | 75 | 15 | 26 | 41 |
| 1972-73 | Los Angeles | 78 | 37 | 30 | 67 |
| 1973-74 | Los Angeles | 75 | 16 | 26 | 42 |
| 1974-75 | Los Angeles | 80 | 13 | 21 | 34 |
| 1975-76 | Los Angeles | 71 | 22 | 21 | 43 |
| 1976-77 | Pittsburgh | 73 | 14 | 27 | 41 |
| 1977-78 | Pittsburgh | 25 | 8 | 12 | 20 |
| | **Totals** | 584 | 152 | 195 | 347 |

**CORRIVEAU, Fred Andre** *Forward*
b. Grand Mere, Que., May 15, 1928

| Season | Club | GP | G | A | Pts. |
|---|---|---|---|---|---|
| 1953-54 | Montreal | 3 | 0 | 1 | 1 |

**CORY, Keith Ross** *Defenseman*
b. Calgary, Alta., Feb. 4, 1957

| Season | Club | GP | G | A | Pts. |
|---|---|---|---|---|---|
| 1979-80 | Winnipeg | 46 | 2 | 9 | 11 |
| 1980 81 | Winnipeg | 5 | 0 | 1 | 1 |
| | **Totals** | 51 | 2 | 10 | 12 |

**COSSETTE, Jacques** *Forward*
b. Rouyn-Noranda, Que., June 20, 1954

| Season | Club | GP | G | A | Pts. |
|---|---|---|---|---|---|
| 1975-76 | Pittsburgh | 7 | 0 | 2 | 2 |
| 1976-77 | Pittsburgh | 19 | 1 | 2 | 3 |
| 1978-79 | Pittsburgh | 38 | 7 | 2 | 9 |
| | **Totals** | 64 | 8 | 6 | 14 |

**COSTELLO, Lester John Thomas** *Forward*
b. South Porcupine, Ont., Feb. 16, 1928

| Season | Club | GP | G | A | Pts. |
|---|---|---|---|---|---|
| 1948-49 | Toronto | 15 | 2 | 3 | 5 |

**COSTELLO, Murray** *Forward*
b. South Porcupine, Ont., Feb. 24, 1934

| Season | Club | GP | G | A | Pts. |
|---|---|---|---|---|---|
| 1953-54 | Chicago | 40 | 3 | 2 | 5 |
| 1954-55 | Boston | 54 | 4 | 11 | 15 |
| 1955-56 | Bos-Det | 65 | 6 | 6 | 12 |
| 1956-57 | Detroit | 3 | 0 | 0 | 0 |
| | **Totals** | 162 | 13 | 19 | 32 |

**COTCH, Charles** *Forward*

| Season | Club | GP | G | A | Pts. |
|---|---|---|---|---|---|
| 1924-25 | Ham-Tor | 11 | 1 | 0 | 1 |

**COTE, Alain** *Forward*
b. Matane, Que., May 3, 1957

| Season | Club | GP | G | A | Pts. |
|---|---|---|---|---|---|
| 1977-78 | Quebec (WHA) | 27 | 3 | 5 | 8 |
| 1978-79 | Quebec (WHA) | 79 | 14 | 13 | 27 |
| 1979-80 | Quebec | 41 | 5 | 11 | 16 |
| 1980-81 | Quebec | 51 | 8 | 18 | 26 |
| 1981-82 | Quebec | 79 | 15 | 16 | 31 |
| 1982-83 | Quebec | 79 | 12 | 28 | 40 |
| | **NHL Totals** | 250 | 40 | 73 | 113 |
| | **WHA Totals** | 106 | 17 | 18 | 35 |

**COTTON, Harold (Baldy)** *Forward*
b. Toronto, Ont., Nov. 5, 1902

| Season | Club | GP | G | A | Pts. |
|---|---|---|---|---|---|
| 1925-26 | Pittsburgh Pi | 33 | 7 | 1 | 8 |
| 1926-27 | Pittsburgh Pi | 35 | 5 | 0 | 5 |
| 1927-28 | Pittsburgh Pi | 42 | 9 | 3 | 12 |
| 1928-29 | PittPi-Tor | 43 | 4 | 4 | 8 |
| 1929-30 | Toronto | 41 | 21 | 17 | 38 |
| 1930-31 | Toronto | 43 | 12 | 17 | 29 |
| 1931-32 | Toronto | 47 | 5 | 13 | 18 |
| 1932-33 | Toronto | 48 | 10 | 11 | 21 |
| 1933-34 | Toronto | 47 | 8 | 14 | 22 |
| 1934-35 | Toronto | 47 | 11 | 14 | 25 |
| 1935-36 | New York A | 45 | 7 | 9 | 16 |
| 1936-37 | New York A | 29 | 2 | 0 | 2 |
| | **Totals** | 500 | 101 | 103 | 204 |

**COUGHLIN, Jack** *Forward*

| Season | Club | GP | G | A | Pts. |
|---|---|---|---|---|---|
| 1917-18 | Toronto A | 6 | 2 | 0 | 2 |
| 1919-20 | Que-Mont | 11 | 0 | 0 | 0 |
| 1920-21 | Hamilton | 2 | 0 | 0 | 0 |
| | **Totals** | 19 | 2 | 0 | 2 |

**COULIS, Tim** *Forward*
b. Kenora, Ont., Feb. 24, 1958

| Season | Club | GP | G | A | Pts. |
|---|---|---|---|---|---|
| 1979-80 | Washington | 19 | 1 | 2 | 3 |

**COULSON, Darcy** *Defenseman*

| Season | Club | GP | G | A | Pts. |
|---|---|---|---|---|---|
| 1930-31 | Philadelphia Q | 31 | 0 | 0 | 0 |

**COULTER, Arthur Edmund** *Defenseman*
b. Winnipeg, Man., May 31, 1909

| Season | Club | GP | G | A | Pts. |
|---|---|---|---|---|---|
| 1931-32 | Chicago | 14 | 0 | 1 | 1 |
| 1932-33 | Chicago | 46 | 3 | 2 | 5 |
| 1933-34 | Chicago | 41 | 5 | 2 | 7 |
| 1934-35 | Chicago | 48 | 4 | 8 | 12 |
| 1935-36 | Chi-NYR | 46 | 1 | 7 | 8 |
| 1936-37 | New York R | 47 | 1 | 5 | 6 |
| 1937-38 | New York R | 43 | 5 | 10 | 15 |
| 1938-39 | New York R | 44 | 4 | 8 | 12 |
| 1939-40 | New York R | 48 | 1 | 9 | 10 |
| 1940-41 | New York R | 35 | 5 | 14 | 19 |
| 1941-42 | New York R | 47 | 1 | 16 | 17 |
| | **Totals** | 459 | 30 | 82 | 112 |

**COURNOYER, Yvan Serge** *Forward*
b. Drummondville, Que., Nov. 22, 1943

| Season | Club | GP | G | A | Pts. |
|---|---|---|---|---|---|
| 1963-64 | Montreal | 5 | 4 | 0 | 4 |
| 1964-65 | Montreal | 55 | 7 | 10 | 17 |
| 1965-66 | Montreal | 65 | 18 | 11 | 29 |
| 1966-67 | Montreal | 69 | 25 | 15 | 40 |
| 1967-68 | Montreal | 64 | 28 | 32 | 60 |
| 1968-69 | Montreal | 76 | 43 | 44 | 87 |
| 1969-70 | Montreal | 72 | 27 | 36 | 63 |
| 1970-71 | Montreal | 65 | 37 | 36 | 73 |
| 1971-72 | Montreal | 73 | 47 | 36 | 83 |
| 1972-73 | Montreal | 67 | 40 | 39 | 79 |
| 1973-74 | Montreal | 67 | 40 | 33 | 73 |
| 1974-75 | Montreal | 76 | 29 | 45 | 74 |
| 1975-76 | Montreal | 71 | 32 | 36 | 68 |
| 1976-77 | Montreal | 60 | 25 | 28 | 53 |
| 1977-78 | Montreal | 68 | 24 | 29 | 53 |
| 1978-79 | Montreal | 15 | 2 | 5 | 7 |
| | **Totals** | 968 | 428 | 435 | 863 |

**COUTU (Couture), William** *Defenseman*
b. Sault Ste. Marie, Ont.

| Season | Club | GP | G | A | Pts. |
|---|---|---|---|---|---|
| 1917-18 | Montreal | 19 | 2 | 0 | 2 |
| 1918-19 | Montreal | 15 | 1 | 1 | 2 |
| 1919-20 | Montreal | 17 | 4 | 0 | 4 |
| 1920-21 | Hamilton | 24 | 8 | 4 | 12 |
| 1921-22 | Montreal | 23 | 4 | 3 | 7 |
| 1922-23 | Montreal | 24 | 5 | 2 | 7 |
| 1923-24 | Montreal | 16 | 3 | 1 | 4 |
| 1924-25 | Montreal | 28 | 3 | 2 | 5 |
| 1925-26 | Montreal | 33 | 2 | 4 | 6 |
| 1926-27 | Boston | 40 | 1 | 1 | 2 |
| | **Totals** | 239 | 33 | 18 | 51 |

**COUTURE, Gerald Joseph Wilfred Arthur**
*Forward*
b. Saskatoon, Sask., Aug. 6, 1925

| Season | Club | GP | G | A | Pts. |
|---|---|---|---|---|---|
| 1945-46 | Detroit | 43 | 3 | 7 | 10 |
| 1946-47 | Detroit | 30 | 5 | 10 | 15 |
| 1947-48 | Detroit | 19 | 3 | 6 | 9 |
| 1948-49 | Detroit | 51 | 19 | 10 | 29 |
| 1949-50 | Detroit | 70 | 24 | 7 | 31 |
| 1950-51 | Detroit | 53 | 7 | 6 | 13 |
| 1951-52 | Montreal | 10 | 0 | 1 | 1 |
| 1952-53 | Chicago | 70 | 19 | 18 | 37 |
| 1953-54 | Chicago | 40 | 6 | 5 | 11 |
| | **Totals** | 356 | 86 | 70 | 156 |

**COUTURE, Rosario (Lolo)** *Forward*
b. St. Boniface, Man., July 24, 1905

| Season | Club | GP | G | A | Pts. |
|---|---|---|---|---|---|
| 1928-29 | Chicago | 43 | 1 | 3 | 4 |
| 1929-30 | Chicago | 43 | 8 | 8 | 16 |
| 1930-31 | Chicago | 44 | 8 | 11 | 19 |
| 1931-32 | Chicago | 48 | 9 | 9 | 18 |
| 1932-33 | Chicago | 46 | 10 | 7 | 17 |
| 1933-34 | Chicago | 48 | 5 | 8 | 13 |
| 1934-35 | Chicago | 47 | 7 | 9 | 16 |
| 1935-36 | Montreal | 10 | 0 | 1 | 1 |
| | **Totals** | 329 | 48 | 56 | 104 |

**COWICK, Robert Bruce** *Forward*
b. Victoria, B.C., Aug. 18, 1951

| Season | Club | GP | G | A | Pts. |
|---|---|---|---|---|---|
| 1974-75 | Washington | 65 | 5 | 6 | 11 |
| 1975-76 | St Louis | 5 | 0 | 0 | 0 |
| | **Totals** | 70 | 5 | 6 | 11 |

**COWLEY, William Mailes** *Forward*
b. Bristol, Que., June 12, 1912

| Season | Club | GP | G | A | Pts. |
|---|---|---|---|---|---|
| 1934-35 | St Louis E | 43 | 5 | 7 | 12 |
| 1935-36 | Boston | 48 | 11 | 10 | 21 |
| 1936-37 | Boston | 46 | 13 | 22 | 35 |
| 1937-38 | Boston | 48 | 17 | 22 | 39 |
| 1938-39 | Boston | 34 | 8 | 34 | 42 |
| 1939-40 | Boston | 48 | 13 | 27 | 40 |
| 1940-41 | Boston | 46 | 17 | 45 | 62 |
| 1941-42 | Boston | 28 | 4 | 23 | 27 |
| 1942-43 | Boston | 48 | 27 | 45 | 72 |
| 1943-44 | Boston | 36 | 30 | 41 | 71 |
| 1944-45 | Boston | 49 | 25 | 40 | 65 |
| 1945-46 | Boston | 26 | 12 | 12 | 24 |
| 1946-47 | Boston | 51 | 13 | 25 | 38 |
| | **Totals** | 551 | 195 | 353 | 548 |

**COX, Daniel Smith** *Forward*
b. Little Current, Ont., Oct. 12, 1903

| Season | Club | GP | G | A | Pts. |
|---|---|---|---|---|---|
| 1926-27 | Toronto | 14 | 0 | 1 | 1 |
| 1927-28 | Toronto | 41 | 9 | 6 | 15 |
| 1928-29 | Toronto | 42 | 12 | 7 | 19 |
| 1929-30 | Tor-Ott | 42 | 4 | 6 | 10 |
| 1930-31 | Ottawa | 44 | 9 | 12 | 21 |
| 1931-32 | Detroit | 48 | 4 | 6 | 10 |
| 1932-33 | Ottawa | 48 | 4 | 7 | 11 |
| 1933-34 | Ott-NYR | 41 | 5 | 4 | 9 |
| | **Totals** | 320 | 47 | 49 | 96 |

**CRASHLEY, William Barton (Bart)**
*Defenseman*
b. Toronto, Ont., June 15, 1946

| Season | Club | GP | G | A | Pts. |
|---|---|---|---|---|---|
| 1965-66 | Detroit | 1 | 0 | 0 | 0 |
| 1966-67 | Detroit | 2 | 0 | 0 | 0 |
| 1967-68 | Detroit | 57 | 2 | 14 | 16 |
| 1968-69 | Detroit | 1 | 0 | 0 | 0 |
| 1972-73 | Los Angeles (WHA) | 70 | 18 | 27 | 45 |
| 1973-74 | Los Angeles (WHA) | 78 | 4 | 26 | 30 |
| 1974-75 | KC-Det | 75 | 5 | 21 | 26 |
| 1975-76 | Los Angeles | 4 | 0 | 1 | 1 |
| | **NHL Totals** | 140 | 7 | 36 | 43 |
| | **WHA Totals** | 148 | 22 | 53 | 75 |

| Season | Club | GP | G | A | Pts. |
|---|---|---|---|---|---|

**CRAVEN, Murray** *Forward*
b. Medicine Hat, Alta., July 20, 1964

| Season | Club | GP | G | A | Pts. |
|---|---|---|---|---|---|
| 1982-83 | Detroit | 31 | 4 | 7 | 11 |

**CRAWFORD, Marc** *Forward*
b. Belleville, Ont., Feb. 13, 1961

| | | | | | |
|---|---|---|---|---|---|
| 1981-82 | Vancouver | 40 | 4 | 8 | 12 |
| 1982-83 | Vancouver | 41 | 4 | 5 | 9 |
| **Totals** | | 81 | 8 | 13 | 21 |

**CRAWFORD, Robert** *Forward*
b. New York, N.Y., May 27, 1960

| | | | | | |
|---|---|---|---|---|---|
| 1980-81 | Colorado | 15 | 1 | 3 | 4 |
| 1982-83 | Detroit | 1 | 0 | 0 | 0 |
| **Totals** | | 16 | 1 | 3 | 4 |

**CRAWFORD, Robert Remi** *Forward*
b. Belleville, Ont., Apr. 6, 1959

| | | | | | |
|---|---|---|---|---|---|
| 1979-80 | St Louis | 8 | 1 | 0 | 1 |
| 1981-82 | St Louis | 3 | 0 | 1 | 1 |
| 1982-83 | St Louis | 27 | 5 | 9 | 14 |
| **Totals** | | 38 | 6 | 10 | 16 |

**CRAWFORD, Samuel Russell (Rusty)**
*Forward*
b. Cardinal, Ont., Nov. 7, 1884

| | | | | | |
|---|---|---|---|---|---|
| 1917-18 | Tor-Ott | 20 | 3 | 0 | 3 |
| 1918-19 | Toronto | 18 | 0 | 0 | 0 |
| **Totals** | | 38 | 3 | 0 | 3 |

**CREIGHTON, David Theodore** *Forward*
b. Port Arthur, Ont., June 24, 1930

| | | | | | |
|---|---|---|---|---|---|
| 1948-49 | Boston | 12 | 1 | 3 | 4 |
| 1949-50 | Boston | 64 | 18 | 13 | 31 |
| 1950-51 | Boston | 56 | 5 | 4 | 9 |
| 1951-52 | Boston | 49 | 20 | 17 | 37 |
| 1952-53 | Boston | 45 | 8 | 8 | 16 |
| 1953-54 | Boston | 69 | 20 | 20 | 40 |
| 1954-55 | Tor-Chi | 63 | 9 | 8 | 17 |
| 1955-56 | New York R | 70 | 20 | 31 | 51 |
| 1956-57 | New York R | 70 | 18 | 21 | 39 |
| 1957-58 | New York R | 70 | 17 | 35 | 52 |
| 1958-59 | Toronto | 34 | 3 | 9 | 12 |
| 1959-60 | Toronto | 14 | 1 | 5 | 6 |
| **Totals** | | 616 | 140 | 174 | 314 |

**CREIGHTON, James (Jimmy)** *Forward*

| | | | | | |
|---|---|---|---|---|---|
| 1930-31 | Detroit | 9 | 1 | 0 | 1 |

**CRESSMAN, Dave** *Forward*
b. Kitchener, Ont., Jan. 2, 1950

| | | | | | |
|---|---|---|---|---|---|
| 1974-75 | Minnesota | 5 | 2 | 0 | 2 |
| 1975-76 | Minnesota | 80 | 4 | 8 | 12 |
| **Totals** | | 85 | 6 | 8 | 14 |

**CRESSMAN, Glen** *Forward*
b. Peterborough, Ont., Aug. 29, 1934

| | | | | | |
|---|---|---|---|---|---|
| 1956-57 | Montreal | 4 | 0 | 0 | 0 |

**CRISP, Terrance Arthur** *Forward*
b. Parry Sound, Ont., May 28, 1943

| | | | | | |
|---|---|---|---|---|---|
| 1965-66 | Boston | 3 | 0 | 0 | 0 |
| 1967-68 | St Louis | 73 | 9 | 20 | 29 |
| 1968-69 | St Louis | 57 | 6 | 9 | 15 |
| 1969-70 | St Louis | 26 | 5 | 6 | 11 |
| 1970-71 | St Louis | 54 | 5 | 11 | 16 |
| 1971-72 | St Louis | 75 | 13 | 18 | 31 |
| 1972-73 | NYI-Phil | 66 | 5 | 21 | 26 |
| 1973-74 | Philadelphia | 71 | 10 | 21 | 31 |
| 1974-75 | Philadelphia | 71 | 8 | 19 | 27 |
| 1975-76 | Philadelphia | 38 | 6 | 9 | 15 |
| 1976-77 | Philadelphia | 2 | 0 | 0 | 0 |
| **Totals** | | 536 | 67 | 134 | 201 |

**CROMBEEN, Michael Joseph** *Forward*
b. Sarnia, Ont., Apr. 16, 1957

| | | | | | |
|---|---|---|---|---|---|
| 1977-78 | Cleveland | 48 | 3 | 4 | 7 |
| 1978-79 | St Louis | 37 | 3 | 8 | 11 |
| 1979-80 | St Louis | 71 | 10 | 12 | 22 |
| 1980-81 | St Louis | 66 | 9 | 14 | 23 |
| 1981-82 | St Louis | 71 | 19 | 8 | 27 |
| 1982-83 | St Louis | 80 | 6 | 11 | 17 |
| **Totals** | | 373 | 50 | 57 | 107 |

**CROSSETT, Stanley** *Defenseman*

| | | | | | |
|---|---|---|---|---|---|
| 1930-31 | Philadelphia Q | 24 | 0 | 0 | 0 |

**CROSSMAN, Douglas** *Defenseman*
b. Peterborough, Ont., May 30, 1960

| | | | | | |
|---|---|---|---|---|---|
| 1980-81 | Chicago | 9 | 0 | 2 | 2 |
| 1981-82 | Chicago | 70 | 12 | 28 | 40 |
| 1982-83 | Chicago | 80 | 13 | 40 | 53 |
| **Totals** | | 159 | 25 | 70 | 95 |

**CROTEAU, Gary Paul** *Forward*
b. Sudbury, Ont., June 20, 1946

| | | | | | |
|---|---|---|---|---|---|
| 1968-69 | Los Angeles | 11 | 5 | 1 | 6 |
| 1969-70 | LA-Det | 13 | 0 | 2 | 2 |
| 1970-71 | California | 74 | 15 | 28 | 43 |
| 1971-72 | California | 73 | 12 | 12 | 24 |
| 1972-73 | California | 47 | 6 | 15 | 21 |
| 1973-74 | California | 76 | 14 | 21 | 35 |
| 1974-75 | Kansas City | 77 | 8 | 11 | 19 |
| 1975-76 | Kansas City | 79 | 19 | 14 | 33 |
| 1976-77 | Colorado | 78 | 24 | 27 | 51 |
| 1977-78 | Colorado | 62 | 17 | 22 | 39 |
| 1978-79 | Colorado | 79 | 23 | 18 | 41 |
| 1979-80 | Colorado | 15 | 1 | 4 | 5 |
| **Totals** | | 684 | 144 | 175 | 319 |

**CROWDER, Bruce** *Forward*
b. Essex, Ont., Mar. 25, 1957

| | | | | | |
|---|---|---|---|---|---|
| 1981-82 | Boston | 63 | 16 | 11 | 27 |
| 1982-83 | Boston | 80 | 21 | 19 | 40 |
| **Totals** | | 143 | 37 | 30 | 67 |

**CROWDER, Keith Scott** *Forward*
b. Windsor, Ont., Jan. 6, 1959

| | | | | | |
|---|---|---|---|---|---|
| 1978-79 | Birmingham (WHA) | 5 | 1 | 0 | 1 |
| 1980-81 | Boston | 47 | 13 | 12 | 25 |
| 1981-82 | Boston | 71 | 23 | 21 | 44 |
| 1982-83 | Boston | 74 | 35 | 39 | 74 |
| **NHL Totals** | | 192 | 71 | 72 | 143 |
| **WHA Totals** | | 5 | 1 | 0 | 1 |

**CROZIER, Joseph Richard** *Defenseman*
b. Winnipeg, Man., Feb. 19, 1929

| | | | | | |
|---|---|---|---|---|---|
| 1959-60 | Toronto | 5 | 0 | 3 | 3 |

**CRUTCHFIELD, Nelson (Nels)**
*Defenseman-Forward*
b. Knowlton, Que., July 12, 1911

| | | | | | |
|---|---|---|---|---|---|
| 1934-35 | Montreal | — | 5 | 5 | 10 |

**CULLEN, Brian Joseph** *Forward*
b. Ottawa, Ont., Nov. 11, 1933

| | | | | | |
|---|---|---|---|---|---|
| 1954-55 | Toronto | 27 | 3 | 5 | 8 |
| 1955-56 | Toronto | 21 | 2 | 6 | 8 |
| 1956-57 | Toronto | 46 | 8 | 12 | 20 |
| 1957-58 | Toronto | 67 | 20 | 23 | 43 |
| 1958-59 | Toronto | 59 | 4 | 14 | 18 |
| 1959-60 | New York R | 64 | 8 | 21 | 29 |
| 1960-61 | New York R | 42 | 11 | 19 | 30 |
| **Totals** | | 326 | 56 | 100 | 156 |

**CULLEN, Charles Francis (Barry)** *Forward*
b. Ottawa, Ont., June 16, 1935

| | | | | | |
|---|---|---|---|---|---|
| 1955-56 | Toronto | 3 | 0 | 0 | 0 |
| 1956-57 | Toronto | 51 | 6 | 10 | 16 |
| 1957-58 | Toronto | 70 | 16 | 25 | 41 |
| 1958-59 | Toronto | 40 | 6 | 8 | 14 |
| 1959-60 | Detroit | 55 | 4 | 9 | 13 |
| **Totals** | | 219 | 32 | 52 | 84 |

**CULLEN, Raymond Murray** *Forward*
b. Ottawa, Ont., Sept. 20, 1941

| | | | | | |
|---|---|---|---|---|---|
| 1965-66 | New York R | 8 | 1 | 3 | 4 |
| 1966-67 | Detroit | 27 | 8 | 8 | 16 |
| 1967-68 | Minnesota | 67 | 28 | 25 | 53 |
| 1968-69 | Minnesota | 67 | 26 | 38 | 64 |
| 1969-70 | Minnesota | 74 | 17 | 28 | 45 |
| 1970-71 | Vancouver | 70 | 12 | 21 | 33 |
| **Totals** | | 313 | 92 | 123 | 215 |

**CUMMINS, Barry Kenneth** *Defenseman*
b. Regina, Sask., Jan. 25, 1949

| | | | | | |
|---|---|---|---|---|---|
| 1973-74 | California | 36 | 1 | 2 | 3 |

**CUNNEYWORTH, Randy** *Forward*
b. Etobicoke, Ont., May 10, 1961

| | | | | | |
|---|---|---|---|---|---|
| 1981-82 | Buffalo | 20 | 2 | 4 | 6 |

**CUNNINGHAM, James** *Forward*
b. St. Paul, Minn., Aug. 15, 1956

| | | | | | |
|---|---|---|---|---|---|
| 1977-78 | Philadelphia | 1 | 0 | 0 | 0 |

**CUNNINGHAM, Leslie Roy** *Forward*
b. Calgary, Alta., Oct. 4, 1913

| | | | | | |
|---|---|---|---|---|---|
| 1936-37 | New York A | 23 | 1 | 8 | 9 |
| 1939-40 | Chicago | 37 | 6 | 11 | 17 |
| **Totals** | | 60 | 7 | 19 | 26 |

**CUNNINGHAM, Robert Gordon** *Forward*
b. Welland, Ont., Feb. 26, 1941

| | | | | | |
|---|---|---|---|---|---|
| 1960-61 | New York R | 3 | 0 | 1 | 1 |
| 1961-62 | New York R | 1 | 0 | 0 | 0 |
| **Totals** | | 4 | 0 | 1 | 1 |

**CUPOLO, William Donald** *Forward*
b. Niagara Falls, Ont., Jan. 8, 1924

| | | | | | |
|---|---|---|---|---|---|
| 1944-45 | Boston | 47 | 11 | 13 | 24 |

**CURRIE, Glen** *Forward*
b. Montreal, Que., July 18, 1958

| | | | | | |
|---|---|---|---|---|---|
| 1979-80 | Washington | 32 | 2 | 0 | 2 |
| 1980-81 | Washington | 40 | 5 | 13 | 18 |
| 1981-82 | Washington | 43 | 7 | 7 | 14 |
| 1982-83 | Washington | 68 | 11 | 28 | 39 |
| **Totals** | | 183 | 25 | 48 | 73 |

**CURRIE, Hugh Roy** *Defenseman*
b. Saskatoon, Sask., Oct. 22, 1925

| | | | | | |
|---|---|---|---|---|---|
| 1950-51 | Montreal | 1 | 0 | 0 | 0 |

**CURRIE, Tony** *Forward*
b. Sydney Mines, N.S., Nov. 12, 1957

| | | | | | |
|---|---|---|---|---|---|
| 1977-78 | St Louis | 22 | 4 | 5 | 9 |
| 1978-79 | St Louis | 36 | 4 | 15 | 19 |
| 1979-80 | St Louis | 40 | 19 | 14 | 33 |
| 1980-81 | St Louis | 61 | 23 | 32 | 55 |
| 1981-82 | StL-Van | 60 | 23 | 25 | 48 |
| 1982-83 | Vancouver | 8 | 1 | 1 | 2 |
| **Totals** | | 227 | 74 | 92 | 166 |

**CURRY, Floyd James (Busher)** *Forward*
b. Chapleu, Ont., Aug. 11, 1925

| | | | | | |
|---|---|---|---|---|---|
| 1947-48 | Montreal | 31 | 1 | 5 | 6 |
| 1949-50 | Montreal | 49 | 8 | 8 | 16 |
| 1950-51 | Montreal | 69 | 13 | 14 | 27 |
| 1951-52 | Montreal | 64 | 20 | 18 | 38 |
| 1952-53 | Montreal | 68 | 16 | 6 | 22 |
| 1953-54 | Montreal | 70 | 13 | 8 | 21 |
| 1954-55 | Montreal | 68 | 11 | 10 | 21 |
| 1955-56 | Montreal | 70 | 14 | 18 | 32 |
| 1956-57 | Montreal | 70 | 7 | 9 | 16 |
| 1957-58 | Montreal | 42 | 2 | 3 | 5 |
| **Totals** | | 601 | 105 | 99 | 204 |

**CURTIS, Paul Edwin** *Defenseman*
b. Peterborough, Ont., Sept. 29, 1947

| | | | | | |
|---|---|---|---|---|---|
| 1969-70 | Montreal | 1 | 0 | 0 | 0 |
| 1970-71 | Los Angeles | 64 | 1 | 13 | 14 |
| 1971-72 | Los Angeles | 64 | 1 | 12 | 13 |
| 1972-73 | LA-StL | 56 | 1 | 9 | 10 |
| 1974-75 | Baltimore (WHA) | 76 | 4 | 15 | 19 |
| **NHL Totals** | | 185 | 3 | 34 | 37 |
| **WHA Totals** | | 76 | 4 | 15 | 19 |

**CUSHENAN, Ian Robertson** *Defenseman*
b. Hamilton, Ont., Nov. 29, 1933

| Season | Club | GP | G | A | Pts. |
|---|---|---|---|---|---|
| 1956-57 | Chicago | 11 | 0 | 0 | 0 |
| 1957-58 | Chicago | 61 | 2 | 8 | 10 |
| 1958-59 | Montreal | 35 | 1 | 2 | 3 |
| 1959-60 | New York R | 17 | 0 | 1 | 1 |
| 1963-64 | Detroit | 5 | 0 | 0 | 0 |
| | **Totals** | 129 | 3 | 11 | 14 |

**CUSSON, Jean** *Forward*
b. Verdun, Que., Oct. 5, 1942

| Season | Club | GP | G | A | Pts. |
|---|---|---|---|---|---|
| 1967-68 | Oakland | 2 | 0 | 0 | 0 |

**CYR, Denis** *Forward*
b. Verdun, Que., Feb. 4, 1961

| Season | Club | GP | G | A | Pts. |
|---|---|---|---|---|---|
| 1980-81 | Calgary | 10 | 1 | 4 | 5 |
| 1981-82 | Calgary | 45 | 12 | 10 | 22 |
| 1982-83 | Calg-Chi | 52 | 8 | 9 | 17 |
| | **Totals** | 107 | 21 | 23 | 44 |

**CYR, Paul** *Forward*
b. Port Alberni, B.C., Oct. 31, 1963

| Season | Club | GP | G | A | Pts. |
|---|---|---|---|---|---|
| 1982-83 | Buffalo | 36 | 15 | 12 | 27 |

**DAHLSTROM, Carl (Cully)** *Forward*
b. Minneapolis, Minn., July 3, 1913

| Season | Club | GP | G | A | Pts. |
|---|---|---|---|---|---|
| 1937-38 | Chicago | 48 | 10 | 9 | 19 |
| 1938-39 | Chicago | 48 | 6 | 14 | 20 |
| 1939-40 | Chicago | 45 | 11 | 19 | 30 |
| 1940-41 | Chicago | 40 | 11 | 14 | 25 |
| 1941-42 | Chicago | 33 | 13 | 14 | 27 |
| 1942-43 | Chicago | 38 | 11 | 13 | 24 |
| 1943-44 | Chicago | 50 | 20 | 22 | 42 |
| 1944-45 | Chicago | 40 | 6 | 13 | 19 |
| | **Totals** | 342 | 88 | 118 | 206 |

**DAIGLE, Roland Alain** *Forward*
b. Cap-de-la-Madeline, Que., Aug. 24, 1954

| Season | Club | GP | G | A | Pts. |
|---|---|---|---|---|---|
| 1974-75 | Chicago | 52 | 5 | 4 | 9 |
| 1975-76 | Chicago | 71 | 15 | 9 | 24 |
| 1976-77 | Chicago | 73 | 12 | 8 | 20 |
| 1977-78 | Chicago | 53 | 6 | 6 | 12 |
| 1978-79 | Chicago | 74 | 11 | 14 | 25 |
| 1979-80 | Chicago | 66 | 7 | 9 | 16 |
| | **Totals** | 399 | 56 | 50 | 106 |

**DAILEY, Robert Scott** *Defenseman*
b. Kingston, Ont., May 3, 1953

| Season | Club | GP | G | A | Pts. |
|---|---|---|---|---|---|
| 1973-74 | Vancouver | 76 | 7 | 17 | 24 |
| 1974-75 | Vancouver | 70 | 12 | 36 | 48 |
| 1975-76 | Vancouver | 67 | 15 | 24 | 39 |
| 1976-77 | Van-Phil | 76 | 9 | 30 | 39 |
| 1977-78 | Philadelphia | 76 | 21 | 36 | 57 |
| 1978-79 | Philadelphia | 70 | 9 | 30 | 39 |
| 1979-80 | Philadelphia | 61 | 13 | 26 | 39 |
| 1980-81 | Philadelphia | 53 | 7 | 27 | 34 |
| 1981-82 | Philadelphia | 12 | 1 | 5 | 6 |
| | **Totals** | 571 | 94 | 231 | 325 |

**DALEY, Patrick Lloyd** *Forward*
b. Marieville, France, Mar. 27, 1959

| Season | Club | GP | G | A | Pts. |
|---|---|---|---|---|---|
| 1979-80 | Winnipeg | 5 | 1 | 0 | 1 |
| 1980-81 | Winnipeg | 7 | 0 | 0 | 0 |
| | **Totals** | 12 | 1 | 0 | 1 |

**DAME, Aurella N. (Bunny)** *Forward*
b. Edmonton, Alta.

| Season | Club | GP | G | A | Pts. |
|---|---|---|---|---|---|
| 1941-42 | Montreal | 34 | 2 | 5 | 7 |

**DAMORE, Henry** *Forward*
b. Niagara Falls, Ont., July 17, 1918

| Season | Club | GP | G | A | Pts. |
|---|---|---|---|---|---|
| 1943-44 | New York R | 4 | 1 | 0 | 1 |

**DAOUST, Dan** *Forward*
b. Kirkland Lake, Ont., Feb. 29, 1960

| Season | Club | GP | G | A | Pts. |
|---|---|---|---|---|---|
| 1982-83 | Mont-Tor | 52 | 18 | 34 | 52 |

**DARRAGH, Harold Edward** *Forward*
b. Ottawa, Ont., Sept. 13, 1902

| Season | Club | GP | G | A | Pts. |
|---|---|---|---|---|---|
| 1925-26 | Pittsburgh Pi | 35 | 10 | 7 | 17 |
| 1926-27 | Pittsburgh Pi | 42 | 12 | 3 | 15 |
| 1927-28 | Pittsburgh Pi | 44 | 13 | 2 | 15 |
| 1928-29 | Pittsburgh Pi | 43 | 9 | 3 | 12 |
| 1929-30 | Pittsburgh Pi | 42 | 15 | 17 | 32 |
| 1930-31 | PhilQ-Bos | 35 | 3 | 5 | 8 |
| 1931-32 | Toronto | 48 | 5 | 10 | 15 |
| 1932-33 | Toronto | 19 | 1 | 2 | 3 |
| | **Totals** | 308 | 68 | 49 | 117 |

**DARRAGH, John Proctor (Jack)** *Forward*
b. Cornwall, Ont., Dec. 4, 1890

| Season | Club | GP | G | A | Pts. |
|---|---|---|---|---|---|
| 1917-18 | Ottawa | 18 | 14 | 0 | 14 |
| 1918-19 | Ottawa | 14 | 12 | 1 | 13 |
| 1919-20 | Ottawa | 22 | 22 | 5 | 27 |
| 1920-21 | Ottawa | 24 | 11 | 8 | 19 |
| 1922-23 | Ottawa | 24 | 7 | 7 | 14 |
| 1923-24 | Ottawa | 18 | 2 | 0 | 2 |
| | **Totals** | 120 | 68 | 21 | 89 |

**DAVID, Richard** *Forward*
b. Notre Dame de la Salette, Que., Apr. 8, 1958

| Season | Club | GP | G | A | Pts. |
|---|---|---|---|---|---|
| 1978-79 | Quebec (WHA) | 14 | 0 | 4 | 4 |
| 1979-80 | Quebec | 10 | 0 | 0 | 0 |
| 1981-82 | Quebec | 5 | 1 | 1 | 2 |
| 1982-83 | Quebec | 16 | 3 | 3 | 6 |
| | **NHL Totals** | 31 | 3 | 3 | 8 |
| | **WHA Totals** | 14 | 0 | 4 | 4 |

**DAVIDSON, Gordon John** *Defenseman*
b. Stratton, Ont., Aug. 5, 1919

| Season | Club | GP | G | A | Pts. |
|---|---|---|---|---|---|
| 1942-43 | New York R | 35 | 2 | 3 | 5 |
| 1943-44 | New York R | 16 | 1 | 3 | 4 |
| | **Totals** | 51 | 3 | 6 | 9 |

**DAVIDSON, Robert E.** *Forward*
b. Toronto, Ont., Feb. 10, 1912

| Season | Club | GP | G | A | Pts. |
|---|---|---|---|---|---|
| 1934-35 | Toronto | 5 | 0 | 0 | 0 |
| 1935-36 | Toronto | 35 | 4 | 4 | 8 |
| 1936-37 | Toronto | 46 | 8 | 7 | 15 |
| 1937-38 | Toronto | 48 | 3 | 17 | 20 |
| 1938-39 | Toronto | 47 | 4 | 10 | 14 |
| 1939-40 | Toronto | 48 | 8 | 18 | 26 |
| 1940-41 | Toronto | 37 | 3 | 6 | 9 |
| 1941-42 | Toronto | 37 | 6 | 20 | 26 |
| 1942-43 | Toronto | 50 | 13 | 23 | 36 |
| 1943-44 | Toronto | 47 | 19 | 28 | 47 |
| 1944-45 | Toronto | 50 | 17 | 18 | 35 |
| 1945-46 | Toronto | 41 | 9 | 9 | 18 |
| | **Totals** | 491 | 94 | 160 | 254 |

**DAVIE, Robert H. (Pinkle)** *Defenseman*
b. Beausejour, Man., Sept. 12, 1912

| Season | Club | GP | G | A | Pts. |
|---|---|---|---|---|---|
| 1933-34 | Boston | 6 | 0 | 0 | 0 |
| 1934-35 | Boston | 31 | 0 | 1 | 1 |
| 1935-36 | Boston | 2 | 0 | 0 | 0 |
| | **Totals** | 39 | 0 | 1 | 1 |

**DAVIS, Kim** *Forward*
b. Flin Flon, Man., Oct. 31, 1957

| Season | Club | GP | G | A | Pts. |
|---|---|---|---|---|---|
| 1977-78 | Pittsburgh | 1 | 0 | 0 | 0 |
| 1978-79 | Pittsburgh | 1 | 1 | 0 | 1 |
| 1979-80 | Pittsburgh | 24 | 3 | 7 | 10 |
| 1980-81 | Pitt-Tor | 10 | 1 | 0 | 1 |
| | **Totals** | 36 | 5 | 7 | 12 |

**DAVIS, Lorne Austin** *Forward*
b. Regina, Sask., July 20, 1930

| Season | Club | GP | G | A | Pts. |
|---|---|---|---|---|---|
| 1951-52 | Montreal | 3 | 1 | 1 | 2 |
| 1953-54 | Montreal | 37 | 6 | 4 | 10 |
| 1954-55 | Chi-Det | 30 | 0 | 5 | 5 |
| 1955-56 | Boston | 15 | 0 | 1 | 1 |
| 1959-60 | Boston | 10 | 1 | 1 | 2 |
| | **Totals** | 95 | 8 | 12 | 20 |

**DAVIS, Malcolm Sterling** *Forward*
b. Lockeport, N.S., Oct. 10, 1956

| Season | Club | GP | G | A | Pts. |
|---|---|---|---|---|---|
| 1978-79 | Detroit | 6 | 0 | 0 | 0 |
| 1979-80 | Detroit | 5 | 2 | 0 | 2 |
| 1982-83 | Buffalo | 24 | 8 | 12 | 22 |
| | **Totals** | 35 | 10 | 12 | 22 |

**DAVIS, Robert** *Defenseman*
b. Lachine, Que.

| Season | Club | GP | G | A | Pts. |
|---|---|---|---|---|---|
| 1932-33 | Detroit | 2 | 0 | 0 | 0 |

**DAVISON, Murray** *Defenseman*
b. Brantford, Ont., June 10, 1938

| Season | Club | GP | G | A | Pts. |
|---|---|---|---|---|---|
| 1965-66 | Boston | 1 | 0 | 0 | 0 |

**DAWES, Robert James** *Defenseman-Forward*
b. Saskatoon, Sask., Nov. 29, 1924

| Season | Club | GP | G | A | Pts. |
|---|---|---|---|---|---|
| 1946-47 | Toronto | 1 | 0 | 0 | 0 |
| 1948-49 | Toronto | 5 | 1 | 0 | 1 |
| 1949-50 | Toronto | 11 | 1 | 2 | 3 |
| 1950-51 | Montreal | 15 | 0 | 5 | 5 |
| | **Totals** | 32 | 2 | 7 | 9 |

**DAY, Clarence Henry (Happy)** *Defenseman*
b. Owen Sound, Ont., June 14, 1901

| Season | Club | GP | G | A | Pts. |
|---|---|---|---|---|---|
| 1924-25 | Toronto | 26 | 10 | 12 | 22 |
| 1925-26 | Toronto | 36 | 14 | 2 | 16 |
| 1926-27 | Toronto | 44 | 11 | 5 | 16 |
| 1927-28 | Toronto | 22 | 9 | 8 | 17 |
| 1928-29 | Toronto | 44 | 6 | 6 | 12 |
| 1929-30 | Toronto | 43 | 7 | 14 | 21 |
| 1930-31 | Toronto | 44 | 1 | 13 | 14 |
| 1931-32 | Toronto | 47 | 7 | 8 | 15 |
| 1932-33 | Toronto | 47 | 6 | 14 | 20 |
| 1933-34 | Toronto | 48 | 9 | 10 | 19 |
| 1934-35 | Toronto | 45 | 2 | 4 | 6 |
| 1935-36 | Toronto | 44 | 1 | 13 | 14 |
| 1936-37 | Toronto | 48 | 3 | 4 | 7 |
| 1937-38 | New York A | 43 | 0 | 3 | 3 |
| | **Totals** | 581 | 86 | 116 | 202 |

**DEA, William Fraser** *Forward*
b. Edmonton, Alta., Apr. 3, 1933

| Season | Club | GP | G | A | Pts. |
|---|---|---|---|---|---|
| 1953-54 | New York R | 14 | 1 | 1 | 2 |
| 1956-57 | Detroit | 09 | 15 | 15 | 30 |
| 1957-58 | Det-Chi | 63 | 9 | 12 | 21 |
| 1967-68 | Pittsburgh | 73 | 16 | 12 | 28 |
| 1968-69 | Pittsburgh | 66 | 10 | 8 | 18 |
| 1969-70 | Detroit | 70 | 10 | 3 | 13 |
| 1970-71 | Detroit | 42 | 6 | 3 | 9 |
| | **Totals** | 397 | 67 | 54 | 121 |

**DEACON, Donald** *Forward*
b. Regina, Sask., June 2, 1913

| Season | Club | GP | G | A | Pts. |
|---|---|---|---|---|---|
| 1936-37 | Detroit | 4 | 0 | 0 | 0 |
| 1938-39 | Detroit | 6 | 1 | 3 | 4 |
| 1939-40 | Detroit | 17 | 5 | 1 | 6 |
| | **Totals** | 27 | 6 | 4 | 10 |

**DEADMARSH, Ernest Charles (Butch)**
*Forward*
b. Trail, B.C., Apr. 5, 1950

| Season | Club | GP | G | A | Pts. |
|---|---|---|---|---|---|
| 1970-71 | Buffalo | 10 | 0 | 0 | 0 |
| 1971-72 | Buffalo | 12 | 1 | 1 | 2 |
| 1972-73 | Buf-Atl | 53 | 2 | 1 | 3 |
| 1973-74 | Atlanta | 42 | 6 | 1 | 7 |
| 1974-75 | Kansas City | 20 | 3 | 2 | 5 |
| 1974-75 | Vancouver (WHA) | 38 | 7 | 8 | 15 |
| 1975-76 | Calgary (WHA) | 79 | 26 | 28 | 54 |
| 1976-77 | Minn-Calg (WHA) | 73 | 22 | 21 | 43 |
| 1977-78 | Edm-Cin (WHA) | 65 | 8 | 9 | 17 |
| | **NHL Totals** | 134 | 12 | 5 | 17 |
| | **WHA Totals** | 255 | 63 | 66 | 129 |

| Season | Club | GP | G | A | Pts. |
|---|---|---|---|---|---|
| **DEAN, Barry James** *Forward* | | | | | |
| b. Maple Creek, Sask., Feb. 26, 1955 | | | | | |
| 1975-76 | Phoenix (WHA) | 71 | 9 | 25 | 34 |
| 1976-77 | Colorado | 79 | 14 | 25 | 39 |
| 1977-78 | Philadelphia | 56 | 7 | 18 | 25 |
| 1978-79 | Philadelphia | 30 | 4 | 13 | 17 |
| | **NHL Totals** | 165 | 25 | 56 | 81 |
| | **WHA Totals** | 71 | 9 | 25 | 34 |

| Season | Club | GP | G | A | Pts. |
|---|---|---|---|---|---|
| **DEBENEDET, Flavio Nelso** *Forward* | | | | | |
| b. Cardenona, Italy, Dec. 31, 1947 | | | | | |
| 1973-74 | Detroit | 15 | 4 | 1 | 5 |
| 1974-75 | Pittsburgh | 31 | 6 | 3 | 9 |
| | **Totals** | 46 | 10 | 4 | 14 |

| Season | Club | GP | G | A | Pts. |
|---|---|---|---|---|---|
| **DeBLOIS, Lucien** *Forward* | | | | | |
| b. Joliette, Que., June 21, 1957 | | | | | |
| 1977-78 | New York R | 71 | 22 | 8 | 30 |
| 1978-79 | New York R | 62 | 11 | 17 | 28 |
| 1979-80 | NYR-Col | 76 | 27 | 20 | 47 |
| 1980-81 | Colorado | 74 | 26 | 16 | 42 |
| 1981-82 | Winnipeg | 65 | 25 | 27 | 52 |
| 1982-83 | Winnipeg | 79 | 27 | 27 | 54 |
| | **Totals** | 427 | 138 | 115 | 253 |

| Season | Club | GP | G | A | Pts. |
|---|---|---|---|---|---|
| **DEBOL, David** *Forward* | | | | | |
| b. St. Clair Shores, Mich., Mar. 27, 1956 | | | | | |
| 1977-78 | Cincinnati (WHA) | 9 | 3 | 2 | 5 |
| 1978-79 | Cincinnati (WHA) | 59 | 10 | 27 | 37 |
| 1979-80 | Hartford | 48 | 12 | 14 | 26 |
| 1980-81 | Hartford | 44 | 14 | 12 | 26 |
| | **NHL Totals** | 92 | 26 | 26 | 52 |
| | **WHA Totals** | 68 | 13 | 29 | 42 |

| Season | Club | GP | G | A | Pts. |
|---|---|---|---|---|---|
| **DELMONTE, Armand Romeo (Dutch)** | | | | | |
| *Forward* | | | | | |
| b. Timmins, Ont., June 3, 1927 | | | | | |
| 1945-46 | Boston | 1 | 0 | 0 | 0 |

| Season | Club | GP | G | A | Pts. |
|---|---|---|---|---|---|
| **DELORME, Gilbert** *Defenseman* | | | | | |
| b. Longueil, Que., Mar. 23, 1961 | | | | | |
| 1981-82 | Montreal | 60 | 3 | 8 | 11 |
| 1982-83 | Montreal | 78 | 12 | 21 | 33 |
| | **Totals** | 138 | 15 | 29 | 44 |

| Season | Club | GP | G | A | Pts. |
|---|---|---|---|---|---|
| **DELORME, Ronald Elmer** *Forward* | | | | | |
| b. North Battleford, Sask., Sept. 3, 1955 | | | | | |
| 1975-76 | Denver (WHA) | 22 | 1 | 3 | 4 |
| 1976-77 | Colorado | 29 | 6 | 4 | 10 |
| 1977-78 | Colorado | 68 | 10 | 11 | 21 |
| 1978-79 | Colorado | 77 | 20 | 8 | 28 |
| 1979-80 | Colorado | 75 | 19 | 24 | 43 |
| 1980-81 | Colorado | 65 | 11 | 16 | 27 |
| 1981-82 | Vancouver | 59 | 9 | 8 | 17 |
| 1982-83 | Vancouver | 56 | 5 | 8 | 13 |
| | **NHL Totals** | 429 | 80 | 79 | 159 |
| | **WHA Totals** | 22 | 1 | 3 | 4 |

| Season | Club | GP | G | A | Pts. |
|---|---|---|---|---|---|
| **DeLORY, Valentine Arthur** *Forward* | | | | | |
| b. Toronto, Ont., Feb. 14, 1927 | | | | | |
| 1948-49 | New York R | 1 | 0 | 0 | 0 |

| Season | Club | GP | G | A | Pts. |
|---|---|---|---|---|---|
| **DELPARTE, Guy Philipp** *Forward* | | | | | |
| b. Prince Albert, Sask., Aug. 30, 1949 | | | | | |
| 1976-77 | Colorado | 48 | 1 | 8 | 9 |

| Season | Club | GP | G | A | Pts. |
|---|---|---|---|---|---|
| **DELVECCHIO, Alexander Peter (Alex)** | | | | | |
| *Forward* | | | | | |
| b. Ft. William, Ont., Dec. 4, 1931 | | | | | |
| 1950-51 | Detroit | 1 | 0 | 0 | 0 |
| 1951-52 | Detroit | 65 | 15 | 22 | 37 |
| 1952-53 | Detroit | 70 | 16 | 43 | 59 |
| 1953-54 | Detroit | 69 | 11 | 18 | 29 |
| 1954-55 | Detroit | 69 | 17 | 31 | 48 |
| 1955-56 | Detroit | 70 | 25 | 26 | 51 |
| 1956-57 | Detroit | 48 | 16 | 25 | 41 |
| 1957-58 | Detroit | 70 | 21 | 38 | 59 |
| 1958-59 | Detroit | 70 | 19 | 35 | 54 |
| 1959-60 | Detroit | 70 | 19 | 28 | 47 |
| 1960-61 | Detroit | 70 | 27 | 35 | 62 |
| 1961-62 | Detroit | 70 | 26 | 43 | 69 |
| 1962-63 | Detroit | 70 | 20 | 44 | 64 |
| 1963-64 | Detroit | 70 | 23 | 30 | 53 |
| 1964-65 | Detroit | 68 | 25 | 42 | 67 |
| 1965-66 | Detroit | 70 | 31 | 38 | 69 |
| 1966-67 | Detroit | 70 | 17 | 38 | 55 |
| 1967-68 | Detroit | 74 | 22 | 48 | 70 |
| 1968-69 | Detroit | 72 | 25 | 58 | 83 |
| 1969-70 | Detroit | 73 | 21 | 47 | 68 |
| 1970-71 | Detroit | 77 | 21 | 34 | 55 |
| 1971-72 | Detroit | 75 | 20 | 45 | 65 |
| 1972-73 | Detroit | 77 | 18 | 53 | 71 |
| 1973-74 | Detroit | 11 | 1 | 4 | 5 |
| | **Totals** | 1549 | 456 | 825 | 1281 |

| Season | Club | GP | G | A | Pts. |
|---|---|---|---|---|---|
| **DeMARCO, Albert (Ab)** *Forward* | | | | | |
| b. North Bay, Ont., May 10, 1916 | | | | | |
| 1938-39 | Chicago | — | 1 | 0 | 1 |
| 1939-40 | Chicago | — | 0 | 5 | 5 |
| 1942-43 | Tor-Bos | 7 | 4 | 2 | 6 |
| 1943-44 | Bos-NYR | 39 | 14 | 19 | 33 |
| 1944-45 | New York R | 50 | 24 | 30 | 54 |
| 1945-46 | New York R | 50 | 20 | 27 | 47 |
| 1946-47 | New York R | 44 | 9 | 10 | 19 |
| | **Totals** | — | 72 | 93 | 165 |

| Season | Club | GP | G | A | Pts. |
|---|---|---|---|---|---|
| **DeMARCO, Albert Thomas (Ab) Jr.** | | | | | |
| *Defenseman* | | | | | |
| b. North Bay, Ont., Feb. 27, 1949 | | | | | |
| 1969-70 | New York R | 3 | 0 | 0 | 0 |
| 1970-71 | New York R | 2 | 0 | 1 | 1 |
| 1971-72 | New York R | 48 | 4 | 7 | 11 |
| 1972-73 | NYR-StL | 65 | 8 | 22 | 30 |
| 1973-74 | StL-Pitt | 57 | 10 | 21 | 31 |
| 1974-75 | Pitt-Van | 69 | 12 | 15 | 27 |
| 1976-76 | Van-LA | 64 | 7 | 11 | 18 |
| 1976-77 | Los Angeles | 33 | 3 | 3 | 6 |
| 1978-79 | Boston | 3 | 0 | 0 | 0 |
| | **Totals** | 344 | 44 | 80 | 124 |

| Season | Club | GP | G | A | Pts. |
|---|---|---|---|---|---|
| **DEMERS, Antonio (Tony)** *Forward* | | | | | |
| b. Chambly Bassin, Que., July 22, 1917 | | | | | |
| 1937-38 | Montreal | 6 | 0 | 0 | 0 |
| 1939-40 | Montreal | 14 | 2 | 3 | 5 |
| 1940-41 | Montreal | 46 | 13 | 10 | 23 |
| 1941-42 | Montreal | 7 | 3 | 4 | 7 |
| 1942-43 | Montreal | 9 | 2 | 5 | 7 |
| 1943-44 | New York R | 1 | 0 | 0 | 0 |
| | **Totals** | 83 | 20 | 22 | 42 |

| Season | Club | GP | G | A | Pts. |
|---|---|---|---|---|---|
| **DENIS, Jean Paul (Johnny)** *Forward* | | | | | |
| b. Montreal, Que., Feb. 28, 1924 | | | | | |
| 1946-47 | New York R | 6 | 0 | 1 | 1 |
| 1949-50 | New York R | 4 | 0 | 1 | 1 |
| | **Totals** | 10 | 0 | 2 | 2 |

| Season | Club | GP | G | A | Pts. |
|---|---|---|---|---|---|
| **DENIS, Louis Gilbert (Lulu)** *Forward* | | | | | |
| b. Vonda, Sask., June 7, 1928 | | | | | |
| 1949-50 | Montreal | 2 | 0 | 1 | 1 |
| 1950-51 | Montreal | 1 | 0 | 0 | 0 |
| | **Totals** | 3 | 0 | 1 | 1 |

| Season | Club | GP | G | A | Pts. |
|---|---|---|---|---|---|
| **DENNENY, Corbett** *Forward* | | | | | |
| b. Cornwall, Ont., 1894 | | | | | |
| 1917-18 | Toronto | 21 | 20 | 0 | 20 |
| 1918-19 | Toronto | 16 | 7 | 3 | 10 |
| 1919-20 | Toronto | 23 | 23 | 12 | 35 |
| 1920-21 | Toronto | 20 | 17 | 6 | 23 |
| 1921-22 | Toronto | 24 | 19 | 7 | 26 |
| 1922-23 | Ottawa | 1 | 1 | 0 | 1 |
| 1923-24 | Hamilton | 23 | 0 | 0 | 0 |
| 1926-27 | Toronto | 29 | 7 | 1 | 8 |
| 1927-28 | Chicago | 18 | 5 | 0 | 5 |
| | **Totals** | 175 | 99 | 29 | 128 |

| Season | Club | GP | G | A | Pts. |
|---|---|---|---|---|---|
| **DENNENY, Cyril Joseph (Cy)** *Forward* | | | | | |
| b. Farran's Point, Ont., Dec. 23, 1891 | | | | | |
| 1917-18 | Ottawa | 22 | 36 | 0 | 36 |
| 1918-19 | Ottawa | 18 | 18 | 4 | 22 |
| 1919-20 | Ottawa | 22 | 16 | 2 | 18 |

| Season | Club | GP | G | A | Pts. |
|---|---|---|---|---|---|
| 1920-21 | Ottawa | 24 | 34 | 5 | 39 |
| 1921-22 | Ottawa | 22 | 27 | 12 | 39 |
| 1922-23 | Ottawa | 24 | 21 | 10 | 31 |
| 1923-24 | Ottawa | 21 | 22 | 1 | 23 |
| 1924-25 | Ottawa | 28 | 27 | 15 | 42 |
| 1925-26 | Ottawa | 36 | 24 | 12 | 36 |
| 1926-27 | Ottawa | 44 | 17 | 6 | 23 |
| 1927-28 | Ottawa | 44 | 3 | 0 | 3 |
| 1928-29 | Boston | 23 | 1 | 2 | 3 |
| | **Totals** | 328 | 246 | 69 | 315 |

| Season | Club | GP | G | A | Pts. |
|---|---|---|---|---|---|
| **DENNIS, Norman Marshall** *Forward* | | | | | |
| b. Aurora, Ont., Dec. 10, 1942 | | | | | |
| 1968-69 | St Louis | 2 | 0 | 0 | 0 |
| 1969-70 | St Louis | 5 | 3 | 0 | 3 |
| 1970-71 | St Louis | 4 | 0 | 0 | 0 |
| 1971-72 | St Louis | 1 | 0 | 0 | 0 |
| | **Totals** | 12 | 3 | 0 | 3 |

| Season | Club | GP | G | A | Pts. |
|---|---|---|---|---|---|
| **DENOIRD, Gerald** *Forward* | | | | | |
| 1922-23 | Toronto | 15 | 0 | 0 | 0 |

| Season | Club | GP | G | A | Pts. |
|---|---|---|---|---|---|
| **DERLAGO, William Anthony** *Forward* | | | | | |
| b. Birtle, Man., Aug. 25, 1958 | | | | | |
| 1978-79 | Vancouver | 9 | 4 | 4 | 8 |
| 1979-80 | Van-Tor | 77 | 16 | 27 | 43 |
| 1980-81 | Toronto | 80 | 35 | 39 | 74 |
| 1981-82 | Toronto | 75 | 34 | 50 | 84 |
| 1982-83 | Toronto | 58 | 13 | 24 | 37 |
| | **Totals** | 299 | 102 | 144 | 246 |

| Season | Club | GP | G | A | Pts. |
|---|---|---|---|---|---|
| **DESAULNIERS, Gerald** *Forward* | | | | | |
| b. Shawinigan Falls, Que., Dec. 31, 1928 | | | | | |
| 1950-51 | Montreal | 3 | 0 | 1 | 1 |
| 1952-53 | Montreal | 2 | 0 | 1 | 1 |
| 1953-54 | Montreal | 3 | 0 | 0 | 0 |
| | **Totals** | 8 | 0 | 2 | 2 |

| Season | Club | GP | G | A | Pts. |
|---|---|---|---|---|---|
| **DESILETS, Joffre Wilfred** *Forward* | | | | | |
| b. Capreal, Ont., Apr. 16, 1915 | | | | | |
| 1935-36 | Montreal | 38 | 7 | 6 | 13 |
| 1936-37 | Montreal | 48 | 7 | 12 | 19 |
| 1937-38 | Montreal | 32 | 6 | 7 | 13 |
| 1938-39 | Chicago | 48 | 11 | 13 | 24 |
| 1939-40 | Chicago | 26 | 6 | 7 | 13 |
| | **Totals** | 192 | 37 | 45 | 82 |

| Season | Club | GP | G | A | Pts. |
|---|---|---|---|---|---|
| **DESJARDINS, Victor A.** *Forward* | | | | | |
| b. Sault Ste. Marie, Mich., July 4, 1900 | | | | | |
| 1930-31 | Chicago | 38 | 3 | 12 | 15 |
| 1931-32 | New York R | 48 | 3 | 3 | 6 |
| | **Totals** | 86 | 6 | 15 | 21 |

| Season | Club | GP | G | A | Pts. |
|---|---|---|---|---|---|
| **DESLAURIERS, Jacques** *Defenseman* | | | | | |
| b. Montreal, Que., Sept. 3, 1928 | | | | | |
| 1955-56 | Montreal | 2 | 0 | 0 | 0 |

| Season | Club | GP | G | A | Pts. |
|---|---|---|---|---|---|
| **DEVINE, Kevin** *Forward* | | | | | |
| b. Charlottetown, P.E.I., Dec. 9, 1954 | | | | | |
| 1982-83 | New York I | 2 | 0 | 1 | 1 |

| Season | Club | GP | G | A | Pts. |
|---|---|---|---|---|---|
| **DEWAR, Thomas** *Defenseman* | | | | | |
| b. Frobisher, Sask., June 10, 1913 | | | | | |
| 1943-44 | New York R | 9 | 0 | 2 | 2 |

| Season | Club | GP | G | A | Pts. |
|---|---|---|---|---|---|
| **DEWSBURY, Albert Percy** *Defenseman* | | | | | |
| b. Goodrich, Ont., Apr. 12, 1926 | | | | | |
| 1946-47 | Detroit | 23 | 2 | 1 | 3 |
| 1949-50 | Detroit | 11 | 2 | 2 | 4 |
| 1950-51 | Chicago | 67 | 5 | 14 | 19 |
| 1951-52 | Chicago | 69 | 7 | 17 | 24 |
| 1952-53 | Chicago | 69 | 5 | 16 | 21 |
| 1953-54 | Chicago | 69 | 6 | 15 | 21 |
| 1954-55 | Chicago | 2 | 0 | 1 | 1 |
| 1955-56 | Chicago | 37 | 3 | 12 | 15 |
| | **Totals** | 347 | 30 | 78 | 108 |

**DHEERE, Marcel Albert (Ching)** *Forward*
b. St. Boniface, Man., Dec. 19, 1920

| Season | Club | GP | G | A | Pts. |
|---|---|---|---|---|---|
| 1942-43 | Montreal | 11 | 1 | 2 | 3 |

**DIACHUK, Edward** *Forward*
b. Vegreville, Alta., Aug. 16, 1936

| 1960-61 | Detroit | 12 | 0 | 0 | 0 |
|---|---|---|---|---|---|

**DICK, Harry** *Defenseman*
b. Port Colborne, Ont., Nov. 22, 1922

| 1946-47 | Chicago | 14 | 0 | 1 | 1 |
|---|---|---|---|---|---|

**DICKENS, Ernest Leslie** *Defenseman*
b. Winnipeg, Man., June 25, 1921

| 1941-42 | Toronto | 10 | 2 | 2 | 4 |
|---|---|---|---|---|---|
| 1945-46 | Toronto | 15 | 1 | 3 | 4 |
| 1947-48 | Chicago | 54 | 5 | 15 | 20 |
| 1948-49 | Chicago | 59 | 2 | 3 | 5 |
| 1949-50 | Chicago | 70 | 0 | 13 | 13 |
| 1950-51 | Chicago | 70 | 2 | 8 | 10 |
| | **Totals** | 278 | 12 | 44 | 56 |

**DICKENSON, John Herbert (Herb)** *Forward*
b. Mount Hope, Ont., June 11, 1931

| 1951-52 | New York R | 37 | 14 | 13 | 27 |
|---|---|---|---|---|---|
| 1952-53 | New York R | 11 | 4 | 4 | 8 |
| | **Totals** | 48 | 18 | 17 | 35 |

**DILL, Robert Edward** *Defenseman*
b. St. Paul, Minn., Apr. 25, 1920

| 1943-44 | New York R | 28 | 6 | 10 | 16 |
|---|---|---|---|---|---|
| 1944-45 | New York R | 48 | 9 | 5 | 14 |
| | **Totals** | 76 | 15 | 15 | 30 |

**DILLABOUGH, Robert Wellington** *Forward*
b. Belleville, Ont., Apr. 14, 1941

| 1961-62 | Detroit | 5 | 0 | 0 | 0 |
|---|---|---|---|---|---|
| 1964-65 | Detroit | 4 | 0 | 0 | 0 |
| 1965-66 | Boston | 53 | 7 | 13 | 20 |
| 1966-67 | Boston | 60 | 6 | 12 | 18 |
| 1967-68 | Pittsburgh | 47 | 7 | 12 | 19 |
| 1968-69 | Pitt-Oak | 62 | 7 | 12 | 19 |
| 1969-70 | Oakland | 52 | 5 | 5 | 10 |
| 1972-73 | Cleveland (WHA) | 72 | 8 | 8 | 16 |
| | **NHL Totals** | 283 | 32 | 54 | 86 |
| | **WHA Totals** | 72 | 8 | 8 | 16 |

**DILLON, Cecil Graham** *Forward*
b. Toledo, Ohio, Apr. 26, 1908

| 1930-31 | New York R | 25 | 7 | 3 | 10 |
|---|---|---|---|---|---|
| 1931-32 | New York R | 48 | 23 | 15 | 38 |
| 1932-33 | New York R | 48 | 21 | 10 | 31 |
| 1933-34 | New York R | 48 | 13 | 26 | 39 |
| 1934-35 | New York R | 48 | 25 | 9 | 34 |
| 1935-36 | New York R | 48 | 18 | 14 | 32 |
| 1936-37 | New York R | 48 | 20 | 11 | 31 |
| 1937-38 | New York R | 48 | 21 | 18 | 39 |
| 1938-39 | New York R | 48 | 12 | 15 | 27 |
| 1939-40 | Detroit | 44 | 7 | 10 | 17 |
| | **Totals** | 453 | 167 | 131 | 298 |

**DILLON, Gary Kevin** *Forward*
b. Toronto, Ont., Feb. 28, 1959

| 1980-81 | Colorado | 13 | 1 | 1 | 2 |
|---|---|---|---|---|---|

**DILLON, Gerald Wayne** *Forward*
b. Toronto, Ont., May 25, 1955

| 1973-74 | Toronto (WHA) | 71 | 30 | 35 | 65 |
|---|---|---|---|---|---|
| 1974-75 | Toronto (WHA) | 77 | 29 | 66 | 95 |
| 1975-76 | New York R | 79 | 21 | 24 | 45 |
| 1976-77 | New York R | 78 | 17 | 29 | 46 |
| 1977-78 | New York R | 59 | 5 | 13 | 18 |
| 1978-79 | Winnipeg | 13 | 0 | 0 | 0 |
| | **NHL Totals** | 229 | 43 | 66 | 109 |
| | **WHA Totals** | 148 | 59 | 101 | 160 |

**DINEEN, Gary** *Forward*
b. Montreal, Que., Dec. 24, 1943

| 1968-69 | Minnesota | 4 | 0 | 1 | 1 |
|---|---|---|---|---|---|

**DINEEN, Gord** *Defenseman*
b. Toronto, Ont., Sept. 21, 1962

| 1982-83 | New York I | 2 | 0 | 0 | 0 |
|---|---|---|---|---|---|

**DINEEN, William Patrick** *Forward*
b. Arvida, Que., Sept. 18, 1932

| 1953-54 | Detroit | 70 | 17 | 8 | 25 |
|---|---|---|---|---|---|
| 1954-55 | Detroit | 69 | 10 | 9 | 19 |
| 1955-56 | Detroit | 70 | 12 | 7 | 19 |
| 1956-57 | Detroit | 51 | 6 | 7 | 13 |
| 1957-58 | Det-Chi | 63 | 6 | 13 | 19 |
| | **Totals** | 323 | 51 | 44 | 95 |

**DINSMORE, Charles (Dinny)** *Forward*
b. Toronto, Ont., July 23, 1903

| 1924-25 | Montreal M | 30 | 2 | 1 | 3 |
|---|---|---|---|---|---|
| 1925-26 | Montreal M | 33 | 3 | 1 | 4 |
| 1926-27 | Montreal M | 28 | 1 | 0 | 1 |
| 1929-30 | Montreal M | 9 | 0 | 0 | 0 |
| | **Totals** | 100 | 6 | 2 | 8 |

**DIONNE, Marcel Elphege** *Forward*
b. Drummondville, Que., Aug. 3, 1951

| 1971-72 | Detroit | 78 | 28 | 49 | 77 |
|---|---|---|---|---|---|
| 1972-73 | Detroit | 77 | 40 | 50 | 90 |
| 1973-74 | Detroit | 74 | 24 | 54 | 78 |
| 1974-75 | Detroit | 80 | 47 | 74 | 121 |
| 1975-76 | Los Angeles | 80 | 40 | 54 | 94 |
| 1976-77 | Los Angeles | 80 | 53 | 69 | 122 |
| 1977-78 | Los Angeles | 70 | 36 | 43 | 79 |
| 1978-79 | Los Angeles | 80 | 59 | 71 | 130 |
| 1979-80 | Los Angeles | 80 | 53 | 84 | 137 |
| 1980-81 | Los Angeles | 80 | 58 | 77 | 135 |
| 1981-82 | Los Angeles | 78 | 50 | 67 | 117 |
| 1982-83 | Los Angeles | 80 | 56 | 51 | 107 |
| | **Totals** | 937 | 544 | 743 | 1287 |

**DOAK, Gary Walter** *Defenseman*
b. Goderich, Ont., Feb. 26, 1946

| 1965-66 | Det-Bos | 24 | 0 | 8 | 8 |
|---|---|---|---|---|---|
| 1966-67 | Boston | 29 | 0 | 1 | 1 |
| 1967-68 | Boston | 59 | 2 | 10 | 12 |
| 1968-69 | Boston | 23 | 3 | 3 | 6 |
| 1969-70 | Boston | 44 | 1 | 7 | 8 |
| 1970-71 | Vancouver | 77 | 2 | 10 | 12 |
| 1971-72 | NYR-Van | 55 | 1 | 11 | 12 |
| 1972-73 | Det-Bos | 49 | 0 | 5 | 5 |
| 1973-74 | Boston | 69 | 0 | 4 | 4 |
| 1974-75 | Boston | 40 | 0 | 0 | 0 |
| 1975-76 | Boston | 58 | 1 | 6 | 7 |
| 1976-77 | Boston | 76 | 3 | 13 | 16 |
| 1977-78 | Boston | 61 | 4 | 13 | 17 |
| 1978-79 | Boston | 63 | 6 | 11 | 17 |
| 1979-80 | Boston | 52 | 0 | 5 | 5 |
| 1980-81 | Boston | 11 | 0 | 0 | 0 |
| | **Totals** | 789 | 23 | 107 | 130 |

**DOBSON, James** *Forward*
b. Winnipeg, Man., Feb. 29, 1960

| 1979-80 | Minnesota | 1 | 0 | 0 | 0 |
|---|---|---|---|---|---|
| 1980-81 | Minnesota | 1 | 0 | 0 | 0 |
| 1981-82 | Minn-Col | 9 | 0 | 0 | 0 |
| | **Totals** | 11 | 0 | 0 | 0 |

**DOHERTY, Fred** *Forward*

| 1918-19 | Montreal M | 3 | 0 | 0 | 0 |
|---|---|---|---|---|---|

**DONALDSON, Robert Gary** *Forward*
b. Trail, B.C., July 15, 1952

| 1973-74 | Chicago | 1 | 0 | 0 | 0 |
|---|---|---|---|---|---|
| 1976-77 | Houston (WHA) | 5 | 0 | 0 | 0 |
| | **NHL Totals** | 1 | 0 | 0 | 0 |
| | **WHA Totals** | 5 | 0 | 0 | 0 |

**DONNELLY, Babe** *Defenseman*
b. Sault Ste. Marie, Ont., Dec. 22, 1895

| 1926-27 | Montreal M | 33 | 0 | 1 | 1 |
|---|---|---|---|---|---|

**DORAN, John Michael (Red)** *Defenseman*
b. Belleville, Ont., May 24, 1911

| 1933-34 | New York A | 39 | 1 | 4 | 5 |
|---|---|---|---|---|---|
| 1935-36 | New York A | 26 | 4 | 2 | 6 |
| 1936-37 | New York A | 23 | 0 | 1 | 1 |
| 1937-38 | Detroit | 7 | 0 | 0 | 0 |
| 1939-40 | Montreal C | 6 | 0 | 3 | 3 |
| | **Totals** | 101 | 5 | 10 | 15 |

**DORAN, Lloyd George** *Forward*
b. South Porcupine, Ont., Jan. 10, 1921

| 1946-47 | Detroit | 26 | 3 | 2 | 5 |
|---|---|---|---|---|---|

**DORATY, Kenneth Edward** *Forward*
b. Stittsville, Ont., June 23, 1906

| 1926-27 | Chicago | 20 | 0 | 0 | 0 |
|---|---|---|---|---|---|
| 1932-33 | Toronto | 38 | 5 | 11 | 16 |
| 1933-34 | Toronto | 34 | 9 | 10 | 19 |
| 1934-35 | Toronto | 11 | 1 | 4 | 5 |
| 1937-38 | Detroit | 3 | 0 | 1 | 1 |
| | **Totals** | 106 | 15 | 26 | 41 |

**DORE, Andre Hector** *Defenseman*
b. Montreal, Que., Feb. 2, 1958

| 1978-79 | New York R | 2 | 0 | 0 | 0 |
|---|---|---|---|---|---|
| 1979-80 | New York R | 2 | 0 | 0 | 0 |
| 1980-81 | New York R | 15 | 1 | 3 | 4 |
| 1981-82 | New York R | 56 | 4 | 16 | 20 |
| 1982-83 | NYR-StL | 77 | 5 | 27 | 32 |
| | **Totals** | 152 | 10 | 46 | 56 |

**DOREY, Robert James (Jim)** *Defenseman*
b. Kingston, Ont., Aug. 17, 1947

| 1968-69 | Toronto | 61 | 8 | 22 | 30 |
|---|---|---|---|---|---|
| 1969-70 | Toronto | 46 | 6 | 11 | 17 |
| 1970-71 | Toronto | 74 | 7 | 22 | 29 |
| 1971-72 | Tor-NYR | 51 | 4 | 19 | 23 |
| 1972-73 | New England (WHA) | 75 | 7 | 56 | 63 |
| 1973-74 | New England (WHA) | 77 | 6 | 40 | 46 |
| 1974-75 | NE-Tor (WHA) | 74 | 16 | 40 | 56 |
| 1975-76 | Toronto (WHA) | 74 | 9 | 51 | 60 |
| 1976-77 | Quebec (WHA) | 73 | 13 | 34 | 47 |
| 1977-78 | Quebec (WHA) | 26 | 1 | 9 | 10 |
| 1978-79 | Quebec (WHA) | 32 | 0 | 2 | 2 |
| | **NHL Totals** | 232 | 25 | 74 | 99 |
| | **WHA Totals** | 431 | 52 | 232 | 284 |

**DORNHOEFER, Gerhardt Otto (Gary)**
*Forward*
b. Kitchener, Ont., Feb. 2, 1943

| 1963-64 | Boston | 32 | 12 | 10 | 22 |
|---|---|---|---|---|---|
| 1964-65 | Boston | 20 | 0 | 1 | 1 |
| 1965-66 | Boston | 10 | 0 | 1 | 1 |
| 1966-67 | Philadelphia | 65 | 13 | 30 | 43 |
| 1967-68 | Philadelphia | 60 | 8 | 16 | 24 |
| 1969-70 | Philadelphia | 65 | 26 | 29 | 55 |
| 1970-71 | Philadelphia | 57 | 20 | 20 | 40 |
| 1971-72 | Philadelphia | 75 | 17 | 32 | 49 |
| 1972-73 | Philadelphia | 77 | 30 | 49 | 79 |
| 1973-74 | Philadelphia | 57 | 11 | 39 | 50 |
| 1974-75 | Philadelphia | 69 | 17 | 27 | 44 |
| 1975-76 | Philadelphia | 74 | 28 | 35 | 63 |
| 1976-77 | Philadelphia | 79 | 25 | 34 | 59 |
| 1977-78 | Philadelphia | 47 | 7 | 5 | 12 |
| | **Totals** | 787 | 214 | 328 | 542 |

**DOROHOY, Edward** *Forward*
b. Medicine Hat, Alta., Mar. 13, 1929

| 1948-49 | Montreal | 16 | 0 | 0 | 0 |
|---|---|---|---|---|---|

**DOUGLAS, Jordy Paul** *Forward*
b. Winnipeg, Man., Jan. 20, 1958

| 1978-79 | New England (WHA) | 51 | 6 | 10 | 16 |
|---|---|---|---|---|---|
| 1979-80 | Hartford | 77 | 33 | 24 | 57 |
| 1980-81 | Hartford | 55 | 13 | 9 | 22 |
| 1981-82 | Hartford | 33 | 10 | 7 | 17 |
| 1982-83 | Minnesota | 68 | 13 | 14 | 27 |
| | **NHL Totals** | 233 | 69 | 54 | 123 |
| | **WHA Totals** | 51 | 6 | 10 | 16 |

| Season | Club | GP | G | A | Pts. |
|--------|------|----|----|----|------|

**DOUGLAS, Kent Gemmell** *Defenseman*
b. Cobalt, Ont., Feb. 6, 1936

| Season | Club | GP | G | A | Pts. |
|--------|------|----|----|----|------|
| 1962-63 | Toronto | 70 | 7 | 15 | 22 |
| 1963-64 | Toronto | 43 | 0 | 1 | 1 |
| 1964-65 | Toronto | 67 | 5 | 23 | 28 |
| 1965-66 | Toronto | 64 | 6 | 14 | 20 |
| 1966-67 | Toronto | 39 | 2 | 12 | 14 |
| 1967-68 | Oak-Det | 76 | 11 | 21 | 32 |
| 1968-69 | Detroit | 69 | 2 | 29 | 31 |
| 1972-73 | New York (WHA) | 60 | 3 | 15 | 18 |
| | **NHL Totals** | 428 | 33 | 115 | 148 |
| | **WHA Totals** | 60 | 3 | 15 | 18 |

**DOUGLAS, Leslie** *Forward*
b. Perth, Ont., Dec. 5, 1918

| Season | Club | GP | G | A | Pts. |
|--------|------|----|----|----|------|
| 1940-41 | Detroit | 18 | 1 | 2 | 3 |
| 1942-43 | Detroit | 21 | 5 | 8 | 13 |
| 1945-46 | Detroit | 1 | 0 | 0 | 0 |
| 1946-47 | Detroit | 12 | 0 | 2 | 2 |
| | **Totals** | 52 | 6 | 12 | 18 |

**DOWNIE, David M.** *Forward*
b. Burk's Falls, Ont., Mar. 11, 1909

| Season | Club | GP | G | A | Pts. |
|--------|------|----|----|----|------|
| 1932-33 | Toronto | — | 0 | 1 | 1 |

**DRAPER, Bruce** *Forward*
b. Toronto, Ont., Oct. 2, 1940

| Season | Club | GP | G | A | Pts. |
|--------|------|----|----|----|------|
| 1962-63 | Toronto | 1 | 0 | 0 | 0 |

**DRILLON, Gordon Arthur** *Forward*
b. Moncton, N.B., Oct. 23, 1914

| Season | Club | GP | G | A | Pts. |
|--------|------|----|----|----|------|
| 1936-37 | Toronto | 41 | 16 | 17 | 33 |
| 1937-38 | Toronto | 48 | 26 | 26 | 52 |
| 1938-39 | Toronto | 40 | 18 | 16 | 34 |
| 1939-40 | Toronto | 43 | 21 | 19 | 40 |
| 1940-41 | Toronto | 42 | 23 | 21 | 44 |
| 1941-42 | Toronto | 48 | 23 | 18 | 41 |
| 1942-43 | Montreal | 49 | 28 | 22 | 50 |
| | **Totals** | 311 | 155 | 139 | 294 |

**DRISCOLL, Peter John** *Forward*
b. Kingston, Ont., Oct. 27, 1954

| Season | Club | GP | G | A | Pts. |
|--------|------|----|----|----|------|
| 1974-75 | Vancouver (WHA) | 21 | 3 | 2 | 5 |
| 1975-76 | Calgary (WHA) | 75 | 16 | 18 | 34 |
| 1976-77 | Calgary (WHA) | 76 | 23 | 29 | 52 |
| 1977-78 | Que-Ind (WHA) | 77 | 28 | 28 | 56 |
| 1978-79 | Ind-Edm (WHA) | 77 | 20 | 24 | 44 |
| 1979-80 | Edmonton | 39 | 1 | 5 | 6 |
| 1980-81 | Edmonton | 21 | 2 | 3 | 5 |
| | **NHL Totals** | 60 | 3 | 8 | 11 |
| | **WHA Totals** | 326 | 90 | 101 | 191 |

**DROUILLARD, Clarence (Clare)** *Forward*
b. Windsor, Ont., Mar. 2, 1914

| Season | Club | GP | G | A | Pts. |
|--------|------|----|----|----|------|
| 1937-38 | Detroit | 10 | 0 | 1 | 1 |

**DROLET, Rene Georges** *Forward*
b. Quebec, Que., Nov. 13, 1944

| Season | Club | GP | G | A | Pts. |
|--------|------|----|----|----|------|
| 1971-72 | Philadelphia | 1 | 0 | 0 | 0 |
| 1974-75 | Detroit | 1 | 0 | 0 | 0 |
| | **Totals** | 2 | 0 | 0 | 0 |

**DROUIN, Jude** *Forward*
b. Mont-Louis, Que., Oct. 28, 1948

| Season | Club | GP | G | A | Pts. |
|--------|------|----|----|----|------|
| 1968-69 | Montreal | 9 | 0 | 1 | 1 |
| 1969-70 | Montreal | 3 | 0 | 0 | 0 |
| 1970-71 | Minnesota | 75 | 16 | 52 | 68 |
| 1971-72 | Minnesota | 63 | 13 | 43 | 56 |
| 1972-73 | Minnesota | 78 | 27 | 46 | 73 |
| 1973-74 | Minnesota | 65 | 19 | 24 | 43 |
| 1974-75 | Minn-NYI | 78 | 18 | 36 | 54 |
| 1975-76 | New York I | 76 | 21 | 41 | 62 |
| 1976-77 | New York I | 78 | 24 | 29 | 53 |
| 1977-78 | New York I | 56 | 5 | 17 | 22 |
| 1979-80 | Winnipeg | 78 | 8 | 16 | 24 |
| 1980-81 | Winnipeg | 7 | 0 | 0 | 0 |
| | **Totals** | 666 | 151 | 305 | 456 |

**DROUIN, Paul Emile (Polly)** *Forward*
b. Ottawa, Ont., Jan. 1916

| Season | Club | GP | G | A | Pts. |
|--------|------|----|----|----|------|
| 1935-36 | Montreal | 30 | 1 | 8 | 9 |
| 1936-37 | Montreal | 4 | 0 | 0 | 0 |
| 1937-38 | Montreal | 31 | 7 | 13 | 20 |
| 1938-39 | Montreal | 28 | 7 | 11 | 18 |
| 1939-40 | Montreal | 42 | 4 | 11 | 15 |
| 1940-41 | Montreal | 21 | 4 | 7 | 11 |
| | **Totals** | 156 | 23 | 50 | 73 |

**DRUMMOND, James** *Defenseman*
b. Toronto, Ont., Oct. 20, 1918

| Season | Club | GP | G | A | Pts. |
|--------|------|----|----|----|------|
| 1944-45 | New York R | 2 | 0 | 0 | 0 |

**DRURY, Herbert** *Defenseman-Forward*
b. 1895

| Season | Club | GP | G | A | Pts. |
|--------|------|----|----|----|------|
| 1925-26 | Pittsburgh Pi | 33 | 6 | 2 | 8 |
| 1926-27 | Pittsburgh Pi | 42 | 5 | 1 | 6 |
| 1927-28 | Pittsburgh Pi | 43 | 6 | 4 | 10 |
| 1928-29 | Pittsburgh Pi | 44 | 5 | 4 | 9 |
| 1929-30 | Pittsburgh Pi | 27 | 2 | 0 | 2 |
| 1930-31 | Philadelphia Q | 24 | 0 | 2 | 2 |
| | **Totals** | 213 | 24 | 13 | 37 |

**DUBE, Joseph Gilles** *Forward*
b. Sherbrooke, Que., June 2, 1927

| Season | Club | GP | G | A | Pts. |
|--------|------|----|----|----|------|
| 1949-50 | Montreal | 12 | 1 | 2 | 3 |

**DUBE, Normand** *Forward*
b. Sherbrooke, Que., Sept. 12, 1951

| Season | Club | GP | G | A | Pts. |
|--------|------|----|----|----|------|
| 1974-75 | Kansas City | 56 | 8 | 10 | 18 |
| 1975-76 | Kansas City | 1 | 0 | 0 | 0 |
| 1976-77 | Quebec (WHA) | 39 | 15 | 18 | 33 |
| 1977-78 | Quebec (WHA) | 73 | 16 | 31 | 47 |
| 1978-79 | Quebec (WHA) | 36 | 2 | 13 | 15 |
| | **Totals** | 205 | 41 | 72 | 113 |

**DUCHESNE, Gaetan** *Forward*
b. Quebec City, Que., July 11, 1961

| Season | Club | GP | G | A | Pts. |
|--------|------|----|----|----|------|
| 1981-82 | Washington | 74 | 9 | 14 | 23 |
| 1982-83 | Washington | 77 | 18 | 19 | 37 |
| | **Totals** | 151 | 27 | 33 | 60 |

**DUDLEY, Richard Clarence (Rick)** *Forward*
b. Toronto, Ont., Jan. 31, 1949

| Season | Club | GP | G | A | Pts. |
|--------|------|----|----|----|------|
| 1972-73 | Buffalo | 6 | 0 | 1 | 1 |
| 1973-74 | Buffalo | 67 | 13 | 13 | 26 |
| 1974-75 | Buffalo | 78 | 31 | 39 | 70 |
| 1975-76 | Cincinnati (WHA) | 74 | 43 | 38 | 81 |
| 1976-77 | Cincinnati (WHA) | 77 | 41 | 47 | 88 |
| 1977-78 | Cincinnati (WHA) | 72 | 30 | 41 | 71 |
| 1978-79 | Cincinnati (WHA) | 47 | 17 | 20 | 37 |
| 1978-79 | Buffalo | 24 | 5 | 6 | 11 |
| 1979-80 | Buffalo | 66 | 11 | 22 | 33 |
| 1980-81 | Buf-Winn | 68 | 15 | 18 | 33 |
| | **NHL Totals** | 309 | 75 | 99 | 174 |
| | **WHA Totals** | 270 | 131 | 146 | 277 |

**DUFF, Terrance Richard (Dick)** *Forward*
b. Kirkland Lake, Ont., Feb. 18, 1936

| Season | Club | GP | G | A | Pts. |
|--------|------|----|----|----|------|
| 1954-55 | Toronto | 3 | 0 | 0 | 0 |
| 1955-56 | Toronto | 69 | 18 | 19 | 37 |
| 1956-57 | Toronto | 70 | 26 | 14 | 40 |
| 1957-58 | Toronto | 65 | 26 | 23 | 49 |
| 1958-59 | Toronto | 69 | 29 | 24 | 53 |
| 1959-60 | Toronto | 67 | 19 | 22 | 41 |
| 1960-61 | Toronto | 67 | 16 | 17 | 33 |
| 1961-62 | Toronto | 51 | 17 | 20 | 37 |
| 1962-63 | Toronto | 69 | 16 | 19 | 35 |
| 1963-64 | Tor-NYR | 66 | 11 | 14 | 25 |
| 1964-65 | NYR-Mont | 69 | 12 | 16 | 28 |
| 1965-66 | Montreal | 63 | 21 | 24 | 45 |
| 1966-67 | Montreal | 51 | 12 | 11 | 23 |
| 1967-68 | Montreal | 66 | 25 | 21 | 46 |
| 1968-69 | Montreal | 68 | 19 | 21 | 40 |
| 1969-70 | Mont-LA | 49 | 6 | 9 | 15 |
| 1970-71 | LA-Buf | 60 | 8 | 13 | 21 |
| 1971-72 | Buffalo | 8 | 2 | 2 | 4 |
| | **Totals** | 1030 | 283 | 289 | 572 |

**DUFOUR, Luc** *Forward*
b. Chicoutimi, Que., Feb. 13, 1963

| Season | Club | GP | G | A | Pts. |
|--------|------|----|----|----|------|
| 1982-83 | Boston | 73 | 14 | 11 | 25 |

**DUFOUR, Marc** *Forward*
b. Trois-Rivieres, Que., Sept. 11, 1941

| Season | Club | GP | G | A | Pts. |
|--------|------|----|----|----|------|
| 1963-64 | New York R | 10 | 1 | 0 | 1 |
| 1964-65 | New York R | 2 | 0 | 0 | 0 |
| 1968-69 | Los Angeles | 2 | 0 | 0 | 0 |
| | **Totals** | 14 | 1 | 0 | 1 |

**DUGGAN, Jack** *Defenseman*

| Season | Club | GP | G | A | Pts. |
|--------|------|----|----|----|------|
| 1925-26 | Ottawa | 27 | 0 | 0 | 0 |

**DUGUAY, Ronald** *Forward*
b. Sudbury, Ont., July 6, 1957

| Season | Club | GP | G | A | Pts. |
|--------|------|----|----|----|------|
| 1977-78 | New York R | 71 | 20 | 20 | 40 |
| 1978-79 | New York R | 79 | 27 | 36 | 63 |
| 1979-80 | New York R | 73 | 28 | 22 | 50 |
| 1980-81 | New York R | 50 | 17 | 21 | 38 |
| 1981-82 | New York R | 72 | 40 | 36 | 76 |
| 1982-83 | New York R | 72 | 19 | 25 | 44 |
| | **Totals** | 417 | 151 | 160 | 311 |

**DUGUID, Lorne Wallace** *Forward*
b. Bolton, Ont., Apr. 4, 1910

| Season | Club | GP | G | A | Pts. |
|--------|------|----|----|----|------|
| 1931-32 | Montreal M | 15 | 0 | 0 | 0 |
| 1932-33 | Montreal M | 48 | 4 | 7 | 11 |
| 1933-34 | Montreal M | 5 | 0 | 1 | 1 |
| 1934-35 | Detroit | 33 | 3 | 3 | 6 |
| 1935-36 | Boston | 35 | 1 | 4 | 5 |
| 1936-37 | Boston | 2 | 1 | 0 | 1 |
| | **Totals** | 138 | 9 | 15 | 24 |

**DUMART, Woodrow Wilson Clarence (Woody and Porky)** *Forward*
b. Kitchener, Ont., Dec. 23, 1916

| Season | Club | GP | G | A | Pts. |
|--------|------|----|----|----|------|
| 1935-36 | Boston | 1 | 0 | 0 | 0 |
| 1936-37 | Boston | 17 | 4 | 4 | 8 |
| 1937-38 | Boston | 48 | 13 | 14 | 27 |
| 1938-39 | Boston | 46 | 14 | 15 | 29 |
| 1939-40 | Boston | 48 | 22 | 21 | 43 |
| 1940-41 | Boston | 40 | 18 | 15 | 33 |
| 1941-42 | Boston | 35 | 14 | 15 | 29 |
| 1945-46 | Boston | 50 | 22 | 12 | 34 |
| 1946-47 | Boston | 60 | 24 | 28 | 52 |
| 1947-48 | Boston | 59 | 21 | 16 | 37 |
| 1948-49 | Boston | 59 | 11 | 12 | 23 |
| 1949-50 | Boston | 69 | 14 | 25 | 39 |
| 1950-51 | Boston | 70 | 20 | 21 | 41 |
| 1951-52 | Boston | 39 | 5 | 8 | 13 |
| 1952-53 | Boston | 62 | 5 | 9 | 14 |
| 1953-54 | Boston | 69 | 4 | 3 | 7 |
| | **Totals** | 772 | 211 | 218 | 429 |

**DUNCAN, Arthur** *Defenseman*

| Season | Club | GP | G | A | Pts. |
|--------|------|----|----|----|------|
| 1926-27 | Detroit | 33 | 3 | 2 | 5 |
| 1927-28 | Toronto | 43 | 7 | 5 | 12 |
| 1928-29 | Toronto | 39 | 4 | 4 | 8 |
| 1920-30 | Toronto | 38 | 4 | 5 | 9 |
| 1930-31 | Toronto | 2 | 0 | 0 | 0 |
| | **Totals** | 155 | 18 | 16 | 34 |

**DUNLAP, Frank** *Forward*

| Season | Club | GP | G | A | Pts. |
|--------|------|----|----|----|------|
| 1943-44 | Toronto | 5 | 0 | 1 | 1 |

**DUNLOP, Blake Robert** *Forward*
b. Hamilton, Ont., Apr. 4, 1953

| Season | Club | GP | G | A | Pts. |
|--------|------|----|----|----|------|
| 1973-74 | Minnesota | 12 | 0 | 0 | 0 |
| 1974-75 | Minnesota | 52 | 9 | 18 | 27 |
| 1975-76 | Minnesota | 33 | 9 | 11 | 20 |
| 1976-77 | Minnesota | 3 | 0 | 1 | 1 |
| 1977-78 | Philadelphia | 3 | 0 | 1 | 1 |
| 1978-79 | Philadelphia | 66 | 20 | 28 | 48 |
| 1979-80 | St Louis | 72 | 18 | 27 | 45 |
| 1980-81 | St Louis | 80 | 20 | 67 | 87 |
| 1981-82 | St Louis | 77 | 25 | 53 | 78 |
| 1982-83 | St Louis | 78 | 22 | 44 | 66 |
| | **Totals** | 476 | 123 | 250 | 373 |

| Season | Club | GP | G | A | Pts. |
|---|---|---|---|---|---|

**DUNN, David George** *Defenseman*
b. Wapella, Sask., Aug. 19, 1948

| Season | Club | GP | G | A | Pts. |
|---|---|---|---|---|---|
| 1973-74 | Vancouver | 68 | 11 | 22 | 33 |
| 1974-75 | Van-Tor | 73 | 3 | 11 | 14 |
| 1975-76 | Toronto | 43 | 0 | 8 | 8 |
| 1976-77 | Winnipeg (WHA) | 40 | 3 | 11 | 14 |
| 1977-78 | Winnipeg (WHA) | 66 | 6 | 20 | 26 |
| | **NHL Totals** | 184 | 14 | 41 | 55 |
| | **WHA Totals** | 106 | 9 | 31 | 40 |

**DUNN, Richard L.** *Defenseman*
b. Boston, Mass., May 12, 1957

| Season | Club | GP | G | A | Pts. |
|---|---|---|---|---|---|
| 1977-78 | Buffalo | 25 | 0 | 3 | 3 |
| 1978-79 | Buffalo | 24 | 0 | 3 | 3 |
| 1979-80 | Buffalo | 80 | 7 | 31 | 38 |
| 1980-81 | Buffalo | 79 | 7 | 42 | 49 |
| 1981-82 | Buffalo | 72 | 7 | 19 | 26 |
| 1982-83 | Calgary | 80 | 3 | 11 | 14 |
| | **Totals** | 360 | 24 | 109 | 133 |

**DUPERE, Denis Gilles** *Forward*
b. Jonquiere, Que., June 21, 1948

| Season | Club | GP | G | A | Pts. |
|---|---|---|---|---|---|
| 1970-71 | Toronto | 20 | 1 | 2 | 3 |
| 1971-72 | Toronto | 77 | 7 | 10 | 17 |
| 1972-73 | Toronto | 61 | 13 | 23 | 36 |
| 1973-74 | Toronto | 34 | 8 | 9 | 17 |
| 1974-75 | Wash-StL | 75 | 23 | 21 | 44 |
| 1975-76 | Kansas City | 43 | 6 | 8 | 14 |
| 1976-77 | Colorado | 57 | 7 | 11 | 18 |
| 1977-78 | Colorado | 54 | 15 | 15 | 30 |
| | **Totals** | 421 | 80 | 99 | 179 |

**DUPONT, Andre (Moose)** *Defenseman*
b. Trois-Rivières, Que., July 27, 1949

| Season | Club | GP | G | A | Pts. |
|---|---|---|---|---|---|
| 1970-71 | New York R | 7 | 1 | 2 | 3 |
| 1971-72 | St Louis | 60 | 3 | 10 | 13 |
| 1972-73 | StL-Phil | 71 | 4 | 26 | 30 |
| 1973-74 | Philadelphia | 75 | 3 | 20 | 23 |
| 1974-75 | Philadelphia | 80 | 11 | 21 | 32 |
| 1975-76 | Philadelphia | 75 | 9 | 27 | 36 |
| 1976-77 | Philadelphia | 69 | 10 | 19 | 29 |
| 1977-78 | Philadelphia | 69 | 2 | 12 | 14 |
| 1978-79 | Philadelphia | 77 | 3 | 9 | 12 |
| 1979-80 | Philadelphia | 58 | 1 | 7 | 8 |
| 1980-81 | Quebec | 63 | 5 | 8 | 13 |
| 1981-82 | Quebec | 60 | 4 | 12 | 16 |
| 1982-83 | Quebec | 46 | 3 | 12 | 15 |
| | **Totals** | 810 | 59 | 185 | 244 |

**DUPONT, Jerome** *Defenseman*
b. Ottawa, Ont., Feb. 21, 1962

| Season | Club | GP | G | A | Pts. |
|---|---|---|---|---|---|
| 1981-82 | Chicago | 34 | 0 | 4 | 4 |
| 1982-83 | Chicago | 1 | 0 | 0 | 0 |
| | **Totals** | 35 | 0 | 4 | 4 |

**DUPONT, Normand** *Forward*
b. Montreal, Que., Feb. 5, 1957

| Season | Club | GP | G | A | Pts. |
|---|---|---|---|---|---|
| 1979-80 | Montreal | 35 | 1 | 3 | 4 |
| 1980-81 | Winnipeg | 80 | 27 | 26 | 53 |
| 1981-82 | Winnipeg | 62 | 13 | 25 | 38 |
| 1982-83 | Winnipeg | 39 | 7 | 16 | 23 |
| | **Totals** | 216 | 48 | 70 | 118 |

**DURBANO, Harry Steven (Steve)**
*Defenseman*
b. Toronto, Ont., Dec. 12, 1951

| Season | Club | GP | G | A | Pts. |
|---|---|---|---|---|---|
| 1972-73 | St Louis | 49 | 3 | 18 | 21 |
| 1973-74 | StL-Pitt | 69 | 8 | 19 | 27 |
| 1974-75 | Pittsburgh | 1 | 0 | 1 | 1 |
| 1975-76 | Pitt-KC | 69 | 1 | 19 | 20 |
| 1976-77 | Colorado | 19 | 0 | 2 | 2 |
| 1977-78 | Birmingham (WHA) | 45 | 6 | 4 | 10 |
| 1978-79 | St Louis | 13 | 1 | 1 | 2 |
| | **NHL Totals** | 220 | 13 | 60 | 73 |
| | **WHA Totals** | 45 | 6 | 4 | 10 |

**DURIS, Vitezslav** *Defenseman*
b. Pizen, Czechoslovakia., Jan. 5, 1954

| Season | Club | GP | G | A | Pts. |
|---|---|---|---|---|---|
| 1980-81 | Toronto | 57 | 1 | 12 | 13 |
| 1982-83 | Toronto | 32 | 2 | 8 | 10 |
| | **Totals** | 89 | 3 | 20 | 23 |

**DUSSAULT, Joseph Normand (Norm)**
*Forward*
b. Springfield, Mass., Sept. 26, 1925

| Season | Club | GP | G | A | Pts. |
|---|---|---|---|---|---|
| 1947-48 | Montreal | 28 | 5 | 10 | 15 |
| 1948-49 | Montreal | 47 | 9 | 8 | 17 |
| 1940-50 | Montreal | 67 | 13 | 24 | 37 |
| 1950-51 | Montreal | 64 | 4 | 20 | 24 |
| | **Totals** | 206 | 31 | 62 | 93 |

**DUTKOWSKI, Laudes (Duke)** *Defenseman*
b. Regina, Sask., Aug. 31, 1902

| Season | Club | GP | G | A | Pts. |
|---|---|---|---|---|---|
| 1926-27 | Chicago | 34 | 3 | 2 | 5 |
| 1929-30 | Chicago | 44 | 7 | 10 | 17 |
| 1930-31 | New York A | 39 | 2 | 4 | 6 |
| 1932-33 | New York A | 48 | 4 | 7 | 11 |
| 1933-34 | Chi-NYA-NYR | 43 | 0 | 7 | 7 |
| | **Totals** | 208 | 16 | 30 | 46 |

**DUTTON, Mervyn (Red)** *Defenseman*
b. Russell, Man., July 23, 1898

| Season | Club | GP | G | A | Pts. |
|---|---|---|---|---|---|
| 1926-27 | Montreal M | 43 | 4 | 4 | 8 |
| 1927-28 | Montreal M | 42 | 7 | 6 | 13 |
| 1928-29 | Montreal M | 44 | 1 | 3 | 4 |
| 1929-30 | Montreal M | 44 | 3 | 13 | 16 |
| 1930-31 | New York A | 44 | 1 | 11 | 12 |
| 1931-32 | New York A | 47 | 3 | 5 | 8 |
| 1932-33 | New York A | 42 | 0 | 2 | 2 |
| 1933-34 | New York A | 48 | 2 | 8 | 10 |
| 1934-35 | New York A | 48 | 3 | 7 | 10 |
| 1935-36 | New York A | 46 | 5 | 8 | 13 |
| | **Totals** | 448 | 29 | 67 | 96 |

**DVORAK, Miroslav** *Defenseman*
b. Czechoslovakia, Oct. 11, 1951

| Season | Club | GP | G | A | Pts. |
|---|---|---|---|---|---|
| 1982-83 | Philadelphia | 80 | 4 | 33 | 37 |

**DWYER, Michael** *Forward*
b. Brampton, Ont., Sept. 16, 1957

| Season | Club | GP | G | A | Pts. |
|---|---|---|---|---|---|
| 1978-79 | Colorado | 12 | 2 | 3 | 5 |
| 1979-80 | Colorado | 10 | 0 | 0 | 0 |
| 1980-81 | Calgary | 4 | 0 | 1 | 1 |
| 1981-82 | Calgary | 5 | 0 | 2 | 2 |
| | **Totals** | 31 | 2 | 6 | 8 |

**DYCK, Henry Richard** *Forward*
b. Saskatoon, Sask., Sept. 5, 1912

| Season | Club | GP | G | A | Pts. |
|---|---|---|---|---|---|
| 1943-44 | New York R | 1 | 0 | 0 | 0 |

**DYE, Cecil Henry (Babe)** *Forward*
b. Hamilton, Ont., May 13, 1898

| Season | Club | GP | G | A | Pts. |
|---|---|---|---|---|---|
| 1919-20 | Toronto | 21 | 12 | 3 | 15 |
| 1920-21 | Tor-Ham | 24 | 35 | 2 | 37 |
| 1921-22 | Toronto | 24 | 30 | 7 | 37 |
| 1922-23 | Toronto | 22 | 26 | 11 | 37 |
| 1923-24 | Toronto | 19 | 17 | 2 | 19 |
| 1924-25 | Toronto | 29 | 38 | 6 | 44 |
| 1925-26 | Toronto | 31 | 18 | 5 | 23 |
| 1926-27 | Chicago | 41 | 25 | 5 | 30 |
| 1927-28 | Chicago | 10 | 0 | 0 | 0 |
| 1928-29 | New York A | 42 | 1 | 0 | 1 |
| 1930-31 | Toronto | 6 | 0 | 0 | 0 |
| | **Totals** | 269 | 202 | 41 | 243 |

**DYTE, John (Jack)** *Defenseman*
b. Kingston, Ont., Oct. 13, 1918

| Season | Club | GP | G | A | Pts. |
|---|---|---|---|---|---|
| 1943-44 | Chicago | 27 | 1 | 0 | 1 |

**EAGLES, Mike** *Forward*
b. Sussex, N.B., March 7, 1963

| Season | Club | GP | G | A | Pts. |
|---|---|---|---|---|---|
| 1982-83 | Quebec | 2 | 0 | 0 | 0 |

**EATOUGH, Jeff** *Forward*
b. Toronto, Ont., June 2, 1963

| Season | Club | GP | G | A | Pts. |
|---|---|---|---|---|---|
| 1981-82 | Buffalo | 1 | 0 | 0 | 0 |

**EAVES, Michael Gordon** *Forward*
b. Denver, Colo., June 10, 1956

| Season | Club | GP | G | A | Pts. |
|---|---|---|---|---|---|
| 1978-79 | Minnesota | 3 | 0 | 0 | 0 |
| 1979-80 | Minnesota | 56 | 18 | 28 | 46 |
| 1980-81 | Minnesota | 48 | 10 | 24 | 34 |
| 1981-82 | Minnesota | 25 | 11 | 10 | 21 |
| 1982-83 | Minnesota | 75 | 16 | 16 | 32 |
| | **Totals** | 207 | 55 | 78 | 133 |

**EAVES, Murray** *Forward*
b. Calgary, Alta., May 10, 1960

| Season | Club | GP | G | A | Pts. |
|---|---|---|---|---|---|
| 1980-81 | Winnipeg | 12 | 1 | 2 | 3 |
| 1981-82 | Winnipeg | 2 | 0 | 0 | 0 |
| 1982-83 | Winnipeg | 26 | 2 | 7 | 9 |
| | **Totals** | 40 | 3 | 9 | 12 |

**ECCLESTONE, Timothy James** *Forward*
b. Toronto, Ont., Sept. 24, 1947

| Season | Club | GP | G | A | Pts. |
|---|---|---|---|---|---|
| 1967-68 | St Louis | 50 | 6 | 8 | 14 |
| 1968-69 | St Louis | 68 | 11 | 23 | 34 |
| 1969-70 | St Louis | 65 | 16 | 21 | 37 |
| 1970-71 | StL-Det | 74 | 19 | 34 | 53 |
| 1971-72 | Detroit | 72 | 18 | 35 | 53 |
| 1972-73 | Detroit | 78 | 18 | 30 | 48 |
| 1973-74 | Det-Tor | 60 | 9 | 19 | 28 |
| 1974-75 | Det-Atl | 67 | 14 | 22 | 36 |
| 1975-76 | Atlanta | 69 | 6 | 21 | 27 |
| 1976-77 | Atlanta | 78 | 9 | 18 | 27 |
| 1977-78 | Atlanta | 11 | 0 | 2 | 2 |
| | **Totals** | 692 | 126 | 233 | 359 |

**EDBERG, Rolf Arne** *Forward*
b. Stockholm, Sweden, Sept. 29, 1950

| Season | Club | GP | G | A | Pts. |
|---|---|---|---|---|---|
| 1978-79 | Washington | 76 | 14 | 27 | 41 |
| 1979-80 | Washington | 63 | 23 | 23 | 46 |
| 1980-81 | Washington | 45 | 8 | 8 | 16 |
| | **Totals** | 184 | 45 | 58 | 103 |

**EDDOLLS, Frank Herbert** *Defenseman*
b. Lachine, Que., July 5, 1921

| Season | Club | GP | G | A | Pts. |
|---|---|---|---|---|---|
| 1944-45 | Montreal | 43 | 5 | 8 | 13 |
| 1945-46 | Montreal | 8 | 0 | 1 | 1 |
| 1946-47 | Montreal | 6 | 0 | 0 | 0 |
| 1947-48 | New York R | 58 | 6 | 13 | 19 |
| 1948-49 | New York R | 34 | 4 | 2 | 6 |
| 1949-50 | New York R | 57 | 2 | 6 | 8 |
| 1950-51 | New York R | 68 | 3 | 8 | 11 |
| 1951-52 | New York R | 42 | 3 | 5 | 8 |
| | **Totals** | 316 | 23 | 43 | 66 |

**EDESTRAND, Darryl** *Defenseman*
b. Strathroy, Ont., Nov. 6, 1945

| Season | Club | GP | G | A | Pts. |
|---|---|---|---|---|---|
| 1967-68 | St Louis | 12 | 0 | 0 | 0 |
| 1969-70 | Philadelphia | 2 | 0 | 0 | 0 |
| 1971-72 | Pittsburgh | 77 | 10 | 23 | 33 |
| 1972-73 | Pittsburgh | 78 | 15 | 24 | 39 |
| 1973-74 | Pitt-Bos | 55 | 3 | 8 | 11 |
| 1947-75 | Boston | 68 | 1 | 9 | 10 |
| 1975-76 | Boston | 77 | 4 | 17 | 21 |
| 1976-77 | Boston | 17 | 0 | 3 | 3 |
| 1977-78 | Bos-LA | 14 | 0 | 2 | 2 |
| 1978-79 | Los Angeles | 55 | 1 | 4 | 5 |
| | **Totals** | 455 | 34 | 90 | 124 |

**EDMUNDSON, Garry Frank** *Forward*
b. Sexsmith, Alta., May 6, 1932

| Season | Club | GP | G | A | Pts. |
|---|---|---|---|---|---|
| 1951-52 | Montreal | 1 | 0 | 0 | 0 |
| 1959-60 | Toronto | 39 | 4 | 6 | 10 |
| 1960-61 | Toronto | 3 | 0 | 0 | 0 |
| | **Totals** | 43 | 4 | 6 | 10 |

**EDUR, Thomas** *Defenseman*
b. Toronto, Ont., Nov. 18, 1954

| Season | Club | GP | G | A | Pts. |
|---|---|---|---|---|---|
| 1973-74 | Cleveland (WHA) | 76 | 7 | 31 | 38 |
| 1974-75 | Cleveland (WHA) | 61 | 3 | 20 | 23 |
| 1975-76 | Cleveland (WHA) | 80 | 7 | 28 | 35 |
| 1976-77 | Colorado | 80 | 7 | 25 | 32 |
| 1977-78 | Colorado | 78 | 10 | 45 | 55 |
| | **NHL Totals** | 158 | 17 | 70 | 87 |
| | **WHA Totals** | 217 | 17 | 79 | 96 |

| Season | Club | GP | G | A | Pts. |
|---|---|---|---|---|---|

**EGAN, Martin Joseph (Pat)** *Defenseman*
b. Blackie, Alta., Apr. 25, 1918

| Season | Club | GP | G | A | Pts. |
|---|---|---|---|---|---|
| 1939-40 | New York A | 8 | 4 | 3 | 7 |
| 1940-41 | New York A | 39 | 4 | 9 | 13 |
| 1941-42 | Brooklyn | 48 | 8 | 20 | 28 |
| 1943-44 | Det-Bos | 48 | 15 | 28 | 43 |
| 1944-45 | Boston | 48 | 7 | 15 | 22 |
| 1945-46 | Boston | 41 | 8 | 10 | 18 |
| 1946-47 | Boston | 60 | 7 | 18 | 25 |
| 1947-48 | Boston | 60 | 8 | 11 | 19 |
| 1948-49 | Boston | 60 | 6 | 18 | 24 |
| 1949-50 | New York R | 70 | 5 | 11 | 16 |
| 1950-51 | New York R | 70 | 5 | 10 | 15 |
| | **Totals** | 552 | 77 | 153 | 230 |

**EGERS, John Richard (Jack)** *Forward*
b. Sudbury, Ont., Jan. 28, 1949

| Season | Club | GP | G | A | Pts. |
|---|---|---|---|---|---|
| 1969-70 | New York R | 6 | 3 | 0 | 3 |
| 1970-71 | New York R | 60 | 7 | 10 | 17 |
| 1971-72 | NYR-StL | 80 | 23 | 26 | 49 |
| 1972-73 | St Louis | 78 | 24 | 24 | 48 |
| 1973-74 | StL-NYR | 34 | 1 | 4 | 5 |
| 1974-75 | Washington | 14 | 3 | 2 | 5 |
| 1975-76 | Washington | 12 | 3 | 3 | 6 |
| | **Totals** | 284 | 64 | 69 | 133 |

**EHMAN, Gerald Joseph** *Forward*
b. Cudworth, Sask., Nov. 3, 1932

| Season | Club | GP | G | A | Pts. |
|---|---|---|---|---|---|
| 1957-58 | Boston | 1 | 1 | 0 | 1 |
| 1958-59 | Det-Tor | 44 | 12 | 14 | 26 |
| 1959-60 | Toronto | 69 | 12 | 16 | 28 |
| 1960-61 | Toronto | 14 | 1 | 1 | 2 |
| 1963-64 | Toronto | 4 | 1 | 1 | 2 |
| 1967-68 | Oakland | 73 | 19 | 25 | 44 |
| 1968-69 | Oakland | 70 | 21 | 24 | 45 |
| 1969-70 | Oakland | 76 | 11 | 19 | 30 |
| 1970-71 | California | 78 | 18 | 18 | 36 |
| | **Totals** | 429 | 96 | 118 | 214 |

**ELDEBRINK, Anders** *Defenseman*
b. Kalix, Sweden, Dec. 11, 1960

| Season | Club | GP | G | A | Pts. |
|---|---|---|---|---|---|
| 1981-82 | Vancouver | 38 | 1 | 8 | 9 |
| 1982-83 | Van-Que | 17 | 2 | 3 | 5 |
| | **Totals** | 55 | 3 | 11 | 14 |

**ELIK, Boris (Bo)** *Forward*
b. Geraldton, Ont., Oct. 17, 1929

| Season | Club | GP | G | A | Pts. |
|---|---|---|---|---|---|
| 1962-63 | Detroit | 3 | 0 | 0 | 0 |

**ELLIOTT, Fred** *Forward*

| Season | Club | GP | G | A | Pts. |
|---|---|---|---|---|---|
| 1928-29 | Ottawa | — | 2 | 0 | 2 |

**ELLIS, Ronald John Edward (Ron)** *Forward*
b. Lindsay, Ont., Jan. 8, 1945

| Season | Club | GP | G | A | Pts. |
|---|---|---|---|---|---|
| 1963-64 | Toronto | 1 | 0 | 0 | 0 |
| 1964-65 | Toronto | 62 | 23 | 16 | 39 |
| 1965-66 | Toronto | 70 | 19 | 23 | 42 |
| 1966-67 | Toronto | 67 | 22 | 23 | 45 |
| 1967-68 | Toronto | 74 | 28 | 20 | 48 |
| 1968-69 | Toronto | 72 | 25 | 21 | 46 |
| 1969-70 | Toronto | 76 | 35 | 19 | 54 |
| 1970-71 | Toronto | 78 | 24 | 29 | 53 |
| 1971-72 | Toronto | 78 | 23 | 24 | 47 |
| 1972-73 | Toronto | 77 | 22 | 29 | 51 |
| 1973-74 | Toronto | 70 | 23 | 25 | 48 |
| 1974-75 | Toronto | 79 | 32 | 29 | 61 |
| 1977-78 | Toronto | 80 | 26 | 24 | 50 |
| 1978-79 | Toronto | 63 | 16 | 12 | 28 |
| | **Totals** | 947 | 318 | 294 | 612 |

**ELORANTA, Kari** *Defenseman*
b. Lahti, Finland, Apr. 29, 1956

| Season | Club | GP | G | A | Pts. |
|---|---|---|---|---|---|
| 1981-82 | Cal-StL | 31 | 1 | 12 | 13 |
| 1982-83 | Calgary | 80 | 4 | 40 | 44 |
| | **Totals** | 111 | 5 | 52 | 57 |

**EMMS, Leighton (Happy)**
*Defenseman-Forward*
b. Barrie, Ont., Jan 16, 1905

| Season | Club | GP | G | A | Pts. |
|---|---|---|---|---|---|
| 1926-27 | Montreal M | 8 | 0 | 0 | 0 |
| 1927-28 | Montreal M | 10 | 0 | 1 | 1 |

| Season | Club | GP | G | A | Pts. |
|---|---|---|---|---|---|
| 1930-31 | New York A | 44 | 5 | 4 | 9 |
| 1931-32 | NYA-Det | 43 | 6 | 9 | 15 |
| 1932-33 | Detroit | 43 | 9 | 13 | 22 |
| 1933-34 | Detroit | 45 | 7 | 7 | 14 |
| 1934-35 | New York A | 40 | 3 | 3 | 6 |
| 1935-36 | New York A | 32 | 1 | 5 | 6 |
| 1936-37 | New York A | 46 | 4 | 8 | 12 |
| 1937-38 | New York A | 20 | 1 | 3 | 4 |
| | **Totals** | 331 | 36 | 53 | 89 |

**ENGBLOM, Brian Paul** *Defenseman*
b. Winnipeg, Man., Jan 27, 1955

| Season | Club | GP | G | A | Pts. |
|---|---|---|---|---|---|
| 1977-78 | Montreal | 28 | 1 | 2 | 3 |
| 1978-79 | Montreal | 62 | 3 | 11 | 14 |
| 1979-80 | Montreal | 70 | 3 | 20 | 23 |
| 1980-81 | Montreal | 80 | 3 | 25 | 28 |
| 1981-82 | Montreal | 76 | 4 | 29 | 33 |
| 1982-83 | Washington | 73 | 5 | 22 | 27 |
| | **Totals** | 389 | 19 | 109 | 128 |

**ENGELE, Jerome Wilfred** *Defenseman*
b. Humboldt, Sask., Nov. 26, 1950

| Season | Club | GP | G | A | Pts. |
|---|---|---|---|---|---|
| 1975-76 | Minnesota | 17 | 0 | 1 | 1 |
| 1976-77 | Minnesota | 31 | 1 | 7 | 8 |
| 1977-78 | Minnesota | 52 | 1 | 5 | 6 |
| | **Totals** | 100 | 2 | 13 | 15 |

**ERICKSON, Autry Raymond** *Defenseman*
b. Lethbridge, Alta., Jan. 25, 1938

| Season | Club | GP | G | A | Pts. |
|---|---|---|---|---|---|
| 1959-60 | Boston | 58 | 1 | 6 | 7 |
| 1960-61 | Boston | 68 | 2 | 6 | 8 |
| 1962-63 | Chicago | 3 | 0 | 0 | 0 |
| 1963-64 | Chicago | 31 | 0 | 1 | 1 |
| 1967-68 | Oakland | 65 | 4 | 11 | 15 |
| 1969-70 | Oakland | 1 | 0 | 0 | 0 |
| | **Totals** | 226 | 7 | 24 | 31 |

**ERICKSON, Grant Charles** *Forward*
b. Pierceland, Sask., Apr. 28, 1947

| Season | Club | GP | G | A | Pts. |
|---|---|---|---|---|---|
| 1968-69 | Boston | 2 | 1 | 0 | 1 |
| 1969-70 | Minnesota | 4 | 0 | 0 | 0 |
| 1972-73 | Cleveland (WHA) | 77 | 15 | 29 | 44 |
| 1973-74 | Cleveland (WHA) | 78 | 23 | 27 | 50 |
| 1974-75 | Cleveland (WHA) | 78 | 12 | 15 | 27 |
| 1975-76 | Phoenix (WHA) | 33 | 4 | 7 | 11 |
| | **NHL Totals** | 6 | 1 | 0 | 1 |
| | **WHA Totals** | 266 | 54 | 78 | 132 |

**ERIKSSON, Bengt Roland** *Forward*
b. Storatuna, Sweden, Mar. 1, 1954

| Season | Club | GP | G | A | Pts. |
|---|---|---|---|---|---|
| 1976-77 | Minnesota | 80 | 25 | 44 | 69 |
| 1977-78 | Minnesota | 78 | 21 | 39 | 60 |
| 1978-79 | Vancouver | 35 | 2 | 12 | 14 |
| 1978-79 | Winnipeg (WHA) | 33 | 5 | 10 | 15 |
| | **NHL Totals** | 193 | 48 | 95 | 143 |
| | **WHA Totals** | 33 | 5 | 10 | 15 |

**ERIKSSON, Thomas** *Defenseman*
b. Stockholm, Sweden, Oct. 16, 1959

| Season | Club | GP | G | A | Pts. |
|---|---|---|---|---|---|
| 1980-81 | Philadelphia | 24 | 1 | 10 | 11 |
| 1981-82 | Philadelphia | 1 | 0 | 0 | 0 |
| | **Totals** | 25 | 1 | 10 | 11 |

**ESPOSITO, Phil** *Forward*
b. Sault Ste. Marie, Ont., Feb. 20, 1942

| Season | Club | GP | G | A | Pts. |
|---|---|---|---|---|---|
| 1963-64 | Chicago | 27 | 3 | 2 | 5 |
| 1964-65 | Chicago | 70 | 23 | 32 | 55 |
| 1965-66 | Chicago | 69 | 27 | 26 | 53 |
| 1966-67 | Chicago | 69 | 21 | 40 | 61 |
| 1967-68 | Boston | 74 | 35 | 49 | 84 |
| 1968-69 | Boston | 74 | 49 | 77 | 126 |
| 1969-70 | Boston | 76 | 43 | 56 | 99 |
| 1970-71 | Boston | 78 | 76 | 76 | 152 |
| 1971-72 | Boston | 76 | 66 | 67 | 133 |
| 1972-73 | Boston | 78 | 55 | 75 | 130 |
| 1973-74 | Boston | 78 | 68 | 77 | 145 |
| 1974-75 | Boston | 79 | 61 | 66 | 127 |
| 1975-76 | Bos-NYR | 74 | 35 | 48 | 83 |
| 1976-77 | New York R | 80 | 34 | 46 | 80 |
| 1977-78 | New York R | 79 | 38 | 43 | 81 |
| 1978-79 | New York R | 80 | 42 | 36 | 78 |

| Season | Club | GP | G | A | Pts. |
|---|---|---|---|---|---|
| 1979-80 | New York R | 80 | 34 | 44 | 78 |
| 1980-81 | New York R | 41 | 7 | 13 | 20 |
| | **Totals** | 1282 | 717 | 873 | 1590 |

**EVANS, Christopher Bruce** *Defenseman*
b. Toronto, Ont., Sept. 14, 1946

| Season | Club | GP | G | A | Pts. |
|---|---|---|---|---|---|
| 1969-70 | Toronto | 2 | 0 | 0 | 0 |
| 1971-72 | Buf-StL | 63 | 6 | 18 | 24 |
| 1972-73 | St Louis | 77 | 9 | 12 | 21 |
| 1973-74 | StL-Det | 77 | 4 | 9 | 13 |
| 1974-75 | KC-StL | 22 | 0 | 3 | 3 |
| 1975-76 | Calgary (WHA) | 75 | 3 | 20 | 23 |
| 1976-77 | Calgary (WHA) | 81 | 7 | 27 | 34 |
| | **NHL Totals** | 241 | 19 | 42 | 61 |
| | **WHA Totals** | 156 | 10 | 47 | 57 |

**EVANS, Daryl Tomas** *Forward*
b. Toronto, Ont., Jan. 12, 1961

| Season | Club | GP | G | A | Pts. |
|---|---|---|---|---|---|
| 1981-82 | Los Angeles | 14 | 2 | 6 | 8 |
| 1982-83 | Los Angeles | 80 | 18 | 22 | 40 |
| | **Totals** | 94 | 20 | 28 | 48 |

**EVANS, John Paul** *Forward*
b. Toronto, Ont., May 2, 1954

| Season | Club | GP | G | A | Pts. |
|---|---|---|---|---|---|
| 1978-79 | Philadelphia | 44 | 6 | 5 | 11 |
| 1980-81 | Philadelphia | 1 | 0 | 0 | 0 |
| 1982-83 | Philadelphia | 58 | 8 | 20 | 28 |
| | **Totals** | 103 | 14 | 25 | 39 |

**EVANS, Paul Edward Vincent** *Forward*
b. Peterborough, Ont., Feb. 24, 1955

| Season | Club | GP | G | A | Pts. |
|---|---|---|---|---|---|
| 1976-77 | Toronto | 7 | 1 | 1 | 2 |
| 1977-78 | Toronto | 4 | 0 | 0 | 0 |
| | **Totals** | 1 | 1 | 0 | 2 |

**EVANS, Stewart (Stu)** *Defenseman*
b. Ottawa, Ont., June 19, 1908

| Season | Club | GP | G | A | Pts. |
|---|---|---|---|---|---|
| 1930-31 | Detroit | 37 | 1 | 4 | 5 |
| 1932-33 | Detroit | 48 | 2 | 6 | 8 |
| 1933-34 | Det-MontM | 48 | 4 | 2 | 6 |
| 1934-35 | Montreal M | 45 | 5 | 7 | 12 |
| 1935-36 | Montreal M | 48 | 3 | 5 | 8 |
| 1936-37 | Montreal M | 47 | 6 | 7 | 13 |
| 1937-38 | Montreal M | 48 | 5 | 11 | 16 |
| 1938-39 | Montreal | 43 | 2 | 7 | 9 |
| | **Totals** | 364 | 28 | 49 | 77 |

**EVANS, William John
(Jack and Tex)** *Defenseman*
b. Garnant, South Wales, Apr. 21, 1928

| Season | Club | GP | G | A | Pts. |
|---|---|---|---|---|---|
| 1948-49 | New York R | 3 | 0 | 0 | 0 |
| 1949-50 | New York R | 2 | 0 | 0 | 0 |
| 1950-51 | New York R | 49 | 1 | 0 | 1 |
| 1951-52 | New York R | 52 | 1 | 6 | 7 |
| 1953-54 | New York R | 44 | 4 | 4 | 8 |
| 1954-55 | New York R | 47 | 0 | 5 | 5 |
| 1955-56 | New York R | 70 | 2 | 9 | 11 |
| 1956-57 | New York R | 66 | 3 | 6 | 9 |
| 1957-58 | New York R | 70 | 4 | 8 | 12 |
| 1958-59 | Chicago | 70 | 1 | 8 | 9 |
| 1959-60 | Chicago | 68 | 0 | 4 | 4 |
| 1960-61 | Chicago | 69 | 0 | 8 | 8 |
| 1961-62 | Chicago | 70 | 3 | 14 | 17 |
| 1962-63 | Chicago | 68 | 0 | 8 | 8 |
| | **Totals** | 752 | 19 | 80 | 99 |

**EZINICKI, William (Wild Bill)** *Forward*
b. Winnipeg, Man., Mar. 11, 1924

| Season | Club | GP | G | A | Pts. |
|---|---|---|---|---|---|
| 1944-45 | Toronto | 8 | 1 | 4 | 5 |
| 1945-46 | Toronto | 24 | 4 | 8 | 12 |
| 1946-47 | Toronto | 60 | 17 | 20 | 37 |
| 1947-48 | Toronto | 60 | 11 | 20 | 31 |
| 1948-49 | Toronto | 52 | 13 | 15 | 28 |
| 1949-50 | Toronto | 67 | 10 | 12 | 22 |
| 1950-51 | Boston | 53 | 16 | 19 | 35 |
| 1951-52 | Boston | 28 | 5 | 5 | 10 |
| 1954-55 | New York R | 16 | 2 | 2 | 4 |
| | **Totals** | 368 | 79 | 105 | 184 |

| Season | Club | GP | G | A | Pts. |
|---|---|---|---|---|---|
| **FAHEY, John Trevor**  *Forward* | | | | | |
| b. New Waterford, N.S., Jan. 4, 1944 | | | | | |
| 1964-65 | New York R | 1 | 0 | 0 | 0 |
| | | | | | |
| **FAIRBAIRN, William John (Bill)**  *Forward* | | | | | |
| b. Brandon, Man., Jan. 7, 1947 | | | | | |
| 1968-69 | New York R | 1 | 0 | 0 | 0 |
| 1969-70 | New York R | 76 | 23 | 33 | 56 |
| 1970-71 | New York R | 56 | 7 | 23 | 30 |
| 1971-72 | New York R | 78 | 22 | 37 | 59 |
| 1972-73 | New York R | 78 | 30 | 33 | 63 |
| 1973-74 | New York R | 78 | 18 | 44 | 62 |
| 1974-75 | New York R | 80 | 24 | 37 | 61 |
| 1975-76 | New York R | 80 | 13 | 15 | 28 |
| 1976-77 | NYR-Minn | 60 | 10 | 22 | 32 |
| 1977-78 | Minn-StL | 66 | 14 | 17 | 31 |
| 1978-79 | St Louis | 5 | 1 | 0 | 1 |
| | **Totals** | 658 | 162 | 261 | 423 |
| | | | | | |
| **FALKENBERG, Robert Arthur**  *Defenseman* | | | | | |
| b. Stettler, Alta., Jan. 1, 1946 | | | | | |
| 1966-67 | Detroit | 16 | 1 | 1 | 2 |
| 1967-68 | Detroit | 20 | 0 | 3 | 3 |
| 1968-69 | Detroit | 5 | 0 | 0 | 0 |
| 1970-71 | Detroit | 9 | 0 | 1 | 1 |
| 1971-72 | Detroit | 4 | 0 | 0 | 0 |
| 1972-73 | Alberta (WHA) | 77 | 6 | 23 | 29 |
| 1973-74 | Edmonton (WHA) | 78 | 3 | 14 | 17 |
| 1974-75 | San Diego (WHA) | 78 | 2 | 18 | 20 |
| 1975-76 | San Diego (WHA) | 79 | 3 | 13 | 16 |
| 1976-77 | San Diego (WHA) | 64 | 0 | 6 | 6 |
| 1977-78 | Edmonton (WHA) | 2 | 0 | 0 | 0 |
| | **NHL Totals** | 54 | 1 | 5 | 6 |
| | **WHA Totals** | 378 | 14 | 74 | 88 |
| | | | | | |
| **FARRANT, Walter (Whitey)**  *Forward* | | | | | |
| b. Toronto, Ont., Aug. 12, 1913 | | | | | |
| 1943-44 | Chicago | 1 | 0 | 0 | 0 |
| | | | | | |
| **FARRISH, David Allan**  *Defenseman* | | | | | |
| b. Wingham, Ont., Aug. 1, 1956 | | | | | |
| 1976-77 | New York R | 80 | 2 | 17 | 19 |
| 1977-78 | New York R | 66 | 3 | 5 | 8 |
| 1978-79 | New York R | 71 | 1 | 19 | 20 |
| 1979-80 | Que-Tor | 24 | 1 | 8 | 9 |
| 1980-81 | Toronto | 74 | 2 | 18 | 20 |
| 1982-83 | Toronto | 56 | 4 | 24 | 28 |
| | **Totals** | 371 | 13 | 91 | 104 |
| | | | | | |
| **FASHOWAY, Gordon**  *Forward* | | | | | |
| b. Portage la Prairie, Man., June 16, 1926 | | | | | |
| 1950-51 | Chicago | 13 | 3 | 2 | 5 |
| | | | | | |
| **FAUBERT, Mario**  *Defenseman* | | | | | |
| b. Valleyfield, Que., Dec. 2, 1954 | | | | | |
| 1974-75 | Pittsburgh | 10 | 1 | 0 | 1 |
| 1975-76 | Pittsburgh | 21 | 1 | 8 | 9 |
| 1976-77 | Pittsburgh | 47 | 2 | 11 | 13 |
| 1977-78 | Pittsburgh | 18 | 0 | 6 | 6 |
| 1979-80 | Pittsburgh | 49 | 5 | 13 | 18 |
| 1980-81 | Pittsburgh | 72 | 8 | 44 | 52 |
| 1981-82 | Pittsburgh | 14 | 4 | 8 | 12 |
| | **Totals** | 231 | 21 | 90 | 111 |
| | | | | | |
| **FAULKNER, Alexander Selm**  *Forward* | | | | | |
| b. Bishops Falls, Nfld., May 21, 1936 | | | | | |
| 1961-62 | Toronto | 1 | 0 | 0 | 0 |
| 1962-63 | Detroit | 70 | 10 | 10 | 20 |
| 1963-64 | Detroit | 30 | 5 | 7 | 12 |
| | **Totals** | 101 | 15 | 17 | 32 |
| | | | | | |
| **FEAMSTER, David Allan**  *Defenseman* | | | | | |
| b. Detroit, Mich., Sept. 10, 1958 | | | | | |
| 1981-82 | Chicago | 29 | 0 | 2 | 2 |
| 1982-83 | Chicago | 78 | 6 | 12 | 18 |
| | **Totals** | 107 | 6 | 14 | 20 |

| Season | Club | GP | G | A | Pts. |
|---|---|---|---|---|---|
| **FEATHERSTONE, Anthony James**  *Forward* | | | | | |
| b. Toronto, Ont., July 31, 1949 | | | | | |
| 1969-70 | Oakland | 9 | 0 | 1 | 1 |
| 1970-71 | California | 67 | 8 | 8 | 16 |
| 1973-74 | Minnesota | 54 | 9 | 12 | 21 |
| 1974-75 | Toronto (WHA) | 76 | 25 | 38 | 63 |
| 1975-76 | Toronto (WHA) | 32 | 4 | 7 | 11 |
| | **NHL Totals** | 130 | 17 | 21 | 38 |
| | **WHA Totals** | 108 | 29 | 45 | 74 |
| | | | | | |
| **FEDERKO, Bernard Allan**  *Forward* | | | | | |
| b. Foam Lake, Sask., May 12, 1956 | | | | | |
| 1976-77 | St Louis | 31 | 14 | 9 | 23 |
| 1977-78 | St Louis | 72 | 17 | 24 | 41 |
| 1978-79 | St Louis | 74 | 31 | 64 | 95 |
| 1979-80 | St Louis | 79 | 38 | 56 | 94 |
| 1980-81 | St Louis | 78 | 31 | 73 | 104 |
| 1981-82 | St Louis | 74 | 30 | 62 | 92 |
| 1982-83 | St Louis | 75 | 24 | 60 | 84 |
| | **Totals** | 483 | 185 | 348 | 533 |
| | | | | | |
| **FELTRIN, Anthony Louis**  *Defenseman* | | | | | |
| b. Ladysmith, B.C., Dec. 6, 1961 | | | | | |
| 1980-81 | Pittsburgh | 2 | 0 | 0 | 0 |
| 1981-82 | Pittsburgh | 4 | 0 | 0 | 0 |
| 1982-83 | Pittsburgh | 32 | 3 | 3 | 6 |
| | **Totals** | 38 | 3 | 3 | 6 |
| | | | | | |
| **FENYVES, Dave**  *Defenseman* | | | | | |
| b. Dunnville, Ont., Apr. 29, 1960 | | | | | |
| 1982-83 | Buffalo | 24 | 0 | 8 | 8 |
| | | | | | |
| **FERGUS, Tom Joseph**  *Forward* | | | | | |
| b. Chicago, Ill., June 16, 1962 | | | | | |
| 1981-82 | Boston | 61 | 15 | 24 | 39 |
| 1982-83 | Boston | 80 | 28 | 35 | 63 |
| | **Totals** | 141 | 43 | 59 | 102 |
| | | | | | |
| **FERGUSON, George**  *Forward* | | | | | |
| b. Trenton, Ont., Aug. 22, 1952 | | | | | |
| 1972-73 | Toronto | 72 | 10 | 13 | 23 |
| 1973-74 | Toronto | 16 | 0 | 4 | 4 |
| 1974-75 | Toronto | 69 | 19 | 30 | 49 |
| 1975-76 | Toronto | 79 | 12 | 32 | 44 |
| 1976-77 | Toronto | 50 | 9 | 15 | 24 |
| 1977-78 | Toronto | 73 | 7 | 16 | 23 |
| 1978-79 | Pittsburgh | 80 | 21 | 29 | 50 |
| 1979-80 | Pittsburgh | 73 | 21 | 28 | 49 |
| 1980-81 | Pittsburgh | 79 | 25 | 18 | 43 |
| 1981-82 | Pittsburgh | 71 | 22 | 31 | 53 |
| 1982-83 | Pitt-Minn | 72 | 8 | 12 | 20 |
| | **Totals** | 734 | 154 | 228 | 382 |
| | | | | | |
| **FERGUSON, John Bowie**  *Forward* | | | | | |
| b. Vancouver, B.C., Sept. 5, 1938 | | | | | |
| 1963-64 | Montreal | 59 | 18 | 27 | 45 |
| 1964-65 | Montreal | 69 | 17 | 27 | 44 |
| 1965-66 | Montreal | 65 | 11 | 14 | 25 |
| 1966-67 | Montreal | 67 | 20 | 22 | 42 |
| 1967-68 | Montreal | 61 | 15 | 18 | 33 |
| 1968-69 | Montreal | 71 | 29 | 23 | 52 |
| 1969-70 | Montreal | 48 | 19 | 13 | 32 |
| 1970-71 | Montreal | 60 | 16 | 14 | 30 |
| | **Totals** | 500 | 145 | 158 | 303 |
| | | | | | |
| **FERGUSON, Lorne Robert**  *Forward* | | | | | |
| b. Palmerston, Ont., May 26, 1930 | | | | | |
| 1949-50 | Boston | 3 | 1 | 1 | 2 |
| 1950-51 | Boston | 70 | 16 | 17 | 33 |
| 1951-52 | Boston | 27 | 3 | 4 | 7 |
| 1954-55 | Boston | 69 | 20 | 14 | 34 |
| 1955-56 | Bos-Det | 63 | 15 | 12 | 27 |
| 1956-57 | Detroit | 70 | 13 | 10 | 23 |
| 1957-58 | Det-Chi | 53 | 7 | 12 | 19 |
| 1958-59 | Chicago | 67 | 7 | 10 | 17 |
| | **Totals** | 422 | 82 | 80 | 162 |

| Season | Club | GP | G | A | Pts. |
|---|---|---|---|---|---|
| **FERGUSON, Norman Gerald**  *Forward* | | | | | |
| b. Sydney, N.S., Oct. 16, 1945 | | | | | |
| 1968-69 | Oakland | 76 | 34 | 20 | 54 |
| 1969-70 | Oakland | 72 | 11 | 9 | 20 |
| 1970-71 | California | 54 | 14 | 17 | 31 |
| 1971-72 | California | 77 | 14 | 20 | 34 |
| 1972-73 | New York (WHA) | 56 | 28 | 40 | 68 |
| 1973-74 | Jersey (WHA) | 75 | 15 | 21 | 36 |
| 1974-75 | San Diego (WHA) | 78 | 36 | 33 | 69 |
| 1975-76 | San Diego (WHA) | 79 | 37 | 37 | 74 |
| 1976-77 | San Diego (WHA) | 77 | 39 | 32 | 71 |
| | **NHL Totals** | 279 | 73 | 66 | 139 |
| | **WHA Totals** | 365 | 155 | 163 | 318 |
| | | | | | |
| **FIDLER, Michael Edward**  *Forward* | | | | | |
| b. Everett, Mass., Aug. 19, 1956 | | | | | |
| 1976-77 | Cleveland | 46 | 17 | 16 | 33 |
| 1977-78 | Cleveland | 78 | 28 | 23 | 51 |
| 1978-79 | Minnesota | 59 | 23 | 26 | 49 |
| 1979-80 | Minnesota | 24 | 5 | 4 | 9 |
| 1980-81 | Minn-Hart | 58 | 14 | 21 | 35 |
| 1981-82 | Hartford | 2 | 0 | 1 | 1 |
| 1982-83 | Chicago | 4 | 2 | 1 | 3 |
| | **Totals** | 271 | 84 | 97 | 181 |
| | | | | | |
| **FIELD, Wilfred Spence**  *Defenseman* | | | | | |
| b. Winnipeg, Man., Apr. 29, 1915 | | | | | |
| 1936-37 | New York A | 2 | 0 | 0 | 0 |
| 1938-39 | New York A | 47 | 1 | 3 | 4 |
| 1949-40 | New York A | 45 | 1 | 3 | 4 |
| 1940-41 | New York A | 36 | 5 | 6 | 11 |
| 1941-42 | Brooklyn | 41 | 6 | 9 | 15 |
| 1944-45 | Mont-Chi | 48 | 4 | 4 | 8 |
| | **Totals** | 219 | 17 | 25 | 42 |
| | | | | | |
| **FIELDER, Guyle Abner**  *Forward* | | | | | |
| b. Potlach, Idaho, Nov. 21, 1930 | | | | | |
| 1950-51 | Chicago | 3 | 0 | 0 | 0 |
| 1957-58 | Detroit | 6 | 0 | 0 | 0 |
| | **Totals** | 9 | 0 | 0 | 0 |
| | | | | | |
| **FILLION, Marcel**  *Forward* | | | | | |
| b. Thetford Mines, Que., May 28, 1923 | | | | | |
| 1944-45 | Boston | 1 | 0 | 0 | 0 |
| | | | | | |
| **FILLION, Robert Louis**  *Forward* | | | | | |
| b. Thetford Mines, Que., July 12, 1921 | | | | | |
| 1943-44 | Montreal | 41 | 7 | 23 | 30 |
| 1944-45 | Montreal | 31 | 6 | 8 | 14 |
| 1945-46 | Montreal | 50 | 10 | 6 | 16 |
| 1946-47 | Montreal | 57 | 6 | 3 | 9 |
| 1947-48 | Montreal | 32 | 9 | 9 | 18 |
| 1948-49 | Montreal | 59 | 3 | 9 | 12 |
| | **Totals** | 270 | 41 | 58 | 99 |
| | | | | | |
| **FILMORE, Thomas**  *Forward* | | | | | |
| b. Thamesford, Ont., 1906 | | | | | |
| 1930-31 | Detroit | 39 | 6 | 2 | 8 |
| 1931-32 | Det-NYA | 40 | 8 | 6 | 14 |
| 1932-33 | New York A | 35 | 1 | 4 | 5 |
| 1933-34 | Boston | 3 | 0 | 0 | 0 |
| | **Totals** | 117 | 15 | 12 | 27 |
| | | | | | |
| **FINKBEINER, Lloyd**  *Forward* | | | | | |
| b. Guelph, Ont., Mar. 12, 1920 | | | | | |
| 1940-41 | New York A | — | 0 | 0 | 0 |
| | | | | | |
| **FINNEY, Joseph Sidney (Sid)**  *Forward* | | | | | |
| b. Banbridge, Ireland, May 1, 1929 | | | | | |
| 1951-52 | Chicago | 35 | 6 | 5 | 11 |
| 1952-53 | Chicago | 18 | 4 | 2 | 6 |
| 1953-54 | Chicago | 6 | 0 | 0 | 0 |
| | **Totals** | 59 | 10 | 7 | 17 |
| | | | | | |
| **FINNIGAN, Edward**  *Forward* | | | | | |
| b. Shawville, Que. | | | | | |
| 1934-35 | St Louis E | 12 | 1 | 1 | 2 |
| 1935-36 | Boston | 3 | 0 | 0 | 0 |
| | **Totals** | 15 | 1 | 1 | 2 |

**FINNIGAN, Frank** *Forward*
b. Shawville, Que., July 9, 1903

| Season | Club | GP | G | A | Pts. |
|---|---|---|---|---|---|
| 1923-24 | Ottawa | 4 | 0 | 0 | 0 |
| 1924-25 | Ottawa | 29 | 0 | 0 | 0 |
| 1925-26 | Ottawa | 36 | 2 | 0 | 2 |
| 1926-27 | Ottawa | 36 | 15 | 1 | 16 |
| 1927-28 | Ottawa | 38 | 20 | 5 | 25 |
| 1928-29 | Ottawa | 44 | 15 | 4 | 19 |
| 1929-30 | Ottawa | 43 | 21 | 15 | 36 |
| 1930-31 | Ottawa | 44 | 9 | 8 | 17 |
| 1931-32 | Toronto | 47 | 8 | 13 | 21 |
| 1932-33 | Ottawa | 45 | 4 | 14 | 18 |
| 1933-34 | Ottawa | 48 | 10 | 10 | 20 |
| 1934-35 | StLE-Tor | 45 | 7 | 5 | 12 |
| 1935-36 | Toronto | 48 | 2 | 6 | 8 |
| 1936-37 | Toronto | 48 | 2 | 7 | 9 |
| | **Totals** | 555 | 115 | 88 | 203 |

**FISCHER, Ronald Alexander** *Defenseman*
b. Merritt, B.C., Apr. 12, 1959

| Season | Club | GP | G | A | Pts. |
|---|---|---|---|---|---|
| 1981-82 | Buffalo | 15 | 0 | 7 | 7 |
| 1982-83 | Buffalo | 3 | 0 | 0 | 0 |
| | **Totals** | 18 | 0 | 7 | 7 |

**FISHER, Alvin** *Forward*

| Season | Club | GP | G | A | Pts. |
|---|---|---|---|---|---|
| 1924-25 | Toronto | 9 | 1 | 0 | 1 |

**FISHER, Duncan Robert** *Forward*
b. Regina, Sask., Aug. 30, 1927

| Season | Club | GP | G | A | Pts. |
|---|---|---|---|---|---|
| 1948-49 | New York R | 60 | 9 | 16 | 25 |
| 1949-50 | New York R | 70 | 12 | 21 | 33 |
| 1950-51 | NYR-Bos | 65 | 9 | 20 | 29 |
| 1951-52 | Boston | 65 | 15 | 12 | 27 |
| 1952-53 | Boston | 7 | 0 | 1 | 1 |
| 1958-59 | Detroit | 8 | 0 | 0 | 0 |
| | **Totals** | 275 | 45 | 70 | 115 |

**FISHER, Joseph** *Forward*
b. Medicine Hat, Alta., July 4, 1916

| Season | Club | GP | G | A | Pts. |
|---|---|---|---|---|---|
| 1939-40 | Detroit | 32 | 2 | 4 | 6 |
| 1940-41 | Detroit | 27 | 5 | 8 | 13 |
| 1941-42 | Detroit | 3 | 0 | 0 | 0 |
| 1942-43 | Detroit | 1 | 1 | 0 | 1 |
| | **Totals** | 63 | 8 | 12 | 20 |

**FITCHNER, Robert Douglas** *Forward*
b. Sudbury, Ont., Dec. 22, 1950

| Season | Club | GP | G | A | Pts. |
|---|---|---|---|---|---|
| 1973-74 | Edmonton (WHA) | 31 | 1 | 2 | 3 |
| 1974-75 | Indianapolis (WHA) | 78 | 11 | 19 | 30 |
| 1975-76 | Ind-Que (WHA) | 73 | 22 | 25 | 47 |
| 1976-77 | Quebec (WHA) | 81 | 29 | 30 | 59 |
| 1977-78 | Quebec (WHA) | 72 | 15 | 28 | 43 |
| 1978-79 | Quebec (WHA) | 79 | 10 | 35 | 45 |
| 1979-80 | Quebec | 70 | 11 | 20 | 31 |
| 1980-81 | Quebec | 8 | 1 | 0 | 1 |
| | **NHL Totals** | 78 | 12 | 20 | 32 |
| | **WHA Totals** | 414 | 88 | 139 | 227 |

**FITZPATRICK, Alexander Stewart (Sandy)**
*Forward*
b. Paisley, Scotland, Dec. 22, 1944

| Season | Club | GP | G | A | Pts. |
|---|---|---|---|---|---|
| 1964-64 | New York R | 4 | 0 | 0 | 0 |
| 1967-68 | Minnesota | 18 | 3 | 6 | 9 |
| | **Totals** | 22 | 3 | 6 | 9 |

**FITZPATRICK, Ross** *Forward*
b. Penticton, B.C., Oct. 7, 1960

| Season | Club | GP | G | A | Pts. |
|---|---|---|---|---|---|
| 1982-83 | Philadelphia | 1 | 0 | 0 | 0 |

**FLAMAN, Ferdinand Charles (Fernie)**
*Defenseman*
b. Dysart, Sask., Jan. 25, 1927

| Season | Club | GP | G | A | Pts. |
|---|---|---|---|---|---|
| 1944-45 | Boston | 1 | 0 | 0 | 0 |
| 1945-46 | Boston | 1 | 0 | 0 | 0 |
| 1946-47 | Boston | 23 | 1 | 4 | 5 |
| 1947-48 | Boston | 56 | 4 | 6 | 10 |
| 1948-49 | Boston | 60 | 4 | 12 | 16 |
| 1949-50 | Boston | 69 | 2 | 5 | 7 |
| 1950-51 | Bos-Tor | 53 | 3 | 7 | 10 |
| 1951-52 | Toronto | 61 | 0 | 7 | 7 |
| 1952-53 | Toronto | 66 | 2 | 6 | 8 |
| 1953-54 | Toronto | 62 | 0 | 8 | 8 |
| 1954-55 | Boston | 70 | 4 | 14 | 18 |
| 1955-56 | Boston | 62 | 4 | 17 | 21 |
| 1956-57 | Boston | 68 | 6 | 25 | 31 |
| 1957-58 | Boston | 66 | 0 | 15 | 15 |
| 1958-59 | Boston | 70 | 0 | 21 | 21 |
| 1959-60 | Boston | 60 | 2 | 18 | 20 |
| 1960-61 | Boston | 62 | 2 | 9 | 11 |
| | **Totals** | 910 | 34 | 174 | 208 |

**FLEMING, Reginald Stephen**
*Defenseman-Forward*
b. Montreal, Que., Apr. 21, 1936

| Season | Club | GP | G | A | Pts. |
|---|---|---|---|---|---|
| 1959-60 | Montreal | 3 | 0 | 0 | 0 |
| 1960-61 | Chicago | 66 | 4 | 4 | 8 |
| 1961-62 | Chicago | 70 | 7 | 9 | 16 |
| 1962-63 | Chicago | 64 | 7 | 7 | 14 |
| 1963-64 | Chicago | 61 | 3 | 6 | 9 |
| 1964-65 | Boston | 67 | 18 | 23 | 41 |
| 1965-66 | Bos-NYR | 69 | 14 | 20 | 34 |
| 1966-67 | New York R | 61 | 15 | 16 | 31 |
| 1967-68 | New York R | 73 | 17 | 7 | 24 |
| 1968-69 | New York R | 72 | 8 | 12 | 20 |
| 1969-70 | Philadelphia | 65 | 9 | 18 | 27 |
| 1970-71 | Buffalo | 78 | 6 | 10 | 16 |
| 1972-73 | Chicago (WHA) | 75 | 23 | 45 | 68 |
| 1973-74 | Chicago (WHA) | 45 | 2 | 12 | 14 |
| | **NHL Totals** | 749 | 108 | 132 | 240 |
| | **WHA Totals** | 120 | 25 | 57 | 82 |

**FLESCH** *Forward*

| Season | Club | GP | G | A | Pts. |
|---|---|---|---|---|---|
| 1920-21 | Hamilton | 1 | 0 | 0 | 0 |

**FLESCH, John Patrick** *Forward*
b. Sudbury, Ont., July 15, 1953

| Season | Club | GP | G | A | Pts. |
|---|---|---|---|---|---|
| 1974-75 | Minnesota | 57 | 8 | 15 | 23 |
| 1975-76 | Minnesota | 33 | 3 | 2 | 5 |
| 1977-78 | Pittsburgh | 29 | 7 | 5 | 12 |
| 1979-80 | Colorado | 5 | 0 | 1 | 1 |
| | **Totals** | 124 | 18 | 23 | 41 |

**FLETT, William Myer (Cowboy)** *Forward*
b. Vermillion, Alta., July 21, 1943

| Season | Club | GP | G | A | Pts. |
|---|---|---|---|---|---|
| 1967-68 | Los Angeles | 73 | 26 | 20 | 46 |
| 1968-69 | Los Angeles | 72 | 24 | 25 | 49 |
| 1969-70 | Los Angeles | 69 | 14 | 18 | 32 |
| 1970-71 | Los Angeles | 64 | 13 | 24 | 37 |
| 1971-72 | LA-Phil | 76 | 18 | 22 | 40 |
| 1972-73 | Philadelphia | 69 | 43 | 31 | 74 |
| 1973-74 | Philadelphia | 67 | 17 | 27 | 44 |
| 1974-75 | Toronto | 77 | 15 | 25 | 40 |
| 1975-76 | Atlanta | 78 | 23 | 17 | 40 |
| 1976-77 | Atlanta | 24 | 4 | 4 | 8 |
| 1976-77 | Edmonton (WHA) | 48 | 34 | 20 | 54 |
| 1977-78 | Edmonton (WHA) | 74 | 41 | 28 | 69 |
| 1978-79 | Edmonton (WHA) | 73 | 28 | 36 | 64 |
| 1979-80 | Edmonton | 20 | 5 | 2 | 7 |
| | **NHL Totals** | 689 | 202 | 215 | 417 |
| | **WHA Totals** | 194 | 103 | 84 | 187 |

**FLOCKHART, Robert Walter** *Forward*
b. Sicamous, B.C., Feb. 6, 1956

| Season | Club | GP | G | A | Pts. |
|---|---|---|---|---|---|
| 1976-77 | Vancouver | 5 | 0 | 0 | 0 |
| 1977-78 | Vancouver | 24 | 0 | 1 | 1 |
| 1978-79 | Vancouver | 14 | 1 | 1 | 2 |
| 1979-80 | Minnesota | 10 | 1 | 3 | 4 |
| 1980-81 | Minnesota | 2 | 0 | 0 | 0 |
| | **Totals** | 55 | 2 | 5 | 7 |

**FLOCKHART, Ronald** *Forward*
b. Smithers, B.C., Oct. 10, 1960

| Season | Club | GP | G | A | Pts. |
|---|---|---|---|---|---|
| 1980-81 | Philadelphia | 14 | 3 | 7 | 10 |
| 1981-82 | Philadelphia | 72 | 33 | 39 | 72 |
| 1982-83 | Philadelphia | 73 | 29 | 31 | 60 |
| | **Totals** | 159 | 65 | 77 | 142 |

**FLOYD, Larry** *Forward*
b. Peterborough, Ont., May 1, 1961

| Season | Club | GP | G | A | Pts. |
|---|---|---|---|---|---|
| 1982-83 | New Jersey | 5 | 1 | 0 | 1 |

**FOGOLIN, Lee Joseph** *Defenseman*
b. Chicago, Ill., Feb. 7, 1955

| Season | Club | GP | G | A | Pts. |
|---|---|---|---|---|---|
| 1974-75 | Buffalo | 50 | 2 | 2 | 4 |
| 1975-76 | Buffalo | 58 | 0 | 9 | 9 |
| 1976-77 | Buffalo | 71 | 3 | 15 | 18 |
| 1977-78 | Buffalo | 76 | 0 | 23 | 23 |
| 1978-79 | Buffalo | 74 | 3 | 19 | 22 |
| 1979-80 | Edmonton | 80 | 5 | 10 | 15 |
| 1980-81 | Edmonton | 80 | 13 | 17 | 30 |
| 1981-82 | Edmonton | 80 | 4 | 25 | 29 |
| 1982-83 | Edmonton | 72 | 0 | 18 | 18 |
| | **Totals** | 641 | 30 | 138 | 168 |

**FOGOLIN, Lidio John (Lee)** *Defenseman*
b. Fort William, Ont., Feb. 27, 1926

| Season | Club | GP | G | A | Pts. |
|---|---|---|---|---|---|
| 1948-49 | Detroit | 43 | 1 | 2 | 3 |
| 1949-50 | Detroit | 64 | 4 | 8 | 12 |
| 1950-51 | Det-Chi | 54 | 3 | 11 | 14 |
| 1951-52 | Chicago | 69 | 0 | 9 | 9 |
| 1952-53 | Chicago | 70 | 2 | 8 | 10 |
| 1953-54 | Chicago | 68 | 0 | 1 | 1 |
| 1954-55 | Chicago | 9 | 0 | 1 | 1 |
| 1955-56 | Chicago | 51 | 0 | 8 | 8 |
| | **Totals** | 428 | 10 | 48 | 58 |

**FOLCO, Peter Kevin** *Defenseman*
b. Montreal, Que., Aug. 13, 1953

| Season | Club | GP | G | A | Pts. |
|---|---|---|---|---|---|
| 1973-74 | Vancouver | 2 | 0 | 0 | 0 |
| 1975-76 | Toronto (WHA) | 19 | 1 | 8 | 9 |
| 1976-77 | Birmingham (WHA) | 2 | 0 | 0 | 0 |
| | **NHL Totals** | 2 | 0 | 0 | 0 |
| | **WHA Totals** | 21 | 1 | 8 | 9 |

**FOLEY, Gerald James** *Forward*
b. Ware, Mass., Sept. 22, 1932

| Season | Club | GP | G | A | Pts. |
|---|---|---|---|---|---|
| 1954-55 | Toronto | 4 | 0 | 0 | 0 |
| 1956-57 | New York R | 69 | 7 | 9 | 16 |
| 1957-58 | New York R | 68 | 2 | 5 | 7 |
| 1968-69 | Los Angeles | 1 | 0 | 0 | 0 |
| | **Totals** | 142 | 9 | 14 | 23 |

**FOLEY, Gilbert Anthony (Rick)** *Defenseman*
b. Niagara Falls, Ont., Sept. 22, 1945

| Season | Club | GP | G | A | Pts. |
|---|---|---|---|---|---|
| 1970-71 | Chicago | 2 | 0 | 1 | 1 |
| 1971-72 | Philadelphia | 58 | 11 | 25 | 36 |
| 1973-74 | Detroit | 7 | 0 | 0 | 0 |
| | **Totals** | 67 | 11 | 26 | 37 |

**FOLIGNO, Mike Anthony** *Forward*
b. Sudbury, Ont., Jan. 29, 1959

| Season | Club | GP | G | A | Pts. |
|---|---|---|---|---|---|
| 1979-80 | Detroit | 80 | 36 | 35 | 71 |
| 1980-81 | Detroit | 80 | 28 | 35 | 63 |
| 1981-82 | Det-Buf | 82 | 33 | 44 | 77 |
| 1982-83 | Buffalo | 66 | 22 | 25 | 47 |
| | **Totals** | 308 | 119 | 139 | 258 |

**FOLK, William Joseph** *Defenseman*
b. Regina, Sask., July 11, 1927

| Season | Club | GP | G | A | Pts. |
|---|---|---|---|---|---|
| 1951-52 | Detroit | 4 | 0 | 0 | 0 |
| 1952-53 | Detroit | 8 | 0 | 0 | 0 |
| | **Totals** | 12 | 0 | 0 | 0 |

**FONTAINE, Leonard Joseph** *Forward*
b. Quebec City, Que., Feb. 25, 1948

| Season | Club | GP | G | A | Pts. |
|---|---|---|---|---|---|
| 1972-73 | Detroit | 39 | 8 | 10 | 18 |
| 1973-74 | Detroit | 7 | 0 | 1 | 1 |
| 1974-75 | Michigan (WHA) | 21 | 1 | 8 | 9 |
| | **NHL Totals** | 46 | 8 | 11 | 19 |
| | **WHA Totals** | 21 | 1 | 8 | 9 |

**FONTAS, Jon** *Forward*
b. Arlington, Mass., Apr. 16, 1955

| Season | Club | GP | G | A | Pts. |
|---|---|---|---|---|---|
| 1979-80 | Minnesota | 1 | 0 | 0 | 0 |
| 1980-81 | Minnesota | 1 | 0 | 0 | 0 |
| | **Totals** | 2 | 0 | 0 | 0 |

**FONTEYNE, Valere Ronald** *Forward*
b. Wetaskiwin, Alta., Dec. 2, 1933

| Season | Club | GP | G | A | Pts. |
|---|---|---|---|---|---|
| 1959-60 | Detroit | 69 | 4 | 7 | 11 |
| 1960-61 | Detroit | 66 | 6 | 11 | 17 |
| 1961-62 | Detroit | 70 | 5 | 5 | 10 |
| 1962-63 | Detroit | 67 | 6 | 14 | 20 |
| 1963-64 | New York R | 69 | 7 | 18 | 25 |
| 1964-65 | NYR-Det | 43 | 2 | 6 | 8 |
| 1965-66 | Detroit | 59 | 5 | 10 | 15 |
| 1966-67 | Detroit | 28 | 1 | 1 | 2 |
| 1967-68 | Pittsburgh | 69 | 6 | 28 | 34 |
| 1968-69 | Pittsburgh | 74 | 12 | 17 | 29 |
| 1969-70 | Pittsburgh | 68 | 11 | 15 | 26 |
| 1970-71 | Pittsburgh | 70 | 4 | 9 | 13 |
| 1971-72 | Pittsburgh | 68 | 6 | 13 | 19 |
| 1972-73 | Edmonton (WHA) | 71 | 7 | 32 | 39 |
| 1973-74 | Edmonton (WHA) | 72 | 9 | 13 | 22 |
| | **NHL Totals** | 820 | 75 | 154 | 229 |
| | **WHA Totals** | 143 | 16 | 45 | 61 |

**FONTINATO, Louis (The Leaper)**
*Defenseman*
b. Guelph, Ont., Jan. 20, 1932

| Season | Club | GP | G | A | Pts. |
|---|---|---|---|---|---|
| 1954-55 | New York R | 27 | 2 | 2 | 4 |
| 1955-56 | New York R | 70 | 3 | 15 | 18 |
| 1956-57 | New York R | 70 | 3 | 12 | 15 |
| 1957-58 | New York R | 70 | 3 | 8 | 11 |
| 1958-59 | New York R | 64 | 7 | 6 | 13 |
| 1959-60 | New York R | 64 | 2 | 11 | 13 |
| 1960-61 | New York R | 53 | 2 | 3 | 5 |
| 1961-62 | Montreal | 55 | 2 | 13 | 15 |
| 1962-63 | Montreal | 63 | 2 | 6 | 8 |
| | **Totals** | 536 | 26 | 76 | 102 |

**FORBES, David Stephen** *Forward*
b. Montreal, Que., Nov. 16, 1948

| Season | Club | GP | G | A | Pts. |
|---|---|---|---|---|---|
| 1973-74 | Boston | 63 | 10 | 16 | 26 |
| 1974-75 | Boston | 69 | 18 | 12 | 30 |
| 1975-76 | Boston | 79 | 16 | 13 | 29 |
| 1976-77 | Boston | 73 | 9 | 11 | 20 |
| 1977-78 | Washington | 77 | 11 | 11 | 22 |
| 1978-79 | Washington | 2 | 0 | 1 | 1 |
| 1978-79 | Cincinnati (WHA) | 73 | 6 | 5 | 11 |
| | **NHL Totals** | 363 | 64 | 64 | 128 |
| | **WHA Totals** | 73 | 6 | 5 | 11 |

**FOREY, Conley Michael** *Forward*
b. Montreal, Que., Oct. 18, 1950

| Season | Club | GP | G | A | Pts. |
|---|---|---|---|---|---|
| 1973-74 | St. Louis | 4 | 0 | 0 | 0 |

**FORBES, Michael D.** *Defenseman*
b. Brampton, Ont., Sept. 20, 1957

| Season | Club | GP | G | A | Pts. |
|---|---|---|---|---|---|
| 1977-78 | Boston | 32 | 0 | 4 | 4 |
| 1979-80 | Edmonton | 2 | 0 | 0 | 0 |
| | **Totals** | 35 | 0 | 4 | 4 |

**FORSEY, Jack** *Forward*

| Season | Club | GP | G | A | Pts. |
|---|---|---|---|---|---|
| 1942-43 | Toronto | 19 | 7 | 9 | 16 |

**FORSLAND, Gus** *Forward*
b. Fort William, Ont., Apr. 25, 1908

| Season | Club | GP | G | A | Pts. |
|---|---|---|---|---|---|
| 1932-33 | Ottawa | 48 | 4 | 9 | 13 |

**FORSYTH, Alex** *Forward*
b. Galt, Ont., Jan. 6, 1955

| Season | Club | GP | G | A | Pts. |
|---|---|---|---|---|---|
| 1976-77 | Washington | 1 | 0 | 0 | 0 |

**FORTIER, Charles** *Forward*

| Season | Club | GP | G | A | Pts. |
|---|---|---|---|---|---|
| 1923-24 | Montreal | 1 | 0 | 0 | 0 |

**FORTIER, David Edward** *Defenseman*
b. Sudbury, Ont., June 17, 1951

| Season | Club | GP | G | A | Pts. |
|---|---|---|---|---|---|
| 1972-73 | Toronto | 23 | 1 | 4 | 5 |
| 1974-75 | New York I | 65 | 6 | 12 | 18 |
| 1975-76 | New York I | 59 | 0 | 2 | 2 |
| 1976-77 | Vancouver | 58 | 1 | 3 | 4 |
| 1977-78 | Indianapolis (WHA) | 54 | 1 | 15 | 16 |
| | **NHL Totals** | 215 | 8 | 21 | 29 |
| | **WHA Totals** | 54 | 1 | 15 | 16 |

**FORTIN, Raymond Henri** *Defenseman*
b. Drummondville, Que., Mar. 11, 1941

| Season | Club | GP | G | A | Pts. |
|---|---|---|---|---|---|
| 1967-68 | St Louis | 24 | 0 | 2 | 2 |
| 1968-69 | St Louis | 11 | 1 | 0 | 1 |
| 1969-70 | St Louis | 57 | 1 | 4 | 5 |
| | **Totals** | 92 | 2 | 6 | 8 |

**FOSTER, Dwight Alexander** *Forward*
b. Toronto, Ont., Apr. 2, 1957

| Season | Club | GP | G | A | Pts. |
|---|---|---|---|---|---|
| 1977-78 | Boston | 14 | 2 | 1 | 3 |
| 1978-79 | Boston | 44 | 11 | 13 | 24 |
| 1979-80 | Boston | 57 | 10 | 28 | 38 |
| 1980-81 | Boston | 77 | 24 | 28 | 52 |
| 1981-82 | Colorado | 70 | 12 | 19 | 31 |
| 1982-83 | NJ-Det | 62 | 17 | 22 | 39 |
| | **Totals** | 324 | 76 | 111 | 187 |

**FOSTER, Harry C. (Yip)** *Defenseman*
b. Guelph, Ont., Nov. 25, 1907

| Season | Club | GP | G | A | Pts. |
|---|---|---|---|---|---|
| 1929-30 | New York R | 31 | 0 | 0 | 0 |
| 1931-31 | Boston | 31 | 1 | 2 | 3 |
| 1933-34 | Detroit | 6 | 0 | 0 | 0 |
| 1934-35 | Detroit | 13 | 2 | 0 | 2 |
| | **Totals** | 81 | 3 | 2 | 5 |

**FOSTER, Herbert Stanley** *Forward*
b. Brockville, Ont., Aug. 9, 1913

| Season | Club | GP | G | A | Pts. |
|---|---|---|---|---|---|
| 1940-41 | New York R | 4 | 1 | 0 | 1 |
| 1947-48 | New York R | 1 | 0 | 0 | 0 |
| | **Totals** | 5 | 1 | 0 | 1 |

**FOTIU, Nicholas Evlampios** *Forward*
b. Staten Island, N.Y., May 25, 1952

| Season | Club | GP | G | A | Pts. |
|---|---|---|---|---|---|
| 1974-75 | New England (WHA) | 61 | 2 | 2 | 4 |
| 1975-76 | New England (WHA) | 49 | 3 | 2 | 5 |
| 1976-77 | New York R | 70 | 4 | 8 | 12 |
| 1977-78 | New York R | 59 | 2 | 7 | 9 |
| 1978-79 | New York R | 71 | 3 | 5 | 8 |
| 1979-80 | Hartford | 74 | 10 | 8 | 18 |
| 1980-81 | Hart-NYR | 69 | 9 | 9 | 18 |
| 1981-82 | New York R | 70 | 8 | 10 | 18 |
| 1982-83 | New York R | 72 | 8 | 13 | 21 |
| | **NHL Totals** | 485 | 44 | 60 | 104 |
| | **WHA Totals** | 110 | 5 | 4 | 9 |

**FOWLER, James** *Defenseman*
b. Toronto, Ont., Apr. 6, 1915

| Season | Club | GP | G | A | Pts. |
|---|---|---|---|---|---|
| 1936-37 | Toronto | 48 | 7 | 11 | 18 |
| 1937-38 | Toronto | 48 | 10 | 12 | 22 |
| 1938-39 | Toronto | 39 | 1 | 6 | 7 |
| | **Totals** | 135 | 18 | 29 | 47 |

**FOWLER, Thomas** *Forward*
b. Winnipeg, Man., May 18, 1924

| Season | Club | GP | G | A | Pts. |
|---|---|---|---|---|---|
| 1946-47 | Chicago | 24 | 0 | 1 | 1 |

**FOX, Gregory Brent** *Defenseman*
b. Port McNeil, B.C., Aug. 12, 1953

| Season | Club | GP | G | A | Pts. |
|---|---|---|---|---|---|
| 1977-78 | Atlanta | 16 | 1 | 2 | 3 |
| 1978-79 | Atl-Chi | 78 | 0 | 17 | 17 |
| 1979-80 | Chicago | 71 | 4 | 11 | 15 |
| 1980-81 | Chicago | 75 | 3 | 16 | 19 |
| 1981-82 | Chicago | 79 | 2 | 19 | 21 |
| 1982-83 | Chicago | 76 | 0 | 13 | 13 |
| | **Totals** | 395 | 10 | 78 | 88 |

**FOX, James Charles** *Forward*
b. Coniston, Ont., May 18, 1960

| Season | Club | GP | G | A | Pts. |
|---|---|---|---|---|---|
| 1980-81 | Los Angeles | 71 | 18 | 25 | 43 |
| 1981-82 | Los Angeles | 77 | 30 | 38 | 68 |
| 1982-83 | Los Angeles | 77 | 28 | 40 | 68 |
| | **Totals** | 225 | 76 | 103 | 179 |

**FOYSTON, Frank C.** *Forward*
b. Minesing, Ont., Feb. 2, 1891

| Season | Club | GP | G | A | Pts. |
|---|---|---|---|---|---|
| 1926-27 | Detroit | 42 | 10 | 5 | 15 |
| 1927-28 | Detroit | 24 | 7 | 2 | 9 |
| | **Totals** | 66 | 17 | 7 | 24 |

**FRAMPTON, Robert Percy James** *Forward*
b. Toronto, Ont., Jan. 20, 1929

| Season | Club | GP | G | A | Pts. |
|---|---|---|---|---|---|
| 1949-50 | Montreal | 2 | 0 | 0 | 0 |

**FRANCESCHETTI, Lou** *Forward*
b. Toronto, Ont., Apr. 28, 1958

| Season | Club | GP | G | A | Pts. |
|---|---|---|---|---|---|
| 1981-82 | Washington | 30 | 2 | 10 | 12 |

**FRANCIS, Robert** *Forward*
b. North Battleford, Sask., Dec. 5, 1958

| Season | Club | GP | G | A | Pts. |
|---|---|---|---|---|---|
| 1982-83 | Detroit | 14 | 2 | 0 | 2 |

**FRANCIS, Ronald** *Forward*
b. Sault Ste. Marie, Mar. 1, 1963

| Season | Club | GP | G | A | Pts. |
|---|---|---|---|---|---|
| 1981-82 | Hartford | 59 | 25 | 43 | 68 |
| 1982-83 | Hartford | 79 | 31 | 59 | 90 |
| | **Totals** | 138 | 56 | 102 | 158 |

**FRASER, Curt M.** *Forward*
b. Cincinnati, Ohio, Jan. 12, 1958

| Season | Club | GP | G | A | Pts. |
|---|---|---|---|---|---|
| 1978-79 | Vancouver | 78 | 16 | 19 | 35 |
| 1979-80 | Vancouver | 78 | 17 | 25 | 42 |
| 1980-81 | Vancouver | 77 | 25 | 24 | 49 |
| 1981-82 | Vancouver | 79 | 28 | 39 | 67 |
| 1982-83 | Van-Chi | 74 | 12 | 20 | 32 |
| | **Totals** | 386 | 98 | 127 | 225 |

**FRASER, Jack** *Forward*

| Season | Club | GP | G | A | Pts. |
|---|---|---|---|---|---|
| 1923-24 | Hamilton | 1 | 0 | 0 | 0 |

**FRASER, Archibald McKay (Archie)** *Forward*
b. Souris, Man., Feb. 9, 1914

| Season | Club | GP | G | A | Pts. |
|---|---|---|---|---|---|
| 1943-44 | New York R | 3 | 0 | 1 | 1 |

**FRASER, Gordon** *Defenseman*
b. Pembroke, Ont.

| Season | Club | GP | G | A | Pts. |
|---|---|---|---|---|---|
| 1926-27 | Chicago | 44 | 14 | 6 | 20 |
| 1927-28 | Detroit | 41 | 4 | 2 | 6 |
| 1928-29 | Detroit | 14 | 0 | 0 | 0 |
| 1929-30 | Mont-PittPi | 40 | 6 | 4 | 10 |
| 1930-31 | Philadelphia Q | 5 | 0 | 0 | 0 |
| | **Totals** | 144 | 24 | 12 | 36 |

**FRASER, Harvey** *Forward*
b. Souris, Man., Oct. 14, 1918

| Season | Club | GP | G | A | Pts. |
|---|---|---|---|---|---|
| 1944-45 | Chicago | 21 | 5 | 4 | 9 |

**FREDERICKSON, Frank** *Forward*
b. Winnipeg, Man., 1895

| Season | Club | GP | G | A | Pts. |
|---|---|---|---|---|---|
| 1926-27 | Det-Bos | 41 | 18 | 13 | 31 |
| 1927-28 | Boston | 41 | 10 | 4 | 14 |
| 1928-29 | Bos-PittPi | 42 | 6 | 8 | 14 |
| 1929-30 | Pittsburgh Pi | 9 | 4 | 7 | 11 |
| 1930-31 | Detroit | 24 | 1 | 2 | 3 |
| | **Totals** | 157 | 39 | 34 | 73 |

**FREW, Irvine** *Defenseman*
b. Kilsyth, Scotland, Aug. 16, 1907

| Season | Club | GP | G | A | Pts. |
|---|---|---|---|---|---|
| 1933-34 | Montreal M | 32 | 2 | 1 | 3 |
| 1934-35 | St Louis E | 48 | 0 | 2 | 2 |
| 1935-36 | Montreal | 18 | 0 | 2 | 2 |
| | **Totals** | 98 | 2 | 5 | 7 |

**FRIDGEN, Dan** *Forward*
b. Arnprior, Ont., May 18, 1959

| Season | Club | GP | G | A | Pts. |
|---|---|---|---|---|---|
| 1981-82 | Hartford | 2 | 0 | 1 | 1 |
| 1982-83 | Hartford | 11 | 2 | 2 | 4 |
| | **Totals** | 13 | 2 | 3 | 5 |

**FRIEST, Ronald** *Forward*
b. Windsor, Ont., Nov. 4, 1958

| Season | Club | GP | G | A | Pts. |
|---|---|---|---|---|---|
| 1980-81 | Minnesota | 4 | 1 | 0 | 1 |
| 1981-82 | Minnesota | 10 | 0 | 0 | 0 |
| 1982-83 | Minnesota | 50 | 6 | 7 | 13 |
| | **Totals** | 64 | 7 | 7 | 14 |

**FRIG, Leonard Elroy** *Defenseman*
b. Lethbridge, Alta., Oct. 23, 1950

| Season | Club | GP | G | A | Pts. |
|---|---|---|---|---|---|
| 1973-74 | Chicago | 66 | 4 | 10 | 14 |
| 1974-75 | California | 80 | 3 | 17 | 20 |
| 1975-76 | California | 62 | 3 | 12 | 15 |
| 1976-77 | Cleveland | 66 | 2 | 7 | 9 |
| 1977-78 | St Louis | 30 | 1 | 3 | 4 |
| 1979-80 | St Louis | 7 | 0 | 2 | 2 |
| | **Totals** | 311 | 13 | 51 | 64 |

**FROST, Harry** *Forward*
b. Keer Lake, Ont., Aug. 17, 1914

| Season | Club | GP | G | A | Pts. |
|---|---|---|---|---|---|
| 1938-39 | Boston | | 0 | 0 | 0 |

**FRYCER, Miroslav** *Forward*
b. Ostrava, Czechoslovakia, Sept. 27, 1959

| Season | Club | GP | G | A | Pts. |
|---|---|---|---|---|---|
| 1981-82 | Que-Tor | 59 | 24 | 23 | 47 |
| 1982-83 | Toronto | 67 | 25 | 30 | 55 |
| | **Totals** | 126 | 49 | 53 | 102 |

**FRYDAY, Robert George** *Forward*
b. Toronto, Ont., Dec. 5, 1927

| Season | Club | GP | G | A | Pts. |
|---|---|---|---|---|---|
| 1951-52 | Montreal | 3 | 0 | 0 | 0 |

**FTOREK, Robert Brian (Robbie)** *Forward*
b. Needham, Mass., Jan. 2, 1952

| Season | Club | GP | G | A | Pts. |
|---|---|---|---|---|---|
| 1972-73 | Detroit | 3 | 0 | 0 | 0 |
| 1973-74 | Detroit | 12 | 2 | 5 | 7 |
| 1974-75 | Phoenix (WHA) | 53 | 31 | 37 | 68 |
| 1975-76 | Phoenix (WHA) | 80 | 41 | 72 | 113 |
| 1976-77 | Phoenix (WHA) | 80 | 46 | 71 | 117 |
| 1977-78 | Cincinnati (WHA) | 80 | 59 | 50 | 109 |
| 1978-79 | Cincinnati (WHA) | 80 | 39 | 77 | 116 |
| 1979-80 | Quebec | 52 | 18 | 33 | 51 |
| 1980-81 | Quebec | 78 | 24 | 49 | 73 |
| 1981-82 | Que-NYR | 49 | 9 | 33 | 42 |
| 1982-83 | New York R | 61 | 12 | 19 | 31 |
| | **NHL Totals** | 343 | 63 | 134 | 197 |
| | **WHA Totals** | 385 | 218 | 312 | 530 |

**FULLAN, Lawrence** *Forward*
b. Toronto, Ont., Aug. 11, 1949

| Season | Club | GP | G | A | Pts. |
|---|---|---|---|---|---|
| 1974-75 | Washington | 4 | 1 | 0 | 1 |

**GADSBY, William Alexander** *Defenseman*
b. Calgary, Alta., Aug. 8, 1927

| Season | Club | GP | G | A | Pts. |
|---|---|---|---|---|---|
| 1946-47 | Chicago | 48 | 8 | 10 | 18 |
| 1947-48 | Chicago | 60 | 6 | 10 | 16 |
| 1948-49 | Chicago | 50 | 3 | 10 | 13 |
| 1949-50 | Chicago | 70 | 10 | 24 | 34 |
| 1950-51 | Chicago | 25 | 3 | 7 | 10 |
| 1951-52 | Chicago | 59 | 7 | 15 | 22 |
| 1952-53 | Chicago | 68 | 2 | 20 | 22 |
| 1953-54 | Chicago | 70 | 12 | 29 | 41 |
| 1954-55 | Chi-NYR | 70 | 11 | 13 | 24 |
| 1955-56 | New York R | 70 | 9 | 42 | 51 |
| 1956-57 | New York R | 70 | 4 | 37 | 41 |
| 1957-58 | New York R | 65 | 14 | 32 | 46 |
| 1958-59 | New York R | 70 | 5 | 46 | 51 |
| 1959-60 | New York R | 65 | 9 | 22 | 31 |
| 1960-61 | New York R | 65 | 9 | 26 | 35 |
| 1961-62 | Detroit | 70 | 7 | 30 | 37 |
| 1962-63 | Detroit | 70 | 4 | 24 | 28 |
| 1963-64 | Detroit | 64 | 2 | 16 | 18 |
| 1964-65 | Detroit | 61 | 0 | 12 | 12 |
| 1965-66 | Detroit | 58 | 5 | 12 | 17 |
| | **Totals** | 1248 | 130 | 437 | 567 |

**GAGE, Joseph William** *Forward*
b. Toronto, Ont., Nov. 29, 1959

| Season | Club | GP | G | A | Pts. |
|---|---|---|---|---|---|
| 1980-81 | Detroit | 16 | 2 | 2 | 4 |
| 1981-82 | Detroit | 31 | 9 | 9 | 18 |
| | **Totals** | 47 | 11 | 11 | 22 |

**GAGNE, Arthur** *Forward*

| Season | Club | GP | G | A | Pts. |
|---|---|---|---|---|---|
| 1926-27 | Montreal | 44 | 14 | 3 | 17 |
| 1927-28 | Montreal | 44 | 20 | 10 | 30 |
| 1928-29 | Montreal | 44 | 7 | 3 | 10 |
| 1929-30 | Bos-Ott | 38 | 6 | 5 | 11 |
| 1930-31 | Ottawa | 44 | 19 | 11 | 30 |
| 1931-32 | Detroit | 13 | 1 | 1 | 2 |
| | **Totals** | 227 | 67 | 33 | 100 |


**GAGNE, Paul** *Forward*
b. Iroquois Falls, Ont., Feb. 6, 1962

| Season | Club | GP | G | A | Pts. |
|---|---|---|---|---|---|
| 1980-81 | Colorado | 61 | 25 | 16 | 41 |
| 1981-82 | Colorado | 59 | 10 | 12 | 22 |
| 1982-83 | New Jersey | 53 | 14 | 15 | 29 |
| | **Totals** | 173 | 49 | 43 | 92 |

**GAGNE, Pierre** *Forward*
b. North Bay, Ont., June 5, 1940

| Season | Club | GP | G | A | Pts. |
|---|---|---|---|---|---|
| 1959-60 | Boston | 2 | 0 | 0 | 0 |

**GAGNON, Germain** *Forward*
b. Chicoutimi, Que., Dec. 9, 1942

| Season | Club | GP | G | A | Pts. |
|---|---|---|---|---|---|
| 1971-72 | Montreal | 4 | 0 | 0 | 0 |
| 1972-73 | New York I | 63 | 12 | 29 | 41 |
| 1973-74 | New York I | 76 | 11 | 28 | 39 |
| 1974-75 | Chicago | 80 | 16 | 35 | 51 |
| 1975-76 | Kansas City | 31 | 1 | 9 | 10 |
| | **Totals** | 254 | 40 | 101 | 141 |

**GAGNON, John (Black Cat)** *Forward*
b. Chicoutimi, Que., June 8, 1905

| Season | Club | GP | G | A | Pts. |
|---|---|---|---|---|---|
| 1930-31 | Montreal | 41 | 18 | 7 | 25 |
| 1931-32 | Montreal | 48 | 19 | 18 | 37 |
| 1932-33 | Montreal | 48 | 12 | 23 | 35 |
| 1933-34 | Montreal | 48 | 9 | 15 | 24 |
| 1934-35 | Bos-Mont | 47 | 2 | 6 | 8 |
| 1935-36 | Montreal | 48 | 7 | 9 | 16 |
| 1936-37 | Montreal | 48 | 20 | 16 | 36 |
| 1937-38 | Montreal | 47 | 13 | 17 | 30 |
| 1938-39 | Montreal | 45 | 12 | 22 | 34 |
| 1939-40 | Mont-NYR | 34 | 8 | 8 | 16 |
| | **Totals** | 454 | 120 | 141 | 261 |

**GAINEY, Robert Michael (Bob)** *Forward*
b. Peterborough, Ont., Dec. 13, 1953

| Season | Club | GP | G | A | Pts. |
|---|---|---|---|---|---|
| 1973-74 | Montreal | 66 | 3 | 7 | 10 |
| 1974-75 | Montreal | 80 | 17 | 20 | 37 |
| 1975-76 | Montreal | 78 | 15 | 13 | 28 |
| 1976-77 | Montreal | 80 | 14 | 19 | 33 |
| 1977-78 | Montreal | 66 | 15 | 16 | 31 |
| 1978-79 | Montreal | 79 | 20 | 18 | 38 |
| 1979-80 | Montreal | 64 | 14 | 19 | 33 |
| 1980-81 | Montreal | 78 | 23 | 24 | 47 |
| 1981-82 | Montreal | 79 | 21 | 24 | 45 |
| 1982-83 | Montreal | 80 | 12 | 18 | 30 |
| | **Totals** | 750 | 134 | 178 | 332 |

**GAINOR, Norman (Dutch)** *Forward*
b. Calgary, Alta., Apr. 10, 1904

| Season | Club | GP | G | A | Pts. |
|---|---|---|---|---|---|
| 1927-28 | Boston | 41 | 8 | 4 | 12 |
| 1928-29 | Boston | 44 | 14 | 5 | 19 |
| 1929-30 | Boston | 42 | 18 | 31 | 49 |
| 1930-31 | Boston | 35 | 8 | 3 | 11 |
| 1931-32 | New York R | 46 | 3 | 9 | 12 |
| 1932-33 | Ottawa | 2 | 0 | 0 | 0 |
| 1934-35 | Montreal M | 35 | 0 | 4 | 4 |
| | **Totals** | 245 | 51 | 56 | 107 |

**GALARNEAU, Michel** *Forward*
b. Montreal, Que., Mar. 1, 1961

| Season | Club | GP | G | A | Pts. |
|---|---|---|---|---|---|
| 1980-81 | Hartford | 30 | 2 | 6 | 8 |
| 1981-82 | Hartford | 10 | 0 | 0 | 0 |
| 1982-83 | Hartford | 38 | 5 | 4 | 9 |
| | **Totals** | 78 | 7 | 10 | 17 |

**GALBRAITH, Percival (Perk)** *Forward*
b. Toronto, Ont., 1899

| Season | Club | GP | G | A | Pts. |
|---|---|---|---|---|---|
| 1926-27 | Boston | 41 | 9 | 8 | 17 |
| 1927-28 | Boston | 43 | 6 | 5 | 11 |
| 1928-29 | Boston | 38 | 2 | 1 | 3 |
| 1929-30 | Boston | 44 | 7 | 9 | 16 |
| 1930-31 | Boston | 44 | 2 | 3 | 5 |
| 1931-32 | Boston | 48 | 2 | 1 | 3 |
| 1932-33 | Boston | 48 | 1 | 2 | 3 |
| 1933-34 | Boston | 46 | 2 | 0 | 2 |
| | **Totals** | 352 | 31 | 29 | 60 |


**GALLAGHER, John** *Defenseman*
b. Kenora, Ont., Jan. 19, 1909

| Season | Club | GP | G | A | Pts. |
|---|---|---|---|---|---|
| 1930-31 | Montreal M | 36 | 4 | 2 | 6 |
| 1931-32 | Montreal M | 19 | 1 | 0 | 1 |
| 1932-33 | MontM-Det | 43 | 4 | 6 | 10 |
| 1936-37 | Det-NYA | 20 | 1 | 0 | 1 |
| 1937-38 | New York A | 46 | 3 | 6 | 9 |
| 1938-39 | New York A | 43 | 1 | 5 | 6 |
| | **Totals** | 207 | 14 | 19 | 33 |

**GALLIMORE, James** *Forward*
b. Edmonton, Alta., Nov. 28, 1957

| Season | Club | GP | G | A | Pts. |
|---|---|---|---|---|---|
| 1977-78 | Minnesota | 2 | 0 | 0 | 0 |

**GALLINGER, Donald Calvin** *Forward*
b. Port Colborne, Ont., Apr. 10, 1925

| Season | Club | GP | G | A | Pts. |
|---|---|---|---|---|---|
| 1942-43 | Boston | 48 | 14 | 20 | 34 |
| 1943-44 | Boston | 23 | 13 | 5 | 18 |
| 1945-46 | Boston | 50 | 17 | 23 | 40 |
| 1946-47 | Boston | 47 | 11 | 19 | 30 |
| 1947-48 | Boston | 54 | 10 | 21 | 31 |
| | **Totals** | 222 | 65 | 88 | 153 |

**GAMBLE, Richard Frank** *Forward*
b. Moncton, N.B., Nov. 16, 1928

| Season | Club | GP | G | A | Pts. |
|---|---|---|---|---|---|
| 1950-51 | Montreal | 1 | 0 | 0 | 0 |
| 1951-52 | Montreal | 64 | 23 | 17 | 40 |
| 1952-53 | Montreal | 69 | 11 | 13 | 24 |
| 1953-54 | Montreal | 32 | 4 | 8 | 12 |
| 1954-55 | Chi-Mont | 14 | 2 | 0 | 2 |
| 1955-56 | Montreal | 12 | 0 | 3 | 3 |
| 1965-66 | Toronto | 2 | 1 | 0 | 1 |
| 1966-67 | Toronto | 1 | 0 | 0 | 0 |
| | **Totals** | 195 | 41 | 41 | 82 |

**GAMBUCCI, Gary Allan** *Forward*
b. Hibbing, Minn., Sept. 27, 1946

| Season | Club | GP | G | A | Pts. |
|---|---|---|---|---|---|
| 1971-72 | Minnesota | 9 | 1 | 0 | 1 |
| 1973-74 | Minnesota | 42 | 1 | 7 | 8 |
| 1974-75 | Minnesota (WHA) | 68 | 19 | 18 | 37 |
| 1975-76 | Minnesota (WHA) | 45 | 10 | 6 | 16 |
| | **NHL Totals** | 51 | 2 | 7 | 9 |
| | **WHA Totals** | 113 | 29 | 24 | 53 |

**GANS, Dave** *Forward*
b. Brantford, Ont., June 6, 1964

| Season | Club | GP | G | A | Pts. |
|---|---|---|---|---|---|
| 1982-83 | Los Angeles | 3 | 0 | 0 | 0 |

**GARDINER, Herbert Martin** *Defenseman*
b. Winnipeg, Man., May 8, 1891

| Season | Club | GP | G | A | Pts. |
|---|---|---|---|---|---|
| 1926-27 | Montreal | 44 | 6 | 6 | 12 |
| 1927-28 | Montreal | 44 | 4 | 3 | 7 |
| 1928-29 | Chi-Mont | 13 | 0 | 0 | 0 |
| | **Totals** | 101 | 10 | 9 | 19 |

**GARDNER, Calvin Pearly** *Forward*
b. Transcona, Man., Oct. 30, 1924

| Season | Club | GP | G | A | Pts. |
|---|---|---|---|---|---|
| 1945-46 | New York R | 16 | 8 | 2 | 10 |
| 1946-47 | New York R | 52 | 13 | 16 | 29 |
| 1947-48 | New York R | 58 | 7 | 18 | 25 |
| 1948-49 | Toronto | 53 | 13 | 22 | 35 |
| 1949-50 | Toronto | 30 | 7 | 19 | 26 |
| 1950-51 | Toronto | 66 | 23 | 28 | 51 |
| 1951-52 | Toronto | 70 | 15 | 26 | 41 |
| 1952-53 | Chicago | 70 | 11 | 24 | 35 |
| 1953-54 | Boston | 70 | 14 | 20 | 34 |
| 1954-55 | Boston | 70 | 16 | 22 | 38 |
| 1955-56 | Boston | 70 | 15 | 21 | 36 |
| 1956-57 | Boston | 70 | 12 | 20 | 32 |
| | **Totals** | 695 | 154 | 238 | 392 |

**GARDNER, David Calvin (Dave)** *Forward*
b. Toronto, Ont., Aug. 23, 1952

| Season | Club | GP | G | A | Pts. |
|---|---|---|---|---|---|
| 1972-73 | Montreal | 5 | 1 | 1 | 2 |
| 1973-74 | Mont-StL | 46 | 6 | 12 | 18 |
| 1974-75 | StL-Cal | 74 | 16 | 22 | 38 |
| 1975-76 | California | 74 | 16 | 32 | 48 |
| 1976-77 | Cleveland | 76 | 16 | 22 | 38 |
| 1977-78 | Cleveland | 75 | 19 | 25 | 44 |
| 1979-80 | Philadelphia | 2 | 1 | 1 | 2 |
| | **Totals** | 352 | 75 | 115 | 190 |

**GARDNER, Paul Malone** *Forward*
b. Fort Erie, Ont., Mar. 5, 1956

| Season | Club | GP | G | A | Pts. |
|---|---|---|---|---|---|
| 1976-77 | Colorado | 60 | 30 | 29 | 59 |
| 1977-78 | Colorado | 46 | 30 | 22 | 52 |
| 1978-79 | Col-Tor | 75 | 30 | 28 | 58 |
| 1979-80 | Toronto | 45 | 11 | 13 | 24 |
| 1980-81 | Pittsburgh | 62 | 34 | 40 | 74 |
| 1981-82 | Pittsburgh | 59 | 36 | 33 | 69 |
| 1982-83 | Pittsburgh | 70 | 28 | 27 | 55 |
| | **Totals** | 417 | 199 | 192 | 391 |

**GARDNER, William Scott** *Forward*
b. Toronto, Ont., May 19, 1960

| Season | Club | GP | G | A | Pts. |
|---|---|---|---|---|---|
| 1980-81 | Chicago | 1 | 0 | 0 | 0 |
| 1981-82 | Chicago | 69 | 8 | 15 | 23 |
| 1982-83 | Chicago | 77 | 15 | 25 | 40 |
| | **Totals** | 147 | 23 | 40 | 63 |

**GARE, Daniel Mirl (Danny)** *Forward*
b. Nelson, B.C., May 14, 1954

| Season | Club | GP | G | A | Pts. |
|---|---|---|---|---|---|
| 1974-75 | Buffalo | 78 | 31 | 31 | 62 |
| 1975-76 | Buffalo | 79 | 50 | 23 | 73 |
| 1976-77 | Buffalo | 35 | 11 | 15 | 26 |
| 1977-78 | Buffalo | 69 | 39 | 38 | 77 |
| 1978-79 | Buffalo | 71 | 27 | 40 | 67 |
| 1979-80 | Buffalo | 76 | 56 | 33 | 89 |
| 1980-81 | Buffalo | 73 | 46 | 39 | 85 |
| 1981-82 | Buf-Det | 59 | 20 | 24 | 44 |
| 1982-83 | Detroit | 79 | 26 | 35 | 61 |
| | **Totals** | 619 | 306 | 278 | 584 |

**GARIEPY, Raymond** *Defenseman*
b. Toronto, Ont., Sept. 4, 1928

| Season | Club | GP | G | A | Pts. |
|---|---|---|---|---|---|
| 1953-54 | Boston | 35 | 1 | 6 | 7 |
| 1955-56 | Toronto | 1 | 0 | 0 | 0 |
| | **Totals** | 36 | 1 | 6 | 7 |

**GARLAND, Stephen Scott** *Forward*
b. Regina, Sask., May 16, 1952

| Season | Club | GP | G | A | Pts. |
|---|---|---|---|---|---|
| 1975-76 | Toronto | 16 | 4 | 3 | 7 |
| 1976-77 | Toronto | 69 | 9 | 20 | 29 |
| 1978-79 | Los Angeles | 6 | 0 | 1 | 1 |
| | **Totals** | 91 | 13 | 24 | 37 |

**GARNER, Rob** *Forward*
b. Weston, Ont., Aug. 17, 1958

| Season | Club | GP | G | A | Pts. |
|---|---|---|---|---|---|
| 1982-83 | Pittsburgh | 1 | 0 | 0 | 0 |

**GARRETT, Dudley (Red)** *Defenseman*
b. Toronto, Ont., July 24, 1924

| Season | Club | GP | G | A | Pts. |
|---|---|---|---|---|---|
| 1942-43 | New York R | 23 | 1 | 1 | 2 |

**GARTNER, Michael Alfred** *Forward*
b. Ottawa, Ont., Oct. 29, 1959

| Season | Club | GP | G | A | Pts. |
|---|---|---|---|---|---|
| 1979-80 | Washington | 77 | 36 | 32 | 68 |
| 1980-81 | Washington | 80 | 48 | 46 | 94 |
| 1981-82 | Washington | 80 | 35 | 45 | 80 |
| 1982-83 | Washington | 73 | 38 | 38 | 76 |
| | **Totals** | 310 | 157 | 161 | 318 |

**GASSOFF, Robert Allen** *Defenseman*
b. Quesnel, B.C., Apr. 17, 1953

| Season | Club | GP | G | A | Pts. |
|---|---|---|---|---|---|
| 1973-74 | St Louis | 28 | 0 | 3 | 3 |
| 1974-75 | St Louis | 60 | 4 | 14 | 18 |
| 1975-76 | St Louis | 80 | 1 | 12 | 13 |
| 1976-77 | St Louis | 77 | 6 | 18 | 24 |
| | **Totals** | 245 | 11 | 47 | 58 |

**GASSOFF, Howard Bradley** *Forward*
b. Quesnel, B.C., Nov. 13, 1955

| Season | Club | GP | G | A | Pts. |
|---|---|---|---|---|---|
| 1975-76 | Vancouver | 4 | 0 | 0 | 0 |
| 1976-77 | Vancouver | 37 | 6 | 4 | 10 |
| 1977-78 | Vancouver | 47 | 9 | 6 | 15 |
| 1978-79 | Vancouver | 34 | 4 | 7 | 11 |
| | **Totals** | 122 | 19 | 17 | 36 |

**GATZOS, Steve** *Forward*
b. Toronto, Ont., June 22, 1961

| Season | Club | GP | G | A | Pts. |
|---|---|---|---|---|---|
| 1981-82 | Pittsburgh | 16 | 6 | 8 | 14 |
| 1982-83 | Pittsburgh | 44 | 6 | 7 | 13 |
| | **Totals** | 60 | 12 | 15 | 27 |

**GAUDREAULT, Armand Gerard** *Forward*
b. Lake St. John, Que., July 14, 1921

| Season | Club | GP | G | A | Pts. |
|---|---|---|---|---|---|
| 1944-45 | Boston | 44 | 15 | 9 | 24 |

**GAUDREAULT, Leonard (Leo)** *Forward*
b. Chicoutimi, Que.

| Season | Club | GP | G | A | Pts. |
|---|---|---|---|---|---|
| 1927-28 | Montreal | 32 | 6 | 2 | 8 |
| 1928-29 | Montreal | 11 | 0 | 0 | 0 |
| 1932-33 | Montreal | 24 | 2 | 2 | 4 |
| | **Totals** | 67 | 8 | 4 | 12 |

**GAULIN, Jean-Marc** *Forward*
b. Balve, Allemagne, Mar. 3, 1962

| Season | Club | GP | G | A | Pts. |
|---|---|---|---|---|---|
| 1982-83 | Quebec | 1 | 0 | 0 | 0 |

**GAUTHIER, Jean Phillipe** *Defenseman*
b. Montreal, Que., Apr. 29, 1937

| Season | Club | GP | G | A | Pts. |
|---|---|---|---|---|---|
| 1960-61 | Montreal | 4 | 0 | 1 | 1 |
| 1961-62 | Montreal | 12 | 0 | 1 | 1 |
| 1962-63 | Montreal | 65 | 1 | 17 | 18 |
| 1963-64 | Montreal | 1 | 0 | 0 | 0 |
| 1965-66 | Montreal | 2 | 0 | 0 | 0 |
| 1966-67 | Montreal | 2 | 0 | 0 | 0 |
| 1967-68 | Philadelphia | 65 | 5 | 7 | 12 |
| 1968-69 | Boston | 11 | 0 | 2 | 2 |
| 1969-70 | Montreal | 4 | 0 | 0 | 0 |
| 1972-73 | New York (WHA) | 31 | 2 | 1 | 3 |
| | **NHL Totals** | 166 | 6 | 28 | 34 |
| | **WHA Totals** | 31 | 2 | 1 | 3 |

**GAUTHIER, Rene Fernand (Fern)** *Forward*
b. Chicoutimi, Que., Aug. 31, 1919

| Season | Club | GP | G | A | Pts. |
|---|---|---|---|---|---|
| 1943-44 | New York R | 33 | 14 | 10 | 24 |
| 1944-45 | Montreal | 50 | 18 | 13 | 31 |
| 1945-46 | Detroit | 30 | 9 | 8 | 17 |
| 1946-47 | Detroit | 40 | 1 | 12 | 13 |
| 1947-48 | Detroit | 35 | 1 | 5 | 6 |
| 1948-49 | Detroit | 41 | 3 | 2 | 5 |
| | **Totals** | 229 | 46 | 50 | 96 |

**GAVIN, Robert Stewart** *Forward*
b. Ottawa, Ont., Mar. 15, 1960

| Season | Club | GP | G | A | Pts. |
|---|---|---|---|---|---|
| 1980-81 | Toronto | 14 | 1 | 2 | 3 |
| 1981-82 | Toronto | 38 | 5 | 6 | 11 |
| 1982-83 | Toronto | 63 | 6 | 5 | 11 |
| | **Totals** | 115 | 12 | 13 | 25 |

**GEE, George** *Forward*
b. Stratford, Ont., June 28, 1922

| Season | Club | GP | G | A | Pts. |
|---|---|---|---|---|---|
| 1945-46 | Chicago | 35 | 14 | 15 | 29 |
| 1946-47 | Chicago | 60 | 20 | 20 | 40 |
| 1947-48 | Chicago | 60 | 14 | 25 | 39 |
| 1948-49 | Chi-Det | 51 | 7 | 14 | 21 |
| 1949-50 | Detroit | 69 | 17 | 21 | 38 |
| 1950-51 | Detroit | 70 | 17 | 20 | 37 |
| 1951-52 | Chicago | 70 | 18 | 31 | 49 |
| 1952-53 | Chicago | 67 | 18 | 21 | 39 |
| 1953-54 | Chicago | 69 | 10 | 16 | 26 |
| | **Totals** | 551 | 135 | 183 | 318 |

**GELDART, Gary Daniel** *Defenseman*
b. Moncton, N.B., June 14, 1950

| Season | Club | GP | G | A | Pts. |
|---|---|---|---|---|---|
| 1970-71 | Minnesota | 4 | 0 | 0 | 0 |

**GENDRON, Jean-Guy (Smitty)** *Forward*
b. Montreal, Que., Aug. 30, 1934

| Season | Club | GP | G | A | Pts. |
|---|---|---|---|---|---|
| 1955-56 | New York R | 63 | 5 | 7 | 12 |
| 1956-57 | New York R | 70 | 9 | 6 | 15 |
| 1957-58 | New York R | 70 | 10 | 17 | 27 |
| 1958-59 | Boston | 60 | 15 | 9 | 24 |
| 1959-60 | Boston | 67 | 24 | 11 | 35 |
| 1960-61 | Bos-Mont | 66 | 10 | 19 | 29 |
| 1961-62 | New York R | 69 | 14 | 11 | 25 |
| 1962-63 | Boston | 66 | 21 | 22 | 43 |
| 1963-64 | Boston | 54 | 5 | 13 | 18 |
| 1967-68 | Philadelphia | 1 | 0 | 1 | 1 |
| 1968-69 | Philadelphia | 74 | 20 | 35 | 55 |
| 1969-70 | Philadelphia | 71 | 23 | 21 | 44 |
| 1970-71 | Philadelphia | 76 | 20 | 16 | 36 |
| 1971-72 | Philadelphia | 56 | 6 | 13 | 19 |
| 1972-73 | Quebec (WHA) | 63 | 17 | 33 | 50 |
| 1973-74 | Quebec (WHA) | 64 | 11 | 8 | 19 |
| | **NHL Totals** | 859 | 182 | 201 | 383 |
| | **WHA Totals** | 127 | 28 | 41 | 69 |

**GEOFFRION, Bernard Joseph Andre (Boom-Boom and Boomer)** *Forward*
b. Montreal, Que., Feb. 14, 1931

| Season | Club | GP | G | A | Pts. |
|---|---|---|---|---|---|
| 1950-51 | Montreal | 18 | 8 | 6 | 14 |
| 1951-52 | Montreal | 67 | 30 | 24 | 54 |
| 1952-53 | Montreal | 65 | 22 | 17 | 39 |
| 1953-54 | Montreal | 54 | 29 | 25 | 54 |
| 1954-55 | Montreal | 70 | 38 | 37 | 75 |
| 1955-56 | Montreal | 59 | 29 | 33 | 62 |
| 1956-57 | Montreal | 41 | 19 | 21 | 40 |
| 1957-58 | Montreal | 42 | 27 | 23 | 50 |
| 1958-59 | Montreal | 59 | 22 | 44 | 66 |
| 1959-60 | Montreal | 59 | 30 | 41 | 71 |
| 1960-61 | Montreal | 64 | 50 | 45 | 95 |
| 1961-62 | Montreal | 62 | 23 | 36 | 59 |
| 1962-63 | Montreal | 51 | 23 | 18 | 41 |
| 1963-64 | Montreal | 55 | 21 | 18 | 39 |
| 1966-67 | New York R | 58 | 17 | 25 | 42 |
| 1967-68 | New York R | 59 | 5 | 16 | 21 |
| | **Totals** | 883 | 393 | 429 | 822 |

**GEOFFRION, Daniel** *Forward*
b. Montreal, Que., Jan. 24, 1958

| Season | Club | GP | G | A | Pts. |
|---|---|---|---|---|---|
| 1978-79 | Quebec (WHA) | 77 | 12 | 14 | 26 |
| 1979-80 | Montreal | 32 | 0 | 6 | 6 |
| 1980-81 | Winnipeg | 78 | 20 | 26 | 46 |
| | **NHL Totals** | 100 | 20 | 32 | 52 |
| | **WHL Totals** | 77 | 12 | 14 | 26 |

**GERAN, George Pierce (Jerry)** *Forward*
b. Holyoke, Mass., Aug. 3, 1896

| Season | Club | GP | G | A | Pts. |
|---|---|---|---|---|---|
| 1917-18 | Montreal W | 4 | 0 | 0 | 0 |
| 1925-26 | Boston | 33 | 5 | 1 | 6 |
| | **Totals** | 37 | 5 | 1 | 6 |

**GERARD, Edward George** *Defenseman*
b. Ottawa, Ont., Feb. 22, 1890

| Season | Club | GP | G | A | Pts. |
|---|---|---|---|---|---|
| 1917-18 | Ottawa | 21 | 13 | 0 | 13 |
| 1918-19 | Ottawa | 18 | 4 | 6 | 10 |
| 1919-20 | Ottawa | 21 | 9 | 3 | 12 |
| 1920-21 | Ottawa | 24 | 11 | 4 | 15 |
| 1921-22 | Ottawa | 21 | 7 | 9 | 16 |
| 1922-23 | Ottawa | 23 | 6 | 8 | 14 |
| | **Totals** | 128 | 50 | 30 | 80 |

**GETLIFFE, Raymond** *Forward*
b. Galt, Ont., Apr. 3, 1914

| Season | Club | GP | G | A | Pts. |
|---|---|---|---|---|---|
| 1935-36 | Boston | 1 | 0 | 0 | 0 |
| 1936-37 | Boston | 47 | 16 | 15 | 31 |
| 1937-38 | Boston | 35 | 11 | 13 | 24 |
| 1938-39 | Boston | 41 | 10 | 12 | 22 |
| 1939-40 | Montreal | 46 | 11 | 12 | 23 |
| 1940-41 | Montreal | 39 | 15 | 10 | 25 |
| 1941-42 | Montreal | 45 | 11 | 15 | 26 |
| 1942-43 | Montreal | 50 | 18 | 28 | 46 |
| 1943-44 | Montreal | 44 | 28 | 25 | 53 |
| 1944-45 | Montreal | 41 | 16 | 7 | 23 |
| | **Totals** | 389 | 136 | 137 | 273 |

**GIALLONARDO, Mario** *Defenseman*
b. Toronto, Ont., Sept. 23, 1957

| Season | Club | GP | G | A | Pts. |
|---|---|---|---|---|---|
| 1979-80 | Colorado | 8 | 0 | 1 | 1 |
| 1980-81 | Colorado | 15 | 0 | 2 | 2 |
| | **Totals** | 23 | 0 | 3 | 3 |

**GIBBS, Barry Paul** *Defenseman*
 b. Lloydminster, Sask., Sept. 28, 1948

| Season | Club | GP | G | A | Pts. |
|---|---|---|---|---|---|
| 1967-68 | Boston | 16 | 0 | 0 | 0 |
| 1968-69 | Boston | 8 | 0 | 0 | 0 |
| 1969-70 | Minnesota | 56 | 3 | 13 | 16 |
| 1970-71 | Minnesota | 68 | 5 | 15 | 20 |
| 1971-72 | Minnesota | 75 | 4 | 20 | 24 |
| 1972-73 | Minnesota | 63 | 10 | 24 | 34 |
| 1973-74 | Minnesota | 76 | 9 | 29 | 38 |
| 1974-75 | Minn-Atl | 76 | 7 | 33 | 40 |
| 1975-76 | Atlanta | 76 | 8 | 21 | 29 |
| 1976-77 | Atlanta | 66 | 1 | 16 | 17 |
| 1977-78 | Atl-StL | 78 | 7 | 17 | 24 |
| 1978-79 | St Louis | 76 | 2 | 27 | 29 |
| 1979-80 | Los Angeles | 63 | 2 | 9 | 11 |
| | **Totals** | 797 | 58 | 224 | 282 |

**GIBSON, Douglas John (Doug)** *Forward*
 b. Peterborough, Ont., Sept. 28, 1953

| Season | Club | GP | G | A | Pts. |
|---|---|---|---|---|---|
| 1973-74 | Boston | 2 | 0 | 0 | 0 |
| 1975-76 | Boston | 50 | 7 | 18 | 25 |
| 1977-78 | Washington | 11 | 2 | 1 | 3 |
| 1978-79 | Winnipeg (WHA) | 9 | 0 | 1 | 1 |
| | **NHL Totals** | 63 | 9 | 19 | 28 |
| | **WHA Totals** | 9 | 0 | 1 | 1 |

**GIBSON, John William** *Defenseman*
 b. St. Catharines, Ont., June 2, 1959

| Season | Club | GP | G | A | Pts. |
|---|---|---|---|---|---|
| 1980-81 | Los Angeles | 4 | 0 | 0 | 0 |
| 1981-82 | LA-Tor | 33 | 0 | 2 | 2 |
| | **Totals** | 37 | 0 | 2 | 2 |

**GIESEBRECHT, Roy (Gus)** *Forward*
 b. Petawawa, Ont., Sept. 14, 1918

| Season | Club | GP | G | A | Pts. |
|---|---|---|---|---|---|
| 1938-39 | Detroit | 29 | 10 | 10 | 20 |
| 1939-40 | Detroit | 30 | 4 | 7 | 11 |
| 1940-41 | Detroit | 43 | 7 | 18 | 25 |
| 1941-42 | Detroit | 34 | 6 | 16 | 22 |
| | **Totals** | 136 | 27 | 51 | 78 |

**GILBERT, Edward Ferguson** *Forward*
 b. Hamilton, Ont., Mar. 12, 1952

| Season | Club | GP | G | A | Pts. |
|---|---|---|---|---|---|
| 1974-75 | Kansas City | 80 | 16 | 22 | 38 |
| 1975-76 | KC-Pitt | 79 | 5 | 9 | 14 |
| 1976-77 | Pittsburgh | 7 | 0 | 0 | 0 |
| | **Totals** | 166 | 21 | 31 | 52 |

**GILBERT, Greg Scott** *Forward*
 b. Mississauga, Ont., Jan. 22, 1962

| Season | Club | GP | G | A | Pts. |
|---|---|---|---|---|---|
| 1981-82 | New York I | 1 | 1 | 0 | 1 |
| 1982-83 | New York I | 45 | 8 | 11 | 19 |
| | **Totals** | 46 | 9 | 11 | 20 |

**GILBERT, Jeannot Elmourt** *Forward*
 b. Grande Baie, Que., Dec. 29, 1940

| Season | Club | GP | G | A | Pts. |
|---|---|---|---|---|---|
| 1962-63 | Boston | 5 | 0 | 0 | 0 |
| 1964-65 | Boston | 4 | 0 | 1 | 1 |
| 1973-74 | Quebec (WHA) | 75 | 17 | 39 | 56 |
| 1974-75 | Quebec (WHA) | 58 | 7 | 21 | 28 |
| | **NHL Totals** | 9 | 0 | 1 | 1 |
| | **WHA Totals** | 133 | 24 | 60 | 84 |

**GILBERT, Rodrique Gabriel** *Forward*
 b. Montreal, Que., July 1, 1941

| Season | Club | GP | G | A | Pts. |
|---|---|---|---|---|---|
| 1960-61 | New York R | 1 | 0 | 1 | 1 |
| 1961-62 | New York R | 1 | 0 | 0 | 0 |
| 1962-63 | New York R | 70 | 11 | 20 | 31 |
| 1963-64 | New York R | 70 | 24 | 40 | 64 |
| 1964-65 | New York R | 70 | 25 | 36 | 61 |
| 1965-66 | New York R | 34 | 10 | 15 | 25 |
| 1966-67 | New York R | 64 | 28 | 18 | 46 |
| 1967-68 | New York R | 73 | 29 | 48 | 77 |
| 1968-69 | New York R | 66 | 28 | 49 | 77 |
| 1969-70 | New York R | 72 | 16 | 37 | 53 |
| 1970-71 | New York R | 78 | 30 | 31 | 61 |
| 1971-72 | New York R | 73 | 43 | 54 | 97 |
| 1972-73 | New York R | 76 | 25 | 59 | 84 |
| 1973-74 | New York R | 75 | 36 | 41 | 77 |
| 1974-75 | New York R | 76 | 36 | 61 | 97 |
| 1975-76 | New York R | 70 | 36 | 50 | 86 |
| 1976-77 | New York R | 77 | 27 | 48 | 75 |
| 1977-78 | New York R | 19 | 2 | 7 | 9 |
| | **Totals** | 1065 | 406 | 615 | 1021 |

**GILBERTSON, Stan** *Forward*
 b. Duluth, Minn., Oct. 29, 1944

| Season | Club | GP | G | A | Pts. |
|---|---|---|---|---|---|
| 1971-72 | California | 78 | 16 | 16 | 32 |
| 1972-73 | California | 66 | 6 | 15 | 21 |
| 1973-74 | California | 76 | 18 | 12 | 30 |
| 1974-75 | Cal-Wash | 62 | 13 | 15 | 28 |
| 1975-76 | Wash-Pitt | 79 | 26 | 22 | 48 |
| 1976-77 | Pittsburgh | 67 | 6 | 9 | 15 |
| | **Totals** | 428 | 85 | 89 | 174 |

**GILES, Curt** *Defenseman*
 b. Humboldt, Sask., Nov. 30, 1958

| Season | Club | GP | G | A | Pts. |
|---|---|---|---|---|---|
| 1979-80 | Minnesota | 37 | 2 | 7 | 9 |
| 1980-81 | Minnesota | 67 | 5 | 22 | 27 |
| 1981-82 | Minnesota | 74 | 3 | 12 | 15 |
| 1982-83 | Minnesota | 76 | 2 | 21 | 23 |
| | **Totals** | 254 | 12 | 62 | 74 |

**GILHEN, Randy** *Forward*
 b. Zweibrucken, W. Germany, June 13, 1963

| Season | Club | GP | G | A | Pts. |
|---|---|---|---|---|---|
| 1982-83 | Hartford | 2 | 0 | 1 | 1 |

**GILLEN, Donald** *Forward*
 b. Dodsland, Sask., Dec. 24, 1960

| Season | Club | GP | G | A | Pts. |
|---|---|---|---|---|---|
| 1979-80 | Philadelphia | 1 | 1 | 0 | 1 |
| 1981-82 | Hartford | 34 | 1 | 4 | 5 |
| | **Totals** | 35 | 2 | 4 | 6 |

**GILLIES, Clark** *Forward*
 b. Moose Jaw, Sask., Apr. 7, 1954

| Season | Club | GP | G | A | Pts. |
|---|---|---|---|---|---|
| 1974-75 | New York I | 80 | 25 | 22 | 47 |
| 1975-76 | New York I | 80 | 34 | 27 | 61 |
| 1976-77 | New York I | 70 | 33 | 22 | 55 |
| 1977-78 | New York I | 80 | 35 | 50 | 85 |
| 1978-79 | New York I | 75 | 35 | 56 | 91 |
| 1979-80 | New York I | 73 | 19 | 35 | 54 |
| 1980-81 | New York I | 80 | 33 | 45 | 78 |
| 1981-82 | New York I | 79 | 38 | 39 | 77 |
| 1982-83 | New York I | 70 | 21 | 20 | 41 |
| | **Totals** | 677 | 273 | 316 | 589 |

**GILLIS, Jere Alan** *Forward*
 b. Bend, Ont., Jan. 18, 1957

| Season | Club | GP | G | A | Pts. |
|---|---|---|---|---|---|
| 1977-78 | Vancouver | 79 | 23 | 18 | 41 |
| 1978-79 | Vancouver | 78 | 13 | 12 | 25 |
| 1979-80 | Vancouver | 67 | 13 | 17 | 30 |
| 1980-81 | Van-NYR | 46 | 10 | 14 | 24 |
| 1981-82 | NYR-Que | 38 | 5 | 10 | 15 |
| 1982-83 | Buffalo | 3 | 0 | 0 | 0 |
| | **Totals** | 311 | 64 | 71 | 135 |

**GILLIS, Michael David** *Forward*
 b. Sudbury, Ont., Dec. 1, 1958

| Season | Club | GP | G | A | Pts. |
|---|---|---|---|---|---|
| 1978-79 | Colorado | 30 | 1 | 7 | 8 |
| 1979-80 | Colorado | 40 | 4 | 5 | 9 |
| 1980-81 | Col-Bos | 68 | 13 | 11 | 24 |
| 1981-82 | Boston | 53 | 9 | 8 | 17 |
| 1982-83 | Boston | 5 | 0 | 1 | 1 |
| | **Totals** | 196 | 27 | 32 | 59 |

**GILLIS, Paul** *Forward*
 b. Toronto, Ont., Dec. 21, 1963

| Season | Club | GP | G | A | Pts. |
|---|---|---|---|---|---|
| 1982-83 | Quebec | 7 | 0 | 2 | 2 |

**GINGRAS, Gaston Reginald** *Defenseman*
 b. Temiscamingue, Que., Feb. 13, 1959

| Season | Club | GP | G | A | Pts. |
|---|---|---|---|---|---|
| 1978-79 | Birmingham (WHA) | 60 | 13 | 21 | 34 |
| 1979-80 | Montreal | 34 | 3 | 7 | 10 |
| 1980-81 | Montreal | 55 | 5 | 16 | 21 |
| 1981-82 | Montreal | 34 | 6 | 18 | 24 |
| 1982-83 | Mont-Tor | 67 | 11 | 26 | 37 |
| | **NHL Totals** | 190 | 25 | 67 | 92 |
| | **WHA Totals** | 60 | 13 | 21 | 34 |

**GIRARD, Kenneth** *Forward*
 b. Toronto, Ont., Dec. 8, 1936

| Season | Club | GP | G | A | Pts. |
|---|---|---|---|---|---|
| 1956-57 | Toronto | 3 | 0 | 1 | 1 |
| 1957-58 | Toronto | 3 | 0 | 0 | 0 |
| 1959-60 | Toronto | 1 | 0 | 0 | 0 |
| | **Totals** | 7 | 0 | 1 | 1 |

**GIRARD, Robert** *Forward*
 b. Montreal, Que., Apr. 12, 1949

| Season | Club | GP | G | A | Pts. |
|---|---|---|---|---|---|
| 1975-76 | California | 80 | 16 | 26 | 42 |
| 1976-77 | Cleveland | 68 | 11 | 10 | 21 |
| 1977-78 | Clev-Wash | 77 | 9 | 18 | 27 |
| 1978-79 | Washington | 79 | 9 | 15 | 24 |
| 1979-80 | Washington | 1 | 0 | 0 | 0 |
| | **Totals** | 305 | 45 | 69 | 114 |

**GIROUX, Arthur** *Forward*
 b. Strathmore, Alta., June 6, 1908

| Season | Club | GP | G | A | Pts. |
|---|---|---|---|---|---|
| 1932-33 | Montreal | 40 | 5 | 2 | 7 |
| 1934-35 | Boston | 10 | 1 | 0 | 1 |
| 1935-36 | Detroit | 4 | 0 | 2 | 2 |
| | **Totals** | 54 | 6 | 4 | 10 |

**GIROUX, Larry Douglas** *Defenseman*
 b. Weyburn, Sask., Aug. 28, 1951

| Season | Club | GP | G | A | Pts. |
|---|---|---|---|---|---|
| 1973-74 | St Louis | 74 | 15 | 17 | 32 |
| 1974-75 | KC-Det | 60 | 2 | 26 | 28 |
| 1975-76 | Detroit | 10 | 1 | 1 | 2 |
| 1976-77 | Detroit | 2 | 0 | 0 | 0 |
| 1977-78 | Detroit | 5 | 0 | 3 | 3 |
| 1978-79 | St Louis | 73 | 5 | 22 | 27 |
| 1979-80 | StL-Hart | 50 | 2 | 5 | 7 |
| | **Totals** | 274 | 25 | 74 | 99 |

**GIROUS, Pierre** *Forward*
 b. Brownsburg, Que., Nov. 17, 1955

| Season | Club | GP | G | A | Pts. |
|---|---|---|---|---|---|
| 1982-83 | Los Angeles | 6 | 1 | 0 | 1 |

**GLADNEY, Bob** *Defenseman*
 b. Come-by-Chance, Nfld., Aug. 27, 1957

| Season | Club | GP | G | A | Pts. |
|---|---|---|---|---|---|
| 1982-83 | Los Angeles | 1 | 0 | 0 | 0 |

**GLADU, Joseph Jean Paul** *Forward*
 b. St. Hyacinthe, Que., June 20, 1922

| Season | Club | GP | G | A | Pts. |
|---|---|---|---|---|---|
| 1944-45 | Boston | 40 | 6 | 14 | 20 |

**GLENNIE, Brian Alexander** *Defenseman*
 b. Toronto, Ont., Aug. 29, 1946

| Season | Club | GP | G | A | Pts. |
|---|---|---|---|---|---|
| 1969-70 | Toronto | 52 | 1 | 14 | 15 |
| 1970-71 | Toronto | 54 | 0 | 8 | 8 |
| 1971-72 | Toronto | 61 | 2 | 8 | 10 |
| 1972-73 | Toronto | 44 | 1 | 10 | 11 |
| 1973-74 | Toronto | 65 | 4 | 18 | 22 |
| 1974-75 | Toronto | 63 | 1 | 7 | 8 |
| 1975-76 | Toronto | 69 | 0 | 8 | 8 |
| 1976-77 | Toronto | 69 | 1 | 10 | 11 |
| 1977-78 | Toronto | 77 | 2 | 15 | 17 |
| 1978-79 | Los Angeles | 18 | 2 | 2 | 4 |
| | **Totals** | 572 | 14 | 100 | 114 |

**GLOOR, Daniel Harold** *Forward*
 b. Mitchell, Ont., Dec. 4, 1952

| Season | Club | GP | G | A | Pts. |
|---|---|---|---|---|---|
| 1973-74 | Vancouver | 2 | 0 | 0 | 0 |

**GLOVER, Frederick Austin** *Forward*
 b. Toronto, Ont., Jan. 5, 1928

| Season | Club | GP | G | A | Pts. |
|---|---|---|---|---|---|
| 1949-50 | Detroit | 7 | 0 | 0 | 0 |
| 1951-52 | Detroit | 54 | 9 | 9 | 18 |
| 1952-53 | Chicago | 31 | 4 | 2 | 6 |
| | **Totals** | 92 | 13 | 11 | 24 |

**GLOVER, Howard Edward** *Forward*
 b. Toronto, Ont., Feb. 14, 1935

| Season | Club | GP | G | A | Pts. |
|---|---|---|---|---|---|
| 1958-59 | Chicago | 13 | 0 | 1 | 1 |
| 1960-61 | Detroit | 66 | 21 | 8 | 29 |
| 1961-62 | Detroit | 39 | 7 | 8 | 15 |
| 1963-64 | New York R | 25 | 1 | 0 | 1 |
| 1968-69 | Montreal | 1 | 0 | 0 | 0 |
| | **Totals** | 144 | 29 | 17 | 46 |

| Season | Club | GP | G | A | Pts. |
|---|---|---|---|---|---|
| **GODDEN, Ernie Alfred** *Forward* | | | | | |
| b. Keswick, Ont., Mar. 13, 1961 | | | | | |
| 1981-82 | Toronto | 5 | 1 | 1 | 2 |
| **GODFREY, Warren Edward (Rocky)** | | | | | |
| *Defenseman* | | | | | |
| b. Toronto, Ont., Mar. 23, 1931 | | | | | |
| 1952-53 | Boston | 60 | 1 | 13 | 14 |
| 1953-54 | Boston | 70 | 5 | 9 | 14 |
| 1954-55 | Boston | 62 | 1 | 17 | 18 |
| 1955-56 | Detroit | 67 | 2 | 6 | 8 |
| 1956-57 | Detroit | 69 | 1 | 8 | 9 |
| 1957-58 | Detroit | 67 | 2 | 16 | 18 |
| 1958-59 | Detroit | 69 | 6 | 4 | 10 |
| 1959-60 | Detroit | 69 | 5 | 9 | 14 |
| 1960-61 | Detroit | 63 | 3 | 16 | 19 |
| 1961-62 | Detroit | 70 | 4 | 13 | 17 |
| 1962-63 | Boston | 66 | 2 | 9 | 11 |
| 1963-64 | Detroit | 4 | 0 | 0 | 0 |
| 1964-65 | Detroit | 11 | 0 | 0 | 0 |
| 1965-66 | Detroit | 26 | 0 | 4 | 4 |
| 1966-67 | Detroit | 2 | 0 | 0 | 0 |
| 1967-68 | Detroit | 12 | 0 | 1 | 1 |
| | **Totals** | 787 | 32 | 125 | 157 |
| **GODIN, H. Gabriel (Sam)** *Forward* | | | | | |
| b. Rockland, Ont., Sept. 20, 1909 | | | | | |
| 1927-28 | Ottawa | 18 | 0 | 0 | 0 |
| 1928-29 | Ottawa | 25 | 2 | 1 | 3 |
| 1933-34 | Montreal | 36 | 2 | 2 | 4 |
| | **Totals** | 79 | 4 | 3 | 7 |
| **GODIN, Joseph Alain Eddy** *Forward* | | | | | |
| b. Donnacona, Que., Mar. 29, 1957 | | | | | |
| 1977-78 | Washington | 18 | 3 | 3 | 6 |
| 1978-79 | Washington | 9 | 0 | 3 | 3 |
| | **Totals** | 27 | 3 | 6 | 9 |
| **GOEGAN, Peter John** *Defenseman* | | | | | |
| b. Fort William, Ont., Mar. 6, 1934 | | | | | |
| 1957-58 | Detroit | 14 | 0 | 2 | 2 |
| 1958-59 | Detroit | 67 | 1 | 11 | 12 |
| 1959-60 | Detroit | 21 | 3 | 0 | 3 |
| 1960-61 | Detroit | 67 | 5 | 29 | 34 |
| 1961-62 | Det-NYR | 46 | 5 | 7 | 12 |
| 1962-63 | Detroit | 62 | 1 | 8 | 9 |
| 1963-64 | Detroit | 12 | 0 | 0 | 0 |
| 1964-65 | Detroit | 4 | 1 | 0 | 1 |
| 1965-66 | Detroit | 13 | 0 | 2 | 2 |
| 1966-67 | Detroit | 31 | 2 | 6 | 8 |
| 1967-68 | Minnesota | 46 | 1 | 2 | 3 |
| | **Totals** | 383 | 19 | 67 | 86 |
| **GOLDHAM, Robert John** *Defenseman* | | | | | |
| b. Georgetown, Ont., May 12, 1922 | | | | | |
| 1941-42 | Toronto | 19 | 4 | 7 | 11 |
| 1945-46 | Toronto | 49 | 7 | 14 | 21 |
| 1946-47 | Toronto | 11 | 1 | 1 | 2 |
| 1947-48 | Chicago | 38 | 2 | 9 | 11 |
| 1948-49 | Chicago | 60 | 1 | 10 | 11 |
| 1949-50 | Chicago | 67 | 2 | 10 | 12 |
| 1950-51 | Detroit | 61 | 5 | 18 | 23 |
| 1951-52 | Detroit | 69 | 0 | 14 | 14 |
| 1952-53 | Detroit | 70 | 1 | 13 | 14 |
| 1953-54 | Detroit | 69 | 1 | 15 | 16 |
| 1954-55 | Detroit | 69 | 1 | 16 | 17 |
| 1955-56 | Detroit | 68 | 3 | 16 | 19 |
| | **Totals** | 650 | 28 | 143 | 171 |
| **GOLDSWORTHY, Leroy D.** | | | | | |
| *Defenseman-Forward* | | | | | |
| b. Two Harbors, Minn., Oct. 18, 1908 | | | | | |
| 1929-30 | New York R | 44 | 4 | 1 | 5 |
| 1930-31 | Detroit | 12 | 1 | 0 | 1 |
| 1932-33 | Detroit | 25 | 3 | 6 | 9 |
| 1933-34 | Chicago | 27 | 3 | 3 | 6 |
| 1934-35 | Montreal | 40 | 20 | 9 | 29 |
| 1935-36 | Montreal | 47 | 15 | 11 | 26 |
| 1936-37 | Boston | 47 | 8 | 6 | 14 |
| 1937-38 | Boston | 46 | 9 | 10 | 19 |
| 1938-39 | New York A | 48 | 3 | 11 | 14 |
| | **Totals** | 336 | 66 | 57 | 123 |

| Season | Club | GP | G | A | Pts. |
|---|---|---|---|---|---|
| **GOLDSWORTHY, William Alfred** | | | | | |
| *Forward* | | | | | |
| b. Waterloo, Ont., Aug. 24, 1944 | | | | | |
| 1964-65 | Boston | 2 | 0 | 0 | 0 |
| 1965-66 | Boston | 13 | 3 | 1 | 4 |
| 1966-67 | Boston | 18 | 3 | 5 | 8 |
| 1967-68 | Minnesota | 68 | 14 | 19 | 33 |
| 1968-69 | Minnesota | 68 | 14 | 10 | 24 |
| 1969-70 | Minnesota | 75 | 36 | 29 | 65 |
| 1970-71 | Minnesota | 77 | 34 | 31 | 65 |
| 1971-72 | Minnesota | 78 | 31 | 31 | 62 |
| 1972-73 | Minnesota | 75 | 27 | 33 | 60 |
| 1973-74 | Minnesota | 74 | 48 | 26 | 74 |
| 1974-75 | Minnesota | 71 | 37 | 35 | 72 |
| 1975-76 | Minnesota | 68 | 24 | 22 | 46 |
| 1976-77 | Minn-NYR | 77 | 12 | 15 | 27 |
| 1977-78 | New York R | 7 | 0 | 1 | 1 |
| 1977-78 | Indianapolis (WHA) | 32 | 8 | 10 | 18 |
| 1978-79 | Edmonton (WHA) | 17 | 4 | 2 | 6 |
| | **NHL Totals** | 771 | 283 | 258 | 541 |
| | **WHA Totals** | 49 | 12 | 12 | 24 |
| **GOLDUP, Glenn Michael** *Forward* | | | | | |
| b. St. Catharines, Ont., Apr. 26, 1953 | | | | | |
| 1973-74 | Montreal | 6 | 0 | 0 | 0 |
| 1974-75 | Montreal | 9 | 0 | 1 | 1 |
| 1975-76 | Montreal | 3 | 0 | 0 | 0 |
| 1976-77 | Los Angeles | 28 | 7 | 6 | 13 |
| 1977-78 | Los Angeles | 66 | 14 | 18 | 32 |
| 1978-79 | Los Angeles | 73 | 15 | 22 | 37 |
| 1979-80 | Los Angeles | 55 | 10 | 11 | 21 |
| 1980-81 | Los Angeles | 39 | 6 | 9 | 15 |
| 1981-82 | Los Angeles | 2 | 0 | 0 | 0 |
| | **Totals** | 281 | 52 | 67 | 119 |
| **GOLDUP, Henry (Hank)** *Forward* | | | | | |
| b. Kingston, Ont., Oct. 29, 1918 | | | | | |
| 1939-40 | Toronto | 21 | 6 | 4 | 10 |
| 1940-41 | Toronto | 26 | 10 | 5 | 15 |
| 1941-42 | Toronto | 44 | 12 | 18 | 30 |
| 1942-43 | Tor-NYR | 44 | 12 | 27 | 39 |
| 1944-45 | New York R | 48 | 17 | 25 | 42 |
| 1945-46 | New York R | 19 | 6 | 1 | 7 |
| | **Totals** | 202 | 63 | 80 | 143 |
| **GOODEN, William Francis Charles** *Forward* | | | | | |
| b. Winnipeg, Man., Sept. 8, 1923 | | | | | |
| 1942-43 | New York R | 12 | 0 | 3 | 3 |
| 1943-44 | New York R | 41 | 9 | 8 | 17 |
| | **Totals** | 53 | 9 | 11 | 20 |
| **GOODENOUGH, Larry J.** *Defenseman* | | | | | |
| b. Toronto, Ont., Jan. 19, 1953 | | | | | |
| 1974-75 | Philadelphia | 20 | 3 | 9 | 12 |
| 1975-76 | Philadelphia | 77 | 8 | 34 | 42 |
| 1976-77 | Phil-Van | 62 | 6 | 17 | 23 |
| 1977-78 | Vancouver | 42 | 1 | 6 | 7 |
| 1978-79 | Vancouver | 36 | 4 | 9 | 13 |
| 1979-80 | Vancouver | 5 | 0 | 2 | 2 |
| | **Totals** | 242 | 22 | 77 | 99 |
| **GOODFELLOW, Ebenezer Ralston (Ebbie)** | | | | | |
| *Defenseman-Forward* | | | | | |
| b. Ottawa, Ont., Apr. 9, 1907 | | | | | |
| 1929-30 | Detroit | 44 | 17 | 17 | 34 |
| 1930-31 | Detroit | 44 | 25 | 23 | 48 |
| 1931-32 | Detroit | 48 | 14 | 16 | 30 |
| 1932-33 | Detroit | 41 | 12 | 8 | 20 |
| 1933-34 | Detroit | 48 | 13 | 13 | 26 |
| 1934-35 | Detroit | 48 | 12 | 24 | 36 |
| 1935-36 | Detroit | 48 | 5 | 18 | 23 |
| 1936-37 | Detroit | 48 | 9 | 16 | 25 |
| 1937-38 | Detroit | 30 | 0 | 7 | 7 |
| 1938-39 | Detroit | 48 | 8 | 8 | 16 |
| 1939-40 | Detroit | 43 | 11 | 17 | 28 |
| 1940-41 | Detroit | 47 | 5 | 17 | 22 |
| 1941-42 | Detroit | 8 | 2 | 2 | 4 |
| 1942-43 | Detroit | 11 | 1 | 4 | 5 |
| | **Totals** | 556 | 134 | 190 | 324 |

| Season | Club | GP | G | A | Pts. |
|---|---|---|---|---|---|
| **GORDON, K. Fred** *Forward* | | | | | |
| 1926-27 | Detroit | 38 | 5 | 5 | 10 |
| 1927-28 | Boston | 43 | 3 | 2 | 5 |
| | **Totals** | 81 | 8 | 7 | 15 |
| **GORDON, John (Jackie)** *Forward* | | | | | |
| b. Winnipeg, Man., Mar. 3, 1928 | | | | | |
| 1948-49 | New York R | 31 | 3 | 9 | 12 |
| 1949-50 | New York R | 1 | 0 | 0 | 0 |
| 1950-51 | New York R | 4 | 0 | 1 | 1 |
| | **Totals** | 36 | 3 | 10 | 13 |
| **GORENCE, Thomas** *Forward* | | | | | |
| b. St. Paul, Minn., Mar. 11, 1957 | | | | | |
| 1978-79 | Philadelphia | 42 | 13 | 6 | 19 |
| 1979-80 | Philadelphia | 51 | 8 | 13 | 21 |
| 1980-81 | Philadelphia | 79 | 24 | 18 | 42 |
| 1981-82 | Philadelphia | 66 | 5 | 8 | 13 |
| 1982-83 | Philadelphia | 53 | 7 | 7 | 14 |
| | **Totals** | 291 | 57 | 52 | 109 |
| **GORING, Robert Thomas (Butch)** *Forward* | | | | | |
| b. St. Boniface, Man., Oct. 22, 1949 | | | | | |
| 1969-70 | Los Angeles | 59 | 13 | 23 | 36 |
| 1970-71 | Los Angeles | 19 | 2 | 5 | 7 |
| 1971-72 | Los Angeles | 74 | 21 | 29 | 50 |
| 1972-73 | Los Angeles | 67 | 28 | 31 | 59 |
| 1973-74 | Los Angeles | 70 | 28 | 33 | 61 |
| 1974-75 | Los Angeles | 60 | 27 | 33 | 60 |
| 1975-76 | Los Angeles | 80 | 33 | 40 | 73 |
| 1976-77 | Los Angeles | 78 | 30 | 55 | 85 |
| 1977-78 | Los Angeles | 80 | 37 | 36 | 73 |
| 1978-79 | Los Angeles | 80 | 36 | 51 | 87 |
| 1979-80 | LA-NYI | 81 | 26 | 53 | 79 |
| 1980-81 | New York I | 78 | 23 | 37 | 60 |
| 1981-82 | New York I | 67 | 15 | 17 | 32 |
| 1982-83 | New York I | 75 | 19 | 20 | 39 |
| | **Totals** | 968 | 338 | 463 | 801 |
| **GORMAN, David Peter** *Forward* | | | | | |
| b. Oshawa, Ont., Apr. 8, 1955 | | | | | |
| 1974-75 | Phoenix (WHA) | 13 | 3 | 5 | 8 |
| 1975-76 | Phoenix (WHA) | 67 | 11 | 20 | 31 |
| 1976-77 | Phoe-Birm (WHA) | 57 | 9 | 13 | 22 |
| 1977-78 | Birmingham (WHA) | 63 | 19 | 21 | 40 |
| 1978-79 | Birmingham (WHA) | 60 | 14 | 24 | 38 |
| 1979-80 | Atlanta | 3 | 0 | 0 | 0 |
| | **NHL Totals** | 3 | 0 | 0 | 0 |
| | **WHA Totals** | 260 | 56 | 83 | 139 |
| **GORMAN, Edwin** *Defenseman* | | | | | |
| 1924-25 | Ottawa | 30 | 11 | 3 | 14 |
| 1925-26 | Ottawa | 23 | 2 | 1 | 3 |
| 1926-27 | Ottawa | 39 | 1 | 0 | 1 |
| 1927-28 | Toronto | 19 | 0 | 1 | 1 |
| | **Totals** | 111 | 14 | 5 | 19 |
| **GOSSELIN, Benoit** *Forward* | | | | | |
| b. Montreal, Que., July 19, 1957 | | | | | |
| 1977-78 | New York R | 7 | 0 | 0 | 0 |
| **GOTTSELIG, John P.** *Forward* | | | | | |
| b. Odessa, Russia, June 24, 1906 | | | | | |
| 1928-29 | Chicago | 44 | 5 | 3 | 8 |
| 1929-30 | Chicago | 39 | 21 | 4 | 25 |
| 1930-31 | Chicago | 42 | 20 | 12 | 32 |
| 1931-32 | Chicago | 44 | 13 | 15 | 28 |
| 1932-33 | Chicago | 41 | 11 | 11 | 22 |
| 1933-34 | Chicago | 48 | 16 | 14 | 30 |
| 1934-35 | Chicago | 48 | 19 | 18 | 37 |
| 1935-36 | Chicago | 41 | 14 | 15 | 29 |
| 1936-37 | Chicago | 47 | 9 | 21 | 30 |
| 1937-38 | Chicago | 48 | 13 | 19 | 32 |
| 1938-39 | Chicago | 48 | 16 | 23 | 39 |
| 1939-40 | Chicago | 39 | 8 | 15 | 23 |
| 1940-41 | Chicago | 5 | 1 | 4 | 5 |
| 1942-43 | Chicago | 10 | 2 | 6 | 8 |
| 1943-44 | Chicago | 45 | 8 | 15 | 23 |
| 1944-45 | Chicago | 1 | 0 | 0 | 0 |
| | **Totals** | 590 | 176 | 195 | 371 |

| Season | Club | GP | G | A | Pts. |
|---|---|---|---|---|---|

**GOULD, John Milton** *Forward*
b. Alliston, Ont., Apr. 11, 1949

| Season | Club | GP | G | A | Pts. |
|---|---|---|---|---|---|
| 1971-72 | Buffalo | 2 | 1 | 0 | 1 |
| 1972-73 | Buffalo | 8 | 0 | 1 | 1 |
| 1973-74 | Buf-Van | 75 | 13 | 12 | 25 |
| 1974-75 | Vancouver | 78 | 34 | 31 | 65 |
| 1975-76 | Vancouver | 70 | 32 | 27 | 59 |
| 1976-77 | Van-Atl | 79 | 15 | 23 | 38 |
| 1977-78 | Atlanta | 79 | 19 | 28 | 47 |
| 1978-79 | Atlanta | 61 | 8 | 7 | 15 |
| 1979-80 | Buffalo | 52 | 9 | 9 | 18 |
| | **Totals** | 504 | 131 | 138 | 269 |

**GOULD, Larry Stephen** *Forward*
b. Beeton, Ont., Aug. 16, 1952

| Season | Club | GP | G | A | Pts. |
|---|---|---|---|---|---|
| 1973-74 | Vancouver | 2 | 0 | 0 | 0 |

**GOULD, Robert** *Forward*
b. Petrolia, Ont., Sept. 2, 1957

| Season | Club | GP | G | A | Pts. |
|---|---|---|---|---|---|
| 1979-80 | Atlanta | 1 | 0 | 0 | 0 |
| 1980-81 | Calgary | 3 | 0 | 0 | 0 |
| 1981-82 | Calg-Wash | 76 | 21 | 13 | 34 |
| 1982-83 | Washington | 80 | 22 | 18 | 40 |
| | **Totals** | 160 | 43 | 31 | 74 |

**GOULET, Michel** *Forward*
b. Peribonqua, Que., Apr. 21, 1960

| Season | Club | GP | G | A | Pts. |
|---|---|---|---|---|---|
| 1978-79 | Birmingham (WHA) | 78 | 28 | 30 | 58 |
| 1979-80 | Quebec | 77 | 22 | 32 | 54 |
| 1980-81 | Quebec | 76 | 32 | 39 | 71 |
| 1981-82 | Quebec | 80 | 42 | 42 | 84 |
| 1982-83 | Quebec | 80 | 57 | 48 | 105 |
| | **NHL Totals** | 313 | 153 | 161 | 314 |
| | **WHA Totals** | 78 | 28 | 30 | 58 |

**GOUPILLE, Clifford (Red)** *Defenseman*
b. Trois-Rivieres, Que., Sept. 2, 1915

| Season | Club | GP | G | A | Pts. |
|---|---|---|---|---|---|
| 1935-36 | Montreal | 4 | 0 | 0 | 0 |
| 1936-37 | Montreal | 4 | 0 | 0 | 0 |
| 1937-38 | Montreal | 47 | 4 | 5 | 9 |
| 1938-39 | Montreal | 18 | 0 | 2 | 2 |
| 1939-40 | Montreal | 48 | 2 | 10 | 12 |
| 1940-41 | Montreal | 48 | 3 | 6 | 9 |
| 1941-42 | Montreal | 47 | 1 | 5 | 6 |
| 1942-43 | Montreal | 6 | 2 | 0 | 2 |
| | **Totals** | 222 | 12 | 28 | 40 |

**GOYER, Gerald** *Forward*
b. Belleville, Ont., Oct. 20, 1936

| Season | Club | GP | G | A | Pts. |
|---|---|---|---|---|---|
| 1967-68 | Chicago | 40 | 1 | 2 | 3 |

**GOYETTE, Joseph George Phillipe** *Forward*
b. Lachine, Que., Oct. 31, 1933

| Season | Club | GP | G | A | Pts. |
|---|---|---|---|---|---|
| 1956-57 | Montreal | 14 | 3 | 4 | 7 |
| 1957-58 | Montreal | 70 | 9 | 37 | 46 |
| 1958-59 | Montreal | 63 | 10 | 18 | 28 |
| 1959-60 | Montreal | 65 | 21 | 22 | 43 |
| 1960-61 | Montreal | 62 | 7 | 4 | 11 |
| 1961-62 | Montreal | 69 | 7 | 27 | 34 |
| 1962-63 | Montreal | 32 | 5 | 8 | 13 |
| 1963-64 | New York R | 67 | 24 | 41 | 65 |
| 1964-65 | New York R | 52 | 12 | 34 | 46 |
| 1965-66 | New York R | 60 | 11 | 31 | 42 |
| 1966-67 | New York R | 70 | 12 | 49 | 61 |
| 1967-68 | New York R | 73 | 25 | 40 | 65 |
| 1968-69 | New York R | 67 | 13 | 32 | 45 |
| 1969-70 | St Louis | 72 | 29 | 49 | 78 |
| 1970-71 | Buffalo | 60 | 15 | 46 | 61 |
| 1971-72 | Buf-NYR | 45 | 4 | 25 | 29 |
| | **Totals** | 941 | 207 | 467 | 674 |

**GRABOSKI, Anthony** *Defenseman*
b. Timmins, Ont., May 29, 1916

| Season | Club | GP | G | A | Pts. |
|---|---|---|---|---|---|
| 1940-41 | Montreal | 34 | 4 | 3 | 7 |
| 1941-42 | Montreal | 23 | 2 | 5 | 7 |
| 1942-43 | Montreal | 9 | 0 | 2 | 2 |
| | **Totals** | 66 | 6 | 10 | 16 |

**GRACIE, Robert J.** *Forward*
b. North Bay, Ont., Nov. 8, 1911

| Season | Club | GP | G | A | Pts. |
|---|---|---|---|---|---|
| 1930-31 | Toronto | 8 | 4 | 2 | 6 |
| 1931-32 | Toronto | 48 | 13 | 8 | 21 |
| 1932-33 | Toronto | 48 | 9 | 13 | 22 |
| 1933-34 | Bos-NYA | 49 | 6 | 12 | 18 |
| 1934-35 | NYA-MontM | 48 | 12 | 9 | 21 |
| 1935-36 | Montreal M | 48 | 11 | 14 | 25 |
| 1936-37 | Montreal M | 47 | 11 | 25 | 36 |
| 1937-38 | Montreal M | 48 | 12 | 19 | 31 |
| 1938-39 | MontM-Chi | 38 | 4 | 7 | 11 |
| | **Totals** | 382 | 82 | 109 | 191 |

**GRADIN, Thomas** *Forward*
b. Solleftea, Sweden, Feb. 18, 1956

| Season | Club | GP | G | A | Pts. |
|---|---|---|---|---|---|
| 1978-79 | Vancouver | 76 | 20 | 31 | 51 |
| 1979-80 | Vancouver | 80 | 30 | 45 | 75 |
| 1980-81 | Vancouver | 79 | 21 | 48 | 69 |
| 1981-82 | Vancouver | 76 | 37 | 49 | 86 |
| 1982-83 | Vancouver | 80 | 32 | 54 | 86 |
| | **Totals** | 391 | 140 | 227 | 367 |

**GRAHAM, Edward Dixon (Teddy)**
*Defenseman*
b. Owen Sound, Ont., June 30, 1906

| Season | Club | GP | G | A | Pts. |
|---|---|---|---|---|---|
| 1927-28 | Chicago | 19 | 1 | 0 | 1 |
| 1929-30 | Chicago | 26 | 1 | 2 | 3 |
| 1930-31 | Chicago | 44 | 0 | 7 | 7 |
| 1931-32 | Chicago | 48 | 0 | 3 | 3 |
| 1932-33 | Chicago | 48 | 3 | 8 | 11 |
| 1933-34 | MontM-Det | 44 | 3 | 1 | 4 |
| 1934-35 | Det-StLE | 39 | 0 | 2 | 2 |
| 1935-36 | Boston | 48 | 4 | 1 | 5 |
| 1936-37 | New York A | 32 | 2 | 1 | 3 |
| | **Totals** | 348 | 14 | 25 | 39 |

**GRAHAM, Leth** *Defenseman*
b. 1894

| Season | Club | GP | G | A | Pts. |
|---|---|---|---|---|---|
| 1920-21 | Ottawa | 13 | 0 | 0 | 0 |
| 1921-22 | Ottawa | 2 | 2 | 0 | 2 |
| 1922-23 | Hamilton | 4 | 1 | 0 | 1 |
| 1923-24 | Ottawa | 3 | 0 | 0 | 0 |
| 1924-25 | Ottawa | 3 | 0 | 0 | 0 |
| 1925-26 | Ottawa | 1 | 0 | 0 | 0 |
| | **Totals** | 26 | 3 | 0 | 3 |

**GRAHAM, Pat Thomas** *Forward*
b. Toronto, Ont., May 25, 1961

| Season | Club | GP | G | A | Pts. |
|---|---|---|---|---|---|
| 1981-82 | Pittsburgh | 42 | 6 | 8 | 14 |
| 1982-83 | Pittsburgh | 20 | 1 | 5 | 6 |
| | **Totals** | 62 | 7 | 13 | 20 |

**GRAHAM, Rodney Douglas** *Forward*
b. London, Ont., Aug. 19, 1946

| Season | Club | GP | G | A | Pts. |
|---|---|---|---|---|---|
| 1974-75 | Boston | 14 | 2 | 1 | 3 |

**GRANT, Daniel Frederick** *Forward*
b. Fredericton, N.B., Feb. 21, 1946

| Season | Club | GP | G | A | Pts. |
|---|---|---|---|---|---|
| 1965-66 | Montreal | 1 | 0 | 0 | 0 |
| 1967-68 | Montreal | 22 | 3 | 4 | 7 |
| 1968-69 | Minnesota | 75 | 34 | 31 | 65 |
| 1969-70 | Minnesota | 76 | 29 | 28 | 57 |
| 1970-71 | Minnesota | 78 | 34 | 23 | 57 |
| 1971-72 | Minnesota | 78 | 18 | 25 | 43 |
| 1972-73 | Minnesota | 78 | 32 | 35 | 67 |
| 1973-74 | Minnesota | 78 | 29 | 35 | 64 |
| 1974-75 | Detroit | 80 | 50 | 37 | 87 |
| 1975-76 | Detroit | 39 | 10 | 13 | 23 |
| 1976-77 | Detroit | 42 | 2 | 10 | 12 |
| 1977-78 | Det-LA | 54 | 12 | 21 | 33 |
| 1978-79 | Los Angeles | 35 | 10 | 11 | 21 |
| | **Totals** | 736 | 263 | 273 | 536 |

**GRATTON, Normand Lionel (Norm)** *Forward*
b. LaSalle, Que., Dec. 22, 1950

| Season | Club | GP | G | A | Pts. |
|---|---|---|---|---|---|
| 1971-72 | New York R | 3 | 0 | 1 | 1 |
| 1972-73 | Atl-Buf | 50 | 9 | 11 | 20 |
| 1973-74 | Buffalo | 57 | 6 | 11 | 17 |

| Season | Club | GP | G | A | Pts. |
|---|---|---|---|---|---|
| 1974-75 | Buf-Minn | 59 | 17 | 18 | 35 |
| 1975-76 | Minnesota | 32 | 7 | 3 | 10 |
| | **Totals** | 201 | 39 | 44 | 83 |

**GRAVELLE, Joseph Gerard Leo** *Forward*
b. Aylmer, Que., June 10, 1925

| Season | Club | GP | G | A | Pts. |
|---|---|---|---|---|---|
| 1946-47 | Montreal | 53 | 16 | 14 | 30 |
| 1947-48 | Montreal | 15 | 0 | 0 | 0 |
| 1948-49 | Montreal | 36 | 4 | 6 | 10 |
| 1949-50 | Montreal | 70 | 19 | 10 | 29 |
| 1950-51 | Mont-Det | 49 | 5 | 4 | 9 |
| | **Totals** | 223 | 44 | 34 | 78 |

**GRAVES, Hilliard** *Forward*
b. Saint John, N.B., Oct. 18, 1950

| Season | Club | GP | G | A | Pts. |
|---|---|---|---|---|---|
| 1970-71 | California | 14 | 0 | 0 | 0 |
| 1972-73 | California | 75 | 27 | 25 | 52 |
| 1973-74 | California | 64 | 11 | 18 | 29 |
| 1974-75 | California | 67 | 10 | 19 | 29 |
| 1975-76 | Atlanta | 80 | 19 | 30 | 49 |
| 1976-77 | Atl-Van | 79 | 18 | 25 | 43 |
| 1977-78 | Vancouver | 80 | 21 | 26 | 47 |
| 1978-79 | Vancouver | 62 | 11 | 15 | 26 |
| 1979-80 | Winnipeg | 35 | 1 | 5 | 6 |
| | **Totals** | 556 | 118 | 163 | 281 |

**GRAY, Alexander** *Forward*
b. Glasgow, Scotland, June 21, 1899

| Season | Club | GP | G | A | Pts. |
|---|---|---|---|---|---|
| 1927-28 | New York R | 43 | 7 | 0 | 7 |
| 1928-29 | Toronto | 7 | 0 | 0 | 0 |
| | **Totals** | 50 | 7 | 0 | 7 |

**GRAY, Terence Stanley** *Forward*
b. Montreal, Que., Mar. 21, 1938

| Season | Club | GP | G | A | Pts. |
|---|---|---|---|---|---|
| 1961-62 | Boston | 42 | 8 | 7 | 15 |
| 1963-64 | Montreal | 4 | 0 | 0 | 0 |
| 1967-68 | Los Angeles | 65 | 12 | 16 | 28 |
| 1968-69 | St Louis | 8 | 4 | 0 | 4 |
| 1969-70 | St Louis | 28 | 2 | 5 | 7 |
| | **Totals** | 147 | 26 | 28 | 54 |

**GREEN, Edward Joseph (Ted)** *Defenseman*
b. St. Boniface, Man., Mar. 23, 1940

| Season | Club | GP | G | A | Pts. |
|---|---|---|---|---|---|
| 1960-61 | Boston | 1 | 0 | 0 | 0 |
| 1961-62 | Boston | 66 | 3 | 8 | 11 |
| 1962-63 | Boston | 70 | 1 | 11 | 12 |
| 1963-64 | Boston | 70 | 4 | 10 | 14 |
| 1964-65 | Boston | 70 | 8 | 27 | 35 |
| 1965-66 | Boston | 27 | 5 | 13 | 18 |
| 1966-67 | Boston | 47 | 6 | 10 | 16 |
| 1967-68 | Boston | 72 | 7 | 36 | 43 |
| 1968-69 | Boston | 65 | 8 | 38 | 46 |
| 1970-71 | Boston | 78 | 5 | 37 | 42 |
| 1971-72 | Boston | 54 | 1 | 16 | 17 |
| 1972-73 | New England (WHA) | 78 | 16 | 30 | 46 |
| 1973-74 | New England (WHA) | 75 | 7 | 26 | 33 |
| 1974-75 | New England (WHA) | 57 | 6 | 14 | 20 |
| 1975-76 | Winnipeg (WHA) | 79 | 5 | 23 | 28 |
| 1976-77 | Winnipeg (WHA) | 70 | 4 | 21 | 25 |
| 1977-78 | Winnipeg (WHA) | 73 | 4 | 22 | 26 |
| 1978-79 | Winnipeg (WHA) | 20 | 0 | 2 | 2 |
| | **NHL Totals** | 620 | 48 | 206 | 254 |
| | **WHA Totals** | 452 | 42 | 138 | 180 |

**GREEN, Redvers** *Forward*
b. Sudbury, Ont.

| Season | Club | GP | G | A | Pts. |
|---|---|---|---|---|---|
| 1923-24 | Hamilton | 23 | 11 | 0 | 11 |
| 1924-25 | Hamilton | 30 | 19 | 4 | 23 |
| 1925-26 | New York A | 35 | 13 | 4 | 17 |
| 1926-27 | New York A | 43 | 10 | 4 | 14 |
| 1927-28 | New York A | 40 | 6 | 1 | 7 |
| 1928-29 | Boston | 22 | 0 | 0 | 0 |
| | **Totals** | 193 | 59 | 13 | 72 |

**GREEN, Richard Douglas** *Defenseman*
b. Belleville, Ont., Feb. 20, 1956

| Season | Club | GP | G | A | Pts. |
|---|---|---|---|---|---|
| 1976-77 | Washington | 45 | 3 | 12 | 15 |
| 1977-78 | Washington | 60 | 5 | 14 | 19 |
| 1978-79 | Washington | 71 | 8 | 33 | 41 |
| 1979-80 | Washington | 71 | 4 | 20 | 24 |

| Season | Club | GP | G | A | Pts. |
|---|---|---|---|---|---|
| 1980-81 | Washington | 65 | 8 | 23 | 31 |
| 1981-82 | Washington | 65 | 3 | 25 | 28 |
| 1982-83 | Montreal | 66 | 2 | 24 | 26 |
| | **Totals** | 443 | 33 | 151 | 184 |

**GREEN, Wilfred (Shorty)** *Forward*
b. Sudbury, Ont., July 17, 1896

| Season | Club | GP | G | A | Pts. |
|---|---|---|---|---|---|
| 1923-24 | Hamilton | 22 | 7 | 2 | 9 |
| 1924-25 | Hamilton | 28 | 18 | 1 | 19 |
| 1925-26 | New York A | 33 | 6 | 4 | 10 |
| 1926-27 | New York A | 21 | 2 | 1 | 3 |
| | **Totals** | 104 | 33 | 8 | 41 |

**GREGG, Randy** *Defenseman*
b. Edmonton, Alta., Feb. 7, 1955

| Season | Club | GP | G | A | Pts. |
|---|---|---|---|---|---|
| 1982-83 | Edmonton | 80 | 6 | 22 | 28 |

**GREIG, Bruce** *Forward*
b. High River, Alta., May 9, 1953

| Season | Club | GP | G | A | Pts. |
|---|---|---|---|---|---|
| 1973-74 | California | 1 | 0 | 0 | 0 |
| 1974-75 | California | 8 | 0 | 1 | 1 |
| 1976-77 | Calgary (WHA) | 7 | 1 | 1 | 2 |
| 1977-78 | Cincinnati (WHA) | 32 | 3 | 1 | 4 |
| 1978-79 | Indianapolis (WHA) | 21 | 3 | 7 | 10 |
| | **NHL Totals** | 9 | 0 | 1 | 1 |
| | **WHA Totals** | 60 | 7 | 9 | 16 |

**GRENIER, Lucien S. J.** *Forward*
b. Malartic, Que., Nov. 3, 1946

| Season | Club | GP | G | A | Pts. |
|---|---|---|---|---|---|
| 1969-70 | Montreal | 23 | 2 | 3 | 5 |
| 1970-71 | Los Angeles | 68 | 9 | 7 | 16 |
| 1971-72 | Los Angeles | 60 | 3 | 4 | 7 |
| | **Totals** | 151 | 14 | 14 | 28 |

**GRENIER, Richard** *Forward*
b. Montreal, Que., Sept. 18, 1952

| Season | Club | GP | G | A | Pts. |
|---|---|---|---|---|---|
| 1972-73 | New York I | 10 | 1 | 1 | 2 |
| 1976-77 | Quebec (WHA) | 34 | 11 | 9 | 20 |
| | **NHL Totals** | 10 | 1 | 1 | 2 |
| | **WHA Totals** | 34 | 11 | 9 | 20 |

**GRESCHNER, Ronald S.** *Defenseman*
b. Goodsoil, Sask., Dec. 22, 1954

| Season | Club | GP | G | A | Pts. |
|---|---|---|---|---|---|
| 1974-75 | New York R | 70 | 8 | 37 | 45 |
| 1975-76 | New York R | 77 | 6 | 21 | 27 |
| 1976-77 | New York R | 80 | 11 | 36 | 47 |
| 1977-78 | New York R | 78 | 24 | 48 | 72 |
| 1978-79 | New York R | 60 | 17 | 36 | 53 |
| 1979-80 | New York R | 76 | 21 | 37 | 58 |
| 1980-81 | New York R | 74 | 27 | 41 | 68 |
| 1981-82 | New York R | 29 | 5 | 11 | 16 |
| 1982-83 | New York R | 10 | 3 | 5 | 8 |
| | **Totals** | 554 | 122 | 272 | 394 |

**GRETZKY, Wayne** *Forward*
b. Brantford, Ont., Jan. 26, 1961

| Season | Club | GP | G | A | Pts. |
|---|---|---|---|---|---|
| 1978-79 | Ind-Edm (WHA) | 80 | 46 | 64 | 110 |
| 1979-80 | Edmonton | 79 | 51 | 125 | 137 |
| 1980-81 | Edmonton | 80 | 55 | 109 | 164 |
| 1981-82 | Edmonton | 80 | 92 | 120 | 212 |
| 1982-83 | Edmonton | 80 | 71 | 125 | 196 |
| | **NHL Totals** | 319 | 269 | 440 | 709 |
| | **WHA Totals** | 80 | 46 | 64 | 110 |

**GRIGOR, George** *Forward*
b. Edinburgh, Scotland

| Season | Club | GP | G | A | Pts. |
|---|---|---|---|---|---|
| 1943-44 | Chicago | 2 | 1 | 0 | 1 |

**GRISDALE, John Russel** *Defenseman*
b. Toronto, Ont., Aug. 23, 1948

| Season | Club | GP | G | A | Pts. |
|---|---|---|---|---|---|
| 1972-73 | Toronto | 49 | 1 | 7 | 8 |
| 1974-75 | Tor-Van | 60 | 1 | 12 | 13 |
| 1975-76 | Vancouver | 38 | 2 | 6 | 8 |
| 1976-77 | Vancouver | 20 | 0 | 2 | 2 |
| 1977-78 | Vancouver | 42 | 0 | 9 | 9 |
| 1978-79 | Vancouver | 41 | 0 | 3 | 3 |
| | **Totals** | 250 | 4 | 39 | 43 |

**GROGHEN, Maurice (Moe)** *Forward*
b. Montreal, Que., Nov. 19, 1914

| Season | Club | GP | G | A | Pts. |
|---|---|---|---|---|---|
| 1937-38 | Montreal M | 16 | 0 | 0 | 0 |

**GRONSDAHL, Lloyd Gilford** *Forward*
b. Norquay, Sask., May 10, 1921

| Season | Club | GP | G | A | Pts. |
|---|---|---|---|---|---|
| 1941-42 | Boston | 10 | 1 | 2 | 3 |

**GROSS, Lloyd** *Forward*
b. Kitchener, Ont., Sept. 15, 1907

| Season | Club | GP | G | A | Pts. |
|---|---|---|---|---|---|
| 1926-27 | Toronto | 6 | 1 | 1 | 2 |
| 1933-34 | NYA-Bos-Det | 43 | 9 | 4 | 13 |
| 1934-35 | Detroit | 6 | 1 | 0 | 1 |
| | **Totals** | 55 | 11 | 5 | 16 |

**GROSSO, Donald (Count)** *Forward*
b. Sault Ste. Marie, Ont., Apr. 12, 1915

| Season | Club | GP | G | A | Pts. |
|---|---|---|---|---|---|
| 1938-39 | Detroit | 1 | 1 | 1 | 2 |
| 1939-40 | Detroit | 29 | 2 | 3 | 5 |
| 1940-41 | Detroit | 45 | 8 | 7 | 15 |
| 1941-42 | Detroit | 48 | 23 | 30 | 53 |
| 1942-43 | Detroit | 50 | 15 | 17 | 32 |
| 1943-44 | Detroit | 42 | 16 | 31 | 47 |
| 1944-45 | Det-Chi | 41 | 15 | 16 | 31 |
| 1945-46 | Chicago | 47 | 7 | 10 | 17 |
| 1946-47 | Boston | 33 | 0 | 2 | 2 |
| | **Totals** | 336 | 87 | 117 | 204 |

**GROSVENAR, Leonard (Len)** *Forward*
b. Ottawa, Ont.

| Season | Club | GP | G | A | Pts. |
|---|---|---|---|---|---|
| 1927-28 | Ottawa | 43 | 1 | 2 | 3 |
| 1928-29 | Ottawa | 43 | 3 | 2 | 5 |
| 1929-30 | Ottawa | 15 | 0 | 3 | 3 |
| 1930-31 | Ottawa | 33 | 5 | 4 | 9 |
| 1931-32 | New York A | 12 | 0 | 0 | 0 |
| 1932-33 | Montreal | 4 | 0 | 0 | 0 |
| | **Totals** | 150 | 9 | 11 | 20 |

**GRUEN, Daniel Patrick** *Forward*
b. Thunder Bay, Ont., June 26, 1952

| Season | Club | GP | G | A | Pts. |
|---|---|---|---|---|---|
| 1972-73 | Detroit | 2 | 0 | 0 | 0 |
| 1973-74 | Detroit | 18 | 1 | 3 | 4 |
| 1974-75 | Mich-Winn (WHA) | 66 | 19 | 28 | 47 |
| 1975-76 | Cleveland (WHA) | 80 | 26 | 24 | 50 |
| 1976-77 | Minn-Calg (WHA) | 35 | 11 | 9 | 20 |
| 1976-77 | Colorado | 29 | 8 | 10 | 18 |
| | **NHL Totals** | 49 | 9 | 13 | 22 |
| | **WHA Totals** | 181 | 56 | 61 | 117 |

**GRUHL, Scott Kenneth** *Forward*
b. Port Colborne, Ont., Sept. 13, 1959

| Season | Club | GP | G | A | Pts. |
|---|---|---|---|---|---|
| 1981-82 | Los Angeles | 7 | 2 | 1 | 3 |
| 1982-83 | Los Angeles | 7 | 0 | 2 | 2 |
| | **Totals** | 14 | 2 | 3 | 5 |

**GRYP, Robert Douglas** *Forward*
b. Chatham, Ont., May 6, 1950

| Season | Club | GP | G | A | Pts. |
|---|---|---|---|---|---|
| 1973-74 | Boston | 1 | 0 | 0 | 0 |
| 1974-75 | Washington | 27 | 5 | 8 | 13 |
| 1975-76 | Washington | 46 | 6 | 5 | 11 |
| | **Totals** | 74 | 11 | 13 | 24 |

**GUEVREMONT, Jocelyn Marcel Josh**
*Defenseman*
b. Montreal, Que., Mar. 1, 1951

| Season | Club | GP | G | A | Pts. |
|---|---|---|---|---|---|
| 1971-72 | Vancouver | 75 | 13 | 38 | 51 |
| 1972-73 | Vancouver | 78 | 16 | 26 | 42 |
| 1973-74 | Vancouver | 72 | 15 | 24 | 39 |
| 1974-75 | Van-Buf | 66 | 7 | 25 | 32 |
| 1975-76 | Buffalo | 80 | 12 | 40 | 52 |
| 1976-77 | Buffalo | 80 | 9 | 29 | 38 |
| 1977-78 | Buffalo | 66 | 7 | 28 | 35 |
| 1978-79 | Buffalo | 34 | 3 | 8 | 11 |
| 1979-80 | New York R | 20 | 2 | 5 | 7 |
| | **Totals** | 571 | 84 | 223 | 307 |

**GUIDOLIN, Aldo Reno** *Defenseman-Forward*
b. Forks of Credit, Ont., June 6, 1932

| Season | Club | GP | G | A | Pts. |
|---|---|---|---|---|---|
| 1952-53 | New York R | 30 | 4 | 4 | 8 |
| 1953-54 | New York R | 68 | 2 | 6 | 8 |
| 1954-55 | New York R | 70 | 2 | 5 | 7 |
| 1955-56 | New York R | 14 | 1 | 0 | 1 |
| | **Totals** | 182 | 9 | 15 | 24 |

**GUIDOLIN, Armand (Bep)** *Forward*
b. Thorold, Ont., Dec. 9, 1925

| Season | Club | GP | G | A | Pts. |
|---|---|---|---|---|---|
| 1942-43 | Boston | 42 | 7 | 15 | 22 |
| 1943-44 | Boston | 47 | 17 | 25 | 42 |
| 1945-46 | Boston | 50 | 15 | 17 | 32 |
| 1946-47 | Boston | 56 | 10 | 13 | 23 |
| 1947-48 | Detroit | 58 | 12 | 10 | 22 |
| 1948-49 | Det-Chi | 60 | 4 | 17 | 21 |
| 1949-50 | Chicago | 70 | 17 | 34 | 51 |
| 1950-51 | Chicago | 69 | 12 | 22 | 34 |
| 1951-52 | Chicago | 67 | 13 | 18 | 31 |
| | **Totals** | 519 | 107 | 171 | 278 |

**GUINDON, Robert Pierre** *Forward*
b. Labelle, Que., Nov. 19, 1950

| Season | Club | GP | G | A | Pts. |
|---|---|---|---|---|---|
| 1972-73 | Quebec (WHA) | 71 | 28 | 28 | 56 |
| 1973-74 | Quebec (WHA) | 77 | 31 | 39 | 70 |
| 1974-75 | Quebec (WHA) | 69 | 12 | 18 | 30 |
| 1975-76 | Winnipeg (WHA) | 29 | 3 | 3 | 6 |
| 1976-77 | Winnipeg (WHA) | 69 | 10 | 17 | 27 |
| 1977-78 | Winnipeg (WHA) | 77 | 20 | 22 | 42 |
| 1978-79 | Winnipeg (WHA) | 71 | 8 | 18 | 26 |
| 1979-80 | Winnipeg | 6 | 0 | 1 | 1 |
| | **NHL Totals** | 6 | 0 | 1 | 1 |
| | **WHA Totals** | 463 | 112 | 145 | 257 |

**GUSTAFSSON, Bengt-Ake** *Forward*
b. Karlskoga, Sweden, Mar. 23, 1958

| Season | Club | GP | G | A | Pts. |
|---|---|---|---|---|---|
| 1979-80 | Washington | 80 | 22 | 38 | 60 |
| 1980-81 | Washington | 72 | 21 | 34 | 55 |
| 1981-82 | Washington | 70 | 26 | 34 | 60 |
| 1982-83 | Washington | 67 | 22 | 42 | 64 |
| | **Totals** | 289 | 91 | 148 | 239 |

**GUSTAVSSON, Peter** *Forward*
b. Bollebygd, Sweden, Mar. 30, 1958

| Season | Club | GP | G | A | Pts. |
|---|---|---|---|---|---|
| 1981-82 | Colorado | 2 | 0 | 0 | 0 |

**HABSCHEID, Marc Joseph** *Forward*
b. Swift Current, Sask., Mar. 1, 1963

| Season | Club | GP | G | A | Pts. |
|---|---|---|---|---|---|
| 1981-82 | Edmonton | 7 | 1 | 3 | 4 |
| 1982-83 | Edmonton | 32 | 3 | 10 | 13 |
| | **Totals** | 39 | 4 | 13 | 17 |

**HADDON, Lloyd Ward** *Defenseman*
b. Sarnia, Ont., Aug. 10, 1938

| Season | Club | GP | G | A | Pts. |
|---|---|---|---|---|---|
| 1959-60 | Detroit | 8 | 0 | 0 | 0 |

**HADFIELD, Victor Edward** *Forward*
b. Oakville, Ont., Oct. 4, 1940

| Season | Club | GP | G | A | Pts. |
|---|---|---|---|---|---|
| 1961-62 | New York R | 44 | 3 | 1 | 4 |
| 1962-63 | New York R | 36 | 5 | 6 | 11 |
| 1963-64 | New York R | 69 | 14 | 11 | 25 |
| 1964-65 | New York R | 70 | 18 | 20 | 38 |
| 1965-66 | New York R | 67 | 16 | 19 | 35 |
| 1966-67 | New York R | 69 | 13 | 20 | 33 |
| 1967-68 | New York R | 59 | 20 | 19 | 39 |
| 1968-69 | New York R | 73 | 26 | 40 | 66 |
| 1969-70 | New York R | 71 | 20 | 34 | 54 |
| 1970-71 | New York R | 63 | 22 | 22 | 44 |
| 1971-72 | New York R | 78 | 50 | 56 | 106 |
| 1972-73 | New York R | 63 | 28 | 34 | 62 |
| 1973-74 | New York R | 77 | 27 | 28 | 55 |
| 1974-75 | Pittsburgh | 78 | 31 | 42 | 73 |
| 1975-76 | Pittsburgh | 76 | 30 | 35 | 65 |
| 1976-77 | Pittsburgh | 9 | 0 | 2 | 2 |
| | **Totals** | 1002 | 323 | 389 | 712 |

**HAGGERTY, James** *Forward*
b. Port Arthur, Ont., Apr. 14, 1914

| Season | Club | GP | G | A | Pts. |
|---|---|---|---|---|---|
| 1941-42 | Montreal | 5 | 1 | 1 | 2 |

| Season | Club | GP | G | A | Pts. |
|---|---|---|---|---|---|
| **HAGMAN, Matti Risto** *Forward* | | | | | |
| b. Helsinki, Finland, Sept. 21, 1955 | | | | | |
| 1976-77 | Boston | 75 | 11 | 17 | 28 |
| 1977-78 | Boston | 15 | 4 | 1 | 5 |
| 1977-78 | Quebec (WHA) | 53 | 25 | 31 | 56 |
| 1980-81 | Edmonton | 75 | 20 | 33 | 53 |
| 1981-82 | Edmonton | 72 | 21 | 38 | 59 |
| | **NHL Totals** | 237 | 56 | 89 | 145 |
| | **WHA Totals** | 53 | 25 | 31 | 56 |
| **HAJT, William Albert** *Defenseman* | | | | | |
| b. Borden, Sask., Nov. 18, 1951 | | | | | |
| 1973-74 | Buffalo | 6 | 0 | 2 | 2 |
| 1974-75 | Buffalo | 76 | 3 | 26 | 29 |
| 1975-76 | Buffalo | 80 | 6 | 21 | 27 |
| 1976-77 | Buffalo | 79 | 6 | 20 | 26 |
| 1977-78 | Buffalo | 76 | 4 | 18 | 22 |
| 1978-79 | Buffalo | 40 | 3 | 8 | 11 |
| 1979-80 | Buffalo | 75 | 4 | 12 | 16 |
| 1980-81 | Buffalo | 68 | 2 | 19 | 21 |
| 1981-82 | Buffalo | 65 | 2 | 9 | 11 |
| 1982-83 | Buffalo | 72 | 3 | 12 | 15 |
| | **Totals** | 637 | 33 | 147 | 170 |
| **HAKANSSON, Anders** *Forward* | | | | | |
| b. Munfors, Sweden, Apr. 27, 1956 | | | | | |
| 1981-82 | Minnesota | 72 | 12 | 4 | 16 |
| 1982-83 | Minn-Pitt | 67 | 9 | 12 | 21 |
| | **Totals** | 139 | 21 | 16 | 37 |
| **HALDERSON, Harold (Slim)** *Forward* | | | | | |
| b. Winnipeg, Man., Jan. 6, 1900 | | | | | |
| 1926-27 | Tor-Det | 44 | 3 | 2 | 5 |
| **HALE, Larry James** *Defenseman* | | | | | |
| b. Summerland, B.C., Oct. 9, 1941 | | | | | |
| 1968-69 | Philadelphia | 67 | 3 | 16 | 19 |
| 1969-70 | Philadelphia | 53 | 1 | 9 | 10 |
| 1970-71 | Philadelphia | 70 | 1 | 11 | 12 |
| 1971-72 | Philadelphia | 6 | 0 | 1 | 1 |
| 1972-73 | Houston (WHA) | 68 | 4 | 26 | 30 |
| 1973-74 | Houston (WHA) | 69 | 2 | 14 | 16 |
| 1974-75 | Houston (WHA) | 76 | 2 | 18 | 20 |
| 1975-76 | Houston (WHA) | 77 | 1 | 14 | 15 |
| 1976-77 | Houston (WHA) | 67 | 0 | 14 | 14 |
| 1977-78 | Houston (WHA) | 56 | 2 | 11 | 13 |
| | **NHL Totals** | 196 | 5 | 37 | 42 |
| | **WHA Totals** | 413 | 11 | 97 | 108 |
| **HALEY, Leonard Frank** *Forward* | | | | | |
| b. Edmonton, Alta., Sept. 15, 1931 | | | | | |
| 1959-60 | Detroit | 27 | 1 | 2 | 3 |
| 1960-61 | Detroit | 3 | 1 | 0 | 1 |
| | **Totals** | 30 | 2 | 2 | 4 |
| **HALL, Del Allison** *Forward* | | | | | |
| b. Peterborough, Ont., May 7, 1949 | | | | | |
| 1972-73 | California | 6 | 0 | 0 | 0 |
| 1973-74 | California | 2 | 0 | 2 | 2 |
| 1975-76 | Phoenix (WHA) | 80 | 47 | 44 | 91 |
| 1976-77 | Phoenix (WHA) | 80 | 38 | 41 | 79 |
| 1977-78 | Cin-Edm (WHA) | 26 | 4 | 3 | 7 |
| | **NHL Totals** | 8 | 0 | 2 | 2 |
| | **WHA Totals** | 186 | 89 | 88 | 177 |
| **HALL, Gary Wayne** *Forward* | | | | | |
| b. Melita, Man., May 22, 1939 | | | | | |
| 1960-61 | New York R | 4 | 0 | 0 | 0 |
| **HALL, Joseph Henry** *Defenseman* | | | | | |
| b. Stratfordshire, England, May 3, 1882 | | | | | |
| 1917-18 | Montreal | 20 | 8 | 0 | 8 |
| 1918-19 | Montreal | 17 | 7 | 1 | 8 |
| | **Totals** | 37 | 15 | 1 | 16 |
| **HALL, Murray Winston** *Forward* | | | | | |
| b. Kirkland Lake, Ont., Nov. 24, 1940 | | | | | |
| 1961-62 | Chicago | 2 | 0 | 0 | 0 |
| 1963-64 | Chicago | 23 | 2 | 0 | 2 |
| 1965-66 | Detroit | 1 | 0 | 0 | 0 |
| 1966-67 | Detroit | 12 | 4 | 3 | 7 |
| 1967-68 | Minnesota | 17 | 2 | 1 | 3 |
| 1970-71 | Vancouver | 77 | 21 | 38 | 59 |
| 1971-72 | Vancouver | 32 | 6 | 6 | 12 |
| 1972-73 | Houston (WHA) | 76 | 28 | 42 | 70 |
| 1973-74 | Houston (WHA) | 78 | 30 | 28 | 58 |
| 1974-75 | Houston (WHA) | 78 | 18 | 29 | 47 |
| 1975-76 | Houston (WHA) | 80 | 20 | 26 | 46 |
| | **NHL Totals** | 164 | 35 | 48 | 83 |
| | **WHA Totals** | 312 | 96 | 125 | 221 |
| **HALL, Robert** *Forward* | | | | | |
| 1925-26 | New York A | 8 | 0 | 0 | 0 |
| **HALLIDAY, Milton** *Defenseman-Forward* | | | | | |
| b. Ottawa, Ont. | | | | | |
| 1926-27 | Ottawa | 36 | 1 | 0 | 1 |
| 1927-28 | Ottawa | 13 | 0 | 0 | 0 |
| 1928-29 | Ottawa | 16 | 0 | 0 | 0 |
| | **Totals** | 65 | 1 | 0 | 1 |
| **HALLIN, Mats** *Froward* | | | | | |
| b. Eskilstuna, Sweden, Mar. 19, 1958 | | | | | |
| 1982-83 | New York I | 30 | 7 | 7 | 14 |
| **HALWARD, Douglas Robert** *Defenseman* | | | | | |
| b. Toronto, Ont., Nov. 1, 1955 | | | | | |
| 1975-76 | Boston | 22 | 1 | 5 | 6 |
| 1976-77 | Boston | 18 | 2 | 2 | 4 |
| 1977-78 | Boston | 25 | 0 | 2 | 2 |
| 1978-79 | Los Angeles | 27 | 1 | 5 | 6 |
| 1979-80 | Los Angeles | 63 | 11 | 45 | 56 |
| 1980-81 | LA-Van | 58 | 4 | 16 | 20 |
| 1981-82 | Vancouver | 37 | 4 | 13 | 17 |
| 1982-83 | Vancouver | 75 | 19 | 33 | 52 |
| | **Totals** | 325 | 43 | 121 | 163 |
| **HAMEL, Gilles** *Forward* | | | | | |
| b. Asbestos, Que., Mar. 18, 1960 | | | | | |
| 1980-81 | Buffalo | 51 | 10 | 9 | 19 |
| 1981-82 | Buffalo | 16 | 2 | 7 | 9 |
| 1982-83 | Buffalo | 66 | 22 | 20 | 42 |
| | **Totals** | 133 | 34 | 36 | 70 |
| **HAMEL, Herbert (Hap)** *Forward* | | | | | |
| 1930-31 | Toronto | — | 0 | 0 | 0 |
| **HAMEL, Jean** *Defenseman* | | | | | |
| b. Asbestos, Que., June 6, 1952 | | | | | |
| 1972-73 | St Louis | 55 | 2 | 7 | 9 |
| 1973-74 | StL-Det | 45 | 1 | 4 | 5 |
| 1974-75 | Detroit | 80 | 5 | 19 | 24 |
| 1975-76 | Detroit | 77 | 3 | 9 | 12 |
| 1976-77 | Detroit | 71 | 1 | 10 | 11 |
| 1977-78 | Detroit | 32 | 2 | 6 | 8 |
| 1978-79 | Detroit | 52 | 2 | 4 | 6 |
| 1979-80 | Detroit | 49 | 1 | 4 | 5 |
| 1980-81 | Detroit | 68 | 5 | 7 | 12 |
| 1981-82 | Quebec | 40 | 1 | 6 | 7 |
| 1982-83 | Quebec | 51 | 2 | 7 | 9 |
| | **Totals** | 620 | 25 | 83 | 108 |
| **HAMILL, Robert George (Red)** *Forward* | | | | | |
| b. Toronto, Ont., Jan. 11, 1917 | | | | | |
| 1937-38 | Boston | 6 | 0 | 1 | 1 |
| 1938-39 | Boston | 6 | 0 | 1 | 1 |
| 1939-40 | Boston | 30 | 10 | 8 | 18 |
| 1940-41 | Boston | 8 | 0 | 1 | 1 |
| 1941-42 | Bos-Chi | 43 | 24 | 12 | 36 |
| 1942-43 | Chicago | 50 | 28 | 16 | 44 |
| 1945-46 | Chicago | 38 | 20 | 17 | 37 |
| 1946-47 | Chicago | 60 | 21 | 19 | 40 |
| 1947-48 | Chicago | 60 | 11 | 13 | 24 |
| 1948-49 | Chicago | 57 | 8 | 4 | 12 |
| 1949-50 | Chicago | 59 | 6 | 2 | 8 |
| 1950-51 | Chicago | 2 | 0 | 0 | 0 |
| | **Totals** | 419 | 128 | 94 | 222 |
| **HAMILTON, Allan Guy** *Defenseman* | | | | | |
| b. Flin Flon, Man., Aug. 20, 1946 | | | | | |
| 1965-66 | New York R | 4 | 0 | 0 | 0 |
| 1967-68 | New York R | 2 | 0 | 0 | 0 |
| 1968-69 | New York R | 16 | 0 | 0 | 0 |
| 1969-70 | New York R | 59 | 0 | 5 | 5 |
| 1970-71 | Buffalo | 69 | 2 | 28 | 30 |
| 1971-72 | Buffalo | 76 | 4 | 30 | 34 |
| 1972-73 | Alberta (WHA) | 78 | 11 | 50 | 61 |
| 1973-74 | Edmonton (WHA) | 78 | 14 | 45 | 59 |
| 1974-75 | Edmonton (WHA) | 25 | 1 | 13 | 14 |
| 1975-76 | Edmonton (WHA) | 54 | 2 | 32 | 34 |
| 1976-77 | Edmonton (WHA) | 81 | 8 | 37 | 45 |
| 1977-78 | Edmonton (WHA) | 59 | 11 | 43 | 54 |
| 1978-79 | Edmonton (WHA) | 80 | 6 | 38 | 44 |
| 1979-80 | Edmonton | 31 | 4 | 15 | 19 |
| | **NHL Totals** | 257 | 10 | 78 | 88 |
| | **WHA Totals** | 455 | 53 | 258 | 311 |
| **HAMILTON, Charles (Chuck)** *Defenseman* | | | | | |
| b. Kirkland Lake, Ont., Jan. 18, 1939 | | | | | |
| 1961-62 | Montreal | 1 | 0 | 0 | 0 |
| 1972-73 | St Louis | 3 | 0 | 2 | 2 |
| | **Totals** | 4 | 0 | 2 | 2 |
| **HAMILTON, James** *Forward* | | | | | |
| b. Barrie, Ont., Jan. 18, 1957 | | | | | |
| 1977-78 | Pittsburgh | 25 | 2 | 4 | 6 |
| 1978-79 | Pittsburgh | 2 | 0 | 0 | 0 |
| 1979-80 | Pittsburgh | 10 | 2 | 0 | 2 |
| 1980-81 | Pittsburgh | 20 | 1 | 6 | 7 |
| 1981-82 | Pittsburgh | 11 | 5 | 3 | 8 |
| 1982-83 | Pittsburgh | 5 | 0 | 2 | 2 |
| | **Totals** | 73 | 10 | 15 | 25 |
| **HAMILTON, John McIvor (Jackie)** *Forward* | | | | | |
| b. Trenton, Ont., June 2, 1925 | | | | | |
| 1942-43 | Toronto | 11 | 1 | 1 | 2 |
| 1943-44 | Toronto | 49 | 20 | 17 | 37 |
| 1945-46 | Toronto | 40 | 7 | 9 | 16 |
| | **Totals** | 100 | 28 | 27 | 55 |
| **HAMILTON, Reginald** *Defenseman* | | | | | |
| b. Toronto, Ont., Apr. 29, 1914 | | | | | |
| 1936-37 | Toronto | 39 | 3 | 7 | 10 |
| 1937-38 | Toronto | 45 | 1 | 4 | 5 |
| 1938-39 | Toronto | 48 | 0 | 7 | 7 |
| 1939-40 | Toronto | 23 | 2 | 2 | 4 |
| 1940-41 | Toronto | 45 | 3 | 12 | 15 |
| 1941-42 | Toronto | 22 | 0 | 4 | 4 |
| 1942-43 | Toronto | 49 | 4 | 22 | 26 |
| 1943-44 | Toronto | 39 | 4 | 12 | 16 |
| 1944-45 | Toronto | 50 | 3 | 12 | 15 |
| 1945-46 | Chicago | 48 | 1 | 7 | 8 |
| 1946-47 | Chicago | 10 | 0 | 3 | 3 |
| | **Totals** | 418 | 21 | 92 | 113 |
| **HAMMARSTROM, Hans Inge** *Forward* | | | | | |
| b. Sundsvall, Sweden, Jan. 20, 1948 | | | | | |
| 1973-74 | Toronto | 66 | 20 | 23 | 43 |
| 1974-75 | Toronto | 69 | 21 | 20 | 41 |
| 1975-76 | Toronto | 76 | 19 | 21 | 40 |
| 1976-77 | Toronto | 78 | 24 | 17 | 41 |
| 1977-78 | Tor-StL | 73 | 20 | 20 | 40 |
| 1978-79 | St Louis | 65 | 12 | 22 | 34 |
| | **Totals** | 427 | 116 | 123 | 239 |
| **HAMPSON, Edward George (Ted)** *Forward* | | | | | |
| b. Togo, Sask., Dec. 11, 1936 | | | | | |
| 1959-60 | Toronto | 41 | 2 | 8 | 10 |
| 1960-61 | New York R | 69 | 6 | 14 | 20 |
| 1961-62 | New York R | 68 | 4 | 24 | 28 |
| 1962-63 | New York R | 46 | 4 | 2 | 6 |
| 1963-64 | Detroit | 7 | 0 | 1 | 1 |
| 1964-65 | Detroit | 1 | 0 | 0 | 0 |
| 1966-67 | Detroit | 65 | 13 | 35 | 48 |
| 1967-68 | Det-Oak | 71 | 17 | 37 | 54 |
| 1968-69 | Oakland | 76 | 26 | 49 | 75 |
| 1969-70 | Oakland | 76 | 17 | 35 | 52 |
| 1970-71 | Cal-Minn | 78 | 14 | 26 | 40 |

| Season | Club | GP | G | A | Pts. |
|---|---|---|---|---|---|
| 1971-72 | Minnesota | 78 | 5 | 14 | 19 |
| 1972-73 | Minnesota (WHA) | 76 | 17 | 45 | 62 |
| 1973-74 | Minnesota (WHA) | 77 | 17 | 38 | 55 |
| 1974-75 | Minnesota (WHA) | 78 | 17 | 36 | 53 |
| | **NHL Totals** | 676 | 108 | 245 | 353 |
| | **WHA Totals** | 231 | 51 | 119 | 170 |

**HAMPSON, Gord** *Forward*
b. Vancouver, B.C., Feb. 13, 1959

| Season | Club | GP | G | A | Pts. |
|---|---|---|---|---|---|
| 1982-83 | Calgary | 4 | 0 | 0 | 0 |

**HAMPTON, Richard Charles**
*Defenseman-Forward*
b. King, Ont., June 14, 1956

| Season | Club | GP | G | A | Pts. |
|---|---|---|---|---|---|
| 1974-75 | California | 78 | 8 | 17 | 25 |
| 1975-76 | California | 73 | 14 | 37 | 51 |
| 1976-77 | Cleveland | 57 | 16 | 24 | 40 |
| 1977-78 | Cleveland | 77 | 18 | 18 | 36 |
| 1978-79 | Los Angeles | 49 | 3 | 17 | 20 |
| 1979-80 | Los Angeles | 3 | 0 | 0 | 0 |
| | **Totals** | 337 | 59 | 113 | 172 |

**HANGSLEBEN, Alan** *Defenseman*
b. Warroad, Minn., Feb. 22, 1953

| Season | Club | GP | G | A | Pts. |
|---|---|---|---|---|---|
| 1974-75 | New England (WHA) | 26 | 0 | 5 | 5 |
| 1975-76 | New England (WHA) | 78 | 2 | 23 | 25 |
| 1976-77 | New England (WHA) | 74 | 13 | 9 | 22 |
| 1977-78 | New England (WHA) | 79 | 11 | 18 | 29 |
| 1978-79 | New England (WHA) | 77 | 10 | 19 | 29 |
| 1979-80 | Hart-Wash | 74 | 13 | 22 | 35 |
| 1980-81 | Washington | 74 | 5 | 19 | 24 |
| 1981-82 | Wash-LA | 35 | 3 | 7 | 10 |
| | **NHL Totals** | 183 | 21 | 48 | 69 |
| | **WHA Totals** | 334 | 36 | 74 | 110 |

**HANNA, John** *Defenseman*
b. Sydney, N.S., Apr. 5, 1935

| Season | Club | GP | G | A | Pts. |
|---|---|---|---|---|---|
| 1958-59 | New York R | 70 | 1 | 10 | 11 |
| 1959-60 | New York R | 61 | 4 | 8 | 12 |
| 1960-61 | New York R | 46 | 1 | 8 | 9 |
| 1963-64 | Montreal | 6 | 0 | 0 | 0 |
| 1967-68 | Philadelphia | 15 | 0 | 0 | 0 |
| 1972-73 | Cleveland (WHA) | 66 | 6 | 20 | 26 |
| | **NHL Totals** | 198 | 6 | 26 | 32 |
| | **WHA Totals** | 66 | 6 | 20 | 26 |

**HANNAN, David** *Forward*
b. Sudbury, Ont., Nov. 26, 1961

| Season | Club | GP | G | A | Pts. |
|---|---|---|---|---|---|
| 1981-82 | Pittsburgh | 1 | 0 | 0 | 0 |
| 1982-83 | Pittsburgh | 74 | 11 | 22 | 33 |
| | **Totals** | 75 | 11 | 22 | 33 |

**HANNIGAN, John Gordon** *Forward*
b. Schumacher, Ont., Jan. 19, 1929

| Season | Club | GP | G | A | Pts. |
|---|---|---|---|---|---|
| 1952-53 | Toronto | 65 | 17 | 18 | 35 |
| 1953-54 | Toronto | 35 | 4 | 4 | 8 |
| 1954-55 | Toronto | 13 | 0 | 2 | 2 |
| 1955-56 | Toronto | 48 | 8 | 7 | 15 |
| | **Totals** | 161 | 29 | 31 | 60 |

**HANNIGAN, Patrick Edward** *Forward*
b. Timmins, Ont., Mar. 5, 1936

| Season | Club | GP | G | A | Pts. |
|---|---|---|---|---|---|
| 1959-60 | Toronto | 1 | 0 | 0 | 0 |
| 1960-61 | New York R | 53 | 11 | 9 | 20 |
| 1961-62 | New York R | 56 | 8 | 14 | 22 |
| 1967-68 | Philadelphia | 65 | 11 | 15 | 26 |
| 1968-69 | Philadelphia | 7 | 0 | 1 | 1 |
| | **Totals** | 182 | 30 | 39 | 69 |

**HANNIGAN, Raymond James** *Forward*
b. Schumacher, Ont., July 14, 1927

| Season | Club | GP | G | A | Pts. |
|---|---|---|---|---|---|
| 1948-49 | Toronto | 3 | 0 | 0 | 0 |

**HANSEN, Richard John** *Forward*
b. Bronx, N.Y., Oct. 30, 1955

| Season | Club | GP | G | A | Pts. |
|---|---|---|---|---|---|
| 1976-77 | New York I | 4 | 1 | 0 | 1 |
| 1977-78 | New York I | 2 | 0 | 0 | 0 |


| Season | Club | GP | G | A | Pts. |
|---|---|---|---|---|---|
| 1978-79 | New York I | 12 | 1 | 6 | 7 |
| 1981-82 | St Louis | 2 | 0 | 2 | 2 |
| | **Totals** | 20 | 2 | 8 | 10 |

**HANSON, David** *Defenseman*
b. Cumberland, Wis., Apr. 12, 1954

| Season | Club | GP | G | A | Pts. |
|---|---|---|---|---|---|
| 1976-77 | Minn-NE (WHA) | 8 | 0 | 2 | 2 |
| 1977-78 | Birmingham (WHA) | 42 | 7 | 16 | 23 |
| 1978-79 | Birmingham (WHA) | 53 | 6 | 22 | 28 |
| 1978-79 | Detroit | 11 | 0 | 0 | 0 |
| 1979-80 | Minnesota | 22 | 1 | 1 | 2 |
| | **NHL Totals** | 33 | 1 | 1 | 2 |
| | **WHA Totals** | 103 | 13 | 40 | 53 |

**HANSON, Emil** *Defenseman*
b. Centerville, S. Dak., Nov. 18, 1907

| Season | Club | GP | G | A | Pts. |
|---|---|---|---|---|---|
| 1932-33 | Detroit | — | 0 | 0 | 0 |

**HARBARUK, Mikolaj Nicholas (Nick)**
*Forward*
b. Drohiczyn, Poland, Aug. 16, 1943

| Season | Club | GP | G | A | Pts. |
|---|---|---|---|---|---|
| 1969-70 | Pittsburgh | 74 | 5 | 17 | 22 |
| 1970-71 | Pittsburgh | 78 | 13 | 12 | 25 |
| 1971-72 | Pittsburgh | 78 | 12 | 17 | 29 |
| 1972-73 | Pittsburgh | 78 | 10 | 15 | 25 |
| 1973-74 | St Louis | 56 | 5 | 14 | 19 |
| 1974-75 | Indianapolis (WHA) | 78 | 20 | 23 | 43 |
| 1975-76 | Indianapolis (WHA) | 76 | 23 | 19 | 42 |
| 1976-77 | Indianapolis (WHA) | 27 | 2 | 2 | 4 |
| | **NHL Totals** | 364 | 45 | 75 | 120 |
| | **WHA Totals** | 181 | 45 | 44 | 89 |

**HARDY, Jocelyn Joseph (Joe)** *Forward*
b. Kenogami, Que., Dec. 5, 1945

| Season | Club | GP | G | A | Pts. |
|---|---|---|---|---|---|
| 1969-70 | Oakland | 23 | 5 | 4 | 9 |
| 1970-71 | California | 40 | 4 | 10 | 14 |
| 1972-73 | Cleveland (WHA) | 72 | 17 | 33 | 50 |
| 1973-74 | Chicago (WHA) | 77 | 24 | 35 | 59 |
| 1974-75 | Chi-Ind-SD (WHA) | 61 | 5 | 26 | 31 |
| | **NHL Totals** | 63 | 9 | 14 | 23 |
| | **WHA Totals** | 210 | 46 | 94 | 140 |

**HARDY, Mark Lea** *Defenseman*
b. Semaden, Switzerland, Feb. 1, 1959

| Season | Club | GP | G | A | Pts. |
|---|---|---|---|---|---|
| 1979-80 | Los Angeles | 15 | 0 | 1 | 1 |
| 1980-81 | Los Angeles | 77 | 5 | 20 | 25 |
| 1981-82 | Los Angeles | 77 | 6 | 39 | 45 |
| 1982-83 | Los Angeles | 74 | 5 | 34 | 39 |
| | **Totals** | 243 | 16 | 94 | 110 |

**HARGREAVES, James Albert** *Defenseman*
b. Winnipeg, Man., May 2, 1950

| Season | Club | GP | G | A | Pts. |
|---|---|---|---|---|---|
| 1970-71 | Vancouver | 7 | 0 | 1 | 1 |
| 1972-73 | Vancouver | 59 | 1 | 6 | 7 |
| 1973-74 | Winnipeg (WHA) | 53 | 1 | 4 | 5 |
| 1974-75 | Ind-SD (WHA) | 78 | 10 | 15 | 25 |
| | **NHL Totals** | 66 | 1 | 7 | 8 |
| | **WHA Totals** | 131 | 11 | 19 | 30 |

**HARMON, David Glen** *Defenseman*
b. Holland, Man., Jan. 2, 1921

| Season | Club | GP | G | A | Pts. |
|---|---|---|---|---|---|
| 1942-43 | Montreal | 27 | 5 | 9 | 14 |
| 1943-44 | Montreal | 43 | 5 | 16 | 21 |
| 1944-45 | Montreal | 42 | 5 | 8 | 13 |
| 1945-46 | Montreal | 49 | 7 | 10 | 17 |
| 1946-47 | Montreal | 57 | 5 | 9 | 14 |
| 1947-48 | Montreal | 56 | 10 | 4 | 14 |
| 1948-49 | Montreal | 59 | 8 | 12 | 20 |
| 1949-50 | Montreal | 62 | 3 | 16 | 19 |
| 1950-51 | Montreal | 57 | 2 | 12 | 14 |
| | **Totals** | 452 | 50 | 96 | 146 |

**HARMS, John** *Forward*
b. Saskatoon, Sask., Apr. 29, 1925

| Season | Club | GP | G | A | Pts. |
|---|---|---|---|---|---|
| 1943-44 | Chicago | 1 | 0 | 0 | 0 |
| 1944-45 | Chicago | 43 | 5 | 5 | 10 |
| | **Totals** | 44 | 5 | 5 | 10 |


**HARNOTT, Walter (Happy)** *Forward*
b. Montreal, Que., Sept. 24, 1912

| Season | Club | GP | G | A | Pts. |
|---|---|---|---|---|---|
| 1933-34 | Boston | 5 | 0 | 0 | 0 |

**HARPER, Terrance Victor (Terry)**
*Defenseman*
b. Regina, Sask., Jan. 27, 1940

| Season | Club | GP | G | A | Pts. |
|---|---|---|---|---|---|
| 1962-63 | Montreal | 14 | 1 | 1 | 2 |
| 1963-64 | Montreal | 70 | 2 | 15 | 17 |
| 1964-65 | Montreal | 62 | 0 | 7 | 7 |
| 1965-66 | Montreal | 69 | 1 | 11 | 12 |
| 1966-67 | Montreal | 56 | 0 | 16 | 16 |
| 1967-68 | Montreal | 57 | 3 | 8 | 11 |
| 1968-69 | Montreal | 21 | 0 | 3 | 3 |
| 1969-70 | Montreal | 75 | 4 | 18 | 22 |
| 1970-71 | Montreal | 78 | 1 | 21 | 22 |
| 1971-72 | Montreal | 52 | 2 | 12 | 14 |
| 1972-73 | Los Angeles | 77 | 1 | 8 | 9 |
| 1973-74 | Los Angeles | 77 | 0 | 17 | 17 |
| 1974-75 | Los Angeles | 80 | 5 | 21 | 26 |
| 1975-76 | Detroit | 69 | 8 | 25 | 33 |
| 1976-77 | Detroit | 52 | 4 | 8 | 12 |
| 1977-78 | Detroit | 80 | 2 | 17 | 19 |
| 1978-79 | Detroit | 51 | 0 | 6 | 6 |
| 1979-80 | St Louis | 11 | 1 | 5 | 6 |
| 1980-81 | Colorado | 15 | 0 | 2 | 2 |
| | **Totals** | 1066 | 35 | 221 | 256 |

**HARRER, Tim** *Forward*
b. Bloomington, Minn., May 10, 1957

| Season | Club | GP | G | A | Pts. |
|---|---|---|---|---|---|
| 1982-83 | Calgary | 3 | 0 | 0 | 0 |

**HARRINGTON, Leland (Hugo)** *Forward*
b. Melrose, Mass.

| Season | Club | GP | G | A | Pts. |
|---|---|---|---|---|---|
| 1925-26 | Boston | 36 | 7 | 2 | 9 |
| 1927-28 | Boston | 22 | 1 | 0 | 1 |
| 1932-33 | Montreal | 24 | 1 | 1 | 2 |
| | **Totals** | 82 | 9 | 3 | 12 |

**HARRIS, Edward Alexander (Ted)**
*Defenseman*
b. Winnipeg, Man., July 18, 1936

| Season | Club | GP | G | A | Pts. |
|---|---|---|---|---|---|
| 1963-64 | Montreal | 4 | 0 | 1 | 1 |
| 1964-65 | Montreal | 68 | 1 | 14 | 15 |
| 1965-66 | Montreal | 53 | 0 | 13 | 13 |
| 1966-67 | Montreal | 65 | 2 | 16 | 18 |
| 1967-68 | Montreal | 67 | 5 | 16 | 21 |
| 1968-69 | Montreal | 76 | 7 | 18 | 25 |
| 1969-70 | Montreal | 74 | 3 | 17 | 20 |
| 1970-71 | Minnesota | 78 | 2 | 13 | 15 |
| 1971-72 | Minnesota | 78 | 2 | 15 | 17 |
| 1972-73 | Minnesota | 78 | 7 | 23 | 30 |
| 1973-74 | Minn-Det-Stl. | 77 | 0 | 16 | 16 |
| 1974-75 | Philadelphia | 70 | 1 | 6 | 7 |
| | **Totals** | 788 | 30 | 168 | 198 |

**HARRIS, Fred (Smokey)** *Forward*

| Season | Club | GP | G | A | Pts. |
|---|---|---|---|---|---|
| 1924-25 | Boston | 6 | 3 | 1 | 4 |

**HARRIS, George Francis (Duke)** *Forward*
b. Sarnia, Ont., Feb. 25, 1942

| Season | Club | GP | G | A | Pts. |
|---|---|---|---|---|---|
| 1967-68 | Minn-Tor | 26 | 1 | 4 | 5 |
| 1972-73 | Houston (WHA) | 75 | 30 | 12 | 42 |
| 1973-74 | Chicago (WHA) | 64 | 14 | 16 | 30 |
| 1974-75 | Chicago (WHA) | 54 | 9 | 19 | 28 |
| | **NHL Totals** | 26 | 1 | 4 | 5 |
| | **WHA Totals** | 193 | 53 | 47 | 100 |

**HARRIS, Henry (Smokey)** *Forward*

| Season | Club | GP | G | A | Pts. |
|---|---|---|---|---|---|
| 1930-31 | Boston | 32 | 2 | 4 | 6 |

**HARRIS, Hugh Thomas** *Forward*
b. Toronto, Ont., June 7, 1948

| Season | Club | GP | G | A | Pts. |
|---|---|---|---|---|---|
| 1972-73 | Buffalo | 60 | 12 | 26 | 38 |
| 1973-74 | New England (WHA) | 75 | 24 | 28 | 52 |
| 1974-75 | Phoe-Van (WHA) | 80 | 33 | 44 | 77 |
| 1975-76 | Cal-Ind (WHA) | 71 | 17 | 36 | 53 |
| 1976-77 | Indianapolis (WHA) | 46 | 21 | 35 | 56 |
| 1977-78 | Indianapolis (WHA) | 18 | 1 | 7 | 8 |
| | **NHL Totals** | 60 | 12 | 26 | 38 |
| | **WHA Totals** | 290 | 96 | 150 | 246 |

## HARRIS, Ronald Thomas
*Defenseman-Forward*
b. Verdun, Que., June 30, 1942

| Season | Club | GP | G | A | Pts. |
|---|---|---|---|---|---|
| 1962-63 | Detroit | 1 | 0 | 1 | 1 |
| 1963-64 | Detroit | 3 | 0 | 0 | 0 |
| 1967-68 | Oakland | 54 | 4 | 6 | 10 |
| 1968-69 | Detroit | 73 | 3 | 13 | 16 |
| 1969-70 | Detroit | 72 | 2 | 19 | 21 |
| 1970-71 | Detroit | 42 | 2 | 8 | 10 |
| 1971-72 | Detroit | 61 | 1 | 10 | 11 |
| 1972-73 | Atl-NYR | 70 | 5 | 14 | 19 |
| 1973-74 | New York R | 63 | 2 | 12 | 14 |
| 1974-75 | New York R | 34 | 1 | 7 | 8 |
| 1975-76 | New York R | 3 | 0 | 1 | 1 |
| **Totals** | | 476 | 20 | 91 | 111 |

## HARRIS, William Edward (Billy) *Forward*
b. Toronto, Ont., Jan. 29, 1952

| Season | Club | GP | G | A | Pts. |
|---|---|---|---|---|---|
| 1972-73 | New York I | 78 | 28 | 22 | 50 |
| 1973-74 | New York I | 78 | 23 | 27 | 50 |
| 1974-75 | New York I | 80 | 25 | 37 | 62 |
| 1975-76 | New York I | 80 | 32 | 38 | 70 |
| 1976-77 | New York I | 80 | 24 | 43 | 67 |
| 1977-78 | New York I | 80 | 22 | 38 | 60 |
| 1978-79 | New York I | 80 | 15 | 39 | 54 |
| 1979-80 | NYI-LA | 78 | 19 | 18 | 37 |
| 1980-81 | Los Angeles | 80 | 20 | 29 | 49 |
| 1981-82 | LA-Tor | 36 | 3 | 3 | 6 |
| 1982-83 | Toronto | 76 | 11 | 19 | 30 |
| **Totals** | | 826 | 222 | 313 | 535 |

## HARRIS, William Edward *Forward*
b. Toronto, Ont., July 29, 1935

| Season | Club | GP | G | A | Pts. |
|---|---|---|---|---|---|
| 1955-56 | Toronto | 70 | 9 | 13 | 22 |
| 1956-57 | Toronto | 23 | 4 | 6 | 10 |
| 1957-58 | Toronto | 68 | 16 | 28 | 44 |
| 1958-59 | Toronto | 70 | 22 | 30 | 52 |
| 1959-60 | Toronto | 70 | 13 | 25 | 38 |
| 1960-61 | Toronto | 66 | 12 | 27 | 39 |
| 1961-62 | Toronto | 67 | 15 | 10 | 25 |
| 1962-63 | Toronto | 65 | 8 | 24 | 32 |
| 1963-64 | Toronto | 63 | 6 | 12 | 18 |
| 1964-65 | Toronto | 48 | 1 | 6 | 7 |
| 1965-66 | Detroit | 24 | 1 | 4 | 5 |
| 1967-68 | Oakland | 62 | 12 | 17 | 29 |
| 1968-69 | Oak-Pitt | 73 | 7 | 17 | 24 |
| **Totals** | | 769 | 126 | 219 | 345 |

## HARRISON, Edward Francis *Forward*
b. Mimico, Ont., July 25, 1927

| Season | Club | GP | G | A | Pts. |
|---|---|---|---|---|---|
| 1947-48 | Boston | 52 | 6 | 7 | 13 |
| 1948-49 | Boston | 59 | 5 | 5 | 10 |
| 1949-50 | Boston | 70 | 14 | 12 | 26 |
| 1950-51 | Bos-NYR | 13 | 2 | 0 | 2 |
| **Totals** | | 194 | 27 | 24 | 51 |

## HARRISON, James David *Forward*
b. Bonnyville, Alta., July 9, 1947

| Season | Club | GP | G | A | Pts. |
|---|---|---|---|---|---|
| 1968-69 | Boston | 16 | 1 | 2 | 3 |
| 1969-70 | Bos-Tor | 54 | 10 | 11 | 21 |
| 1970-71 | Toronto | 78 | 13 | 20 | 33 |
| 1971-72 | Toronto | 66 | 19 | 17 | 36 |
| 1972-73 | Alberta (WHA) | 66 | 39 | 47 | 86 |
| 1973-74 | Edmonton (WHA) | 47 | 24 | 45 | 69 |
| 1974-75 | Cleveland (WHA) | 60 | 20 | 22 | 42 |
| 1975-76 | Cleveland (WHA) | 59 | 34 | 38 | 72 |
| 1976-77 | Chicago | 60 | 18 | 23 | 41 |
| 1977-78 | Chicago | 26 | 2 | 8 | 10 |
| 1978-79 | Chicago | 21 | 4 | 5 | 9 |
| 1979-80 | Edmonton | 3 | 0 | 0 | 0 |
| **NHL Totals** | | 324 | 67 | 86 | 153 |
| **WHA Totals** | | 232 | 117 | 152 | 269 |

## HART, Gerald William *Defenseman*
b. Flin Flon, Man., Jan. 1, 1948

| Season | Club | GP | G | A | Pts. |
|---|---|---|---|---|---|
| 1968-69 | Detroit | 1 | 0 | 0 | 0 |
| 1969-70 | Detroit | 3 | 0 | 0 | 0 |
| 1970-71 | Detroit | 64 | 2 | 7 | 9 |
| 1971-72 | Detroit | 3 | 0 | 0 | 0 |
| 1972-73 | New York I | 47 | 1 | 11 | 12 |
| 1973-74 | New York I | 70 | 1 | 10 | 11 |
| 1974-75 | New York I | 71 | 4 | 14 | 18 |
| 1975-76 | New York I | 80 | 6 | 18 | 24 |
| 1976-77 | New York I | 80 | 4 | 18 | 22 |
| 1977-78 | New York I | 78 | 2 | 23 | 25 |
| 1978-79 | New York I | 50 | 2 | 14 | 16 |
| 1979-80 | Quebec | 71 | 3 | 23 | 26 |
| 1980-81 | Que-StL | 69 | 4 | 11 | 15 |
| 1981-82 | St Louis | 35 | 0 | 1 | 1 |
| 1982-83 | St Louis | 8 | 0 | 0 | 0 |
| **Totals** | | 730 | 29 | 150 | 179 |

## HART, Harold *Forward*

| Season | Club | GP | G | A | Pts. |
|---|---|---|---|---|---|
| 1926-27 | Detroit | — | 0 | 0 | 0 |

## HART, Wilfred (Gizzy) *Forward*
b. Weyburn, Sask., June 1, 1902

| Season | Club | GP | G | A | Pts. |
|---|---|---|---|---|---|
| 1926-27 | Montreal | 38 | 3 | 3 | 6 |
| 1927-28 | Montreal | 44 | 3 | 2 | 5 |
| 1932-33 | Montreal | 18 | 0 | 3 | 3 |
| **Totals** | | 100 | 6 | 8 | 14 |

## HARTSBURG, Craig *Defenseman*
b. Stratford, Ont., June 29, 1959

| Season | Club | GP | G | A | Pts. |
|---|---|---|---|---|---|
| 1978-79 | Birmingham (WHA) | 77 | 9 | 40 | 49 |
| 1979-80 | Minnesota | 79 | 14 | 30 | 44 |
| 1980-81 | Minnesota | 74 | 13 | 30 | 43 |
| 1981-82 | Minnesota | 76 | 17 | 60 | 77 |
| 1982-83 | Minnesota | 78 | 12 | 50 | 62 |
| **NHL Totals** | | 307 | 56 | 170 | 226 |
| **WHA Totals** | | 77 | 9 | 40 | 49 |

## HARVEY, Douglas Norman *Defenseman*
b. Montreal, Que., Dec. 19, 1924

| Season | Club | GP | G | A | Pts. |
|---|---|---|---|---|---|
| 1947-48 | Montreal | 35 | 4 | 4 | 8 |
| 1948-49 | Montreal | 55 | 3 | 13 | 16 |
| 1949-50 | Montreal | 70 | 4 | 20 | 24 |
| 1950-51 | Montreal | 70 | 5 | 24 | 29 |
| 1951-52 | Montreal | 68 | 6 | 23 | 29 |
| 1952-53 | Montreal | 69 | 4 | 30 | 34 |
| 1953-54 | Montreal | 68 | 8 | 29 | 37 |
| 1954-55 | Montreal | 70 | 6 | 43 | 49 |
| 1955-56 | Montreal | 62 | 5 | 39 | 44 |
| 1956-57 | Montreal | 70 | 6 | 44 | 50 |
| 1957-58 | Montreal | 68 | 9 | 32 | 41 |
| 1958-59 | Montreal | 61 | 4 | 16 | 20 |
| 1959-60 | Montreal | 66 | 6 | 21 | 27 |
| 1960-61 | Montreal | 58 | 6 | 33 | 39 |
| 1961-62 | New York R | 69 | 6 | 24 | 30 |
| 1962-63 | New York R | 68 | 4 | 35 | 39 |
| 1963-64 | New York R | 14 | 0 | 2 | 2 |
| 1966-67 | Detroit | 2 | 0 | 0 | 0 |
| 1968-69 | St Louis | 70 | 2 | 20 | 22 |
| **Totals** | | 1113 | 88 | 452 | 540 |

## HARVEY, Frederick (Buster) *Forward*
b. Fredericton, N.B., Apr. 2, 1950

| Season | Club | GP | G | A | Pts. |
|---|---|---|---|---|---|
| 1970-71 | Minnesota | 59 | 12 | 8 | 20 |
| 1972-73 | Minnesota | 68 | 21 | 34 | 55 |
| 1973-74 | Minnesota | 72 | 16 | 17 | 33 |
| 1974-75 | Atlanta | 79 | 17 | 27 | 44 |
| 1975-76 | Atl-KC-Det | 75 | 13 | 21 | 34 |
| 1976-77 | Detroit | 54 | 11 | 11 | 22 |
| **Totals** | | 407 | 90 | 118 | 208 |

## HARVEY, Lionel Hugh *Forward*
b. Kingston, Ont., June 25, 1949

| Season | Club | GP | G | A | Pts. |
|---|---|---|---|---|---|
| 1974-75 | Kansas City | 8 | 0 | 0 | 0 |
| 1975-76 | Kansas City | 10 | 1 | 1 | 2 |
| **Totals** | | 18 | 1 | 1 | 2 |

## HASSARD, Robert Harry *Forward*
b. Lloydminster, Sask., Mar. 26, 1929

| Season | Club | GP | G | A | Pts. |
|---|---|---|---|---|---|
| 1949-50 | Toronto | 1 | 0 | 0 | 0 |
| 1950-51 | Toronto | 12 | 0 | 1 | 1 |
| 1952-53 | Toronto | 70 | 8 | 23 | 31 |
| 1953-54 | Toronto | 26 | 1 | 4 | 5 |
| 1954-55 | Chicago | 17 | 0 | 0 | 0 |
| **Totals** | | 126 | 9 | 28 | 37 |

## HATOUM, Edward *Forward*
b. Beirut, Lebanon, Dec. 7, 1947

| Season | Club | GP | G | A | Pts. |
|---|---|---|---|---|---|
| 1968-69 | Detroit | 16 | 2 | 1 | 3 |
| 1969-70 | Detroit | 5 | 0 | 2 | 2 |
| 1970-71 | Vancouver | 26 | 1 | 3 | 4 |
| 1972-73 | Chicago (WHA) | 15 | 1 | 1 | 2 |
| 1973-74 | Vancouver (WHA) | 37 | 3 | 12 | 15 |
| **NHL Totals** | | 47 | 3 | 6 | 9 |
| **WHA Totals** | | 52 | 4 | 13 | 17 |

## HAWERCHUK, Dale *Forward*
b. Toronto, Ont., Apr. 4, 1963

| Season | Club | GP | G | A | Pts. |
|---|---|---|---|---|---|
| 1981-82 | Winnipeg | 80 | 45 | 58 | 103 |
| 1982-83 | Winnipeg | 79 | 40 | 51 | 91 |
| **Totals** | | 159 | 85 | 109 | 194 |

## HAWORTH, Alan Joseph Gordon *Forward*
b. Drummondville, Que., Sept. 1, 1960

| Season | Club | GP | G | A | Pts. |
|---|---|---|---|---|---|
| 1980-81 | Buffalo | 49 | 16 | 20 | 36 |
| 1981-82 | Buffalo | 57 | 21 | 18 | 39 |
| 1982-83 | Washington | 74 | 23 | 27 | 50 |
| **Totals** | | 180 | 60 | 65 | 125 |

## HAWORTH, Gordon J. *Forward*
b. Drummondville, Que., Feb. 20, 1932

| Season | Club | GP | G | A | Pts. |
|---|---|---|---|---|---|
| 1952-53 | New York R | 2 | 0 | 1 | 1 |

## HAWRYLIW, Neil *Forward*
b. Fielding, Sask., Nov. 9, 1955

| Season | Club | GP | G | A | Pts. |
|---|---|---|---|---|---|
| 1981-82 | New York I | 1 | 0 | 0 | 0 |

## HAY, George William *Forward*
b. Listowel, Ont., Jan. 10, 1898

| Season | Club | GP | G | A | Pts. |
|---|---|---|---|---|---|
| 1926-27 | Chicago | 35 | 14 | 8 | 22 |
| 1927-28 | Detroit | 42 | 22 | 13 | 35 |
| 1928-29 | Detroit | 39 | 11 | 8 | 19 |
| 1929-30 | Detroit | 44 | 18 | 15 | 33 |
| 1930-31 | Detroit | 44 | 8 | 10 | 18 |
| 1932-33 | Detroit | 35 | 1 | 6 | 7 |
| **Totals** | | 239 | 74 | 60 | 134 |

## HAY, James Alexander (Red-Eye)
*Defenseman*
b. Saskatoon, Sask., May 15, 1931

| Season | Club | GP | G | A | Pts. |
|---|---|---|---|---|---|
| 1952-53 | Detroit | 42 | 1 | 4 | 5 |
| 1953-54 | Detroit | 12 | 0 | 0 | 0 |
| 1954-55 | Detroit | 21 | 0 | 1 | 1 |
| **Totals** | | 75 | 1 | 5 | 6 |

## HAYEK, Peter *Defenseman*
b. Minneapolis, Minn., Nov. 16, 1957

| Season | Club | GP | G | A | Pts. |
|---|---|---|---|---|---|
| 1981-82 | Minnesota | 1 | 0 | 0 | 0 |

## HAY, William Charles (Red) *Forward*
b. Saskatoon, Sask., Dec. 8, 1935

| Season | Club | GP | G | A | Pts. |
|---|---|---|---|---|---|
| 1959-60 | Chicago | 70 | 18 | 37 | 55 |
| 1960-61 | Chicago | 69 | 11 | 48 | 59 |
| 1961-62 | Chicago | 60 | 11 | 52 | 63 |
| 1962-63 | Chicago | 64 | 12 | 33 | 45 |
| 1963-64 | Chicago | 70 | 23 | 33 | 56 |
| 1964-65 | Chicago | 69 | 11 | 26 | 37 |
| 1965-66 | Chicago | 68 | 20 | 31 | 51 |
| 1966-67 | Chicago | 36 | 7 | 13 | 20 |
| **Totals** | | 506 | 113 | 273 | 386 |

## HAYMES, Paul *Forward*
b. Montreal, Que., Mar. 1, 1910

| Season | Club | GP | G | A | Pts. |
|---|---|---|---|---|---|
| 1930-31 | Montreal M | 19 | 1 | 0 | 1 |
| 1931-32 | Montreal M | 12 | 1 | 0 | 1 |
| 1932-33 | Montreal M | 48 | 16 | 25 | 41 |
| 1933-34 | Montreal M | 44 | 5 | 4 | 9 |
| 1934-35 | MontM-Bos | 40 | 5 | 5 | 10 |
| 1935-36 | Montreal | 48 | 5 | 19 | 24 |
| 1936-37 | Montreal | 47 | 8 | 18 | 26 |
| 1937-38 | Montreal | 48 | 13 | 22 | 35 |
| 1938-39 | Montreal | 47 | 5 | 33 | 38 |
| 1939-40 | Montreal | 23 | 2 | 8 | 10 |
| 1940-41 | Montreal | 7 | 0 | 0 | 0 |
| **Totals** | | 383 | 61 | 134 | 195 |

| Season | Club | GP | G | A | Pts. |
|--------|------|----|----|----|----|
| **HAZLETT, Steven** *Forward* | | | | | |
| b. Sarnia, Ont., Dec. 12, 1957 | | | | | |
| 1979-80 | Vancouver | 1 | 0 | 0 | 0 |
| **HEADLEY, Fern** *Forward* | | | | | |
| b. March 2, 1901 | | | | | |
| 1924-25 | Bos-Mont | 27 | 1 | 1 | 2 |
| **HEALEY, Richard Thomas** *Defenseman* | | | | | |
| b. Vancouver, B.C., Mar. 12, 1938 | | | | | |
| 1960-61 | Detroit | 1 | 0 | 0 | 0 |
| **HEASLIP, Mark Patrick** *Forward* | | | | | |
| b. Duluth, Minn., Dec. 26, 1951 | | | | | |
| 1976-77 | New York R | 19 | 1 | 0 | 1 |
| 1977-78 | New York R | 29 | 5 | 10 | 15 |
| 1978-79 | New York R | 69 | 4 | 9 | 13 |
| | **Totals** | 117 | 10 | 19 | 29 |
| **HEBENTON, Andrew Alex** *Forward* | | | | | |
| b. Winnipeg, Man., Oct. 3, 1929 | | | | | |
| 1955-56 | New York R | 70 | 24 | 14 | 38 |
| 1956-57 | New York R | 70 | 21 | 23 | 44 |
| 1957-58 | New York R | 70 | 21 | 24 | 45 |
| 1958-59 | New York R | 70 | 33 | 29 | 62 |
| 1959-60 | New York R | 70 | 19 | 27 | 46 |
| 1960-61 | New York R | 70 | 26 | 28 | 54 |
| 1961-62 | New York R | 70 | 18 | 24 | 42 |
| 1962-63 | New York R | 70 | 15 | 22 | 37 |
| 1963-64 | Boston | 70 | 12 | 11 | 23 |
| | **Totals** | 630 | 189 | 202 | 391 |
| **HEDBERG, Anders** *Forward* | | | | | |
| b. Ornskoldsvik, Sweden, Feb. 25, 1951 | | | | | |
| 1974-75 | Winnipeg (WHA) | 65 | 53 | 47 | 100 |
| 1975-76 | Winnipeg (WHA) | 76 | 50 | 55 | 105 |
| 1976-77 | Winnipeg (WHA) | 68 | 70 | 61 | 131 |
| 1977-78 | Winnipeg (WHA) | 77 | 63 | 59 | 122 |
| 1978-79 | New York R | 80 | 33 | 45 | 78 |
| 1979-80 | New York R | 80 | 32 | 39 | 71 |
| 1980-81 | New York R | 80 | 30 | 40 | 70 |
| 1981-82 | New York R | 4 | 0 | 1 | 1 |
| 1982-83 | New York R | 78 | 25 | 34 | 59 |
| | **NHL Totals** | 321 | 120 | 159 | 279 |
| | **WHA Totals** | 286 | 236 | 222 | 458 |
| **HEFFERNAN, Frank** *Forward* | | | | | |
| 1919-20 | Toronto | 17 | 0 | 0 | 0 |
| **HEFFERNAN, Gerald** *Forward* | | | | | |
| b. Montreal, Que., July 24, 1916 | | | | | |
| 1941-42 | Montreal | 40 | 5 | 15 | 20 |
| 1943-44 | Montreal | 43 | 28 | 20 | 48 |
| | **Totals** | 83 | 33 | 35 | 68 |
| **HEINDL, William Wayne (Bill)** *Forward* | | | | | |
| b. Sherbrooke, Que., May 13, 1946 | | | | | |
| 1970-71 | Minnesota | 12 | 1 | 1 | 2 |
| 1971-72 | Minnesota | 2 | 0 | 0 | 0 |
| 1972-73 | New York R | 4 | 1 | 0 | 1 |
| 1973-74 | Cleveland (WHA) | 67 | 4 | 14 | 18 |
| | **NHL Totals** | 18 | 2 | 1 | 3 |
| | **WHA Totals** | 67 | 4 | 14 | 18 |
| **HEINRICH, Lionel Grant** | | | | | |
| *Defenseman-Forward* | | | | | |
| b. Churchbridge, Sask., Apr. 20, 1934 | | | | | |
| 1955-56 | Boston | 35 | 1 | 1 | 2 |
| **HEISKALA, Earl W.** *Forward* | | | | | |
| b. Kirkland Lake, Ont., Nov. 30, 1942 | | | | | |
| 1968-69 | Philadelphia | 21 | 3 | 3 | 6 |
| 1969-70 | Philadelphia | 65 | 8 | 7 | 15 |
| 19/0-/1 | Philadelphia | 41 | 2 | 1 | 3 |
| 1972-73 | Los Angeles (WHA) | 70 | 12 | 17 | 29 |
| 1973-74 | Los Angeles (WHA) | 24 | 2 | 6 | 8 |
| | **NHL Totals** | 127 | 13 | 11 | 24 |
| | **WHA Totals** | 94 | 14 | 23 | 37 |

| Season | Club | GP | G | A | Pts. |
|--------|------|----|----|----|----|
| **HELANDER, Peter** *Defenseman* | | | | | |
| b. Stockholm, Sweden, Dec. 4, 1951 | | | | | |
| 1982-83 | Los Angeles | 7 | 0 | 1 | 1 |
| **HELLER, Ehrhardt Henry (Ott)** *Defenseman* | | | | | |
| b. Kitchener, Ont., June 2, 1910 | | | | | |
| 1931-32 | New York R | 21 | 2 | 2 | 4 |
| 1932-33 | New York R | 40 | 5 | 7 | 12 |
| 1933-34 | New York R | 48 | 2 | 5 | 7 |
| 1934-35 | New York R | 47 | 3 | 11 | 14 |
| 1935-36 | New York R | 43 | 2 | 11 | 13 |
| 1936-37 | New York R | 48 | 5 | 12 | 17 |
| 1937-38 | New York R | 48 | 2 | 14 | 16 |
| 1938-39 | New York R | 48 | 0 | 23 | 23 |
| 1939-40 | New York R | 47 | 5 | 14 | 19 |
| 1940-41 | New York R | 48 | 2 | 16 | 18 |
| 1941-42 | New York R | 35 | 6 | 5 | 11 |
| 1942-43 | New York R | 45 | 4 | 14 | 18 |
| 1943-44 | New York R | 50 | 8 | 27 | 35 |
| 1944-45 | New York R | 45 | 7 | 12 | 19 |
| 1945-46 | New York R | 34 | 2 | 3 | 5 |
| | **Totals** | 647 | 55 | 176 | 231 |
| **HELMAN, Harry** *Defenseman* | | | | | |
| 1922-23 | Ottawa | 24 | 0 | 0 | 0 |
| 1923-24 | Ottawa | 17 | 1 | 0 | 1 |
| 1924-25 | Ottawa | 1 | 0 | 0 | 0 |
| | **Totals** | 42 | 1 | 0 | 1 |
| **HEMMERLING, Elmer C. (Tony)** *Forward* | | | | | |
| b. Landis, Sask., May 15, 1914 | | | | | |
| 1935-36 | New York A | 3 | 0 | 0 | 0 |
| 1936-37 | New York A | 19 | 3 | 3 | 6 |
| | **Totals** | 22 | 3 | 3 | 6 |
| **HENDERSON, Archie** *Forward* | | | | | |
| b. Calgary, Alta., Feb. 17, 1957 | | | | | |
| 1980-81 | Washington | 7 | 1 | 0 | 1 |
| 1981-82 | Minnesota | 1 | 0 | 0 | 0 |
| 1982-83 | Hartford | 15 | 2 | 1 | 3 |
| | **Totals** | 23 | 3 | 1 | 4 |
| **HENDERSON, John Murray (Moe)** | | | | | |
| *Defenseman* | | | | | |
| b. Toronto, Ont., Sept. 5, 1921 | | | | | |
| 1944-45 | Boston | 5 | 0 | 1 | 1 |
| 1945-46 | Boston | 48 | 4 | 11 | 15 |
| 1946-47 | Boston | 57 | 5 | 12 | 17 |
| 1947-48 | Boston | 49 | 6 | 8 | 14 |
| 1948-49 | Boston | 60 | 2 | 9 | 11 |
| 1949-50 | Boston | 64 | 3 | 8 | 11 |
| 1950-51 | Boston | 66 | 4 | 7 | 11 |
| 1951-52 | Boston | 56 | 0 | 6 | 6 |
| | **Totals** | 405 | 24 | 62 | 86 |
| **HENDERSON, Paul Garnet** *Forward* | | | | | |
| b. Kincardine, Ont., Jan. 28, 1943 | | | | | |
| 1962-63 | Detroit | 2 | 0 | 0 | 0 |
| 1963-64 | Detroit | 32 | 3 | 3 | 6 |
| 1964-65 | Detroit | 70 | 8 | 13 | 21 |
| 1965-66 | Detroit | 69 | 22 | 24 | 46 |
| 1966-67 | Detroit | 46 | 21 | 19 | 40 |
| 1967-68 | Det-Tor | 63 | 18 | 26 | 44 |
| 1968-69 | Toronto | 74 | 27 | 32 | 59 |
| 1969-70 | Toronto | 67 | 20 | 22 | 42 |
| 1970-71 | Toronto | 72 | 30 | 30 | 60 |
| 1971-72 | Toronto | 73 | 38 | 19 | 57 |
| 1972-73 | Toronto | 40 | 18 | 16 | 34 |
| 1973-74 | Toronto | 69 | 24 | 31 | 55 |
| 1974-75 | Toronto (WHA) | 58 | 30 | 33 | 63 |
| 1975-76 | Toronto (WHA) | 65 | 26 | 29 | 55 |
| 1976-77 | Birmingham (WHA) | 81 | 23 | 25 | 48 |
| 1977-78 | Birmingham (WHA) | 80 | 37 | 29 | 66 |
| 1978-79 | Birmingham (WHA) | 76 | 24 | 27 | 51 |
| 1979-80 | Atlanta | 30 | 7 | 6 | 13 |
| | **NHL Totals** | 707 | 236 | 241 | 477 |
| | **WHA Totals** | 360 | 140 | 143 | 283 |

| Season | Club | GP | G | A | Pts. |
|--------|------|----|----|----|----|
| **HENDRICKSON, John Gunnard** *Defenseman* | | | | | |
| b. Kingston, Ont., Dec. 5, 1936 | | | | | |
| 1957-58 | Detroit | 1 | 0 | 0 | 0 |
| 1958-59 | Detroit | 3 | 0 | 0 | 0 |
| 1961-62 | Detroit | 1 | 0 | 0 | 0 |
| | **Totals** | 5 | 0 | 0 | 0 |
| **HENNING, Lorne Edward** *Forward* | | | | | |
| b. Melfort, Sask., Feb. 22, 1952 | | | | | |
| 1972-73 | New York I | 63 | 7 | 19 | 26 |
| 1973-74 | New York I | 60 | 12 | 15 | 27 |
| 1974-75 | New York I | 61 | 5 | 6 | 11 |
| 1975-76 | New York I | 80 | 7 | 10 | 17 |
| 1976-77 | New York I | 80 | 13 | 18 | 31 |
| 1977-78 | New York I | 79 | 12 | 15 | 27 |
| 1978-79 | New York I | 73 | 13 | 20 | 33 |
| 1979-80 | New York I | 39 | 3 | 6 | 9 |
| 1980-81 | New York I | 9 | 1 | 2 | 3 |
| | **Totals** | 544 | 73 | 111 | 184 |
| **HENRY, Camille (Eel)** *Forward* | | | | | |
| b. Quebec City, Que., Jan. 31, 1933 | | | | | |
| 1953-54 | New York R | 66 | 24 | 15 | 39 |
| 1954-55 | New York R | 21 | 5 | 2 | 7 |
| 1956-57 | New York R | 36 | 14 | 15 | 29 |
| 1957-58 | New York R | 70 | 32 | 24 | 56 |
| 1958-59 | New York R | 70 | 23 | 35 | 58 |
| 1959-60 | New York R | 49 | 12 | 15 | 27 |
| 1960-61 | New York R | 53 | 28 | 25 | 53 |
| 1961-62 | New York R | 60 | 23 | 15 | 38 |
| 1962-63 | New York R | 60 | 37 | 23 | 60 |
| 1963-64 | New York R | 68 | 29 | 26 | 55 |
| 1964-65 | NYR-Chi | 70 | 26 | 18 | 44 |
| 1967-68 | New York R | 36 | 8 | 12 | 20 |
| 1968-69 | St Louis | 64 | 17 | 22 | 39 |
| 1969-70 | St Louis | 4 | 1 | 2 | 3 |
| | **Totals** | 817 | 279 | 249 | 528 |
| **HERBERTS, James** *Defenseman-Forward* | | | | | |
| b. Collingwood, Ont., 1897 | | | | | |
| 1924-25 | Boston | 30 | 17 | 5 | 22 |
| 1925-26 | Boston | 36 | 26 | 5 | 31 |
| 1926-27 | Boston | 34 | 15 | 7 | 22 |
| 1927-28 | Bos-Tor | 43 | 15 | 4 | 19 |
| 1928-29 | Detroit | 40 | 9 | 5 | 14 |
| 1929-30 | Detroit | 23 | 1 | 3 | 4 |
| | **Totals** | 206 | 83 | 29 | 112 |
| **HERCHENRATTER, Arthur** *Forward* | | | | | |
| b. Kitchener, Ont., Nov. 24, 1917 | | | | | |
| 1940-41 | Detroit | 9 | 1 | 2 | 3 |
| **HERGERT, Fred** *Forward* | | | | | |
| b. Calgary, Alta., Jan. 29, 1913 | | | | | |
| 1934-35 | New York A | 19 | 1 | 5 | 6 |
| 1935-36 | New York A | 1 | 0 | 0 | 0 |
| | **Totals** | 20 | 1 | 5 | 6 |
| **HERGESHEIMER, Philip** *Forward* | | | | | |
| b. Winnipeg, Man., July 9, 1914 | | | | | |
| 1939-40 | Chicago | — | 9 | 11 | 20 |
| 1940-41 | Chicago | — | 8 | 16 | 24 |
| 1941-42 | Chi-Bos | 26 | 3 | 11 | 14 |
| 1942-43 | Chicago | 9 | 1 | 3 | 4 |
| | **Totals** | — | 21 | 41 | 62 |
| **HERGESHEIMER, Walter Edgar** *Forward* | | | | | |
| b. Winnipeg, Man., Jan 8, 1927 | | | | | |
| 1951-52 | New York R | 68 | 26 | 12 | 38 |
| 1952-53 | New York R | 70 | 30 | 29 | 59 |
| 1953-54 | New York R | 66 | 27 | 16 | 43 |
| 1954-55 | New York R | 14 | 4 | 2 | 6 |
| 1955-56 | New York R | 70 | 22 | 18 | 40 |
| 1956-57 | Chicago | 41 | 2 | 8 | 10 |
| 1958-59 | New York R | 22 | 3 | 0 | 3 |
| | **Totals** | 351 | 114 | 85 | 199 |

| Season | Club | GP | G | A | Pts. |
|---|---|---|---|---|---|

**HERON, Robert (Red)** *Forward*
b. Toronto, Ont., Dec. 31, 1917

| Season | Club | GP | G | A | Pts. |
|---|---|---|---|---|---|
| 1938-39 | Toronto | 6 | 0 | 0 | 0 |
| 1939-40 | Toronto | 42 | 11 | 12 | 23 |
| 1940-41 | Toronto | 35 | 9 | 5 | 14 |
| 1941-42 | NYA-Mont | 23 | 1 | 2 | 3 |
| | **Totals** | 106 | 21 | 19 | 40 |

**HESS, Robert George** *Defenseman*
b. Middleton, N.S., May 19, 1955

| Season | Club | GP | G | A | Pts. |
|---|---|---|---|---|---|
| 1974-75 | St Louis | 76 | 9 | 30 | 39 |
| 1975-76 | St Louis | 78 | 9 | 23 | 32 |
| 1976-77 | St Louis | 53 | 4 | 18 | 22 |
| 1977-78 | St Louis | 55 | 2 | 12 | 14 |
| 1978-79 | St Louis | 27 | 3 | 4 | 7 |
| 1980-81 | St Louis | 4 | 0 | 0 | 0 |
| 1981-82 | Buffalo | 33 | 0 | 8 | 8 |
| | **Totals** | 326 | 27 | 95 | 122 |

**HEXIMER, Orville Russell (Obs)** *Forward*
b. Niagara Falls, Ont., Feb. 16, 1910

| Season | Club | GP | G | A | Pts. |
|---|---|---|---|---|---|
| 1929-30 | New York R | 19 | 1 | 0 | 1 |
| 1932-33 | Boston | 48 | 7 | 5 | 12 |
| 1934-35 | New York A | 17 | 5 | 2 | 7 |
| | **Totals** | 84 | 13 | 7 | 20 |

**HEXTALL, Bryan Aldwyn** *Forward*
b. Grenfell, Sask., July 31, 1913

| Season | Club | GP | G | A | Pts. |
|---|---|---|---|---|---|
| 1936-37 | New York R | 1 | 0 | 1 | 1 |
| 1937-38 | New York R | 48 | 17 | 4 | 21 |
| 1938-39 | New York R | 48 | 20 | 15 | 35 |
| 1939-40 | New York R | 48 | 24 | 15 | 39 |
| 1940-41 | New York R | 48 | 26 | 18 | 44 |
| 1941-42 | New York R | 48 | 24 | 32 | 56 |
| 1942-43 | New York R | 50 | 27 | 32 | 59 |
| 1943-44 | New York R | 50 | 21 | 33 | 54 |
| 1945-46 | New York R | 3 | 0 | 1 | 1 |
| 1946-47 | New York R | 60 | 21 | 10 | 31 |
| 1947-48 | New York R | 43 | 8 | 14 | 22 |
| | **Totals** | 447 | 188 | 175 | 363 |

**HEXTALL, Bryan Lee** *Forward*
b. Winnipeg, Man., May 23, 1941

| Season | Club | GP | G | A | Pts. |
|---|---|---|---|---|---|
| 1962-63 | New York R | 21 | 0 | 2 | 2 |
| 1969-70 | Pittsburgh | 66 | 12 | 19 | 31 |
| 1970-71 | Pittsburgh | 76 | 16 | 32 | 48 |
| 1971-72 | Pittsburgh | 78 | 20 | 24 | 44 |
| 1972-73 | Pittsburgh | 78 | 21 | 33 | 54 |
| 1973-74 | Pitt-Atl | 77 | 4 | 11 | 15 |
| | **Totals** | 396 | 73 | 121 | 194 |

**HEXTALL, Dennis Harold** *Forward*
b. Winnipeg, Man., Apr. 17, 1943

| Season | Club | GP | G | A | Pts. |
|---|---|---|---|---|---|
| 1968-69 | New York R | 13 | 1 | 4 | 5 |
| 1969-70 | Los Angeles | 28 | 5 | 7 | 12 |
| 1970-71 | California | 78 | 21 | 31 | 52 |
| 1971-72 | Minnesota | 33 | 6 | 10 | 16 |
| 1972-73 | Minnesota | 78 | 30 | 52 | 82 |
| 1973-74 | Minnesota | 78 | 20 | 62 | 82 |
| 1974-75 | Minnesota | 80 | 17 | 57 | 74 |
| 1975-76 | Minn-Det | 76 | 16 | 44 | 60 |
| 1976-77 | Detroit | 78 | 14 | 32 | 46 |
| 1977-78 | Detroit | 78 | 16 | 33 | 49 |
| 1978-79 | Det-Wash | 46 | 6 | 17 | 23 |
| 1979-80 | Washington | 15 | 1 | 1 | 2 |
| | **Totals** | 681 | 153 | 350 | 503 |

**HEYLIGER, Victor** *Forward*
b. Boston, Mass., Sept. 26, 1911

| Season | Club | GP | G | A | Pts. |
|---|---|---|---|---|---|
| 1943-44 | Chicago | 26 | 2 | 3 | 5 |

**HICKE, Ernest Allen** *Forward*
b. Regina, Sask., Nov. 7, 1947

| Season | Club | GP | G | A | Pts. |
|---|---|---|---|---|---|
| 1970-71 | California | 78 | 22 | 25 | 47 |
| 1971-72 | California | 68 | 11 | 12 | 23 |
| 1972-73 | Atl-NYI | 59 | 14 | 23 | 37 |
| 1973-74 | New York I | 55 | 6 | 7 | 13 |
| 1974-75 | NYI-Minn | 62 | 17 | 19 | 36 |
| 1975-76 | Minnesota | 80 | 23 | 19 | 42 |
| 1976-77 | Minnesota | 77 | 30 | 20 | 50 |
| 1977-78 | Los Angeles | 41 | 9 | 15 | 24 |
| | **Totals** | 520 | 132 | 140 | 272 |

**HICKE, William Lawrence** *Forward*
b. Regina, Sask., Mar. 31, 1938

| Season | Club | GP | G | A | Pts. |
|---|---|---|---|---|---|
| 1959-60 | Montreal | 43 | 3 | 10 | 13 |
| 1960-61 | Montreal | 70 | 18 | 27 | 45 |
| 1961-62 | Montreal | 70 | 20 | 31 | 51 |
| 1962-63 | Montreal | 70 | 17 | 22 | 39 |
| 1963-64 | Montreal | 48 | 11 | 9 | 20 |
| 1964-65 | Mont-NYR | 57 | 6 | 12 | 18 |
| 1965-66 | New York R | 49 | 9 | 18 | 27 |
| 1966-67 | New York R | 48 | 3 | 4 | 7 |
| 1967-68 | Oakland | 52 | 21 | 19 | 40 |
| 1968-69 | Oakland | 67 | 25 | 36 | 61 |
| 1969-70 | Oakland | 69 | 15 | 29 | 44 |
| 1970-71 | California | 74 | 18 | 17 | 35 |
| 1971-72 | Pittsburgh | 12 | 2 | 0 | 2 |
| 1972-73 | Edmonton (WHA) | 73 | 14 | 24 | 38 |
| | **NHL Totals** | 729 | 168 | 234 | 402 |
| | **WHA Totals** | 73 | 14 | 24 | 38 |

**HICKEY, Greg** *Forward*
b. Toronto, Ont., Mar. 8, 1955

| Season | Club | GP | G | A | Pts. |
|---|---|---|---|---|---|
| 1977-78 | New York R | 1 | 0 | 0 | 0 |

**HICKEY, Patrick Joseph** *Forward*
b. Brantford, Ont., May 15, 1953

| Season | Club | GP | G | A | Pts. |
|---|---|---|---|---|---|
| 1973-74 | Toronto (WHA) | 78 | 26 | 29 | 55 |
| 1974-75 | Toronto (WHA) | 74 | 34 | 34 | 68 |
| 1975-76 | New York R | 70 | 14 | 22 | 36 |
| 1976-77 | New York R | 80 | 23 | 17 | 40 |
| 1977-78 | New York R | 80 | 40 | 33 | 73 |
| 1978-79 | New York R | 80 | 34 | 41 | 75 |
| 1979-80 | NYR-Col-Tor | 76 | 31 | 27 | 58 |
| 1980-81 | Toronto | 72 | 16 | 33 | 49 |
| 1981-82 | Tor-NYR-Que | 61 | 15 | 15 | 30 |
| 1982-83 | St Louis | 1 | 0 | 0 | 0 |
| | **NHL Totals** | 520 | 173 | 188 | 361 |
| | **WHA Totals** | 152 | 60 | 63 | 123 |

**HICKS, Doug** *Defenseman*
b. Cold Lake, Alta., May 28, 1955

| Season | Club | GP | G | A | Pts. |
|---|---|---|---|---|---|
| 1974-75 | Minnesota | 80 | 6 | 12 | 18 |
| 1975-76 | Minnesota | 80 | 5 | 13 | 18 |
| 1976-77 | Minnesota | 79 | 5 | 14 | 19 |
| 1977-78 | Minn-Chi | 74 | 3 | 16 | 19 |
| 1978-79 | Chicago | 44 | 1 | 8 | 9 |
| 1979-80 | Edmonton | 78 | 9 | 31 | 40 |
| 1980-81 | Edmonton | 59 | 5 | 16 | 21 |
| 1981-82 | Edm-Wash | 61 | 3 | 21 | 24 |
| 1982-83 | Washington | 6 | 0 | 0 | 0 |
| | **Totals** | 561 | 37 | 131 | 168 |

**HICKS, Glenn** *Forward*
b. Red Deer, Alta., Aug. 28, 1958

| Season | Club | GP | G | A | Pts. |
|---|---|---|---|---|---|
| 1978-79 | Winnipeg (WHA) | 69 | 6 | 10 | 16 |
| 1979-80 | Detroit | 50 | 1 | 2 | 3 |
| 1980-81 | Detroit | 58 | 5 | 10 | 15 |
| | **NHL Totals** | 108 | 6 | 12 | 18 |
| | **WHA Totals** | 69 | 6 | 10 | 16 |

**HICKS, Harold** *Defenseman*
b. Ottawa, Ont., Dec. 10, 1900

| Season | Club | GP | G | A | Pts. |
|---|---|---|---|---|---|
| 1928-29 | Montreal M | 44 | 2 | 0 | 2 |
| 1929-30 | Detroit | 30 | 3 | 2 | 5 |
| 1930-31 | Detroit | 16 | 0 | 0 | 0 |
| | **Totals** | 90 | 5 | 2 | 7 |

**HICKS, Wayne Wilson** *Forward*
b. Aberdeen, Wash., Apr. 9, 1937

| Season | Club | GP | G | A | Pts. |
|---|---|---|---|---|---|
| 1960-61 | Chicago | 1 | 0 | 0 | 0 |
| 1962-63 | Boston | 65 | 7 | 9 | 16 |
| 1963-64 | Montreal | 2 | 0 | 0 | 0 |
| 1967-68 | Phil-Pitt | 47 | 6 | 14 | 20 |
| | **Totals** | 115 | 13 | 23 | 36 |

**HIGGINS, Paul** *Forward*
b. St. John, N.B., Jan. 13, 1962

| Season | Club | GP | G | A | Pts. |
|---|---|---|---|---|---|
| 1981-82 | Toronto | 3 | 0 | 0 | 0 |
| 1982-83 | Toronto | 22 | 0 | 0 | 0 |
| | **Totals** | 25 | 0 | 0 | 0 |

**HIGGINS, Tim Ray** *Forward*
b. Ottawa, Ont., Feb. 7, 1958

| Season | Club | GP | G | A | Pts. |
|---|---|---|---|---|---|
| 1978-79 | Chicago | 36 | 7 | 16 | 23 |
| 1979-80 | Chicago | 74 | 13 | 12 | 25 |
| 1980-81 | Chicago | 78 | 24 | 35 | 59 |
| 1981-82 | Chicago | 74 | 20 | 30 | 50 |
| 1982-83 | Chicago | 64 | 14 | 9 | 23 |
| | **Totals** | 326 | 78 | 102 | 180 |

**HILDEBRAND, Issac Bruce (Ike)** *Forward*
b. Winnipeg, Man., May 27, 1927

| Season | Club | GP | G | A | Pts. |
|---|---|---|---|---|---|
| 1953-54 | NYR-Chi | 38 | 7 | 11 | 18 |
| 1954-55 | Chicago | 3 | 0 | 0 | 0 |
| | **Totals** | 41 | 7 | 11 | 18 |

**HILL, Alan Douglas** *Forward*
b. Nanaimo, B.C., Apr. 22, 1955

| Season | Club | GP | G | A | Pts. |
|---|---|---|---|---|---|
| 1976-77 | Philadelphia | 9 | 2 | 4 | 6 |
| 1977-78 | Philadelphia | 3 | 0 | 0 | 0 |
| 1978-79 | Philadelphia | 31 | 5 | 11 | 16 |
| 1979-80 | Philadelphia | 61 | 16 | 10 | 26 |
| 1980-81 | Philadelphia | 57 | 10 | 15 | 25 |
| 1981-82 | Philadelphia | 41 | 6 | 13 | 19 |
| | **Totals** | 202 | 39 | 53 | 92 |

**HILL, Brian Nelson** *Forward*
b. Regina, Sask., Jan. 12, 1957

| Season | Club | GP | G | A | Pts. |
|---|---|---|---|---|---|
| 1979-80 | Hartford | 19 | 1 | 1 | 2 |

**HILL, John Melvin (Sudden Death)** *Forward*
b. Glenboro, Man., Feb. 15, 1914

| Season | Club | GP | G | A | Pts. |
|---|---|---|---|---|---|
| 1937-38 | Boston | 6 | 2 | 0 | 2 |
| 1938-39 | Boston | 46 | 10 | 10 | 20 |
| 1939-40 | Boston | 38 | 9 | 11 | 20 |
| 1940-41 | Boston | 41 | 5 | 4 | 9 |
| 1941-42 | Brooklyn | 47 | 14 | 23 | 37 |
| 1942-43 | Toronto | 49 | 17 | 27 | 44 |
| 1943-44 | Toronto | 17 | 9 | 10 | 19 |
| 1944-45 | Toronto | 45 | 18 | 17 | 35 |
| 1945-46 | Toronto | 35 | 5 | 7 | 12 |
| | **Totals** | 324 | 89 | 109 | 198 |

**HILLER, Wilbert Carl (Dutch)** *Forward*
b. Kitchener, Ont., May 11, 1915

| Season | Club | GP | G | A | Pts. |
|---|---|---|---|---|---|
| 1937-38 | New York R | 9 | 0 | 1 | 1 |
| 1938-39 | New York R | 48 | 10 | 19 | 29 |
| 1939-40 | New York R | 48 | 13 | 19 | 32 |
| 1940-41 | NYR-Det | 45 | 8 | 10 | 18 |
| 1941-42 | Det-Bos | 50 | 7 | 10 | 17 |
| 1942-43 | Bos-Mont | 42 | 8 | 6 | 14 |
| 1943-44 | New York R | 50 | 18 | 22 | 40 |
| 1944-45 | Montreal | 48 | 20 | 16 | 36 |
| 1945-46 | Montreal | 45 | 7 | 11 | 18 |
| | **Totals** | 385 | 91 | 114 | 205 |

**HILLIER, Randy George** *Defenseman*
b. Toronto, Ont., Mar. 30, 1960

| Season | Club | GP | G | A | Pts. |
|---|---|---|---|---|---|
| 1981-82 | Boston | 25 | 0 | 8 | 8 |
| 1982-83 | Boston | 70 | 0 | 10 | 10 |
| | **Totals** | 95 | 0 | 18 | 18 |

**HILLMAN, Floyd Arthur** *Defenseman*
b. Ruthven, Ont., Nov. 19, 1933

| Season | Club | GP | G | A | Pts. |
|---|---|---|---|---|---|
| 1956-57 | Boston | 6 | 0 | 0 | 0 |

**HILLMAN, Larry Morley** *Defenseman*
b. Kirkland Lake, Ont., Feb. 5, 1937

| Season | Club | GP | G | A | Pts. |
|---|---|---|---|---|---|
| 1954-55 | Detroit | 6 | 0 | 0 | 0 |
| 1955-56 | Detroit | 47 | 0 | 3 | 3 |
| 1956-57 | Detroit | 16 | 1 | 2 | 3 |
| 1957-58 | Boston | 70 | 3 | 19 | 22 |
| 1958-59 | Boston | 55 | 3 | 10 | 13 |
| 1959-60 | Boston | 2 | 0 | 1 | 1 |
| 1960-61 | Toronto | 62 | 3 | 10 | 13 |
| 1961-62 | Toronto | 5 | 0 | 0 | 0 |
| 1962-63 | Toronto | 5 | 0 | 0 | 0 |
| 1963-64 | Toronto | 33 | 0 | 4 | 4 |
| 1964-65 | Toronto | 2 | 0 | 0 | 0 |
| 1965-66 | Toronto | 48 | 3 | 25 | 28 |
| 1966-67 | Toronto | 55 | 4 | 19 | 23 |

| Season | Club | GP | G | A | Pts. |
|---|---|---|---|---|---|
| 1967-68 | Toronto | 55 | 3 | 17 | 20 |
| 1968-69 | Minn-Mont | 37 | 1 | 10 | 11 |
| 1969-70 | Philadelphia | 76 | 5 | 26 | 31 |
| 1970-71 | Philadelphia | 73 | 3 | 13 | 16 |
| 1971-72 | LA-Buf | 65 | 2 | 13 | 15 |
| 1972-73 | Buffalo | 78 | 5 | 24 | 29 |
| 1973-74 | Cleveland (WHA) | 44 | 5 | 21 | 26 |
| 1974-75 | Cleveland (WHA) | 77 | 0 | 16 | 16 |
| | **NHL Totals** | 790 | 36 | 196 | 232 |
| | **WHA Totals** | 121 | 5 | 37 | 42 |

**HILLMAN, Wayne James** *Defenseman*
b. Kirkland Lake, Ont., Nov. 13, 1938

| Season | Club | GP | G | A | Pts. |
|---|---|---|---|---|---|
| 1961-62 | Chicago | 19 | 0 | 2 | 2 |
| 1962-63 | Chicago | 67 | 3 | 5 | 8 |
| 1963-64 | Chicago | 59 | 1 | 4 | 5 |
| 1964-65 | Chi-NYR | 41 | 1 | 8 | 9 |
| 1965-66 | New York R | 68 | 3 | 17 | 20 |
| 1966-67 | New York R | 67 | 2 | 12 | 14 |
| 1967-68 | New York R | 62 | 0 | 5 | 5 |
| 1968-69 | Minnesota | 50 | 0 | 8 | 8 |
| 1969-70 | Philadelphia | 68 | 3 | 5 | 8 |
| 1970-71 | Philadelphia | 69 | 5 | 7 | 12 |
| 1971-72 | Philadelphia | 47 | 0 | 3 | 3 |
| 1972-73 | Philadelphia | 74 | 0 | 10 | 10 |
| 1973-74 | Cleveland (WHA) | 66 | 1 | 7 | 8 |
| 1974-75 | Cleveland (WHA) | 60 | 2 | 9 | 11 |
| | **NHL Totals** | 691 | 18 | 86 | 104 |
| | **WHA Totals** | 126 | 3 | 16 | 19 |

**HILLWORTH, John** *Defenseman*
b. Jasper, Alta., May 23, 1957

| Season | Club | GP | G | A | Pts. |
|---|---|---|---|---|---|
| 1977-78 | Detroit | 5 | 0 | 0 | 0 |
| 1978-79 | Detroit | 37 | 1 | 1 | 2 |
| 1979-80 | Detroit | 15 | 0 | 0 | 0 |
| | **Totals** | 57 | 1 | 1 | 2 |

**HIMES, Norman** *Forward*
b. Galt, Ont., Apr. 13, 1903

| Season | Club | GP | G | A | Pts. |
|---|---|---|---|---|---|
| 1926-27 | New York A | 41 | 9 | 2 | 11 |
| 1927-28 | New York A | 43 | 14 | 5 | 19 |
| 1928-29 | New York A | 43 | 10 | 0 | 10 |
| 1929-30 | New York A | 44 | 28 | 22 | 50 |
| 1930-31 | New York A | 44 | 15 | 9 | 24 |
| 1931-32 | New York A | 47 | 7 | 21 | 28 |
| 1932-33 | New York A | 48 | 9 | 25 | 34 |
| 1933-34 | New York A | 48 | 9 | 16 | 25 |
| 1934-35 | New York A | 41 | 5 | 13 | 18 |
| | **Totals** | 399 | 106 | 113 | 219 |

**HINDMARCH, David** *Forward*
b. Vancouver, B.C., Oct. 15, 1958

| Season | Club | GP | G | A | Pts. |
|---|---|---|---|---|---|
| 1980-81 | Calgary | 1 | 1 | 0 | 1 |
| 1981-82 | Calgary | 9 | 3 | 0 | 3 |
| 1982-83 | Calgary | 60 | 11 | 12 | 23 |
| | **Totals** | 70 | 15 | 12 | 27 |

**HINSE, Andre Joseph Charles** *Forward*
b. Trois-Rivières, Que., Apr. 19, 1945

| Season | Club | GP | G | A | Pts. |
|---|---|---|---|---|---|
| 1967-68 | Toronto | 4 | 0 | 0 | 0 |
| 1973-74 | Houston (WHA) | 69 | 24 | 56 | 80 |
| 1974-75 | Houston (WHA) | 75 | 39 | 47 | 86 |
| 1975-76 | Houston (WHA) | 70 | 35 | 38 | 73 |
| | **NHL Totals** | 4 | 0 | 0 | 0 |
| | **WHA Totals** | 214 | 98 | 141 | 239 |

**HINTON, Daniel Anthony** *Forward*
b. Toronto, Ont., May 24, 1953

| Season | Club | GP | G | A | Pts. |
|---|---|---|---|---|---|
| 1976-77 | Chicago | 14 | 0 | 0 | 0 |

**HIRSCHFELD, John Albert (Bert)** *Forward*
b. Halifax, N.S., Mar. 1, 1929

| Season | Club | GP | G | A | Pts. |
|---|---|---|---|---|---|
| 1949-50 | Montreal | 13 | 1 | 2 | 3 |
| 1950-51 | Montreal | 20 | 0 | 2 | 2 |
| | **Totals** | 33 | 1 | 4 | 5 |

**HISLOP, James Donald** *Forward*
b. Sarnia, Ont., Jan. 20, 1954

| Season | Club | GP | G | A | Pts. |
|---|---|---|---|---|---|
| 1976-77 | Cincinnati (WHA) | 46 | 7 | 19 | 26 |
| 1977-78 | Cincinnati (WHA) | 80 | 24 | 43 | 67 |


| Season | Club | GP | G | A | Pts. |
|---|---|---|---|---|---|
| 1978-79 | Cincinnati (WHA) | 80 | 30 | 40 | 70 |
| 1979-80 | Quebec | 80 | 19 | 20 | 39 |
| 1980-81 | Que-Calg | 79 | 25 | 31 | 56 |
| 1981-82 | Calgary | 80 | 16 | 25 | 41 |
| 1982-83 | Calgary | 79 | 14 | 19 | 33 |
| | **NHL Totals** | 318 | 74 | 95 | 169 |
| | **WHA Totals** | 206 | 61 | 102 | 163 |

**HITCHMAN, Lionel (Fred)** *Defenseman*
b. Toronto, Ont., 1903

| Season | Club | GP | G | A | Pts. |
|---|---|---|---|---|---|
| 1922-23 | Ottawa | 3 | 0 | 1 | 1 |
| 1923-24 | Ottawa | 24 | 2 | 6 | 8 |
| 1924-25 | Ott-Bos | 30 | 3 | 0 | 3 |
| 1925-26 | Boston | 36 | 7 | 4 | 11 |
| 1926-27 | Boston | 40 | 3 | 6 | 9 |
| 1927-28 | Boston | 43 | 5 | 3 | 8 |
| 1928-29 | Boston | 37 | 1 | 0 | 1 |
| 1929-30 | Boston | 39 | 2 | 7 | 9 |
| 1930-31 | Boston | 43 | 0 | 2 | 2 |
| 1931-32 | Boston | 48 | 4 | 3 | 7 |
| 1932-33 | Boston | 41 | 0 | 1 | 1 |
| 1933-34 | Boston | 29 | 1 | 0 | 1 |
| | **Totals** | 413 | 28 | 33 | 61 |

**HLINKA, Ivan** *Forward*
b. Most, Czechoslovakia, Jan. 26, 1950

| Season | Club | GP | G | A | Pts. |
|---|---|---|---|---|---|
| 1981-82 | Vancouver | 72 | 23 | 37 | 60 |
| 1982-83 | Vancouver | 65 | 19 | 44 | 63 |
| | **Totals** | 137 | 42 | 81 | 123 |

**HODGE, Kenneth Raymond (Ken)** *Forward*
b. Birmingham, England, June 25, 1944

| Season | Club | GP | G | A | Pts. |
|---|---|---|---|---|---|
| 1964-65 | Chicago | 1 | 0 | 0 | 0 |
| 1965-66 | Chicago | 63 | 6 | 17 | 23 |
| 1966-67 | Chicago | 69 | 10 | 25 | 35 |
| 1967-68 | Boston | 74 | 25 | 31 | 56 |
| 1968-69 | Boston | 75 | 45 | 45 | 90 |
| 1969-70 | Boston | 72 | 25 | 29 | 54 |
| 1970-71 | Boston | 78 | 43 | 62 | 105 |
| 1971-72 | Boston | 60 | 16 | 40 | 56 |
| 1972-73 | Boston | 73 | 37 | 44 | 81 |
| 1973-74 | Boston | 76 | 50 | 55 | 105 |
| 1974-75 | Boston | 72 | 23 | 43 | 66 |
| 1975-76 | Boston | 72 | 25 | 36 | 61 |
| 1976-77 | New York R | 78 | 21 | 41 | 62 |
| 1977-78 | New York R | 18 | 2 | 4 | 6 |
| | **Totals** | 881 | 328 | 472 | 800 |

**HODGSON, Richard** *Defenseman*
b. Medicine Hat, Alta., May 23, 1956

| Season | Club | GP | G | A | Pts. |
|---|---|---|---|---|---|
| 1979-80 | Hartford | 6 | 0 | 0 | 0 |

**HODGSON, Theodore James** *Forward*
b. Hobbema, Alta., June 30, 1945

| Season | Club | GP | G | A | Pts. |
|---|---|---|---|---|---|
| 1966-67 | Boston | 4 | 0 | 0 | 0 |
| 1972-73 | Cleveland (WHA) | 74 | 15 | 23 | 38 |
| 1973-74 | Clev-LA (WHA) | 33 | 3 | 11 | 14 |
| | **NHL Totals** | 4 | 0 | 0 | 0 |
| | **WHA Totals** | 107 | 18 | 34 | 52 |

**HOEKSTRA, Cecil Thomas** *Forward*
b. Winnipeg, Man., Apr. 2, 1935

| Season | Club | GP | G | A | Pts. |
|---|---|---|---|---|---|
| 1959-60 | Montreal | 4 | 0 | 0 | 0 |

**HOEKSTRA, Edward Adrian** *Forward*
b. Winnipeg, Man., Nov. 4, 1937

| Season | Club | GP | G | A | Pts. |
|---|---|---|---|---|---|
| 1967-68 | Philadelphia | 70 | 15 | 21 | 36 |
| 1972-73 | Houston (WHA) | 78 | 11 | 28 | 39 |
| 1973-74 | Houston (WHA) | 19 | 2 | 0 | 2 |
| | **NHL Totals** | 70 | 15 | 21 | 36 |
| | **WHA Totals** | 97 | 13 | 28 | 41 |

**HOENE, Phil George** *Forward*
b. Duluth, Minn., Mar. 15, 1949

| Season | Club | GP | G | A | Pts. |
|---|---|---|---|---|---|
| 1972-73 | Los Angeles | 4 | 0 | 1 | 1 |
| 1973-74 | Los Angeles | 31 | 2 | 3 | 5 |
| 1974-75 | Los Angeles | 2 | 0 | 0 | 0 |
| | **Totals** | 37 | 2 | 4 | 6 |


**HOFFINGER, Victor** *Defenseman*

| Season | Club | GP | G | A | Pts. |
|---|---|---|---|---|---|
| 1927-28 | Chicago | 15 | 0 | 1 | 1 |
| 1928-29 | Chicago | 10 | 0 | 0 | 0 |
| | **Totals** | 25 | 0 | 1 | 1 |

**HOFFMAN, Mike** *Forward*
b. Cambridge, Ont., Feb. 26, 1963

| Season | Club | GP | G | A | Pts. |
|---|---|---|---|---|---|
| 1982-83 | Hartford | 2 | 0 | 1 | 1 |

**HOFFMEYER, Robert Frank** *Defenseman*
b. Dodsland, Sask., July 27, 1955

| Season | Club | GP | G | A | Pts. |
|---|---|---|---|---|---|
| 1977-78 | Chicago | 5 | 0 | 1 | 1 |
| 1978-79 | Chicago | 6 | 0 | 2 | 2 |
| 1981-82 | Philadelphia | 57 | 7 | 20 | 27 |
| 1982-83 | Philadelphia | 35 | 2 | 11 | 13 |
| | **Totals** | 103 | 9 | 34 | 43 |

**HOGABOAM, William Harold (Bill)** *Forward*
b. Swift Current, Sask., Sept. 5, 1949

| Season | Club | GP | G | A | Pts. |
|---|---|---|---|---|---|
| 1972-73 | Atl-Det | 6 | 1 | 0 | 1 |
| 1973-74 | Detroit | 47 | 18 | 23 | 41 |
| 1974-75 | Detroit | 60 | 14 | 27 | 41 |
| 1975-76 | Det-Minn | 68 | 28 | 23 | 51 |
| 1976-77 | Minnesota | 73 | 10 | 15 | 25 |
| 1977-78 | Minnesota | 8 | 1 | 2 | 3 |
| 1978-79 | Minn-Det | 28 | 5 | 7 | 12 |
| 1979-80 | Detroit | 42 | 3 | 12 | 15 |
| | **Totals** | 332 | 80 | 109 | 189 |

**HOGANSON, Dale Gordon (Red)**
*Defenseman*
b. North Battleford, Sask., July 8, 1949

| Season | Club | GP | G | A | Pts. |
|---|---|---|---|---|---|
| 1969-70 | Los Angeles | 49 | 1 | 7 | 8 |
| 1970-71 | Los Angeles | 70 | 4 | 10 | 14 |
| 1971-72 | LA-Mont | 31 | 1 | 2 | 3 |
| 1972-73 | Montreal | 26 | 0 | 2 | 2 |
| 1973-74 | Quebec (WHA) | 62 | 8 | 33 | 41 |
| 1974-75 | Quebec (WHA) | 78 | 9 | 35 | 44 |
| 1975-76 | Quebec (WHA) | 45 | 3 | 14 | 17 |
| 1976-77 | Birmingham (WHA) | 81 | 7 | 48 | 55 |
| 1977-78 | Birmingham (WHA) | 43 | 1 | 12 | 13 |
| 1978-79 | Quebec (WHA) | 69 | 2 | 19 | 21 |
| 1979-80 | Quebec | 77 | 4 | 36 | 40 |
| 1980-81 | Quebec | 61 | 3 | 14 | 17 |
| 1981-82 | Quebec | 30 | 0 | 6 | 6 |
| | **NHL Totals** | 344 | 13 | 77 | 90 |
| | **WHA Totals** | 378 | 30 | 161 | 191 |

**HOLBROOK, Terry Eugene** *Forward*
b. Petrolia, Ont., July 11, 1950

| Season | Club | GP | G | A | Pts. |
|---|---|---|---|---|---|
| 1972-73 | Minnesota | 21 | 2 | 3 | 5 |
| 1973-74 | Minnesota | 22 | 1 | 3 | 4 |
| 1974-75 | Cleveland (WHA) | 78 | 10 | 13 | 23 |
| 1975-76 | Cleveland (WHA) | 15 | 1 | 2 | 3 |
| | **NHL Totals** | 43 | 3 | 6 | 9 |
| | **WHA Totals** | 93 | 11 | 15 | 26 |

**HOLLAND, Jerry Allan** *Forward*
b. Beaverlodge, Alta., Aug. 25, 1954

| Season | Club | GP | G | A | Pts. |
|---|---|---|---|---|---|
| 1974-75 | New York R | 1 | 1 | 0 | 1 |
| 1975-76 | New York R | 36 | 7 | 4 | 11 |
| 1977-78 | Edmonton (WHA) | 22 | 2 | 1 | 3 |
| | **NHL Totals** | 37 | 8 | 4 | 12 |
| | **WHA Totals** | 22 | 2 | 1 | 3 |

**HOLLETT, William (Flash)**
*Defenseman-Forward*
b. North Sydney, N.S., Apr. 13, 1912

| Season | Club | GP | G | A | Pts. |
|---|---|---|---|---|---|
| 1933-34 | Tor-Ott | 34 | 7 | 4 | 11 |
| 1934-35 | Toronto | 48 | 10 | 16 | 26 |
| 1935-36 | Tor-Bos | 17 | 2 | 6 | 8 |
| 1936-37 | Boston | 48 | 3 | 7 | 10 |
| 1937-38 | Boston | 48 | 4 | 10 | 14 |
| 1938-39 | Boston | 44 | 10 | 17 | 27 |
| 1939-40 | Boston | 44 | 10 | 18 | 28 |
| 1940-41 | Boston | 41 | 9 | 15 | 24 |
| 1941-42 | Boston | 48 | 19 | 14 | 33 |
| 1942-43 | Boston | 50 | 19 | 25 | 44 |
| 1943-44 | Bos-Det | 52 | 15 | 19 | 34 |
| 1944-45 | Detroit | 50 | 20 | 21 | 41 |
| 1945-46 | Detroit | 38 | 4 | 9 | 13 |
| | **Totals** | 562 | 132 | 181 | 313 |

| Season | Club | GP | G | A | Pts. |
|--------|------|----|----|----|------|

**HOLLINGWORTH, Gordon (Bucky)**
*Defenseman*
  b. Verdun, Que., July 24, 1933

| Season | Club | GP | G | A | Pts. |
|--------|------|----|----|----|------|
| 1954-55 | Chicago | 70 | 3 | 9 | 12 |
| 1955-56 | Detroit | 41 | 0 | 2 | 2 |
| 1956-57 | Detroit | 25 | 0 | 1 | 1 |
| 1957-58 | Detroit | 27 | 1 | 2 | 3 |
| | **Totals** | 163 | 4 | 14 | 18 |

**HOLMES, Charles Frank** *Forward*
  b. Edmonton, Alta., Sept. 21, 1934

| Season | Club | GP | G | A | Pts. |
|--------|------|----|----|----|------|
| 1958-59 | Detroit | 15 | 0 | 3 | 3 |
| 1961-62 | Detroit | 8 | 1 | 0 | 1 |
| | **Totals** | 23 | 1 | 3 | 4 |

**HOLMES, Louis** *Forward*
  b. Edmonton, Alta., Jan. 29, 1911

| Season | Club | GP | G | A | Pts. |
|--------|------|----|----|----|------|
| 1931-32 | Det-Chi | 41 | 2 | 4 | 6 |
| 1932-33 | Chicago | 15 | 0 | 0 | 0 |
| | **Totals** | 56 | 2 | 4 | 6 |

**HOLMES, Warren** *Forward*
  b. Beeton, Ont., Feb. 18, 1957

| Season | Club | GP | G | A | Pts. |
|--------|------|----|----|----|------|
| 1981-82 | Los Angeles | 3 | 0 | 2 | 2 |
| 1982-83 | Los Angeles | 39 | 8 | 16 | 24 |
| | **Totals** | 42 | 8 | 18 | 26 |

**HOLMES, William** *Forward*
  b. Weyburn, Sask., 1899

| Season | Club | GP | G | A | Pts. |
|--------|------|----|----|----|------|
| 1925-26 | Montreal | 9 | 1 | 0 | 1 |
| 1929-30 | New York A | — | 5 | 4 | 9 |
| | **Totals** | — | 6 | 4 | 10 |

**HOLMGREN, Paul Howard** *Forward*
  b. St. Paul, Minn., Dec. 2, 1955

| Season | Club | GP | G | A | Pts. |
|--------|------|----|----|----|------|
| 1975-76 | Minnesota (WHA) | 51 | 14 | 16 | 30 |
| 1975-76 | Philadelphia | 1 | 0 | 0 | 0 |
| 1976-77 | Philadelphia | 59 | 14 | 12 | 26 |
| 1977-78 | Philadelphia | 62 | 16 | 18 | 34 |
| 1978-79 | Philadelphia | 57 | 19 | 10 | 29 |
| 1979-80 | Philadelphia | 74 | 30 | 35 | 65 |
| 1980-81 | Philadelphia | 77 | 22 | 37 | 59 |
| 1981-82 | Philadelphia | 41 | 9 | 22 | 31 |
| 1982-83 | Philadelphia | 77 | 19 | 24 | 43 |
| | **NHL Totals** | 448 | 129 | 158 | 287 |
| | **WHA Totals** | 51 | 14 | 16 | 30 |

**HOLOTA, John** *Forward*
  b. Hamilton, Ont., Feb. 25, 1921

| Season | Club | GP | G | A | Pts. |
|--------|------|----|----|----|------|
| 1942-43 | Detroit | 12 | 2 | 0 | 2 |
| 1945-46 | Detroit | 3 | 0 | 0 | 0 |
| | **Totals** | 15 | 2 | 0 | 2 |

**HOLST, Greg** *Forward*
  b. Montreal, Que., Feb. 21, 1954

| Season | Club | GP | G | A | Pts. |
|--------|------|----|----|----|------|
| 1975-76 | New York R | 2 | 0 | 0 | 0 |
| 1976-77 | New York R | 5 | 0 | 0 | 0 |
| | **Totals** | 7 | 0 | 0 | 0 |

**HOLT, Gareth Ray** *Forward*
  b. Sarnia, Ont., Nov. 1, 1952

| Season | Club | GP | G | A | Pts. |
|--------|------|----|----|----|------|
| 1973-74 | California | 1 | 0 | 0 | 0 |
| 1974-75 | California | 1 | 0 | 1 | 1 |
| 1975-76 | California | 48 | 6 | 5 | 11 |
| 1976-77 | Cleveland | 2 | 0 | 1 | 1 |
| 1977-78 | St Louis | 49 | 7 | 4 | 11 |
| | **Totals** | 101 | 13 | 11 | 24 |

**HOLT, Steward Randall** *Defenseman*
  b. Pembroke, Ont., Jan. 15, 1953

| Season | Club | GP | G | A | Pts. |
|--------|------|----|----|----|------|
| 1974-75 | Chicago | 12 | 0 | 1 | 1 |
| 1975-76 | Chicago | 12 | 0 | 0 | 0 |
| 1976-77 | Chicago | 12 | 0 | 3 | 3 |
| 1977-78 | Chi-Clev | 54 | 1 | 4 | 5 |
| 1978-79 | Van-LA | 58 | 1 | 9 | 10 |
| 1979-80 | Los Angeles | 42 | 0 | 1 | 1 |
| 1980-81 | Calgary | 48 | 0 | 5 | 5 |

| Season | Club | GP | G | A | Pts. |
|--------|------|----|----|----|------|
| 1981-82 | Calg-Wash | 61 | 2 | 6 | 8 |
| 1982-83 | Washington | 70 | 0 | 8 | 8 |
| | **Totals** | 369 | 4 | 37 | 41 |

**HOLWEY, Albert R. (Toots)** *Defenseman*
  b. Toronto, Ont., Sept. 24, 1902

| Season | Club | GP | G | A | Pts. |
|--------|------|----|----|----|------|
| 1923-24 | Toronto | 6 | 1 | 0 | 1 |
| 1924-25 | Toronto | 25 | 2 | 2 | 4 |
| 1925-26 | Tor-MontM | 29 | 0 | 0 | 0 |
| 1926-27 | Montreal M | 13 | 0 | 0 | 0 |
| 1928-29 | Pittsburgh | 44 | 4 | 0 | 4 |
| | **Totals** | 117 | 7 | 2 | 9 |

**HOMENUKE, Ron** *Forward*
  b. Hazelton, B.C., Jan. 5, 1952

| Season | Club | GP | G | A | Pts. |
|--------|------|----|----|----|------|
| 1972-73 | Vancouver | 1 | 0 | 0 | 0 |

**HOPKINS, Dean** *Forward*
  b. Cobourg, Ont., June 6, 1959

| Season | Club | GP | G | A | Pts. |
|--------|------|----|----|----|------|
| 1979-80 | Los Angeles | 60 | 8 | 6 | 14 |
| 1980-81 | Los Angeles | 57 | 8 | 18 | 26 |
| 1981-82 | Los Angeles | 41 | 2 | 13 | 15 |
| 1982-83 | Los Angeles | 49 | 5 | 12 | 17 |
| | **Totals** | 207 | 23 | 49 | 72 |

**HOPKINS, Larry Harold** *Forward*
  b. Oshawa, Ont., Mar. 17, 1954

| Season | Club | GP | G | A | Pts. |
|--------|------|----|----|----|------|
| 1977-78 | Toronto | 2 | 0 | 0 | 0 |
| 1979-80 | Winnipeg | 5 | 0 | 0 | 0 |
| 1981-82 | Winnipeg | 41 | 10 | 15 | 25 |
| 1982-83 | Winnipeg | 12 | 3 | 1 | 4 |
| | **Totals** | 60 | 13 | 16 | 29 |

**HORBUL, Douglas George** *Forward*
  b. Nokomis, Sask., July 27, 1952

| Season | Club | GP | G | A | Pts. |
|--------|------|----|----|----|------|
| 1974-75 | Kansas City | 4 | 1 | 0 | 1 |

**HORDY, Michael** *Defenseman*
  b. Thunder Bay, Ont., Oct. 10, 1956

| Season | Club | GP | G | A | Pts. |
|--------|------|----|----|----|------|
| 1978-79 | New York I | 2 | 0 | 0 | 0 |
| 1979-80 | New York I | 9 | 0 | 0 | 0 |
| | **Totals** | 11 | 0 | 0 | 0 |

**HORECK, Peter** *Forward*
  b. Massey, Ont., June 15, 1923

| Season | Club | GP | G | A | Pts. |
|--------|------|----|----|----|------|
| 1944-45 | Chicago | 50 | 20 | 16 | 36 |
| 1945-46 | Chicago | 50 | 20 | 21 | 41 |
| 1946-47 | Chi-Det | 56 | 16 | 19 | 35 |
| 1947-48 | Detroit | 50 | 12 | 17 | 29 |
| 1948-49 | Detroit | 60 | 14 | 16 | 30 |
| 1949-50 | Boston | 34 | 5 | 5 | 10 |
| 1950-51 | Boston | 66 | 10 | 13 | 23 |
| 1951-52 | Chicago | 60 | 9 | 11 | 20 |
| | **Totals** | 426 | 106 | 118 | 224 |

**HORNE, George (Shorty)** *Forward*

| Season | Club | GP | G | A | Pts. |
|--------|------|----|----|----|------|
| 1925-26 | Montreal M | 13 | 0 | 0 | 0 |
| 1928-29 | Toronto | 39 | 9 | 3 | 12 |
| | **Totals** | 52 | 9 | 3 | 12 |

**HORNER, George Reginald (Red)**
*Defenseman*
  b. Lynden, Ont., May 29, 1909

| Season | Club | GP | G | A | Pts. |
|--------|------|----|----|----|------|
| 1928-29 | Toronto | 22 | 0 | 0 | 0 |
| 1929-30 | Toronto | 33 | 2 | 7 | 9 |
| 1930-31 | Toronto | 42 | 1 | 11 | 12 |
| 1931-32 | Toronto | 42 | 7 | 9 | 16 |
| 1932-33 | Toronto | 48 | 3 | 8 | 11 |
| 1933-34 | Toronto | 40 | 11 | 10 | 21 |
| 1934-35 | Toronto | 46 | 4 | 8 | 12 |
| 1935-36 | Toronto | 43 | 2 | 9 | 11 |
| 1936-37 | Toronto | 48 | 3 | 9 | 12 |
| 1937-38 | Toronto | 47 | 4 | 20 | 24 |
| 1938-39 | Toronto | 48 | 4 | 10 | 14 |
| 1939-40 | Toronto | 31 | 1 | 9 | 10 |
| | **Totals** | 490 | 42 | 110 | 152 |

**HORNUNG, Larry John** *Defenseman*
  b. Gravelbourg, Sask., Nov. 10, 1945

| Season | Club | GP | G | A | Pts. |
|--------|------|----|----|----|------|
| 1970-71 | St Louis | 1 | 0 | 0 | 0 |
| 1971-72 | St Louis | 47 | 2 | 9 | 11 |
| 1972-73 | Winnipeg (WHA) | 77 | 13 | 45 | 58 |
| 1973-74 | Winnipeg (WHA) | 51 | 4 | 19 | 23 |
| 1974-75 | Winnipeg (WHA) | 69 | 7 | 25 | 32 |
| 1975-76 | Winnipeg (WHA) | 76 | 3 | 18 | 21 |
| 1976-77 | Edm-SD (WHA) | 79 | 6 | 10 | 16 |
| | **NHL Totals** | 48 | 2 | 9 | 11 |
| | **WHA Totals** | 352 | 33 | 117 | 150 |

**HORTON, Myles Gilbert (Tim)**
*Defenseman-Forward*
  b. Cochrane, Ont., Jan. 12, 1930

| Season | Club | GP | G | A | Pts. |
|--------|------|----|----|----|------|
| 1949-50 | Toronto | 1 | 0 | 0 | 0 |
| 1951-52 | Toronto | 4 | 0 | 0 | 0 |
| 1952-53 | Toronto | 70 | 2 | 14 | 16 |
| 1953-54 | Toronto | 70 | 7 | 24 | 31 |
| 1954-55 | Toronto | 67 | 5 | 9 | 14 |
| 1955-56 | Toronto | 35 | 0 | 5 | 5 |
| 1956-57 | Toronto | 66 | 6 | 19 | 25 |
| 1957-58 | Toronto | 53 | 6 | 20 | 26 |
| 1958-59 | Toronto | 70 | 5 | 21 | 26 |
| 1959-60 | Toronto | 70 | 3 | 29 | 32 |
| 1960-61 | Toronto | 57 | 6 | 15 | 21 |
| 1961-62 | Toronto | 70 | 10 | 28 | 38 |
| 1962-63 | Toronto | 70 | 6 | 19 | 25 |
| 1963-64 | Toronto | 70 | 9 | 20 | 29 |
| 1964-65 | Toronto | 70 | 12 | 16 | 28 |
| 1965-66 | Toronto | 70 | 6 | 22 | 28 |
| 1966-67 | Toronto | 70 | 8 | 17 | 25 |
| 1967-68 | Toronto | 69 | 4 | 23 | 27 |
| 1968-69 | Toronto | 74 | 11 | 29 | 40 |
| 1969-70 | Tor-NYR | 74 | 4 | 24 | 28 |
| 1970-71 | New York R | 78 | 2 | 18 | 20 |
| 1971-72 | Pittsburgh | 44 | 2 | 9 | 11 |
| 1972-73 | Buffalo | 69 | 1 | 16 | 17 |
| 1973-74 | Buffalo | 55 | 0 | 6 | 6 |
| | **Totals** | 1446 | 115 | 403 | 518 |

**HORVATH, Bronco Joseph** *Forward*
  b. Port Colborne, Ont., Mar. 12, 1930

| Season | Club | GP | G | A | Pts. |
|--------|------|----|----|----|------|
| 1955-56 | New York R | 66 | 12 | 17 | 29 |
| 1956-57 | NYR-Mont | 8 | 1 | 2 | 3 |
| 1957-58 | Boston | 67 | 30 | 36 | 66 |
| 1958-59 | Boston | 45 | 19 | 20 | 39 |
| 1959-60 | Boston | 68 | 39 | 41 | 80 |
| 1960-61 | Boston | 47 | 15 | 15 | 30 |
| 1961-62 | Chicago | 69 | 17 | 29 | 46 |
| 1962-63 | NYR-Tor | 50 | 7 | 19 | 26 |
| 1967-68 | Minnesota | 14 | 1 | 6 | 7 |
| | **Totals** | 434 | 141 | 185 | 326 |

**HOSPODAR, Edward David** *Defenseman*
  b. Bowling Green, Ohio, Feb. 9, 1959

| Season | Club | GP | G | A | Pts. |
|--------|------|----|----|----|------|
| 1979-80 | New York R | 20 | 0 | 1 | 1 |
| 1980-81 | New York R | 61 | 5 | 14 | 19 |
| 1981-82 | New York R | 41 | 3 | 8 | 11 |
| 1982-83 | Hartford | 72 | 1 | 9 | 10 |
| | **Totals** | 194 | 9 | 32 | 41 |

**HOTHAM, Gregory** *Defenseman*
  b. London, Ont., Mar. 7, 1956

| Season | Club | GP | G | A | Pts. |
|--------|------|----|----|----|------|
| 1979-80 | Toronto | 46 | 3 | 10 | 13 |
| 1980-81 | Toronto | 11 | 1 | 1 | 2 |
| 1981-82 | Tor-Pitt | 28 | 4 | 6 | 10 |
| 1982-83 | Pittsburgh | 58 | 2 | 30 | 32 |
| | **Totals** | 143 | 10 | 47 | 57 |

**HOUDE, Claude** *Defenseman*
  b. Drummondville, Que., Nov. 8, 1947

| Season | Club | GP | G | A | Pts. |
|--------|------|----|----|----|------|
| 1974-75 | Kansas City | 34 | 3 | 4 | 7 |
| 1975-76 | Kansas City | 25 | 0 | 2 | 2 |
| | **Totals** | 59 | 3 | 6 | 9 |

**HOULE, Rejean** *Forward*
  b. Rouyne, Que., Oct. 25, 1949

| Season | Club | GP | G | A | Pts. |
|--------|------|----|----|----|------|
| 1969-70 | Montreal | 9 | 0 | 1 | 1 |
| 1970-71 | Montreal | 66 | 10 | 9 | 19 |
| 1971-72 | Montreal | 77 | 11 | 17 | 28 |

| Season | Club | GP | G | A | Pts. |
|---|---|---|---|---|---|
| 1972-73 | Montreal | 72 | 13 | 35 | 48 |
| 1973-74 | Quebec (WHA) | 69 | 27 | 35 | 62 |
| 1974-75 | Quebec (WHA) | 64 | 40 | 52 | 92 |
| 1975-76 | Quebec (WHA) | 81 | 51 | 52 | 103 |
| 1976-77 | Montreal | 65 | 22 | 30 | 52 |
| 1977-78 | Montreal | 76 | 30 | 28 | 58 |
| 1978-79 | Montreal | 66 | 17 | 34 | 51 |
| 1979-80 | Montreal | 60 | 18 | 27 | 45 |
| 1980-81 | Montreal | 77 | 27 | 31 | 58 |
| 1981-82 | Montreal | 51 | 11 | 32 | 43 |
| 1982-83 | Montreal | 16 | 2 | 3 | 5 |
| | **NHL Totals** | 635 | 161 | 247 | 408 |
| | **WHA Totals** | 214 | 118 | 139 | 257 |

**HOUSLEY, Phil**  *Defenseman*
b. St. Paul, Minn., Mar. 9, 1964

| Season | Club | GP | G | A | Pts. |
|---|---|---|---|---|---|
| 1982-83 | Buffalo | 77 | 19 | 47 | 66 |

**HOUSTON, Kenneth**  *Forward*
b. Dresden, Ont., Sept. 15, 1953

| Season | Club | GP | G | A | Pts. |
|---|---|---|---|---|---|
| 1975-76 | Atlanta | 38 | 5 | 6 | 11 |
| 1976-77 | Atlanta | 78 | 20 | 24 | 44 |
| 1977-78 | Atlanta | 74 | 22 | 16 | 38 |
| 1978-79 | Atlanta | 80 | 21 | 31 | 52 |
| 1979-80 | Atlanta | 80 | 23 | 31 | 54 |
| 1980-81 | Calgary | 42 | 15 | 15 | 30 |
| 1981-82 | Calgary | 70 | 22 | 22 | 44 |
| 1982-83 | Washington | 71 | 25 | 14 | 39 |
| | **Totals** | 533 | 153 | 159 | 312 |

**HOWARD, Jack Francis**  *Defenseman*
b. London, Ont., Oct. 15, 1915

| Season | Club | GP | G | A | Pts. |
|---|---|---|---|---|---|
| 1936-37 | Toronto | 2 | 0 | 0 | 0 |

**HOWATT, Gary**  *Forward*
b. Grand Center, Alta., Sept. 26, 1952

| Season | Club | GP | G | A | Pts. |
|---|---|---|---|---|---|
| 1972-73 | New York I | 8 | 0 | 1 | 1 |
| 1973-74 | New York I | 78 | 6 | 11 | 17 |
| 1974-75 | New York I | 77 | 18 | 30 | 48 |
| 1975-76 | New York I | 80 | 21 | 13 | 34 |
| 1976-77 | New York I | 70 | 13 | 15 | 28 |
| 1977-78 | New York I | 61 | 7 | 12 | 19 |
| 1978-79 | New York I | 75 | 16 | 12 | 28 |
| 1979-80 | New York I | 77 | 8 | 11 | 19 |
| 1980-81 | New York I | 70 | 4 | 15 | 19 |
| 1981-82 | Hartford | 80 | 18 | 32 | 50 |
| 1982-83 | New Jersey | 38 | 1 | 4 | 5 |
| | **Totals** | 714 | 112 | 156 | 268 |

**HOWE, Gordon (Gordie)**  *Forward*
b. Floral, Sask., Mar. 31, 1928

| Season | Club | GP | G | A | Pts. |
|---|---|---|---|---|---|
| 1946-47 | Detroit | 58 | 7 | 15 | 22 |
| 1947-48 | Detroit | 60 | 16 | 28 | 44 |
| 1948-49 | Detroit | 40 | 12 | 25 | 37 |
| 1949-50 | Detroit | 70 | 35 | 33 | 68 |
| 1950-51 | Detroit | 70 | 43 | 43 | 86 |
| 1951-52 | Detroit | 70 | 47 | 39 | 86 |
| 1952-53 | Detroit | 70 | 49 | 46 | 95 |
| 1953-54 | Detroit | 70 | 33 | 48 | 81 |
| 1954-55 | Detroit | 64 | 29 | 33 | 62 |
| 1955-56 | Detroit | 70 | 38 | 41 | 79 |
| 1956-57 | Detroit | 70 | 44 | 45 | 89 |
| 1957-58 | Detroit | 64 | 33 | 44 | 77 |
| 1958-59 | Detroit | 70 | 32 | 46 | 78 |
| 1959-60 | Detroit | 70 | 28 | 45 | 73 |
| 1960-61 | Detroit | 64 | 23 | 49 | 72 |
| 1961-62 | Detroit | 70 | 33 | 44 | 77 |
| 1962-63 | Detroit | 70 | 38 | 48 | 86 |
| 1963-64 | Detroit | 69 | 26 | 47 | 73 |
| 1964-65 | Detroit | 70 | 29 | 47 | 76 |
| 1965-66 | Detroit | 70 | 29 | 46 | 75 |
| 1966-67 | Detroit | 69 | 25 | 40 | 65 |
| 1967-68 | Detroit | 74 | 39 | 43 | 82 |
| 1968-69 | Detroit | 76 | 44 | 59 | 103 |
| 1969-70 | Detroit | 76 | 31 | 40 | 71 |
| 1970-71 | Detroit | 63 | 23 | 29 | 52 |
| 1973-74 | Houston (WHA) | 70 | 31 | 69 | 100 |
| 1974-75 | Houston (WHA) | 75 | 34 | 65 | 99 |
| 1975-76 | Houston (WHA) | 78 | 32 | 70 | 102 |
| 1976-77 | Houston (WHA) | 62 | 24 | 44 | 68 |
| 1977-78 | New England (WHA) | 76 | 34 | 62 | 96 |
| 1978-79 | New England (WHA) | 58 | 19 | 24 | 43 |
| 1979-80 | Hartford | 80 | 15 | 26 | 41 |
| | **NHL Totals** | 1767 | 801 | 1040 | 1850 |
| | **WHA Totals** | 419 | 174 | 334 | 508 |

**HOWE, Mark Steven**  *Forward*
b. Detroit, Mich., May 28, 1955

| Season | Club | GP | G | A | Pts. |
|---|---|---|---|---|---|
| 1973-74 | Houston (WHA) | 76 | 38 | 41 | 79 |
| 1974-75 | Houston (WHA) | 74 | 36 | 40 | 76 |
| 1975-76 | Houston (WHA) | 72 | 39 | 37 | 76 |
| 1976-77 | Houston (WHA) | 57 | 23 | 52 | 75 |
| 1977-78 | New England (WHA) | 70 | 30 | 61 | 91 |
| 1978-79 | New England (WHA) | 77 | 42 | 65 | 107 |
| 1979-80 | Hartford | 74 | 24 | 56 | 80 |
| 1980-81 | Hartford | 63 | 19 | 46 | 65 |
| 1981-82 | Hartford | 76 | 8 | 45 | 53 |
| 1982-83 | Philadelphia | 76 | 20 | 47 | 67 |
| | **NHL Totals** | 289 | 71 | 194 | 265 |
| | **WHA Totals** | 426 | 208 | 296 | 504 |

**HOWE, Marty Gordon**  *Defenseman*
b. Detroit, Mich., Feb. 18, 1954

| Season | Club | GP | G | A | Pts. |
|---|---|---|---|---|---|
| 1973-74 | Houston (WHA) | 73 | 4 | 20 | 24 |
| 1974-75 | Houston (WHA) | 75 | 13 | 21 | 34 |
| 1975-76 | Houston (WHA) | 80 | 14 | 23 | 37 |
| 1976-77 | Houston (WHA) | 80 | 17 | 28 | 45 |
| 1977-78 | New England (WHA) | 75 | 10 | 10 | 20 |
| 1978-79 | New England (WHA) | 66 | 9 | 15 | 24 |
| 1979-80 | Hartford | 6 | 0 | 1 | 1 |
| 1980-81 | Hartford | 12 | 0 | 1 | 1 |
| 1981-82 | Hartford | 13 | 0 | 4 | 4 |
| 1982-83 | Boston | 78 | 1 | 11 | 12 |
| | **NHL Totals** | 109 | 1 | 17 | 18 |
| | **WHA Totals** | 449 | 67 | 117 | 184 |

**HOWE, Sydney Harris**  *Forward*
b. Ottawa, Ont., Sept. 18, 1911

| Season | Club | GP | G | A | Pts. |
|---|---|---|---|---|---|
| 1929-30 | Ottawa | 12 | 1 | 1 | 2 |
| 1930-31 | Philadelphia Q | 44 | 9 | 11 | 20 |
| 1931-32 | Toronto | 3 | 0 | 0 | 0 |
| 1932-33 | Ottawa | 48 | 12 | 12 | 24 |
| 1933-34 | Ottawa | 42 | 13 | 7 | 20 |
| 1934-35 | StLE-Det | 50 | 22 | 25 | 47 |
| 1935-36 | Detroit | 48 | 16 | 14 | 30 |
| 1936-37 | Detroit | 45 | 17 | 10 | 27 |
| 1937-38 | Detroit | 48 | 8 | 19 | 27 |
| 1938-39 | Detroit | 48 | 16 | 20 | 36 |
| 1939-40 | Detroit | 46 | 14 | 23 | 37 |
| 1940-41 | Detroit | 48 | 20 | 24 | 44 |
| 1941-42 | Detroit | 48 | 16 | 19 | 35 |
| 1942-43 | Detroit | 50 | 20 | 35 | 55 |
| 1943-44 | Detroit | 40 | 32 | 28 | 60 |
| 1944-45 | Detroit | 46 | 17 | 36 | 53 |
| 1945-46 | Detroit | 26 | 4 | 7 | 11 |
| | **Totals** | 692 | 237 | 291 | 528 |

**HOWE, Victor Stanley**  *Forward*
b. Saskatoon, Sask., Nov. 2, 1929

| Season | Club | GP | G | A | Pts. |
|---|---|---|---|---|---|
| 1950-51 | New York R | 3 | 1 | 0 | 1 |
| 1953-54 | New York R | 1 | 0 | 0 | 0 |
| 1954-55 | New York R | 29 | 2 | 4 | 6 |
| | **Totals** | 33 | 3 | 4 | 7 |

**HOWELL, Henry Vernon (Harry)**  *Defenseman*
b. Hamilton, Ont., Dec. 28, 1932

| Season | Club | GP | G | A | Pts. |
|---|---|---|---|---|---|
| 1952-53 | New York R | 67 | 3 | 8 | 11 |
| 1953-54 | New York R | 67 | 7 | 9 | 16 |
| 1954-55 | New York R | 70 | 2 | 14 | 16 |
| 1955-56 | New York R | 70 | 3 | 15 | 18 |
| 1956-57 | New York R | 65 | 2 | 10 | 12 |
| 1957-58 | New York R | 70 | 4 | 7 | 11 |
| 1958-59 | New York R | 70 | 4 | 10 | 14 |
| 1959-60 | New York R | 67 | 7 | 6 | 13 |
| 1960-61 | New York R | 70 | 7 | 10 | 17 |
| 1961-62 | New York R | 66 | 6 | 15 | 21 |
| 1962-63 | New York R | 70 | 5 | 20 | 25 |
| 1963-64 | New York R | 70 | 5 | 31 | 36 |
| 1964-65 | New York R | 68 | 2 | 22 | 24 |
| 1965-66 | New York R | 70 | 4 | 29 | 33 |
| 1966-67 | New York R | 70 | 12 | 28 | 40 |
| 1967-68 | New York R | 74 | 5 | 24 | 29 |
| 1968-69 | New York R | 56 | 4 | 7 | 11 |
| 1969-70 | Oakland | 55 | 4 | 16 | 20 |
| 1970-71 | Cal-LA | 46 | 3 | 17 | 20 |
| 1971-72 | Los Angeles | 77 | 1 | 17 | 18 |
| 1972-73 | Los Angeles | 73 | 4 | 11 | 15 |
| | **Totals** | 1411 | 94 | 324 | 418 |

**HOWELL, Ronald**  *Defenseman-Forward*
b. Hamilton, Ont., Dec. 4, 1935

| Season | Club | GP | G | A | Pts. |
|---|---|---|---|---|---|
| 1954-55 | New York R | 3 | 0 | 0 | 0 |
| 1955-56 | New York R | 1 | 0 | 0 | 0 |
| | **Totals** | 4 | 0 | 0 | 0 |

**HOWSE, Donald Gordon**  *Forward*
b. Grand Falls, Nfld., July 28, 1952

| Season | Club | GP | G | A | Pts. |
|---|---|---|---|---|---|
| 1979-80 | Los Angeles | 33 | 2 | 5 | 7 |

**HOYDA, David Allan**  *Forward*
b. Edmonton, Alta., May 20, 1957

| Season | Club | GP | G | A | Pts. |
|---|---|---|---|---|---|
| 1977-78 | Philadelphia | 41 | 1 | 3 | 4 |
| 1978-79 | Philadelphia | 67 | 3 | 13 | 16 |
| 1979-80 | Winnipeg | 15 | 1 | 1 | 2 |
| 1980-81 | Winnipeg | 9 | 1 | 0 | 1 |
| | **Totals** | 132 | 6 | 17 | 23 |

**HRECKOSY, David John**  *Forward*
b. Winnipeg, Man., Nov. 1, 1951

| Season | Club | GP | G | A | Pts. |
|---|---|---|---|---|---|
| 1973-74 | California | 2 | 0 | 0 | 0 |
| 1974-75 | California | 72 | 29 | 14 | 43 |
| 1975-76 | Cal-StL | 51 | 12 | 8 | 20 |
| 1976-77 | St Louis | 15 | 1 | 2 | 3 |
| | **Totals** | 145 | 42 | 24 | 66 |

**HRYCUIK, James Peter**  *Forward*
b. Rostern, Sask., Oct. 7, 1949

| Season | Club | GP | G | A | Pts. |
|---|---|---|---|---|---|
| 1974-75 | Washington | 21 | 5 | 5 | 10 |

**HRYMNAK, Stephen**  *Defenseman*
b. Port Arthur, Ont., Mar. 3, 1926

| Season | Club | GP | G | A | Pts. |
|---|---|---|---|---|---|
| 1951-52 | Chicago | 18 | 2 | 1 | 3 |

**HRYNEWICH, Tim**  *Forward*
b. Leamington, Ont., Oct. 2, 1963

| Season | Club | GP | G | A | Pts. |
|---|---|---|---|---|---|
| 1982-83 | Pittsburgh | 30 | 2 | 3 | 5 |

**HUARD, Roland**  *Forward*

| Season | Club | GP | G | A | Pts. |
|---|---|---|---|---|---|
| 1930-31 | Toronto | 1 | 1 | 0 | 1 |

**HUBER, Wilhelm Heinrich**  *Defenseman*
b. Strasskirchen, Germany, Jan. 15, 1958

| Season | Club | GP | G | A | Pts. |
|---|---|---|---|---|---|
| 1978-79 | Detroit | 68 | 7 | 24 | 31 |
| 1979-80 | Detroit | 76 | 17 | 23 | 40 |
| 1980-81 | Detroit | 80 | 15 | 34 | 49 |
| 1981-82 | Detroit | 74 | 15 | 30 | 45 |
| 1982-83 | Detroit | 74 | 14 | 19 | 33 |
| | **Totals** | 372 | 68 | 130 | 198 |

**HUBICK, Gregory Wayne**  *Defenseman*
b. Strasbourg, Germany, Nov. 12, 1951

| Season | Club | GP | G | A | Pts. |
|---|---|---|---|---|---|
| 1975-76 | Toronto | 72 | 6 | 8 | 14 |
| 1979-80 | Vancouver | 5 | 0 | 1 | 1 |
| | **Totals** | 77 | 6 | 9 | 15 |

**HUCK, Francis (Fran)**  *Forward*
b. Regina, Sask., Dec. 4, 1945

| Season | Club | GP | G | A | Pts. |
|---|---|---|---|---|---|
| 1969-70 | Montreal | 2 | 0 | 0 | 0 |
| 1970-71 | Mont-StL | 34 | 8 | 10 | 18 |
| 1972-73 | St Louis | 58 | 16 | 20 | 36 |
| 1973-74 | Winnipeg (WHA) | 74 | 26 | 48 | 74 |
| 1974-75 | Minnesota (WHA) | 78 | 22 | 45 | 67 |
| | **NHL Totals** | 94 | 24 | 30 | 54 |
| | **WHA Totals** | 152 | 48 | 93 | 141 |

**HUCUL, Frederick Albert**  *Defenseman*
b. Tubrose, Sask., Dec. 4, 1931

| Season | Club | GP | G | A | Pts. |
|---|---|---|---|---|---|
| 1950-51 | Chicago | 3 | 1 | 0 | 1 |
| 1951-52 | Chicago | 34 | 3 | 7 | 10 |
| 1952-53 | Chicago | 57 | 5 | 7 | 12 |
| 1953-54 | Chicago | 27 | 0 | 3 | 3 |
| 1967-68 | St Louis | 43 | 2 | 13 | 15 |
| | **Totals** | 164 | 11 | 30 | 41 |

**HUDDY, Charles William** *Defenseman*
b. Toronto, Ont., June 2, 1959

| Season | Club | GP | G | A | Pts. |
|---|---|---|---|---|---|
| 1980-81 | Edmonton | 12 | 2 | 5 | 7 |
| 1981-82 | Edmonton | 41 | 4 | 11 | 15 |
| 1982-83 | Edmonton | 76 | 20 | 37 | 57 |
| | **Totals** | 129 | 26 | 53 | 79 |

**HUDSON, Alexander** *Defenseman*
b. Winnipeg, Man., Dec. 31, 1955

| Season | Club | GP | G | A | Pts. |
|---|---|---|---|---|---|
| 1978-79 | Pittsburgh | 2 | 0 | 0 | 0 |

**HUDSON, David Richard (Dave)** *Forward*
b. St. Thomas, Ont., Dec. 28, 1949

| Season | Club | GP | G | A | Pts. |
|---|---|---|---|---|---|
| 1972-73 | New York I | 69 | 12 | 19 | 31 |
| 1973-74 | New York I | 63 | 2 | 10 | 12 |
| 1974-75 | Kansas City | 70 | 9 | 32 | 41 |
| 1975-76 | Kansas City | 74 | 11 | 20 | 31 |
| 1976-77 | Colorado | 73 | 15 | 21 | 36 |
| 1977-78 | Colorado | 60 | 10 | 22 | 32 |
| | **Totals** | 412 | 59 | 124 | 183 |

**HUDSON, Ronald** *Forward*
b. Timmins, Ont., Apr. 18, 1914

| Season | Club | GP | G | A | Pts. |
|---|---|---|---|---|---|
| 1937-38 | Detroit | 32 | 5 | 2 | 7 |
| 1939-40 | Detroit | 1 | 0 | 0 | 0 |
| | **Totals** | 33 | 5 | 2 | 7 |

**HUGGINS, Allan** *Forward*
b. Toronto, Ont.

| Season | Club | GP | G | A | Pts. |
|---|---|---|---|---|---|
| 1930-31 | Montreal M | 18 | 1 | 1 | 2 |

**HUGHES, Albert** *Forward*
b. Collingwood, Ont.

| Season | Club | GP | G | A | Pts. |
|---|---|---|---|---|---|
| 1930-31 | New York A | 44 | 5 | 7 | 12 |
| 1931-32 | New York A | 18 | 1 | 1 | 2 |
| | **Totals** | 62 | 6 | 8 | 14 |

**HUGHES, Brenton Alexander** *Defenseman*
b. Bowmanville, Ont., June 17, 1943

| Season | Club | GP | G | A | Pts. |
|---|---|---|---|---|---|
| 1967-68 | Los Angeles | 44 | 4 | 10 | 14 |
| 1968-69 | Los Angeles | 72 | 2 | 19 | 21 |
| 1969-70 | Los Angeles | 52 | 1 | 7 | 8 |
| 1970-71 | Philadelphia | 30 | 1 | 10 | 11 |
| 1971-72 | Philadelphia | 63 | 2 | 20 | 22 |
| 1972-73 | Phil-StL | 37 | 3 | 12 | 15 |
| 1973-74 | StL-Det | 71 | 1 | 21 | 22 |
| 1974-75 | Kansas City | 66 | 1 | 18 | 19 |
| 1975-76 | San Diego (WHA) | 78 | 7 | 28 | 35 |
| 1976-77 | San Diego (WHA) | 62 | 4 | 13 | 17 |
| 1977-78 | Birmingham (WHA) | 80 | 9 | 35 | 44 |
| 1978-79 | Birmingham (WHA) | 48 | 3 | 3 | 6 |
| | **NHL Totals** | 435 | 15 | 117 | 132 |
| | **WHA Totals** | 268 | 23 | 79 | 102 |

**HUGHES, Frank** *Forward*
b. Fernie, B.C., Oct. 1, 1949

| Season | Club | GP | G | A | Pts. |
|---|---|---|---|---|---|
| 1971-72 | California | 5 | 0 | 0 | 0 |
| 1972-73 | Houston (WHA) | 72 | 22 | 19 | 41 |
| 1973-74 | Houston (WHA) | 73 | 42 | 42 | 84 |
| 1974-75 | Houston (WHA) | 76 | 48 | 35 | 83 |
| 1975-76 | Houston (WHA) | 80 | 32 | 45 | 77 |
| 1976-77 | Hou-Phoe (WHA) | 75 | 27 | 37 | 64 |
| 1977-78 | Houston (WHA) | 11 | 3 | 2 | 5 |
| | **NHL Totals** | 5 | 0 | 0 | 0 |
| | **WHA Totals** | 387 | 174 | 180 | 354 |

**HUGHES, Howard Duncan** *Forward*
b. St. Boniface, Man., Apr. 4, 1939

| Season | Club | GP | G | A | Pts. |
|---|---|---|---|---|---|
| 1967-68 | Los Angeles | 74 | 9 | 14 | 23 |
| 1968-69 | Los Angeles | 73 | 16 | 14 | 30 |
| 1969-70 | Los Angeles | 21 | 0 | 4 | 4 |
| | **Totals** | 168 | 25 | 32 | 57 |

**HUGHES, J. (Rusty)** *Defenseman*

| Season | Club | GP | G | A | Pts. |
|---|---|---|---|---|---|
| 1929-30 | Detroit | 38 | 0 | 1 | 1 |

**HUGHES, John F.** *Defenseman*
b. Somerville, Mass., July 20, 1957

| Season | Club | GP | G | A | Pts. |
|---|---|---|---|---|---|
| 1980-81 | Colorado | 38 | 2 | 5 | 7 |
| 1981-82 | Colorado | 8 | 0 | 0 | 0 |
| | **Totals** | 46 | 2 | 5 | 7 |


**HUGHES, John Spencer** *Defenseman*
b. Charlottetown, P.E.I., Mar. 18, 1954

| Season | Club | GP | G | A | Pts. |
|---|---|---|---|---|---|
| 1974-75 | Phoenix (WHA) | 72 | 4 | 25 | 29 |
| 1975-76 | Cincinnati (WHA) | 79 | 3 | 34 | 37 |
| 1976-77 | Cincinnati (WHA) | 79 | 3 | 27 | 30 |
| 1977-78 | Houston (WHA) | 79 | 3 | 25 | 28 |
| 1978-79 | Ind-Edm (WHA) | 63 | 5 | 19 | 24 |
| 1979-80 | Vancouver | 52 | 2 | 11 | 13 |
| 1980-81 | Edmonton | 18 | 0 | 3 | 3 |
| | **NHL Totals** | 70 | 2 | 14 | 16 |
| | **WHA Totals** | 372 | 18 | 130 | 148 |

**HUGHES, Patrick** *Forward*
b. Calgary, Alta., Mar. 25, 1955

| Season | Club | GP | G | A | Pts. |
|---|---|---|---|---|---|
| 1977-78 | Montreal | 3 | 0 | 0 | 0 |
| 1978-79 | Montreal | 41 | 9 | 8 | 17 |
| 1979-80 | Pittsburgh | 76 | 18 | 14 | 32 |
| 1980-81 | Pitt-Edm | 60 | 10 | 9 | 19 |
| 1981-82 | Edmonton | 68 | 24 | 22 | 46 |
| 1982-83 | Edmonton | 80 | 25 | 20 | 45 |
| | **Totals** | 328 | 86 | 73 | 159 |

**HULL, Dennis William** *Forward*
b. Point Anne, Ont., Nov. 19, 1944

| Season | Club | GP | G | A | Pts. |
|---|---|---|---|---|---|
| 1964-65 | Chicago | 55 | 10 | 4 | 14 |
| 1965-66 | Chicago | 25 | 1 | 5 | 6 |
| 1966-67 | Chicago | 70 | 25 | 17 | 42 |
| 1967-68 | Chicago | 74 | 18 | 15 | 33 |
| 1968-69 | Chicago | 72 | 30 | 34 | 64 |
| 1969-70 | Chicago | 76 | 17 | 35 | 52 |
| 1970-71 | Chicago | 78 | 40 | 26 | 66 |
| 1971-72 | Chicago | 78 | 30 | 39 | 69 |
| 1972-73 | Chicago | 78 | 39 | 51 | 90 |
| 1973-74 | Chicago | 74 | 29 | 39 | 68 |
| 1974-75 | Chicago | 69 | 16 | 21 | 37 |
| 1975-76 | Chicago | 80 | 27 | 39 | 66 |
| 1976-77 | Chicago | 75 | 16 | 17 | 33 |
| 1977-78 | Detroit | 55 | 5 | 9 | 14 |
| | **Totals** | 959 | 303 | 351 | 654 |

**HULL, Robert Marvin** *Forward*
b. Point Anne, Ont., Jan. 3, 1939

| Season | Club | GP | G | A | Pts. |
|---|---|---|---|---|---|
| 1957-58 | Chicago | 70 | 13 | 34 | 47 |
| 1958-59 | Chicago | 70 | 18 | 32 | 50 |
| 1959-60 | Chicago | 70 | 39 | 42 | 81 |
| 1960-61 | Chicago | 67 | 31 | 25 | 56 |
| 1961-62 | Chicago | 70 | 50 | 34 | 84 |
| 1962-63 | Chicago | 65 | 31 | 31 | 62 |
| 1963-64 | Chicago | 70 | 43 | 44 | 87 |
| 1964-65 | Chicago | 61 | 39 | 32 | 71 |
| 1965-66 | Chicago | 65 | 54 | 43 | 97 |
| 1966-67 | Chicago | 66 | 52 | 28 | 80 |
| 1967-68 | Chicago | 71 | 44 | 31 | 75 |
| 1968-69 | Chicago | 74 | 58 | 49 | 107 |
| 1969-70 | Chicago | 61 | 38 | 29 | 67 |
| 1970-71 | Chicago | 78 | 44 | 52 | 96 |
| 1971-72 | Chicago | 78 | 50 | 43 | 93 |
| 1972-73 | Winnipeg (WHA) | 63 | 51 | 52 | 103 |
| 1973-74 | Winnipeg (WHA) | 75 | 53 | 42 | 95 |
| 1974-75 | Winnipeg (WHA) | 78 | 77 | 65 | 142 |
| 1975-76 | Winnipeg (WHA) | 80 | 53 | 70 | 123 |
| 1976-77 | Winnipeg (WHA) | 34 | 21 | 32 | 53 |
| 1977-78 | Winnipeg (WHA) | 77 | 46 | 71 | 117 |
| 1978-79 | Winnipeg (WHA) | 4 | 2 | 3 | 5 |
| 1979-80 | Winn-Hart | 27 | 6 | 11 | 17 |
| | **NHL Totals** | 1063 | 610 | 560 | 1170 |
| | **WHA Totals** | 411 | 303 | 335 | 638 |

**HUNT, Frederick Tennyson** *Forward*
b. Brantford, Ont., Jan. 17, 1918

| Season | Club | GP | G | A | Pts. |
|---|---|---|---|---|---|
| 1940-41 | New York A | 15 | 2 | 5 | 7 |
| 1944-45 | New York R | 44 | 13 | 9 | 22 |
| | **Totals** | 59 | 15 | 14 | 29 |

**HUNTER, Dale Robert** *Forward*
b. Oil Springs, Ont., July 31, 1960

| Season | Club | GP | G | A | Pts. |
|---|---|---|---|---|---|
| 1980-81 | Quebec | 80 | 19 | 44 | 63 |
| 1981-82 | Quebec | 80 | 22 | 50 | 72 |
| 1982-83 | Quebec | 80 | 17 | 46 | 63 |
| | **Totals** | 240 | 58 | 140 | 198 |


**HUNTER, David** *Forward*
b. Petrolia, Ont., Jan. 1, 1958

| Season | Club | GP | G | A | Pts. |
|---|---|---|---|---|---|
| 1978-79 | Edmonton (WHA) | 72 | 7 | 25 | 32 |
| 1979-80 | Edmonton | 80 | 12 | 31 | 43 |
| 1980-81 | Edmonton | 78 | 12 | 16 | 28 |
| 1981-82 | Edmonton | 63 | 16 | 22 | 38 |
| 1982-83 | Edmonton | 80 | 13 | 18 | 31 |
| | **NHL Totals** | 301 | 53 | 87 | 140 |
| | **WHA Totals** | 72 | 7 | 25 | 32 |

**HUNTER, Mark** *Forward*
b. Petrolia, Que., Nov. 12, 1962

| Season | Club | GP | G | A | Pts. |
|---|---|---|---|---|---|
| 1981-82 | Montreal | 71 | 18 | 11 | 29 |
| 1982-83 | Montreal | 31 | 8 | 8 | 16 |
| | **Totals** | 102 | 26 | 19 | 45 |

**HUNTER, Tim Robert** *Defenseman*
b. Calgary, Alta., Sept. 10, 1960

| Season | Club | GP | G | A | Pts. |
|---|---|---|---|---|---|
| 1981-82 | Calgary | 2 | 0 | 0 | 0 |
| 1982-83 | Calgary | 16 | 1 | 0 | 1 |
| | **Totals** | 18 | 1 | 0 | 1 |

**HURAS, Larry Robert** *Defenseman*
b. Listowel, Ont., July 8, 1955

| Season | Club | GP | G | A | Pts. |
|---|---|---|---|---|---|
| 1976-77 | New York R | 1 | 0 | 0 | 0 |

**HURLBURT, Robert George** *Forward*
b. Toronto, Ont., May 1, 1950

| Season | Club | GP | G | A | Pts. |
|---|---|---|---|---|---|
| 1974-75 | Vancouver | 1 | 0 | 0 | 0 |

**HURLEY, Paul Michael** *Defenseman*
b. Melrose, Mass., July 12, 1946

| Season | Club | GP | G | A | Pts. |
|---|---|---|---|---|---|
| 1968-69 | Boston | 1 | 0 | 1 | 1 |
| 1972-73 | New England (WHA) | 78 | 3 | 15 | 18 |
| 1973-74 | New England (WHA) | 52 | 3 | 11 | 14 |
| 1974-75 | New England (WHA) | 75 | 3 | 26 | 29 |
| 1975-76 | NE-Edm (WHA) | 72 | 1 | 18 | 19 |
| 1976-77 | Calgary (WHA) | 34 | 0 | 6 | 6 |
| | **NHL Totals** | 1 | 0 | 1 | 1 |
| | **WHA Totals** | 311 | 10 | 76 | 86 |

**HURST, Ronald** *Forward*
b. Toronto, Ont., May 18, 1931

| Season | Club | GP | G | A | Pts. |
|---|---|---|---|---|---|
| 1955-56 | Toronto | 50 | 7 | 5 | 12 |
| 1956-57 | Toronto | 14 | 2 | 2 | 4 |
| | **Totals** | 64 | 9 | 7 | 16 |

**HUSTON, Ronald Earle (Ron)** *Forward*
b. Manitou, Man., Apr. 8, 1945

| Season | Club | GP | G | A | Pts. |
|---|---|---|---|---|---|
| 1973-74 | California | 23 | 3 | 10 | 13 |
| 1974-75 | California | 56 | 12 | 21 | 33 |
| 1975-76 | Phoenix (WHA) | 79 | 22 | 44 | 66 |
| 1976-77 | Phoenix (WHA) | 80 | 20 | 39 | 59 |
| | **NHL Totals** | 79 | 15 | 31 | 46 |
| | **WHA Totals** | 159 | 42 | 83 | 125 |

**HUTCHINSON, Ronald Wayne** *Forward*
b. Flin Flon, Man., Oct. 24, 1936

| Season | Club | GP | G | A | Pts. |
|---|---|---|---|---|---|
| 1960-61 | New York R | 9 | 0 | 0 | 0 |

**HUTCHISON, David Joseph** *Defenseman*
b. London, Ont., May 2, 1952

| Season | Club | GP | G | A | Pts. |
|---|---|---|---|---|---|
| 1972-73 | Philadelphia (WHA) | 28 | 0 | 2 | 2 |
| 1973-74 | Vancouver (WHA) | 69 | 0 | 13 | 13 |
| 1974-75 | Los Angeles | 68 | 0 | 6 | 6 |
| 1975-76 | Los Angeles | 50 | 0 | 10 | 10 |
| 1976-77 | Los Angeles | 70 | 6 | 11 | 17 |
| 1977-78 | Los Angeles | 44 | 0 | 10 | 10 |
| 1978-79 | Toronto | 79 | 4 | 15 | 19 |
| 1979-80 | Tor-Chi | 69 | 1 | 11 | 12 |
| 1980-81 | Chicago | 59 | 2 | 9 | 11 |
| 1981-82 | Chicago | 46 | 5 | 18 | 23 |
| 1982-83 | New Jersey | 32 | 1 | 4 | 5 |
| | **NHL Totals** | 517 | 19 | 94 | 113 |
| | **WHA Totals** | 97 | 0 | 15 | 15 |

**HUTTON, William David** *Defenseman*
b. Calgary, Alta., Jan. 28, 1910

| Season | Club | GP | G | A | Pts. |
|---|---|---|---|---|---|
| 1929-30 | Bos-Ott | 33 | 2 | 1 | 3 |
| 1930-31 | PhilQ-Bos | 30 | 1 | 1 | 2 |
| | **Totals** | 63 | 3 | 2 | 5 |

| Season | Club | GP | G | A | Pts. |
|---|---|---|---|---|---|
| **HYLAND, Harry M.** *Forward* | | | | | |
| b. Montreal, Que., Jan. 2, 1889 | | | | | |
| 1917-18 | MontW-Ott | 16 | 14 | 0 | 14 |
| **HYNES, David** *Forward* | | | | | |
| b. Cambridge, Mass., Apr. 17, 1951 | | | | | |
| 1973-74 | Boston | 3 | 0 | 0 | 0 |
| 1974-75 | Boston | 19 | 4 | 0 | 4 |
| 1976-77 | New England (WHA) | 22 | 5 | 4 | 9 |
| | **NHL Totals** | 22 | 4 | 0 | 4 |
| | **WHA Totals** | 22 | 5 | 4 | 9 |
| **IHNACAK, Peter** *Forward* | | | | | |
| b. Czechoslovakia, 1957 | | | | | |
| 1982-83 | Toronto | 80 | 28 | 38 | 66 |
| **IMLACH, Brent** *Forward* | | | | | |
| b. Toronto, Ont., Nov. 16, 1946 | | | | | |
| 1965-66 | Toronto | 2 | 0 | 0 | 0 |
| 1966-67 | Toronto | 1 | 0 | 0 | 0 |
| | **Totals** | 3 | 0 | 0 | 0 |
| **INGARFIELD, Earl Thompson** *Forward* | | | | | |
| b. Lethbridge, Alta., Oct. 25, 1934 | | | | | |
| 1958-59 | New York R | 35 | 1 | 2 | 3 |
| 1959-60 | New York R | 20 | 1 | 2 | 3 |
| 1960-61 | New York R | 66 | 13 | 21 | 34 |
| 1961-62 | New York R | 70 | 26 | 31 | 57 |
| 1962-63 | New York R | 69 | 19 | 24 | 43 |
| 1963-64 | New York R | 63 | 15 | 11 | 26 |
| 1964-65 | New York R | 69 | 15 | 13 | 28 |
| 1965-66 | New York R | 68 | 20 | 16 | 36 |
| 1966-67 | New York R | 67 | 12 | 22 | 34 |
| 1967-68 | Pittsburgh | 50 | 15 | 22 | 37 |
| 1968-69 | Pitt-Oak | 66 | 16 | 30 | 46 |
| 1969-70 | Oakland | 54 | 21 | 24 | 45 |
| 1970-71 | California | 49 | 5 | 8 | 13 |
| | **Totals** | 746 | 179 | 226 | 405 |
| **INGARFIELD, Earl Thompson Jr.** *Forward* | | | | | |
| b. New York, N.Y., Jan. 30, 1959 | | | | | |
| 1979-80 | Atlanta | 1 | 0 | 0 | 0 |
| 1980-81 | Calg-Det | 38 | 4 | 4 | 8 |
| | **Totals** | 39 | 4 | 4 | 8 |
| **INGLIS, William John** *Forward* | | | | | |
| b. Ottawa, Ont., May 11, 1943 | | | | | |
| 1967-68 | Los Angeles | 12 | 1 | 1 | 2 |
| 1968-69 | Los Angeles | 10 | 0 | 1 | 1 |
| 1970-71 | Buffalo | 14 | 0 | 1 | 1 |
| | **Totals** | 36 | 1 | 3 | 4 |
| **INGOLSBY, Jack** *Defenseman-Forward* | | | | | |
| b. Toronto, Ont., June 21, 1924 | | | | | |
| 1942-43 | Toronto | 8 | 0 | 1 | 1 |
| 1943-44 | Toronto | 21 | 5 | 0 | 5 |
| | **Totals** | 29 | 5 | 1 | 6 |
| **INGRAM, Frank** *Forward* | | | | | |
| b. Craven, Sask., Sept. 17, 1907 | | | | | |
| 1924-25 | Boston | 1 | 0 | 0 | 0 |
| 1929-30 | Chicago | 35 | 6 | 10 | 16 |
| 1930-31 | Chicago | 44 | 17 | 4 | 21 |
| 1931-32 | Chicago | 19 | 1 | 2 | 3 |
| | **Totals** | 99 | 24 | 16 | 40 |
| **INGRAM, Ronald Walter** *Defenseman* | | | | | |
| b. Toronto, Ont., July 5, 1933 | | | | | |
| 1956-57 | Chicago | 45 | 1 | 6 | 7 |
| 1963-64 | Det-NYR | 66 | 4 | 9 | 13 |
| 1964-65 | New York R | 3 | 0 | 0 | 0 |
| | **Totals** | 114 | 5 | 15 | 20 |
| **IRVIN, James Dickinson (Dick)** *Forward* | | | | | |
| b. Limestone Ridge, Ont., July 19, 1892 | | | | | |
| 1926-27 | Chicago | 43 | 18 | 18 | 36 |
| 1927-28 | Chicago | 12 | 5 | 4 | 9 |
| 1928-29 | Chicago | 39 | 6 | 1 | 7 |
| | **Totals** | 94 | 29 | 23 | 52 |

| Season | Club | GP | G | A | Pts. |
|---|---|---|---|---|---|
| **IRVINE, Edward Amos (Ted)** *Forward* | | | | | |
| b. Winnipeg, Man., Dec. 8, 1944 | | | | | |
| 1963-64 | Boston | 1 | 0 | 0 | 0 |
| 1967-68 | Los Angeles | 73 | 18 | 22 | 40 |
| 1968-69 | Los Angeles | 76 | 15 | 24 | 39 |
| 1969-70 | LA-NYR | 75 | 11 | 16 | 27 |
| 1970-71 | New York R | 76 | 20 | 18 | 38 |
| 1971-72 | New York R | 78 | 15 | 21 | 36 |
| 1972-73 | New York R | 53 | 8 | 12 | 20 |
| 1973-74 | New York R | 75 | 26 | 20 | 46 |
| 1974-75 | New York R | 79 | 17 | 17 | 34 |
| 1975-76 | St Louis | 69 | 10 | 13 | 23 |
| 1976-77 | St Louis | 69 | 14 | 14 | 28 |
| | **Totals** | 724 | 154 | 177 | 331 |
| **IRWIN, Ivan Duane** *Defenseman* | | | | | |
| b. Chicago, Ill., Mar. 13, 1927 | | | | | |
| 1952-53 | Montreal | 4 | 0 | 1 | 1 |
| 1953-54 | New York R | 56 | 2 | 12 | 14 |
| 1954-55 | New York R | 60 | 0 | 13 | 13 |
| 1955-56 | New York R | 34 | 0 | 1 | 1 |
| 1957-58 | New York R | 1 | 0 | 0 | 0 |
| | **Totals** | 155 | 2 | 27 | 29 |
| **ISAKSSON, Ulf** *Forward* | | | | | |
| b. Norfunda, Sweden, Mar. 19, 1954 | | | | | |
| 1982-83 | Los Angeles | 50 | 7 | 15 | 22 |
| **JACKSON, Arthur** *Forward* | | | | | |
| b. Toronto, Ont., Dec. 15, 1915 | | | | | |
| 1934-35 | Toronto | 20 | 1 | 3 | 4 |
| 1935-36 | Toronto | 48 | 5 | 15 | 20 |
| 1936-37 | Toronto | 14 | 2 | 0 | 2 |
| 1937-38 | Boston | 48 | 9 | 3 | 12 |
| 1938-39 | New York A | 48 | 12 | 13 | 25 |
| 1939-40 | Boston | 46 | 7 | 18 | 25 |
| 1940-41 | Boston | 48 | 17 | 15 | 32 |
| 1941-42 | Boston | 47 | 6 | 18 | 24 |
| 1942-43 | Boston | 50 | 22 | 31 | 53 |
| 1943-44 | Boston | 49 | 28 | 41 | 69 |
| 1944-45 | Bos-Tor | 50 | 14 | 21 | 35 |
| | **Totals** | 468 | 123 | 178 | 301 |
| **JACKSON, Donald Clinton** *Defenseman* | | | | | |
| b. Minneapolis, Minn., Sept. 2, 1956 | | | | | |
| 1977-78 | Minnesota | 2 | 0 | 0 | 0 |
| 1978-79 | Minnesota | 5 | 0 | 0 | 0 |
| 1979-80 | Minnesota | 10 | 0 | 4 | 4 |
| 1980-81 | Minnesota | 10 | 0 | 3 | 3 |
| 1981-82 | Edmonton | 8 | 0 | 0 | 0 |
| 1982-83 | Edmonton | 71 | 2 | 8 | 10 |
| | **Totals** | 106 | 2 | 15 | 17 |
| **JACKSON, Harold Russell** *Defenseman* | | | | | |
| b. Cedar Springs, Ont., Aug. 1, 1918 | | | | | |
| 1936-37 | Chicago | 38 | 1 | 3 | 4 |
| 1937-38 | Chicago | 3 | 0 | 0 | 0 |
| 1940-41 | Detroit | 1 | 0 | 0 | 0 |
| 1942-43 | Detroit | 4 | 0 | 4 | 4 |
| 1943-44 | Detroit | 50 | 7 | 12 | 19 |
| 1944-45 | Detroit | 50 | 5 | 6 | 11 |
| 1945-46 | Detroit | 36 | 3 | 4 | 7 |
| 1946-47 | Detroit | 37 | 1 | 5 | 6 |
| | **Totals** | 219 | 17 | 34 | 51 |
| **JACKSON, Harvey (Busher)** *Forward* | | | | | |
| b. Toronto, Ont., Jan. 17, 1911 | | | | | |
| 1929-30 | Toronto | 31 | 12 | 6 | 18 |
| 1930-31 | Toronto | 43 | 18 | 13 | 31 |
| 1931-32 | Toronto | 48 | 28 | 25 | 53 |
| 1932-33 | Toronto | 48 | 27 | 17 | 44 |
| 1933-34 | Toronto | 38 | 20 | 18 | 38 |
| 1934-35 | Toronto | 42 | 22 | 22 | 44 |
| 1935-36 | Toronto | 47 | 11 | 11 | 22 |
| 1936-37 | Toronto | 46 | 21 | 19 | 40 |
| 1937-38 | Toronto | 48 | 17 | 17 | 34 |
| 1938-39 | Toronto | 41 | 10 | 17 | 27 |
| 1939-40 | New York A | 43 | 12 | 8 | 20 |
| 1940-41 | New York A | 46 | 8 | 18 | 26 |
| 1941-42 | Boston | 26 | 5 | 7 | 12 |
| 1942-43 | Boston | 44 | 19 | 15 | 34 |
| 1943-44 | Boston | 42 | 11 | 21 | 32 |
| | **Totals** | 633 | 241 | 234 | 475 |

| Season | Club | GP | G | A | Pts. |
|---|---|---|---|---|---|
| **JACKSON, Jim** *Forward* | | | | | |
| b. Oshawa, Ont., Feb. 1, 1960 | | | | | |
| 1982-83 | Calgary | 48 | 8 | 12 | 20 |
| **JACKSON, John Alexander** *Defenseman* | | | | | |
| b. Windsor, Ont., May 3, 1925 | | | | | |
| 1946-47 | Chicago | 48 | 2 | 5 | 7 |
| **JACKSON, Lloyd** *Forward* | | | | | |
| b. Ottawa, Ont., Jan. 7, 1912 | | | | | |
| 1936-37 | New York A | 11 | 1 | 1 | 2 |
| **JACKSON, Stanton** *Forward* | | | | | |
| 1921-22 | Toronto | 1 | 0 | 0 | 0 |
| 1923-24 | Toronto | 21 | 1 | 1 | 2 |
| 1924-25 | Tor-Bos | 27 | 5 | 0 | 5 |
| 1925-26 | Boston | 28 | 3 | 3 | 6 |
| 1926-27 | Ottawa | 7 | 0 | 0 | 0 |
| | **Totals** | 84 | 9 | 4 | 13 |
| **JACKSON, Walter (Red)** *Forward* | | | | | |
| b. Winnipeg, Man. | | | | | |
| 1932-33 | New York A | 34 | 10 | 2 | 12 |
| 1933-34 | New York A | 47 | 6 | 9 | 15 |
| 1935-36 | Boston | 2 | 0 | 0 | 0 |
| | **Totals** | 83 | 16 | 11 | 27 |
| **JACOBS** | | | | | |
| 1918-19 | Toronto | 1 | 0 | 0 | 0 |
| **JACOBS, Timothy James** *Defenseman* | | | | | |
| b. Espanola, Ont., Mar. 28, 1952 | | | | | |
| 1975-76 | California | 46 | 0 | 10 | 10 |
| **JALONEN, Kari** *Forward* | | | | | |
| b. Oulu, Finland, Jan. 6, 1960 | | | | | |
| 1982-83 | Calgary | 25 | 9 | 3 | 12 |
| **JAMES, Gerald Edwin** *Forward* | | | | | |
| b. Regina, Sask., Oct. 22, 1934 | | | | | |
| 1954-55 | Toronto | 1 | 0 | 0 | 0 |
| 1955-56 | Toronto | 46 | 3 | 3 | 6 |
| 1956-57 | Toronto | 53 | 4 | 12 | 16 |
| 1957-58 | Toronto | 15 | 3 | 2 | 5 |
| 1959-60 | Toronto | 34 | 4 | 9 | 13 |
| | **Totals** | 149 | 14 | 26 | 40 |
| **JAMES, Valmore** *Forward* | | | | | |
| b. Ocala, Fla., Feb. 14, 1957 | | | | | |
| 1981-82 | Buffalo | 7 | 0 | 0 | 0 |
| **JAMIESON, James** *Defenseman* | | | | | |
| b. Brantford, Ont., Mar. 21, 1922 | | | | | |
| 1943-44 | New York R | 1 | 0 | 1 | 1 |
| **JANKOWSKI, Louis Casimer** *Forward* | | | | | |
| b. Regina, Sask., June 27, 1931 | | | | | |
| 1950-51 | Detroit | 1 | 0 | 1 | 1 |
| 1952-53 | Detroit | 22 | 1 | 2 | 3 |
| 1953-54 | Chicago | 68 | 15 | 13 | 28 |
| 1954-55 | Chicago | 36 | 3 | 2 | 5 |
| | **Totals** | 127 | 19 | 18 | 37 |
| **JARRETT, Douglas William** *Defenseman* | | | | | |
| b. London, Ont., Apr. 22, 1944 | | | | | |
| 1964-65 | Chicago | 46 | 2 | 15 | 17 |
| 1965-66 | Chicago | 66 | 4 | 12 | 16 |
| 1966-67 | Chicago | 70 | 5 | 21 | 26 |
| 1967-68 | Chicago | 74 | 4 | 19 | 23 |
| 1968-69 | Chicago | 69 | 0 | 13 | 13 |
| 1969-70 | Chicago | 72 | 4 | 20 | 24 |
| 1970-71 | Chicago | 51 | 1 | 12 | 13 |
| 1971-72 | Chicago | 78 | 6 | 23 | 29 |
| 1972-73 | Chicago | 49 | 2 | 11 | 13 |
| 1973-74 | Chicago | 67 | 5 | 11 | 16 |
| 1974-75 | Chicago | 79 | 5 | 21 | 26 |
| 1975-76 | New York R | 45 | 0 | 4 | 4 |
| 1976-77 | New York R | 9 | 0 | 0 | 0 |
| | **Totals** | 775 | 38 | 182 | 220 |

**JARRETT, Gary Walter** *Forward*
b. Toronto, Ont., Sept. 3, 1942

| Season | Club | GP | G | A | Pts. |
|---|---|---|---|---|---|
| 1960-61 | Toronto | 1 | 0 | 0 | 0 |
| 1966-67 | Detroit | 4 | 0 | 0 | 0 |
| 1967-68 | Detroit | 68 | 18 | 21 | 39 |
| 1968-69 | Oakland | 63 | 22 | 23 | 45 |
| 1969-70 | Oakland | 75 | 12 | 19 | 31 |
| 1970-71 | California | 75 | 15 | 19 | 34 |
| 1971-72 | California | 55 | 5 | 10 | 15 |
| 1972-73 | Cleveland (WHA) | 77 | 40 | 38 | 78 |
| 1973-74 | Cleveland (WHA) | 75 | 31 | 39 | 70 |
| 1974-75 | Cleveland (WHA) | 77 | 17 | 24 | 41 |
| 1975-76 | Cleveland (WHA) | 69 | 16 | 17 | 33 |
| | NHL Totals | 341 | 72 | 92 | 164 |
| | WHA Totals | 298 | 104 | 118 | 222 |

**JARRY, Pierre Joseph Reynald** *Forward*
b. Montreal, Que., Mar. 30, 1949

| Season | Club | GP | G | A | Pts. |
|---|---|---|---|---|---|
| 1971-72 | NYR-Tor | 52 | 6 | 7 | 13 |
| 1972-73 | Toronto | 74 | 19 | 18 | 37 |
| 1973-74 | Tor-Det | 64 | 17 | 31 | 48 |
| 1974-75 | Detroit | 39 | 8 | 13 | 21 |
| 1975-76 | Minnesota | 59 | 21 | 18 | 39 |
| 1976-77 | Minnesota | 21 | 8 | 13 | 21 |
| 1977-78 | Minnesota | 35 | 9 | 17 | 26 |
| | Totals | 344 | 88 | 117 | 205 |

**JARVIS, Douglas** *Forward*
b. Peterborough, Ont., Mar. 24, 1955

| Season | Club | GP | G | A | Pts. |
|---|---|---|---|---|---|
| 1975-76 | Montreal | 80 | 5 | 30 | 35 |
| 1976-77 | Montreal | 80 | 16 | 22 | 38 |
| 1977-78 | Montreal | 80 | 11 | 28 | 39 |
| 1978-79 | Montreal | 80 | 10 | 13 | 23 |
| 1979-80 | Montreal | 80 | 13 | 11 | 24 |
| 1980-81 | Montreal | 80 | 16 | 22 | 38 |
| 1981-82 | Montreal | 80 | 20 | 28 | 48 |
| 1982-83 | Washington | 80 | 8 | 22 | 30 |
| | Totals | 640 | 99 | 176 | 275 |

**JARVIS, James (Bud)** *Forward*
b. Fort William, Ont., Dec. 7, 1907

| Season | Club | GP | G | A | Pts. |
|---|---|---|---|---|---|
| 1929-30 | Pittsburgh Pi | 44 | 11 | 8 | 19 |
| 1930-31 | Philadelphia Q | 44 | 5 | 7 | 12 |
| 1936-37 | Toronto | 24 | 1 | 0 | 1 |
| | Totals | 112 | 17 | 15 | 32 |

**JARVIS, Wesley** *Forward*
b. Toronto, Ont., May 30, 1958

| Season | Club | GP | G | A | Pts. |
|---|---|---|---|---|---|
| 1979-80 | Washington | 63 | 11 | 15 | 26 |
| 1980-81 | Washington | 55 | 9 | 14 | 23 |
| 1981-82 | Washington | 26 | 1 | 12 | 13 |
| 1982-83 | Minnesota | 3 | 0 | 0 | 0 |
| | Totals | 147 | 21 | 41 | 62 |

**JEFFREY, Lawrence Joseph (Larry)** *Forward*
b. Goderich, Ont., Oct. 12, 1940

| Season | Club | GP | G | A | Pts. |
|---|---|---|---|---|---|
| 1961-62 | Detroit | 18 | 5 | 3 | 8 |
| 1962-63 | Detroit | 53 | 5 | 11 | 16 |
| 1963-64 | Detroit | 58 | 10 | 18 | 28 |
| 1964-65 | Detroit | 41 | 4 | 2 | 6 |
| 1965-66 | Toronto | 20 | 1 | 1 | 2 |
| 1966-67 | Toronto | 56 | 11 | 17 | 28 |
| 1967-68 | New York R | 47 | 2 | 4 | 6 |
| 1968-69 | New York R | 75 | 1 | 6 | 7 |
| | Totals | 368 | 39 | 62 | 101 |

**JENKINS, Roger** *Defenseman*
b. Appleton, Wis., Nov. 18, 1911

| Season | Club | GP | G | A | Pts. |
|---|---|---|---|---|---|
| 1930-31 | Chicago | 31 | 0 | 1 | 1 |
| 1932-33 | Chicago | 46 | 3 | 10 | 13 |
| 1933-34 | Chicago | 48 | 2 | 2 | 4 |
| 1934-35 | Montreal | 45 | 4 | 6 | 10 |
| 1935-36 | Boston | 40 | 2 | 6 | 8 |
| 1936-37 | Mont-NYA | 37 | 1 | 4 | 5 |
| 1937-38 | Chicago | 37 | 1 | 8 | 9 |
| 1938-39 | Chi-NYA | 41 | 2 | 2 | 4 |
| | Totals | 325 | 15 | 39 | 54 |

**JENNINGS, Joseph W. (Bill)** *Forward*
b. Toronto, Ont., June 28, 1917

| Season | Club | GP | G | A | Pts. |
|---|---|---|---|---|---|
| 1940-41 | Detroit | 12 | 1 | 5 | 6 |
| 1941-42 | Detroit | 16 | 2 | 1 | 3 |


| Season | Club | GP | G | A | Pts. |
|---|---|---|---|---|---|
| 1942-43 | Detroit | 8 | 3 | 3 | 6 |
| 1943-44 | Detroit | 33 | 6 | 11 | 17 |
| 1944-45 | Boston | 39 | 20 | 13 | 33 |
| | Totals | 108 | 32 | 33 | 65 |

**JENSEN, Steven Allan** *Forward*
b. Minneapolis, Minn., Apr. 14, 1955

| Season | Club | GP | G | A | Pts. |
|---|---|---|---|---|---|
| 1975-76 | Minnesota | 19 | 7 | 6 | 13 |
| 1976-77 | Minnesota | 78 | 22 | 23 | 45 |
| 1977-78 | Minnesota | 74 | 13 | 17 | 30 |
| 1978-79 | Los Angeles | 72 | 23 | 8 | 31 |
| 1979-80 | Los Angeles | 76 | 21 | 15 | 36 |
| 1980-81 | Los Angeles | 74 | 19 | 19 | 38 |
| 1981-82 | Los Angeles | 45 | 8 | 19 | 27 |
| | Totals | 438 | 113 | 107 | 220 |

**JEREMIAH, Edward J.** *Defenseman-Forward*
b. Worcester, Mass., Nov. 4, 1905

| Season | Club | GP | G | A | Pts. |
|---|---|---|---|---|---|
| 1931-32 | NYA-Bos | 8 | 0 | 1 | 1 |

**JERWA, Frank** *Defenseman-Forward*
b. Bankhead, Alta., Feb. 28, 1910

| Season | Club | GP | G | A | Pts. |
|---|---|---|---|---|---|
| 1931-32 | Boston | 28 | 4 | 5 | 9 |
| 1932-33 | Boston | 31 | 3 | 4 | 7 |
| 1933-34 | Boston | 8 | 0 | 0 | 0 |
| | Totals | 67 | 7 | 9 | 16 |

**JERWA, Joseph** *Defenseman*
b. Bankhead, Alta., Jan. 20, 1908

| Season | Club | GP | G | A | Pts. |
|---|---|---|---|---|---|
| 1930-31 | New York R | 33 | 4 | 7 | 11 |
| 1931-32 | Boston | 12 | 0 | 0 | 0 |
| 1934-35 | Bos-StL | 21 | 4 | 7 | 11 |
| 1935-36 | New York A | 47 | 9 | 12 | 21 |
| 1936-37 | Bos-NYA | 46 | 9 | 13 | 22 |
| 1937-38 | New York A | 48 | 3 | 14 | 17 |
| 1938-39 | New York A | 47 | 4 | 12 | 16 |
| | Totals | 254 | 33 | 65 | 98 |

**JIRIK, Jaroslav** *Forward*
b. Vojnuv, Mestac, Czechoslovakia, Dec. 10, 1939

| Season | Club | GP | G | A | Pts. |
|---|---|---|---|---|---|
| 1969-70 | St Louis | 3 | 0 | 0 | 0 |

**JOANETTE, Rosario (Kit)** *Forward*
b. Valleyfield, Que., Aug. 27, 1915

| Season | Club | GP | G | A | Pts. |
|---|---|---|---|---|---|
| 1944-45 | Montreal | 2 | 0 | 1 | 1 |

**JODZIO, Richard Joseph** *Forward*
b. Edmonton, Alta., June 3, 1954

| Season | Club | GP | G | A | Pts. |
|---|---|---|---|---|---|
| 1974-75 | Vancouver (WHA) | 44 | 1 | 3 | 4 |
| 1975-76 | Calgary (WHA) | 47 | 10 | 7 | 17 |
| 1976-77 | Calgary (WHA) | 46 | 4 | 6 | 10 |
| 1977-78 | Col-Clev | 70 | 2 | 8 | 10 |
| | NHL Totals | 70 | 2 | 8 | 10 |
| | WHA Totals | 137 | 15 | 16 | 31 |

**JOHANSEN, Trevor Daniel** *Defenseman*
b. Thunder Bay, Ont., Mar. 30, 1957

| Season | Club | GP | G | A | Pts. |
|---|---|---|---|---|---|
| 1977-78 | Toronto | 79 | 2 | 14 | 16 |
| 1978-79 | Tor-Col | 51 | 2 | 7 | 9 |
| 1979-80 | Colorado | 62 | 3 | 8 | 11 |
| 1980-81 | Colorado | 35 | 0 | 7 | 7 |
| 1981-82 | LA-Tor | 59 | 4 | 10 | 14 |
| | Totals | 286 | 11 | 46 | 57 |

**JOHANSSON, Bjorn** *Defenseman*
b. Orebo, Sweden, Jan. 15, 1956

| Season | Club | GP | G | A | Pts. |
|---|---|---|---|---|---|
| 1976-77 | Cleveland | 10 | 1 | 1 | 2 |
| 1977-78 | Cleveland | 5 | 0 | 0 | 0 |
| | Totals | 15 | 1 | 1 | 2 |

**JOHNS, Donald Ernest** *Defenseman*
b. St. George, Ont., Dec. 13, 1937

| Season | Club | GP | G | A | Pts. |
|---|---|---|---|---|---|
| 1960-61 | New York R | 63 | 1 | 7 | 8 |
| 1962-63 | New York R | 6 | 0 | 4 | 4 |
| 1963-64 | New York R | 57 | 1 | 9 | 10 |
| 1964-65 | New York R | 22 | 0 | 1 | 1 |
| 1965-66 | Montreal | 1 | 0 | 0 | 0 |
| 1967-68 | Minnesota | 4 | 0 | 0 | 0 |
| | Totals | 153 | 2 | 21 | 23 |


**JOHNSON, Allan Edmund** *Forward*
b. Winnipeg, Man., Mar. 30, 1935

| Season | Club | GP | G | A | Pts. |
|---|---|---|---|---|---|
| 1956-57 | Montreal | 2 | 0 | 1 | 1 |
| 1960-61 | Detroit | 70 | 16 | 21 | 37 |
| 1961-62 | Detroit | 31 | 5 | 6 | 11 |
| 1962-63 | Detroit | 2 | 0 | 0 | 0 |
| | Totals | 105 | 21 | 28 | 49 |

**JOHNSON, Daniel Douglas**
b. Winnipegosis, Man., Oct. 1, 1944

| Season | Club | GP | G | A | Pts. |
|---|---|---|---|---|---|
| 1969-70 | Toronto | 1 | 0 | 0 | 0 |
| 1970-71 | Vancouver | 66 | 15 | 11 | 26 |
| 1971-72 | Det-Van | 54 | 3 | 8 | 11 |
| 1972-73 | Winnipeg (WHA) | 77 | 19 | 23 | 42 |
| 1973-74 | Winnipeg (WHA) | 78 | 16 | 21 | 37 |
| 1974-75 | Winnipeg (WHA) | 78 | 18 | 14 | 32 |
| | NHL Totals | 121 | 18 | 19 | 37 |
| | WHA Totals | 233 | 53 | 58 | 111 |

**JOHNSON, Earl O.** *Forward*
b. Fort Francis, Ont., June 28, 1931

| Season | Club | GP | G | A | Pts. |
|---|---|---|---|---|---|
| 1953-54 | Detroit | 1 | 0 | 0 | 0 |

**JOHNSON, Ivan Wilfred (Ching)** *Defenseman*
b. Winnipeg, Man., Dec. 7, 1897

| Season | Club | GP | G | A | Pts. |
|---|---|---|---|---|---|
| 1926-27 | New York R | 27 | 3 | 2 | 5 |
| 1927-28 | New York R | 43 | 10 | 6 | 16 |
| 1928-29 | New York R | 9 | 0 | 3 | 6 |
| 1929-30 | New York R | 30 | 3 | 3 | 6 |
| 1930-31 | New York R | 44 | 2 | 6 | 8 |
| 1931-32 | New York R | 47 | 3 | 10 | 13 |
| 1932-33 | New York R | 48 | 8 | 9 | 17 |
| 1933-34 | New York R | 48 | 2 | 6 | 8 |
| 1934-35 | New York R | 26 | 2 | 3 | 5 |
| 1935-36 | New York R | 47 | 5 | 3 | 8 |
| 1936-37 | New York R | 34 | 0 | 0 | 0 |
| 1937-38 | New York A | — | 0 | 0 | 0 |
| | Totals | — | 38 | 48 | 86 |

**JOHNSON, Mark** *Forward*
b. Madison, Wis., Sept. 22, 1957

| Season | Club | GP | G | A | Pts. |
|---|---|---|---|---|---|
| 1979-80 | Pittsburgh | 17 | 3 | 5 | 8 |
| 1980-81 | Pittsburgh | 73 | 10 | 23 | 33 |
| 1981-82 | Pitt-Minn | 56 | 12 | 13 | 25 |
| 1982-83 | Hartford | 73 | 31 | 38 | 69 |
| | Totals | 219 | 56 | 79 | 135 |

**JOHNSON, Norman B.** *Forward*
b. Moose Jaw, Sask., Nov. 27, 1932

| Season | Club | GP | G | A | Pts. |
|---|---|---|---|---|---|
| 1957-58 | Boston | 15 | 2 | 3 | 5 |
| 1958-59 | Bos-Chi | 46 | 3 | 17 | 20 |
| | Totals | 61 | 5 | 20 | 25 |

**JOHNSON, Norman James (Jim)** *Forward*
b. Winnipeg, Man., Nov. 7, 1942

| Season | Club | GP | G | A | Pts. |
|---|---|---|---|---|---|
| 1964-65 | New York R | 1 | 0 | 0 | 0 |
| 1965-66 | New York R | 5 | 1 | 0 | 1 |
| 1966-67 | New York R | 2 | 0 | 0 | 0 |
| 1967-68 | Philadelphia | 13 | 2 | 1 | 3 |
| 1968-69 | Philadelphia | 69 | 17 | 27 | 44 |
| 1969-70 | Philadelphia | 72 | 18 | 30 | 48 |
| 1970-71 | Philadelphia | 66 | 16 | 29 | 45 |
| 1971-72 | Phil-LA | 76 | 21 | 24 | 45 |
| 1972-73 | Minnesota (WHA) | 33 | 9 | 14 | 23 |
| 1973-74 | Minnesota (WHA) | 71 | 15 | 39 | 54 |
| 1974-75 | Minnesota (WHA) | 11 | 1 | 3 | 4 |
| | NHL Totals | 302 | 75 | 111 | 186 |
| | WHA Totals | 115 | 25 | 56 | 81 |

**JOHNSON, Terrance** *Defenseman*
b. Calgary, Alta., Nov. 28, 1958

| Season | Club | GP | G | A | Pts. |
|---|---|---|---|---|---|
| 1979-80 | Quebec | 3 | 0 | 0 | 0 |
| 1980-81 | Quebec | 13 | 0 | 1 | 1 |
| 1981-82 | Quebec | 6 | 0 | 1 | 1 |
| 1982-83 | Quebec | 3 | 0 | 0 | 0 |
| | Totals | 25 | 0 | 2 | 2 |

**JOHNSON, Thomas Christian** *Defenseman*
b. Baldur, Man., Feb. 18, 1928

| Season | Club | GP | G | A | Pts. |
|---|---|---|---|---|---|
| 1947-48 | Montreal | 1 | 0 | 0 | 0 |
| 1950-51 | Montreal | 70 | 2 | 8 | 10 |

| Season | Club | GP | G | A | Pts. |
|---|---|---|---|---|---|
| 1951-52 | Montreal | 67 | 0 | 7 | 7 |
| 1952-53 | Montreal | 70 | 3 | 8 | 11 |
| 1953-54 | Montreal | 70 | 7 | 11 | 18 |
| 1954-55 | Montreal | 70 | 6 | 19 | 25 |
| 1955-56 | Montreal | 64 | 3 | 10 | 13 |
| 1956-57 | Montreal | 70 | 4 | 11 | 15 |
| 1957-58 | Montreal | 66 | 8 | 13 | 21 |
| 1958-59 | Montreal | 70 | 10 | 29 | 39 |
| 1959-60 | Montreal | 64 | 4 | 25 | 29 |
| 1960-61 | Montreal | 70 | 1 | 15 | 16 |
| 1961-62 | Montreal | 62 | 1 | 18 | 19 |
| 1962-63 | Montreal | 43 | 3 | 5 | 8 |
| 1963-64 | Boston | 70 | 4 | 21 | 25 |
| 1964-65 | Boston | 51 | 0 | 9 | 9 |
| **Totals** | | 978 | 56 | 209 | 265 |

**JOHNSON, Virgil** *Defenseman*
b. Minneapolis, Minn., Mar. 4, 1912

| Season | Club | GP | G | A | Pts. |
|---|---|---|---|---|---|
| 1937-38 | Chicago | 25 | 1 | 0 | 1 |
| 1943-44 | Chicago | 48 | 1 | 8 | 9 |
| 1944-45 | Chicago | 2 | 0 | 1 | 1 |
| **Totals** | | 75 | 2 | 9 | 11 |

**JOHNSON, William** *Forward*
b. Winnipeg, Man., Apr. 16, 1928

| Season | Club | GP | G | A | Pts. |
|---|---|---|---|---|---|
| 1949-50 | Toronto | 1 | 0 | 0 | 0 |

**JOHNSTON, Bernard** *Forward*
b. Toronto, Ont., Sept. 15, 1956

| Season | Club | GP | G | A | Pts. |
|---|---|---|---|---|---|
| 1979-80 | Hartford | 32 | 8 | 13 | 21 |
| 1980-81 | Hartford | 25 | 4 | 11 | 15 |
| **Totals** | | 57 | 12 | 24 | 36 |

**JOHNSTON, George Joseph (Wingy)**
*Forward*
b. St. Charles, Man., July 30, 1920

| Season | Club | GP | G | A | Pts. |
|---|---|---|---|---|---|
| 1941-42 | Chicago | 2 | 2 | 0 | 2 |
| 1942-43 | Chicago | 30 | 10 | 7 | 17 |
| 1945-46 | Chicago | 16 | 5 | 4 | 9 |
| 1946-47 | Colorado | 10 | 3 | 1 | 4 |
| **Totals** | | 58 | 20 | 12 | 32 |

**JOHNSTON, John** *Defenseman*
b. Hamilton, Ont., Feb. 28, 1958

| Season | Club | GP | G | A | Pts. |
|---|---|---|---|---|---|
| 1980-81 | Washington | 2 | 0 | 0 | 0 |
| 1981-82 | Washington | 6 | 0 | 0 | 0 |
| **Totals** | | 8 | 0 | 0 | 0 |

**JOHNSTON, Joseph John (Joey)** *Forward*
b. Peterborough, Ont., Mar. 3, 1949

| Season | Club | GP | G | A | Pts. |
|---|---|---|---|---|---|
| 1968-69 | Minnesota | 12 | 1 | 0 | 1 |
| 1971-72 | California | 77 | 15 | 17 | 32 |
| 1972-73 | California | 71 | 28 | 21 | 49 |
| 1973-74 | California | 78 | 27 | 40 | 67 |
| 1974-75 | California | 62 | 14 | 23 | 37 |
| 1975-76 | Chicago | 32 | 0 | 5 | 5 |
| **Totals** | | 332 | 85 | 106 | 191 |

**JOHNSTON, Larry Marshall** *Forward*
b. Birch Hills, Sask., June 6, 1941

| Season | Club | GP | G | A | Pts. |
|---|---|---|---|---|---|
| 1967-68 | Minnesota | 7 | 0 | 0 | 0 |
| 1968-69 | Minnesota | 13 | 0 | 0 | 0 |
| 1969-70 | Minnesota | 28 | 0 | 5 | 5 |
| 1970-71 | California | 1 | 0 | 0 | 0 |
| 1971-72 | California | 74 | 2 | 11 | 13 |
| 1972-73 | California | 78 | 10 | 20 | 30 |
| 1973-74 | California | 50 | 2 | 16 | 18 |
| **Totals** | | 251 | 14 | 52 | 66 |

**JOHNSTON, Lawrence Roy** *Defenseman*
b. Kitchener, Ont., July 20, 1943

| Season | Club | GP | G | A | Pts. |
|---|---|---|---|---|---|
| 1967-68 | Los Angeles | 4 | 0 | 0 | 0 |
| 1971-72 | Detroit | 65 | 4 | 20 | 24 |
| 1972-73 | Detroit | 73 | 1 | 12 | 13 |
| 1973-74 | Detroit | 65 | 2 | 12 | 14 |
| 1974-75 | Michigan (WHA) | 49 | 0 | 9 | 9 |
| 1974-75 | Kansas City | 16 | 0 | 7 | 7 |
| 1975-76 | Kansas City | 72 | 2 | 10 | 12 |
| 1976-77 | Colorado | 25 | 0 | 3 | 3 |
| **NHL Totals** | | 320 | 9 | 64 | 73 |
| **WHA Totals** | | 49 | 0 | 9 | 9 |

**JOHNSTON, Randy John** *Defenseman*
b. Brampton, Ont., June 2, 1958

| Season | Club | GP | G | A | Pts. |
|---|---|---|---|---|---|
| 1979-80 | New York I | 4 | 0 | 0 | 0 |

**JOHNSTONE, Edward Lavern** *Forward*
b. Brandon, Man., Mar. 2, 1954

| Season | Club | GP | G | A | Pts. |
|---|---|---|---|---|---|
| 1974-75 | Michigan (WHA) | 23 | 4 | 4 | 8 |
| 1975-76 | New York R | 10 | 2 | 1 | 3 |
| 1977-78 | New York R | 53 | 13 | 13 | 26 |
| 1978-79 | New York R | 30 | 5 | 3 | 8 |
| 1979-80 | New York R | 78 | 14 | 21 | 35 |
| 1980-81 | New York R | 80 | 30 | 38 | 68 |
| 1981-82 | New York R | 68 | 30 | 28 | 58 |
| 1982-83 | New York R | 52 | 15 | 21 | 36 |
| **NHL Totals** | | 371 | 109 | 125 | 234 |
| **WHA Totals** | | 23 | 4 | 4 | 8 |

**JOHNSTONE, Robert Ross** *Defenseman*
b. Montreal, Que., Apr. 7, 1926

| Season | Club | GP | G | A | Pts. |
|---|---|---|---|---|---|
| 1943-44 | Toronto | 18 | 2 | 0 | 2 |
| 1944-45 | Toronto | 24 | 3 | 4 | 7 |
| **Totals** | | 42 | 5 | 4 | 9 |

**JOLIAT, Aurel Emile** *Forward*
b. Ottawa, Ont., Aug. 29, 1901

| Season | Club | GP | G | A | Pts. |
|---|---|---|---|---|---|
| 1922-23 | Montreal | 24 | 13 | 9 | 22 |
| 1923-24 | Montreal | 24 | 15 | 5 | 20 |
| 1924-25 | Montreal | 24 | 29 | 11 | 40 |
| 1925-26 | Montreal | 35 | 17 | 9 | 26 |
| 1926-27 | Montreal | 43 | 14 | 4 | 18 |
| 1927-28 | Montreal | 44 | 28 | 11 | 39 |
| 1928-29 | Montreal | 44 | 12 | 5 | 17 |
| 1929-30 | Montreal | 42 | 19 | 12 | 31 |
| 1930-31 | Montreal | 43 | 13 | 22 | 35 |
| 1931-32 | Montreal | 48 | 15 | 24 | 39 |
| 1932-33 | Montreal | 48 | 18 | 21 | 39 |
| 1933-34 | Montreal | 48 | 22 | 15 | 37 |
| 1934-35 | Montreal | 48 | 17 | 12 | 29 |
| 1935-36 | Montreal | 48 | 15 | 8 | 23 |
| 1936-37 | Montreal | 47 | 17 | 15 | 32 |
| 1937-38 | Montreal | 44 | 6 | 7 | 13 |
| **Totals** | | 654 | 270 | 190 | 460 |

**JOLIAT, Rene (Bobby)** *Forward*

| Season | Club | GP | G | A | Pts. |
|---|---|---|---|---|---|
| 1924-25 | Montreal | 1 | 0 | 0 | 0 |

**JOLY, Gregory James** *Defenseman*
b. Calgary, Alta., May 30, 1954

| Season | Club | GP | G | A | Pts. |
|---|---|---|---|---|---|
| 1974-75 | Washington | 44 | 1 | 7 | 8 |
| 1975-76 | Washington | 54 | 8 | 17 | 25 |
| 1976-77 | Detroit | 53 | 1 | 11 | 12 |
| 1977-78 | Detroit | 79 | 7 | 20 | 27 |
| 1978-79 | Detroit | 20 | 0 | 4 | 4 |
| 1979-80 | Detroit | 59 | 3 | 10 | 13 |
| 1980-81 | Detroit | 17 | 0 | 2 | 2 |
| 1981-82 | Detroit | 37 | 1 | 5 | 6 |
| 1982-83 | Detroit | 2 | 0 | 0 | 0 |
| **Totals** | | 365 | 21 | 76 | 97 |

**JOLY, Yvan Rene** *Forward*
b. Hawkesbury, Ont., Feb. 6, 1960

| Season | Club | GP | G | A | Pts. |
|---|---|---|---|---|---|
| 1980-81 | Montreal | 1 | 0 | 0 | 0 |
| 1982-83 | Montreal | 1 | 0 | 0 | 0 |
| **Totals** | | 2 | 0 | 0 | 0 |

**JONATHAN, Stanley Carl** *Forward*
b. Oshweken, Ont., Sept. 5, 1955

| Season | Club | GP | G | A | Pts. |
|---|---|---|---|---|---|
| 1975-76 | Boston | 1 | 0 | 0 | 0 |
| 1976-77 | Boston | 69 | 17 | 13 | 30 |
| 1977-78 | Boston | 68 | 27 | 25 | 52 |
| 1978-79 | Boston | 33 | 6 | 9 | 15 |
| 1979-80 | Boston | 79 | 21 | 19 | 40 |
| 1980-81 | Boston | 74 | 14 | 24 | 38 |
| 1981-82 | Boston | 67 | 6 | 17 | 23 |
| 1982-83 | Bos-Pitt | 20 | 0 | 3 | 3 |
| **Totals** | | 411 | 91 | 110 | 201 |

**JONES, Alvin Bernard (Buck)** *Defenseman*
b. Owen Sound, Ont., Aug. 17, 1919

| Season | Club | GP | G | A | Pts. |
|---|---|---|---|---|---|
| 1938-39 | Detroit | 11 | 0 | 1 | 1 |
| 1939-40 | Detroit | 2 | 0 | 0 | 0 |
| 1941-42 | Detroit | 21 | 2 | 1 | 3 |
| 1942-43 | Toronto | 16 | 0 | 0 | 0 |
| **Totals** | | 50 | 2 | 2 | 4 |

**JONES, James Harrison** *Forward*
b. Woodbridge, Ont., Jan. 2, 1953

| Season | Club | GP | G | A | Pts. |
|---|---|---|---|---|---|
| 1973-74 | Vancouver (WHA) | 18 | 3 | 2 | 5 |
| 1974-75 | Vancouver (WHA) | 63 | 11 | 7 | 18 |
| 1977-78 | Toronto | 78 | 4 | 9 | 13 |
| 1978-79 | Toronto | 69 | 9 | 9 | 18 |
| 1979-80 | Toronto | 1 | 0 | 0 | 0 |
| **NHL Totals** | | 148 | 13 | 18 | 31 |
| **WHA Totals** | | 81 | 14 | 9 | 23 |

**JONES, James William (Jim)** *Defenseman*
b. Espanola, Ont., July 27, 1949

| Season | Club | GP | G | A | Pts. |
|---|---|---|---|---|---|
| 1971-72 | California | 2 | 0 | 0 | 0 |

**JONES, Robert Charles** *Forward*
b. Espanola, Ont., Nov. 27, 1945

| Season | Club | GP | G | A | Pts. |
|---|---|---|---|---|---|
| 1968-69 | New York R | 2 | 0 | 0 | 0 |
| 1972-73 | LA-NY (WHA) | 76 | 13 | 19 | 32 |
| 1973-74 | New Jersey (WHA) | 78 | 17 | 28 | 45 |
| 1974-75 | Baltimore (WHA) | 5 | 0 | 1 | 1 |
| 1975-76 | Indianapolis (WHA) | 2 | 0 | 0 | 0 |
| **NHL Totals** | | 2 | 0 | 0 | 0 |
| **WHA Totals** | | 161 | 30 | 48 | 78 |

**JONES, Ronald Perry (Ron)** *Defenseman*
b. Vermillion, Alta., Apr. 11, 1951

| Season | Club | GP | G | A | Pts. |
|---|---|---|---|---|---|
| 1971-72 | Boston | 1 | 0 | 0 | 0 |
| 1972-73 | Boston | 7 | 0 | 0 | 0 |
| 1973-74 | Pittsburgh | 25 | 0 | 3 | 3 |
| 1974-75 | Washington | 19 | 1 | 1 | 2 |
| 1975-76 | Washington | 2 | 0 | 0 | 0 |
| **Totals** | | 54 | 1 | 4 | 5 |

**JONSSON, Tomas** *Defenseman*
b. Falun, Sweden, Apr. 12, 1960

| Season | Club | GP | G | A | Pts. |
|---|---|---|---|---|---|
| 1981-82 | New York I | 70 | 9 | 25 | 34 |
| 1982-83 | New York I | 72 | 13 | 35 | 48 |
| **Totals** | | 142 | 22 | 60 | 82 |

**JOYAL, Edward Abel** *Forward*
b. Edmonton, Alta., May 8, 1940

| Season | Club | GP | G | A | Pts. |
|---|---|---|---|---|---|
| 1962-63 | Detroit | 14 | 2 | 8 | 10 |
| 1963-64 | Detroit | 47 | 10 | 7 | 17 |
| 1964-65 | Detroit | 46 | 8 | 14 | 22 |
| 1965-66 | Toronto | 14 | 0 | 2 | 2 |
| 1967-68 | Los Angeles | 74 | 23 | 34 | 57 |
| 1968-69 | Los Angeles | 73 | 33 | 19 | 52 |
| 1969-70 | Los Angeles | 59 | 18 | 22 | 40 |
| 1970-71 | Los Angeles | 69 | 20 | 21 | 41 |
| 1971-72 | LA-Phil | 70 | 14 | 7 | 21 |
| 1972-73 | Alberta (WHA) | 71 | 22 | 16 | 38 |
| 1973-74 | Edmonton (WHA) | 45 | 8 | 10 | 18 |
| 1974-75 | Edmonton (WHA) | 78 | 22 | 25 | 47 |
| **NHL Totals** | | 466 | 128 | 134 | 262 |
| **WHA Totals** | | 194 | 52 | 51 | 103 |

**JUCKES, Winston Bryan (Bing)** *Forward*
b. Hamiota, Man., June 14, 1926

| Season | Club | GP | G | A | Pts. |
|---|---|---|---|---|---|
| 1947-48 | New York R | 2 | 0 | 0 | 0 |
| 1949-50 | New York R | 14 | 2 | 1 | 3 |
| **Totals** | | 16 | 2 | 1 | 3 |

**JUZDA, William** *Defenseman*
b. Winnipeg, Man., Oct. 29, 1920

| Season | Club | GP | G | A | Pts. |
|---|---|---|---|---|---|
| 1940-41 | New York R | 5 | 0 | 0 | 0 |
| 1941-42 | New York R | 45 | 4 | 8 | 12 |
| 1945-46 | New York R | 32 | 1 | 3 | 4 |
| 1946-47 | New York R | 45 | 3 | 5 | 8 |
| 1947-48 | New York R | 60 | 3 | 9 | 12 |
| 1948-49 | Toronto | 38 | 1 | 2 | 3 |
| 1949-50 | Toronto | 62 | 1 | 14 | 15 |
| 1950-51 | Toronto | 65 | 0 | 9 | 9 |
| 1951-52 | Toronto | 46 | 1 | 4 | 5 |
| **Totals** | | 398 | 14 | 54 | 68 |

| Season | Club | GP | G | A | Pts. |
|---|---|---|---|---|---|

**KABEL, Robert Gerald** *Forward*
b. Dauphin, Man., Nov. 11, 1934

| Season | Club | GP | G | A | Pts. |
|---|---|---|---|---|---|
| 1959-60 | New York R | 44 | 5 | 11 | 16 |
| 1960-61 | New York R | 4 | 0 | 2 | 2 |
| | Totals | 48 | 5 | 13 | 18 |

**KACHUR, Edward Charles** *Forward*
b. Fort William, Ont., Apr. 22, 1934

| Season | Club | GP | G | A | Pts. |
|---|---|---|---|---|---|
| 1956-57 | Chicago | 34 | 5 | 7 | 12 |
| 1957-58 | Chicago | 62 | 5 | 7 | 12 |
| | Totals | 96 | 10 | 14 | 24 |

**KAISER, Vernon Charles** *Forward*
b. Preston, Ont., Sept. 28, 1925

| Season | Club | GP | G | A | Pts. |
|---|---|---|---|---|---|
| 1950-51 | Montreal | 50 | 7 | 5 | 12 |

**KALBFLIESH, Walter (Jeff)** *Defenseman*
b. New Hamberg, Ont., Dec. 18, 1911

| Season | Club | GP | G | A | Pts. |
|---|---|---|---|---|---|
| 1933-34 | Ottawa | 23 | 0 | 4 | 4 |
| 1934-35 | St Louis E | 3 | 0 | 0 | 0 |
| 1935-36 | New York A | 4 | 0 | 0 | 0 |
| 1936-37 | New York A | 6 | 0 | 0 | 0 |
| | Totals | 36 | 0 | 4 | 4 |

**KALETA, Alexander (Killer)** *Forward*
b. Canmore, Alta., Nov. 29, 1919

| Season | Club | GP | G | A | Pts. |
|---|---|---|---|---|---|
| 1941-42 | Chicago | 48 | 7 | 21 | 28 |
| 1945-46 | Chicago | 49 | 19 | 27 | 46 |
| 1946-47 | Chicago | 57 | 24 | 20 | 44 |
| 1947-48 | Chicago | 52 | 10 | 16 | 26 |
| 1948-49 | New York R | 56 | 12 | 19 | 31 |
| 1949-50 | New York R | 67 | 17 | 14 | 31 |
| 1950-51 | New York R | 58 | 3 | 4 | 7 |
| | Totals | 387 | 92 | 121 | 213 |

**KALLUR, Anders** *Forward*
b. Ludrika, Sweden, July 6, 1952

| Season | Club | GP | G | A | Pts. |
|---|---|---|---|---|---|
| 1979-80 | New York I | 76 | 22 | 30 | 52 |
| 1980-81 | New York I | 78 | 36 | 28 | 64 |
| 1981-82 | New York I | 58 | 18 | 22 | 40 |
| 1982-83 | New York I | 55 | 6 | 8 | 14 |
| | Totals | 267 | 82 | 88 | 170 |

**KAMINSKY, Max** *Forward*
b. Niagara Falls, Ont., Apr. 19, 1913

| Season | Club | GP | G | A | Pts. |
|---|---|---|---|---|---|
| 1933-34 | Ottawa | 38 | 9 | 17 | 26 |
| 1934-35 | Boston | 50 | 12 | 15 | 27 |
| 1935-36 | Boston | 36 | 1 | 2 | 3 |
| 1936-37 | Montreal | 6 | 0 | 0 | 0 |
| | Totals | 130 | 22 | 34 | 56 |

**KAMPMAN, Rudolph (Bingo)** *Defenseman*
b. Kitchener, Ont., Mar. 12, 1914

| Season | Club | GP | G | A | Pts. |
|---|---|---|---|---|---|
| 1937-38 | Toronto | 32 | 1 | 2 | 3 |
| 1938-39 | Toronto | 41 | 2 | 8 | 10 |
| 1939-40 | Toronto | 39 | 6 | 9 | 15 |
| 1940-41 | Toronto | 38 | 1 | 4 | 5 |
| 1941-42 | Toronto | 38 | 4 | 7 | 11 |
| | Totals | 189 | 14 | 30 | 44 |

**KANE, Francis Joseph** *Defenseman*
b. Stratford, Ont., Jan. 19, 1924

| Season | Club | GP | G | A | Pts. |
|---|---|---|---|---|---|
| 1943-44 | Detroit | 2 | 0 | 0 | 0 |

**KANNEGIESSER, Gordon Cameron (Gord)**
*Defenseman*
b. North Bay, Ont., Dec. 21, 1945

| Season | Club | GP | G | A | Pts. |
|---|---|---|---|---|---|
| 1967-68 | St Louis | 19 | 0 | 1 | 1 |
| 1971-72 | St Louis | 4 | 0 | 0 | 0 |
| 1972-73 | Houston (WHA) | 45 | 0 | 10 | 10 |
| | NHL Totals | 23 | 0 | 1 | 1 |
| | WHA Totals | 45 | 0 | 10 | 10 |

**KANNEGIESSER, Sheldon Bruce**
*Defenseman*
b. North Bay, Ont., Aug. 15, 1947

| Season | Club | GP | G | A | Pts. |
|---|---|---|---|---|---|
| 1970-71 | Pittsburgh | 18 | 0 | 2 | 2 |
| 1971-72 | Pittsburgh | 54 | 2 | 4 | 6 |

| Season | Club | GP | G | A | Pts. |
|---|---|---|---|---|---|
| 1972-73 | Pitt-NYR | 6 | 0 | 1 | 1 |
| 1973-74 | NYR-LA | 63 | 4 | 20 | 24 |
| 1974-75 | Los Angeles | 74 | 2 | 23 | 25 |
| 1975-76 | Los Angeles | 70 | 4 | 9 | 13 |
| 1976-77 | Los Angeles | 39 | 1 | 1 | 2 |
| 1977-78 | Vancouver | 42 | 1 | 7 | 8 |
| | Totals | 366 | 14 | 67 | 81 |

**KARLANDER, Allan David (Al)** *Forward*
b. Lac la Hache, B.C., Nov. 5, 1946

| Season | Club | GP | G | A | Pts. |
|---|---|---|---|---|---|
| 1969-70 | Detroit | 41 | 5 | 10 | 15 |
| 1970-71 | Detroit | 23 | 1 | 4 | 5 |
| 1971-72 | Detroit | 71 | 15 | 20 | 35 |
| 1972-73 | Detroit | 77 | 15 | 22 | 37 |
| 1973-74 | New England (WHA) | 77 | 20 | 41 | 61 |
| 1974-75 | New England (WHA) | 51 | 7 | 14 | 21 |
| 1975-76 | Indianapolis (WHA) | 79 | 19 | 26 | 45 |
| 1976-77 | Indianapolis (WHA) | 65 | 17 | 28 | 45 |
| | NHL Totals | 212 | 36 | 56 | 92 |
| | WHA Totals | 272 | 63 | 109 | 172 |

**KASPER, Stephen Neil** *Forward*
b. Montreal, Que., Sept. 28, 1961

| Season | Club | GP | G | A | Pts. |
|---|---|---|---|---|---|
| 1980-81 | Boston | 76 | 21 | 35 | 56 |
| 1981-82 | Boston | 73 | 20 | 31 | 51 |
| 1982-83 | Boston | 24 | 2 | 6 | 8 |
| | Totals | 173 | 43 | 72 | 115 |

**KASZYCKI, Michael** *Forward*
b. Milton, Ont., Feb. 27, 1956

| Season | Club | GP | G | A | Pts. |
|---|---|---|---|---|---|
| 1977-78 | New York I | 58 | 13 | 29 | 42 |
| 1978-79 | New York I | 71 | 16 | 18 | 34 |
| 1979-80 | NYI-Wash-Tor | 69 | 12 | 18 | 30 |
| 1980-81 | Toronto | 6 | 0 | 2 | 2 |
| 1982-83 | Toronto | 22 | 1 | 13 | 14 |
| | Totals | 226 | 42 | 80 | 122 |

**KEA, Adrian Joseph (Ed)** *Defenseman*
b. Weesp, Holland, Jan. 19, 1948

| Season | Club | GP | G | A | Pts. |
|---|---|---|---|---|---|
| 1973-74 | Atlanta | 3 | 0 | 2 | 2 |
| 1974-75 | Atlanta | 50 | 1 | 9 | 10 |
| 1975-76 | Atlanta | 78 | 8 | 19 | 27 |
| 1976-77 | Atlanta | 72 | 4 | 21 | 25 |
| 1977-78 | Atlanta | 60 | 3 | 23 | 26 |
| 1978-79 | Atlanta | 53 | 6 | 18 | 24 |
| 1979-80 | St Louis | 69 | 3 | 16 | 19 |
| 1980-81 | St Louis | 74 | 3 | 18 | 21 |
| 1981-82 | St Louis | 78 | 2 | 14 | 16 |
| 1982-83 | St Louis | 46 | 0 | 5 | 5 |
| | Totals | 583 | 30 | 145 | 175 |

**KEARNS, Dennis McAleer** *Defenseman*
b. Kingston, Ont., Sept. 27, 1945

| Season | Club | GP | G | A | Pts. |
|---|---|---|---|---|---|
| 1971-72 | Vancouver | 73 | 3 | 26 | 29 |
| 1972-73 | Vancouver | 72 | 4 | 33 | 37 |
| 1973-74 | Vancouver | 52 | 4 | 13 | 17 |
| 1974-75 | Vancouver | 49 | 1 | 11 | 12 |
| 1975-76 | Vancouver | 80 | 5 | 46 | 51 |
| 1976-77 | Vancouver | 80 | 5 | 55 | 60 |
| 1977-78 | Vancouver | 80 | 4 | 43 | 47 |
| 1978-79 | Vancouver | 78 | 3 | 31 | 34 |
| 1979-80 | Vancouver | 67 | 1 | 18 | 19 |
| 1980-81 | Vancouver | 46 | 1 | 14 | 15 |
| | Totals | 677 | 31 | 290 | 321 |

**KEATING, John R. (Jack)** *Forward*
b. Newcastle, N.B.

| Season | Club | GP | G | A | Pts. |
|---|---|---|---|---|---|
| 1931-32 | New York A | 22 | 5 | 3 | 8 |
| 1932-33 | New York A | 13 | 0 | 2 | 2 |
| | Totals | 35 | 5 | 5 | 10 |

**KEATING, John Thomas** *Forward*
b. Kitchener, Ont., Oct. 9, 1916

| Season | Club | GP | G | A | Pts. |
|---|---|---|---|---|---|
| 1938-39 | Detroit | 1 | 1 | 0 | 1 |
| 1939-40 | Detroit | 11 | 2 | 0 | 2 |
| | Totals | 12 | 3 | 0 | 3 |

**KEATING, Mike** *Forward*
b. Toronto, Ont., Jan 21, 1957

| Season | Club | GP | G | A | Pts. |
|---|---|---|---|---|---|
| 1977-78 | New York R | 1 | 0 | 0 | 0 |

**KEATS, Gordon (Duke)** *Forward*
b. Montreal, Que., Mar. 1, 1895

| Season | Club | GP | G | A | Pts. |
|---|---|---|---|---|---|
| 1926-27 | Bos-Det | 42 | 16 | 8 | 24 |
| 1927-28 | Det-Chi | 38 | 14 | 10 | 24 |
| 1928-29 | Chicago | 3 | 0 | 1 | 1 |
| | Totals | 83 | 30 | 19 | 49 |

**KEELING, Melville, Sidney (Butch)** *Forward*
b. Owen Sound, Ont., Aug. 10, 1905

| Season | Club | GP | G | A | Pts. |
|---|---|---|---|---|---|
| 1926-27 | Toronto | 30 | 11 | 2 | 13 |
| 1927-28 | Toronto | 41 | 10 | 6 | 16 |
| 1928-29 | New York R | 43 | 6 | 3 | 9 |
| 1929-30 | New York R | 44 | 19 | 7 | 26 |
| 1930-31 | New York R | 44 | 13 | 9 | 22 |
| 1931-32 | New York R | 48 | 17 | 3 | 20 |
| 1932-33 | New York R | 47 | 8 | 6 | 14 |
| 1933-34 | New York R | 48 | 15 | 5 | 20 |
| 1934-35 | New York R | 47 | 15 | 4 | 19 |
| 1935-36 | New York R | 47 | 13 | 5 | 18 |
| 1936-37 | New York R | 48 | 22 | 4 | 26 |
| 1937-38 | New York R | 39 | 8 | 9 | 17 |
| | Totals | 526 | 157 | 63 | 220 |

**KEENAN, Lawrence Christopher** *Forward*
b. North Bay, Ont., Oct. 1, 1940

| Season | Club | GP | G | A | Pts. |
|---|---|---|---|---|---|
| 1961-62 | Toronto | 2 | 0 | 0 | 0 |
| 1967-68 | St Louis | 40 | 12 | 8 | 20 |
| 1968-69 | St Louis | 47 | 5 | 9 | 14 |
| 1969-70 | St Louis | 56 | 10 | 23 | 33 |
| 1970-71 | StL-Buf | 61 | 8 | 23 | 31 |
| 1971-72 | Buf-Phil | 28 | 3 | 1 | 4 |
| | Totals | 234 | 38 | 64 | 102 |

**KEHOE, Ricky Thomas (Rick)** *Forward*
b. Windsor, Ont., July 15, 1951

| Season | Club | GP | G | A | Pts. |
|---|---|---|---|---|---|
| 1971-72 | Toronto | 38 | 8 | 8 | 16 |
| 1972-73 | Toronto | 77 | 33 | 42 | 75 |
| 1973-74 | Toronto | 69 | 18 | 22 | 40 |
| 1974-75 | Pittsburgh | 76 | 32 | 31 | 63 |
| 1975-76 | Pittsburgh | 71 | 29 | 47 | 76 |
| 1976-77 | Pittsburgh | 80 | 30 | 27 | 57 |
| 1977-78 | Pittsburgh | 70 | 29 | 21 | 50 |
| 1978-79 | Pittsburgh | 57 | 27 | 18 | 45 |
| 1979-80 | Pittsburgh | 79 | 30 | 30 | 60 |
| 1980-81 | Pittsburgh | 80 | 55 | 33 | 88 |
| 1981-82 | Pittsburgh | 71 | 33 | 52 | 85 |
| 1982-83 | Pittsburgh | 75 | 29 | 36 | 65 |
| | Totals | 843 | 353 | 367 | 720 |

**KELLER, Ralph** *Defenseman*
b. Wilkie, Sask., Feb. 6, 1936

| Season | Club | GP | G | A | Pts. |
|---|---|---|---|---|---|
| 1962-63 | New York R | 3 | 1 | 0 | 1 |

**KELLGREN, Christer** *Forward*
b. Gothenburg, Sweden, Aug. 15, 1958

| Season | Club | GP | G | A | Pts. |
|---|---|---|---|---|---|
| 1981-82 | Colorado | 5 | 0 | 0 | 0 |

**KELLY, Dave** *Forward*
b. Chatham, Ont., Sept. 20, 1952

| Season | Club | GP | G | A | Pts. |
|---|---|---|---|---|---|
| 1976-77 | Detroit | 16 | 2 | 0 | 2 |

**KELLY, John Paul** *Forward*
b. Edmonton, Alta., Nov. 15, 1959

| Season | Club | GP | G | A | Pts. |
|---|---|---|---|---|---|
| 1979-80 | Los Angeles | 40 | 2 | 5 | 7 |
| 1980-81 | Los Angeles | 19 | 3 | 6 | 9 |
| 1981-82 | Los Angeles | 70 | 12 | 11 | 23 |
| 1982-83 | Los Angeles | 65 | 16 | 15 | 31 |
| | Totals | 194 | 33 | 37 | 70 |

**KELLY, John Robert** *Forward*
b. Fort Williams, Ont., June 6, 1946

| Season | Club | GP | G | A | Pts. |
|---|---|---|---|---|---|
| 1973-74 | StL-Pitt | 67 | 16 | 18 | 34 |
| 1974-75 | Pittsburgh | 69 | 27 | 24 | 51 |
| 1975-76 | Pittsburgh | 77 | 25 | 30 | 55 |
| 1976-77 | Pittsburgh | 74 | 10 | 21 | 31 |
| 1977-78 | Chicago | 75 | 7 | 11 | 18 |
| 1978-79 | Chicago | 63 | 2 | 5 | 7 |
| | Totals | 425 | 87 | 109 | 196 |

| Season | Club | GP | G | A | Pts. |
|---|---|---|---|---|---|

**KELLY, Leonard Patrick (Red)**
*Defenseman-Forward*
b. Simcoe, Ont., July 9, 1927

| Season | Club | GP | G | A | Pts. |
|---|---|---|---|---|---|
| 1947-48 | Detroit | 60 | 6 | 14 | 20 |
| 1948-49 | Detroit | 59 | 5 | 11 | 16 |
| 1949-50 | Detroit | 70 | 15 | 25 | 40 |
| 1950-51 | Detroit | 70 | 17 | 37 | 54 |
| 1951-52 | Detroit | 67 | 16 | 31 | 47 |
| 1952-53 | Detroit | 70 | 19 | 27 | 46 |
| 1953-54 | Detroit | 62 | 16 | 33 | 49 |
| 1954-55 | Detroit | 70 | 15 | 30 | 45 |
| 1955-56 | Detroit | 70 | 16 | 34 | 50 |
| 1956-57 | Detroit | 70 | 10 | 25 | 35 |
| 1957-58 | Detroit | 61 | 13 | 18 | 31 |
| 1958-59 | Detroit | 67 | 8 | 13 | 21 |
| 1959-60 | Det-Tor | 68 | 12 | 17 | 29 |
| 1960-61 | Toronto | 64 | 20 | 50 | 70 |
| 1961-62 | Toronto | 58 | 22 | 27 | 49 |
| 1962-63 | Toronto | 66 | 20 | 40 | 60 |
| 1963-64 | Toronto | 70 | 11 | 34 | 45 |
| 1964-65 | Toronto | 70 | 18 | 28 | 46 |
| 1965-66 | Toronto | 63 | 8 | 24 | 32 |
| 1966-67 | Toronto | 61 | 14 | 24 | 38 |
| | **Totals** | 1316 | 281 | 542 | 823 |

**KELLY, Peter Cameron** *Forward*
b. Winnipeg, Man., May 22, 1913

| Season | Club | GP | G | A | Pts. |
|---|---|---|---|---|---|
| 1934-35 | St Louis E | 25 | 3 | 10 | 13 |
| 1935-36 | Detroit | 46 | 6 | 8 | 14 |
| 1936-37 | Detroit | 47 | 5 | 4 | 9 |
| 1937-38 | Detroit | 9 | 0 | 1 | 1 |
| 1938-39 | Detroit | 32 | 4 | 9 | 13 |
| 1940-41 | New York A | 11 | 3 | 5 | 8 |
| 1941-42 | Brooklyn | 7 | 0 | 1 | 1 |
| | **Totals** | 177 | 21 | 38 | 59 |

**KELLY, Regis J. (Pep)** *Forward*
b. North Bay, Ont., Jan. 17, 1914

| Season | Club | GP | G | A | Pts. |
|---|---|---|---|---|---|
| 1934-35 | Toronto | 47 | 11 | 8 | 19 |
| 1935-36 | Toronto | 42 | 11 | 8 | 19 |
| 1936-37 | Tor-Chi | 45 | 15 | 4 | 19 |
| 1937-38 | Toronto | 43 | 9 | 10 | 19 |
| 1938-39 | Toronto | 48 | 11 | 11 | 22 |
| 1939-40 | New York A | 34 | 11 | 9 | 20 |
| 1940-41 | Chicago | 21 | 5 | 3 | 8 |
| 1941-42 | Brooklyn | 8 | 1 | 0 | 1 |
| | **Totals** | 288 | 74 | 53 | 127 |

**KELLY, Robert James (Bob)** *Forward*
b. Oakville, Ont., Nov. 25, 1950

| Season | Club | GP | G | A | Pts. |
|---|---|---|---|---|---|
| 1970-71 | Philadelphia | 76 | 14 | 18 | 32 |
| 1971-72 | Philadelphia | 78 | 14 | 15 | 29 |
| 1972-73 | Philadelphia | 77 | 10 | 11 | 21 |
| 1973-74 | Philadelphia | 65 | 4 | 10 | 14 |
| 1974-75 | Philadelphia | 67 | 11 | 18 | 29 |
| 1975-76 | Philadelphia | 79 | 12 | 8 | 20 |
| 1976-77 | Philadelphia | 73 | 22 | 24 | 46 |
| 1977-78 | Philadelphia | 74 | 19 | 13 | 32 |
| 1978-79 | Philadelphia | 77 | 7 | 31 | 38 |
| 1979-80 | Philadelphia | 75 | 15 | 20 | 35 |
| 1980-81 | Washington | 80 | 26 | 36 | 62 |
| 1981-82 | Washington | 16 | 0 | 4 | 4 |
| | **Totals** | 837 | 154 | 208 | 362 |

**KEMP, Kevin Glen** *Defenseman*
b. Ottawa, Ont., May 3, 1954

| Season | Club | GP | G | A | Pts. |
|---|---|---|---|---|---|
| 1980-81 | Hartford | 3 | 0 | 0 | 0 |

**KEMP, Stanley** *Defenseman*
b. Hamilton, Ont., Mar. 2, 1924

| Season | Club | GP | G | A | Pts. |
|---|---|---|---|---|---|
| 1948-49 | Toronto | 1 | 0 | 0 | 0 |

**KENDALL, William** *Forward*
b. Winnipeg, Man., Apr. 1, 1910

| Season | Club | GP | G | A | Pts. |
|---|---|---|---|---|---|
| 1933-34 | Chicago | 21 | 3 | 0 | 3 |
| 1934-35 | Chicago | 47 | 6 | 4 | 10 |
| 1935-36 | Chicago | 22 | 2 | 1 | 3 |
| 1936-37 | Chi-Tor | 32 | 5 | 4 | 9 |
| 1937-38 | Chicago | 9 | 0 | 1 | 1 |
| | **Totals** | 131 | 16 | 10 | 26 |

**KENNEDY, Dean** *Defenseman*
b. Redvers, Sask., Jan. 18, 1963

| Season | Club | GP | G | A | Pts. |
|---|---|---|---|---|---|
| 1982-83 | Los Angeles | 55 | 0 | 12 | 12 |

**KENNEDY, Forbes Taylor** *Forward*
b. Dorchester, N.B., Aug. 18, 1935

| Season | Club | GP | G | A | Pts. |
|---|---|---|---|---|---|
| 1956-57 | Chicago | 69 | 8 | 13 | 21 |
| 1957-58 | Detroit | 70 | 11 | 16 | 27 |
| 1958-59 | Detroit | 67 | 1 | 4 | 5 |
| 1959-60 | Detroit | 17 | 1 | 2 | 3 |
| 1961-62 | Detroit | 14 | 1 | 0 | 1 |
| 1962-63 | Boston | 49 | 12 | 18 | 30 |
| 1963-64 | Boston | 70 | 8 | 17 | 25 |
| 1964-65 | Boston | 52 | 6 | 4 | 10 |
| 1965-66 | Boston | 50 | 4 | 6 | 10 |
| 1967-68 | Philadelphia | 73 | 10 | 18 | 28 |
| 1968-69 | Phil-Tor | 72 | 8 | 9 | 17 |
| | **Totals** | 580 | 70 | 107 | 177 |

**KENNEDY, Theodore S. (Teeder)** *Forward*
b. Humberstone, Ont., Dec. 12, 1925

| Season | Club | GP | G | A | Pts. |
|---|---|---|---|---|---|
| 1942-43 | Toronto | 2 | 0 | 1 | 1 |
| 1943-44 | Toronto | 49 | 26 | 23 | 49 |
| 1944-45 | Toronto | 49 | 29 | 25 | 54 |
| 1945-46 | Toronto | 21 | 3 | 2 | 5 |
| 1946-47 | Toronto | 60 | 28 | 32 | 60 |
| 1947-48 | Toronto | 60 | 25 | 21 | 46 |
| 1948-49 | Toronto | 59 | 18 | 21 | 39 |
| 1949-50 | Toronto | 53 | 20 | 24 | 44 |
| 1950-51 | Toronto | 63 | 18 | 43 | 61 |
| 1951-52 | Toronto | 70 | 19 | 33 | 52 |
| 1952-53 | Toronto | 43 | 14 | 23 | 37 |
| 1953-54 | Toronto | 67 | 15 | 23 | 38 |
| 1954-55 | Toronto | 70 | 10 | 42 | 52 |
| 1955-56 | Toronto | 30 | 6 | 16 | 22 |
| | **Totals** | 696 | 231 | 329 | 560 |

**KENNY, William Ernest** *Defenseman*
b. Vermillion, Alta., Aug. 23, 1907

| Season | Club | GP | G | A | Pts. |
|---|---|---|---|---|---|
| 1930-31 | New York R | 6 | 0 | 0 | 0 |
| 1934-35 | Chicago | 4 | 0 | 0 | 0 |
| | **Totals** | 10 | 0 | 0 | 0 |

**KEON, David Michael (Dave)** *Forward*
b. Noranda, Que., Mar. 22, 1940

| Season | Club | GP | G | A | Pts. |
|---|---|---|---|---|---|
| 1960-61 | Toronto | 70 | 20 | 25 | 45 |
| 1961-62 | Toronto | 64 | 26 | 35 | 61 |
| 1962-63 | Toronto | 68 | 28 | 28 | 56 |
| 1963-64 | Toronto | 70 | 23 | 37 | 60 |
| 1964-65 | Toronto | 65 | 21 | 29 | 50 |
| 1965-66 | Toronto | 69 | 24 | 30 | 54 |
| 1966-67 | Toronto | 66 | 19 | 33 | 52 |
| 1967-68 | Toronto | 67 | 11 | 37 | 48 |
| 1968-69 | Toronto | 75 | 27 | 34 | 61 |
| 1969-70 | Toronto | 72 | 32 | 30 | 62 |
| 1970-71 | Toronto | 76 | 38 | 38 | 76 |
| 1971-72 | Toronto | 72 | 18 | 30 | 48 |
| 1972-73 | Toronto | 76 | 37 | 36 | 73 |
| 1973-74 | Toronto | 74 | 25 | 28 | 53 |
| 1974-75 | Toronto | 78 | 16 | 43 | 59 |
| 1975-76 | Minn-Ind (WHA) | 69 | 29 | 45 | 74 |
| 1976-77 | Minn-NE (WHA) | 76 | 27 | 63 | 90 |
| 1977-78 | New England (WHA) | 77 | 24 | 38 | 62 |
| 1978-79 | New England (WHA) | 79 | 22 | 43 | 65 |
| 1979-80 | Hartford | 76 | 10 | 52 | 62 |
| 1980-81 | Hartford | 80 | 13 | 34 | 47 |
| 1981-82 | Hartford | 78 | 8 | 11 | 19 |
| | **NHL Totals** | 1296 | 396 | 590 | 986 |
| | **WHA Totals** | 301 | 102 | 189 | 291 |

**KERR, Reginald John** *Forward*
b. Oxbow, Sask., Oct. 16, 1957

| Season | Club | GP | G | A | Pts. |
|---|---|---|---|---|---|
| 1977-78 | Clev-Chi | 9 | 0 | 4 | 4 |
| 1978-79 | Chicago | 73 | 16 | 24 | 40 |
| 1979-80 | Chicago | 49 | 9 | 8 | 17 |
| 1980-81 | Chicago | 70 | 30 | 30 | 60 |
| 1981-82 | Chicago | 59 | 11 | 28 | 39 |
| 1982-83 | Chicago | Z | Z | Z | Z |
| | **Totals** | 260 | 66 | 94 | 160 |

**KERR, Tim** *Forward*
b. Windsor, Ont., Jan. 5, 1960

| Season | Club | GP | G | A | Pts. |
|---|---|---|---|---|---|
| 1980-81 | Philadelphia | 68 | 22 | 23 | 45 |
| 1981-82 | Philadelphia | 61 | 21 | 30 | 51 |
| 1982-83 | Philadelphia | 24 | 11 | 8 | 19 |
| | **Totals** | 153 | 54 | 61 | 115 |

**KESSELL, Richard John (Rick)** *Forward*
b. Toronto, Ont., July 27, 1949

| Season | Club | GP | G | A | Pts. |
|---|---|---|---|---|---|
| 1969-70 | Pittsburgh | 8 | 1 | 2 | 3 |
| 1970-71 | Pittsburgh | 6 | 0 | 2 | 2 |
| 1971-72 | Pittsburgh | 3 | 0 | 1 | 1 |
| 1972-73 | Pittsburgh | 66 | 1 | 13 | 14 |
| 1973-74 | California | 51 | 2 | 6 | 8 |
| | **Totals** | 134 | 4 | 24 | 28 |

**KETOLA, Veli** *Forward*
b. Pori, Finland, Mar. 28, 1948

| Season | Club | GP | G | A | Pts. |
|---|---|---|---|---|---|
| 1981-82 | Colorado | 44 | 9 | 5 | 14 |

**KETTER, Kerry Kenneth** *Defenseman*
b. Prince George, B.C., Sept. 20, 1947

| Season | Club | GP | G | A | Pts. |
|---|---|---|---|---|---|
| 1972-73 | Atlanta | 41 | 0 | 2 | 2 |

**KIESSLING, Udo** *Defenseman*
b. Crimmitschau, Germany, May 21, 1955

| Season | Club | GP | G | A | Pts. |
|---|---|---|---|---|---|
| 1981-82 | Minnesota | 1 | 0 | 0 | 0 |

**KILREA, Brian Blair** *Forward*
b. Ottawa, Ont., Oct. 21, 1934

| Season | Club | GP | G | A | Pts. |
|---|---|---|---|---|---|
| 1957-58 | Detroit | 1 | 0 | 0 | 0 |
| 1967-68 | Los Angeles | 25 | 3 | 5 | 8 |
| | **Totals** | 26 | 3 | 5 | 8 |

**KILREA, Hector J.** *Forward*
b. Blackburn, Ont., June 11, 1907

| Season | Club | GP | G | A | Pts. |
|---|---|---|---|---|---|
| 1925-26 | Ottawa | 35 | 5 | 0 | 5 |
| 1926-27 | Ottawa | 42 | 11 | 7 | 18 |
| 1927-28 | Ottawa | 43 | 19 | 4 | 23 |
| 1928-29 | Ottawa | 38 | 5 | 7 | 12 |
| 1929-30 | Ottawa | 44 | 36 | 22 | 58 |
| 1930-31 | Ottawa | 44 | 14 | 8 | 22 |
| 1931-32 | Detroit | 47 | 13 | 3 | 16 |
| 1932-33 | Ottawa | 47 | 14 | 8 | 22 |
| 1933-34 | Toronto | 43 | 10 | 13 | 23 |
| 1934-35 | Toronto | 46 | 11 | 13 | 24 |
| 1935-36 | Detroit | 48 | 6 | 17 | 23 |
| 1936-37 | Detroit | 48 | 6 | 9 | 15 |
| 1937-38 | Detroit | 48 | 9 | 9 | 18 |
| 1938-39 | Detroit | 48 | 8 | 9 | 17 |
| 1939-40 | Detroit | 12 | 0 | 0 | 0 |
| | **Totals** | 633 | 167 | 129 | 296 |

**KILREA, Kenneth Armstrong** *Forward*
b. Ottawa, Ont., Jan. 16, 1919

| Season | Club | GP | G | A | Pts. |
|---|---|---|---|---|---|
| 1938-39 | Detroit | 1 | 0 | 0 | 0 |
| 1939-40 | Detroit | 40 | 10 | 8 | 18 |
| 1940-41 | Detroit | 15 | 2 | 0 | 2 |
| 1941-42 | Detroit | 21 | 3 | 12 | 15 |
| 1943-44 | Detroit | 14 | 1 | 3 | 4 |
| | **Totals** | 91 | 16 | 23 | 39 |

**KILREA, Walter Charles** *Forward*
b. Ottawa, Ont., Feb. 18, 1909

| Season | Club | GP | G | A | Pts. |
|---|---|---|---|---|---|
| 1929-30 | Ottawa | 38 | 4 | 2 | 6 |
| 1930-31 | Philadelphia Q | 44 | 8 | 12 | 20 |
| 1931-32 | New York A | 48 | 3 | 8 | 11 |
| 1932-33 | Ott-MontM | 51 | 5 | 12 | 17 |
| 1933-34 | Montreal M | 45 | 3 | 1 | 4 |
| 1934-35 | Detroit | 3 | 0 | 0 | 0 |
| 1935-36 | Detroit | 48 | 4 | 10 | 14 |
| 1936-37 | Detroit | 47 | 8 | 13 | 21 |
| 1937-38 | Detroit | 5 | 0 | 0 | 0 |
| | **Totals** | 329 | 35 | 58 | 93 |

**KINDRACHUK, Orest** *Forward*
b. Nanton, Alta., Sept. 14, 1950

| Season | Club | GP | G | A | Pts. |
|---|---|---|---|---|---|
| 1972-73 | Philadelphia | 2 | 0 | 0 | 0 |
| 1973-74 | Philadelphia | 71 | 11 | 30 | 41 |
| 1974-75 | Philadelphia | 60 | 10 | 21 | 31 |
| 1975-76 | Philadelphia | 76 | 26 | 49 | 75 |
| 1976-77 | Philadelphia | 78 | 15 | 36 | 51 |
| 1977-78 | Philadelphia | 73 | 17 | 45 | 62 |
| 1978-79 | Pittsburgh | 79 | 18 | 42 | 60 |
| 1979-80 | Pittsburgh | 52 | 17 | 29 | 46 |
| 1980-81 | Pittsburgh | 13 | 3 | 9 | 12 |
| 1981-82 | Washington | 4 | 1 | 0 | 1 |
| | **Totals** | 508 | 118 | 261 | 379 |

| Season | Club | GP | G | A | Pts. |
|---|---|---|---|---|---|

**KING, Frank Edward** *Forward*
b. Toronto, Ont., Mar. 7, 1929

| Season | Club | GP | G | A | Pts. |
|---|---|---|---|---|---|
| 1950-51 | Montreal | 10 | 1 | 0 | 1 |

**KING, Wayne Gordon** *Forward*
b. Midland, Ont., Sept. 4, 1951

| Season | Club | GP | G | A | Pts. |
|---|---|---|---|---|---|
| 1973-74 | California | 2 | 0 | 0 | 0 |
| 1974-75 | California | 25 | 4 | 7 | 11 |
| 1975-76 | California | 46 | 1 | 11 | 12 |
| | **Totals** | **73** | **5** | **18** | **23** |

**KINSELLA, Brian** *Forward*
b. Barrie, Ont., Feb. 11, 1954

| Season | Club | GP | G | A | Pts. |
|---|---|---|---|---|---|
| 1975-76 | Washington | 4 | 0 | 1 | 1 |
| 1976-77 | Washington | 6 | 0 | 0 | 0 |
| | **Totals** | **10** | **0** | **1** | **1** |

**KINSELLA, Thomas Raymond (Ray)** *Forward*
b. Ottawa, Ont., Jan. 27, 1911

| Season | Club | GP | G | A | Pts. |
|---|---|---|---|---|---|
| 1930-31 | Ottawa | 13 | 0 | 0 | 0 |

**KIRK, Robert Hunter** *Forward*
b. Belfast, Ireland, Aug. 8, 1910

| Season | Club | GP | G | A | Pts. |
|---|---|---|---|---|---|
| 1937-38 | New York R | 39 | 4 | 8 | 12 |

**KIRKPATRICK, Robert Drynan** *Forward*
b. Regina, Sask., Dec. 1, 1915

| Season | Club | GP | G | A | Pts. |
|---|---|---|---|---|---|
| 1942-43 | New York R | 49 | 12 | 12 | 24 |

**KIRTON, Mark Robert** *Forward*
b. Regina, Sask., Feb. 3, 1958

| Season | Club | GP | G | A | Pts. |
|---|---|---|---|---|---|
| 1979-80 | Toronto | 2 | 1 | 0 | 1 |
| 1980-81 | Tor-Det | 61 | 18 | 13 | 31 |
| 1981-82 | Detroit | 74 | 14 | 28 | 42 |
| 1982-83 | Det-Van | 41 | 5 | 7 | 12 |
| | **Totals** | **178** | **38** | **48** | **86** |

**KISIO, Kelly** *Forward*
b. Wetaskwin, Alta., Sept. 18, 1959

| Season | Club | GP | G | A | Pts. |
|---|---|---|---|---|---|
| 1982-83 | Detroit | 15 | 4 | 3 | 7 |

**KITCHEN, C. Hobie** *Defenseman-Forward*
b. Toronto, Ont.

| Season | Club | GP | G | A | Pts. |
|---|---|---|---|---|---|
| 1925-26 | Montreal M | 30 | 5 | 2 | 7 |
| 1926-27 | Detroit | 17 | 0 | 2 | 2 |
| | **Totals** | **47** | **5** | **4** | **9** |

**KITCHEN, Michael Elivin** *Defenseman*
b. Newmarket, Ont., Feb. 1, 1956

| Season | Club | GP | G | A | Pts. |
|---|---|---|---|---|---|
| 1976-77 | Colorado | 60 | 1 | 8 | 9 |
| 1977-78 | Colorado | 61 | 2 | 17 | 19 |
| 1978-79 | Colorado | 53 | 1 | 4 | 5 |
| 1979-80 | Colorado | 42 | 1 | 6 | 7 |
| 1980-81 | Colorado | 75 | 1 | 7 | 8 |
| 1981-82 | Colorado | 63 | 1 | 8 | 9 |
| 1982-83 | New Jersey | 77 | 4 | 8 | 12 |
| | **Totals** | **431** | **11** | **58** | **69** |

**KITCHEN, William** *Defenseman*
b. Schomberg, Ont., Oct. 2, 1960

| Season | Club | GP | G | A | Pts. |
|---|---|---|---|---|---|
| 1981-82 | Montreal | 1 | 0 | 0 | 0 |
| 1982-83 | Montreal | 8 | 0 | 0 | 0 |
| | **Totals** | **9** | **0** | **0** | **0** |

**KLASSEN, Ralph L.** *Forward*
b. Humboldt, Ont., Sept. 15, 1955

| Season | Club | GP | G | A | Pts. |
|---|---|---|---|---|---|
| 1975-76 | California | 71 | 6 | 15 | 21 |
| 1976-77 | Cleveland | 80 | 14 | 18 | 32 |
| 1977-78 | Clev-Col | 57 | 8 | 10 | 18 |
| 1978-79 | Colorado | 64 | 6 | 13 | 19 |
| 1979-80 | St Louis | 80 | 9 | 16 | 25 |
| 1980-81 | St Louis | 66 | 6 | 12 | 18 |
| 1981-82 | St Louis | 45 | 3 | 7 | 10 |
| 1982-83 | St Louis | 29 | 0 | 2 | 2 |
| | **Totals** | **492** | **52** | **93** | **145** |

**KLEIN, James Lloyd (Dede)** *Forward*
b. Saskatoon, Sask., Jan. 13, 1910

| Season | Club | GP | G | A | Pts. |
|---|---|---|---|---|---|
| 1928-29 | Boston | 8 | 1 | 0 | 1 |
| 1931-32 | Boston | 5 | 1 | 0 | 1 |
| 1932-33 | New York A | 15 | 2 | 2 | 4 |
| 1933-34 | New York A | 48 | 13 | 9 | 22 |
| 1934-35 | New York A | 29 | 7 | 3 | 10 |
| 1935-36 | New York A | 42 | 4 | 8 | 12 |
| 1936-37 | New York A | 14 | 2 | 1 | 3 |
| 1937-38 | New York A | 3 | 0 | 1 | 1 |
| | **Totals** | **164** | **30** | **24** | **54** |

**KLEINENDORST, Scot** *Defenseman*
b. Grand Rapids, Minn., Jan. 16, 1960

| Season | Club | GP | G | A | Pts. |
|---|---|---|---|---|---|
| 1982-83 | New York R. | 30 | 2 | 9 | 11 |

**KLINGBEIL, Ernest** *Forward*

| Season | Club | GP | G | A | Pts. |
|---|---|---|---|---|---|
| 1936-37 | Chicago | 5 | 1 | 2 | 3 |

**KLUKAY, Joseph Francis** *Forward*
b. Sault Ste. Marie, Ont., Nov. 6, 1922

| Season | Club | GP | G | A | Pts. |
|---|---|---|---|---|---|
| 1946-47 | Toronto | 55 | 9 | 20 | 29 |
| 1947-48 | Toronto | 59 | 15 | 15 | 30 |
| 1948-49 | Toronto | 45 | 11 | 10 | 21 |
| 1949-50 | Toronto | 70 | 15 | 16 | 31 |
| 1950-51 | Toronto | 70 | 14 | 16 | 30 |
| 1951-52 | Toronto | 43 | 4 | 8 | 12 |
| 1952-53 | Boston | 70 | 13 | 16 | 29 |
| 1953-54 | Boston | 70 | 20 | 17 | 37 |
| 1954-55 | Bos-Tor | 66 | 8 | 8 | 16 |
| 1955-56 | Toronto | 18 | 0 | 1 | 1 |
| | **Totals** | **566** | **109** | **127** | **236** |

**KLUZAK, Gord** *Defenseman*
b. Climax, Sask., Mar. 4, 1964

| Season | Club | GP | G | A | Pts. |
|---|---|---|---|---|---|
| 1982-83 | Boston | 70 | 1 | 6 | 7 |

**KNIBBS, William Arthur** *Forward*
b. Toronto, Ont., Jan. 24, 1942

| Season | Club | GP | G | A | Pts. |
|---|---|---|---|---|---|
| 1964-65 | Boston | 53 | 7 | 10 | 17 |

**KNOTT, William Earl (Nick)**
*Defenseman-Forward*
b. Kingston, Ont., July 23, 1920

| Season | Club | GP | G | A | Pts. |
|---|---|---|---|---|---|
| 1941-42 | Brooklyn | 14 | 3 | 1 | 4 |

**KNOX, Paul** *Forward*

| Season | Club | GP | G | A | Pts. |
|---|---|---|---|---|---|
| 1954-55 | Toronto | 1 | 0 | 0 | 0 |

**KOMADOSKI, Neil G.** *Defenseman*
b. Winnipeg, Man., Nov. 5, 1951

| Season | Club | GP | G | A | Pts. |
|---|---|---|---|---|---|
| 1972-73 | Los Angeles | 62 | 1 | 8 | 9 |
| 1973-74 | Los Angeles | 68 | 2 | 4 | 6 |
| 1974-75 | Los Angeles | 75 | 4 | 12 | 16 |
| 1975-76 | Los Angeles | 80 | 3 | 15 | 18 |
| 1976-77 | Los Angeles | 68 | 3 | 9 | 12 |
| 1977-78 | LA-StL | 58 | 2 | 14 | 16 |
| 1978-79 | St Louis | 42 | 1 | 2 | 3 |
| 1979-80 | St Louis | 49 | 0 | 12 | 12 |
| | **Totals** | **509** | **16** | **76** | **92** |

**KONIK, George Samuel** *Defenseman-Forward*
b. Flin Flon, Man., May 4, 1938

| Season | Club | GP | G | A | Pts. |
|---|---|---|---|---|---|
| 1967-68 | Pittsburgh | 52 | 7 | 8 | 15 |
| 1972-73 | Minnesota (WHA) | 54 | 4 | 12 | 16 |
| | **NHL Totals** | **52** | **7** | **8** | **15** |
| | **WHA Totals** | **54** | **4** | **12** | **16** |

**KONROYD, Stephen Mark** *Defenseman*
b. Scarborough, Ont., Feb. 10, 1961

| Season | Club | GP | G | A | Pts. |
|---|---|---|---|---|---|
| 1980-81 | Calgary | 4 | 0 | 0 | 0 |
| 1981-82 | Calgary | 63 | 3 | 14 | 17 |
| 1982-83 | Calgary | 79 | 4 | 13 | 17 |
| | **Totals** | **146** | **7** | **27** | **34** |

**KONTOS, Chris** *Forward*
b. Toronto, Ont., Dec. 10, 1963

| Season | Club | GP | G | A | Pts. |
|---|---|---|---|---|---|
| 1982-83 | New York R | 44 | 8 | 7 | 15 |

**KOPAK, Russell** *Forward*
b. Edmonton, Alta., Apr. 26, 1924

| Season | Club | GP | G | A | Pts. |
|---|---|---|---|---|---|
| 1943-44 | Boston | 24 | 7 | 9 | 16 |

**KORAB, Gerald Joseph (Jerry)** *Forward*
b. Sault Ste. Marie, Ont., Sept. 15, 1948

| Season | Club | GP | G | A | Pts. |
|---|---|---|---|---|---|
| 1970-71 | Chicago | 46 | 4 | 14 | 18 |
| 1971-72 | Chicago | 73 | 9 | 5 | 14 |
| 1972-73 | Chicago | 77 | 12 | 15 | 27 |
| 1973-74 | Van-Buf | 76 | 10 | 19 | 29 |
| 1974-75 | Buffalo | 79 | 12 | 44 | 56 |
| 1975-76 | Buffalo | 65 | 13 | 28 | 41 |
| 1976-77 | Buffalo | 77 | 14 | 33 | 47 |
| 1977-78 | Buffalo | 77 | 7 | 34 | 41 |
| 1978-79 | Buffalo | 78 | 11 | 40 | 51 |
| 1979-80 | Buf-LA | 54 | 2 | 12 | 14 |
| 1980-81 | Los Angeles | 78 | 9 | 43 | 52 |
| 1981-82 | Los Angeles | 50 | 5 | 13 | 18 |
| 1982-83 | Los Angeles | 72 | 3 | 26 | 29 |
| | **Totals** | **902** | **111** | **326** | **437** |

**KORN, James A.** *Defenseman*
b. Hopkins, Minn., July 28, 1957

| Season | Club | GP | G | A | Pts. |
|---|---|---|---|---|---|
| 1979-80 | Detroit | 63 | 5 | 13 | 18 |
| 1980-81 | Detroit | 63 | 5 | 15 | 20 |
| 1981-82 | Det-Tor | 70 | 2 | 10 | 12 |
| 1982-83 | Toronto | 80 | 8 | 21 | 29 |
| | **Totals** | **276** | **20** | **59** | **79** |

**KORNEY, Michael Wayne**
*Defenseman-Forward*
b. Dauphin, Man., Sept. 15, 1953

| Season | Club | GP | G | A | Pts. |
|---|---|---|---|---|---|
| 1973-74 | Detroit | 2 | 0 | 0 | 0 |
| 1974-75 | Detroit | 30 | 8 | 2 | 10 |
| 1975-76 | Detroit | 27 | 1 | 7 | 8 |
| 1978-79 | New York R | 18 | 0 | 1 | 1 |
| | **Totals** | **77** | **9** | **10** | **19** |

**KOROLL, Clifford Eugene (Cliff)** *Forward*
b. Canora, Sask., Oct. 1, 1946

| Season | Club | GP | G | A | Pts. |
|---|---|---|---|---|---|
| 1969-70 | Chicago | 73 | 18 | 19 | 37 |
| 1970-71 | Chicago | 72 | 16 | 34 | 50 |
| 1971-72 | Chicago | 76 | 22 | 23 | 45 |
| 1972-73 | Chicago | 77 | 33 | 24 | 57 |
| 1973-74 | Chicago | 78 | 21 | 25 | 46 |
| 1974-75 | Chicago | 80 | 27 | 32 | 59 |
| 1975-76 | Chicago | 80 | 25 | 33 | 58 |
| 1976-77 | Chicago | 80 | 15 | 26 | 41 |
| 1977-78 | Chicago | 73 | 16 | 15 | 31 |
| 1978-79 | Chicago | 78 | 12 | 19 | 31 |
| 1979-80 | Chicago | 47 | 3 | 4 | 7 |
| | **Totals** | **814** | **208** | **254** | **462** |

**KOTANEN, Elno R. (Dick)** *Defenseman*
b. Port Arthur, Ont., Nov. 18, 1925

| Season | Club | GP | G | A | Pts. |
|---|---|---|---|---|---|
| 1948-49 | New York R | 1 | 0 | 1 | 1 |
| 1950-51 | New York R | 1 | 0 | 0 | 0 |
| | **Totals** | **2** | **0** | **1** | **1** |

**KOTSOPOULOS, Christopher** *Defenseman*
b. Toronto, Ont., Nov. 27, 1958

| Season | Club | GP | G | A | Pts. |
|---|---|---|---|---|---|
| 1980-81 | New York R | 54 | 4 | 12 | 16 |
| 1981-82 | Hartford | 68 | 13 | 20 | 33 |
| 1982-83 | Hartford | 68 | 6 | 24 | 30 |
| | **Totals** | **190** | **23** | **56** | **79** |

**KOWAL, Joseph Douglas** *Forward*
b. Toronto, Ont., Feb. 3, 1956

| Season | Club | GP | G | A | Pts. |
|---|---|---|---|---|---|
| 1976-77 | Buffalo | 16 | 0 | 5 | 5 |
| 1977-78 | Buffalo | 6 | 0 | 0 | 0 |
| | **Totals** | **22** | **0** | **5** | **5** |

**KOZAK, Donald** *Forward*
b. Edmonton, Alta., Feb. 2, 1952

| Season | Club | GP | G | A | Pts. |
|---|---|---|---|---|---|
| 1972-73 | Los Angeles | 72 | 14 | 6 | 20 |
| 1973-74 | Los Angeles | 76 | 21 | 14 | 35 |
| 1974-75 | Los Angeles | 77 | 16 | 15 | 31 |
| 1975-76 | Los Angeles | 62 | 20 | 24 | 44 |
| 1976-77 | Los Angeles | 79 | 15 | 17 | 32 |

| Season | Club | GP | G | A | Pts. |
|---|---|---|---|---|---|
| 1977-78 | Los Angeles | 43 | 8 | 5 | 13 |
| 1978-79 | Vancouver | 28 | 2 | 5 | 7 |
| | Totals | 437 | 96 | 86 | 182 |

**KOZAK, Lester** *Forward*
b. Yorkton, Sask., Oct. 28, 1940

| Season | Club | GP | G | A | Pts. |
|---|---|---|---|---|---|
| 1961-62 | Toronto | 12 | 1 | 0 | 1 |

**KRAFTCHECK, Stephen S.** *Defenseman*
b. Tinturn, Ont., Mar. 3, 1929

| Season | Club | GP | G | A | Pts. |
|---|---|---|---|---|---|
| 1950-51 | Boston | 22 | 0 | 0 | 0 |
| 1951-52 | New York R | 58 | 8 | 9 | 17 |
| 1952-53 | New York R | 69 | 2 | 9 | 11 |
| 1958-59 | Toronto | 8 | 1 | 0 | 1 |
| | Totals | 157 | 11 | 18 | 29 |

**KRAKE, Philip Gordon (Skip)** *Forward*
b. North Battleford, Sask., Oct. 14, 1943

| Season | Club | GP | G | A | Pts. |
|---|---|---|---|---|---|
| 1963-64 | Boston | 2 | 0 | 0 | 0 |
| 1965-66 | Boston | 2 | 0 | 0 | 0 |
| 1966-67 | Boston | 15 | 6 | 2 | 8 |
| 1967-68 | Boston | 68 | 5 | 7 | 12 |
| 1968-69 | Los Angeles | 30 | 3 | 9 | 12 |
| 1969-70 | Los Angeles | 58 | 5 | 17 | 22 |
| 1970-71 | Buffalo | 74 | 4 | 5 | 9 |
| 1972-73 | Cleveland (WHA) | 28 | 9 | 10 | 19 |
| 1973-74 | Cleveland (WHA) | 69 | 20 | 36 | 56 |
| 1974-75 | Cleveland (WHA) | 71 | 15 | 23 | 38 |
| 1975-76 | Edmonton (WHA) | 41 | 8 | 8 | 16 |
| | NHL Totals | 249 | 23 | 40 | 63 |
| | WHA Totals | 209 | 52 | 77 | 129 |

**KROL, Joseph** *Forward*
b. Winnipeg, Man., Aug. 13, 1915

| Season | Club | GP | G | A | Pts. |
|---|---|---|---|---|---|
| 1936-37 | New York R | 1 | 0 | 0 | 0 |
| 1938-39 | New York R | 1 | 1 | 1 | 2 |
| 1941-42 | Brooklyn | 24 | 9 | 3 | 12 |
| | Totals | 26 | 10 | 4 | 14 |

**KROOK, Kevin** *Defenseman*
b. Cold Lake, Alta., Apr. 5, 1958

| Season | Club | GP | G | A | Pts. |
|---|---|---|---|---|---|
| 1978-79 | Colorado | 3 | 0 | 0 | 0 |

**KRULICKI, James John (Jim)** *Forward*
b. Kitchener, Ont., Mar. 9, 1948

| Season | Club | GP | G | A | Pts. |
|---|---|---|---|---|---|
| 1970-71 | NYR-Det | 41 | 0 | 3 | 3 |

**KRUSHELNYSKI, Michael** *Forward*
b. Montreal, Que., Apr. 27, 1960

| Season | Club | GP | G | A | Pts. |
|---|---|---|---|---|---|
| 1981-82 | Boston | 17 | 3 | 3 | 6 |
| 1982-83 | Boston | 79 | 23 | 42 | 65 |
| | Totals | 96 | 26 | 45 | 71 |

**KRYSKOW, David Roy (Dave)** *Forward*
b. Edmonton, Alta., Dec. 25, 1951

| Season | Club | GP | G | A | Pts. |
|---|---|---|---|---|---|
| 1972-73 | Chicago | 11 | 1 | 0 | 1 |
| 1973-74 | Chicago | 72 | 7 | 12 | 19 |
| 1974-75 | Wash-Det | 69 | 10 | 19 | 29 |
| 1975-76 | Atlanta | 79 | 15 | 25 | 40 |
| 1976-77 | Calgary (WHA) | 45 | 16 | 17 | 33 |
| 1977-78 | Winnipeg (WHA) | 71 | 20 | 21 | 41 |
| | NHL Totals | 231 | 33 | 56 | 89 |
| | WHA Totals | 116 | 36 | 38 | 74 |

**KRYZANOWSKI, Edward Lloyd** *Defenseman*
b. Fort Francis, Ont., Nov. 14, 1925

| Season | Club | GP | G | A | Pts. |
|---|---|---|---|---|---|
| 1948-49 | Boston | 36 | 1 | 3 | 4 |
| 1949-50 | Boston | 59 | 6 | 10 | 16 |
| 1950-51 | Boston | 69 | 3 | 6 | 9 |
| 1061 52 | Boston | 70 | 5 | 3 | 8 |
| 1952-53 | Chicago | 5 | 0 | 0 | 0 |
| | Totals | 239 | 15 | 22 | 37 |

**KUHN, Gordon (Doggie)** *Forward*
b. Truro, N.S.

| Season | Club | GP | G | A | Pts. |
|---|---|---|---|---|---|
| 1932-33 | New York A | 9 | 1 | 1 | 2 |

**KUKULOWICZ, Adolph Frank (Aggie)** *Forward*
b. Winnipeg, Man., Apr. 2, 1933

| Season | Club | GP | G | A | Pts. |
|---|---|---|---|---|---|
| 1952-53 | New York R | 3 | 1 | 0 | 1 |
| 1953-54 | New York R | 1 | 0 | 0 | 0 |
| | Totals | 4 | 1 | 0 | 1 |

**KULAK, Stuart** *Forward*
b. Edmonton, Alta., Mar. 10, 1963

| Season | Club | GP | G | A | Pts. |
|---|---|---|---|---|---|
| 1982-83 | Vancouver | 4 | 1 | 1 | 2 |

**KULLMAN, Arnold Edwin** *Forward*
b. Winnipeg, Man., Oct. 9, 1927

| Season | Club | GP | G | A | Pts. |
|---|---|---|---|---|---|
| 1947-48 | Boston | 1 | 0 | 0 | 0 |
| 1949-50 | Boston | 12 | 0 | 1 | 1 |
| | Totals | 13 | 0 | 1 | 1 |

**KULLMAN, Edward George** *Forward*
b. Winnipeg, Man., Dec. 12, 1923

| Season | Club | GP | G | A | Pts. |
|---|---|---|---|---|---|
| 1947-48 | New York R | 51 | 15 | 17 | 32 |
| 1948-49 | New York R | 18 | 4 | 5 | 9 |
| 1950-51 | New York R | 70 | 14 | 18 | 32 |
| 1951-52 | New York R | 64 | 11 | 10 | 21 |
| 1952-53 | New York R | 70 | 8 | 10 | 18 |
| 1953-54 | New York R | 70 | 4 | 10 | 14 |
| | Totals | 343 | 56 | 70 | 126 |

**KUNTZ, Alan Robert** *Forward*
b. Toronto, Ont., June 4, 1919

| Season | Club | GP | G | A | Pts. |
|---|---|---|---|---|---|
| 1941-42 | New York R | 31 | 10 | 11 | 21 |
| 1945-46 | New York R | 14 | 0 | 1 | 1 |
| | Totals | 45 | 10 | 12 | 22 |

**KUNTZ, Murray Robert** *Forward*
b. Ottawa, Ont., Dec. 19, 1945

| Season | Club | GP | G | A | Pts. |
|---|---|---|---|---|---|
| 1974-75 | St Louis | 7 | 1 | 2 | 3 |

**KURRI, Jari** *Forward*
b. Helsinki, Finland, May 18, 1960

| Season | Club | GP | G | A | Pts. |
|---|---|---|---|---|---|
| 1980-81 | Edmonton | 75 | 32 | 43 | 75 |
| 1981-82 | Edmonton | 71 | 32 | 54 | 86 |
| 1982-83 | Edmonton | 80 | 45 | 59 | 104 |
| | Totals | 226 | 109 | 156 | 265 |

**KURTENBACH, Orland John** *Forward*
b. Cudworth, Sask., Sept. 7, 1936

| Season | Club | GP | G | A | Pts. |
|---|---|---|---|---|---|
| 1960-61 | New York R | 10 | 0 | 6 | 6 |
| 1961-62 | Boston | 8 | 0 | 0 | 0 |
| 1963-64 | Boston | 70 | 12 | 25 | 37 |
| 1964-65 | Boston | 64 | 6 | 20 | 26 |
| 1965-66 | Toronto | 70 | 9 | 6 | 15 |
| 1966-67 | New York R | 60 | 11 | 25 | 36 |
| 1967-68 | New York R | 73 | 15 | 20 | 35 |
| 1968-69 | New York R | 2 | 0 | 0 | 0 |
| 1969-70 | New York R | 53 | 4 | 10 | 14 |
| 1970-71 | Vancouver | 52 | 21 | 32 | 53 |
| 1971-72 | Vancouver | 78 | 24 | 37 | 61 |
| 1972-73 | Vancouver | 47 | 9 | 19 | 28 |
| 1973-74 | Vancouver | 52 | 8 | 13 | 21 |
| | Totals | 639 | 119 | 213 | 332 |

**KUZYK, Kenneth Michael** *Forward*
b. Toronto, Ont., Aug. 11, 1953

| Season | Club | GP | G | A | Pts. |
|---|---|---|---|---|---|
| 1976-77 | Cleveland | 13 | 0 | 5 | 5 |
| 1977-78 | Cleveland | 28 | 5 | 4 | 9 |
| | Totals | 41 | 5 | 9 | 14 |

**KWONG, Lawrence (King)** *Forward*
b. Vernon, B.C., June 17, 1923

| Season | Club | GP | G | A | Pts. |
|---|---|---|---|---|---|
| 1947-48 | New York R | 1 | 0 | 0 | 0 |

**KYLE, Walter Lawrence (Gus)** *Defenseman*
b. Dysart, Sask., Sept. 11, 1923

| Season | Club | GP | G | A | Pts. |
|---|---|---|---|---|---|
| 1949-50 | New York R | 70 | 3 | 5 | 8 |
| 1950-51 | New York R | 64 | 2 | 3 | 5 |
| 1951-52 | Boston | 69 | 1 | 12 | 13 |
| | Totals | 203 | 6 | 20 | 26 |

**KYLE, William** *Forward*
b. Dysart, Sask., Dec. 23, 1924

| Season | Club | GP | G | A | Pts. |
|---|---|---|---|---|---|
| 1949-50 | New York R | 2 | 0 | 0 | 0 |
| 1950-51 | New York R | 1 | 0 | 3 | 3 |
| | Totals | 3 | 0 | 3 | 3 |

**KYTE, Jim** *Defenseman*
b. Ottawa, Ont., Mar. 21, 1964

| Season | Club | GP | G | A | Pts. |
|---|---|---|---|---|---|
| 1982-83 | Winnipeg | 2 | 0 | 0 | 0 |

**LABADIE, Joseph G. Michel (Mike)** *Forward*
b. St. Francois d'Assisi, Que., Aug. 17, 1932

| Season | Club | GP | G | A | Pts. |
|---|---|---|---|---|---|
| 1952-53 | New York R | 3 | 0 | 0 | 0 |

**LABATTE, Neil Joseph Henry** *Defenseman*
b. Toronto, Ont., Apr. 24, 1957

| Season | Club | GP | G | A | Pts. |
|---|---|---|---|---|---|
| 1978-79 | St Louis | 22 | 0 | 2 | 2 |
| 1981-82 | St Louis | 4 | 0 | 0 | 0 |
| | Totals | 26 | 0 | 2 | 2 |

**L'ABBE, Maurice Joseph (Moe)** *Forward*
b. Montreal, Que., Aug. 12, 1947

| Season | Club | GP | G | A | Pts. |
|---|---|---|---|---|---|
| 1972-73 | Chicago | 5 | 0 | 1 | 1 |

**LABINE, Leo Gerald** *Forward*
b. Haileybury, Ont., July 22, 1931

| Season | Club | GP | G | A | Pts. |
|---|---|---|---|---|---|
| 1951-52 | Boston | 15 | 2 | 4 | 6 |
| 1952-53 | Boston | 51 | 8 | 15 | 23 |
| 1953-54 | Boston | 68 | 16 | 19 | 35 |
| 1954-55 | Boston | 67 | 24 | 18 | 42 |
| 1955-56 | Boston | 68 | 16 | 18 | 34 |
| 1956-57 | Boston | 67 | 18 | 29 | 47 |
| 1957-58 | Boston | 62 | 7 | 14 | 21 |
| 1958-59 | Boston | 70 | 9 | 23 | 32 |
| 1959-60 | Boston | 63 | 16 | 28 | 44 |
| 1960-61 | Bos-Det | 64 | 9 | 21 | 30 |
| 1961-62 | Detroit | 47 | 3 | 4 | 7 |
| | Totals | 642 | 128 | 193 | 321 |

**LABOSSIERE, Gordon William** *Forward*
b. St. Boniface, Man., Jan. 2, 1940

| Season | Club | GP | G | A | Pts. |
|---|---|---|---|---|---|
| 1963-64 | New York R | 15 | 0 | 0 | 0 |
| 1964-65 | New York R | 1 | 0 | 0 | 0 |
| 1967-68 | Los Angeles | 68 | 13 | 27 | 40 |
| 1968-69 | Los Angeles | 48 | 10 | 18 | 28 |
| 1970-71 | LA-Minn | 74 | 19 | 14 | 33 |
| 1971-72 | Minnesota | 9 | 2 | 3 | 5 |
| 1972-73 | Houston (WHA) | 77 | 36 | 60 | 96 |
| 1973-74 | Houston (WHA) | 67 | 19 | 36 | 55 |
| 1974-75 | Houston (WHA) | 76 | 23 | 34 | 57 |
| 1975-76 | Houston (WHA) | 80 | 24 | 32 | 56 |
| | NHL Totals | 215 | 44 | 62 | 106 |
| | WHA Totals | 300 | 102 | 162 | 264 |

**LABOVITCH, Max** *Forward*
b. Winnipeg, Man., Jan. 18, 1924

| Season | Club | GP | G | A | Pts. |
|---|---|---|---|---|---|
| 1943-44 | New York R | 5 | 0 | 0 | 0 |

**LABRAATEN, Daniel** *Forward*
b. Lesland, Sweden, June 9, 1951

| Season | Club | GP | G | A | Pts. |
|---|---|---|---|---|---|
| 1976-77 | Winnipeg (WHA) | 64 | 24 | 27 | 51 |
| 1977-78 | Winnipeg (WHA) | 47 | 18 | 16 | 34 |
| 1978-79 | Detroit | 78 | 19 | 19 | 38 |
| 1979-80 | Detroit | 76 | 30 | 27 | 57 |
| 1980-81 | Det-Calg | 71 | 12 | 15 | 27 |
| 1981-82 | Calgary | 43 | 10 | 12 | 22 |
| | NHL Totals | 268 | 71 | 73 | 144 |
| | WHA Totals | 111 | 42 | 43 | 85 |

**LABRE, Yvon Jules** *Defenseman*
b. Sudbury, Ont., Nov. 29, 1949

| Season | Club | GP | G | A | Pts. |
|---|---|---|---|---|---|
| 1970-71 | Pittsburgh | 21 | 1 | 1 | 2 |
| 1973-74 | Pittsburgh | 16 | 1 | 2 | 3 |
| 1974-75 | Washington | 76 | 4 | 23 | 27 |
| 1975-76 | Washington | 80 | 2 | 20 | 22 |
| 1976-77 | Washington | 62 | 3 | 11 | 14 |
| 1977-78 | Washington | 22 | 0 | 8 | 8 |
| 1978-79 | Washington | 51 | 1 | 13 | 14 |
| 1979-80 | Washington | 18 | 0 | 5 | 5 |
| 1980-81 | Washington | 25 | 2 | 4 | 6 |
| | Totals | 371 | 14 | 87 | 101 |

| Season | Club | GP | G | A | Pts. |
|---|---|---|---|---|---|
| **LABRIE, Guy** *Defenseman* | | | | | |
| b. St. Charles Bellechase, Que., Aug. 11, 1920 | | | | | |
| 1943-44 | Boston | 15 | 2 | 7 | 9 |
| 1944-45 | New York R | 27 | 2 | 2 | 4 |
| | **Totals** | 42 | 4 | 9 | 13 |
| **LACH, Elmer James** *Forward* | | | | | |
| b. Nokomis, Sask., Jan. 22, 1918 | | | | | |
| 1940-41 | Montreal | 43 | 7 | 14 | 21 |
| 1941-42 | Montreal | 1 | 0 | 1 | 1 |
| 1942-43 | Montreal | 45 | 18 | 40 | 58 |
| 1943-44 | Montreal | 48 | 24 | 48 | 72 |
| 1944-45 | Montreal | 50 | 26 | 54 | 80 |
| 1945-46 | Montreal | 50 | 13 | 34 | 47 |
| 1946-47 | Montreal | 31 | 14 | 16 | 30 |
| 1947-48 | Montreal | 60 | 30 | 31 | 61 |
| 1948-49 | Montreal | 36 | 11 | 18 | 29 |
| 1949-50 | Montreal | 64 | 15 | 33 | 48 |
| 1950-51 | Montreal | 65 | 21 | 24 | 45 |
| 1951-52 | Montreal | 70 | 15 | 50 | 65 |
| 1952-53 | Montreal | 53 | 16 | 25 | 41 |
| 1953-54 | Montreal | 48 | 5 | 20 | 25 |
| | **Totals** | 664 | 215 | 408 | 623 |
| **LACHANCE, Michel** *Defenseman* | | | | | |
| b. Quebec City, Que., Apr. 11, 1955 | | | | | |
| 1978-79 | Colorado | 21 | 0 | 4 | 4 |
| **LACOMBE, Francois** *Defenseman* | | | | | |
| b. Lachine, Que., Feb. 24, 1948 | | | | | |
| 1968-69 | Oakland | 72 | 2 | 16 | 18 |
| 1969-70 | Oakland | 2 | 0 | 0 | 0 |
| 1970-71 | Buffalo | 1 | 0 | 1 | 1 |
| 1972-73 | Quebec (WHA) | 62 | 10 | 18 | 28 |
| 1973-74 | Quebec (WHA) | 71 | 9 | 26 | 35 |
| 1974-75 | Quebec (WHA) | 55 | 7 | 17 | 24 |
| 1975-76 | Calgary (WHA) | 71 | 3 | 28 | 31 |
| 1976-77 | Quebec (WHA) | 81 | 5 | 22 | 27 |
| 1977-78 | Quebec (WHA) | 22 | 1 | 7 | 8 |
| 1978-79 | Quebec (WHA) | 78 | 3 | 21 | 24 |
| 1979-80 | Quebec | 3 | 0 | 0 | 0 |
| | **NHL Totals** | 78 | 2 | 17 | 19 |
| | **WHA Totals** | 440 | 38 | 139 | 177 |
| **LACROIX, Andre Joseph** *Forward* | | | | | |
| b. Lauzon, Que., June 5, 1945 | | | | | |
| 1967-68 | Philadelphia | 18 | 6 | 8 | 14 |
| 1968-69 | Philadelphia | 75 | 24 | 32 | 56 |
| 1969-70 | Philadelphia | 74 | 22 | 36 | 58 |
| 1970-71 | Philadelphia | 78 | 20 | 22 | 42 |
| 1971-72 | Chicago | 51 | 4 | 7 | 11 |
| 1972-73 | Philadelphia (WHA) | 78 | 50 | 74 | 124 |
| 1973-74 | New Jersey (WHA) | 78 | 31 | 80 | 111 |
| 1974-75 | San Diego (WHA) | 78 | 41 | 106 | 147 |
| 1975-76 | San Diego (WHA) | 80 | 29 | 72 | 101 |
| 1976-77 | San Diego (WHA) | 81 | 32 | 82 | 114 |
| 1977-78 | Houston (WHA) | 78 | 36 | 77 | 113 |
| 1978-79 | New England (WHA) | 78 | 32 | 56 | 88 |
| 1979-80 | Hartford | 29 | 3 | 14 | 17 |
| | **NHL Totals** | 325 | 79 | 119 | 198 |
| | **WHA Totals** | 551 | 251 | 547 | 798 |
| **LACROIX, Pierre** *Defenseman* | | | | | |
| b. Quebec City, Que., Apr. 11, 1959 | | | | | |
| 1979-80 | Quebec | 76 | 9 | 21 | 30 |
| 1980-81 | Quebec | 61 | 5 | 34 | 39 |
| 1981-82 | Quebec | 68 | 4 | 23 | 27 |
| 1982-83 | Que-Hart | 69 | 6 | 30 | 36 |
| | **Totals** | 274 | 24 | 108 | 132 |
| **LADOUCEUR, Randy** *Defenseman* | | | | | |
| b. Brockville, Ont., June 30, 1960 | | | | | |
| 1982-83 | Detroit | 27 | 0 | 4 | 4 |
| **LAFLEUR, Guy Damien** *Forward* | | | | | |
| b. Thurso, Que., Sept. 20, 1951 | | | | | |
| 1971-72 | Montreal | 73 | 29 | 35 | 64 |
| 1972-73 | Montreal | 70 | 28 | 27 | 55 |
| 1973-74 | Montreal | 73 | 21 | 35 | 56 |
| 1974-75 | Montreal | 70 | 53 | 66 | 119 |
| 1975-76 | Montreal | 80 | 56 | 69 | 125 |

| Season | Club | GP | G | A | Pts. |
|---|---|---|---|---|---|
| 1976-77 | Montreal | 80 | 56 | 80 | 136 |
| 1977-78 | Montreal | 78 | 60 | 72 | 132 |
| 1978-79 | Montreal | 80 | 52 | 77 | 129 |
| 1979-80 | Montreal | 74 | 50 | 75 | 125 |
| 1980-81 | Montreal | 51 | 27 | 43 | 70 |
| 1981-82 | Montreal | 66 | 27 | 57 | 84 |
| 1982-83 | Montreal | 68 | 27 | 49 | 76 |
| | **Totals** | 863 | 486 | 685 | 1171 |
| **LaFLEUR, Rene** *Forward* | | | | | |
| 1924-25 | Montreal | 1 | 0 | 0 | 0 |
| **LaFORCE, Ernest** *Defenseman* | | | | | |
| b. Montreal, Que., June 23, 1916 | | | | | |
| 1942-43 | Montreal | 1 | 0 | 0 | 0 |
| **LAFORGE, Claude Roger** *Forward* | | | | | |
| b. Sorel, Que., July 1, 1936 | | | | | |
| 1957-58 | Montreal | 5 | 0 | 0 | 0 |
| 1958-59 | Detroit | 57 | 2 | 5 | 7 |
| 1960-61 | Detroit | 10 | 1 | 0 | 1 |
| 1961-62 | Detroit | 38 | 10 | 9 | 19 |
| 1963-64 | Detroit | 17 | 2 | 3 | 5 |
| 1964-65 | Detroit | 1 | 0 | 0 | 0 |
| 1967-68 | Philadelphia | 63 | 9 | 16 | 25 |
| 1968-69 | Philadelphia | 2 | 0 | 0 | 0 |
| | **Totals** | 193 | 24 | 33 | 57 |
| **LAFRAMBOISE, Peter** *Forward* | | | | | |
| b. Ottawa, Ont., Jan. 18, 1950 | | | | | |
| 1971-72 | California | 5 | 0 | 0 | 0 |
| 1972-73 | California | 77 | 16 | 25 | 41 |
| 1973-74 | California | 65 | 7 | 7 | 14 |
| 1974-75 | Wash-Pitt | 80 | 10 | 23 | 33 |
| 1976-77 | Edmonton (WHA) | 17 | 0 | 5 | 5 |
| | **NHL Totals** | 217 | 33 | 55 | 88 |
| | **WHA Totals** | 17 | 0 | 5 | 5 |
| **LaFRANCE, Adelard** *Forward* | | | | | |
| b. Chapleau, Ont., Jan. 13, 1912 | | | | | |
| 1933-34 | Montreal | 3 | 0 | 0 | 0 |
| **LaFRANCE, Leo** *Forward* | | | | | |
| 1926-27 | Montreal | 4 | 0 | 0 | 0 |
| 1927-28 | Chicago | 29 | 2 | 0 | 2 |
| | **Totals** | 33 | 2 | 0 | 2 |
| **LAFRENIERE, Roger J.** *Forward* | | | | | |
| b. Montreal, Que., July 24, 1942 | | | | | |
| 1962-63 | Detroit | 3 | 0 | 0 | 0 |
| 1972-73 | St Louis | 10 | 0 | 0 | 0 |
| | **Totals** | 13 | 0 | 0 | 0 |
| **LAGACE, Jean-Guy** *Defenseman* | | | | | |
| b. L'Abord a Plouffe, Que., Feb. 5, 1945 | | | | | |
| 1968-69 | Pittsburgh | 17 | 0 | 1 | 1 |
| 1970-71 | Buffalo | 3 | 0 | 0 | 0 |
| 1972-73 | Pittsburgh | 31 | 1 | 5 | 6 |
| 1973-74 | Pittsburgh | 31 | 2 | 6 | 8 |
| 1974-75 | Pitt-KC | 46 | 3 | 17 | 20 |
| 1975-76 | Kansas City | 69 | 3 | 10 | 13 |
| 1976-77 | Birmingham (WHA) | 78 | 2 | 25 | 27 |
| | **NHL Totals** | 197 | 9 | 39 | 48 |
| | **WHA Totals** | 78 | 2 | 25 | 27 |
| **LAIDLAW, Thomas** *Defenseman* | | | | | |
| b. Brampton, Ont., Apr. 15, 1958 | | | | | |
| 1980-81 | New York R | 80 | 6 | 23 | 29 |
| 1981-82 | New York R | 79 | 3 | 18 | 21 |
| 1982-83 | New York R | 80 | 0 | 10 | 10 |
| | **Totals** | 239 | 9 | 51 | 60 |
| **LAIRD, Robbie** *Forward* | | | | | |
| b. Regina, Sask., Dec. 29, 1954 | | | | | |
| 1979-80 | | 1 | 0 | 0 | 0 |
| **LAJEUNESSE, Serge** *Defenseman* | | | | | |
| b. Montreal, Que., June 11, 1950 | | | | | |
| 1970-71 | Detroit | 62 | 1 | 3 | 4 |
| 1971-72 | Detroit | 7 | 0 | 0 | 0 |

| Season | Club | GP | G | A | Pts. |
|---|---|---|---|---|---|
| 1972-73 | Detroit | 28 | 0 | 1 | 1 |
| 1973-74 | Philadelphia | 1 | 0 | 0 | 0 |
| 1974-75 | Philadelphia | 5 | 0 | 0 | 0 |
| | **Totals** | 106 | 1 | 4 | 5 |
| **LALANDE, Hector** *Forward* | | | | | |
| b. North Bay, Ont., Nov. 24, 1934 | | | | | |
| 1953-54 | Chicago | 2 | 0 | 0 | 0 |
| 1955-56 | Chicago | 65 | 8 | 18 | 26 |
| 1956-57 | Chicago | 50 | 11 | 17 | 28 |
| 1957-58 | Chi-Det | 34 | 2 | 4 | 6 |
| | **Totals** | 151 | 21 | 39 | 60 |
| **LALONDE, Edouard (Newsy)** | | | | | |
| *Defenseman-Forward* | | | | | |
| b. Cornwall, Ont., Oct. 31, 1887 | | | | | |
| 1917-18 | Montreal | 14 | 23 | 0 | 23 |
| 1918-19 | Montreal | 17 | 23 | 9 | 32 |
| 1919-20 | Montreal | 23 | 36 | 6 | 42 |
| 1920-21 | Montreal | 24 | 33 | 8 | 41 |
| 1921-22 | Montreal | 20 | 9 | 4 | 13 |
| 1926-27 | New York A | 1 | 0 | 0 | 0 |
| | **Totals** | 99 | 124 | 27 | 151 |
| **LALONDE, Robert Patrick (Bobby)** *Forward* | | | | | |
| b. Montreal, Que., Mar. 27, 1951 | | | | | |
| 1971-72 | Vancouver | 27 | 1 | 5 | 6 |
| 1972-73 | Vancouver | 77 | 20 | 27 | 47 |
| 1973-74 | Vancouver | 36 | 3 | 4 | 7 |
| 1974-75 | Vancouver | 74 | 17 | 30 | 47 |
| 1975-76 | Vancouver | 71 | 14 | 36 | 50 |
| 1976-77 | Vancouver | 68 | 17 | 15 | 32 |
| 1977-78 | Atlanta | 73 | 14 | 23 | 37 |
| 1978-79 | Atlanta | 78 | 24 | 32 | 56 |
| 1979-80 | Atl-Bos | 74 | 10 | 26 | 36 |
| 1980-81 | Boston | 62 | 4 | 12 | 16 |
| 1981-82 | Calgary | 1 | 0 | 0 | 0 |
| | **Totals** | 641 | 124 | 210 | 334 |
| **LALONDE, Ronald** *Forward* | | | | | |
| b. Toronto, Ont., Oct. 30, 1952 | | | | | |
| 1972-73 | Pittsburgh | 9 | 0 | 0 | 0 |
| 1973-74 | Pittsburgh | 73 | 10 | 17 | 27 |
| 1974-75 | Pitt-Wash | 74 | 12 | 17 | 29 |
| 1975-76 | Washington | 80 | 9 | 10 | 19 |
| 1976-77 | Washington | 76 | 12 | 17 | 29 |
| 1977-78 | Washington | 67 | 1 | 5 | 6 |
| 1978-79 | Washington | 18 | 1 | 3 | 4 |
| | **Totals** | 397 | 45 | 69 | 114 |
| **LAMB, Joseph Gordon** *Forward* | | | | | |
| b. Sussex, N.B., June 18, 1906 | | | | | |
| 1927-28 | Montreal M | 21 | 8 | 5 | 13 |
| 1928-29 | MontM-Ott | 36 | 4 | 1 | 5 |
| 1929-30 | Ottawa | 44 | 29 | 20 | 49 |
| 1930-31 | Ottawa | 44 | 11 | 14 | 25 |
| 1931-32 | New York A | 48 | 14 | 11 | 25 |
| 1932-33 | Boston | 42 | 11 | 8 | 19 |
| 1933-34 | Boston | 48 | 10 | 15 | 25 |
| 1934-35 | Mont-StLE | 38 | 14 | 14 | 28 |
| 1935-36 | Montreal M | 35 | 0 | 3 | 3 |
| 1936-37 | New York A | 48 | 3 | 9 | 12 |
| 1937-38 | NYA-Det | 39 | 4 | 1 | 5 |
| | **Totals** | 443 | 108 | 101 | 209 |
| **LAMBERT, Yvon Pierre** *Forward* | | | | | |
| b. Drummondville, Que., May 20, 1950 | | | | | |
| 1972-73 | Montreal | 1 | 0 | 0 | 0 |
| 1973-74 | Montreal | 60 | 6 | 10 | 16 |
| 1974-75 | Montreal | 80 | 32 | 35 | 67 |
| 1975-76 | Montreal | 80 | 32 | 35 | 67 |
| 1976-77 | Montreal | 79 | 24 | 28 | 52 |
| 1977-78 | Montreal | 77 | 18 | 22 | 40 |
| 1978-79 | Montreal | 79 | 26 | 40 | 66 |
| 1979-80 | Montreal | 77 | 21 | 32 | 53 |
| 1980-81 | Montreal | 73 | 22 | 32 | 54 |
| 1981-82 | Buffalo | 77 | 25 | 39 | 64 |
| | **Totals** | 683 | 206 | 273 | 479 |

| Season | Club | GP | G | A | Pts. |
|---|---|---|---|---|---|
| **LAMBY, Richard A.** *Defenseman* | | | | | |
| b. Auburn, Mass., May 3, 1955 | | | | | |
| 1978-79 | St Louis | 9 | 0 | 4 | 4 |
| 1979-80 | St Louis | 12 | 0 | 1 | 1 |
| 1980-81 | St Louis | 1 | 0 | 0 | 0 |
| **Totals** | | 22 | 0 | 5 | 5 |
| **LAMIRANCE, Jean Paul** *Defenseman* | | | | | |
| b. Shawinigan Falls, Que., Aug. 21, 1923 | | | | | |
| 1946-47 | New York R | 14 | 1 | 1 | 2 |
| 1947-48 | New York R | 18 | 0 | 1 | 1 |
| 1949-50 | New York R | 16 | 4 | 3 | 7 |
| 1954-55 | Montreal | 1 | 0 | 0 | 0 |
| **Totals** | | 49 | 5 | 5 | 10 |
| **LAMOUREUX, Leo Peter** *Defenseman* | | | | | |
| b. Espanola, Ont., Oct. 1, 1916 | | | | | |
| 1941-42 | Montreal | 1 | 0 | 0 | 0 |
| 1942-43 | Montreal | 46 | 2 | 16 | 18 |
| 1943-44 | Montreal | 44 | 8 | 23 | 31 |
| 1944-45 | Montreal | 49 | 2 | 22 | 24 |
| 1945-46 | Montreal | 45 | 5 | 7 | 12 |
| 1946-47 | Montreal | 50 | 2 | 11 | 13 |
| **Totals** | | 235 | 19 | 79 | 98 |
| **LAMPMAN, Michael** *Forward* | | | | | |
| b. Lakewood, Calif., Apr. 20, 1950 | | | | | |
| 1972-73 | St Louis | 18 | 2 | 3 | 5 |
| 1973-74 | StL-Van | 29 | 2 | 0 | 2 |
| 1975-76 | Washington | 27 | 7 | 12 | 19 |
| 1976-77 | Washington | 22 | 6 | 5 | 11 |
| **Totals** | | 96 | 17 | 20 | 37 |
| **LANCIEN, John Gordon (Jack)** *Defenseman* | | | | | |
| b. Regina, Sask., June 14, 1923 | | | | | |
| 1946-47 | New York R | 1 | 0 | 0 | 0 |
| 1949-50 | New York R | 43 | 0 | 4 | 5 |
| 1950-51 | New York R | 19 | 0 | 1 | 1 |
| **Totals** | | 63 | 1 | 5 | 6 |
| **LANE, Gordon** *Defenseman* | | | | | |
| b. Brandon, Man., Mar. 31, 1953 | | | | | |
| 1975-76 | Washington | 3 | 1 | 0 | 1 |
| 1976-77 | Washington | 80 | 2 | 15 | 17 |
| 1977-78 | Washington | 69 | 2 | 9 | 11 |
| 1978-79 | Washington | 64 | 3 | 15 | 18 |
| 1979-80 | Wash-NYI | 74 | 4 | 18 | 22 |
| 1980-81 | New York I | 60 | 3 | 9 | 12 |
| 1981-82 | New York I | 51 | 0 | 13 | 13 |
| 1982-83 | New York I | 44 | 3 | 4 | 7 |
| **Totals** | | 445 | 18 | 83 | 101 |
| **LANE, Myles J.** *Defenseman* | | | | | |
| b. Melrose, Mass., Oct. 2, 1905 | | | | | |
| 1928-29 | New York R | 24 | 2 | 0 | 2 |
| 1929-30 | Boston | 3 | 0 | 0 | 0 |
| 1933-34 | Boston | 25 | 2 | 1 | 3 |
| **Totals** | | 52 | 4 | 1 | 5 |
| **LANGDON, Stephen Murray** *Forward* | | | | | |
| b. Toronto, Ont., Dec. 23, 1953 | | | | | |
| 1974-75 | Boston | 1 | 0 | 1 | 1 |
| 1975-76 | Boston | 4 | 0 | 0 | 0 |
| 1977-78 | Boston | 2 | 0 | 0 | 0 |
| **Totals** | | 7 | 0 | 1 | 1 |
| **LANGELLE, Peter** *Forward* | | | | | |
| b. Winnipeg, Man., Nov. 4, 1917 | | | | | |
| 1938-39 | Toronto | 2 | 1 | 0 | 1 |
| 1939-40 | Toronto | 39 | 7 | 14 | 21 |
| 1940-41 | Toronto | 47 | 4 | 15 | 19 |
| 1941-42 | Toronto | 48 | 10 | 22 | 32 |
| **Totals** | | 136 | 22 | 51 | 73 |
| **LANGEVIN, David** *Defenseman* | | | | | |
| b. St. Paul, Minn., May 15, 1954 | | | | | |
| 1976-77 | Edmonton (WHA) | 77 | 7 | 16 | 23 |
| 1977-78 | Edmonton (WHA) | 62 | 6 | 22 | 28 |

| Season | Club | GP | G | A | Pts. |
|---|---|---|---|---|---|
| 1978-79 | Edmonton (WHA) | 77 | 6 | 21 | 27 |
| 1979-80 | New York I | 76 | 3 | 13 | 16 |
| 1980-81 | New York I | 75 | 1 | 16 | 17 |
| 1981-82 | New York I | 73 | 1 | 20 | 21 |
| 1982-83 | New York I | 73 | 4 | 17 | 21 |
| **NHL Totals** | | 297 | 9 | 66 | 75 |
| **WHA Totals** | | 216 | 19 | 59 | 78 |
| **LANGLAIS, Joseph Alfred Alain** *Forward* | | | | | |
| b. Chicoutimi, Que., Oct. 9, 1950 | | | | | |
| 1974-75 | Minnesota | 11 | 1 | 1 | 2 |
| **LANGLOIS, Albert (Junior)** *Defenseman* | | | | | |
| b. Magog, Que., Nov. 6, 1934 | | | | | |
| 1957-58 | Montreal | 1 | 0 | 0 | 0 |
| 1958-59 | Montreal | 48 | 0 | 3 | 3 |
| 1959-60 | Montreal | 67 | 1 | 14 | 15 |
| 1960-61 | Montreal | 61 | 1 | 12 | 13 |
| 1961-62 | New York R | 69 | 7 | 18 | 25 |
| 1962-63 | New York R | 60 | 2 | 14 | 16 |
| 1963-64 | NYR-Det | 61 | 5 | 8 | 13 |
| 1964-65 | Detroit | 65 | 1 | 12 | 13 |
| 1965-66 | Boston | 65 | 4 | 10 | 14 |
| **Totals** | | 497 | 21 | 91 | 112 |
| **LANGLOIS, Charles** *Defenseman* | | | | | |
| b. Lotbiniere, Que., Aug. 25, 1894 | | | | | |
| 1924-25 | Hamilton | 30 | 6 | 1 | 7 |
| 1925-26 | New York A | 36 | 9 | 1 | 10 |
| 1926-27 | NYA-PittPi | 45 | 7 | 1 | 8 |
| 1927-28 | PittPi-MontM | 40 | 0 | 0 | 0 |
| **Totals** | | 151 | 22 | 3 | 25 |
| **LANGWAY, Rod Corry** *Defenseman* | | | | | |
| b. Maag, Taiwan, May 3, 1957 | | | | | |
| 1977-78 | Birmingham (WHA) | 52 | 3 | 18 | 21 |
| 1978-79 | Montreal | 45 | 3 | 4 | 7 |
| 1979-80 | Montreal | 77 | 7 | 29 | 36 |
| 1980-81 | Montreal | 80 | 11 | 34 | 45 |
| 1981-82 | Montreal | 66 | 5 | 34 | 39 |
| 1982-83 | Washington | 80 | 3 | 29 | 32 |
| **NHL Totals** | | 348 | 29 | 130 | 159 |
| **WHA Totals** | | 52 | 3 | 18 | 21 |
| **LANYON, Edward George (Ted)** *Defenseman* | | | | | |
| b. Winnipeg, Man., June 11, 1939 | | | | | |
| 1967-68 | Pittsburgh | 5 | 0 | 0 | 0 |
| **LANZ, Rick Roman** *Defenseman* | | | | | |
| b. Karlouyvary, Czechoslovakia, Sept. 16, 1961 | | | | | |
| 1980-81 | Vancouver | 76 | 7 | 22 | 29 |
| 1981-82 | Vancouver | 39 | 3 | 11 | 14 |
| 1982-83 | Vancouver | 74 | 10 | 38 | 48 |
| **Totals** | | 189 | 20 | 71 | 91 |
| **LAPERRIERE, J. Jacques** *Defenseman* | | | | | |
| b. Rouyn, Que., Nov. 22, 1941 | | | | | |
| 1962-63 | Montreal | 6 | 0 | 2 | 2 |
| 1963-64 | Montreal | 65 | 2 | 28 | 30 |
| 1964-65 | Montreal | 67 | 5 | 22 | 27 |
| 1965-66 | Montreal | 57 | 6 | 25 | 31 |
| 1966-67 | Montreal | 61 | 0 | 20 | 20 |
| 1967-68 | Montreal | 72 | 4 | 21 | 25 |
| 1968-69 | Montreal | 69 | 5 | 26 | 31 |
| 1969-70 | Montreal | 73 | 6 | 31 | 37 |
| 1970-71 | Montreal | 49 | 0 | 16 | 16 |
| 1971-72 | Montreal | 73 | 3 | 25 | 28 |
| 1972-73 | Montreal | 57 | 7 | 16 | 23 |
| 1973-74 | Montreal | 42 | 2 | 10 | 12 |
| **Totals** | | 691 | 40 | 242 | 282 |
| **LAPOINTE, Guy Gerard** *Defenseman* | | | | | |
| b. Montreal, Que., Mar. 18, 1948 | | | | | |
| 1968-69 | Montreal | 1 | 0 | 0 | 0 |
| 1969-70 | Montreal | 5 | 0 | 0 | 0 |
| 1970-71 | Montreal | 78 | 15 | 29 | 44 |
| 1971-72 | Montreal | 69 | 11 | 38 | 49 |
| 1972-73 | Montreal | 76 | 19 | 35 | 54 |
| 1973-74 | Montreal | 71 | 13 | 40 | 53 |
| 1974-75 | Montreal | 80 | 28 | 47 | 75 |

| Season | Club | GP | G | A | Pts. |
|---|---|---|---|---|---|
| 1975-76 | Montreal | 77 | 21 | 47 | 68 |
| 1976-77 | Montreal | 77 | 25 | 51 | 76 |
| 1977-78 | Montreal | 49 | 13 | 29 | 42 |
| 1978-79 | Montreal | 69 | 13 | 42 | 55 |
| 1979-80 | Montreal | 45 | 6 | 20 | 26 |
| 1980-81 | Montreal | 33 | 1 | 9 | 10 |
| 1981-82 | Mont-StL | 55 | 1 | 25 | 26 |
| 1982-83 | St Louis | 54 | 3 | 23 | 26 |
| **Totals** | | 839 | 169 | 435 | 604 |
| **LAPOINTE, Richard Paul** *Defenseman* | | | | | |
| b. Victoria, B.C., Aug. 2, 1955 | | | | | |
| 1975-76 | Detroit | 80 | 10 | 23 | 33 |
| 1976-77 | Det-Phil | 71 | 3 | 19 | 22 |
| 1977-78 | Philadelphia | 47 | 4 | 16 | 20 |
| 1978-79 | Philadelphia | 77 | 3 | 18 | 21 |
| 1979-80 | St Louis | 80 | 6 | 19 | 25 |
| 1980-81 | St Louis | 80 | 8 | 25 | 33 |
| 1981-82 | St Louis | 71 | 2 | 20 | 22 |
| 1982-83 | Quebec | 43 | 2 | 9 | 11 |
| **Totals** | | 549 | 38 | 149 | 187 |
| **LAPRADE, Edgar Louis** *Forward* | | | | | |
| b. Mine Center, Ont., Oct. 10, 1919 | | | | | |
| 1945-46 | New York R | 49 | 15 | 19 | 34 |
| 1946-47 | New York R | 58 | 15 | 25 | 40 |
| 1947-48 | New York R | 59 | 13 | 34 | 47 |
| 1948-49 | New York R | 56 | 18 | 12 | 30 |
| 1949-50 | New York R | 60 | 22 | 22 | 44 |
| 1950-51 | New York R | 42 | 10 | 13 | 23 |
| 1951-52 | New York R | 70 | 9 | 29 | 38 |
| 1952-53 | New York R | 11 | 2 | 1 | 3 |
| 1953-54 | New York R | 35 | 1 | 6 | 7 |
| 1954-55 | New York R | 60 | 3 | 11 | 14 |
| **Totals** | | 500 | 108 | 172 | 280 |
| **LaPRAIRIE, Ben (Bun)** *Defenseman* | | | | | |
| 1936-37 | Chicago | 6 | 0 | 0 | 0 |
| **LARIVIERE, Garry Joseph** *Defenseman* | | | | | |
| b. St. Catharines, Ont., Dec. 6, 1954 | | | | | |
| 1974-75 | Phoenix (WHA) | 4 | 0 | 1 | 1 |
| 1975-76 | Phoenix (WHA) | 79 | 7 | 17 | 24 |
| 1976-77 | Phoe-Que (WHA) | 76 | 7 | 26 | 33 |
| 1977-78 | Quebec (WHA) | 80 | 7 | 49 | 56 |
| 1978-79 | Quebec (WHA) | 50 | 5 | 33 | 38 |
| 1979-80 | Quebec | 75 | 2 | 19 | 21 |
| 1980-81 | Que-Edm | 65 | 3 | 15 | 18 |
| 1981-82 | Edmonton | 62 | 1 | 21 | 22 |
| 1982-83 | Edmonton | 17 | 0 | 2 | 2 |
| **NHL Totals** | | 219 | 6 | 57 | 63 |
| **WHA Totals** | | 289 | 26 | 126 | 152 |
| **LARMER, Jeff** *Forward* | | | | | |
| b. Peterborough, Ont., Nov. 10, 1962 | | | | | |
| 1981-82 | Colorado | 8 | 1 | 1 | 2 |
| 1982-83 | New Jersey | 65 | 21 | 24 | 45 |
| **Totals** | | 73 | 22 | 25 | 47 |
| **LARMER, Steve Donald** *Forward* | | | | | |
| b. Peterborough, Ont., June 16, 1961 | | | | | |
| 1980-81 | Chicago | 4 | 0 | 1 | 1 |
| 1981-82 | Chicago | 3 | 0 | 0 | 0 |
| 1982-83 | Chicago | 80 | 43 | 47 | 90 |
| **Totals** | | 87 | 43 | 48 | 91 |
| **LAROCHELLE, Wildor** *Forward* | | | | | |
| b. Sorel, Que., Sept. 3, 1906 | | | | | |
| 1925-26 | Montreal | 33 | 2 | 1 | 3 |
| 1926-27 | Montreal | 41 | 0 | 1 | 1 |
| 1927-28 | Montreal | 40 | 3 | 1 | 4 |
| 1928-29 | Montreal | 2 | 0 | 0 | 0 |
| 1929-30 | Montreal | 44 | 14 | 11 | 15 |
| 1930-31 | Montreal | 40 | 8 | 5 | 13 |
| 1931-32 | Montreal | 40 | 18 | 8 | 20 |
| 1932-33 | Montreal | 47 | 11 | 4 | 15 |
| 1933-34 | Montreal | 48 | 16 | 11 | 27 |
| 1934-35 | Montreal | 48 | 9 | 19 | 28 |
| 1935-36 | Mont-Chi | 40 | 2 | 3 | 5 |
| 1935-36 | Chicago | 43 | 9 | 10 | 19 |
| **Totals** | | 474 | 92 | 74 | 166 |

| Season | Club | GP | G | A | Pts. |
|---|---|---|---|---|---|
| **LAROSE, Charles** *Forward* | | | | | |
| 1925-26 | Boston | 6 | 0 | 0 | 0 |
| **LAROSE, Claude** *Forward* | | | | | |
| b. St. Jean, Que., May 17, 1955 | | | | | |
| 1975-76 | Cincinnati (WHA) | 79 | 28 | 24 | 52 |
| 1976-77 | Cincinnati (WHA) | 81 | 30 | 46 | 76 |
| 1977-78 | Cin-Ind (WHA) | 79 | 25 | 36 | 61 |
| 1978-79 | Indianapolis (WHA) | 13 | 5 | 8 | 13 |
| 1979-80 | New York R | 25 | 4 | 7 | 11 |
| | NHL Totals | 25 | 4 | 7 | 11 |
| | WHA Totals | 252 | 88 | 114 | 202 |
| **LAROSE, Claude David** *Forward* | | | | | |
| b. Hearst, Ont., Mar. 2, 1942 | | | | | |
| 1962-63 | Montreal | 4 | 0 | 0 | 0 |
| 1963-64 | Montreal | 21 | 1 | 1 | 2 |
| 1964-65 | Montreal | 68 | 21 | 16 | 37 |
| 1965-66 | Montreal | 64 | 15 | 18 | 33 |
| 1966-67 | Montreal | 69 | 19 | 16 | 35 |
| 1967-68 | Montreal | 42 | 2 | 9 | 11 |
| 1968-69 | Minnesota | 67 | 25 | 37 | 62 |
| 1969-70 | Minnesota | 75 | 24 | 23 | 47 |
| 1970-71 | Montreal | 64 | 10 | 13 | 23 |
| 1971-72 | Montreal | 77 | 20 | 18 | 38 |
| 1972-73 | Montreal | 73 | 11 | 23 | 34 |
| 1973-74 | Montreal | 39 | 17 | 7 | 24 |
| 1974-75 | Mont-StL | 64 | 11 | 19 | 30 |
| 1975-76 | St Louis | 67 | 13 | 25 | 38 |
| 1976-77 | St Louis | 80 | 29 | 19 | 48 |
| 1977-78 | St Louis | 69 | 8 | 13 | 21 |
| | Totals | 943 | 226 | 257 | 483 |
| **LAROUCHE, Pierre** *Forward* | | | | | |
| b. Taschereau, Que., Nov. 16, 1955 | | | | | |
| 1974-75 | Pittsburgh | 79 | 31 | 37 | 68 |
| 1975-76 | Pittsburgh | 76 | 53 | 58 | 111 |
| 1976-77 | Pittsburgh | 65 | 29 | 34 | 63 |
| 1977-78 | Pitt-Mont | 64 | 23 | 37 | 60 |
| 1978-79 | Montreal | 36 | 9 | 13 | 22 |
| 1979-80 | Montreal | 73 | 50 | 41 | 91 |
| 1980-81 | Montreal | 61 | 25 | 28 | 53 |
| 1981-82 | Mont-Hart | 67 | 34 | 37 | 71 |
| 1982-83 | Hartford | 38 | 18 | 22 | 40 |
| | Totals | 529 | 272 | 307 | 579 |
| **LARSON, Norman Lyle** *Forward* | | | | | |
| b. Moose Jaw, Sask., Oct. 13, 1920 | | | | | |
| 1940-41 | New York A | 47 | 9 | 9 | 18 |
| 1941-42 | New York A | 40 | 16 | 9 | 25 |
| 1946-47 | New York R | 1 | 0 | 0 | 0 |
| | Totals | 88 | 25 | 18 | 43 |
| **LARSON, Reed David** *Defenseman* | | | | | |
| b. Minneapolis, Minn., July 30, 1956 | | | | | |
| 1976-77 | Detroit | 14 | 0 | 1 | 1 |
| 1977-78 | Detroit | 75 | 19 | 41 | 60 |
| 1978-79 | Detroit | 79 | 18 | 49 | 67 |
| 1979-80 | Detroit | 80 | 22 | 44 | 66 |
| 1980-81 | Detroit | 78 | 27 | 31 | 58 |
| 1981-82 | Detroit | 80 | 21 | 39 | 60 |
| 1982-83 | Detroit | 80 | 22 | 52 | 74 |
| | Totals | 486 | 129 | 257 | 386 |
| **LATREILLE, Philip J.** *Forward* | | | | | |
| b. Montreal, Que., Apr. 22, 1938 | | | | | |
| 1960-61 | New York R | 4 | 0 | 0 | 0 |
| **LAUGHLIN, Craig** *Forward* | | | | | |
| b. Toronto, Ont., Sept. 19, 1957 | | | | | |
| 1981-82 | Montreal | 36 | 12 | 11 | 23 |
| 1982-83 | Washington | 75 | 17 | 27 | 44 |
| | Totals | 111 | 29 | 38 | 67 |
| **LAUGHTON, Michael Frederic** *Forward* | | | | | |
| b. Nelson, B.C., Feb. 21, 1944 | | | | | |
| 1967-68 | Oakland | 35 | 2 | 6 | 8 |
| 1968-69 | Oakland | 53 | 20 | 23 | 43 |
| 1969-70 | Oakland | 76 | 16 | 19 | 35 |
| 1970-71 | California | 25 | 1 | 0 | 1 |
| 1972-73 | New York (WHA) | 67 | 16 | 20 | 36 |
| 1973-74 | New Jersey (WHA) | 71 | 20 | 18 | 38 |
| 1974-75 | San Diego (WHA) | 65 | 7 | 9 | 16 |
| | NHL Totals | 189 | 39 | 48 | 87 |
| | WHA Totals | 203 | 43 | 47 | 90 |
| **LAURENCE, Don (Red)** *Forward* | | | | | |
| b. Galt, Ont., June 27, 1957 | | | | | |
| 1978-79 | Atlanta | 59 | 14 | 20 | 34 |
| 1979-80 | St Louis | 20 | 1 | 2 | 3 |
| | Totals | 79 | 15 | 22 | 37 |
| **LAVALLEE, Kevin A.** *Forward* | | | | | |
| b. Sudbury, Ont., Sept. 16, 1961 | | | | | |
| 1980-81 | Calgary | 77 | 15 | 20 | 35 |
| 1981-82 | Calgary | 75 | 32 | 29 | 61 |
| 1982-83 | Calgary | 60 | 19 | 16 | 35 |
| | Totals | 212 | 66 | 65 | 131 |
| **LAVENDER, Brian James** *Forward* | | | | | |
| b. Edmonton, Alta., Apr. 20, 1947 | | | | | |
| 1971-72 | St Louis | 46 | 5 | 11 | 16 |
| 1972-73 | NYI-Det | 70 | 8 | 8 | 16 |
| 1973-74 | Detroit | 4 | 0 | 0 | 0 |
| 1974-75 | California | 65 | 3 | 7 | 10 |
| | Totals | 185 | 16 | 26 | 42 |
| **LAVIOLETTE, Jack** *Defenseman-Forward* | | | | | |
| b. Belleville, Ont., July 27, 1879 | | | | | |
| 1917-18 | Montreal | 18 | 2 | 0 | 2 |
| **LAWLESS, Paul** *Forward* | | | | | |
| b. Scarboro, Ont., July 2, 1964 | | | | | |
| 1982-83 | Hartford | 47 | 6 | 9 | 15 |
| **LAWSON, Daniel Michael** *Forward* | | | | | |
| b. Toronto, Ont., Oct. 30, 1947 | | | | | |
| 1967-68 | Detroit | 1 | 0 | 0 | 0 |
| 1968-69 | Det-Minn | 62 | 8 | 10 | 18 |
| 1969-70 | Minnesota | 45 | 9 | 8 | 17 |
| 1970-71 | Minnesota | 33 | 1 | 5 | 6 |
| 1971-72 | Buffalo | 78 | 10 | 6 | 16 |
| 1972-73 | Philadelphia (WHA) | 78 | 61 | 45 | 106 |
| 1973-74 | Vancouver (WHA) | 78 | 50 | 38 | 88 |
| 1974-75 | Vancouver (WHA) | 78 | 33 | 43 | 76 |
| 1975-76 | Calgary (WHA) | 80 | 44 | 52 | 96 |
| 1976-77 | Calg-Winn (WHA) | 78 | 30 | 26 | 56 |
| | NHL Totals | 219 | 28 | 29 | 57 |
| | WHA Totals | 392 | 218 | 204 | 422 |
| **LAYCOE, Harold Richardson** *Defenseman* | | | | | |
| b. Sutherland, Sask., June 23, 1922 | | | | | |
| 1945-46 | New York R | 17 | 0 | 2 | 2 |
| 1946-47 | New York R | 58 | 1 | 12 | 13 |
| 1947-48 | Montreal | 14 | 1 | 2 | 3 |
| 1948-49 | Montreal | 51 | 3 | 5 | 8 |
| 1949-50 | Montreal | 30 | 0 | 2 | 2 |
| 1950-51 | Mont-Bos | 44 | 1 | 3 | 4 |
| 1951-52 | Boston | 70 | 5 | 7 | 12 |
| 1952-53 | Boston | 54 | 2 | 10 | 12 |
| 1953-54 | Boston | 58 | 3 | 16 | 19 |
| 1954-55 | Boston | 70 | 4 | 13 | 17 |
| 1955-56 | Boston | 65 | 5 | 5 | 10 |
| | Totals | 531 | 25 | 77 | 102 |
| **LEACH, Lawrence R** *Forward* | | | | | |
| b. Humboldt, Sask., June 18, 1936 | | | | | |
| 1958-59 | Boston | 29 | 4 | 12 | 16 |
| 1959-60 | Boston | 69 | 7 | 12 | 19 |
| 1961-62 | Boston | 28 | 2 | 5 | 7 |
| | Totals | 126 | 13 | 29 | 42 |
| **LEACH, Reginald Joseph (Reg)** *Forward* | | | | | |
| b. Riverton, Man., Apr. 23, 1950 | | | | | |
| 1970-71 | Boston | 23 | 2 | 4 | 6 |
| 1971-72 | Bos-Cal | 73 | 13 | 20 | 33 |
| 1972-73 | California | 76 | 23 | 12 | 35 |
| 1973-74 | California | 78 | 22 | 24 | 46 |
| 1974-75 | Philadelphia | 80 | 45 | 33 | 78 |
| 1975-76 | Philadelphia | 80 | 61 | 30 | 91 |
| 1976-77 | Philadelphia | 77 | 32 | 14 | 46 |
| 1977-78 | Philadelphia | 72 | 24 | 28 | 52 |
| 1978-79 | Philadelphia | 76 | 34 | 20 | 54 |
| 1979-80 | Philadelphia | 76 | 50 | 26 | 76 |
| 1980-81 | Philadelphia | 79 | 34 | 36 | 70 |
| 1981-82 | Philadelphia | 66 | 26 | 21 | 47 |
| 1982-83 | Detroit | 78 | 15 | 17 | 32 |
| | Totals | 934 | 381 | 285 | 666 |
| **LEBLANC, Fernand** *Forward* | | | | | |
| b. Gaspezie, Que., Jan. 12, 1956 | | | | | |
| 1976-77 | Detroit | 3 | 0 | 0 | 0 |
| 1977-78 | Detroit | 2 | 0 | 0 | 0 |
| 1978-79 | Detroit | 29 | 5 | 6 | 11 |
| | Totals | 34 | 5 | 6 | 11 |
| **LEBLANC, Jean Paul** *Forward* | | | | | |
| b. South Durham, Que., Oct. 20, 1946 | | | | | |
| 1968-69 | Chicago | 6 | 1 | 2 | 3 |
| 1972-73 | Los Angeles (WHA) | 77 | 19 | 50 | 69 |
| 1973-74 | Los Angeles (WHA) | 78 | 20 | 46 | 66 |
| 1974-75 | Baltimore (WHA) | 78 | 16 | 33 | 49 |
| 1975-76 | Denver (WHA) | 15 | 1 | 5 | 6 |
| 1975-76 | Detroit | 46 | 4 | 9 | 13 |
| 1976-77 | Detroit | 74 | 7 | 11 | 18 |
| 1977-78 | Detroit | 3 | 0 | 2 | 2 |
| 1978-79 | Detroit | 24 | 2 | 6 | 8 |
| | NHL Totals | 153 | 14 | 30 | 44 |
| | WHA Totals | 248 | 56 | 134 | 190 |
| **LEBRUN, Albert Ivan** *Defenseman* | | | | | |
| b. Timmins, Ont., Dec. 1, 1940 | | | | | |
| 1960-61 | New York R | 4 | 0 | 2 | 2 |
| 1965-66 | New York R | 2 | 0 | 0 | 0 |
| | Totals | 6 | 0 | 2 | 2 |
| **LECAINE, William Joseph** *Forward* | | | | | |
| b. Moose Jaw, Sask., Mar. 11, 1940 | | | | | |
| 1968-69 | Pittsburgh | 4 | 0 | 0 | 0 |
| **LECLAIR, John Louis (Jackie)** *Forward* | | | | | |
| b. Quebec City, Que., May 30, 1929 | | | | | |
| 1954-55 | Montreal | 59 | 11 | 22 | 33 |
| 1955-56 | Montreal | 54 | 6 | 8 | 14 |
| 1956-57 | Montreal | 47 | 3 | 10 | 13 |
| | Totals | 160 | 20 | 40 | 60 |
| **LECLERC, Renald (Rene)** *Forward* | | | | | |
| b. Ville-de-Vanier, Que., Nov. 12, 1947 | | | | | |
| 1968-69 | Detroit | 43 | 2 | 3 | 5 |
| 1970-71 | Detroit | 44 | 8 | 8 | 16 |
| 1972-73 | Quebec (WHA) | 67 | 24 | 28 | 52 |
| 1973-74 | Quebec (WHA) | 53 | 17 | 27 | 44 |
| 1974-75 | Quebec (WHA) | 73 | 18 | 32 | 50 |
| 1975-76 | Que-Ind (WHA) | 82 | 33 | 38 | 71 |
| 1976-77 | Indianapolis (WHA) | 68 | 25 | 30 | 55 |
| 1977-78 | Indianapolis (WHA) | 60 | 12 | 15 | 27 |
| 1978-79 | Ind-Que (WHA) | 45 | 5 | 7 | 12 |
| | NHL Totals | 87 | 10 | 11 | 21 |
| | WHA Totals | 448 | 134 | 177 | 311 |
| **LECUYER, Douglas J.** *Forward* | | | | | |
| b. Wainwright, Alta., Mar. 10, 1958 | | | | | |
| 1978-79 | Chicago | 2 | 1 | 0 | 1 |
| 1979-80 | Chicago | 53 | 3 | 10 | 13 |
| 1980-81 | Chi-Winn | 59 | 6 | 17 | 23 |
| 1981-82 | Pittsburgh | 12 | 1 | 4 | 5 |
| | Totals | 126 | 11 | 31 | 42 |
| **LEDINGHAM, Walter N.** *Forward* | | | | | |
| b. Weyburn, Sask., Oct. 26, 1950 | | | | | |
| 1972-73 | Chicago | 9 | 0 | 1 | 1 |
| 1974-75 | New York I | 2 | 0 | 1 | 1 |
| 1976-77 | New York I | 4 | 0 | 0 | 0 |
| | Totals | 15 | 0 | 2 | 2 |
| **LEDUC, Albert (Battleship)** *Defenseman* | | | | | |
| b. Valleyfield, Que., July 31, 1901 | | | | | |
| 1925-26 | Montreal | 32 | 10 | 3 | 13 |
| 1926-27 | Montreal | 43 | 5 | 2 | 7 |

| Season | Club | GP | G | A | Pts. |
|---|---|---|---|---|---|
| 1927-28 | Montreal | 43 | 8 | 5 | 13 |
| 1928-29 | Montreal | 43 | 9 | 2 | 11 |
| 1929-30 | Montreal | 44 | 6 | 8 | 14 |
| 1930-31 | Montreal | 44 | 8 | 6 | 14 |
| 1931-32 | Montreal | 41 | 5 | 3 | 8 |
| 1932-33 | Montreal | 48 | 5 | 3 | 8 |
| 1933-34 | NYR-Ott | 42 | 1 | 3 | 4 |
| 1934-35 | Montreal | 4 | 0 | 0 | 0 |
| **Totals** | | 384 | 57 | 35 | 92 |

**LEDUC, Richard Henri (Rich)** *Forward*
b. Ile Perrot, Que., Aug. 24, 1951

| Season | Club | GP | G | A | Pts. |
|---|---|---|---|---|---|
| 1972-73 | Boston | 5 | 1 | 1 | 2 |
| 1973-74 | Boston | 28 | 3 | 3 | 6 |
| 1974-75 | Cleveland (WHA) | 78 | 34 | 31 | 65 |
| 1975-76 | Cleveland (WHA) | 79 | 36 | 22 | 58 |
| 1976-77 | Cincinnati (WHA) | 81 | 52 | 55 | 107 |
| 1977-78 | Cin-Ind (WHA) | 82 | 37 | 46 | 83 |
| 1978-79 | Ind-Que (WHA) | 74 | 35 | 41 | 76 |
| 1979-80 | Quebec | 75 | 21 | 27 | 48 |
| 1980-81 | Quebec | 22 | 3 | 7 | 10 |
| **NHL Totals** | | 130 | 28 | 38 | 66 |
| **WHA Totals** | | 394 | 194 | 195 | 389 |

**LEE, Peter John** *Forward*
b. Ellesmere, England, Jan. 2, 1956

| Season | Club | GP | G | A | Pts. |
|---|---|---|---|---|---|
| 1977-78 | Pittsburgh | 60 | 5 | 13 | 18 |
| 1978-79 | Pittsburgh | 80 | 32 | 26 | 58 |
| 1979-80 | Pittsburgh | 74 | 16 | 29 | 45 |
| 1980-81 | Pittsburgh | 80 | 30 | 34 | 64 |
| 1981-82 | Pittsburgh | 74 | 18 | 16 | 34 |
| 1982-83 | Pittsburgh | 63 | 13 | 13 | 26 |
| **Totals** | | 431 | 114 | 131 | 245 |

**LEFLEY, Bryan Andrew** *Defenseman*
b. Grosse Isle, Man., Oct. 18, 1948

| Season | Club | GP | G | A | Pts. |
|---|---|---|---|---|---|
| 1972-73 | New York I | 63 | 3 | 7 | 10 |
| 1973-74 | New York I | 7 | 0 | 0 | 0 |
| 1974-75 | Kansas City | 29 | 0 | 3 | 3 |
| 1976-77 | Colorado | 58 | 0 | 6 | 6 |
| 1977-78 | Colorado | 71 | 4 | 13 | 17 |
| **Totals** | | 228 | 7 | 29 | 36 |

**LEFLEY, Charles Thomas (Chuck)** *Forward*
b. Winnipeg, Man., Jan. 20, 1950

| Season | Club | GP | G | A | Pts. |
|---|---|---|---|---|---|
| 1971-72 | Montreal | 16 | 0 | 2 | 2 |
| 1972-73 | Montreal | 65 | 21 | 25 | 46 |
| 1973-74 | Montreal | 74 | 23 | 31 | 54 |
| 1974-75 | Mont-StL | 75 | 24 | 28 | 52 |
| 1975-76 | St Louis | 75 | 43 | 42 | 85 |
| 1976-77 | St Louis | 71 | 11 | 30 | 41 |
| 1977-78 | St Louis | 28 | 6 | 6 | 12 |
| **Totals** | | 404 | 128 | 164 | 292 |

**LEGER, Roger** *Defenseman*
b. L'Annonciation, Que., Mar. 26, 1919

| Season | Club | GP | G | A | Pts. |
|---|---|---|---|---|---|
| 1943-44 | New York R | 7 | 1 | 2 | 3 |
| 1946-47 | Montreal | 49 | 4 | 18 | 22 |
| 1947-48 | Montreal | 48 | 4 | 14 | 18 |
| 1948-49 | Montreal | 28 | 6 | 7 | 13 |
| 1949-50 | Montreal | 55 | 3 | 12 | 15 |
| **Totals** | | 187 | 18 | 53 | 71 |

**LEGGE, Barry Graham** *Defenseman*
b. Winnipeg, Man., Oct. 22, 1954

| Season | Club | GP | G | A | Pts. |
|---|---|---|---|---|---|
| 1974-75 | Baltimore (WHA) | 36 | 3 | 18 | 21 |
| 1975-76 | Ott-Clev (WHA) | 75 | 6 | 15 | 21 |
| 1976-77 | Minn-Cin (WHA) | 76 | 7 | 22 | 29 |
| 1977-78 | Cincinnati (WHA) | 78 | 7 | 17 | 24 |
| 1978-79 | Cincinnati (WHA) | 80 | 3 | 8 | 11 |
| 1979-80 | Quebec | 31 | 0 | 3 | 3 |
| 1980-81 | Winnipeg | 38 | 0 | 6 | 6 |
| 1981-82 | Winnipeg | 38 | 1 | 2 | 3 |
| **NHL Totals** | | 107 | 1 | 11 | 12 |
| **WHA Totals** | | 345 | 26 | 80 | 106 |

**LEGGE, Norman Randall (Randy)** *Defenseman*
b. Newmarket, Ont., Dec. 16, 1945

| Season | Club | GP | G | A | Pts. |
|---|---|---|---|---|---|
| 1972-73 | New York R | 12 | 0 | 2 | 2 |
| 1974-75 | Baltimore (WHA) | 78 | 1 | 14 | 15 |
| 1975-76 | Winn-Clev (WHA) | 45 | 1 | 8 | 9 |
| 1976-77 | San Diego (WHA) | 69 | 1 | 9 | 10 |
| **NHL Totals** | | 12 | 0 | 2 | 2 |
| **WHA Totals** | | 192 | 3 | 31 | 34 |

**LEHTONEN, Antero** *Forward*
b. Tampere, Finland, Apr. 12, 1954

| Season | Club | GP | G | A | Pts. |
|---|---|---|---|---|---|
| 1979-80 | Washington | 65 | 9 | 12 | 21 |

**LEHVONEN, Henry** *Defenseman*
b. Sarnia, Ont., Aug. 26, 1950

| Season | Club | GP | G | A | Pts. |
|---|---|---|---|---|---|
| 1974-75 | Kansas City | 4 | 0 | 0 | 0 |

**LEIER, Edward** *Forward*
b. Poland, Nov. 3, 1927

| Season | Club | GP | G | A | Pts. |
|---|---|---|---|---|---|
| 1949-50 | Chicago | 5 | 0 | 1 | 1 |
| 1950-51 | Chicago | 11 | 2 | 0 | 2 |
| **Totals** | | 16 | 2 | 1 | 3 |

**LEINONEN, Mikko** *Forward*
b. Tampere, Finland, July 15, 1955

| Season | Club | GP | G | A | Pts. |
|---|---|---|---|---|---|
| 1981-82 | New York R | 53 | 11 | 19 | 30 |
| 1982-83 | New York R | 78 | 17 | 34 | 51 |
| **Totals** | | 131 | 28 | 53 | 81 |

**LEITER, Robert Edward** *Forward*
b. Winnipeg, Man., Mar. 22, 1941

| Season | Club | GP | G | A | Pts. |
|---|---|---|---|---|---|
| 1962-63 | Boston | 51 | 9 | 13 | 22 |
| 1963-64 | Boston | 56 | 6 | 13 | 19 |
| 1964-65 | Boston | 18 | 3 | 1 | 4 |
| 1965-66 | Boston | 9 | 2 | 1 | 3 |
| 1968-69 | Boston | 1 | 0 | 0 | 0 |
| 1971-72 | Pittsburgh | 78 | 14 | 17 | 31 |
| 1972-73 | Atlanta | 78 | 26 | 34 | 60 |
| 1973-74 | Atlanta | 78 | 26 | 26 | 52 |
| 1974-75 | Atlanta | 52 | 10 | 18 | 28 |
| 1975-76 | Atlanta | 26 | 2 | 3 | 5 |
| **Totals** | | 447 | 98 | 126 | 224 |

**LEMAIRE, Jacques Gerard** *Forward*
b. LaSalle, Que., Sept. 7, 1945

| Season | Club | GP | G | A | Pts. |
|---|---|---|---|---|---|
| 1967-68 | Montreal | 69 | 22 | 20 | 42 |
| 1968-69 | Montreal | 75 | 29 | 34 | 63 |
| 1969-70 | Montreal | 69 | 32 | 28 | 60 |
| 1970-71 | Montreal | 78 | 28 | 28 | 56 |
| 1971-72 | Montreal | 77 | 32 | 49 | 81 |
| 1972-73 | Montreal | 77 | 44 | 51 | 95 |
| 1973-74 | Montreal | 66 | 29 | 38 | 67 |
| 1974-75 | Montreal | 80 | 36 | 56 | 92 |
| 1975-76 | Montreal | 61 | 20 | 32 | 52 |
| 1976-77 | Montreal | 75 | 34 | 41 | 75 |
| 1977-78 | Montreal | 76 | 36 | 61 | 97 |
| 1978-79 | Montreal | 50 | 24 | 31 | 55 |
| **Totals** | | 853 | 366 | 469 | 835 |

**LEMAY, Moe** *Forward*
b. Saskatoon, Sask., Feb. 18, 1962

| Season | Club | GP | G | A | Pts. |
|---|---|---|---|---|---|
| 1981-82 | Vancouver | 5 | 1 | 2 | 3 |
| 1982-83 | Vancouver | 44 | 11 | 9 | 20 |
| **Totals** | | 49 | 12 | 11 | 23 |

**LEMELIN, Roger Marcel** *Defenseman*
b. Iroquois Falls, Ont., Feb. 6, 1954

| Season | Club | GP | G | A | Pts. |
|---|---|---|---|---|---|
| 1974-75 | Kansas City | 8 | 0 | 1 | 1 |
| 1975-76 | Kansas City | 11 | 0 | 0 | 0 |
| 1976-77 | Colorado | 14 | 1 | 1 | 2 |
| 1977-78 | Colorado | 3 | 0 | 0 | 0 |
| **Totals** | | 36 | 1 | 2 | 3 |

**LEMIEUX, Alain** *Forward*
b. Montreal, Que., May 24, 1961

| Season | Club | GP | G | A | Pts. |
|---|---|---|---|---|---|
| 1981-82 | St Louis | 3 | 0 | 1 | 1 |
| 1982-83 | St Louis | 42 | 9 | 25 | 34 |
| **Totals** | | 45 | 9 | 26 | 35 |

**LEMIEUX, Jacques** *Defenseman*
b. Matane, Que., Apr. 8, 1943

| Season | Club | GP | G | A | Pts. |
|---|---|---|---|---|---|
| 1967-68 | Los Angeles | 16 | 0 | 3 | 3 |
| 1969-70 | Los Angeles | 3 | 0 | 1 | 1 |
| **Totals** | | 19 | 0 | 4 | 4 |

**LEMIEUX, Jean Louis** *Defenseman*
b. Noranda, Que., May 31, 1952

| Season | Club | GP | G | A | Pts. |
|---|---|---|---|---|---|
| 1973-74 | Atlanta | 32 | 3 | 5 | 8 |
| 1974-75 | Atlanta | 75 | 3 | 24 | 27 |
| 1975-76 | Atl-Wash | 66 | 10 | 23 | 33 |
| 1976-77 | Washington | 15 | 4 | 4 | 8 |
| 1977-78 | Washington | 16 | 3 | 7 | 10 |
| **Totals** | | 204 | 23 | 63 | 86 |

**LEMIEUX, Real Gaston** *Forward*
b. Victoriaville, Que., Jan. 3, 1945

| Season | Club | GP | G | A | Pts. |
|---|---|---|---|---|---|
| 1966-67 | Detroit | 1 | 0 | 0 | 0 |
| 1967-68 | Los Angeles | 74 | 12 | 23 | 35 |
| 1968-69 | Los Angeles | 75 | 11 | 29 | 40 |
| 1969-70 | NYR-LA | 73 | 6 | 10 | 16 |
| 1970-71 | Los Angeles | 43 | 3 | 6 | 9 |
| 1971-72 | Los Angeles | 78 | 13 | 25 | 38 |
| 1972-73 | Los Angeles | 74 | 5 | 10 | 15 |
| 1973-74 | LA-NYR-Buf | 38 | 1 | 1 | 2 |
| **Totals** | | 456 | 51 | 104 | 155 |

**LEMIEUX, Richard Bernard** *Forward*
b. Temiscamingue, Que., Apr. 19, 1951

| Season | Club | GP | G | A | Pts. |
|---|---|---|---|---|---|
| 1971-72 | Vancouver | 42 | 7 | 9 | 16 |
| 1972-73 | Vancouver | 78 | 17 | 35 | 52 |
| 1973-74 | Vancouver | 72 | 5 | 17 | 22 |
| 1974-75 | Kansas City | 79 | 10 | 20 | 30 |
| 1975-76 | KC-Atl | 3 | 0 | 1 | 1 |
| 1976-77 | Calgary (WHA) | 33 | 6 | 11 | 17 |
| **NHL Totals** | | 274 | 39 | 82 | 121 |
| **WHA Totals** | | 33 | 6 | 11 | 17 |

**LEMIEUX, Robert** *Defenseman*
b. Montreal, Que., Dec. 16, 1944

| Season | Club | GP | G | A | Pts. |
|---|---|---|---|---|---|
| 1967-68 | Oakland | 19 | 0 | 1 | 1 |

**LEPINE, Alfred (Pit)** *Forward*
b. St. Anne de Bellevue, Que., July 31, 1901

| Season | Club | GP | G | A | Pts. |
|---|---|---|---|---|---|
| 1925-26 | Montreal | 27 | 9 | 1 | 10 |
| 1926-27 | Montreal | 44 | 16 | 1 | 17 |
| 1927-28 | Montreal | 20 | 4 | 1 | 5 |
| 1928-29 | Montreal | 44 | 6 | 1 | 7 |
| 1929-30 | Montreal | 44 | 24 | 9 | 33 |
| 1930-31 | Montreal | 44 | 17 | 7 | 24 |
| 1931-32 | Montreal | 48 | 19 | 11 | 30 |
| 1932-33 | Montreal | 46 | 8 | 8 | 16 |
| 1933-34 | Montreal | 48 | 10 | 8 | 18 |
| 1934-35 | Montreal | 48 | 12 | 19 | 31 |
| 1935-36 | Montreal | 32 | 6 | 10 | 16 |
| 1936-37 | Montreal | 34 | 7 | 8 | 15 |
| 1937-38 | Montreal | 47 | 5 | 14 | 19 |
| **Totals** | | 526 | 143 | 98 | 241 |

**LEPINE, Hector** *Forward*

| Season | Club | GP | G | A | Pts. |
|---|---|---|---|---|---|
| 1925-26 | Montreal | 33 | 5 | 2 | 7 |

**LESIEUR, Arthur** *Defenseman*
b. Fall River, Mass., Sept. 13, 1907

| Season | Club | GP | G | A | Pts. |
|---|---|---|---|---|---|
| 1928-29 | Chi-Mont | 17 | 0 | 0 | 0 |
| 1930-31 | Montreal | 21 | 2 | 0 | 2 |
| 1931-32 | Montreal | 24 | 1 | 2 | 3 |
| 1935-36 | Montreal | 38 | 1 | 0 | 1 |
| **Totals** | | 100 | 4 | 2 | 6 |

**LESUK, William Anton (Bill)** *Forward*
b. Moose Jaw, Sask., Nov. 1, 1946

| Season | Club | GP | G | A | Pts. |
|---|---|---|---|---|---|
| 1968-69 | Boston | 5 | 0 | 1 | 1 |
| 1969-70 | Boston | 3 | 0 | 0 | 0 |
| 1970-71 | Philadelphia | 78 | 17 | 19 | 36 |
| 1971-72 | Phil-LA | 72 | 11 | 16 | 27 |
| 1972-73 | Los Angeles | 67 | 6 | 14 | 20 |
| 1973-74 | Los Angeles | 35 | 2 | 1 | 3 |
| 1974-75 | Washington | 79 | 8 | 11 | 19 |
| 1975-76 | Winnipeg (WHA) | 81 | 15 | 21 | 36 |
| 1976-77 | Winnipeg (WHA) | 78 | 14 | 27 | 41 |
| 1977-78 | Winnipeg (WHA) | 80 | 9 | 18 | 27 |
| 1978-79 | Winnipeg (WHA) | 79 | 17 | 15 | 32 |
| 1979-80 | Winnipeg | 49 | 0 | 1 | 1 |
| **NHL Totals** | | 388 | 44 | 63 | 107 |
| **WHA Totals** | | 318 | 55 | 81 | 136 |

## LESWICK, Anthony Joseph  *Forward*
b. Humboldt, Sask., Mar. 17, 1923

| Season | Club | GP | G | A | Pts. |
|---|---|---|---|---|---|
| 1945-46 | New York R | 50 | 15 | 9 | 24 |
| 1946-47 | New York R | 59 | 27 | 14 | 41 |
| 1947-48 | New York R | 60 | 24 | 16 | 40 |
| 1948-49 | New York R | 60 | 13 | 14 | 27 |
| 1949-50 | New York R | 69 | 19 | 25 | 44 |
| 1950-51 | New York R | 70 | 15 | 11 | 26 |
| 1951-52 | Detroit | 70 | 9 | 10 | 19 |
| 1952-53 | Detroit | 70 | 15 | 12 | 27 |
| 1953-54 | Detroit | 70 | 6 | 18 | 24 |
| 1954-55 | Detroit | 70 | 10 | 17 | 27 |
| 1955-56 | Chicago | 70 | 11 | 11 | 22 |
| 1957-58 | Detroit | 11 | 1 | 2 | 3 |
| | **Totals** | 729 | 165 | 159 | 324 |

## LESWICK, Jack  *Forward*

| Season | Club | GP | G | A | Pts. |
|---|---|---|---|---|---|
| 1933-34 | Chicago | 37 | 1 | 7 | 8 |

## LESWICK, Peter Paul  *Forward*
b. Saskatoon, Sask., July 12, 1917

| Season | Club | GP | G | A | Pts. |
|---|---|---|---|---|---|
| 1936-37 | New York A | 1 | 1 | 0 | 1 |
| 1944-45 | Boston | 2 | 0 | 0 | 0 |
| | **Totals** | 3 | 1 | 0 | 1 |

## LEVANDOSKI, Joseph Thomas  *Forward*
b. Cobalt, Ont., Mar. 17, 1922

| Season | Club | GP | G | A | Pts. |
|---|---|---|---|---|---|
| 1946-47 | New York R | 8 | 1 | 1 | 2 |

## LEVEILLE, Normand  *Forward*
b. Montreal, Que., Jan. 10, 1963

| Season | Club | GP | G | A | Pts. |
|---|---|---|---|---|---|
| 1981-82 | Boston | 65 | 14 | 19 | 33 |
| 1982-83 | Boston | 9 | 3 | 6 | 9 |
| | **Totals** | 74 | 17 | 25 | 42 |

## LEVER, Donald Richard  *Forward*
b. S. Porcupine, Ont., Nov. 14, 1952

| Season | Club | GP | G | A | Pts. |
|---|---|---|---|---|---|
| 1972-73 | Vancouver | 78 | 12 | 26 | 38 |
| 1973-74 | Vancouver | 78 | 23 | 25 | 48 |
| 1974-75 | Vancouver | 80 | 38 | 30 | 68 |
| 1975-76 | Vancouver | 80 | 25 | 40 | 65 |
| 1976-77 | Vancouver | 80 | 27 | 30 | 57 |
| 1977-78 | Vancouver | 75 | 17 | 32 | 49 |
| 1978-79 | Vancouver | 71 | 23 | 21 | 44 |
| 1979-80 | Van-Atl | 79 | 35 | 33 | 68 |
| 1980-81 | Calgary | 62 | 26 | 31 | 57 |
| 1981-82 | Calg-Col | 82 | 30 | 39 | 69 |
| 1982-83 | New Jersey | 79 | 23 | 30 | 53 |
| | **Totals** | 844 | 279 | 337 | 616 |

## LEVIE, Craig Dean  *Defenseman*
b. Calgary, Alta., Aug. 17, 1959

| Season | Club | GP | G | A | Pts. |
|---|---|---|---|---|---|
| 1981-82 | Winnipeg | 40 | 4 | 9 | 13 |
| 1982-83 | Winnipeg | 22 | 4 | 5 | 9 |
| | **Totals** | 62 | 8 | 14 | 22 |

## LEVINSKY, Alexander (Mine Boy)
*Defenseman*
b. Syracuse, N.Y., Feb. 2, 1910

| Season | Club | GP | G | A | Pts. |
|---|---|---|---|---|---|
| 1930-31 | Toronto | 8 | 0 | 1 | 1 |
| 1931-32 | Toronto | 47 | 5 | 5 | 10 |
| 1932-33 | Toronto | 48 | 1 | 4 | 5 |
| 1933-34 | Toronto | 47 | 5 | 11 | 16 |
| 1934-35 | NYR-Chi | 43 | 3 | 8 | 11 |
| 1935-36 | Chicago | 48 | 1 | 7 | 8 |
| 1936-37 | Chicago | 48 | 0 | 8 | 8 |
| 1937-38 | Chicago | 48 | 3 | 2 | 5 |
| 1938-39 | Chicago | 30 | 1 | 3 | 4 |
| | **Totals** | 367 | 19 | 49 | 68 |

## LEVO, Tapio  *Defenseman*
b. Pori, Finland, Sept. 24, 1955

| Season | Club | GP | G | A | Pts. |
|---|---|---|---|---|---|
| 1981-82 | Colorado | 34 | 9 | 13 | 22 |
| 1982-83 | New Jersey | 73 | 7 | 40 | 47 |
| | **Totals** | 107 | 16 | 53 | 69 |

## LEWICKI, Daniel  *Forward*
b. Fort William, Ont., Mar. 12, 1931

| Season | Club | GP | G | A | Pts. |
|---|---|---|---|---|---|
| 1950-51 | Toronto | 61 | 16 | 18 | 34 |
| 1951-52 | Toronto | 51 | 4 | 9 | 13 |

| Season | Club | GP | G | A | Pts. |
|---|---|---|---|---|---|
| 1952-53 | Toronto | 4 | 1 | 3 | 4 |
| 1953-54 | Toronto | 7 | 0 | 1 | 1 |
| 1954-55 | New York R | 70 | 29 | 24 | 53 |
| 1955-56 | New York R | 70 | 18 | 27 | 45 |
| 1956-57 | New York R | 70 | 18 | 20 | 38 |
| 1957-58 | New York R | 70 | 11 | 19 | 30 |
| 1958-59 | Chicago | 58 | 8 | 14 | 22 |
| | **Totals** | 461 | 105 | 135 | 240 |

## LEWIS, David Rodney  *Defenseman*
b. Kindersley, Sask., July 3, 1953

| Season | Club | GP | G | A | Pts. |
|---|---|---|---|---|---|
| 1973-74 | New York I | 66 | 2 | 15 | 17 |
| 1974-75 | New York I | 78 | 5 | 14 | 19 |
| 1975-76 | New York I | 73 | 0 | 19 | 19 |
| 1976-77 | New York I | 79 | 4 | 24 | 28 |
| 1977-78 | New York I | 77 | 3 | 11 | 14 |
| 1978-79 | New York I | 79 | 5 | 18 | 23 |
| 1979-80 | NYI-LA | 73 | 6 | 17 | 23 |
| 1980-81 | Los Angeles | 67 | 1 | 12 | 13 |
| 1981-82 | Los Angeles | 64 | 1 | 13 | 14 |
| 1982-83 | Los Angeles | 79 | 2 | 10 | 12 |
| | **Totals** | 735 | 29 | 153 | 182 |

## LEWIS, Douglas  *Forward*
b. Winnipeg, Man., Mar. 3, 1921

| Season | Club | GP | G | A | Pts. |
|---|---|---|---|---|---|
| 1946-47 | Montreal | 3 | 0 | 0 | 0 |

## LEWIS, Herbert A.  *Forward*
b. Calgary, Alta., Apr. 17, 1906

| Season | Club | GP | G | A | Pts. |
|---|---|---|---|---|---|
| 1928-29 | Detroit | 36 | 9 | 5 | 14 |
| 1929-30 | Detroit | 44 | 20 | 11 | 31 |
| 1930-31 | Detroit | 43 | 15 | 6 | 21 |
| 1931-32 | Detroit | 48 | 5 | 14 | 19 |
| 1932-33 | Detroit | 48 | 20 | 14 | 34 |
| 1933-34 | Detroit | 43 | 16 | 15 | 31 |
| 1934-35 | Detroit | 47 | 16 | 27 | 43 |
| 1935-36 | Detroit | 45 | 14 | 23 | 37 |
| 1936-37 | Detroit | 45 | 14 | 18 | 32 |
| 1937-38 | Detroit | 43 | 13 | 18 | 31 |
| 1938-39 | Detroit | 42 | 6 | 10 | 16 |
| | **Totals** | 484 | 148 | 161 | 309 |

## LEWIS, Robert Dale  *Forward*
b. Edmonton, Alta., July 28, 1952

| Season | Club | GP | G | A | Pts. |
|---|---|---|---|---|---|
| 1975-76 | New York R | 8 | 0 | 0 | 0 |

## LEY, Richard Norman (Ricky)  *Defenseman*
b. Orillia, Ont., Nov. 2, 1948

| Season | Club | GP | G | A | Pts. |
|---|---|---|---|---|---|
| 1968-69 | Toronto | 38 | 1 | 11 | 12 |
| 1969-70 | Toronto | 48 | 2 | 13 | 15 |
| 1970-71 | Toronto | 76 | 4 | 16 | 20 |
| 1971-72 | Toronto | 67 | 1 | 14 | 15 |
| 1972-73 | New England (WHA) | 76 | 3 | 27 | 30 |
| 1973-74 | New England (WHA) | 72 | 6 | 35 | 41 |
| 1974-75 | New England (WHA) | 62 | 6 | 36 | 42 |
| 1975-76 | New England (WHA) | 67 | 8 | 30 | 38 |
| 1976-77 | New England (WHA) | 55 | 2 | 21 | 23 |
| 1977-78 | New England (WHA) | 73 | 3 | 41 | 44 |
| 1978-79 | New England (WHA) | 73 | 7 | 20 | 27 |
| 1979-80 | Hartford | 65 | 4 | 16 | 20 |
| 1980-81 | Hartford | 16 | 0 | 2 | 2 |
| | **NHL Totals** | 310 | 12 | 72 | 84 |
| | **WHA Totals** | 478 | 35 | 210 | 245 |

## LIBETT, Lynn Nicholas (Nick)  *Forward*
b. Stratford, Ont., Dec. 9, 1945

| Season | Club | GP | G | A | Pts. |
|---|---|---|---|---|---|
| 1967-68 | Detroit | 22 | 2 | 1 | 3 |
| 1968-69 | Detroit | 75 | 10 | 14 | 24 |
| 1969-70 | Detroit | 76 | 20 | 20 | 40 |
| 1970-71 | Detroit | 78 | 16 | 13 | 29 |
| 1971-72 | Detroit | 77 | 31 | 22 | 53 |
| 1972-73 | Detroit | 78 | 19 | 34 | 53 |
| 1973-74 | Detroit | 67 | 24 | 24 | 48 |
| 1974-75 | Detroit | 80 | 23 | 28 | 51 |
| 1975-76 | Detroit | 80 | 20 | 26 | 46 |
| 1976-77 | Detroit | 80 | 14 | 27 | 41 |
| 1977-78 | Detroit | 80 | 23 | 22 | 45 |
| 1978-79 | Detroit | 68 | 15 | 19 | 34 |
| 1979-80 | Pittsburgh | 78 | 14 | 12 | 26 |
| 1980-81 | Pittsburgh | 43 | 6 | 6 | 12 |
| | **Totals** | 982 | 237 | 268 | 505 |

## LICARI, Anthony  *Forward*
b. Ottawa, Ont., Apr. 9, 1921

| Season | Club | GP | G | A | Pts. |
|---|---|---|---|---|---|
| 1946-47 | Detroit | 9 | 0 | 1 | 1 |

## LIDDINGTON, Robert Allen (Bob)  *Forward*
b. Calgary, Alta., Sept. 15, 1948

| Season | Club | GP | G | A | Pts. |
|---|---|---|---|---|---|
| 1970-71 | Toronto | 11 | 0 | 1 | 1 |
| 1972-73 | Chicago (WHA) | 78 | 20 | 11 | 31 |
| 1973-74 | Chicago (WHA) | 73 | 26 | 21 | 47 |
| 1974-75 | Chicago (WHA) | 78 | 23 | 18 | 41 |
| 1975-76 | Ott-Hou (WHA) | 37 | 7 | 8 | 15 |
| 1976-77 | Phoenix (WHA) | 80 | 20 | 24 | 44 |
| | **NHL Totals** | 11 | 0 | 1 | 1 |
| | **WHA Totals** | 346 | 96 | 82 | 178 |

## LINDGREN, Lars  *Defenseman*
b. Pitea, Sweden, Oct. 12, 1952

| Season | Club | GP | G | A | Pts. |
|---|---|---|---|---|---|
| 1978-79 | Vancouver | 64 | 2 | 19 | 21 |
| 1979-80 | Vancouver | 73 | 5 | 30 | 35 |
| 1980-81 | Vancouver | 52 | 4 | 18 | 22 |
| 1981-82 | Vancouver | 75 | 5 | 16 | 21 |
| 1982-83 | Vancouver | 64 | 6 | 14 | 20 |
| | **Totals** | 328 | 22 | 97 | 119 |

## LINDSAY, Robert Blake Theodore (Ted)
*Forward*
b. Renfrew, Ont., July 29, 1925

| Season | Club | GP | G | A | Pts. |
|---|---|---|---|---|---|
| 1944-45 | Detroit | 45 | 17 | 6 | 23 |
| 1945-46 | Detroit | 47 | 7 | 10 | 17 |
| 1946-47 | Detroit | 59 | 27 | 15 | 42 |
| 1947-48 | Detroit | 60 | 33 | 19 | 52 |
| 1948-49 | Detroit | 50 | 26 | 28 | 54 |
| 1949-50 | Detroit | 69 | 23 | 55 | 78 |
| 1950-51 | Detroit | 67 | 24 | 35 | 59 |
| 1951-52 | Detroit | 70 | 30 | 39 | 69 |
| 1952-53 | Detroit | 70 | 32 | 39 | 71 |
| 1953-54 | Detroit | 70 | 26 | 36 | 62 |
| 1954-55 | Detroit | 49 | 19 | 19 | 38 |
| 1955-56 | Detroit | 67 | 27 | 23 | 50 |
| 1956-57 | Detroit | 70 | 30 | 55 | 85 |
| 1957-58 | Chicago | 68 | 15 | 24 | 39 |
| 1958-59 | Chicago | 70 | 22 | 36 | 58 |
| 1959-60 | Chicago | 68 | 7 | 19 | 26 |
| 1964-65 | Detroit | 68 | 14 | 14 | 28 |
| | **Totals** | 1068 | 379 | 472 | 851 |

## LINDSTROM, Bo Morgan Willy  *Forward*
b. Grunns, Sweden, May 5, 1951

| Season | Club | GP | G | A | Pts. |
|---|---|---|---|---|---|
| 1975-76 | Winnipeg (WHA) | 81 | 23 | 36 | 59 |
| 1976-77 | Winnipeg (WHA) | 79 | 44 | 36 | 80 |
| 1977-78 | Winnipeg (WHA) | 77 | 30 | 30 | 60 |
| 1978-79 | Winnipeg (WHA) | 79 | 26 | 36 | 62 |
| 1979-80 | Winnipeg | 79 | 23 | 26 | 49 |
| 1980-81 | Winnipeg | 72 | 22 | 13 | 35 |
| 1981-82 | Winnipeg | 74 | 32 | 27 | 59 |
| 1982-83 | Winn-Edm | 73 | 26 | 30 | 56 |
| | **NHL Totals** | 298 | 103 | 96 | 199 |
| | **WHA Totals** | 316 | 123 | 138 | 261 |

## LINSEMAN, Ken  *Forward*
b. Kingston, Ont., Aug. 11, 1958

| Season | Club | GP | G | A | Pts. |
|---|---|---|---|---|---|
| 1977-78 | Birmingham (WHA) | 71 | 38 | 38 | 76 |
| 1978-79 | Philadelphia | 30 | 5 | 20 | 25 |
| 1979-80 | Philadelphia | 80 | 22 | 57 | 79 |
| 1980-81 | Philadelphia | 51 | 17 | 30 | 47 |
| 1981-82 | Philadelphia | 79 | 24 | 68 | 92 |
| 1982-83 | Edmonton | 72 | 33 | 42 | 75 |
| | **NHL Totals** | 312 | 101 | 217 | 318 |
| | **WHA Totals** | 71 | 38 | 38 | 76 |

## LISCOMBE, Harry Carlyle (Carl)  *Forward*
b. Perth, Ont., May 17, 1915

| Season | Club | GP | G | A | Pts. |
|---|---|---|---|---|---|
| 1937-38 | Detroit | 41 | 14 | 10 | 24 |
| 1938-39 | Detroit | 48 | 8 | 18 | 26 |
| 1939-40 | Detroit | 25 | 2 | 7 | 9 |
| 1940-41 | Detroit | 33 | 10 | 10 | 20 |
| 1941-42 | Detroit | 47 | 13 | 17 | 30 |
| 1942-43 | Detroit | 50 | 19 | 23 | 42 |
| 1943-44 | Detroit | 50 | 36 | 37 | 73 |
| 1944-45 | Detroit | 42 | 23 | 9 | 32 |
| 1945-46 | Detroit | 44 | 12 | 9 | 21 |
| | **Totals** | 380 | 137 | 140 | 277 |

| Season | Club | GP | G | A | Pts. |
|---|---|---|---|---|---|
| **LITZENBERGER, Edward C. J.** *Forward* | | | | | |
| b. Neudorf, Sask., July 15, 1932 | | | | | |
| 1952-53 | Montreal | 2 | 1 | 0 | 1 |
| 1953-54 | Montreal | 3 | 0 | 0 | 0 |
| 1954-55 | Mont-Chi | 73 | 23 | 28 | 51 |
| 1955-56 | Chicago | 70 | 10 | 29 | 39 |
| 1956-57 | Chicago | 70 | 32 | 32 | 64 |
| 1957-58 | Chicago | 70 | 32 | 30 | 62 |
| 1958-59 | Chicago | 70 | 33 | 44 | 77 |
| 1959-60 | Chicago | 52 | 12 | 18 | 30 |
| 1960-61 | Chicago | 62 | 10 | 22 | 32 |
| 1961-62 | Det-Tor | 69 | 18 | 22 | 40 |
| 1962-63 | Toronto | 58 | 5 | 13 | 18 |
| 1963-64 | Toronto | 19 | 2 | 0 | 2 |
| | **Totals** | 618 | 178 | 238 | 416 |
| **LOCAS, Jacques** *Forward* | | | | | |
| b. Pointe aux Trembles, Que., Feb. 12, 1926 | | | | | |
| 1947-58 | Montreal | 56 | 7 | 8 | 15 |
| 1948-59 | Montreal | 3 | 0 | 0 | 0 |
| | **Totals** | 59 | 7 | 8 | 15 |
| **LOCHEAD, William Alexander** *Forward* | | | | | |
| b. Forest, Ont., Oct. 13, 1954 | | | | | |
| 1974-75 | Detroit | 65 | 16 | 12 | 28 |
| 1975-76 | Detroit | 53 | 9 | 11 | 20 |
| 1976-77 | Detroit | 61 | 16 | 14 | 30 |
| 1977-78 | Detroit | 77 | 20 | 16 | 36 |
| 1978-79 | Det-Col | 67 | 8 | 9 | 17 |
| 1979-80 | New York R | 7 | 0 | 0 | 0 |
| | **Totals** | 330 | 69 | 62 | 131 |
| **LOCKING, Norman** *Forward* | | | | | |
| b. Owen Sound, Ont., May 24, 1911 | | | | | |
| 1934-35 | Chicago | 38 | 2 | 5 | 7 |
| 1935-36 | Chicago | 14 | 0 | 1 | 1 |
| | **Totals** | 52 | 2 | 6 | 8 |
| **LOFTHOUSE, Mark** *Forward* | | | | | |
| b. New Westminster, B.C., Apr. 21, 1957 | | | | | |
| 1977-78 | Washington | 18 | 2 | 1 | 3 |
| 1978-79 | Washington | 52 | 13 | 10 | 23 |
| 1979-80 | Washington | 68 | 15 | 18 | 33 |
| 1980-81 | Washington | 3 | 1 | 1 | 2 |
| 1981-82 | Detroit | 12 | 3 | 4 | 7 |
| 1982-83 | Detroit | 28 | 8 | 4 | 12 |
| | **Totals** | 181 | 42 | 38 | 80 |
| **LOGAN, David George** *Defenseman* | | | | | |
| b. Montreal, Que., July 2, 1954 | | | | | |
| 1975-76 | Chicago | 2 | 0 | 0 | 0 |
| 1976-77 | Chicago | 34 | 0 | 2 | 2 |
| 1977-78 | Chicago | 54 | 1 | 5 | 6 |
| 1978-79 | Chicago | 76 | 1 | 14 | 15 |
| 1979-80 | Chi-Van | 45 | 3 | 8 | 11 |
| 1980-81 | Vancouver | 7 | 0 | 0 | 0 |
| | **Totals** | 218 | 5 | 29 | 34 |
| **LOISELLE, Claude** *Forward* | | | | | |
| b. Ottawa, Ont., May 29, 1963 | | | | | |
| 1981-82 | Detroit | 4 | 1 | 0 | 1 |
| 1982-83 | Detroit | 18 | 2 | 0 | 2 |
| | **Totals** | 22 | 3 | 0 | 3 |
| **LONG, Barry Kenneth** *Defenseman* | | | | | |
| b. Brantford, Ont., Jan. 3, 1949 | | | | | |
| 1972-73 | Los Angeles | 70 | 2 | 13 | 15 |
| 1973-74 | Los Angeles | 60 | 3 | 19 | 22 |
| 1974-75 | Edmonton (WHA) | 78 | 20 | 40 | 60 |
| 1975-76 | Edmonton (WHA) | 78 | 10 | 32 | 42 |
| 1976-77 | Edm-Winn (WHA) | 73 | 9 | 39 | 48 |
| 1977-78 | Winnipeg (WHA) | 78 | 7 | 24 | 31 |
| 1978-79 | Winnipeg (WHA) | 79 | 5 | 36 | 41 |
| 1979-80 | Detroit | 80 | 0 | 17 | 17 |
| 1980-81 | Winnipeg | 65 | 6 | 17 | 23 |
| 1981-82 | Winnipeg | 5 | 0 | 2 | 2 |
| | **NHL Totals** | 280 | 11 | 68 | 79 |
| | **WHA Totals** | 386 | 51 | 171 | 222 |

| Season | Club | GP | G | A | Pts. |
|---|---|---|---|---|---|
| **LONSBERRY, David Ross** *Forward* | | | | | |
| b. Humboldt, Sask., Feb. 7, 1947 | | | | | |
| 1966-67 | Boston | 8 | 0 | 1 | 1 |
| 1967-68 | Boston | 19 | 2 | 2 | 4 |
| 1968-69 | Boston | 6 | 0 | 0 | 0 |
| 1969-70 | Los Angeles | 76 | 20 | 22 | 42 |
| 1970-71 | Los Angeles | 76 | 25 | 28 | 53 |
| 1971-72 | LA-Phil | 82 | 16 | 21 | 37 |
| 1972-73 | Philadelphia | 77 | 21 | 29 | 50 |
| 1973-74 | Philadelphia | 75 | 32 | 19 | 51 |
| 1974-75 | Philadelphia | 80 | 24 | 25 | 49 |
| 1975-76 | Philadelphia | 80 | 19 | 28 | 47 |
| 1976-77 | Philadelphia | 75 | 23 | 32 | 55 |
| 1977-78 | Philadelphia | 78 | 18 | 30 | 48 |
| 1978-79 | Pittsburgh | 80 | 24 | 22 | 46 |
| 1979-80 | Pittsburgh | 76 | 15 | 18 | 33 |
| 1980-81 | Pittsburgh | 80 | 17 | 33 | 50 |
| | **Totals** | 968 | 256 | 310 | 566 |
| **LORENTZ, James Peter (Jim)** *Forward* | | | | | |
| b. Waterloo, Ont., May 1, 1947 | | | | | |
| 1968-69 | Boston | 11 | 1 | 3 | 4 |
| 1969-70 | Boston | 68 | 7 | 16 | 23 |
| 1970-71 | St Louis | 76 | 19 | 21 | 40 |
| 1971-72 | StL-NYR-Buf | 52 | 10 | 15 | 25 |
| 1972-73 | Buffalo | 78 | 27 | 35 | 62 |
| 1973-74 | Buffalo | 78 | 23 | 31 | 54 |
| 1974-75 | Buffalo | 72 | 25 | 45 | 70 |
| 1975-76 | Buffalo | 75 | 17 | 24 | 41 |
| 1976-77 | Buffalo | 79 | 23 | 33 | 56 |
| 1977-78 | Buffalo | 70 | 9 | 15 | 24 |
| | **Totals** | 659 | 161 | 238 | 399 |
| **LORIMER, Robert Roy** *Defenseman* | | | | | |
| b. Toronto, Ont., Aug. 25, 1953 | | | | | |
| 1976-77 | New York I | 1 | 0 | 1 | 1 |
| 1977-78 | New York I | 5 | 1 | 0 | 1 |
| 1978-79 | New York I | 67 | 3 | 18 | 21 |
| 1979-80 | New York I | 74 | 3 | 16 | 19 |
| 1980-81 | New York I | 73 | 1 | 12 | 13 |
| 1981-82 | Colorado | 79 | 5 | 15 | 20 |
| 1982-83 | New Jersey | 66 | 3 | 10 | 13 |
| | **Totals** | 365 | 16 | 72 | 88 |
| **LORRAIN, Rodrique** *Forward* | | | | | |
| b. Buckingham, Que., July 1915 | | | | | |
| 1935-36 | Montreal | 1 | 0 | 0 | 0 |
| 1936-37 | Montreal | 47 | 3 | 6 | 9 |
| 1937-38 | Montreal | 48 | 13 | 19 | 32 |
| 1938-39 | Montreal | 38 | 10 | 9 | 19 |
| 1939-40 | Montreal | 41 | 1 | 5 | 6 |
| 1941-42 | Montreal | 4 | 1 | 0 | 1 |
| | **Totals** | 179 | 28 | 39 | 67 |
| **LOUGHLIN, Clem** *Defenseman* | | | | | |
| b. Carroll, Man., 1894 | | | | | |
| 1926-27 | Detroit | 31 | 7 | 3 | 10 |
| 1927-28 | Detroit | 43 | 1 | 2 | 3 |
| 1928-29 | Chicago | 24 | 0 | 1 | 1 |
| | **Totals** | 98 | 8 | 6 | 14 |
| **LOUGHLIN, Wilfred** *Defenseman-Forward* | | | | | |
| 1923-24 | Toronto | 14 | 0 | 0 | 0 |
| **LOWDERMILK, Dwayne Kenneth** *Defenseman* | | | | | |
| b. Burnaby, B.C., Jan. 9, 1958 | | | | | |
| 1980-81 | Washington | 2 | 0 | 1 | 1 |
| **LOWE, Norman E. (Odie)** *Forward* | | | | | |
| b. Winnipeg, Man., Apr. 15, 1928 | | | | | |
| 1948-49 | New York R | 1 | 0 | 0 | 0 |
| 1949-50 | New York R | 3 | 1 | 1 | 2 |
| | **Totals** | 4 | 1 | 1 | 2 |
| **LOWE, Kevin Hugh** *Defenseman* | | | | | |
| b. Hawkesbury, Ont., Apr. 15, 1959 | | | | | |
| 1979-80 | Edmonton | 64 | 2 | 19 | 21 |
| 1980-81 | Edmonton | 79 | 10 | 24 | 34 |

| Season | Club | GP | G | A | Pts. |
|---|---|---|---|---|---|
| 1981-82 | Edmonton | 80 | 9 | 31 | 40 |
| 1982-83 | Edmonton | 80 | 6 | 34 | 40 |
| | **Totals** | 303 | 27 | 108 | 135 |
| **LOWE, Ross Robert** *Forward* | | | | | |
| b. Oshawa, Ont., Sept. 21, 1928 | | | | | |
| 1949-50 | Boston | 3 | 0 | 0 | 0 |
| 1950-51 | Bos-Mont | 43 | 5 | 3 | 8 |
| 1951-52 | Montreal | 31 | 1 | 5 | 6 |
| | **Totals** | 77 | 6 | 8 | 14 |
| **LOWERY, Gerald** *Forward* | | | | | |
| b. Ottawa, Ont. | | | | | |
| 1927-28 | Toronto | 25 | 6 | 5 | 11 |
| 1928-29 | Tor-PittPi | 44 | 5 | 12 | 17 |
| 1929-30 | Pittsburgh Pi | 44 | 16 | 14 | 30 |
| 1930-31 | Philadelphia Q | 43 | 13 | 14 | 27 |
| 1931-32 | Chicago | 48 | 8 | 3 | 11 |
| 1932-33 | Ottawa | 7 | 0 | 0 | 0 |
| | **Totals** | 211 | 48 | 48 | 96 |
| **LOWREY, Eddie** *Defenseman* | | | | | |
| b. 1894 | | | | | |
| 1917-18 | Ottawa | 11 | 0 | 0 | 0 |
| 1918-19 | Ottawa | 10 | 0 | 0 | 0 |
| 1920-21 | Hamilton | 3 | 0 | 0 | 0 |
| | **Totals** | 24 | 0 | 0 | 0 |
| **LOWREY, Frank (Frock)** *Forward* | | | | | |
| b. Ottawa, Ont. | | | | | |
| 1924-25 | Montreal M | 28 | 0 | 0 | 0 |
| 1925-26 | MontM-PittPi | 26 | 1 | 0 | 1 |
| | **Totals** | 54 | 1 | 0 | 1 |
| **LUCAS, Daniel Kenneth** *Forward* | | | | | |
| b. Powell River, B.C., Feb. 28, 1958 | | | | | |
| 1978-79 | Philadelphia | 6 | 1 | 0 | 1 |
| **LUCAS, David** *Defenseman* | | | | | |
| b. Downeyville, Ont., Mar. 22, 1932 | | | | | |
| 1962-63 | Detroit | 1 | 0 | 0 | 0 |
| **LUCE, Donald Harold** *Forward* | | | | | |
| b. London, Ont., Oct. 2, 1948 | | | | | |
| 1969-70 | New York R | 12 | 1 | 2 | 3 |
| 1970-71 | NYR-Det | 67 | 3 | 12 | 15 |
| 1971-72 | Buffalo | 78 | 11 | 8 | 19 |
| 1972-73 | Buffalo | 78 | 18 | 25 | 43 |
| 1973-74 | Buffalo | 75 | 26 | 31 | 57 |
| 1974-75 | Buffalo | 80 | 33 | 43 | 76 |
| 1975-76 | Buffalo | 77 | 21 | 49 | 70 |
| 1976-77 | Buffalo | 80 | 26 | 43 | 69 |
| 1977-78 | Buffalo | 78 | 26 | 35 | 61 |
| 1978-79 | Buffalo | 79 | 26 | 35 | 61 |
| 1979-80 | Buffalo | 80 | 14 | 29 | 43 |
| 1980-81 | Buf-LA | 71 | 16 | 13 | 29 |
| 1981-82 | Toronto | 39 | 4 | 4 | 8 |
| | **Totals** | 894 | 225 | 329 | 554 |
| **LUDVIG, Jan** *Forward* | | | | | |
| b. Liberic, Czechoslovakia, Sept. 17, 1961 | | | | | |
| 1982-83 | New Jersey | 51 | 7 | 10 | 17 |
| **LUDWIG, Craig Lee** *Defenseman* | | | | | |
| b. Eagle River, Wis., Mar. 15, 1961 | | | | | |
| 1982-83 | Montreal | 80 | 0 | 25 | 25 |
| **LUDZIK, Steve** *Forward* | | | | | |
| b. Toronto, Ont., Apr. 3, 1961 | | | | | |
| 1981-82 | Chicago | 8 | 2 | 1 | 3 |
| 1982-83 | Chicago | 66 | 6 | 19 | 25 |
| | **Totals** | 74 | 8 | 20 | 28 |
| **LUPUL, Gary John** *Forward* | | | | | |
| b. Powell River, B.C., Apr. 4, 1959 | | | | | |
| 1979-80 | Vancouver | 51 | 9 | 11 | 20 |
| 1980-81 | Vancouver | 7 | 0 | 2 | 2 |
| 1981-82 | Vancouver | 41 | 10 | 7 | 17 |
| 1982-83 | Vancouver | 40 | 18 | 10 | 28 |
| | **Totals** | 139 | 37 | 30 | 67 |

**LUKOWICH, Bernard Joseph** *Forward*
b. North Battleford, Sask., Mar. 18, 1952

| Season | Club | GP | G | A | Pts. |
|---|---|---|---|---|---|
| 1973-74 | Pittsburgh | 53 | 9 | 10 | 19 |
| 1974-75 | St Louis | 26 | 4 | 5 | 9 |
| 1975-76 | Calgary (WHA) | 15 | 5 | 2 | 7 |
| 1976-77 | Calgary (WHA) | 6 | 0 | 1 | 1 |
| | **NHL Totals** | 79 | 13 | 15 | 28 |
| | **WHA Totals** | 21 | 5 | 3 | 8 |

**LUKOWICH, Morris** *Forward*
b. Saskatoon, Sask., June 1, 1956

| Season | Club | GP | G | A | Pts. |
|---|---|---|---|---|---|
| 1976-77 | Houston (WHA) | 62 | 27 | 18 | 45 |
| 1977-78 | Houston (WHA) | 80 | 40 | 35 | 75 |
| 1978-79 | Houston (WHA) | 80 | 65 | 34 | 99 |
| 1979-80 | Winnipeg | 78 | 35 | 39 | 74 |
| 1980-81 | Winnipeg | 80 | 33 | 34 | 67 |
| 1981-82 | Winnipeg | 77 | 43 | 49 | 92 |
| 1982-83 | Winnipeg | 69 | 22 | 21 | 43 |
| | **NHL Totals** | 304 | 133 | 143 | 276 |
| | **WHA Totals** | 222 | 132 | 87 | 219 |

**LUKSA, Charles** *Defenseman*
b. Toronto, Ont., Feb. 19, 1954

| Season | Club | GP | G | A | Pts. |
|---|---|---|---|---|---|
| 1978-79 | Cincinnati (WHA) | 78 | 8 | 12 | 20 |
| 1979-80 | Hartford | 8 | 0 | 1 | 1 |
| | **NHL Totals** | 8 | 0 | 1 | 1 |
| | **WHA Totals** | 78 | 8 | 12 | 20 |

**LUMLEY, David** *Forward*
b. Toronto, Ont., Sept. 1, 1954

| Season | Club | GP | G | A | Pts. |
|---|---|---|---|---|---|
| 1978-79 | Montreal | 3 | 0 | 0 | 0 |
| 1979-80 | Edmonton | 80 | 20 | 38 | 58 |
| 1980-81 | Edmonton | 53 | 7 | 9 | 16 |
| 1981-82 | Edmonton | 66 | 32 | 42 | 74 |
| 1982-83 | Edmonton | 72 | 13 | 24 | 37 |
| | **Totals** | 274 | 72 | 113 | 185 |

**LUND, Pentti Alexander (Penny)** *Forward*
b. Helsinki, Finland, Dec. 6, 1925

| Season | Club | GP | G | A | Pts. |
|---|---|---|---|---|---|
| 1948-49 | New York R | 59 | 14 | 16 | 30 |
| 1949-50 | New York R | 64 | 18 | 9 | 27 |
| 1950-51 | New York R | 59 | 4 | 16 | 20 |
| 1951-52 | Boston | 23 | 0 | 5 | 5 |
| 1952-53 | Boston | 54 | 8 | 9 | 17 |
| | **Totals** | 259 | 44 | 55 | 99 |

**LUNDBERG, Brian** *Defenseman*
b. Burnaby, B.C., June 5, 1960

| Season | Club | GP | G | A | Pts. |
|---|---|---|---|---|---|
| 1982-83 | Pittsburgh | 1 | 0 | 0 | 0 |

**LUNDE, Leonard Melvin** *Forward*
b. Campbell River, Alta., Nov. 13, 1936

| Season | Club | GP | G | A | Pts. |
|---|---|---|---|---|---|
| 1958-59 | Detroit | 68 | 14 | 12 | 26 |
| 1959-60 | Detroit | 66 | 6 | 17 | 23 |
| 1960-61 | Detroit | 53 | 6 | 12 | 18 |
| 1961-62 | Detroit | 23 | 2 | 9 | 11 |
| 1962-63 | Chicago | 60 | 6 | 22 | 28 |
| 1965-66 | Chicago | 24 | 4 | 7 | 11 |
| 1967-68 | Minnesota | 7 | 0 | 1 | 1 |
| 1970-71 | Vancouver | 20 | 1 | 3 | 4 |
| | **Totals** | 321 | 39 | 83 | 122 |

**LUNDHOLM, Bengt** *Forward*
b. Falun, Sweden, Aug. 4, 1955

| Season | Club | GP | G | A | Pts. |
|---|---|---|---|---|---|
| 1981-82 | Winnipeg | 66 | 14 | 30 | 44 |
| 1982-83 | Winnipeg | 58 | 14 | 28 | 42 |
| | **Totals** | 124 | 28 | 58 | 86 |

**LUNDRIGAN, Joseph Roche (Joe)**
*Defenseman*
b. Corner Brook, Nfld., Sept. 12, 1948

| Season | Club | GP | G | A | Pts. |
|---|---|---|---|---|---|
| 1972-73 | Toronto | 49 | 2 | 7 | 9 |
| 1974-75 | Washington | 3 | 0 | 0 | 0 |
| | **Totals** | 52 | 2 | 7 | 9 |


**LUNDSTROM, Tord** *Forward*
b. Kiruna, Sweden, Mar. 4, 1945

| Season | Club | GP | G | A | Pts. |
|---|---|---|---|---|---|
| 1973-74 | Detroit | 11 | 1 | 1 | 2 |

**LUNDY, Patrick Anthony** *Forward*
b. Saskatoon, Sask., May 31, 1924

| Season | Club | GP | G | A | Pts. |
|---|---|---|---|---|---|
| 1945-46 | Detroit | 4 | 3 | 2 | 5 |
| 1946-47 | Detroit | 59 | 17 | 17 | 34 |
| 1947-48 | Detroit | 11 | 4 | 1 | 5 |
| 1948-49 | Detroit | 15 | 4 | 3 | 7 |
| 1950-51 | Chicago | 61 | 9 | 9 | 18 |
| | **Totals** | 150 | 37 | 32 | 69 |

**LUPIEN, Gilles** *Defenseman*
b. Lacute, Que., Apr. 20, 1954

| Season | Club | GP | G | A | Pts. |
|---|---|---|---|---|---|
| 1977-78 | Montreal | 46 | 1 | 3 | 4 |
| 1978-79 | Montreal | 72 | 1 | 9 | 10 |
| 1979-80 | Montreal | 56 | 1 | 7 | 8 |
| 1980-81 | Pitt-Hart | 51 | 2 | 5 | 7 |
| 1981-82 | Hartford | 1 | 0 | 1 | 1 |
| | **Totals** | 226 | 5 | 25 | 30 |

**LYLE, George** *Forward*
b. North Vancouver, B.C., Nov. 24, 1953

| Season | Club | GP | G | A | Pts. |
|---|---|---|---|---|---|
| 1976-77 | New England (WHA) | 75 | 39 | 33 | 72 |
| 1977-78 | New England (WHA) | 68 | 30 | 24 | 54 |
| 1978-79 | New England (WHA) | 59 | 17 | 18 | 35 |
| 1979-80 | Detroit | 27 | 7 | 4 | 11 |
| 1980-81 | Detroit | 31 | 10 | 14 | 24 |
| 1981-82 | Det-Hart | 25 | 3 | 14 | 17 |
| 1982-83 | Hartford | 16 | 4 | 6 | 10 |
| | **NHL Totals** | 99 | 24 | 38 | 62 |
| | **WHA Totals** | 202 | 86 | 75 | 161 |

**LYNCH, John Alan (Jack)** *Defenseman*
b. Toronto, Ont., May 28, 1952

| Season | Club | GP | G | A | Pts. |
|---|---|---|---|---|---|
| 1972-73 | Pittsburgh | 47 | 1 | 18 | 19 |
| 1973-74 | Pitt-Det | 52 | 5 | 24 | 29 |
| 1974-75 | Det-Wash | 70 | 3 | 20 | 23 |
| 1975-76 | Washington | 79 | 9 | 13 | 22 |
| 1976-77 | Washington | 75 | 5 | 25 | 30 |
| 1977-78 | Washington | 29 | 1 | 8 | 9 |
| 1978-79 | Washington | 30 | 2 | 6 | 8 |
| | **Totals** | 382 | 26 | 114 | 140 |

**LYNN, Victor Ivan** *Defenseman-Forward*
b. Saskatoon, Sask., Jan. 26, 1925

| Season | Club | GP | G | A | Pts. |
|---|---|---|---|---|---|
| 1943-44 | Detroit | 3 | 0 | 0 | 0 |
| 1945-46 | Montreal | 2 | 0 | 0 | 0 |
| 1946-47 | Toronto | 31 | 6 | 14 | 20 |
| 1947-48 | Toronto | 60 | 12 | 22 | 34 |
| 1948-49 | Toronto | 52 | 7 | 9 | 16 |
| 1949-50 | Toronto | 70 | 7 | 13 | 20 |
| 1950-51 | Boston | 56 | 14 | 6 | 20 |
| 1951-52 | Boston | 12 | 2 | 2 | 4 |
| 1952-53 | Chicago | 29 | 0 | 10 | 10 |
| 1953-54 | Chicago | 11 | 1 | 0 | 1 |
| | **Totals** | 326 | 49 | 76 | 125 |

**LYON, Steve** *Forward*
b. Toronto, Ont., May 16, 1952

| Season | Club | GP | G | A | Pts. |
|---|---|---|---|---|---|
| 1976-77 | Pittsburgh | 3 | 0 | 0 | 0 |

**LYONS, Ronald** *Forward*

| Season | Club | GP | G | A | Pts. |
|---|---|---|---|---|---|
| 1930-31 | Phil-Bos | 34 | 2 | 4 | 6 |

**LYSIAK, Thomas James** *Forward*
b. High Prairie, Alta., Apr. 22, 1953

| Season | Club | GP | G | A | Pts. |
|---|---|---|---|---|---|
| 1973-74 | Atlanta | 77 | 19 | 45 | 64 |
| 1974-75 | Atlanta | 77 | 25 | 52 | 77 |
| 1975-76 | Atlanta | 80 | 31 | 51 | 82 |
| 1976-77 | Atlanta | 79 | 30 | 51 | 81 |
| 1977-78 | Atlanta | 80 | 27 | 42 | 69 |
| 1978-79 | Atl-Chi | 66 | 23 | 45 | 68 |
| 1979-80 | Chicago | 77 | 26 | 43 | 69 |
| 1980-81 | Chicago | 72 | 21 | 55 | 76 |
| 1981-82 | Chicago | 71 | 32 | 50 | 82 |
| 1982-83 | Chicago | 61 | 23 | 38 | 61 |
| | **Totals** | 740 | 257 | 472 | 729 |


**MacADAM, Reginald Alan** *Forward*
b. Charlottestown, P.E.I., Mar. 16, 1952

| Season | Club | GP | G | A | Pts. |
|---|---|---|---|---|---|
| 1973-74 | Philadelphia | 5 | 0 | 0 | 0 |
| 1974-75 | California | 80 | 18 | 25 | 43 |
| 1975-76 | California | 80 | 32 | 31 | 63 |
| 1976-77 | Cleveland | 80 | 22 | 41 | 63 |
| 1977-78 | Cleveland | 80 | 16 | 32 | 48 |
| 1978-79 | Minnesota | 69 | 24 | 34 | 58 |
| 1979-80 | Minnesota | 80 | 42 | 51 | 93 |
| 1980-81 | Minnesota | 78 | 21 | 39 | 60 |
| 1981-82 | Minnesota | 79 | 18 | 43 | 61 |
| 1982-83 | Minnesota | 73 | 11 | 22 | 33 |
| | **Totals** | 704 | 204 | 318 | 522 |

**MacDERMID, Paul** *Forward*
b. Cheslen, Ont., Apr. 14, 1963

| Season | Club | GP | G | A | Pts. |
|---|---|---|---|---|---|
| 1981-82 | Hartford | 3 | 1 | 0 | 1 |
| 1982-83 | Hartford | 7 | 0 | 0 | 0 |
| | **Totals** | 10 | 1 | 0 | 1 |

**MacDONALD, Blair Joseph** *Forward*
b. Cornwall, Ont., Nov. 17, 1953

| Season | Club | GP | G | A | Pts. |
|---|---|---|---|---|---|
| 1973-74 | Edmonton (WHA) | 78 | 21 | 24 | 45 |
| 1974-75 | Edmonton (WHA) | 72 | 22 | 24 | 46 |
| 1975-76 | Edm-Ind (WHA) | 85 | 27 | 16 | 43 |
| 1976-77 | Indianapolis (WHA) | 81 | 34 | 30 | 64 |
| 1977-78 | Edmonton (WHA) | 80 | 34 | 34 | 68 |
| 1978-79 | Edmonton (WHA) | 80 | 34 | 37 | 71 |
| 1979-80 | Edmonton | 80 | 46 | 48 | 94 |
| 1980-81 | Edm-Van | 63 | 24 | 33 | 57 |
| 1981-82 | Vancouver | 59 | 18 | 15 | 33 |
| 1982-83 | Vancouver | 17 | 3 | 4 | 7 |
| | **NHL Totals** | 219 | 91 | 100 | 191 |
| | **WHA Totals** | 476 | 172 | 165 | 337 |

**MacDONALD, Calvin Parker** *Forward*
b. Sydney, N.S., June 14, 1933

| Season | Club | GP | G | A | Pts. |
|---|---|---|---|---|---|
| 1952-53 | Toronto | 1 | 0 | 0 | 0 |
| 1954-55 | Toronto | 62 | 8 | 3 | 11 |
| 1956-57 | New York R | 45 | 7 | 8 | 15 |
| 1957-58 | New York R | 70 | 8 | 10 | 18 |
| 1959-60 | New York R | 4 | 0 | 0 | 0 |
| 1960-61 | Detroit | 70 | 14 | 12 | 26 |
| 1961-62 | Detroit | 31 | 5 | 7 | 12 |
| 1962-63 | Detroit | 69 | 33 | 28 | 61 |
| 1963-64 | Detroit | 68 | 21 | 25 | 46 |
| 1964-65 | Detroit | 69 | 13 | 33 | 46 |
| 1965-66 | Bos-Det | 66 | 11 | 16 | 27 |
| 1966-67 | Detroit | 16 | 3 | 5 | 8 |
| 1967-68 | Minnesota | 69 | 19 | 23 | 42 |
| 1968-69 | Minnesota | 35 | 2 | 9 | 11 |
| | **Totals** | 675 | 144 | 179 | 323 |

**MacDONALD, James Allen Kilby** *Forward*
b. Ottawa, Ont., Sept. 6, 1913

| Season | Club | GP | G | A | Pts. |
|---|---|---|---|---|---|
| 1939-40 | New York R | 44 | 15 | 13 | 28 |
| 1940-41 | New York R | 47 | 5 | 6 | 11 |
| 1943-44 | New York R | 24 | 7 | 9 | 16 |
| 1944-45 | New York R | 36 | 9 | 6 | 15 |
| | **Totals** | 151 | 36 | 34 | 70 |

**MacDONALD, Lowell Wilson** *Forward*
b. New Glasgow, N.S., Aug. 30, 1941

| Season | Club | GP | G | A | Pts. |
|---|---|---|---|---|---|
| 1961-62 | Detroit | 1 | 0 | 0 | 0 |
| 1962-63 | Detroit | 26 | 2 | 1 | 3 |
| 1963-64 | Detroit | 10 | 1 | 4 | 5 |
| 1964-65 | Detroit | 9 | 2 | 1 | 3 |
| 1967-68 | Los Angeles | 74 | 21 | 24 | 45 |
| 1968-69 | Los Angeles | 58 | 14 | 14 | 28 |
| 1970-71 | Pittsburgh | 10 | 0 | 1 | 1 |
| 1972-73 | Pittsburgh | 78 | 34 | 41 | 75 |
| 1973-74 | Pittsburgh | 78 | 43 | 39 | 82 |
| 1974-75 | Pittsburgh | 71 | 27 | 33 | 60 |
| 1975-76 | Pittsburgh | 69 | 30 | 43 | 73 |
| 1976-77 | Pittsburgh | 3 | 1 | 1 | 2 |
| 1977-78 | Pittsburgh | 19 | 5 | 8 | 13 |
| | **Totals** | 506 | 180 | 210 | 390 |

**MacDOUGALL, Kim** *Defenseman*
b. Regina, Sask., Aug. 29, 1954

| Season | Club | GP | G | A | Pts. |
|---|---|---|---|---|---|
| 1974-75 | Minnesota | 1 | 0 | 0 | 0 |

**MACEY, Hubert (Hub)**  *Forward*
b. The Pas, Man., Apr. 13, 1921

| Season | Club | GP | G | A | Pts. |
|---|---|---|---|---|---|
| 1941-42 | New York R | 9 | 3 | 5 | 8 |
| 1942-43 | New York R | 9 | 3 | 3 | 6 |
| 1946-47 | Montreal | 12 | 0 | 1 | 1 |
| | **Totals** | 30 | 6 | 9 | 15 |

**MacFAYDEN, Donald P.**  *Forward*
b. Grossfield, Alta., Mar. 24, 1907

| Season | Club | GP | G | A | Pts. |
|---|---|---|---|---|---|
| 1932-33 | Chicago | 47 | 5 | 9 | 14 |
| 1933-34 | Chicago | 34 | 1 | 3 | 4 |
| 1934-35 | Chicago | 36 | 2 | 5 | 7 |
| 1935-36 | Chicago | 47 | 4 | 16 | 20 |
| | **Totals** | 164 | 12 | 33 | 45 |

**MacGREGOR, Bruce Cameron**  *Forward*
b. Edmonton, Alta., Apr. 26, 1941

| Season | Club | GP | G | A | Pts. |
|---|---|---|---|---|---|
| 1960-61 | Detroit | 12 | 0 | 1 | 1 |
| 1961-62 | Detroit | 65 | 6 | 12 | 18 |
| 1962-63 | Detroit | 67 | 11 | 11 | 22 |
| 1963-64 | Detroit | 63 | 11 | 21 | 32 |
| 1964-65 | Detroit | 66 | 21 | 20 | 41 |
| 1965-66 | Detroit | 70 | 20 | 14 | 34 |
| 1966-67 | Detroit | 70 | 28 | 19 | 47 |
| 1967-68 | Detroit | 71 | 15 | 24 | 39 |
| 1968-69 | Detroit | 69 | 18 | 23 | 41 |
| 1969-70 | Detroit | 73 | 15 | 23 | 38 |
| 1970-71 | Det-NYR | 74 | 18 | 29 | 47 |
| 1971-72 | New York R | 75 | 19 | 21 | 40 |
| 1972-73 | New York R | 52 | 14 | 12 | 26 |
| 1973-74 | New York R | 66 | 17 | 27 | 44 |
| 1974-75 | Edmonton (WHA) | 72 | 24 | 28 | 52 |
| 1975-76 | Edmonton (WHA) | 63 | 13 | 10 | 23 |
| | **NHL Totals** | 893 | 213 | 257 | 470 |
| | **WHA Totals** | 135 | 37 | 38 | 75 |

**MacGREGOR, Randy Kenneth**  *Forward*
b. Cobourg, Ont., July 9, 1953

| Season | Club | GP | G | A | Pts. |
|---|---|---|---|---|---|
| 1981-82 | | 2 | 1 | 1 | 2 |

**MacGUIGAN, Garth Leslie**  *Forward*
b. Charlottestown, P.E.I., Feb. 16, 1956

| Season | Club | GP | G | A | Pts. |
|---|---|---|---|---|---|
| 1979-80 | New York I | 2 | 0 | 0 | 0 |

**MacINNIS, Allan**  *Defenseman*
b. Inverness, N.S., July 11, 1963

| Season | Club | GP | G | A | Pts. |
|---|---|---|---|---|---|
| 1981-82 | Calgary | 2 | 0 | 0 | 0 |
| 1982-83 | Calgary | 14 | 1 | 3 | 4 |
| | **Totals** | 16 | 1 | 3 | 4 |

**MacIVER, Donald**  *Defenseman*
b. Montreal, Que., May 3, 1955

| Season | Club | GP | G | A | Pts. |
|---|---|---|---|---|---|
| 1979-80 | Winnipeg | 6 | 0 | 0 | 0 |

**MacKASEY, Blair**  *Defenseman*
b. Hamilton, Ont., Dec. 13, 1955

| Season | Club | GP | G | A | Pts. |
|---|---|---|---|---|---|
| 1976-77 | Toronto | 1 | 0 | 0 | 0 |

**MacKAY, Calum (Baldy)**  *Forward*
b. Toronto, Ont., Jan. 1, 1927

| Season | Club | GP | G | A | Pts. |
|---|---|---|---|---|---|
| 1946-47 | Detroit | 5 | 0 | 0 | 0 |
| 1948-49 | Detroit | 1 | 0 | 0 | 0 |
| 1949-50 | Montreal | 52 | 8 | 10 | 18 |
| 1950-51 | Montreal | 70 | 18 | 10 | 28 |
| 1951-52 | Montreal | 12 | 0 | 1 | 1 |
| 1953-54 | Montreal | 47 | 10 | 13 | 23 |
| 1954-55 | Montreal | 50 | 14 | 21 | 35 |
| | **Totals** | 237 | 50 | 55 | 105 |

**MacKAY, David**  *Forward*

| Season | Club | GP | G | A | Pts. |
|---|---|---|---|---|---|
| 1940-41 | Chicago | 27 | 3 | 0 | 3 |

**MacKAY, Duncan (Mickey)**  *Forward*
b. Chesley, Ont., May 21, 1894

| Season | Club | GP | G | A | Pts. |
|---|---|---|---|---|---|
| 1926-27 | Chicago | 34 | 14 | 8 | 22 |
| 1927-28 | Chicago | 36 | 17 | 4 | 21 |
| 1928-29 | PittPi-Bos | 39 | 9 | 2 | 11 |
| 1929-30 | Boston | 37 | 4 | 5 | 9 |
| | **Totals** | 146 | 44 | 19 | 63 |


**MacKAY, Murdo John**  *Forward*
b. Fort William, Ont., Aug. 8, 1917

| Season | Club | GP | G | A | Pts. |
|---|---|---|---|---|---|
| 1945-46 | Montreal | 5 | 0 | 1 | 1 |
| 1947-48 | Montreal | 14 | 0 | 2 | 2 |
| | **Totals** | 19 | 0 | 3 | 3 |

**MACKELL, Fleming David**  *Forward*
b. Montreal, Que., Apr. 30, 1929

| Season | Club | GP | G | A | Pts. |
|---|---|---|---|---|---|
| 1947-48 | Toronto | 3 | 0 | 0 | 0 |
| 1948-49 | Toronto | 11 | 1 | 1 | 2 |
| 1949-50 | Toronto | 36 | 7 | 13 | 20 |
| 1950-51 | Toronto | 70 | 12 | 13 | 25 |
| 1951-52 | Tor-Bos | 62 | 3 | 16 | 19 |
| 1952-53 | Boston | 65 | 27 | 17 | 44 |
| 1953-54 | Boston | 67 | 15 | 32 | 47 |
| 1954-55 | Boston | 60 | 11 | 24 | 35 |
| 1955-56 | Boston | 52 | 7 | 9 | 16 |
| 1956-57 | Boston | 65 | 22 | 17 | 39 |
| 1957-58 | Boston | 70 | 20 | 40 | 60 |
| 1958-59 | Boston | 57 | 17 | 23 | 40 |
| 1959-60 | Boston | 47 | 7 | 15 | 22 |
| | **Totals** | 665 | 149 | 220 | 369 |

**MacKENZIE, Barry**  *Defenseman*
b. Toronto, Ont., Aug. 16, 1941

| Season | Club | GP | G | A | Pts. |
|---|---|---|---|---|---|
| 1968-69 | Minnesota | 6 | 0 | 1 | 1 |

**MacKENZIE, William Kenneth**  *Defenseman*
b. Winnipeg, Man., Dec. 12, 1912

| Season | Club | GP | G | A | Pts. |
|---|---|---|---|---|---|
| 1932-33 | Chicago | 36 | 4 | 4 | 8 |
| 1933-34 | Montreal M | 47 | 4 | 3 | 7 |
| 1934-35 | New York R | 20 | 1 | 0 | 1 |
| 1936-37 | MontM-Mont | 49 | 4 | 4 | 8 |
| 1937-38 | Mont-Chi | 46 | 1 | 2 | 3 |
| 1938-39 | Chicago | 47 | 1 | 0 | 1 |
| 1939-40 | Chicago | 19 | 0 | 1 | 1 |
| | **Totals** | 264 | 15 | 14 | 29 |

**MACKEY, Reginald**  *Defenseman*
b. Ottawa, Ont., May 7, 1900

| Season | Club | GP | G | A | Pts. |
|---|---|---|---|---|---|
| 1926-26 | New York R | 34 | 0 | 0 | 0 |

**MACKIE, Howard**  *Defenseman*
b. Kitchener, Ont., Aug. 30, 1913

| Season | Club | GP | G | A | Pts. |
|---|---|---|---|---|---|
| 1936-37 | Detroit | 10 | 1 | 0 | 1 |
| 1937-38 | Detroit | 8 | 0 | 0 | 0 |
| | **Totals** | 18 | 1 | 0 | 1 |

**MacKINNON, Paul**  *Defenseman*
b. Brantford, Ont., Nov. 6, 1958

| Season | Club | GP | G | A | Pts. |
|---|---|---|---|---|---|
| 1978-79 | Winnipeg (WHA) | 73 | 2 | 15 | 17 |
| 1979-80 | Washington | 63 | 1 | 11 | 12 |
| 1980-81 | Washington | 14 | 0 | 0 | 0 |
| 1981-82 | Washington | 39 | 2 | 9 | 11 |
| 1982-83 | Washington | 19 | 2 | 2 | 4 |
| | **NHL Totals** | 135 | 5 | 22 | 27 |
| | **WHA Totals** | 73 | 2 | 15 | 17 |

**MacKINTOSH, Ian Ronald**  *Forward*
b. Selkirk, Man., June 10, 1927

| Season | Club | GP | G | A | Pts. |
|---|---|---|---|---|---|
| 1952-53 | New York R | 4 | 0 | 0 | 0 |

**MacLEAN, Paul**  *Forward*
b. Grostenquin, France, Mar. 9, 1958

| Season | Club | GP | G | A | Pts. |
|---|---|---|---|---|---|
| 1980-81 | St Louis | 1 | 0 | 0 | 0 |
| 1981-82 | Winnipeg | 74 | 36 | 25 | 61 |
| 1982-83 | Winnipeg | 80 | 32 | 44 | 76 |
| | **Totals** | 155 | 68 | 69 | 137 |

**MacLEISH, Richard George (Rick)**  *Forward*
b. Lindsay, Ont., Jan. 3, 1950

| Season | Club | GP | G | A | Pts. |
|---|---|---|---|---|---|
| 1970-71 | Philadelphia | 26 | 2 | 4 | 6 |
| 1971-72 | Philadelphia | 17 | 1 | 2 | 3 |
| 1972-73 | Philadelphia | 78 | 50 | 50 | 100 |
| 1973-74 | Philadelphia | 78 | 32 | 45 | 77 |
| 1974-75 | Philadelphia | 80 | 38 | 41 | 79 |
| 1975-76 | Philadelphia | 51 | 22 | 23 | 45 |
| 1976-77 | Philadelphia | 79 | 49 | 48 | 97 |
| 1977-78 | Philadelphia | 76 | 31 | 39 | 70 |
| 1978-79 | Philadelphia | 71 | 26 | 32 | 58 |
| 1979-80 | Philadelphia | 78 | 31 | 35 | 66 |
| 1980-81 | Philadelphia | 78 | 38 | 36 | 74 |


| Season | Club | GP | G | A | Pts. |
|---|---|---|---|---|---|
| 1981-82 | Pittsburgh | 74 | 19 | 28 | 47 |
| 1982-83 | Pittsburgh | 6 | 0 | 5 | 5 |
| | **Totals** | 792 | 339 | 388 | 727 |

**MacLELLAN, Brian**  *Forward*
b. Guelph, Ont., Oct. 27, 1958

| Season | Club | GP | G | A | Pts. |
|---|---|---|---|---|---|
| 1982-83 | Los Angeles | 8 | 0 | 3 | 3 |

**MacMILLAN, John**  *Forward*
b. Lethbridge, Alta., Oct. 25, 1935

| Season | Club | GP | G | A | Pts. |
|---|---|---|---|---|---|
| 1960-61 | Toronto | 31 | 3 | 5 | 8 |
| 1961-62 | Toronto | 32 | 1 | 0 | 1 |
| 1962-63 | Toronto | 6 | 1 | 1 | 2 |
| 1963-64 | Tor-Det | 33 | 0 | 3 | 3 |
| 1964-65 | Detroit | 3 | 0 | 1 | 1 |
| | **Totals** | 104 | 5 | 10 | 15 |

**MacMILLAN, Robert Lea**  *Forward*
b. Charlottetown, P.E.I., Sept. 13, 1952

| Season | Club | GP | G | A | Pts. |
|---|---|---|---|---|---|
| 1972-73 | Minnesota (WHA) | 75 | 13 | 27 | 40 |
| 1973-74 | Minnesota (WHA) | 78 | 14 | 34 | 48 |
| 1974-75 | New York R | 22 | 1 | 2 | 3 |
| 1975-76 | St Louis | 80 | 20 | 32 | 52 |
| 1976-77 | St Louis | 80 | 19 | 39 | 58 |
| 1977-78 | StL-Atl | 80 | 38 | 33 | 71 |
| 1978-79 | Atlanta | 79 | 37 | 71 | 108 |
| 1979-80 | Atlanta | 77 | 22 | 39 | 61 |
| 1980-81 | Calgary | 77 | 28 | 35 | 63 |
| 1981-82 | Calg-Col | 80 | 22 | 39 | 61 |
| 1982-83 | New Jersey | 71 | 19 | 29 | 48 |
| | **NHL Totals** | 646 | 206 | 319 | 525 |
| | **WHA Totals** | 153 | 27 | 61 | 88 |

**MacMILLAN, William Stewart (Billy)**  *Forward*
b. Charlottetown, P.E.I., Mar. 7, 1943

| Season | Club | GP | G | A | Pts. |
|---|---|---|---|---|---|
| 1970-71 | Toronto | 76 | 22 | 19 | 41 |
| 1971-72 | Toronto | 61 | 10 | 7 | 17 |
| 1972-73 | Atlanta | 78 | 10 | 15 | 25 |
| 1973-74 | New York I | 55 | 4 | 9 | 13 |
| 1974-75 | New York I | 69 | 13 | 12 | 25 |
| 1975-76 | New York I | 64 | 9 | 7 | 16 |
| 1976-77 | New York I | 43 | 6 | 8 | 14 |
| | **Totals** | 446 | 74 | 77 | 151 |

**MacNEIL, Allster Wences**  *Defenseman*
b. Sydney, N.S., Sept. 27, 1935

| Season | Club | GP | G | A | Pts. |
|---|---|---|---|---|---|
| 1955-56 | Toronto | 1 | 0 | 0 | 0 |
| 1956-57 | Toronto | 53 | 4 | 8 | 12 |
| 1957-58 | Toronto | 13 | 0 | 0 | 0 |
| 1959-60 | Toronto | 4 | 0 | 0 | 0 |
| 1961-62 | Montreal | 62 | 1 | 7 | 8 |
| 1962-63 | Chicago | 70 | 2 | 19 | 21 |
| 1963-64 | Chicago | 70 | 5 | 19 | 24 |
| 1964-65 | Chicago | 69 | 3 | 7 | 10 |
| 1965-66 | Chicago | 51 | 0 | 1 | 1 |
| 1966-67 | New York R | 58 | 0 | 4 | 4 |
| 1967-68 | Pittsburgh | 74 | 2 | 10 | 12 |
| | **Totals** | 525 | 17 | 75 | 92 |

**MacNEIL, Stephen Bernard**  *Forward*
by Sudbury, Ont., Mar. 7, 1950

| Season | Club | GP | G | A | Pts. |
|---|---|---|---|---|---|
| 1972-73 | Los Angeles (WHA) | 41 | 4 | 7 | 11 |
| 1973-74 | St. Louis | 4 | 0 | 0 | 0 |
| 1975-76 | Cincinnati (WHA) | 77 | 15 | 12 | 27 |
| | **NHL Totals** | 4 | 0 | 0 | 0 |
| | **WHA Totals** | 118 | 19 | 19 | 38 |

**MACOUN, Jamie**  *Forward*
b. Newmarket, Ont., Aug. 17, 1961

| Season | Club | GP | G | A | Pts. |
|---|---|---|---|---|---|
| 1982-83 | Calgary | 22 | 1 | 4 | 5 |

**MacPHERSON, James Albert (Bud)**
*Defenseman*
b. Edmonton, Alta., Mar. 21, 1927

| Season | Club | GP | G | A | Pts. |
|---|---|---|---|---|---|
| 1948-49 | Montreal | 3 | 0 | 0 | 0 |
| 1950-51 | Montreal | 62 | 0 | 16 | 16 |
| 1951-52 | Montreal | 54 | 2 | 1 | 3 |
| 1952-53 | Montreal | 59 | 2 | 3 | 5 |
| 1953-54 | Montreal | 41 | 0 | 5 | 5 |
| 1954-55 | Montreal | 30 | 1 | 8 | 9 |
| 1956-57 | Montreal | 10 | 0 | 0 | 0 |
| | **Totals** | 259 | 5 | 33 | 38 |

| Season | Club | GP | G | A | Pts. |
|---|---|---|---|---|---|
| **MacSWEYN, Donald Ralph** | *Defenseman* | | | | |
| b. Hawkesbury, Ont., Sept. 8, 1942 | | | | | |
| 1967-68 | Philadelphia | 4 | 0 | 0 | 0 |
| 1968-69 | Philadelphia | 24 | 0 | 4 | 4 |
| 1969-70 | Philadelphia | 17 | 0 | 0 | 0 |
| 1971-72 | Philadelphia | 2 | 0 | 1 | 1 |
| 1972-73 | Los Angeles (WHA) | 78 | 0 | 23 | 23 |
| 1973-74 | LA-Van (WHA) | 69 | 2 | 21 | 23 |
| | **NHL Totals** | 47 | 0 | 5 | 5 |
| | **WHA Totals** | 147 | 2 | 44 | 46 |
| **MacTAVISH, Craig** | *Forward* | | | | |
| b. London, Ont., Aug. 15, 1958 | | | | | |
| 1979-80 | Boston | 46 | 11 | 17 | 28 |
| 1980-81 | Boston | 24 | 3 | 5 | 8 |
| 1981-82 | Boston | 2 | 0 | 1 | 1 |
| 1982-83 | Boston | 75 | 10 | 20 | 30 |
| | **Totals** | 147 | 24 | 43 | 67 |
| **MADIGAN, Cornelius Dennis (Connie)** | | | | | |
| *Defenseman* | | | | | |
| b. Port Arthur, Ont., Oct. 4, 1934 | | | | | |
| 1972-73 | St Louis | 20 | 0 | 3 | 3 |
| **MAGEE, Dean** | *Forward* | | | | |
| b. Rocky Mountain House, Alta., | | | | | |
| Apr. 29, 1955 | | | | | |
| 1977-78 | Minnesota | 7 | 0 | 0 | 0 |
| 1978-79 | Indianapolis (WHA) | 5 | 0 | 1 | 1 |
| | **NHL Totals** | 7 | 0 | 0 | 0 |
| | **WHA Totals** | 5 | 0 | 1 | 1 |
| **MAGGS, Darryl John** | *Defenseman* | | | | |
| b. Victoria, B.C., Apr. 6, 1949 | | | | | |
| 1971-72 | Chicago | 59 | 7 | 4 | 11 |
| 1972-73 | Chi-Cal | 71 | 7 | 15 | 22 |
| 1973-74 | Chicago (WHA) | 78 | 8 | 22 | 30 |
| 1974-75 | Chicago (WHA) | 77 | 6 | 27 | 33 |
| 1975-76 | Ott-Ind (WHA) | 36 | 5 | 16 | 21 |
| 1976-77 | Indianapolis (WHA) | 81 | 16 | 55 | 71 |
| 1977-78 | Ind-Cin (WHA) | 62 | 8 | 20 | 28 |
| 1978-79 | Cincinnati (WHA) | 27 | 4 | 14 | 18 |
| 1979-80 | Toronto | 5 | 0 | 0 | 0 |
| | **NHL Totals** | 135 | 14 | 19 | 33 |
| | **WHA Totals** | 361 | 47 | 154 | 201 |
| **MAGNAN, Marc** | *Forward* | | | | |
| b. Beaumont, Alta., Feb. 17, 1962 | | | | | |
| 1982-83 | Toronto | 4 | 0 | 1 | 1 |
| **MAGNUSON, Keith Arlen** | *Defenseman* | | | | |
| b. Saskatoon, Sask., Apr. 27, 1947 | | | | | |
| 1969-70 | Chicago | 76 | 0 | 24 | 24 |
| 1970-71 | Chicago | 76 | 3 | 20 | 23 |
| 1971-72 | Chicago | 74 | 2 | 19 | 21 |
| 1972-73 | Chicago | 77 | 0 | 19 | 19 |
| 1973-74 | Chicago | 57 | 2 | 11 | 13 |
| 1974-75 | Chicago | 48 | 2 | 12 | 14 |
| 1975-76 | Chicago | 48 | 1 | 6 | 7 |
| 1976-77 | Chicago | 37 | 1 | 6 | 7 |
| 1977-78 | Chicago | 67 | 2 | 4 | 6 |
| 1978-79 | Chicago | 26 | 1 | 4 | 5 |
| 1979-80 | Chicago | 3 | 0 | 0 | 0 |
| | **Totals** | 589 | 14 | 125 | 139 |
| **MAHAFFY, John** | *Forward* | | | | |
| b. Montreal, Que., July 18, 1918 | | | | | |
| 1942-43 | Montreal | 9 | 2 | 5 | 7 |
| 1943-44 | Mont-NYR | 28 | 9 | 20 | 29 |
| | **Totals** | 37 | 11 | 25 | 36 |
| **MAHOVLICH, Francis William (Frank)** | | | | | |
| *Forward* | | | | | |
| b. Timmins, Ont., Jan. 10, 1938 | | | | | |
| 1956-57 | Toronto | 3 | 1 | 0 | 1 |
| 1957-58 | Toronto | 67 | 20 | 16 | 36 |
| 1958-59 | Toronto | 63 | 22 | 27 | 49 |
| 1959-60 | Toronto | 70 | 18 | 21 | 39 |
| 1960-61 | Toronto | 70 | 48 | 36 | 84 |
| 1961-62 | Toronto | 70 | 33 | 38 | 71 |

| Season | Club | GP | G | A | Pts. |
|---|---|---|---|---|---|
| 1962-63 | Toronto | 67 | 36 | 37 | 73 |
| 1963-64 | Toronto | 70 | 26 | 29 | 55 |
| 1964-65 | Toronto | 59 | 23 | 28 | 51 |
| 1965-66 | Toronto | 68 | 32 | 24 | 56 |
| 1966-67 | Toronto | 63 | 18 | 28 | 46 |
| 1967-68 | Tor-Det | 63 | 26 | 26 | 52 |
| 1968-69 | Detroit | 76 | 49 | 29 | 78 |
| 1969-70 | Detroit | 74 | 38 | 32 | 70 |
| 1970-71 | Det-Mont | 73 | 31 | 42 | 73 |
| 1971-72 | Montreal | 76 | 43 | 53 | 96 |
| 1972-73 | Montreal | 78 | 38 | 55 | 93 |
| 1973-74 | Montreal | 71 | 31 | 49 | 80 |
| 1974-75 | Toronto (WHA) | 73 | 38 | 44 | 82 |
| 1975-76 | Toronto (WHA) | 75 | 34 | 55 | 89 |
| 1976-77 | Birmingham (WHA) | 17 | 3 | 20 | 23 |
| 1977-78 | Birmingham (WHA) | 72 | 14 | 24 | 38 |
| | **NHL Totals** | 1181 | 533 | 570 | 1103 |
| | **WHA Totals** | 237 | 89 | 143 | 232 |
| **MAHOVLICH, Peter Joseph** | *Forward* | | | | |
| b. Timmons, Ont., Oct. 10, 1946 | | | | | |
| 1965-66 | Detroit | 3 | 0 | 1 | 1 |
| 1966-67 | Detroit | 34 | 1 | 3 | 4 |
| 1967-68 | Detroit | 15 | 6 | 4 | 10 |
| 1968-69 | Detroit | 30 | 2 | 2 | 4 |
| 1969-70 | Montreal | 36 | 9 | 8 | 17 |
| 1970-71 | Montreal | 78 | 35 | 26 | 61 |
| 1971-72 | Montreal | 75 | 35 | 32 | 67 |
| 1972-73 | Montreal | 61 | 21 | 38 | 59 |
| 1973-74 | Montreal | 78 | 36 | 37 | 73 |
| 1974-75 | Montreal | 80 | 35 | 82 | 117 |
| 1975-76 | Montreal | 80 | 34 | 71 | 105 |
| 1976-77 | Montreal | 76 | 15 | 47 | 62 |
| 1977-78 | Mont-Pitt | 74 | 28 | 41 | 69 |
| 1978-79 | Pittsburgh | 60 | 14 | 39 | 53 |
| 1979-80 | Detroit | 80 | 16 | 50 | 66 |
| 1980-81 | Detroit | 24 | 1 | 4 | 5 |
| | **Totals** | 884 | 288 | 485 | 773 |
| **MAILLEY, Frank** | *Forward* | | | | |
| 1942-43 | Montreal | 1 | 0 | 0 | 0 |
| **MAIR, James McKay (Jim)** | *Defenseman* | | | | |
| b. Schumacher, Ont., May 15, 1946 | | | | | |
| 1970-71 | Philadelphia | 2 | 0 | 0 | 0 |
| 1971-72 | Philadelphia | 2 | 0 | 0 | 0 |
| 1972-73 | NYI-Van | 64 | 3 | 11 | 14 |
| 1973-74 | Vancouver | 6 | 1 | 3 | 4 |
| 1974-75 | Vancouver | 2 | 0 | 1 | 1 |
| | **Totals** | 76 | 4 | 15 | 19 |
| **MAJEAU, Fernand** | *Forward* | | | | |
| b. Verdun, Que., May 3, 1916 | | | | | |
| 1943-44 | Montreal | 44 | 20 | 18 | 38 |
| 1944-45 | Montreal | 12 | 2 | 6 | 8 |
| | **Totals** | 56 | 22 | 24 | 46 |
| **MAKI, Ronald Patrick (Chico)** | *Forward* | | | | |
| b. Sault Ste. Marie, Ont., Aug. 17, 1939 | | | | | |
| 1961-62 | Chicago | 16 | 4 | 6 | 10 |
| 1962-63 | Chicago | 65 | 7 | 17 | 24 |
| 1963-64 | Chicago | 68 | 8 | 14 | 22 |
| 1964-65 | Chicago | 65 | 16 | 24 | 40 |
| 1965-66 | Chicago | 68 | 17 | 31 | 48 |
| 1966-67 | Chicago | 56 | 9 | 29 | 38 |
| 1967-68 | Chicago | 60 | 8 | 16 | 24 |
| 1968-69 | Chicago | 66 | 7 | 21 | 28 |
| 1969-70 | Chicago | 75 | 10 | 24 | 34 |
| 1970-71 | Chicago | 72 | 22 | 26 | 48 |
| 1971-72 | Chicago | 72 | 13 | 34 | 47 |
| 1972-73 | Chicago | 77 | 13 | 19 | 32 |
| 1973-74 | Chicago | 69 | 9 | 25 | 34 |
| 1974-75 | Chicago | 22 | 0 | 6 | 6 |
| | **Totals** | 841 | 143 | 292 | 435 |
| **MAKI, Wayne** | *Forward* | | | | |
| b. Sault Ste. Marie, Ont., Nov. 10, 1944 | | | | | |
| 1967-68 | Chicago | 49 | 5 | 5 | 10 |
| 1968-69 | Chicago | 1 | 0 | 0 | 0 |
| 1969-70 | St Louis | 16 | 2 | 1 | 3 |
| 1970-71 | Vancouver | 78 | 25 | 38 | 63 |

| Season | Club | GP | G | A | Pts. |
|---|---|---|---|---|---|
| 1971-72 | Vancouver | 76 | 22 | 25 | 47 |
| 1972-73 | Vancouver | 26 | 3 | 10 | 13 |
| | **Totals** | 246 | 57 | 79 | 136 |
| **MAKKONEN, Karl** | *Forward* | | | | |
| b. Pori, Finland, Jan. 20, 1955 | | | | | |
| 1979-80 | Edmonton | 9 | 2 | 2 | 4 |
| **MALINOWSKI, Merlin Trevis** | *Forward* | | | | |
| b. North Battleford, Sask., Sept. 27, 1958 | | | | | |
| 1978-79 | Colorado | 54 | 6 | 17 | 23 |
| 1979-80 | Colorado | 10 | 2 | 4 | 6 |
| 1980-81 | Colorado | 69 | 25 | 37 | 62 |
| 1981-82 | Colorado | 69 | 13 | 28 | 41 |
| 1982-83 | NJ-Hart | 80 | 8 | 25 | 33 |
| | **Totals** | 282 | 54 | 111 | 165 |
| **MALONE, Clifford** | *Forward* | | | | |
| b. Quebec City, Que., Sept. 4, 1925 | | | | | |
| 1951-52 | Montreal | 3 | 0 | 0 | 0 |
| **MALONE, Maurice Joseph** | *Forward* | | | | |
| b. Quebec City, Que., Feb. 28, 1890 | | | | | |
| 1917-18 | Montreal | 20 | 44 | 0 | 44 |
| 1918-19 | Montreal | 8 | 7 | 1 | 8 |
| 1919-20 | Quebec | 24 | 39 | 6 | 45 |
| 1920-21 | Hamilton | 20 | 30 | 4 | 34 |
| 1921-22 | Hamilton | 24 | 25 | 7 | 32 |
| 1922-23 | Montreal | 20 | 1 | 0 | 1 |
| 1923-24 | Montreal | 9 | 0 | 0 | 0 |
| | **Totals** | 125 | 146 | 18 | 164 |
| **MALONE, William Gregory** | *Forward* | | | | |
| b. Fredericton, N.B., Mar. 8, 1956 | | | | | |
| 1976-77 | Pittsburgh | 66 | 18 | 19 | 37 |
| 1977-78 | Pittsburgh | 78 | 18 | 43 | 61 |
| 1978-79 | Pittsburgh | 80 | 35 | 30 | 65 |
| 1979-80 | Pittsburgh | 51 | 19 | 32 | 51 |
| 1980-81 | Pittsburgh | 62 | 21 | 29 | 50 |
| 1981-82 | Pittsburgh | 78 | 15 | 24 | 39 |
| 1982-83 | Pittsburgh | 80 | 17 | 44 | 61 |
| | **Totals** | 495 | 143 | 221 | 364 |
| **MALONEY, Daniel Charles (Dan)** | *Forward* | | | | |
| b. Barrie, Ont., Sept. 24, 1950 | | | | | |
| 1970-71 | Chicago | 74 | 12 | 14 | 26 |
| 1972-73 | Chi-LA | 71 | 17 | 24 | 41 |
| 1973-74 | Los Angeles | 65 | 15 | 17 | 32 |
| 1974-75 | Los Angeles | 80 | 27 | 39 | 66 |
| 1975-76 | Detroit | 77 | 27 | 39 | 66 |
| 1976-77 | Detroit | 34 | 13 | 13 | 26 |
| 1977-78 | Det-Tor | 79 | 19 | 33 | 52 |
| 1978-79 | Toronto | 77 | 17 | 36 | 53 |
| 1979-80 | Toronto | 71 | 17 | 16 | 33 |
| 1980-81 | Toronto | 65 | 20 | 21 | 41 |
| 1981-82 | Toronto | 44 | 8 | 7 | 15 |
| | **Totals** | 737 | 192 | 259 | 451 |
| **MALONEY, David Wilfred** | *Defenseman* | | | | |
| b. Kitchener, Ont., July 31, 1956 | | | | | |
| 1974-75 | New York R | 4 | 0 | 2 | 2 |
| 1975-76 | New York R | 21 | 1 | 3 | 4 |
| 1976-77 | New York R | 66 | 3 | 18 | 21 |
| 1977-78 | New York R | 56 | 2 | 19 | 21 |
| 1978-79 | New York R | 76 | 11 | 17 | 28 |
| 1979-80 | New York R | 77 | 12 | 25 | 37 |
| 1980-81 | New York R | 79 | 11 | 36 | 47 |
| 1981-82 | New York R | 64 | 13 | 36 | 49 |
| 1982-83 | New York R | 78 | 8 | 42 | 50 |
| | **Totals** | 521 | 61 | 198 | 259 |
| **MALONEY, Donald** | *Forward* | | | | |
| b. Lindsay, Ont., Sept. 5, 1958 | | | | | |
| 1978-79 | New York R | 28 | 9 | 17 | 26 |
| 1979-80 | New York R | 79 | 25 | 48 | 73 |
| 1980-81 | New York R | 61 | 29 | 23 | 52 |
| 1981-82 | New York R | 54 | 22 | 36 | 58 |
| 1982-83 | New York R | 78 | 29 | 40 | 69 |
| | **Totals** | 300 | 114 | 164 | 278 |

| Season | Club | GP | G | A | Pts. |
|---|---|---|---|---|---|
| **MALONEY, Philip Francis** *Forward* | | | | | |
| b. Ottawa, Ont., Oct. 6, 1927 | | | | | |
| 1949-50 | Boston | 70 | 15 | 31 | 46 |
| 1950-51 | Bos-Tor | 14 | 3 | 0 | 3 |
| 1952-53 | Toronto | 29 | 2 | 6 | 8 |
| 1958-59 | Chicago | 24 | 2 | 2 | 4 |
| 1959-60 | Chicago | 21 | 6 | 4 | 10 |
| | **Totals** | 158 | 28 | 43 | 71 |
| **MALVITA, Raymond William** *Defenseman* | | | | | |
| b. Flin Flon, Man., July 24, 1954 | | | | | |
| 1975-76 | Boston | 2 | 0 | 0 | 0 |
| 1976-77 | Boston | 23 | 2 | 3 | 5 |
| | **Totals** | 25 | 2 | 3 | 5 |
| **MANASTERSKY, Timothy (Tom)** *Defenseman* | | | | | |
| b. Montreal, Que., Mar. 7, 1929 | | | | | |
| 1950-51 | Montreal | 6 | 0 | 0 | 0 |
| **MANCUSO, Felix (Gus)** *Forward* | | | | | |
| b. Niagara, Falls, Ont., Apr. 11, 1913 | | | | | |
| 1937-38 | Montreal | 17 | 1 | 1 | 2 |
| 1938-39 | Montreal | 2 | 0 | 0 | 0 |
| 1939-40 | Montreal | 7 | 0 | 0 | 0 |
| 1942-43 | New York R | 41 | 6 | 8 | 14 |
| | **Totals** | 67 | 7 | 9 | 16 |
| **MANDICH, Dan** *Defenseman* | | | | | |
| b. Brantford, Ont., June 12, 1960 | | | | | |
| 1982-83 | Minnesota | 67 | 3 | 4 | 7 |
| **MANERY, Kris Franklin** *Forward* | | | | | |
| b. Leamington, Ont., Sept. 24, 1954 | | | | | |
| 1977-78 | Cleveland | 78 | 22 | 27 | 49 |
| 1978-79 | Minnesota | 60 | 17 | 19 | 36 |
| 1979-80 | Minn-Van-Winn | 65 | 11 | 9 | 20 |
| 1980-81 | Winnipeg | 47 | 13 | 9 | 22 |
| | **Totals** | 250 | 63 | 64 | 127 |
| **MANERY, Randy Neal** *Defenseman* | | | | | |
| b. Leamington, Ont., Jan. 10, 1949 | | | | | |
| 1970-71 | Detroit | 2 | 0 | 0 | 0 |
| 1971-72 | Detroit | 1 | 0 | 0 | 0 |
| 1972-73 | Atlanta | 78 | 5 | 30 | 35 |
| 1973-74 | Atlanta | 78 | 8 | 29 | 37 |
| 1974-75 | Atlanta | 68 | 5 | 27 | 32 |
| 1975-76 | Atlanta | 80 | 7 | 32 | 39 |
| 1976-77 | Atlanta | 73 | 5 | 24 | 29 |
| 1977-78 | Los Angeles | 79 | 6 | 27 | 33 |
| 1978-79 | Los Angeles | 71 | 8 | 27 | 35 |
| 1979-80 | Los Angeles | 52 | 6 | 10 | 16 |
| | **Totals** | 582 | 50 | 206 | 256 |
| **MANN, James Edward** *Forward* | | | | | |
| b. Montreal, Que., Apr. 17, 1959 | | | | | |
| 1979-80 | Winnipeg | 72 | 3 | 5 | 8 |
| 1980-81 | Winnipeg | 37 | 3 | 3 | 6 |
| 1981-82 | Winnipeg | 37 | 3 | 2 | 5 |
| 1982-83 | Winnipeg | 40 | 0 | 1 | 1 |
| | **Totals** | 186 | 9 | 11 | 20 |
| **MANN, John Edward Kingsley** *Forward* | | | | | |
| b. Winnipeg, Man., July 27, 1919 | | | | | |
| 1943-44 | New York R | 3 | 0 | 0 | 0 |
| 1944-45 | New York R | 6 | 3 | 4 | 7 |
| | **Totals** | 9 | 3 | 4 | 7 |
| **MANN, Kenneth Rose** *Forward* | | | | | |
| b. Hamilton, Ont., Sept. 5, 1953 | | | | | |
| 1975-76 | Detroit | 1 | 0 | 0 | 0 |
| **MANN, Norman** *Forward* | | | | | |
| b. Bradford, England, Mar. 3, 1914 | | | | | |
| 1938-39 | Toronto | 16 | 0 | 0 | 0 |
| 1940-41 | Toronto | 15 | 0 | 3 | 3 |
| | **Totals** | 31 | 3 | 3 | 3 |

| Season | Club | GP | G | A | Pts. |
|---|---|---|---|---|---|
| **MANNERS, Rennison** *Forward* | | | | | |
| 1929-30 | Pittsburgh Pi | 33 | 3 | 2 | 5 |
| 1930-31 | Philadelphia Q | 5 | 0 | 0 | 0 |
| | **Totals** | 38 | 3 | 2 | 5 |
| **MANNO, Robert John** *Defenseman* | | | | | |
| b. Niagara Falls, Ont., Oct. 31, 1956 | | | | | |
| 1976-77 | Vancouver | 2 | 0 | 0 | 0 |
| 1977-78 | Vancouver | 49 | 5 | 14 | 19 |
| 1978-79 | Vancouver | 52 | 5 | 16 | 21 |
| 1979-80 | Vancouver | 40 | 3 | 14 | 17 |
| 1980-81 | Vancouver | 20 | 0 | 11 | 11 |
| 1981-82 | Toronto | 72 | 9 | 41 | 50 |
| | **Totals** | 235 | 22 | 96 | 118 |
| **MANSOM, Raymond Clifton** *Forward* | | | | | |
| b. St. Boniface, Man., Dec. 3, 1926 | | | | | |
| 1947-48 | Boston | 1 | 0 | 0 | 0 |
| 1948-49 | New York R | 1 | 0 | 1 | 1 |
| | **Totals** | 2 | 0 | 1 | 1 |
| **MANTHA, Georges** *Forward* | | | | | |
| b. Lachine, Que., Nov. 29, 1908 | | | | | |
| 1928-29 | Montreal | 21 | 0 | 0 | 0 |
| 1929-30 | Montreal | 44 | 5 | 2 | 7 |
| 1930-31 | Montreal | 44 | 11 | 6 | 17 |
| 1931-32 | Montreal | 48 | 1 | 7 | 8 |
| 1932-33 | Montreal | 43 | 3 | 6 | 9 |
| 1933-34 | Montreal | 44 | 6 | 9 | 15 |
| 1934-35 | Montreal | 42 | 12 | 10 | 22 |
| 1935-36 | Montreal | 35 | 1 | 12 | 13 |
| 1936-37 | Montreal | 47 | 13 | 14 | 27 |
| 1937-38 | Montreal | 47 | 23 | 19 | 42 |
| 1938-39 | Montreal | 25 | 5 | 5 | 10 |
| 1939-40 | Montreal | 42 | 9 | 11 | 20 |
| 1940-41 | Montreal | 6 | 0 | 1 | 1 |
| | **Totals** | 488 | 89 | 102 | 191 |
| **MANTHA, Maurice William (Moe)** | | | | | |
| *Defenseman* | | | | | |
| b. Lakewood, Ohio, Jan. 21, 1961 | | | | | |
| 1980-81 | Winnipeg | 58 | 2 | 23 | 25 |
| 1981-82 | Winnipeg | 25 | 0 | 12 | 12 |
| 1982-83 | Winnipeg | 21 | 2 | 7 | 9 |
| | **Totals** | 104 | 4 | 42 | 46 |
| **MANTHA, Sylvio** *Defenseman* | | | | | |
| b. Montreal, Que., Apr. 14, 1902 | | | | | |
| 1923-24 | Montreal | 24 | 1 | 0 | 1 |
| 1924-25 | Montreal | 30 | 2 | 0 | 2 |
| 1925-26 | Montreal | 34 | 2 | 1 | 3 |
| 1926-27 | Montreal | 43 | 10 | 5 | 15 |
| 1927-28 | Montreal | 43 | 4 | 11 | 15 |
| 1928-29 | Montreal | 44 | 9 | 4 | 13 |
| 1929-30 | Montreal | 44 | 13 | 11 | 24 |
| 1930-31 | Montreal | 44 | 4 | 7 | 11 |
| 1931-32 | Montreal | 47 | 5 | 5 | 10 |
| 1932-33 | Montreal | 48 | 4 | 7 | 11 |
| 1933-34 | Montreal | 48 | 4 | 6 | 10 |
| 1934-35 | Montreal | 47 | 3 | 11 | 14 |
| 1935-36 | Montreal | 42 | 2 | 4 | 6 |
| 1936-37 | Boston | 5 | 0 | 0 | 0 |
| | **Totals** | 543 | 63 | 72 | 135 |
| **MARACLE, Henry Elmer** *Forward* | | | | | |
| b. Ayr, Ont., Sept. 8, 1904 | | | | | |
| 1930-31 | New York R | 11 | 1 | 3 | 4 |
| **MARCETTA, Milan (Mike)** *Forward* | | | | | |
| b. Cadomin, Alta., Sept. 19, 1936 | | | | | |
| 1967-68 | Minnesota | 36 | 4 | 13 | 17 |
| 1968-69 | Minnesota | 18 | 3 | 2 | 5 |
| | **Totals** | 54 | 7 | 15 | 22 |
| **MARCH, Harold C. (Mush)** *Forward* | | | | | |
| b. Sitton, Sask., Oct., 18, 1908 | | | | | |
| 1928-29 | Chicago | 35 | 3 | 3 | 6 |
| 1929-30 | Chicago | 43 | 8 | 7 | 15 |
| 1930-31 | Chicago | 44 | 11 | 6 | 17 |
| 1931-32 | Chicago | 48 | 12 | 10 | 22 |

| Season | Club | GP | G | A | Pts. |
|---|---|---|---|---|---|
| 1932-33 | Chicago | 48 | 9 | 11 | 20 |
| 1933-34 | Chicago | 48 | 4 | 13 | 17 |
| 1934-35 | Chicago | 48 | 13 | 17 | 30 |
| 1935-36 | Chicago | 48 | 16 | 19 | 35 |
| 1936-37 | Chicago | 36 | 11 | 6 | 17 |
| 1937-38 | Chicago | 42 | 11 | 17 | 28 |
| 1938-39 | Chicago | 47 | 10 | 11 | 21 |
| 1939-40 | Chicago | 47 | 9 | 14 | 23 |
| 1940-41 | Chicago | 43 | 8 | 9 | 17 |
| 1941-42 | Chicago | 46 | 6 | 26 | 32 |
| 1942-43 | Chicago | 50 | 7 | 29 | 36 |
| 1943-44 | Chicago | 48 | 10 | 27 | 37 |
| 1944-45 | Chicago | 38 | 5 | 5 | 10 |
| | **Totals** | 759 | 153 | 230 | 383 |
| **MARCHINKO, Brian Nicholas Wayne** | | | | | |
| *Forward* | | | | | |
| b. Weyburn, Sask., Aug. 2, 1948 | | | | | |
| 1970-71 | Toronto | 2 | 0 | 0 | 0 |
| 1971-72 | Toronto | 3 | 0 | 0 | 0 |
| 1972-73 | New York I | 36 | 2 | 6 | 8 |
| 1973-74 | New York I | 6 | 0 | 0 | 0 |
| | **Totals** | 47 | 2 | 6 | 8 |
| **MARCON, Louis Angelo** *Defenseman* | | | | | |
| b. Fort William, Ont., May 28, 1935 | | | | | |
| 1958-59 | Detroit | 21 | 0 | 1 | 1 |
| 1959-60 | Detroit | 38 | 0 | 3 | 3 |
| 1962-63 | Detroit | 1 | 0 | 0 | 0 |
| | **Totals** | 60 | 0 | 4 | 4 |
| **MARCOTTE, Donald M.** *Forward* | | | | | |
| b. Asbestos, Que., Apr. 15, 1947 | | | | | |
| 1965-66 | Boston | 1 | 0 | 0 | 0 |
| 1968-69 | Boston | 7 | 1 | 0 | 1 |
| 1969-70 | Boston | 35 | 9 | 3 | 12 |
| 1970-71 | Boston | 75 | 15 | 13 | 28 |
| 1971-72 | Boston | 47 | 6 | 4 | 10 |
| 1972-73 | Boston | 78 | 24 | 31 | 55 |
| 1973-74 | Boston | 78 | 24 | 31 | 55 |
| 1974-75 | Boston | 80 | 31 | 33 | 64 |
| 1975-76 | Boston | 58 | 16 | 20 | 36 |
| 1976-77 | Boston | 80 | 27 | 18 | 45 |
| 1977-78 | Boston | 77 | 20 | 34 | 54 |
| 1978-79 | Boston | 79 | 20 | 27 | 47 |
| 1979-80 | Boston | 32 | 4 | 11 | 15 |
| 1980-81 | Boston | 72 | 20 | 13 | 33 |
| 1981-82 | Boston | 69 | 13 | 22 | 35 |
| | **Totals** | 868 | 230 | 260 | 490 |
| **MARINI, Hector** *Forward* | | | | | |
| b. Timmins, Ont., Jan. 27, 1957 | | | | | |
| 1978-79 | New York I | 1 | 0 | 0 | 0 |
| 1980-81 | New York I | 14 | 4 | 7 | 11 |
| 1981-82 | New York I | 30 | 4 | 9 | 13 |
| 1982-83 | New Jersey | 77 | 17 | 28 | 45 |
| | **Totals** | 122 | 25 | 44 | 69 |
| **MARIO, Frank George** *Forward* | | | | | |
| b. Esterhazy, Sask., Feb. 25, 1921 | | | | | |
| 1941-42 | Boston | 9 | 1 | 1 | 2 |
| 1944-45 | Boston | 44 | 8 | 18 | 26 |
| | **Totals** | 53 | 9 | 19 | 28 |
| **MARIUCCI, John** *Defenseman* | | | | | |
| b. Eveleth, Minn., May 8, 1916 | | | | | |
| 1940-41 | Chicago | 23 | 0 | 5 | 5 |
| 1941-42 | Chicago | 47 | 5 | 8 | 13 |
| 1945-46 | Chicago | 50 | 3 | 8 | 11 |
| 1946-47 | Chicago | 52 | 2 | 9 | 11 |
| 1947-48 | Chicago | 51 | 1 | 4 | 5 |
| | **Totals** | 223 | 11 | 34 | 45 |
| **MARKELL, John Richard** *Forward* | | | | | |
| b. Cornwall, Ont., Mar. 10, 1956 | | | | | |
| 1979-80 | Winnipeg | 38 | 10 | 7 | 17 |
| 1980-81 | Winnipeg | 14 | 1 | 3 | 4 |
| | **Totals** | 52 | 11 | 10 | 21 |

| Season | Club | GP | G | A | Pts. |
|---|---|---|---|---|---|
| **MARKER, August Solberg (Gus)** *Forward* | | | | | |
| b. Wetaskewin, Alta., 1, 1907 | | | | | |
| 1932-33 | Detroit | 13 | 1 | 1 | 2 |
| 1933-34 | Detroit | 7 | 1 | 0 | 1 |
| 1934-35 | Montreal M | 44 | 11 | 4 | 15 |
| 1935-36 | Montreal M | 48 | 7 | 12 | 19 |
| 1936-37 | Montreal M | 47 | 10 | 12 | 22 |
| 1937-38 | Montreal M | 48 | 9 | 15 | 24 |
| 1938-39 | Toronto | 29 | 9 | 6 | 15 |
| 1939-40 | Toronto | 42 | 10 | 9 | 19 |
| 1940-41 | Toronto | 27 | 4 | 5 | 9 |
| 1941-42 | New York A | 17 | 2 | 5 | 7 |
| | **Totals** | 322 | 64 | 69 | 133 |

| Season | Club | GP | G | A | Pts. |
|---|---|---|---|---|---|
| **MARKHAM, Ray Joseph** *Forward* | | | | | |
| b. Windsor, Ont., Jan. 23, 1958 | | | | | |
| 1979-80 | New York R | 14 | 1 | 1 | 2 |

| Season | Club | GP | G | A | Pts. |
|---|---|---|---|---|---|
| **MARKLE, Jack** *Forward* | | | | | |
| b. Thessalon, Ont., 1909 | | | | | |
| 1935-36 | Toronto | 8 | 0 | 1 | 1 |

| Season | Club | GP | G | A | Pts. |
|---|---|---|---|---|---|
| **MARKS, Jack** *Forward* | | | | | |
| 1917-18 | MontW-Tor | 6 | 0 | 0 | 0 |
| 1919-20 | Quebec | 1 | 0 | 0 | 0 |
| | **Totals** | 7 | 0 | 0 | 0 |

| Season | Club | GP | G | A | Pts. |
|---|---|---|---|---|---|
| **MARKS, John Garrison** *Defenseman* | | | | | |
| b. Hamiota, Man., Mar. 22, 1948 | | | | | |
| 1972-73 | Chicago | 55 | 3 | 10 | 13 |
| 1973-74 | Chicago | 76 | 13 | 18 | 31 |
| 1974-75 | Chicago | 80 | 17 | 30 | 47 |
| 1975-76 | Chicago | 80 | 21 | 23 | 44 |
| 1976-77 | Chicago | 80 | 7 | 15 | 22 |
| 1977-78 | Chicago | 80 | 15 | 22 | 37 |
| 1978-79 | Chicago | 80 | 21 | 24 | 45 |
| 1979-80 | Chicago | 74 | 6 | 15 | 21 |
| 1980-81 | Chicago | 30 | 8 | 6 | 14 |
| 1981-82 | Chicago | 13 | 1 | 0 | 1 |
| | **Totals** | 648 | 112 | 163 | 275 |

| Season | Club | GP | G | A | Pts. |
|---|---|---|---|---|---|
| **MAROIS, Mario** *Defenseman* | | | | | |
| b. Ancienne Lovette, Que., Dec. 15, 1957 | | | | | |
| 1977-78 | New York R | 8 | 1 | 1 | 2 |
| 1978-79 | New York R | 71 | 5 | 26 | 31 |
| 1979-80 | New York R | 79 | 8 | 23 | 31 |
| 1980-81 | NYR-Van-Que | 69 | 5 | 21 | 26 |
| 1981-82 | Quebec | 71 | 11 | 32 | 43 |
| 1982-83 | Quebec | 36 | 2 | 12 | 14 |
| | **Totals** | 334 | 32 | 115 | 147 |

| Season | Club | GP | G | A | Pts. |
|---|---|---|---|---|---|
| **MAROTTE, Jean Gilles** *Defenseman-Forward* | | | | | |
| b. Montreal, Que., June 7, 1945 | | | | | |
| 1965-66 | Boston | 51 | 3 | 17 | 20 |
| 1966-67 | Boston | 67 | 7 | 8 | 15 |
| 1967-68 | Chicago | 73 | 0 | 21 | 21 |
| 1968-69 | Chicago | 68 | 5 | 29 | 34 |
| 1969-70 | Chi-LA | 72 | 5 | 19 | 24 |
| 1970-71 | Los Angeles | 78 | 6 | 27 | 33 |
| 1971-72 | Los Angeles | 72 | 10 | 24 | 34 |
| 1972-73 | Los Angeles | 78 | 6 | 39 | 45 |
| 1973-74 | New York R | 46 | 2 | 17 | 19 |
| 1974-75 | New York R | 77 | 4 | 32 | 36 |
| 1975-76 | New York R | 57 | 4 | 17 | 21 |
| 1976-77 | St Louis | 47 | 3 | 4 | 7 |
| 1977-78 | Cin-Ind (WHA) | 73 | 3 | 20 | 23 |
| | **NHL Totals** | 786 | 58 | 274 | 332 |
| | **WHA Totals** | 73 | 3 | 20 | 23 |

| Season | Club | GP | G | A | Pts. |
|---|---|---|---|---|---|
| **MARQUESS, Clarence Emmett (Mark)** | | | | | |
| *Forward* | | | | | |
| b. Bassano, Alta., Mar. 26, 1925 | | | | | |
| 1946-47 | Boston | 27 | 5 | 4 | 9 |

| Season | Club | GP | G | A | Pts. |
|---|---|---|---|---|---|
| **MARSH, Charles Bradley** *Defenseman* | | | | | |
| b. London, Ont., Mar. 31, 1958 | | | | | |
| 1978-79 | Atlanta | 80 | 0 | 19 | 19 |
| 1979-80 | Atlanta | 80 | 2 | 9 | 11 |
| 1980-81 | Calgary | 80 | 1 | 12 | 13 |
| 1981-82 | Calg-Phil | 83 | 2 | 23 | 25 |
| 1982-83 | Philadelphia | 68 | 2 | 11 | 13 |
| | **Totals** | 391 | 7 | 74 | 81 |

| Season | Club | GP | G | A | Pts. |
|---|---|---|---|---|---|
| **MARSH, Gary Arthur** *Forward* | | | | | |
| b. Toronto, Ont., Mar. 9, 1946 | | | | | |
| 1967-68 | Detroit | 6 | 1 | 3 | 4 |
| 1968-69 | Toronto | 1 | 0 | 0 | 0 |
| | **Totals** | 7 | 1 | 3 | 4 |

| Season | Club | GP | G | A | Pts. |
|---|---|---|---|---|---|
| **MARSH, Peter** *Forward* | | | | | |
| b. Halifax, N.S., Dec. 21, 1956 | | | | | |
| 1976-77 | Cincinnati (WHA) | 76 | 23 | 28 | 51 |
| 1977-78 | Cincinnati (WHA) | 74 | 25 | 25 | 50 |
| 1978-79 | Cincinnati (WHA) | 80 | 43 | 23 | 66 |
| 1979-80 | Winnipeg | 57 | 18 | 20 | 38 |
| 1980-81 | Winn-Chi | 53 | 10 | 13 | 23 |
| 1981-82 | Chicago | 57 | 10 | 18 | 28 |
| 1982-83 | Chicago | 68 | 6 | 14 | 20 |
| | **NHL Totals** | 235 | 44 | 65 | 109 |
| | **WHA Totals** | 230 | 91 | 76 | 167 |

| Season | Club | GP | G | A | Pts. |
|---|---|---|---|---|---|
| **MARSHALL, Albert Leroy (Bert)** *Defenseman* | | | | | |
| b. Kamloops, B.C., Nov. 22, 1943 | | | | | |
| 1965-66 | Detroit | 61 | 0 | 19 | 19 |
| 1966-67 | Detroit | 57 | 0 | 10 | 10 |
| 1967-68 | Det-Oak | 57 | 1 | 9 | 10 |
| 1968-69 | Oakland | 68 | 3 | 15 | 18 |
| 1969-70 | Oakland | 72 | 1 | 15 | 16 |
| 1970-71 | California | 32 | 2 | 6 | 8 |
| 1971-72 | California | 66 | 0 | 14 | 14 |
| 1972-73 | Cal-NYR | 63 | 2 | 6 | 8 |
| 1973-74 | New York I | 69 | 1 | 7 | 8 |
| 1974-75 | New York I | 77 | 2 | 28 | 30 |
| 1975-76 | New York I | 71 | 0 | 16 | 16 |
| 1976-77 | New York I | 72 | 4 | 21 | 25 |
| 1977-78 | New York I | 58 | 0 | 7 | 7 |
| 1978-79 | New York I | 45 | 1 | 8 | 9 |
| | **Totals** | 868 | 17 | 181 | 198 |

| Season | Club | GP | G | A | Pts. |
|---|---|---|---|---|---|
| **MARSHALL, Donald Robert** *Forward* | | | | | |
| b. Verdun, Que., Mar. 23, 1932 | | | | | |
| 1951-52 | Montreal | 1 | 0 | 0 | 0 |
| 1954-55 | Montreal | 39 | 5 | 3 | 8 |
| 1955-56 | Montreal | 66 | 4 | 1 | 5 |
| 1956-57 | Montreal | 70 | 12 | 8 | 20 |
| 1957-58 | Montreal | 68 | 22 | 19 | 41 |
| 1958-59 | Montreal | 70 | 10 | 22 | 32 |
| 1959-60 | Montreal | 70 | 16 | 22 | 38 |
| 1960-61 | Montreal | 70 | 14 | 17 | 31 |
| 1961-62 | Montreal | 66 | 18 | 28 | 46 |
| 1962-63 | Montreal | 65 | 13 | 20 | 33 |
| 1963-64 | New York R | 70 | 11 | 12 | 23 |
| 1964-65 | New York R | 69 | 20 | 15 | 35 |
| 1965-66 | New York R | 69 | 26 | 28 | 54 |
| 1966-67 | New York R | 70 | 24 | 22 | 46 |
| 1967-68 | New York R | 70 | 19 | 30 | 49 |
| 1968-69 | New York R | 74 | 20 | 19 | 39 |
| 1969-70 | New York R | 57 | 9 | 15 | 24 |
| 1970-71 | Buffalo | 62 | 20 | 29 | 49 |
| 1971-72 | Toronto | 50 | 2 | 14 | 16 |
| | **Totals** | 1288 | 265 | 324 | 589 |

| Season | Club | GP | G | A | Pts. |
|---|---|---|---|---|---|
| **MARSHALL, Paul A.** *Forward* | | | | | |
| b. Toronto, Ont., Sept. 7, 1960 | | | | | |
| 1979-80 | Pittsburgh | 46 | 9 | 12 | 21 |
| 1980-81 | Pitt-Tor | 26 | 3 | 2 | 5 |
| 1981-82 | Toronto | 10 | 2 | 2 | 4 |
| 1982-83 | Hartford | 13 | 1 | 2 | 3 |
| | **Totals** | 95 | 15 | 18 | 33 |

| Season | Club | GP | G | A | Pts. |
|---|---|---|---|---|---|
| **MARSHALL, Willmott Charles (Willie)** *Forward* | | | | | |
| b. Kirkland Lake, Ont., Dec. 1, 1931 | | | | | |
| 1952-53 | Toronto | 2 | 0 | 0 | 0 |
| 1954-55 | Toronto | 16 | 1 | 4 | 5 |
| 1955-56 | Toronto | 6 | 0 | 0 | 0 |
| 1958-59 | Toronto | 9 | 0 | 1 | 1 |
| | **Totals** | 33 | 1 | 5 | 6 |

| Season | Club | GP | G | A | Pts. |
|---|---|---|---|---|---|
| **MARSON, Michael Robert** *Forward* | | | | | |
| b. Scarborough, Ont., July 24, 1955 | | | | | |
| 1974-75 | Washington | 76 | 16 | 12 | 28 |
| 1975-76 | Washington | 57 | 4 | 7 | 11 |
| 1976-77 | Washington | 10 | 0 | 1 | 1 |
| 1977-78 | Washington | 46 | 4 | 4 | 8 |
| 1978-79 | Washington | 4 | 0 | 0 | 0 |
| 1979-80 | Los Angeles | 3 | 0 | 0 | 0 |
| | **Totals** | 196 | 24 | 24 | 48 |

| Season | Club | GP | G | A | Pts. |
|---|---|---|---|---|---|
| **MARTIN, Francis William (Frank)** | | | | | |
| *Defenseman* | | | | | |
| b. Cayuga, Ont., May 1, 1933 | | | | | |
| 1952-53 | Boston | 14 | 0 | 2 | 2 |
| 1953-54 | Boston | 68 | 3 | 17 | 20 |
| 1954-55 | Chicago | 66 | 4 | 8 | 12 |
| 1955-56 | Chicago | 61 | 3 | 11 | 14 |
| 1956-57 | Chicago | 70 | 1 | 8 | 9 |
| 1957-58 | Chicago | 3 | 0 | 0 | 0 |
| | **Totals** | 282 | 11 | 46 | 57 |

| Season | Club | GP | G | A | Pts. |
|---|---|---|---|---|---|
| **MARTIN, George Clare** *Defenseman* | | | | | |
| b. Waterloo, Ont., Feb. 25, 1922 | | | | | |
| 1941-42 | Boston | 13 | 0 | 1 | 1 |
| 1946-47 | Boston | 6 | 3 | 0 | 3 |
| 1947-48 | Boston | 59 | 5 | 13 | 18 |
| 1949-50 | Detroit | 64 | 2 | 5 | 7 |
| 1950-51 | Detroit | 50 | 1 | 6 | 7 |
| 1951-52 | Chi-NYR | 45 | 1 | 3 | 4 |
| | **Totals** | 237 | 12 | 28 | 40 |

| Season | Club | GP | G | A | Pts. |
|---|---|---|---|---|---|
| **MARTIN, Hubert Jacques (Pit)** *Forward* | | | | | |
| b. Noranda, Que., Dec. 9, 1943 | | | | | |
| 1961-62 | Detroit | 1 | 0 | 1 | 1 |
| 1963-64 | Detroit | 50 | 9 | 12 | 21 |
| 1964-65 | Detroit | 58 | 8 | 9 | 17 |
| 1965-66 | Det-Bos | 51 | 17 | 12 | 29 |
| 1966-67 | Boston | 70 | 20 | 22 | 42 |
| 1967-68 | Chicago | 63 | 16 | 19 | 35 |
| 1968-69 | Chicago | 76 | 23 | 38 | 61 |
| 1969-70 | Chicago | 73 | 30 | 33 | 63 |
| 1970-71 | Chicago | 62 | 22 | 33 | 55 |
| 1971-72 | Chicago | 78 | 24 | 51 | 75 |
| 1972-73 | Chicago | 78 | 29 | 61 | 90 |
| 1973-74 | Chicago | 78 | 30 | 47 | 77 |
| 1974-75 | Chicago | 70 | 19 | 26 | 45 |
| 1975-76 | Chicago | 80 | 32 | 39 | 71 |
| 1976-77 | Chicago | 75 | 17 | 36 | 53 |
| 1977-78 | Chi-Van | 74 | 16 | 32 | 48 |
| 1978-79 | Vancouver | 64 | 12 | 14 | 26 |
| | **Totals** | 1101 | 324 | 485 | 809 |

| Season | Club | GP | G | A | Pts. |
|---|---|---|---|---|---|
| **MARTIN, Jack** *Forward* | | | | | |
| b. St. Catharines, Ont., Nov. 29, 1940 | | | | | |
| 1960-61 | Toronto | 1 | 0 | 0 | 0 |

| Season | Club | GP | G | A | Pts. |
|---|---|---|---|---|---|
| **MARTIN, Richard Lionel** *Forward* | | | | | |
| b. Verdun, Que., July 26, 1951 | | | | | |
| 1971-72 | Buffalo | 73 | 44 | 30 | 74 |
| 1972-73 | Buffalo | 75 | 37 | 36 | 73 |
| 1973-74 | Buffalo | 78 | 52 | 34 | 86 |
| 1974-75 | Buffalo | 68 | 52 | 43 | 95 |
| 1975-76 | Buffalo | 80 | 49 | 37 | 86 |
| 1976-77 | Buffalo | 66 | 36 | 29 | 65 |
| 1977-78 | Buffalo | 65 | 28 | 35 | 63 |
| 1978-79 | Buffalo | 73 | 32 | 21 | 53 |
| 1979-80 | Buffalo | 80 | 45 | 34 | 79 |
| 1980-81 | Buf-LA | 24 | 8 | 15 | 23 |
| 1981-82 | Los Angeles | 3 | 1 | 3 | 4 |
| | **Totals** | 685 | 384 | 317 | 701 |

| Season | Club | GP | G | A | Pts. |
|---|---|---|---|---|---|
| **MARTIN, Ronald** *Forward* | | | | | |
| b. Calgary, Alta., Aug. 22, 1909 | | | | | |
| 1932-33 | New York A | 46 | 5 | 7 | 12 |
| 1933-34 | New York A | 46 | 8 | 9 | 17 |
| | **Totals** | 92 | 13 | 16 | 29 |

| Season | Club | GP | G | A | Pts. |
|---|---|---|---|---|---|
| **MARTIN, Terry George** *Forward* | | | | | |
| b. Barrie, Ont., Oct. 25, 1955 | | | | | |
| 1975-76 | Buffalo | 1 | 0 | 0 | 0 |
| 1976-77 | Buffalo | 62 | 11 | 12 | 23 |

| Season | Club | GP | G | A | Pts. |
|---|---|---|---|---|---|
| 1977-78 | Buffalo | 21 | 3 | 2 | 5 |
| 1978-79 | Buffalo | 64 | 6 | 8 | 14 |
| 1979-80 | Que-Tor | 40 | 6 | 15 | 21 |
| 1980-81 | Toronto | 69 | 23 | 14 | 37 |
| 1981-82 | Toronto | 72 | 25 | 24 | 49 |
| 1982-83 | Toronto | 76 | 14 | 13 | 27 |
| | **Totals** | 405 | 88 | 88 | 176 |

**MARTIN, Thomas Raymond**  *Forward*
b. Toronto, Ont., Oct. 16, 1947

| Season | Club | GP | G | A | Pts. |
|---|---|---|---|---|---|
| 1967-68 | Toronto | 3 | 1 | 0 | 1 |
| 1972-73 | Ottawa (WHA) | 74 | 19 | 27 | 46 |
| 1973-74 | Toronto (WHA) | 74 | 25 | 32 | 57 |
| 1974-75 | Toronto (WHA) | 64 | 14 | 17 | 31 |
| | **NHL Totals** | 3 | 1 | 0 | 1 |
| | **WHA Totals** | 212 | 58 | 76 | 134 |

**MARTINEAU, Donald Jean**  *Forward*
b. Kimberley, B.C., Apr. 25, 1952

| Season | Club | GP | G | A | Pts. |
|---|---|---|---|---|---|
| 1973-74 | Atlanta | 4 | 0 | 0 | 0 |
| 1974-75 | Minnesota | 76 | 6 | 9 | 15 |
| 1975-76 | Detroit | 9 | 0 | 1 | 1 |
| 1976-77 | Detroit | 1 | 0 | 0 | 0 |
| | **Totals** | 90 | 6 | 10 | 16 |

**MARUK, Dennis John**  *Forward*
b. Toronto, Ont., Nov. 17, 1955

| Season | Club | GP | G | A | Pts. |
|---|---|---|---|---|---|
| 1975-76 | Cleveland | 80 | 30 | 32 | 62 |
| 1976-77 | Cleveland | 80 | 28 | 50 | 78 |
| 1977-78 | Cleveland | 76 | 36 | 35 | 71 |
| 1978-79 | Minn-Wash | 76 | 31 | 59 | 90 |
| 1979-80 | Washington | 27 | 10 | 17 | 27 |
| 1980-81 | Washington | 80 | 50 | 47 | 97 |
| 1981-82 | Washington | 80 | 60 | 76 | 136 |
| 1982-83 | Washington | 80 | 31 | 50 | 81 |
| | **Totals** | 579 | 276 | 366 | 642 |

**MASNICK, Paul Andrew**  *Forward*
b. Regina, Sask., Apr. 14, 1931

| Season | Club | GP | G | A | Pts. |
|---|---|---|---|---|---|
| 1950-51 | Montreal | 43 | 4 | 1 | 5 |
| 1951-52 | Montreal | 15 | 1 | 2 | 3 |
| 1952-53 | Montreal | 53 | 5 | 7 | 12 |
| 1953-54 | Montreal | 50 | 5 | 21 | 26 |
| 1954-55 | Mont-Chi | 30 | 1 | 1 | 2 |
| 1957-58 | Toronto | 41 | 2 | 9 | 11 |
| | **Totals** | 232 | 18 | 41 | 59 |

**MASON, Charles C.**  *Forward*
b. Seaforth, Ont., Feb. 1, 1912

| Season | Club | GP | G | A | Pts. |
|---|---|---|---|---|---|
| 1934-35 | New York R | 46 | 5 | 9 | 14 |
| 1935-36 | New York R | 28 | 1 | 5 | 6 |
| 1938-39 | Chicago | 17 | 1 | 4 | 5 |
| | **Totals** | 91 | 7 | 18 | 25 |

**MASSECAR, George**  *Forward*
b. Niagara Falls, Ont.

| Season | Club | GP | G | A | Pts. |
|---|---|---|---|---|---|
| 1929-30 | New York A | 44 | 7 | 3 | 10 |
| 1930-31 | New York A | 42 | 4 | 7 | 11 |
| 1931-32 | New York A | 15 | 1 | 1 | 2 |
| | **Totals** | 101 | 12 | 11 | 23 |

**MASTERS, James Edward**  *Defenseman*
b. Toronto, Ont., Apr. 14, 1955

| Season | Club | GP | G | A | Pts. |
|---|---|---|---|---|---|
| 1975-76 | St Louis | 7 | 0 | 0 | 0 |
| 1976-77 | St Louis | 16 | 1 | 7 | 8 |
| 1978-79 | St Louis | 10 | 0 | 6 | 6 |
| | **Totals** | 33 | 1 | 13 | 14 |

**MASTERTON, William (Bat)**  *Forward*
b. Winnipeg, Man., Aug. 16, 1938

| Season | Club | GP | G | A | Pts. |
|---|---|---|---|---|---|
| 1967-68 | Minnesota | 38 | 4 | 8 | 12 |

**MATHERS, Frank Sydney**  *Defenseman*
b. Winnipeg, Man., Mar. 29, 1924

| Season | Club | GP | G | A | Pts. |
|---|---|---|---|---|---|
| 1948-49 | Toronto | 15 | 1 | 2 | 3 |
| 1949-50 | Toronto | 6 | 0 | 1 | 1 |
| 1951-52 | Toronto | 2 | 0 | 0 | 0 |
| | **Totals** | 23 | 1 | 3 | 4 |

**MATTE, Joseph**  *Defenseman*
b. 1893

| Season | Club | GP | G | A | Pts. |
|---|---|---|---|---|---|
| 1919-20 | Toronto | 16 | 8 | 2 | 10 |
| 1920-21 | Hamilton | 19 | 7 | 9 | 16 |
| 1921-22 | Hamilton | 20 | 3 | 3 | 6 |
| 1925-26 | Bos-Mont | 9 | 0 | 0 | 0 |
| | **Totals** | 64 | 18 | 14 | 32 |

**MATTE, Joseph**  *Defenseman*
b. Ottawa, Ont., Mar. 3, 1909

| Season | Club | GP | G | A | Pts. |
|---|---|---|---|---|---|
| 1942-43 | Chicago | 12 | 0 | 2 | 2 |

**MATTE, Roland J.**  *Defenseman*
b. Bourget, Ont., Mar. 15, 1909

| Season | Club | GP | G | A | Pts. |
|---|---|---|---|---|---|
| 1929-30 | Detroit | 11 | 0 | 1 | 1 |
| 1942-43 | Chicago | 12 | 0 | 2 | 2 |
| | **Totals** | 23 | 0 | 3 | 3 |

**MATTIUSSI, Richard Arthur**  *Forward*
b. Smooth Rock Falls, Ont., May 1, 1938

| Season | Club | GP | G | A | Pts. |
|---|---|---|---|---|---|
| 1967-68 | Pittsburgh | 32 | 0 | 2 | 2 |
| 1968-69 | Pitt-Oak | 36 | 1 | 11 | 12 |
| 1969-70 | Oakland | 65 | 4 | 10 | 14 |
| 1970-71 | California | 67 | 3 | 8 | 11 |
| | **Totals** | 200 | 8 | 31 | 39 |

**MATZ, John**  *Forward*

| Season | Club | GP | G | A | Pts. |
|---|---|---|---|---|---|
| 1924-25 | Montreal | 30 | 3 | 2 | 5 |

**MAXNER, Wayne Douglas**  *Forward*
b. Halifax, N.S., Sept. 27, 1942

| Season | Club | GP | G | A | Pts. |
|---|---|---|---|---|---|
| 1964-65 | Boston | 54 | 7 | 6 | 13 |
| 1965-66 | Boston | 8 | 1 | 3 | 4 |
| | **Totals** | 62 | 8 | 9 | 17 |

**MAXWELL, Brad Robert**  *Defenseman*
b. Brandon, Man., July 8, 1957

| Season | Club | GP | G | A | Pts. |
|---|---|---|---|---|---|
| 1977-78 | Minnesota | 75 | 18 | 29 | 47 |
| 1978-79 | Minnesota | 70 | 9 | 28 | 37 |
| 1979-80 | Minnesota | 58 | 7 | 30 | 37 |
| 1980-81 | Minnesota | 27 | 3 | 13 | 16 |
| 1981-82 | Minnesota | 51 | 10 | 21 | 31 |
| 1982-83 | Minnesota | 77 | 11 | 28 | 39 |
| | **Totals** | 358 | 58 | 149 | 207 |

**MAXWELL, Bryan Clifford**  *Defenseman*
b. North Bay, Ont., Sept. 7, 1955

| Season | Club | GP | G | A | Pts. |
|---|---|---|---|---|---|
| 1975-76 | Cleveland (WHA) | 73 | 3 | 14 | 17 |
| 1976-77 | Cincinnati (WHA) | 34 | 1 | 8 | 9 |
| 1977-78 | New England (WHA) | 17 | 2 | 1 | 3 |
| 1977-78 | Minnesota | 18 | 2 | 5 | 7 |
| 1978-79 | Minnesota | 25 | 1 | 6 | 7 |
| 1979-80 | St Louis | 57 | 1 | 11 | 12 |
| 1980-81 | St Louis | 40 | 3 | 10 | 13 |
| 1981-82 | Winnipeg | 45 | 1 | 9 | 10 |
| 1982-83 | Winnipeg | 54 | 7 | 13 | 20 |
| | **NHL Totals** | 239 | 15 | 54 | 69 |
| | **WHA Totals** | 124 | 6 | 23 | 29 |

**MAXWELL, Kevin**  *Forward*
b. Edmonton, Alta., Mar. 30, 1960

| Season | Club | GP | G | A | Pts. |
|---|---|---|---|---|---|
| 1980-81 | Minnesota | 6 | 0 | 3 | 3 |
| 1981-82 | Minn-Col | 46 | 6 | 9 | 15 |
| | **Totals** | 52 | 6 | 12 | 18 |

**MAXWELL, Wally**  *Forward*
b. Ottawa, Ont., Aug. 24, 1933

| Season | Club | GP | G | A | Pts. |
|---|---|---|---|---|---|
| 1952-53 | Toronto | 2 | 0 | 0 | 0 |

**MAYER, James Patrick**  *Forward*
b. Capreol, Ont., Oct. 30, 1954

| Season | Club | GP | G | A | Pts. |
|---|---|---|---|---|---|
| 1976-77 | Calgary (WHA) | 21 | 2 | 3 | 5 |
| 1977-78 | New England (WHA) | 51 | 11 | 9 | 20 |
| 1978-79 | Edmonton (WHA) | 2 | 0 | 0 | 0 |
| 1979-80 | New York R | 4 | 0 | 0 | 0 |
| | **NHL Totals** | 4 | 0 | 0 | 0 |
| | **WHA Totals** | 74 | 13 | 12 | 25 |

**MAYER, Sheppard E.**  *Forward*
b. Sturgeon Falls, Ont.

| Season | Club | GP | G | A | Pts. |
|---|---|---|---|---|---|
| 1942-43 | Toronto | 2 | 1 | 2 | 3 |

**MAZUR, Edward Joseph (Spider)**  *Forward*
b. Winnipeg, Man., July 25, 1929

| Season | Club | GP | G | A | Pts. |
|---|---|---|---|---|---|
| 1953-54 | Montreal | 67 | 7 | 14 | 21 |
| 1954-55 | Montreal | 25 | 1 | 5 | 6 |
| 1956-57 | Chicago | 15 | 0 | 1 | 1 |
| | **Totals** | 107 | 8 | 20 | 28 |

**McADAM, Gary**  *Forward*
b. Smith Falls, Ont., Dec. 31, 1955

| Season | Club | GP | G | A | Pts. |
|---|---|---|---|---|---|
| 1975-76 | Buffalo | 31 | 1 | 2 | 3 |
| 1976-77 | Buffalo | 73 | 13 | 16 | 29 |
| 1977-78 | Buffalo | 79 | 19 | 22 | 41 |
| 1978-79 | Buf-Pitt | 68 | 11 | 14 | 25 |
| 1979-80 | Pittsburgh | 78 | 19 | 22 | 41 |
| 1980-81 | Pitt-Det | 74 | 8 | 23 | 31 |
| 1981-82 | Calgary | 46 | 12 | 15 | 27 |
| 1982-83 | Buffalo | 4 | 1 | 0 | 1 |
| | **Totals** | 453 | 84 | 114 | 198 |

**McADAM, Samuel**  *Forward*
b. Sterling, Scotland, May 31, 1908

| Season | Club | GP | G | A | Pts. |
|---|---|---|---|---|---|
| 1930-31 | New York R | 4 | 0 | 0 | 0 |

**McANDREW, Hazen**  *Defenseman*
b. Mayo, Que., Aug. 7, 1917

| Season | Club | GP | G | A | Pts. |
|---|---|---|---|---|---|
| 1941-42 | New York A | 7 | 0 | 1 | 1 |

**McANEELEY, Edward (Ted)**  *Defenseman*
b. Cranbrook, B.C., Nov. 7, 1950

| Season | Club | GP | G | A | Pts. |
|---|---|---|---|---|---|
| 1972-73 | California | 77 | 4 | 13 | 17 |
| 1973-74 | California | 72 | 4 | 20 | 24 |
| 1974-75 | California | 9 | 0 | 2 | 2 |
| | **Totals** | 158 | 8 | 35 | 43 |

**McATEE, Jerome (Jud)**  *Forward*
b. Stratford, Ont., May 2, 1920

| Season | Club | GP | G | A | Pts. |
|---|---|---|---|---|---|
| 1943-44 | Detroit | 1 | 0 | 2 | 2 |
| 1944-45 | Detroit | 44 | 15 | 11 | 26 |
| | **Totals** | 45 | 15 | 13 | 28 |

**McATEE, Norman Joseph**  *Forward*
b. Stratford, Ont., June 28, 1921

| Season | Club | GP | G | A | Pts. |
|---|---|---|---|---|---|
| 1946-47 | Boston | 13 | 0 | 1 | 1 |

**McBURNEY, James**  *Forward*
b. Sault Ste. Marie, Ont., Jan. 3, 1933

| Season | Club | GP | G | A | Pts. |
|---|---|---|---|---|---|
| 1952-53 | Chicago | 1 | 0 | 1 | 1 |

**McCABE, Stanley**  *Defenseman*
b. Ottawa, Ont.

| Season | Club | GP | G | A | Pts. |
|---|---|---|---|---|---|
| 1929-30 | Detroit | 26 | 7 | 3 | 10 |
| 1930-31 | Detroit | 38 | 2 | 1 | 3 |
| 1932-33 | Montreal M | 1 | 0 | 0 | 0 |
| 1933-34 | Montreal M | 7 | 0 | 0 | 0 |
| | **Totals** | 72 | 9 | 4 | 13 |

**McCAFFREY, Albert**  *Defenseman*
b. Listowel, Ont.

| Season | Club | GP | G | A | Pts. |
|---|---|---|---|---|---|
| 1924-25 | Toronto | 30 | 9 | 6 | 15 |
| 1925-26 | Toronto | 36 | 14 | 7 | 21 |
| 1926-27 | Toronto | 43 | 5 | 5 | 10 |
| 1927-28 | Tor-PittPi | 44 | 7 | 4 | 11 |
| 1928-29 | Pittsburgh Pi | 42 | 1 | 0 | 1 |
| 1929-30 | PittPi-Mont | 43 | 4 | 7 | 11 |
| 1930-31 | Montreal | 22 | 2 | 1 | 3 |
| | **Totals** | 260 | 42 | 30 | 72 |

**McCAHILL, John Walter**  *Defenseman*
b. Sarnia, Ont., Dec. 2, 1955

| Season | Club | GP | G | A | Pts. |
|---|---|---|---|---|---|
| 1977-78 | Colorado | 1 | 0 | 0 | 0 |

| Season | Club | GP | G | A | Pts. |
|---|---|---|---|---|---|

**McCAIG, Douglas** *Defenseman*
b. Guelph, Ont., Feb. 24, 1919

| Season | Club | GP | G | A | Pts. |
|---|---|---|---|---|---|
| 1941-42 | Detroit | 9 | 0 | 1 | 1 |
| 1945-46 | Detroit | 6 | 0 | 1 | 1 |
| 1946-47 | Detroit | 47 | 2 | 4 | 6 |
| 1947-48 | Detroit | 29 | 3 | 3 | 6 |
| 1948-49 | Det-Chi | 56 | 1 | 3 | 4 |
| 1949-50 | Chicago | 64 | 0 | 4 | 4 |
| 1950-51 | Chicago | 53 | 2 | 5 | 7 |
| | **Totals** | 264 | 8 | 21 | 29 |

**McCALLUM, Duncan Selby** *Defenseman*
b. Flin Flon, Man., Mar. 29, 1940

| Season | Club | GP | G | A | Pts. |
|---|---|---|---|---|---|
| 1965-66 | New York R | 2 | 0 | 0 | 0 |
| 1967-68 | Pittsburgh | 32 | 0 | 2 | 2 |
| 1968-69 | Pittsburgh | 62 | 5 | 13 | 18 |
| 1969-70 | Pittsburgh | 14 | 0 | 0 | 0 |
| 1970-71 | Pittsburgh | 77 | 9 | 20 | 29 |
| 1972-73 | Houston (WHA) | 69 | 9 | 20 | 29 |
| | **NHL Totals** | 187 | 14 | 35 | 49 |
| | **WHA Totals** | 69 | 9 | 20 | 29 |

**McCALMON, Edward**

| Season | Club | GP | G | A | Pts. |
|---|---|---|---|---|---|
| 1927-28 | Chicago | 21 | 2 | 0 | 2 |
| 1930-31 | Philadelphia Q | 17 | 3 | 0 | 3 |
| | **Totals** | 38 | 5 | 0 | 5 |

**McCANN, Richard Leo (Rick)** *Forward*
b. Hamilton, Ont., May 27, 1944

| Season | Club | GP | G | A | Pts. |
|---|---|---|---|---|---|
| 1967-68 | Detroit | 3 | 0 | 0 | 0 |
| 1968-69 | Detroit | 3 | 0 | 0 | 0 |
| 1969-70 | Detroit | 18 | 0 | 1 | 1 |
| 1970-71 | Detroit | 5 | 0 | 0 | 0 |
| 1971-72 | Detroit | 1 | 0 | 0 | 0 |
| 1974-75 | Detroit | 13 | 1 | 3 | 4 |
| | **Totals** | 43 | 1 | 4 | 5 |

**McCARTHY, Daniel** *Forward*
b. St. Mary's, Ont., Apr. 7, 1958

| Season | Club | GP | G | A | Pts. |
|---|---|---|---|---|---|
| 1980-81 | New York R | 5 | 4 | 0 | 4 |

**McCARTHY, Kevin** *Defenseman*
b. Winnipeg, Man., July 14, 1957

| Season | Club | GP | G | A | Pts. |
|---|---|---|---|---|---|
| 1977-78 | Philadelphia | 62 | 2 | 15 | 17 |
| 1978-79 | Phil-Van | 23 | 1 | 2 | 3 |
| 1979-80 | Vancouver | 79 | 15 | 30 | 45 |
| 1980-81 | Vancouver | 80 | 16 | 37 | 53 |
| 1981-82 | Vancouver | 71 | 6 | 39 | 45 |
| 1982-83 | Vancouver | 74 | 12 | 28 | 40 |
| | **Totals** | 389 | 52 | 151 | 203 |

**McCARTHY, Thomas** *Forward*

| Season | Club | GP | G | A | Pts. |
|---|---|---|---|---|---|
| 1919-20 | Quebec | 12 | 11 | 2 | 13 |
| 1920-21 | Hamilton | 22 | 8 | 1 | 9 |
| | **Totals** | 34 | 19 | 3 | 22 |

**McCARTHY, Tom Joseph** *Forward*
b. Toronto, Ont., July 31, 1960

| Season | Club | GP | G | A | Pts. |
|---|---|---|---|---|---|
| 1979-80 | Minnesota | 68 | 16 | 20 | 36 |
| 1980-81 | Minnesota | 62 | 23 | 25 | 48 |
| 1981-82 | Minnesota | 40 | 12 | 30 | 42 |
| 1982-83 | Minnesota | 80 | 28 | 48 | 76 |
| | **Totals** | 250 | 79 | 123 | 202 |

**McCARTHY, Thomas Patrick Francis**
*Forward*
b. Toronto, Ont., Sept. 15, 1934

| Season | Club | GP | G | A | Pts. |
|---|---|---|---|---|---|
| 1956-57 | Detroit | 3 | 0 | 0 | 0 |
| 1957-58 | Detroit | 18 | 2 | 1 | 3 |
| 1958-59 | Detroit | 15 | 2 | 3 | 5 |
| 1960-61 | Boston | 24 | 4 | 5 | 9 |
| | **Totals** | 60 | 8 | 9 | 17 |

**McCARTNEY, R.**

| Season | Club | GP | G | A | Pts. |
|---|---|---|---|---|---|
| 1932-33 | Montreal | 2 | 0 | 0 | 0 |

**McCASKILL, Edward J. (Ted)** *Forward*
b. Kapuskasing, Ont., Oct. 29, 1936

| Season | Club | GP | G | A | Pts. |
|---|---|---|---|---|---|
| 1967-68 | Minnesota | 4 | 0 | 2 | 2 |
| 1972-73 | Los Angeles (WHA) | 73 | 11 | 11 | 22 |
| | **NHL Totals** | 4 | 0 | 2 | 2 |
| | **WHA Totals** | 73 | 11 | 11 | 22 |

**McCLANAHAN, Rob** *Forward*
b. St. Paul, Minn., Jan. 9, 1958

| Season | Club | GP | G | A | Pts. |
|---|---|---|---|---|---|
| 1979-80 | Buffalo | 13 | 2 | 5 | 7 |
| 1980-81 | Buffalo | 53 | 3 | 12 | 15 |
| 1981-82 | Hart-NYR | 39 | 5 | 12 | 17 |
| 1982-83 | New York R | 78 | 22 | 26 | 48 |
| | **Totals** | 183 | 32 | 55 | 87 |

**McCLELLAND, Kevin** *Forward*
b. Oshawa, Ont., July 4, 1962

| Season | Club | GP | G | A | Pts. |
|---|---|---|---|---|---|
| 1981-82 | Pittsburgh | 10 | 1 | 4 | 5 |
| 1982-83 | Pittsburgh | 38 | 5 | 4 | 9 |
| | **Totals** | 48 | 6 | 8 | 14 |

**McCORD, Dennis Frederick** *Defenseman*
b. Chatham, Ont., July 28, 1951

| Season | Club | GP | G | A | Pts. |
|---|---|---|---|---|---|
| 1973-74 | Vancouver | 3 | 0 | 0 | 0 |

**McCORD, Robert Lomer** *Defenseman*
b. Timmins, Ont., Mar. 20, 1934

| Season | Club | GP | G | A | Pts. |
|---|---|---|---|---|---|
| 1963-64 | Boston | 65 | 1 | 9 | 10 |
| 1964-65 | Boston | 43 | 0 | 6 | 6 |
| 1965-66 | Detroit | 9 | 0 | 2 | 2 |
| 1966-67 | Detroit | 14 | 1 | 2 | 3 |
| 1967-68 | Det-Minn | 73 | 3 | 9 | 12 |
| 1968-69 | Minnesota | 69 | 4 | 17 | 21 |
| 1972-73 | St Louis | 43 | 1 | 13 | 14 |
| | **Totals** | 316 | 10 | 58 | 68 |

**McCORMACK, John Ronald (Goose)**
*Forward*
b. Edmonton, Alta., Aug. 2, 1925

| Season | Club | GP | G | A | Pts. |
|---|---|---|---|---|---|
| 1947-48 | Toronto | 3 | 0 | 1 | 1 |
| 1948-49 | Toronto | 1 | 0 | 0 | 0 |
| 1949-50 | Toronto | 34 | 6 | 5 | 11 |
| 1950-51 | Toronto | 46 | 6 | 7 | 13 |
| 1951-52 | Montreal | 54 | 2 | 10 | 12 |
| 1952-53 | Montreal | 59 | 1 | 9 | 10 |
| 1953-54 | Montreal | 51 | 5 | 10 | 15 |
| 1954-55 | Chicago | 63 | 5 | 7 | 12 |
| | **Totals** | 311 | 25 | 49 | 74 |

**McCOURT, Dale Allen** *Forward*
b. Falconbridge, Ont., Jan. 26, 1957

| Season | Club | GP | G | A | Pts. |
|---|---|---|---|---|---|
| 1977-78 | Detroit | 76 | 33 | 39 | 72 |
| 1978-79 | Detroit | 79 | 28 | 43 | 71 |
| 1979-80 | Detroit | 80 | 31 | 50 | 81 |
| 1980-81 | Detroit | 80 | 30 | 56 | 86 |
| 1981-82 | Det-Buf | 78 | 33 | 36 | 69 |
| 1982-83 | Buffalo | 62 | 20 | 32 | 52 |
| | **Totals** | 455 | 175 | 256 | 431 |

**McCREARY, Vernon Keith** *Forward*
b. Sundridge, Ont., June 19, 1940

| Season | Club | GP | G | A | Pts. |
|---|---|---|---|---|---|
| 1964-65 | Montreal | 9 | 0 | 3 | 3 |
| 1967-68 | Pittsburgh | 70 | 14 | 12 | 26 |
| 1968-69 | Pittsburgh | 70 | 25 | 23 | 48 |
| 1969-70 | Pittsburgh | 60 | 18 | 8 | 26 |
| 1970-71 | Pittsburgh | 59 | 21 | 12 | 33 |
| 1971-72 | Pittsburgh | 33 | 4 | 4 | 8 |
| 1972-73 | Atlanta | 77 | 20 | 21 | 41 |
| 1973-74 | Atlanta | 76 | 18 | 19 | 37 |
| 1974-75 | Atlanta | 78 | 11 | 10 | 21 |
| | **Totals** | 532 | 131 | 112 | 243 |

**McCREARY, William** *Forward*
b. Springfield, Mass., Apr. 15, 1960

| Season | Club | GP | G | A | Pts. |
|---|---|---|---|---|---|
| 1980-81 | Toronto | 12 | 1 | 0 | 1 |

**McCREARY, William Edward** *Forward*
b. Sundridge, Ont., Dec. 2, 1934

| Season | Club | GP | G | A | Pts. |
|---|---|---|---|---|---|
| 1953-54 | New York R | 2 | 0 | 0 | 0 |
| 1954-55 | New York R | 8 | 0 | 2 | 2 |
| 1957-58 | Detroit | 3 | 1 | 0 | 1 |
| 1962-63 | Montreal | 14 | 2 | 3 | 5 |
| 1967-68 | St Louis | 70 | 13 | 13 | 26 |
| 1968-69 | St Louis | 71 | 13 | 17 | 30 |
| 1969-70 | St Louis | 73 | 15 | 17 | 32 |
| 1970-71 | St Louis | 68 | 9 | 10 | 19 |
| | **Totals** | 309 | 53 | 62 | 115 |

**McCREAVY, Patrick Joseph** *Forward*
b. Owen Sound, Ont., Jan. 16, 1918

| Season | Club | GP | G | A | Pts. |
|---|---|---|---|---|---|
| 1938-39 | Boston | 6 | 0 | 0 | 0 |
| 1939-40 | Boston | 2 | 0 | 0 | 0 |
| 1940-41 | Boston | 7 | 0 | 1 | 1 |
| 1941-42 | Bos-Det | 40 | 5 | 9 | 14 |
| | **Totals** | 55 | 5 | 10 | 15 |

**McCREEDY, John** *Forward*
b. Winnipeg, Man., May 23, 1917

| Season | Club | GP | G | A | Pts. |
|---|---|---|---|---|---|
| 1941-42 | Toronto | 47 | 15 | 8 | 23 |
| 1944-45 | Toronto | 17 | 2 | 4 | 6 |
| | **Totals** | 64 | 17 | 12 | 29 |

**McCRIMMON, Byron Brad** *Defenseman*
b. Dodsland, Sask., Mar. 29, 1959

| Season | Club | GP | G | A | Pts. |
|---|---|---|---|---|---|
| 1979-80 | Boston | 72 | 5 | 11 | 16 |
| 1980-81 | Boston | 78 | 11 | 18 | 29 |
| 1981-82 | Boston | 78 | 1 | 8 | 9 |
| 1982-83 | Philadelphia | 79 | 4 | 21 | 25 |
| | **Totals** | 307 | 21 | 58 | 79 |

**McCRIMMON, Jim** *Defenseman*
b. Ponoka, Alta., May 29, 1953

| Season | Club | GP | G | A | Pts. |
|---|---|---|---|---|---|
| 1973-74 | Edmonton (WHA) | 75 | 2 | 3 | 5 |
| 1974-75 | Edmonton (WHA) | 34 | 1 | 5 | 6 |
| 1974-75 | St Louis | 2 | 0 | 0 | 0 |
| | **NHL Totals** | 2 | 0 | 0 | 0 |
| | **WHA Totals** | 109 | 3 | 8 | 11 |

**McCURRY, Francis J. (Duke)** *Forward*

| Season | Club | GP | G | A | Pts. |
|---|---|---|---|---|---|
| 1925-26 | Pittsburgh Pi | 36 | 13 | 4 | 17 |
| 1926-27 | Pittsburgh Pi | 33 | 3 | 3 | 6 |
| 1927-28 | Pittsburgh Pi | 44 | 5 | 3 | 8 |
| 1928-29 | Pittsburgh Pi | 35 | 0 | 1 | 1 |
| | **Totals** | 148 | 21 | 11 | 32 |

**McCUSKER, Red**

| Season | Club | GP | G | A | Pts. |
|---|---|---|---|---|---|
| 1926-27 | Chicago | 1 | 0 | 0 | 0 |

**McCUTCHEON, Brian** *Forward*
b. Toronto, Ont., Aug. 3, 1949

| Season | Club | GP | G | A | Pts. |
|---|---|---|---|---|---|
| 1974-75 | Detroit | 17 | 3 | 1 | 4 |
| 1975-76 | Detroit | 8 | 0 | 0 | 0 |
| 1976-77 | Detroit | 12 | 0 | 0 | 0 |
| | **Totals** | 37 | 3 | 1 | 4 |

**McCUTCHEON, Darwin** *Defenseman*
b. Listowel, Ont., Apr. 19, 1962

| Season | Club | GP | G | A | Pts. |
|---|---|---|---|---|---|
| 1981-82 | Toronto | 1 | 0 | 0 | 0 |

**McDILL, Jeffrey Donald** *Forward*
b. Thunder Bay, Ont., Mar. 16, 1956

| Season | Club | GP | G | A | Pts. |
|---|---|---|---|---|---|
| 1976-77 | Chicago | 1 | 0 | 0 | 0 |

**McDONAGH, William James** *Forward*
b. Rouyn, Que., Apr. 30, 1928

| Season | Club | GP | G | A | Pts. |
|---|---|---|---|---|---|
| 1949-50 | New York R | 4 | 0 | 0 | 0 |

**McDONALD, Alvin Brian (Ab)** *Forward*
b. Winnipeg, Man., Feb. 18, 1936

| Season | Club | GP | G | A | Pts. |
|---|---|---|---|---|---|
| 1958-59 | Montreal | 69 | 13 | 23 | 36 |
| 1959-60 | Montreal | 68 | 9 | 13 | 22 |
| 1960-61 | Mont-Chi | 61 | 17 | 16 | 33 |
| 1961-62 | Chicago | 65 | 22 | 18 | 40 |
| 1962-63 | Chicago | 69 | 20 | 41 | 61 |

| Season | Club | GP | G | A | Pts. |
|---|---|---|---|---|---|
| 1963-64 | Chicago | 70 | 14 | 32 | 46 |
| 1964-65 | Boston | 60 | 9 | 9 | 18 |
| 1965-66 | Detroit | 43 | 6 | 16 | 22 |
| 1966-67 | Detroit | 12 | 2 | 0 | 2 |
| 1967-68 | Pittsburgh | 74 | 22 | 21 | 43 |
| 1968-69 | St Louis | 68 | 21 | 21 | 42 |
| 1969-70 | St Louis | 64 | 25 | 30 | 55 |
| 1970-71 | St Louis | 20 | 0 | 5 | 5 |
| 1971-72 | Detroit | 19 | 2 | 3 | 5 |
| 1972-73 | Winnipeg (WHA) | 77 | 17 | 24 | 41 |
| | **NHL Totals** | 762 | 182 | 248 | 430 |
| | **WHA Totals** | 77 | 17 | 24 | 41 |

**McDONALD, Brian Harold** *Forward*
b. Toronto, Ont., Mar. 23, 1945

| Season | Club | GP | G | A | Pts. |
|---|---|---|---|---|---|
| 1970-71 | Buffalo | 12 | 0 | 0 | 0 |
| 1972-73 | Houston (WHA) | 71 | 20 | 20 | 40 |
| 1973-74 | Los Angeles (WHA) | 56 | 22 | 30 | 52 |
| 1974-75 | Mich-Ind (WHA) | 65 | 17 | 20 | 37 |
| 1975-76 | Indianapolis (WHA) | 62 | 15 | 18 | 33 |
| 1976-77 | Indianapolis (WHA) | 50 | 15 | 13 | 28 |
| | **NHL Totals** | 12 | 0 | 0 | 0 |
| | **WHA Totals** | 304 | 89 | 101 | 190 |

**McDONALD, Byron Russell** *Forward*
b. Assiniboia, Sask., Nov. 21, 1917

| Season | Club | GP | G | A | Pts. |
|---|---|---|---|---|---|
| 1939-40 | Detroit | 37 | 1 | 6 | 7 |
| 1944-45 | Det-Chi | 29 | 7 | 14 | 21 |
| | **Totals** | 66 | 8 | 20 | 28 |

**McDONALD, David B.** *Forward*
b. Winnipeg, Man., Mar. 6, 1960

| Season | Club | GP | G | A | Pts. |
|---|---|---|---|---|---|
| 1981-82 | Hartford | 3 | 0 | 0 | 0 |

**McDONALD, Jack** *Forward*

| Season | Club | GP | G | A | Pts. |
|---|---|---|---|---|---|
| 1917-18 | MontW-Mont | 12 | 12 | 0 | 12 |
| 1918-19 | Montreal | 18 | 8 | 4 | 12 |
| 1919-20 | Quebec | 24 | 7 | 6 | 13 |
| 1920-21 | Mont-Tor | 17 | 0 | 1 | 1 |
| 1921-22 | Montreal | 2 | 0 | 0 | 0 |
| | **Totals** | 73 | 27 | 11 | 38 |

**McDONALD, John A. (Jack)** *Forward*
b. Swan River, Man., Nov. 21, 1921

| Season | Club | GP | G | A | Pts. |
|---|---|---|---|---|---|
| 1943-44 | New York R | 43 | 10 | 9 | 19 |

**McDONALD, Lanny King** *Forward*
b. Hanna, Alta., Feb. 16, 1953

| Season | Club | GP | G | A | Pts. |
|---|---|---|---|---|---|
| 1973-74 | Toronto | 70 | 14 | 16 | 30 |
| 1974-75 | Toronto | 64 | 17 | 27 | 44 |
| 1975-76 | Toronto | 75 | 37 | 56 | 93 |
| 1976-77 | Toronto | 80 | 46 | 44 | 90 |
| 1977-78 | Toronto | 74 | 47 | 40 | 87 |
| 1978-79 | Toronto | 79 | 43 | 42 | 85 |
| 1979-80 | Tor-Col | 81 | 40 | 35 | 75 |
| 1980-81 | Colorado | 80 | 35 | 46 | 81 |
| 1981-82 | Col-Calg | 71 | 40 | 42 | 82 |
| 1982-83 | Calgary | 80 | 66 | 32 | 98 |
| | **Totals** | 754 | 385 | 380 | 765 |

**McDONALD, Robert** *Forward*
b. Toronto, Ont., Jan. 4, 1923

| Season | Club | GP | G | A | Pts. |
|---|---|---|---|---|---|
| 1943-44 | New York R | 1 | 0 | 0 | 0 |

**McDONALD, Terry Grant** *Defenseman*
b. Coquitlam, B.C., June 17, 1955

| Season | Club | GP | G | A | Pts. |
|---|---|---|---|---|---|
| 1975-76 | Kansas City | 8 | 0 | 1 | 1 |

**McDONALD, Wilfred Kennedy (Bucko)**
*Defenseman*
b. Fergus, Ont., Oct. 31, 1911

| Season | Club | GP | G | A | Pts. |
|---|---|---|---|---|---|
| 1934-35 | Detroit | 15 | 1 | 2 | 3 |
| 1935-36 | Detroit | 47 | 4 | 6 | 10 |
| 1936-37 | Detroit | 47 | 3 | 5 | 8 |
| 1937-38 | Detroit | 47 | 3 | 7 | 10 |
| 1938-39 | Det-Tor | 47 | 3 | 3 | 6 |
| 1939-40 | Toronto | 34 | 2 | 5 | 7 |
| 1940-41 | Toronto | 31 | 6 | 11 | 17 |
| 1941-42 | Toronto | 48 | 2 | 19 | 21 |
| 1942-43 | Toronto | 40 | 2 | 11 | 13 |
| 1943-44 | Tor-NYR | 50 | 7 | 10 | 17 |
| 1944-45 | New York R | 40 | 2 | 9 | 11 |
| | **Totals** | 446 | 35 | 88 | 123 |

**McDONNELL, Joe Patrick** *Defenseman*
b. Kitchener, Ont., May 11, 1961

| Season | Club | GP | G | A | Pts. |
|---|---|---|---|---|---|
| 1981-82 | Vancouver | 7 | 0 | 1 | 1 |

**McDONNELL, Moylan** *Defenseman*

| Season | Club | GP | G | A | Pts. |
|---|---|---|---|---|---|
| 1920-21 | Hamilton | 20 | 1 | 1 | 2 |

**McDONOUGH, James Allison (Al)** *Forward*
b. Hamilton, Ont., June 6, 1950

| Season | Club | GP | G | A | Pts. |
|---|---|---|---|---|---|
| 1970-71 | Los Angeles | 6 | 2 | 1 | 3 |
| 1971-72 | LA-Pitt | 68 | 10 | 13 | 23 |
| 1972-73 | Pittsburgh | 78 | 35 | 41 | 76 |
| 1973-74 | Pitt-Atl | 72 | 24 | 31 | 55 |
| 1974-75 | Cleveland (WHA) | 78 | 34 | 30 | 64 |
| 1975-76 | Cleveland (WHA) | 80 | 23 | 22 | 45 |
| 1976-77 | Minnesota (WHA) | 42 | 9 | 21 | 30 |
| 1977-78 | Detroit | 13 | 2 | 2 | 4 |
| | **NHL Totals** | 237 | 73 | 88 | 161 |
| | **WHA Totals** | 200 | 66 | 73 | 139 |

**McDOUGAL, Michael George** *Forward*
b. Port Huron, Mich., Apr. 30, 1958

| Season | Club | GP | G | A | Pts. |
|---|---|---|---|---|---|
| 1978-79 | New York R | 1 | 0 | 0 | 0 |
| 1980-81 | New York R | 2 | 0 | 0 | 0 |
| 1981-82 | Hartford | 3 | 0 | 0 | 0 |
| 1982-83 | Hartford | 55 | 8 | 10 | 18 |
| | **Totals** | 61 | 8 | 10 | 18 |

**McELMURY, James D. (Jim)** *Defenseman*
b. St. Paul, Minn., Oct. 3, 1949

| Season | Club | GP | G | A | Pts. |
|---|---|---|---|---|---|
| 1972-73 | Minnesota | 7 | 0 | 1 | 1 |
| 1974-75 | Kansas City | 78 | 5 | 17 | 22 |
| 1975-76 | Kansas City | 38 | 2 | 6 | 8 |
| 1976-77 | Colorado | 55 | 7 | 23 | 30 |
| 1977-78 | Colorado | 2 | 0 | 0 | 0 |
| | **Totals** | 180 | 14 | 47 | 61 |

**McEWEN, Michael Todd** *Defenseman*
b. Hornepayne, Ont., Aug. 10, 1956

| Season | Club | GP | G | A | Pts. |
|---|---|---|---|---|---|
| 1976-77 | New York R | 80 | 14 | 19 | 33 |
| 1977-78 | New York R | 57 | 5 | 13 | 18 |
| 1978-79 | New York R | 80 | 20 | 38 | 58 |
| 1979-80 | NYR-Col | 76 | 12 | 47 | 59 |
| 1980-81 | Col-NYI | 78 | 11 | 38 | 49 |
| 1981-82 | New York I | 73 | 10 | 39 | 49 |
| 1982-83 | New York I | 42 | 2 | 11 | 13 |
| | **Totals** | 486 | 74 | 205 | 279 |

**McFADDEN, James Alexander** *Forward*
b. Belfast, Ireland, Apr. 15, 1920

| Season | Club | GP | G | A | Pts. |
|---|---|---|---|---|---|
| 1947-48 | Detroit | 60 | 24 | 24 | 48 |
| 1948-49 | Detroit | 55 | 12 | 20 | 32 |
| 1949-50 | Detroit | 68 | 14 | 16 | 30 |
| 1950-51 | Detroit | 70 | 14 | 18 | 32 |
| 1951-52 | Chicago | 70 | 10 | 24 | 34 |
| 1952-53 | Chicago | 70 | 23 | 21 | 44 |
| 1953-54 | Chicago | 19 | 3 | 3 | 6 |
| | **Totals** | 412 | 100 | 126 | 226 |

**McGEOUGH, James** *Forward*
b. Regina, Sask., Apr. 13, 1963

| Season | Club | GP | G | A | Pts. |
|---|---|---|---|---|---|
| 1981-82 | Washington | 4 | 0 | 0 | 0 |

**McGIBBON, Irving** *Forward*

| Season | Club | GP | G | A | Pts. |
|---|---|---|---|---|---|
| 1942-43 | Montreal | 1 | 0 | 0 | 0 |

**McGILL, Jack** *Forward*
b. Ottawa, Ont., Nov. 3, 1910

| Season | Club | GP | G | A | Pts. |
|---|---|---|---|---|---|
| 1934-35 | Montreal | 44 | 9 | 1 | 10 |
| 1935-36 | Montreal | 46 | 13 | 7 | 20 |
| 1936-37 | Montreal | 44 | 5 | 2 | 7 |
| | **Totals** | 134 | 27 | 10 | 37 |

**McGILL, John George (Big Jack)** *Forward*
b. Edmonton, Alta., Sept. 19, 1921

| Season | Club | GP | G | A | Pts. |
|---|---|---|---|---|---|
| 1941-42 | Boston | 13 | 8 | 11 | 19 |
| 1944-45 | Boston | 14 | 4 | 2 | 6 |
| 1945-46 | Boston | 46 | 6 | 14 | 20 |
| 1946-47 | Boston | 24 | 5 | 9 | 14 |
| | **Totals** | 97 | 23 | 36 | 59 |

**McGILL, Robert** *Defenseman*
b. Edmonton, Alta., Apr. 27, 1962

| Season | Club | GP | G | A | Pts. |
|---|---|---|---|---|---|
| 1981-82 | Toronto | 68 | 1 | 10 | 11 |
| 1982-83 | Toronto | 30 | 0 | 0 | 0 |
| | **Totals** | 98 | 1 | 10 | 11 |

**McGREGOR, Donald Alexander (Sandy)**
*Forward*
b. Toronto, Ont., Mar. 30, 1939

| Season | Club | GP | G | A | Pts. |
|---|---|---|---|---|---|
| 1963-64 | New York R | 2 | 0 | 0 | 0 |

**McGUIRE, Frank (Mickey)** *Forward*

| Season | Club | GP | G | A | Pts. |
|---|---|---|---|---|---|
| 1926-27 | Pittsburgh Pi | 29 | 3 | 0 | 3 |
| 1927-28 | Pittsburgh Pi | 4 | 0 | 0 | 0 |
| | **Totals** | 33 | 3 | 0 | 3 |

**McILHARGEY, John Cecil (Jack)**
*Defenseman*
b. Edmonton, Alta., Mar. 7, 1952

| Season | Club | GP | G | A | Pts. |
|---|---|---|---|---|---|
| 1974-75 | Philadelphia | 2 | 0 | 0 | 0 |
| 1975-76 | Philadelphia | 57 | 1 | 2 | 3 |
| 1976-77 | Phil-Van | 61 | 3 | 8 | 11 |
| 1977-78 | Vancouver | 69 | 3 | 5 | 8 |
| 1978-79 | Vancouver | 53 | 2 | 4 | 6 |
| 1979-80 | Van-Phil | 50 | 0 | 6 | 6 |
| 1980-81 | Phil-Hart | 51 | 1 | 6 | 7 |
| 1981-82 | Hartford | 50 | 1 | 5 | 6 |
| | **Totals** | 393 | 11 | 36 | 47 |

**McINENLY, Bert** *Defenseman-Forward*
b. Ottawa, Ont., May 6, 1906

| Season | Club | GP | G | A | Pts. |
|---|---|---|---|---|---|
| 1930-31 | Detroit | 44 | 3 | 5 | 8 |
| 1931-32 | Det-NYA | 46 | 12 | 7 | 19 |
| 1932-33 | Ottawa | 31 | 2 | 2 | 4 |
| 1933-34 | Boston | 8 | 0 | 0 | 0 |
| 1934-35 | Boston | 33 | 2 | 1 | 3 |
| 1935-36 | Boston | 2 | 0 | 0 | 0 |
| | **Totals** | 164 | 19 | 15 | 34 |

**McINTOSH, Bruce** *Defenseman*
b. St. Paul, Minn., Mar. 17, 1949

| Season | Club | GP | G | A | Pts. |
|---|---|---|---|---|---|
| 1972-73 | Minnesota | 2 | 0 | 0 | 0 |

**McINTOSH, Paul** *Defenseman*
b. Listowel, Ont., Mar. 13, 1954

| Season | Club | GP | G | A | Pts. |
|---|---|---|---|---|---|
| 1974-75 | Buffalo | 6 | 0 | 1 | 1 |
| 1975-76 | Buffalo | 42 | 0 | 1 | 1 |
| | **Totals** | 48 | 0 | 2 | 2 |

**McINTYRE, John Archibald** *Forward*
b. Brussels, Ont., Sept. 8, 1930

| Season | Club | GP | G | A | Pts. |
|---|---|---|---|---|---|
| 1949-50 | Boston | 1 | 0 | 1 | 1 |
| 1951-52 | Boston | 52 | 12 | 19 | 31 |
| 1952-53 | Boston | 70 | 7 | 15 | 22 |
| 1953-54 | Chicago | 23 | 8 | 3 | 11 |
| 1954-55 | Chicago | 65 | 16 | 13 | 29 |
| 1955-56 | Chicago | 46 | 10 | 5 | 15 |
| 1956-57 | Chicago | 70 | 18 | 14 | 32 |
| 1957-58 | Chi-Det | 68 | 15 | 11 | 26 |
| 1958-59 | Detroit | 55 | 15 | 14 | 29 |
| 1959-60 | Detroit | 49 | 8 | 7 | 15 |
| | **Totals** | 499 | 109 | 102 | 211 |

**McINTYRE, Lawrence Albert (Larry)** *Forward*
b. Moose Jaw, Sask., July 13, 1949

| Season | Club | GP | G | A | Pts. |
|---|---|---|---|---|---|
| 1969-70 | Toronto | 1 | 0 | 0 | 0 |
| 1972-73 | Toronto | 40 | 0 | 3 | 3 |
| | **Totals** | 41 | 0 | 3 | 3 |

| Season | Club | GP | G | A | Pts. |
|---|---|---|---|---|---|
| **McKAY, Raymond Owen** _Defenseman_ | | | | | |
| b. Edmonton, Alta., Aug. 22, 1946 | | | | | |
| 1968-69 | Chicago | 9 | 0 | 1 | 1 |
| 1969-70 | Chicago | 17 | 0 | 0 | 0 |
| 1970-71 | Chicago | 2 | 0 | 0 | 0 |
| 1971-72 | Buffalo | 39 | 0 | 3 | 3 |
| 1972-73 | Buffalo | 1 | 0 | 0 | 0 |
| 1973-74 | California | 72 | 2 | 12 | 14 |
| 1974-75 | Edmonton (WHA) | 69 | 8 | 20 | 28 |
| 1975-76 | Cleveland (WHA) | 68 | 3 | 10 | 13 |
| 1976-77 | Minn-Birm (WHA) | 61 | 2 | 10 | 12 |
| 1977-78 | Edmonton (WHA) | 14 | 1 | 4 | 5 |
| | **NHL Totals** | 140 | 2 | 16 | 18 |
| | **WHA Totals** | 212 | 14 | 44 | 58 |
| **McKECHNIE, Walter T.** _Forward_ | | | | | |
| b. London, Ont., June 19, 1947 | | | | | |
| 1967-68 | Minnesota | 4 | 0 | 0 | 0 |
| 1968-69 | Minnesota | 58 | 5 | 9 | 14 |
| 1969-70 | Minnesota | 20 | 1 | 3 | 4 |
| 1970-71 | Minnesota | 30 | 3 | 1 | 4 |
| 1971-72 | California | 56 | 11 | 20 | 31 |
| 1972-73 | California | 78 | 16 | 38 | 54 |
| 1973-74 | California | 63 | 23 | 29 | 52 |
| 1974-75 | Bos-Det | 76 | 9 | 14 | 23 |
| 1975-76 | Detroit | 80 | 26 | 56 | 82 |
| 1976-77 | Detroit | 80 | 25 | 34 | 59 |
| 1977-78 | Wash-Clev | 69 | 16 | 23 | 39 |
| 1978-79 | Toronto | 79 | 25 | 36 | 61 |
| 1979-80 | Tor-Col | 71 | 7 | 40 | 47 |
| 1980-81 | Colorado | 53 | 15 | 23 | 38 |
| 1981-82 | Detroit | 74 | 18 | 37 | 55 |
| 1982-83 | Detroit | 64 | 14 | 29 | 43 |
| | **Totals** | 955 | 214 | 392 | 606 |
| **McKEGNEY, Anthony Sylyd** _Forward_ | | | | | |
| b. Montreal, Que., Feb. 15, 1958 | | | | | |
| 1978-79 | Buffalo | 52 | 8 | 14 | 22 |
| 1979-80 | Buffalo | 80 | 23 | 29 | 52 |
| 1980-81 | Buffalo | 80 | 37 | 32 | 69 |
| 1981-82 | Buffalo | 73 | 23 | 29 | 52 |
| 1982-83 | Buffalo | 78 | 36 | 37 | 73 |
| | **Totals** | 363 | 127 | 141 | 268 |
| **McKEGNEY, Ian Robert** _Defenseman_ | | | | | |
| b. Sarnia, Ont., May 7, 1947 | | | | | |
| 1976-77 | Chicago | 3 | 0 | 0 | 0 |
| **McKELL, Jack** _Defenseman_ | | | | | |
| b. 1895 | | | | | |
| 1919-20 | Ottawa | 21 | 2 | 0 | 2 |
| 1920-21 | Ottawa | 21 | 2 | 1 | 3 |
| | **Totals** | 42 | 4 | 1 | 5 |
| **McKENDRY, Alex** _Forward_ | | | | | |
| b. Midland, Ont., Nov. 21, 1956 | | | | | |
| 1977-78 | New York I | 4 | 0 | 0 | 0 |
| 1978-79 | New York I | 4 | 0 | 0 | 0 |
| 1979-80 | New York I | 2 | 0 | 0 | 0 |
| 1980-81 | Calgary | 36 | 3 | 6 | 9 |
| | **Totals** | 46 | 3 | 6 | 9 |
| **McKENNA, Sean** _Forward_ | | | | | |
| b. Asbestos, Que., Mar. 7, 1962 | | | | | |
| 1981-82 | Buffalo | 3 | 0 | 1 | 1 |
| 1982-83 | Buffalo | 46 | 10 | 14 | 24 |
| | **Totals** | 49 | 10 | 15 | 25 |
| **McKENNEY, Donald Hamilton** _Forward_ | | | | | |
| b. Smith Falls, Ont., Apr. 30, 1934 | | | | | |
| 1954-55 | Boston | 69 | 22 | 20 | 42 |
| 1955-56 | Boston | 65 | 10 | 24 | 34 |
| 1956-57 | Boston | 69 | 21 | 39 | 60 |
| 1957-58 | Boston | 70 | 28 | 30 | 58 |
| 1958-59 | Boston | 70 | 32 | 30 | 62 |
| 1959-60 | Boston | 70 | 20 | 49 | 69 |
| 1960-61 | Boston | 68 | 26 | 23 | 49 |
| 1961-62 | Boston | 70 | 22 | 33 | 55 |
| 1962-63 | Bos-NYR | 62 | 22 | 35 | 57 |
| 1963-64 | NYR-Tor | 70 | 18 | 23 | 41 |
| 1964-65 | Toronto | 52 | 6 | 13 | 19 |

| Season | Club | GP | G | A | Pts. |
|---|---|---|---|---|---|
| 1965-66 | Detroit | 24 | 1 | 6 | 7 |
| 1967-68 | St Louis | 39 | 9 | 20 | 29 |
| | **Totals** | 798 | 237 | 345 | 582 |
| **McKENNY, James Claude (Jim)** _Defenseman_ | | | | | |
| b. Ottawa, Ont., Dec. 1, 1946 | | | | | |
| 1965-66 | Toronto | 2 | 0 | 0 | 0 |
| 1966-67 | Toronto | 6 | 1 | 0 | 1 |
| 1967-68 | Toronto | 5 | 1 | 0 | 1 |
| 1968-69 | Toronto | 7 | 0 | 0 | 0 |
| 1969-70 | Toronto | 73 | 11 | 33 | 44 |
| 1970-71 | Toronto | 68 | 4 | 26 | 30 |
| 1971-72 | Toronto | 76 | 5 | 31 | 36 |
| 1972-73 | Toronto | 77 | 11 | 41 | 52 |
| 1973-74 | Toronto | 77 | 14 | 28 | 42 |
| 1974-75 | Toronto | 66 | 8 | 35 | 43 |
| 1975-76 | Toronto | 46 | 10 | 19 | 29 |
| 1976-77 | Toronto | 76 | 14 | 31 | 45 |
| 1977-78 | Toronto | 15 | 2 | 2 | 4 |
| 1978-79 | Minnesota | 10 | 1 | 1 | 2 |
| | **Totals** | 604 | 82 | 247 | 329 |
| **McKENZIE, Brian Stewart** _Forward_ | | | | | |
| b. St. Catharines, Ont., Mar. 16, 1951 | | | | | |
| 1971-72 | Pittsburgh | 6 | 1 | 1 | 2 |
| 1973-74 | Edmonton (WHA) | 78 | 18 | 20 | 38 |
| 1974-75 | Indianapolis (WHA) | 9 | 1 | 0 | 1 |
| | **NHL Totals** | 6 | 1 | 1 | 2 |
| | **WHA Totals** | 87 | 19 | 20 | 39 |
| **McKENZIE, John Albert** _Forward_ | | | | | |
| b. High River, Alta., Dec. 12, 1937 | | | | | |
| 1958-59 | Chicago | 32 | 3 | 4 | 7 |
| 1959-60 | Detroit | 59 | 8 | 12 | 20 |
| 1960-61 | Detroit | 16 | 3 | 1 | 4 |
| 1963-64 | Chicago | 45 | 9 | 9 | 18 |
| 1964-65 | Chicago | 51 | 8 | 10 | 18 |
| 1965-66 | NYR-Bos | 71 | 19 | 14 | 33 |
| 1966-67 | Boston | 69 | 17 | 19 | 36 |
| 1967-68 | Boston | 74 | 28 | 38 | 66 |
| 1968-69 | Boston | 60 | 29 | 27 | 56 |
| 1969-70 | Boston | 72 | 29 | 41 | 70 |
| 1970-71 | Boston | 65 | 31 | 46 | 77 |
| 1971-72 | Boston | 77 | 22 | 47 | 69 |
| 1972-73 | Philadelphia (WHA) | 60 | 28 | 50 | 78 |
| 1973-74 | Vancouver (WHA) | 45 | 14 | 38 | 52 |
| 1974-75 | Vancouver (WHA) | 74 | 23 | 37 | 60 |
| 1975-76 | Minn-Cin (WHA) | 69 | 24 | 36 | 60 |
| 1976-77 | Minn-NE (WHA) | 74 | 28 | 32 | 60 |
| 1977-78 | New England (WHA) | 79 | 27 | 29 | 56 |
| 1978-79 | New England (WHA) | 76 | 19 | 28 | 47 |
| | **NHL Totals** | 691 | 206 | 268 | 474 |
| | **WHA Totals** | 477 | 163 | 250 | 413 |
| **McKINNON, Alexander** _Defenseman_ | | | | | |
| b. Sudbury, Ont. | | | | | |
| 1924-25 | Hamilton | 30 | 8 | 2 | 10 |
| 1925-26 | New York A | 35 | 5 | 3 | 8 |
| 1926-27 | New York A | 42 | 2 | 1 | 3 |
| 1927-28 | Pittsburgh Pi | 43 | 3 | 1 | 4 |
| 1928-29 | Chicago | 44 | 1 | 1 | 2 |
| | **Totals** | 194 | 19 | 8 | 27 |
| **McKINNON, John** _Defenseman_ | | | | | |
| b. Guysborough, N.S., July 15, 1902 | | | | | |
| 1925-26 | Montreal | 2 | 0 | 0 | 0 |
| 1926-27 | Pittsburgh Pi | 44 | 13 | 0 | 13 |
| 1927-28 | Pittsburgh Pi | 43 | 3 | 3 | 6 |
| 1928-29 | Pittsburgh Pi | 39 | 1 | 0 | 1 |
| 1929-30 | Pittsburgh Pi | 41 | 10 | 7 | 17 |
| 1930-31 | Philadelphia Q | 39 | 1 | 1 | 2 |
| | **Totals** | 208 | 28 | 11 | 39 |
| **McKINNON, Robert** _Forward_ | | | | | |
| 1928-29 | Chicago | — | 1 | 1 | 2 |
| **McLEAN, Fred** _Forward_ | | | | | |
| 1919-20 | Quebec | 7 | 0 | 0 | 0 |
| 1920-21 | Hamilton | 2 | 0 | 0 | 0 |
| | **Totals** | 9 | 0 | 0 | 0 |

| Season | Club | GP | G | A | Pts. |
|---|---|---|---|---|---|
| **McLEAN, Jack** _Forward_ | | | | | |
| b. Toronto, Ont., Jan. 31, 1923 | | | | | |
| 1942-43 | Toronto | 27 | 9 | 8 | 17 |
| 1943-44 | Toronto | 32 | 3 | 15 | 18 |
| 1944-45 | Toronto | 8 | 2 | 1 | 3 |
| | **Totals** | 67 | 14 | 24 | 38 |
| **McLEAN, Robert Donald** _Defenseman_ | | | | | |
| b. Niagara Falls, Ont., Jan. 19, 1954 | | | | | |
| 1975-76 | Washington | 9 | 0 | 0 | 0 |
| **McLELLAN, Daniel John** _Forward_ | | | | | |
| b. South Porcupine, Ont., Aug. 6, 1928 | | | | | |
| 1951-52 | Toronto | 2 | 0 | 0 | 0 |
| **McLELLAN, Scott** _Forward_ | | | | | |
| b. Toronto, Ont., Feb. 10, 1963 | | | | | |
| 1982-83 | Boston | 2 | 0 | 0 | 0 |
| **McLENAHAN, Roland Joseph** _Defenseman_ | | | | | |
| b. Fredericton, N.B., Oct. 26, 1921 | | | | | |
| 1945-46 | Detroit | 9 | 2 | 1 | 3 |
| **McLEOD, Allan Sidney** _Defenseman_ | | | | | |
| b. Medicine Hat, Alta., June 17, 1949 | | | | | |
| 1973-74 | Detroit | 26 | 2 | 2 | 4 |
| 1974-75 | Phoenix (WHA) | 77 | 3 | 16 | 19 |
| 1975-76 | Phoenix (WHA) | 80 | 2 | 18 | 20 |
| 1976-77 | Phoe-Hou (WHA) | 80 | 8 | 26 | 34 |
| 1977-78 | Houston (WHA) | 80 | 2 | 22 | 24 |
| | **NHL Totals** | 26 | 2 | 2 | 4 |
| | **WHA Totals** | 317 | 15 | 82 | 97 |
| **McLEOD, Robert John (Jackie)** _Forward_ | | | | | |
| b. Regina, Sask., Apr. 30, 1930 | | | | | |
| 1949-50 | New York R | 38 | 6 | 9 | 15 |
| 1950-51 | New York R | 41 | 5 | 10 | 15 |
| 1951-52 | New York R | 13 | 2 | 3 | 5 |
| 1952-53 | New York R | 3 | 0 | 0 | 0 |
| 1954-55 | New York R | 11 | 1 | 1 | 2 |
| | **Totals** | 106 | 14 | 23 | 37 |
| **McMAHON, Michael Clarence** _Defenseman_ | | | | | |
| b. Brockville, Ont., Feb. 1, 1917 | | | | | |
| 1943-44 | Montreal | 42 | 7 | 17 | 24 |
| 1945-46 | Mont-Bos | 15 | 0 | 1 | 1 |
| | **Totals** | 57 | 7 | 18 | 25 |
| **McMAHON, Michael William** _Defenseman_ | | | | | |
| b. Quebec, Que., Aug. 30, 1941 | | | | | |
| 1963-64 | New York R | 18 | 0 | 1 | 1 |
| 1964-65 | New York R | 1 | 0 | 0 | 0 |
| 1965-66 | New York R | 41 | 0 | 12 | 12 |
| 1967-68 | Minnesota | 74 | 14 | 33 | 47 |
| 1968-69 | Minn-Chi | 63 | 0 | 19 | 19 |
| 1969-70 | Det-Pitt | 14 | 1 | 3 | 4 |
| 1970-71 | Buffalo | 12 | 0 | 0 | 0 |
| 1971-72 | New York R | 1 | 0 | 0 | 0 |
| 1972-73 | Minnesota (WHA) | 75 | 12 | 39 | 51 |
| 1973-74 | Minnesota (WHA) | 71 | 10 | 35 | 45 |
| 1974-75 | Minnesota (WHA) | 64 | 5 | 15 | 20 |
| | **NHL Totals** | 224 | 15 | 68 | 83 |
| | **WHA Totals** | 210 | 27 | 89 | 116 |
| **McMANAMA, Robert S.** _Forward_ | | | | | |
| b. Belmont, Mass., Oct. 7, 1951 | | | | | |
| 1973-74 | Pittsburgh | 47 | 5 | 14 | 19 |
| 1974-75 | Pittsburgh | 40 | 5 | 9 | 14 |
| 1975-76 | Pittsburgh | 12 | 1 | 2 | 3 |
| | **Totals** | 99 | 11 | 25 | 36 |
| **McMANUS, Samuel** _Forward_ | | | | | |
| b. Belfast, Ireland, 1909 | | | | | |
| 1934-35 | Montreal M | 23 | 0 | 1 | 1 |
| 1936-37 | Boston | 1 | 0 | 0 | 0 |
| | **Totals** | 24 | 0 | 1 | 1 |

| Season | Club | GP | G | A | Pts. |
|---|---|---|---|---|---|
| **McNAB, Maxwell Douglas** *Forward* | | | | | |
| b. Watson, Sask., June 21, 1924 | | | | | |
| 1947-48 | Detroit | 12 | 2 | 2 | 4 |
| 1948-49 | Detroit | 51 | 10 | 13 | 23 |
| 1949-50 | Detroit | 65 | 4 | 4 | 8 |
| | **Totals** | 128 | 16 | 19 | 35 |
| **McNAB, Peter Maxwell** *Forward* | | | | | |
| b. Vancouver, B.C., May 8, 1952 | | | | | |
| 1973-74 | Buffalo | 22 | 3 | 6 | 9 |
| 1974-75 | Buffalo | 53 | 22 | 21 | 43 |
| 1975-76 | Buffalo | 79 | 24 | 32 | 56 |
| 1976-77 | Boston | 80 | 38 | 48 | 86 |
| 1977-78 | Boston | 79 | 41 | 39 | 80 |
| 1978-79 | Boston | 76 | 35 | 45 | 80 |
| 1979-80 | Boston | 74 | 40 | 38 | 78 |
| 1980-81 | Boston | 80 | 37 | 46 | 83 |
| 1981-82 | Boston | 80 | 36 | 40 | 76 |
| 1982-83 | Boston | 74 | 22 | 52 | 74 |
| | **Totals** | 697 | 298 | 367 | 665 |
| **McNAMARA, Howard** *Defenseman* | | | | | |
| 1919-20 | Montreal | 11 | 1 | 0 | 1 |
| **McNAUGHTON, George** *Forward* | | | | | |
| 1919-20 | Quebec | 1 | 0 | 0 | 0 |
| **McNEILL, Stuart** *Forward* | | | | | |
| b. Port Arthur, Ont., Sept. 25, 1938 | | | | | |
| 1957-58 | Detroit | 2 | 0 | 0 | 0 |
| 1959-60 | Detroit | 5 | 0 | 0 | 0 |
| | **Totals** | 7 | 0 | 0 | 0 |
| **McNEILL, William Ronald** *Forward* | | | | | |
| b. Edmonton, Alta., Jan. 26, 1936 | | | | | |
| 1956-57 | Detroit | 64 | 5 | 10 | 15 |
| 1957-58 | Detroit | 35 | 5 | 10 | 15 |
| 1958-59 | Detroit | 54 | 2 | 5 | 7 |
| 1959-60 | Detroit | 47 | 5 | 13 | 18 |
| 1962-63 | Detroit | 42 | 3 | 7 | 10 |
| 1963-64 | Detroit | 15 | 1 | 1 | 2 |
| | **Totals** | 257 | 21 | 46 | 67 |
| **McRAE, Basil Paul** *Forward* | | | | | |
| b. Beaverton, Ont., Jan. 1, 1961 | | | | | |
| 1981-82 | Quebec | 20 | 4 | 3 | 7 |
| 1982-83 | Quebec | 22 | 1 | 1 | 2 |
| | **Totals** | 42 | 5 | 4 | 9 |
| **McSHEFFREY, Bryan G.** *Forward* | | | | | |
| b. Eston, Sask., Sept. 25, 1952 | | | | | |
| 1972-73 | Vancouver | 33 | 4 | 4 | 8 |
| 1973-74 | Vancouver | 54 | 9 | 3 | 12 |
| 1974-75 | Buffalo | 3 | 0 | 0 | 0 |
| | **Totals** | 90 | 13 | 7 | 20 |
| **McTAGGERT, James** *Defenseman* | | | | | |
| b. Weyburn, Sask., Mar. 31, 1960 | | | | | |
| 1980-81 | Washington | 52 | 1 | 6 | 7 |
| 1981-82 | Washington | 19 | 2 | 4 | 6 |
| | **Totals** | 71 | 3 | 10 | 13 |
| **McTAVISH, Gordon** *Center* | | | | | |
| b. Guelph, Ont., June 3, 1954 | | | | | |
| 1978-79 | St Louis | 1 | 0 | 0 | 0 |
| 1979-80 | Winnipeg | 10 | 1 | 3 | 4 |
| | **Totals** | 11 | 1 | 3 | 4 |
| **McVEIGH, Charles (Rabbit)** *Forward* | | | | | |
| b. Kenora, Ont., Mar. 29, 1898 | | | | | |
| 1926-27 | Chicago | 43 | 12 | 4 | 16 |
| 1927-28 | Chicago | 39 | 6 | 7 | 13 |
| 1928-29 | New York A | 43 | 6 | 2 | 8 |
| 1929-30 | New York A | 38 | 14 | 14 | 28 |
| 1930-31 | New York A | 44 | 5 | 11 | 16 |
| 1931-32 | New York A | 46 | 12 | 15 | 27 |
| 1932-33 | New York A | 40 | 7 | 12 | 19 |

| Season | Club | GP | G | A | Pts. |
|---|---|---|---|---|---|
| 1933-34 | New York A | 48 | 15 | 12 | 27 |
| 1934-35 | New York A | 48 | 7 | 11 | 18 |
| | **Totals** | 389 | 84 | 88 | 172 |
| **McVICOR, John (Slim)** *Defenseman* | | | | | |
| 1930-31 | Montreal M | 40 | 2 | 4 | 6 |
| 1931-32 | Montreal M | 48 | 0 | 0 | 0 |
| | **Totals** | 88 | 2 | 4 | 6 |
| **MEAGHER, Richard** *Forward* | | | | | |
| b. Belleville, Ont., Nov. 4, 1953 | | | | | |
| 1979-80 | Montreal | 2 | 0 | 0 | 0 |
| 1980-81 | Hartford | 27 | 7 | 10 | 17 |
| 1981-82 | Hartford | 65 | 24 | 19 | 43 |
| 1982-83 | Hart-NJ | 61 | 15 | 14 | 29 |
| | **Totals** | 155 | 46 | 43 | 89 |
| **MEEHAN, Gerald Marcus (Gerry)** *Forward* | | | | | |
| b. Toronto, Ont., Sept. 3, 1946 | | | | | |
| 1968-69 | Tor-Phil | 37 | 0 | 5 | 5 |
| 1970-71 | Buffalo | 77 | 24 | 31 | 55 |
| 1971-72 | Buffalo | 77 | 19 | 27 | 46 |
| 1972-73 | Buffalo | 77 | 31 | 29 | 60 |
| 1973-74 | Buffalo | 72 | 20 | 26 | 46 |
| 1974-75 | Buf-Van-Atl | 74 | 14 | 26 | 40 |
| 1975-76 | Atl-Wash | 80 | 23 | 35 | 58 |
| 1976-77 | Washington | 80 | 28 | 36 | 64 |
| 1977-78 | Washington | 78 | 19 | 24 | 43 |
| 1978-79 | Washington | 18 | 2 | 4 | 6 |
| 1978-79 | Cincinnati (WHA) | 2 | 0 | 0 | 0 |
| | **NHL Totals** | 670 | 180 | 243 | 423 |
| | **WHA Totals** | 2 | 0 | 0 | 0 |
| **MEEKE, Brent Alan** *Defenseman* | | | | | |
| b. Toronto, Ont., Apr. 10, 1952 | | | | | |
| 1972-73 | California | 3 | 0 | 0 | 0 |
| 1973-74 | California | 18 | 1 | 9 | 10 |
| 1974-75 | California | 4 | 0 | 0 | 0 |
| 1975-76 | California | 1 | 0 | 0 | 0 |
| 1976-77 | Cleveland | 49 | 8 | 13 | 21 |
| | **Totals** | 75 | 9 | 22 | 31 |
| **MEEKER, Howard William** *Forward* | | | | | |
| b. Kitchener, Ont., Nov. 4, 1924 | | | | | |
| 1946-47 | Toronto | 55 | 27 | 18 | 45 |
| 1947-48 | Toronto | 58 | 14 | 20 | 34 |
| 1948-49 | Toronto | 30 | 7 | 7 | 14 |
| 1949-50 | Toronto | 70 | 18 | 22 | 40 |
| 1950-51 | Toronto | 49 | 6 | 14 | 20 |
| 1951-52 | Toronto | 54 | 9 | 14 | 23 |
| 1952-53 | Toronto | 25 | 1 | 7 | 8 |
| 1953-54 | Toronto | 5 | 1 | 0 | 1 |
| | **Totals** | 346 | 83 | 102 | 185 |
| **MEEKER, Mike** *Forward* | | | | | |
| b. Kingston, Ont., Feb. 23, 1958 | | | | | |
| 1978-79 | Pittsburgh | 4 | 0 | 0 | 0 |
| **MEEKING, Harry** *Forward* | | | | | |
| b. Kitchener, Ont., Nov. 4, 1894 | | | | | |
| 1917-18 | Toronto | 20 | 10 | 0 | 10 |
| 1918-19 | Toronto | 14 | 7 | 3 | 10 |
| 1926-27 | Bos-Det | 29 | 1 | 0 | 1 |
| | **Totals** | 63 | 18 | 3 | 21 |
| **MEGER, Paul Carl** *Forward* | | | | | |
| b. Watrous, Sask., Feb. 17, 1929 | | | | | |
| 1950-51 | Montreal | 17 | 2 | 4 | 6 |
| 1951-52 | Montreal | 69 | 24 | 18 | 42 |
| 1952-53 | Montreal | 69 | 9 | 17 | 26 |
| 1953-54 | Montreal | 44 | 4 | 9 | 13 |
| 1954-55 | Montreal | 13 | 0 | 4 | 4 |
| | **Totals** | 212 | 39 | 52 | 91 |
| **MEIGHAN, Ron James** *Defenseman* | | | | | |
| b. Montreal, Que., May 26, 1963 | | | | | |
| 1981-82 | Minnesota | 7 | 1 | 1 | 2 |
| 1982-83 | Pittsburgh | 41 | 2 | 6 | 8 |
| | **Totals** | 48 | 3 | 7 | 10 |

| Season | Club | GP | G | A | Pts. |
|---|---|---|---|---|---|
| **MEISSNER, Barrie M.** *Forward* | | | | | |
| b. Unity, Sask., July 26, 1946 | | | | | |
| 1967-68 | Minnesota | 1 | 0 | 0 | 0 |
| 1968-69 | Minnesota | 5 | 0 | 1 | 1 |
| | **Totals** | 6 | 0 | 1 | 1 |
| **MEISSNER, Richard Donald** *Forward* | | | | | |
| b. Kindersley, Sask., Jan. 6, 1940 | | | | | |
| 1959-60 | Boston | 60 | 5 | 6 | 11 |
| 1960-61 | Boston | 9 | 0 | 1 | 1 |
| 1961-62 | Boston | 66 | 3 | 3 | 6 |
| 1963-64 | New York R | 35 | 3 | 5 | 8 |
| 1964-65 | New York R | 1 | 0 | 0 | 0 |
| | **Totals** | 171 | 11 | 15 | 26 |
| **MELIN, Roger Alf** *Forward* | | | | | |
| b. Enkoping, Sweden, Apr. 25, 1956 | | | | | |
| 1980-81 | Minnesota | 1 | 0 | 0 | 0 |
| 1981-82 | Minnesota | 2 | 0 | 0 | 0 |
| | **Totals** | 3 | 0 | 0 | 0 |
| **MELLOR, Thomas Robert** *Defenseman* | | | | | |
| b. Cranston, R.I., Jan. 27, 1950 | | | | | |
| 1973-74 | Detroit | 25 | 2 | 4 | 6 |
| 1974-75 | Detroit | 1 | 0 | 0 | 0 |
| | **Totals** | 26 | 2 | 4 | 6 |
| **MELNYK, Larry Joseph** *Defenseman* | | | | | |
| b. New Westminster, B.C., Feb. 21, 1960 | | | | | |
| 1980-81 | Boston | 26 | 0 | 4 | 4 |
| 1981-82 | Boston | 48 | 0 | 8 | 8 |
| 1982-83 | Boston | 1 | 0 | 0 | 0 |
| | **Totals** | 75 | 0 | 12 | 12 |
| **MELNYK, Michael Gerald (Gerry)** *Forward* | | | | | |
| b. Edmonton, Alta., Sept. 16, 1934 | | | | | |
| 1959-60 | Detroit | 63 | 10 | 10 | 20 |
| 1960-61 | Detroit | 70 | 9 | 16 | 25 |
| 1961-62 | Chicago | 63 | 5 | 16 | 21 |
| 1967-68 | St Louis | 73 | 15 | 35 | 50 |
| | **Totals** | 269 | 39 | 77 | 116 |
| **MELROSE, Barry** *Defenseman* | | | | | |
| b. Kelvington, Sask., July 15, 1956 | | | | | |
| 1976-77 | Cincinnati (WHA) | 29 | 1 | 4 | 5 |
| 1977-78 | Cincinnati (WHA) | 69 | 2 | 9 | 11 |
| 1978-79 | Cincinnati (WHA) | 80 | 2 | 14 | 16 |
| 1979-80 | Winnipeg | 74 | 4 | 6 | 10 |
| 1980-81 | Winn-Tor | 75 | 3 | 6 | 9 |
| 1981-82 | Toronto | 64 | 1 | 5 | 6 |
| 1982-83 | Toronto | 52 | 2 | 5 | 7 |
| | **NHL Totals** | 265 | 10 | 22 | 32 |
| | **WHA Totals** | 178 | 5 | 27 | 32 |
| **MENARD, Hillary** *Defenseman* | | | | | |
| b. Timmins, Ont., Jan. 15, 1934 | | | | | |
| 1953-54 | Chicago | 1 | 0 | 0 | 0 |
| **MENARD, Howard Hubert** *Forward* | | | | | |
| b. Timmins, Ont., Apr. 28, 1942 | | | | | |
| 1963-64 | Detroit | 3 | 0 | 0 | 0 |
| 1967-68 | Los Angeles | 35 | 9 | 15 | 24 |
| 1968-69 | Los Angeles | 56 | 10 | 17 | 27 |
| 1969-70 | Chi-Oak | 57 | 4 | 10 | 14 |
| | **Totals** | 151 | 23 | 42 | 65 |
| **MERCREDI, Victor Dennis** *Forward* | | | | | |
| b. Yellowknife, N.W.T., Mar. 31, 1953 | | | | | |
| 1974-75 | Atlanta | 2 | 0 | 0 | 0 |
| 1975-76 | Calgary (WHA) | 3 | 0 | 0 | 0 |
| | **NHL Totals** | 2 | 0 | 0 | 0 |
| | **WHA Totals** | 3 | 0 | 0 | 0 |
| **MEREDITH, Gregory Paul** *Forward* | | | | | |
| b. Toronto, Ont., Feb. 23, 1958 | | | | | |
| 1980-81 | Calgary | 3 | 1 | 0 | 1 |
| 1982-83 | Calgary | 35 | 5 | 4 | 9 |
| | **Totals** | 38 | 6 | 4 | 10 |

| Season | Club | GP | G | A | Pts. |
|---|---|---|---|---|---|

**MERKOSKY, Glenn**  *Forward*
b. Edmonton, Alta., Apr. 8, 1960

| Season | Club | GP | G | A | Pts. |
|---|---|---|---|---|---|
| 1981-82 | Hartford | 7 | 0 | 0 | 0 |
| 1982-83 | New Jersey | 34 | 4 | 10 | 14 |
| | **Totals** | 41 | 4 | 10 | 14 |

**MERONEK, William (Smiley)**  *Forward*
b. Stony Mountain, Man., Apr. 5, 1917

| Season | Club | GP | G | A | Pts. |
|---|---|---|---|---|---|
| 1939-40 | Montreal | 7 | 2 | 2 | 4 |
| 1942-43 | Montreal | 12 | 3 | 6 | 9 |
| | **Totals** | 19 | 5 | 8 | 13 |

**MERRICK, Leonard Wayne**  *Forward*
b. Sarnia, Ont., Apr. 23, 1952

| Season | Club | GP | G | A | Pts. |
|---|---|---|---|---|---|
| 1972-73 | St Louis | 50 | 10 | 11 | 21 |
| 1973-74 | St Louis | 64 | 20 | 23 | 43 |
| 1974-75 | St Louis | 76 | 28 | 37 | 65 |
| 1975-76 | StL-Cal | 75 | 32 | 35 | 67 |
| 1976-77 | Cleveland | 80 | 18 | 38 | 56 |
| 1977-78 | Clev-NYI | 55 | 12 | 19 | 31 |
| 1978-79 | New York I | 75 | 20 | 21 | 41 |
| 1979-80 | New York I | 70 | 13 | 22 | 35 |
| 1980-81 | New York I | 71 | 16 | 15 | 31 |
| 1981-82 | New York I | 68 | 12 | 27 | 39 |
| 1982-83 | New York I | 59 | 4 | 12 | 16 |
| | **Totals** | 743 | 185 | 260 | 445 |

**MERRILL, Horace**  *Defenseman*
b. 1885

| Season | Club | GP | G | A | Pts. |
|---|---|---|---|---|---|
| 1917-18 | Ottawa | 4 | 0 | 0 | 0 |
| 1919-20 | Ottawa | 7 | 0 | 0 | 0 |
| | **Totals** | 11 | 0 | 0 | 0 |

**MESSIER, Mark Douglas**  *Forward*
b. Edmonton, Alta., Jan. 18, 1961

| Season | Club | GP | G | A | Pts. |
|---|---|---|---|---|---|
| 1978-79 | Ind-Cin (WHA) | 52 | 1 | 10 | 11 |
| 1979-80 | Edmonton | 75 | 12 | 21 | 33 |
| 1980-81 | Edmonton | 72 | 23 | 40 | 63 |
| 1981-82 | Edmonton | 78 | 50 | 38 | 88 |
| 1982-83 | Edmonton | 77 | 48 | 58 | 106 |
| | **NHL Totals** | 302 | 133 | 157 | 290 |
| | **WHA Totals** | 52 | 1 | 10 | 11 |

**MESSIER, Paul Edmond**  *Forward*
b. Nottingham, England, Jan. 27, 1958

| Season | Club | GP | G | A | Pts. |
|---|---|---|---|---|---|
| 1978-79 | Colorado | 9 | 0 | 0 | 0 |

**METZ, Donald Maurice**  *Forward*
b. Wilcox, Sask., Jan. 10, 1916

| Season | Club | GP | G | A | Pts. |
|---|---|---|---|---|---|
| 1939-40 | Toronto | 10 | 1 | 1 | 2 |
| 1940-41 | Toronto | 31 | 4 | 10 | 14 |
| 1941-42 | Toronto | 25 | 2 | 3 | 5 |
| 1945-46 | Toronto | 7 | 1 | 0 | 1 |
| 1946-47 | Toronto | 40 | 4 | 9 | 13 |
| 1947-48 | Toronto | 24 | 4 | 6 | 10 |
| 1948-49 | Toronto | 33 | 4 | 6 | 10 |
| | **Totals** | 170 | 20 | 35 | 55 |

**METZ, Nicholas J.**  *Forward*
b. Wilcox, Sask., Feb. 16, 1914

| Season | Club | GP | G | A | Pts. |
|---|---|---|---|---|---|
| 1934-35 | Toronto | 18 | 2 | 2 | 4 |
| 1935-36 | Toronto | 38 | 14 | 6 | 20 |
| 1936-37 | Toronto | 48 | 9 | 11 | 20 |
| 1937-38 | Toronto | 48 | 15 | 7 | 22 |
| 1938-39 | Toronto | 47 | 11 | 10 | 21 |
| 1939-40 | Toronto | 31 | 6 | 5 | 11 |
| 1940-41 | Toronto | 47 | 14 | 21 | 35 |
| 1941-42 | Toronto | 30 | 11 | 9 | 20 |
| 1944-45 | Toronto | 50 | 22 | 13 | 35 |
| 1945-46 | Toronto | 41 | 11 | 11 | 22 |
| 1946-47 | Toronto | 60 | 12 | 16 | 28 |
| 1947-48 | Toronto | 60 | 4 | 8 | 12 |
| | **Totals** | 518 | 129 | 119 | 248 |

**MICHALUK, Arthur**  *Defenseman*
b. Canmore, Alta., May 4, 1923

| Season | Club | GP | G | A | Pts. |
|---|---|---|---|---|---|
| 1947-48 | Chicago | 5 | 0 | 0 | 0 |

**MICHALUK, John**  *Forward*
b. Canmore, Alta., Nov. 2, 1928

| Season | Club | GP | G | A | Pts. |
|---|---|---|---|---|---|
| 1950-51 | Chicago | 1 | 0 | 0 | 0 |

**MICHAYLUK, David**  *Forward*
b. Wakaw, Sask., May 18, 1962

| Season | Club | GP | G | A | Pts. |
|---|---|---|---|---|---|
| 1981-82 | Philadelphia | 1 | 0 | 0 | 0 |
| 1982-83 | Philadelphia | 13 | 2 | 6 | 8 |
| | **Totals** | 14 | 2 | 6 | 8 |

**MICHELETTI, Joseph Robert**  *Defenseman*
b. Hibbing, Minn., Oct. 24, 1954

| Season | Club | GP | G | A | Pts. |
|---|---|---|---|---|---|
| 1976-77 | Calgary (WHA) | 14 | 3 | 3 | 6 |
| 1977-78 | Edmonton (WHA) | 56 | 14 | 34 | 48 |
| 1978-79 | Edmonton (WHA) | 72 | 14 | 33 | 47 |
| 1979-80 | St Louis | 54 | 2 | 16 | 18 |
| 1980-81 | St Louis | 63 | 4 | 27 | 31 |
| 1981-82 | StL-Col | 41 | 5 | 17 | 22 |
| | **NHL Totals** | 158 | 11 | 60 | 71 |
| | **WHA Totals** | 142 | 31 | 70 | 101 |

**MICKEY, Robert (Larry)**  *Forward*
b. Lacombe, Alta., Oct. 21, 1943

| Season | Club | GP | G | A | Pts. |
|---|---|---|---|---|---|
| 1964-65 | Chicago | 1 | 0 | 0 | 0 |
| 1965-66 | New York R | 7 | 0 | 0 | 0 |
| 1966-67 | New York R | 8 | 0 | 0 | 0 |
| 1967-68 | New York R | 4 | 0 | 2 | 2 |
| 1968-69 | Toronto | 55 | 8 | 19 | 27 |
| 1969-70 | Montreal | 21 | 4 | 4 | 8 |
| 1970-71 | Los Angeles | 65 | 6 | 12 | 18 |
| 1971-72 | Phil-Buf | 18 | 1 | 3 | 4 |
| 1972-73 | Buffalo | 77 | 15 | 9 | 24 |
| 1973-74 | Buffalo | 13 | 3 | 4 | 7 |
| 1974-75 | Buffalo | 23 | 2 | 0 | 2 |
| | **Totals** | 292 | 39 | 53 | 92 |

**MICKOSKI, Nicholas**  *Forward*
b. Winnipeg, Man., Dec. 7, 1927

| Season | Club | GP | G | A | Pts. |
|---|---|---|---|---|---|
| 1948-49 | New York R | 54 | 13 | 9 | 22 |
| 1949-50 | New York R | 45 | 10 | 10 | 20 |
| 1950-51 | New York R | 64 | 20 | 15 | 35 |
| 1951-52 | New York R | 43 | 7 | 13 | 20 |
| 1952-53 | New York R | 70 | 19 | 16 | 35 |
| 1953-54 | New York R | 68 | 19 | 16 | 35 |
| 1954-55 | NYR-Chi | 70 | 10 | 33 | 43 |
| 1955-56 | Chicago | 70 | 19 | 20 | 39 |
| 1956-57 | Chicago | 70 | 16 | 20 | 36 |
| 1957-58 | Chi-Det | 64 | 13 | 18 | 31 |
| 1958-59 | Detroit | 66 | 11 | 15 | 26 |
| 1959-60 | Boston | 18 | 1 | 0 | 1 |
| | **Totals** | 703 | 158 | 185 | 343 |

**MIDDLETON, Richard David**  *Forward*
b. Toronto, Ont., Dec. 4, 1953

| Season | Club | GP | G | A | Pts. |
|---|---|---|---|---|---|
| 1974-75 | New York R | 47 | 22 | 18 | 40 |
| 1975-76 | New York R | 77 | 24 | 26 | 50 |
| 1976-77 | Boston | 72 | 20 | 22 | 42 |
| 1977-78 | Boston | 79 | 25 | 35 | 60 |
| 1978-79 | Boston | 71 | 38 | 48 | 86 |
| 1979-80 | Boston | 80 | 40 | 52 | 92 |
| 1980-81 | Boston | 80 | 44 | 59 | 103 |
| 1981-82 | Boston | 75 | 51 | 43 | 94 |
| 1982-83 | Boston | 80 | 49 | 47 | 96 |
| | **Totals** | 661 | 313 | 350 | 663 |

**MIGAY, Rudolph Joseph**  *Forward*
b. Fort William, Ont., Nov. 18, 1928

| Season | Club | GP | G | A | Pts. |
|---|---|---|---|---|---|
| 1949-50 | Toronto | 18 | 1 | 5 | 6 |
| 1951-52 | Toronto | 19 | 2 | 1 | 3 |
| 1952-53 | Toronto | 40 | 5 | 4 | 9 |
| 1953-54 | Toronto | 70 | 8 | 15 | 23 |
| 1954-55 | Toronto | 67 | 8 | 16 | 24 |
| 1955-56 | Toronto | 70 | 12 | 16 | 28 |
| 1956-57 | Toronto | 66 | 15 | 20 | 35 |
| 1957-58 | Toronto | 48 | 7 | 14 | 21 |
| 1958-59 | Toronto | 19 | 1 | 1 | 2 |
| 1959-60 | Toronto | 1 | 0 | 0 | 0 |
| | **Totals** | 418 | 59 | 92 | 151 |

**MIKITA, Stanley**  *Forward*
b. Sokolce, Czechoslovakia, May 20, 1940

| Season | Club | GP | G | A | Pts. |
|---|---|---|---|---|---|
| 1958-59 | Chicago | 3 | 0 | 1 | 1 |
| 1959-60 | Chicago | 67 | 8 | 18 | 26 |
| 1960-61 | Chicago | 66 | 19 | 34 | 53 |
| 1961-62 | Chicago | 70 | 25 | 52 | 77 |
| 1962-63 | Chicago | 65 | 31 | 45 | 76 |
| 1963-64 | Chicago | 70 | 39 | 50 | 89 |
| 1964-65 | Chicago | 70 | 28 | 59 | 87 |
| 1965-66 | Chicago | 68 | 30 | 48 | 78 |
| 1966-67 | Chicago | 70 | 35 | 62 | 97 |
| 1967-68 | Chicago | 72 | 40 | 47 | 87 |
| 1968-69 | Chicago | 74 | 30 | 67 | 97 |
| 1969-70 | Chicago | 76 | 39 | 47 | 86 |
| 1970-71 | Chicago | 74 | 24 | 48 | 72 |
| 1971-72 | Chicago | 74 | 26 | 39 | 65 |
| 1972-73 | Chicago | 57 | 27 | 56 | 83 |
| 1973-74 | Chicago | 76 | 30 | 50 | 80 |
| 1974-75 | Chicago | 79 | 36 | 50 | 86 |
| 1975-76 | Chicago | 48 | 16 | 41 | 57 |
| 1976-77 | Chicago | 57 | 19 | 30 | 49 |
| 1977-78 | Chicago | 76 | 18 | 41 | 59 |
| 1978-79 | Chicago | 65 | 19 | 36 | 55 |
| 1979-80 | Chicago | 17 | 2 | 5 | 7 |
| | **Totals** | 1394 | 541 | 926 | 1467 |

**MIKKELSON, William Robert (Bill)**  *Forward*
b. Neepawa, Man., May 21, 1948

| Season | Club | GP | G | A | Pts. |
|---|---|---|---|---|---|
| 1971-72 | Los Angeles | 15 | 0 | 1 | 1 |
| 1972-73 | New York I | 72 | 1 | 10 | 11 |
| 1974-75 | Washington | 59 | 3 | 7 | 10 |
| 1976-77 | Washington | 1 | 0 | 0 | 0 |
| | **Totals** | 147 | 4 | 18 | 22 |

**MIKOL, John Stanley (Jim)**
*Defenseman-Forward*
b. Kitchener, Ont., June 11, 1938

| Season | Club | GP | G | A | Pts. |
|---|---|---|---|---|---|
| 1962-63 | Toronto | 4 | 0 | 1 | 1 |
| 1964-65 | New York R | 30 | 1 | 3 | 4 |
| | **Totals** | 34 | 1 | 4 | 5 |

**MILBURY, Michael James**  *Defenseman*
b. Brighton, Mass., June 17, 1952

| Season | Club | GP | G | A | Pts. |
|---|---|---|---|---|---|
| 1975-76 | Boston | 3 | 0 | 0 | 0 |
| 1976-77 | Boston | 77 | 6 | 18 | 24 |
| 1977-78 | Boston | 80 | 8 | 30 | 38 |
| 1978-79 | Boston | 74 | 1 | 34 | 35 |
| 1979-80 | Boston | 72 | 10 | 13 | 23 |
| 1980-81 | Boston | 77 | 0 | 18 | 18 |
| 1981-82 | Boston | 51 | 2 | 10 | 12 |
| 1982-83 | Boston | 78 | 9 | 15 | 24 |
| | **Totals** | 512 | 36 | 138 | 174 |

**MILKS, Herbert (Hib)**  *Defenseman-Forward*
b. Ottawa, Ont., Apr. 1, 1902

| Season | Club | GP | G | A | Pts. |
|---|---|---|---|---|---|
| 1925-26 | Pittsburgh Pi | 36 | 14 | 5 | 19 |
| 1926-27 | Pittsburgh Pi | 44 | 16 | 6 | 22 |
| 1927-28 | Pittsburgh Pi | 44 | 18 | 3 | 21 |
| 1928-29 | Pittsburgh Pi | 44 | 9 | 3 | 12 |
| 1929-30 | Pittsburgh Pi | 41 | 13 | 11 | 24 |
| 1930-31 | Philadelphia Q | 44 | 17 | 6 | 23 |
| 1931-32 | New York R | 45 | 0 | 4 | 4 |
| 1932-33 | Ottawa | 16 | 0 | 3 | 3 |
| | **Totals** | 314 | 87 | 41 | 128 |

**MILLAR, Hugh Alexander**  *Defenseman*
b. Edmonton, Alta., Apr. 3, 1921

| Season | Club | GP | G | A | Pts. |
|---|---|---|---|---|---|
| 1946-47 | Detroit | 4 | 0 | 0 | 0 |

**MILLER, Earl**  *Forward*
b. Regina, Sask.

| Season | Club | GP | G | A | Pts. |
|---|---|---|---|---|---|
| 1927-28 | Chicago | 21 | 1 | 1 | 2 |
| 1928-29 | Chicago | 17 | 1 | 1 | 2 |
| 1929-30 | Chicago | 28 | 11 | 5 | 16 |
| 1930-31 | Chicago | 19 | 3 | 4 | 7 |
| 1931-32 | Toronto | 24 | 3 | 3 | 6 |
| | **Totals** | 109 | 19 | 14 | 33 |

**MILLER, Jack Leslie** *Forward*
b. Delisle, Sask., Sept. 16, 1925

| Season | Club | GP | G | A | Pts. |
|---|---|---|---|---|---|
| 1949-50 | Chicago | 6 | 0 | 0 | 0 |
| 1950-51 | Chicago | 11 | 0 | 0 | 0 |
| | **Totals** | 17 | 0 | 0 | 0 |

**MILLER, Paul Edward** *Forward*
b. Billerca, Mass., Aug. 21, 1959

| Season | Club | GP | G | A | Pts. |
|---|---|---|---|---|---|
| 1981-82 | Colorado | 3 | 0 | 3 | 3 |

**MILLER, Perry Elvin** *Defenseman*
b. Winnipeg, Man., June 24, 1952

| Season | Club | GP | G | A | Pts. |
|---|---|---|---|---|---|
| 1974-75 | Winnipeg (WHA) | 67 | 9 | 19 | 28 |
| 1975-76 | Winn-Minn (WHA) | 60 | 8 | 10 | 18 |
| 1976-77 | Winnipeg (WHA) | 74 | 14 | 31 | 45 |
| 1977-78 | Detroit | 62 | 4 | 17 | 21 |
| 1978-79 | Detroit | 75 | 5 | 23 | 28 |
| 1979-80 | Detroit | 16 | 0 | 3 | 3 |
| 1980-81 | Detroit | 64 | 1 | 8 | 9 |
| | **NHL Totals** | 217 | 10 | 51 | 61 |
| | **WHA Totals** | 201 | 31 | 60 | 91 |

**MILLER, Robert** *Forward*
b. Medford, Mass., Sept. 28, 1956

| Season | Club | GP | G | A | Pts. |
|---|---|---|---|---|---|
| 1977-78 | Boston | 76 | 20 | 20 | 40 |
| 1978-79 | Boston | 77 | 15 | 33 | 48 |
| 1979-80 | Boston | 80 | 16 | 25 | 41 |
| 1980-81 | Bos-Col | 52 | 9 | 5 | 14 |
| 1981-82 | Colorado | 56 | 11 | 20 | 31 |
| | **Totals** | 341 | 71 | 103 | 174 |

**MILLER, Thomas William (Tom)** *Forward*
b. Kitchener, Ont., Mar. 31, 1947

| Season | Club | GP | G | A | Pts. |
|---|---|---|---|---|---|
| 1970-71 | Detroit | 29 | 1 | 7 | 8 |
| 1972-73 | New York I | 69 | 13 | 17 | 30 |
| 1973-74 | New York I | 19 | 2 | 1 | 3 |
| 1974-75 | New York I | 1 | 0 | 0 | 0 |
| | **Totals** | 118 | 16 | 25 | 41 |

**MILLER, Warren** *Forward*
b. South St. Paul, Minn., Jan. 1, 1954

| Season | Club | GP | G | A | Pts. |
|---|---|---|---|---|---|
| 1975-76 | Calgary (WHA) | 3 | 0 | 0 | 0 |
| 1976-77 | Calgary (WHA) | 80 | 23 | 32 | 55 |
| 1977-78 | Edm-Que (WHA) | 78 | 16 | 28 | 44 |
| 1978-79 | New England (WHA) | 77 | 26 | 23 | 49 |
| 1979-80 | New York R | 55 | 7 | 6 | 13 |
| 1980-81 | Hartford | 77 | 22 | 22 | 44 |
| 1981-82 | Hartford | 74 | 10 | 12 | 22 |
| 1982-83 | Hartford | 56 | 1 | 10 | 11 |
| | **NHL Totals** | 262 | 40 | 50 | 90 |
| | **WHA Totals** | 238 | 65 | 83 | 148 |

**MILLER, William** *Forward*
b. Campbellton, N.B., Aug. 1, 1908

| Season | Club | GP | G | A | Pts. |
|---|---|---|---|---|---|
| 1934-35 | Montreal M | 21 | 3 | 0 | 3 |
| 1935-36 | Montreal | 25 | 1 | 2 | 3 |
| 1936-37 | Montreal | 48 | 3 | 1 | 4 |
| | **Totals** | 94 | 7 | 3 | 10 |

**MINOR, Gerald** *Forward*
b. Regina, Sask., Oct. 27, 1958

| Season | Club | GP | G | A | Pts. |
|---|---|---|---|---|---|
| 1979-80 | Vancouver | 5 | 0 | 1 | 1 |
| 1980-81 | Vancouver | 74 | 10 | 14 | 24 |
| 1981-82 | Vancouver | 13 | 0 | 1 | 1 |
| 1982-83 | Vancouver | 39 | 1 | 5 | 6 |
| | **Totals** | 131 | 11 | 21 | 32 |

**MISZUK, John Stanley** *Defenseman*
b. Naliboki, Poland, Sept. 29, 1940

| Season | Club | GP | G | A | Pts. |
|---|---|---|---|---|---|
| 1963-64 | Detroit | 42 | 0 | 2 | 2 |
| 1965-66 | Chicago | 2 | 1 | 1 | 2 |
| 1966-67 | Chicago | 3 | 0 | 0 | 0 |
| 1967-68 | Philadelphia | 74 | 5 | 17 | 22 |
| 1968-69 | Philadelphia | 66 | 1 | 13 | 14 |
| 1969-70 | Minnesota | 50 | 0 | 6 | 6 |
| 1974-75 | Baltimore (WHA) | 66 | 2 | 19 | 21 |

| Season | Club | GP | G | A | Pts. |
|---|---|---|---|---|---|
| 1975-76 | Calgary (WHA) | 69 | 2 | 21 | 23 |
| 1976-77 | Calgary (WHA) | 79 | 2 | 26 | 28 |
| | **NHL Totals** | 237 | 7 | 39 | 46 |
| | **WHA Totals** | 214 | 6 | 66 | 72 |

**MITCHELL, Herbert** *Forward*

| Season | Club | GP | G | A | Pts. |
|---|---|---|---|---|---|
| 1924-25 | Boston | 27 | 3 | 0 | 3 |
| 1925-26 | Boston | 26 | 3 | 0 | 3 |
| | **Totals** | 53 | 6 | 0 | 6 |

**MITCHELL, William** *Defenseman*
b. Toronto, Ont., Sept. 6, 1912

| Season | Club | GP | G | A | Pts. |
|---|---|---|---|---|---|
| 1941-42 | Chicago | 1 | 0 | 0 | 0 |
| 1942-43 | Chicago | 42 | 1 | 1 | 2 |
| 1944-45 | Chicago | 40 | 3 | 4 | 7 |
| | **Totals** | 83 | 4 | 5 | 9 |

**MITCHELL, William Dickie (Red)** *Defenseman*
b. Port Dalhousie, Ont., Feb. 22, 1930

| Season | Club | GP | G | A | Pts. |
|---|---|---|---|---|---|
| 1963-64 | Detroit | 1 | 0 | 0 | 0 |

**MOE, William Carl** *Defenseman*
b. Danvers, Mass., Oct. 2, 1916

| Season | Club | GP | G | A | Pts. |
|---|---|---|---|---|---|
| 1944-45 | New York R | 35 | 2 | 4 | 6 |
| 1945-46 | New York R | 48 | 4 | 4 | 8 |
| 1946-47 | New York R | 59 | 4 | 10 | 14 |
| 1947-48 | New York R | 59 | 1 | 15 | 16 |
| 1948-49 | New York R | 60 | 0 | 9 | 9 |
| | **Totals** | 261 | 11 | 42 | 53 |

**MOFFAT, Lyle Gordon** *Forward*
b. Calgary, Alta., Mar. 19, 1948

| Season | Club | GP | G | A | Pts. |
|---|---|---|---|---|---|
| 1972-73 | Toronto | 1 | 0 | 0 | 0 |
| 1974-75 | Toronto | 22 | 2 | 7 | 9 |
| 1975-76 | Clev-Winn (WHA) | 75 | 17 | 16 | 33 |
| 1976-77 | Winnipeg (WHA) | 74 | 13 | 11 | 24 |
| 1977-78 | Winnipeg (WHA) | 57 | 9 | 16 | 25 |
| 1978-79 | Winnipeg (WHA) | 70 | 14 | 18 | 32 |
| 1979-80 | Winnipeg | 74 | 10 | 9 | 19 |
| | **NHL Totals** | 97 | 12 | 16 | 28 |
| | **WHA Totals** | 276 | 53 | 61 | 114 |

**MOFFAT, Ronald** *Forward*
b. West Hope, N. Dak.

| Season | Club | GP | G | A | Pts. |
|---|---|---|---|---|---|
| 1932-33 | Detroit | 24 | 1 | 1 | 2 |
| 1933-34 | Detroit | 5 | 0 | 0 | 0 |
| 1934-35 | Detroit | 8 | 0 | 0 | 0 |
| | **Totals** | 37 | 1 | 1 | 2 |

**MOHER, Mike** *Forward*
b. Manitowage, Ont., March 26, 1962

| Season | Club | GP | G | A | Pts. |
|---|---|---|---|---|---|
| 1982-83 | New Jersey | 9 | 0 | 1 | 1 |

**MOHNS, Douglas Allen** *Defenseman-Forward*
b. Capreol, Ont., Dec. 13, 1933

| Season | Club | GP | G | A | Pts. |
|---|---|---|---|---|---|
| 1953-54 | Boston | 70 | 13 | 14 | 27 |
| 1954-55 | Boston | 70 | 14 | 18 | 32 |
| 1955-56 | Boston | 64 | 10 | 8 | 18 |
| 1956-57 | Boston | 68 | 6 | 34 | 40 |
| 1957-58 | Boston | 54 | 5 | 16 | 21 |
| 1958-59 | Boston | 47 | 6 | 24 | 30 |
| 1959-60 | Boston | 65 | 20 | 25 | 45 |
| 1960-61 | Boston | 65 | 12 | 21 | 33 |
| 1961-62 | Boston | 69 | 16 | 29 | 45 |
| 1962-63 | Boston | 68 | 7 | 23 | 30 |
| 1963-64 | Boston | 70 | 9 | 17 | 26 |
| 1964-65 | Chicago | 49 | 13 | 20 | 33 |
| 1965-66 | Chicago | 70 | 22 | 27 | 49 |
| 1966-67 | Chicago | 61 | 25 | 35 | 60 |
| 1967-68 | Chicago | 65 | 24 | 29 | 53 |
| 1968-69 | Chicago | 65 | 22 | 19 | 41 |
| 1969-70 | Chicago | 66 | 6 | 27 | 33 |
| 1970-71 | Chi-Minn | 56 | 6 | 11 | 17 |
| 1971-72 | Minnesota | 78 | 6 | 30 | 36 |
| 1972-73 | Minnesota | 67 | 4 | 13 | 17 |
| 1973-74 | Atlanta | 28 | 0 | 3 | 3 |
| 1974-75 | Washington | 75 | 2 | 19 | 21 |
| | **Totals** | 1390 | 248 | 462 | 710 |

**MOHNS, Lloyd Warren** *Defenseman*
b. Petawawa, Ont., July 31, 1921

| Season | Club | GP | G | A | Pts. |
|---|---|---|---|---|---|
| 1943-44 | New York R | 1 | 0 | 0 | 0 |

**MOKOSAK, Carl** *Forward*
b. Fort Saskatchewan, Alta., Sept. 22, 1962

| Season | Club | GP | G | A | Pts. |
|---|---|---|---|---|---|
| 1981-82 | Calgary | 1 | 0 | 1 | 1 |
| 1982-83 | Calgary | 41 | 7 | 6 | 13 |
| | **Totals** | 42 | 7 | 7 | 14 |

**MOLIN, Lars** *Forward*
b. Ornskoldsvik, Sweden, Dec. 3, 1958

| Season | Club | GP | G | A | Pts. |
|---|---|---|---|---|---|
| 1981-82 | Vancouver | 72 | 15 | 31 | 46 |
| 1982-83 | Vancouver | 58 | 12 | 27 | 39 |
| | **Totals** | 130 | 27 | 58 | 85 |

**MOLLER, Michael John** *Forward*
b. Calgary, Alta., June 16, 1962

| Season | Club | GP | G | A | Pts. |
|---|---|---|---|---|---|
| 1980-81 | Buffalo | 5 | 2 | 2 | 4 |
| 1981-82 | Buffalo | 9 | 0 | 0 | 0 |
| 1982-83 | Buffalo | 49 | 6 | 12 | 18 |
| | **Totals** | 63 | 8 | 14 | 22 |

**MOLLER, Randy** *Defenseman*
b. Red Deer, Alta., Aug. 23, 1963

| Season | Club | GP | G | A | Pts. |
|---|---|---|---|---|---|
| 1982-83 | Quebec | 75 | 2 | 12 | 14 |

**MOLYNEAUX, Laurence S.** *Defenseman*
b. West Sutton, Ont., July 8, 1912

| Season | Club | GP | G | A | Pts. |
|---|---|---|---|---|---|
| 1937-38 | New York R | 2 | 0 | 0 | 0 |
| 1938-39 | New York R | 43 | 0 | 1 | 1 |
| | **Totals** | 45 | 0 | 1 | 1 |

**MONAHAN, Garry Michael** *Forward*
b. Barrie, Ont., Oct. 20, 1946

| Season | Club | GP | G | A | Pts. |
|---|---|---|---|---|---|
| 1967-68 | Montreal | 11 | 0 | 0 | 0 |
| 1968-69 | Montreal | 3 | 0 | 0 | 0 |
| 1969-70 | Det-LA | 72 | 3 | 7 | 10 |
| 1970-71 | Toronto | 78 | 15 | 22 | 37 |
| 1971-72 | Toronto | 78 | 14 | 17 | 31 |
| 1972-73 | Toronto | 78 | 13 | 18 | 31 |
| 1973-74 | Toronto | 78 | 9 | 16 | 25 |
| 1974-75 | Tor-Van | 79 | 14 | 20 | 34 |
| 1975-76 | Vancouver | 66 | 16 | 17 | 33 |
| 1976-77 | Vancouver | 76 | 18 | 26 | 44 |
| 1977-78 | Vancouver | 67 | 10 | 19 | 29 |
| 1978-79 | Toronto | 62 | 4 | 7 | 11 |
| | **Totals** | 748 | 116 | 169 | 285 |

**MONAHAN, Hartland Patrick** *Forward*
b. Montreal, Que., Mar. 29, 1951

| Season | Club | GP | G | A | Pts. |
|---|---|---|---|---|---|
| 1973-74 | California | 1 | 0 | 0 | 0 |
| 1974-75 | New York R | 6 | 0 | 1 | 1 |
| 1975-76 | Washington | 80 | 17 | 29 | 46 |
| 1976-77 | Washington | 79 | 23 | 27 | 50 |
| 1977-78 | Pitt-LA | 71 | 12 | 9 | 21 |
| 1979-80 | St Louis | 72 | 5 | 12 | 17 |
| 1980-81 | St Louis | 25 | 4 | 2 | 6 |
| | **Totals** | 334 | 61 | 80 | 141 |

**MONDOU, Armand** *Forward*
b. Yanaska, Que., June 27, 1905

| Season | Club | GP | G | A | Pts. |
|---|---|---|---|---|---|
| 1928-29 | Montreal | 32 | 3 | 4 | 7 |
| 1929-30 | Montreal | 44 | 3 | 5 | 8 |
| 1930-31 | Montreal | 40 | 5 | 4 | 9 |
| 1931-32 | Montreal | 47 | 6 | 12 | 18 |
| 1932-33 | Montreal | 24 | 1 | 3 | 4 |
| 1933-34 | Montreal | 48 | 5 | 3 | 8 |
| 1934-35 | Montreal | 46 | 9 | 15 | 24 |
| 1935-36 | Montreal | 36 | 7 | 11 | 18 |
| 1936-37 | Montreal | 7 | 1 | 1 | 2 |
| 1937-38 | Montreal | 7 | 2 | 4 | 6 |
| 1938-39 | Montreal | 34 | 3 | 7 | 10 |
| 1939-40 | Montreal | 21 | 2 | 2 | 4 |
| | **Totals** | 386 | 47 | 71 | 118 |

| Season | Club | GP | G | A | Pts. |
|---|---|---|---|---|---|
| **MONDOU, Pierre** *Forward* | | | | | |
| b. Sorel, Que., Nov. 27, 1955 | | | | | |
| 1977-78 | Montreal | 71 | 19 | 30 | 49 |
| 1978-79 | Montreal | 77 | 31 | 41 | 72 |
| 1979-80 | Montreal | 75 | 30 | 36 | 66 |
| 1980-81 | Montreal | 57 | 17 | 24 | 41 |
| 1981-82 | Montreal | 73 | 35 | 33 | 68 |
| 1982-83 | Montreal | 76 | 29 | 37 | 66 |
| | **Totals** | **429** | **161** | **201** | **362** |
| **MONGRAIN, Robert** *Forward* | | | | | |
| b. LaSarre, Que., Aug. 31, 1959 | | | | | |
| 1979-80 | Buffalo | 34 | 4 | 6 | 10 |
| 1980-81 | Buffalo | 4 | 0 | 0 | 0 |
| 1981-82 | Buffalo | 24 | 6 | 4 | 10 |
| | **Totals** | **62** | **10** | **10** | **20** |
| **MONTIETH, Henry George (Hank)** *Forward* | | | | | |
| b. Stratford, Ont., Oct. 2, 1945 | | | | | |
| 1968-69 | Detroit | 34 | 1 | 9 | 10 |
| 1969-70 | Detroit | 9 | 0 | 0 | 0 |
| 1970-71 | Detroit | 34 | 4 | 3 | 7 |
| | **Totals** | **77** | **5** | **12** | **17** |
| **MOORE, Richard W. (Dickie)** *Forward* | | | | | |
| b. Montreal, Que., Jan. 6, 1931 | | | | | |
| 1951-52 | Montreal | 33 | 18 | 15 | 33 |
| 1952-53 | Montreal | 18 | 2 | 6 | 8 |
| 1953-54 | Montreal | 13 | 1 | 4 | 5 |
| 1954-55 | Montreal | 67 | 16 | 20 | 36 |
| 1955-56 | Montreal | 70 | 11 | 39 | 50 |
| 1956-57 | Montreal | 70 | 29 | 29 | 58 |
| 1957-58 | Montreal | 70 | 36 | 48 | 84 |
| 1958-59 | Montreal | 70 | 41 | 55 | 96 |
| 1959-60 | Montreal | 62 | 22 | 42 | 64 |
| 1960-61 | Montreal | 57 | 35 | 34 | 69 |
| 1961-62 | Montreal | 57 | 19 | 22 | 41 |
| 1962-63 | Montreal | 67 | 24 | 26 | 50 |
| 1964-65 | Toronto | 38 | 2 | 4 | 6 |
| 1967-68 | St Louis | 27 | 5 | 3 | 8 |
| | **Totals** | **719** | **261** | **347** | **608** |
| **MORAN, Ambrose (Amby)** *Defenseman* | | | | | |
| 1926-27 | Montreal | — | 0 | 0 | 0 |
| 1927-28 | Chicago | — | 1 | 1 | 2 |
| | **Totals** | — | **1** | **1** | **2** |
| **MORENZ, Howarth William (Howie)** *Forward* | | | | | |
| b. Mitchell, Ont., Sept. 21, 1902 | | | | | |
| 1923-24 | Montreal | 24 | 13 | 3 | 16 |
| 2924-25 | Montreal | 30 | 27 | 7 | 34 |
| 1925-26 | Montreal | 31 | 23 | 3 | 26 |
| 1926-27 | Montreal | 44 | 25 | 7 | 32 |
| 1927-28 | Montreal | 43 | 33 | 18 | 51 |
| 1928-29 | Montreal | 42 | 17 | 10 | 27 |
| 1929-30 | Montreal | 44 | 40 | 10 | 50 |
| 1930-31 | Montreal | 39 | 28 | 23 | 51 |
| 1931-32 | Montreal | 48 | 24 | 25 | 49 |
| 1932-33 | Montreal | 46 | 14 | 21 | 35 |
| 1933-34 | Montreal | 39 | 8 | 13 | 21 |
| 1934-35 | Chicago | 48 | 8 | 26 | 34 |
| 1935-36 | Chi-NYR | 42 | 6 | 15 | 21 |
| 1936-37 | Montreal | 30 | 4 | 16 | 20 |
| | **Totals** | **550** | **270** | **197** | **467** |
| **MORETTO, Angelo** *Forward* | | | | | |
| b. Toronto, Ont., Sept. 18, 1953 | | | | | |
| 1976-77 | Cleveland | 5 | 1 | 2 | 3 |
| **MORIN, Pierre (Pete)** *Forward* | | | | | |
| b. Lachine, Que., Dec. 8, 1915 | | | | | |
| 1941-42 | Montreal | — | 10 | 12 | 22 |
| **MORRIS, Bernard** *Forward* | | | | | |
| 1924-25 | Boston | 6 | 2 | 0 | 2 |
| **MORRIS, Elwin Gordon (Moe)** *Defenseman* | | | | | |
| b. Toronto, Ont., Jan. 3, 1921 | | | | | |
| 1943-44 | Toronto | 50 | 12 | 21 | 33 |
| 1944-45 | Toronto | 29 | 0 | 2 | 2 |

| Season | Club | GP | G | A | Pts. |
|---|---|---|---|---|---|
| 1945-46 | Toronto | 38 | 1 | 5 | 6 |
| 1948-49 | New York R | 18 | 0 | 1 | 1 |
| | **Totals** | **137** | **13** | **29** | **42** |
| **MORRISON, David Stuart** *Forward* | | | | | |
| b. Toronto, Ont., June 12, 1962 | | | | | |
| 1980-81 | Los Angeles | 3 | 0 | 0 | 0 |
| 1981-82 | Los Angeles | 4 | 0 | 0 | 0 |
| 1982-83 | Los Angeles | 24 | 3 | 6 | 6 |
| | **Totals** | **31** | **3** | **3** | **6** |
| **MORRISON, Donald Macrae** *Forward* | | | | | |
| b. Saskatoon, Sask., July 14, 1923 | | | | | |
| 1947-48 | Detroit | 40 | 10 | 15 | 25 |
| 1948-49 | Detroit | 13 | 0 | 1 | 1 |
| 1950-51 | Chicago | 59 | 8 | 12 | 20 |
| | **Totals** | **112** | **18** | **28** | **46** |
| **MORRISON, Douglas** *Forward* | | | | | |
| b. Vancouver, B.C., Feb. 1, 1960 | | | | | |
| 1979-80 | Boston | 1 | 0 | 0 | 0 |
| 1980-81 | Boston | 18 | 7 | 3 | 10 |
| 1981-82 | Boston | 3 | 0 | 0 | 0 |
| | **Totals** | **22** | **7** | **3** | **10** |
| **MORRISON, Gary** *Forward* | | | | | |
| b. Detroit, Mich., Nov. 8, 1955 | | | | | |
| 1979-80 | Philadelphia | 3 | 0 | 2 | 2 |
| 1980-81 | Philadelphia | 33 | 1 | 13 | 14 |
| 1981-82 | Philadelphia | 7 | 0 | 0 | 0 |
| | **Totals** | **43** | **1** | **15** | **16** |
| **MORRISON, George Harold** *Forward* | | | | | |
| b. Toronto, Ont., Dec. 24, 1948 | | | | | |
| 1970-71 | St Louis | 73 | 15 | 10 | 25 |
| 1971-72 | St Louis | 42 | 2 | 11 | 13 |
| 1972-73 | Minnesota (WHA) | 70 | 16 | 24 | 40 |
| 1973-74 | Minnesota (WHA) | 73 | 40 | 38 | 78 |
| 1974-75 | Minnesota (WHA) | 76 | 31 | 29 | 60 |
| 1975-76 | Calgary (WHA) | 79 | 25 | 32 | 57 |
| 1976-77 | Calgary (WHA) | 63 | 11 | 19 | 30 |
| | **NHL Totals** | **115** | **17** | **21** | **38** |
| | **WHA Totals** | **361** | **123** | **142** | **265** |
| **MORRISON, James Stewart Hunter (Jim)** *Defenseman* | | | | | |
| b. Montreal, Que., Oct. 11, 1931 | | | | | |
| 1951-52 | Bos-Tor | 31 | 0 | 3 | 3 |
| 1952-53 | Toronto | 56 | 1 | 8 | 9 |
| 1953-54 | Toronto | 60 | 9 | 11 | 20 |
| 1954-55 | Toronto | 70 | 5 | 12 | 17 |
| 1955-56 | Toronto | 63 | 2 | 17 | 19 |
| 1956-57 | Toronto | 63 | 3 | 17 | 20 |
| 1957-58 | Toronto | 70 | 3 | 21 | 24 |
| 1958-59 | Boston | 70 | 8 | 17 | 25 |
| 1959-60 | Detroit | 70 | 3 | 23 | 26 |
| 1960-61 | New York R | 19 | 1 | 6 | 7 |
| 1969-70 | Pittsburgh | 59 | 5 | 15 | 20 |
| 1970-71 | Pittsburgh | 73 | 0 | 10 | 10 |
| | **Totals** | **704** | **40** | **160** | **200** |
| **MORRISON, John (Crutchy)** *Forward* | | | | | |
| 1925-26 | New York A | 18 | 0 | 0 | 0 |
| **MORRISON, Kevin Gregory Joseph** *Defenseman* | | | | | |
| b. Sydney, N.S., Oct. 28, 1949 | | | | | |
| 1974-75 | San Diego (WHA) | 78 | 20 | 61 | 81 |
| 1975-76 | San Diego (WHA) | 80 | 22 | 43 | 65 |
| 1976-77 | San Diego (WHA) | 75 | 8 | 30 | 38 |
| 1977-78 | Indianapolis (WHA) | 75 | 17 | 40 | 57 |
| 1978-79 | Ind-Que (WHA) | 32 | 2 | 7 | 9 |
| 1979-80 | Colorado | 41 | 4 | 11 | 15 |
| | **NHL Totals** | **41** | **4** | **11** | **15** |
| | **WHA Totals** | **340** | **69** | **181** | **250** |
| **MORRISON, Lewis Henry** *Forward* | | | | | |
| b. Gainsborough Sask., Feb. 11, 1948 | | | | | |
| 1969-70 | Philadelphia | 66 | 9 | 10 | 19 |
| 1970-71 | Philadelphia | 78 | 5 | 7 | 12 |

| Season | Club | GP | G | A | Pts. |
|---|---|---|---|---|---|
| 1971-72 | Philadelphia | 58 | 5 | 5 | 10 |
| 1972-73 | Atlanta | 77 | 6 | 9 | 15 |
| 1973-74 | Atlanta | 52 | 1 | 4 | 5 |
| 1974-75 | Wash-Pitt | 70 | 7 | 9 | 16 |
| 1975-76 | Pittsburgh | 78 | 4 | 5 | 9 |
| 1976-77 | Pittsburgh | 76 | 2 | 1 | 3 |
| 1977-78 | Pittsburgh | 8 | 0 | 2 | 2 |
| | **Totals** | **563** | **39** | **52** | **91** |
| **MORRISON, Mark** *Forward* | | | | | |
| b. Prince George, B.C., Mar. 11, 1963 | | | | | |
| 1981-82 | New York R | 9 | 1 | 1 | 2 |
| **MORRISON, Roderick Finlay** *Forward* | | | | | |
| b. Saskatoon, Sask., Oct. 7, 1925 | | | | | |
| 1947-48 | Detroit | 34 | 8 | 7 | 15 |
| **MORROW, Ken** *Defenseman* | | | | | |
| b. Davison, Mich., Oct. 17, 1956 | | | | | |
| 1979-80 | New York I | 18 | 0 | 3 | 3 |
| 1980-81 | New York I | 80 | 2 | 11 | 13 |
| 1981-82 | New York I | 75 | 1 | 18 | 19 |
| 1982-83 | New York I | 79 | 5 | 11 | 16 |
| | **Totals** | **252** | **8** | **43** | **51** |
| **MORTSON, James Angus Gerald (Gus)** *Defenseman* | | | | | |
| b. New Liskeard, Ont., Jan. 24, 1925 | | | | | |
| 1946-47 | Toronto | 60 | 5 | 13 | 18 |
| 1947-48 | Toronto | 58 | 7 | 11 | 18 |
| 1948-49 | Toronto | 60 | 2 | 13 | 15 |
| 1949-50 | Toronto | 68 | 3 | 14 | 17 |
| 1950-51 | Toronto | 60 | 3 | 10 | 13 |
| 1951-52 | Toronto | 65 | 1 | 10 | 11 |
| 1952-53 | Chicago | 68 | 5 | 18 | 23 |
| 1953-54 | Chicago | 68 | 5 | 13 | 18 |
| 1954-55 | Chicago | 65 | 2 | 11 | 13 |
| 1955-56 | Chicago | 52 | 5 | 10 | 15 |
| 1956-57 | Chicago | 70 | 5 | 18 | 23 |
| 1957-58 | Chicago | 67 | 3 | 10 | 13 |
| 1958-59 | Detroit | 36 | 0 | 1 | 1 |
| | **Totals** | **797** | **46** | **152** | **198** |
| **MOSDELL, Kenneth** *Forward* | | | | | |
| b. Montreal, Que., July 13, 1922 | | | | | |
| 1941-42 | Brooklyn | 41 | 7 | 9 | 16 |
| 1944-45 | Montreal | 31 | 12 | 6 | 18 |
| 1945-46 | Montreal | 13 | 2 | 1 | 3 |
| 1946-47 | Montreal | 54 | 5 | 10 | 15 |
| 1947-48 | Montreal | 23 | 1 | 0 | 1 |
| 1948-49 | Montreal | 60 | 17 | 9 | 26 |
| 1949-50 | Montreal | 67 | 15 | 12 | 27 |
| 1950-51 | Montreal | 66 | 13 | 18 | 31 |
| 1951-52 | Montreal | 44 | 5 | 11 | 16 |
| 1952-53 | Montreal | 63 | 5 | 14 | 19 |
| 1953-54 | Montreal | 67 | 22 | 24 | 46 |
| 1954-55 | Montreal | 70 | 22 | 32 | 54 |
| 1955-56 | Montreal | 67 | 13 | 17 | 30 |
| 1956-57 | Chicago | 25 | 2 | 4 | 6 |
| 1957-58 | Montreal | 2 | 0 | 1 | 1 |
| | **Totals** | **693** | **141** | **168** | **309** |
| **MOSIENKO, William** *Forward* | | | | | |
| b. Winnipeg, Man., Nov. 2, 1921 | | | | | |
| 1941-42 | Chicago | 12 | 6 | 8 | 14 |
| 1942-43 | Chicago | 2 | 0 | 2 | 2 |
| 1943-44 | Chicago | 50 | 32 | 38 | 70 |
| 1944-45 | Chicago | 50 | 28 | 26 | 54 |
| 1945-46 | Chicago | 40 | 18 | 30 | 48 |
| 1946-47 | Chicago | 59 | 25 | 27 | 52 |
| 1947-48 | Chicago | 40 | 16 | 9 | 25 |
| 1948-49 | Chicago | 60 | 17 | 25 | 42 |
| 1949-50 | Chicago | 69 | 18 | 28 | 46 |
| 1950-51 | Chicago | 65 | 21 | 15 | 36 |
| 1951-52 | Chicago | 70 | 31 | 22 | 53 |
| 1952-53 | Chicago | 65 | 17 | 20 | 37 |
| 1953-54 | Chicago | 65 | 15 | 19 | 34 |
| 1954-55 | Chicago | 64 | 12 | 15 | 27 |
| | **Totals** | **711** | **258** | **282** | **540** |

| Season | Club | GP | G | A | Pts. |
|---|---|---|---|---|---|
| **MOTT, Morris Kenneth** *Forward* | | | | | |
| b. Creelman, Sask., May 25, 1946 | | | | | |
| 1972-73 | California | 70 | 6 | 7 | 13 |
| 1973-74 | California | 77 | 9 | 17 | 26 |
| 1974-75 | California | 52 | 3 | 8 | 11 |
| 1976-77 | Winnipeg (WHA) | 2 | 0 | 1 | 1 |
| | **NHL Totals** | 199 | 18 | 32 | 50 |
| | **WHA Totals** | 2 | 0 | 1 | 1 |
| **MOTTER, Alexander Everett** *Defenseman* | | | | | |
| b. Melville, Sask., June 20, 1913 | | | | | |
| 1934-35 | Boston | 3 | 0 | 0 | 0 |
| 1935-36 | Boston | 23 | 1 | 4 | 5 |
| 1937-38 | Bos-Det | 32 | 5 | 17 | 22 |
| 1938-39 | Detroit | 44 | 5 | 11 | 16 |
| 1939-40 | Detroit | 37 | 7 | 12 | 19 |
| 1940-41 | Detroit | 48 | 13 | 12 | 25 |
| 1941-42 | Detroit | 30 | 2 | 4 | 6 |
| 1942-43 | Detroit | 50 | 6 | 4 | 10 |
| | **Totals** | 267 | 39 | 64 | 103 |
| **MOXEY, James George** *Forward* | | | | | |
| b. Toronto, Ont., May 28, 1953 | | | | | |
| 1974-75 | California | 47 | 5 | 4 | 9 |
| 1975-76 | California | 44 | 10 | 16 | 26 |
| 1976-77 | Clev-LA | 36 | 7 | 7 | 14 |
| | **Totals** | 127 | 22 | 27 | 49 |
| **MULHERN, Richard Sidney** *Defenseman* | | | | | |
| b. Edmonton, Alta., Mar. 1, 1955 | | | | | |
| 1975-76 | Atlanta | 12 | 1 | 0 | 1 |
| 1976-77 | Atlanta | 79 | 12 | 32 | 44 |
| 1977-78 | Atlanta | 79 | 9 | 23 | 32 |
| 1978-79 | Atl-LA | 73 | 5 | 21 | 26 |
| 1979-80 | LA-Tor | 41 | 0 | 13 | 13 |
| 1980-81 | Winnipeg | 19 | 0 | 4 | 4 |
| | **Totals** | 303 | 27 | 93 | 120 |
| **MULLEN, Brian** *Forward* | | | | | |
| b. New York, N.Y., Mar. 16, 1962 | | | | | |
| 1982-83 | Winnipeg | 80 | 24 | 26 | 50 |
| **MULLEN, Joe** *Forward* | | | | | |
| b. New York N.Y., Feb. 26, 1957 | | | | | |
| 1981-82 | St Louis | 45 | 25 | 34 | 59 |
| 1982-83 | St Louis | 49 | 17 | 30 | 47 |
| | **Totals** | 94 | 42 | 64 | 106 |
| **MULOIN, John Wayne** *Defenseman* | | | | | |
| b. Dryden, Ont., Dec. 24, 1941 | | | | | |
| 1963-64 | Detroit | 3 | 0 | 1 | 1 |
| 1969-70 | Oakland | 71 | 3 | 6 | 9 |
| 1970-71 | Cal-Minn | 73 | 0 | 14 | 14 |
| 1972-73 | Cleveland (WHA) | 67 | 2 | 13 | 15 |
| 1973-74 | Cleveland (WHA) | 76 | 3 | 7 | 10 |
| 1974-75 | Cleveland (WHA) | 78 | 4 | 17 | 21 |
| 1975-76 | Clev-Edm (WHA) | 37 | 1 | 6 | 7 |
| | **NHL Totals** | 147 | 3 | 21 | 24 |
| | **WHA Totals** | 258 | 10 | 43 | 53 |
| **MULVEY, Grant Michael** *Forward* | | | | | |
| b. Sudbury, Ont., Sept. 17, 1956 | | | | | |
| 1974-75 | Chicago | 74 | 7 | 4 | 11 |
| 1975-76 | Chicago | 64 | 11 | 17 | 28 |
| 1976-77 | Chicago | 80 | 10 | 14 | 24 |
| 1977-78 | Chicago | 78 | 14 | 24 | 38 |
| 1978-79 | Chicago | 80 | 19 | 15 | 34 |
| 1979-80 | Chicago | 80 | 39 | 26 | 65 |
| 1980-81 | Chicago | 42 | 18 | 14 | 32 |
| 1981-82 | Chicago | 73 | 30 | 19 | 49 |
| 1982-83 | Chicago | 3 | 0 | 0 | 0 |
| | **Totals** | 574 | 148 | 133 | 281 |
| **MULVEY, Paul Joseph** *Forward* | | | | | |
| b. Sudbury, Ont., Sept. 27, 1958 | | | | | |
| 1978-79 | Washington | 55 | 7 | 4 | 11 |
| 1979-80 | Washington | 77 | 15 | 19 | 34 |
| 1980-81 | Washington | 55 | 7 | 14 | 21 |
| 1981-82 | Pitt-LA | 38 | 1 | 14 | 15 |
| | **Totals** | 225 | 30 | 51 | 81 |

| Season | Club | GP | G | A | Pts. |
|---|---|---|---|---|---|
| **MUMMERY, Harry** *Defenseman* | | | | | |
| 1917-18 | Toronto | 18 | 3 | 0 | 3 |
| 1918-19 | Toronto | 13 | 2 | 0 | 2 |
| 1919-20 | Quebec | 24 | 9 | 6 | 15 |
| 1920-21 | Montreal | 24 | 15 | 5 | 20 |
| 1921-22 | Hamilton | 20 | 4 | 2 | 6 |
| 1922-23 | Hamilton | 7 | 0 | 0 | 0 |
| | **Totals** | 106 | 33 | 13 | 46 |
| **MUNI, Craig** *Defenseman* | | | | | |
| b. Toronto, Ont., July 19, 1962 | | | | | |
| 1981-82 | Toronto | 3 | 0 | 0 | 0 |
| 1982-83 | Toronto | 2 | 0 | 1 | 1 |
| | **Totals** | 5 | 0 | 1 | 1 |
| **MUNRO, Duncan** *Defenseman* | | | | | |
| b. Toronto, Ont. | | | | | |
| 1924-25 | Montreal M | 27 | 5 | 1 | 6 |
| 1925-26 | Montreal M | 33 | 4 | 6 | 10 |
| 1926-27 | Montreal M | 43 | 6 | 5 | 11 |
| 1927-28 | Montreal M | 43 | 5 | 2 | 7 |
| 1928-29 | Montreal M | 1 | 0 | 0 | 0 |
| 1929-30 | Montreal M | 40 | 7 | 2 | 9 |
| 1930-31 | Montreal M | 4 | 0 | 1 | 1 |
| 1931-32 | Montreal | 48 | 1 | 1 | 2 |
| | **Totals** | 239 | 28 | 18 | 46 |
| **MUNRO, Gerald** *Defenseman* | | | | | |
| b. Sault Ste. Marie, Ont., Nov. 20, 1897 | | | | | |
| 1924-25 | Montreal M | 29 | 1 | 0 | 1 |
| 1925-26 | Toronto | 4 | 0 | 0 | 0 |
| | **Totals** | 33 | 1 | 0 | 1 |
| **MURDOCH, Donald Walter** *Forward* | | | | | |
| b. Cranbrook, B.C., Oct. 25, 1956 | | | | | |
| 1976-77 | New York R | 59 | 32 | 24 | 56 |
| 1977-78 | New York R | 66 | 27 | 28 | 55 |
| 1978-79 | New York R | 40 | 15 | 22 | 37 |
| 1979-80 | NYR-Edm | 66 | 28 | 21 | 49 |
| 1980-81 | Edmonton | 40 | 10 | 9 | 19 |
| 1981-82 | Detroit | 49 | 9 | 13 | 22 |
| | **Totals** | 320 | 121 | 117 | 238 |
| **MURDOCH, John Murray** *Forward* | | | | | |
| b. Lucknow, Ont., May 19, 1904 | | | | | |
| 1926-27 | New York R | 44 | 6 | 4 | 10 |
| 1927-28 | New York R | 44 | 7 | 3 | 10 |
| 1928-29 | New York R | 44 | 8 | 6 | 14 |
| 1929-30 | New York R | 44 | 13 | 13 | 26 |
| 1930-31 | New York R | 44 | 7 | 7 | 14 |
| 1931-32 | New York R | 48 | 5 | 16 | 21 |
| 1932-33 | New York R | 48 | 5 | 11 | 16 |
| 1933-34 | New York R | 48 | 17 | 10 | 27 |
| 1934-35 | New York R | 48 | 14 | 15 | 29 |
| 1935-36 | New York R | 48 | 2 | 9 | 11 |
| 1936-37 | New York R | 48 | 0 | 14 | 14 |
| | **Totals** | 508 | 84 | 108 | 192 |
| **MURDOCH, Robert John (Bob)** *Defenseman* | | | | | |
| b. Kirkland Lake, Ont., Nov. 20, 1946 | | | | | |
| 1970-71 | Montreal | 1 | 0 | 2 | 2 |
| 1971-72 | Montreal | 11 | 1 | 1 | 2 |
| 1972-73 | Montreal | 69 | 2 | 22 | 24 |
| 1973-74 | Los Angeles | 76 | 8 | 20 | 28 |
| 1974-75 | Los Angeles | 80 | 13 | 29 | 42 |
| 1975-76 | Los Angeles | 80 | 6 | 29 | 35 |
| 1976-77 | Los Angeles | 70 | 9 | 23 | 32 |
| 1977-78 | Los Angeles | 76 | 2 | 17 | 19 |
| 1978-79 | LA-Atl | 67 | 8 | 23 | 31 |
| 1979-80 | Atlanta | 80 | 5 | 16 | 21 |
| 1980-81 | Calgary | 74 | 3 | 19 | 22 |
| 1981-82 | Calgary | 73 | 3 | 17 | 20 |
| | **Totals** | 757 | 60 | 218 | 278 |
| **MURDOCH, Robert Lovell** *Forward* | | | | | |
| b. Cranbrook, B.C., Jan. 29, 1954 | | | | | |
| 1975-76 | California | 78 | 22 | 27 | 49 |
| 1976-77 | Cleveland | 57 | 23 | 19 | 42 |
| 1977-78 | Cleveland | 71 | 14 | 26 | 40 |
| 1978-79 | St Louis | 54 | 13 | 13 | 26 |
| | **Totals** | 260 | 72 | 85 | 157 |

| Season | Club | GP | G | A | Pts. |
|---|---|---|---|---|---|
| **MURPHY, Brian** *Forward* | | | | | |
| b. Toronto, Ont., Aug. 20, 1947 | | | | | |
| 1974-75 | Detroit | 1 | 0 | 0 | 0 |
| **MURPHY, Lawrence Thomas** *Defenseman* | | | | | |
| b. Scarborough, Ont., Mar. 8, 1961 | | | | | |
| 1980-81 | Los Angeles | 80 | 16 | 60 | 76 |
| 1981-82 | Los Angeles | 79 | 22 | 44 | 66 |
| 1982-83 | Los Angeles | 77 | 14 | 48 | 62 |
| | **Totals** | 236 | 52 | 152 | 204 |
| **MURPHY, Michael John (Mike)** *Forward* | | | | | |
| b. Toronto, Ont., Sept. 12, 1950 | | | | | |
| 1971-72 | St Louis | 63 | 20 | 23 | 43 |
| 1972-73 | StL-NYR | 79 | 22 | 31 | 53 |
| 1973-74 | NYR-LA | 69 | 15 | 17 | 32 |
| 1974-75 | Los Angeles | 78 | 30 | 38 | 68 |
| 1975-76 | Los Angeles | 80 | 26 | 42 | 68 |
| 1976-77 | Los Angeles | 76 | 25 | 36 | 61 |
| 1977-78 | Los Angeles | 72 | 20 | 36 | 56 |
| 1978-79 | Los Angeles | 64 | 16 | 29 | 45 |
| 1979-80 | Los Angeles | 80 | 27 | 22 | 49 |
| 1980-81 | Los Angeles | 68 | 16 | 23 | 39 |
| 1981-82 | Los Angeles | 28 | 5 | 10 | 15 |
| 1982-83 | Los Angeles | 74 | 16 | 11 | 27 |
| | **Totals** | 831 | 238 | 318 | 556 |
| **MURPHY, Robert Ronald (Ron)** *Forward* | | | | | |
| b. Hamilton, Ont., Apr. 10, 1933 | | | | | |
| 1952-53 | New York R | 15 | 3 | 1 | 4 |
| 1953-54 | New York R | 27 | 1 | 3 | 4 |
| 1954-55 | New York R | 66 | 14 | 16 | 30 |
| 1955-56 | New York R | 66 | 16 | 28 | 44 |
| 1956-57 | New York R | 33 | 7 | 12 | 19 |
| 1957-58 | Chicago | 69 | 11 | 17 | 28 |
| 1958-59 | Chicago | 59 | 17 | 30 | 47 |
| 1959-60 | Chicago | 63 | 15 | 21 | 36 |
| 1960-61 | Chicago | 70 | 21 | 19 | 40 |
| 1961-62 | Chicago | 61 | 12 | 16 | 28 |
| 1962-63 | Chicago | 68 | 18 | 16 | 34 |
| 1963-64 | Chicago | 70 | 11 | 8 | 19 |
| 1964-65 | Detroit | 58 | 20 | 19 | 39 |
| 1965-66 | Det-Bos | 34 | 10 | 8 | 18 |
| 1966-67 | Boston | 39 | 11 | 16 | 27 |
| 1967-68 | Boston | 12 | 0 | 1 | 1 |
| 1968-69 | Boston | 60 | 16 | 38 | 54 |
| 1969-70 | Boston | 20 | 2 | 5 | 7 |
| | **Totals** | 890 | 205 | 274 | 479 |
| **MURRAY, Robert** *Defenseman* | | | | | |
| b. Burlington, Ont., July 16, 1948 | | | | | |
| 1973-74 | Atlanta | 62 | 0 | 3 | 3 |
| 1974-75 | Atl-Van | 55 | 4 | 8 | 12 |
| 1975-76 | Vancouver | 65 | 2 | 5 | 7 |
| 1976-77 | Vancouver | 12 | 0 | 0 | 0 |
| | **Totals** | 194 | 6 | 16 | 22 |
| **MURRAY, Robert Frederick** *Defenseman* | | | | | |
| b. Kingston, Ont., Nov. 26, 1954 | | | | | |
| 1975-76 | Chicago | 64 | 1 | 2 | 3 |
| 1976-77 | Chicago | 77 | 10 | 11 | 21 |
| 1977-78 | Chicago | 70 | 14 | 17 | 31 |
| 1978-79 | Chicago | 79 | 19 | 32 | 51 |
| 1979-80 | Chicago | 74 | 16 | 34 | 50 |
| 1980-81 | Chicago | 77 | 13 | 47 | 60 |
| 1981-82 | Chicago | 45 | 8 | 22 | 30 |
| 1982-83 | Chicago | 79 | 7 | 32 | 39 |
| | **Totals** | 565 | 88 | 197 | 285 |
| **MURRAY, Allan** *Defenseman* | | | | | |
| b. Stratford, Ont., Nov. 10, 1908 | | | | | |
| 1933-34 | New York A | 39 | 1 | 1 | 2 |
| 1934-35 | New York A | 43 | 2 | 1 | 3 |
| 1935-36 | New York A | 48 | 1 | 0 | 1 |
| 1936-37 | New York A | 40 | 0 | 2 | 2 |
| 1937-38 | New York A | 47 | 0 | 1 | 1 |
| 1938-39 | New York A | 18 | 0 | 0 | 0 |
| 1939-40 | New York A | 36 | 1 | 4 | 5 |
| | **Totals** | 271 | 5 | 9 | 14 |

| Season | Club | GP | G | A | Pts. |
|---|---|---|---|---|---|

**MURRAY, James Arnold**  *Defenseman*
b. Virden, Man., Nov. 25, 1943

| Season | Club | GP | G | A | Pts. |
|---|---|---|---|---|---|
| 1967-68 | Los Angeles | 30 | 0 | 2 | 2 |

**MURRAY, Kenneth R. (Ken)**  *Defenseman*
b. Toronto, Ont., Jan. 22, 1948

| Season | Club | GP | G | A | Pts. |
|---|---|---|---|---|---|
| 1969-70 | Toronto | 1 | 0 | 1 | 1 |
| 1970-71 | Toronto | 4 | 0 | 0 | 0 |
| 1972-73 | NYI-Det | 71 | 1 | 5 | 6 |
| 1974-75 | Kansas City | 8 | 0 | 2 | 2 |
| 1975-76 | Kansas City | 23 | 0 | 2 | 2 |
| | **Totals** | 107 | 1 | 10 | 11 |

**MURRAY, Leo**  *Forward*
b. Portage La Prairie, Man., Feb. 15, 1902

| Season | Club | GP | G | A | Pts. |
|---|---|---|---|---|---|
| 1932-33 | Montreal | 6 | 0 | 0 | 0 |

**MURRAY, Randall (Randy)**  *Defenseman*
b. Chatham, Ont., Aug. 24, 1945

| Season | Club | GP | G | A | Pts. |
|---|---|---|---|---|---|
| 1969-70 | Toronto | 1 | 0 | 1 | 1 |

**MURRAY, Terry Rodney**  *Defenseman*
b. Shawville, Que., July 20, 1950

| Season | Club | GP | G | A | Pts. |
|---|---|---|---|---|---|
| 1972-73 | California | 23 | 0 | 3 | 3 |
| 1973-74 | California | 58 | 0 | 12 | 12 |
| 1974-75 | California | 9 | 0 | 2 | 2 |
| 1975-76 | Philadelphia | 3 | 0 | 0 | 0 |
| 1976-77 | Phil-Det | 59 | 0 | 20 | 20 |
| 1978-79 | Philadelphia | 5 | 0 | 0 | 0 |
| 1980-81 | Philadelphia | 71 | 1 | 17 | 18 |
| 1981-82 | Washington | 74 | 3 | 22 | 25 |
| | **Totals** | 302 | 4 | 76 | 80 |

**MURRAY, Troy Norman**  *Forward*
b. Calgary, Alta., July 31, 1962

| Season | Club | GP | G | A | Pts. |
|---|---|---|---|---|---|
| 1981-82 | Chicago | 1 | 0 | 0 | 0 |
| 1982-83 | Chicago | 54 | 8 | 8 | 16 |
| | **Totals** | 55 | 8 | 8 | 16 |

**MYERS, Harold Robert (Hap)**  *Defenseman*
b. Edmonton, Alta., July 28, 1947

| Season | Club | GP | G | A | Pts. |
|---|---|---|---|---|---|
| 1970-71 | Buffalo | 13 | 0 | 0 | 0 |

**MYLES, Victor Robert**  *Defenseman*
b. Fairlight, Sask., Nov. 12, 1915

| Season | Club | GP | G | A | Pts. |
|---|---|---|---|---|---|
| 1942-43 | New York R | 45 | 6 | 9 | 15 |

**NACHBAUER, Donald Kenneth**  *Forward*
b. Kitimat, B.C., Jan. 30, 1959

| Season | Club | GP | G | A | Pts. |
|---|---|---|---|---|---|
| 1980-81 | Hartford | 77 | 16 | 17 | 33 |
| 1981-82 | Hartford | 77 | 5 | 21 | 26 |
| 1982-83 | Edmonton | 4 | 0 | 0 | 0 |
| | **Totals** | 158 | 21 | 38 | 59 |

**NAHRGANG, James Herbert**  *Defenseman*
b. Kitchener, Ont., Apr. 17, 1951

| Season | Club | GP | G | A | Pts. |
|---|---|---|---|---|---|
| 1974-75 | Detroit | 1 | 0 | 0 | 0 |
| 1975-76 | Detroit | 3 | 0 | 1 | 1 |
| 1976-77 | Detroit | 53 | 5 | 11 | 16 |
| | **Totals** | 57 | 5 | 12 | 17 |

**NANNE, Louis Vincent (Lou)**  *Defenseman*
b. Sault Ste. Marie, Ont., June 2, 1941

| Season | Club | GP | G | A | Pts. |
|---|---|---|---|---|---|
| 1967-68 | Minnesota | 2 | 0 | 1 | 1 |
| 1968-69 | Minnesota | 41 | 2 | 12 | 14 |
| 1969-70 | Minnesota | 74 | 3 | 20 | 23 |
| 1970-71 | Minnesota | 68 | 5 | 11 | 16 |
| 1971-72 | Minnesota | 78 | 21 | 28 | 49 |
| 1972-73 | Minnesota | 74 | 15 | 20 | 35 |
| 1973-74 | Minnesota | 76 | 11 | 21 | 32 |
| 1974-75 | Minnesota | 49 | 6 | 9 | 15 |
| 1975-76 | Minnesota | 79 | 3 | 14 | 17 |
| 1976-77 | Minnesota | 68 | 2 | 20 | 22 |
| 1977-78 | Minnesota | 26 | 0 | 1 | 1 |
| | **Totals** | 635 | 68 | 157 | 225 |

**NANTAIS, Richard**  *Forward*
b. Repentigny, Que., Oct. 27, 1954

| Season | Club | GP | G | A | Pts. |
|---|---|---|---|---|---|
| 1974-75 | Minnesota | 18 | 4 | 1 | 5 |
| 1975-76 | Minnesota | 5 | 0 | 0 | 0 |
| 1976-77 | Minnesota | 40 | 1 | 3 | 4 |
| | **Totals** | 63 | 5 | 4 | 9 |

**NAPIER, Robert (Mark)**  *Forward*
b. Toronto, Ont., Jan. 28, 1957

| Season | Club | GP | G | A | Pts. |
|---|---|---|---|---|---|
| 1975-76 | Toronto (WHA) | 78 | 43 | 50 | 93 |
| 1976-77 | Birmingham (WHA) | 80 | 60 | 36 | 96 |
| 1977-78 | Birmingham (WHA) | 79 | 33 | 32 | 65 |
| 1978-79 | Montreal | 54 | 11 | 20 | 31 |
| 1979-80 | Montreal | 76 | 16 | 33 | 49 |
| 1980-81 | Montreal | 79 | 35 | 36 | 71 |
| 1981-82 | Montreal | 80 | 40 | 41 | 81 |
| 1982-83 | Montreal | 73 | 40 | 27 | 67 |
| | **NHL Totals** | 362 | 142 | 157 | 299 |
| | **WHA Totals** | 237 | 136 | 118 | 254 |

**NASLUND, Mats**  *Forward*
b. Timra, Sweden, Oct. 31, 1959

| Season | Club | GP | G | A | Pts. |
|---|---|---|---|---|---|
| 1982-83 | Montreal | 74 | 26 | 45 | 71 |

**NATTRASS, Ralph William**  *Defenseman*
b. Gainsboro, Sask., May 26, 1925

| Season | Club | GP | G | A | Pts. |
|---|---|---|---|---|---|
| 1946-47 | Chicago | 35 | 4 | 5 | 9 |
| 1947-48 | Chicago | 60 | 5 | 12 | 17 |
| 1948-49 | Chicago | 60 | 4 | 10 | 14 |
| 1949-50 | Chicago | 69 | 5 | 11 | 16 |
| | **Totals** | 224 | 18 | 38 | 56 |

**NATTRESS, Ric**  *Defenseman*
b. Hamilton, Ont., May 25, 1962

| Season | Club | GP | G | A | Pts. |
|---|---|---|---|---|---|
| 1982-83 | Montreal | 40 | 1 | 3 | 4 |

**NECHAEV, Victor**  *Forward*
b. Siberia, Jan. 18, 1955

| Season | Club | GP | G | A | Pts. |
|---|---|---|---|---|---|
| 1982-83 | Los Angeles | 3 | 1 | 0 | 1 |

**NEDOMANSKY, Vaclav**  *Forward*
b. Hodonin, Czechoslovakia, Mar. 14, 1944

| Season | Club | GP | G | A | Pts. |
|---|---|---|---|---|---|
| 1974-75 | Toronto (WHA) | 78 | 41 | 40 | 81 |
| 1975-76 | Toronto (WHA) | 81 | 56 | 42 | 98 |
| 1976-77 | Birmingham (WHA) | 81 | 36 | 33 | 69 |
| 1977-78 | Birmingham (WHA) | 12 | 2 | 3 | 5 |
| 1977-78 | Detroit | 63 | 11 | 17 | 28 |
| 1978-79 | Detroit | 80 | 38 | 35 | 73 |
| 1979-80 | Detroit | 79 | 35 | 39 | 74 |
| 1980-81 | Detroit | 74 | 12 | 20 | 32 |
| 1981-82 | Detroit | 68 | 12 | 28 | 40 |
| 1982-83 | NYR-StL | 57 | 14 | 17 | 31 |
| | **NHL Totals** | 421 | 122 | 156 | 278 |
| | **WHA Totals** | 252 | 135 | 118 | 253 |

**NEELY, Robert Barry**  *Forward*
b. Sarnia, Ont., Nov. 9, 1953

| Season | Club | GP | G | A | Pts. |
|---|---|---|---|---|---|
| 1973-74 | Toronto | 54 | 5 | 7 | 12 |
| 1974-75 | Toronto | 57 | 5 | 16 | 21 |
| 1975-76 | Toronto | 69 | 9 | 13 | 22 |
| 1976-77 | Toronto | 70 | 17 | 16 | 33 |
| 1977-78 | Tor-Col | 33 | 3 | 7 | 10 |
| | **Totals** | 283 | 39 | 59 | 98 |

**NEILSON, James Anthony (Chief)**
*Defenseman*
b. Big River, Sask., Nov. 28, 1940

| Season | Club | GP | G | A | Pts. |
|---|---|---|---|---|---|
| 1962-63 | New York R | 69 | 5 | 11 | 16 |
| 1963-64 | New York R | 69 | 5 | 24 | 29 |
| 1964-65 | New York R | 62 | 0 | 13 | 13 |
| 1965-66 | New York R | 65 | 4 | 19 | 23 |
| 1966-67 | New York R | 61 | 4 | 11 | 15 |
| 1967-68 | New York R | 67 | 6 | 29 | 35 |
| 1968-69 | New York R | 76 | 10 | 34 | 44 |
| 1969-70 | New York R | 62 | 3 | 20 | 23 |
| 1970-71 | New York R | 77 | 8 | 24 | 32 |
| 1971-72 | New York R | 78 | 7 | 30 | 37 |
| 1972-73 | New York R | 52 | 4 | 16 | 20 |
| 1973-74 | New York R | 72 | 4 | 7 | 11 |
| 1974-75 | California | 72 | 3 | 17 | 20 |
| 1975-76 | California | 26 | 1 | 6 | 7 |

| Season | Club | GP | G | A | Pts. |
|---|---|---|---|---|---|
| 1976-77 | Cleveland | 47 | 3 | 17 | 20 |
| 1977-78 | Cleveland | 68 | 2 | 21 | 23 |
| 1978-79 | Edmonton (WHA) | 35 | 0 | 5 | 5 |
| | **NHL Totals** | 1023 | 69 | 299 | 368 |
| | **WHA Totals** | 35 | 0 | 5 | 5 |

**NELSON, Gordon William**  *Defenseman*
b. Kinisting, Sask., May 10, 1947

| Season | Club | GP | G | A | Pts. |
|---|---|---|---|---|---|
| 1969-70 | Toronto | 3 | 0 | 0 | 0 |

**NESTERENKO, Eric Paul**  *Forward*
b. Flin Flon, Man., Oct. 31, 1933

| Season | Club | GP | G | A | Pts. |
|---|---|---|---|---|---|
| 1951-52 | Toronto | 1 | 0 | 0 | 0 |
| 1952-53 | Toronto | 35 | 10 | 6 | 16 |
| 1953-54 | Toronto | 68 | 14 | 9 | 23 |
| 1954-55 | Toronto | 62 | 15 | 15 | 30 |
| 1955-56 | Toronto | 40 | 4 | 6 | 10 |
| 1956-57 | Chicago | 24 | 8 | 15 | 23 |
| 1957-58 | Chicago | 70 | 20 | 18 | 38 |
| 1958-59 | Chicago | 70 | 16 | 18 | 34 |
| 1959-60 | Chicago | 61 | 13 | 23 | 36 |
| 1960-61 | Chicago | 68 | 19 | 19 | 38 |
| 1961-62 | Chicago | 68 | 15 | 14 | 29 |
| 1962-63 | Chicago | 67 | 12 | 15 | 27 |
| 1963-64 | Chicago | 70 | 7 | 19 | 26 |
| 1964-65 | Chicago | 56 | 14 | 16 | 30 |
| 1965-66 | Chicago | 67 | 15 | 25 | 40 |
| 1966-67 | Chicago | 68 | 14 | 23 | 37 |
| 1967-68 | Chicago | 71 | 11 | 25 | 36 |
| 1968-69 | Chicago | 72 | 15 | 17 | 32 |
| 1969-70 | Chicago | 67 | 16 | 18 | 34 |
| 1970-71 | Chicago | 76 | 8 | 15 | 23 |
| 1971-72 | Chicago | 38 | 4 | 8 | 12 |
| | **Totals** | 1219 | 250 | 324 | 574 |

**NETHERY, Lance**  *Forward*
b. Toronto, Ont., June 28, 1957

| Season | Club | GP | G | A | Pts. |
|---|---|---|---|---|---|
| 1980-81 | New York R | 33 | 11 | 12 | 23 |
| 1981-82 | NYR-Edm | 8 | 0 | 2 | 2 |
| | **Totals** | 41 | 11 | 14 | 25 |

**NEUFELD, Ray Matthew**  *Forward*
b. St. Boniface, Man., Apr. 15, 1959

| Season | Club | GP | G | A | Pts. |
|---|---|---|---|---|---|
| 1979-80 | Hartford | 8 | 1 | 0 | 1 |
| 1980-81 | Hartford | 52 | 5 | 10 | 15 |
| 1981-82 | Hartford | 19 | 4 | 3 | 7 |
| 1982-83 | Hartford | 80 | 26 | 31 | 57 |
| | **Totals** | 159 | 36 | 44 | 80 |

**NEVILLE, Michael**  *Forward*
b. Toronto, Ont.

| Season | Club | GP | G | A | Pts. |
|---|---|---|---|---|---|
| 1917-18 | Toronto | 1 | 1 | 0 | 1 |
| 1924-25 | Toronto | 12 | 1 | 0 | 1 |
| 1925-26 | Toronto | 33 | 3 | 3 | 6 |
| 1930-31 | Toronto | 19 | 1 | 0 | 1 |
| | **Totals** | 65 | 6 | 3 | 9 |

**NEVIN, Robert Frank (Bob)**  *Forward*
b. South Porcupine, Ont., Mar. 18, 1938

| Season | Club | GP | G | A | Pts. |
|---|---|---|---|---|---|
| 1957-58 | Toronto | 4 | 0 | 0 | 0 |
| 1958-59 | Toronto | 2 | 0 | 0 | 0 |
| 1960-61 | Toronto | 68 | 21 | 37 | 58 |
| 1961-62 | Toronto | 69 | 15 | 30 | 45 |
| 1962-63 | Toronto | 58 | 12 | 21 | 33 |
| 1963-64 | Tor-NYR | 63 | 12 | 16 | 28 |
| 1964-65 | New York R | 64 | 16 | 14 | 30 |
| 1965-66 | New York R | 69 | 29 | 33 | 62 |
| 1966-67 | New York R | 67 | 20 | 24 | 44 |
| 1967-68 | New York R | 74 | 28 | 30 | 58 |
| 1968-69 | New York R | 71 | 31 | 25 | 56 |
| 1969-70 | New York R | 68 | 18 | 19 | 37 |
| 1970-71 | New York R | 78 | 21 | 25 | 46 |
| 1971-72 | Minnesota | 72 | 15 | 19 | 34 |
| 1972-73 | Minnesota | 66 | 5 | 13 | 18 |
| 1973-74 | Los Angeles | 78 | 20 | 30 | 50 |
| 1974-75 | Los Angeles | 80 | 31 | 41 | 72 |
| 1975-76 | Los Angeles | 77 | 13 | 42 | 55 |
| | **Totals** | 1128 | 307 | 419 | 726 |

| Season | Club | GP | G | A | Pts. |
|---|---|---|---|---|---|

**NEWELL, Gordon Richard (Rick)**
*Defenseman*
b. Winnipeg, Man., Feb. 18, 1948

| Season | Club | GP | G | A | Pts. |
|---|---|---|---|---|---|
| 1972-73 | Detroit | 3 | 0 | 0 | 0 |
| 1973-74 | Detroit | 3 | 0 | 0 | 0 |
| | **Totals** | 6 | 0 | 0 | 0 |

**NEWMAN, Daniel Kenneth** *Forward*
b. Windsor, Ont., Jan. 26, 1952

| Season | Club | GP | G | A | Pts. |
|---|---|---|---|---|---|
| 1976-77 | New York R | 41 | 9 | 8 | 17 |
| 1977-78 | New York R | 59 | 5 | 13 | 18 |
| 1978-79 | Montreal | 16 | 0 | 2 | 2 |
| 1979-80 | Edmonton | 10 | 3 | 1 | 4 |
| | **Totals** | 126 | 17 | 24 | 41 |

**NEWMAN, John**

| Season | Club | GP | G | A | Pts. |
|---|---|---|---|---|---|
| 1930-31 | Detroit | 10 | 1 | 1 | 2 |

**NICHOLLS, Bernie Irvine** *Forward*
b. Holiburton, Ont., June 24, 1961

| Season | Club | GP | G | A | Pts. |
|---|---|---|---|---|---|
| 1981-82 | Los Angeles | 22 | 14 | 18 | 32 |
| 1982-83 | Los Angeles | 71 | 28 | 22 | 50 |
| | **Totals** | 93 | 42 | 40 | 82 |

**NICHOLSON, Allan Douglas** *Forward*
b. Estevan, Sask., Apr. 26, 1936

| Season | Club | GP | G | A | Pts. |
|---|---|---|---|---|---|
| 1955-56 | Boston | 14 | 0 | 0 | 0 |
| 1956-57 | Boston | 5 | 0 | 1 | 1 |
| | **Totals** | 19 | 0 | 1 | 1 |

**NICHOLSON, Edward George** *Defenseman*
b. Portsmouth, Ont., Sept. 9, 1923

| Season | Club | GP | G | A | Pts. |
|---|---|---|---|---|---|
| 1947-48 | Detroit | 1 | 0 | 0 | 0 |

**NICHOLSON, Graeme Butte** *Defenseman*
b. North Bay, Ont., Jan. 13, 1955

| Season | Club | GP | G | A | Pts. |
|---|---|---|---|---|---|
| 1978-79 | Boston | 1 | 0 | 0 | 0 |
| 1981-82 | Colorado | 41 | 2 | 7 | 9 |
| | **Totals** | 42 | 2 | 7 | 9 |

**NICHOLSON, John Ivan** *Forward*
b. Charlottetown, P.E.I., Sept. 9, 1914

| Season | Club | GP | G | A | Pts. |
|---|---|---|---|---|---|
| 1937-38 | Chicago | 2 | 1 | 0 | 1 |

**NICHOLSON, Neil Andrews** *Defenseman*
b. Saint John, N.B., Sept. 12, 1949

| Season | Club | GP | G | A | Pts. |
|---|---|---|---|---|---|
| 1972-73 | New York I | 30 | 3 | 1 | 4 |
| 1973-74 | New York I | 8 | 0 | 0 | 0 |
| 1974-75 | New York I | 1 | 0 | 0 | 0 |
| | **Totals** | 39 | 3 | 1 | 4 |

**NICHOLSON, Paul** *Forward*
b. London, Ont., Feb. 16, 1954

| Season | Club | GP | G | A | Pts. |
|---|---|---|---|---|---|
| 1974-75 | Washington | 39 | 4 | 5 | 9 |
| 1975-76 | Washington | 14 | 0 | 2 | 2 |
| 1976-77 | Washington | 9 | 0 | 1 | 1 |
| | **Totals** | 62 | 4 | 8 | 12 |

**NICOLSON, Graeme** *Defenseman*
b. North Bay, Ont., July 13, 1958

| Season | Club | GP | G | A | Pts. |
|---|---|---|---|---|---|
| 1982-83 | New York R | 10 | 0 | 0 | 0 |

**NIEKAMP, James Lawrence (Jim)**
*Defenseman*
b. Detroit, Mich., Mar. 11, 1946

| Season | Club | GP | G | A | Pts. |
|---|---|---|---|---|---|
| 1970-71 | Detroit | 24 | 0 | 2 | 2 |
| 1971-72 | Detroit | 5 | 0 | 0 | 0 |
| 1972-73 | Los Angeles (WHA) | 78 | 7 | 22 | 29 |
| 1973-74 | Los Angeles (WHA) | 76 | 2 | 19 | 21 |
| 1974-75 | Phoenix (WHA) | 71 | 2 | 26 | 28 |
| 1975-76 | Phoenix (WHA) | 79 | 4 | 14 | 18 |
| 1976-77 | Phoenix (WHA) | 79 | 1 | 15 | 16 |
| | **NHL Totals** | 29 | 0 | 2 | 2 |
| | **WHA Totals** | 383 | 16 | 96 | 112 |

**NIGHBOR, Frank (Dutch)** *Forward*
b. Pembroke, Ont., Jan. 26, 1893

| Season | Club | GP | G | A | Pts. |
|---|---|---|---|---|---|
| 1917-18 | Ottawa | 9 | 11 | 0 | 11 |
| 1918-19 | Ottawa | 18 | 18 | 4 | 22 |
| 1919-20 | Ottawa | 23 | 26 | 7 | 33 |
| 1920-21 | Ottawa | 24 | 18 | 3 | 21 |
| 1921-22 | Ottawa | 20 | 8 | 8 | 16 |
| 1922-23 | Ottawa | 22 | 11 | 5 | 16 |
| 1923-24 | Ottawa | 20 | 10 | 3 | 13 |
| 1924-25 | Ottawa | 26 | 5 | 2 | 7 |
| 1925-26 | Ottawa | 35 | 12 | 13 | 25 |
| 1926-27 | Ottawa | 38 | 6 | 6 | 12 |
| 1927-28 | Ottawa | 42 | 8 | 5 | 13 |
| 1928-29 | Ottawa | 30 | 1 | 4 | 5 |
| 1929-30 | Ott-Tor | 41 | 2 | 0 | 2 |
| | **Totals** | 348 | 136 | 60 | 196 |

**NIGRO, Frank** *Forward*
b. Richmond Hill, Ont., Feb. 11, 1960

| Season | Club | GP | G | A | Pts. |
|---|---|---|---|---|---|
| 1982-83 | Toronto | 51 | 6 | 15 | 21 |

**NILAN, Christopher John** *Forward*
b. Boston, Mass., Feb. 9, 1958

| Season | Club | GP | G | A | Pts. |
|---|---|---|---|---|---|
| 1979-80 | Montreal | 15 | 0 | 2 | 2 |
| 1980-81 | Montreal | 57 | 7 | 8 | 15 |
| 1981-82 | Montreal | 49 | 7 | 4 | 11 |
| 1982-83 | Montreal | 66 | 6 | 8 | 14 |
| | **Totals** | 187 | 20 | 22 | 42 |

**NILL, James Edward** *Forward*
b. Hanna, Alta., Apr. 11, 1958

| Season | Club | GP | G | A | Pts. |
|---|---|---|---|---|---|
| 1981-82 | StL-Van | 69 | 10 | 14 | 24 |
| 1982-83 | Vancouver | 65 | 7 | 15 | 22 |
| | **Totals** | 134 | 17 | 29 | 46 |

**NILSSON, Kent** *Forward*
b. Nynashamn, Sweden, Aug. 31, 1956

| Season | Club | GP | G | A | Pts. |
|---|---|---|---|---|---|
| 1977-78 | Winnipeg (WHA) | 80 | 42 | 65 | 107 |
| 1978-79 | Winnipeg (WHA) | 78 | 39 | 68 | 107 |
| 1979-80 | Atlanta | 80 | 40 | 53 | 93 |
| 1980-81 | Calgary | 80 | 49 | 82 | 131 |
| 1981-82 | Calgary | 41 | 26 | 29 | 55 |
| 1982-83 | Calgary | 80 | 46 | 58 | 104 |
| | **NHL Totals** | 281 | 161 | 222 | 383 |
| | **WHA Totals** | 158 | 81 | 133 | 214 |

**NILSSON, Ulf Gosta** *Forward*
b. Nynashamn, Sweden, May 11, 1950

| Season | Club | GP | G | A | Pts. |
|---|---|---|---|---|---|
| 1974-75 | Winnipeg (WHA) | 78 | 26 | 94 | 120 |
| 1975-76 | Winnipeg (WHA) | 78 | 38 | 76 | 114 |
| 1976-77 | Winnipeg (WHA) | 71 | 39 | 85 | 124 |
| 1977-78 | Winnipeg (WHA) | 73 | 37 | 89 | 126 |
| 1978-79 | New York R | 59 | 27 | 39 | 66 |
| 1979-80 | New York R | 50 | 14 | 44 | 58 |
| 1980-81 | New York R | 51 | 14 | 25 | 39 |
| 1982-83 | New York R | 10 | 2 | 4 | 6 |
| | **NHL Totals** | 170 | 57 | 112 | 169 |
| | **WHA Totals** | 300 | 140 | 344 | 484 |

**NISTICO, Louis Charles** *Forward*
b. Thunder Bay, Ont., Jan. 25, 1953

| Season | Club | GP | G | A | Pts. |
|---|---|---|---|---|---|
| 1973-74 | Toronto (WHA) | 13 | 1 | 3 | 4 |
| 1974-75 | Toronto (WHA) | 29 | 11 | 11 | 22 |
| 1975-76 | Toronto (WHA) | 65 | 12 | 22 | 34 |
| 1976-77 | Birmingham (WHA) | 79 | 20 | 36 | 56 |
| 1977-78 | Colorado | 3 | 0 | 0 | 0 |
| | **NHL Totals** | 3 | 0 | 0 | 0 |
| | **WHA Totals** | 186 | 44 | 72 | 116 |

**NOBLE, Edward R. (Reg)**
*Defenseman-Forward*
b. Collingwood, Ont., June 23, 1895

| Season | Club | GP | G | A | Pts. |
|---|---|---|---|---|---|
| 1917-18 | Toronto | 20 | 28 | 0 | 28 |
| 1918-19 | Toronto | 17 | 11 | 3 | 14 |
| 1919-20 | Toronto | 24 | 24 | 7 | 31 |
| 1920-21 | Toronto | 24 | 20 | 6 | 26 |
| 1921-22 | Toronto | 24 | 17 | 8 | 25 |
| 1922-23 | Toronto | 24 | 12 | 10 | 22 |
| 1923-24 | Toronto | 23 | 12 | 3 | 15 |
| 1924-25 | Tor-MontM | 30 | 8 | 6 | 14 |
| 1925-26 | Montreal M | 33 | 9 | 9 | 18 |
| 1926-27 | Montreal M | 43 | 3 | 3 | 6 |
| 1927-28 | Detroit | 44 | 6 | 8 | 14 |
| 1928-29 | Detroit | 43 | 6 | 4 | 10 |
| 1929-30 | Detroit | 43 | 6 | 4 | 10 |
| 1930-31 | Detroit | 44 | 2 | 5 | 7 |
| 1931-32 | Detroit | 48 | 3 | 3 | 6 |
| 1932-33 | Montreal M | 25 | 0 | 0 | 0 |
| | **Totals** | 509 | 167 | 79 | 246 |

**NOEL, Claude** *Forward*
b. Kirkland Lake, Ont., Oct. 31, 1955

| Season | Club | GP | G | A | Pts. |
|---|---|---|---|---|---|
| 1979-80 | Washington | 7 | 0 | 0 | 0 |

**NOLAN, Patrick**

| Season | Club | GP | G | A | Pts. |
|---|---|---|---|---|---|
| 1921-22 | Toronto | 2 | 0 | 0 | 0 |

**NOLET, Simon Laurent** *Forward*
b. St. Odilon, Que., Nov. 23, 1941

| Season | Club | GP | G | A | Pts. |
|---|---|---|---|---|---|
| 1967-68 | Philadelphia | 4 | 0 | 0 | 0 |
| 1968-69 | Philadelphia | 35 | 4 | 10 | 14 |
| 1969-70 | Philadelphia | 56 | 22 | 22 | 44 |
| 1970-71 | Philadelphia | 74 | 9 | 19 | 28 |
| 1971-72 | Philadelphia | 67 | 23 | 20 | 43 |
| 1972-73 | Philadelphia | 70 | 16 | 20 | 36 |
| 1973-74 | Philadelphia | 52 | 19 | 17 | 36 |
| 1974-75 | Kansas City | 72 | 26 | 32 | 58 |
| 1975-76 | KC-Pitt | 80 | 19 | 23 | 42 |
| 1976-77 | Colorado | 52 | 12 | 19 | 31 |
| | **Totals** | 562 | 150 | 182 | 332 |

**NORIS, Joseph S. (Joe)** *Defenseman*
b. Denver, Colo., Oct. 26, 1951

| Season | Club | GP | G | A | Pts. |
|---|---|---|---|---|---|
| 1971-72 | Pittsburgh | 35 | 2 | 5 | 7 |
| 1972-73 | St Louis | 2 | 0 | 0 | 0 |
| 1973-74 | Buffalo | 18 | 0 | 0 | 0 |
| 1975-76 | San Diego (WHA) | 80 | 28 | 40 | 68 |
| 1976-77 | San Diego (WHA) | 73 | 35 | 57 | 92 |
| 1977-78 | Birmingham (WHA) | 45 | 9 | 19 | 28 |
| | **NHL Totals** | 55 | 2 | 5 | 7 |
| | **WHA Totals** | 198 | 72 | 116 | 188 |

**NORRISH, Rod** *Forward*
b. Saskatoon, Sask., Nov. 27, 1951

| Season | Club | GP | G | A | Pts. |
|---|---|---|---|---|---|
| 1973-74 | Minnesota | 9 | 2 | 1 | 3 |
| 1974-75 | Minnesota | 12 | 1 | 2 | 3 |
| | **Totals** | 21 | 3 | 3 | 6 |

**NORTHCOTT, Laurence (Baldy)** *Forward*
b. Calgary, Alta., Sept. 7, 1907

| Season | Club | GP | G | A | Pts. |
|---|---|---|---|---|---|
| 1928-29 | Montreal M | 5 | 0 | 0 | 0 |
| 1929-30 | Montreal M | 43 | 10 | 1 | 11 |
| 1930-31 | Montreal M | 22 | 7 | 3 | 10 |
| 1931-32 | Montreal M | 48 | 19 | 6 | 25 |
| 1932-33 | Montreal M | 48 | 22 | 21 | 43 |
| 1933-34 | Montreal | 47 | 20 | 13 | 33 |
| 1934-35 | Montreal | 47 | 9 | 14 | 23 |
| 1935-36 | Montreal M | 48 | 15 | 21 | 36 |
| 1936-37 | Montreal M | 46 | 15 | 14 | 29 |
| 1937-38 | Montreal M | 46 | 11 | 12 | 23 |
| 1938-39 | Chicago | 46 | 5 | 7 | 12 |
| | **Totals** | 446 | 133 | 112 | 245 |

**NORWICH, Craig Richard** *Defenseman*
b. New York, N.Y., Dec. 15, 1955

| Season | Club | GP | G | A | Pts. |
|---|---|---|---|---|---|
| 1977-78 | Cincinnati (WHA) | 65 | 7 | 23 | 30 |
| 1978-79 | Cincinnati (WHA) | 80 | 6 | 51 | 57 |
| 1979-80 | Winnipeg | 70 | 10 | 35 | 45 |
| 1980-81 | StL-Col | 34 | 7 | 23 | 30 |
| | **NHL Totals** | 104 | 17 | 58 | 75 |
| | **WHA Totals** | 145 | 13 | 74 | 87 |

**NORWOOD, Lee Charles** *Defenseman*
b. Oakland, Calif., Feb. 2, 1960

| Season | Club | GP | G | A | Pts. |
|---|---|---|---|---|---|
| 1980-81 | Quebec | 11 | 1 | 1 | 2 |
| 1981-82 | Que-Wash | 28 | 7 | 10 | 17 |
| 1982-83 | Washington | 8 | 0 | 1 | 1 |
| | **Totals** | 47 | 8 | 12 | 20 |

| Season | Club | GP | G | A | Pts. |
|---|---|---|---|---|---|

**NOVY, Milan** *Forward*
   b. Kladno, Czechoslovakia, Sept. 23, 1951

| Season | Club | GP | G | A | Pts. |
|---|---|---|---|---|---|
| 1982-83 | Washington | 73 | 18 | 30 | 48 |

**NOWAK, Henry Stanley** *Forward*
   b. Oshawa, Ont., Nov. 24, 1950

| Season | Club | GP | G | A | Pts. |
|---|---|---|---|---|---|
| 1973-74 | Pittsburgh | 13 | 0 | 0 | 0 |
| 1974-75 | Det-Bos | 77 | 12 | 21 | 33 |
| 1975-76 | Boston | 66 | 7 | 3 | 10 |
| 1976-77 | Boston | 24 | 7 | 5 | 12 |
| | **Totals** | 180 | 26 | 29 | 55 |

**NYKOLUK, Michael** *Forward*
   b. Toronto, Ont., Dec. 11, 1934

| Season | Club | GP | G | A | Pts. |
|---|---|---|---|---|---|
| 1956-57 | Toronto | 32 | 3 | 1 | 4 |

**NYLUND, Gary** *Defenseman*
   b. Surrey, B.C., Oct. 28, 1963

| Season | Club | GP | G | A | Pts. |
|---|---|---|---|---|---|
| 1982-83 | Toronto | 16 | 0 | 3 | 3 |

**NYROP, William** *Defenseman*
   b. Washington, D.C., July 23, 1952

| Season | Club | GP | G | A | Pts. |
|---|---|---|---|---|---|
| 1975-76 | Montreal | 19 | 0 | 3 | 3 |
| 1976-77 | Montreal | 74 | 3 | 19 | 22 |
| 1977-78 | Montreal | 72 | 5 | 21 | 26 |
| 1981-82 | Minnesota | 42 | 4 | 8 | 12 |
| | **Totals** | 207 | 12 | 51 | 63 |

**NYSTROM, Thore Robert (Bob)** *Forward*
   b. Kamloops, B.C., Oct. 10, 1952

| Season | Club | GP | G | A | Pts. |
|---|---|---|---|---|---|
| 1972-73 | New York I | 11 | 1 | 1 | 2 |
| 1973-74 | New York I | 77 | 21 | 20 | 41 |
| 1974-75 | New York I | 76 | 27 | 28 | 55 |
| 1975-76 | New York I | 80 | 23 | 25 | 48 |
| 1976-77 | New York I | 80 | 29 | 27 | 56 |
| 1977-78 | New York I | 80 | 30 | 29 | 59 |
| 1978-79 | New York I | 78 | 19 | 20 | 39 |
| 1979-80 | New York I | 67 | 21 | 18 | 39 |
| 1980-81 | New York I | 79 | 14 | 30 | 44 |
| 1981-82 | New York I | 74 | 22 | 25 | 47 |
| 1982-83 | New York I | 74 | 10 | 20 | 30 |
| | **Totals** | 776 | 217 | 243 | 460 |

**OATMAN, Warren Russell** *Forward*
   b. Tilsonburg, Ont., Feb. 19, 1905

| Season | Club | GP | G | A | Pts. |
|---|---|---|---|---|---|
| 1926-27 | Det-MontM | 39 | 11 | 4 | 15 |
| 1927-28 | Montreal M | 44 | 7 | 4 | 11 |
| 1928-29 | MontM-NYR | 38 | 2 | 1 | 3 |
| | **Totals** | 121 | 20 | 9 | 29 |

**O'BRIEN, Dennis Francis** *Defenseman*
   b. Port Hope, Ont., June 10, 1949

| Season | Club | GP | G | A | Pts. |
|---|---|---|---|---|---|
| 1970-71 | Minnesota | 27 | 3 | 2 | 5 |
| 1971-72 | Minnesota | 70 | 3 | 6 | 9 |
| 1972-73 | Minnesota | 74 | 3 | 11 | 14 |
| 1973-74 | Minnesota | 77 | 5 | 12 | 17 |
| 1974-75 | Minnesota | 56 | 6 | 10 | 16 |
| 1975-76 | Minnesota | 78 | 1 | 14 | 15 |
| 1976-77 | Minnesota | 75 | 6 | 18 | 24 |
| 1977-78 | Minn-Col-Clev-Bos | 68 | 2 | 10 | 12 |
| 1978-79 | Boston | 64 | 2 | 8 | 10 |
| 1979-80 | Boston | 3 | 0 | 0 | 0 |
| | **Totals** | 592 | 31 | 91 | 122 |

**O'BRIEN, Ellard John (Obie)**
*Defenseman-Forward*
   b. St. Catharines, Ont., May 27, 1930

| Season | Club | GP | G | A | Pts. |
|---|---|---|---|---|---|
| 1955-56 | Boston | 2 | 0 | 0 | 0 |

**O'CALLAHAN, Jack** *Defenseman*
   b. Charleston, Mass., July 24, 1957

| Season | Club | GP | G | A | Pts. |
|---|---|---|---|---|---|
| 1982-83 | Chicago | 39 | 0 | 11 | 11 |

**O'CONNELL, Michael Thomas** *Defenseman*
   b. Chicago, Ill., Nov. 25, 1955

| Season | Club | GP | G | A | Pts. |
|---|---|---|---|---|---|
| 1977-78 | Chicago | 6 | 1 | 1 | 2 |
| 1978-79 | Chicago | 48 | 4 | 22 | 26 |
| 1979-80 | Chicago | 78 | 8 | 22 | 30 |
| 1980-81 | Chi-Bos | 82 | 15 | 38 | 53 |

---

| Season | Club | GP | G | A | Pts. |
|---|---|---|---|---|---|
| 1981-82 | Boston | 80 | 5 | 34 | 39 |
| 1982-83 | Boston | 80 | 14 | 39 | 53 |
| | **Totals** | 374 | 47 | 156 | 203 |

**O'CONNOR, Herbert William (Buddy)** *Forward*
   b. Montreal, Que., June 21, 1916

| Season | Club | GP | G | A | Pts. |
|---|---|---|---|---|---|
| 1941-42 | Montreal | 36 | 9 | 16 | 25 |
| 1942-43 | Montreal | 50 | 15 | 43 | 58 |
| 1943-44 | Montreal | 44 | 12 | 42 | 54 |
| 1944-45 | Montreal | 50 | 21 | 23 | 44 |
| 1945-46 | Montreal | 45 | 11 | 11 | 22 |
| 1946-47 | Montreal | 46 | 10 | 20 | 30 |
| 1947-48 | New York R | 60 | 24 | 36 | 60 |
| 1948-49 | New York R | 46 | 11 | 24 | 35 |
| 1949-50 | New York R | 66 | 11 | 22 | 33 |
| 1950-51 | New York R | 66 | 16 | 20 | 36 |
| | **Totals** | 509 | 140 | 257 | 397 |

**ODDLEIFSON, Christopher Roy (Chris)** *Forward*
   b. Brandon, Man., Sept. 7, 1950

| Season | Club | GP | G | A | Pts. |
|---|---|---|---|---|---|
| 1972-73 | Boston | 6 | 0 | 0 | 0 |
| 1973-74 | Bos-Van | 70 | 13 | 16 | 29 |
| 1974-75 | Vancouver | 60 | 16 | 35 | 51 |
| 1975-76 | Vancouver | 80 | 16 | 46 | 62 |
| 1976-77 | Vancouver | 80 | 14 | 26 | 40 |
| 1977-78 | Vancouver | 78 | 17 | 22 | 39 |
| 1978-79 | Vancouver | 67 | 11 | 26 | 37 |
| 1979-80 | Vancouver | 75 | 8 | 20 | 28 |
| 1980-81 | Vancouver | 8 | 0 | 0 | 0 |
| | **Totals** | 524 | 95 | 191 | 286 |

**O'DONNELL, Frederick James (Fred)** *Forward*
   b. Kingston, Ont., Dec. 6, 1949

| Season | Club | GP | G | A | Pts. |
|---|---|---|---|---|---|
| 1972-73 | Boston | 72 | 10 | 4 | 14 |
| 1973-74 | Boston | 43 | 5 | 7 | 12 |
| 1974-75 | New England (WHA) | 76 | 21 | 15 | 36 |
| 1975-76 | New England (WHA) | 79 | 11 | 11 | 22 |
| | **NHL Totals** | 115 | 15 | 11 | 26 |
| | **WHA Totals** | 155 | 32 | 26 | 58 |

**O'DONOGHUE, Donald Francis (Don)** *Forward*
   b. Kingston, Ont., Aug. 27, 1949

| Season | Club | GP | G | A | Pts. |
|---|---|---|---|---|---|
| 1969-70 | Oakland | 68 | 5 | 6 | 11 |
| 1970-71 | California | 43 | 11 | 9 | 20 |
| 1971-72 | California | 14 | 2 | 2 | 4 |
| 1972-73 | Philadelphia (WHA) | 74 | 16 | 23 | 39 |
| 1973-74 | Vancouver (WHA) | 49 | 8 | 6 | 14 |
| 1974-75 | Vancouver (WHA) | 4 | 0 | 0 | 0 |
| | **NHL Totals** | 125 | 18 | 17 | 35 |
| | **WHA Totals** | 127 | 24 | 29 | 53 |

**ODROWSKI, Gerald Bernard**
*Defenseman-Forward*
   b. Trout Creek, Ont., Oct. 4, 1938

| Season | Club | GP | G | A | Pts. |
|---|---|---|---|---|---|
| 1960-61 | Detroit | 68 | 1 | 4 | 5 |
| 1961-62 | Detroit | 69 | 1 | 6 | 7 |
| 1962-63 | Detroit | 1 | 0 | 0 | 0 |
| 1967-68 | Oakland | 42 | 4 | 6 | 10 |
| 1968-69 | Oakland | 74 | 5 | 1 | 6 |
| 1971-72 | St Louis | 55 | 1 | 2 | 3 |
| 1972-73 | Los Angeles (WHA) | 78 | 6 | 31 | 37 |
| 1973-74 | Los Angeles (WHA) | 77 | 4 | 32 | 36 |
| 1974-75 | Phoenix (WHA) | 77 | 5 | 38 | 43 |
| | **NHL Totals** | 309 | 12 | 19 | 31 |
| | **WHA Totals** | 232 | 15 | 101 | 116 |

**O'FLAHERTY, Gerard Joseph** *Forward*
   b. Pittsburgh, Pa., Aug. 31, 1950

| Season | Club | GP | G | A | Pts. |
|---|---|---|---|---|---|
| 1971-72 | Toronto | 2 | 0 | 0 | 0 |
| 1972-73 | Vancouver | 78 | 13 | 17 | 30 |
| 1973-74 | Vancouver | 78 | 22 | 20 | 42 |
| 1974-75 | Vancouver | 80 | 25 | 17 | 42 |
| 1975-76 | Vancouver | 68 | 20 | 18 | 38 |
| 1976-77 | Vancouver | 72 | 12 | 12 | 24 |
| 1977-78 | Vancouver | 59 | 6 | 11 | 17 |
| 1978-79 | Atlanta | 1 | 1 | 0 | 1 |
| | **Totals** | 438 | 99 | 95 | 194 |

---

**O'FLAHERTY, John Benedict (Peanuts)**
*Forward*
   b. Toronto, Ont., Apr. 10, 1918

| Season | Club | GP | G | A | Pts. |
|---|---|---|---|---|---|
| 1940-41 | New York A | — | 4 | 0 | 4 |
| 1941-42 | Brooklyn | 11 | 1 | 1 | 2 |
| | **Totals** | — | 5 | 1 | 6 |

**OGILVIE, Brian Hugh** *Forward*
   b. Stettler, Alta., Jan. 30, 1952

| Season | Club | GP | G | A | Pts. |
|---|---|---|---|---|---|
| 1972-73 | Chicago | 12 | 1 | 2 | 3 |
| 1974-75 | St Louis | 20 | 5 | 5 | 10 |
| 1975-76 | St Louis | 9 | 2 | 1 | 3 |
| 1976-77 | St Louis | 3 | 0 | 0 | 0 |
| 1977-78 | St Louis | 32 | 6 | 8 | 14 |
| 1978-79 | St Louis | 14 | 1 | 5 | 6 |
| | **Totals** | 90 | 15 | 21 | 36 |

**O'GRADY, George**

| Season | Club | GP | G | A | Pts. |
|---|---|---|---|---|---|
| 1917-18 | Montreal W | 4 | 0 | 0 | 0 |

**OGRODNICK, John Alexander** *Forward*
   b. Ottawa, Ont., June 20, 1959

| Season | Club | GP | G | A | Pts. |
|---|---|---|---|---|---|
| 1979-80 | Detroit | 41 | 8 | 24 | 32 |
| 1980-81 | Detroit | 80 | 35 | 35 | 70 |
| 1981-82 | Detroit | 80 | 28 | 26 | 54 |
| 1982-83 | Detroit | 80 | 41 | 44 | 85 |
| | **Totals** | 281 | 122 | 129 | 251 |

**OLIVER, Harold (Harry)** *Forward*
   b. Selkirk, Man., Oct. 26, 1898

| Season | Club | GP | G | A | Pts. |
|---|---|---|---|---|---|
| 1926-27 | Boston | 42 | 18 | 6 | 24 |
| 1927-28 | Boston | 43 | 13 | 5 | 18 |
| 1928-29 | Boston | 43 | 17 | 6 | 23 |
| 1929-30 | Boston | 40 | 16 | 5 | 21 |
| 1930-31 | Boston | 44 | 16 | 14 | 30 |
| 1931-32 | Boston | 42 | 13 | 7 | 20 |
| 1932-33 | Boston | 47 | 11 | 7 | 18 |
| 1933-34 | Boston | 48 | 5 | 9 | 14 |
| 1934-35 | New York A | 47 | 7 | 9 | 16 |
| 1935-36 | New York A | 45 | 9 | 16 | 25 |
| 1936-37 | New York A | 20 | 2 | 1 | 3 |
| | **Totals** | 461 | 127 | 85 | 212 |

**OLIVER, Murray Clifford** *Forward*
   b. Hamilton, Ont., Nov. 14, 1937

| Season | Club | GP | G | A | Pts. |
|---|---|---|---|---|---|
| 1957-58 | Detroit | 1 | 0 | 1 | 1 |
| 1959-60 | Detroit | 54 | 20 | 19 | 39 |
| 1960-61 | Det-Bos | 70 | 17 | 22 | 39 |
| 1961-62 | Boston | 70 | 17 | 29 | 46 |
| 1962-63 | Boston | 65 | 22 | 40 | 62 |
| 1963-64 | Boston | 70 | 24 | 44 | 68 |
| 1964-65 | Boston | 65 | 20 | 23 | 43 |
| 1965-66 | Boston | 70 | 18 | 42 | 60 |
| 1966-67 | Boston | 65 | 9 | 26 | 35 |
| 1967-68 | Toronto | 74 | 16 | 21 | 37 |
| 1968-69 | Toronto | 76 | 14 | 36 | 50 |
| 1969-70 | Toronto | 76 | 14 | 33 | 47 |
| 1970-71 | Minnesota | 61 | 9 | 23 | 32 |
| 1971-72 | Minnesota | 77 | 27 | 29 | 56 |
| 1972-73 | Minnesota | 75 | 11 | 31 | 42 |
| 1973-74 | Minnesota | 78 | 17 | 20 | 37 |
| 1974-75 | Minnesota | 80 | 19 | 15 | 34 |
| | **Totals** | 1127 | 274 | 454 | 728 |

**OLMSTEAD, Murray Bert** *Forward*
   b. Scepter, Sask., Sept. 4, 1926

| Season | Club | GP | G | A | Pts. |
|---|---|---|---|---|---|
| 1948-49 | Chicago | 9 | 0 | 2 | 2 |
| 1949-50 | Chicago | 70 | 20 | 29 | 49 |
| 1950-51 | Chi-Mont | 54 | 18 | 23 | 41 |
| 1951-52 | Montreal | 69 | 7 | 28 | 35 |
| 1952-53 | Montreal | 69 | 17 | 28 | 45 |
| 1953-54 | Montreal | 70 | 15 | 37 | 52 |
| 1954-55 | Montreal | 70 | 10 | 48 | 58 |
| 1955-56 | Montreal | 70 | 14 | 56 | 70 |
| 1956-57 | Montreal | 64 | 15 | 33 | 48 |
| 1957-58 | Montreal | 57 | 9 | 28 | 37 |
| 1958-59 | Toronto | 70 | 10 | 31 | 41 |
| 1959-60 | Toronto | 53 | 15 | 21 | 36 |

| Season | Club | GP | G | A | Pts. |
|---|---|---|---|---|---|
| 1960-61 | Toronto | 67 | 18 | 34 | 52 |
| 1961-62 | Toronto | 56 | 13 | 23 | 36 |
| | **Totals** | 848 | 181 | 421 | 602 |

**OLSON, Dennis** *Forward*
b. Kenora, Ont., Nov. 9, 1934

| Season | Club | GP | G | A | Pts. |
|---|---|---|---|---|---|
| 1957-58 | Detroit | 4 | 0 | 0 | 0 |

**O'NEIL, Paul Joseph** *Forward*
b. Charlestown, Mass., Aug. 24, 1953

| Season | Club | GP | G | A | Pts. |
|---|---|---|---|---|---|
| 1973-74 | Vancouver | 5 | 0 | 0 | 0 |
| 1975-76 | Boston | 1 | 0 | 0 | 0 |
| | **Totals** | 6 | 0 | 0 | 0 |

**O'NEILL, James Beaton (Peggy)** *Forward*
b. Semans, Sask., Apr. 3, 1913

| Season | Club | GP | G | A | Pts. |
|---|---|---|---|---|---|
| 1933-34 | Boston | 23 | 2 | 2 | 4 |
| 1934-35 | Boston | 48 | 2 | 11 | 13 |
| 1935-36 | Boston | 48 | 2 | 11 | 13 |
| 1936-37 | Boston | 21 | 0 | 2 | 2 |
| 1940-41 | Montreal | 12 | 0 | 3 | 3 |
| 1941-42 | Montreal | 4 | 0 | 1 | 1 |
| | **Totals** | 156 | 6 | 30 | 36 |

**O'NEILL, Thomas (Windy)** *Forward*
b. Deseronto, Ont., Sept. 28, 1923

| Season | Club | GP | G | A | Pts. |
|---|---|---|---|---|---|
| 1943-44 | Toronto | 33 | 8 | 7 | 15 |
| 1944-45 | Toronto | 33 | 2 | 5 | 7 |
| | **Totals** | 66 | 10 | 12 | 22 |

**ORBAN, William Terrence** *Forward*
b. Regina, Sask., Feb. 20, 1944

| Season | Club | GP | G | A | Pts. |
|---|---|---|---|---|---|
| 1967-68 | Chicago | 39 | 3 | 2 | 5 |
| 1968-69 | Chi-Minn | 66 | 5 | 11 | 16 |
| 1969-70 | Minnesota | 9 | 0 | 2 | 2 |
| | **Totals** | 114 | 8 | 15 | 23 |

**O'REE, William Eldon (Willie)** *Forward*
b. Fredericton, N.B., Oct. 15, 1935

| Season | Club | GP | G | A | Pts. |
|---|---|---|---|---|---|
| 1957-58 | Boston | 2 | 0 | 0 | 0 |
| 1960-61 | Boston | 43 | 4 | 10 | 14 |
| | **Totals** | 45 | 4 | 10 | 14 |

**O'REILLY, Joseph James Terrence (Terry)**
*Forward*
b. Niagara Falls, Ont., June 7, 1951

| Season | Club | GP | G | A | Pts. |
|---|---|---|---|---|---|
| 1971-72 | Boston | 1 | 1 | 0 | 1 |
| 1972-73 | Boston | 72 | 5 | 22 | 27 |
| 1973-74 | Boston | 76 | 11 | 24 | 35 |
| 1974-75 | Boston | 68 | 15 | 20 | 35 |
| 1975-76 | Boston | 80 | 23 | 27 | 50 |
| 1976-77 | Boston | 79 | 14 | 41 | 55 |
| 1977-78 | Boston | 77 | 29 | 61 | 90 |
| 1978-79 | Boston | 80 | 26 | 51 | 77 |
| 1979-80 | Boston | 71 | 19 | 42 | 61 |
| 1980-81 | Boston | 77 | 8 | 35 | 43 |
| 1981-82 | Boston | 70 | 22 | 30 | 52 |
| 1982-83 | Boston | 19 | 6 | 14 | 20 |
| | **Totals** | 770 | 179 | 367 | 546 |

**ORLANDO, James** *Defenseman*
b. Montreal, Que., Feb. 27, 1916

| Season | Club | GP | G | A | Pts. |
|---|---|---|---|---|---|
| 1936-37 | Detroit | 9 | 0 | 1 | 1 |
| 1937-38 | Detroit | 6 | 0 | 0 | 0 |
| 1939-40 | Detroit | 48 | 1 | 3 | 4 |
| 1940-41 | Detroit | 48 | 1 | 10 | 11 |
| 1941-42 | Detroit | 48 | 1 | 7 | 8 |
| 1942-43 | Detroit | 40 | 3 | 4 | 7 |
| | **Totals** | 199 | 6 | 25 | 31 |

**ORLESKI, David Eugene** *Forward*
b. Edmonton, Alta., Dec. 26, 1959

| Season | Club | GP | G | A | Pts. |
|---|---|---|---|---|---|
| 1980-81 | Montreal | 1 | 0 | 0 | 0 |
| 1981-82 | Montreal | 1 | 0 | 0 | 0 |
| | **Totals** | 2 | 0 | 0 | 0 |

**ORR, Robert Gordon (Bobby)** *Defenseman*
b. Parry Sound, Ont., Mar. 20, 1948

| Season | Club | GP | G | A | Pts. |
|---|---|---|---|---|---|
| 1966-67 | Boston | 61 | 13 | 28 | 41 |
| 1967-68 | Boston | 46 | 11 | 20 | 31 |
| 1968-69 | Boston | 67 | 21 | 43 | 64 |
| 1969-70 | Boston | 76 | 33 | 87 | 120 |
| 1970-71 | Boston | 78 | 37 | 102 | 139 |
| 1971-72 | Boston | 76 | 37 | 80 | 117 |
| 1972-73 | Boston | 63 | 29 | 72 | 101 |
| 1973-74 | Boston | 74 | 32 | 90 | 122 |
| 1974-75 | Boston | 80 | 46 | 89 | 135 |
| 1975-76 | Boston | 10 | 5 | 13 | 18 |
| 1976-77 | Chicago | 20 | 4 | 19 | 23 |
| 1978-79 | Chicago | 6 | 2 | 2 | 4 |
| | **Totals** | 657 | 270 | 645 | 915 |

**OSBORNE, Mark Anatole** *Forward*
b. Toronto, Ont., Aug. 13, 1961

| Season | Club | GP | G | A | Pts. |
|---|---|---|---|---|---|
| 1981-82 | Detroit | 80 | 26 | 41 | 67 |
| 1982-83 | Detroit | 80 | 19 | 24 | 43 |
| | **Totals** | 160 | 45 | 65 | 110 |

**OSBURN, Randoulf Allan** *Forward*
b. Collingwood, Ont., Nov. 26, 1952

| Season | Club | GP | G | A | Pts. |
|---|---|---|---|---|---|
| 1972-73 | Toronto | 26 | 0 | 2 | 2 |
| 1974-75 | Philadelphia | 1 | 0 | 0 | 0 |
| | **Totals** | 27 | 0 | 2 | 2 |

**O'SHEA, Daniel Patrick (Danny)** *Forward*
b. Toronto, Ont., June 15, 1945

| Season | Club | GP | G | A | Pts. |
|---|---|---|---|---|---|
| 1968-69 | Minnesota | 74 | 15 | 34 | 49 |
| 1969-70 | Minnesota | 75 | 10 | 24 | 34 |
| 1970-71 | Minn-Chi | 77 | 18 | 19 | 37 |
| 1971-72 | Chi-StL | 68 | 9 | 12 | 21 |
| 1972-73 | St Louis | 76 | 12 | 26 | 38 |
| 1974-75 | Minnesota (WHA) | 76 | 16 | 25 | 41 |
| | **NHL Totals** | 370 | 64 | 115 | 179 |
| | **WHA Totals** | 76 | 16 | 25 | 41 |

**O'SHEA, Kevin William** *Forward*
b. Toronto, Ont., May 28, 1947

| Season | Club | GP | G | A | Pts. |
|---|---|---|---|---|---|
| 1970-71 | Buffalo | 41 | 4 | 4 | 8 |
| 1971-72 | Buf-StL | 56 | 6 | 9 | 15 |
| 1972-73 | St Louis | 36 | 3 | 5 | 8 |
| 1974-75 | Minnesota (WHA) | 68 | 10 | 10 | 20 |
| | **NHL Totals** | 133 | 13 | 18 | 31 |
| | **WHA Totals** | 68 | 10 | 10 | 20 |

**OUELLETTE, Adelard (Eddie)** *Forward*
b. Ottawa, Ont., Mar. 9, 1911

| Season | Club | GP | G | A | Pts. |
|---|---|---|---|---|---|
| 1935-36 | Chicago | — | 3 | 2 | 5 |

**OUELLETTE, Gerald Adrian** *Forward*
b. Grand Falls, NB., Nov. 1, 1938

| Season | Club | GP | G | A | Pts. |
|---|---|---|---|---|---|
| 1960-61 | Boston | 34 | 5 | 4 | 9 |

**OWCHAR, Dennis** *Defenseman*
b. Dryden, Ont., Mar. 28, 1953

| Season | Club | GP | G | A | Pts. |
|---|---|---|---|---|---|
| 1974-75 | Pittsburgh | 46 | 6 | 11 | 17 |
| 1975-76 | Pittsburgh | 54 | 5 | 12 | 17 |
| 1976-77 | Pittsburgh | 46 | 5 | 18 | 23 |
| 1977-78 | Pitt-Col | 82 | 10 | 31 | 41 |
| 1978-79 | Colorado | 50 | 3 | 13 | 16 |
| 1979-80 | Colorado | 10 | 1 | 0 | 1 |
| | **Totals** | 288 | 30 | 85 | 115 |

**PADDOCK, Alvin John** *Forward*
b. Brandon, Man., June 9, 1954

| Season | Club | GP | G | A | Pts. |
|---|---|---|---|---|---|
| 1975-76 | Washington | 8 | 1 | 1 | 2 |
| 1976-77 | Philadelphia | 5 | 0 | 0 | 0 |
| 1979-80 | Philadelphia | 32 | 3 | 7 | 10 |
| 1980-81 | Quebec | 32 | 2 | 5 | 7 |
| 1982-83 | Philadelphia | 10 | 2 | 1 | 3 |
| | **Totals** | 87 | 8 | 14 | 22 |

**PACHAL, Clayton** *Forward*
b. Yorkton, Sask., Apr. 21, 1956

| Season | Club | GP | G | A | Pts. |
|---|---|---|---|---|---|
| 1976-77 | Boston | 1 | 0 | 0 | 0 |
| 1977-78 | Boston | 10 | 0 | 0 | 0 |
| 1978-79 | Colorado | 24 | 2 | 3 | 5 |
| | **Totals** | 35 | 2 | 3 | 5 |

**PAIEMENT, Rosaire** *Forward*
b. Earlton, Ont., Aug. 12, 1945

| Season | Club | GP | G | A | Pts. |
|---|---|---|---|---|---|
| 1967-68 | Philadelphia | 7 | 1 | 0 | 1 |
| 1968-69 | Philadelphia | 27 | 2 | 4 | 6 |
| 1969-70 | Philadelphia | 9 | 1 | 1 | 2 |
| 1970-71 | Vancouver | 78 | 34 | 28 | 62 |
| 1971-72 | Vancouver | 69 | 10 | 19 | 29 |
| 1972-73 | Chicago (WHA) | 78 | 33 | 36 | 69 |
| 1973-74 | Chicago (WHA) | 78 | 30 | 43 | 73 |
| 1974-75 | Chicago (WHA) | 78 | 26 | 48 | 74 |
| 1975-76 | New England (WHA) | 80 | 28 | 43 | 71 |
| 1976-77 | NE-Ind (WHA) | 80 | 23 | 27 | 50 |
| 1977-78 | Indianapolis (WHA) | 61 | 6 | 24 | 30 |
| | **NHL Totals** | 190 | 48 | 52 | 100 |
| | **WHA Totals** | 455 | 146 | 221 | 367 |

**PAIEMENT, Wilfrid, Jr.** *Forward*
b. Earlton, Ont., Oct. 16, 1955

| Season | Club | GP | G | A | Pts. |
|---|---|---|---|---|---|
| 1974-75 | Kansas City | 78 | 26 | 13 | 39 |
| 1975-76 | Kansas City | 57 | 21 | 22 | 43 |
| 1976-77 | Colorado | 78 | 41 | 40 | 81 |
| 1977-78 | Colorado | 80 | 31 | 56 | 87 |
| 1978-79 | Colorado | 65 | 24 | 36 | 60 |
| 1979-80 | Col-Tor | 75 | 30 | 44 | 74 |
| 1980-81 | Toronto | 77 | 40 | 57 | 97 |
| 1981-82 | Tor-Que | 77 | 25 | 46 | 71 |
| 1982-83 | Quebec | 80 | 26 | 38 | 64 |
| | **Totals** | 667 | 264 | 352 | 616 |

**PALANGIO, Peter** *Forward*
b. North Bay, Ont., Sept. 10, 1909

| Season | Club | GP | G | A | Pts. |
|---|---|---|---|---|---|
| 1926-27 | Montreal | 6 | 0 | 0 | 0 |
| 1927-28 | Detroit | 14 | 3 | 0 | 3 |
| 1928-29 | Montreal | 2 | 0 | 0 | 0 |
| 1936-37 | Chicago | 30 | 8 | 9 | 17 |
| 1937-38 | Chicago | 19 | 2 | 1 | 3 |
| | **Totals** | 71 | 13 | 10 | 23 |

**PALAZZARI, Aldo** *Forward*
b. Eveleth, Minn., July 25, 1918

| Season | Club | GP | G | A | Pts. |
|---|---|---|---|---|---|
| 1943-44 | Bos-NYR | 35 | 8 | 3 | 11 |

**PALAZZARI, Douglas John** *Forward*
b. Eveleth, Minn., Nov. 3, 1952

| Season | Club | GP | G | A | Pts. |
|---|---|---|---|---|---|
| 1974-75 | St Louis | 73 | 14 | 17 | 31 |
| 1976-77 | St Louis | 12 | 1 | 0 | 1 |
| 1977-78 | St Louis | 3 | 1 | 0 | 1 |
| 1978-79 | St Louis | 20 | 2 | 3 | 5 |
| | **Totals** | 108 | 18 | 20 | 38 |

**PALMER, Brad Donald** *Forward*
b. Duncan, B.C., Sept. 14, 1961

| Season | Club | GP | G | A | Pts. |
|---|---|---|---|---|---|
| 1980-81 | Minnesota | 23 | 4 | 4 | 8 |
| 1981-82 | Minnesota | 72 | 22 | 23 | 45 |
| 1982-83 | Boston | 73 | 6 | 11 | 17 |
| | **Totals** | 168 | 32 | 38 | 70 |

**PALMER, Robert Ross** *Defenseman*
b. Sarnia, Ont., Sept. 10, 1956

| Season | Club | GP | G | A | Pts. |
|---|---|---|---|---|---|
| 1977-78 | Los Angeles | 48 | 0 | 3 | 3 |
| 1978-79 | Los Angeles | 78 | 4 | 41 | 45 |
| 1979-80 | Los Angeles | 78 | 4 | 36 | 40 |
| 1980-81 | Los Angeles | 13 | 0 | 4 | 4 |
| 1981-82 | Los Angeles | 5 | 0 | 2 | 2 |
| 1982-83 | New Jersey | 60 | 1 | 10 | 11 |
| | **Totals** | 282 | 9 | 96 | 105 |

**PANAGABKO, Edwin Arnold** *Forward*
b. Norquay, Sask., May 17, 1934

| Season | Club | GP | G | A | Pts. |
|---|---|---|---|---|---|
| 1955-56 | Boston | 28 | 0 | 3 | 3 |
| 1956-57 | Boston | 1 | 0 | 0 | 0 |
| | **Totals** | 29 | 0 | 3 | 3 |

**PAPIKE, Joseph** *Forward*
b. Eveleth, Minn., Mar. 28, 1915

| Season | Club | GP | G | A | Pts. |
|---|---|---|---|---|---|
| 1940-41 | Chicago | 9 | 2 | 2 | 4 |
| 1941-42 | Chicago | 9 | 1 | 0 | 1 |
| 1944-45 | Chicago | 2 | 0 | 1 | 1 |
| | **Totals** | 20 | 3 | 3 | 6 |

**PAPPIN, James Joseph (Jim)** *Forward*
b. Copper Cliff, Ont., Sept. 10, 1939

| Season | Club | GP | G | A | Pts. |
|---|---|---|---|---|---|
| 1963-64 | Toronto | 50 | 11 | 8 | 19 |
| 1964-65 | Toronto | 44 | 9 | 9 | 18 |
| 1965-66 | Toronto | 7 | 0 | 3 | 3 |
| 1966-67 | Toronto | 64 | 21 | 11 | 32 |
| 1967-68 | Toronto | 58 | 13 | 15 | 28 |
| 1968-69 | Chicago | 75 | 30 | 40 | 70 |
| 1969-70 | Chicago | 66 | 28 | 25 | 53 |
| 1970-71 | Chicago | 58 | 22 | 23 | 45 |
| 1971-72 | Chicago | 64 | 27 | 21 | 48 |
| 1972-73 | Chicago | 76 | 41 | 51 | 92 |
| 1973-74 | Chicago | 78 | 32 | 41 | 73 |
| 1974-75 | Chicago | 71 | 36 | 27 | 63 |
| 1975-76 | California | 32 | 6 | 13 | 19 |
| 1976-77 | Cleveland | 24 | 2 | 8 | 10 |
| | **Totals** | 767 | 278 | 295 | 573 |

**PARADISE, Robert Harvey (Bob)**
*Defenseman*
b. St. Paul, Minn., Apr. 22, 1944

| Season | Club | GP | G | A | Pts. |
|---|---|---|---|---|---|
| 1971-72 | Minnesota | 6 | 0 | 0 | 0 |
| 1972-73 | Atlanta | 71 | 1 | 7 | 8 |
| 1973-74 | Atl-Pitt | 56 | 2 | 8 | 10 |
| 1974-75 | Pittsburgh | 78 | 3 | 15 | 18 |
| 1975-76 | Pitt-Wash | 57 | 0 | 8 | 8 |
| 1976-77 | Washington | 22 | 0 | 5 | 5 |
| 1977-78 | Pittsburgh | 64 | 2 | 10 | 12 |
| 1978-79 | Pittsburgh | 14 | 0 | 1 | 1 |
| | **Totals** | 368 | 8 | 54 | 62 |

**PARGETER, George William** *Forward*
b. Calgary, Alta., Feb. 24, 1923

| Season | Club | GP | G | A | Pts. |
|---|---|---|---|---|---|
| 1946-57 | Montreal | 4 | 0 | 0 | 0 |

**PARISE, Jean Paul (JP)** *Forward*
b. Smooth Rock Falls, Ont., Dec. 11, 1941

| Season | Club | GP | G | A | Pts. |
|---|---|---|---|---|---|
| 1965-66 | Boston | 3 | 0 | 0 | 0 |
| 1966-67 | Boston | 18 | 2 | 2 | 4 |
| 1967-68 | Tor-Minn | 44 | 11 | 17 | 29 |
| 1968-69 | Minnesota | 76 | 22 | 27 | 49 |
| 1969-70 | Minnesota | 74 | 24 | 48 | 72 |
| 1970-71 | Minnesota | 73 | 11 | 23 | 34 |
| 1971-72 | Minnesota | 71 | 19 | 18 | 37 |
| 1972-73 | Minnesota | 78 | 27 | 48 | 75 |
| 1973-74 | Minnesota | 78 | 18 | 37 | 55 |
| 1974-75 | Minn-NYI | 79 | 23 | 32 | 55 |
| 1975-76 | New York I | 80 | 22 | 35 | 57 |
| 1976-77 | New York I | 80 | 25 | 31 | 56 |
| 1977-78 | NYI-Clev | 79 | 21 | 29 | 50 |
| 1978-79 | Minnesota | 57 | 13 | 9 | 22 |
| | **Totals** | 890 | 238 | 356 | 594 |

**PARIZEAU, Michel Gerard (Mike)** *Forward*
b. Montreal, Que., Apr. 9, 1948

| Season | Club | GP | G | A | Pts. |
|---|---|---|---|---|---|
| 1971-72 | StL-Phil | 58 | 3 | 14 | 17 |
| 1972-73 | Quebec (WHA) | 75 | 25 | 48 | 73 |
| 1973-74 | Quebec (WHA) | 78 | 26 | 34 | 60 |
| 1974-75 | Quebec (WHA) | 78 | 28 | 46 | 74 |
| 1975-76 | Que-Ind (WHA) | 81 | 25 | 42 | 67 |
| 1976-77 | Indianapolis (WHA) | 75 | 18 | 37 | 55 |
| 1977-78 | Indianapolis (WHA) | 70 | 13 | 27 | 40 |
| 1978-79 | Ind-Cin (WHA) | 52 | 7 | 18 | 25 |
| | **NHL Totals** | 58 | 3 | 14 | 17 |
| | **WHA Totals** | 509 | 145 | 252 | 394 |

**PARK, Douglas Bradford (Brad)** *Defenseman*
b. Toronto, Ont., July 6, 1948

| Season | Club | GP | G | A | Pts. |
|---|---|---|---|---|---|
| 1968-69 | New York R | 54 | 3 | 23 | 26 |
| 1969-70 | New York R | 60 | 11 | 26 | 37 |
| 1970-71 | New York R | 68 | 7 | 37 | 44 |
| 1971-72 | New York R | 75 | 24 | 49 | 73 |
| 1972-73 | New York R | 52 | 10 | 43 | 53 |
| 1973-74 | New York R | 78 | 25 | 57 | 82 |
| 1974-75 | New York R | 65 | 13 | 44 | 57 |
| 1975-76 | NYR-Bos | 56 | 18 | 41 | 59 |
| 1976-77 | Boston | 77 | 12 | 55 | 67 |
| 1977-78 | Boston | 80 | 22 | 57 | 79 |


| Season | Club | GP | G | A | Pts. |
|---|---|---|---|---|---|
| 1978-79 | Boston | 40 | 7 | 32 | 39 |
| 1979-80 | Boston | 32 | 5 | 16 | 21 |
| 1980-81 | Boston | 78 | 14 | 52 | 66 |
| 1981-82 | Boston | 75 | 14 | 42 | 56 |
| 1982-83 | Boston | 76 | 10 | 26 | 36 |
| | **Totals** | 966 | 195 | 600 | 795 |

**PARKES, Ernest (Ernie)** *Forward*

| Season | Club | GP | G | A | Pts. |
|---|---|---|---|---|---|
| 1924-25 | Montreal | 17 | 0 | 0 | 0 |

**PARSON, George** *Forward*
b. Toronto, Ont., June 28, 1914

| Season | Club | GP | G | A | Pts. |
|---|---|---|---|---|---|
| 1936-37 | Toronto ML | 5 | 0 | 0 | 0 |
| 1937-38 | Toronto | 30 | 5 | 6 | 11 |
| 1938-39 | Toronto | 43 | 7 | 7 | 14 |
| | **Totals** | 78 | 12 | 13 | 25 |

**PATERSON, Joseph** *Forward*
b. Toronto, Ont., June 25, 1960

| Season | Club | GP | G | A | Pts. |
|---|---|---|---|---|---|
| 1980-81 | Detroit | 38 | 2 | 5 | 7 |
| 1981-82 | Detroit | 3 | 0 | 0 | 0 |
| 1982-83 | Detroit | 33 | 2 | 1 | 3 |
| | **Totals** | 74 | 4 | 6 | 10 |

**PATERSON, Mark** *Defenseman*
b. Ottawa, Ont., Feb. 22, 1964

| Season | Club | GP | G | A | Pts. |
|---|---|---|---|---|---|
| 1982-83 | Hartford | 2 | 0 | 0 | 0 |

**PATERSON, Rick David** *Forward*
b. Kingston, Ont., Feb. 10, 1958

| Season | Club | GP | G | A | Pts. |
|---|---|---|---|---|---|
| 1979-80 | Chicago | 11 | 0 | 2 | 2 |
| 1980-81 | Chicago | 49 | 8 | 2 | 10 |
| 1981-82 | Chicago | 48 | 4 | 7 | 11 |
| 1982-83 | Chicago | 79 | 14 | 9 | 23 |
| | **Totals** | 187 | 26 | 20 | 46 |

**PATEY, Doug** *Forward*
b. Toronto, Ont., Dec. 28, 1956

| Season | Club | GP | G | A | Pts. |
|---|---|---|---|---|---|
| 1976-77 | Washington | 37 | 3 | 1 | 4 |
| 1977-78 | Washington | 2 | 0 | 1 | 1 |
| 1978-79 | Washington | 6 | 1 | 0 | 1 |
| | **Totals** | 45 | 4 | 2 | 6 |

**PATEY, Larry James** *Forward*
b. Toronto, Ont., Mar. 19, 1953

| Season | Club | GP | G | A | Pts. |
|---|---|---|---|---|---|
| 1973-74 | California | 1 | 0 | 0 | 0 |
| 1974-75 | California | 79 | 25 | 20 | 45 |
| 1975-76 | Cal-StL | 71 | 12 | 10 | 22 |
| 1976-77 | St Louis | 80 | 21 | 29 | 50 |
| 1977-78 | St Louis | 78 | 15 | 19 | 34 |
| 1978-79 | St Louis | 78 | 17 | 17 | 34 |
| 1979-80 | St Louis | 80 | 22 | 23 | 45 |
| 1980-81 | St Louis | 70 | 14 | 12 | 26 |
| 1981-82 | St Louis | 67 | 9 | 12 | 21 |
| | **Totals** | 604 | 135 | 142 | 277 |

**PATRICK, Craig** *Forward*
b. Detroit, Mich., May 20, 1946

| Season | Club | GP | G | A | Pts. |
|---|---|---|---|---|---|
| 1971-72 | California | 59 | 8 | 3 | 11 |
| 1972-73 | California | 71 | 20 | 22 | 42 |
| 1973-74 | California | 59 | 10 | 20 | 30 |
| 1974-75 | St Louis | 43 | 6 | 9 | 15 |
| 1975-76 | Kansas Rity | 80 | 17 | 18 | 35 |
| 1976-77 | Minnesota (WHA) | 30 | 6 | 11 | 17 |
| 1976-77 | Washington | 28 | 7 | 10 | 17 |
| 1977-78 | Washington | 44 | 1 | 7 | 8 |
| 1978-79 | Washington | 3 | 1 | 1 | 2 |
| | **Totals** | 417 | 76 | 101 | 177 |

**PATRICK, Frederick Murray (Muzz)**
*Defenseman*
b. Victoria, B.C., June 28, 1916

| Season | Club | GP | G | A | Pts. |
|---|---|---|---|---|---|
| 1937-38 | New York R | 1 | 0 | 2 | 2 |
| 1938-39 | New York R | 48 | 1 | 10 | 11 |
| 1939-40 | New York R | 46 | 2 | 4 | 6 |
| 1940-41 | New York R | 47 | 2 | 8 | 10 |
| 1945-46 | New York R | 24 | 0 | 2 | 2 |
| | **Totals** | 166 | 5 | 26 | 31 |


**PATRICK, Glenn Curtis** *Defenseman*
b. New York, N.Y., Apr. 26, 1950

| Season | Club | GP | G | A | Pts. |
|---|---|---|---|---|---|
| 1973-74 | St Louis | 1 | 0 | 0 | 0 |
| 1974-75 | California | 2 | 0 | 0 | 0 |
| 1976-77 | Cleveland | 35 | 2 | 3 | 5 |
| 1976-77 | Edmonton (WHA) | 23 | 0 | 4 | 4 |
| | **NHL Totals** | 38 | 2 | 3 | 5 |
| | **WHA Totals** | 23 | 0 | 4 | 4 |

**PATRICK, Lester** *Defenseman*
b. Drummondville, Que., Dec. 30, 1883

| Season | Club | GP | G | A | Pts. |
|---|---|---|---|---|---|
| 1926-27 | New York R | 1 | 0 | 0 | 0 |

**PATRICK, Lynn** *Forward*
b. Victoria, B.C., Feb. 3, 1912

| Season | Club | GP | G | A | Pts. |
|---|---|---|---|---|---|
| 1934-35 | New York R | 48 | 9 | 13 | 22 |
| 1935-36 | New York R | 48 | 11 | 14 | 25 |
| 1936-37 | New York R | 45 | 8 | 16 | 24 |
| 1937-38 | New York R | 48 | 15 | 19 | 34 |
| 1938-39 | New York R | 35 | 8 | 21 | 29 |
| 1939-40 | New York R | 48 | 12 | 16 | 28 |
| 1940-41 | New York R | 48 | 20 | 24 | 44 |
| 1941-42 | New York R | 47 | 32 | 22 | 54 |
| 1942-43 | New York R | 50 | 22 | 39 | 61 |
| 1945-46 | New York R | 38 | 8 | 6 | 14 |
| | **Totals** | 455 | 145 | 190 | 335 |

**PATRICK, Stephen Gary** *Forward*
b. Winnipeg, Man., Feb. 4, 1961

| Season | Club | GP | G | A | Pts. |
|---|---|---|---|---|---|
| 1980-81 | Buffalo | 30 | 1 | 7 | 8 |
| 1981-82 | Buffalo | 41 | 8 | 8 | 16 |
| 1982-83 | Buffalo | 56 | 9 | 13 | 22 |
| | **Totals** | 127 | 18 | 28 | 46 |

**PATTERSON, Dennis G.** *Defenseman*
b. Peterborough, Ont., Jan. 9, 1950

| Season | Club | GP | G | A | Pts. |
|---|---|---|---|---|---|
| 1974-75 | Kansas City | 66 | 1 | 5 | 6 |
| 1975-76 | Kansas City | 69 | 5 | 16 | 21 |
| 1976-77 | Edmonton (WHA) | 23 | 0 | 2 | 2 |
| 1979-80 | Philadelphia | 3 | 0 | 1 | 1 |
| | **NHL Totals** | 138 | 6 | 22 | 28 |
| | **WHA Totals** | 23 | 0 | 2 | 2 |

**PATTERSON, George F. (Paddy)** *Forward*
b. Kingston, Ont., May 22, 1906

| Season | Club | GP | G | A | Pts. |
|---|---|---|---|---|---|
| 1926-27 | Toronto | 17 | 4 | 2 | 6 |
| 1927-28 | Tor-Mont | 28 | 1 | 1 | 2 |
| 1928-29 | Montreal | 44 | 4 | 5 | 9 |
| 1929-30 | New York A | 39 | 13 | 4 | 17 |
| 1930-31 | New York A | 44 | 8 | 6 | 14 |
| 1931-32 | New York A | 20 | 6 | 0 | 6 |
| 1932-33 | New York A | 41 | 12 | 7 | 19 |
| 1933-34 | NYA-Bos | 20 | 3 | 1 | 4 |
| 1934-35 | Det-StLE | 16 | 0 | 1 | 1 |
| | **Totals** | 269 | 51 | 27 | 78 |

**PAVELICH, Mark** *Forward*
b. Eveleth, Minn., Feb. 28, 1958

| Season | Club | GP | G | A | Pts. |
|---|---|---|---|---|---|
| 1981-82 | New York R | 79 | 33 | 43 | 76 |
| 1982-83 | New York R | 78 | 37 | 38 | 75 |
| | **Totals** | 157 | 70 | 81 | 151 |

**PAVELICH, Martin Nicholas** *Forward*
b. Sault Ste. Marie, Ont., Nov. 6, 1927

| Season | Club | GP | G | A | Pts. |
|---|---|---|---|---|---|
| 1947-48 | Detroit | 41 | 4 | 8 | 12 |
| 1948-49 | Detroit | 60 | 10 | 16 | 26 |
| 1949-50 | Detroit | 65 | 8 | 15 | 23 |
| 1950-51 | Detroit | 67 | 9 | 20 | 29 |
| 1951-52 | Detroit | 68 | 17 | 19 | 36 |
| 1952-53 | Detroit | 64 | 13 | 20 | 33 |
| 1953-54 | Detroit | 65 | 9 | 20 | 29 |
| 1954-55 | Detroit | 70 | 15 | 15 | 30 |
| 1955-56 | Detroit | 70 | 5 | 13 | 18 |
| 1956-57 | Detroit | 64 | 3 | 13 | 16 |
| | **Totals** | 634 | 93 | 159 | 252 |

**PAVESE, James Peter** *Defenseman*
b. New York, N.Y., June 8, 1962

| Season | Club | GP | G | A | Pts. |
|---|---|---|---|---|---|
| 1981-82 | St Louis | 42 | 2 | 9 | 11 |
| 1982-83 | St Louis | 24 | 0 | 2 | 2 |
| | **Totals** | 66 | 2 | 11 | 13 |

| Season | Club | GP | G | A | Pts. |
|---|---|---|---|---|---|
| **PAYER** | | | | | |
| 1917-18 | Montreal | 1 | 0 | 0 | 0 |

**PAYNE, Steven John** *Forward*
b. Toronto, Ont., Aug. 16, 1958

| Season | Club | GP | G | A | Pts. |
|---|---|---|---|---|---|
| 1978-79 | Minnesota | 70 | 23 | 17 | 40 |
| 1979-80 | Minnesota | 80 | 42 | 43 | 85 |
| 1981-82 | Minnesota | 74 | 33 | 44 | 77 |
| 1982-83 | Minnesota | 80 | 30 | 39 | 69 |
| | **Totals** | 304 | 128 | 143 | 271 |

**PEARSON, George Alexander Melvin (Mel)** *Forward*
b. Flin Flon, Man., Apr. 29, 1938

| Season | Club | GP | G | A | Pts. |
|---|---|---|---|---|---|
| 1959-60 | New York R | 23 | 1 | 5 | 6 |
| 1961-62 | New York R | 3 | 0 | 0 | 0 |
| 1962-63 | New York R | 5 | 1 | 0 | 1 |
| 1964-65 | New York R | 5 | 0 | 0 | 0 |
| 1967-68 | Pittsburgh | 2 | 0 | 1 | 1 |
| 1972-73 | Minnesota (WHA) | 70 | 8 | 12 | 20 |
| | **NHL Totals** | 38 | 2 | 6 | 8 |
| | **WHA Totals** | 70 | 8 | 12 | 20 |

**PEDERSON, Barry Alan** *Forward*
b. Big River, Sask., Mar. 13, 1961

| Season | Club | GP | G | A | Pts. |
|---|---|---|---|---|---|
| 1980-81 | Boston | 9 | 1 | 4 | 5 |
| 1981-82 | Boston | 80 | 44 | 48 | 92 |
| 1982-83 | Boston | 77 | 46 | 61 | 107 |
| | **Totals** | 166 | 91 | 113 | 204 |

**PELLETIER, Joseph Georges Roger** *Defenseman*
b. Montreal, Que., June 22, 1945

| Season | Club | GP | G | A | Pts. |
|---|---|---|---|---|---|
| 1967-68 | Philadelphia | 1 | 0 | 0 | 0 |

**PELOFFY, Andre** *Forward*
b. Sete, France, Feb. 25, 1951

| Season | Club | GP | G | A | Pts. |
|---|---|---|---|---|---|
| 1974-75 | Washington | 9 | 0 | 0 | 0 |
| 1977-78 | New England (WHA) | 10 | 2 | 0 | 2 |
| | **NHL Totals** | 9 | 0 | 0 | 0 |
| | **WHA Totals** | 10 | 2 | 0 | 2 |

**PELYK, Michael Joseph** *Defenseman*
b. Toronto, Ont., Sept. 29, 1947

| Season | Club | GP | G | A | Pts. |
|---|---|---|---|---|---|
| 1967-68 | Toronto | 24 | 0 | 3 | 3 |
| 1968-69 | Toronto | 65 | 3 | 9 | 12 |
| 1969-70 | Toronto | 36 | 1 | 3 | 4 |
| 1970-71 | Toronto | 73 | 5 | 21 | 26 |
| 1971-72 | Toronto | 46 | 1 | 4 | 5 |
| 1972-73 | Toronto | 72 | 3 | 16 | 19 |
| 1973-74 | Toronto | 71 | 12 | 19 | 31 |
| 1974-75 | Vancouver (WHA) | 75 | 14 | 26 | 40 |
| 1975-76 | Cincinnati (WHA) | 75 | 10 | 23 | 33 |
| 1976-77 | Toronto | 13 | 0 | 2 | 2 |
| 1977-78 | Toronto | 41 | 1 | 11 | 12 |
| | **NHL Totals** | 441 | 26 | 88 | 114 |
| | **WHA Totals** | 150 | 24 | 49 | 73 |

**PENNINGTON, Clifford** *Forward*
b. Winnipeg, Man., Apr. 18, 1940

| Season | Club | GP | G | A | Pts. |
|---|---|---|---|---|---|
| 1960-61 | Montreal | 4 | 1 | 0 | 1 |
| 1961-62 | Boston | 70 | 9 | 32 | 41 |
| 1962-63 | Boston | 27 | 7 | 10 | 17 |
| | **Totals** | 101 | 17 | 42 | 59 |

**PEPLINSKI, James Desmond** *Forward*
b. Renfrew, Ont., Oct. 24, 1960

| Season | Club | GP | G | A | Pts. |
|---|---|---|---|---|---|
| 1980-81 | Calgary | 80 | 13 | 25 | 38 |
| 1981-82 | Calgary | 74 | 30 | 37 | 67 |
| 1982-83 | Calgary | 80 | 15 | 26 | 41 |
| | **Totals** | 234 | 58 | 88 | 146 |

**PERLINI, Fred** *Forward*
b. Sault Ste Marie, Ont., Apr. 12, 1962

| Season | Club | GP | G | A | Pts. |
|---|---|---|---|---|---|
| 1981-82 | Toronto | 7 | 2 | 3 | 5 |

**PERREAULT, Fernand** *Forward*
b. Chambly Basin, Que., Mar. 31, 1927

| Season | Club | GP | G | A | Pts. |
|---|---|---|---|---|---|
| 1947-48 | New York R | 2 | 0 | 0 | 0 |
| 1949-50 | New York R | 1 | 0 | 0 | 0 |
| | **Totals** | 3 | 0 | 0 | 0 |

**PERREAULT, Gilbert** *Forward*
b. Victoriaville, Que., Nov. 13, 1950

| Season | Club | GP | G | A | Pts. |
|---|---|---|---|---|---|
| 1970-71 | Buffalo | 78 | 38 | 34 | 72 |
| 1971-72 | Buffalo | 76 | 26 | 48 | 74 |
| 1972-73 | Buffalo | 78 | 28 | 60 | 88 |
| 1973-74 | Buffalo | 55 | 18 | 33 | 51 |
| 1974-75 | Buffalo | 68 | 39 | 57 | 96 |
| 1975-76 | Buffalo | 80 | 44 | 69 | 113 |
| 1976-77 | Buffalo | 80 | 39 | 56 | 95 |
| 1977-78 | Buffalo | 79 | 41 | 48 | 89 |
| 1978-79 | Buffalo | 79 | 27 | 58 | 85 |
| 1979-80 | Buffalo | 80 | 40 | 66 | 106 |
| 1980-81 | Buffalo | 56 | 20 | 39 | 59 |
| 1981-82 | Buffalo | 62 | 31 | 42 | 73 |
| 1982-83 | Buffalo | 77 | 30 | 46 | 76 |
| | **Totals** | 948 | 421 | 656 | 1077 |

**PERSSON, Stefan** *Defenseman*
b. Bjurholm, Sweden, Dec. 22, 1954

| Season | Club | GP | G | A | Pts. |
|---|---|---|---|---|---|
| 1977-78 | New York I | 66 | 6 | 50 | 56 |
| 1978-79 | New York I | 78 | 10 | 56 | 66 |
| 1979-80 | New York I | 73 | 4 | 35 | 39 |
| 1980-81 | New York I | 80 | 9 | 52 | 61 |
| 1981-82 | New York I | 70 | 6 | 37 | 43 |
| 1982-83 | New York I | 70 | 4 | 25 | 29 |
| | **Totals** | 639 | 39 | 255 | 294 |

**PERRY, Brian Thomas** *Forward*
b. Aldershot, England, Apr. 6, 1944

| Season | Club | GP | G | A | Pts. |
|---|---|---|---|---|---|
| 1968-69 | Oakland | 61 | 10 | 21 | 31 |
| 1969-70 | Oakland | 34 | 6 | 8 | 14 |
| 1970-71 | Buffalo | 1 | 0 | 0 | 0 |
| 1972-73 | New York (WHA) | 74 | 13 | 20 | 33 |
| 1973-74 | New Jersey (WHA) | 71 | 20 | 11 | 31 |
| | **NHL Totals** | 96 | 16 | 29 | 45 |
| | **WHA Totals** | 145 | 33 | 31 | 64 |

**PESUT, George Mathew** *Defenseman*
b. Saskatoon, Sask., June 17, 1953

| Season | Club | GP | G | A | Pts. |
|---|---|---|---|---|---|
| 1974-75 | California | 47 | 0 | 13 | 13 |
| 1975-76 | California | 45 | 3 | 9 | 12 |
| 1976-77 | Calgary (WHA) | 17 | 2 | 0 | 2 |
| | **NHL Totals** | 92 | 3 | 22 | 25 |
| | **WHA Totals** | 17 | 2 | 0 | 2 |

**PETERS, Frank J.** *Defenseman*
b. Rouses Point, N.Y., June 5, 1905

| Season | Club | GP | G | A | Pts. |
|---|---|---|---|---|---|
| 1930-31 | New York R | 44 | 0 | 0 | 0 |

**PETERS, Garry Lorne** *Forward*
b. Regina, Sask., Oct. 9, 1942

| Season | Club | GP | G | A | Pts. |
|---|---|---|---|---|---|
| 1964-65 | Montreal | 13 | 0 | 2 | 2 |
| 1965-66 | New York R | 63 | 7 | 3 | 10 |
| 1966-67 | Montreal | 4 | 0 | 1 | 1 |
| 1967-68 | Philadelphia | 31 | 7 | 5 | 12 |
| 1968-69 | Philadelphia | 66 | 8 | 6 | 14 |
| 1969-70 | Philadelphia | 59 | 6 | 10 | 16 |
| 1970-71 | Philadelphia | 73 | 6 | 7 | 13 |
| 1971-72 | Boston | 2 | 0 | 0 | 0 |
| 1972-73 | New York (WHA) | 23 | 2 | 7 | 9 |
| | **NHL Totals** | 311 | 34 | 34 | 68 |
| | **WHA Totals** | 23 | 2 | 7 | 9 |

**PETERS, James Meldrum** *Forward*
b. Verdun, Que., Oct. 2, 1922

| Season | Club | GP | G | A | Pts. |
|---|---|---|---|---|---|
| 1945-46 | Montreal | 47 | 11 | 19 | 30 |
| 1946-47 | Montreal | 60 | 11 | 13 | 24 |
| 1947-48 | Mont-Bos | 59 | 13 | 18 | 31 |
| 1948-49 | Boston | 60 | 16 | 15 | 31 |
| 1949-50 | Detroit | 70 | 14 | 16 | 30 |
| 1950-51 | Detroit | 68 | 17 | 21 | 38 |
| 1951-52 | Chicago | 70 | 15 | 21 | 36 |
| 1952-53 | Chicago | 69 | 22 | 19 | 41 |
| 1953-54 | Chi-Det | 71 | 6 | 8 | 14 |
| | **Totals** | 574 | 125 | 150 | 275 |

**PETERS, James Stephen, Jr. (Jim)** *Forward*
b. Montreal, Que., June 20, 1944

| Season | Club | GP | G | A | Pts. |
|---|---|---|---|---|---|
| 1964-65 | Detroit | 1 | 0 | 0 | 0 |
| 1965-66 | Detroit | 6 | 1 | 1 | 2 |
| 1966-67 | Detroit | 2 | 0 | 0 | 0 |
| 1967-68 | Detroit | 45 | 5 | 6 | 11 |
| 1968-69 | Los Angeles | 76 | 10 | 15 | 25 |
| 1969-70 | Los Angeles | 74 | 15 | 9 | 24 |
| 1972-73 | Los Angeles | 77 | 4 | 5 | 9 |
| 1973-74 | Los Angeles | 75 | 2 | 0 | 2 |
| 1974-75 | Los Angeles | 3 | 0 | 0 | 0 |
| | **Totals** | 359 | 37 | 36 | 73 |

**PETERS, Steve Alan** *Forward*
b. Peterborough, Ont., Jan. 23, 1960

| Season | Club | GP | G | A | Pts. |
|---|---|---|---|---|---|
| 1979-80 | Colorado | 2 | 0 | 1 | 1 |

**PETERSON, Brent Ronald** *Forward*
b. Calgary, Alta., Feb. 15, 1958

| Season | Club | GP | G | A | Pts. |
|---|---|---|---|---|---|
| 1978-79 | Detroit | 5 | 0 | 0 | 0 |
| 1979-80 | Detroit | 18 | 1 | 2 | 3 |
| 1980-81 | Detroit | 53 | 6 | 18 | 24 |
| 1981-82 | Det-Buf | 61 | 10 | 5 | 15 |
| 1982-83 | Buffalo | 75 | 13 | 24 | 37 |
| | **Totals** | 212 | 30 | 49 | 79 |

**PETIT, Michel** *Defenseman*
b. St. Malo, Que., Feb. 12, 1964

| Season | Club | GP | G | A | Pts. |
|---|---|---|---|---|---|
| 1982-83 | Vancouver | 2 | 0 | 0 | 0 |

**PETTERSSON, Jorgen** *Forward*
b. Gothenburg, Sweden, July 11, 1956

| Season | Club | GP | G | A | Pts. |
|---|---|---|---|---|---|
| 1980-81 | St Louis | 62 | 37 | 36 | 73 |
| 1981-82 | St Louis | 77 | 38 | 31 | 69 |
| 1982-83 | St Louis | 74 | 35 | 38 | 73 |
| | **Totals** | 213 | 110 | 105 | 215 |

**PETTINGER, Eric (Cowboy)** *Forward*
b. Regina, Sask.

| Season | Club | GP | G | A | Pts. |
|---|---|---|---|---|---|
| 1928-29 | Bos-Tor | 42 | 3 | 3 | 6 |
| 1929-30 | Toronto | 43 | 4 | 9 | 13 |
| 1930-31 | Ottawa | 13 | 0 | 0 | 0 |
| | **Totals** | 98 | 7 | 12 | 19 |

**PETTINGER, Gordon Robinson** *Forward*
b. Regina, Sask., Nov. 17, 1911

| Season | Club | GP | G | A | Pts. |
|---|---|---|---|---|---|
| 1932-33 | New York R | 35 | 1 | 2 | 3 |
| 1933-34 | Detroit | — | 3 | 14 | 17 |
| 1934-35 | Detroit | — | 2 | 3 | 5 |
| 1935-36 | Detroit | — | 8 | 7 | 15 |
| 1936-37 | Detroit | — | 7 | 15 | 22 |
| 1937-38 | Det-Bos | — | 8 | 13 | 21 |
| 1938-39 | Boston | — | 11 | 14 | 25 |
| 1939-40 | Boston | — | 2 | 6 | 8 |
| | **Totals** | — | 42 | 74 | 116 |

**PHILLIPOFF, Harold** *Forward*
b. Kamsock, Sask., July 14, 1956

| Season | Club | GP | G | A | Pts. |
|---|---|---|---|---|---|
| 1977-78 | Atlanta | 67 | 17 | 36 | 53 |
| 1978-79 | Atl-Chi | 65 | 9 | 21 | 30 |
| 1979-80 | Chicago | 9 | 0 | 0 | 0 |
| | **Totals** | 141 | 26 | 57 | 83 |

**PHILLIPS, Charles** *Defenseman*
b. Toronto, Ont., May 19, 1917

| Season | Club | GP | G | A | Pts. |
|---|---|---|---|---|---|
| 1942-43 | Montreal | 17 | 0 | 0 | 0 |

**PHILLIPS, Merlyn J. (Bill)** *Forward*
b. Toronto, Ont., 1896

| Season | Club | GP | G | A | Pts. |
|---|---|---|---|---|---|
| 1925-26 | Montreal M | 12 | 3 | 1 | 4 |
| 1926-27 | Montreal M | 43 | 15 | 1 | 16 |
| 1927-28 | Montreal M | 40 | 7 | 5 | 12 |
| 1928-29 | Montreal M | 42 | 6 | 5 | 11 |
| 1929-30 | Montreal M | 44 | 13 | 10 | 23 |
| 1930-31 | Montreal M | 43 | 6 | 1 | 7 |
| 1931-32 | Montreal M | 46 | 1 | 1 | 2 |
| 1932-33 | New York A | 32 | 1 | 7 | 8 |
| | **Totals** | 302 | 52 | 31 | 83 |

**PHILLIPS, W. J. (Batt)** *Forward*
b. Carleton Place, Ont.

| Season | Club | GP | G | A | Pts. |
|---|---|---|---|---|---|
| 1926-27 | Montreal M | 26 | 1 | 1 | 2 |
| 1929-30 | Montreal M | 1 | 0 | 0 | 0 |
| | **Totals** | 27 | 1 | 1 | 2 |

## PICARD, Jean-Noel Yves (Noel)  *Defenseman*
b. Montreal, Que., Dec. 25, 1938

| Season | Club | GP | G | A | Pts. |
|---|---|---|---|---|---|
| 1964-65 | Montreal | 16 | 0 | 7 | 7 |
| 1967-68 | St Louis | 66 | 1 | 10 | 11 |
| 1968-69 | St Louis | 67 | 5 | 19 | 24 |
| 1969-70 | St Louis | 39 | 1 | 4 | 5 |
| 1970-71 | St Louis | 75 | 3 | 8 | 11 |
| 1971-72 | St Louis | 15 | 1 | 5 | 6 |
| 1972-73 | StL-Atl | 57 | 1 | 10 | 11 |
| **Totals** | | 335 | 12 | 63 | 75 |

## PICARD, Robert Rene Joseph  *Defenseman*
b. Montreal, Que., May 25, 1957

| Season | Club | GP | G | A | Pts. |
|---|---|---|---|---|---|
| 1977-78 | Washington | 75 | 10 | 27 | 37 |
| 1978-79 | Washington | 77 | 21 | 44 | 65 |
| 1979-80 | Washington | 78 | 11 | 43 | 54 |
| 1980-81 | Tor-Mont | 67 | 8 | 21 | 29 |
| 1981-82 | Montreal | 62 | 2 | 26 | 28 |
| 1982-83 | Montreal | 64 | 7 | 31 | 38 |
| **Totals** | | 423 | 59 | 192 | 251 |

## PICARD, Roger  *Forward*
b. Montreal, Que., Jan. 13, 1933

| Season | Club | GP | G | A | Pts. |
|---|---|---|---|---|---|
| 1967-68 | St Louis | 15 | 2 | 2 | 4 |

## PICHETTE, Dave  *Defenseman*
b. Grand Falls, Nfld., Feb. 4, 1960

| Season | Club | GP | G | A | Pts. |
|---|---|---|---|---|---|
| 1980-81 | Quebec | 46 | 4 | 16 | 20 |
| 1981-82 | Quebec | 67 | 7 | 30 | 37 |
| 1982-83 | Quebec | 53 | 3 | 21 | 24 |
| **Totals** | | 166 | 14 | 67 | 81 |

## PICKETTS, Fred Harold (Hal)  *Forward*
b. Asquith, Sask., Apr. 22, 1909

| Season | Club | GP | G | A | Pts. |
|---|---|---|---|---|---|
| 1933-34 | New York A | 47 | 3 | 1 | 4 |

## PIDHIRNEY, Harry  *Forward*
b. Toronto, Ont., Mar. 5, 1928

| Season | Club | GP | G | A | Pts. |
|---|---|---|---|---|---|
| 1957-58 | Boston | 2 | 0 | 0 | 0 |

## PIERCE, Randy Stephen  *Forward*
b. Arnprior, Ont., Nov. 23, 1957

| Season | Club | GP | G | A | Pts. |
|---|---|---|---|---|---|
| 1977-78 | Colorado | 35 | 9 | 10 | 19 |
| 1978-79 | Colorado | 70 | 19 | 17 | 36 |
| 1979-80 | Colorado | 75 | 16 | 23 | 39 |
| 1980-81 | Colorado | 55 | 9 | 21 | 30 |
| 1981-82 | Colorado | 5 | 0 | 0 | 0 |
| 1982-83 | New Jersey | 3 | 0 | 0 | 0 |
| **Totals** | | 243 | 53 | 71 | 124 |

## PIERSON, John Frederick  *Forward*
b. Winnipeg, Man., July 21, 1925

| Season | Club | GP | G | A | Pts. |
|---|---|---|---|---|---|
| 1946-47 | Boston | 5 | 0 | 0 | 0 |
| 1947-48 | Boston | 15 | 4 | 2 | 6 |
| 1948-49 | Boston | 59 | 22 | 21 | 43 |
| 1949-50 | Boston | 57 | 27 | 25 | 52 |
| 1950-51 | Boston | 70 | 19 | 19 | 38 |
| 1951-52 | Boston | 68 | 20 | 30 | 50 |
| 1952-53 | Boston | 49 | 14 | 15 | 29 |
| 1953-54 | Boston | 68 | 21 | 19 | 40 |
| 1955-56 | Boston | 33 | 11 | 14 | 25 |
| 1956-57 | Boston | 68 | 13 | 26 | 39 |
| 1957-58 | Boston | 53 | 2 | 2 | 4 |
| **Totals** | | 545 | 153 | 173 | 326 |

## PIKE, Alfred  *Forward*
b. Winnipeg, Man., Sept. 15, 1917

| Season | Club | GP | G | A | Pts. |
|---|---|---|---|---|---|
| 1939-40 | New York R | 47 | 8 | 9 | 17 |
| 1940-41 | New York R | 48 | 6 | 13 | 19 |
| 1941-42 | New York R | 34 | 8 | 19 | 27 |
| 1942-43 | New York R | 41 | 6 | 16 | 22 |
| 1945-46 | New York R | 33 | 7 | 9 | 16 |
| 1946-47 | New York R | 31 | 7 | 11 | 18 |
| **Totals** | | 234 | 42 | 77 | 119 |

## PILOTE, Joseph Albert Pierre Paul  *Defenseman*
b. Kenogami, Que., Dec. 11, 1931

| Season | Club | GP | G | A | Pts. |
|---|---|---|---|---|---|
| 1955-56 | Chicago | 20 | 3 | 5 | 8 |
| 1956-57 | Chicago | 70 | 3 | 14 | 17 |
| 1957-58 | Chicago | 70 | 6 | 24 | 30 |
| 1958-59 | Chicago | 70 | 7 | 30 | 37 |
| 1959-60 | Chicago | 70 | 7 | 38 | 45 |
| 1960-61 | Chicago | 70 | 6 | 29 | 35 |
| 1961-62 | Chicago | 59 | 7 | 35 | 42 |
| 1962-63 | Chicago | 59 | 8 | 18 | 26 |
| 1963-64 | Chicago | 70 | 7 | 46 | 53 |
| 1964-65 | Chicago | 68 | 14 | 45 | 59 |
| 1965-66 | Chicago | 51 | 2 | 34 | 36 |
| 1966-67 | Chicago | 70 | 6 | 46 | 52 |
| 1967-68 | Chicago | 74 | 1 | 36 | 37 |
| 1968-69 | Toronto | 69 | 3 | 18 | 21 |
| **Totals** | | 890 | 80 | 418 | 498 |

## PINDER, Allen Gerald (Gerry)  *Forward*
b. Saskatoon, Sask., Sept. 15, 1948

| Season | Club | GP | G | A | Pts. |
|---|---|---|---|---|---|
| 1969-70 | Chicago | 75 | 19 | 20 | 39 |
| 1970-71 | Chicago | 74 | 13 | 18 | 31 |
| 1971-72 | California | 74 | 23 | 31 | 54 |
| 1972-73 | Cleveland (WHA) | 78 | 30 | 36 | 66 |
| 1973-74 | Cleveland (WHA) | 73 | 23 | 33 | 56 |
| 1974-75 | Cleveland (WHA) | 74 | 13 | 28 | 41 |
| 1975-76 | Cleveland (WHA) | 79 | 21 | 30 | 51 |
| 1976-77 | San Diego (WHA) | 44 | 6 | 13 | 19 |
| 1977-78 | Edmonton (WHA) | 5 | 0 | 1 | 1 |
| **NHL Totals** | | 223 | 55 | 69 | 124 |
| **WHA Totals** | | 353 | 93 | 141 | 234 |

## PIRUS, Joseph Alexander  *Forward*
b. Toronto, Ont., Jan. 12, 1955

| Season | Club | GP | G | A | Pts. |
|---|---|---|---|---|---|
| 1976-77 | Minnesota | 79 | 20 | 17 | 37 |
| 1977-78 | Minnesota | 61 | 9 | 6 | 15 |
| 1978-79 | Minnesota | 15 | 1 | 3 | 4 |
| 1979-80 | Detroit | 4 | 0 | 2 | 2 |
| **Totals** | | 159 | 30 | 28 | 58 |

## PITRE, Didier  *Forward*
b. Sault Ste. Marie, Ont., 1884

| Season | Club | GP | G | A | Pts. |
|---|---|---|---|---|---|
| 1917-18 | Montreal | 19 | 17 | 0 | 17 |
| 1918-19 | Montreal | 17 | 14 | 4 | 18 |
| 1919-20 | Montreal | 22 | 15 | 7 | 22 |
| 1920-21 | Montreal | 23 | 15 | 1 | 16 |
| 1921-22 | Montreal | 23 | 2 | 3 | 5 |
| 1922-23 | Montreal | 23 | 1 | 2 | 3 |
| **Totals** | | 127 | 64 | 17 | 81 |

## PLAGER, Barclay Graham  *Defenseman*
b. Kirkland Lake, Ont., Mar. 25, 1941

| Season | Club | GP | G | A | Pts. |
|---|---|---|---|---|---|
| 1967-68 | St Louis | 49 | 5 | 15 | 20 |
| 1968-69 | St Louis | 61 | 4 | 26 | 30 |
| 1969-70 | St Louis | 75 | 6 | 26 | 32 |
| 1970-71 | St Louis | 69 | 4 | 20 | 24 |
| 1971-72 | St Louis | 78 | 7 | 22 | 29 |
| 1972-73 | St Louis | 68 | 8 | 25 | 33 |
| 1973-74 | St Louis | 72 | 6 | 20 | 26 |
| 1974-75 | St Louis | 76 | 4 | 24 | 28 |
| 1975-76 | St Louis | 64 | 0 | 8 | 8 |
| 1976-77 | St Louis | 2 | 0 | 1 | 1 |
| **Totals** | | 614 | 44 | 187 | 231 |

## PLAGER, Robert Bryan (Bob)  *Defenseman*
b. Kirkland Lake, Ont., Mar. 11, 1943

| Season | Club | GP | G | A | Pts. |
|---|---|---|---|---|---|
| 1964-65 | New York R | 10 | 0 | 0 | 0 |
| 1965-66 | New York R | 18 | 0 | 5 | 5 |
| 1966-67 | New York R | 1 | 0 | 0 | 0 |
| 1967-68 | St Louis | 53 | 2 | 5 | 7 |
| 1968-69 | St Louis | 32 | 0 | 7 | 7 |
| 1969-70 | St Louis | 64 | 3 | 11 | 14 |
| 1970-71 | St Louis | 70 | 1 | 19 | 20 |
| 1971-72 | St Louis | 50 | 4 | 7 | 11 |
| 1972-73 | St Louis | 77 | 2 | 31 | 33 |
| 1973-74 | St Louis | 61 | 3 | 10 | 13 |
| 1974-75 | St Louis | 73 | 1 | 14 | 15 |
| 1975-76 | St Louis | 63 | 3 | 8 | 11 |
| 1976-77 | St Louis | 54 | 1 | 9 | 10 |
| 1977-78 | St Louis | 18 | 0 | 0 | 0 |
| **Totals** | | 644 | 20 | 126 | 146 |

## PLAGER, William Ronald (Bill)  *Defenseman*
b. Kirkland Lake, Ont., July 6, 1945

| Season | Club | GP | G | A | Pts. |
|---|---|---|---|---|---|
| 1967-68 | Minnesota | 32 | 0 | 2 | 2 |
| 1968-69 | St Louis | 2 | 0 | 0 | 0 |
| 1969-70 | St Louis | 24 | 1 | 4 | 5 |
| 1970-71 | St Louis | 36 | 0 | 3 | 3 |
| 1971-72 | St Louis | 65 | 1 | 11 | 12 |
| 1972-73 | Atlanta | 76 | 2 | 11 | 13 |
| 1973-74 | Minnesota | 1 | 0 | 0 | 0 |
| 1974-75 | Minnesota | 7 | 0 | 0 | 0 |
| 1975-76 | Minnesota | 20 | 0 | 3 | 3 |
| **Totals** | | 263 | 4 | 34 | 38 |

## PLAMONDON, Gerard Roger  *Forward*
b. Sherbrooke, Que., Jan. 5, 1925

| Season | Club | GP | G | A | Pts. |
|---|---|---|---|---|---|
| 1945-46 | Montreal | 6 | 0 | 2 | 2 |
| 1947-48 | Montreal | 3 | 1 | 1 | 2 |
| 1948-49 | Montreal | 27 | 5 | 5 | 10 |
| 1949-50 | Montreal | 37 | 1 | 5 | 6 |
| 1950-51 | Montreal | 1 | 0 | 0 | 0 |
| **Totals** | | 74 | 7 | 13 | 20 |

## PLANTE, Pierre Renald  *Forward*
b. Valleyfield, Que., May 14, 1951

| Season | Club | GP | G | A | Pts. |
|---|---|---|---|---|---|
| 1971-72 | Philadelphia | 24 | 1 | 0 | 1 |
| 1972-73 | Phil-StL | 51 | 12 | 16 | 28 |
| 1973-74 | St Louis | 78 | 26 | 28 | 54 |
| 1974-75 | St Louis | 80 | 34 | 32 | 66 |
| 1975-76 | St Louis | 74 | 14 | 19 | 33 |
| 1976-77 | St Louis | 76 | 18 | 20 | 38 |
| 1977-78 | Chicago | 77 | 10 | 18 | 28 |
| 1978-79 | New York R | 70 | 6 | 25 | 31 |
| 1979-80 | Quebec | 69 | 4 | 14 | 18 |
| **Totals** | | 599 | 125 | 172 | 297 |

## PLANTERY, Mark P.  *Defenseman*
b. St. Catharines, Ont., Aug. 14, 1959

| Season | Club | GP | G | A | Pts. |
|---|---|---|---|---|---|
| 1980-81 | Winnipeg | 25 | 1 | 5 | 6 |

## PLAXTON, Hugh  *Forward*
b. Barrie, Ont., May 16, 1904

| Season | Club | GP | G | A | Pts. |
|---|---|---|---|---|---|
| 1932-33 | Montreal M | — | 1 | 2 | 3 |

## PLAYFAIR, Larry William  *Defenseman*
b. Fort St. James, B.C., June 23, 1958

| Season | Club | GP | G | A | Pts. |
|---|---|---|---|---|---|
| 1978-79 | Buffalo | 26 | 0 | 3 | 3 |
| 1979-80 | Buffalo | 79 | 2 | 10 | 12 |
| 1980-81 | Buffalo | 75 | 3 | 9 | 12 |
| 1981-82 | Buffalo | 77 | 6 | 10 | 16 |
| 1982-83 | Buffalo | 79 | 4 | 13 | 17 |
| **Totals** | | 336 | 15 | 45 | 60 |

## PLEAU, Lawrence Winslow  *Forward*
b. Lynn, Mass., June 29, 1947

| Season | Club | GP | G | A | Pts. |
|---|---|---|---|---|---|
| 1969-70 | Montreal | 20 | 1 | 0 | 1 |
| 1970-71 | Montreal | 19 | 1 | 5 | 6 |
| 1971-72 | Montreal | 55 | 7 | 10 | 17 |
| 1972-73 | New England (WHA) | 78 | 39 | 48 | 87 |
| 1973-74 | New England (WHA) | 77 | 26 | 43 | 69 |
| 1974-75 | New England (WHA) | 78 | 30 | 34 | 64 |
| 1975-76 | New England (WHA) | 75 | 29 | 45 | 74 |
| 1976-77 | New England (WHA) | 78 | 11 | 21 | 32 |
| 1977-78 | New England (WHA) | 54 | 16 | 18 | 34 |
| 1978-79 | New England (WHA) | 28 | 6 | 6 | 12 |
| **NHL Totals** | | 94 | 9 | 15 | 24 |
| **WHA Totals** | | 468 | 157 | 215 | 372 |

## PLETT, Willi  *Forward*
b. Paraguay, South America, June 7, 1955

| Season | Club | GP | G | A | Pts. |
|---|---|---|---|---|---|
| 1975-76 | Atlanta | 4 | 0 | 0 | 0 |
| 1976-77 | Atlanta | 64 | 33 | 23 | 56 |
| 1977-78 | Atlanta | 78 | 22 | 21 | 43 |
| 1978-79 | Atlanta | 74 | 23 | 20 | 43 |
| 1979-80 | Atlanta | 76 | 13 | 19 | 32 |
| 1980-81 | Calgary | 78 | 38 | 30 | 68 |
| 1981-82 | Calgary | 78 | 21 | 36 | 57 |
| 1982-83 | Minnesota | 71 | 25 | 14 | 39 |
| **Totals** | | 523 | 175 | 163 | 338 |

## PLUMB, Rob  *Forward*
b. Kingston, Ont., Aug. 29, 1957

| Season | Club | GP | G | A | Pts. |
|---|---|---|---|---|---|
| 1977-78 | Detroit | 7 | 2 | 1 | 3 |
| 1978-79 | Detroit | 7 | 1 | 1 | 2 |
| **Totals** | | 14 | 3 | 2 | 5 |

| Season | Club | GP | G | A | Pts. |
|---|---|---|---|---|---|
| **PLUMB, Ronald William** *Defenseman* | | | | | |
| b. Kingston, Ont., July 17, 1950 | | | | | |
| 1972-73 | Philadelphia (WHA) | 78 | 10 | 41 | 51 |
| 1973-74 | Vancouver (WHA) | 75 | 6 | 32 | 38 |
| 1974-75 | San Diego (WHA) | 78 | 10 | 38 | 48 |
| 1975-76 | Cincinnati (WHA) | 80 | 10 | 36 | 46 |
| 1976-77 | Cincinnati (WHA) | 79 | 11 | 58 | 69 |
| 1977-78 | New England (WHA) | 27 | 1 | 9 | 10 |
| 1978-79 | New England (WHA) | 78 | 4 | 16 | 20 |
| 1979-80 | Hartford | 26 | 3 | 4 | 7 |
| | **NHL Totals** | 26 | 3 | 4 | 7 |
| | **WHA Totals** | 495 | 52 | 230 | 282 |
| **POCZA, Harvie D.** *Forward* | | | | | |
| b. Lethbridge, Alta., Sept. 22, 1959 | | | | | |
| 1979-80 | Washington | 1 | 0 | 0 | 0 |
| 1981-82 | Washington | 2 | 0 | 0 | 0 |
| | **Totals** | 3 | 0 | 0 | 0 |
| **PODDUBNY, Walter Michael** *Forward* | | | | | |
| b. Thunder Bay, Ont., Feb. 14, 1960 | | | | | |
| 1981-82 | Edm-Tor | 15 | 3 | 4 | 7 |
| 1982-83 | Toronto | 72 | 28 | 31 | 59 |
| | **Totals** | 87 | 31 | 35 | 66 |
| **PODOLSKY, Nelson** *Forward* | | | | | |
| b. Winnipeg, Man., Dec. 19, 1925 | | | | | |
| 1948-49 | Detroit | 1 | 0 | 0 | 0 |
| **POETA, Anthony Joseph** *Forward* | | | | | |
| b. North Bay, Ont., Mar. 4, 1933 | | | | | |
| 1951-52 | Chicago | 1 | 0 | 0 | 0 |
| **POILE, Donald B.** *Forward* | | | | | |
| b. Fort William, Ont., June 1, 1932 | | | | | |
| 1954-55 | Detroit | 4 | 0 | 0 | 0 |
| 1957-58 | Detroit | 62 | 7 | 9 | 16 |
| | **Totals** | 66 | 7 | 9 | 16 |
| **POILE, Norman Robert (Bud)** *Forward* | | | | | |
| b. Fort William, Ont., Feb. 10, 1924 | | | | | |
| 1942-43 | Toronto | 48 | 16 | 19 | 35 |
| 1943-44 | Toronto | 11 | 6 | 8 | 14 |
| 1945-46 | Toronto | 9 | 1 | 8 | 9 |
| 1946-47 | Toronto | 59 | 19 | 17 | 36 |
| 1947-48 | Tor-Chi | 58 | 25 | 29 | 54 |
| 1948-49 | Chi-Det | 60 | 21 | 21 | 42 |
| 1949-50 | NYR-Bos | 66 | 19 | 20 | 39 |
| | **Totals** | 311 | 107 | 122 | 229 |
| **POIRIER, Gordon** *Forward* | | | | | |
| b. Maple Creek, Sask., Oct. 27, 1913 | | | | | |
| 1939-40 | Montreal | 10 | 0 | 1 | 1 |
| **POLANIC, Thomas Joseph** *Defenseman* | | | | | |
| b. Toronto, Ont., Apr. 2, 1943 | | | | | |
| 1969-70 | Minnesota | 16 | 0 | 2 | 2 |
| 1970-71 | Minnesota | 3 | 0 | 0 | 0 |
| | **Totals** | 19 | 0 | 2 | 2 |
| **POLICH, John** *Forward* | | | | | |
| b. Hibbing, Minn., July 8, 1916 | | | | | |
| 1939-40 | New York R | 1 | 0 | 0 | 0 |
| 1940-41 | New York R | 2 | 0 | 1 | 1 |
| | **Totals** | 3 | 0 | 1 | 1 |
| **POLICH, Michael D.** *Forward* | | | | | |
| b. Hibbing, Minn., Dec. 19, 1952 | | | | | |
| 1977-78 | Montreal | 1 | 0 | 0 | 0 |
| 1978-79 | Minnesota | 73 | 6 | 10 | 16 |
| 1979-80 | Minnesota | 78 | 10 | 14 | 24 |
| 1980-81 | Minnesota | 74 | 8 | 5 | 13 |
| | **Totals** | 226 | 24 | 29 | 53 |
| **POLIS, Gregory Linn (Greg)** *Forward* | | | | | |
| b. Westlock, Alta., Aug. 8, 1950 | | | | | |
| 1970-71 | Pittsburgh | 61 | 18 | 15 | 33 |
| 1971-72 | Pittsburgh | 76 | 30 | 19 | 49 |

| Season | Club | GP | G | A | Pts. |
|---|---|---|---|---|---|
| 1972-73 | Pittsburgh | 78 | 26 | 23 | 49 |
| 1973-74 | Pitt-StL | 78 | 22 | 25 | 47 |
| 1974-75 | New York R | 76 | 26 | 15 | 41 |
| 1975-76 | New York R | 79 | 15 | 21 | 36 |
| 1976-77 | New York R | 77 | 16 | 23 | 39 |
| 1977-78 | New York R | 37 | 7 | 16 | 23 |
| 1978-79 | NYR-Wash | 25 | 13 | 7 | 20 |
| 1979-80 | Washington | 28 | 1 | 5 | 6 |
| | **Totals** | 615 | 174 | 169 | 343 |
| **POLIZIANI, Daniel** *Forward* | | | | | |
| b. Sydney, N.S., Jan. 8, 1935 | | | | | |
| 1958-59 | Boston | 1 | 0 | 0 | 0 |
| **POLONICH, Dennis Daniel** *Forward* | | | | | |
| b. Foam Lake, Sask., Dec. 4, 1953 | | | | | |
| 1974-75 | Detroit | 4 | 0 | 0 | 0 |
| 1975-76 | Detroit | 57 | 11 | 12 | 23 |
| 1976-77 | Detroit | 79 | 18 | 28 | 46 |
| 1977-78 | Detroit | 79 | 16 | 19 | 35 |
| 1978-79 | Detroit | 62 | 10 | 12 | 22 |
| 1979-80 | Detroit | 66 | 2 | 8 | 10 |
| 1980-81 | Detroit | 32 | 2 | 2 | 4 |
| 1981-82 | Detroit | 11 | 0 | 1 | 1 |
| | **Totals** | 390 | 59 | 82 | 141 |
| **POPEIN, Lawrence Thomas (Larry)** *Forward* | | | | | |
| b. Yorkton, Sask., Aug. 11, 1930 | | | | | |
| 1954-55 | New York R | 70 | 11 | 17 | 28 |
| 1955-56 | New York R | 64 | 14 | 25 | 39 |
| 1956-57 | New York R | 67 | 11 | 19 | 30 |
| 1957-58 | New York R | 70 | 12 | 22 | 34 |
| 1958-59 | New York R | 61 | 13 | 21 | 34 |
| 1959-60 | New York R | 66 | 14 | 22 | 36 |
| 1960-61 | New York R | 4 | 0 | 1 | 1 |
| 1967-68 | Oakland | 47 | 5 | 14 | 19 |
| | **Totals** | 449 | 80 | 141 | 221 |
| **POPIEL, Poul Peter (Paul)** *Defenseman* | | | | | |
| b. Sollested, Denmark, Feb. 28, 1943 | | | | | |
| 1965-66 | Boston | 3 | 0 | 1 | 1 |
| 1967-68 | Los Angeles | 1 | 0 | 0 | 0 |
| 1968-69 | Detroit | 62 | 2 | 13 | 15 |
| 1969-70 | Detroit | 32 | 0 | 4 | 4 |
| 1970-71 | Vancouver | 78 | 10 | 22 | 32 |
| 1971-72 | Vancouver | 38 | 1 | 1 | 2 |
| 1972-73 | Houston (WHA) | 73 | 16 | 48 | 64 |
| 1973-74 | Houston (WHA) | 78 | 7 | 41 | 48 |
| 1974-75 | Houston (WHA) | 78 | 11 | 53 | 64 |
| 1975-76 | Houston (WHA) | 78 | 10 | 36 | 46 |
| 1976-77 | Houston (WHA) | 80 | 12 | 56 | 68 |
| 1977-78 | Houston (WHA) | 80 | 6 | 31 | 37 |
| 1979-80 | Edmonton | 10 | 0 | 0 | 0 |
| | **NHL Totals** | 224 | 13 | 41 | 54 |
| | **WHA Totals** | 467 | 62 | 265 | 327 |
| **PORTLAND, John Frederick** *Defenseman* | | | | | |
| b. Collingwood, Ont., July 30, 1912 | | | | | |
| 1933-34 | Montreal | 31 | 0 | 2 | 2 |
| 1934-35 | Mont-Bos | 20 | 1 | 1 | 2 |
| 1935-36 | Boston | 2 | 0 | 0 | 0 |
| 1936-37 | Boston | 46 | 2 | 4 | 6 |
| 1937-38 | Boston | 48 | 0 | 5 | 5 |
| 1938-39 | Boston | 48 | 4 | 5 | 9 |
| 1939-40 | Bos-Chi | 50 | 1 | 9 | 10 |
| 1940-41 | Chi-Mont | 47 | 2 | 7 | 9 |
| 1941-42 | Montreal | 46 | 2 | 9 | 11 |
| 1942-43 | Montreal | 49 | 3 | 14 | 17 |
| | **Totals** | 387 | 15 | 56 | 71 |
| **PORVARI, Jukka** *Forward* | | | | | |
| b. Tampere, Finland, Jan. 19, 1954 | | | | | |
| 1981-82 | Colorado | 31 | 2 | 6 | 8 |
| 1982-83 | New Jersey | 8 | 1 | 3 | 4 |
| | **Totals** | 39 | 3 | 9 | 12 |
| **POTVIN, Denis Charles** *Defenseman* | | | | | |
| b. Ottawa, Ont., Oct. 29, 1953 | | | | | |
| 1973-74 | New York I | 77 | 17 | 37 | 54 |
| 1974-75 | New York I | 79 | 21 | 55 | 76 |
| 1975-76 | New York I | 78 | 31 | 67 | 98 |

| Season | Club | GP | G | A | Pts. |
|---|---|---|---|---|---|
| 1976-77 | New York I | 80 | 25 | 55 | 80 |
| 1977-78 | New York I | 80 | 30 | 64 | 94 |
| 1978-79 | New York I | 73 | 31 | 70 | 101 |
| 1979-80 | New York I | 31 | 8 | 33 | 41 |
| 1980-81 | New York I | 74 | 20 | 56 | 76 |
| 1981-82 | New York I | 60 | 24 | 37 | 61 |
| 1982-83 | New York I | 69 | 12 | 54 | 66 |
| | **Totals** | 701 | 219 | 528 | 747 |
| **POTVIN, Jean Rene** *Defenseman* | | | | | |
| b. Ottawa, Ont., Mar. 25, 1949 | | | | | |
| 1970-71 | Los Angeles | 4 | 1 | 3 | 4 |
| 1971-72 | LA-Phil | 68 | 5 | 15 | 20 |
| 1972-73 | Phil-NYI | 46 | 3 | 12 | 15 |
| 1973-74 | New York I | 78 | 5 | 23 | 28 |
| 1974-75 | New York I | 73 | 9 | 24 | 33 |
| 1975-76 | New York I | 78 | 17 | 55 | 72 |
| 1976-77 | New York I | 79 | 10 | 36 | 46 |
| 1977-78 | NYI-Clev | 74 | 4 | 24 | 28 |
| 1978-79 | Minnesota | 64 | 5 | 16 | 21 |
| 1979-80 | New York I | 32 | 2 | 13 | 15 |
| 1980-81 | New York I | 18 | 2 | 3 | 5 |
| | **Totals** | 614 | 63 | 224 | 287 |
| **POULIN, Daniel** *Defenseman* | | | | | |
| b. Robertsville, Que., Sept. 19, 1957 | | | | | |
| 1981-82 | Minnesota | 3 | 1 | 1 | 2 |
| 1982-83 | Philadelphia | 2 | 2 | 0 | 2 |
| | **Totals** | 5 | 3 | 1 | 4 |
| **POUZAR, Jaroslav** *Forward* | | | | | |
| b. Czechoslovakia, Jan. 23, 1952 | | | | | |
| 1982-83 | Edmonton | 74 | 15 | 18 | 33 |
| **POWELL, Raymond Henry** *Forward* | | | | | |
| b. Timmins, Ont., Nov. 16, 1925 | | | | | |
| 1950-51 | Chicago | 31 | 7 | 15 | 22 |
| **POWIS, Geoffrey Charles** *Forward* | | | | | |
| b. Winnipeg, Man., June 14, 1945 | | | | | |
| 1967-68 | Chicago | 2 | 0 | 0 | 0 |
| **POWIS, Trevor Lynn** *Forward* | | | | | |
| b. Saskatoon, Sask., Apr. 19, 1949 | | | | | |
| 1973-74 | Chicago | 57 | 8 | 13 | 21 |
| 1974-75 | Kansas City | 73 | 11 | 20 | 31 |
| 1975-76 | Calgary (WHA) | 21 | 4 | 10 | 14 |
| 1976-77 | Calgary (WHA) | 63 | 30 | 30 | 60 |
| 1977-78 | Ind-Winn (WHA) | 69 | 16 | 25 | 41 |
| | **NHL Totals** | 130 | 19 | 33 | 52 |
| | **WHA Totals** | 153 | 50 | 65 | 115 |
| **PRATT, Jack** *Defenseman* | | | | | |
| b. Edinburgh, Scotland | | | | | |
| 1930-31 | Boston | 32 | 2 | 0 | 2 |
| 1931-32 | Boston | 6 | 0 | 0 | 0 |
| | **Totals** | 38 | 2 | 0 | 2 |
| **PRATT, Kelly Edward** *Forward* | | | | | |
| b. High Prairie, Alta., Feb. 8, 1953 | | | | | |
| 1973-74 | Winnipeg (WHA) | 46 | 4 | 6 | 10 |
| 1974-75 | Pittsburgh | 22 | 0 | 6 | 6 |
| | **NHL Totals** | 22 | 0 | 6 | 6 |
| | **WHA Totals** | 46 | 4 | 6 | 10 |
| **PRATT, Tracy Arnold** *Defenseman* | | | | | |
| b. New York, N.Y., Mar. 8, 1943 | | | | | |
| 1967-68 | Oakland | 34 | 0 | 5 | 5 |
| 1968-69 | Pittsburgh | 18 | 0 | 5 | 5 |
| 1969-70 | Pittsburgh | 65 | 5 | 7 | 12 |
| 1970-71 | Buffalo | 76 | 1 | 7 | 8 |
| 1971-72 | Buffalo | 27 | 0 | 10 | 10 |
| 1972-73 | Buffalo | 74 | 1 | 15 | 16 |
| 1973-74 | Buf-Van | 78 | 3 | 15 | 18 |
| 1974-75 | Vancouver | 79 | 5 | 17 | 22 |
| 1975-76 | Vancouver | 52 | 1 | 5 | 6 |
| 1976-77 | Col-Tor | 77 | 1 | 11 | 12 |
| | **Totals** | 580 | 17 | 97 | 114 |

**PRATT, Walter (Babe)** *Defenseman*
b. Stony Mountain, Man., Jan. 7, 1916

| Season | Club | GP | G | A | Pts. |
|---|---|---|---|---|---|
| 1935-36 | New York R | 17 | 1 | 1 | 2 |
| 1936-37 | New York R | 47 | 8 | 7 | 15 |
| 1937-38 | New York R | 47 | 5 | 14 | 19 |
| 1938-39 | New York R | 48 | 2 | 19 | 21 |
| 1939-40 | New York R | 48 | 4 | 13 | 17 |
| 1940-41 | New York R | 47 | 3 | 17 | 20 |
| 1941-42 | New York R | 47 | 4 | 24 | 28 |
| 1942-43 | NYR-Tor | 44 | 12 | 27 | 39 |
| 1943-44 | Toronto | 50 | 17 | 40 | 57 |
| 1944-45 | Toronto | 50 | 18 | 23 | 41 |
| 1945-46 | Toronto | 41 | 5 | 20 | 25 |
| 1946-47 | Boston | 31 | 4 | 4 | 8 |
| | **Totals** | **517** | **83** | **209** | **292** |

**PRENTICE, Dean Sutherland** *Forward*
b. Schumacher, Ont., Oct. 5, 1932

| Season | Club | GP | G | A | Pts. |
|---|---|---|---|---|---|
| 1952-53 | New York R | 55 | 6 | 3 | 9 |
| 1953-54 | New York R | 52 | 4 | 13 | 17 |
| 1954-55 | New York R | 70 | 16 | 15 | 31 |
| 1955-56 | New York R | 70 | 24 | 18 | 42 |
| 1956-57 | New York R | 68 | 19 | 23 | 42 |
| 1957-58 | New York R | 38 | 13 | 9 | 22 |
| 1958-59 | New York R | 70 | 17 | 33 | 50 |
| 1959-60 | New York R | 70 | 32 | 34 | 66 |
| 1960-61 | New York R | 56 | 20 | 25 | 45 |
| 1961-62 | New York R | 68 | 22 | 38 | 60 |
| 1962-63 | NYR-Bos | 68 | 19 | 34 | 53 |
| 1963-64 | Boston | 70 | 23 | 16 | 39 |
| 1964-65 | Boston | 31 | 14 | 9 | 23 |
| 1965-66 | Bos-Det | 69 | 13 | 31 | 44 |
| 1966-67 | Detroit | 68 | 23 | 22 | 45 |
| 1967-68 | Detroit | 69 | 17 | 38 | 55 |
| 1968-69 | Detroit | 74 | 14 | 20 | 34 |
| 1969-70 | Pittsburgh | 75 | 26 | 25 | 51 |
| 1970-71 | Pittsburgh | 69 | 21 | 17 | 38 |
| 1971-72 | Minnesota | 71 | 20 | 27 | 47 |
| 1972-73 | Minnesota | 73 | 26 | 16 | 42 |
| 1973-74 | Minnesota | 24 | 2 | 3 | 5 |
| | **Totals** | **1378** | **391** | **469** | **860** |

**PRENTICE, Eric Dayton** *Forward*
b. Schumacher, Ont., Aug. 22, 1926

| Season | Club | GP | G | A | Pts. |
|---|---|---|---|---|---|
| 1943-44 | Toronto | 5 | 0 | 0 | 0 |

**PRESTON, Richard John** *Forward*
b. Regina, Sask., May 22, 1952

| Season | Club | GP | G | A | Pts. |
|---|---|---|---|---|---|
| 1974-75 | Houston (WHA) | 78 | 20 | 21 | 41 |
| 1975-76 | Houston (WHA) | 77 | 22 | 33 | 55 |
| 1976-77 | Houston (WHA) | 80 | 38 | 41 | 79 |
| 1977-78 | Houston (WHA) | 73 | 25 | 25 | 50 |
| 1978-79 | Winnipeg (WHA) | 80 | 28 | 32 | 60 |
| 1979-80 | Chicago | 80 | 31 | 30 | 61 |
| 1980-81 | Chicago | 47 | 7 | 14 | 21 |
| 1981-82 | Chicago | 75 | 15 | 28 | 43 |
| 1982-83 | Chicago | 79 | 25 | 28 | 53 |
| | **NHL Totals** | **281** | **78** | **100** | **178** |
| | **WHA Totals** | **388** | **133** | **152** | **285** |

**PRESTON, Yves** *Forward*
b. Montreal, Que., June 14, 1956

| Season | Club | GP | G | A | Pts. |
|---|---|---|---|---|---|
| 1978-79 | Philadelphia | 9 | 3 | 1 | 4 |
| 1980-81 | Philadelphia | 19 | 4 | 2 | 6 |
| | **Totals** | **28** | **7** | **3** | **10** |

**PRICE** *Forward*

| Season | Club | GP | G | A | Pts. |
|---|---|---|---|---|---|
| 1919-20 | Ottawa | 1 | 0 | 0 | 0 |

**PRICE, Garry Noel** *Defenseman*
b. Brockville, Ont., Dec. 9, 1935

| Season | Club | GP | G | A | Pts. |
|---|---|---|---|---|---|
| 1957-58 | Toronto | 1 | 0 | 0 | 0 |
| 1958-59 | Toronto | 28 | 0 | 0 | 0 |
| 1959-60 | New York R | 6 | 0 | 0 | 0 |
| 1960-61 | New York R | 1 | 0 | 0 | 0 |
| 1961-62 | Detroit | 20 | 0 | 1 | 1 |
| 1965-66 | Montreal | 15 | 0 | 6 | 6 |
| 1966-67 | Montreal | 24 | 0 | 3 | 3 |
| 1967-68 | Pittsburgh | 70 | 6 | 27 | 33 |
| 1968-69 | Pittsburgh | 73 | 2 | 18 | 20 |
| 1970-71 | Los Angeles | 62 | 1 | 19 | 20 |
| 1972-73 | Atlanta | 54 | 1 | 13 | 14 |
| 1973-74 | Atlanta | 62 | 0 | 13 | 13 |


| Season | Club | GP | G | A | Pts. |
|---|---|---|---|---|---|
| 1974-75 | Atlanta | 80 | 4 | 14 | 18 |
| 1975-76 | Atlanta | 3 | 0 | 0 | 0 |
| | **Totals** | **499** | **14** | **114** | **128** |

**PRICE, John Rees** *Defenseman*
b. Gooderich, Ont., May 8, 1932

| Season | Club | GP | G | A | Pts. |
|---|---|---|---|---|---|
| 1951-52 | Chicago | 1 | 0 | 0 | 0 |
| 1952-53 | Chicago | 10 | 0 | 0 | 0 |
| 1953-54 | Chicago | 46 | 4 | 6 | 10 |
| | **Totals** | **57** | **4** | **6** | **10** |

**PRICE, Shaun Patrick** *Defenseman*
b. Nelson, B.C., Mar. 24, 1955

| Season | Club | GP | G | A | Pts. |
|---|---|---|---|---|---|
| 1974-75 | Vancouver (WHA) | 68 | 5 | 29 | 34 |
| 1975-76 | New York I | 4 | 0 | 2 | 2 |
| 1976-77 | New York I | 71 | 3 | 22 | 25 |
| 1977-78 | New York I | 52 | 2 | 10 | 12 |
| 1978-79 | New York I | 55 | 3 | 11 | 14 |
| 1979-80 | Edmonton | 75 | 11 | 21 | 32 |
| 1980-81 | Edm-Pitt | 63 | 8 | 34 | 42 |
| 1982-83 | Pitt-Que | 52 | 2 | 13 | 15 |
| | **NHL Totals** | **372** | **29** | **113** | **142** |
| | **WHA Totals** | **68** | **5** | **29** | **34** |

**PRICE, Thomas Edward** *Defenseman*
b. Toronto, Ont., July 12, 1954

| Season | Club | GP | G | A | Pts. |
|---|---|---|---|---|---|
| 1974-75 | California | 3 | 0 | 0 | 0 |
| 1975-76 | California | 5 | 0 | 0 | 0 |
| 1976-77 | Clev-Pitt | 9 | 0 | 2 | 2 |
| 1977-78 | Pittsburgh | 10 | 0 | 0 | 0 |
| 1978-79 | Pittsburgh | 2 | 0 | 0 | 0 |
| | **Totals** | **29** | **0** | **2** | **2** |

**PRIMEAU, A. Joseph (Joe)** *Forward*
b. Lindsay, Ont., Jan. 29, 1906

| Season | Club | GP | G | A | Pts. |
|---|---|---|---|---|---|
| 1927-28 | Toronto | 2 | 0 | 0 | 0 |
| 1928-29 | Toronto | 6 | 0 | 1 | 1 |
| 1929-30 | Toronto | 43 | 5 | 21 | 26 |
| 1930-31 | Toronto | 38 | 9 | 32 | 41 |
| 1931-32 | Toronto | 46 | 13 | 37 | 50 |
| 1932-33 | Toronto | 48 | 11 | 21 | 32 |
| 1933-34 | Toronto | 45 | 14 | 32 | 46 |
| 1934-35 | Toronto | 37 | 10 | 20 | 30 |
| 1935-36 | Toronto | 45 | 4 | 13 | 17 |
| | **Totals** | **310** | **66** | **177** | **243** |

**PRINGLE, Ellis** *Defenseman*
b. Toronto, Ont.

| Season | Club | GP | G | A | Pts. |
|---|---|---|---|---|---|
| 1930-31 | New York A | — | 0 | 0 | 0 |

**PRODGERS, George (Goldie)** *Defenseman*
b. 1892

| Season | Club | GP | G | A | Pts. |
|---|---|---|---|---|---|
| 1919-20 | Toronto | 16 | 8 | 6 | 14 |
| 1920-21 | Hamilton | 23 | 18 | 8 | 26 |
| 1921-22 | Hamilton | 24 | 15 | 4 | 19 |
| 1922-23 | Hamilton | 23 | 13 | 3 | 16 |
| 1923-24 | Hamilton | 23 | 9 | 1 | 10 |
| 1924-25 | Hamilton | 1 | 0 | 0 | 0 |
| 1925-26 | Montreal | — | 0 | 0 | 0 |
| | **Totals** | **—** | **63** | **22** | **85** |

**PRONOVOST, Joseph Armand Andre** *Forward*
b. Shawinigan Falls, Que., July 9, 1936

| Season | Club | GP | G | A | Pts. |
|---|---|---|---|---|---|
| 1956-57 | Montreal | 64 | 10 | 11 | 21 |
| 1957-58 | Montreal | 66 | 16 | 12 | 28 |
| 1958-59 | Montreal | 70 | 9 | 14 | 23 |
| 1959-60 | Montreal | 69 | 12 | 19 | 31 |
| 1960-61 | Mont-Bos | 68 | 12 | 16 | 28 |
| 1961-62 | Boston | 70 | 15 | 8 | 23 |
| 1962-63 | Bos-Det | 68 | 13 | 7 | 20 |
| 1963-64 | Detroit | 70 | 7 | 16 | 23 |
| 1964-65 | Detroit | 3 | 0 | 1 | 1 |
| 1967-68 | Minnesota | 8 | 0 | 0 | 0 |
| | **Totals** | **556** | **94** | **104** | **198** |

**PRONOVOST, Joseph Jean Denis** *Forward*
b. Shawinigan Falls, Que., Dec. 18, 1945

| Season | Club | GP | G | A | Pts. |
|---|---|---|---|---|---|
| 1968-69 | Pittsburgh | 76 | 16 | 25 | 41 |
| 1969-70 | Pittsburgh | 72 | 20 | 21 | 41 |


| Season | Club | GP | G | A | Pts. |
|---|---|---|---|---|---|
| 1970-71 | Pittsburgh | 78 | 21 | 24 | 45 |
| 1971-72 | Pittsburgh | 68 | 30 | 23 | 53 |
| 1972-73 | Pittsburgh | 66 | 21 | 22 | 43 |
| 1973-74 | Pittsburgh | 77 | 40 | 32 | 72 |
| 1974-75 | Pittsburgh | 78 | 43 | 32 | 75 |
| 1975-76 | Pittsburgh | 80 | 52 | 52 | 104 |
| 1976-77 | Pittsburgh | 79 | 33 | 31 | 64 |
| 1977-78 | Pittsburgh | 79 | 40 | 25 | 65 |
| 1978-79 | Atlanta | 75 | 28 | 39 | 67 |
| 1979-80 | Atlanta | 80 | 24 | 19 | 43 |
| 1980-81 | Washington | 80 | 22 | 36 | 58 |
| 1981-82 | Washington | 10 | 1 | 2 | 3 |
| | **Totals** | **998** | **391** | **383** | **774** |

**PRONOVOST, Joseph Rene Marcel** *Defenseman*
b. Lac la Tortue, Que., June 15, 1930

| Season | Club | GP | G | A | Pts. |
|---|---|---|---|---|---|
| 1950-51 | Detroit | 37 | 1 | 6 | 7 |
| 1951-52 | Detroit | 69 | 7 | 11 | 18 |
| 1952-53 | Detroit | 68 | 8 | 19 | 27 |
| 1953-54 | Detroit | 57 | 6 | 12 | 18 |
| 1954-55 | Detroit | 70 | 9 | 25 | 34 |
| 1955-56 | Detroit | 68 | 4 | 13 | 17 |
| 1956-57 | Detroit | 70 | 7 | 9 | 16 |
| 1957-58 | Detroit | 62 | 2 | 18 | 20 |
| 1958-59 | Detroit | 69 | 11 | 21 | 32 |
| 1959-60 | Detroit | 69 | 7 | 17 | 24 |
| 1960-61 | Detroit | 70 | 6 | 11 | 17 |
| 1961-62 | Detroit | 70 | 4 | 14 | 18 |
| 1962-63 | Detroit | 69 | 4 | 9 | 13 |
| 1963-64 | Detroit | 67 | 3 | 17 | 20 |
| 1964-65 | Detroit | 68 | 1 | 15 | 16 |
| 1965-66 | Toronto | 54 | 2 | 8 | 10 |
| 1966-67 | Toronto | 58 | 2 | 12 | 14 |
| 1967-68 | Toronto | 70 | 3 | 17 | 20 |
| 1968-69 | Toronto | 34 | 1 | 2 | 3 |
| 1969-70 | Toronto | 7 | 0 | 1 | 1 |
| | **Totals** | **1206** | **88** | **257** | **345** |

**PROPP, Brian Philip** *Forward*
b. Lanigan, Sask., Feb. 15, 1959

| Season | Club | GP | G | A | Pts. |
|---|---|---|---|---|---|
| 1979-80 | Philadelphia | 80 | 34 | 41 | 75 |
| 1980-81 | Philadelphia | 79 | 26 | 40 | 66 |
| 1981-82 | Philadelphia | 80 | 44 | 47 | 91 |
| 1982-83 | Philadelphia | 80 | 40 | 42 | 82 |
| | **Totals** | **319** | **144** | **170** | **314** |

**PROVOST, Claude** *Forward*
b. Montreal, Que., Sept. 17, 1933

| Season | Club | GP | G | A | Pts. |
|---|---|---|---|---|---|
| 1955-56 | Montreal | 60 | 13 | 16 | 29 |
| 1956-57 | Montreal | 67 | 16 | 14 | 30 |
| 1957-58 | Montreal | 70 | 19 | 32 | 51 |
| 1958-59 | Montreal | 69 | 16 | 22 | 38 |
| 1959-60 | Montreal | 70 | 17 | 29 | 46 |
| 1960-61 | Montreal | 49 | 11 | 4 | 15 |
| 1961-62 | Montreal | 70 | 33 | 29 | 62 |
| 1962-63 | Montreal | 67 | 20 | 30 | 50 |
| 1963-64 | Montreal | 68 | 15 | 17 | 32 |
| 1964-65 | Montreal | 70 | 27 | 37 | 64 |
| 1965-66 | Montreal | 70 | 19 | 36 | 55 |
| 1966-67 | Montreal | 64 | 11 | 13 | 24 |
| 1967-68 | Montreal | 73 | 14 | 30 | 44 |
| 1968-69 | Montreal | 73 | 13 | 15 | 28 |
| 1969-70 | Montreal | 65 | 10 | 11 | 21 |
| | **Totals** | **1005** | **254** | **335** | **589** |

**PRYSTAI, Metro** *Forward*
b. Yorkton, Sask., Nov. 7, 1927

| Season | Club | GP | G | A | Pts. |
|---|---|---|---|---|---|
| 1947-48 | Chicago | 54 | 7 | 11 | 18 |
| 1948-49 | Chicago | 59 | 12 | 7 | 19 |
| 1949-50 | Chicago | 65 | 29 | 22 | 51 |
| 1950-51 | Detroit | 62 | 20 | 17 | 37 |
| 1951-52 | Detroit | 69 | 21 | 22 | 43 |
| 1952-53 | Detroit | 70 | 16 | 34 | 50 |
| 1953-54 | Detroit | 70 | 12 | 15 | 27 |
| 1954-55 | Det-Chi | 69 | 13 | 16 | 29 |
| 1955-56 | Chi-Det | 71 | 13 | 19 | 32 |
| 1956-57 | Detroit | 70 | 7 | 15 | 22 |
| 1957-58 | Detroit | 15 | 1 | 1 | 2 |
| | **Totals** | **674** | **151** | **179** | **330** |

| Season | Club | GP | G | A | Pts. |
|---|---|---|---|---|---|

**PULFORD, Robert Jesse (Bob)** *Forward*
b. Newton Robinson, Ont., Mar. 31, 1936

| Season | Club | GP | G | A | Pts. |
|---|---|---|---|---|---|
| 1956-57 | Toronto | 65 | 11 | 11 | 22 |
| 1957-58 | Toronto | 70 | 14 | 17 | 31 |
| 1958-59 | Toronto | 70 | 23 | 14 | 37 |
| 1959-60 | Toronto | 70 | 24 | 28 | 52 |
| 1960-61 | Toronto | 40 | 11 | 18 | 29 |
| 1961-62 | Toronto | 70 | 18 | 21 | 39 |
| 1962-63 | Toronto | 70 | 19 | 25 | 44 |
| 1963-64 | Toronto | 70 | 18 | 30 | 48 |
| 1964-65 | Toronto | 65 | 19 | 20 | 39 |
| 1965-66 | Toronto | 70 | 28 | 28 | 56 |
| 1966-67 | Toronto | 67 | 17 | 28 | 45 |
| 1967-68 | Toronto | 74 | 20 | 30 | 50 |
| 1968-69 | Toronto | 72 | 11 | 23 | 34 |
| 1969-70 | Toronto | 74 | 18 | 19 | 37 |
| 1970-71 | Los Angeles | 59 | 17 | 26 | 43 |
| 1971-72 | Los Angeles | 73 | 13 | 24 | 37 |
| **Totals** | | 1079 | 281 | 362 | 643 |

**PULKKINEN, David Joel John (Dave)**
*Defenseman*
b. Kapuskasing, Ont., May 18, 1949

| Season | Club | GP | G | A | Pts. |
|---|---|---|---|---|---|
| 1972-73 | New York I | 2 | 0 | 0 | 0 |

**PURPUR, Clifford (Fido)** *Forward*
b. Grand Forks, N.D., Sept. 26, 1916

| Season | Club | GP | G | A | Pts. |
|---|---|---|---|---|---|
| 1934-35 | St Louis E | 26 | 2 | 1 | 3 |
| 1941-42 | Chicago | 8 | 0 | 0 | 0 |
| 1942-43 | Chicago | 50 | 13 | 16 | 29 |
| 1943-44 | Chicago | 40 | 9 | 10 | 19 |
| 1944-45 | Chi-Det | 21 | 2 | 7 | 9 |
| **Totals** | | 145 | 26 | 34 | 60 |

**PUSIE, Jean Baptiste** *Defenseman*
b. Montreal, Que., Oct. 15, 1910

| Season | Club | GP | G | A | Pts. |
|---|---|---|---|---|---|
| 1930-31 | Montreal | 6 | 0 | 0 | 0 |
| 1931-32 | Montreal | 1 | 0 | 0 | 0 |
| 1933-34 | New York R | 19 | 0 | 2 | 2 |
| 1934-35 | Boston | 9 | 1 | 0 | 1 |
| 1935-36 | Montreal | 31 | 0 | 2 | 2 |
| **Totals** | | 66 | 1 | 4 | 5 |

**PYATT, Frederick Nelson** *Forward*
b. Port Arthur, Ont., Sept. 9, 1953

| Season | Club | GP | G | A | Pts. |
|---|---|---|---|---|---|
| 1973-74 | Detroit | 5 | 0 | 0 | 0 |
| 1974-75 | Det-Wash | 25 | 6 | 4 | 10 |
| 1975-76 | Washington | 77 | 26 | 23 | 49 |
| 1976-77 | Colorado | 77 | 23 | 22 | 45 |
| 1977-78 | Colorado | 71 | 9 | 12 | 21 |
| 1978-79 | Colorado | 28 | 2 | 2 | 4 |
| 1979-80 | Colorado | 13 | 5 | 0 | 5 |
| **Totals** | | 296 | 71 | 63 | 134 |

**QUACKENBUSH, Hubert George (Bill)**
*Defenseman*
b. Toronto, Ont., Mar. 2, 1922

| Season | Club | GP | G | A | Pts. |
|---|---|---|---|---|---|
| 1942-43 | Detroit | 10 | 1 | 1 | 2 |
| 1943-44 | Detroit | 43 | 4 | 14 | 18 |
| 1944-45 | Detroit | 50 | 7 | 14 | 21 |
| 1945-46 | Detroit | 48 | 11 | 10 | 21 |
| 1946-47 | Detroit | 44 | 5 | 17 | 22 |
| 1947-48 | Detroit | 58 | 6 | 16 | 22 |
| 1948-49 | Detroit | 60 | 6 | 17 | 23 |
| 1949-50 | Boston | 70 | 8 | 17 | 25 |
| 1950-51 | Boston | 70 | 5 | 24 | 29 |
| 1951-52 | Boston | 69 | 2 | 17 | 19 |
| 1952-53 | Boston | 69 | 2 | 16 | 18 |
| 1953-54 | Boston | 45 | 0 | 17 | 17 |
| 1954-55 | Boston | 68 | 2 | 20 | 22 |
| 1955-56 | Boston | 70 | 3 | 22 | 25 |
| **Totals** | | 774 | 62 | 222 | 284 |

**QUACKENBUSH, Maxwell Joseph**
*Defenseman*
b. Toronto, Ont., Aug. 29, 1928

| Season | Club | GP | G | A | Pts. |
|---|---|---|---|---|---|
| 1950-51 | Boston | 47 | 4 | 6 | 10 |
| 1951-52 | Chicago | 14 | 0 | 1 | 1 |
| **Totals** | | 61 | 4 | 7 | 11 |

**QUENNEVILLE, Leo** *Forward*
b. St. Anicet, Que., June 15, 1900

| Season | Club | GP | G | A | Pts. |
|---|---|---|---|---|---|
| 1929-30 | New York R | 25 | 0 | 3 | 3 |

**QUENNEVILLE, Joel Norman** *Defenseman*
b. Windsor, Ont., Sept. 15, 1958

| Season | Club | GP | G | A | Pts. |
|---|---|---|---|---|---|
| 1978-79 | Toronto | 61 | 2 | 9 | 11 |
| 1979-80 | Tor-Col | 67 | 6 | 11 | 17 |
| 1980-81 | Colorado | 71 | 10 | 24 | 34 |
| 1981-82 | Colorado | 64 | 5 | 10 | 15 |
| 1982-83 | New Jersey | 74 | 5 | 12 | 17 |
| **Totals** | | 337 | 28 | 66 | 94 |

**QUILTY, John Francis** *Forward*
b. Ottawa, Ont., Jan. 21, 1921

| Season | Club | GP | G | A | Pts. |
|---|---|---|---|---|---|
| 1940-41 | Montreal | 48 | 18 | 16 | 34 |
| 1941-42 | Montreal | 48 | 12 | 12 | 24 |
| 1946-47 | Montreal | 3 | 1 | 1 | 2 |
| 1947-48 | Mont-Bos | 26 | 5 | 5 | 10 |
| **Totals** | | 125 | 36 | 34 | 70 |

**QUINN, John Brian Patrick (Pat)** *Defenseman*
b. Hamilton, Ont., Jan. 19, 1943

| Season | Club | GP | G | A | Pts. |
|---|---|---|---|---|---|
| 1968-69 | Toronto | 40 | 2 | 7 | 9 |
| 1969-70 | Toronto | 59 | 0 | 5 | 5 |
| 1970-71 | Vancouver | 76 | 2 | 11 | 13 |
| 1971-72 | Vancouver | 57 | 2 | 3 | 5 |
| 1972-73 | Atlanta | 78 | 2 | 18 | 20 |
| 1973-74 | Atlanta | 77 | 5 | 27 | 32 |
| 1974-75 | Atlanta | 80 | 2 | 19 | 21 |
| 1975-76 | Atlanta | 80 | 2 | 11 | 13 |
| 1976-77 | Atlanta | 59 | 1 | 12 | 13 |
| **Totals** | | 606 | 18 | 113 | 131 |

**RADLEY, Harry John (Yip)** *Defenseman*
b. Ottawa, Ont., June 27, 1910

| Season | Club | GP | G | A | Pts. |
|---|---|---|---|---|---|
| 1936-37 | Montreal | 16 | 0 | 1 | 1 |

**RAGLAN, Clarence Eldon (Rags)**
*Defenseman*
b. Pembroke, Ont., Sept. 4, 1927

| Season | Club | GP | G | A | Pts. |
|---|---|---|---|---|---|
| 1950-51 | Detroit | 33 | 3 | 1 | 4 |
| 1951-52 | Chicago | 35 | 0 | 5 | 5 |
| 1952-53 | Chicago | 32 | 1 | 3 | 4 |
| **Totals** | | 100 | 4 | 9 | 13 |

**RALEIGH, James Donald (Bones)** *Forward*
b. Kenora, Ont., June 27, 1926

| Season | Club | GP | G | A | Pts. |
|---|---|---|---|---|---|
| 1943-44 | New York R | 15 | 2 | 2 | 4 |
| 1947-48 | New York R | 52 | 6 | 11 | 33 |
| 1948-49 | New York R | 41 | 10 | 16 | 26 |
| 1949-50 | New York R | 70 | 12 | 25 | 37 |
| 1950-51 | New York R | 64 | 15 | 24 | 39 |
| 1951-52 | New York R | 70 | 19 | 42 | 61 |
| 1952-53 | New York R | 55 | 4 | 18 | 22 |
| 1953-54 | New York R | 70 | 15 | 30 | 45 |
| 1954-55 | New York R | 69 | 8 | 32 | 40 |
| 1955-56 | New York R | 29 | 1 | 12 | 13 |
| **Totals** | | 534 | 101 | 219 | 320 |

**RAMAGE, George Rob** *Defenseman*
b. Byron, Ont., Jan. 11, 1959

| Season | Club | GP | G | A | Pts. |
|---|---|---|---|---|---|
| 1978-79 | Birmingham (WHA) | 80 | 12 | 36 | 48 |
| 1979-80 | Colorado | 75 | 8 | 20 | 28 |
| 1980-81 | Colorado | 79 | 20 | 42 | 62 |
| 1981-82 | Colorado | 80 | 13 | 29 | 42 |
| 1982-83 | St Louis | 78 | 16 | 35 | 51 |
| **NHL Totals** | | 312 | 57 | 126 | 183 |
| **WHA Totals** | | 80 | 12 | 36 | 48 |

**RAMSAY, Craig E.** *Forward*
b. Weston, Ont., Mar. 17, 1951

| Season | Club | GP | G | A | Pts. |
|---|---|---|---|---|---|
| 1971-72 | Buffalo | 57 | 6 | 10 | 16 |
| 1972-73 | Buffalo | 76 | 11 | 17 | 28 |
| 1973-74 | Buffalo | 78 | 20 | 26 | 46 |
| 1974-75 | Buffalo | 80 | 26 | 38 | 64 |
| 1975-76 | Buffalo | 80 | 22 | 49 | 71 |
| 1976-77 | Buffalo | 80 | 20 | 41 | 61 |
| 1977-78 | Buffalo | 80 | 28 | 43 | 71 |
| 1978-79 | Buffalo | 80 | 26 | 31 | 57 |
| 1979-80 | Buffalo | 80 | 21 | 39 | 60 |
| 1980-81 | Buffalo | 80 | 24 | 35 | 59 |
| 1981-82 | Buffalo | 80 | 16 | 35 | 51 |
| 1982-83 | Buffalo | 64 | 11 | 18 | 29 |
| **Totals** | | 915 | 231 | 382 | 613 |

**RAMSEY, Beattie** *Defenseman*

| Season | Club | GP | G | A | Pts. |
|---|---|---|---|---|---|
| 1927-28 | Toronto | 43 | 0 | 2 | 2 |

**RAMSEY, Les** *Forward*
b. Montreal, Que., July 1, 1920

| Season | Club | GP | G | A | Pts. |
|---|---|---|---|---|---|
| 1944-45 | Chicago | 11 | 2 | 2 | 4 |

**RAMSEY, Michael Allen** *Defenseman*
b. Minneapolis, Minn., Dec. 3, 1960

| Season | Club | GP | G | A | Pts. |
|---|---|---|---|---|---|
| 1979-80 | Buffalo | 13 | 1 | 6 | 7 |
| 1980-81 | Buffalo | 72 | 3 | 14 | 17 |
| 1981-82 | Buffalo | 80 | 7 | 23 | 30 |
| 1982-83 | Buffalo | 77 | 8 | 30 | 38 |
| **Totals** | | 242 | 19 | 73 | 92 |

**RAMSEY, Wayne** *Defenseman*
b. Hamiota, Man., Jan. 31, 1957

| Season | Club | GP | G | A | Pts. |
|---|---|---|---|---|---|
| 1977-78 | Buffalo | 2 | 0 | 0 | 0 |

**RANDALL, Kenneth** *Defenseman*

| Season | Club | GP | G | A | Pts. |
|---|---|---|---|---|---|
| 1917-18 | Toronto | 20 | 12 | 0 | 12 |
| 1918-19 | Toronto | 14 | 7 | 6 | 13 |
| 1919-20 | Toronto | 21 | 10 | 7 | 17 |
| 1920-21 | Toronto | 21 | 6 | 1 | 7 |
| 1921-22 | Toronto | 24 | 10 | 6 | 16 |
| 1922-23 | Toronto | 24 | 3 | 5 | 8 |
| 1923-24 | Hamilton | 24 | 7 | 1 | 8 |
| 1924-25 | Hamilton | 30 | 8 | 0 | 8 |
| 1925-26 | New York A | 34 | 4 | 2 | 6 |
| 1926-27 | New York A | 5 | 0 | 0 | 0 |
| **Totals** | | 217 | 67 | 28 | 95 |

**RANIERI, George Dominic** *Forward*
b. Toronto, Ont., Jan. 14, 1936

| Season | Club | GP | G | A | Pts. |
|---|---|---|---|---|---|
| 1956-57 | Boston | 2 | 0 | 0 | 0 |

**RATELLE, Joseph Gilbert Yvon Jean**
*Forward*
b. Lac St. Jean, Que., Oct. 3, 1940

| Season | Club | GP | G | A | Pts. |
|---|---|---|---|---|---|
| 1960-61 | New York R | 3 | 2 | 1 | 3 |
| 1961-62 | New York R | 31 | 4 | 8 | 12 |
| 1962-63 | New York R | 48 | 11 | 9 | 20 |
| 1963-64 | New York R | 15 | 0 | 7 | 7 |
| 1964-65 | New York R | 54 | 14 | 21 | 35 |
| 1965-66 | New York R | 67 | 21 | 30 | 51 |
| 1966-67 | New York R | 41 | 6 | 5 | 11 |
| 1967-68 | New York R | 74 | 32 | 46 | 78 |
| 1968-69 | New York R | 75 | 32 | 46 | 78 |
| 1969-70 | New York R | 75 | 32 | 42 | 74 |
| 1970-71 | New York R | 78 | 26 | 46 | 72 |
| 1971-72 | New York R | 63 | 46 | 63 | 109 |
| 1972-73 | New York R | 78 | 41 | 53 | 94 |
| 1973-74 | New York R | 68 | 28 | 39 | 67 |
| 1974-75 | New York R | 79 | 36 | 55 | 91 |
| 1975-76 | NYR-Bos | 80 | 36 | 69 | 105 |
| 1976-77 | Boston | 78 | 33 | 61 | 94 |
| 1977-78 | Boston | 80 | 25 | 59 | 84 |
| 1978-79 | Boston | 80 | 27 | 45 | 72 |
| 1979-80 | Boston | 67 | 28 | 45 | 73 |
| 1980-81 | Boston | 47 | 11 | 26 | 37 |
| **Totals** | | 1281 | 491 | 776 | 1267 |

**RATHWELL, John Donald** *Forward*
b. Temiskaming, Que., Aug. 12, 1947

| Season | Club | GP | G | A | Pts. |
|---|---|---|---|---|---|
| 1974-75 | Boston | 1 | 0 | 0 | 0 |

**RAUSSE, Errol A.** *Forward*
b. Quesnel, B.C., May 18, 1959

| Season | Club | GP | G | A | Pts. |
|---|---|---|---|---|---|
| 1979-80 | Washington | 24 | 6 | 2 | 8 |
| 1980-81 | Washington | 5 | 1 | 1 | 2 |
| 1981-82 | Washington | 2 | 0 | 0 | 0 |
| **Totals** | | 31 | 7 | 3 | 10 |

| Season | Club | GP | G | A | Pts. |
|---|---|---|---|---|---|
| **RAUTAKALLIO, Pekka** *Defenseman* | | | | | |
| b. Pori, Finland, July 25, 1953 | | | | | |
| 1975-76 | Phoenix (WHA) | 73 | 11 | 39 | 50 |
| 1976-77 | Phoenix (WHA) | 78 | 4 | 31 | 35 |
| 1979-80 | Atlanta | 79 | 5 | 25 | 30 |
| 1980-81 | Calgary | 76 | 11 | 45 | 56 |
| 1981-82 | Calgary | 80 | 17 | 51 | 68 |
| | **NHL Totals** | 235 | 33 | 121 | 154 |
| | **WHA Totals** | 151 | 15 | 70 | 85 |
| **RAVLICH, Matthew Joseph** *Defenseman* | | | | | |
| b. Sault Ste. Marie, Ont., July 12, 1938 | | | | | |
| 1962-63 | Boston | 2 | 1 | 0 | 1 |
| 1964-65 | Chicago | 61 | 3 | 16 | 19 |
| 1965-66 | Chicago | 62 | 0 | 16 | 16 |
| 1966-67 | Chicago | 62 | 0 | 3 | 3 |
| 1968-69 | Chicago | 60 | 2 | 12 | 14 |
| 1969-70 | Det-LA | 67 | 3 | 13 | 16 |
| 1970-71 | Los Angeles | 66 | 3 | 16 | 19 |
| 1971-72 | Boston | 25 | 0 | 1 | 1 |
| 1972-73 | Boston | 5 | 0 | 1 | 1 |
| 1973-74 | Boston | 50 | 4 | 20 | 24 |
| | **Totals** | 460 | 16 | 98 | 114 |
| **RAYMOND, Armand** *Defenseman* | | | | | |
| b. Mechanicsville, N.Y., Jan. 12, 1913 | | | | | |
| 1939-40 | Montreal | 11 | 0 | 1 | 1 |
| **RAYMOND, Paul Marcel** *Forward* | | | | | |
| b. Montreal, Que., Feb. 27, 1913 | | | | | |
| 1932-33 | Montreal | 16 | 0 | 0 | 0 |
| 1933-34 | Montreal | 29 | 1 | 0 | 1 |
| 1934-35 | Montreal | 20 | 1 | 1 | 2 |
| 1937-38 | Montreal | 11 | 0 | 2 | 2 |
| | **Totals** | 76 | 2 | 3 | 5 |
| **READ, Melvin Dean (Pee Wee)** *Forward* | | | | | |
| b. Montreal, Que., Apr. 10, 1922 | | | | | |
| 1946-47 | New York R | 6 | 0 | 0 | 0 |
| **REARDON, Kenneth Joseph** *Defenseman* | | | | | |
| b. Winnipeg, Man., Apr. 1, 1921 | | | | | |
| 1940-41 | Montreal | 34 | 2 | 8 | 10 |
| 1941-42 | Montreal | 41 | 3 | 12 | 15 |
| 1945-46 | Montreal | 43 | 5 | 4 | 9 |
| 1946-47 | Montreal | 52 | 5 | 17 | 22 |
| 1947-48 | Montreal | 58 | 7 | 15 | 22 |
| 1948-49 | Montreal | 46 | 3 | 13 | 16 |
| 1949-50 | Montreal | 67 | 1 | 27 | 28 |
| | **Totals** | 341 | 26 | 96 | 122 |
| **REARDON, Terrance George** | | | | | |
| *Defenseman-Forward* | | | | | |
| b. Winnipeg, Man., Apr. 6, 1919 | | | | | |
| 1939-40 | Boston | 4 | 0 | 0 | 0 |
| 1940-41 | Boston | 35 | 6 | 5 | 11 |
| 1941-42 | Montreal | 33 | 17 | 17 | 34 |
| 1942-43 | Montreal | 13 | 6 | 6 | 12 |
| 1945-46 | Boston | 49 | 12 | 11 | 23 |
| 1946-47 | Boston | 60 | 6 | 14 | 20 |
| | **Totals** | 194 | 47 | 53 | 100 |
| **REAUME, Marc Avellin** *Defenseman* | | | | | |
| b. Lasalle, Ont., Feb. 7, 1934 | | | | | |
| 1954-55 | Toronto | 1 | 0 | 0 | 0 |
| 1955-56 | Toronto | 48 | 0 | 12 | 12 |
| 1956-57 | Toronto | 63 | 6 | 14 | 20 |
| 1957-58 | Toronto | 68 | 1 | 7 | 8 |
| 1958-59 | Toronto | 51 | 1 | 5 | 6 |
| 1959-60 | Tor-Det | 45 | 0 | 2 | 2 |
| 1960-61 | Detroit | 38 | 0 | 1 | 1 |
| 1963-64 | Montreal | 3 | 0 | 0 | 0 |
| 1970-71 | Vancouver | 27 | 0 | 2 | 2 |
| | **Totals** | 344 | 8 | 43 | 51 |
| **REAY, William Tulip** *Forward* | | | | | |
| b. Winnipeg, Man., Aug. 21, 1918 | | | | | |
| 1943-44 | Detroit | 2 | 2 | 0 | 2 |
| 1944-45 | Detroit | 2 | 0 | 0 | 0 |
| 1945-46 | Montreal | 44 | 17 | 12 | 29 |

| Season | Club | GP | G | A | Pts. |
|---|---|---|---|---|---|
| 1946-47 | Montreal | 59 | 22 | 20 | 42 |
| 1947-48 | Montreal | 60 | 6 | 14 | 20 |
| 1948-49 | Montreal | 60 | 22 | 23 | 45 |
| 1949-50 | Montreal | 68 | 19 | 26 | 45 |
| 1950-51 | Montreal | 60 | 6 | 18 | 24 |
| 1951-52 | Montreal | 68 | 7 | 34 | 41 |
| 1952-53 | Montreal | 56 | 4 | 15 | 19 |
| | **Totals** | 479 | 105 | 162 | 267 |
| **REDAHL, Gordon** *Forward* | | | | | |
| b. Kinistino, Sask., Aug. 28, 1935 | | | | | |
| 1958-59 | Boston | 18 | 0 | 1 | 1 |
| **REDDING, George** *Defenseman* | | | | | |
| 1924-25 | Boston | 27 | 3 | 2 | 5 |
| 1925-26 | Boston | 8 | 0 | 0 | 0 |
| | **Totals** | 35 | 3 | 2 | 5 |
| **REDMOND, Michael Edward (Mickey)** | | | | | |
| *Forward* | | | | | |
| b. Kirkland Lake, Ont., Dec. 27, 1947 | | | | | |
| 1967-68 | Montreal | 41 | 6 | 5 | 11 |
| 1968-69 | Montreal | 65 | 9 | 15 | 24 |
| 1969-70 | Montreal | 75 | 27 | 27 | 54 |
| 1970-71 | Mont-Det | 61 | 20 | 23 | 43 |
| 1971-72 | Detroit | 78 | 42 | 29 | 71 |
| 1972-73 | Detroit | 76 | 52 | 41 | 93 |
| 1973-74 | Detroit | 76 | 51 | 26 | 77 |
| 1974-75 | Detroit | 29 | 15 | 12 | 27 |
| 1975-76 | Detroit | 37 | 11 | 17 | 28 |
| | **Totals** | 538 | 233 | 195 | 428 |
| **REDMOND, Richard John (Dick)** *Defenseman* | | | | | |
| b. Kirkland Lake, Ont., Aug. 14, 1949 | | | | | |
| 1969-70 | Minnesota | 7 | 0 | 1 | 1 |
| 1970-71 | Minn-Cal | 20 | 2 | 6 | 8 |
| 1971-72 | California | 74 | 10 | 35 | 45 |
| 1972-73 | Cal-Chi | 76 | 12 | 32 | 44 |
| 1973-74 | Chicago | 76 | 17 | 42 | 59 |
| 1974-75 | Chicago | 80 | 14 | 43 | 57 |
| 1975-76 | Chicago | 53 | 9 | 27 | 36 |
| 1976-77 | Chicago | 80 | 22 | 25 | 47 |
| 1977-78 | StL-Atl | 70 | 11 | 22 | 33 |
| 1978-79 | Boston | 64 | 7 | 26 | 33 |
| 1979-80 | Boston | 76 | 14 | 33 | 47 |
| 1980-81 | Boston | 78 | 15 | 20 | 35 |
| 1981-82 | Boston | 17 | 0 | 0 | 0 |
| | **Totals** | 771 | 133 | 312 | 445 |
| **REEDS, Mark** *Forward* | | | | | |
| b. Burlington, Ont., Jan. 24, 1960 | | | | | |
| 1981-82 | St Louis | 9 | 1 | 3 | 4 |
| 1982-83 | St Louis | 20 | 5 | 14 | 19 |
| | **Totals** | 29 | 6 | 17 | 23 |
| **REGAN, Lawrence Emmett** *Forward* | | | | | |
| b. North Bay, Ont., Aug. 9, 1930 | | | | | |
| 1956-57 | Boston | 69 | 14 | 19 | 33 |
| 1957-58 | Boston | 59 | 11 | 28 | 39 |
| 1958-59 | Bos-Tor | 68 | 9 | 27 | 36 |
| 1959-60 | Toronto | 47 | 4 | 16 | 20 |
| 1960-61 | Toronto | 37 | 3 | 5 | 8 |
| | **Totals** | 280 | 41 | 95 | 136 |
| **REGAN, William Donald** *Defenseman* | | | | | |
| b. Creighton Mines, Ont., Dec. 11, 1908 | | | | | |
| 1929-30 | New York R | 10 | 0 | 0 | 0 |
| 1930-31 | New York R | 42 | 2 | 1 | 3 |
| 1932-33 | New York A | 15 | 1 | 1 | 2 |
| | **Totals** | 67 | 3 | 2 | 5 |
| **REGIER, Darcy** *Defenseman* | | | | | |
| b. Swift Current, Sask., Nov. 27, 1956 | | | | | |
| 1977-78 | Cleveland | 15 | 0 | 1 | 1 |
| 1982-83 | New York I | 6 | 0 | 0 | 0 |
| | **Totals** | 21 | 0 | 1 | 1 |

| Season | Club | GP | G | A | Pts. |
|---|---|---|---|---|---|
| **REIBEL, Earl (Dutch)** *Forward* | | | | | |
| b. Kitchener, Ont., July 21, 1930 | | | | | |
| 1953-54 | Detroit | 69 | 15 | 33 | 48 |
| 1954-55 | Detroit | 70 | 25 | 41 | 66 |
| 1955-56 | Detroit | 68 | 17 | 39 | 56 |
| 1956-57 | Detroit | 70 | 13 | 23 | 36 |
| 1957-58 | Det-Chi | 69 | 8 | 17 | 25 |
| 1958-59 | Boston | 63 | 6 | 8 | 14 |
| | **Totals** | 409 | 84 | 161 | 245 |
| **REID, Allen Thomas (Tom)** *Defenseman* | | | | | |
| b. Fort Erie, Ont., June 24, 1946 | | | | | |
| 1967-68 | Chicago | 56 | 0 | 4 | 4 |
| 1968-69 | Chi-Minn | 48 | 0 | 7 | 7 |
| 1969-70 | Minnesota | 66 | 1 | 7 | 8 |
| 1970-71 | Minnesota | 73 | 3 | 14 | 17 |
| 1971-72 | Minnesota | 78 | 6 | 15 | 21 |
| 1972-73 | Minnesota | 60 | 1 | 13 | 14 |
| 1973-74 | Minnesota | 76 | 4 | 19 | 23 |
| 1974-75 | Minnesota | 74 | 1 | 5 | 6 |
| 1975-76 | Minnesota | 69 | 0 | 15 | 15 |
| 1976-77 | Minnesota | 65 | 0 | 8 | 8 |
| 1977-78 | Minnesota | 36 | 1 | 6 | 7 |
| | **Totals** | 701 | 17 | 113 | 130 |
| **REID, David** *Forward* | | | | | |
| b. Toronto, Ont., Jan. 11, 1934 | | | | | |
| 1952-53 | Toronto | 2 | 0 | 0 | 0 |
| 1954-55 | Toronto | 1 | 0 | 0 | 0 |
| 1955-56 | Toronto | 4 | 0 | 0 | 0 |
| | **Totals** | 7 | 0 | 0 | 0 |
| **REID, Gordon J.** *Defenseman* | | | | | |
| b. Mt. Albert, Ont., Feb. 19, 1912 | | | | | |
| 1936-37 | New York A | — | 0 | 0 | 0 |
| **REID, Reginald S.** | | | | | |
| 1924-25 | Toronto | 28 | 2 | 0 | 2 |
| 1925-26 | Toronto | 12 | 0 | 0 | 0 |
| | **Totals** | 40 | 2 | 0 | 2 |
| **REIGLE, Edmond (Rags)** *Defenseman* | | | | | |
| b. Winnipeg, Man., June 19, 1924 | | | | | |
| 1950-51 | Boston | 17 | 0 | 2 | 2 |
| **REINHART, Paul** *Defenseman* | | | | | |
| b. Kitchener, Ont., Jan. 8, 1960 | | | | | |
| 1979-80 | Atlanta | 79 | 9 | 38 | 47 |
| 1980-81 | Calgary | 74 | 18 | 49 | 67 |
| 1981-82 | Calgary | 62 | 13 | 48 | 61 |
| 1982-83 | Calgary | 78 | 17 | 58 | 75 |
| | **Totals** | 293 | 57 | 193 | 250 |
| **REINIKKA, Oliver Mathias (Rocco)** *Forward* | | | | | |
| b. Shuswap, B.C., Aug. 2, 1901 | | | | | |
| 1926-27 | New York R | 16 | 0 | 0 | 0 |
| **REISE, Leo Charles, Jr.** *Defenseman* | | | | | |
| b. Stoney Creek, Ont., June 7, 1922 | | | | | |
| 1945-46 | Chicago | 6 | 0 | 0 | 0 |
| 1946-47 | Chi-Det | 48 | 4 | 6 | 10 |
| 1947-48 | Detroit | 58 | 5 | 4 | 9 |
| 1948-49 | Detroit | 59 | 3 | 7 | 10 |
| 1949-50 | Detroit | 70 | 4 | 17 | 21 |
| 1950-51 | Detroit | 68 | 5 | 16 | 21 |
| 1951-52 | Detroit | 54 | 0 | 11 | 11 |
| 1952-53 | New York R | 61 | 4 | 15 | 19 |
| 1953-54 | New York R | 70 | 3 | 5 | 8 |
| | **Totals** | 494 | 28 | 81 | 109 |
| **REISE, Leo Charles, Sr.** *Defenseman* | | | | | |
| b. Pembroke, Ont., June 1, 1892 | | | | | |
| 1920-21 | Hamilton | 6 | 2 | 0 | 2 |
| 1921-22 | Hamilton | 24 | 9 | 14 | 23 |
| 1922-23 | Hamilton | 24 | 6 | 6 | 12 |
| 1923-24 | Hamilton | 4 | 0 | 0 | 0 |
| 1926-27 | New York A | 40 | 7 | 6 | 13 |
| 1927-28 | New York A | 43 | 8 | 1 | 9 |

| Season | Club | GP | G | A | Pts. |
|---|---|---|---|---|---|
| 1928-29 | New York A | 44 | 4 | 1 | 5 |
| 1929-30 | New York R | 14 | 0 | 1 | 1 |
| | **Totals** | 199 | 36 | 29 | 65 |

**RENAUD, Mark** *Defenseman*
b. Windsor, Ont., Feb. 21, 1959

| Season | Club | GP | G | A | Pts. |
|---|---|---|---|---|---|
| 1979-80 | Hartford | 13 | 0 | 2 | 2 |
| 1980-81 | Hartford | 4 | 1 | 0 | 1 |
| 1981-82 | Hartford | 48 | 1 | 17 | 18 |
| 1982-83 | Hartford | 77 | 3 | 28 | 31 |
| | **Totals** | 142 | 5 | 47 | 52 |

**RIBBLE, Patrick Wayne** *Defenseman*
b. Leamington, Ont., Apr. 26, 1954

| Season | Club | GP | G | A | Pts. |
|---|---|---|---|---|---|
| 1975-76 | Atlanta | 3 | 0 | 0 | 0 |
| 1976-77 | Atlanta | 23 | 2 | 2 | 4 |
| 1977-78 | Atlanta | 80 | 5 | 12 | 17 |
| 1978-79 | Atl-Chi | 78 | 6 | 19 | 25 |
| 1979-80 | Chi-Tor-Wash | 55 | 2 | 9 | 11 |
| 1980-81 | Washington | 67 | 3 | 15 | 18 |
| 1981-82 | Wash-Calg | 15 | 1 | 2 | 3 |
| 1982-83 | Calgary | 28 | 0 | 1 | 1 |
| | **Totals** | 349 | 19 | 60 | 79 |

**RICHARD, Jacques** *Forward*
b. Quebec City, Que., Oct. 7, 1952

| Season | Club | GP | G | A | Pts. |
|---|---|---|---|---|---|
| 1972-73 | Atlanta | 74 | 13 | 18 | 31 |
| 1973-74 | Atlanta | 78 | 27 | 16 | 43 |
| 1974-75 | Atlanta | 63 | 17 | 12 | 29 |
| 1975-76 | Buffalo | 73 | 12 | 23 | 35 |
| 1976-77 | Buffalo | 21 | 2 | 0 | 2 |
| 1978-79 | Buffalo | 61 | 10 | 15 | 25 |
| 1979-80 | Quebec | 14 | 3 | 12 | 15 |
| 1980-81 | Quebec | 78 | 52 | 51 | 103 |
| 1981-82 | Quebec | 59 | 15 | 26 | 41 |
| 1982-83 | Quebec | 35 | 9 | 14 | 23 |
| | **Totals** | 556 | 160 | 187 | 347 |

**RICHARD, Joseph Henri (Pocket Rocket)**
*Forward*
b. Montreal, Que., Feb. 29, 1936

| Season | Club | GP | G | A | Pts. |
|---|---|---|---|---|---|
| 1955-56 | Montreal | 64 | 19 | 21 | 40 |
| 1956-57 | Montreal | 63 | 18 | 36 | 54 |
| 1957-58 | Montreal | 67 | 28 | 52 | 80 |
| 1958-59 | Montreal | 63 | 21 | 30 | 51 |
| 1959-60 | Montreal | 70 | 30 | 43 | 73 |
| 1960-61 | Montreal | 70 | 24 | 44 | 68 |
| 1961-62 | Montreal | 54 | 21 | 29 | 50 |
| 1962-63 | Montreal | 67 | 23 | 50 | 73 |
| 1963-64 | Montreal | 66 | 14 | 39 | 53 |
| 1964-65 | Montreal | 53 | 23 | 29 | 52 |
| 1965-66 | Montreal | 62 | 22 | 39 | 61 |
| 1966-67 | Montreal | 65 | 21 | 34 | 55 |
| 1967-68 | Montreal | 54 | 9 | 19 | 28 |
| 1968-69 | Montreal | 64 | 15 | 37 | 52 |
| 1969-70 | Montreal | 62 | 16 | 36 | 52 |
| 1970-71 | Montreal | 75 | 12 | 37 | 49 |
| 1971-72 | Montreal | 75 | 12 | 32 | 44 |
| 1972-73 | Montreal | 71 | 8 | 35 | 43 |
| 1973-74 | Montreal | 75 | 19 | 36 | 55 |
| 1974-75 | Montreal | 16 | 3 | 10 | 13 |
| | **Totals** | 1256 | 358 | 688 | 1046 |

**RICHARD, Joseph Henri Maurice (Rocket)**
*Forward*
b. Montreal, Que., Aug. 4, 1921

| Season | Club | GP | G | A | Pts. |
|---|---|---|---|---|---|
| 1942-43 | Montreal | 16 | 5 | 6 | 11 |
| 1943-44 | Montreal | 46 | 32 | 22 | 54 |
| 1944-45 | Montreal | 50 | 50 | 23 | 73 |
| 1945-46 | Montreal | 50 | 27 | 21 | 48 |
| 1946-47 | Montreal | 60 | 45 | 26 | 71 |
| 1947-48 | Montreal | 53 | 28 | 25 | 53 |
| 1948-49 | Montreal | 59 | 20 | 18 | 38 |
| 1949-50 | Montreal | 70 | 43 | 22 | 65 |
| 1950-51 | Montreal | 65 | 42 | 24 | 66 |
| 1951-52 | Montreal | 48 | 27 | 17 | 44 |
| 1952-53 | Montreal | 70 | 28 | 33 | 61 |
| 1953-54 | Montreal | 70 | 37 | 30 | 67 |
| 1954-55 | Montreal | 67 | 38 | 36 | 74 |
| 1955-56 | Montreal | 70 | 38 | 33 | 71 |
| 1956-57 | Montreal | 63 | 33 | 29 | 62 |
| 1957-58 | Montreal | 28 | 15 | 19 | 34 |

| Season | Club | GP | G | A | Pts. |
|---|---|---|---|---|---|
| 1958-59 | Montreal | 42 | 17 | 21 | 38 |
| 1959-60 | Montreal | 51 | 19 | 16 | 35 |
| | **Totals** | 978 | 544 | 421 | 965 |

**RICHARDSON, David George** *Forward*
b. St. Boniface, Man., Dec. 11, 1940

| Season | Club | GP | G | A | Pts. |
|---|---|---|---|---|---|
| 1963-64 | New York R | 34 | 3 | 1 | 4 |
| 1964-65 | New York R | 7 | 0 | 1 | 1 |
| 1965-66 | Chicago | 3 | 0 | 0 | 0 |
| 1967-68 | Detroit | 1 | 0 | 0 | 0 |
| | **Totals** | 45 | 3 | 2 | 5 |

**RICHARDSON, Glen Gordon** *Forward*
b. Barrie, Ont., Sept. 20, 1955

| Season | Club | GP | G | A | Pts. |
|---|---|---|---|---|---|
| 1975-76 | Vancouver | 24 | 3 | 6 | 9 |

**RICHARDSON, Kenneth William** *Forward*
b. North Bay, Ont., Apr. 12, 1951

| Season | Club | GP | G | A | Pts. |
|---|---|---|---|---|---|
| 1974-75 | St Louis | 21 | 5 | 7 | 12 |
| 1977-78 | St Louis | 12 | 2 | 5 | 7 |
| 1978-79 | St Louis | 16 | 1 | 1 | 2 |
| | **Totals** | 49 | 8 | 13 | 21 |

**RICHER, Robert Roger (Bob)** *Forward*
b. Cowansville, Que., Mar. 5, 1951

| Season | Club | GP | G | A | Pts. |
|---|---|---|---|---|---|
| 1972-73 | Buffalo | 3 | 0 | 0 | 0 |

**RICHTER, Dave** *Defenseman*
b. St. Boniface, Man., Apr. 8, 1960

| Season | Club | GP | G | A | Pts. |
|---|---|---|---|---|---|
| 1981-82 | Minnesota | 3 | 0 | 0 | 0 |
| 1982-83 | Minnesota | 6 | 0 | 0 | 0 |
| | **Totals** | 9 | 0 | 0 | 0 |

**RILEY, Jack** *Forward*
b. Berckenia, Ireland, Dec. 29, 1910

| Season | Club | GP | G | A | Pts. |
|---|---|---|---|---|---|
| 1933-34 | Montreal | 48 | 6 | 11 | 17 |
| 1934-35 | Montreal | 47 | 4 | 11 | 15 |
| | **Totals** | 95 | 10 | 22 | 32 |

**RILEY, James** *Defenseman*

| Season | Club | GP | G | A | Pts. |
|---|---|---|---|---|---|
| 1926-27 | Det-Chi | 15 | 0 | 2 | 2 |

**RILEY, James William** *Forward*
b. Amherst, N.S., Sept. 20, 1950

| Season | Club | GP | G | A | Pts. |
|---|---|---|---|---|---|
| 1974-75 | Washington | 1 | 0 | 0 | 0 |
| 1976-77 | Washington | 43 | 13 | 14 | 27 |
| 1977-78 | Washington | 57 | 13 | 12 | 25 |
| 1978-79 | Washington | 24 | 2 | 2 | 4 |
| 1979-80 | Winnipeg | 14 | 3 | 2 | 5 |
| | **Totals** | 139 | 31 | 30 | 61 |

**RIOPELLE, Howard Joseph (Rip)** *Forward*
b. Ottawa, Ont., Jan. 30, 1922

| Season | Club | GP | G | A | Pts. |
|---|---|---|---|---|---|
| 1947-48 | Montreal | 55 | 5 | 2 | 7 |
| 1948-49 | Montreal | 48 | 10 | 6 | 16 |
| 1949-50 | Montreal | 66 | 12 | 8 | 20 |
| | **Totals** | 169 | 27 | 16 | 43 |

**RIOUX, Pierre** *Forward*
b. Quebec City, Que., Feb. 1, 1962

| Season | Club | GP | G | A | Pts. |
|---|---|---|---|---|---|
| 1982-83 | Calgary | 14 | 1 | 2 | 3 |

**RIPLEY, Victor Merrick** *Forward*
b. Elgin, Ont., May 30, 1906

| Season | Club | GP | G | A | Pts. |
|---|---|---|---|---|---|
| 1928-29 | Chicago | 39 | 11 | 2 | 13 |
| 1929-30 | Chicago | 38 | 8 | 8 | 16 |
| 1930-31 | Chicago | 39 | 8 | 4 | 12 |
| 1931-32 | Chicago | 48 | 12 | 6 | 18 |
| 1932-33 | Chi-Bos | 40 | 4 | 9 | 13 |
| 1933-34 | Bos-NYR | 48 | 7 | 13 | 20 |
| 1934-35 | NYR-StLE | 35 | 1 | 7 | 8 |
| | **Totals** | 287 | 51 | 49 | 100 |

**RISEBROUGH, Douglas** *Forward*
b. Guelph, Ont., Jan. 29, 1954

| Season | Club | GP | G | A | Pts. |
|---|---|---|---|---|---|
| 1974-75 | Montreal | 64 | 15 | 32 | 47 |
| 1975-76 | Montreal | 80 | 16 | 28 | 44 |

| Season | Club | GP | G | A | Pts. |
|---|---|---|---|---|---|
| 1976-77 | Montreal | 78 | 22 | 38 | 60 |
| 1977-78 | Montreal | 72 | 18 | 23 | 41 |
| 1978-79 | Montreal | 48 | 10 | 15 | 25 |
| 1979-80 | Montreal | 44 | 8 | 10 | 18 |
| 1980-81 | Montreal | 48 | 13 | 21 | 34 |
| 1981-82 | Montreal | 59 | 15 | 18 | 33 |
| 1982-83 | Calgary | 71 | 21 | 37 | 58 |
| | **Totals** | 564 | 138 | 222 | 360 |

**RISSLING, Gary Daniel** *Forward*
b. Saskatoon, Sask., Aug. 8, 1956

| Season | Club | GP | G | A | Pts. |
|---|---|---|---|---|---|
| 1978-79 | Washington | 26 | 3 | 3 | 6 |
| 1979-80 | Washington | 11 | 0 | 1 | 1 |
| 1980-81 | Pittsburgh | 25 | 1 | 0 | 1 |
| 1981-82 | Pittsburgh | 16 | 0 | 0 | 0 |
| 1982-83 | Pittsburgh | 40 | 5 | 4 | 9 |
| | **Totals** | 118 | 9 | 8 | 17 |

**RITCHIE, David** *Defenseman*

| Season | Club | GP | G | A | Pts. |
|---|---|---|---|---|---|
| 1917-18 | MontW-Ott | 17 | 9 | 0 | 9 |
| 1918-19 | Toronto | 4 | 0 | 0 | 0 |
| 1919-20 | Quebec | 21 | 6 | 3 | 9 |
| 1920-21 | Montreal | 5 | 0 | 0 | 0 |
| 1924-25 | Montreal | 5 | 0 | 0 | 0 |
| 1925-26 | Montreal | 2 | 0 | 0 | 0 |
| | **Totals** | 54 | 15 | 3 | 18 |

**RITCHIE, Robert** *Forward*
b. Laverlocheve, Que., Feb. 20, 1955

| Season | Club | GP | G | A | Pts. |
|---|---|---|---|---|---|
| 1976-77 | Phil-Det | 18 | 6 | 2 | 8 |
| 1977-78 | Detroit | 11 | 2 | 2 | 4 |
| | **Totals** | 29 | 8 | 4 | 12 |

**RITSON, Alexander Clive (Alex)** *Forward*
b. Peace River, Alta., Mar. 7, 1922

| Season | Club | GP | G | A | Pts. |
|---|---|---|---|---|---|
| 1944-45 | New York R | 1 | 0 | 0 | 0 |

**RITTINGER, Alan Wilbur** *Forward*
b. Regina, Sask., Jan. 28, 1925

| Season | Club | GP | G | A | Pts. |
|---|---|---|---|---|---|
| 1943-44 | Boston | 19 | 3 | 7 | 10 |

**RIVARD, Joseph Robert (Bob)** *Forward*
b. Sherbrooke, Que., Aug. 1, 1939

| Season | Club | GP | G | A | Pts. |
|---|---|---|---|---|---|
| 1967-68 | Pittsburgh | 27 | 5 | 12 | 17 |

**RIVERS, George (Gus)** *Forward*
b. Winnipeg, Man., Nov. 19, 1909

| Season | Club | GP | G | A | Pts. |
|---|---|---|---|---|---|
| 1929-30 | Montreal | 19 | 1 | 0 | 1 |
| 1930-31 | Montreal | 44 | 2 | 5 | 7 |
| 1931-32 | Montreal | 25 | 1 | 0 | 1 |
| | **Totals** | 88 | 4 | 5 | 9 |

**RIVERS, John Wayne** *Forward*
b. Hamilton, Ont., Feb. 1, 1942

| Season | Club | GP | G | A | Pts. |
|---|---|---|---|---|---|
| 1961-62 | Detroit | 2 | 0 | 0 | 0 |
| 1963-64 | Boston | 12 | 2 | 7 | 9 |
| 1964-65 | Boston | 58 | 6 | 17 | 23 |
| 1965-66 | Boston | 2 | 1 | 1 | 2 |
| 1966-67 | Boston | 8 | 2 | 1 | 3 |
| 1967-68 | St Louis | 22 | 4 | 4 | 8 |
| 1968-69 | New York R | 4 | 0 | 0 | 0 |
| 1972-73 | New York (WHA) | 75 | 37 | 40 | 77 |
| 1973-74 | New Jersey (WHA) | 73 | 30 | 27 | 57 |
| 1974-75 | San Diego (WHA) | 78 | 54 | 53 | 107 |
| 1975-76 | San Diego (WHA) | 71 | 19 | 25 | 44 |
| 1976-77 | San Diego (WHA) | 60 | 18 | 31 | 49 |
| | **NHL Totals** | 108 | 15 | 30 | 45 |
| | **WHA Totals** | 357 | 158 | 176 | 334 |

**RIZZUTO, Garth Alexander** *Forward*
b. Trail, B.C., Sept. 11, 1947

| Season | Club | GP | G | A | Pts. |
|---|---|---|---|---|---|
| 1970-71 | Vancouver | 37 | 3 | 4 | 7 |
| 1972-73 | Winnipeg (WHA) | 63 | 10 | 10 | 20 |
| | **NHL Totals** | 37 | 3 | 4 | 7 |
| | **WHA Totals** | 63 | 10 | 10 | 20 |

**ROACH, Mickey** *Forward*
b. Boston, Mass., 1895

| Season | Club | GP | G | A | Pts. |
|---|---|---|---|---|---|
| 1919-20 | Toronto | 20 | 10 | 2 | 12 |
| 1920-21 | Tor-Ham | 22 | 9 | 7 | 16 |
| 1921-22 | Hamilton | 24 | 14 | 3 | 17 |
| 1922-23 | Hamilton | 23 | 17 | 8 | 25 |
| 1923-24 | Hamilton | 21 | 5 | 3 | 8 |
| 1924-25 | Hamilton | 30 | 6 | 4 | 10 |
| 1925-26 | New York A | 25 | 3 | 0 | 3 |
| 1926-27 | New York A | 44 | 11 | 0 | 11 |
| | **Totals** | 209 | 75 | 27 | 102 |

**ROBERT, Claude** *Forward*
b. Montreal, Que., Aug. 10, 1928

| Season | Club | GP | G | A | Pts. |
|---|---|---|---|---|---|
| 1950-51 | Montreal | 23 | 1 | 0 | 1 |

**ROBERT, Rene Paul** *Forward*
b. Trois-Rivières, Que., Dec. 31, 1948

| Season | Club | GP | G | A | Pts. |
|---|---|---|---|---|---|
| 1970-71 | Toronto | 5 | 0 | 0 | 0 |
| 1971-72 | Pitt-Buf | 61 | 13 | 14 | 27 |
| 1972-73 | Buffalo | 75 | 40 | 43 | 83 |
| 1973-74 | Buffalo | 76 | 21 | 44 | 65 |
| 1974-75 | Buffalo | 74 | 40 | 60 | 100 |
| 1975-76 | Buffalo | 72 | 35 | 52 | 87 |
| 1976-77 | Buffalo | 80 | 33 | 40 | 73 |
| 1977-78 | Buffalo | 67 | 25 | 48 | 73 |
| 1978-79 | Buffalo | 68 | 22 | 40 | 62 |
| 1979-80 | Colorado | 69 | 28 | 35 | 63 |
| 1980-81 | Col-Tor | 42 | 14 | 18 | 32 |
| 1981-82 | Toronto | 55 | 13 | 24 | 37 |
| | **Totals** | 744 | 284 | 418 | 702 |

**ROBERTO, Philip Joseph** *Forward*
b. Niagara Falls, Ont., Jan. 1, 1949

| Season | Club | GP | G | A | Pts. |
|---|---|---|---|---|---|
| 1969-70 | Montreal | 8 | 0 | 1 | 1 |
| 1970-71 | Montreal | 39 | 14 | 7 | 21 |
| 1971-72 | StL-Mont | 76 | 15 | 15 | 30 |
| 1972-73 | St Louis | 77 | 20 | 22 | 42 |
| 1973-74 | St Louis | 15 | 1 | 1 | 2 |
| 1974-75 | StL-Det | 53 | 13 | 29 | 42 |
| 1975-76 | Det-KC | 74 | 8 | 22 | 30 |
| 1976-77 | Col-Clev | 43 | 4 | 9 | 13 |
| 1977-78 | Birmingham (WHA) | 53 | 8 | 20 | 28 |
| | **NHL Totals** | 385 | 75 | 106 | 181 |
| | **WHA Totals** | 53 | 8 | 20 | 28 |

**ROBERTS, Douglas William (Doug)**
*Defenseman*
b. Detroit, Mich., Oct. 28, 1942

| Season | Club | GP | G | A | Pts. |
|---|---|---|---|---|---|
| 1965-66 | Detroit | 1 | 0 | 0 | 0 |
| 1966-67 | Detroit | 13 | 3 | 1 | 4 |
| 1967-68 | Detroit | 37 | 8 | 9 | 17 |
| 1968-69 | Oakland | 76 | 1 | 19 | 20 |
| 1969-70 | Oakland | 76 | 6 | 25 | 31 |
| 1970-71 | California | 78 | 4 | 13 | 17 |
| 1971-72 | Boston | 3 | 1 | 0 | 1 |
| 1972-73 | Boston | 45 | 4 | 7 | 11 |
| 1973-74 | Detroit | 64 | 12 | 26 | 38 |
| 1974-75 | Detroit | 26 | 4 | 4 | 8 |
| 1975-76 | New England (WHA) | 76 | 4 | 13 | 17 |
| 1976-77 | New England (WHA) | 64 | 3 | 18 | 21 |
| | **NHL Totals** | 419 | 43 | 104 | 147 |
| | **WHA Totals** | 140 | 7 | 31 | 38 |

**ROBERTS, Gordon** *Defenseman*
b. Detroit, Mich., Oct. 2, 1957

| Season | Club | GP | G | A | Pts. |
|---|---|---|---|---|---|
| 1975-76 | New England (WHA) | 77 | 3 | 19 | 22 |
| 1976-77 | New England (WHA) | 77 | 13 | 33 | 46 |
| 1977-78 | New England (WHA) | 78 | 15 | 46 | 61 |
| 1978-79 | New England (WHA) | 79 | 11 | 46 | 57 |
| 1979-80 | Hartford | 80 | 8 | 28 | 36 |
| 1980-81 | Hart-Minn | 77 | 8 | 42 | 50 |
| 1981-82 | Minnesota | 79 | 4 | 30 | 34 |
| 1982-83 | Minnesota | 80 | 3 | 41 | 44 |
| | **NHL Totals** | 316 | 23 | 141 | 164 |
| | **WHA Totals** | 311 | 42 | 144 | 186 |

**ROBERTS, James Drew** *Forward*
b. Toronto, Ont., June 8, 1956

| Season | Club | GP | G | A | Pts. |
|---|---|---|---|---|---|
| 1976-77 | Minnesota | 53 | 11 | 8 | 19 |
| 1977-78 | Minnesota | 42 | 4 | 14 | 18 |
| 1978-79 | Minnesota | 11 | 2 | 1 | 3 |
| | **Totals** | 106 | 17 | 23 | 40 |


**ROBERTS, James Wilfred (Jim)**
*Defenseman-Forward*
b. Toronto, Ont., Apr. 9, 1940

| Season | Club | GP | G | A | Pts. |
|---|---|---|---|---|---|
| 1963-64 | Montreal | 15 | 0 | 1 | 1 |
| 1964-65 | Montreal | 70 | 3 | 10 | 13 |
| 1965-66 | Montreal | 70 | 5 | 5 | 10 |
| 1966-67 | Montreal | 63 | 3 | 0 | 3 |
| 1967-68 | St Louis | 74 | 14 | 23 | 37 |
| 1968-69 | St Louis | 72 | 14 | 19 | 33 |
| 1969-70 | St Louis | 76 | 13 | 17 | 30 |
| 1970-71 | St Louis | 72 | 13 | 18 | 31 |
| 1971-72 | StL-Mont | 77 | 12 | 22 | 34 |
| 1972-73 | Montreal | 77 | 14 | 18 | 32 |
| 1973-74 | Montreal | 67 | 8 | 16 | 24 |
| 1974-75 | Montreal | 79 | 5 | 13 | 18 |
| 1975-76 | Montreal | 74 | 13 | 8 | 21 |
| 1976-77 | Montreal | 45 | 5 | 14 | 19 |
| 1977-78 | Montreal | 75 | 4 | 10 | 14 |
| | **Totals** | 1006 | 126 | 194 | 320 |

**ROBERTSON, Fred** *Defenseman*
b. Carlisle, England, Oct. 22, 1911

| Season | Club | GP | G | A | Pts. |
|---|---|---|---|---|---|
| 1931-32 | Toronto | 8 | 0 | 0 | 0 |
| 1933-34 | Detroit | 20 | 1 | 0 | 1 |
| | **Totals** | 28 | 1 | 0 | 1 |

**ROBERTSON, Geordie** *Forward*
b. Victoria, B.C., Aug. 1, 1959

| Season | Club | GP | G | A | Pts. |
|---|---|---|---|---|---|
| 1982-83 | Buffalo | 5 | 1 | 2 | 3 |

**ROBERTSON, George Thomas** *Forward*
b. Winnipeg, Man., May 11, 1928

| Season | Club | GP | G | A | Pts. |
|---|---|---|---|---|---|
| 1947-48 | Montreal | 1 | 0 | 0 | 0 |
| 1948-49 | Montreal | 30 | 2 | 5 | 7 |
| | **Totals** | 31 | 2 | 5 | 7 |

**ROBERTSON, Torrie Andrew** *Forward*
b. Victoria, B.C., Aug. 2, 1961

| Season | Club | GP | G | A | Pts. |
|---|---|---|---|---|---|
| 1980-81 | Washington | 3 | 0 | 0 | 0 |
| 1981-82 | Washington | 54 | 8 | 13 | 21 |
| 1982-83 | Washington | 5 | 2 | 0 | 2 |
| | **Totals** | 62 | 10 | 13 | 23 |

**ROBIDOUX, Florent** *Forward*
b. Treberne, Man., May 5, 1960

| Season | Club | GP | G | A | Pts. |
|---|---|---|---|---|---|
| 1980-81 | Chicago | 36 | 6 | 2 | 8 |
| 1981-82 | Chicago | 4 | 1 | 2 | 3 |
| | **Totals** | 40 | 7 | 4 | 11 |

**ROBINSON, Douglas Garnet (Doug)** *Forward*
b. St. Catharines, Ont., Aug. 27, 1940

| Season | Club | GP | G | A | Pts. |
|---|---|---|---|---|---|
| 1964-65 | Chi-NYR | 61 | 10 | 23 | 33 |
| 1965-66 | New York R | 51 | 8 | 12 | 20 |
| 1966-67 | New York R | 1 | 0 | 0 | 0 |
| 1967-68 | Los Angeles | 34 | 9 | 9 | 18 |
| 1968-69 | Los Angeles | 31 | 2 | 10 | 12 |
| 1970-71 | Los Angeles | 61 | 15 | 13 | 28 |
| | **Totals** | 239 | 44 | 67 | 111 |

**ROBINSON, Earle** *Forward*
b. Montreal, Que., Mar. 11, 1907

| Season | Club | GP | G | A | Pts. |
|---|---|---|---|---|---|
| 1928-29 | Montreal M | 38 | 2 | 1 | 3 |
| 1929-30 | Montreal M | 31 | 1 | 2 | 3 |
| 1931-32 | Montreal M | 26 | 0 | 3 | 3 |
| 1932-33 | Montreal M | 44 | 15 | 9 | 24 |
| 1933-34 | Montreal M | 47 | 12 | 16 | 28 |
| 1934-35 | Montreal M | 48 | 17 | 18 | 35 |
| 1935-36 | Montreal M | 39 | 6 | 14 | 20 |
| 1936-37 | Montreal M | 47 | 16 | 18 | 34 |
| 1937-38 | Montreal M | 39 | 4 | 7 | 11 |
| 1938-39 | Chicago | 47 | 9 | 6 | 15 |
| 1939-40 | Montreal | 11 | 1 | 4 | 5 |
| | **Totals** | 417 | 83 | 98 | 181 |

**ROBINSON, Larry Clark** *Defenseman*
b. Winchester, Ont., June 2, 1951

| Season | Club | GP | G | A | Pts. |
|---|---|---|---|---|---|
| 1972-73 | Montreal | 36 | 2 | 4 | 6 |
| 1973-74 | Montreal | 78 | 6 | 20 | 26 |
| 1974-75 | Montreal | 80 | 14 | 47 | 61 |
| 1975-76 | Montreal | 80 | 10 | 30 | 40 |
| 1976-77 | Montreal | 77 | 19 | 66 | 85 |


| Season | Club | GP | G | A | Pts. |
|---|---|---|---|---|---|
| 1977-78 | Montreal | 80 | 13 | 52 | 65 |
| 1978-79 | Montreal | 67 | 16 | 45 | 61 |
| 1979-80 | Montreal | 72 | 14 | 61 | 75 |
| 1980-81 | Montreal | 65 | 12 | 38 | 50 |
| 1981-82 | Montreal | 71 | 12 | 47 | 59 |
| 1982-83 | Montreal | 71 | 14 | 49 | 63 |
| | **Totals** | 777 | 132 | 459 | 591 |

**ROBINSON, Morris** *Defenseman*
b. Winchester, Ont., May 29, 1957

| Season | Club | GP | G | A | Pts. |
|---|---|---|---|---|---|
| 1979-80 | Montreal | 1 | 0 | 0 | 0 |

**ROBITAILLE, Michael James David (Mike)**
*Defenseman*
b. Midland, Ont., Feb. 12, 1948

| Season | Club | GP | G | A | Pts. |
|---|---|---|---|---|---|
| 1969-70 | New York R | 4 | 0 | 0 | 0 |
| 1970-71 | NYR-Det | 34 | 5 | 9 | 14 |
| 1971-72 | Buffalo | 31 | 2 | 10 | 12 |
| 1972-73 | Buffalo | 65 | 4 | 17 | 21 |
| 1973-74 | Buffalo | 71 | 2 | 18 | 20 |
| 1974-75 | Buf-Van | 66 | 2 | 23 | 25 |
| 1975-76 | Vancouver | 71 | 8 | 19 | 27 |
| 1976-77 | Vancouver | 40 | 0 | 9 | 9 |
| | **Totals** | 382 | 23 | 105 | 128 |

**ROCHE, Desse** *Forward*
b. Prescott, Ont., Feb. 1, 1907

| Season | Club | GP | G | A | Pts. |
|---|---|---|---|---|---|
| 1930-31 | Montreal M | — | 0 | 1 | 1 |
| 1932-33 | Ottawa | — | 3 | 6 | 9 |
| 1933-34 | Ottawa | — | 14 | 10 | 24 |
| 1934-35 | Detroit | — | 3 | 1 | 4 |
| | **Totals** | — | 20 | 18 | 38 |

**ROCHE, Earl** *Forward*
b. Prescott, Ont., Feb. 22, 1910

| Season | Club | GP | G | A | Pts. |
|---|---|---|---|---|---|
| 1930-31 | Montreal M | 42 | 2 | 0 | 2 |
| 1931-32 | Montreal M | 2 | 0 | 0 | 0 |
| 1932-33 | Bos-Ott | 29 | 4 | 5 | 9 |
| 1933-34 | Ottawa | 45 | 13 | 16 | 29 |
| 1934-35 | StLE-Det | 34 | 6 | 6 | 12 |
| | **Totals** | 152 | 25 | 27 | 52 |

**ROCHE, Ernest Charles** *Defenseman*
b. Montreal, Que., Feb. 4, 1930

| Season | Club | GP | G | A | Pts. |
|---|---|---|---|---|---|
| 1950-51 | Montreal | 4 | 0 | 0 | 0 |

**ROCHEFORT, David Joseph** *Forward*
b. Red Deer, Alta., July 22, 1946

| Season | Club | GP | G | A | Pts. |
|---|---|---|---|---|---|
| 1966-67 | Detroit | 1 | 0 | 0 | 0 |

**ROCHEFORT, Leon Joseph Fernand**
*Forward*
b. Cap de la Madelaine, Que., May 4, 1939

| Season | Club | GP | G | A | Pts. |
|---|---|---|---|---|---|
| 1960-61 | New York R | 1 | 0 | 0 | 0 |
| 1962-63 | New York R | 23 | 5 | 4 | 9 |
| 1963-64 | Montreal | 3 | 0 | 0 | 0 |
| 1964-65 | Montreal | 9 | 2 | 0 | 2 |
| 1965-66 | Montreal | 1 | 0 | 1 | 1 |
| 1966-67 | Montreal | 27 | 9 | 7 | 16 |
| 1967-68 | Philadelphia | 74 | 21 | 21 | 42 |
| 1968-69 | Philadelphia | 65 | 14 | 21 | 35 |
| 1969-70 | Los Angeles | 76 | 9 | 23 | 32 |
| 1970-71 | Montreal | 57 | 5 | 10 | 15 |
| 1971-72 | Detroit | 64 | 17 | 12 | 29 |
| 1972-73 | Det-Atl | 74 | 11 | 22 | 33 |
| 1973-74 | Atlanta | 56 | 10 | 12 | 22 |
| 1974-75 | Vancouver | 76 | 18 | 11 | 29 |
| 1975-76 | Vancouver | 11 | 0 | 3 | 3 |
| | **Totals** | 617 | 121 | 147 | 268 |

**ROCHEFORT, Normand** *Defenseman*
b. Trois-Rivières, Que., Jan. 28, 1961

| Season | Club | GP | G | A | Pts. |
|---|---|---|---|---|---|
| 1980-81 | Quebec | 56 | 3 | 7 | 10 |
| 1981-82 | Quebec | 72 | 4 | 14 | 18 |
| 1982-83 | Quebec | 62 | 6 | 17 | 23 |
| | **Totals** | 190 | 13 | 38 | 51 |

**ROCKBURN, Harvey** *Defenseman*
b. —

| Season | Club | GP | G | A | Pts. |
|---|---|---|---|---|---|
| 1929-30 | Detroit | 37 | 4 | 0 | 4 |
| 1930-31 | Detroit | 43 | 0 | 1 | 1 |
| 1932-33 | Ottawa | 17 | 0 | 1 | 1 |
| | **Totals** | 97 | 4 | 2 | 6 |

| Season | Club | GP | G | A | Pts. |
|---|---|---|---|---|---|
| **RODDEN, Edmund Anthony** *Forward* | | | | | |
| b. Toronto, Ont., Mar. 22, 1901 | | | | | |
| 1926-27 | Chicago | 19 | 3 | 3 | 6 |
| 1927-28 | Chi-Tor | 42 | 3 | 8 | 11 |
| 1928-29 | Boston | 13 | 0 | 0 | 0 |
| 1930-31 | New York R | 24 | 0 | 3 | 3 |
| | **Totals** | 98 | 6 | 14 | 20 |
| **ROGERS, Alfred John** *Forward* | | | | | |
| b. Paradise Hill, Alta., Apr. 10, 1953 | | | | | |
| 1973-74 | Minnesota | 10 | 2 | 4 | 6 |
| 1974-75 | Minnesota | 4 | 0 | 0 | 0 |
| | **Totals** | 14 | 2 | 4 | 6 |
| **ROGERS, Michael** *Forward* | | | | | |
| b. Calgary, Alta., Oct. 24, 1954 | | | | | |
| 1974-75 | Edmonton (WHA) | 78 | 35 | 48 | 83 |
| 1975-76 | Edm-NE (WHA) | 80 | 30 | 29 | 59 |
| 1976-77 | New England (WHA) | 78 | 25 | 57 | 82 |
| 1977-78 | New England (WHA) | 80 | 28 | 43 | 71 |
| 1978-79 | New England (WHA) | 80 | 27 | 45 | 72 |
| 1979-80 | Hartford | 80 | 44 | 61 | 105 |
| 1980-81 | Hartford | 80 | 40 | 65 | 105 |
| 1981-82 | New York R | 80 | 38 | 65 | 103 |
| 1982-83 | New York R | 71 | 29 | 47 | 76 |
| | **NHL Totals** | 311 | 151 | 238 | 389 |
| | **WHA Totals** | 396 | 145 | 222 | 367 |
| **ROLFE, Dale Roland** *Defenseman* | | | | | |
| b. Timmins, Ont., Apr. 30, 1940 | | | | | |
| 1959-60 | Boston | 3 | 0 | 0 | 0 |
| 1967-68 | Los Angeles | 68 | 3 | 13 | 16 |
| 1968-69 | Los Angeles | 75 | 3 | 19 | 22 |
| 1969-70 | LA-Det | 75 | 3 | 18 | 21 |
| 1970-71 | Det-NYR | 58 | 3 | 16 | 19 |
| 1971-72 | New York R | 68 | 2 | 14 | 16 |
| 1972-73 | New York R | 72 | 7 | 25 | 32 |
| 1973-74 | New York R | 48 | 3 | 12 | 15 |
| 1974-75 | New York R | 42 | 1 | 8 | 9 |
| | **Totals** | 509 | 25 | 125 | 150 |
| **ROMANCHYCH, Larry Brian** *Forward* | | | | | |
| b. Vancouver, B.C., Sept. 7, 1949 | | | | | |
| 1970-71 | Chicago | 10 | 0 | 2 | 2 |
| 1972-73 | Atlanta | 70 | 18 | 30 | 48 |
| 1973-74 | Atlanta | 73 | 22 | 29 | 51 |
| 1974-75 | Atlanta | 53 | 8 | 12 | 20 |
| 1975-76 | Atlanta | 67 | 16 | 19 | 35 |
| 1976-77 | Atlanta | 25 | 4 | 5 | 9 |
| | **Totals** | 298 | 68 | 97 | 165 |
| **ROMBOUGH, Douglas George (Doug)** *Forward* | | | | | |
| b. Fergus, Ont., July 8, 1950 | | | | | |
| 1972-73 | Buffalo | 5 | 2 | 0 | 2 |
| 1973-74 | Buf-NYI | 58 | 9 | 10 | 19 |
| 1974-75 | NYI-Minn | 68 | 11 | 15 | 26 |
| 1975-76 | Minnesota | 19 | 2 | 2 | 4 |
| | **Totals** | 150 | 24 | 27 | 51 |
| **ROMNES, Elwin N. (Doc)** *Forward* | | | | | |
| b. White Bear, Minn., Jan. 1, 1909 | | | | | |
| 1930-31 | Chicago | 30 | 5 | 7 | 12 |
| 1931-32 | Chicago | 18 | 1 | 0 | 1 |
| 1932-33 | Chicago | 47 | 10 | 12 | 22 |
| 1933-34 | Chicago | 47 | 8 | 21 | 29 |
| 1934-35 | Chicago | 35 | 10 | 14 | 24 |
| 1935-36 | Chicago | 48 | 13 | 25 | 38 |
| 1936-37 | Chicago | 28 | 4 | 14 | 18 |
| 1937-38 | Chicago | 44 | 10 | 22 | 32 |
| 1938-39 | Chi-Tor | 48 | 7 | 20 | 27 |
| 1939-40 | New York A | 15 | 0 | 1 | 1 |
| | **Totals** | 360 | 68 | 136 | 204 |
| **RONAN, Erskine (Skene)** *Forward* | | | | | |
| 1918-19 | Ottawa | 11 | 0 | 0 | 0 |
| **RONSON, Leonard Keith** *Forward* | | | | | |
| b. Brantford, Ont., July 8, 1936 | | | | | |
| 1960-61 | New York R | 13 | 2 | 1 | 3 |
| 1968-69 | Oakland | 5 | 0 | 0 | 0 |
| | **Totals** | 18 | 2 | 1 | 3 |
| **RONTY, Paul** *Forward* | | | | | |
| b. Toronto, Ont., June 12, 1928 | | | | | |
| 1947-48 | Boston | 24 | 3 | 11 | 14 |
| 1948-49 | Boston | 60 | 20 | 29 | 49 |
| 1949-50 | Boston | 70 | 23 | 36 | 59 |
| 1950-51 | Boston | 71 | 10 | 22 | 32 |
| 1951-52 | New York R | 65 | 12 | 31 | 43 |
| 1952-53 | New York R | 70 | 16 | 38 | 54 |
| 1953-54 | New York R | 70 | 13 | 33 | 46 |
| 1954-55 | Montreal | 59 | 4 | 11 | 15 |
| | **Totals** | 488 | 101 | 211 | 312 |
| **ROOT, Bill** *Defenseman* | | | | | |
| b. Toronto, Ont., Sept. 6, 1959 | | | | | |
| 1982-83 | Montreal | 46 | 2 | 3 | 5 |
| **ROSS, Arthur Howey** *Defenseman* | | | | | |
| b. Naughton, Ont., Jan. 13, 1886 | | | | | |
| 1917-18 | Montreal W | 3 | 1 | 0 | 1 |
| **ROSS, James** *Defenseman* | | | | | |
| b. Edinburgh, Scotland, May 20, 1926 | | | | | |
| 1951-52 | New York R | 51 | 2 | 9 | 11 |
| 1952-53 | New York R | 11 | 0 | 2 | 2 |
| | **Totals** | 62 | 2 | 11 | 13 |
| **ROSSIGNOL, Roland** *Forward* | | | | | |
| b. Edmundston, N.B., Oct. 18, 1921 | | | | | |
| 1943-44 | Detroit | 1 | 0 | 1 | 1 |
| 1944-45 | Montreal | 5 | 2 | 2 | 4 |
| 1945-46 | Detroit | 8 | 1 | 2 | 3 |
| | **Totals** | 14 | 3 | 5 | 8 |
| **ROTA, Darcy Irwin** *Forward* | | | | | |
| b. Vancouver, B.C., Feb. 16, 1953 | | | | | |
| 1973-74 | Chicago | 74 | 21 | 12 | 33 |
| 1974-75 | Chicago | 78 | 22 | 22 | 44 |
| 1975-76 | Chicago | 79 | 20 | 17 | 37 |
| 1976-77 | Chicago | 76 | 24 | 22 | 46 |
| 1977-78 | Chicago | 78 | 17 | 20 | 37 |
| 1978-79 | Chi-Atl | 76 | 22 | 22 | 44 |
| 1979-80 | Atl-Van | 70 | 15 | 14 | 29 |
| 1980-81 | Vancouver | 80 | 25 | 31 | 56 |
| 1981-82 | Vancouver | 51 | 20 | 20 | 40 |
| 1982-83 | Vancouver | 73 | 42 | 39 | 81 |
| | **Totals** | 735 | 228 | 219 | 447 |
| **ROTA, Randy Frank** *Forward* | | | | | |
| b. Creston, B.C., Aug. 16, 1950 | | | | | |
| 1972-73 | Montreal | 2 | 1 | 1 | 2 |
| 1973-74 | Los Angeles | 58 | 10 | 6 | 16 |
| 1974-75 | Kansas City | 80 | 15 | 18 | 33 |
| 1975-76 | Kansas City | 71 | 12 | 14 | 26 |
| 1976-77 | Colorado | 1 | 0 | 0 | 0 |
| 1976-77 | Edmonton (WHA) | 40 | 9 | 6 | 15 |
| 1977-78 | Edmonton (WHA) | 53 | 8 | 22 | 30 |
| | **NHL Totals** | 212 | 38 | 39 | 77 |
| | **WHA Totals** | 93 | 17 | 28 | 45 |
| **ROTHSCHILD, Samuel (Sammy)** *Forward* | | | | | |
| b. Sudbury, Ont., Oct. 16, 1899 | | | | | |
| 1924-25 | Montreal M | 27 | 5 | 4 | 9 |
| 1925-26 | Montreal M | 33 | 2 | 1 | 3 |
| 1926-27 | Montreal M | 22 | 1 | 1 | 2 |
| 1927-28 | New York A | 17 | 0 | 0 | 0 |
| | **Totals** | 99 | 8 | 6 | 14 |
| **ROULSTON, Thomas** *Forward* | | | | | |
| b. Winnipeg, Man., Nov. 20, 1957 | | | | | |
| 1980-81 | Edmonton | 11 | 1 | 1 | 2 |
| 1981-82 | Edmonton | 35 | 11 | 3 | 14 |
| 1982-83 | Edmonton | 67 | 19 | 21 | 40 |
| | **Totals** | 113 | 31 | 25 | 56 |
| **ROULSTON, William Orville (Rolly)** *Defenseman* | | | | | |
| b. Toronto, Ont., Apr. 12, 1911 | | | | | |
| 1935-36 | Detroit | 1 | 0 | 0 | 0 |
| 1936-37 | Detroit | 21 | 0 | 5 | 5 |
| 1937-38 | Detroit | 2 | 0 | 1 | 1 |
| | **Totals** | 24 | 0 | 6 | 6 |
| **ROUSSEAU, Guy** *Forward* | | | | | |
| b. Montreal, Que., Dec. 21, 1934 | | | | | |
| 1954-55 | Montreal | 2 | 0 | 1 | 1 |
| 1956-57 | Montreal | 2 | 0 | 0 | 0 |
| | **Totals** | 4 | 0 | 1 | 1 |
| **ROUSSEAU, Joseph Jean-Paul Robert (Bobby)** *Forward* | | | | | |
| b. Montreal, Que., July 26, 1940 | | | | | |
| 1960-61 | Montreal | 15 | 1 | 2 | 3 |
| 1961-62 | Montreal | 70 | 21 | 24 | 45 |
| 1962-63 | Montreal | 62 | 19 | 18 | 37 |
| 1963-64 | Montreal | 70 | 25 | 31 | 56 |
| 1964-65 | Montreal | 66 | 12 | 35 | 47 |
| 1965-66 | Montreal | 70 | 30 | 48 | 78 |
| 1966-67 | Montreal | 68 | 19 | 44 | 63 |
| 1967-68 | Montreal | 74 | 19 | 46 | 65 |
| 1968-69 | Montreal | 76 | 30 | 40 | 70 |
| 1969-70 | Montreal | 72 | 24 | 34 | 58 |
| 1970-71 | Minnesota | 63 | 4 | 20 | 24 |
| 1971-72 | New York R | 78 | 21 | 36 | 57 |
| 1972-73 | New York R | 78 | 8 | 37 | 45 |
| 1973-74 | New York R | 72 | 10 | 41 | 51 |
| 1974-75 | New York R | 8 | 2 | 2 | 4 |
| | **Totals** | 942 | 245 | 458 | 703 |
| **ROUSSEAU, Roland** *Defenseman* | | | | | |
| b. Montreal, Que., Dec. 1, 1929 | | | | | |
| 1952-53 | Montreal | 2 | 0 | 0 | 0 |
| **ROWE, Robert (Bobby)** *Defenseman* | | | | | |
| 1924-25 | Boston | 4 | 1 | 0 | 1 |
| **ROWE, Ronald Nicklas** *Forward* | | | | | |
| b. Toronto, Ont., Nov. 30, 1924 | | | | | |
| 1947-48 | New York R | 5 | 1 | 0 | 1 |
| **ROWE, Thomas John** *Forward* | | | | | |
| b. Lynn, Mass., May 23, 1956 | | | | | |
| 1976-77 | Washington | 12 | 1 | 2 | 3 |
| 1977-78 | Washington | 63 | 13 | 8 | 21 |
| 1978-79 | Washington | 69 | 31 | 30 | 61 |
| 1979-80 | Wash-Hart | 61 | 16 | 21 | 37 |
| 1980-81 | Hartford | 74 | 13 | 28 | 41 |
| 1981-82 | Washington | 27 | 5 | 1 | 6 |
| 1982-83 | Detroit | 51 | 6 | 10 | 16 |
| | **Totals** | 357 | 85 | 100 | 185 |
| **ROZZINI, Gino** *Forward* | | | | | |
| b. Shawinigan Falls, Que., Oct. 24, 1918 | | | | | |
| 1944-45 | Boston | 31 | 5 | 10 | 15 |
| **RUELLE, Bernard Edward** *Forward* | | | | | |
| b. Haughton, Mich., Nov. 23, 1920 | | | | | |
| 1943-44 | Detroit | 2 | 1 | 0 | 1 |
| **RUFF, Lindy Cameron** *Defenseman* | | | | | |
| b. Warburg, Alta., Feb. 17, 1960 | | | | | |
| 1979-80 | Buffalo | 63 | 5 | 14 | 19 |
| 1980-81 | Buffalo | 65 | 8 | 18 | 26 |
| 1981-82 | Buffalo | 79 | 16 | 32 | 48 |
| 1982-83 | Buffalo | 60 | 12 | 17 | 29 |
| | **Totals** | 267 | 41 | 81 | 122 |
| **RUHNKE, Kent** *Forward* | | | | | |
| b. Toronto, Ont., Sept. 18, 1952 | | | | | |
| 1975-76 | Boston | 2 | 0 | 1 | 1 |
| 1976-77 | Winnipeg (WHA) | 51 | 11 | 11 | 22 |
| 1977-78 | Winnipeg (WHA) | 21 | 8 | 9 | 17 |
| | **NHL Totals** | 2 | 0 | 1 | 1 |
| | **WHA Totals** | 72 | 19 | 20 | 39 |

| Season | Club | GP | G | A | Pts. |
|---|---|---|---|---|---|
| **RUNGE, Paul** *Forward* | | | | | |
| b. Edmonton, Alta., Sept. 10, 1909 | | | | | |
| 1930-31 | Boston | 1 | 0 | 0 | 0 |
| 1931-32 | Boston | 14 | 0 | 1 | 1 |
| 1933-34 | Montreal M | 4 | 0 | 0 | 0 |
| 1934-35 | Montreal | 3 | 0 | 0 | 0 |
| 1935-36 | Mont-Bos | 45 | 8 | 4 | 12 |
| 1936-37 | Mont-MontM | 34 | 5 | 10 | 15 |
| 1937-38 | Montreal M | 39 | 5 | 7 | 12 |
| | Totals | 140 | 18 | 22 | 40 |
| **RUOTSALAINEN, Reijo** *Defenseman* | | | | | |
| b. Oulu, Finland, Apr. 1, 1960 | | | | | |
| 1981-82 | New York R | 78 | 18 | 38 | 56 |
| 1982-83 | New York R | 77 | 16 | 53 | 69 |
| | Totals | 155 | 34 | 91 | 125 |
| **RUPP, Duane Edward Franklin** *Defenseman* | | | | | |
| b. Macnutt, Sask., Mar. 29, 1938 | | | | | |
| 1962-63 | New York R | 2 | 0 | 0 | 0 |
| 1964-65 | Toronto | 2 | 0 | 0 | 0 |
| 1965-66 | Toronto | 2 | 0 | 1 | 1 |
| 1966-67 | Toronto | 3 | 0 | 0 | 0 |
| 1967-68 | Toronto | 71 | 1 | 8 | 9 |
| 1968-69 | Minn-Pitt | 59 | 5 | 11 | 16 |
| 1969-70 | Pittsburgh | 64 | 2 | 14 | 16 |
| 1970-71 | Pittsburgh | 59 | 5 | 28 | 33 |
| 1971-72 | Pittsburgh | 34 | 4 | 18 | 22 |
| 1972-73 | Pittsburgh | 78 | 7 | 13 | 20 |
| 1974-75 | Vancouver (WHA) | 73 | 3 | 26 | 29 |
| 1975-76 | Calgary (WHA) | 42 | 0 | 16 | 16 |
| | NHL Totals | 374 | 24 | 93 | 117 |
| | WHA Totals | 115 | 3 | 42 | 45 |
| **RUSKOWSKI, Terry Wallace** *Forward* | | | | | |
| b. Prince Albert, Sask., Dec. 31, 1954 | | | | | |
| 1974-75 | Houston (WHA) | 71 | 10 | 36 | 46 |
| 1975-76 | Houston (WHA) | 65 | 14 | 35 | 49 |
| 1976-77 | Houston (WHA) | 80 | 24 | 60 | 84 |
| 1977-78 | Houston (WHA) | 78 | 15 | 57 | 72 |
| 1978-79 | Winnipeg (WHA) | 75 | 20 | 66 | 86 |
| 1979-80 | Chicago | 74 | 15 | 55 | 70 |
| 1980-81 | Chicago | 72 | 8 | 51 | 59 |
| 1981-82 | Chicago | 60 | 7 | 30 | 37 |
| 1982-83 | Chi-LA | 76 | 14 | 32 | 46 |
| | NHL Totals | 282 | 44 | 168 | 212 |
| | WHA Totals | 369 | 83 | 254 | 337 |
| **RUSSELL, Churchill Davidson** *Forward* | | | | | |
| b. Winnipeg, Man., Mar. 16, 1923 | | | | | |
| 1945-46 | New York R | 17 | 0 | 5 | 5 |
| 1946-47 | New York R | 54 | 20 | 8 | 28 |
| 1947-48 | New York R | 19 | 0 | 3 | 3 |
| | Totals | 90 | 20 | 16 | 36 |
| **RUSSELL, Phillip Douglas (Phil)** | | | | | |
| *Defenseman* | | | | | |
| b. Edmonton, Alta., July 1, 1952 | | | | | |
| 1972-73 | Chicago | 76 | 6 | 19 | 25 |
| 1973-74 | Chicago | 75 | 10 | 25 | 35 |
| 1974-75 | Chicago | 80 | 5 | 24 | 29 |
| 1975-76 | Chicago | 74 | 9 | 29 | 38 |
| 1976-77 | Chicago | 76 | 9 | 36 | 45 |
| 1977-78 | Chicago | 57 | 6 | 20 | 26 |
| 1978-79 | Chi-Atl | 79 | 9 | 29 | 38 |
| 1979-80 | Atlanta | 80 | 5 | 31 | 36 |
| 1980-81 | Calgary | 80 | 6 | 23 | 29 |
| 1981-82 | Calgary | 71 | 4 | 25 | 29 |
| 1982-83 | Calgary | 78 | 13 | 18 | 31 |
| | Totals | 826 | 82 | 279 | 361 |
| **SABOURIN, Gary Bruce** *Forward* | | | | | |
| b. Parry Sound, Ont., Dec. 4, 1943 | | | | | |
| 1967-68 | St Louis | 50 | 13 | 10 | 23 |
| 1968-69 | St Louis | 75 | 25 | 23 | 48 |
| 1969-70 | St Louis | 72 | 28 | 14 | 42 |
| 1970-71 | St Louis | 59 | 14 | 17 | 31 |
| 1971-72 | St Louis | 77 | 28 | 17 | 45 |
| 1972-73 | St Louis | 76 | 21 | 27 | 48 |
| 1973-74 | St Louis | 54 | 7 | 23 | 30 |
| 1974-75 | Toronto | 55 | 5 | 18 | 23 |

| Season | Club | GP | G | A | Pts. |
|---|---|---|---|---|---|
| 1975-76 | California | 76 | 21 | 28 | 49 |
| 1976-77 | Cleveland | 33 | 7 | 11 | 18 |
| | Totals | 627 | 169 | 188 | 357 |
| **SABOURIN, Robert** *Forward* | | | | | |
| b. Sudbury, Ont., Mar. 17, 1933 | | | | | |
| 1951-52 | Toronto | 1 | 0 | 0 | 0 |
| **SACHARUK, Lawrence William** *Defenseman* | | | | | |
| b. Saskatoon, Sask., Oct. 16, 1952 | | | | | |
| 1972-73 | New York R | 8 | 1 | 0 | 1 |
| 1973-74 | New York R | 23 | 2 | 4 | 6 |
| 1974-75 | St Louis | 76 | 20 | 22 | 42 |
| 1975-76 | New York R | 42 | 6 | 7 | 13 |
| 1976-77 | New York R | 2 | 0 | 0 | 0 |
| 1978-79 | Indianapolis (WHA) | 15 | 2 | 9 | 11 |
| | NHL Totals | 151 | 29 | 33 | 62 |
| | WHA Totals | 15 | 2 | 9 | 11 |
| **SAGANIUK, Rocky** *Forward* | | | | | |
| b. Myman, Alta., Oct. 15, 1957 | | | | | |
| 1978-79 | Toronto | 16 | 3 | 5 | 8 |
| 1979-80 | Toronto | 75 | 24 | 23 | 47 |
| 1980-81 | Toronto | 71 | 12 | 18 | 30 |
| 1981-82 | Toronto | 65 | 17 | 16 | 33 |
| 1982-83 | Toronto | 3 | 0 | 0 | 0 |
| | Totals | 230 | 56 | 62 | 118 |
| **ST. LAURENT, Andre** *Forward* | | | | | |
| b. Rouyn-Noranda, Que., Feb. 16, 1953 | | | | | |
| 1973-74 | New York I | 42 | 5 | 9 | 14 |
| 1974-75 | New York I | 78 | 14 | 27 | 41 |
| 1975-76 | New York I | 67 | 9 | 17 | 26 |
| 1976-77 | New York I | 72 | 10 | 13 | 23 |
| 1977-78 | NYI-Det | 79 | 31 | 39 | 70 |
| 1978-79 | Detroit | 76 | 18 | 31 | 49 |
| 1979-80 | Los Angeles | 77 | 6 | 24 | 30 |
| 1980-81 | Los Angeles | 22 | 10 | 6 | 16 |
| 1981-82 | LA-Pitt | 34 | 10 | 9 | 19 |
| 1982-83 | Pittsburgh | 70 | 13 | 9 | 22 |
| | Totals | 617 | 126 | 184 | 310 |
| **ST. LAURENT, Dollard Herve** *Defenseman* | | | | | |
| b. Verdun, Que., May 12, 1929 | | | | | |
| 1950-51 | Montreal | 3 | 0 | 0 | 0 |
| 1951-52 | Montreal | 40 | 3 | 10 | 13 |
| 1952-53 | Montreal | 54 | 2 | 6 | 8 |
| 1953-54 | Montreal | 53 | 3 | 12 | 15 |
| 1954-55 | Montreal | 58 | 3 | 14 | 17 |
| 1955-56 | Montreal | 46 | 4 | 9 | 13 |
| 1956-57 | Montreal | 64 | 1 | 11 | 12 |
| 1957-58 | Montreal | 65 | 3 | 20 | 23 |
| 1958-59 | Chicago | 70 | 4 | 8 | 12 |
| 1959-60 | Chicago | 68 | 4 | 13 | 17 |
| 1960-61 | Chicago | 67 | 2 | 17 | 19 |
| 1961-62 | Chicago | 64 | 0 | 13 | 13 |
| | Totals | 652 | 29 | 133 | 162 |
| **ST. MARSEILLE, Francis Leo (Frank)** | | | | | |
| *Forward* | | | | | |
| b. Levack, Ont., Dec. 14, 1939 | | | | | |
| 1967-68 | St Louis | 57 | 16 | 16 | 32 |
| 1968-69 | St Louis | 72 | 12 | 26 | 38 |
| 1969-70 | St Louis | 74 | 16 | 43 | 59 |
| 1970-71 | St Louis | 77 | 19 | 32 | 51 |
| 1971-72 | St Louis | 78 | 16 | 36 | 52 |
| 1972-73 | StL-LA | 74 | 14 | 22 | 36 |
| 1973-74 | Los Angeles | 78 | 14 | 36 | 50 |
| 1974-75 | Los Angeles | 80 | 17 | 36 | 53 |
| 1975-76 | Los Angeles | 68 | 10 | 16 | 26 |
| 1976-77 | Los Angeles | 49 | 6 | 22 | 28 |
| | Totals | 707 | 140 | 285 | 425 |
| **ST. SAUVEUR, Claude** *Forward* | | | | | |
| b. Sherbroke, Que., Jan. 2, 1952 | | | | | |
| 1972-73 | Philadelphia (WHA) | 2 | 1 | 0 | 1 |
| 1973-74 | Vancouver (WHA) | 70 | 38 | 30 | 68 |
| 1974-75 | Vancouver (WHA) | 76 | 24 | 23 | 47 |
| 1975-76 | Atlanta | 74 | 24 | 24 | 48 |
| 1976-77 | Calg-Edm (WHA) | 32 | 5 | 10 | 15 |

| Season | Club | GP | G | A | Pts. |
|---|---|---|---|---|---|
| 1977-78 | Indianapolis (WHA) | 72 | 36 | 42 | 78 |
| 1978-79 | Ind-Cin (WHA) | 33 | 8 | 7 | 15 |
| | NHL Totals | 74 | 24 | 24 | 48 |
| | WHA Totals | 285 | 112 | 112 | 224 |
| **SALESKI, Donald Patrick (Don)** *Forward* | | | | | |
| b. Moose Jaw, Sask., Nov. 10, 1949 | | | | | |
| 1971-72 | Philadelphia | 1 | 0 | 0 | 0 |
| 1972-73 | Philadelphia | 78 | 12 | 9 | 21 |
| 1973-74 | Philadelphia | 77 | 15 | 25 | 40 |
| 1974-75 | Philadelphia | 63 | 10 | 18 | 28 |
| 1975-76 | Philadelphia | 78 | 21 | 26 | 47 |
| 1976-77 | Philadelphia | 74 | 22 | 16 | 38 |
| 1977-78 | Philadelphia | 70 | 27 | 18 | 45 |
| 1978-79 | Phil-Col | 51 | 13 | 5 | 18 |
| 1979-80 | Colorado | 51 | 8 | 8 | 16 |
| | Totals | 543 | 128 | 125 | 253 |
| **SALMING, Anders Borje** *Defenseman* | | | | | |
| b. Kiruna, Sweden, Apr. 17, 1951 | | | | | |
| 1973-74 | Toronto | 76 | 5 | 34 | 39 |
| 1974-75 | Toronto | 60 | 12 | 25 | 37 |
| 1975-76 | Toronto | 78 | 16 | 41 | 57 |
| 1976-77 | Toronto | 76 | 12 | 66 | 78 |
| 1977-78 | Toronto | 80 | 16 | 60 | 76 |
| 1978-79 | Toronto | 78 | 17 | 56 | 73 |
| 1979-80 | Toronto | 74 | 19 | 52 | 71 |
| 1980-81 | Toronto | 72 | 5 | 61 | 66 |
| 1981-82 | Toronto | 69 | 12 | 44 | 56 |
| 1982-83 | Toronto | 69 | 7 | 38 | 45 |
| | Totals | 732 | 121 | 487 | 608 |
| **SALOVAARA, John Barry** *Defenseman* | | | | | |
| b. Cookesville, Ont., Jan. 7, 1948 | | | | | |
| 1974-75 | Detroit | 27 | 0 | 2 | 2 |
| 1975-76 | Detroit | 63 | 2 | 11 | 13 |
| | Totals | 90 | 2 | 13 | 15 |
| **SAMIS, Philip Lawrence** *Defenseman* | | | | | |
| b. Edmonton, Alta., Dec. 28, 1927 | | | | | |
| 1949-50 | Toronto | 2 | 0 | 0 | 0 |
| **SANDERSON, Derek Michael (Turk)** *Forward* | | | | | |
| b. Niagara Falls, Ont., June 16, 1946 | | | | | |
| 1965-66 | Boston | 2 | 0 | 0 | 0 |
| 1966-67 | Boston | 2 | 0 | 0 | 0 |
| 1967-68 | Boston | 71 | 24 | 25 | 49 |
| 1968-69 | Boston | 61 | 26 | 22 | 48 |
| 1969-70 | Boston | 50 | 18 | 23 | 41 |
| 1970-71 | Boston | 71 | 29 | 34 | 63 |
| 1971-72 | Boston | 78 | 25 | 33 | 58 |
| 1972-73 | Philadelphia (WHA) | 8 | 3 | 3 | 6 |
| 1972-73 | Boston | 25 | 5 | 10 | 15 |
| 1973-74 | Boston | 29 | 8 | 12 | 20 |
| 1974-75 | New York R | 75 | 25 | 25 | 50 |
| 1975-76 | NYR-StL | 73 | 24 | 43 | 67 |
| 1976-77 | StL-Van | 48 | 15 | 22 | 37 |
| 1977-78 | Pittsburgh | 13 | 3 | 1 | 4 |
| | NHL Totals | 598 | 202 | 250 | 452 |
| | WHA Totals | 8 | 3 | 3 | 6 |
| **SANDFORD, Edward Michael** *Forward* | | | | | |
| b. New Toronto, Ont., Aug. 20, 1928 | | | | | |
| 1947-48 | Boston | 59 | 10 | 15 | 25 |
| 1948-49 | Boston | 56 | 16 | 20 | 36 |
| 1949-50 | Boston | 17 | 1 | 4 | 5 |
| 1950-51 | Boston | 51 | 10 | 13 | 23 |
| 1951-52 | Boston | 65 | 13 | 12 | 25 |
| 1952-53 | Boston | 61 | 14 | 21 | 35 |
| 1953-54 | Boston | 70 | 16 | 31 | 47 |
| 1954-55 | Boston | 60 | 14 | 20 | 34 |
| 1955-56 | Det-Chi | 61 | 12 | 9 | 21 |
| | Totals | 500 | 106 | 145 | 251 |
| **SANDS, Charles Henry** *Forward* | | | | | |
| b. Fort William, Ont., Mar. 23, 1910 | | | | | |
| 1932-33 | Toronto | 3 | 0 | 3 | 3 |
| 1933-34 | Toronto | 45 | 8 | 8 | 16 |
| 1934-35 | Toronto | 41 | 15 | 12 | 27 |
| 1935-36 | Boston | 40 | 6 | 4 | 10 |
| 1936-37 | Boston | 47 | 18 | 5 | 23 |

| Season | Club | GP | G | A | Pts. |
|---|---|---|---|---|---|
| 1937-38 | Boston | 46 | 17 | 12 | 29 |
| 1938-39 | Boston | 37 | 7 | 5 | 12 |
| 1939-40 | Montreal | 47 | 9 | 20 | 29 |
| 1940-41 | Montreal | 43 | 5 | 13 | 18 |
| 1941-42 | Montreal | 39 | 11 | 16 | 27 |
| 1942-43 | Montreal | 31 | 3 | 9 | 12 |
| 1943-44 | New York R | 9 | 0 | 2 | 2 |
| | Totals | 428 | 99 | 109 | 208 |

**SARGENT, Gary Alan** *Defenseman*
b. Red Lake, Minn., Feb. 8, 1954

| | | | | | |
|---|---|---|---|---|---|
| 1975-76 | Los Angeles | 63 | 8 | 16 | 24 |
| 1976-77 | Los Angeles | 80 | 14 | 40 | 54 |
| 1977-78 | Los Angeles | 72 | 7 | 34 | 41 |
| 1978-79 | Minnesota | 79 | 12 | 32 | 44 |
| 1979-80 | Minnesota | 52 | 13 | 21 | 34 |
| 1980-81 | Minnesota | 23 | 4 | 7 | 11 |
| 1981-82 | Minnesota | 15 | 0 | 5 | 5 |
| 1982-83 | Minnesota | 18 | 3 | 6 | 9 |
| | Totals | 402 | 61 | 161 | 222 |

**SARNER, Craig Brian** *Forward*
b. St. Paul, Minn., June 20, 1949

| | | | | | |
|---|---|---|---|---|---|
| 1974-75 | Boston | 7 | 0 | 0 | 0 |

**SARRAZIN, Richard (Dick)** *Forward*
b. St. Gabriel de Brandon, Que., Jan. 22, 1946

| | | | | | |
|---|---|---|---|---|---|
| 1968-69 | Philadelphia | 54 | 16 | 30 | 46 |
| 1969-70 | Philadelphia | 18 | 1 | 1 | 2 |
| 1971-72 | Philadelphia | 28 | 3 | 4 | 7 |
| 1972-73 | NE-Chi (WHA) | 68 | 7 | 15 | 22 |
| | NHL Totals | 100 | 20 | 35 | 55 |
| | WHA Totals | 68 | 7 | 15 | 22 |

**SASKAMOOSE, Fred** *Forward*
b. Sandy Lake Reserve, Sask., Dec. 24, 1934

| | | | | | |
|---|---|---|---|---|---|
| 1953-54 | Chicago | 11 | 0 | 0 | 0 |

**SATHER, Glen Cameron** *Forward*
b. High River, Alta., Sept. 2, 1943

| | | | | | |
|---|---|---|---|---|---|
| 1966-67 | Boston | 5 | 0 | 0 | 0 |
| 1967-68 | Boston | 65 | 8 | 12 | 20 |
| 1968-69 | Boston | 76 | 4 | 11 | 15 |
| 1969-70 | Pittsburgh | 76 | 12 | 14 | 26 |
| 1970-71 | Pitt-NYR | 77 | 10 | 3 | 13 |
| 1971-72 | New York R | 76 | 5 | 9 | 14 |
| 1972-73 | New York R | 77 | 11 | 15 | 26 |
| 1973-74 | NYR-StL | 71 | 15 | 29 | 44 |
| 1974-75 | Montreal | 63 | 6 | 10 | 16 |
| 1975-76 | Minnesota | 72 | 9 | 10 | 19 |
| 1976-77 | Edmonton (WHA) | 81 | 19 | 34 | 53 |
| | NHL Totals | 658 | 80 | 113 | 193 |
| | WHA Totals | 81 | 19 | 34 | 53 |

**SAUNDERS, Bernie** *Forward*
b. Montreal, Que., June 21, 1956

| | | | | | |
|---|---|---|---|---|---|
| 1979-80 | Quebec | 4 | 0 | 0 | 0 |
| 1980-81 | Quebec | 6 | 0 | 1 | 1 |
| | Totals | 10 | 0 | 1 | 1 |

**SAUNDERS, Theodore (Ted)** *Forward*
b. Ottawa, Ont., Aug. 29, 1911

| | | | | | |
|---|---|---|---|---|---|
| 1933-34 | Ottawa | 49 | 1 | 3 | 4 |

**SAUVE, Jean-Francois** *Forward*
b. Ste. Genevieve, Que., Jan. 23, 1960

| | | | | | |
|---|---|---|---|---|---|
| 1980-81 | Buffalo | 20 | 5 | 9 | 14 |
| 1981-82 | Buffalo | 69 | 19 | 36 | 55 |
| 1982-83 | Buffalo | 9 | 0 | 4 | 4 |
| | Totals | 98 | 24 | 49 | 73 |

**SAVAGE, Gordon (Tony)** *Defenseman*
b. Calgary, Alta., July 18, 1906

| | | | | | |
|---|---|---|---|---|---|
| 1934-35 | Bos-Mont | 49 | 1 | 5 | 6 |

**SAVARD, Andre** *Forward*
b. Temiscamingue, Que., Sept. 2, 1953

| | | | | | |
|---|---|---|---|---|---|
| 1973-74 | Boston | 72 | 16 | 14 | 30 |
| 1974-75 | Boston | 77 | 19 | 25 | 44 |

| Season | Club | GP | G | A | Pts. |
|---|---|---|---|---|---|
| 1975-76 | Boston | 79 | 17 | 23 | 40 |
| 1976-77 | Buffalo | 80 | 25 | 35 | 60 |
| 1977-78 | Buffalo | 80 | 19 | 20 | 39 |
| 1978-79 | Buffalo | 65 | 18 | 22 | 40 |
| 1979-80 | Buffalo | 33 | 3 | 10 | 13 |
| 1980-81 | Buffalo | 79 | 31 | 43 | 74 |
| 1981-82 | Buffalo | 62 | 18 | 20 | 38 |
| 1982-83 | Buffalo | 68 | 16 | 25 | 41 |
| | Totals | 695 | 182 | 237 | 419 |

**SAVARD, Denis Joseph** *Forward*
b. Pointe Gatineau, Que., Feb. 4, 1961

| | | | | | |
|---|---|---|---|---|---|
| 1980-81 | Chicago | 76 | 28 | 47 | 75 |
| 1981-82 | Chicago | 80 | 32 | 87 | 119 |
| 1982-83 | Chicago | 78 | 35 | 85 | 120 |
| | Totals | 234 | 95 | 219 | 314 |

**SAVARD, Jean** *Forward*
b. Verdun, Que., Apr. 26, 1957

| | | | | | |
|---|---|---|---|---|---|
| 1977-78 | Chicago | 31 | 7 | 11 | 18 |
| 1978-79 | Chicago | 11 | 0 | 1 | 1 |
| 1979-80 | Hartford | 1 | 0 | 0 | 0 |
| | Totals | 43 | 7 | 12 | 19 |

**SAVARD, Serge A.** *Defenseman*
b. Montreal, Que., Jan 22, 1946

| | | | | | |
|---|---|---|---|---|---|
| 1966-67 | Montreal | 2 | 0 | 0 | 0 |
| 1967-68 | Montreal | 67 | 2 | 13 | 15 |
| 1968-69 | Montreal | 74 | 8 | 23 | 31 |
| 1969-70 | Montreal | 64 | 12 | 19 | 31 |
| 1970-71 | Montreal | 37 | 5 | 10 | 15 |
| 1971-72 | Montreal | 23 | 1 | 8 | 9 |
| 1972-73 | Montreal | 74 | 7 | 32 | 39 |
| 1973-74 | Montreal | 67 | 4 | 14 | 18 |
| 1974-75 | Montreal | 80 | 20 | 40 | 60 |
| 1975-76 | Montreal | 71 | 8 | 39 | 47 |
| 1976-77 | Montreal | 78 | 9 | 33 | 42 |
| 1977-78 | Montreal | 77 | 8 | 34 | 42 |
| 1978-79 | Montreal | 80 | 7 | 26 | 33 |
| 1979-80 | Montreal | 46 | 5 | 8 | 13 |
| 1980-81 | Montreal | 77 | 4 | 13 | 17 |
| 1981-82 | Winnipeg | 47 | 2 | 5 | 7 |
| 1982-83 | Winnipeg | 76 | 4 | 16 | 20 |
| | Totals | 1040 | 106 | 333 | 439 |

**SCAMURRA, Peter Vincent** *Defenseman*
b. Buffalo, N.Y., Feb. 23, 1955

| | | | | | |
|---|---|---|---|---|---|
| 1975-76 | Washington | 58 | 2 | 13 | 15 |
| 1976-77 | Washington | 21 | 0 | 2 | 2 |
| 1978-79 | Washington | 30 | 3 | 5 | 8 |
| 1979-80 | Washington | 23 | 3 | 5 | 8 |
| | Totals | 132 | 8 | 25 | 33 |

**SCHAEFER, Paul**

| | | | | | |
|---|---|---|---|---|---|
| 1936-37 | Chicago | — | 0 | 0 | 0 |

**SCHAMEHORN, Kevin Dean** *Forward*
b. Calgary, Alta., July 28, 1956

| | | | | | |
|---|---|---|---|---|---|
| 1976-77 | Detroit | 3 | 0 | 0 | 0 |
| 1979-80 | Detroit | 2 | 0 | 0 | 0 |
| 1980-81 | Los Angeles | 5 | 0 | 0 | 0 |
| | Totals | 10 | 0 | 0 | 0 |

**SCHELLA, John Edward** *Defenseman*
b. Port Arthur, Ont., May 9, 1947

| | | | | | |
|---|---|---|---|---|---|
| 1970-71 | Vancouver | 38 | 0 | 5 | 5 |
| 1971-72 | Vancouver | 77 | 2 | 13 | 15 |
| 1972-73 | Houston (WHA) | 77 | 2 | 24 | 26 |
| 1973-74 | Houston (WHA) | 73 | 12 | 19 | 31 |
| 1974-75 | Houston (WHA) | 78 | 10 | 42 | 52 |
| 1975-76 | Houston (WHA) | 74 | 6 | 32 | 38 |
| 1976-77 | Houston (WHA) | 20 | 0 | 6 | 6 |
| 1977-78 | Houston (WHA) | 63 | 9 | 20 | 29 |
| | NHL Totals | 115 | 2 | 18 | 20 |
| | WHA Totals | 385 | 39 | 143 | 182 |

**SCHERZA, Charles (Chuck)** *Forward*
b. Brandon, Man., Feb. 15, 1923

| | | | | | |
|---|---|---|---|---|---|
| 1943-44 | Bos-NYR | 14 | 4 | 3 | 7 |
| 1944-45 | New York R | 22 | 2 | 3 | 5 |
| | Totals | 36 | 6 | 6 | 12 |

**SCHINKEL, Kenneth Calvin (Ken)** *Forward*
b. Jansen, Sask., Nov. 27, 1932

| | | | | | |
|---|---|---|---|---|---|
| 1959-60 | New York R | 69 | 13 | 16 | 29 |
| 1960-61 | New York R | 38 | 2 | 6 | 8 |
| 1961-62 | New York R | 65 | 7 | 21 | 28 |
| 1962-63 | New York R | 69 | 6 | 9 | 15 |
| 1963-64 | New York R | 4 | 0 | 0 | 0 |
| 1966-67 | New York R | 20 | 6 | 3 | 9 |
| 1967-68 | Pittsburgh | 57 | 14 | 25 | 39 |
| 1968-69 | Pittsburgh | 76 | 18 | 34 | 52 |
| 1969-70 | Pittsburgh | 72 | 20 | 25 | 45 |
| 1970-71 | Pittsburgh | 50 | 15 | 19 | 34 |
| 1971-72 | Pittsburgh | 74 | 15 | 30 | 45 |
| 1972-73 | Pittsburgh | 42 | 11 | 10 | 21 |
| | Totals | 636 | 127 | 198 | 325 |

**SCHLIEBENER, Andreus** *Defenseman*
b. Ottawa, Ont., Aug. 16, 1962

| | | | | | |
|---|---|---|---|---|---|
| 1981-82 | Vancouver | 22 | 0 | 1 | 1 |

**SCHMAUTZ, Clifford Harvey (Cliff)** *Forward*
b. Saskatoon, Sask., Mar. 17, 1939

| | | | | | |
|---|---|---|---|---|---|
| 1970-71 | Buf-Phil | 56 | 13 | 19 | 32 |

**SCHMAUTZ, Robert James (Bob)** *Forward*
b. Saskatoon, Sask., Mar. 28, 1945

| | | | | | |
|---|---|---|---|---|---|
| 1967-68 | Chicago | 13 | 3 | 2 | 5 |
| 1968-69 | Chicago | 63 | 9 | 7 | 16 |
| 1970-71 | Vancouver | 26 | 5 | 5 | 10 |
| 1971-72 | Vancouver | 60 | 12 | 13 | 25 |
| 1972-73 | Vancouver | 77 | 38 | 33 | 71 |
| 1973-74 | Van-Bos | 76 | 33 | 32 | 65 |
| 1974-75 | Boston | 56 | 21 | 30 | 51 |
| 1975-76 | Boston | 75 | 28 | 34 | 62 |
| 1976-77 | Boston | 57 | 23 | 29 | 52 |
| 1977-78 | Boston | 54 | 27 | 27 | 54 |
| 1978-79 | Boston | 65 | 20 | 22 | 42 |
| 1979-80 | Bos-Edm-Col | 69 | 25 | 18 | 43 |
| 1980-81 | Vancouver | 73 | 27 | 34 | 61 |
| | Totals | 764 | 271 | 286 | 557 |

**SCHMIDT, Clarence** *Forward*
b. 1923

| | | | | | |
|---|---|---|---|---|---|
| 1943-44 | Boston | 7 | 1 | 0 | 1 |

**SCHMIDT, John R.** *Forward*
b. Odessa, Sask., Nov. 11, 1924

| | | | | | |
|---|---|---|---|---|---|
| 1942-43 | Boston | 45 | 6 | 7 | 13 |

**SCHMIDT, Joseph** *Forward*

| | | | | | |
|---|---|---|---|---|---|
| 1943-44 | Boston | 2 | 0 | 0 | 0 |

**SCHMIDT, Milton Conrad** *Forward*
b. Kitchener, Ont., Mar. 5, 1918

| | | | | | |
|---|---|---|---|---|---|
| 1936-37 | Boston | 26 | 2 | 8 | 10 |
| 1937-38 | Boston | 44 | 13 | 14 | 27 |
| 1938-39 | Boston | 41 | 15 | 17 | 32 |
| 1939-40 | Boston | 48 | 22 | 30 | 52 |
| 1940-41 | Boston | 45 | 13 | 25 | 38 |
| 1941-42 | Boston | 36 | 14 | 21 | 35 |
| 1945-46 | Boston | 48 | 13 | 18 | 31 |
| 1946-47 | Boston | 59 | 27 | 35 | 62 |
| 1947-48 | Boston | 33 | 9 | 17 | 26 |
| 1948-49 | Boston | 44 | 10 | 22 | 32 |
| 1949-50 | Boston | 68 | 19 | 22 | 41 |
| 1950-51 | Boston | 62 | 22 | 39 | 61 |
| 1951-52 | Boston | 69 | 21 | 29 | 50 |
| 1952-53 | Boston | 68 | 11 | 23 | 34 |
| 1953-54 | Boston | 62 | 14 | 18 | 32 |
| 1954-55 | Boston | 23 | 4 | 8 | 12 |
| | Totals | 776 | 229 | 346 | 575 |

**SCHNARR, Werner** *Forward*

| | | | | | |
|---|---|---|---|---|---|
| 1924-25 | Boston | 24 | 0 | 0 | 0 |
| 1925-26 | Boston | 1 | 0 | 0 | 0 |
| | Totals | 25 | 0 | 0 | 0 |

**SCHOCK, Daniel Patrick (Danny)** *Forward*
b. Terrace Bay, Ont., Dec. 30, 1948

| | | | | | |
|---|---|---|---|---|---|
| 1970-71 | Bos-Phil | 20 | 1 | 2 | 3 |

| Season | Club | GP | G | A | Pts. |
|---|---|---|---|---|---|

**SCHOCK, Ronald Lawrence (Ron)** *Forward*
b. Chapleau, Ont., Dec. 19, 1943

| Season | Club | GP | G | A | Pts. |
|---|---|---|---|---|---|
| 1963-64 | Boston | 5 | 1 | 2 | 3 |
| 1964-65 | Boston | 33 | 4 | 7 | 11 |
| 1965-66 | Boston | 24 | 2 | 2 | 4 |
| 1966-67 | Boston | 66 | 10 | 20 | 30 |
| 1967-68 | St Louis | 55 | 9 | 9 | 18 |
| 1968-69 | St Louis | 67 | 12 | 27 | 39 |
| 1969-70 | Pittsburgh | 76 | 8 | 21 | 29 |
| 1970-71 | Pittsburgh | 71 | 14 | 26 | 40 |
| 1971-72 | Pittsburgh | 77 | 17 | 29 | 46 |
| 1972-73 | Pittsburgh | 78 | 13 | 36 | 49 |
| 1973-74 | Pittsburgh | 77 | 14 | 29 | 43 |
| 1974-75 | Pittsburgh | 80 | 23 | 63 | 86 |
| 1975-76 | Pittsburgh | 80 | 18 | 44 | 62 |
| 1976-77 | Pittsburgh | 80 | 17 | 32 | 49 |
| 1977-78 | Buffalo | 40 | 4 | 4 | 8 |
| | **Totals** | 909 | 166 | 351 | 517 |

**SCHOENFELD, James Grant (Jim)**
*Defenseman*
b. Galt, Ont., Sept. 4, 1952

| Season | Club | GP | G | A | Pts. |
|---|---|---|---|---|---|
| 1972-73 | Buffalo | 66 | 4 | 15 | 19 |
| 1973-74 | Buffalo | 28 | 1 | 8 | 9 |
| 1974-75 | Buffalo | 68 | 1 | 19 | 20 |
| 1975-76 | Buffalo | 56 | 2 | 22 | 24 |
| 1976-77 | Buffalo | 65 | 7 | 25 | 32 |
| 1977-78 | Buffalo | 60 | 2 | 20 | 22 |
| 1978-79 | Buffalo | 46 | 8 | 17 | 25 |
| 1979-80 | Buffalo | 77 | 9 | 27 | 36 |
| 1980-81 | Buffalo | 71 | 8 | 25 | 33 |
| 1981-82 | Buf-Det | 52 | 8 | 11 | 19 |
| 1982-83 | Detroit | 57 | 1 | 10 | 11 |
| | **Totals** | 646 | 51 | 199 | 250 |

**SCHOFIELD, Dwight** *Defenseman*
b. Waltham, Mass., Mar. 25, 1956

| Season | Club | GP | G | A | Pts. |
|---|---|---|---|---|---|
| 1976-77 | Detroit | 3 | 1 | 0 | 1 |
| 1982-83 | Montreal | 2 | 0 | 0 | 0 |
| | **Totals** | 5 | 1 | 0 | 1 |

**SCHRINER, David (Sweeney)** *Forward*
b. Calgary, Alta., Nov. 30, 1911

| Season | Club | GP | G | A | Pts. |
|---|---|---|---|---|---|
| 1934-35 | New York A | 48 | 18 | 22 | 40 |
| 1935-36 | New York A | 48 | 19 | 26 | 45 |
| 1936-37 | New York A | 48 | 21 | 25 | 46 |
| 1937-38 | New York A | 48 | 21 | 17 | 38 |
| 1938-39 | New York A | 48 | 13 | 31 | 44 |
| 1939-40 | Toronto | 39 | 11 | 15 | 26 |
| 1940-41 | Toronto | 48 | 24 | 14 | 38 |
| 1941-42 | Toronto | 47 | 20 | 16 | 36 |
| 1942-43 | Toronto | 37 | 19 | 17 | 36 |
| 1944-45 | Toronto | 26 | 22 | 15 | 37 |
| 1945-46 | Toronto | 47 | 13 | 6 | 19 |
| | **Totals** | 484 | 201 | 204 | 405 |

**SCHULTZ, David William (Dave)** *Forward*
b. Waldheim, Sask., Oct. 14, 1949

| Season | Club | GP | G | A | Pts. |
|---|---|---|---|---|---|
| 1971-72 | Philadelphia | 1 | 0 | 0 | 0 |
| 1972-73 | Philadelphia | 76 | 9 | 12 | 21 |
| 1973-74 | Philadelphia | 73 | 20 | 16 | 36 |
| 1974-75 | Philadelphia | 76 | 9 | 17 | 26 |
| 1975-76 | Philadelphia | 71 | 13 | 19 | 32 |
| 1976-77 | Los Angeles | 76 | 10 | 20 | 30 |
| 1977-78 | LA-Pitt | 74 | 11 | 25 | 36 |
| 1978-79 | Pitt-Buf | 75 | 6 | 12 | 18 |
| 1979-80 | Buffalo | 13 | 1 | 0 | 1 |
| | **Totals** | 535 | 79 | 121 | 200 |

**SCHURMAN, Maynard** *Forward*
b. Summerdale, P.E.I., July 16, 1957

| Season | Club | GP | G | A | Pts. |
|---|---|---|---|---|---|
| 1979-80 | Hartford | 7 | 0 | 0 | 0 |

**SCHUTT, Rodney** *Forward*
b. Bancroft, Ont., Oct. 13, 1956

| Season | Club | GP | G | A | Pts. |
|---|---|---|---|---|---|
| 1977-78 | Montreal | 2 | 0 | 0 | 0 |
| 1978-79 | Pittsburgh | 74 | 24 | 21 | 45 |
| 1979-80 | Pittsburgh | 73 | 18 | 21 | 39 |
| 1980-81 | Pittsburgh | 80 | 25 | 35 | 60 |
| 1981-82 | Pittsburgh | 35 | 8 | 12 | 20 |
| 1982-83 | Pittsburgh | 5 | 0 | 0 | 0 |
| | **Totals** | 269 | 75 | 89 | 164 |

**SCLISIZZI, James Enio** *Forward*
b. Milton, Ont., Aug. 1, 1925

| Season | Club | GP | G | A | Pts. |
|---|---|---|---|---|---|
| 1947-48 | Detroit | 4 | 1 | 0 | 1 |
| 1948-49 | Detroit | 50 | 9 | 8 | 17 |
| 1949-50 | Detroit | 4 | 0 | 0 | 0 |
| 1951-52 | Detroit | 9 | 2 | 1 | 3 |
| 1952-53 | Chicago | 14 | 0 | 2 | 2 |
| | **Totals** | 81 | 12 | 11 | 23 |

**SCOTT, Ganton** *Defenseman*

| Season | Club | GP | G | A | Pts. |
|---|---|---|---|---|---|
| 1922-23 | Toronto | 17 | 0 | 0 | 0 |
| 1923-24 | Tor-Ham | 8 | 0 | 0 | 0 |
| 1924-25 | Montreal M | 28 | 1 | 1 | 2 |
| 1926-27 | Toronto | 1 | 0 | 0 | 0 |
| | **Totals** | 54 | 1 | 1 | 2 |

**SCOTT, Lawrence (Laurie)** *Forward*
b. South River, Ont., June 19, 1900

| Season | Club | GP | G | A | Pts. |
|---|---|---|---|---|---|
| 1926-27 | New York A | 39 | 6 | 2 | 8 |
| 1927-28 | New York R | 23 | 0 | 1 | 1 |
| | **Totals** | 62 | 6 | 3 | 9 |

**SCRUTON, Howard** *Defenseman*
b. Toronto, Ont., Oct. 6, 1962

| Season | Club | GP | G | A | Pts. |
|---|---|---|---|---|---|
| 1982-83 | Los Angeles | 4 | 0 | 4 | 4 |

**SECORD, Alan** *Forward*
b. Sudbury, Ont., Mar. 3, 1958

| Season | Club | GP | G | A | Pts. |
|---|---|---|---|---|---|
| 1978-79 | Boston | 71 | 16 | 7 | 23 |
| 1979-80 | Boston | 77 | 23 | 16 | 39 |
| 1980-81 | Bos-Chi | 59 | 13 | 12 | 25 |
| 1981-82 | Chicago | 80 | 44 | 31 | 75 |
| 1982-83 | Chicago | 80 | 54 | 32 | 86 |
| | **Totals** | 367 | 150 | 98 | 248 |

**SEDLBAUER, Ronald Andrew** *Forward*
b. Burlington, Ont., Oct. 22, 1954

| Season | Club | GP | G | A | Pts. |
|---|---|---|---|---|---|
| 1974-75 | Vancouver | 26 | 3 | 4 | 7 |
| 1975-76 | Vancouver | 56 | 19 | 13 | 32 |
| 1976-77 | Vancouver | 70 | 18 | 20 | 38 |
| 1977-78 | Vancouver | 62 | 18 | 12 | 30 |
| 1978-79 | Vancouver | 79 | 40 | 16 | 56 |
| 1979-80 | Van-Chi | 77 | 23 | 14 | 37 |
| 1980-81 | Chi-Tor | 60 | 22 | 7 | 29 |
| | **Totals** | 430 | 143 | 86 | 229 |

**SEGUIN, Daniel G.** *Forward*
b. Sudbury, Ont., June 7, 1948

| Season | Club | GP | G | A | Pts. |
|---|---|---|---|---|---|
| 1970-71 | Minn-Van | 36 | 1 | 6 | 7 |
| 1973-74 | Vancouver | 1 | 1 | 0 | 1 |
| | **Totals** | 37 | 2 | 6 | 8 |

**SEIBERT, Earl Walter** *Defenseman*
b. Kitchener, Ont., Dec. 7, 1911

| Season | Club | GP | G | A | Pts. |
|---|---|---|---|---|---|
| 1931-32 | New York R | 44 | 4 | 6 | 10 |
| 1932-33 | New York R | 45 | 2 | 3 | 5 |
| 1933-34 | New York R | 48 | 13 | 10 | 23 |
| 1934-35 | New York R | 48 | 6 | 19 | 25 |
| 1935-36 | NYR-Chi | 41 | 5 | 9 | 14 |
| 1936-37 | Chicago | 43 | 9 | 6 | 15 |
| 1937-38 | Chicago | 48 | 8 | 13 | 21 |
| 1938-39 | Chicago | 48 | 4 | 11 | 15 |
| 1939-40 | Chicago | 37 | 3 | 7 | 10 |
| 1940-41 | Chicago | 44 | 3 | 17 | 20 |
| 1941-42 | Chicago | 45 | 7 | 14 | 21 |
| 1942-43 | Chicago | 44 | 5 | 27 | 32 |
| 1943-44 | Chicago | 50 | 8 | 25 | 33 |
| 1944-45 | Chi-Det | 47 | 12 | 17 | 29 |
| 1945-46 | Detroit | 18 | 0 | 3 | 3 |
| | **Totals** | 650 | 89 | 187 | 276 |

**SEILING, Richard James** *Forward*
b. Elmira, Ont., Dec. 15, 1957

| Season | Club | GP | G | A | Pts. |
|---|---|---|---|---|---|
| 1977-78 | Buffalo | 80 | 19 | 19 | 38 |
| 1978-79 | Buffalo | 78 | 20 | 22 | 42 |
| 1979-80 | Buffalo | 80 | 25 | 35 | 60 |
| 1980-81 | Buffalo | 74 | 30 | 27 | 57 |
| 1981-82 | Buffalo | 57 | 22 | 25 | 47 |
| 1982-83 | Buffalo | 75 | 19 | 22 | 41 |
| | **Totals** | 444 | 135 | 150 | 285 |

**SEILING, Rodney Albert (Rod)** *Defenseman*
b. Elmira, Ont., Nov. 14, 1944

| Season | Club | GP | G | A | Pts. |
|---|---|---|---|---|---|
| 1962-63 | Toronto | 1 | 0 | 1 | 1 |
| 1963-64 | New York R | 2 | 0 | 1 | 1 |
| 1964-65 | New York R | 68 | 4 | 22 | 26 |
| 1965-66 | New York R | 52 | 5 | 10 | 15 |
| 1966-67 | New York R | 12 | 1 | 1 | 2 |
| 1967-68 | New York R | 71 | 5 | 11 | 16 |
| 1968-69 | New York R | 73 | 4 | 17 | 21 |
| 1969-70 | New York R | 76 | 5 | 21 | 26 |
| 1970-71 | New York R | 68 | 5 | 22 | 27 |
| 1971-72 | New York R | 78 | 5 | 36 | 41 |
| 1972-73 | New York R | 72 | 9 | 33 | 42 |
| 1973-74 | New York R | 68 | 7 | 23 | 30 |
| 1974-75 | NYR-Wash-Tor | 65 | 5 | 13 | 18 |
| 1975-76 | Toronto | 77 | 3 | 16 | 19 |
| 1976-77 | St Louis | 79 | 3 | 26 | 29 |
| 1977-78 | St Louis | 78 | 1 | 11 | 12 |
| 1978-79 | StL-Atl | 39 | 0 | 5 | 5 |
| | **Totals** | 979 | 62 | 269 | 331 |

**SELBY, Robert Briton (Brit)** *Forward*
b. Kingston, Ont., Mar. 27, 1945

| Season | Club | GP | G | A | Pts. |
|---|---|---|---|---|---|
| 1964-65 | Toronto | 3 | 2 | 0 | 2 |
| 1965-66 | Toronto | 61 | 14 | 13 | 27 |
| 1966-67 | Toronto | 6 | 1 | 1 | 2 |
| 1967-68 | Philadelphia | 56 | 15 | 15 | 30 |
| 1968-69 | Phil-Tor | 77 | 12 | 15 | 27 |
| 1969-70 | Toronto | 74 | 10 | 13 | 23 |
| 1970-71 | Tor-StL | 67 | 1 | 5 | 6 |
| 1971-72 | St Louis | 6 | 0 | 0 | 0 |
| 1972-73 | Que-NE (WHA) | 72 | 13 | 30 | 43 |
| | **NHL Totals** | 350 | 55 | 62 | 117 |
| | **WHA Totals** | 72 | 13 | 30 | 43 |

**SELWOOD, Bradley, Wayne (Brad)**
*Defenseman*
b. Leamington, Ont., Mar. 18, 1948

| Season | Club | GP | G | A | Pts. |
|---|---|---|---|---|---|
| 1970-71 | Toronto | 28 | 2 | 10 | 12 |
| 1971-72 | Toronto | 72 | 4 | 17 | 21 |
| 1972-73 | New England (WHA) | 75 | 13 | 21 | 34 |
| 1973-74 | New England (WHA) | 76 | 9 | 28 | 37 |
| 1974-75 | New England (WHA) | 77 | 4 | 35 | 39 |
| 1975-76 | New England (WHA) | 40 | 2 | 10 | 12 |
| 1976-77 | New England (WHA) | 41 | 4 | 12 | 16 |
| 1977-78 | New England (WHA) | 80 | 6 | 25 | 31 |
| 1978-79 | New England (WHA) | 42 | 4 | 12 | 16 |
| 1979-80 | Los Angeles | 63 | 1 | 13 | 14 |
| | **NHL Totals** | 163 | 7 | 40 | 47 |
| | **WHA Totals** | 431 | 42 | 143 | 185 |

**SEMENKO, David** *Forward*
b. Winnipeg, Man., July 12, 1957

| Season | Club | GP | G | A | Pts. |
|---|---|---|---|---|---|
| 1977-78 | Edmonton (WHA) | 65 | 6 | 6 | 12 |
| 1978-79 | Edmonton (WHA) | 77 | 10 | 14 | 24 |
| 1979-80 | Edmonton | 67 | 6 | 7 | 13 |
| 1980-81 | Edmonton | 58 | 11 | 8 | 19 |
| 1981-82 | Edmonton | 59 | 12 | 12 | 24 |
| 1982-83 | Edmonton | 75 | 12 | 15 | 27 |
| | **NHL Totals** | 259 | 41 | 42 | 83 |
| | **WHA Totals** | 142 | 16 | 20 | 36 |

**SENICK, George** *Forward*
b. Saskatoon, Sask., Sept. 16, 1929

| Season | Club | GP | G | A | Pts. |
|---|---|---|---|---|---|
| 1952-53 | New York R | 13 | 2 | 3 | 5 |

**SERAFINI, Ronald William** *Defenseman*
b. Detroit, Mich., Oct. 31, 1953

| Season | Club | GP | G | A | Pts. |
|---|---|---|---|---|---|
| 1973-74 | California | 2 | 0 | 0 | 0 |

**SHACK, Edward Steven Phillip (Eddie)**
*Forward*
b. Sudbury, Sask., Feb. 11, 1937

| Season | Club | GP | G | A | Pts. |
|---|---|---|---|---|---|
| 1958-59 | New York R | 67 | 7 | 14 | 21 |
| 1959-60 | New York R | 62 | 8 | 10 | 18 |
| 1960-61 | NYR-Tor | 67 | 15 | 16 | 31 |
| 1961-62 | Toronto | 44 | 7 | 14 | 21 |
| 1962-63 | Toronto | 63 | 16 | 9 | 25 |
| 1963-64 | Toronto | 64 | 11 | 10 | 21 |
| 1964-65 | Toronto | 67 | 5 | 9 | 14 |
| 1965-66 | Toronto | 63 | 26 | 17 | 43 |
| 1966-67 | Toronto | 63 | 11 | 14 | 25 |
| 1967-68 | Boston | 70 | 23 | 19 | 42 |

| Season | Club | GP | G | A | Pts. |
|---|---|---|---|---|---|
| 1968-69 | Boston | 50 | 11 | 11 | 22 |
| 1969-70 | Los Angeles | 73 | 22 | 12 | 34 |
| 1970-71 | LA-Buf | 67 | 27 | 19 | 46 |
| 1971-72 | Buf-Pitt | 68 | 16 | 23 | 39 |
| 1972-73 | Pittsburgh | 74 | 25 | 20 | 45 |
| 1973-74 | Toronto | 59 | 7 | 8 | 15 |
| 1974-75 | Toronto | 26 | 2 | 1 | 3 |
| | **Totals** | 1047 | 239 | 226 | 465 |

**SHACK, Joseph** *Forward*
b. Winnipeg, Man., Dec. 8, 1916

| Season | Club | GP | G | A | Pts. |
|---|---|---|---|---|---|
| 1942-43 | New York R | 20 | 5 | 9 | 14 |
| 1944-45 | New York R | 50 | 4 | 18 | 22 |
| | **Totals** | 70 | 9 | 27 | 36 |

**SHAKES, Paul Steven** *Defenseman*
b. Collingwood, Ont., Sept. 4, 1952

| Season | Club | GP | G | A | Pts. |
|---|---|---|---|---|---|
| 1973-74 | California | 21 | 0 | 4 | 4 |

**SHANAHAN, Sean Bryan** *Forward*
b. Toronto, Ont., Feb. 8, 1951

| Season | Club | GP | G | A | Pts. |
|---|---|---|---|---|---|
| 1975-76 | Montreal | 4 | 0 | 0 | 0 |
| 1976-77 | Colorado | 30 | 1 | 3 | 4 |
| 1977-78 | Boston | 6 | 0 | 0 | 0 |
| 1978-79 | Cincinnati (WHA) | 4 | 0 | 0 | 0 |
| | **NHL Totals** | 40 | 1 | 3 | 4 |
| | **WHA Totals** | 4 | 0 | 0 | 0 |

**SHAND, David Alistair** *Defenseman*
b. Cold Lake, Alta., Aug. 11, 1956

| Season | Club | GP | G | A | Pts. |
|---|---|---|---|---|---|
| 1976-77 | Atlanta | 55 | 5 | 11 | 16 |
| 1977-78 | Atlanta | 80 | 2 | 23 | 25 |
| 1978-79 | Atlanta | 79 | 4 | 22 | 26 |
| 1979-80 | Atlanta | 74 | 3 | 7 | 10 |
| 1980-81 | Toronto | 47 | 0 | 4 | 4 |
| 1982-83 | Toronto | 1 | 0 | 1 | 1 |
| | **Totals** | 336 | 14 | 68 | 82 |

**SHANNON, Charles Kitchener** *Defenseman*
b. Campbellford, Ont., Mar. 22, 1916

| Season | Club | GP | G | A | Pts. |
|---|---|---|---|---|---|
| 1936-37 | Montreal M | 31 | 9 | 7 | 16 |
| 1937-38 | Montreal M | 36 | 0 | 3 | 3 |
| 1939-40 | New York A | 4 | 0 | 0 | 0 |
| | **Totals** | 71 | 9 | 10 | 19 |

**SHANNON, Gerald (Jerry)** *Forward*
b. Campbellford, Ont., Oct. 25, 1910

| Season | Club | GP | G | A | Pts. |
|---|---|---|---|---|---|
| 1933-34 | Ottawa | 48 | 11 | 15 | 26 |
| 1934-35 | StLE-Bos | 42 | 3 | 3 | 6 |
| 1935-36 | Boston | 23 | 0 | 1 | 1 |
| | **Totals** | 113 | 14 | 19 | 33 |

**SHARPLEY, Glen Stuart** *Forward*
b. York, Ont., Sept. 6, 1956

| Season | Club | GP | G | A | Pts. |
|---|---|---|---|---|---|
| 1976-77 | Minnesota | 80 | 25 | 32 | 57 |
| 1977-78 | Minnesota | 79 | 22 | 33 | 55 |
| 1978-79 | Minnesota | 80 | 19 | 34 | 53 |
| 1979-80 | Minnesota | 51 | 20 | 27 | 47 |
| 1980-81 | Minn-Chi | 63 | 22 | 28 | 50 |
| 1981-82 | Chicago | 36 | 9 | 7 | 16 |
| | **Totals** | 389 | 117 | 161 | 278 |

**SHAW, David** *Defenseman*
b. St. Thomas, Ont., May 25, 1964

| Season | Club | GP | G | A | Pts. |
|---|---|---|---|---|---|
| 1982-83 | Quebec | 2 | 0 | 0 | 0 |

**SHAY, Norman** *Forward*

| Season | Club | GP | G | A | Pts. |
|---|---|---|---|---|---|
| 1924-25 | Boston | 18 | 1 | 1 | 2 |
| 1925-26 | Bos-Tor | 35 | 4 | 1 | 5 |
| | **Totals** | 53 | 5 | 2 | 7 |

**SHEA, Francis (Pat)** *Defenseman*
b. Potlach, Idaho, Oct. 29, 1912

| Season | Club | GP | G | A | Pts. |
|---|---|---|---|---|---|
| 1931-32 | Chicago | 10 | 0 | 1 | 1 |

**SHEDDEN, Douglas** *Forward*
b. Wallaceburg, Ont., Apr. 26, 1961

| Season | Club | GP | G | A | Pts. |
|---|---|---|---|---|---|
| 1981-82 | Pittsburgh | 38 | 10 | 15 | 25 |
| 1982-83 | Pittsburgh | 80 | 24 | 43 | 67 |
| | **Totals** | 118 | 34 | 58 | 92 |

**SHEEHAN, Robert Richard (Bobby)** *Forward*
b. Weymouth, Mass., Jan. 11, 1949

| Season | Club | GP | G | A | Pts. |
|---|---|---|---|---|---|
| 1969-70 | Montreal | 16 | 2 | 1 | 3 |
| 1970-71 | Montreal | 29 | 6 | 5 | 11 |
| 1971-72 | California | 78 | 20 | 26 | 46 |
| 1972-73 | New York (WHA) | 75 | 35 | 53 | 88 |
| 1973-74 | NJ-Edm (WHA) | 60 | 13 | 11 | 24 |
| 1974-75 | Edmonton (WHA) | 77 | 19 | 39 | 58 |
| 1975-76 | Chicago | 78 | 11 | 20 | 31 |
| 1976-77 | Detroit | 34 | 5 | 4 | 9 |
| 1977-78 | Indianapolis (WHA) | 29 | 8 | 7 | 15 |
| 1979-80 | Colorado | 30 | 3 | 4 | 7 |
| 1980-81 | Colorado | 41 | 1 | 3 | 4 |
| 1981-82 | Los Angeles | 4 | 0 | 0 | 0 |
| | **NHL Totals** | 310 | 48 | 63 | 111 |
| | **WHA Totals** | 241 | 75 | 110 | 185 |

**SHEEHY, Timothy Kane** *Forward*
b. Ft. Francis, Ont., Sept. 3, 1948

| Season | Club | GP | G | A | Pts. |
|---|---|---|---|---|---|
| 1972-73 | New England (WHA) | 78 | 33 | 38 | 71 |
| 1973-74 | New England (WHA) | 77 | 29 | 29 | 58 |
| 1974-75 | NE-Edm (WHA) | 81 | 28 | 33 | 61 |
| 1975-76 | Edmonton (WHA) | 81 | 34 | 31 | 65 |
| 1976-77 | Edm-Birm (WHA) | 78 | 41 | 29 | 70 |
| 1977-78 | Birm-NE (WHA) | 40 | 8 | 11 | 19 |
| 1977-78 | Detroit | 15 | 0 | 0 | 0 |
| 1979-80 | Hartford | 12 | 2 | 1 | 3 |
| | **NHL Totals** | 27 | 2 | 1 | 3 |
| | **WHA Totals** | 435 | 173 | 171 | 344 |

**SHELTON, Douglas** *Forward*
b. Woodstock, Ont., June 27, 1945

| Season | Club | GP | G | A | Pts. |
|---|---|---|---|---|---|
| 1967-68 | Chicago | 5 | 0 | 1 | 1 |

**SHEPPARD, Frank** *Forward*
b. Montreal, Que., Oct. 19, 1907

| Season | Club | GP | G | A | Pts. |
|---|---|---|---|---|---|
| 1927-28 | Detroit | 8 | 1 | 1 | 2 |

**SHEPPARD, Gregory Wayne (Greg)** *Forward*
b. North Battleford, Sask., Apr. 23, 1949

| Season | Club | GP | G | A | Pts. |
|---|---|---|---|---|---|
| 1972-73 | Boston | 64 | 24 | 26 | 50 |
| 1973-74 | Boston | 75 | 16 | 31 | 47 |
| 1974-75 | Boston | 76 | 30 | 48 | 78 |
| 1975-76 | Boston | 70 | 31 | 43 | 74 |
| 1976-77 | Boston | 77 | 31 | 36 | 67 |
| 1977-78 | Boston | 54 | 23 | 36 | 59 |
| 1978-79 | Pittsburgh | 60 | 15 | 22 | 37 |
| 1979-80 | Pittsburgh | 70 | 13 | 24 | 37 |
| 1980-81 | Pittsburgh | 47 | 11 | 17 | 28 |
| 1981-82 | Pittsburgh | 58 | 11 | 10 | 21 |
| | **Totals** | 657 | 205 | 293 | 498 |

**SHEPPARD, Jake O. (Johnny)** *Forward*
b. Montreal, Que., Oct. 19, 1907

| Season | Club | GP | G | A | Pts. |
|---|---|---|---|---|---|
| 1926-27 | Detroit | 44 | 13 | 8 | 21 |
| 1927-28 | Detroit | 43 | 10 | 10 | 20 |
| 1928-29 | New York A | 47 | 5 | 4 | 9 |
| 1929-30 | New York A | 39 | 14 | 15 | 29 |
| 1930-31 | New York A | 44 | 5 | 8 | 13 |
| 1931-32 | New York A | 5 | 1 | 0 | 1 |
| 1932-33 | New York A | 47 | 17 | 9 | 26 |
| 1933-34 | Bos-Chi | 43 | 3 | 4 | 7 |
| | **Totals** | 309 | 68 | 58 | 126 |

**SHERF, John** *Forward*
b. Calumet, Mich., Apr. 8, 1914

| Season | Club | GP | G | A | Pts. |
|---|---|---|---|---|---|
| 1935-36 | Detroit | 1 | 0 | 0 | 0 |
| 1936-37 | Detroit | 1 | 0 | 0 | 0 |
| 1937-38 | Det-NYA | 6 | 0 | 0 | 0 |
| 1938-39 | Detroit | 3 | 0 | 0 | 0 |
| 1943-44 | Detroit | 8 | 0 | 0 | 0 |
| | **Totals** | 19 | 0 | 0 | 0 |

**SHERO, Frederick Alexander** *Defenseman*
b. Winnipeg, Man., Oct. 23, 1925

| Season | Club | GP | G | A | Pts. |
|---|---|---|---|---|---|
| 1947-48 | New York R | 19 | 1 | 0 | 1 |
| 1948-49 | New York R | 59 | 3 | 6 | 9 |
| 1949-50 | New York R | 67 | 2 | 8 | 10 |
| | **Totals** | 145 | 6 | 14 | 20 |

**SHERRITT, Gordon Ephraim** *Defenseman*
b. Oakville, Man., Apr. 8, 1922

| Season | Club | GP | G | A | Pts. |
|---|---|---|---|---|---|
| 1943-44 | Detroit | 8 | 0 | 0 | 0 |

**SHEWCHUK, John Michael** *Defenseman*
b. Brantford, Ont., June 19, 1917

| Season | Club | GP | G | A | Pts. |
|---|---|---|---|---|---|
| 1938-39 | Boston | 6 | 0 | 0 | 0 |
| 1939-40 | Boston | 47 | 2 | 4 | 6 |
| 1940-41 | Boston | 20 | 2 | 2 | 4 |
| 1941-42 | Boston | 22 | 2 | 0 | 2 |
| 1942-43 | Boston | 48 | 2 | 6 | 8 |
| 1944-45 | Boston | 47 | 1 | 7 | 8 |
| | **Totals** | 190 | 9 | 19 | 28 |

**SHIBICKY, Alexi (Alex)** *Forward*
b. Winnipeg, Man., May 19, 1914

| Season | Club | GP | G | A | Pts. |
|---|---|---|---|---|---|
| 1935-36 | New York R | 18 | 4 | 2 | 6 |
| 1936-37 | New York R | 47 | 14 | 8 | 22 |
| 1937-38 | New York R | 43 | 17 | 18 | 35 |
| 1938-39 | New York R | 43 | 24 | 9 | 33 |
| 1939-40 | New York R | 43 | 11 | 21 | 32 |
| 1940-41 | New York R | 40 | 10 | 14 | 24 |
| 1941-42 | New York R | 45 | 20 | 14 | 34 |
| 1945-46 | New York R | 33 | 10 | 5 | 15 |
| | **Totals** | 322 | 110 | 91 | 201 |

**SHIELDS, Allen** *Defenseman*
b. Ottawa, Ont., May 10, 1907

| Season | Club | GP | G | A | Pts. |
|---|---|---|---|---|---|
| 1927-28 | Ottawa | 7 | 0 | 1 | 1 |
| 1928-29 | Ottawa | 42 | 0 | 1 | 1 |
| 1929-30 | Ottawa | 44 | 6 | 3 | 9 |
| 1930-31 | Philadelphia Q | 43 | 7 | 3 | 10 |
| 1931-32 | New York A | 48 | 4 | 1 | 5 |
| 1932-33 | Ottawa | 48 | 7 | 4 | 11 |
| 1933-34 | Ottawa | 47 | 4 | 7 | 11 |
| 1934-35 | Montreal M | 42 | 4 | 8 | 12 |
| 1935-36 | Montreal M | 45 | 2 | 7 | 9 |
| 1936-37 | NYA-Bos | 48 | 3 | 4 | 7 |
| 1937-38 | Montreal M | 48 | 5 | 7 | 12 |
| | **Totals** | 462 | 42 | 46 | 88 |

**SHILL, John Walker (Jack)** *Forward*
b. Toronto, Ont., Jan. 12, 1913

| Season | Club | GP | G | A | Pts. |
|---|---|---|---|---|---|
| 1933-34 | Toronto | 7 | 0 | 1 | 1 |
| 1934-35 | Boston | 46 | 4 | 4 | 8 |
| 1935-36 | Toronto | 3 | 0 | 1 | 1 |
| 1936-37 | Toronto | 32 | 4 | 4 | 8 |
| 1937-38 | NYA-Chi | 45 | 5 | 6 | 11 |
| 1938-39 | Chicago | 28 | 2 | 4 | 6 |
| | **Totals** | 161 | 15 | 20 | 35 |

**SHILL, William Roy** *Forward*
b. Toronto, Ont., Mar. 6, 1923

| Season | Club | GP | G | A | Pts. |
|---|---|---|---|---|---|
| 1942-43 | Boston | 7 | 4 | 1 | 5 |
| 1945-46 | Boston | 45 | 15 | 12 | 27 |
| 1946-47 | Boston | 27 | 2 | 0 | 2 |
| | **Totals** | 79 | 21 | 13 | 34 |

**SHINSKE, Richard Charles** *Forward*
b. Weyburn, Sask., May 31, 1955

| Season | Club | GP | G | A | Pts. |
|---|---|---|---|---|---|
| 1976-77 | Cleveland | 5 | 0 | 0 | 0 |
| 1977-78 | Cleveland | 47 | 5 | 12 | 17 |
| 1978-79 | St Louis | 11 | 0 | 4 | 4 |
| | **Totals** | 63 | 5 | 16 | 21 |

**SHIRES, James Arthur (Jim)** *Forward*
b. Edmonton, Alta., Nov. 15, 1945

| Season | Club | GP | G | A | Pts. |
|---|---|---|---|---|---|
| 1970-71 | Detroit | 20 | 2 | 1 | 3 |
| 1971-72 | St Louis | 18 | 0 | 3 | 3 |
| 1972-73 | Pittsburgh | 18 | 1 | 2 | 3 |
| | **Totals** | 56 | 3 | 6 | 9 |

| Season | Club | GP | G | A | Pts. |
|---|---|---|---|---|---|
| **SHMYR, Paul** *Defenseman* | | | | | |
| | b. Cudworth, Sask., Jan. 28, 1946 | | | | |
| 1968-69 | Chicago | 3 | 1 | 0 | 1 |
| 1969-70 | Chicago | 24 | 0 | 4 | 4 |
| 1970-71 | Chicago | 57 | 1 | 12 | 13 |
| 1971-72 | California | 69 | 6 | 21 | 27 |
| 1972-73 | Cleveland (WHA) | 73 | 5 | 43 | 48 |
| 1973-74 | Cleveland (WHA) | 78 | 13 | 31 | 44 |
| 1974-75 | Cleveland (WHA) | 49 | 7 | 14 | 21 |
| 1975-76 | Cleveland (WHA) | 70 | 6 | 44 | 50 |
| 1976-77 | San Diego (WHA) | 81 | 13 | 37 | 50 |
| 1977-78 | Edmonton (WHA) | 80 | 9 | 40 | 49 |
| 1978-79 | Edmonton (WHA) | 80 | 8 | 39 | 47 |
| 1979-80 | Minnesota | 63 | 3 | 15 | 18 |
| 1980-81 | Minnesota | 61 | 1 | 9 | 10 |
| 1981-82 | Hartford | 66 | 1 | 11 | 12 |
| | **NHL Totals** | 343 | 13 | 72 | 85 |
| | **WHA Totals** | 511 | 61 | 248 | 309 |
| **SHORE, Edward William** *Defenseman* | | | | | |
| | b. St. Qu'Appelle-Cupar, Sask., | | | | |
| | Nov. 25, 1902 | | | | |
| 1926-27 | Boston | 40 | 12 | 6 | 18 |
| 1927-28 | Boston | 43 | 11 | 6 | 17 |
| 1928-29 | Boston | 39 | 12 | 7 | 19 |
| 1929-30 | Boston | 42 | 12 | 19 | 31 |
| 1930-31 | Boston | 44 | 15 | 16 | 31 |
| 1931-32 | Boston | 45 | 9 | 13 | 22 |
| 1932-33 | Boston | 48 | 8 | 27 | 35 |
| 1933-34 | Boston | 30 | 2 | 10 | 12 |
| 1934-35 | Boston | 48 | 7 | 26 | 33 |
| 1935-36 | Boston | 45 | 3 | 16 | 19 |
| 1936-37 | Boston | 20 | 3 | 1 | 4 |
| 1937-38 | Boston | 48 | 3 | 14 | 17 |
| 1938-39 | Boston | 44 | 4 | 14 | 18 |
| 1939-40 | Bos-NYA | 14 | 4 | 4 | 8 |
| | **Totals** | 550 | 105 | 179 | 284 |
| **SHORE, Sam Hamilton (Hamby)** *Defenseman* | | | | | |
| | b. Ottawa, Ont., 1886 | | | | |
| 1917-18 | Ottawa | 18 | 3 | 0 | 3 |
| **SHORT, Steven** *Forward* | | | | | |
| | b. Roseville, Minn., Apr. 6, 1954 | | | | |
| 1977-78 | Los Angeles | 5 | 0 | 0 | 0 |
| 1978-79 | Detroit | 1 | 0 | 0 | 0 |
| | **Totals** | 6 | 0 | 0 | 0 |
| **SHUTT, Stephen John (Steve)** *Forward* | | | | | |
| | b. Toronto, Ont., July 1, 1952 | | | | |
| 1972-73 | Montreal | 50 | 8 | 8 | 16 |
| 1973-74 | Montreal | 70 | 15 | 20 | 35 |
| 1974-75 | Montreal | 77 | 30 | 35 | 65 |
| 1975-76 | Montreal | 80 | 45 | 34 | 79 |
| 1976-77 | Montreal | 80 | 60 | 45 | 105 |
| 1977-78 | Montreal | 80 | 49 | 37 | 86 |
| 1978-79 | Montreal | 72 | 37 | 40 | 77 |
| 1979-80 | Montreal | 77 | 47 | 42 | 89 |
| 1980-81 | Montreal | 77 | 35 | 38 | 73 |
| 1981-82 | Montreal | 57 | 31 | 24 | 55 |
| 1982-83 | Montreal | 78 | 35 | 22 | 57 |
| | **Totals** | 798 | 392 | 345 | 737 |
| **SIEBERT, Albert Charles (Babe)** | | | | | |
| | *Defenseman-Forward* | | | | |
| | b. Plattsville, Que., Jan. 14, 1904 | | | | |
| 1925-26 | Montreal M | 35 | 16 | 8 | 24 |
| 1926-27 | Montreal M | 42 | 5 | 3 | 8 |
| 1927-28 | Montreal M | 40 | 8 | 9 | 17 |
| 1928-29 | Montreal M | 39 | 3 | 5 | 8 |
| 1929-30 | Montreal M | 41 | 14 | 19 | 33 |
| 1930-31 | Montreal M | 42 | 16 | 12 | 28 |
| 1931-32 | Montreal M | 48 | 21 | 18 | 39 |
| 1932-33 | New York R | 42 | 9 | 10 | 19 |
| 1933-34 | NYR-Bos | 45 | 5 | 7 | 12 |
| 1934-35 | Boston | 48 | 6 | 18 | 24 |
| 1935-36 | Boston | 45 | 12 | 9 | 21 |
| 1936-37 | Montreal | 44 | 8 | 20 | 28 |
| 1937-38 | Montreal | 37 | 8 | 11 | 19 |
| 1938-39 | Montreal | 44 | 9 | 7 | 16 |
| | **Totals** | 592 | 140 | 156 | 296 |

| Season | Club | GP | G | A | Pts. |
|---|---|---|---|---|---|
| **SILK, David** *Forward* | | | | | |
| | b. Situate, Mass., Jan. 1, 1958 | | | | |
| 1979-80 | New York R | 2 | 0 | 0 | 0 |
| 1980-81 | New York R | 59 | 14 | 12 | 26 |
| 1981-82 | New York R | 64 | 15 | 20 | 35 |
| 1982-83 | New York R | 16 | 1 | 1 | 2 |
| | **Totals** | 141 | 30 | 33 | 63 |
| **SILTALA, Michael** *Forward* | | | | | |
| | b. Toronto, Ont., Aug. 5, 1963 | | | | |
| 1981-82 | Washington | 3 | 1 | 0 | 1 |
| **SILTANEN, Risto** *Defenseman* | | | | | |
| | b. Tampere, Finland, Oct. 31, 1958 | | | | |
| 1978-79 | Edmonton (WHA) | 20 | 3 | 4 | 7 |
| 1979-80 | Edmonton | 64 | 6 | 29 | 35 |
| 1980-81 | Edmonton | 79 | 17 | 36 | 53 |
| 1981-82 | Edmonton | 63 | 15 | 48 | 63 |
| 1982-83 | Hartford | 74 | 5 | 25 | 30 |
| | **NHL Totals** | 280 | 43 | 138 | 181 |
| | **WHA Totals** | 20 | 3 | 4 | 7 |
| **SIMMER, Charles Robert** *Forward* | | | | | |
| | b. Terrace Bay, Ont., Mar. 20, 1954 | | | | |
| 1974-75 | California | 35 | 8 | 13 | 21 |
| 1975-76 | California | 21 | 1 | 1 | 2 |
| 1976-77 | Cleveland | 24 | 2 | 0 | 2 |
| 1977-78 | Los Angeles | 3 | 0 | 0 | 0 |
| 1978-79 | Los Angeles | 38 | 21 | 27 | 48 |
| 1979-80 | Los Angeles | 64 | 56 | 45 | 101 |
| 1980-81 | Los Angeles | 65 | 56 | 49 | 105 |
| 1981-82 | Los Angeles | 50 | 15 | 24 | 39 |
| 1982-83 | Los Angeles | 80 | 29 | 51 | 80 |
| | **Totals** | 380 | 188 | 210 | 398 |
| **SIMMONS, Allan Kenneth** *Defenseman* | | | | | |
| | b. Winnipeg, Man., Sept. 25, 1951 | | | | |
| 1971-72 | California | 1 | 0 | 0 | 0 |
| 1973-74 | Boston | 3 | 0 | 0 | 0 |
| 1975-76 | Boston | 7 | 0 | 1 | 1 |
| | **Totals** | 11 | 0 | 1 | 1 |
| **SIMON, John Cullen (Cully)** *Defenseman* | | | | | |
| | b. Brockville, Ont., May 8, 1918 | | | | |
| 1942-43 | Detroit | 34 | 1 | 1 | 2 |
| 1943-44 | Detroit | 46 | 3 | 7 | 10 |
| 1944-45 | Det-Chi | 50 | 0 | 3 | 3 |
| | **Totals** | 130 | 4 | 11 | 15 |
| **SIMON, Thain Andrew** *Defenseman* | | | | | |
| | b. Brockville, Ont., Apr. 24, 1922 | | | | |
| 1946-47 | Detroit | 3 | 0 | 0 | 0 |
| **SIMPSON, Clifford Vernon** *Forward* | | | | | |
| | b. Toronto, Ont., Apr. 4, 1923 | | | | |
| 1946-47 | Detroit | 6 | 0 | 1 | 1 |
| **SIMPSON, Harold Joseph (Bullet Joe)** | | | | | |
| | *Defenseman* | | | | |
| | b. Selkirk, Man. | | | | |
| 1925-26 | New York A | 32 | 2 | 2 | 4 |
| 1926-27 | New York A | 43 | 4 | 2 | 6 |
| 1927-28 | New York A | 24 | 2 | 0 | 2 |
| 1928-29 | New York A | 43 | 3 | 2 | 5 |
| 1929-30 | New York A | 44 | 8 | 13 | 21 |
| 1930-31 | New York A | 42 | 2 | 0 | 2 |
| | **Totals** | 228 | 21 | 19 | 40 |
| **SIMPSON, Robert** *Forward* | | | | | |
| | b. Caughnawaga, Que., Nov. 17, 1956 | | | | |
| 1976-77 | Atlanta | 72 | 13 | 10 | 23 |
| 1977-78 | Atlanta | 55 | 10 | 8 | 18 |
| 1979-80 | St Louis | 18 | 2 | 2 | 4 |
| 1981-82 | Pittsburgh | 26 | 9 | 9 | 18 |
| 1982-83 | Pittsburgh | 4 | 1 | 0 | 1 |
| | **Totals** | 175 | 35 | 29 | 64 |

| Season | Club | GP | G | A | Pts. |
|---|---|---|---|---|---|
| **SIMS, Allan Eugene** *Defenseman* | | | | | |
| | b. Toronto, Ont., Apr. 18, 1953 | | | | |
| 1973-74 | Boston | 77 | 3 | 9 | 12 |
| 1974-75 | Boston | 75 | 4 | 8 | 12 |
| 1975-76 | Boston | 48 | 4 | 3 | 7 |
| 1976-77 | Boston | 1 | 0 | 0 | 0 |
| 1977-78 | Boston | 43 | 2 | 8 | 10 |
| 1978-79 | Boston | 67 | 9 | 20 | 29 |
| 1979-80 | Hartford | 76 | 10 | 31 | 41 |
| 1980-81 | Hartford | 80 | 16 | 36 | 52 |
| 1981-82 | Los Angeles | 8 | 1 | 1 | 2 |
| 1982-83 | Los Angeles | 1 | 0 | 0 | 0 |
| | **Totals** | 476 | 49 | 116 | 165 |
| **SINCLAIR, Reginald Alexander** *Forward* | | | | | |
| | b. Lachine, Que., Mar. 6, 1925 | | | | |
| 1950-51 | New York R | 70 | 18 | 21 | 39 |
| 1951-52 | New York R | 69 | 20 | 10 | 30 |
| 1952-53 | Detroit | 69 | 11 | 12 | 23 |
| | **Totals** | 208 | 49 | 43 | 92 |
| **SINGBUSH, Alexander (Alex)** *Defenseman* | | | | | |
| | b. Winnipeg, Man., 1915 | | | | |
| 1940-41 | Montreal | 32 | 0 | 5 | 5 |
| **SINISALO, Ilkka** *Forward* | | | | | |
| | b. Helsinki, Finland, July 10, 1958 | | | | |
| 1981-82 | Philadelphia | 66 | 15 | 22 | 37 |
| 1982-83 | Philadelphia | 61 | 21 | 29 | 50 |
| | **Totals** | 127 | 36 | 51 | 87 |
| **SIROIS, Robert** *Forward* | | | | | |
| | b. Montreal, Que., Feb. 6, 1954 | | | | |
| 1974-75 | Philadelphia | 3 | 1 | 0 | 1 |
| 1975-76 | Phil-Wash | 44 | 10 | 19 | 29 |
| 1976-77 | Washington | 45 | 13 | 22 | 35 |
| 1977-78 | Washington | 72 | 24 | 37 | 61 |
| 1978-79 | Washington | 73 | 29 | 25 | 54 |
| 1979-80 | Washington | 49 | 15 | 17 | 32 |
| | **Totals** | 286 | 92 | 120 | 212 |
| **SITTLER, Darryl Glen** *Forward* | | | | | |
| | b. Kitchener, Ont., Sept. 18, 1950 | | | | |
| 1970-71 | Toronto | 49 | 10 | 8 | 18 |
| 1971-72 | Toronto | 74 | 15 | 17 | 32 |
| 1972-73 | Toronto | 78 | 29 | 48 | 77 |
| 1973-74 | Toronto | 78 | 38 | 46 | 84 |
| 1974-75 | Toronto | 72 | 36 | 44 | 80 |
| 1975-76 | Toronto | 79 | 41 | 59 | 100 |
| 1976-77 | Toronto | 73 | 38 | 52 | 90 |
| 1977-78 | Toronto | 80 | 45 | 72 | 117 |
| 1978-79 | Toronto | 70 | 36 | 51 | 87 |
| 1979-80 | Toronto | 73 | 40 | 57 | 97 |
| 1980-81 | Toronto | 80 | 43 | 53 | 96 |
| 1981-82 | Tor-Phil | 73 | 32 | 38 | 70 |
| 1982-83 | Philadelphia | 80 | 43 | 40 | 83 |
| | **Totals** | 959 | 446 | 585 | 1031 |
| **SJOBERG, Lars-Erik** *Defenseman* | | | | | |
| | b. Falun, Sweden, Apr. 5, 1944 | | | | |
| 1974-75 | Winnipeg (WHA) | 75 | 7 | 53 | 60 |
| 1975-76 | Winnipeg (WHA) | 81 | 5 | 36 | 41 |
| 1976-77 | Winnipeg (WHA) | 52 | 2 | 38 | 40 |
| 1977-78 | Winnipeg (WHA) | 78 | 11 | 39 | 50 |
| 1978-79 | Winnipeg (WHA) | 9 | 0 | 3 | 3 |
| 1979-80 | Winnipeg | 79 | 7 | 27 | 34 |
| | **NHL Totals** | 79 | 7 | 27 | 34 |
| | **WHA Totals** | 295 | 25 | 169 | 194 |
| **SKILTON, Raymond** *Defenseman* | | | | | |
| | | | | | |
| 1917-18 | Montreal W | 1 | 0 | 0 | 0 |
| **SKINNER, Alf** *Forward* | | | | | |
| | | | | | |
| 1917-18 | Toronto | 19 | 13 | 0 | 13 |
| 1918-19 | Toronto | 17 | 12 | 3 | 15 |
| 1924-25 | Bos-Mont M | 27 | 1 | 1 | 2 |
| 1925-26 | Pittsburgh Pi | 7 | 0 | 0 | 0 |
| | **Totals** | 60 | 26 | 4 | 30 |

| Season | Club | GP | G | A | Pts. |
|---|---|---|---|---|---|

**SKINNER, Larry Foster**  *Forward*
b. Vancouver, B.C., Apr. 21, 1956

| Season | Club | GP | G | A | Pts. |
|---|---|---|---|---|---|
| 1976-77 | Colorado | 19 | 4 | 5 | 9 |
| 1977-78 | Colorado | 14 | 3 | 5 | 8 |
| 1978-79 | Colorado | 12 | 3 | 2 | 5 |
| 1979-80 | Colorado | 2 | 0 | 0 | 0 |
| | **Totals** | 47 | 10 | 12 | 22 |

**SKOV, Glen Frederick**  *Forward*
b. Wheatley, Ont., Jan. 26, 1931

| Season | Club | GP | G | A | Pts. |
|---|---|---|---|---|---|
| 1949-50 | Detroit | 2 | 0 | 0 | 0 |
| 1950-51 | Detroit | 19 | 7 | 6 | 13 |
| 1951-52 | Detroit | 70 | 12 | 14 | 26 |
| 1952-53 | Detroit | 70 | 12 | 15 | 27 |
| 1953-54 | Detroit | 70 | 17 | 10 | 27 |
| 1954-55 | Detroit | 70 | 14 | 16 | 30 |
| 1955-56 | Chicago | 70 | 7 | 20 | 27 |
| 1956-57 | Chicago | 67 | 14 | 28 | 42 |
| 1957-58 | Chicago | 70 | 17 | 18 | 35 |
| 1958-59 | Chicago | 70 | 3 | 5 | 8 |
| 1959-60 | Chicago | 69 | 3 | 4 | 7 |
| 1960-61 | Montreal | 3 | 0 | 0 | 0 |
| | **Totals** | 650 | 106 | 136 | 242 |

**SLEAVER, John**  *Forward*
b. Copper Cliff, Ont., Aug. 18, 1934

| Season | Club | GP | G | A | Pts. |
|---|---|---|---|---|---|
| 1953-54 | Chicago | 1 | 0 | 0 | 0 |
| 1956-57 | Chicago | 12 | 1 | 0 | 1 |
| | **Totals** | 13 | 1 | 0 | 1 |

**SLEIGHER, Louis**  *Forward*
b. Nouvelle, Que., Oct. 23, 1958

| Season | Club | GP | G | A | Pts. |
|---|---|---|---|---|---|
| 1978-79 | Birmingham (WHA) | 62 | 26 | 12 | 38 |
| 1979-80 | Quebec | 2 | 0 | 1 | 1 |
| 1981-82 | Quebec | 8 | 0 | 0 | 0 |
| 1982-83 | Quebec | 51 | 14 | 10 | 24 |
| | **NHL Totals** | 61 | 14 | 11 | 25 |
| | **WHA Total** | 62 | 26 | 12 | 38 |

**SLOAN, Aloysius Martin (Tod)**  *Forward*
b. Vinton, Que., Nov. 30, 1927

| Season | Club | GP | G | A | Pts. |
|---|---|---|---|---|---|
| 1947-48 | Toronto | 1 | 0 | 0 | 0 |
| 1948-49 | Toronto | 29 | 3 | 4 | 7 |
| 1950-51 | Toronto | 70 | 31 | 25 | 56 |
| 1951-52 | Toronto | 68 | 25 | 23 | 48 |
| 1952-53 | Toronto | 70 | 15 | 10 | 25 |
| 1953-54 | Toronto | 67 | 11 | 32 | 43 |
| 1954-55 | Toronto | 63 | 13 | 15 | 28 |
| 1955-56 | Toronto | 70 | 37 | 29 | 66 |
| 1956-57 | Toronto | 52 | 14 | 21 | 35 |
| 1957-58 | Toronto | 59 | 13 | 25 | 38 |
| 1958-59 | Chicago | 59 | 27 | 35 | 62 |
| 1959-60 | Chicago | 70 | 20 | 20 | 40 |
| 1960-61 | Chicago | 67 | 11 | 23 | 34 |
| | **Totals** | 745 | 220 | 262 | 482 |

**SLOBODIAN, Peter Paul**  *Defenseman*
b. Dauphin, Man., Apr. 24, 1918

| Season | Club | GP | G | A | Pts. |
|---|---|---|---|---|---|
| 1940-41 | New York A | 40 | 3 | 2 | 5 |

**SLOWINSKI, Edward Stanley**  *Forward*
b. Winnipeg, Man., Nov. 18, 1922

| Season | Club | GP | G | A | Pts. |
|---|---|---|---|---|---|
| 1947-48 | Det-NYR | 38 | 6 | 5 | 11 |
| 1948-49 | New York R | 20 | 1 | 1 | 2 |
| 1949-50 | New York R | 63 | 14 | 23 | 37 |
| 1950-51 | New York R | 69 | 14 | 18 | 32 |
| 1951-52 | New York R | 64 | 21 | 22 | 43 |
| 1952-53 | New York R | 37 | 2 | 5 | 7 |
| | **Totals** | 291 | 58 | 74 | 132 |

**SLY, Darryl Hayward**  *Defenseman*
b. Collingwood, Ont., Apr. 3, 1939

| Season | Club | GP | G | A | Pts. |
|---|---|---|---|---|---|
| 1965-66 | Toronto | 2 | 0 | 0 | 0 |
| 1967-68 | Toronto | 17 | 0 | 0 | 0 |
| 1969-70 | Minnesota | 29 | 1 | 0 | 1 |
| 1970-71 | Vancouver | 31 | 0 | 2 | 2 |
| | **Totals** | 79 | 1 | 2 | 3 |

**SMAIL, Douglas**  *Forward*
b. Moose Jaw, Sask., Sept. 2, 1957

| Season | Club | GP | G | A | Pts. |
|---|---|---|---|---|---|
| 1980-81 | Winnipeg | 30 | 10 | 8 | 18 |
| 1981-82 | Winnipeg | 72 | 17 | 18 | 35 |
| 1982-83 | Winnipeg | 80 | 15 | 29 | 44 |
| | **Totals** | 182 | 42 | 55 | 97 |

**SMART, Alexander (Alex)**  *Forward*
b. Brandon, Man., May 29, 1918

| Season | Club | GP | G | A | Pts. |
|---|---|---|---|---|---|
| 1942-43 | Montreal | 8 | 5 | 2 | 7 |

**SMEDSMO, Dale Darwin**  *Forward*
b. Roseau, Minn., Apr. 23, 1951

| Season | Club | GP | G | A | Pts. |
|---|---|---|---|---|---|
| 1972-73 | Toronto | 4 | 0 | 0 | 0 |
| 1975-76 | Cincinnati (WHA) | 66 | 8 | 14 | 22 |
| 1976-77 | NE-Cin (WHA) | 38 | 2 | 5 | 7 |
| 1977-78 | Indianapolis (WHA) | 6 | 0 | 3 | 3 |
| | **NHL Totals** | 4 | 0 | 0 | 0 |
| | **WHA Totals** | 110 | 10 | 22 | 32 |

**SMILLIE, Donald**  *Forward*

| Season | Club | GP | G | A | Pts. |
|---|---|---|---|---|---|
| 1933-34 | Boston | 13 | 2 | 2 | 4 |

**SMITH, Alexander (Alex)**  *Defenseman*
b. Liverpool, England, Apr. 2, 1905

| Season | Club | GP | G | A | Pts. |
|---|---|---|---|---|---|
| 1924-25 | Ottawa | 7 | 0 | 0 | 0 |
| 1925-26 | Ottawa | 36 | 0 | 0 | 0 |
| 1926-27 | Ottawa | 42 | 4 | 1 | 5 |
| 1927-28 | Ottawa | 44 | 9 | 4 | 13 |
| 1928-29 | Ottawa | 44 | 1 | 7 | 8 |
| 1929-30 | Ottawa | 43 | 2 | 6 | 8 |
| 1930-31 | Ottawa | 37 | 5 | 6 | 11 |
| 1931-32 | Detroit | 48 | 6 | 8 | 14 |
| 1932-33 | Ott-Bos | 49 | 7 | 4 | 11 |
| 1933-34 | Boston | 45 | 4 | 6 | 10 |
| 1934-35 | New York A | 48 | 3 | 8 | 11 |
| | **Totals** | 443 | 41 | 50 | 91 |

**SMITH, Arthur**
b. 1907

| Season | Club | GP | G | A | Pts. |
|---|---|---|---|---|---|
| 1927-28 | Toronto | 15 | 5 | 3 | 8 |
| 1928-29 | Toronto | 43 | 5 | 0 | 5 |
| 1929-30 | Toronto | 43 | 3 | 3 | 6 |
| 1930-31 | Ottawa | 43 | 2 | 4 | 6 |
| | **Totals** | 144 | 15 | 10 | 25 |

**SMITH, Barry Edward**  *Forward*
b. Surrey, B.C., Apr. 25, 1955

| Season | Club | GP | G | A | Pts. |
|---|---|---|---|---|---|
| 1975-76 | Boston | 19 | 1 | 0 | 1 |
| 1979-80 | Colorado | 33 | 2 | 3 | 5 |
| 1980-81 | Colorado | 62 | 4 | 4 | 8 |
| | **Totals** | 114 | 7 | 7 | 14 |

**SMITH, Brad Allan**  *Forward*
b. Windsor, Ont., Apr. 13, 1958

| Season | Club | GP | G | A | Pts. |
|---|---|---|---|---|---|
| 1978-79 | Vancouver | 2 | 0 | 0 | 0 |
| 1979-80 | Van-Atl | 23 | 1 | 3 | 4 |
| 1980-81 | Calg-Det | 65 | 12 | 6 | 18 |
| 1981-82 | Detroit | 33 | 2 | 0 | 2 |
| 1982-83 | Detroit | 1 | 0 | 0 | 0 |
| | **Totals** | 124 | 15 | 9 | 24 |

**SMITH, Brian Desmond**  *Forward*
b. Ottawa, Ont., Sept. 6, 1940

| Season | Club | GP | G | A | Pts. |
|---|---|---|---|---|---|
| 1967-68 | Los Angeles | 58 | 10 | 9 | 19 |
| 1968-69 | Minnesota | 9 | 0 | 1 | 1 |
| 1972-73 | Houston (WHA) | 48 | 7 | 6 | 13 |
| | **NHL Totals** | 67 | 10 | 10 | 20 |
| | **WHA Totals** | 48 | 7 | 6 | 13 |

**SMITH, Brian Stuart**  *Forward*
b. Creighton Mines, Ont., Dec. 6, 1937

| Season | Club | GP | G | A | Pts. |
|---|---|---|---|---|---|
| 1957-58 | Detroit | 4 | 0 | 1 | 1 |
| 1959-60 | Detroit | 31 | 2 | 5 | 7 |
| 1960-61 | Detroit | 26 | 0 | 2 | 2 |
| | **Totals** | 61 | 2 | 8 | 10 |

**SMITH, Carl David**  *Forward*
b. Cache Bay, Ont., Sept. 18, 1917

| Season | Club | GP | G | A | Pts. |
|---|---|---|---|---|---|
| 1943-44 | Detroit | 7 | 1 | 1 | 2 |

**SMITH, Clinton James (Snuffy)**  *Forward*
b. Assiniboia, Sask., Dec. 12, 1913

| Season | Club | GP | G | A | Pts. |
|---|---|---|---|---|---|
| 1936-37 | New York R | 2 | 1 | 0 | 1 |
| 1937-38 | New York R | 48 | 14 | 23 | 37 |
| 1938-39 | New York R | 48 | 21 | 20 | 41 |
| 1939-40 | New York R | 41 | 8 | 16 | 24 |
| 1940-41 | New York R | 48 | 14 | 11 | 25 |
| 1941-42 | New York R | 47 | 10 | 24 | 34 |
| 1942-43 | New York R | 47 | 12 | 21 | 33 |
| 1943-44 | Chicago | 50 | 23 | 49 | 72 |
| 1944-45 | Chicago | 50 | 23 | 31 | 54 |
| 1945-46 | Chicago | 50 | 26 | 24 | 50 |
| 1946-47 | Chicago | 52 | 9 | 17 | 26 |
| | **Totals** | 483 | 161 | 236 | 397 |

**SMITH, Dallas Earl**  *Defenseman*
b. Hamiota, Man., Oct. 10, 1941

| Season | Club | GP | G | A | Pts. |
|---|---|---|---|---|---|
| 1959-60 | Boston | 5 | 1 | 1 | 2 |
| 1960-61 | Boston | 70 | 1 | 9 | 10 |
| 1961-62 | Boston | 7 | 0 | 0 | 0 |
| 1965-66 | Boston | 2 | 0 | 0 | 0 |
| 1966-67 | Boston | 33 | 0 | 1 | 1 |
| 1967-68 | Boston | 74 | 4 | 23 | 27 |
| 1968-69 | Boston | 75 | 4 | 24 | 28 |
| 1969-70 | Boston | 75 | 7 | 17 | 24 |
| 1970-71 | Boston | 73 | 7 | 38 | 45 |
| 1971-72 | Boston | 78 | 8 | 22 | 30 |
| 1972-73 | Boston | 78 | 4 | 27 | 31 |
| 1973-74 | Boston | 77 | 6 | 21 | 27 |
| 1974-75 | Boston | 79 | 3 | 20 | 23 |
| 1975-76 | Boston | 77 | 7 | 25 | 32 |
| 1977-78 | New York R | 29 | 1 | 4 | 5 |
| | **Totals** | 832 | 53 | 232 | 285 |

**SMITH, Dalton Joseph (Nakina)**  *Forward*
b. Cache Bay, Ont., July 26, 1915

| Season | Club | GP | G | A | Pts. |
|---|---|---|---|---|---|
| 1943-44 | Detroit | 10 | 1 | 2 | 3 |

**SMITH, Derek Robert**  *Forward*
b. Quebec, Que., July 31, 1954

| Season | Club | GP | G | A | Pts. |
|---|---|---|---|---|---|
| 1976-77 | Buffalo | 5 | 0 | 0 | 0 |
| 1977-78 | Buffalo | 36 | 3 | 3 | 6 |
| 1978-79 | Buffalo | 43 | 14 | 12 | 26 |
| 1979-80 | Buffalo | 79 | 24 | 39 | 63 |
| 1980-81 | Buffalo | 69 | 21 | 43 | 64 |
| 1981-82 | Buf-Det | 61 | 9 | 15 | 24 |
| 1982-83 | Detroit | 42 | 7 | 4 | 11 |
| | **Totals** | 335 | 78 | 116 | 194 |

**SMITH, Desmond Patrick**  *Defenseman*
b. Ottawa, Ont., Feb. 22, 1914

| Season | Club | GP | G | A | Pts. |
|---|---|---|---|---|---|
| 1937-38 | Montreal M | — | 3 | 1 | 4 |
| 1938-39 | Montreal | — | 3 | 3 | 6 |
| 1939-40 | Chi-Bos | — | 3 | 6 | 9 |
| 1940-41 | Boston | — | 6 | 8 | 14 |
| 1941-42 | Boston | 48 | 7 | 7 | 14 |
| | **Totals** | — | 22 | 25 | 47 |

**SMITH, Donald**  *Forward*
b. 1889

| Season | Club | GP | G | A | Pts. |
|---|---|---|---|---|---|
| 1919-20 | Montreal | 10 | 1 | 0 | 1 |

**SMITH, Donald Arthur**  *Forward*
b. Regina, Sask., May 4, 1929

| Season | Club | GP | G | A | Pts. |
|---|---|---|---|---|---|
| 1949-50 | New York R | 11 | 1 | 1 | 2 |

**SMITH, Douglas**  *Forward*
b. Ottawa, Ont., May 17, 1963

| Season | Club | GP | G | A | Pts. |
|---|---|---|---|---|---|
| 1981-82 | Los Angeles | 80 | 16 | 14 | 30 |
| 1982-83 | Los Angeles | 42 | 11 | 11 | 22 |
| | **Totals** | 122 | 27 | 25 | 52 |

**SMITH, George**

| Season | Club | GP | G | A | Pts. |
|---|---|---|---|---|---|
| 1921-22 | Toronto | 9 | 0 | 0 | 0 |

**SMITH, Glen**

| Season | Club | GP | G | A | Pts. |
|---|---|---|---|---|---|
| 1950-51 | Chicago | 2 | 0 | 0 | 0 |

**SMITH, Gordon Joseph**  *Defenseman*
b. Perth, Ont., Nov. 17, 1949

| Season | Club | GP | G | A | Pts. |
|---|---|---|---|---|---|
| 1974-75 | Washington | 63 | 3 | 8 | 11 |
| 1975-76 | Washington | 25 | 1 | 2 | 3 |
| 1976-77 | Washington | 79 | 1 | 12 | 13 |
| 1977-78 | Washington | 80 | 4 | 7 | 11 |
| 1978-79 | Washington | 39 | 0 | 1 | 1 |
| 1979-80 | Winnipeg | 13 | 0 | 0 | 0 |
| | Totals | 299 | 9 | 30 | 39 |

**SMITH, Gregory James**  *Defenseman*
b. Ponoka, Alta., July 8, 1955

| Season | Club | GP | G | A | Pts. |
|---|---|---|---|---|---|
| 1975-76 | California | 1 | 0 | 1 | 1 |
| 1976-77 | Cleveland | 74 | 9 | 17 | 26 |
| 1977-78 | Cleveland | 80 | 7 | 30 | 37 |
| 1978-79 | Minnesota | 80 | 5 | 27 | 32 |
| 1979-80 | Minnesota | 55 | 5 | 13 | 18 |
| 1980-81 | Minnesota | 74 | 5 | 21 | 26 |
| 1981-82 | Detroit | 69 | 10 | 22 | 32 |
| 1982-83 | Detroit | 73 | 4 | 26 | 30 |
| | Totals | 306 | 45 | 157 | 202 |

**SMITH, Kenneth Alvin**  *Forward*
b. Moose Jaw, Sask., May 8, 1924

| Season | Club | GP | G | A | Pts. |
|---|---|---|---|---|---|
| 1944-45 | Boston | 49 | 20 | 14 | 34 |
| 1945-46 | Boston | 23 | 2 | 6 | 8 |
| 1946-47 | Boston | 60 | 14 | 7 | 21 |
| 1947-48 | Boston | 60 | 11 | 12 | 23 |
| 1948-49 | Boston | 59 | 20 | 20 | 40 |
| 1949-50 | Boston | 66 | 10 | 31 | 41 |
| 1950-51 | Boston | 14 | 1 | 3 | 4 |
| | Totals | 331 | 78 | 93 | 171 |

**SMITH, Reginald Joseph (Hooley)**
*Defenseman-Forward*
b. Toronto, Ont., Jan. 7, 1905

| Season | Club | GP | G | A | Pts. |
|---|---|---|---|---|---|
| 1924-25 | Ottawa | 30 | 10 | 3 | 13 |
| 1925-26 | Ottawa | 28 | 16 | 9 | 25 |
| 1926-27 | Ottawa | 43 | 9 | 6 | 15 |
| 1927-28 | Montreal M | 34 | 14 | 5 | 19 |
| 1928-29 | Montreal M | 41 | 10 | 9 | 19 |
| 1929-30 | Montreal M | 42 | 21 | 9 | 30 |
| 1930-31 | Montreal M | 39 | 12 | 14 | 26 |
| 1931-32 | Montreal M | 43 | 11 | 33 | 44 |
| 1932-33 | Montreal M | 48 | 20 | 21 | 41 |
| 1933-34 | Montreal M | 47 | 18 | 19 | 37 |
| 1934-35 | Montreal M | 46 | 5 | 22 | 27 |
| 1935-36 | Montreal M | 47 | 19 | 19 | 38 |
| 1936-37 | Boston | 44 | 8 | 10 | 18 |
| 1937-38 | New York A | 47 | 10 | 10 | 20 |
| 1938-39 | New York A | 48 | 8 | 11 | 19 |
| 1939-40 | New York A | 47 | 7 | 8 | 15 |
| 1940-41 | New York A | 41 | 2 | 7 | 9 |
| | Totals | 715 | 200 | 215 | 415 |

**SMITH, Richard Allan (Rick)**  *Defenseman*
b. Kingston, Ont., June 29, 1948

| Season | Club | GP | G | A | Pts. |
|---|---|---|---|---|---|
| 1968-69 | Boston | 48 | 0 | 5 | 5 |
| 1969-70 | Boston | 69 | 2 | 8 | 10 |
| 1970-71 | Boston | 67 | 4 | 19 | 23 |
| 1971-72 | Bos-Cal | 78 | 3 | 16 | 19 |
| 1972-73 | California | 64 | 9 | 24 | 33 |
| 1973-74 | Minnesota (WHA) | 71 | 10 | 28 | 38 |
| 1974-75 | Minnesota (WHA) | 78 | 9 | 29 | 38 |
| 1975-76 | Minnesota (WHA) | 51 | 1 | 32 | 33 |
| 1975-76 | St Louis | 24 | 1 | 7 | 8 |
| 1976-77 | StL-Bos | 64 | 6 | 17 | 23 |
| 1977-78 | Boston | 79 | 7 | 29 | 36 |
| 1978-79 | Boston | 65 | 7 | 18 | 25 |
| 1979-80 | Boston | 78 | 8 | 18 | 26 |
| 1980-81 | Det-Wash | 51 | 5 | 6 | 11 |
| | NHL Totals | 687 | 52 | 167 | 219 |
| | WHA Totals | 200 | 20 | 89 | 109 |

**SMITH, Robert David**  *Forward*
b. North Sydney, N.S., Feb. 12, 1958

| Season | Club | GP | G | A | Pts. |
|---|---|---|---|---|---|
| 1978-79 | Minnesota | 80 | 30 | 44 | 74 |
| 1979-80 | Minnesota | 61 | 27 | 56 | 83 |


| Season | Club | GP | G | A | Pts. |
|---|---|---|---|---|---|
| 1980-81 | Minnesota | 78 | 29 | 64 | 93 |
| 1981-82 | Minnesota | 80 | 43 | 71 | 114 |
| 1982-83 | Minnesota | 77 | 24 | 53 | 77 |
| | Totals | 376 | 153 | 288 | 441 |

**SMITH, Rodger**  *Defenseman*
b. 1898

| Season | Club | GP | G | A | Pts. |
|---|---|---|---|---|---|
| 1925-26 | Pittsburgh Pi | 36 | 9 | 1 | 10 |
| 1926-27 | Pittsburgh Pi | 37 | 4 | 0 | 4 |
| 1927-28 | Pittsburgh Pi | 42 | 1 | 0 | 1 |
| 1928-29 | Pittsburgh Pi | 44 | 4 | 2 | 6 |
| 1929-30 | Pittsburgh Pi | 43 | 2 | 1 | 3 |
| 1930-31 | Philadelphia Q | 8 | 0 | 0 | 0 |
| | Totals | 210 | 20 | 4 | 24 |

**SMITH, Ronald Floyd**  *Forward*
b. Perth, Ont., May 16, 1935

| Season | Club | GP | G | A | Pts. |
|---|---|---|---|---|---|
| 1954-55 | Boston | 3 | 0 | 1 | 1 |
| 1956-57 | Boston | 23 | 0 | 0 | 0 |
| 1960-6 | New York R | 29 | 5 | 9 | 14 |
| 1962-63 | Detroit | 51 | 9 | 17 | 26 |
| 1963-64 | Detroit | 52 | 18 | 13 | 31 |
| 1964-65 | Detroit | 67 | 16 | 29 | 45 |
| 1965-66 | Detroit | 66 | 21 | 28 | 49 |
| 1966-67 | Detroit | 54 | 11 | 14 | 25 |
| 1967-68 | Det-Tor | 63 | 24 | 22 | 46 |
| 1968-69 | Toronto | 64 | 15 | 19 | 34 |
| 1969-70 | Toronto | 61 | 4 | 14 | 18 |
| 1970-71 | Buffalo | 77 | 6 | 11 | 17 |
| 1971-72 | Buffalo | 6 | 0 | 1 | 1 |
| | Totals | 616 | 129 | 178 | 307 |

**SMITH, Ronald Robert (Ron)**  *Defenseman*
b. Port Hope, Ont., Nov. 19, 1952

| Season | Club | GP | G | A | Pts. |
|---|---|---|---|---|---|
| 1972-73 | New York I | 11 | 1 | 1 | 2 |

**SMITH, Sidney James**  *Forward*
b. Toronto, Ont., July 11, 1925

| Season | Club | GP | G | A | Pts. |
|---|---|---|---|---|---|
| 1946-47 | Toronto | 14 | 2 | 1 | 3 |
| 1947-48 | Toronto | 31 | 7 | 10 | 17 |
| 1948-49 | Toronto | 1 | 0 | 0 | 0 |
| 1949-50 | Toronto | 68 | 22 | 23 | 45 |
| 1950-51 | Toronto | 70 | 30 | 21 | 51 |
| 1951-52 | Toronto | 70 | 27 | 30 | 57 |
| 1952-53 | Toronto | 70 | 20 | 19 | 39 |
| 1953-54 | Toronto | 70 | 22 | 16 | 38 |
| 1954-55 | Toronto | 70 | 33 | 21 | 54 |
| 1955-56 | Toronto | 55 | 4 | 17 | 21 |
| 1956-57 | Toronto | 70 | 17 | 24 | 41 |
| 1957-58 | Toronto | 12 | 2 | 1 | 3 |
| | Totals | 601 | 186 | 183 | 369 |

**SMITH, Stanford George**  *Forward*
b. Coal Creek, B.C., Aug. 13, 1917

| Season | Club | GP | G | A | Pts. |
|---|---|---|---|---|---|
| 1939-40 | New York R | 1 | 0 | 0 | 0 |
| 1940-41 | New York R | 8 | 2 | 1 | 3 |
| | Totals | 9 | 2 | 1 | 3 |

**SMITH, Steve**  *Defenseman*
b. Trenton, Ont., Apr. 4, 1963

| Season | Club | GP | G | A | Pts. |
|---|---|---|---|---|---|
| 1981-82 | Philadelphia | 8 | 0 | 1 | 1 |

**SMITH, Stuart**  *Forward*

| Season | Club | GP | G | A | Pts. |
|---|---|---|---|---|---|
| 1940-41 | Montreal | — | 2 | 1 | 3 |
| 1941-42 | Montreal | — | 0 | 1 | 1 |
| | Totals | — | 2 | 2 | 4 |

**SMITH, Stuart Gordon**  *Defenseman*
b. Toronto, Ont., Mar. 17, 1960

| Season | Club | GP | G | A | Pts. |
|---|---|---|---|---|---|
| 1980-81 | Hartford | 38 | 1 | 7 | 8 |
| 1981-82 | Hartford | 17 | 0 | 3 | 3 |
| 1982-83 | Hartford | 18 | 1 | 0 | 1 |
| | Totals | 73 | 2 | 10 | 12 |

**SMITH, Thomas J.**  *Forward*
b. Ottawa, Ont., Sept. 27, 1885

| Season | Club | GP | G | A | Pts. |
|---|---|---|---|---|---|
| 1919-20 | Quebec | 10 | 0 | 0 | 0 |


**SMITH, Wayne**  *Defenseman*
b. Kamsack, Sask., Feb. 12, 1943

| Season | Club | GP | G | A | Pts. |
|---|---|---|---|---|---|
| 1966-67 | Chicago | 2 | 1 | 1 | 2 |

**SMRKE, John**  *Forward*
b. Chicoutimi, Que., Feb. 25, 1956

| Season | Club | GP | G | A | Pts. |
|---|---|---|---|---|---|
| 1977-78 | St Louis | 18 | 2 | 4 | 6 |
| 1978-79 | St Louis | 55 | 6 | 8 | 14 |
| 1979-80 | Quebec | 30 | 3 | 5 | 8 |
| | Totals | 103 | 11 | 17 | 28 |

**SMRKE, Stanley**  *Forward*
b. Belgrade, Yugoslavia, Sept. 2, 1928

| Season | Club | GP | G | A | Pts. |
|---|---|---|---|---|---|
| 1956-57 | Montreal | 4 | 0 | 0 | 0 |
| 1957-58 | Montreal | 5 | 0 | 3 | 3 |
| | Totals | 9 | 0 | 3 | 3 |

**SMYL, Stanley Phillip**  *Forward*
b. Glendon, Alta., Jan. 28, 1958

| Season | Club | GP | G | A | Pts. |
|---|---|---|---|---|---|
| 1978-79 | Vancouver | 62 | 14 | 24 | 38 |
| 1979-80 | Vancouver | 77 | 31 | 47 | 78 |
| 1980-81 | Vancouver | 80 | 25 | 38 | 63 |
| 1981-82 | Vancouver | 80 | 34 | 44 | 78 |
| 1982-83 | Vancouver | 74 | 38 | 50 | 88 |
| | Totals | 373 | 142 | 203 | 345 |

**SMYLIE, Roderick (Rod)**  *Defenseman-Forward*

| Season | Club | GP | G | A | Pts. |
|---|---|---|---|---|---|
| 1920-21 | Toronto | 23 | 2 | 0 | 2 |
| 1921-22 | Toronto | 21 | 0 | 0 | 0 |
| 1922-23 | Toronto | 2 | 0 | 0 | 0 |
| 1923-24 | Ottawa | 14 | 1 | 1 | 2 |
| 1924-25 | Toronto | 11 | 0 | 0 | 0 |
| 1925-26 | Toronto | 5 | 0 | 0 | 0 |
| | Totals | 76 | 3 | 1 | 4 |

**SNELL, Harold Edward**  *Forward*
b. Ottawa, Ont., May 28, 1946

| Season | Club | GP | G | A | Pts. |
|---|---|---|---|---|---|
| 1973-74 | Pittsburgh | 55 | 4 | 12 | 16 |
| 1974-75 | KC-Det | 49 | 3 | 6 | 9 |
| | Totals | 104 | 7 | 18 | 25 |

**SNELL, Ronald Wayne**  *Forward*
b. Regina, Sask., Aug. 11, 1948

| Season | Club | GP | G | A | Pts. |
|---|---|---|---|---|---|
| 1968-69 | Pittsburgh | 4 | 3 | 1 | 4 |
| 1969-70 | Pittsburgh | 3 | 0 | 1 | 1 |
| 1973-74 | Winnipeg (WHA) | 70 | 24 | 25 | 49 |
| 1974-75 | Winnipeg (WHA) | 20 | 0 | 0 | 0 |
| | NHL Totals | 7 | 3 | 2 | 5 |
| | WHA Totals | 90 | 24 | 25 | 49 |

**SNEPSTS, Harold John**  *Defenseman*
b. Edmonton, Alta., Oct. 24, 1954

| Season | Club | GP | G | A | Pts. |
|---|---|---|---|---|---|
| 1974-75 | Vancouver | 27 | 1 | 2 | 3 |
| 1975-76 | Vancouver | 78 | 3 | 15 | 18 |
| 1976-77 | Vancouver | 79 | 4 | 18 | 22 |
| 1977-78 | Vancouver | 75 | 4 | 16 | 20 |
| 1978-79 | Vancouver | 76 | 7 | 24 | 31 |
| 1979-80 | Vancouver | 79 | 3 | 20 | 23 |
| 1980-81 | Vancouver | 76 | 3 | 16 | 19 |
| 1981-82 | Vancouver | 68 | 3 | 14 | 17 |
| 1982-83 | Vancouver | 46 | 2 | 8 | 10 |
| | Totals | 604 | 30 | 133 | 163 |

**SNOW, William Alexander (Sandy)**  *Forward*
b. Dokin, N.S., Nov. 11, 1946

| Season | Club | GP | G | A | Pts. |
|---|---|---|---|---|---|
| 1968-69 | Detroit | 3 | 0 | 0 | 0 |

**SOBCHUK, Dennis James**  *Forward*
b. Lang, Sask., Jan. 12, 1954

| Season | Club | GP | G | A | Pts. |
|---|---|---|---|---|---|
| 1974-75 | Phoenix (WHA) | 78 | 32 | 45 | 77 |
| 1975-76 | Cincinnati (WHA) | 79 | 32 | 40 | 72 |
| 1976-77 | Cincinnati (WHA) | 81 | 44 | 52 | 96 |
| 1977-78 | Cin-Edm (WHA) | 36 | 11 | 12 | 23 |
| 1978-79 | Edmonton (WHA) | 74 | 26 | 37 | 63 |

| Season | Club | GP | G | A | Pts. |
|---|---|---|---|---|---|
| 1979-80 | Detroit | 33 | 4 | 6 | 10 |
| 1982-83 | Quebec | 2 | 1 | 0 | 1 |
| | **NHL Totals** | 35 | 5 | 6 | 11 |
| | **WHA Totals** | 348 | 145 | 186 | 331 |

**SOBCHUK, Eugene** *Forward*
b. Lang, Sask., Jan. 2, 1951

| Season | Club | GP | G | A | Pts. |
|---|---|---|---|---|---|
| 1973-74 | Vancouver | 1 | 0 | 0 | 0 |
| 1974-75 | Phoenix (WHA) | 3 | 1 | 0 | 1 |
| 1975-76 | Cincinnati (WHA) | 78 | 24 | 18 | 42 |
| | **NHL Totals** | 1 | 0 | 0 | 0 |
| | **WHA Totals** | 81 | 25 | 18 | 43 |

**SOLHEIM, Kenneth Lawrence** *Forward*
b. Hythe, Alta., Mar. 27, 1961

| Season | Club | GP | G | A | Pts. |
|---|---|---|---|---|---|
| 1980-81 | Chi-Minn | 10 | 4 | 1 | 5 |
| 1981-82 | Minnesota | 29 | 4 | 5 | 9 |
| 1982-83 | Minn-Det | 35 | 2 | 4 | 6 |
| | **Totals** | 74 | 10 | 10 | 20 |

**SOLINGER, Robert Edward** *Forward*
b. Star City, Sask., Dec. 23, 1925

| Season | Club | GP | G | A | Pts. |
|---|---|---|---|---|---|
| 1951-52 | Toronto | 24 | 5 | 3 | 8 |
| 1952-53 | Toronto | 19 | 1 | 1 | 2 |
| 1953-54 | Toronto | 39 | 3 | 2 | 5 |
| 1954-55 | Toronto | 17 | 1 | 5 | 6 |
| | **Totals** | 98 | 10 | 11 | 21 |

**SOMERS, Arthur E.** *Forward*
b. Winnipeg, Man., Jan. 17, 1904

| Season | Club | GP | G | A | Pts. |
|---|---|---|---|---|---|
| 1929-30 | Chicago | 44 | 11 | 13 | 24 |
| 1930-31 | Chicago | 33 | 3 | 6 | 9 |
| 1931-32 | New York R | 48 | 11 | 15 | 26 |
| 1932-33 | New York R | 48 | 7 | 15 | 22 |
| 1933-34 | New York R | 8 | 1 | 2 | 3 |
| 1934-35 | New York R | 41 | 0 | 5 | 5 |
| 1949-50 | New York R | 55 | 4 | 4 | 8 |
| | **Totals** | 277 | 37 | 60 | 97 |

**SOMMER, Roy** *Forward*
b. Oakland, Calif., Apr. 5, 1957

| Season | Club | GP | G | A | Pts. |
|---|---|---|---|---|---|
| 1980-81 | Edmonton | 3 | 1 | 0 | 1 |

**SONGIN, Thomas David** *Forward*
b. Norwood, Mass., Dec. 20, 1953

| Season | Club | GP | G | A | Pts. |
|---|---|---|---|---|---|
| 1978-79 | Boston | 17 | 3 | 1 | 4 |
| 1979-80 | Boston | 17 | 1 | 3 | 4 |
| 1980-81 | Boston | 9 | 1 | 1 | 2 |
| | **Totals** | 43 | 5 | 5 | 10 |

**SONMOR, Glen Robert** *Forward*
b. Moose Jaw, Sask., Apr. 22, 1929

| Season | Club | GP | G | A | Pts. |
|---|---|---|---|---|---|
| 1953-54 | New York R | 15 | 2 | 0 | 2 |
| 1954-55 | New York R | 13 | 0 | 0 | 0 |
| | **Totals** | 28 | 2 | 0 | 2 |

**SORRELL, John Arthur** *Forward*
b. Chesterville, Ont., Jan. 16, 1906

| Season | Club | GP | G | A | Pts. |
|---|---|---|---|---|---|
| 1930-31 | Detroit | 40 | 9 | 7 | 16 |
| 1931-32 | Detroit | 48 | 8 | 5 | 13 |
| 1932-33 | Detroit | 48 | 14 | 10 | 24 |
| 1933-34 | Detroit | 48 | 21 | 10 | 31 |
| 1934-35 | Detroit | 47 | 20 | 16 | 36 |
| 1935-36 | Detroit | 47 | 13 | 15 | 28 |
| 1936-37 | Detroit | 48 | 8 | 16 | 24 |
| 1937-38 | Det-NYA | 39 | 11 | 9 | 20 |
| 1938-39 | New York A | 46 | 13 | 9 | 22 |
| 1939-40 | New York A | 48 | 8 | 16 | 24 |
| 1940-41 | New York A | 30 | 2 | 6 | 8 |
| | **Totals** | 489 | 127 | 119 | 246 |

**SPARROW, Emory (Spunk)** *Forward*
b. Chesterville, Ont., Jan. 16, 1906

| Season | Club | GP | G | A | Pts. |
|---|---|---|---|---|---|
| 1924-25 | Boston | 6 | 0 | 0 | 0 |

**SPECK, Frederick Edmondstone (Fred)**
*Forward*
b. Thorold, Ont., July 22, 1947

| Season | Club | GP | G | A | Pts. |
|---|---|---|---|---|---|
| 1968-69 | Detroit | 5 | 0 | 0 | 0 |
| 1969-70 | Detroit | 5 | 0 | 0 | 0 |
| 1971-72 | Vancouver | 18 | 1 | 2 | 3 |
| 1972-73 | Minn-LA (WHA) | 75 | 16 | 29 | 45 |
| | **NHL Totals** | 28 | 1 | 2 | 3 |
| | **WHA Totals** | 75 | 16 | 29 | 45 |

**SPEER, Francis William (Bill)** *Defenseman*
b. Lindsay, Ont., Mar. 20, 1942

| Season | Club | GP | G | A | Pts. |
|---|---|---|---|---|---|
| 1967-68 | Pittsburgh | 68 | 3 | 13 | 16 |
| 1968-69 | Pittsburgh | 34 | 1 | 4 | 5 |
| 1969-70 | Boston | 27 | 1 | 3 | 4 |
| 1970-71 | Boston | 1 | 0 | 0 | 0 |
| 1972-73 | New York (WHA) | 69 | 3 | 23 | 26 |
| | **NHL Totals** | 130 | 5 | 20 | 25 |
| | **WHA Totals** | 69 | 3 | 23 | 26 |

**SPENCER, Brian Roy** *Forward*
b. Fort St. James, B.C., Sept. 3, 1949

| Season | Club | GP | G | A | Pts. |
|---|---|---|---|---|---|
| 1969-70 | Toronto | 9 | 0 | 0 | 0 |
| 1970-71 | Toronto | 50 | 9 | 15 | 24 |
| 1971-72 | Toronto | 36 | 1 | 5 | 6 |
| 1972-73 | New York I | 78 | 14 | 24 | 38 |
| 1973-74 | NYI-Buf | 67 | 8 | 18 | 26 |
| 1974-75 | Buffalo | 73 | 12 | 29 | 41 |
| 1975-76 | Buffalo | 77 | 13 | 26 | 39 |
| 1976-77 | Buffalo | 77 | 14 | 15 | 29 |
| 1977-78 | Pittsburgh | 79 | 9 | 11 | 20 |
| 1978-79 | Pittsburgh | 7 | 0 | 0 | 0 |
| | **Totals** | 553 | 80 | 143 | 223 |

**SPENCER, Irvin James (Spinner)**
*Defenseman-Forward*
b. Sudbury, Ont., Dec. 4, 1937

| Season | Club | GP | G | A | Pts. |
|---|---|---|---|---|---|
| 1959-60 | New York R | 32 | 1 | 2 | 3 |
| 1960-61 | New York R | 56 | 1 | 8 | 9 |
| 1961-62 | New York R | 43 | 2 | 10 | 12 |
| 1962-63 | Boston | 69 | 5 | 17 | 22 |
| 1963-64 | Detroit | 25 | 3 | 0 | 3 |
| 1967-68 | Detroit | 5 | 0 | 1 | 1 |
| 1972-73 | Philadelphia (WHA) | 54 | 2 | 27 | 29 |
| | **NHL Totals** | 228 | 12 | 38 | 50 |
| | **WHA Totals** | 54 | 2 | 27 | 29 |

**SPEYER, Christopher** *Defenseman*
b. Toronto, Ont., June 1906

| Season | Club | GP | G | A | Pts. |
|---|---|---|---|---|---|
| 1923-24 | Toronto | 3 | 0 | 0 | 0 |
| 1924-25 | Toronto | 2 | 0 | 0 | 0 |
| 1933-34 | New York A | 9 | 0 | 0 | 0 |
| | **Totals** | 14 | 0 | 0 | 0 |

**SPRING, Donald Neil** *Defenseman*
b. Maracaibo, Venezuela, June 15, 1959

| Season | Club | GP | G | A | Pts. |
|---|---|---|---|---|---|
| 1980-81 | Winnipeg | 80 | 1 | 18 | 19 |
| 1981-82 | Winnipeg | 78 | 0 | 16 | 16 |
| 1982-83 | Winnipeg | 80 | 0 | 16 | 16 |
| | **Totals** | 238 | 1 | 50 | 51 |

**SPRING, Franklin Patrick** *Forward*
b. Cranbrook, B.C., Oct. 19, 1949

| Season | Club | GP | G | A | Pts. |
|---|---|---|---|---|---|
| 1969-70 | Boston | 1 | 0 | 0 | 0 |
| 1973-74 | St Louis | 2 | 0 | 0 | 0 |
| 1974-75 | StL-Cal | 31 | 3 | 8 | 11 |
| 1975-76 | California | 1 | 0 | 2 | 2 |
| 1976-77 | Cleveland | 26 | 11 | 10 | 21 |
| 1977-78 | Indianapolis (WHA) | 13 | 2 | 4 | 6 |
| | **NHL Totals** | 61 | 14 | 20 | 34 |
| | **WHA Totals** | 13 | 2 | 4 | 6 |

**SPRING, Jesse** *Defenseman*
b. Toronto, Ont.

| Season | Club | GP | G | A | Pts. |
|---|---|---|---|---|---|
| 1923-24 | Hamilton | 20 | 3 | 2 | 5 |
| 1924-25 | Hamilton | 29 | 2 | 0 | 2 |
| 1925-26 | Pittsburgh Pi | 32 | 5 | 0 | 5 |
| 1926-27 | Toronto | 2 | 0 | 0 | 0 |

| Season | Club | GP | G | A | Pts. |
|---|---|---|---|---|---|
| 1928-29 | Pittsburgh Pi | 32 | 0 | 0 | 0 |
| 1929-30 | Pittsburgh Pi | 22 | 1 | 0 | 1 |
| | **Totals** | 137 | 11 | 2 | 13 |

**SPRUCE, Andrew William** *Forward*
b. London, Ont., Apr. 17, 1954

| Season | Club | GP | G | A | Pts. |
|---|---|---|---|---|---|
| 1976-77 | Vancouver | 51 | 9 | 6 | 15 |
| 1977-78 | Colorado | 74 | 19 | 21 | 40 |
| 1978-79 | Colorado | 47 | 3 | 15 | 18 |
| | **Totals** | 172 | 31 | 42 | 73 |

**STACKHOUSE, Ronald Lorne (Ron)**
*Defenseman*
b. Haliburton, Ont., Aug. 26, 1949

| Season | Club | GP | G | A | Pts. |
|---|---|---|---|---|---|
| 1970-71 | California | 78 | 8 | 24 | 32 |
| 1971-72 | Cal-Det | 79 | 6 | 28 | 34 |
| 1972-73 | Detroit | 78 | 5 | 29 | 34 |
| 1973-74 | Det-Pitt | 69 | 6 | 29 | 35 |
| 1974-75 | Pittsburgh | 72 | 15 | 45 | 60 |
| 1975-76 | Pittsburgh | 80 | 11 | 60 | 71 |
| 1976-77 | Pittsburgh | 80 | 7 | 34 | 41 |
| 1977-78 | Pittsburgh | 50 | 5 | 15 | 20 |
| 1978-79 | Pittsburgh | 75 | 10 | 33 | 43 |
| 1979-80 | Pittsburgh | 78 | 6 | 27 | 33 |
| 1980-81 | Pittsburgh | 74 | 6 | 29 | 35 |
| 1981-82 | Pittsburgh | 76 | 2 | 19 | 21 |
| | **Totals** | 889 | 87 | 372 | 459 |

**STACKHOUSE, Theodore** *Defenseman*

| Season | Club | GP | G | A | Pts. |
|---|---|---|---|---|---|
| 1921-22 | Toronto | 12 | 0 | 0 | 0 |

**STALEY, Allan (Red)** *Forward*
b. Regina, Sask., Sept. 21, 1928

| Season | Club | GP | G | A | Pts. |
|---|---|---|---|---|---|
| 1948-49 | New York R | 1 | 0 | 1 | 1 |

**STAMLER, Lorne Alexander** *Forward*
b. Winnipeg, Man., Aug. 9, 1951

| Season | Club | GP | G | A | Pts. |
|---|---|---|---|---|---|
| 1976-77 | Los Angeles | 7 | 2 | 1 | 3 |
| 1977-78 | Los Angeles | 2 | 0 | 0 | 0 |
| 1978-79 | Toronto | 45 | 4 | 3 | 7 |
| 1979-80 | Winnipeg | 62 | 8 | 7 | 15 |
| | **Totals** | 116 | 14 | 11 | 25 |

**STANDING, George Michael** *Forward*
b. Toronto, Ont., Aug. 3, 1941

| Season | Club | GP | G | A | Pts. |
|---|---|---|---|---|---|
| 1967-68 | Minnesota | 2 | 0 | 0 | 0 |

**STANFIELD, Frederic William (Fred)** *Forward*
b. Toronto, Ont., May 4, 1944

| Season | Club | GP | G | A | Pts. |
|---|---|---|---|---|---|
| 1964-65 | Chicago | 58 | 7 | 10 | 17 |
| 1965-66 | Chicago | 39 | 2 | 2 | 4 |
| 1966-67 | Chicago | 10 | 1 | 0 | 1 |
| 1967-68 | Boston | 73 | 20 | 44 | 64 |
| 1968-69 | Boston | 71 | 25 | 29 | 54 |
| 1969-70 | Boston | 73 | 23 | 35 | 58 |
| 1970-71 | Boston | 75 | 24 | 52 | 76 |
| 1971-72 | Boston | 78 | 23 | 56 | 79 |
| 1972-73 | Boston | 78 | 20 | 58 | 78 |
| 1973-74 | Minnesota | 71 | 16 | 28 | 44 |
| 1974-75 | Minn-Buf | 72 | 20 | 39 | 59 |
| 1975-76 | Buffalo | 80 | 18 | 30 | 48 |
| 1976-77 | Buffalo | 79 | 9 | 14 | 23 |
| 1977-78 | Buffalo | 57 | 3 | 8 | 11 |
| | **Totals** | 914 | 211 | 405 | 616 |

**STANFIELD, James Boviard (Jim)** *Forward*
b. Toronto, Ont., Jan. 1, 1947

| Season | Club | GP | G | A | Pts. |
|---|---|---|---|---|---|
| 1969-70 | Los Angeles | 1 | 0 | 0 | 0 |
| 1970-71 | Los Angeles | 2 | 0 | 0 | 0 |
| 1971-72 | Los Angeles | 4 | 0 | 1 | 1 |
| | **Totals** | 7 | 0 | 1 | 1 |

**STANKIEWICZ, Edward** *Forward*
b. Kitchener, Ont., Dec. 1, 1929

| Season | Club | GP | G | A | Pts. |
|---|---|---|---|---|---|
| 1953-54 | Detroit | 1 | 0 | 0 | 0 |
| 1955-56 | Detroit | 5 | 0 | 0 | 0 |
| | **Totals** | 6 | 0 | 0 | 0 |

| Season | Club | GP | G | A | Pts. |
|---|---|---|---|---|---|
| **STANKIEWICZ, Myron (Mike)** *Forward* | | | | | |
| b. Kitchener, Ont., Dec. 4, 1935 | | | | | |
| 1968-69 | StL-Phil | 35 | 0 | 7 | 7 |
| **STANLEY, Allan Herbert** *Defenseman* | | | | | |
| b. Timmins, Ont., Mar. 1, 1926 | | | | | |
| 1948-49 | New York R | 40 | 2 | 8 | 10 |
| 1949-50 | New York R | 55 | 4 | 4 | 8 |
| 1950-51 | New York R | 70 | 7 | 14 | 21 |
| 1951-52 | New York R | 50 | 5 | 14 | 19 |
| 1952-53 | New York R | 70 | 5 | 12 | 17 |
| 1953-54 | New York R | 10 | 0 | 2 | 2 |
| 1954-55 | NYR-Chi | 64 | 10 | 16 | 26 |
| 1955-56 | Chicago | 59 | 4 | 14 | 18 |
| 1956-57 | Boston | 60 | 6 | 25 | 31 |
| 1957-58 | Boston | 69 | 6 | 25 | 31 |
| 1958-59 | Toronto | 70 | 1 | 22 | 23 |
| 1959-60 | Toronto | 64 | 10 | 23 | 33 |
| 1960-61 | Toronto | 68 | 9 | 25 | 34 |
| 1961-62 | Toronto | 60 | 9 | 26 | 35 |
| 1962-63 | Toronto | 61 | 4 | 15 | 19 |
| 1963-64 | Toronto | 70 | 6 | 21 | 27 |
| 1964-65 | Toronto | 64 | 2 | 15 | 17 |
| 1965-66 | Toronto | 59 | 4 | 14 | 18 |
| 1966-67 | Toronto | 53 | 1 | 12 | 13 |
| 1967-68 | Toronto | 64 | 1 | 13 | 14 |
| 1968-69 | Philadelphia | 64 | 4 | 13 | 17 |
| | **Totals** | 1244 | 100 | 333 | 433 |
| **STANLEY, Russell (Barney)** *Forward* | | | | | |
| b. Paisley, Ont., June 1, 1893 | | | | | |
| 1927-28 | Chicago | 2 | 0 | 0 | 0 |
| **STANOWSKI, Walter Peter** *Defenseman* | | | | | |
| b. Winnipeg, Man., Apr. 28, 1919 | | | | | |
| 1939-40 | Toronto | 27 | 2 | 7 | 9 |
| 1940-41 | Toronto | 47 | 7 | 14 | 21 |
| 1941-42 | Toronto | 24 | 1 | 7 | 8 |
| 1944-45 | Toronto | 34 | 2 | 9 | 11 |
| 1945-46 | Toronto | 45 | 3 | 10 | 13 |
| 1946-47 | Toronto | 51 | 3 | 16 | 19 |
| 1947-48 | Toronto | 54 | 2 | 11 | 13 |
| 1948-49 | New York R | 60 | 1 | 8 | 9 |
| 1949-50 | New York R | 37 | 1 | 1 | 2 |
| 1950-51 | New York R | 49 | 1 | 5 | 6 |
| | **Totals** | 428 | 23 | 88 | 111 |
| **STAPLETON, Patrick James (Pat)** | | | | | |
| *Defenseman* | | | | | |
| b. Sarnia, Ont., July 4, 1940 | | | | | |
| 1961-62 | Boston | 69 | 2 | 5 | 7 |
| 1962-63 | Boston | 21 | 0 | 3 | 3 |
| 1965-66 | Chicago | 55 | 4 | 30 | 34 |
| 1966-67 | Chicago | 70 | 3 | 31 | 34 |
| 1967-68 | Chicago | 67 | 4 | 34 | 38 |
| 1968-69 | Chicago | 75 | 6 | 50 | 56 |
| 1969-70 | Chicago | 49 | 4 | 38 | 42 |
| 1970-71 | Chicago | 76 | 7 | 44 | 51 |
| 1971-72 | Chicago | 78 | 3 | 38 | 41 |
| 1972-73 | Chicago | 75 | 10 | 21 | 31 |
| 1973-74 | Chicago (WHA) | 78 | 6 | 52 | 58 |
| 1974-75 | Chicago (WHA) | 68 | 4 | 30 | 34 |
| 1975-76 | Indianapolis (WHA) | 80 | 4 | 40 | 44 |
| 1976-77 | Indianapolis (WHA) | 81 | 8 | 45 | 53 |
| 1977-78 | Cincinnati (WHA) | 65 | 4 | 45 | 49 |
| | **NHL Totals** | 635 | 43 | 294 | 337 |
| | **WHA Totals** | 372 | 26 | 212 | 238 |
| **STARR, Harold** *Defenseman* | | | | | |
| b. Ottawa, Ont., July 8, 1905 | | | | | |
| 1929-30 | Ottawa | 28 | 2 | 1 | 3 |
| 1930-31 | Ottawa | 35 | 2 | 1 | 3 |
| 1931-32 | Montreal M | 47 | 1 | 2 | 3 |
| 1932-33 | Ott-Mont | 46 | 0 | 0 | 0 |
| 1934-35 | Det-NYR | 33 | 1 | 1 | 2 |
| 1935-36 | New York R | 15 | 0 | 0 | 0 |
| | **Totals** | 204 | 6 | 5 | 11 |
| **STARR, Wilfrid Peter** *Forward* | | | | | |
| b. Winnipeg, Man., July 22, 1909 | | | | | |
| 1932-33 | New York A | 26 | 4 | 3 | 7 |
| 1933-34 | Detroit | 28 | 2 | 2 | 4 |

| Season | Club | GP | G | A | Pts. |
|---|---|---|---|---|---|
| 1934-35 | Detroit | 24 | 1 | 1 | 2 |
| 1935-36 | Detroit | 9 | 1 | 0 | 1 |
| | **Totals** | 87 | 8 | 6 | 14 |
| **STASIUK, Victor John** *Forward* | | | | | |
| b. Lethbridge, Alta., May 23, 1929 | | | | | |
| 1949-50 | Chicago | 17 | 1 | 1 | 2 |
| 1950-51 | Chi-Det | 70 | 8 | 13 | 21 |
| 1951-52 | Detroit | 58 | 5 | 9 | 14 |
| 1952-53 | Detroit | 3 | 0 | 0 | 0 |
| 1953-54 | Detroit | 42 | 5 | 2 | 7 |
| 1954-55 | Detroit | 59 | 8 | 11 | 19 |
| 1955-56 | Boston | 59 | 19 | 18 | 37 |
| 1956-57 | Boston | 64 | 24 | 16 | 40 |
| 1957-58 | Boston | 70 | 21 | 35 | 56 |
| 1958-59 | Boston | 70 | 27 | 33 | 60 |
| 1959-60 | Boston | 69 | 29 | 39 | 68 |
| 1960-61 | Bos-Det | 69 | 15 | 38 | 53 |
| 1961-62 | Detroit | 59 | 15 | 28 | 43 |
| 1962-63 | Detroit | 36 | 6 | 11 | 17 |
| | **Totals** | 745 | 183 | 254 | 437 |
| **STASTNY, Anton** *Forward* | | | | | |
| b. Bratislavia, Czechoslovakia, Aug. 5, 1959 | | | | | |
| 1980-81 | Quebec | 80 | 39 | 46 | 85 |
| 1981-82 | Quebec | 68 | 26 | 46 | 72 |
| 1982-83 | Quebec | 79 | 32 | 60 | 92 |
| | **Totals** | 227 | 97 | 152 | 249 |
| **STASTNY, Marian** *Forward* | | | | | |
| b. Bratislavia, Czechoslovakia, Jan. 8, 1953 | | | | | |
| 1981-82 | Quebec | 74 | 35 | 54 | 89 |
| 1982-83 | Quebec | 60 | 36 | 43 | 79 |
| | **Totals** | 134 | 71 | 97 | 168 |
| **STASTNY, Peter** *Forward* | | | | | |
| b. Bratislavia, Czechoslovakia, Sept. 18, 1956 | | | | | |
| 1980-81 | Quebec | 77 | 39 | 70 | 109 |
| 1981-82 | Quebec | 80 | 46 | 93 | 139 |
| 1982-83 | Quebec | 75 | 47 | 77 | 124 |
| | **Totals** | 232 | 132 | 240 | 372 |
| **STEEN, Anders** *Forward* | | | | | |
| b. Nykoping, Sweden, Apr. 28, 1955 | | | | | |
| 1980-81 | Winnipeg | 42 | 5 | 11 | 16 |
| **STEEN, Thomas** *Forward* | | | | | |
| b. Tockmark, Sweden, June 8, 1960 | | | | | |
| 1981-82 | Winnipeg | 73 | 15 | 29 | 44 |
| 1982-83 | Winnipeg | 75 | 26 | 33 | 59 |
| | **Totals** | 148 | 41 | 62 | 103 |
| **STEFANSKI, Ed Stanley Michael (Bud)** | | | | | |
| *Forward* | | | | | |
| b. South Porcupine, Ont., Apr. 28, 1955 | | | | | |
| 1977-78 | New York R | 1 | 0 | 0 | 0 |
| **STEFANIW, Morris Alexander** *Forward* | | | | | |
| b. North Battleford, Sask., Jan. 10, 1948 | | | | | |
| 1972-73 | Atlanta | 13 | 1 | 1 | 2 |
| **STEMKOWSKI, Peter David** *Forward* | | | | | |
| b. Winnipeg, Man., Aug. 25, 1943 | | | | | |
| 1963-64 | Toronto | 1 | 0 | 0 | 0 |
| 1964-65 | Toronto | 36 | 5 | 15 | 20 |
| 1965-66 | Toronto | 56 | 4 | 12 | 16 |
| 1966-67 | Toronto | 68 | 13 | 22 | 35 |
| 1967-68 | Tor-Det | 73 | 10 | 21 | 31 |
| 1968-69 | Detroit | 71 | 21 | 31 | 52 |
| 1969-70 | Detroit | 76 | 25 | 24 | 49 |
| 1970-71 | Det-NYR | 78 | 18 | 31 | 49 |
| 1971-72 | New York R | 59 | 11 | 17 | 28 |
| 1972-73 | New York R | 78 | 22 | 37 | 59 |
| 1973-74 | New York R | 78 | 25 | 45 | 70 |
| 1974-75 | New York R | 77 | 24 | 35 | 59 |
| 1975-76 | New York R | 75 | 13 | 28 | 41 |

| Season | Club | GP | G | A | Pts. |
|---|---|---|---|---|---|
| 1976-77 | New York R | 61 | 2 | 13 | 15 |
| 1977-78 | Los Angeles | 80 | 13 | 18 | 31 |
| | **Totals** | 967 | 206 | 349 | 555 |
| **STENLUND, Vern** *Forward* | | | | | |
| b. Thunder Bay, Ont., Nov. 4, 1956 | | | | | |
| 1976-77 | Cleveland | 4 | 0 | 0 | 0 |
| **STEPHENS, Philip** *Defenseman* | | | | | |
| b. 1895 | | | | | |
| 1917-18 | Montreal W | 4 | 1 | 0 | 1 |
| 1921-22 | Montreal | 4 | 0 | 0 | 0 |
| | **Totals** | 8 | 1 | 0 | 1 |
| **STEPHENSON, Robert** *Forward* | | | | | |
| b. Saskatoon, Sask., Feb. 1, 1954 | | | | | |
| 1978-79 | Birmingham (WHA) | 80 | 12 | 36 | 48 |
| 1979-80 | Hart-Tor | 18 | 2 | 3 | 5 |
| | **NHL Totals** | 18 | 2 | 3 | 5 |
| | **WHA Totals** | 80 | 12 | 36 | 48 |
| **STERNER, Ulf** *Forward* | | | | | |
| b. Deje, Sweden, Feb. 11, 1941 | | | | | |
| 1964-65 | New York R | 4 | 0 | 0 | 0 |
| **STEVENS, Paul** *Defenseman* | | | | | |
| b. 1925-26 Boston | 17 | 0 | 0 | 0 |
| 1925-26 | Boston | 17 | 0 | 0 | 0 |
| **STEVENS, Scott** *Defenseman* | | | | | |
| b. Kitchener, Ont., Apr. 1, 1954 | | | | | |
| 1982-83 | Washington | 77 | 9 | 16 | 25 |
| **STEWART, Blair James** *Forward* | | | | | |
| b. Winnipeg, Man., Mar. 15, 1953 | | | | | |
| 1973-74 | Detroit | 17 | 0 | 4 | 4 |
| 1974-75 | Det-Wash | 21 | 1 | 5 | 6 |
| 1975-76 | Washington | 74 | 13 | 14 | 27 |
| 1976-77 | Washington | 34 | 5 | 2 | 7 |
| 1977-78 | Washington | 8 | 0 | 1 | 1 |
| 1978-79 | Washington | 45 | 7 | 12 | 19 |
| 1979-80 | Quebec | 30 | 8 | 6 | 14 |
| | **Totals** | 229 | 34 | 44 | 78 |
| **STEWART, James Gaye** *Forward* | | | | | |
| b. Fort William, Ont., June 28, 1923 | | | | | |
| 1942-43 | Toronto | 48 | 24 | 23 | 47 |
| 1945-46 | Toronto | 50 | 37 | 15 | 52 |
| 1946-47 | Toronto | 60 | 19 | 14 | 33 |
| 1947-48 | Tor-Chi | 61 | 27 | 29 | 56 |
| 1948-49 | Chicago | 54 | 20 | 18 | 38 |
| 1949-50 | Chicago | 70 | 24 | 19 | 43 |
| 1950-51 | Detroit | 67 | 18 | 13 | 31 |
| 1951-52 | New York R | 69 | 15 | 25 | 40 |
| 1952-53 | NYR-Mont | 23 | 1 | 3 | 4 |
| | **Totals** | 502 | 185 | 159 | 344 |
| **STEWART, John Alexander** *Forward* | | | | | |
| b. Eriksdale, Man., May 16, 1950 | | | | | |
| 1970-71 | Pittsburgh | 15 | 2 | 1 | 3 |
| 1971-72 | Pittsburgh | 25 | 2 | 8 | 10 |
| 1972-73 | Atlanta | 68 | 17 | 17 | 34 |
| 1973-74 | Atlanta | 74 | 18 | 15 | 33 |
| 1974-75 | California | 76 | 19 | 19 | 38 |
| 1975-76 | Cleveland (WHA) | 79 | 12 | 21 | 33 |
| 1976-77 | Minn-Birm (WHA) | 16 | 3 | 3 | 6 |
| | **NHL Totals** | 258 | 58 | 60 | 118 |
| | **WHA Totals** | 95 | 15 | 24 | 39 |
| **STEWART, John Christopher** *Forward* | | | | | |
| b. Toronto, Ont., Jan. 2, 1954 | | | | | |
| 1974-75 | Cleveland (WHA) | 59 | 4 | 7 | 11 |
| 1975-76 | Cleveland (WHA) | 42 | 2 | 9 | 11 |
| 1976-77 | Birmingham (WHA) | 52 | 17 | 24 | 41 |
| 1977-78 | Birmingham (WHA) | 48 | 13 | 26 | 39 |
| 1978-79 | Birmingham (WHA) | 70 | 24 | 26 | 50 |
| 1979-80 | Quebec | 2 | 0 | 0 | 0 |
| | **NHL Totals** | 2 | 0 | 0 | 0 |
| | **WHA Totals** | 271 | 60 | 92 | 152 |

| Season | Club | GP | G | A | Pts. |
|---|---|---|---|---|---|

**STEWART, John Sherratt (Black Jack)** *Defenseman*
b. Pilot Mound, Man., May 6, 1917

| Season | Club | GP | G | A | Pts. |
|---|---|---|---|---|---|
| 1938-39 | Detroit | 33 | 0 | 1 | 1 |
| 1939-40 | Detroit | 47 | 1 | 0 | 1 |
| 1940-41 | Detroit | 47 | 2 | 6 | 8 |
| 1941-42 | Detroit | 44 | 4 | 7 | 11 |
| 1942-43 | Detroit | 44 | 2 | 9 | 11 |
| 1945-46 | Detroit | 47 | 4 | 11 | 15 |
| 1946-47 | Detroit | 55 | 5 | 9 | 14 |
| 1947-48 | Detroit | 60 | 5 | 14 | 19 |
| 1948-49 | Detroit | 60 | 4 | 11 | 15 |
| 1949-50 | Detroit | 66 | 3 | 11 | 14 |
| 1950-51 | Chicago | 26 | 0 | 2 | 2 |
| 1951-52 | Chicago | 37 | 1 | 3 | 4 |
| | **Totals** | 566 | 31 | 84 | 115 |

**STEWART, Kenneth** *Defenseman*
b. Port Arthur, Ont., 1915

| Season | Club | GP | G | A | Pts. |
|---|---|---|---|---|---|
| 1941-42 | Chicago | — | 1 | 1 | 2 |

**STEWART, Nelson Robert (Old Poison)** *Forward*
b. Montreal, Que., Dec. 29, 1902

| Season | Club | GP | G | A | Pts. |
|---|---|---|---|---|---|
| 1925-26 | Montreal M | 36 | 34 | 8 | 42 |
| 1926-27 | Montreal M | 43 | 17 | 4 | 21 |
| 1927-28 | Montreal M | 41 | 27 | 7 | 34 |
| 1928-29 | Montreal M | 44 | 21 | 8 | 29 |
| 1929-30 | Montreal M | 44 | 39 | 16 | 55 |
| 1930-31 | Montreal M | 42 | 25 | 14 | 39 |
| 1931-32 | Montreal M | 38 | 22 | 11 | 33 |
| 1932-33 | Boston | 47 | 18 | 18 | 36 |
| 1933-34 | Boston | 48 | 21 | 17 | 38 |
| 1934-35 | Boston | 47 | 21 | 18 | 39 |
| 1935-36 | New York A | 48 | 14 | 15 | 29 |
| 1936-37 | Bos-NYA | 43 | 23 | 12 | 35 |
| 1937-38 | New York A | 48 | 19 | 17 | 36 |
| 1938-39 | New York A | 46 | 16 | 19 | 35 |
| 1939-40 | New York A | 35 | 7 | 7 | 14 |
| | **Totals** | 650 | 324 | 191 | 515 |

**STEWART, Paul** *Forward*
b. Boston, Mass., Mar. 21, 1954

| Season | Club | GP | G | A | Pts. |
|---|---|---|---|---|---|
| 1976-77 | Edmonton (WHA) | 2 | 0 | 0 | 0 |
| 1977-78 | Cincinnati (WHA) | 40 | 1 | 5 | 6 |
| 1978-79 | Cincinnati (WHA) | 23 | 2 | 1 | 3 |
| 1979-80 | Quebec | 21 | 2 | 0 | 2 |
| | **NHL Totals** | 21 | 2 | 0 | 2 |
| | **WHA Totals** | 65 | 3 | 6 | 9 |

**STEWART, Ralph Donald** *Forward*
b. Fort William, Ont., Dec. 2, 1948

| Season | Club | GP | G | A | Pts. |
|---|---|---|---|---|---|
| 1970-71 | Vancouver | 3 | 0 | 1 | 1 |
| 1972-73 | New York I | 31 | 4 | 10 | 14 |
| 1973-74 | New York I | 67 | 23 | 20 | 43 |
| 1974-75 | New York I | 70 | 16 | 24 | 40 |
| 1975-76 | New York I | 31 | 6 | 7 | 13 |
| 1976-77 | Vancouver | 34 | 6 | 8 | 14 |
| 1977-78 | Vancouver | 16 | 2 | 3 | 5 |
| | **Totals** | 252 | 57 | 73 | 130 |

**STEWART, Robert Harold (Bob)** *Defenseman*
b. Charlottetown, P.E.I., Nov. 10, 1950

| Season | Club | GP | G | A | Pts. |
|---|---|---|---|---|---|
| 1971-72 | Bos-Cal | 24 | 1 | 2 | 3 |
| 1972-73 | California | 63 | 4 | 17 | 21 |
| 1973-74 | California | 47 | 2 | 5 | 7 |
| 1974-75 | California | 67 | 5 | 12 | 17 |
| 1975-76 | California | 76 | 4 | 17 | 21 |
| 1976-77 | Cleveland | 73 | 1 | 12 | 13 |
| 1977-78 | Cleveland | 72 | 2 | 15 | 17 |
| 1978-79 | St Louis | 78 | 5 | 13 | 18 |
| 1979-80 | StL-Pitt | 75 | 3 | 8 | 11 |
| | **Totals** | 575 | 27 | 101 | 128 |

**STEWART, Ronald George (Ron)** *Defenseman-Forward*
b. Calgary, Alta., July 11, 1932

| Season | Club | GP | G | A | Pts. |
|---|---|---|---|---|---|
| 1952-53 | Toronto | 70 | 13 | 22 | 35 |
| 1953-54 | Toronto | 70 | 14 | 11 | 25 |
| 1954-55 | Toronto | 53 | 14 | 5 | 19 |
| 1955-56 | Toronto | 69 | 13 | 14 | 27 |
| 1956-57 | Toronto | 65 | 15 | 20 | 35 |
| 1957-58 | Toronto | 70 | 15 | 24 | 39 |
| 1958-59 | Toronto | 70 | 21 | 13 | 34 |
| 1959-60 | Toronto | 67 | 14 | 20 | 34 |
| 1960-61 | Toronto | 51 | 13 | 12 | 25 |
| 1961-62 | Toronto | 60 | 8 | 9 | 17 |
| 1962-63 | Toronto | 63 | 16 | 16 | 32 |
| 1963-64 | Toronto | 65 | 14 | 5 | 19 |
| 1964-65 | Toronto | 65 | 16 | 11 | 27 |
| 1965-66 | Boston | 70 | 20 | 16 | 36 |
| 1966-67 | Boston | 56 | 14 | 10 | 24 |
| 1967-68 | StL-NYR | 74 | 14 | 12 | 26 |
| 1968-69 | New York R | 75 | 18 | 11 | 29 |
| 1969-70 | New York R | 76 | 14 | 10 | 24 |
| 1970-71 | New York R | 76 | 5 | 6 | 11 |
| 1971-72 | Van-NYR | 55 | 3 | 3 | 6 |
| 1972-73 | NYR-NYI | 33 | | 3 | 5 |
| | **Totals** | 1353 | 276 | 253 | 529 |

**STEWART, William Donald** *Defenseman*
b. Toronto, Ont., Oct. 6, 1957

| Season | Club | GP | G | A | Pts. |
|---|---|---|---|---|---|
| 1977-78 | Buffalo | 13 | 2 | 0 | 2 |
| 1978-79 | Buffalo | 68 | 1 | 17 | 18 |
| 1979-80 | St Louis | 60 | 2 | 21 | 23 |
| 1981-82 | St Louis | 22 | 0 | 5 | 5 |
| 1982-83 | St Louis | 7 | 0 | 0 | 0 |
| | **Totals** | 170 | 5 | 43 | 48 |

**STODDARD, John Edward** *Forward*
b. Stony Creek, Ont., Sept. 26, 1926

| Season | Club | GP | G | A | Pts. |
|---|---|---|---|---|---|
| 1951-52 | New York R | 20 | 4 | 2 | 6 |
| 1952-53 | New York R | 60 | 12 | 13 | 25 |
| | **Totals** | 80 | 16 | 15 | 31 |

**STONE, Stephen George** *Forward*
b. Toronto, Ont., Sept. 26, 1952

| Season | Club | GP | G | A | Pts. |
|---|---|---|---|---|---|
| 1973-74 | Vancouver | 2 | 0 | 0 | 0 |

**STOLTZ, Roland** *Forward*
b. Oeverkalix, Sweden, Aug. 15, 1954

| Season | Club | GP | G | A | Pts. |
|---|---|---|---|---|---|
| 1981-82 | Washington | 14 | 2 | 2 | 4 |

**STOUGHTON, Blaine** *Forward*
b. Gilbert Plains, Man., Mar. 13, 1953

| Season | Club | GP | G | A | Pts. |
|---|---|---|---|---|---|
| 1973-74 | Pittsburgh | 34 | 5 | 6 | 11 |
| 1974-75 | Toronto | 78 | 23 | 14 | 37 |
| 1975-76 | Toronto | 43 | 6 | 11 | 17 |
| 1976-77 | Cincinnati (WHA) | 81 | 52 | 52 | 104 |
| 1977-78 | Cin-Ind (WHA) | 77 | 19 | 26 | 45 |
| 1978-79 | Ind-NE (WHA) | 61 | 18 | 12 | 30 |
| 1979-80 | Hartford | 80 | 56 | 44 | 100 |
| 1980-81 | Hartford | 71 | 43 | 30 | 73 |
| 1981-82 | Hartford | 80 | 52 | 39 | 91 |
| 1982-83 | Hartford | 72 | 45 | 31 | 76 |
| | **NHL Totals** | 458 | 230 | 175 | 405 |
| | **WHA Totals** | 219 | 89 | 90 | 179 |

**STRAIN, Neil Gilbert** *Forward*
b. Kenora, Ont., Feb. 24, 1926

| Season | Club | GP | G | A | Pts. |
|---|---|---|---|---|---|
| 1952-53 | New York R | 52 | 11 | 13 | 24 |

**STRATE, Gordon Lynn** *Defenseman*
b. Edmonton, Alta., May 28, 1935

| Season | Club | GP | G | A | Pts. |
|---|---|---|---|---|---|
| 1956-57 | Detroit | 5 | 0 | 0 | 0 |
| 1957-58 | Detroit | 45 | 0 | 0 | 0 |
| 1958-59 | Detroit | 11 | 0 | 0 | 0 |
| | **Totals** | 61 | 0 | 0 | 0 |

**STRATTON, Arthur** *Forward*
b. Winnipeg, Man., Oct. 8, 1935

| Season | Club | GP | G | A | Pts. |
|---|---|---|---|---|---|
| 1959-60 | New York R | 18 | 2 | 5 | 7 |
| 1963-64 | Detroit | 5 | 0 | 3 | 3 |
| 1965-66 | Chicago | 2 | 0 | 0 | 0 |
| 1967-68 | Pitt-Phil | 70 | 16 | 25 | 41 |
| | **Totals** | 95 | 18 | 33 | 51 |

**STROBEL, Arthur George** *Forward*
b. Regina, Sask., Nov. 28, 1922

| Season | Club | GP | G | A | Pts. |
|---|---|---|---|---|---|
| 1943-44 | New York R | 7 | 0 | 0 | 0 |

**STRONG, Ken,** *Forward*
b. Toronto, Ont., May 9, 1963

| Season | Club | GP | G | A | Pts. |
|---|---|---|---|---|---|
| 1982-83 | Toronto | 2 | 0 | 0 | 0 |

**STRUEBY, Todd** *Forward*
b. Linnigan, Sask., June 15, 1963

| Season | Club | GP | G | A | Pts. |
|---|---|---|---|---|---|
| 1981-82 | Edmonton | 3 | 0 | 0 | 0 |
| 1982-83 | Edmonton | 1 | 0 | 0 | 0 |
| | **Totals** | 4 | 0 | 0 | 0 |

**STUART, William (Red)** *Defenseman*
b. Amherst, N.S., 1899

| Season | Club | GP | G | A | Pts. |
|---|---|---|---|---|---|
| 1920-21 | Toronto | 18 | 2 | 1 | 3 |
| 1921-22 | Toronto | 24 | 3 | 6 | 9 |
| 1922-23 | Toronto | 23 | 7 | 3 | 10 |
| 1923-24 | Toronto | 24 | 4 | 3 | 7 |
| 1924-25 | Tor-Bos | 29 | 5 | 2 | 7 |
| 1925-26 | Boston | 35 | 6 | 1 | 7 |
| 1926-27 | Boston | 42 | 3 | 1 | 4 |
| | **Totals** | 195 | 30 | 17 | 47 |

**STUMPF, Robert** *Defenseman*
b. Milo, Alta., Apr. 25, 1953

| Season | Club | GP | G | A | Pts. |
|---|---|---|---|---|---|
| 1974-75 | StL-Pitt | 10 | 1 | 1 | 2 |

**STURGEON, Peter Alexander** *Forward*
b. Whitehorse, Yuk., Feb. 12, 1954

| Season | Club | GP | G | A | Pts. |
|---|---|---|---|---|---|
| 1979-80 | Colorado | 2 | 0 | 0 | 0 |
| 1980-81 | Colorado | 4 | 0 | 1 | 1 |
| | **Totals** | 6 | 0 | 1 | 1 |

**SUIKKANEN, Kai** *Defenseman*
b. Opiskelija, Finland, Sept. 29, 1960

| Season | Club | GP | G | A | Pts. |
|---|---|---|---|---|---|
| 1981-82 | Buffalo | 1 | 0 | 0 | 0 |
| 1982-83 | Buffalo | 1 | 0 | 0 | 0 |
| | **Totals** | 2 | 0 | 0 | 0 |

**SULLIMAN, Simon Douglas** *Forward*
b. Glace Bay, N.S., Aug. 29, 1959

| Season | Club | GP | G | A | Pts. |
|---|---|---|---|---|---|
| 1979-80 | New York R | 31 | 4 | 7 | 11 |
| 1980-81 | New York R | 32 | 4 | 1 | 5 |
| 1981-82 | Hartford | 77 | 29 | 40 | 69 |
| 1982-83 | Hartford | 77 | 22 | 19 | 41 |
| | **Totals** | 217 | 59 | 67 | 126 |

**SULLIVAN, Barry Carter** *Forward*
b. Preston, Ont., Sept. 21, 1926

| Season | Club | GP | G | A | Pts. |
|---|---|---|---|---|---|
| 1947-48 | Detroit | 1 | 0 | 0 | 0 |

**SULLIVAN, Bob** *Forward*
b. Noranda, Que., Nov. 29, 1957

| Season | Club | GP | G | A | Pts. |
|---|---|---|---|---|---|
| 1982-83 | Hartford | 62 | 18 | 19 | 37 |

**SULLIVAN, Frank Taylor (Sully)** *Defenseman*
b. Toronto, Ont., June 16, 1929

| Season | Club | GP | G | A | Pts. |
|---|---|---|---|---|---|
| 1949-50 | Toronto | 1 | 0 | 0 | 0 |
| 1952-53 | Toronto | 5 | 0 | 0 | 0 |
| 1954-55 | Chicago | 1 | 0 | 0 | 0 |
| 1955-56 | Chicago | 1 | 0 | 0 | 0 |
| | **Totals** | 8 | 0 | 0 | 0 |

**SULLIVAN, George James (Red)** *Forward*
b. Peterborough, Ont., Dec. 24, 1929

| Season | Club | GP | G | A | Pts. |
|---|---|---|---|---|---|
| 1949-50 | Boston | 3 | 0 | 1 | 1 |
| 1951-52 | Boston | 67 | 12 | 12 | 24 |
| 1952-53 | Boston | 32 | 3 | 8 | 11 |
| 1954-55 | Chicago | 70 | 19 | 42 | 61 |
| 1955-56 | Chicago | 63 | 14 | 26 | 40 |
| 1956-57 | New York R | 42 | 6 | 17 | 23 |
| 1957-58 | New York R | 70 | 11 | 35 | 46 |
| 1958-59 | New York R | 70 | 21 | 42 | 63 |
| 1959-60 | New York R | 70 | 12 | 25 | 37 |
| 1960-61 | New York R | 70 | 9 | 31 | 40 |
| | **Totals** | 557 | 107 | 239 | 346 |

| Season | Club | GP | G | A | Pts. |
|---|---|---|---|---|---|

**SULLIVAN, Peter Gerald** *Forward*
b. Toronto, Ont., July 25, 1951

| Season | Club | GP | G | A | Pts. |
|---|---|---|---|---|---|
| 1975-76 | Winnipeg (WHA) | 78 | 32 | 39 | 71 |
| 1976-77 | Winnipeg (WHA) | 78 | 31 | 52 | 83 |
| 1977-78 | Winnipeg (WHA) | 77 | 16 | 39 | 55 |
| 1978-79 | Winnipeg (WHA) | 80 | 46 | 40 | 86 |
| 1979-80 | Winnipeg | 79 | 24 | 35 | 59 |
| 1980-81 | Winnipeg | 47 | 4 | 19 | 23 |
| | **NHL Totals** | 126 | 28 | 54 | 82 |
| | **WHA Totals** | 313 | 125 | 170 | 295 |

**SUMMERHILL, William Arthur (Pee Wee)**
*Forward*
b. Toronto, Ont., July 9, 1915

| Season | Club | GP | G | A | Pts. |
|---|---|---|---|---|---|
| 1938-39 | Montreal | 43 | 6 | 10 | 16 |
| 1939-40 | Montreal | 13 | 3 | 2 | 5 |
| 1941-42 | Brooklyn | 16 | 5 | 5 | 10 |
| | **Totals** | 72 | 14 | 17 | 31 |

**SUNDSTROM, Patrik** *Forward*
b. Skellefteaa, Sweden, Dec. 14, 1961

| Season | Club | GP | G | A | Pts. |
|---|---|---|---|---|---|
| 1982-83 | Vancouver | 74 | 23 | 23 | 46 |

**SUOMI, Al** *Forward*

| Season | Club | GP | G | A | Pts. |
|---|---|---|---|---|---|
| 1936-37 | Chicago | 5 | 0 | 0 | 0 |

**SUTHERLAND, Ronald** *Defenseman*
b. Eston, Sask., Feb. 8, 1913

| Season | Club | GP | G | A | Pts. |
|---|---|---|---|---|---|
| 1931-32 | Boston | 2 | 0 | 0 | 0 |

**SUTHERLAND, William Fraser (Bill)** *Forward*
b. Regina, Sask., Nov. 10, 1934

| Season | Club | GP | G | A | Pts. |
|---|---|---|---|---|---|
| 1967-68 | Philadelphia | 60 | 20 | 9 | 29 |
| 1968-69 | Tor-Phil | 56 | 14 | 8 | 22 |
| 1969-70 | Philadelphia | 51 | 15 | 17 | 32 |
| 1970-71 | Phil-StL | 69 | 19 | 20 | 39 |
| 1971-72 | StL-Det | 14 | 2 | 4 | 6 |
| 1972-73 | Winnipeg (WHA) | 49 | 6 | 16 | 22 |
| | **NHL Totals** | 250 | 70 | 58 | 128 |
| | **WHA Totals** | 49 | 6 | 16 | 22 |

**SUTTER, Brent Bolin** *Forward*
b. Viking, Alta., June 10, 1962

| Season | Club | GP | G | A | Pts. |
|---|---|---|---|---|---|
| 1980-81 | New York I | 3 | 2 | 2 | 4 |
| 1981-82 | New York I | 43 | 21 | 22 | 43 |
| 1982-83 | New York I | 80 | 21 | 19 | 40 |
| | **Totals** | 126 | 44 | 43 | 87 |

**SUTTER, Brian Louis Allen** *Forward*
b. Viking, Alta., Oct. 7, 1956

| Season | Club | GP | G | A | Pts. |
|---|---|---|---|---|---|
| 1976-77 | St Louis | 35 | 4 | 10 | 14 |
| 1977-78 | St Louis | 78 | 9 | 13 | 22 |
| 1978-79 | St Louis | 77 | 41 | 39 | 80 |
| 1979-80 | St Louis | 71 | 23 | 35 | 58 |
| 1980-81 | St Louis | 78 | 35 | 34 | 69 |
| 1981-82 | St Louis | 74 | 39 | 36 | 75 |
| 1982-83 | St Louis | 79 | 46 | 30 | 76 |
| | **Totals** | 492 | 197 | 197 | 394 |

**SUTTER, Darryl John** *Forward*
b. Viking, Alta., Aug. 19, 1958

| Season | Club | GP | G | A | Pts. |
|---|---|---|---|---|---|
| 1979-80 | Chicago | 8 | 2 | 0 | 2 |
| 1980-81 | Chicago | 76 | 40 | 22 | 62 |
| 1981-82 | Chicago | 40 | 23 | 12 | 35 |
| 1982-83 | Chicago | 80 | 31 | 30 | 61 |
| | **Totals** | 204 | 96 | 64 | 160 |

**SUTTER, Duane Calvin** *Forward*
b. Viking, Alta., Mar. 16, 1960

| Season | Club | GP | G | A | Pts. |
|---|---|---|---|---|---|
| 1979-80 | New York I | 56 | 15 | 9 | 24 |
| 1980-81 | New York I | 23 | 7 | 11 | 18 |
| 1981-82 | New York I | 77 | 18 | 35 | 53 |
| 1982-83 | New York I | 75 | 13 | 19 | 32 |
| | **Totals** | 231 | 53 | 74 | 127 |

**SUTTER, Rich** *Forward*
b. Viking, Alta., Dec. 2, 1963

| Season | Club | GP | G | A | Pts. |
|---|---|---|---|---|---|
| 1982-83 | Pittsburgh | 4 | 0 | 0 | 0 |

**SUTTER, Ron** *Forward*
b. Viking, Alta., Dec. 2, 1963

| Season | Club | GP | G | A | Pts. |
|---|---|---|---|---|---|
| 1982-83 | Philadelphia | 10 | 1 | 1 | 2 |

**SUZOR, Mark Joseph** *Defenseman*
b. Windsor, Ont., Nov. 5, 1956

| Season | Club | GP | G | A | Pts. |
|---|---|---|---|---|---|
| 1976-77 | Philadelphia | 4 | 0 | 1 | 1 |
| 1977-78 | Colorado | 60 | 4 | 15 | 19 |
| | **Totals** | 64 | 4 | 16 | 20 |

**SVENSSON, Leif** *Defenseman*
b. Harnosand, Sweden, July 8, 1951

| Season | Club | GP | G | A | Pts. |
|---|---|---|---|---|---|
| 1978-79 | Washington | 74 | 2 | 29 | 31 |
| 1979-80 | Washington | 47 | 4 | 11 | 15 |
| | **Totals** | 121 | 6 | 40 | 46 |

**SWAIN, Garth Frederick Arthur (Gary)**
*Forward*
b. Welland, Ont., Sept. 11, 1947

| Season | Club | GP | G | A | Pts. |
|---|---|---|---|---|---|
| 1968-69 | Pittsburgh | 9 | 1 | 1 | 2 |
| 1974-75 | New England (WHA) | 66 | 7 | 15 | 22 |
| 1975-76 | New England (WHA) | 79 | 10 | 16 | 26 |
| 1976-77 | New England (WHA) | 26 | 5 | 2 | 7 |
| | **NHL Totals** | 9 | 1 | 1 | 2 |
| | **WHA Totals** | 171 | 22 | 33 | 55 |

**SWARBRICK, George Raymond** *Forward*
b. Moose Jaw, Sask., Feb. 16, 1942

| Season | Club | GP | G | A | Pts. |
|---|---|---|---|---|---|
| 1967-68 | Oakland | 49 | 13 | 5 | 18 |
| 1968-69 | Oak-Pitt | 69 | 4 | 19 | 23 |
| 1969-70 | Pittsburgh | 12 | 0 | 1 | 1 |
| 1970-71 | Philadelphia | 2 | 0 | 0 | 0 |
| | **Totals** | 132 | 17 | 25 | 42 |

**SWEENEY, William** *Forward*
b. Guelph, Ont., Jan. 30, 1937

| Season | Club | GP | G | A | Pts. |
|---|---|---|---|---|---|
| 1959-60 | New York R | 4 | 1 | 0 | 1 |

**SYKES, Phil** *Forward*
b. Dawson Creek, B.C., May 18, 1959

| Season | Club | GP | G | A | Pts. |
|---|---|---|---|---|---|
| 1982-83 | Los Angeles | 7 | 2 | 0 | 2 |

**SYKES, Robert John William** *Forward*
b. Sudbury, Ont., Sept. 26, 1951

| Season | Club | GP | G | A | Pts. |
|---|---|---|---|---|---|
| 1974-75 | Toronto | 2 | 0 | 0 | 0 |

**SZURA, Joseph Boleslaw** *Forward*
b. Fort William, Ont., Dec. 18, 1938

| Season | Club | GP | G | A | Pts. |
|---|---|---|---|---|---|
| 1967-68 | Oakland | 20 | 1 | 3 | 4 |
| 1968-69 | Oakland | 70 | 9 | 12 | 21 |
| 1972-73 | Los Angeles (WHA) | 73 | 13 | 32 | 45 |
| | **NHL Totals** | 90 | 10 | 15 | 25 |
| | **WHA Totals** | 73 | 13 | 32 | 45 |

**TAFT, John Philip** *Defenseman*
b. Minneapolis, Minn., Mar. 8, 1954

| Season | Club | GP | G | A | Pts. |
|---|---|---|---|---|---|
| 1978-79 | Detroit | 15 | 0 | 2 | 2 |

**TALAFOUS, Dean Charles** *Forward*
b. Duluth, Minn., Aug. 25, 1953

| Season | Club | GP | G | A | Pts. |
|---|---|---|---|---|---|
| 1974-75 | Atl-Minn | 61 | 9 | 21 | 30 |
| 1975-76 | Minnesota | 79 | 18 | 30 | 48 |
| 1976-77 | Minnesota | 80 | 22 | 27 | 49 |
| 1977-78 | Minnesota | 75 | 13 | 16 | 29 |
| 1978-79 | New York R | 68 | 13 | 16 | 29 |
| 1979-80 | New York R | 55 | 10 | 20 | 30 |
| 1980-81 | New York R | 50 | 13 | 17 | 30 |
| 1981-82 | New York R | 29 | 6 | 7 | 13 |
| | **Totals** | 497 | 104 | 154 | 258 |

**TALBOT, Jean Guy** *Defenseman*
b. Cap de la Madeleine, Que., July 11, 1932

| Season | Club | GP | G | A | Pts. |
|---|---|---|---|---|---|
| 1954-55 | Montreal | 3 | 0 | 1 | 1 |
| 1955-56 | Montreal | 66 | 1 | 13 | 14 |
| 1956-57 | Montreal | 59 | 0 | 13 | 13 |
| 1957-58 | Montreal | 55 | 4 | 15 | 19 |
| 1958-59 | Montreal | 69 | 4 | 17 | 21 |
| 1959-60 | Montreal | 69 | 1 | 14 | 15 |
| 1960-61 | Montreal | 70 | 5 | 26 | 31 |
| 1961-62 | Montreal | 70 | 5 | 42 | 47 |
| 1962-63 | Montreal | 70 | 3 | 22 | 25 |
| 1963-64 | Montreal | 66 | 1 | 13 | 14 |
| 1964-65 | Montreal | 67 | 8 | 14 | 22 |
| 1965-66 | Montreal | 59 | 1 | 14 | 15 |
| 1966-67 | Montreal | 68 | 3 | 5 | 8 |
| 1967-68 | Minn-Det-StL | 59 | 0 | 7 | 7 |
| 1968-69 | St Louis | 69 | 5 | 4 | 9 |
| 1969-70 | St Louis | 75 | 2 | 15 | 17 |
| 1970-71 | StL-Buf | 62 | 0 | 7 | 7 |
| | **Totals** | 1056 | 43 | 242 | 285 |

**TALLON, Michael Dale Lee** *Defenseman*
b. Noranda, Que., Oct. 19, 1950

| Season | Club | GP | G | A | Pts. |
|---|---|---|---|---|---|
| 1970-71 | Vancouver | 78 | 14 | 42 | 56 |
| 1971-72 | Vancouver | 69 | 17 | 27 | 44 |
| 1972-73 | Vancouver | 75 | 13 | 24 | 37 |
| 1973-74 | Chicago | 65 | 15 | 19 | 34 |
| 1974-75 | Chicago | 35 | 5 | 10 | 15 |
| 1975-76 | Chicago | 80 | 15 | 47 | 62 |
| 1976-77 | Chicago | 70 | 5 | 16 | 21 |
| 1977-78 | Chicago | 75 | 4 | 20 | 24 |
| 1978-79 | Pittsburgh | 63 | 5 | 24 | 29 |
| 1979-80 | Pittsburgh | 32 | 5 | 9 | 14 |
| | **Totals** | 642 | 98 | 238 | 336 |

**TAMBELLINI, Steven Anthony** *Forward*
b. Trail, B.C., May 14, 1958

| Season | Club | GP | G | A | Pts. |
|---|---|---|---|---|---|
| 1978-79 | New York I | 1 | 0 | 0 | 0 |
| 1979-80 | New York I | 45 | 5 | 8 | 13 |
| 1980-81 | NYI-Col | 74 | 25 | 29 | 54 |
| 1981-82 | Colorado | 79 | 29 | 30 | 59 |
| 1982-83 | New Jersey | 73 | 25 | 18 | 43 |
| | **Totals** | 272 | 84 | 85 | 169 |

**TANGUAY, Christian** *Forward*
b. Beauport, Que., Aug. 4, 1962

| Season | Club | GP | G | A | Pts. |
|---|---|---|---|---|---|
| 1981-82 | Quebec | 2 | 0 | 0 | 0 |

**TANNAHILL, Donald Andrew (Don)** *Forward*
b. Penetang, Ont., Feb. 21, 1949

| Season | Club | GP | G | A | Pts. |
|---|---|---|---|---|---|
| 1972-73 | Vancouver | 78 | 22 | 21 | 43 |
| 1973-74 | Vancouver | 33 | 8 | 12 | 20 |
| 1974-75 | Minnesota (WHA) | 72 | 23 | 30 | 53 |
| 1975-76 | Calgary (WHA) | 78 | 25 | 24 | 49 |
| 1976-77 | Calgary (WHA) | 72 | 10 | 22 | 32 |
| | **NHL Totals** | 111 | 30 | 33 | 63 |
| | **WHA Totals** | 222 | 58 | 76 | 134 |

**TANTI, Tony** *Forward*
b. Toronto, Ont., Sept. 7, 1963

| Season | Club | GP | G | A | Pts. |
|---|---|---|---|---|---|
| 1982-83 | Chi-Van | 40 | 9 | 8 | 17 |

**TARDIF, Marc** *Forward*
b. Granby, Que., June 12, 1949

| Season | Club | GP | G | A | Pts. |
|---|---|---|---|---|---|
| 1969-70 | Montreal | 18 | 3 | 2 | 5 |
| 1970-71 | Montreal | 76 | 19 | 30 | 49 |
| 1971-72 | Montreal | 75 | 31 | 22 | 53 |
| 1972-73 | Montreal | 76 | 25 | 25 | 50 |
| 1973-74 | Los Angeles (WHA) | 75 | 40 | 30 | 70 |
| 1974-75 | Mich-Que (WHA) | 76 | 50 | 39 | 89 |
| 1975-76 | Quebec (WHA) | 81 | 71 | 77 | 148 |
| 1976-77 | Quebec (WHA) | 62 | 49 | 60 | 109 |
| 1977-78 | Quebec (WHA) | 78 | 65 | 89 | 154 |
| 1978-79 | Quebec (WHA) | 74 | 41 | 55 | 96 |
| 1979-80 | Quebec | 58 | 33 | 35 | 68 |
| 1980-81 | Quebec | 63 | 23 | 31 | 54 |
| 1981-82 | Quebec | 75 | 39 | 31 | 70 |
| 1982-83 | Quebec | 76 | 21 | 31 | 52 |
| | **NHL Totals** | 317 | 194 | 207 | 401 |
| | **WHA Totals** | 446 | 316 | 350 | 666 |

| Season | Club | GP | G | A | Pts. |
|---|---|---|---|---|---|
| **TATCHELL, Spencer Harry** *Defenseman* | | | | | |
| b. Lloydminster, Sask., July 16, 1924 | | | | | |
| 1942-43 | New York R | 1 | 0 | 0 | 0 |
| | | | | | |
| **TAYLOR, David Andrew** *Forward* | | | | | |
| b. Levack, Ont., Dec. 4, 1955 | | | | | |
| 1977-78 | Los Angeles | 64 | 22 | 21 | 43 |
| 1978-79 | Los Angeles | 78 | 43 | 48 | 91 |
| 1979-80 | Los Angeles | 61 | 37 | 53 | 90 |
| 1980-81 | Los Angeles | 72 | 47 | 65 | 112 |
| 1981-82 | Los Angeles | 78 | 39 | 67 | 106 |
| 1982-83 | Los Angeles | 46 | 21 | 37 | 58 |
| | Totals | 399 | 209 | 291 | 500 |
| | | | | | |
| **TAYLOR, Edward Wray (Ted)** *Forward* | | | | | |
| b. Brandon, Man., Feb. 25, 1942 | | | | | |
| 1964-65 | New York R | 4 | 0 | 0 | 0 |
| 1965-66 | New York R | 4 | 0 | 1 | 1 |
| 1966-67 | Detroit | 2 | 0 | 0 | 0 |
| 1967-68 | Minnesota | 31 | 3 | 5 | 8 |
| 1970-71 | Vancouver | 56 | 11 | 16 | 27 |
| 1971-72 | Vancouver | 69 | 9 | 13 | 22 |
| 1972-73 | Houston (WHA) | 72 | 34 | 42 | 76 |
| 1973-74 | Houston (WHA) | 75 | 21 | 23 | 44 |
| 1974-75 | Houston (WHA) | 73 | 26 | 27 | 53 |
| 1975-76 | Houston (WHA) | 68 | 15 | 26 | 41 |
| 1976-77 | Houston (WHA) | 78 | 16 | 35 | 51 |
| 1977-78 | Houston (WHA) | 54 | 11 | 11 | 22 |
| | NHL Totals | 166 | 23 | 35 | 58 |
| | WHA Totals | 420 | 123 | 164 | 287 |
| | | | | | |
| **TAYLOR, Harry** *Defenseman* | | | | | |
| b. St. James, Man., Mar. 28, 1926 | | | | | |
| 1946-47 | Toronto | 9 | 0 | 2 | 2 |
| 1948-49 | Toronto | 42 | 4 | 7 | 11 |
| 1951-52 | Chicago | 15 | 1 | 1 | 2 |
| | Totals | 66 | 5 | 10 | 15 |
| | | | | | |
| **TAYLOR, Mark** *Forward* | | | | | |
| b. Vancouver, B.C., Jan. 26, 1958 | | | | | |
| 1981-82 | Philadelphia | 2 | 0 | 0 | 0 |
| 1982-83 | Philadelphia | 61 | 8 | 25 | 33 |
| | Totals | 63 | 8 | 25 | 33 |
| | | | | | |
| **TAYLOR, Ralph F. (Bouncer)** *Defenseman* | | | | | |
| b. Toronto, Ont., Oct. 2, 1905 | | | | | |
| 1927-38 | Chicago | 22 | 1 | 1 | 2 |
| 1928-29 | Chicago | 38 | 0 | 0 | 0 |
| 1929-30 | Chi-NYR | 40 | 3 | 0 | 3 |
| | Totals | 100 | 4 | 1 | 5 |
| | | | | | |
| **TAYLOR, Robert** *Forward* | | | | | |
| b. Newton, Mass., Aug. 12, 1904 | | | | | |
| 1929-30 | Boston | — | 0 | 0 | 0 |
| | | | | | |
| **TAYLOR, William Gordon** *Forward* | | | | | |
| b. Winnipeg, Man., Oct. 14, 1942 | | | | | |
| 1964-65 | New York R | 2 | 0 | 0 | 0 |
| | | | | | |
| **TAYLOR, William James** *Forward* | | | | | |
| b. Winnipeg, Man., May 3, 1919 | | | | | |
| 1939-40 | Toronto | 43 | 4 | 6 | 10 |
| 1940-41 | Toronto | 48 | 9 | 26 | 35 |
| 1941-42 | Toronto | 48 | 12 | 26 | 38 |
| 1942-43 | Toronto | 50 | 18 | 42 | 60 |
| 1945-46 | Toronto | 48 | 23 | 18 | 41 |
| 1946-47 | Detroit | 60 | 17 | 46 | 63 |
| 1947-48 | Bos-NYR | 41 | 4 | 16 | 20 |
| | Totals | 338 | 87 | 180 | 267 |
| | | | | | |
| **TEAL, Allen Leslie (Skip)** *Forward* | | | | | |
| b. Ridgeway, Ont., July 17, 1933 | | | | | |
| 1954-55 | Boston | 1 | 0 | 0 | 0 |
| | | | | | |
| **TEAL, Victor** *Forward* | | | | | |
| b. St. Catharines, Ont., Aug. 10, 1949 | | | | | |
| 1973-74 | New York I | 1 | 0 | 0 | 0 |
| | | | | | |
| **TERBENCHE, Paul Frederick** | | | | | |
| *Defenseman-Forward* | | | | | |
| b. Cobourg, Ont., Sept. 16, 1945 | | | | | |
| 1967-68 | Chicago | 68 | 3 | 7 | 10 |
| 1970-71 | Buffalo | 3 | 0 | 0 | 0 |
| 1971-72 | Buffalo | 9 | 0 | 0 | 0 |
| 1972-73 | Buffalo | 42 | 0 | 7 | 7 |
| 1973-74 | Buffalo | 67 | 2 | 12 | 14 |
| 1974-75 | Vancouver (WHA) | 60 | 3 | 14 | 17 |
| 1975-76 | Calgary (WHA) | 58 | 2 | 4 | 6 |
| 1976-77 | Calgary (WHA) | 80 | 9 | 24 | 33 |
| 1977-78 | Birmingham (WHA) | 11 | 1 | 0 | 1 |
| 1978-79 | Winnipeg (WHA) | 68 | 3 | 22 | 25 |
| | NHL Totals | 189 | 5 | 26 | 31 |
| | WHA Totals | 277 | 18 | 64 | 82 |
| | | | | | |
| **TERRION, Greg Patrick** *Forward* | | | | | |
| b. Peterborough, Ont., May 2, 1960 | | | | | |
| 1980-81 | Los Angeles | 73 | 12 | 25 | 37 |
| 1981-82 | Los Angeles | 61 | 15 | 22 | 37 |
| 1982-83 | Toronto | 74 | 16 | 16 | 32 |
| | Totals | 208 | 43 | 63 | 106 |
| | | | | | |
| **TESSIER, Orval Ray** *Forward* | | | | | |
| b. Cornwall, Ont., June 30, 1933 | | | | | |
| 1954-55 | Montreal | 4 | 0 | 0 | 0 |
| 1955-56 | Boston | 23 | 2 | 3 | 5 |
| 1960-61 | Boston | 32 | 3 | 4 | 7 |
| | Totals | 59 | 5 | 7 | 12 |
| | | | | | |
| **THEBERGE, Greg Ray** *Defenseman* | | | | | |
| b. Peterborough, Ont., Sept. 3, 1959 | | | | | |
| 1979-80 | Washington | 12 | 0 | 1 | 1 |
| 1980-81 | Washington | 1 | 1 | 0 | 1 |
| 1981-82 | Washington | 57 | 5 | 32 | 37 |
| 1982-83 | Washington | 70 | 8 | 28 | 36 |
| | Totals | 140 | 14 | 61 | 75 |
| | | | | | |
| **THERRIEN, Gaston** *Defenseman* | | | | | |
| b. Montreal, Que., May 27, 1960 | | | | | |
| 1980-81 | Quebec | 3 | 0 | 1 | 1 |
| 1981-82 | Quebec | 14 | 0 | 7 | 7 |
| 1982-83 | Quebec | 5 | 0 | 0 | 0 |
| | Totals | 22 | 0 | 8 | 8 |
| | | | | | |
| **THIBEAULT, Lawrence Lorrain (Larry)** | | | | | |
| *Forward* | | | | | |
| b. Charletone, Ont., Oct. 2, 1918 | | | | | |
| 1944-45 | Detroit | 4 | 0 | 2 | 2 |
| 1945-46 | Montreal | 1 | 0 | 0 | 0 |
| | Totals | 5 | 0 | 2 | 2 |
| | | | | | |
| **THOMAS, Cyril James (Cy)** *Forward* | | | | | |
| b. Dowlais, Wales, Aug. 5, 1926 | | | | | |
| 1947-48 | Chi-Tor | 14 | 2 | 2 | 4 |
| | | | | | |
| **THOMAS, Reginald Kenneth** *Forward* | | | | | |
| b. Lambeth, Ont., Apr. 21, 1953 | | | | | |
| 1973-74 | Los Angeles (WHA) | 72 | 14 | 21 | 35 |
| 1974-75 | Baltimore (WHA) | 50 | 8 | 13 | 21 |
| 1975-76 | Indianapolis (WHA) | 80 | 23 | 17 | 40 |
| 1976-77 | Indianapolis (WHA) | 79 | 25 | 30 | 55 |
| 1977-78 | Ind-Cin (WHA) | 67 | 19 | 18 | 37 |
| 1978-79 | Cincinnati (WHA) | 80 | 32 | 39 | 71 |
| 1979-80 | Quebec | 39 | 9 | 7 | 16 |
| | NHL Totals | 39 | 9 | 7 | 16 |
| | WHA Totals | 428 | 121 | 138 | 259 |
| | | | | | |
| **THOMPSON, Clifford** *Defenseman* | | | | | |
| b. Winchester, Mass., Dec. 9, 1918 | | | | | |
| 1941-42 | Boston | 6 | 0 | 0 | 0 |
| 1948-49 | Boston | 10 | 0 | 1 | 1 |
| | Totals | 16 | 0 | 1 | 1 |
| | | | | | |
| **THOMPSON, Kenneth** | | | | | |
| 1917-18 | Montreal W | 1 | 0 | 0 | 0 |
| | | | | | |
| **THOMPSON, Loran Errol** *Forward* | | | | | |
| b. Summerside, P.E.I., May 28, 1950 | | | | | |
| 1970-71 | Toronto | 1 | 0 | 0 | 0 |
| 1972-73 | Toronto | 68 | 13 | 19 | 32 |
| 1973-74 | Toronto | 56 | 7 | 8 | 15 |
| 1974-75 | Toronto | 65 | 25 | 17 | 42 |
| 1975-76 | Toronto | 75 | 43 | 37 | 80 |
| 1976-77 | Toronto | 41 | 21 | 16 | 37 |
| 1977-78 | Tor-Det | 73 | 22 | 23 | 45 |
| 1978-79 | Detroit | 70 | 23 | 31 | 54 |
| 1979-80 | Detroit | 77 | 34 | 14 | 48 |
| 1980-81 | Det-Pitt | 73 | 20 | 20 | 40 |
| | Totals | 599 | 208 | 185 | 393 |
| | | | | | |
| **THOMPSON, Paul Ivan** *Forward* | | | | | |
| b. Calgary, Alta., Nov. 2, 1906 | | | | | |
| 1926-27 | New York R | 43 | 7 | 3 | 10 |
| 1927-28 | New York R | 41 | 4 | 4 | 8 |
| 1928-29 | New York R | 44 | 10 | 7 | 17 |
| 1929-30 | New York R | 44 | 7 | 12 | 19 |
| 1930-31 | New York R | 44 | 7 | 7 | 14 |
| 1931-32 | Chicago | 48 | 8 | 14 | 22 |
| 1932-33 | Chicago | 48 | 13 | 20 | 33 |
| 1933-34 | Chicago | 48 | 20 | 16 | 36 |
| 1934-35 | Chicago | 48 | 16 | 23 | 39 |
| 1935-36 | Chicago | 45 | 17 | 23 | 40 |
| 1936-37 | Chicago | 47 | 17 | 18 | 35 |
| 1937-38 | Chicago | 48 | 22 | 22 | 44 |
| 1938-39 | Chicago | 33 | 5 | 10 | 15 |
| | Totals | 581 | 153 | 179 | 332 |
| | | | | | |
| **THOMS, William D.** *Forward* | | | | | |
| b. Newmarket, Ont., Mar. 5, 1910 | | | | | |
| 1932-33 | Toronto | 29 | 3 | 9 | 12 |
| 1933-34 | Toronto | 47 | 8 | 18 | 26 |
| 1934-35 | Toronto | 47 | 9 | 13 | 22 |
| 1935-36 | Toronto | 48 | 23 | 15 | 38 |
| 1936-37 | Toronto | 48 | 10 | 9 | 19 |
| 1937-38 | Toronto | 48 | 14 | 24 | 38 |
| 1938-39 | Tor-Chi | 48 | 7 | 15 | 22 |
| 1939-40 | Chicago | 47 | 9 | 13 | 22 |
| 1940-41 | Chicago | 47 | 13 | 19 | 32 |
| 1941-42 | Chicago | 47 | 15 | 30 | 45 |
| 1942-43 | Chicago | 47 | 15 | 28 | 43 |
| 1943-44 | Chicago | 7 | 3 | 5 | 8 |
| 1944-45 | Chi-Bos | 38 | 6 | 8 | 14 |
| | Totals | 548 | 135 | 206 | 341 |
| | | | | | |
| **THOMSON, Floyd Harvey** *Forward* | | | | | |
| b. Sudbury, Ont., June 14, 1949 | | | | | |
| 1971-72 | St Louis | 49 | 4 | 6 | 10 |
| 1972-73 | St Louis | 75 | 14 | 20 | 34 |
| 1973-74 | St Louis | 77 | 11 | 22 | 33 |
| 1974-75 | St Louis | 77 | 9 | 27 | 36 |
| 1975-76 | St Louis | 58 | 8 | 10 | 18 |
| 1976-77 | St Louis | 58 | 7 | 8 | 15 |
| 1977-78 | St Louis | 6 | 1 | 1 | 2 |
| 1979-80 | St Louis | 11 | 2 | 3 | 5 |
| | Totals | 411 | 56 | 97 | 153 |
| | | | | | |
| **THOMSON, James Richard** *Defenseman* | | | | | |
| b. Winnipeg, Man., Feb. 23, 1927 | | | | | |
| 1945-46 | Toronto | 5 | 0 | 1 | 1 |
| 1946-47 | Toronto | 60 | 2 | 14 | 16 |
| 1947-48 | Toronto | 59 | 0 | 29 | 29 |
| 1948-49 | Toronto | 60 | 4 | 16 | 20 |
| 1949-50 | Toronto | 70 | 0 | 13 | 13 |
| 1950-51 | Toronto | 69 | 3 | 33 | 36 |
| 1951-52 | Toronto | 70 | 0 | 25 | 25 |
| 1952-53 | Toronto | 69 | 0 | 22 | 22 |
| 1953-54 | Toronto | 61 | 2 | 24 | 26 |
| 1954-55 | Toronto | 70 | 4 | 12 | 16 |
| 1955-56 | Toronto | 62 | 0 | 7 | 7 |
| 1956-57 | Toronto | 62 | 0 | 12 | 12 |
| 1957-58 | Chicago | 70 | 4 | 7 | 11 |
| | Totals | 787 | 19 | 215 | 234 |
| | | | | | |
| **THOMSON, John F.** *Defenseman* | | | | | |
| b. Bixbridge, England, Jan. 31, 1918 | | | | | |
| 1939-40 | New York A | 12 | 1 | 1 | 2 |
| 1940-41 | New York A | 3 | 0 | 0 | 0 |
| | Totals | 15 | 1 | 1 | 2 |

| Season | Club | GP | G | A | Pts. |
|---|---|---|---|---|---|
| **THOMPSON, Rhys G.** *Defenseman* b. Toronto, Ont., Aug. 9, 1918 | | | | | |
| 1939-40 | Montreal | 7 | 0 | 0 | 0 |
| 1942-43 | Toronto | 18 | 0 | 2 | 2 |
| | **Totals** | 25 | 0 | 2 | 2 |
| **THOMSON, William Ferguson** *Forward* b. Ayrshire, Scotland, Mar. 23, 1914 | | | | | |
| 1938-39 | Detroit | 3 | 0 | 0 | 0 |
| 1943-44 | Chi-Det | 6 | 2 | 2 | 4 |
| | **Totals** | 9 | 2 | 2 | 4 |
| **THORSTEINSON, Joseph** *Forward* b. Winnipeg, Man. | | | | | |
| 1932-33 | New York A | 4 | 0 | 0 | 0 |
| **THURIER, Alfred Michael (Fred)** *Forward* b. Granby, Que., Jan. 11, 1918 | | | | | |
| 1940-41 | New York A | 3 | 2 | 1 | 3 |
| 1941-42 | Brooklyn | 27 | 7 | 7 | 14 |
| 1944-45 | New York R | 50 | 16 | 19 | 35 |
| | **Totals** | 80 | 25 | 27 | 52 |
| **THURLBY, Thomas Newman** *Defenseman* b. Kingston, Ont., Nov. 9, 1938 | | | | | |
| 1967-68 | Oakland | 20 | 1 | 1 | 2 |
| **TIMGREN, Raymond Charles** *Forward* b. Windsor, Ont., Sept. 29, 1928 | | | | | |
| 1948-49 | Toronto | 36 | 3 | 12 | 15 |
| 1949-50 | Toronto | 68 | 7 | 18 | 25 |
| 1950-51 | Toronto | 70 | 1 | 9 | 10 |
| 1951-52 | Toronto | 50 | 2 | 4 | 6 |
| 1952-53 | Toronto | 12 | 0 | 0 | 0 |
| 1954-55 | Tor-Chi | 15 | 1 | 1 | 2 |
| | **Totals** | 251 | 14 | 44 | 58 |
| **TITANIC, Morris S.** *Forward* b. Toronto, Ont., Jan. 7, 1953 | | | | | |
| 1974-75 | Buffalo | 17 | 0 | 0 | 0 |
| 1975-76 | Buffalo | 2 | 0 | 0 | 0 |
| | **Totals** | 19 | 0 | 0 | 0 |
| **TKACZUK, Walter Robert** *Forward* b. Emstedetten, Germany, Sept. 29, 1947 | | | | | |
| 1967-68 | New York R | 2 | 0 | 0 | 0 |
| 1968-69 | New York R | 71 | 12 | 24 | 36 |
| 1969-70 | New York R | 76 | 27 | 50 | 77 |
| 1970-71 | New York R | 77 | 26 | 49 | 75 |
| 1971-72 | New York R | 76 | 24 | 42 | 66 |
| 1972-73 | New York R | 76 | 27 | 39 | 66 |
| 1973-74 | New York R | 71 | 21 | 42 | 63 |
| 1974-75 | New York R | 62 | 11 | 25 | 36 |
| 1975-76 | New York R | 78 | 8 | 28 | 36 |
| 1976-77 | New York R | 80 | 12 | 38 | 50 |
| 1977-78 | New York R | 80 | 26 | 40 | 66 |
| 1978-79 | New York R | 77 | 15 | 27 | 42 |
| 1979-80 | New York R | 76 | 12 | 25 | 37 |
| 1980-81 | New York R | 43 | 6 | 22 | 28 |
| | **Totals** | 945 | 227 | 451 | 678 |
| **TOAL, Michael James** *Forward* b. Red Deer, Alta., Mar. 23, 1959 | | | | | |
| 1979-80 | Edmonton | 3 | 0 | 0 | 0 |
| **TONELLI, John** *Forward* b. Hamilton, Ont., Mar. 23, 1957 | | | | | |
| 1975-76 | Houston (WHA) | 79 | 17 | 14 | 31 |
| 1976-77 | Houston (WHA) | 80 | 24 | 31 | 55 |
| 1977-78 | Houston (WHA) | 65 | 23 | 41 | 64 |
| 1978-79 | New York I | 73 | 17 | 39 | 56 |
| 1979-80 | New York I | 77 | 14 | 30 | 44 |
| 1980-81 | New York I | 70 | 20 | 32 | 52 |
| 1981-82 | New York I | 80 | 35 | 58 | 93 |
| 1982-83 | New York I | 76 | 31 | 40 | 71 |
| | **NHL Totals** | 376 | 117 | 199 | 316 |
| | **WHA Totals** | 224 | 64 | 86 | 150 |

| Season | Club | GP | G | A | Pts. |
|---|---|---|---|---|---|
| **TOOKEY, Timothy Raymond** *Forward* b. Edmonton, Alta., Aug. 29, 1960 | | | | | |
| 1980-81 | Washington | 20 | 10 | 13 | 23 |
| 1981-82 | Washington | 28 | 8 | 8 | 16 |
| 1982-83 | Quebec | 12 | 1 | 6 | 7 |
| | **Totals** | 160 | 19 | 27 | 46 |
| **TOPPAZZINI, Gerald (Topper)** *Forward* b. Copper Cliff, Ont., July 29, 1931 | | | | | |
| 1952-53 | Boston | 69 | 10 | 13 | 23 |
| 1953-54 | Bos-Chi | 51 | 5 | 8 | 13 |
| 1954-55 | Chicago | 70 | 9 | 18 | 27 |
| 1955-56 | Det-Bos | 68 | 8 | 14 | 22 |
| 1956-57 | Boston | 55 | 15 | 23 | 38 |
| 1957-58 | Boston | 64 | 25 | 24 | 49 |
| 1958-59 | Boston | 70 | 21 | 23 | 44 |
| 1959-60 | Boston | 69 | 12 | 33 | 45 |
| 1960-61 | Boston | 67 | 15 | 35 | 50 |
| 1961-62 | Boston | 70 | 19 | 31 | 50 |
| 1962-63 | Boston | 65 | 17 | 18 | 35 |
| 1963-64 | Boston | 65 | 7 | 4 | 11 |
| | **Totals** | 783 | 163 | 244 | 407 |
| **TOPPAZZINI, Zellio Peter** *Forward* b. Copper Cliff, Ont., Jan. 5, 1930 | | | | | |
| 1948-49 | Boston | 5 | 1 | 1 | 2 |
| 1949-50 | Boston | 36 | 5 | 5 | 10 |
| 1950-51 | Bos-NYR | 59 | 14 | 14 | 28 |
| 1951-52 | New York R | 16 | 1 | 1 | 2 |
| 1956-57 | Chicago | 7 | 0 | 0 | 0 |
| | **Totals** | 123 | 21 | 21 | 42 |
| **TOUHEY, William** *Forward* b. Ottawa, Ont., Mar. 23, 1906 | | | | | |
| 1927-28 | Montreal M | 26 | 2 | 0 | 2 |
| 1928-29 | Ottawa | 44 | 9 | 3 | 12 |
| 1929-30 | Ottawa | 44 | 10 | 3 | 13 |
| 1930-31 | Ottawa | 44 | 15 | 15 | 30 |
| 1931-32 | Boston | 28 | 5 | 4 | 9 |
| 1932-33 | Ottawa | 48 | 12 | 7 | 19 |
| 1933-34 | Ottawa | 48 | 12 | 8 | 20 |
| | **Totals** | 282 | 65 | 40 | 105 |
| **TOUPIN, Jacques (Jack)** *Forward* b. Trois-Rivières, Que. | | | | | |
| 1943-44 | Chicago | 8 | 1 | 2 | 3 |
| **TOWNSEND, Arthur** | | | | | |
| 1926-27 | Chicago | 1 | 0 | 0 | 0 |
| **TRADER, Larry** *Defenseman* b. Barry's Bay, Ont., July 7, 1963 | | | | | |
| 1982-83 | Detroit | 15 | 0 | 2 | 2 |
| **TRAINOR, Thomas Weston (Wes)** *Forward* b. Charlottetown, P.E.I., Sept. 11, 1922 | | | | | |
| 1948-49 | New York R | 17 | 1 | 2 | 3 |
| **TRAPP, Albert Robert (Bob)** *Defenseman* b. 1898 | | | | | |
| 1926-27 | Chicago | 44 | 4 | 2 | 6 |
| 1927-28 | Chicago | 34 | 0 | 2 | 2 |
| | **Totals** | 78 | 4 | 4 | 8 |
| **TRAUB, Percy (Puss)** *Defenseman* | | | | | |
| 1926-27 | Chicago | 37 | 0 | 2 | 2 |
| 1927-28 | Detroit | 44 | 3 | 1 | 4 |
| 1928-29 | Detroit | 43 | 0 | 0 | 0 |
| | **Totals** | 124 | 3 | 3 | 6 |
| **TREMBLAY, Brent Francis** *Defenseman* b. North Bay, Ont., Nov. 1, 1957 | | | | | |
| 1978-79 | Washington | 1 | 0 | 0 | 0 |
| 1979-80 | Washington | 9 | 1 | 0 | 1 |
| | **Totals** | 10 | 1 | 0 | 1 |

| Season | Club | GP | G | A | Pts. |
|---|---|---|---|---|---|
| **TREMBLAY, Gilles** *Forward* b. Montmorency, Que., Dec. 18, 1938 | | | | | |
| 1960-61 | Montreal | 45 | 7 | 11 | 18 |
| 1961-62 | Montreal | 70 | 32 | 22 | 54 |
| 1962-63 | Montreal | 60 | 25 | 24 | 49 |
| 1963-64 | Montreal | 61 | 22 | 15 | 37 |
| 1964-65 | Montreal | 26 | 9 | 7 | 16 |
| 1965-66 | Montreal | 70 | 27 | 21 | 48 |
| 1966-67 | Montreal | 62 | 13 | 19 | 32 |
| 1967-68 | Montreal | 71 | 23 | 28 | 51 |
| 1968-69 | Montreal | 44 | 10 | 15 | 25 |
| | **Totals** | 509 | 168 | 162 | 330 |
| **TREMBLAY, Jean-Claude (J.C.)** *Defenseman* b. Bagotville, Que., Jan. 22, 1939 | | | | | |
| 1959-60 | Montreal | 11 | 0 | 1 | 1 |
| 1960-61 | Montreal | 29 | 1 | 3 | 4 |
| 1961-62 | Montreal | 70 | 3 | 17 | 20 |
| 1962-63 | Montreal | 69 | 1 | 17 | 18 |
| 1963-64 | Montreal | 70 | 5 | 16 | 21 |
| 1964-65 | Montreal | 68 | 3 | 17 | 20 |
| 1965-66 | Montreal | 59 | 6 | 29 | 35 |
| 1966-67 | Montreal | 60 | 8 | 26 | 34 |
| 1967-68 | Montreal | 73 | 4 | 26 | 30 |
| 1968-69 | Montreal | 75 | 7 | 32 | 39 |
| 1969-70 | Montreal | 58 | 2 | 19 | 21 |
| 1970-71 | Montreal | 76 | 11 | 52 | 63 |
| 1971-72 | Montreal | 76 | 6 | 51 | 57 |
| 1972-73 | Quebec (WHA) | 75 | 14 | 75 | 89 |
| 1973-74 | Quebec (WHA) | 68 | 9 | 44 | 53 |
| 1974-75 | Quebec (WHA) | 68 | 16 | 56 | 72 |
| 1975-76 | Quebec (WHA) | 80 | 12 | 77 | 89 |
| 1976-77 | Quebec (WHA) | 53 | 4 | 31 | 35 |
| 1977-78 | Quebec (WHA) | 54 | 5 | 37 | 42 |
| 1978-79 | Quebec (WHA) | 56 | 6 | 38 | 44 |
| | **NHL Totals** | 794 | 57 | 306 | 363 |
| | **WHA Totals** | 454 | 66 | 358 | 424 |
| **TREMBLAY, Marcel** *Forward* b. Winnipeg, Man., July 4, 1915 | | | | | |
| 1938-39 | Montreal | 10 | 0 | 2 | 2 |
| **TREMBLAY, Mario** *Forward* b. Alma, Que., Sept. 2, 1956 | | | | | |
| 1974-75 | Montreal | 63 | 21 | 18 | 39 |
| 1975-76 | Montreal | 71 | 11 | 16 | 27 |
| 1976-77 | Montreal | 74 | 18 | 28 | 46 |
| 1977-78 | Montreal | 56 | 10 | 14 | 24 |
| 1978-79 | Montreal | 76 | 30 | 29 | 59 |
| 1979-80 | Montreal | 77 | 16 | 26 | 42 |
| 1980-81 | Montreal | 77 | 25 | 38 | 63 |
| 1981-82 | Montreal | 80 | 33 | 40 | 73 |
| 1982-83 | Montreal | 80 | 30 | 37 | 67 |
| | **Totals** | 654 | 194 | 246 | 440 |
| **TREMBLAY, Nils** *Forward* b. Quebec City, Que., July 26, 1923 | | | | | |
| 1944-45 | Montreal | 1 | 0 | 1 | 1 |
| 1945-46 | Montreal | 2 | 0 | 0 | 0 |
| | **Totals** | 3 | 0 | 1 | 1 |
| **TRIMPER, Timothy Edward** *Forward* b. Windsor, Ont., Sept. 28, 1959 | | | | | |
| 1979-80 | Chicago | 30 | 6 | 10 | 16 |
| 1980-81 | Winnipeg | 56 | 15 | 14 | 29 |
| 1981-82 | Winnipeg | 74 | 8 | 8 | 16 |
| 1982-83 | Winnipeg | 5 | 0 | 0 | 0 |
| | **Totals** | 165 | 29 | 32 | 61 |
| **TROTTIER, Bryan John** *Forward* b. Val Marie, Sask., July 17, 1956 | | | | | |
| 1975-76 | New York I | 80 | 32 | 63 | 95 |
| 1976-77 | New York I | 76 | 30 | 42 | 72 |
| 1977-78 | New York I | 77 | 46 | 77 | 123 |
| 1978-79 | New York I | 76 | 47 | 87 | 134 |
| 1979-80 | New York I | 78 | 42 | 62 | 104 |
| 1980-81 | New York I | 73 | 31 | 72 | 103 |

| Season | Club | GP | G | A | Pts. |
|---|---|---|---|---|---|
| 1981-82 | New York I | 80 | 50 | 79 | 129 |
| 1982-83 | New York I | 80 | 34 | 55 | 89 |
| **Totals** | | 620 | 312 | 537 | 849 |

**TROTTIER, David T.** *Forward*
b. Pembroke, Ont., June 25, 1906

| Season | Club | GP | G | A | Pts. |
|---|---|---|---|---|---|
| 1928-29 | Montreal M | 36 | 2 | 4 | 6 |
| 1929-30 | Montreal M | 42 | 17 | 10 | 27 |
| 1930-31 | Montreal M | 41 | 9 | 8 | 17 |
| 1931-32 | Montreal M | 48 | 26 | 18 | 44 |
| 1932-33 | Montreal M | 48 | 16 | 15 | 31 |
| 1933-34 | Montreal M | 48 | 9 | 17 | 26 |
| 1934-35 | Montreal M | 34 | 10 | 9 | 19 |
| 1935-36 | Montreal M | 44 | 10 | 10 | 20 |
| 1936-37 | Montreal M | 42 | 12 | 11 | 23 |
| 1937-38 | Montreal M | 46 | 9 | 10 | 19 |
| 1938-39 | Detroit | 12 | 1 | 1 | 2 |
| **Totals** | | 441 | 121 | 113 | 234 |

**TROTTIER, Guy** *Forward*
b. Hull, Que., Apr. 1, 1941

| Season | Club | GP | G | A | Pts. |
|---|---|---|---|---|---|
| 1968-69 | New York R | 2 | 0 | 0 | 0 |
| 1970-71 | Toronto | 61 | 19 | 5 | 24 |
| 1971-72 | Toronto | 52 | 9 | 12 | 21 |
| 1972-73 | Ottawa (WHA) | 72 | 26 | 32 | 58 |
| 1973-74 | Toronto (WHA) | 71 | 27 | 35 | 62 |
| 1974-75 | Tor-Mich (WHA) | 23 | 7 | 6 | 13 |
| **NHL Totals** | | 115 | 28 | 17 | 45 |
| **WHA Totals** | | 166 | 60 | 73 | 133 |

**TRUDEL, Louis Napoleon** *Forward*
b. Salem, Mass., July 21, 1913

| Season | Club | GP | G | A | Pts. |
|---|---|---|---|---|---|
| 1933-34 | Chicago | 34 | 1 | 3 | 4 |
| 1934-35 | Chicago | 47 | 11 | 11 | 22 |
| 1935-36 | Chicago | 46 | 3 | 4 | 7 |
| 1936-37 | Chicago | 42 | 6 | 12 | 18 |
| 1937-38 | Chicago | 42 | 6 | 16 | 22 |
| 1938-39 | Montreal | 31 | 8 | 13 | 21 |
| 1939-40 | Montreal | 47 | 12 | 7 | 19 |
| 1940-41 | Montreal | 16 | 2 | 3 | 5 |
| **Totals** | | 305 | 49 | 69 | 118 |

**TRUDELL, Rene Joseph** *Forward*
b. Mariapolis, Man., Jan. 31, 1919

| Season | Club | GP | G | A | Pts. |
|---|---|---|---|---|---|
| 1945-46 | New York R | 16 | 3 | 5 | 8 |
| 1946-47 | New York R | 59 | 8 | 16 | 24 |
| 1947-48 | New York R | 54 | 13 | 7 | 20 |
| **Totals** | | 129 | 24 | 28 | 52 |

**TUDOR, Robert Alan** *Forward*
b. Cupur, Sask., June 30, 1956

| Season | Club | GP | G | A | Pts. |
|---|---|---|---|---|---|
| 1978-79 | Vancouver | 24 | 4 | 4 | 8 |
| 1979-80 | Vancouver | 2 | 0 | 0 | 0 |
| 1982-83 | St Louis | 2 | 0 | 0 | 0 |
| **Totals** | | 28 | 4 | 4 | 8 |

**TURLIK, Gordon** *Forward*
b. Mickel, B.C., Sept. 17, 1939

| Season | Club | GP | G | A | Pts. |
|---|---|---|---|---|---|
| 1959-60 | Boston | 2 | 0 | 0 | 0 |

**TURNBULL, Ian Wayne** *Defenseman*
b. Montreal, Que., Dec. 22, 1953

| Season | Club | GP | G | A | Pts. |
|---|---|---|---|---|---|
| 1973-74 | Toronto | 78 | 8 | 27 | 35 |
| 1974-75 | Toronto | 22 | 6 | 7 | 13 |
| 1975-76 | Toronto | 76 | 20 | 36 | 56 |
| 1976-77 | Toronto | 80 | 22 | 57 | 79 |
| 1977-78 | Toronto | 77 | 14 | 47 | 61 |
| 1978-79 | Toronto | 80 | 12 | 15 | 27 |
| 1979-80 | Toronto | 75 | 11 | 28 | 39 |
| 1980-81 | Toronto | 80 | 19 | 47 | 66 |
| 1981-82 | Tor-LA | 54 | 11 | 17 | 28 |
| 1982-83 | Pittsburgh | 6 | 0 | 0 | 0 |
| **Totals** | | 628 | 123 | 281 | 404 |

**TURNBULL, Perry John** *Forward*
b. Rimbey, Alta., Mar. 9, 1959

| Season | Club | GP | G | A | Pts. |
|---|---|---|---|---|---|
| 1979-80 | St Louis | 80 | 16 | 19 | 35 |
| 1980-81 | St Louis | 75 | 34 | 22 | 56 |
| 1981-82 | St Louis | 79 | 33 | 26 | 59 |
| 1982-83 | St Louis | 79 | 32 | 15 | 47 |
| **Totals** | | 313 | 115 | 82 | 197 |

**TURNBULL, Randy Layne** *Defenseman*
b. Bentley, Alta., Feb. 7, 1962

| Season | Club | GP | G | A | Pts. |
|---|---|---|---|---|---|
| 1981-82 | Calgary | 2 | 0 | 0 | 0 |
| **Totals** | | 2 | 0 | 0 | 0 |

**TURNER, Dean Cameron** *Defenseman*
b. Dearborn, Mich., June 22, 1958

| Season | Club | GP | G | A | Pts. |
|---|---|---|---|---|---|
| 1978-79 | New York R | 1 | 0 | 0 | 0 |
| 1979-80 | Colorado | 27 | 1 | 0 | 1 |
| 1980-81 | Colorado | 4 | 0 | 0 | 0 |
| 1982-83 | Los Angeles | 3 | 0 | 0 | 0 |
| **Totals** | | 35 | 1 | 0 | 1 |

**TURNER, Robert George** *Defenseman*
b. Regina, Sask., Jan. 31, 1943

| Season | Club | GP | G | A | Pts. |
|---|---|---|---|---|---|
| 1955-56 | Montreal | 33 | 1 | 4 | 5 |
| 1956-57 | Montreal | 58 | 1 | 4 | 5 |
| 1957-58 | Montreal | 68 | 0 | 3 | 3 |
| 1958-59 | Montreal | 68 | 4 | 24 | 28 |
| 1959-60 | Montreal | 54 | 0 | 9 | 9 |
| 1960-61 | Montreal | 60 | 2 | 2 | 4 |
| 1961-62 | Chicago | 69 | 8 | 2 | 10 |
| 1962-63 | Chicago | 70 | 3 | 3 | 6 |
| **Totals** | | 478 | 19 | 51 | 70 |

**TUSTIN, Norman Robert** *Forward*
b. Regina, Sask., Jan. 3, 1919

| Season | Club | GP | G | A | Pts. |
|---|---|---|---|---|---|
| 1941-42 | New York R | 18 | 2 | 4 | 6 |

**TUTEN, Audley K.** *Defenseman*
b. Enterprise, Alta., Jan. 14, 1915

| Season | Club | GP | G | A | Pts. |
|---|---|---|---|---|---|
| 1941-42 | Chicago | 5 | 1 | 1 | 2 |
| 1942-43 | Chicago | 34 | 3 | 7 | 10 |
| **Totals** | | 39 | 4 | 8 | 12 |

**TYDEY, Alex** *Forward*
b. Vancouver, B.C., Jan. 5, 1955

| Season | Club | GP | G | A | Pts. |
|---|---|---|---|---|---|
| 1975-76 | San Diego (WHA) | 74 | 16 | 11 | 27 |
| 1976-77 | Buffalo | 3 | 0 | 0 | 0 |
| 1977-78 | Buffalo | 1 | 0 | 0 | 0 |
| 1979-80 | Buffalo | 5 | 0 | 0 | 0 |
| **NHL Totals** | | 9 | 0 | 0 | 0 |
| **WHA Totals** | | 74 | 16 | 11 | 27 |

**UBRIACO, Eugene Stephen** *Forward*
b. Sault Ste. Marie, Ont., Dec. 26, 1937

| Season | Club | GP | G | A | Pts. |
|---|---|---|---|---|---|
| 1967-68 | Pittsburgh | 65 | 18 | 15 | 33 |
| 1968-69 | Pitt-Oak | 75 | 19 | 18 | 37 |
| 1969-70 | Oak-Chi | 37 | 2 | 2 | 4 |
| **Totals** | | 177 | 39 | 35 | 74 |

**ULLMAN, Norman Victor Alexander** *Forward*
b. Provost, Alta., Dec. 26, 1935

| Season | Club | GP | G | A | Pts. |
|---|---|---|---|---|---|
| 1955-56 | Detroit | 66 | 9 | 9 | 18 |
| 1956-57 | Detroit | 64 | 16 | 36 | 52 |
| 1957-58 | Detroit | 69 | 23 | 28 | 51 |
| 1958-59 | Detroit | 69 | 22 | 36 | 58 |
| 1959-60 | Detroit | 70 | 24 | 34 | 58 |
| 1960-61 | Detroit | 70 | 28 | 42 | 70 |
| 1961-62 | Detroit | 70 | 26 | 38 | 64 |
| 1962-63 | Detroit | 70 | 26 | 30 | 56 |
| 1963-64 | Detroit | 61 | 21 | 30 | 51 |
| 1964-65 | Detroit | 70 | 42 | 41 | 83 |
| 1965-66 | Detroit | 70 | 31 | 41 | 72 |
| 1966-67 | Detroit | 68 | 26 | 44 | 70 |
| 1967-68 | Det-Tor | 71 | 35 | 37 | 72 |
| 1968-69 | Toronto | 75 | 35 | 42 | 77 |
| 1969-70 | Toronto | 74 | 18 | 42 | 60 |
| 1970-71 | Toronto | 73 | 34 | 51 | 85 |
| 1971-72 | Toronto | 77 | 23 | 50 | 73 |
| 1972-73 | Toronto | 65 | 20 | 35 | 55 |
| 1973-74 | Toronto | 78 | 22 | 47 | 69 |
| 1974-75 | Toronto | 80 | 9 | 26 | 35 |
| 1975-76 | Edmonton (WHA) | 77 | 31 | 56 | 87 |
| 1976-77 | Edmonton (WHA) | 67 | 16 | 27 | 43 |
| **NHL Totals** | | 1410 | 490 | 739 | 1229 |
| **WHA Totals** | | 144 | 47 | 83 | 130 |

**UNGER, Garry Douglas** *Forward*
b. Edmonton, Alta., Dec. 7, 1947

| Season | Club | GP | G | A | Pts. |
|---|---|---|---|---|---|
| 1967-68 | Tor-Det | 28 | 6 | 11 | 17 |
| 1968-69 | Detroit | 76 | 24 | 20 | 44 |
| 1969-70 | Detroit | 76 | 42 | 24 | 66 |
| 1970-71 | Det-StL | 79 | 28 | 28 | 56 |
| 1971-72 | St Louis | 78 | 36 | 34 | 70 |
| 1972-73 | St Louis | 78 | 41 | 39 | 80 |
| 1973-74 | St Louis | 78 | 33 | 35 | 68 |
| 1974-75 | St Louis | 80 | 36 | 44 | 80 |
| 1975-76 | St Louis | 80 | 39 | 44 | 83 |
| 1976-77 | St Louis | 80 | 30 | 27 | 57 |
| 1977-78 | St Louis | 80 | 32 | 20 | 52 |
| 1978-79 | St Louis | 80 | 30 | 26 | 56 |
| 1979-80 | Atlanta | 79 | 17 | 16 | 33 |
| 1980-81 | LA-Edm | 71 | 10 | 10 | 20 |
| 1981-82 | Edmonton | 46 | 7 | 13 | 20 |
| 1982-83 | Edmonton | 16 | 2 | 0 | 2 |
| **Totals** | | 1105 | 413 | 391 | 804 |

**VADNAIS, Carol Marcel** *Defenseman-Forward*
b. Montreal, Que., Sept. 25, 1945

| Season | Club | GP | G | A | Pts. |
|---|---|---|---|---|---|
| 1966-67 | Montreal | 11 | 0 | 3 | 3 |
| 1967-68 | Montreal | 31 | 1 | 1 | 2 |
| 1968-69 | Oakland | 76 | 15 | 27 | 42 |
| 1969-70 | Oakland | 76 | 24 | 20 | 44 |
| 1970-71 | California | 42 | 10 | 16 | 26 |
| 1971-72 | Cal-Bos | 68 | 18 | 26 | 44 |
| 1972-73 | Boston | 78 | 7 | 24 | 31 |
| 1973-74 | Boston | 78 | 16 | 43 | 59 |
| 1974-75 | Boston | 79 | 18 | 56 | 74 |
| 1975-76 | Bos-NYR | 76 | 22 | 35 | 57 |
| 1976-77 | New York R | 74 | 11 | 37 | 48 |
| 1977-78 | New York R | 80 | 6 | 40 | 46 |
| 1978-79 | New York R | 77 | 8 | 37 | 45 |
| 1979-80 | New York R | 66 | 3 | 20 | 23 |
| 1980-81 | New York R | 74 | 3 | 20 | 23 |
| 1981-82 | New York R | 50 | 5 | 6 | 11 |
| 1982-83 | New Jersey | 51 | 2 | 7 | 9 |
| **Totals** | | 1087 | 169 | 418 | 587 |

**VAIL, Eric Douglas** *Forward*
b. Timmins, Ont., Sept. 16, 1953

| Season | Club | GP | G | A | Pts. |
|---|---|---|---|---|---|
| 1973-74 | Atlanta | 23 | 2 | 9 | 11 |
| 1974-75 | Atlanta | 72 | 39 | 21 | 60 |
| 1975-76 | Atlanta | 60 | 16 | 31 | 47 |
| 1976-77 | Atlanta | 78 | 32 | 39 | 71 |
| 1977-78 | Atlanta | 79 | 22 | 36 | 58 |
| 1978-79 | Atlanta | 80 | 35 | 48 | 83 |
| 1979-80 | Atlanta | 77 | 28 | 25 | 53 |
| 1980-81 | Calgary | 64 | 28 | 36 | 64 |
| 1981-82 | Calg-Det | 58 | 14 | 15 | 29 |
| **Totals** | | 591 | 216 | 260 | 476 |

**VAIL, Melville (Sparky)** *Defenseman*
b. Meaford, Ont., July 5, 1906

| Season | Club | GP | G | A | Pts. |
|---|---|---|---|---|---|
| 1928-29 | New York R | 18 | 3 | 0 | 3 |
| 1929-30 | New York R | 32 | 1 | 1 | 2 |
| **Totals** | | 50 | 4 | 1 | 5 |

**VAIVE, Rick Claude** *Forward*
b. Ottawa, Ont., May 14, 1959

| Season | Club | GP | G | A | Pts. |
|---|---|---|---|---|---|
| 1978-79 | Birmingham (WHA) | 75 | 26 | 33 | 59 |
| 1979-80 | Van-Tor | 69 | 22 | 15 | 37 |
| 1980-81 | Toronto | 75 | 33 | 29 | 62 |
| 1981-82 | Toronto | 77 | 54 | 35 | 89 |
| 1982-83 | Toronto | 78 | 51 | 28 | 79 |
| **NHL Totals** | | 299 | 160 | 107 | 267 |
| **WHA Totals** | | 75 | 26 | 33 | 59 |

**VALENTINE, Christopher William** *Forward*
b. Belleville, Ont., Dec. 6, 1961

| Season | Club | GP | G | A | Pts. |
|---|---|---|---|---|---|
| 1981-82 | Washington | 60 | 30 | 37 | 67 |
| 1982-83 | Washington | 23 | 7 | 10 | 17 |
| **Totals** | | 83 | 37 | 47 | 84 |

| Season | Club | GP | G | A | Pts. |
|---|---|---|---|---|---|

**VALIQUETTE, John Joseph (Jack)** *Forward*
b. St. Thomas, Ont., Mar. 18, 1956

| Season | Club | GP | G | A | Pts. |
|---|---|---|---|---|---|
| 1974-75 | Toronto | 1 | 0 | 0 | 0 |
| 1975-76 | Toronto | 45 | 10 | 23 | 33 |
| 1976-77 | Toronto | 66 | 15 | 30 | 45 |
| 1977-78 | Toronto | 60 | 8 | 13 | 21 |
| 1978-79 | Colorado | 76 | 23 | 34 | 57 |
| 1979-80 | Colorado | 77 | 25 | 25 | 50 |
| 1980-81 | Colorado | 25 | 3 | 9 | 12 |
| | **Totals** | **350** | **84** | **134** | **218** |

**VAN BOXMEER, John Martin** *Defenseman*
b. Petrolia, Ont., Nov. 20, 1952

| Season | Club | GP | G | A | Pts. |
|---|---|---|---|---|---|
| 1973-74 | Montreal | 20 | 1 | 4 | 5 |
| 1974-75 | Montreal | 9 | 0 | 2 | 2 |
| 1975-76 | Montreal | 46 | 6 | 11 | 17 |
| 1976-77 | Mont-Col | 45 | 2 | 12 | 14 |
| 1977-78 | Colorado | 80 | 12 | 42 | 54 |
| 1978-79 | Colorado | 76 | 9 | 34 | 43 |
| 1979-80 | Buffalo | 80 | 11 | 40 | 51 |
| 1980-81 | Buffalo | 80 | 18 | 51 | 69 |
| 1981-82 | Buffalo | 69 | 14 | 54 | 68 |
| 1982-83 | Buffalo | 65 | 6 | 21 | 27 |
| | **Totals** | **570** | **79** | **271** | **350** |

**VAN IMPE, Edward Charles** *Defenseman*
b. Saskatoon, Sask., May 27, 1940

| Season | Club | GP | G | A | Pts. |
|---|---|---|---|---|---|
| 1966-67 | Chicago | 61 | 8 | 11 | 19 |
| 1967-68 | Philadelphia | 67 | 4 | 13 | 17 |
| 1968-69 | Philadelphia | 68 | 7 | 12 | 19 |
| 1969-70 | Philadelphia | 65 | 0 | 10 | 10 |
| 1970-71 | Philadelphia | 77 | 0 | 11 | 11 |
| 1971-72 | Philadelphia | 73 | 4 | 9 | 13 |
| 1972-73 | Philadelphia | 72 | 1 | 11 | 12 |
| 1973-74 | Philadelphia | 77 | 2 | 16 | 18 |
| 1974-75 | Philadelphia | 78 | 1 | 17 | 18 |
| 1975-76 | Phil-Pitt | 52 | 0 | 13 | 13 |
| 1976-77 | Pittsburgh | 10 | 0 | 3 | 3 |
| | **Totals** | **700** | **27** | **126** | **153** |

**VASKO, Elmer (Moose)** *Defenseman*
b. Duparquet, Que., Dec. 11, 1935

| Season | Club | GP | G | A | Pts. |
|---|---|---|---|---|---|
| 1956-57 | Chicago | 64 | 3 | 12 | 15 |
| 1957-58 | Chicago | 59 | 6 | 20 | 26 |
| 1958-59 | Chicago | 63 | 6 | 10 | 16 |
| 1959-60 | Chicago | 69 | 3 | 27 | 30 |
| 1960-61 | Chicago | 63 | 4 | 18 | 22 |
| 1961-62 | Chicago | 61 | 2 | 22 | 24 |
| 1962-63 | Chicago | 64 | 4 | 9 | 13 |
| 1963-64 | Chicago | 70 | 2 | 18 | 20 |
| 1964-65 | Chicago | 69 | 1 | 10 | 11 |
| 1965-66 | Chicago | 56 | 1 | 7 | 8 |
| 1967-68 | Minnesota | 70 | 1 | 6 | 7 |
| 1968-69 | Minnesota | 72 | 1 | 7 | 8 |
| 1969-70 | Minnesota | 3 | 0 | 0 | 0 |
| | **Totals** | **783** | **34** | **166** | **200** |

**VASKO, Richard John** *Defenseman*
b. St. Catharines, Ont., Jan. 12, 1957

| Season | Club | GP | G | A | Pts. |
|---|---|---|---|---|---|
| 1977-78 | Detroit | 3 | 0 | 0 | 0 |
| 1979-80 | Detroit | 8 | 0 | 0 | 0 |
| 1980-81 | Detroit | 20 | 3 | 7 | 10 |
| | **Totals** | **31** | **3** | **7** | **10** |

**VAUTOUR, Yvon** *Forward*
b. St. John, B.C., Sept. 10, 1956

| Season | Club | GP | G | A | Pts. |
|---|---|---|---|---|---|
| 1979-80 | New York I | 17 | 3 | 1 | 4 |
| 1980-81 | Colorado | 74 | 15 | 19 | 34 |
| 1981-82 | Colorado | 14 | 1 | 2 | 3 |
| 1982-83 | New Jersey | 52 | 4 | 7 | 11 |
| | **Totals** | **157** | **23** | **29** | **52** |

**VAYDIK, Gregory** *Forward*
b. Yellowknife, N.W.T., Oct. 9, 1955

| Season | Club | GP | G | A | Pts. |
|---|---|---|---|---|---|
| 1976-77 | Chicago | 5 | 0 | 0 | 0 |

**VEITCH, Darren William** *Defenseman*
b. Saskatoon, Sask., Apr. 24, 1960

| Season | Club | GP | G | A | Pts. |
|---|---|---|---|---|---|
| 1980-81 | Washington | 59 | 4 | 21 | 25 |
| 1981-82 | Washington | 67 | 9 | 44 | 53 |
| 1982-83 | Washington | 10 | 0 | 8 | 8 |
| | **Totals** | **136** | **13** | **73** | **86** |

**VELISCHEK, Randy** *Defenseman*
b. Montreal, Que., Feb. 10, 1962

| Season | Club | GP | G | A | Pts. |
|---|---|---|---|---|---|
| 1982-83 | Minnesota | 3 | 0 | 0 | 0 |

**VENASKY, Victor William (Vic)** *Forward*
b. Thunder Bay, Ont., June 3, 1951

| Season | Club | GP | G | A | Pts. |
|---|---|---|---|---|---|
| 1972-73 | Los Angeles | 77 | 15 | 19 | 34 |
| 1973-74 | Los Angeles | 32 | 6 | 5 | 11 |
| 1974-75 | Los Angeles | 17 | 1 | 2 | 3 |
| 1975-76 | Los Angeles | 80 | 18 | 26 | 44 |
| 1976-77 | Los Angeles | 80 | 14 | 26 | 40 |
| 1977-78 | Los Angeles | 71 | 3 | 10 | 13 |
| 1978-79 | Los Angeles | 73 | 4 | 13 | 17 |
| | **Totals** | **430** | **61** | **101** | **162** |

**VENERUZZO, Gary Raymond** *Forward*
b. Fort William, Ont., June 28, 1943

| Season | Club | GP | G | A | Pts. |
|---|---|---|---|---|---|
| 1967-68 | St Louis | 5 | 1 | 1 | 2 |
| 1971-72 | St Louis | 2 | 0 | 0 | 0 |
| 1972-73 | Los Angeles (WHA) | 78 | 43 | 30 | 73 |
| 1973-74 | Los Angeles (WHA) | 78 | 39 | 29 | 68 |
| 1974-75 | Baltimore (WHA) | 77 | 33 | 27 | 60 |
| 1975-76 | Cin-Phoe (WHA) | 75 | 22 | 26 | 48 |
| 1976-77 | San Diego (WHA) | 40 | 14 | 11 | 25 |
| | **NHL Totals** | **7** | **1** | **1** | **2** |
| | **WHA Totals** | **348** | **151** | **123** | **274** |

**VERBEEK, Pat** *Forward*
b. Sarnia, Ont., May 24, 1964

| Season | Club | GP | G | A | Pts. |
|---|---|---|---|---|---|
| 1982-83 | New Jersey | 6 | 3 | 2 | 5 |

**VERVERGAERT, Dennis Andrew** *Forward*
b. Hamilton, Ont., Mar. 30, 1953

| Season | Club | GP | G | A | Pts. |
|---|---|---|---|---|---|
| 1973-74 | Vancouver | 78 | 26 | 31 | 57 |
| 1974-75 | Vancouver | 57 | 19 | 32 | 51 |
| 1975-76 | Vancouver | 80 | 37 | 34 | 71 |
| 1976-77 | Vancouver | 79 | 27 | 18 | 45 |
| 1977-78 | Vancouver | 80 | 21 | 33 | 54 |
| 1978-79 | Van-Phil | 72 | 18 | 24 | 42 |
| 1979-80 | Philadelphia | 58 | 14 | 17 | 31 |
| 1980-81 | Washington | 79 | 14 | 27 | 41 |
| | **Totals** | **583** | **176** | **216** | **392** |

**VEYSEY, Sid** *Forward*
b. Sherbrooke, Que., July 3, 1955

| Season | Club | GP | G | A | Pts. |
|---|---|---|---|---|---|
| 1977-78 | Vancouver | 1 | 0 | 0 | 0 |

**VICKERS, Stephen James (Steve)** *Forward*
b. Toronto, Ont., Apr. 21, 1951

| Season | Club | GP | G | A | Pts. |
|---|---|---|---|---|---|
| 1972-73 | New York R | 61 | 30 | 23 | 53 |
| 1973-74 | New York R | 75 | 34 | 24 | 58 |
| 1974-75 | New York R | 80 | 41 | 48 | 89 |
| 1975-76 | New York R | 80 | 30 | 53 | 83 |
| 1976-77 | New York R | 75 | 22 | 31 | 53 |
| 1977-78 | New York R | 79 | 19 | 44 | 63 |
| 1978-79 | New York R | 66 | 13 | 34 | 47 |
| 1979-80 | New York R | 75 | 29 | 33 | 62 |
| 1980-81 | New York R | 73 | 19 | 39 | 58 |
| 1981-82 | New York R | 34 | 9 | 11 | 20 |
| | **Totals** | **698** | **246** | **340** | **586** |

**VIGNEAULT, Alain** *Defenseman*
b. Quebec City, Que., May 14, 1961

| Season | Club | GP | G | A | Pts. |
|---|---|---|---|---|---|
| 1981-82 | St Louis | 14 | 1 | 2 | 3 |
| 1982-83 | St Louis | 28 | 1 | 3 | 4 |
| | **Totals** | **42** | **2** | **5** | **7** |

**VIPOND, Peter** *Forward*
b. Oshawa, Ont., Dec. 18, 1949

| Season | Club | GP | G | A | Pts. |
|---|---|---|---|---|---|
| 1972-73 | California | 2 | 0 | 0 | 0 |

**VIRTA, Hannu** *Defenseman*
b. Turku, Finland, Mar. 22, 1963

| Season | Club | GP | G | A | Pts. |
|---|---|---|---|---|---|
| 1981-82 | Buffalo | 3 | 0 | 1 | 1 |
| 1982-83 | Buffalo | 74 | 13 | 24 | 37 |
| | **Totals** | **77** | **13** | **25** | **38** |

**VOLCAN, Michael Stephen** *Defenseman*
b. Edmonton, Alta., Mar. 3, 1962

| Season | Club | GP | G | A | Pts. |
|---|---|---|---|---|---|
| 1980-81 | Hartford | 40 | 2 | 11 | 13 |
| 1981-82 | Hartford | 26 | 1 | 5 | 6 |
| 1982-83 | Hartford | 68 | 4 | 13 | 17 |
| | **Totals** | **134** | **7** | **29** | **36** |

**VOLMAR, Douglas Steven (Doug)** *Forward*
b. Cleveland, Ohio, Jan. 9, 1945

| Season | Club | GP | G | A | Pts. |
|---|---|---|---|---|---|
| 1970-71 | Detroit | 2 | 0 | 1 | 1 |
| 1971-72 | Detroit | 39 | 9 | 5 | 14 |
| 1972-73 | Los Angeles | 21 | 4 | 2 | 6 |
| 1974-75 | San Diego (WHA) | 10 | 0 | 1 | 1 |
| | **NHL Totals** | **62** | **13** | **8** | **21** |
| | **WHA Totals** | **10** | **0** | **1** | **1** |

**VOSS, Carl Potter** *Forward*
b. Chelsea, Mass., Jan. 6, 1907

| Season | Club | GP | G | A | Pts. |
|---|---|---|---|---|---|
| 1926-27 | Toronto | 9 | 0 | 0 | 0 |
| 1928-29 | Toronto | 2 | 0 | 0 | 0 |
| 1932-33 | NYR-Det | 48 | 8 | 15 | 23 |
| 1933-34 | Det-Ott | 47 | 7 | 18 | 25 |
| 1934-35 | St Louis E | 48 | 13 | 18 | 31 |
| 1935-36 | New York A | 45 | 3 | 9 | 12 |
| 1936-37 | Montreal M | 21 | 0 | 2 | 2 |
| 1937-38 | Chicago | 37 | 3 | 8 | 11 |
| | **Totals** | **257** | **34** | **70** | **104** |

**WADDELL, Donald** *Defenseman*
b. Detroit, Mich., Aug. 19, 1958

| Season | Club | GP | G | A | Pts. |
|---|---|---|---|---|---|
| 1980-81 | Los Angeles | 1 | 0 | 0 | 0 |

**WAITE, Frank E. (Deacon)** *Forward*
b. Qu'Appelle, Sask., Apr. 9, 1906

| Season | Club | GP | G | A | Pts. |
|---|---|---|---|---|---|
| 1930-31 | New York R | 17 | 1 | 3 | 4 |

**WALKER, Howard** *Defenseman*
b. Grande Prairie, Alta., Aug. 5, 1958

| Season | Club | GP | G | A | Pts. |
|---|---|---|---|---|---|
| 1980-81 | Washington | 64 | 2 | 11 | 13 |
| 1981-82 | Washington | 16 | 0 | 2 | 2 |
| 1982-83 | Calgary | 3 | 0 | 0 | 0 |
| | **Totals** | **83** | **2** | **13** | **15** |

**WALKER, John Phillip (Jack)** *Forward*
b. Silver Mountain, Ont., Nov. 28, 1888

| Season | Club | GP | G | A | Pts. |
|---|---|---|---|---|---|
| 1926-27 | Detroit | 39 | 3 | 4 | 7 |
| 1927-28 | Detroit | 39 | 2 | 4 | 6 |
| | **Totals** | **78** | **5** | **8** | **13** |

**WALKER, Kurt** *Defenseman*
b. Weymouth, Mass., June 10, 1954

| Season | Club | GP | G | A | Pts. |
|---|---|---|---|---|---|
| 1975-76 | Toronto | 5 | 0 | 0 | 0 |
| 1976-77 | Toronto | 26 | 2 | 3 | 5 |
| 1977-78 | Toronto | 40 | 2 | 2 | 4 |
| | **Totals** | **71** | **4** | **5** | **9** |

**WALL, Robert James Albert (Bob)**
*Defenseman-Forward*
b. Richmond Hill, Ont., Dec. 1, 1942

| Season | Club | GP | G | A | Pts. |
|---|---|---|---|---|---|
| 1964-65 | Detroit | 1 | 0 | 0 | 0 |
| 1965-66 | Detroit | 8 | 1 | 1 | 2 |
| 1966-67 | Detroit | 31 | 2 | 2 | 4 |
| 1967-68 | Los Angeles | 71 | 5 | 18 | 23 |
| 1968-69 | Los Angeles | 71 | 13 | 13 | 26 |
| 1969-70 | Los Angeles | 70 | 5 | 13 | 18 |
| 1970-71 | St Louis | 25 | 2 | 4 | 6 |
| 1971-72 | Detroit | 45 | 2 | 4 | 6 |
| 1972-73 | Alberta (WHA) | 78 | 16 | 29 | 45 |
| 1973-74 | Edmonton (WHA) | 74 | 6 | 31 | 37 |
| 1974-75 | San Diego (WHA) | 33 | 0 | 9 | 9 |
| 1975-76 | San Diego (WHA) | 68 | 1 | 20 | 21 |
| | **NHL Totals** | **322** | **30** | **55** | **85** |
| | **WHA Totals** | **253** | **23** | **89** | **112** |

**WALKER, Russell** *Forward*
b. Red Deer, Alta., May 24, 1953

| Season | Club | GP | G | A | Pts. |
|---|---|---|---|---|---|
| 1973-74 | Cleveland (WHA) | 76 | 15 | 14 | 29 |
| 1974-75 | Cleveland (WHA) | 66 | 14 | 11 | 25 |

| Season | Club | GP | G | A | Pts. |
|---|---|---|---|---|---|
| 1975-76 | Cleveland (WHA) | 72 | 23 | 15 | 38 |
| 1976-77 | Los Angeles | 16 | 1 | 0 | 1 |
| 1977-78 | Los Angeles | 1 | 0 | 0 | 0 |
| | **NHL Totals** | 17 | 1 | 0 | 1 |
| | **WHA Totals** | 214 | 52 | 40 | 92 |

**WALLIN, Peter**  *Forward*
b. Stockholm, Sweden, Apr. 30, 1957

| Season | Club | GP | G | A | Pts. |
|---|---|---|---|---|---|
| 1980-81 | New York R | 12 | 1 | 5 | 6 |
| 1981-82 | New York R | 40 | 2 | 9 | 11 |
| | **Totals** | 52 | 3 | 14 | 17 |

**WALSH, James**  *Defenseman*
b. Norfolk, Va., Oct. 26, 1956

| Season | Club | GP | G | A | Pts. |
|---|---|---|---|---|---|
| 1981-82 | Buffalo | 4 | 0 | 1 | 1 |

**WALTER, Ryan William**  *Forward*
b. New Westminster, B.C., Apr. 23, 1958

| Season | Club | GP | G | A | Pts. |
|---|---|---|---|---|---|
| 1978-79 | Washington | 69 | 28 | 28 | 56 |
| 1979-80 | Washington | 80 | 24 | 42 | 66 |
| 1980-81 | Washington | 80 | 24 | 44 | 68 |
| 1981-82 | Washington | 78 | 38 | 49 | 87 |
| 1982-83 | Montreal | 80 | 29 | 46 | 75 |
| | **Totals** | 387 | 143 | 209 | 352 |

**WALTON, Michael Robert**  *Forward*
b. Kirkland Lake, Ont., Jan. 3, 1945

| Season | Club | GP | G | A | Pts. |
|---|---|---|---|---|---|
| 1965-66 | Toronto | 6 | 1 | 3 | 4 |
| 1966-67 | Toronto | 31 | 7 | 10 | 17 |
| 1967-68 | Toronto | 73 | 30 | 29 | 59 |
| 1968-69 | Toronto | 66 | 22 | 21 | 43 |
| 1969-70 | Toronto | 58 | 21 | 34 | 55 |
| 1970-71 | Tor-Bos | 45 | 6 | 15 | 21 |
| 1971-72 | Boston | 76 | 28 | 28 | 56 |
| 1972-73 | Boston | 56 | 25 | 22 | 47 |
| 1973-74 | Minnesota (WHA) | 78 | 57 | 60 | 117 |
| 1974-75 | Minnesota (WHA) | 75 | 48 | 45 | 93 |
| 1975-76 | Minnesota (WHA) | 58 | 31 | 40 | 71 |
| 1975-76 | Vancouver | 10 | 8 | 8 | 16 |
| 1976-77 | Vancouver | 40 | 7 | 24 | 31 |
| 1977-78 | Vancouver | 65 | 29 | 37 | 66 |
| 1978-79 | StL-Bos-Chi | 62 | 17 | 16 | 33 |
| | **NHL Totals** | 588 | 201 | 247 | 448 |
| | **WHA Totals** | 211 | 136 | 145 | 281 |

**WALTON, Robert Charles**  *Forward*
b. Ottawa, Ont., Aug. 5, 1917

| Season | Club | GP | G | A | Pts. |
|---|---|---|---|---|---|
| 1943-44 | Montreal | 4 | 0 | 0 | 0 |

**WAPPEL, Gordon Alexander**  *Defenseman*
b. Regina, Sask., July 26, 1958

| Season | Club | GP | G | A | Pts. |
|---|---|---|---|---|---|
| 1979-80 | Atlanta | 2 | 0 | 0 | 0 |
| 1980-81 | Calgary | 7 | 0 | 1 | 1 |
| 1981-82 | Calgary | 11 | 1 | 0 | 1 |
| | **Totals** | 20 | 1 | 1 | 2 |

**WARD, Donald Joseph**  *Defenseman*
b. Sarnia, Ont., Oct. 19, 1935

| Season | Club | GP | G | A | Pts. |
|---|---|---|---|---|---|
| 1957-58 | Chicago | 3 | 0 | 0 | 0 |
| 1959-60 | Boston | 31 | 0 | 1 | 1 |
| | **Totals** | 34 | 0 | 1 | 1 |

**WARD, James W.**  *Forward*
b. Fort William, Ont., Sept. 1, 1906

| Season | Club | GP | G | A | Pts. |
|---|---|---|---|---|---|
| 1927-28 | Montreal M | 42 | 10 | 2 | 12 |
| 1928-29 | Montreal M | 43 | 14 | 8 | 22 |
| 1929-30 | Montreal M | 44 | 10 | 7 | 17 |
| 1930-31 | Montreal M | 41 | 14 | 8 | 22 |
| 1931-32 | Montreal M | 48 | 19 | 19 | 38 |
| 1932-33 | Montreal M | 48 | 16 | 17 | 33 |
| 1933-34 | Montreal M | 48 | 14 | 9 | 23 |
| 1934-35 | Montreal M | 41 | 9 | 6 | 15 |
| 1935-36 | Montreal M | 48 | 12 | 19 | 31 |
| 1936-37 | Montreal M | 40 | 14 | 14 | 28 |
| 1937-38 | Montreal M | 48 | 11 | 15 | 26 |
| 1938-39 | Montreal | 36 | 4 | 3 | 7 |
| | **Totals** | 527 | 147 | 127 | 274 |

| Season | Club | GP | G | A | Pts. |
|---|---|---|---|---|---|

**WARD, Joseph Michael**  *Forward*
b. Sarnia, Ont., Feb. 11, 1961

| Season | Club | GP | G | A | Pts. |
|---|---|---|---|---|---|
| 1980-81 | Colorado | 4 | 0 | 0 | 0 |

**WARD, Ronald Leon**  *Forward*
b. Cornwall, Ont., Sept. 12, 1944

| Season | Club | GP | G | A | Pts. |
|---|---|---|---|---|---|
| 1969-70 | Toronto | 18 | 0 | 1 | 1 |
| 1971-72 | Vancouver | 71 | 2 | 4 | 6 |
| 1972-73 | New York (WHA) | 77 | 51 | 67 | 118 |
| 1973-74 | Van-LA-Clev (WHA) | 70 | 33 | 28 | 61 |
| 1974-75 | Cleveland (WHA) | 73 | 30 | 32 | 62 |
| 1975-76 | Cleveland (WHA) | 75 | 32 | 50 | 82 |
| 1976-77 | Min-Win-Calg (WHA) | 64 | 24 | 33 | 57 |
| | **NHL Totals** | 89 | 2 | 5 | 7 |
| | **WHA Totals** | 359 | 170 | 210 | 380 |

**WARES, Edward**  *Forward*
b. Calgary, Alta., Mar. 19, 1915

| Season | Club | GP | G | A | Pts. |
|---|---|---|---|---|---|
| 1936-37 | New York R | 2 | 2 | 0 | 2 |
| 1937-38 | Detroit | 21 | 9 | 7 | 16 |
| 1938-39 | Detroit | 30 | 8 | 8 | 16 |
| 1939-40 | Detroit | 33 | 2 | 6 | 8 |
| 1940-41 | Detroit | 42 | 10 | 16 | 26 |
| 1941-42 | Detroit | 43 | 9 | 29 | 38 |
| 1942-43 | Detroit | 47 | 12 | 18 | 30 |
| 1945-46 | Chicago | 45 | 4 | 11 | 15 |
| 1946-47 | Chicago | 60 | 4 | 7 | 11 |
| | **Totals** | 321 | 60 | 102 | 162 |

**WARNER, James Francis**  *Forward*
b. Minneapolis, Minn., Mar. 26, 1954

| Season | Club | GP | G | A | Pts. |
|---|---|---|---|---|---|
| 1979-80 | Hartford | 32 | 0 | 3 | 3 |

**WARNER, Robert Norman**  *Defenseman*
b. Grimsby, Ont., Dec. 13, 1950

| Season | Club | GP | G | A | Pts. |
|---|---|---|---|---|---|
| 1976-77 | Toronto | 10 | 1 | 1 | 2 |

**WARWICK, Grant David (Knobby)**  *Forward*
b. Regina, Sask., Oct. 11, 1921

| Season | Club | GP | G | A | Pts. |
|---|---|---|---|---|---|
| 1941-42 | New York R | 44 | 16 | 17 | 33 |
| 1942-43 | New York R | 50 | 17 | 18 | 35 |
| 1943-44 | New York R | 18 | 8 | 9 | 17 |
| 1944-45 | New York R | 42 | 20 | 22 | 42 |
| 1945-46 | New York R | 45 | 19 | 18 | 37 |
| 1946-47 | New York R | 54 | 20 | 20 | 40 |
| 1947-48 | NYR-Bos | 58 | 23 | 17 | 40 |
| 1948-49 | Boston | 58 | 22 | 15 | 37 |
| 1949-50 | Montreal | 30 | 2 | 6 | 8 |
| | **Totals** | 399 | 147 | 142 | 289 |

**WARWICK, William Harvey**  *Forward*
b. Regina, Sask., Nov. 17, 1924

| Season | Club | GP | G | A | Pts. |
|---|---|---|---|---|---|
| 1942-43 | New York R | 1 | 0 | 1 | 1 |
| 1943-44 | New York R | 13 | 3 | 2 | 5 |
| | **Totals** | 14 | 3 | 3 | 6 |

**WASNIE, Nicholas**  *Forward*
b. Winnipeg, Man., Jan 1, 1904

| Season | Club | GP | G | A | Pts. |
|---|---|---|---|---|---|
| 1927-28 | Chicago | 15 | 1 | 0 | 1 |
| 1929-30 | Montreal | 44 | 12 | 11 | 23 |
| 1930-31 | Montreal | 44 | 9 | 2 | 11 |
| 1931-32 | Montreal | 48 | 10 | 2 | 13 |
| 1932-33 | New York A | 46 | 11 | 12 | 23 |
| 1933-34 | Ottawa | 35 | 11 | 6 | 17 |
| 1934-35 | St Louis E | 12 | 3 | 1 | 4 |
| | **Totals** | 244 | 57 | 34 | 91 |

**WATSON, Bryan Joseph**  *Defenseman*
b. Bancroft, Ont., Nov. 14, 1942

| Season | Club | GP | G | A | Pts. |
|---|---|---|---|---|---|
| 1963-64 | Montreal | 39 | 0 | 2 | 2 |
| 1964-65 | Montreal | 5 | 0 | 1 | 1 |
| 1965-66 | Detroit | 70 | 2 | 7 | 9 |
| 1966-67 | Detroit | 48 | 0 | 1 | 1 |
| 1967-68 | Montreal | 12 | 0 | 1 | 1 |
| 1968-69 | Oak-Pitt | 68 | 2 | 7 | 9 |
| 1969-70 | Pittsburgh | 61 | 1 | 9 | 10 |
| 1970-71 | Pittsburgh | 43 | 2 | 6 | 8 |
| 1971-72 | Pittsburgh | 75 | 3 | 17 | 20 |

| Season | Club | GP | G | A | Pts. |
|---|---|---|---|---|---|
| 1972-73 | Pittsburgh | 69 | 1 | 17 | 18 |
| 1973-74 | Pitt-StL-Det | 70 | 1 | 9 | 10 |
| 1974-75 | Detroit | 70 | 1 | 13 | 14 |
| 1975-76 | Detroit | 79 | 0 | 18 | 18 |
| 1976-77 | Det-Wash | 70 | 1 | 15 | 16 |
| 1977-78 | Washington | 79 | 3 | 11 | 14 |
| 1978-79 | Washington | 20 | 0 | 1 | 1 |
| 1978-79 | Cincinnati (WHA) | 21 | 0 | 2 | 2 |
| | **NHL Totals** | 878 | 17 | 135 | 152 |
| | **WHA Totals** | 21 | 0 | 2 | 2 |

**WATSON, David**  *Forward*
b. Kirkland, Ont., May 19, 1958

| Season | Club | GP | G | A | Pts. |
|---|---|---|---|---|---|
| 1979-80 | Colorado | 5 | 0 | 0 | 0 |
| 1980-81 | Colorado | 13 | 0 | 1 | 1 |
| | **Totals** | 18 | 0 | 1 | 1 |

**WATSON, Harry Percival**  *Forward*
b. Saskatoon, Sask., May 6, 1923

| Season | Club | GP | G | A | Pts. |
|---|---|---|---|---|---|
| 1941-42 | Brooklyn | 47 | 10 | 8 | 18 |
| 1942-43 | Detroit | 50 | 13 | 18 | 31 |
| 1945-46 | Detroit | 44 | 14 | 10 | 24 |
| 1946-47 | Toronto | 44 | 19 | 15 | 34 |
| 1947-48 | Toronto | 57 | 21 | 20 | 41 |
| 1948-49 | Toronto | 60 | 26 | 19 | 45 |
| 1949-50 | Toronto | 60 | 19 | 16 | 35 |
| 1950-51 | Toronto | 68 | 18 | 19 | 37 |
| 1951-52 | Toronto | 70 | 22 | 17 | 39 |
| 1952-53 | Toronto | 63 | 16 | 8 | 24 |
| 1953-54 | Toronto | 70 | 21 | 7 | 28 |
| 1954-55 | Tor-Chi | 51 | 15 | 17 | 32 |
| 1955-56 | Chicago | 55 | 11 | 14 | 25 |
| 1956-57 | Chicago | 70 | 11 | 19 | 30 |
| | **Totals** | 809 | 236 | 207 | 443 |

**WATSON, James Charles (Jim)**  *Defenseman*
b. Smithers, B.C., Aug. 19, 1952

| Season | Club | GP | G | A | Pts. |
|---|---|---|---|---|---|
| 1972-73 | Philadelphia | 4 | 0 | 1 | 1 |
| 1973-74 | Philadelphia | 78 | 2 | 18 | 20 |
| 1974-75 | Philadelphia | 68 | 7 | 18 | 25 |
| 1975-76 | Philadelphia | 79 | 2 | 34 | 36 |
| 1976-77 | Philadelphia | 71 | 3 | 23 | 26 |
| 1977-78 | Philadelphia | 71 | 5 | 12 | 17 |
| 1978-79 | Philadelphia | 77 | 9 | 13 | 22 |
| 1979-80 | Philadelphia | 71 | 5 | 18 | 23 |
| 1980-81 | Philadelphia | 18 | 2 | 2 | 4 |
| 1981-82 | Philadelphia | 76 | 3 | 9 | 12 |
| | **Totals** | 613 | 38 | 148 | 186 |

**WATSON, James Arthur (Jim)**  *Defenseman*
b. Malartic, Que., June 28, 1943

| Season | Club | GP | G | A | Pts. |
|---|---|---|---|---|---|
| 1963-64 | Detroit | 1 | 0 | 0 | 0 |
| 1964-65 | Detroit | 1 | 0 | 0 | 0 |
| 1965-66 | Detroit | 2 | 0 | 0 | 0 |
| 1967-68 | Detroit | 61 | 0 | 3 | 3 |
| 1968-69 | Detroit | 8 | 0 | 1 | 1 |
| 1969-70 | Detroit | 4 | 0 | 0 | 0 |
| 1970-71 | Buffalo | 78 | 2 | 9 | 11 |
| 1971-72 | Buffalo | 66 | 2 | 6 | 8 |
| 1972-73 | Los Angeles (WHA) | 75 | 5 | 15 | 20 |
| 1973-74 | Los Angeles (WHA) | 71 | 0 | 11 | 11 |
| 1974-75 | Chicago (WHA) | 57 | 3 | 6 | 9 |
| | **NHL Totals** | 221 | 4 | 19 | 23 |
| | **WHA Totals** | 203 | 8 | 32 | 40 |

**WATSON, Joseph John (Joe)**  *Defenseman*
b. Smithers, B.C., July 6, 1943

| Season | Club | GP | G | A | Pts. |
|---|---|---|---|---|---|
| 1964-65 | Boston | 4 | 0 | 1 | 1 |
| 1966-67 | Boston | 69 | 2 | 13 | 15 |
| 1967-68 | Philadelphia | 73 | 5 | 14 | 19 |
| 1968-69 | Philadelphia | 60 | 2 | 8 | 10 |
| 1969-70 | Philadelphia | 54 | 3 | 11 | .14 |
| 1970-71 | Philadelphia | 57 | 3 | 7 | 10 |
| 1971-72 | Philadelphia | 65 | 3 | 7 | 10 |
| 1972-73 | Philadelphia | 63 | 2 | 24 | 26 |
| 1973-74 | Philadelphia | 74 | 1 | 17 | 18 |
| 1974-75 | Philadelphia | 80 | 6 | 17 | 23 |
| 1975-76 | Philadelphia | 78 | 2 | 22 | 24 |
| 1976-77 | Philadelphia | 77 | 4 | 26 | 30 |
| 1977-78 | Philadelphia | 65 | 5 | 9 | 14 |
| 1978-79 | Colorado | 16 | 0 | 2 | 2 |
| | **Totals** | 835 | 38 | 178 | 216 |

**WATSON, Phillipe Henri** *Forward*
b. Montreal, Que., Oct. 24, 1914

| Season | Club | GP | G | A | Pts. |
|---|---|---|---|---|---|
| 1935-36 | New York R | 24 | 0 | 2 | 2 |
| 1936-37 | New York R | 48 | 11 | 17 | 28 |
| 1937-38 | New York R | 48 | 7 | 25 | 32 |
| 1938-39 | New York R | 48 | 15 | 22 | 37 |
| 1939-40 | New York R | 48 | 7 | 28 | 35 |
| 1940-41 | New York R | 40 | 11 | 25 | 36 |
| 1941-42 | New York R | 48 | 15 | 37 | 52 |
| 1942-43 | New York R | 46 | 14 | 28 | 42 |
| 1943-44 | Montreal | 44 | 17 | 32 | 49 |
| 1944-45 | New York R | 45 | 11 | 8 | 19 |
| 1945-46 | New York R | 49 | 12 | 14 | 26 |
| 1946-47 | New York R | 48 | 6 | 12 | 18 |
| 1947-48 | New York R | 54 | 18 | 15 | 33 |
| | **Totals** | 590 | 144 | 265 | 409 |

**WATTERS, Timothy J.** *Defenseman*
b. Kamloops, B.C., July 25, 1959

| Season | Club | GP | G | A | Pts. |
|---|---|---|---|---|---|
| 1981-82 | Winnipeg | 69 | 2 | 22 | 24 |
| 1982-83 | Winnipeg | 77 | 5 | 18 | 23 |
| | **Totals** | 146 | 7 | 40 | 47 |

**WEBSTER, Donald** *Forward*
b. Toronto, Ont., July 3, 1924

| Season | Club | GP | G | A | Pts. |
|---|---|---|---|---|---|
| 1943-44 | Toronto | 27 | 7 | 6 | 13 |

**WEBSTER, John Robert (Chick)** *Forward*
b. Toronto, Ont., Nov. 3, 1921

| Season | Club | GP | G | A | Pts. |
|---|---|---|---|---|---|
| 1949-50 | New York R | 14 | 0 | 0 | 0 |

**WEBSTER, Thomas Ronald (Tom)** *Forward*
b. Kirkland Lake, Ont., Oct. 4, 1948

| Season | Club | GP | G | A | Pts. |
|---|---|---|---|---|---|
| 1968-69 | Boston | 9 | 0 | 2 | 2 |
| 1969-70 | Boston | 2 | 0 | 1 | 1 |
| 1970-71 | Detroit | 78 | 30 | 37 | 67 |
| 1971-72 | Det-Cal | 12 | 3 | 2 | 5 |
| 1972-73 | New England (WHA) | 77 | 53 | 50 | 103 |
| 1973-74 | New England (WHA) | 64 | 43 | 27 | 70 |
| 1974-75 | New England (WHA) | 66 | 40 | 24 | 64 |
| 1975-76 | New England (WHA) | 55 | 33 | 50 | 83 |
| 1976-77 | New England (WHA) | 70 | 36 | 49 | 85 |
| 1977-78 | New England (WHA) | 20 | 15 | 5 | 20 |
| 1979-80 | Detroit | 1 | 0 | 0 | 0 |
| | **NHL Totals** | 102 | 33 | 42 | 75 |
| | **WHA Totals** | 352 | 220 | 205 | 425 |

**WEILAND, Ralph C. (Cooney)** *Forward*
b. Egmondville, Ont., Nov. 5, 1904

| Season | Club | GP | G | A | Pts. |
|---|---|---|---|---|---|
| 1928-29 | Boston | 42 | 11 | 7 | 18 |
| 1929-30 | Boston | 44 | 43 | 30 | 73 |
| 1930-31 | Boston | 44 | 25 | 13 | 38 |
| 1931-32 | Boston | 46 | 14 | 12 | 26 |
| 1932-33 | Ottawa | 48 | 16 | 11 | 27 |
| 1933-34 | Ott-Det | 48 | 13 | 19 | 32 |
| 1934-35 | Detroit | 48 | 13 | 25 | 38 |
| 1935-36 | Boston | 48 | 14 | 13 | 27 |
| 1936-37 | Boston | 48 | 6 | 9 | 15 |
| 1937-38 | Boston | 48 | 11 | 12 | 23 |
| 1938-39 | Boston | 45 | 7 | 9 | 16 |
| | **Totals** | 509 | 173 | 160 | 333 |

**WEIR, Stanley Brian (Stan)** *Forward*
b. Ponoka, Alta., Mar. 17, 1952

| Season | Club | GP | G | A | Pts. |
|---|---|---|---|---|---|
| 1972-73 | California | 78 | 15 | 24 | 39 |
| 1973-74 | California | 58 | 9 | 7 | 16 |
| 1974-75 | California | 80 | 18 | 27 | 45 |
| 1975-76 | Toronto | 64 | 19 | 32 | 51 |
| 1976-77 | Toronto | 65 | 11 | 19 | 30 |
| 1977-78 | Toronto | 30 | 12 | 5 | 17 |
| 1978-79 | Edmonton (WHA) | 68 | 31 | 30 | 61 |
| 1979-80 | Edmonton | 79 | 33 | 33 | 66 |
| 1980-81 | Edmonton | 70 | 12 | 20 | 32 |
| 1981-82 | Edm-Col | 61 | 5 | 16 | 21 |
| 1982-83 | Detroit | 57 | 5 | 24 | 29 |
| | **Totals** | 642 | 139 | 207 | 346 |

**WEIR, Wally** *Defenseman*
b. Verdun, Que., June 3, 1954

| Season | Club | GP | G | A | Pts. |
|---|---|---|---|---|---|
| 1976-77 | Quebec (WHA) | 69 | 3 | 17 | 20 |
| 1977-78 | Quebec (WHA) | 13 | 0 | 0 | 0 |


| Season | Club | GP | G | A | Pts. |
|---|---|---|---|---|---|
| 1978-79 | Quebec (WHA) | 68 | 2 | 7 | 9 |
| 1979-80 | Quebec | 73 | 3 | 12 | 15 |
| 1980-81 | Quebec | 54 | 6 | 8 | 14 |
| 1981-82 | Quebec | 62 | 3 | 5 | 8 |
| 1982-83 | Quebec | 58 | 5 | 11 | 16 |
| | **NHL Totals** | 247 | 17 | 36 | 53 |
| | **WHA Totals** | 150 | 5 | 24 | 29 |

**WELLINGTON, Duke** *Defenseman*

| Season | Club | GP | G | A | Pts. |
|---|---|---|---|---|---|
| 1919-20 | Quebec | 1 | 0 | 0 | 0 |

**WELLS, Gordon Jay** *Defenseman*
b. Paris, Ont., May 18, 1959

| Season | Club | GP | G | A | Pts. |
|---|---|---|---|---|---|
| 1979-80 | Los Angeles | 43 | 0 | 0 | 0 |
| 1980-81 | Los Angeles | 72 | 5 | 13 | 18 |
| 1981-82 | Los Angeles | 60 | 1 | 8 | 9 |
| 1982-83 | Los Angeles | 69 | 3 | 12 | 15 |
| | **Totals** | 244 | 9 | 33 | 42 |

**WENSINK, John** *Forward*
b. Cornwall, Ont., Apr. 1, 1953

| Season | Club | GP | G | A | Pts. |
|---|---|---|---|---|---|
| 1973-74 | St Louis | 3 | 0 | 0 | 0 |
| 1976-77 | Boston | 23 | 4 | 6 | 10 |
| 1977-78 | Boston | 80 | 16 | 20 | 36 |
| 1978-79 | Boston | 76 | 28 | 18 | 46 |
| 1979-80 | Boston | 69 | 9 | 11 | 20 |
| 1980-81 | Quebec | 56 | 6 | 3 | 9 |
| 1981-82 | Colorado | 57 | 5 | 3 | 8 |
| 1982-83 | New Jersey | 42 | 2 | 7 | 9 |
| | **Totals** | 406 | 70 | 68 | 138 |

**WENTWORTH, Marvin (Cy)** *Defenseman*
b. Grimsby, Ont., Jan. 24, 1905

| Season | Club | GP | G | A | Pts. |
|---|---|---|---|---|---|
| 1927-28 | Chicago | 43 | 5 | 5 | 10 |
| 1928-29 | Chicago | 44 | 2 | 1 | 3 |
| 1929-30 | Chicago | 37 | 3 | 4 | 7 |
| 1930-31 | Chicago | 44 | 4 | 4 | 8 |
| 1931-32 | Chicago | 48 | 3 | 10 | 13 |
| 1932-33 | Montreal M | 47 | 4 | 10 | 14 |
| 1933-34 | Montreal M | 48 | 2 | 5 | 7 |
| 1934-35 | Montreal M | 48 | 4 | 9 | 13 |
| 1935-36 | Montreal M | 48 | 4 | 5 | 9 |
| 1936-37 | Montreal M | 43 | 3 | 4 | 7 |
| 1937-38 | Montreal M | 48 | 4 | 5 | 9 |
| 1938-39 | Montreal | 45 | 0 | 3 | 3 |
| 1939-40 | Montreal | 32 | 1 | 3 | 4 |
| | **Totals** | 575 | 39 | 68 | 107 |

**WESLEY, Trevor Blake** *Defenseman*
b. Red Deer, Alta., July 10, 1959

| Season | Club | GP | G | A | Pts. |
|---|---|---|---|---|---|
| 1979-80 | Philadelphia | 2 | 0 | 1 | 1 |
| 1980-81 | Philadelphia | 50 | 3 | 7 | 10 |
| 1981-82 | Hartford | 78 | 9 | 18 | 27 |
| 1982-83 | Hart-Que | 74 | 4 | 9 | 13 |
| | **Totals** | 204 | 16 | 35 | 51 |

**WESTFALL, Vernon Edwin (Ed)** *Forward*
b. Belleville, Ont., Sept. 19, 1940

| Season | Club | GP | G | A | Pts. |
|---|---|---|---|---|---|
| 1961-62 | Boston | 63 | 2 | 9 | 11 |
| 1962-63 | Boston | 48 | 1 | 11 | 12 |
| 1963-64 | Boston | 55 | 1 | 5 | 6 |
| 1964-65 | Boston | 68 | 12 | 15 | 27 |
| 1965-66 | Boston | 59 | 9 | 21 | 30 |
| 1966-67 | Boston | 70 | 12 | 24 | 36 |
| 1967-68 | Boston | 73 | 14 | 22 | 36 |
| 1968-69 | Boston | 70 | 18 | 24 | 42 |
| 1969-70 | Boston | 72 | 14 | 22 | 36 |
| 1970-71 | Boston | 78 | 25 | 34 | 59 |
| 1971-72 | Boston | 71 | 18 | 26 | 44 |
| 1972-73 | New York I | 67 | 15 | 31 | 46 |
| 1973-74 | New York I | 68 | 19 | 23 | 42 |
| 1974-75 | New York I | 73 | 22 | 33 | 55 |
| 1975-76 | New York I | 80 | 25 | 31 | 56 |
| 1976-77 | New York I | 79 | 14 | 33 | 47 |
| 1977-78 | New York I | 71 | 5 | 19 | 24 |
| 1978-79 | New York I | 55 | 5 | 11 | 16 |
| | **Totals** | 1220 | 231 | 394 | 625 |

**WHARRAM, Kenneth Malcolm (Ken)** *Forward*
b. Ferris, Ont., July 2, 1933

| Season | Club | GP | G | A | Pts. |
|---|---|---|---|---|---|
| 1951-52 | Chicago | 1 | 0 | 0 | 0 |
| 1953-54 | Chicago | 29 | 1 | 7 | 8 |


| Season | Club | GP | G | A | Pts. |
|---|---|---|---|---|---|
| 1955-56 | Chicago | 3 | 0 | 0 | 0 |
| 1958-59 | Chicago | 66 | 10 | 9 | 19 |
| 1959-60 | Chicago | 59 | 14 | 11 | 25 |
| 1960-61 | Chicago | 64 | 18 | 29 | 45 |
| 1961-62 | Chicago | 62 | 14 | 23 | 37 |
| 1962-63 | Chicago | 55 | 20 | 18 | 38 |
| 1963-64 | Chicago | 70 | 39 | 32 | 71 |
| 1964-65 | Chicago | 68 | 24 | 20 | 44 |
| 1965-66 | Chicago | 69 | 26 | 17 | 43 |
| 1966-67 | Chicago | 70 | 31 | 34 | 65 |
| 1967-68 | Chicago | 74 | 27 | 42 | 69 |
| 1968-69 | Chicago | 76 | 30 | 39 | 69 |
| | **Totals** | 766 | 252 | 281 | 533 |

**WHARTON, Thomas (Len)** *Defenseman*
b. Winnipeg, Man., Dec. 13, 1927

| Season | Club | GP | G | A | Pts. |
|---|---|---|---|---|---|
| 1944-45 | New York R | 1 | 0 | 0 | 0 |

**WHELDEN, Donald** *Defenseman*
b. Falmouth, Mass., Dec. 28, 1954

| Season | Club | GP | G | A | Pts. |
|---|---|---|---|---|---|
| 1974-75 | St Louis | 2 | 0 | 0 | 0 |

**WHELTON, William** *Defenseman*
b. Everett, Mass., Aug. 28, 1959

| Season | Club | GP | G | A | Pts. |
|---|---|---|---|---|---|
| 1980-81 | Winnipeg | 2 | 0 | 0 | 0 |

**WHITE, Anthony Raymond** *Forward*
b. Grand Falls, Nfld., June 16, 1954

| Season | Club | GP | G | A | Pts. |
|---|---|---|---|---|---|
| 1974-75 | Washington | 5 | 0 | 2 | 2 |
| 1975-76 | Washington | 80 | 25 | 17 | 42 |
| 1976-77 | Washington | 72 | 12 | 9 | 21 |
| 1977-78 | Washington | 1 | 0 | 0 | 0 |
| 1979-80 | Minnesota | 6 | 0 | 0 | 0 |
| | **Totals** | 164 | 37 | 28 | 65 |

**WHITE, Leonard Arthur (Moe)** *Forward*
b. Verdun, Que., July 28, 1919

| Season | Club | GP | G | A | Pts. |
|---|---|---|---|---|---|
| 1945-46 | Montreal | 4 | 0 | 1 | 1 |

**WHITE, Sherman** *Forward*
b. Amherst, N.S., May 12, 1923

| Season | Club | GP | G | A | Pts. |
|---|---|---|---|---|---|
| 1946-47 | New York R | 1 | 0 | 0 | 0 |
| 1949-50 | New York R | 3 | 0 | 2 | 2 |
| | **Totals** | 4 | 0 | 2 | 2 |

**WHITE, Wilfred Belmont (Tex)** *Forward*
b. 1901

| Season | Club | GP | G | A | Pts. |
|---|---|---|---|---|---|
| 1925-26 | Pittsburgh Pi | 35 | 7 | 1 | 8 |
| 1926-27 | Pittsburgh Pi | 43 | 5 | 4 | 9 |
| 1927-28 | Pittsburgh Pi | 44 | 5 | 1 | 6 |
| 1928-29 | PittPi-NYA | 43 | 5 | 5 | 10 |
| 1929-30 | Pittsburgh Pi | 29 | 8 | 1 | 9 |
| 1930-31 | Philadelphia Q | 9 | 3 | 0 | 3 |
| | **Totals** | 203 | 33 | 12 | 45 |

**WHITE, William Earl (Bill)** *Defenseman*
b. Toronto, Ont., Aug. 26, 1939

| Season | Club | GP | G | A | Pts. |
|---|---|---|---|---|---|
| 1967-68 | Los Angeles | 74 | 11 | 27 | 38 |
| 1968-69 | Los Angeles | 75 | 5 | 28 | 33 |
| 1969-70 | LA-Chi | 61 | 4 | 16 | 20 |
| 1970-71 | Chicago | 67 | 4 | 21 | 25 |
| 1971-72 | Chicago | 76 | 7 | 22 | 29 |
| 1972-73 | Chicago | 72 | 9 | 38 | 47 |
| 1973-74 | Chicago | 69 | 5 | 31 | 36 |
| 1974-75 | Chicago | 51 | 4 | 23 | 27 |
| 1975-76 | Chicago | 59 | 1 | 9 | 10 |
| | **Totals** | 604 | 50 | 215 | 265 |

**WHITELAW, Robert** *Defenseman*
b. Motherwell, Scotland, Oct. 5, 1916

| Season | Club | GP | G | A | Pts. |
|---|---|---|---|---|---|
| 1940-41 | Detroit | 23 | 0 | 2 | 2 |
| 1941-42 | Detroit | 9 | 0 | 0 | 0 |
| | **Totals** | 32 | 0 | 2 | 2 |

**WHITLOCK, Robert Angus (Bob)** *Forward*
b. Charlottetown, P.E.I., July 16, 1949

| Season | Club | GP | G | A | Pts. |
|---|---|---|---|---|---|
| 1969-70 | Minnesota | 1 | 0 | 0 | 0 |
| 1972-73 | Chicago (WHA) | 77 | 23 | 28 | 51 |
| 1973-74 | Chi-LA (WHA) | 46 | 20 | 29 | 49 |

| Season | Club | GP | G | A | Pts. |
|---|---|---|---|---|---|
| 1974-75 | Indianapolis (WHA) | 73 | 31 | 26 | 57 |
| 1975-76 | Indianapolis (WHA) | 30 | 7 | 15 | 22 |
| | **NHL Totals** | 1 | 0 | 0 | 0 |
| | **WHA Totals** | 226 | 81 | 98 | 179 |

**WICKENHEISER, Douglas Peter** *Forward*
b. Regina, Sask., Mar. 30, 1961

| Season | Club | GP | G | A | Pts. |
|---|---|---|---|---|---|
| 1980-81 | Montreal | 41 | 7 | 8 | 15 |
| 1981-82 | Montreal | 56 | 12 | 23 | 35 |
| 1982-83 | Montreal | 78 | 25 | 30 | 55 |
| | **Totals** | 175 | 44 | 61 | 105 |

**WIDING, Juha Markku (Whitey)** *Forward*
b. Uleaborg, Finland, July 4, 1947

| Season | Club | GP | G | A | Pts. |
|---|---|---|---|---|---|
| 1969-70 | NYR-LA | 48 | 7 | 9 | 16 |
| 1970-71 | Los Angeles | 78 | 25 | 40 | 65 |
| 1971-72 | Los Angeles | 78 | 27 | 28 | 55 |
| 1972-73 | Los Angeles | 77 | 16 | 54 | 70 |
| 1973-74 | Los Angeles | 71 | 27 | 30 | 57 |
| 1974-75 | Los Angeles | 80 | 26 | 34 | 60 |
| 1975-76 | Los Angeles | 67 | 7 | 15 | 22 |
| 1976-77 | LA-Clev | 76 | 9 | 16 | 25 |
| 1977-78 | Edmonton (WHA) | 71 | 18 | 24 | 42 |
| | **NHL Totals** | 575 | 144 | 226 | 370 |
| | **WHA Totals** | 71 | 18 | 24 | 42 |

**WIEBE, Arthur Walter Ronald** *Defenseman*
b. Rosthern, Sask., Sept. 28, 1913

| Season | Club | GP | G | A | Pts. |
|---|---|---|---|---|---|
| 1932-33 | Chicago | 4 | 0 | 0 | 0 |
| 1934-35 | Chicago | 42 | 2 | 1 | 3 |
| 1935-36 | Chicago | 46 | 1 | 0 | 1 |
| 1936-37 | Chicago | 43 | 0 | 2 | 2 |
| 1937-38 | Chicago | 43 | 0 | 3 | 3 |
| 1938-39 | Chicago | 47 | 1 | 2 | 3 |
| 1939-40 | Chicago | 47 | 2 | 2 | 4 |
| 1940-41 | Chicago | 45 | 3 | 2 | 5 |
| 1941-42 | Chicago | 43 | 2 | 4 | 6 |
| 1942-43 | Chicago | 33 | 1 | 7 | 8 |
| 1943-44 | Chicago | 21 | 2 | 4 | 6 |
| | **Totals** | 414 | 14 | 27 | 41 |

**WILCOX, Archibald** *Defenseman*
b. Montreal, Que., May 9, 1903

| Season | Club | GP | G | A | Pts. |
|---|---|---|---|---|---|
| 1929-30 | Montreal M | 42 | 3 | 5 | 8 |
| 1930-31 | Montreal M | 39 | 2 | 2 | 4 |
| 1931-32 | Montreal M | 48 | 3 | 3 | 6 |
| 1932-33 | Montreal M | 47 | 0 | 3 | 3 |
| 1933-34 | MontM-Bos | 24 | 0 | 1 | 1 |
| 1934-35 | St Louis | 8 | 0 | 0 | 0 |
| | **Totals** | 208 | 8 | 14 | 22 |

**WILCOX, Barry** *Forward*
b. New Westminster, B.C., Apr. 23, 1948

| Season | Club | GP | G | A | Pts. |
|---|---|---|---|---|---|
| 1972-73 | Vancouver | 31 | 3 | 2 | 5 |

**WILDER, Archibald (Archie)** *Forward*
b. Melville, Sask., Apr. 30, 1917

| Season | Club | GP | G | A | Pts. |
|---|---|---|---|---|---|
| 1940-41 | Detroit | 18 | 0 | 2 | 2 |

**WILEY, James Thomas (Jim)** *Forward*
b. Sault Ste. Marie, Ont., Apr. 28, 1950

| Season | Club | GP | G | A | Pts. |
|---|---|---|---|---|---|
| 1972-73 | Pittsburgh | 4 | 0 | 1 | 1 |
| 1973-74 | Pittsburgh | 22 | 0 | 3 | 3 |
| 1974-75 | Vancouver | 1 | 0 | 0 | 0 |
| 1975-76 | Vancouver | 2 | 0 | 0 | 0 |
| 1976-77 | Vancouver | 34 | 4 | 6 | 10 |
| | **Totals** | 63 | 4 | 10 | 14 |

**WILKENSON, John** *Defenseman*

| Season | Club | GP | G | A | Pts. |
|---|---|---|---|---|---|
| 1943-44 | Boston | 9 | 0 | 0 | 0 |

**WILKINS, Barry James** *Forward*
b. Toronto, Ont., Feb. 28, 1947

| Season | Club | GP | G | A | Pts. |
|---|---|---|---|---|---|
| 1966-67 | Boston | 1 | 0 | 0 | 0 |
| 1968-69 | Boston | 1 | 1 | 0 | 1 |
| 1969-70 | Boston | 6 | 0 | 0 | 0 |
| 1970-71 | Vancouver | 70 | 5 | 18 | 23 |
| 1971-72 | Vancouver | 45 | 2 | 5 | 7 |

| Season | Club | GP | G | A | Pts. |
|---|---|---|---|---|---|
| 1972-73 | Vancouver | 76 | 11 | 17 | 28 |
| 1973-74 | Vancouver | 78 | 3 | 28 | 31 |
| 1974-75 | Van-Pitt | 66 | 5 | 30 | 35 |
| 1975-76 | Pittsburgh | 75 | 0 | 27 | 27 |
| 1976-77 | Edmonton (WHA) | 51 | 4 | 24 | 28 |
| 1977-78 | Indianapolis (WHA) | 79 | 2 | 21 | 23 |
| | **NHL Totals** | 418 | 27 | 125 | 152 |
| | **WHA Totals** | 130 | 6 | 45 | 51 |

**WILLARD, Rod** *Forward*
b. Cornwall, Ont., May 1, 1960

| Season | Club | GP | G | A | Pts. |
|---|---|---|---|---|---|
| 1982-83 | Toronto | 1 | 0 | 0 | 0 |

**WILLIAMS, Burr** *Defenseman*
b. Okemah, Okla., Aug. 30, 1909

| Season | Club | GP | G | A | Pts. |
|---|---|---|---|---|---|
| 1933-34 | Detroit | 4 | 0 | 1 | 1 |
| 1934-35 | StLE-Bos | 18 | 0 | 0 | 0 |
| 1936-37 | Detroit | 2 | 0 | 0 | 0 |
| | **Totals** | 24 | 0 | 1 | 1 |

**WILLIAMS, David James (Tiger)** *Forward*
b. Weyburn, Sask., Feb. 3, 1954

| Season | Club | GP | G | A | Pts. |
|---|---|---|---|---|---|
| 1974-75 | Toronto | 42 | 10 | 19 | 29 |
| 1975-76 | Toronto | 78 | 21 | 19 | 40 |
| 1976-77 | Toronto | 77 | 18 | 25 | 43 |
| 1977-78 | Toronto | 78 | 19 | 31 | 50 |
| 1978-79 | Toronto | 77 | 19 | 20 | 39 |
| 1979-80 | Tor-Van | 58 | 30 | 23 | 53 |
| 1980-81 | Vancouver | 77 | 35 | 27 | 62 |
| 1981-82 | Vancouver | 77 | 17 | 21 | 38 |
| 1982-83 | Vancouver | 68 | 8 | 13 | 21 |
| | **Totals** | 632 | 177 | 198 | 375 |

**WILLIAMS, Frederick Richard** *Forward*
b. Saskatoon, Sask., July 1, 1956

| Season | Club | GP | G | A | Pts. |
|---|---|---|---|---|---|
| 1976-77 | Detroit | 44 | 2 | 5 | 7 |

**WILLIAMS, Gordon James** *Forward*
b. Saskatoon, Sask., Apr. 10, 1960

| Season | Club | GP | G | A | Pts. |
|---|---|---|---|---|---|
| 1981-82 | Philadelphia | 1 | 0 | 0 | 0 |
| 1982-83 | Philadelphia | 1 | 0 | 0 | 0 |
| | **Totals** | 2 | 0 | 0 | 0 |

**WILLIAMS, Thomas Charles (Tom)** *Forward*
b. Windsor, Ont., Feb. 7, 1951

| Season | Club | GP | G | A | Pts. |
|---|---|---|---|---|---|
| 1971-72 | New York R | 3 | 0 | 0 | 0 |
| 1972-73 | New York R | 10 | 0 | 1 | 1 |
| 1973-74 | NYR-LA | 60 | 12 | 19 | 31 |
| 1974-75 | Los Angeles | 74 | 24 | 22 | 46 |
| 1975-76 | Los Angeles | 70 | 19 | 20 | 39 |
| 1976-77 | Los Angeles | 80 | 35 | 39 | 74 |
| 1977-78 | Los Angeles | 58 | 15 | 22 | 37 |
| 1978-79 | Los Angeles | 44 | 10 | 15 | 25 |
| | **Totals** | 399 | 115 | 138 | 253 |

**WILLIAMS, Thomas Mark (Tom)** *Forward*
b. Duluth, Minn., Apr. 17, 1940

| Season | Club | GP | G | A | Pts. |
|---|---|---|---|---|---|
| 1961-62 | Boston | 26 | 6 | 6 | 12 |
| 1962-63 | Boston | 69 | 23 | 20 | 43 |
| 1963-64 | Boston | 37 | 8 | 15 | 23 |
| 1964-65 | Boston | 65 | 13 | 21 | 34 |
| 1965-66 | Boston | 70 | 16 | 22 | 38 |
| 1966-67 | Boston | 29 | 8 | 13 | 21 |
| 1967-68 | Boston | 68 | 18 | 32 | 50 |
| 1968-69 | Boston | 26 | 4 | 7 | 11 |
| 1969-70 | Minnesota | 75 | 15 | 52 | 67 |
| 1970-71 | Minn-Cal | 59 | 17 | 23 | 40 |
| 1971-72 | California | 32 | 3 | 9 | 12 |
| 1972-73 | New England (WHA) | 69 | 10 | 21 | 31 |
| 1973-74 | New England (WHA) | 70 | 21 | 37 | 58 |
| 1974-75 | Washington | 73 | 22 | 36 | 58 |
| 1975-76 | Washington | 34 | 8 | 13 | 21 |
| | **NHL Totals** | 663 | 161 | 269 | 430 |
| | **WHA Totals** | 139 | 31 | 58 | 89 |

**WILLIAMS, Warren Milton** *Forward*
b. Duluth, Minn., Sept. 11, 1952

| Season | Club | GP | G | A | Pts. |
|---|---|---|---|---|---|
| 1973-74 | St Louis | 31 | 3 | 10 | 13 |
| 1974-75 | California | 63 | 11 | 21 | 32 |

| Season | Club | GP | G | A | Pts. |
|---|---|---|---|---|---|
| 1975-76 | California | 14 | 0 | 4 | 4 |
| 1976-77 | Edmonton (WHA) | 29 | 3 | 10 | 13 |
| | **NHL Totals** | 108 | 14 | 35 | 49 |
| | **WHA Totals** | 29 | 3 | 10 | 13 |

**WILLSON, Donald Arthur** *Forward*
b. Chatham, Ont., Jan. 1, 1914

| Season | Club | GP | G | A | Pts. |
|---|---|---|---|---|---|
| 1937-38 | Montreal | 18 | 2 | 7 | 9 |
| 1938-39 | Montreal | 4 | 0 | 0 | 0 |
| | **Totals** | 22 | 2 | 7 | 9 |

**WILSON, Behn Bevan** *Defenseman*
b. Toronto, Ont., Dec. 19, 1958

| Season | Club | GP | G | A | Pts. |
|---|---|---|---|---|---|
| 1978-79 | Philadelphia | 80 | 13 | 36 | 49 |
| 1979-80 | Philadelphia | 61 | 9 | 25 | 34 |
| 1980-81 | Philadelphia | 77 | 16 | 47 | 63 |
| 1981-82 | Philadelphia | 59 | 13 | 23 | 36 |
| 1982-83 | Philadelphia | 62 | 8 | 24 | 32 |
| | **Totals** | 339 | 59 | 155 | 214 |

**WILSON, Bertwin Hilliard** *Forward*
b. Orangeville, Ont., Oct. 17, 1949

| Season | Club | GP | G | A | Pts. |
|---|---|---|---|---|---|
| 1973-74 | New York R | 5 | 1 | 1 | 2 |
| 1974-75 | New York R | 61 | 5 | 1 | 6 |
| 1975-76 | StL-LA | 58 | 2 | 3 | 5 |
| 1976-77 | Los Angeles | 77 | 4 | 3 | 7 |
| 1977-78 | Los Angeles | 79 | 7 | 16 | 23 |
| 1978-79 | Los Angeles | 73 | 9 | 10 | 19 |
| 1979-80 | Los Angeles | 75 | 4 | 3 | 7 |
| 1980-81 | Calgary | 50 | 5 | 7 | 12 |
| | **Totals** | 478 | 37 | 44 | 81 |

**WILSON, Carol (Cully)** *Forward*
b. 1893

| Season | Club | GP | G | A | Pts. |
|---|---|---|---|---|---|
| 1919-20 | Toronto | 23 | 21 | 5 | 26 |
| 1920-21 | Tor-Mont | 17 | 8 | 2 | 10 |
| 1921-22 | Hamilton | 23 | 7 | 9 | 16 |
| 1922-23 | Hamilton | 23 | 16 | 3 | 19 |
| 1926-27 | Chicago | 39 | 8 | 4 | 12 |
| | **Totals** | 125 | 60 | 23 | 83 |

**WILSON, Douglas, Jr.** *Defenseman*
b. Ottawa, Ont., July 5, 1957

| Season | Club | GP | G | A | Pts. |
|---|---|---|---|---|---|
| 1977-78 | Chicago | 77 | 14 | 20 | 34 |
| 1978-79 | Chicago | 56 | 5 | 21 | 26 |
| 1979-80 | Chicago | 73 | 12 | 49 | 61 |
| 1980-81 | Chicago | 76 | 12 | 39 | 51 |
| 1981-82 | Chicago | 76 | 39 | 46 | 85 |
| 1982-83 | Chicago | 74 | 18 | 51 | 69 |
| | **Totals** | 432 | 100 | 226 | 326 |

**WILSON, Gerald** *Forward*
b. Edmonton, Alta., Apr. 10, 1937

| Season | Club | GP | G | A | Pts. |
|---|---|---|---|---|---|
| 1956-57 | Montreal | 3 | 0 | 0 | 0 |

**WILSON, John Edward** *Forward*
b. Kincardine, Ont., June 14, 1929

| Season | Club | GP | G | A | Pts. |
|---|---|---|---|---|---|
| 1949-50 | Detroit | 1 | 0 | 0 | 0 |
| 1951-52 | Detroit | 28 | 4 | 5 | 9 |
| 1952-53 | Detroit | 70 | 23 | 19 | 42 |
| 1953-54 | Detroit | 70 | 17 | 17 | 34 |
| 1954-55 | Detroit | 70 | 12 | 15 | 27 |
| 1955-56 | Chicago | 70 | 24 | 9 | 33 |
| 1956-57 | Detroit | 70 | 18 | 30 | 48 |
| 1957-58 | Detroit | 70 | 12 | 27 | 39 |
| 1958-59 | Detroit | 70 | 11 | 17 | 28 |
| 1959-60 | Toronto | 70 | 15 | 16 | 31 |
| 1960-61 | Tor-NYR | 59 | 14 | 13 | 27 |
| 1961-62 | New York R | 40 | 11 | 3 | 14 |
| | **Totals** | 688 | 161 | 171 | 332 |

**WILSON, Lawrence** *Forward*
b. Kincardine, Ont., Oct. 23, 1930

| Season | Club | GP | G | A | Pts. |
|---|---|---|---|---|---|
| 1949-50 | Detroit | 1 | 0 | 0 | 0 |
| 1951-52 | Detroit | 5 | 0 | 0 | 0 |
| 1952-53 | Detroit | 15 | 0 | 4 | 4 |
| 1953-54 | Chicago | 66 | 9 | 33 | 42 |
| 1954-55 | Chicago | 63 | 12 | 11 | 23 |
| 1955-56 | Chicago | 2 | 0 | 0 | 0 |
| | **Totals** | 152 | 21 | 48 | 69 |

| Season | Club | GP | G | A | Pts. |
|---|---|---|---|---|---|
| **WILSON, Murray Charles** *Forward* | | | | | |
| b. Ottawa, Ont., Aug. 3, 1951 | | | | | |
| 1972-73 | Montreal | 52 | 18 | 9 | 27 |
| 1973-74 | Montreal | 72 | 17 | 14 | 31 |
| 1974-75 | Montreal | 73 | 24 | 18 | 42 |
| 1975-76 | Montreal | 59 | 11 | 24 | 35 |
| 1976-77 | Montreal | 60 | 13 | 14 | 27 |
| 1977-78 | Montreal | 12 | 0 | 1 | 1 |
| 1978-79 | Los Angeles | 58 | 11 | 15 | 26 |
| | **Totals** | 386 | 94 | 95 | 189 |
| **WILSON, Richard Gordon** *Defenseman* | | | | | |
| b. Prince Albert, Sask., Aug. 10, 1950 | | | | | |
| 1973-74 | Montreal | 21 | 0 | 2 | 2 |
| 1974-75 | St Louis | 76 | 2 | 5 | 7 |
| 1975-76 | St Louis | 65 | 1 | 6 | 7 |
| 1976-77 | Detroit | 77 | 3 | 13 | 16 |
| | **Totals** | 239 | 6 | 26 | 32 |
| **WILSON, Richard William** *Defenseman* | | | | | |
| b. Long Beach, Calif., June 17, 1962 | | | | | |
| 1981-82 | St Louis | 48 | 3 | 18 | 21 |
| 1982-83 | St Louis | 56 | 3 | 11 | 14 |
| | **Totals** | 104 | 6 | 29 | 35 |
| **WILSON, Robert Wayne** *Defenseman* | | | | | |
| b. Sudbury, Ont., Feb. 18, 1934 | | | | | |
| 1953-54 | Chicago | 1 | 0 | 0 | 0 |
| **WILSON, Roger Sidney** *Defenseman* | | | | | |
| b. Sudbury, Ont., Sept. 18, 1946 | | | | | |
| 1974-75 | Chicago | 7 | 0 | 2 | 2 |
| **WILSON, Ronald Lawrence** | | | | | |
| *Defenseman-Forward* | | | | | |
| b. Windsor, Ont., May 28, 1955 | | | | | |
| 1977-78 | Toronto | 13 | 2 | 1 | 3 |
| 1978-79 | Toronto | 46 | 5 | 12 | 17 |
| 1979-80 | Toronto | 5 | 0 | 2 | 2 |
| | **Totals** | 64 | 7 | 15 | 22 |
| **WILSON, Ronald Lee** *Forward* | | | | | |
| b. Toronto, Ont., May 13, 1956 | | | | | |
| 1979-80 | Winnipeg | 79 | 21 | 36 | 57 |
| 1980-81 | Winnipeg | 77 | 18 | 33 | 51 |
| 1981-82 | Winnipeg | 39 | 3 | 13 | 16 |
| 1982-83 | Winnipeg | 12 | 6 | 3 | 9 |
| | **Totals** | 207 | 48 | 85 | 133 |
| **WILSON, Wallace Lloyd** *Forward* | | | | | |
| b. Berwick, N.S., May 25, 1921 | | | | | |
| 1947-48 | Boston | 53 | 11 | 8 | 19 |
| **WING, Murray Allan** *Defenseman* | | | | | |
| b. Thunder Bay, Ont., Oct. 14, 1950 | | | | | |
| 1973-74 | Detroit | 1 | 0 | 1 | 1 |
| **WISEMAN, Edward Randall** *Forward* | | | | | |
| b. Newcastle, N.B., Dec. 28, 1912 | | | | | |
| 1932-33 | Detroit | 43 | 8 | 8 | 16 |
| 1933-34 | Detroit | 48 | 5 | 9 | 14 |
| 1934-35 | Detroit | 39 | 11 | 13 | 24 |
| 1935-36 | New York A | 45 | 12 | 16 | 28 |
| 1936-37 | New York A | 44 | 14 | 19 | 33 |
| 1937-38 | New York A | 48 | 18 | 14 | 32 |
| 1938-39 | New York A | 47 | 12 | 21 | 33 |
| 1939-40 | NYA-Bos | 49 | 7 | 19 | 26 |
| 1940-41 | Boston | 48 | 16 | 24 | 40 |
| 1941-42 | Boston | 45 | 12 | 22 | 34 |
| | **Totals** | 456 | 115 | 165 | 280 |
| **WISTE, James Andrew (Jim)** *Forward* | | | | | |
| b. Moose Jaw, Sask., Feb. 18, 1946 | | | | | |
| 1968-69 | Chicago | 3 | 0 | 0 | 0 |
| 1969-70 | Chicago | 26 | 0 | 8 | 8 |
| 1970-71 | Vancouver | 23 | 1 | 2 | 3 |
| 1972-73 | Cleveland (WHA) | 70 | 28 | 43 | 71 |

| Season | Club | GP | G | A | Pts. |
|---|---|---|---|---|---|
| 1973-74 | Cleveland (WHA) | 76 | 23 | 35 | 58 |
| 1974-75 | Indianapolis (WHA) | 75 | 13 | 28 | 41 |
| | **NHL Totals** | 52 | 1 | 10 | 11 |
| | **WHA Totals** | 221 | 64 | 106 | 170 |
| **WITHERSPOON, James Douglas** | | | | | |
| *Defenseman* | | | | | |
| b. Toronto, Ont., Oct. 3, 1951 | | | | | |
| 1975-76 | Los Angeles | 2 | 0 | 0 | 0 |
| **WITIUK, Stephen (Steve)** *Forward* | | | | | |
| b. Winnipeg, Man., Jan. 8, 1929 | | | | | |
| 1951-52 | Chicago | 33 | 3 | 8 | 11 |
| **WOCHY, Stephen** *Forward* | | | | | |
| b. Fort William, Ont., Dec. 25, 1922 | | | | | |
| 1944-45 | Detroit | 49 | 19 | 20 | 39 |
| 1946-47 | Detroit | 5 | 0 | 0 | 0 |
| | **Totals** | 54 | 19 | 20 | 39 |
| **WOIT, Benedict Francis** *Defenseman* | | | | | |
| b. Fort William, Ont., Jan. 7, 1928 | | | | | |
| 1950-51 | Detroit | 2 | 0 | 0 | 0 |
| 1951-52 | Detroit | 58 | 3 | 8 | 11 |
| 1952-53 | Detroit | 70 | 1 | 5 | 6 |
| 1953-54 | Detroit | 70 | 0 | 2 | 2 |
| 1954-55 | Detroit | 62 | 2 | 3 | 5 |
| 1955-56 | Chicago | 63 | 1 | 8 | 9 |
| 1956-57 | Chicago | 9 | 0 | 0 | 0 |
| | **Totals** | 234 | 7 | 26 | 33 |
| **WOLF, Bennett Martin** *Defenseman* | | | | | |
| b. Kitchener, Ont., Oct. 23, 1959 | | | | | |
| 1980-81 | Pittsburgh | 24 | 0 | 1 | 1 |
| 1981-82 | Pittsburgh | 1 | 0 | 0 | 0 |
| 1982-83 | Pittsburgh | 5 | 0 | 0 | 0 |
| | **Totals** | 30 | 0 | 1 | 1 |
| **WONG, Michael Anthony** *Forward* | | | | | |
| b. Minneapolis, Minn., Jan. 14, 1955 | | | | | |
| 1975-76 | Detroit | 22 | 1 | 1 | 2 |
| **WOOD, Robert** *Defenseman* | | | | | |
| b. Lethbridge, Alta., July 9, 1930 | | | | | |
| 1950-51 | New York R | 1 | 0 | 0 | 0 |
| **WOODS, Paul William** *Forward* | | | | | |
| b. Hespeler, Ont., Apr. 12, 1955 | | | | | |
| 1977-78 | Detroit | 80 | 19 | 23 | 42 |
| 1978-79 | Detroit | 80 | 14 | 23 | 37 |
| 1979-80 | Detroit | 79 | 6 | 20 | 26 |
| 1980-81 | Detroit | 67 | 8 | 16 | 24 |
| 1981-82 | Detroit | 75 | 10 | 17 | 27 |
| 1982-83 | Detroit | 63 | 13 | 20 | 33 |
| | **Totals** | 444 | 70 | 119 | 189 |
| **WOYTOWICH, Robert Ivan** *Defenseman* | | | | | |
| b. Winnipeg, Man., Aug. 18, 1941 | | | | | |
| 1964-65 | Boston | 21 | 2 | 10 | 12 |
| 1965-66 | Boston | 68 | 2 | 17 | 19 |
| 1966-67 | Boston | 64 | 2 | 7 | 9 |
| 1967-68 | Minnesota | 66 | 4 | 17 | 21 |
| 1968-69 | Pittsburgh | 71 | 9 | 20 | 29 |
| 1969-70 | Pittsburgh | 68 | 8 | 25 | 33 |
| 1970-71 | Pittsburgh | 78 | 4 | 22 | 26 |
| 1971-72 | Pitt-LA | 67 | 1 | 8 | 9 |
| 1972-73 | Winnipeg (WHA) | 62 | 2 | 4 | 6 |
| 1973-74 | Winnipeg (WHA) | 72 | 6 | 28 | 34 |
| 1974-75 | Winn-Ind (WHA) | 66 | 0 | 12 | 12 |
| | **NHL Totals** | 503 | 32 | 126 | 158 |
| | **WHA Totals** | 200 | 8 | 44 | 52 |
| **WRIGHT, John Gilbert** *Forward* | | | | | |
| b. Toronto, Ont., Nov. 9, 1948 | | | | | |
| 1972-73 | Vancouver | 71 | 10 | 27 | 37 |
| 1973-74 | Van-StL | 52 | 6 | 9 | 15 |
| 1974-75 | Kansas City | 4 | 0 | 0 | 0 |
| | **Totals** | 127 | 16 | 36 | 52 |

| Season | Club | GP | G | A | Pts. |
|---|---|---|---|---|---|
| **WRIGHT, Keith Edward** *Forward* | | | | | |
| b. Newmarket, Ont., Apr. 13, 1944 | | | | | |
| 1967-68 | Philadelphia | 1 | 0 | 0 | 0 |
| **WRIGHT, Larry Dale** *Forward* | | | | | |
| b. Regina, Sask., Oct. 8, 1951 | | | | | |
| 1971-72 | Philadelphia | 27 | 0 | 1 | 1 |
| 1972-73 | Philadelphia | 9 | 0 | 1 | 1 |
| 1974-75 | California | 2 | 0 | 0 | 0 |
| 1975-76 | Philadelphia | 2 | 1 | 0 | 1 |
| 1977-78 | Detroit | 66 | 3 | 6 | 9 |
| | **Totals** | 106 | 4 | 8 | 12 |
| **WYCHERLEY, Ralph (Bus)** *Forward* | | | | | |
| b. Saskatoon, Sask., Feb. 26, 1920 | | | | | |
| 1940-41 | New York A | 25 | 4 | 5 | 9 |
| 1941-42 | Brooklyn | 2 | 0 | 2 | 2 |
| | **Totals** | 27 | 4 | 7 | 11 |
| **WYLIE, Duane Steven** *Forward* | | | | | |
| b. Spokane, Wash., Nov. 10, 1950 | | | | | |
| 1974-75 | Chicago | 6 | 1 | 3 | 4 |
| 1976-77 | Chicago | 8 | 2 | 0 | 2 |
| | **Totals** | 14 | 3 | 3 | 6 |
| **WYLIE, William Vance (Wiggy)** *Forward* | | | | | |
| b. Galt, Ont., July 15, 1928 | | | | | |
| 1950-51 | New York R | 1 | 0 | 0 | 0 |
| **WYROZUB, William Randall (Randy)** *Forward* | | | | | |
| b. Lacombe, Alta., Apr. 8, 1950 | | | | | |
| 1970-71 | Buffalo | 16 | 2 | 2 | 4 |
| 1971-72 | Buffalo | 34 | 3 | 4 | 7 |
| 1972-73 | Buffalo | 45 | 3 | 3 | 6 |
| 1973-74 | Buffalo | 5 | 0 | 1 | 1 |
| 1975-76 | Indianapolis (WHA) | 55 | 11 | 14 | 25 |
| | **NHL Totals** | 100 | 8 | 10 | 18 |
| | **WHA Totals** | 55 | 11 | 14 | 25 |
| **YACKEL, Kenneth James** *Forward* | | | | | |
| b. St. Paul, Minn., Mar. 5, 1932 | | | | | |
| 1958-59 | Boston | 6 | 0 | 0 | 0 |
| **YAREMCHUK, Gary** *Forward* | | | | | |
| b. Edmonton, Alta., Aug. 15, 1961 | | | | | |
| 1981-82 | Toronto | 18 | 0 | 3 | 3 |
| 1982-83 | Toronto | 3 | 0 | 0 | 0 |
| | **Totals** | 21 | 0 | 3 | 3 |
| **YOUNG, Brian Donald** *Defenseman* | | | | | |
| b. Jasper, Alta., Oct. 2, 1958 | | | | | |
| 1980-81 | Chicago | 8 | 0 | 2 | 2 |
| **YOUNG, Douglas** *Defenseman* | | | | | |
| b. Medicine Hat, Alta., Oct. 1, 1908 | | | | | |
| 1931-32 | Detroit | 47 | 10 | 2 | 12 |
| 1932-33 | Detroit | 48 | 5 | 6 | 11 |
| 1933-34 | Detroit | 47 | 4 | 0 | 4 |
| 1934-35 | Detroit | 48 | 4 | 6 | 10 |
| 1935-36 | Detroit | 47 | 5 | 12 | 17 |
| 1936-37 | Detroit | 11 | 0 | 0 | 0 |
| 1937-38 | Detroit | 48 | 3 | 5 | 8 |
| 1938-39 | Detroit | 42 | 1 | 5 | 6 |
| 1939-40 | Montreal | 47 | 3 | 9 | 12 |
| 1940-41 | Montreal | 3 | 0 | 0 | 0 |
| | **Totals** | 388 | 35 | 45 | 80 |
| **YOUNG, Howard John Edward** *Defenseman* | | | | | |
| b. Toronto, Ont., Aug. 2, 1937 | | | | | |
| 1960-61 | Detroit | 29 | 0 | 8 | 8 |
| 1961-62 | Detroit | 31 | 0 | 2 | 2 |
| 1962-63 | Detroit | 64 | 4 | 5 | 9 |
| 1963-64 | Chicago | 39 | 0 | 7 | 7 |
| 1966-67 | Detroit | 44 | 3 | 14 | 17 |
| 1967-68 | Detroit | 62 | 2 | 17 | 19 |
| 1968-69 | Chicago | 57 | 3 | 7 | 10 |
| 1974-75 | Phoe-Winn (WHA) | 72 | 16 | 22 | 38 |
| | **NHL Totals** | 326 | 12 | 60 | 72 |
| | **WHA Totals** | 72 | 16 | 22 | 38 |

**YOUNG, Timothy Michael**  *Forward*
b. Scarborough, Ont., Feb. 22, 1955

| Season | Club | GP | G | A | Pts. |
|---|---|---|---|---|---|
| 1975-76 | Minnesota | 63 | 18 | 33 | 51 |
| 1976-77 | Minnesota | 80 | 29 | 66 | 95 |
| 1977-78 | Minnesota | 78 | 23 | 35 | 58 |
| 1978-79 | Minnesota | 73 | 24 | 32 | 56 |
| 1979-80 | Minnesota | 77 | 31 | 43 | 74 |
| 1980-81 | Minnesota | 74 | 25 | 41 | 66 |
| 1981-82 | Minnesota | 49 | 10 | 31 | 41 |
| 1982-83 | Minnesota | 70 | 18 | 35 | 53 |
| | **Totals** | 564 | 178 | 316 | 484 |

**YOUNG, Warren**  *Forward*
b. Toronto, Ont., Jan. 11, 1956

| Season | Club | GP | G | A | Pts. |
|---|---|---|---|---|---|
| 1981-82 | Minnesota | 1 | 0 | 0 | 0 |
| 1982-83 | Minnesota | 4 | 1 | 1 | 2 |
| | **Totals** | 5 | 1 | 1 | 2 |

**YOUNGHANS, Thomas A.**  *Forward*
b. St. Paul, Minn., Jan. 22, 1953

| Season | Club | GP | G | A | Pts. |
|---|---|---|---|---|---|
| 1976-77 | Minnesota | 78 | 8 | 6 | 14 |
| 1977-78 | Minnesota | 72 | 10 | 8 | 18 |
| 1978-79 | Minnesota | 76 | 8 | 10 | 18 |
| 1979-80 | Minnesota | 79 | 10 | 6 | 16 |
| 1980-81 | Minnesota | 74 | 4 | 6 | 10 |
| 1981-82 | Minn-NYR | 50 | 4 | 5 | 9 |
| | **Totals** | 429 | 44 | 41 | 85 |

**ZAHARKO, Miles**  *Defenseman*
b. Mannville, Alta., Apr. 30, 1957

| Season | Club | GP | G | A | Pts. |
|---|---|---|---|---|---|
| 1977-78 | Atlanta | 71 | 1 | 19 | 20 |
| 1978-79 | Chicago | 1 | 0 | 0 | 0 |

**ZAINE, Rodney Carl (Rod)**  *Forwrd*
b. Ottawa, Ont., May 18, 1946

| Season | Club | GP | G | A | Pts. |
|---|---|---|---|---|---|
| 1970-71 | Pittsburgh | 37 | 8 | 5 | 13 |
| 1971-72 | Buffalo | 24 | 2 | 1 | 3 |
| 1972-73 | Chicago (WHA) | 74 | 3 | 14 | 17 |
| 1973-74 | Chicago (WHA) | 77 | 5 | 13 | 18 |
| 1974-75 | Chicago (WHA) | 68 | 3 | 6 | 9 |
| | **NHL Totals** | 61 | 10 | 6 | 16 |
| | **WHA Totals** | 219 | 11 | 33 | 44 |

**ZANUSSI, Ronald Kenneth**  *Forward*
b. Toronto, Ont., Aug. 31, 1956

| Season | Club | GP | G | A | Pts. |
|---|---|---|---|---|---|
| 1977-78 | Minnesota | 68 | 15 | 17 | 32 |
| 1978-79 | Minnesota | 63 | 14 | 16 | 30 |
| 1979-80 | Minnesota | 72 | 14 | 31 | 45 |
| 1980-81 | Minn-Tor | 53 | 9 | 11 | 20 |
| 1981-82 | Toronto | 43 | 0 | 8 | 8 |
| | **Totals** | 299 | 52 | 83 | 135 |

**ZANUSSI, Joseph Lawrence**  *Defenseman*
b. Rossland, B.C., Sept. 25, 1947

| Season | Club | GP | G | A | Pts. |
|---|---|---|---|---|---|
| 1972-73 | Winnipeg (WHA) | 73 | 4 | 21 | 25 |
| 1973-74 | Winnipeg (WHA) | 76 | 3 | 22 | 25 |
| 1974-75 | New York R | 8 | 0 | 2 | 2 |
| 1975-76 | Boston | 60 | 1 | 7 | 8 |
| 1976-77 | Bos-StL | 19 | 0 | 4 | 4 |
| | **NHL Totals** | 87 | 1 | 13 | 14 |
| | **WHA Totals** | 149 | 7 | 43 | 50 |

**ZEIDEL, Lawrence**  *Defenseman*
b. Montreal, Que., June 1, 1928

| Season | Club | GP | G | A | Pts. |
|---|---|---|---|---|---|
| 1951-52 | Detroit | 19 | 1 | 0 | 1 |
| 1952-53 | Detroit | 9 | 0 | 0 | 0 |
| 1953-54 | Chicago | 64 | 1 | 6 | 7 |
| 1967-68 | Philadelphia | 57 | 1 | 10 | 11 |
| 1968-69 | Philadelphia | 9 | 0 | 0 | 0 |
| | **Totals** | 158 | 3 | 16 | 19 |

**ZENIUK, Edward**  *Defenseman*
b. Landis, Sask., Mar. 8, 1933

| Season | Club | GP | G | A | Pts. |
|---|---|---|---|---|---|
| 1954-55 | Detroit | 2 | 0 | 0 | 0 |

**ZETTERSTROM, Lars**  *Defenseman*
b. Stockholm, Sweden, Nov. 6, 1953

| Season | Club | GP | G | A | Pts. |
|---|---|---|---|---|---|
| 1978-79 | Vancouver | 14 | 0 | 1 | 1 |

**ZOBROSKY, Martin**

| Season | Club | GP | G | A | Pts. |
|---|---|---|---|---|---|
| 1944-45 | Chicago | 1 | 0 | 0 | 0 |

**ZUKE, Michael**  *Forward*
b. Sault Ste. Marie, Ont., Apr. 16, 1954

| Season | Club | GP | G | A | Pts. |
|---|---|---|---|---|---|
| 1976-77 | Indianapolis (WHA) | 15 | 3 | 4 | 7 |
| 1977-78 | Edmonton (WHA) | 71 | 23 | 34 | 57 |
| 1978-79 | St Louis | 34 | 9 | 17 | 26 |
| 1979-80 | St Louis | 69 | 22 | 42 | 64 |
| 1980-81 | St Louis | 74 | 24 | 44 | 68 |
| 1981-82 | St Louis | 76 | 13 | 40 | 53 |
| 1982-83 | St Louis | 43 | 8 | 16 | 24 |
| | **NHL Totals** | 296 | 76 | 159 | 235 |
| | **WHA Totals** | 86 | 26 | 38 | 64 |

**ZUNICH, Ralph (Ricky)**  *Defenseman*
b. Calumet, Mich., Nov. 24, 1910

| Season | Club | GP | G | A | Pts. |
|---|---|---|---|---|---|
| 1943-44 | Detroit | 2 | 0 | 0 | 0 |

| Season | Club | GP | G | A | Pts. |
|---|---|---|---|---|---|
| 1980-81 | Chicago | 42 | 3 | 11 | 14 |
| 1981-82 | Chicago | 15 | 1 | 2 | 3 |
| | **Totals** | 129 | 5 | 32 | 37 |

# GOALIES

| Season | Club | GP | GA | SO | Avg. |
|---|---|---|---|---|---|
| **ABBOT, George** | | | | | |
| 1943-44 | Boston | 1 | 7 | 0 | 7.00 |
| **ADAMS, John Matthew** | | | | | |
| b. Port Arthur, Ont., July 27, 1946 | | | | | |
| 1972-73 | Boston | 14 | 39 | 1 | 3.00 |
| 1974-75 | Washington | 8 | 46 | 0 | 6.90 |
| | **Totals** | 22 | 85 | 1 | 4.32 |
| **AIKEN, John** | | | | | |
| b. Arlington, Mass., Jan. 1, 1932 | | | | | |
| 1957-58 | Montreal | 1 | 6 | 0 | 6.00 |
| **AITKENHEAD, Andrew** | | | | | |
| b. Glasgow, Scotland, Mar. 6, 1904 | | | | | |
| 1932-33 | New York R | 48 | 107 | 3 | 2.23 |
| 1933-34 | New York R | 48 | 113 | 7 | 2.35 |
| 1934-35 | New York R | 10 | 37 | 1 | 3.70 |
| | **Totals** | 106 | 257 | 11 | 2.42 |
| **ALMAS, Ralph Clayton (Red)** | | | | | |
| b. Saskatoon, Sask., April, 26, 1924 | | | | | |
| 1946-47 | Detroit | 1 | 5 | 0 | 5.00 |
| 1950-51 | Chicago | 1 | 5 | 0 | 5.00 |
| 1952-53 | Detroit | 1 | 3 | 0 | 3.00 |
| | **Totals** | 3 | 13 | 0 | 4.33 |
| **ANDERSON, Lawrence Lorne** | | | | | |
| b. Renfrew, Ont., July 26, 1931 | | | | | |
| 1951-52 | New York R | 3 | 18 | 0 | 6.00 |
| **ASTROM, Hardy** | | | | | |
| b. Skelleftea, Sweden, Mar. 29, 1951 | | | | | |
| 1977-78 | New York R | 4 | 14 | 0 | 3.50 |
| 1979-80 | Colorado | 49 | 161 | 0 | 3.75 |
| 1980-81 | Colorado | 30 | 102 | 0 | 3.76 |
| | **Totals** | 83 | 277 | 0 | 3.73 |
| **BAKER, Steven** | | | | | |
| b. Boston, Mass., May 6, 1957 | | | | | |
| 1979-80 | New York R | 27 | 79 | 1 | 3.41 |
| 1980-81 | New York R | 21 | 73 | 2 | 3.48 |
| 1981-82 | New York R | 6 | 33 | 0 | 6.03 |
| 1982-83 | New York R | 3 | 5 | 0 | 2.94 |
| | **Totals** | 57 | 190 | 3 | 3.70 |
| **BANNERMAN, Murray** | | | | | |
| b. Fort Francis, Ont., Apr. 27, 1957 | | | | | |
| 1977-78 | Vancouver | 1 | 0 | 0 | 0.00 |
| 1980-81 | Chicago | 15 | 62 | 0 | 4.30 |
| 1981-82 | Chicago | 29 | 116 | 1 | 4.17 |
| 1982-83 | Chicago | 41 | 127 | 4 | 3.10 |
| | **Totals** | 86 | 305 | 1 | 3.65 |
| **BARON, Marco Joseph** | | | | | |
| b. Montreal, Que., Apr. 8, 1959 | | | | | |
| 1979-80 | Boston | 1 | 2 | 0 | 3.00 |
| 1980-81 | Boston | 10 | 24 | 0 | 2.84 |
| 1981-82 | Boston | 44 | 144 | 1 | 3.44 |
| 1982-83 | Boston | 9 | 33 | 0 | 3.84 |
| | **Totals** | 64 | 203 | 1 | 3.41 |

| Season | Club | GP | GA | SO | Avg. |
|---|---|---|---|---|---|
| **BASSEN, Henry (Hank)** | | | | | |
| b. Calgary, Alta., Dec. 6, 1932 | | | | | |
| 1954-55 | Chicago | 21 | 63 | 0 | 3.00 |
| 1955-56 | Chicago | 12 | 42 | 1 | 3.50 |
| 1960-61 | Detroit | 35 | 102 | 0 | 2.97 |
| 1961-62 | Detroit | 27 | 76 | 3 | 2.81 |
| 1962-63 | Detroit | 17 | 53 | 0 | 3.18 |
| 1963-64 | Detroit | 1 | 4 | 0 | 4.00 |
| 1965-66 | Detroit | 7 | 17 | 0 | 2.55 |
| 1966-67 | Detroit | 7 | 22 | 0 | 3.30 |
| 1967-68 | Pittsburgh | 22 | 62 | 1 | 2.82 |
| | **Totals** | 149 | 441 | 5 | 2.97 |
| **BASTIEN, Aldege (Baz)** | | | | | |
| b. Timmins, Ont., Aug. 29, 1920 | | | | | |
| 1945-46 | Toronto | 5 | 20 | 0 | 4.00 |
| **BAUMAN, Garry Glenwood** | | | | | |
| b. Innisfail, Alta., July 21, 1940 | | | | | |
| 1966-67 | Montreal | 2 | 5 | 0 | 2.50 |
| 1967-68 | Minnesota | 22 | 75 | 0 | 3.41 |
| 1968-69 | Minnesota | 5 | 22 | 0 | 4.40 |
| | **Totals** | 29 | 102 | 0 | 3.52 |
| **BEAUPRE, Donald William** | | | | | |
| b. Waterloo, Ont., Sept. 19, 1961 | | | | | |
| 1980-81 | Minnesota | 44 | 138 | 0 | 3.20 |
| 1981-82 | Minnesota | 29 | 101 | 0 | 3.71 |
| 1982-83 | Minnesota | 36 | 120 | 0 | 3.58 |
| | **Totals** | 109 | 359 | 0 | 3.46 |
| **BEDARD, James Arthur** | | | | | |
| b. Niagara Falls, Ont., Nov. 14, 1956 | | | | | |
| 1977-78 | Washington | 43 | 152 | 1 | 3.66 |
| 1978-79 | Washington | 30 | 126 | 0 | 4.34 |
| | **Totals** | 73 | 278 | 1 | 3.94 |
| **BELANGER, Yves** | | | | | |
| b. Baie Comeau, Que., Sept. 30, 1952 | | | | | |
| 1974-75 | St Louis | 11 | 29 | 1 | 2.72 |
| 1975-76 | St Louis | 31 | 113 | 0 | 3.85 |
| 1976-77 | St Louis | 3 | 7 | 0 | 3.00 |
| 1977-78 | StL-Atl | 20 | 70 | 1 | 3.89 |
| 1978-79 | Atlanta | 5 | 21 | 0 | 6.92 |
| 1979-80 | Boston | 8 | 19 | 0 | 3.48 |
| | **Totals** | 78 | 259 | 2 | 3.76 |
| **BELHUMEUR, Michel** | | | | | |
| b. Sorel, Que., Sept. 2, 1949 | | | | | |
| 1972-73 | Philadelphia | 23 | 60 | 0 | 3.22 |
| 1974-75 | Washington | 35 | 162 | 0 | 5.36 |
| 1975-76 | Washington | 7 | 32 | 0 | 5.09 |
| | **Totals** | 65 | 254 | 0 | 4.61 |
| **BELL, Gordon** | | | | | |
| b. Portage la Prairie, Man., Mar. 13, 1925 | | | | | |
| 1945-46 | Toronto | 8 | 31 | 0 | 3.87 |
| **BENEDICT, Clinton (Benny)** | | | | | |
| b. Ottawa, Ont., 1891 | | | | | |
| 1917-18 | Ottawa | 22 | 114 | 1 | 5.18 |
| 1918-19 | Ottawa | 18 | 53 | 2 | 2.94 |

| Season | Club | GP | GA | SO | Avg. |
|---|---|---|---|---|---|
| 1919-20 | Ottawa | 24 | 68 | 5 | 2.67 |
| 1920-21 | Ottawa | 24 | 75 | 2 | 3.13 |
| 1921-22 | Ottawa | 24 | 84 | 2 | 3.50 |
| 1922-23 | Ottawa | 24 | 54 | 4 | 2.25 |
| 1923-24 | Ottawa | 22 | 45 | 3 | 2.04 |
| 1924-25 | Montreal M | 30 | 65 | 2 | 2.17 |
| 1925-26 | Montreal M | 36 | 73 | 6 | 2.03 |
| 1926-27 | Montreal M | 44 | 68 | 13 | 1.54 |
| 1927-28 | Montreal M | 44 | 77 | 6 | 1.75 |
| 1928-29 | Montreal M | 37 | 57 | 11 | 1.54 |
| 1929-30 | Montreal M | 15 | 41 | 0 | 2.73 |
| | **Totals** | 364 | 874 | 57 | 2.37 |
| **BENNETT, Harvey A.** | | | | | |
| b. Edington, Sask., July 23, 1925 | | | | | |
| 1944-45 | Boston | 24 | 103 | 0 | 4.29 |
| **BERNHARDT, Tim** | | | | | |
| b. Sarnia, Ont., Apr. 19, 1958 | | | | | |
| 1982-83 | Calgary | 6 | 21 | 0 | 4.50 |
| **BEVERIDGE, William S.** | | | | | |
| b. Ottawa, Ont., July 1, 1909 | | | | | |
| 1929-30 | Detroit | 39 | 114 | 2 | 2.92 |
| 1930-31 | Ottawa | 8 | 32 | 0 | 4.00 |
| 1932-33 | Ottawa | 35 | 95 | 5 | 2.71 |
| 1933-34 | Ottawa | 48 | 143 | 3 | 2.98 |
| 1934-35 | St Louis E | 48 | 144 | 2 | 3.00 |
| 1935-36 | Montreal M | 32 | 71 | 1 | 2.22 |
| 1936-37 | Montreal M | 21 | 46 | 1 | 2.19 |
| 1937-38 | Montreal M | 48 | 149 | 2 | 3.10 |
| 1942-43 | New York R | 17 | 89 | 1 | 5.24 |
| | **Totals** | 296 | 883 | 17 | 2.98 |
| **BIBEAULT, Paul** | | | | | |
| b. Montreal, Que., Apr. 13, 1919 | | | | | |
| 1940-41 | Montreal | 4 | 15 | 0 | 3.75 |
| 1941-42 | Montreal | 38 | 131 | 1 | 3.47 |
| 1942-43 | Montreal | 50 | 191 | 1 | 3.82 |
| 1943-44 | Toronto | 29 | 87 | 5 | 3.00 |
| 1944-45 | Boston | 26 | 116 | 0 | 4.46 |
| 1945-46 | Bos-Mont | 26 | 75 | 2 | 2.88 |
| 1946-47 | Chicago | 41 | 170 | 1 | 4.14 |
| | **Totals** | 214 | 785 | 10 | 3.67 |
| **BINETTE, Andre** | | | | | |
| b. Montreal, Que., Dec. 2, 1933 | | | | | |
| 1954-55 | Montreal | 1 | 4 | 0 | 4.00 |
| **BINKLEY, Leslie John (Les)** | | | | | |
| b. Owen Sound, Ont., June 6, 1936 | | | | | |
| 1967-68 | Pittsburgh | 54 | 151 | 6 | 2.88 |
| 1968-69 | Pittsburgh | 50 | 158 | 0 | 3.29 |
| 1969-70 | Pittsburgh | 27 | 79 | 3 | 3.22 |
| 1970-71 | Pittsburgh | 34 | 89 | 2 | 2.85 |
| 1971-72 | Pittsburgh | 31 | 98 | 0 | 3.51 |
| 1972-73 | Ottawa (WHA) | 30 | 106 | 0 | 3.72 |
| 1973-74 | Toronto (WHA) | 27 | 77 | 1 | 3.27 |
| 1974-75 | Toronto (WHA) | 17 | 47 | 0 | 3.65 |
| 1975-76 | Toronto (WHA) | 7 | 32 | 0 | 5.73 |
| | **NHL Totals** | 196 | 575 | 11 | 3.12 |
| | **WHA Totals** | 81 | 262 | 1 | 3.72 |

| Season | Club | GP | GA | SO | Avg. |
|---|---|---|---|---|---|
| **BITTNER, Richard J.** | | | | | |
| b. New Haven, Conn., Jan. 12, 1922 | | | | | |
| 1949-50 | Boston | 1 | 3 | 0 | 3.00 |
| | | | | | |
| **BLAKE, Michael W.** | | | | | |
| b. Kitchener, Ont., Apr. 6, 1956 | | | | | |
| 1981-82 | Los Angeles | 2 | 2 | 0 | 2.35 |
| 1982-83 | Los Angeles | 9 | 30 | 0 | 4.17 |
| | **Totals** | 11 | 32 | 0 | 3.98 |
| | | | | | |
| **BOISVERT, Gilles** | | | | | |
| b. Trois-Rivières, Que., Feb. 15, 1933 | | | | | |
| 1959-60 | Detroit | 3 | 9 | 0 | 3.00 |
| | | | | | |
| **BOUCHARD, Daniel Hector** | | | | | |
| b. Val d'Or, Que., Dec. 12, 1950 | | | | | |
| 1972-73 | Atlanta | 34 | 100 | 2 | 3.09 |
| 1973-74 | Atlanta | 46 | 123 | 5 | 2.77 |
| 1974-75 | Atlanta | 40 | 111 | 3 | 2.77 |
| 1975-76 | Atlanta | 47 | 113 | 2 | 2.54 |
| 1976-77 | Atlanta | 42 | 139 | 1 | 3.51 |
| 1977-78 | Atlanta | 58 | 153 | 2 | 2.75 |
| 1978-79 | Atlanta | 64 | 201 | 4 | 3.33 |
| 1979-80 | Atlanta | 53 | 163 | 4 | 3.18 |
| 1980-81 | Calg-Que | 43 | 143 | 2 | 3.43 |
| 1981-82 | Quebec | 60 | 230 | 1 | 3.86 |
| 1982-83 | Quebec | 50 | 197 | 1 | 4.01 |
| | **Totals** | 537 | 1673 | 24 | 3.23 |
| | | | | | |
| **BOURQUE, Claude Hennessey** | | | | | |
| b. Oxford, N.S., Mar. 31, 1915 | | | | | |
| 1938-39 | Montreal | 25 | 69 | 2 | 2.76 |
| 1939-40 | Mont-Det | 37 | 123 | 3 | 3.32 |
| | **Totals** | 62 | 192 | 5 | 3.10 |
| | | | | | |
| **BOUTIN, Roland** | | | | | |
| b. Westlock, Alta., Nov. 6, 1957 | | | | | |
| 1978-79 | Washington | 2 | 10 | 0 | 6.67 |
| 1979-80 | Washington | 18 | 54 | 0 | 3.50 |
| 1980-81 | Washington | 2 | 11 | 0 | 5.50 |
| | **Totals** | 22 | 75 | 0 | 3.96 |
| | | | | | |
| **BOUVRETTE, Lionel** | | | | | |
| b. Hawsbury, Ont., June 10, 1914 | | | | | |
| 1942-43 | New York R | 1 | 6 | 0 | 6.00 |
| | | | | | |
| **BOWER, John William (China Wall)** | | | | | |
| b. Prince Albert, Sask., Nov. 8, 1924 | | | | | |
| 1953-54 | New York R | 70 | 182 | 5 | 2.60 |
| 1954-55 | New York R | 5 | 13 | 0 | 2.60 |
| 1956-57 | New York R | 2 | 7 | 0 | 3.50 |
| 1958-59 | Toronto | 39 | 107 | 3 | 2.74 |
| 1959-60 | Toronto | 66 | 180 | 5 | 2.73 |
| 1960-61 | Toronto | 58 | 145 | 2 | 2.50 |
| 1961-62 | Toronto | 59 | 152 | 2 | 2.58 |
| 1962-63 | Toronto | 42 | 110 | 1 | 2.62 |
| 1963-64 | Toronto | 50 | 106 | 5 | 2.12 |
| 1964-65 | Toronto | 34 | 81 | 3 | 2.38 |
| 1965-66 | Toronto | 34 | 75 | 3 | 2.25 |
| 1966-67 | Toronto | 24 | 63 | 2 | 2.63 |
| 1967-68 | Toronto | 38 | 84 | 4 | 2.25 |
| 1968-69 | Toronto | 13 | 37 | 2 | 2.85 |
| 1969-70 | Toronto | 1 | 5 | 0 | 5.00 |
| | **Totals** | 535 | 1347 | 37 | 2.53 |
| | | | | | |
| **BRIMSEK, Francis Charles (Mr. Zero)** | | | | | |
| b. Eveleth, Minn., Sept. 26, 1915 | | | | | |
| 1938-39 | Boston | 43 | 69 | 10 | 1.60 |
| 1939-40 | Boston | 48 | 98 | 6 | 2.04 |
| 1940-41 | Boston | 48 | 102 | 6 | 2.12 |
| 1941-42 | Boston | 47 | 112 | 3 | 2.38 |
| 1942-43 | Boston | 50 | 176 | 1 | 3.52 |
| 1945-46 | Boston | 34 | 111 | 2 | 3.26 |
| 1946-47 | Boston | 60 | 175 | 3 | 2.91 |
| 1947-48 | Boston | 60 | 168 | 3 | 2.82 |
| 1948-49 | Boston | 54 | 147 | 1 | 2.72 |
| 1949-50 | Chicago | 70 | 244 | 5 | 3.48 |
| | **Totals** | 478 | 1402 | 40 | 2.94 |
| | | | | | |
| **BRODA, Walter (Turk)** | | | | | |
| b. Brandon, Man., May 15, 1914 | | | | | |
| 1936-37 | Toronto | 45 | 106 | 3 | 2.35 |
| 1937-38 | Toronto | 48 | 127 | 6 | 2.64 |
| 1938-39 | Toronto | 48 | 107 | 8 | 2.23 |
| 1939-40 | Toronto | 47 | 108 | 4 | 2.30 |
| 1940-41 | Toronto | 48 | 99 | 4 | 2.06 |
| 1941-42 | Toronto | 48 | 136 | 6 | 2.83 |
| 1942-43 | Toronto | 50 | 159 | 1 | 3.18 |
| 1945-46 | Toronto | 15 | 53 | 0 | 3.53 |
| 1946-47 | Toronto | 60 | 172 | 4 | 2.86 |
| 1947-48 | Toronto | 60 | 143 | 5 | 2.38 |
| 1948-49 | Toronto | 60 | 161 | 5 | 2.68 |
| 1949-50 | Toronto | 68 | 167 | 9 | 2.45 |
| 1950-51 | Toronto | 31 | 68 | 6 | 2.19 |
| 1951-52 | Toronto | 1 | 3 | 0 | 3.00 |
| | **Totals** | 630 | 1611 | 61 | 2.56 |
| | | | | | |
| **BRODERICK, Kenneth Lorne** | | | | | |
| b. Toronto, Ont., Feb. 16, 1942 | | | | | |
| 1969-70 | Minnesota | 7 | 26 | 0 | 4.33 |
| 1973-74 | Boston | 5 | 16 | 0 | 3.20 |
| 1974-75 | Boston | 15 | 32 | 1 | 2.39 |
| 1976-77 | Edmonton (WHA) | 40 | 134 | 4 | 3.49 |
| 1977-78 | Edm-Que (WHA) | 32 | 125 | 0 | 4.41 |
| | **NHL Totals** | 27 | 74 | 1 | 3.03 |
| | **WHA Totals** | 72 | 259 | 4 | 3.88 |
| | | | | | |
| **BRODERICK, Len** | | | | | |
| b. Toronto, Ont., Oct. 11, 1930 | | | | | |
| 1957-58 | Montreal | 1 | 2 | 0 | 2.00 |
| | | | | | |
| **BRODEUR, Richard** | | | | | |
| b. Longeuil, Que., Sept. 15, 1952 | | | | | |
| 1972-73 | Quebec (WHA) | 24 | 102 | 0 | 4.75 |
| 1973-74 | Quebec (WHA) | 30 | 89 | 1 | 3.32 |
| 1974-75 | Quebec (WHA) | 51 | 188 | 0 | 3.84 |
| 1975-76 | Quebec (WHA) | 69 | 244 | 2 | 3.69 |
| 1976-77 | Quebec (WHA) | 53 | 167 | 2 | 3.45 |
| 1977-78 | Quebec (WHA) | 36 | 121 | 0 | 3.70 |
| 1978-79 | Quebec (WHA) | 42 | 126 | 3 | 3.11 |
| 1979-80 | New York I | 2 | 6 | 0 | 4.50 |
| 1980-81 | Vancouver | 52 | 177 | 0 | 3.51 |
| 1981-82 | Vancouver | 52 | 168 | 2 | 3.35 |
| 1982-83 | Vancouver | 58 | 208 | 0 | 3.79 |
| | **NHL Totals** | 164 | 559 | 2 | 3.57 |
| | **WHA Totals** | 305 | 1037 | 8 | 3.64 |
| | | | | | |
| **BROMLEY, Gary Bert** | | | | | |
| b. Edmonton, Alta., Jan. 19, 1950 | | | | | |
| 1973-74 | Buffalo | 12 | 33 | 0 | 3.31 |
| 1974-75 | Buffalo | 50 | 144 | 4 | 3.10 |
| 1975-76 | Buffalo | 1 | 7 | 0 | 7.00 |
| 1976-77 | Calgary (WHA) | 28 | 79 | 0 | 3.83 |
| 1977-78 | Winnipeg (WHA) | 39 | 124 | 1 | 3.30 |
| 1978-79 | Vancouver | 38 | 136 | 2 | 3.81 |
| 1979-80 | Vancouver | 15 | 43 | 1 | 3.00 |
| 1980-81 | Vancouver | 20 | 62 | 0 | 3.80 |
| | **NHL Totals** | 136 | 425 | 7 | 3.43 |
| | **WHA Totals** | 67 | 205 | 1 | 3.53 |
| | | | | | |
| **BROOKS, Arthur** | | | | | |
| 1917-18 | Toronto | 3 | 18 | 0 | 6.00 |
| | | | | | |
| **BROOKS, Donald Ross** | | | | | |
| b. Toronto, Ont., Oct. 17, 1937 | | | | | |
| 1972-73 | Boston | 16 | 40 | 1 | 2.64 |
| 1973-74 | Boston | 21 | 46 | 3 | 2.36 |
| 1974-75 | Boston | 17 | 48 | 0 | 2.98 |
| | **Totals** | 54 | 134 | 4 | 2.64 |
| | | | | | |
| **BROPHY, Frank** | | | | | |
| 1919-20 | Quebec | 21 | 151 | 0 | 7.18 |
| | | | | | |
| **BROWN, Andrew Conrad (Andy)** | | | | | |
| b. Hamilton, Ont., Feb. 15, 1944 | | | | | |
| 1971-72 | Detroit | 10 | 37 | 0 | 3.96 |
| 1972-73 | Det-Pitt | 16 | 61 | 0 | 4.27 |
| 1973-74 | Pittsburgh | 36 | 115 | 1 | 3.53 |
| 1974-75 | Indianapolis (WHA) | 52 | 206 | 2 | 4.15 |
| 1975-76 | Indianapolis (WHA) | 24 | 82 | 1 | 3.60 |
| 1976-77 | Indianapolis (WHA) | 10 | 26 | 0 | 3.63 |
| | **NHL Totals** | 62 | 213 | 1 | 3.79 |
| | **WHA Totals** | 86 | 314 | 3 | 3.95 |
| | | | | | |
| **BROWN, Kenneth Murray (Ken)** | | | | | |
| b. Port Arthur, Ont., Dec. 19, 1948 | | | | | |
| 1970-71 | Chicago | 1 | 1 | 0 | 3.33 |
| 1972-73 | Alberta (WHA) | 20 | 63 | 1 | 3.65 |
| 1974-75 | Edmonton (WHA) | 33 | 86 | 2 | 3.47 |
| | **NHL Totals** | 1 | 1 | 0 | 3.33 |
| | **WHA Totals** | 53 | 149 | 3 | 3.54 |
| | | | | | |
| **BULLOCK, Bruce John** | | | | | |
| b. Toronto, Ont., May 9, 1949 | | | | | |
| 1972-73 | Vancouver | 14 | 67 | 0 | 4.79 |
| 1974-75 | Vancouver | 1 | 4 | 0 | 4.00 |
| 1976-77 | Vancouver | 1 | 3 | 0 | 6.67 |
| | **Totals** | 16 | 74 | 0 | 4.79 |
| | | | | | |
| **BUZINSKI, Stephen** | | | | | |
| b. Dunblane, Sask., Oct. 15, 1917 | | | | | |
| 1942-43 | New York R | 9 | 55 | 0 | 6.11 |
| | | | | | |
| **CALEY, Donald Thomas** | | | | | |
| b. Dauphin, Man., Oct. 9, 1945 | | | | | |
| 1967-68 | St Louis | 1 | 3 | 0 | 6.00 |
| | | | | | |
| **CAPRICE, Frank** | | | | | |
| b. Hamilton, Ont., May 2, 1962 | | | | | |
| 1982-83 | Vancouver | 1 | 3 | 0 | 9.00 |
| | | | | | |
| **CARON, Jacques Joseph** | | | | | |
| b. Noranda, Que., Apr. 21, 1939 | | | | | |
| 1967-68 | Los Angeles | 1 | 4 | 0 | 4.00 |
| 1968-69 | Los Angeles | 3 | 9 | 0 | 3.86 |
| 1971-72 | St Louis | 28 | 68 | 1 | 2.52 |
| 1972-73 | St Louis | 30 | 92 | 1 | 3.53 |
| 1973-74 | Vancouver | 10 | 38 | 0 | 4.90 |
| 1975-76 | Cleveland (WHA) | 2 | 8 | 0 | 3.69 |
| 1976-77 | Cincinnati (WHA) | 24 | 62 | 3 | 2.83 |
| | **NHL Totals** | 72 | 211 | 2 | 3.29 |
| | **WHA Totals** | 26 | 70 | 3 | 2.91 |
| | | | | | |
| **CARTER, Lyle Dwight** | | | | | |
| b. Truro, N.S., Apr. 29, 1945 | | | | | |
| 1971-72 | California | 12 | 50 | 0 | 4.16 |
| | | | | | |
| **CHABOT, Lorne** | | | | | |
| b. Montreal, Que., Oct. 5, 1900 | | | | | |
| 1926-27 | New York R | 36 | 56 | 10 | 1.56 |
| 1927-28 | New York R | 44 | 79 | 11 | 1.80 |
| 1928-29 | Toronto | 43 | 67 | 12 | 1.56 |
| 1929-30 | Toronto | 41 | 110 | 6 | 2.68 |
| 1930-31 | Toronto | 37 | 80 | 6 | 2.16 |
| 1931-32 | Toronto | 44 | 109 | 4 | 2.48 |
| 1932-33 | Toronto | 48 | 111 | 5 | 2.31 |
| 1933-34 | Montreal | 47 | 101 | 8 | 2.15 |
| 1934-35 | Chicago | 48 | 88 | 8 | 1.83 |
| 1935-36 | Montreal M | 16 | 35 | 2 | 2.19 |
| 1936-37 | New York A | 6 | 25 | 1 | 4.17 |
| | **Totals** | 410 | 861 | 73 | 2.10 |
| | | | | | |
| **CHADWICK, Edwin Walter** | | | | | |
| b. Fergus, Ont., May 8, 1933 | | | | | |
| 1955-56 | Toronto | 5 | 3 | 2 | 0.60 |
| 1956-57 | Toronto | 70 | 192 | 5 | 2.74 |
| 1957-58 | Toronto | 70 | 226 | 4 | 2.23 |
| 1958-59 | Toronto | 31 | 93 | 3 | 3.00 |
| 1959-60 | Toronto | 4 | 15 | 0 | 3.75 |
| 1961-62 | Boston | 4 | 22 | 0 | 5.50 |
| | **Totals** | 184 | 551 | 14 | 2.99 |

**CHEEVERS, Gerald Michael (Cheesy)**
b. St. Catharines, Ont., Dec. 2, 1940

| Season | Club | GP | GA | SO | Avg. |
|---|---|---|---|---|---|
| 1961-62 | Toronto | 2 | 7 | 0 | 3.50 |
| 1965-66 | Boston | 7 | 34 | 0 | 6.00 |
| 1966-67 | Boston | 22 | 72 | 1 | 3.33 |
| 1967-68 | Boston | 47 | 125 | 3 | 2.83 |
| 1968-69 | Boston | 52 | 145 | 3 | 2.80 |
| 1969-70 | Boston | 41 | 108 | 4 | 2.72 |
| 1970-71 | Boston | 40 | 109 | 3 | 2.72 |
| 1971-72 | Boston | 41 | 101 | 2 | 2.50 |
| 1972-73 | Cleveland (WHA) | 52 | 149 | 5 | 2.83 |
| 1973-74 | Cleveland (WHA) | 59 | 180 | 4 | 3.03 |
| 1974-75 | Cleveland (WHA) | 52 | 167 | 4 | 3.26 |
| 1975-76 | Cleveland (WHA) | 28 | 95 | 1 | 3.58 |
| 1975-76 | Boston | 15 | 41 | 1 | 2.73 |
| 1976-77 | Boston | 45 | 137 | 3 | 3.04 |
| 1977-78 | Boston | 21 | 48 | 1 | 2.65 |
| 1978-79 | Boston | 43 | 132 | 1 | 3.16 |
| 1979-80 | Boston | 42 | 116 | 4 | 2.81 |
| | NHL Totals | 418 | 1175 | 26 | 2.89 |
| | WHA Totals | 191 | 591 | 14 | 3.11 |

**CLEGHORN, Ogilvie (Odie)**
b. Montreal, Que., 1891

| Season | Club | GP | GA | SO | Avg. |
|---|---|---|---|---|---|
| 1925-26 | Pittsburgh Pi | 1 | 2 | 0 | 2.00 |

**CLOUTIER, Jacques**
b. Noranda, Que., Jan. 3, 1960

| Season | Club | GP | GA | SO | Avg. |
|---|---|---|---|---|---|
| 1981-82 | Buffalo | 7 | 13 | 0 | 2.51 |
| 1982-83 | Buffalo | 25 | 81 | 0 | 3.50 |
| | Totals | 32 | 94 | 0 | 3.32 |

**COLVIN, Les**
b. Oshawa, Ont., Feb. 8, 1921

| Season | Club | GP | GA | SO | Avg. |
|---|---|---|---|---|---|
| 1948-49 | Boston | 1 | 4 | 0 | 4.00 |

**CONNELL, Alex (The Ottawa Fireman)**
b. Oshawa, Ont., Feb. 8, 1901

| Season | Club | GP | GA | SO | Avg. |
|---|---|---|---|---|---|
| 1924-25 | Ottawa | 30 | 66 | 7 | 2.20 |
| 1925-26 | Ottawa | 36 | 39 | 16 | 1.08 |
| 1926-27 | Ottawa | 44 | 69 | 13 | 1.57 |
| 1927-28 | Ottawa | 44 | 57 | 15 | 1.30 |
| 1928-29 | Ottawa | 44 | 68 | 7 | 1.55 |
| 1929-30 | Ottawa | 44 | 118 | 3 | 2.68 |
| 1930-31 | Ottawa | 36 | 110 | 3 | 3.06 |
| 1931-32 | Detroit | 48 | 108 | 6 | 2.25 |
| 1932-33 | Ottawa | 44 | 36 | 1 | 2.57 |
| 1933-34 | New York A | 1 | 2 | 0 | 2.00 |
| 1934-35 | Montreal M | 48 | 92 | 9 | 1.92 |
| 1936-37 | Montreal M | 27 | 64 | 2 | 2.37 |
| | Totals | 416 | 829 | 82 | 1.99 |

**CORSI, James**
b. Montreal, Que., June 19, 1954

| Season | Club | GP | GA | SO | Avg. |
|---|---|---|---|---|---|
| 1977-78 | Quebec (WHA) | 23 | 82 | 0 | 4.52 |
| 1978-79 | Quebec (WHA) | 40 | 126 | 3 | 3.30 |
| 1979-80 | Edmonton | 26 | 83 | 0 | 3.65 |
| | NHL Totals | 26 | 83 | 0 | 3.65 |
| | WHA Totals | 63 | 208 | 3 | 3.69 |

**COURTEAU, Maurice Laurent**
b. Quebec City, Que., Feb. 18, 1918

| Season | Club | GP | GA | SO | Avg. |
|---|---|---|---|---|---|
| 1943-44 | Boston | 6 | 33 | 0 | 5.50 |

**COX, Abbie**

| Season | Club | GP | GA | SO | Avg. |
|---|---|---|---|---|---|
| 1929-30 | Montreal M | 1 | 2 | 0 | 2.00 |
| 1933-34 | Det-NYA | 2 | 7 | 0 | 3.50 |
| 1935-36 | Montreal | 1 | 1 | 0 | 1.00 |
| | Totals | 4 | 10 | 0 | 2.50 |

**CRAIG, James**
b. North Easton, Mass., May 31, 1957

| Season | Club | GP | GA | SO | Avg. |
|---|---|---|---|---|---|
| 1979-80 | Atlanta | 4 | 13 | 0 | 3.79 |
| 1980-81 | Boston | 23 | 78 | 0 | 3.68 |
| | Totals | 27 | 91 | 0 | 3.69 |

**CRHA, Jiri**
b. Pardubice, Czechoslovakia, Apr. 13, 1950

| Season | Club | GP | GA | SO | Avg. |
|---|---|---|---|---|---|
| 1979-80 | Toronto | 15 | 50 | 0 | 3.61 |
| 1980-81 | Toronto | 54 | 211 | 0 | 4.07 |
| | Totals | 69 | 261 | 0 | 3.97 |


**CROZIER, Roger Allan**
b. Bracebridge, Ont., Mar. 16, 1942

| Season | Club | GP | GA | SO | Avg. |
|---|---|---|---|---|---|
| 1963-64 | Detroit | 15 | 51 | 2 | 3.40 |
| 1964-65 | Detroit | 70 | 168 | 6 | 2.42 |
| 1965-66 | Detroit | 64 | 173 | 7 | 2.78 |
| 1966-67 | Detroit | 58 | 182 | 4 | 3.35 |
| 1967-68 | Detroit | 34 | 95 | 1 | 3.31 |
| 1968-69 | Detroit | 38 | 101 | 0 | 3.33 |
| 1969-70 | Detroit | 34 | 83 | 0 | 2.65 |
| 1970-71 | Buffalo | 44 | 135 | 1 | 3.68 |
| 1971-72 | Buffalo | 63 | 214 | 2 | 3.51 |
| 1972-73 | Buffalo | 49 | 121 | 3 | 2.76 |
| 1973-74 | Buffalo | 12 | 39 | 0 | 3.80 |
| 1974-75 | Buffalo | 23 | 55 | 3 | 2.62 |
| 1975-76 | Buffalo | 11 | 27 | 1 | 2.61 |
| 1976-77 | Washington | 3 | 2 | 0 | 1.17 |
| | Totals | 518 | 1446 | 30 | 3.04 |

**CUDE, Wilfred**
b. Barry, Wales, July 4, 1910

| Season | Club | GP | GA | SO | Avg. |
|---|---|---|---|---|---|
| 1930-31 | Philadelphia Q | 29 | 127 | 1 | 4.38 |
| 1931-32 | Boston | 2 | 6 | 1 | 3.00 |
| 1933-34 | Det-Mont | 30 | 47 | 5 | 1.57 |
| 1934-35 | Montreal | 48 | 145 | 1 | 3.02 |
| 1935-36 | Montreal | 47 | 122 | 6 | 2.60 |
| 1936-37 | Montreal | 44 | 99 | 5 | 2.25 |
| 1937-38 | Montreal | 47 | 126 | 3 | 2.68 |
| 1938-39 | Montreal | 23 | 77 | 2 | 3.35 |
| 1939-40 | Montreal | 7 | 24 | 0 | 3.43 |
| 1940-41 | Montreal | 3 | 13 | 0 | 4.33 |
| | Totals | 280 | 786 | 24 | 2.81 |

**CUTTS, Donald Edward**
b. Edmonton, Alta., Feb. 24, 1953

| Season | Club | GP | GA | SO | Avg. |
|---|---|---|---|---|---|
| 1979-80 | Edmonton | 6 | 16 | 0 | 3.57 |

**CYR, Claude**
b. Montreal, Que., Mar. 27, 1939

| Season | Club | GP | GA | SO | Avg. |
|---|---|---|---|---|---|
| 1958-59 | Montreal | 1 | 1 | 0 | 1.00 |

**DALEY, Thomas Joseph (Joe)**
b. Winnipeg, Man., Feb. 20, 1943

| Season | Club | GP | GA | SO | Avg. |
|---|---|---|---|---|---|
| 1968-69 | Pittsburgh | 29 | 87 | 2 | 3.22 |
| 1969-70 | Pittsburgh | 9 | 26 | 0 | 2.95 |
| 1970-71 | Buffalo | 38 | 128 | 1 | 3.70 |
| 1971-72 | Detroit | 29 | 85 | 0 | 3.14 |
| 1972-73 | Winnipeg (WHA) | 29 | 83 | 2 | 2.89 |
| 1973-74 | Winnipeg (WHA) | 41 | 163 | 0 | 3.99 |
| 1974-75 | Winnipeg (WHA) | 51 | 175 | 1 | 3.62 |
| 1975-76 | Winnipeg (WHA) | 62 | 171 | 5 | 2.84 |
| 1976-77 | Winnipeg (WHA) | 65 | 206 | 3 | 3.24 |
| 1977-78 | Winnipeg (WHA) | 37 | 114 | 1 | 3.30 |
| 1978-79 | Winnipeg (WHA) | 23 | 90 | 0 | 4.30 |
| | NHL Totals | 105 | 326 | 3 | 3.35 |
| | WHA Totals | 308 | 1002 | 12 | 3.37 |

**DAMORE, Nicholas J.**
b. Niagara Falls, Ont., July 10, 1916

| Season | Club | GP | GA | SO | Avg. |
|---|---|---|---|---|---|
| 1941-42 | Boston | 1 | 3 | 0 | 3.00 |

**DAVIDSON, John Arthur**
b. Ottawa, Ont., Feb. 27, 1953

| Season | Club | GP | GA | SO | Avg. |
|---|---|---|---|---|---|
| 1973-74 | St Louis | 39 | 118 | 0 | 3.08 |
| 1974-75 | St Louis | 40 | 144 | 0 | 3.66 |
| 1975-76 | New York R | 56 | 212 | 3 | 3.97 |
| 1976-77 | New York R | 39 | 125 | 1 | 3.54 |
| 1977-78 | New York R | 34 | 98 | 1 | 3.18 |
| 1978-79 | New York R | 39 | 131 | 0 | 3.52 |
| 1979-80 | New York R | 41 | 122 | 2 | 3.17 |
| 1980-81 | New York R | 10 | 48 | 0 | 5.14 |
| 1981-82 | New York R | 1 | 1 | 0 | 1.00 |
| 1982-83 | New York R | 2 | 5 | 0 | 2.50 |
| | Totals | 301 | 1004 | 0 | 3.52 |

**DeCOURCY, Robert Philip**
b. Toronto, Ont., June 12, 1927

| Season | Club | GP | GA | SO | Avg. |
|---|---|---|---|---|---|
| 1947-48 | New York R | 1 | 6 | 0 | 6.00 |

**DeFELICE, Norman**
b. Schumacher, Ont., Jan. 19, 1933

| Season | Club | GP | GA | SO | Avg. |
|---|---|---|---|---|---|
| 1956-57 | Boston | 10 | 30 | 0 | 3.00 |


**DeJORDY, Denis Emile**
b. St. Hyacinthe, Que., Nov. 12, 1938

| Season | Club | GP | GA | SO | Avg. |
|---|---|---|---|---|---|
| 1962-63 | Chicago | 5 | 12 | 0 | 2.48 |
| 1963-64 | Chicago | 6 | 19 | 0 | 3.35 |
| 1964-65 | Chicago | 30 | 74 | 3 | 2.52 |
| 1966-67 | Chicago | 44 | 104 | 4 | 2.46 |
| 1967-68 | Chicago | 50 | 128 | 4 | 2.80 |
| 1968-69 | Chicago | 53 | 156 | 2 | 3.14 |
| 1969-70 | Chi-LA | 31 | 87 | 0 | 3.06 |
| 1970-71 | Los Angeles | 60 | 214 | 1 | 3.80 |
| 1971-72 | LA-Mont | 12 | 48 | 0 | 4.62 |
| 1972-73 | Detroit | 24 | 83 | 1 | 3.74 |
| 1973-74 | Detroit | 1 | 4 | 0 | 12.00 |
| | Totals | 316 | 929 | 15 | 3.12 |

**DESJARDINS, Gerald Ferdinand**
b. Sudbury, Ont., July 22, 1944

| Season | Club | GP | GA | SO | Avg. |
|---|---|---|---|---|---|
| 1968-69 | Los Angeles | 60 | 190 | 4 | 3.26 |
| 1969-70 | LA-Chicago | 47 | 167 | 3 | 3.72 |
| 1970-71 | Chicago | 22 | 49 | 0 | 2.41 |
| 1971-72 | Chicago | 6 | 21 | 0 | 3.50 |
| 1972-73 | New York I | 44 | 195 | 0 | 4.68 |
| 1973-74 | New York I | 36 | 101 | 0 | 3.12 |
| 1974-75 | Baltimore (WHA) | 41 | 162 | 0 | 4.26 |
| 1974-75 | Buffalo | 9 | 25 | 0 | 2.78 |
| 1975-76 | Buffalo | 55 | 161 | 2 | 2.95 |
| 1976-77 | Buffalo | 49 | 126 | 3 | 2.63 |
| 1977-78 | Buffalo | 3 | 7 | 0 | 3.78 |
| | NHL Totals | 331 | 1042 | 12 | 3.29 |
| | WHA Totals | 41 | 162 | 0 | 4.26 |

**DICKIE, William**
b. Chicago

| Season | Club | GP | GA | SO | Avg. |
|---|---|---|---|---|---|
| 1941-42 | Chicago | 1 | 3 | 0 | 3.00 |

**DION, Conrad (Connie)**
b. St. Remi de Tingwick, Que., Aug. 11, 1918

| Season | Club | GP | GA | SO | Avg. |
|---|---|---|---|---|---|
| 1943-44 | Detroit | 26 | 80 | 0 | 3.07 |
| 1944-45 | Detroit | 12 | 39 | 0 | 3.25 |
| | Totals | 38 | 119 | 0 | 3.13 |

**DION, Michel**
b. Granby, Que., Feb. 11, 1954

| Season | Club | GP | GA | SO | Avg. |
|---|---|---|---|---|---|
| 1974-75 | Indianapolis (WHA) | 1 | 4 | 0 | 4.00 |
| 1975-76 | Indianapolis (WHA) | 31 | 85 | 0 | 2.74 |
| 1976-77 | Indianapolis (WHA) | 42 | 128 | 1 | 3.36 |
| 1977-78 | Cincinnati (WHA) | 45 | 140 | 4 | 3.57 |
| 1978-79 | Cincinnati (WHA) | 30 | 93 | 0 | 3.32 |
| 1979-80 | Quebec | 50 | 171 | 2 | 3.70 |
| 1980-81 | Que-Winn | 26 | 122 | 0 | 5.07 |
| 1981-82 | Pittsburgh | 62 | 226 | 0 | 3.79 |
| 1982-83 | Pittsburgh | 49 | 198 | 0 | 3.97 |
| | NHL Totals | 187 | 717 | 2 | 4.06 |
| | WHA Totals | 149 | 450 | 5 | 3.28 |

**DOLSON, Clarence (Dolly)**

| Season | Club | GP | GA | SO | Avg. |
|---|---|---|---|---|---|
| 1928-29 | Detroit | 44 | 63 | 10 | 1.43 |
| 1929-30 | Detroit | 5 | 19 | 0 | 3.80 |
| 1930-31 | Detroit | 44 | 105 | 6 | 2.39 |
| | Totals | 93 | 187 | 16 | 2.01 |

**DRYDEN, David Murray**
b. Hamilton, Ont., Sept. 5, 1941

| Season | Club | GP | GA | SO | Avg. |
|---|---|---|---|---|---|
| 1961-62 | New York R | 1 | 3 | 0 | 4.50 |
| 1965-66 | Chicago | 11 | 23 | 0 | 3.05 |
| 1967-68 | Chicago | 27 | 69 | 1 | 3.26 |
| 1968-69 | Chicago | 30 | 79 | 3 | 3.20 |
| 1970-71 | Buffalo | 10 | 23 | 1 | 3.37 |
| 1971-72 | Buffalo | 20 | 68 | 0 | 3.97 |
| 1972-73 | Buffalo | 37 | 89 | 3 | 2.65 |
| 1973-74 | Buffalo | 53 | 148 | 1 | 2.97 |
| 1974-75 | Chicago (WHA) | 45 | 176 | 1 | 3.87 |
| 1975-76 | Edmonton (WHA) | 62 | 235 | 1 | 3.95 |
| 1976-77 | Edmonton (WHA) | 24 | 77 | 1 | 3.26 |
| 1977-78 | Edmonton (WHA) | 48 | 150 | 2 | 3.49 |
| 1978-79 | Edmonton (WHA) | 63 | 170 | 3 | 2.89 |
| 1979-80 | Edmonton | 14 | 53 | 0 | 4.27 |
| | NHL Totals | 203 | 555 | 9 | 3.19 |
| | WHA Totals | 242 | 808 | 8 | 3.51 |

**DRYDEN, Kenneth Wayne (Ken)**
b. Hamilton, Ont., Aug. 8, 1947

| Season | Club | GP | GA | SO | Avg. |
|---|---|---|---|---|---|
| 1970-71 | Montreal | 6 | 9 | 0 | 1.65 |
| 1971-72 | Montreal | 64 | 142 | 8 | 2.24 |
| 1972-73 | Montreal | 54 | 119 | 6 | 2.26 |
| 1974-75 | Montreal | 56 | 149 | 4 | 2.69 |
| 1975-76 | Montreal | 62 | 121 | 8 | 2.03 |
| 1976-77 | Montreal | 56 | 117 | 10 | 2.14 |
| 1977-78 | Montreal | 52 | 105 | 5 | 2.05 |
| 1978-79 | Montreal | 47 | 108 | 5 | 2.30 |
| | Totals | 397 | 870 | 46 | 2.23 |

**DUMAS, Michel Joseph**
b. St. Antoine-de-Pontbriand, Que., July 8, 1949

| Season | Club | GP | GA | SO | Avg. |
|---|---|---|---|---|---|
| 1974-75 | Chicago | 3 | 7 | 0 | 3.47 |
| 1976-77 | Chicago | 5 | 17 | 0 | 4.23 |
| | Totals | 8 | 24 | 0 | 3.98 |

**DURNAN, William Ronald**
b. Toronto, Ont., Jan. 22, 1915

| Season | Club | GP | GA | SO | Avg. |
|---|---|---|---|---|---|
| 1943-44 | Montreal | 50 | 109 | 2 | 2.18 |
| 1944-45 | Montreal | 50 | 121 | 1 | 2.42 |
| 1945-46 | Montreal | 40 | 104 | 4 | 2.60 |
| 1946-47 | Montreal | 60 | 138 | 4 | 2.30 |
| 1947-48 | Montreal | 59 | 162 | 5 | 2.74 |
| 1948-49 | Montreal | 60 | 126 | 10 | 2.10 |
| 1949-50 | Montreal | 64 | 141 | 8 | 2.20 |
| | Totals | 383 | 901 | 34 | 2.35 |

**DYCK, Edwin Paul**
b. Warman, Sask., Oct. 29, 1950

| Season | Club | GP | GA | SO | Avg. |
|---|---|---|---|---|---|
| 1971-72 | Vancouver | 12 | 35 | 0 | 3.66 |
| 1972-73 | Vancouver | 25 | 98 | 1 | 4.53 |
| 1973-74 | Vancouver | 12 | 45 | 0 | 4.63 |
| 1974-75 | Indianapolis (WHA) | 32 | 123 | 0 | 4.36 |
| | NHL Totals | 49 | 178 | 1 | 4.35 |
| | WHA Totals | 32 | 123 | 0 | 4.36 |

**EDWARDS, Allen Roy**
b. Seneca Township, Ont., Mar. 12, 1937

| Season | Club | GP | GA | SO | Avg. |
|---|---|---|---|---|---|
| 1967-68 | Detroit | 41 | 127 | 0 | 3.50 |
| 1968-69 | Detroit | 40 | 89 | 4 | 2.54 |
| 1969-70 | Detroit | 47 | 116 | 2 | 2.59 |
| 1970-71 | Detroit | 37 | 119 | 0 | 3.39 |
| 1971-72 | Pittsburgh | 15 | 36 | 0 | 2.55 |
| 1972-73 | Detroit | 52 | 132 | 6 | 2.63 |
| 1973-74 | Detroit | 4 | 18 | 0 | 5.78 |
| | Totals | 236 | 637 | 12 | 2.92 |

**EDWARDS, Donald Laurie**
b. Hamilton, Ont., Sept. 28, 1955

| Season | Club | GP | GA | SO | Avg. |
|---|---|---|---|---|---|
| 1976-77 | Buffalo | 25 | 62 | 2 | 2.51 |
| 1977-78 | Buffalo | 72 | 185 | 5 | 2.64 |
| 1978-79 | Buffalo | 54 | 159 | 2 | 3.02 |
| 1979-80 | Buffalo | 49 | 125 | 2 | 2.57 |
| 1980-81 | Buffalo | 45 | 133 | 3 | 2.96 |
| 1981-82 | Buffalo | 62 | 205 | 0 | 3.51 |
| 1982-83 | Calgary | 39 | 148 | 1 | 4.02 |
| | Totals | 346 | 1017 | 15 | 3.02 |

**EDWARDS, Gary William**
b. Toronto, Ont., Oct. 5, 1947

| Season | Club | GP | GA | SO | Avg. |
|---|---|---|---|---|---|
| 1968-69 | St Louis | 1 | 0 | 0 | 0.00 |
| 1969-70 | St Louis | 1 | 4 | 0 | 4.00 |
| 1971-72 | Los Angeles | 44 | 150 | 2 | 3.59 |
| 1972-73 | Los Angeles | 27 | 94 | 1 | 3.62 |
| 1973-74 | Los Angeles | 18 | 50 | 1 | 3.23 |
| 1974-75 | Los Angeles | 27 | 61 | 3 | 2.34 |
| 1975-76 | Los Angeles | 29 | 103 | 0 | 3.55 |
| 1976-77 | LA-Clev | 27 | 107 | 2 | 4.28 |
| 1977-78 | Cleveland | 30 | 128 | 0 | 4.52 |
| 1978-79 | Minnesota | 25 | 83 | 0 | 3.72 |
| 1979-80 | Minnesota | 26 | 82 | 0 | 3.20 |
| 1980-81 | Edmonton | 15 | 44 | 0 | 3.62 |
| 1981-82 | StL-Pitt | 16 | 67 | 1 | 4.79 |
| | Totals | 286 | 973 | 10 | 3.65 |

**EDWARDS, Marvin Wayne**
b. St. Catharines, Ont., Aug. 15, 1935

| Season | Club | GP | GA | SO | Avg. |
|---|---|---|---|---|---|
| 1968-69 | Pittsburgh | 1 | 3 | 0 | 3.00 |
| 1969-70 | Toronto | 25 | 77 | 1 | 3.25 |
| 1972-73 | California | 21 | 87 | 1 | 4.32 |
| 1973-74 | California | 14 | 51 | 0 | 3.92 |
| | Totals | 61 | 218 | 2 | 3.77 |

**ELLACOTT, Ken**
b. Paris, Ont., Mar. 3, 1959

| Season | Club | GP | GA | SO | Avg. |
|---|---|---|---|---|---|
| 1982-83 | Vancouver | 12 | 41 | 0 | 4.43 |

**ESPOSITO, Anthony James (Tony)**
b. Sault Ste. Marie, Ont., Apr. 23, 1943

| Season | Club | GP | GA | SO | Avg. |
|---|---|---|---|---|---|
| 1968-69 | Montreal | 13 | 34 | 2 | 2.73 |
| 1969-70 | Chicago | 63 | 136 | 15 | 2.17 |
| 1970-71 | Chicago | 57 | 126 | 6 | 2.27 |
| 1971-72 | Chicago | 48 | 82 | 9 | 1.76 |
| 1972-73 | Chicago | 56 | 140 | 4 | 2.51 |
| 1973-74 | Chicago | 70 | 141 | 10 | 2.04 |
| 1974-75 | Chicago | 71 | 193 | 6 | 2.74 |
| 1975-76 | Chicago | 68 | 198 | 4 | 2.97 |
| 1976-77 | Chicago | 69 | 234 | 2 | 3.45 |
| 1977-78 | Chicago | 64 | 168 | 5 | 2.63 |
| 1978-79 | Chicago | 63 | 206 | 4 | 3.27 |
| 1979-80 | Chicago | 69 | 205 | 6 | 2.97 |
| 1980-81 | Chicago | 66 | 246 | 0 | 3.75 |
| 1981-82 | Chicago | 52 | 231 | 1 | 4.52 |
| 1982-83 | Chicago | 39 | 135 | 1 | 3.46 |
| | Totals | 868 | 2475 | 75 | 2.88 |

**EVANS, Claude**
b. Longueuil, Que., Apr. 28, 1933

| Season | Club | GP | GA | SO | Avg. |
|---|---|---|---|---|---|
| 1954-55 | Montreal | 3 | 12 | 0 | 4.00 |
| 1957-58 | Boston | 1 | 4 | 0 | 4.00 |
| | Totals | 4 | 16 | 0 | 4.00 |

**FARR, Norman Richard (Rocky)**
b. Toronto, Ont., Apr. 7, 1947

| Season | Club | GP | GA | SO | Avg. |
|---|---|---|---|---|---|
| 1972-73 | Buffalo | 1 | 3 | 0 | 6.21 |
| 1973-74 | Buffalo | 11 | 25 | 0 | 3.13 |
| 1974-75 | Buffalo | 7 | 14 | 0 | 3.94 |
| | Totals | 19 | 42 | 0 | 3.49 |

**FAVELL, Douglas Robert**
b. St. Catharines, Ont., Apr. 5, 1945

| Season | Club | GP | GA | SO | Avg. |
|---|---|---|---|---|---|
| 1967-68 | Philadelphia | 37 | 83 | 4 | 2.27 |
| 1968-69 | Philadelphia | 21 | 71 | 1 | 3.56 |
| 1969-70 | Philadelphia | 15 | 43 | 1 | 3.15 |
| 1970-71 | Philadelphia | 44 | 108 | 2 | 2.66 |
| 1971-72 | Philadelphia | 54 | 140 | 5 | 2.80 |
| 1972-73 | Philadelphia | 44 | 114 | 3 | 2.83 |
| 1973-74 | Toronto | 32 | 79 | 0 | 2.71 |
| 1974-75 | Toronto | 39 | 145 | 1 | 4.05 |
| 1975-76 | Toronto | 3 | 15 | 0 | 5.63 |
| 1976-77 | Colorado | 30 | 105 | 0 | 3.90 |
| 1977-78 | Colorado | 47 | 159 | 1 | 3.58 |
| 1978-79 | Colorado | 7 | 34 | 0 | 5.37 |
| | Totals | 373 | 1096 | 18 | 3.16 |

**FORBES, Vernon (Jake)**
b. Toronto, Ont.

| Season | Club | GP | GA | SO | Avg. |
|---|---|---|---|---|---|
| 1919-20 | Toronto | 5 | 21 | 0 | 4.20 |
| 1920-21 | Toronto | 20 | 78 | 0 | 3.90 |
| 1922-23 | Hamilton | 24 | 110 | 0 | 4.58 |
| 1923-24 | Hamilton | 24 | 70 | 1 | 2.92 |
| 1924-25 | Hamilton | 30 | 61 | 6 | 2.03 |
| 1925-26 | New York A | 36 | 89 | 2 | 2.47 |
| 1926-27 | New York A | 44 | 91 | 8 | 2.07 |
| 1927-28 | New York A | 16 | 51 | 2 | 3.19 |
| 1928-29 | New York A | 1 | 3 | 0 | 3.00 |
| 1929-30 | New York A | 1 | 1 | 0 | 1.00 |
| 1930-31 | Philadelphia Q | 2 | 7 | 0 | 3.50 |
| 1931-32 | New York A | 6 | 16 | 0 | 2.67 |
| 1932-33 | New York A | 1 | 2 | 0 | 2.00 |
| | Totals | 210 | 600 | 19 | 2.86 |

**FOWLER, Norman (Hec)**

| Season | Club | GP | GA | SO | Avg. |
|---|---|---|---|---|---|
| 1924-25 | Boston | 7 | 43 | 0 | 6.14 |

**FUHR, Grant**
b. Edmonton, Alta., Sept. 21, 1962

| Season | Club | GP | GA | SO | Avg. |
|---|---|---|---|---|---|
| 1981-82 | Edmonton | 48 | 157 | 0 | 3.31 |
| 1982-83 | Edmonton | 32 | 129 | 0 | 4.29 |
| | Totals | 80 | 286 | 0 | 3.69 |

**FRANCIS, Emile Percy (Cat)**
b. North Battleford, Sask., Sept. 13, 1926

| Season | Club | GP | GA | SO | Avg. |
|---|---|---|---|---|---|
| 1946-47 | Chicago | 19 | 104 | 0 | 5.47 |
| 1947-48 | Chicago | 54 | 183 | 1 | 3.39 |
| 1948-49 | New York R | 2 | 4 | 0 | 2.00 |
| 1949-50 | New York R | 1 | 8 | 0 | 8.00 |
| 1950-51 | New York R | 5 | 14 | 0 | 2.80 |
| 1951-52 | New York R | 14 | 42 | 0 | 3.00 |
| | Totals | 95 | 355 | 1 | 3.74 |

**FRANKS, James Reginald**
b. Melville, Sask., Nov. 8, 1914

| Season | Club | GP | GA | SO | Avg. |
|---|---|---|---|---|---|
| 1937-38 | Detroit | 1 | 3 | 0 | 3.00 |
| 1942-43 | New York R | 23 | 103 | 0 | 4.48 |
| 1943-44 | Det-Bos | 18 | 75 | 1 | 4.17 |
| | Totals | 42 | 181 | 1 | 4.31 |

**FREDERICK, Raymond**
b. Fort Francis, Ont., July 31, 1929

| Season | Club | GP | GA | SO | Avg. |
|---|---|---|---|---|---|
| 1954-55 | Chicago | 5 | 22 | 0 | 4.40 |

**FROESE, Bob**
b. St. Catharines, Ont., June 30, 1958

| Season | Club | GP | GA | SO | Avg. |
|---|---|---|---|---|---|
| 1982-83 | Philadelphia | 24 | 59 | 4 | 2.52 |

**GAMBLE, Bruce George**
b. Port Arthur, Ont., May 24, 1938

| Season | Club | GP | GA | SO | Avg. |
|---|---|---|---|---|---|
| 1958-59 | New York R | 2 | 6 | 0 | 3.00 |
| 1960-61 | Boston | 52 | 195 | 0 | 3.75 |
| 1961-62 | Boston | 28 | 123 | 1 | 4.39 |
| 1965-66 | Toronto | 10 | 21 | 4 | 2.51 |
| 1966-67 | Toronto | 23 | 67 | 0 | 3.39 |
| 1967-68 | Toronto | 41 | 85 | 5 | 2.31 |
| 1968-69 | Toronto | 61 | 161 | 3 | 2.80 |
| 1969-70 | Toronto | 52 | 156 | 5 | 3.06 |
| 1970-71 | Tor-Phil | 34 | 120 | 2 | 3.78 |
| 1971-72 | Philadelphia | 24 | 58 | 2 | 2.93 |
| | Totals | 327 | 992 | 22 | 3.23 |

**GARDINER, Charles Robert (Chuck)**
b. Edinburgh, Scotland, Dec. 31, 1904

| Season | Club | GP | GA | SO | Avg. |
|---|---|---|---|---|---|
| 1927-28 | Chicago | 40 | 114 | 3 | 2.85 |
| 1928-29 | Chicago | 44 | 85 | 6 | 1.93 |
| 1929-30 | Chicago | 44 | 111 | 3 | 2.52 |
| 1930-31 | Chicago | 44 | 78 | 12 | 1.77 |
| 1931-32 | Chicago | 48 | 101 | 4 | 2.10 |
| 1932-33 | Chicago | 48 | 101 | 5 | 2.10 |
| 1933-34 | Chicago | 48 | 83 | 10 | 1.73 |
| | Totals | 316 | 673 | 43 | 2.13 |

**GARDINER, Wilbert (Bert)**
b. Saskatoon, Sask., Mar. 25, 1913

| Season | Club | GP | GA | SO | Avg. |
|---|---|---|---|---|---|
| 1935-36 | New York R | 1 | 1 | 0 | 1.00 |
| 1940-41 | Montreal | 42 | 119 | 2 | 2.83 |
| 1941-42 | Montreal | 10 | 42 | 0 | 4.20 |
| 1942-43 | Chicago | 50 | 180 | 1 | 3.60 |
| 1943-44 | Boston | 41 | 212 | 1 | 5.17 |
| | Totals | 144 | 554 | 4 | 3.85 |

**GARDNER, George Edward (Bud)**
b. Lachine, Que., Oct. 8, 1942

| Season | Club | GP | GA | SO | Avg. |
|---|---|---|---|---|---|
| 1965-66 | Detroit | 1 | 1 | 0 | 1.00 |
| 1966-67 | Detroit | 11 | 36 | 0 | 3.86 |
| 1967-68 | Detroit | 12 | 32 | 0 | 3.60 |
| 1970-71 | Vancouver | 18 | 52 | 0 | 3.38 |
| 1971-72 | Vancouver | 24 | 86 | 0 | 4.17 |
| 1972-73 | Los Angeles (WHA) | 49 | 149 | 1 | 3.79 |
| 1973-74 | LA-Van (WHA) | 30 | 138 | 0 | 4.84 |
| | NHL Totals | 66 | 207 | 0 | 3.75 |
| | WHA Totals | 79 | 287 | 1 | 4.23 |

## GARRETT, John Murdoch
b. Trenton, Ont., June 17, 1951

| Season | Club | GP | GA | SO | Avg. |
|---|---|---|---|---|---|
| 1973-74 | Minnesota (WHA) | 40 | 137 | 1 | 3.59 |
| 1974-75 | Minnesota (WHA) | 58 | 180 | 2 | 3.28 |
| 1975-76 | Toronto (WHA) | 57 | 210 | 3 | 3.38 |
| 1976-77 | Birmingham (WHA) | 65 | 224 | 4 | 3.53 |
| 1977-78 | Birmingham (WHA) | 58 | 210 | 2 | 3.81 |
| 1978-79 | NE (WHA) | 41 | 149 | 2 | 3.58 |
| 1979-80 | Hartford | 52 | 202 | 0 | 3.98 |
| 1980-81 | Hartford | 54 | 241 | 0 | 4.59 |
| 1981-82 | Hart-Que | 28 | 125 | 0 | 4.64 |
| 1982-83 | Que-Van | 34 | 112 | 1 | 3.56 |
| | **NHL Totals** | 168 | 680 | 1 | 4.20 |
| | **WHA Totals** | 323 | 1110 | 14 | 3.52 |

## GATHERUM, David L.
b. Fort William, Ont., Mar. 28, 1932

| Season | Club | GP | GA | SO | Avg. |
|---|---|---|---|---|---|
| 1953-54 | Detroit | 3 | 3 | 1 | 1.00 |

## GAUTHIER, Paul
b. Winnipeg, Man.

| Season | Club | GP | GA | SO | Avg. |
|---|---|---|---|---|---|
| 1937-38 | Montreal | 1 | 2 | 0 | 2.00 |

## GELINEAU, John Edward (Jack)
b. Toronto, Ont., Nov. 11, 1924

| Season | Club | GP | GA | SO | Avg. |
|---|---|---|---|---|---|
| 1948-49 | Boston | 4 | 12 | 0 | 3.00 |
| 1949-50 | Boston | 67 | 220 | 3 | 3.28 |
| 1950-51 | Boston | 70 | 197 | 4 | 2.81 |
| 1953-54 | Chicago | 2 | 18 | 0 | 9.00 |
| | **Totals** | 143 | 447 | 7 | 3.13 |

## GIACOMIN, Edward
b. Sudbury, Ont., June 6, 1939

| Season | Club | GP | GA | SO | Avg. |
|---|---|---|---|---|---|
| 1965-66 | New York R | 36 | 128 | 0 | 3.66 |
| 1966-67 | New York R | 68 | 173 | 9 | 2.61 |
| 1967-68 | New York R | 66 | 160 | 8 | 2.44 |
| 1968-69 | New York R | 70 | 175 | 7 | 2.55 |
| 1969-70 | New York R | 70 | 163 | 6 | 2.36 |
| 1970-71 | New York R | 45 | 95 | 8 | 2.15 |
| 1971-72 | New York R | 44 | 115 | 1 | 2.70 |
| 1972-73 | New York R | 43 | 125 | 4 | 2.91 |
| 1973-74 | New York R | 56 | 168 | 5 | 3.07 |
| 1974-75 | New York R | 37 | 120 | 1 | 3.48 |
| 1975-76 | NYR-Det | 33 | 119 | 2 | 3.61 |
| 1976-77 | Detroit | 33 | 107 | 3 | 3.58 |
| 1977-78 | Detroit | 9 | 27 | 0 | 3.14 |
| | **Totals** | 610 | 1675 | 54 | 2.82 |

## GILBERT, Gilles Joseph
b. St. Esprit, Que., Mar. 31, 1949

| Season | Club | GP | GA | SO | Avg. |
|---|---|---|---|---|---|
| 1969-70 | Minnesota | 1 | 6 | 0 | 6.00 |
| 1970-71 | Minnesota | 17 | 59 | 0 | 3.80 |
| 1971-72 | Minnesota | 4 | 11 | 0 | 3.02 |
| 1972-73 | Minnesota | 22 | 67 | 2 | 3.05 |
| 1973-74 | Boston | 54 | 158 | 6 | 2.95 |
| 1974-75 | Boston | 53 | 158 | 3 | 3.13 |
| 1975-76 | Boston | 55 | 151 | 3 | 2.90 |
| 1976-77 | Boston | 34 | 97 | 1 | 2.85 |
| 1977-78 | Boston | 25 | 56 | 2 | 2.53 |
| 1978-79 | Boston | 23 | 74 | 0 | 3.54 |
| 1979-80 | Boston | 33 | 88 | 1 | 2.73 |
| 1980-81 | Detroit | 48 | 175 | 0 | 4.01 |
| 1981-82 | Detroit | 27 | 105 | 0 | 4.26 |
| 1982-83 | Detroit | 20 | 85 | 0 | 4.49 |
| | **Totals** | 416 | 1290 | 18 | 3.27 |

## GILL, Andre
b. Sorel, Que., Sept. 19, 1941

| Season | Club | GP | GA | SO | Avg. |
|---|---|---|---|---|---|
| 1967-68 | Boston | 5 | 13 | 1 | 2.89 |
| 1972-73 | Chicago (WHA) | 33 | 118 | 0 | 4.14 |
| 1973-74 | Chicago (WHA) | 13 | 46 | 0 | 3.44 |
| | **NHL Totals** | 5 | 13 | 1 | 2.89 |
| | **WHA Totals** | 46 | 164 | 0 | 3.92 |

## GOODMAN, Paul
b. Selkirk, Man., Nov. 4, 1909

| Season | Club | GP | GA | SO | Avg. |
|---|---|---|---|---|---|
| 1939-40 | Chicago | 31 | 62 | 4 | 2.00 |
| 1940-41 | Chicago | 21 | 55 | 2 | 2.61 |
| | **Totals** | 52 | 117 | 6 | 2.25 |

## GRAHAME, Ronald
b. Victoria, B.C., June 7, 1950

| Season | Club | GP | GA | SO | Avg. |
|---|---|---|---|---|---|
| 1973-74 | Houston (WHA) | 4 | 5 | 1 | 1.20 |
| 1974-75 | Houston (WHA) | 43 | 131 | 4 | 3.03 |
| 1975-76 | Houston (WHA) | 57 | 182 | 3 | 3.27 |
| 1976-77 | Houston (WHA) | 39 | 107 | 4 | 2.74 |
| 1977-78 | Boston | 40 | 107 | 3 | 2.76 |
| 1978-79 | Los Angeles | 34 | 136 | 0 | 4.21 |
| 1979-80 | Los Angeles | 26 | 98 | 2 | 4.19 |
| 1980-81 | LA-Que | 14 | 68 | 0 | 5.11 |
| | **NHL Totals** | 114 | 409 | 5 | 3.79 |
| | **WHA Totals** | 143 | 425 | 12 | 2.99 |

## GRANT, Benjamin Cameron
b. Owen Sound, Ont., July 14, 1909

| Season | Club | GP | GA | SO | Avg. |
|---|---|---|---|---|---|
| 1928-29 | Toronto | 1 | 2 | 0 | 2.00 |
| 1929-30 | NYA-Tor | 10 | 39 | 0 | 3.90 |
| 1930-31 | Toronto | 7 | 19 | 2 | 2.71 |
| 1931-32 | Toronto | 4 | 18 | 0 | 4.50 |
| 1933-34 | New York A | 5 | 18 | 1 | 3.60 |
| 1943-44 | Tor-Bos | 21 | 93 | 0 | 4.43 |
| | **Totals** | 48 | 189 | 3 | 3.94 |

## GRANT, Doug Munro
b. Corner Brook, Nfld., July 27, 1948

| Season | Club | GP | GA | SO | Avg. |
|---|---|---|---|---|---|
| 1973-74 | Detroit | 37 | 140 | 1 | 4.16 |
| 1974-75 | Detroit | 7 | 34 | 0 | 5.37 |
| 1975-76 | Detroit | 2 | 8 | 0 | 4.00 |
| 1976-77 | St Louis | 17 | 50 | 1 | 3.13 |
| 1977-78 | St Louis | 9 | 24 | 0 | 2.88 |
| 1978-79 | St Louis | 4 | 23 | 0 | 7.26 |
| 1979-80 | St Louis | 1 | 1 | 0 | 1.94 |
| | **Totals** | 77 | 280 | 2 | 4.00 |

## GRATTON, Gilles
b. LaSalle, Que., July 28, 1952

| Season | Club | GP | GA | SO | Avg. |
|---|---|---|---|---|---|
| 1972-73 | Ottawa (WHA) | 51 | 187 | 0 | 3.71 |
| 1973-74 | Toronto (WHA) | 57 | 188 | 2 | 3.53 |
| 1974-75 | Toronto (WHA) | 52 | 185 | 2 | 3.85 |
| 1975-76 | St Louis | 6 | 11 | 0 | 2.49 |
| 1976-77 | New York R | 41 | 143 | 0 | 4.22 |
| | **NHL Totals** | 47 | 154 | 0 | 4.02 |
| | **WHA Totals** | 160 | 560 | 4 | 3.69 |

## GRAY, Gerald Robert (Gerry)
b. Brantford, Ont., Jan. 28, 1948

| Season | Club | GP | GA | SO | Avg. |
|---|---|---|---|---|---|
| 1970-71 | Detroit | 7 | 30 | 0 | 4.73 |
| 1972-73 | New York I | 1 | 5 | 0 | 5.00 |
| | **Totals** | 8 | 35 | 0 | 4.81 |

## GRAY, Harrison Leroy
b. Calgary, Alta., Sept. 5, 1941

| Season | Club | GP | GA | SO | Avg. |
|---|---|---|---|---|---|
| 1963-64 | Detroit | 1 | 5 | 0 | 7.50 |

## HAINSWORTH, George
b. Toronto, Ont., June 26, 1895

| Season | Club | GP | GA | SO | Avg. |
|---|---|---|---|---|---|
| 1926-27 | Montreal | 44 | 67 | 14 | 1.52 |
| 1927-28 | Montreal | 44 | 48 | 13 | 1.09 |
| 1928-29 | Montreal | 44 | 43 | 22 | 0.98 |
| 1929-30 | Montreal | 42 | 108 | 4 | 2.57 |
| 1930-31 | Montreal | 44 | 89 | 8 | 2.02 |
| 1931-32 | Montreal | 48 | 111 | 6 | 2.31 |
| 1932-33 | Montreal | 48 | 115 | 7 | 2.40 |
| 1933-34 | Toronto | 48 | 119 | 3 | 2.48 |
| 1934-35 | Toronto | 48 | 111 | 6 | 2.31 |
| 1935-36 | Toronto | 48 | 106 | 8 | 2.21 |
| 1936-37 | Tor-Mont | 7 | 21 | 0 | 3.00 |
| | **Totals** | 465 | 938 | 91 | 2.02 |

## HALL, Glenn Henry
b. Humboldt, Sask., Oct. 3, 1931

| Season | Club | GP | GA | SO | Avg. |
|---|---|---|---|---|---|
| 1952-53 | Detroit | 6 | 10 | 1 | 1.67 |
| 1954-55 | Detroit | 2 | 2 | 0 | 1.00 |
| 1955-56 | Detroit | 70 | 148 | 12 | 2.11 |
| 1956-57 | Detroit | 70 | 157 | 4 | 2.24 |
| 1957-58 | Chicago | 70 | 202 | 7 | 2.88 |
| 1958-59 | Chicago | 70 | 208 | 1 | 2.97 |
| 1959-60 | Chicago | 70 | 180 | 6 | 2.57 |
| 1960-61 | Chicago | 70 | 180 | 6 | 2.57 |
| 1961-62 | Chicago | 70 | 186 | 9 | 2.65 |
| 1962-63 | Chicago | 66 | 166 | 5 | 2.54 |
| 1963-64 | Chicago | 65 | 148 | 7 | 2.30 |
| 1964-65 | Chicago | 41 | 99 | 4 | 2.43 |
| 1965-66 | Chicago | 63 | 164 | 4 | 2.63 |
| 1966-67 | Chicago | 28 | 66 | 2 | 2.38 |
| 1967-68 | St Louis | 48 | 118 | 5 | 2.48 |
| 1968-69 | St Louis | 40 | 85 | 8 | 2.17 |
| 1969-70 | St Louis | 17 | 49 | 1 | 2.91 |
| 1970-71 | St Louis | 29 | 71 | 2 | 2.41 |
| | **Totals** | 895 | 2239 | 84 | 2.51 |

## HAMEL, Pierre
b. Montreal, Que., Sept. 16, 1952

| Season | Club | GP | GA | SO | Avg. |
|---|---|---|---|---|---|
| 1974-75 | Toronto | 4 | 18 | 0 | 5.54 |
| 1978-79 | Toronto | 1 | 0 | 0 | 0.00 |
| 1979-80 | Winnipeg | 35 | 130 | 0 | 4.01 |
| 1980-81 | Winnipeg | 29 | 128 | 0 | 4.73 |
| | **Totals** | 69 | 276 | 0 | 4.40 |

## HANLON, Glen
b. Brandon, Man., Feb. 20, 1957

| Season | Club | GP | GA | SO | Avg. |
|---|---|---|---|---|---|
| 1977-78 | Vancouver | 4 | 9 | 0 | 2.70 |
| 1978-79 | Vancouver | 31 | 94 | 3 | 3.10 |
| 1979-80 | Vancouver | 57 | 193 | 0 | 3.47 |
| 1980-81 | Vancouver | 17 | 59 | 1 | 4.44 |
| 1981-82 | Van-StL | 30 | 114 | 1 | 4.06 |
| 1982-83 | StL-NYR | 35 | 117 | 0 | 3.81 |
| | **Totals** | 174 | 584 | 5 | 3.62 |

## HARRISON, Paul Douglas
b. Timmins, Ont., Feb. 11, 1955

| Season | Club | GP | GA | SO | Avg. |
|---|---|---|---|---|---|
| 1975-76 | Minnesota | 6 | 28 | 0 | 5.47 |
| 1976-77 | Minnesota | 2 | 11 | 0 | 5.50 |
| 1977-78 | Minnesota | 27 | 99 | 1 | 3.82 |
| 1978-79 | Toronto | 25 | 82 | 1 | 3.51 |
| 1979-80 | Toronto | 30 | 110 | 0 | 4.42 |
| 1981-82 | Buf-Pitt | 19 | 78 | 0 | 5.04 |
| | **Totals** | 109 | 408 | 2 | 4.22 |

## HAYWARD, Brian
b. Georgetown, Ont., June 25, 1960

| Season | Club | GP | GA | SO | Avg. |
|---|---|---|---|---|---|
| 1982-83 | Winnipeg | 24 | 89 | 1 | 3.71 |

## HEAD, Donald Charles
b. Mount Dennis, Ont., June 30, 1933

| Season | Club | GP | GA | SO | Avg. |
|---|---|---|---|---|---|
| 1961-62 | Boston | 38 | 161 | 2 | 4.24 |

## HEBERT, Samuel
b. 1894

| Season | Club | GP | GA | SO | Avg. |
|---|---|---|---|---|---|
| 1917-18 | Tor-Ott | 2 | 15 | 0 | 7.50 |
| 1923-24 | Ottawa | 2 | 9 | 0 | 4.50 |
| | **Totals** | 4 | 24 | 0 | 6.00 |

## HEINZ, Richard
b. Essex, Ont., May 30, 1955

| Season | Club | GP | GA | SO | Avg. |
|---|---|---|---|---|---|
| 1980-81 | St Louis | 4 | 8 | 0 | 2.18 |
| 1981-82 | StL-Van | 12 | 44 | 1 | 4.31 |
| 1982-83 | St Louis | 9 | 24 | 1 | 4.30 |
| | **Totals** | 25 | 76 | 1 | 4.11 |

## HENDERSON, John Duncan (Long John)
b. Toronto, Ont., Mar. 25, 1933

| Season | Club | GP | GA | SO | Avg. |
|---|---|---|---|---|---|
| 1954-55 | Boston | 44 | 109 | 5 | 2.40 |
| 1955-56 | Boston | 1 | 4 | 0 | 4.00 |
| | **Totals** | 45 | 113 | 5 | 2.51 |

## HENRY, Gordon David (Red)
b. Owen Sound, Ont., Aug. 17, 1926

| Season | Club | GP | GA | SO | Avg. |
|---|---|---|---|---|---|
| 1948-49 | Boston | 1 | 0 | 1 | 0.00 |
| 1949-50 | Boston | 2 | 5 | 0 | 2.50 |
| | **Totals** | 3 | 5 | 1 | 1.67 |

## HENRY, Samuel James (Sugar Jim)
b. Winnipeg, Man., Oct. 23, 1920

| Season | Club | GP | GA | SO | Avg. |
|---|---|---|---|---|---|
| 1941-42 | New York R | 48 | 143 | 2 | 2.98 |
| 1945-46 | New York R | 11 | 41 | 1 | 3.73 |
| 1946-47 | New York R | 2 | 9 | 0 | 4.50 |
| 1947-48 | New York R | 48 | 153 | 2 | 3.19 |

| Season | Club | GP | GA | SO | Avg. |
|--------|------|----|----|----|------|
| 1948-49 | Chicago | 60 | 211 | 0 | 3.52 |
| 1951-52 | Boston | 70 | 176 | 7 | 2.51 |
| 1952-53 | Boston | 70 | 172 | 8 | 2.46 |
| 1953-54 | Boston | 70 | 181 | 8 | 2.58 |
| 1954-55 | Boston | 26 | 79 | 1 | 3.00 |
| **Totals** | | 405 | 1165 | 29 | 2.88 |

**HERRON, Denis**
b. Chambly, Que., June 18, 1952

| Season | Club | GP | GA | SO | Avg. |
|--------|------|----|----|----|------|
| 1972-73 | Pittsburgh | 18 | 55 | 2 | 3.41 |
| 1973-74 | Pittsburgh | 5 | 18 | 0 | 4.15 |
| 1974-75 | Pitt-KC | 25 | 91 | 0 | 3.93 |
| 1975-76 | Kansas City | 64 | 243 | 0 | 4.03 |
| 1976-77 | Pittsburgh | 34 | 94 | 1 | 2.94 |
| 1977-78 | Pittsburgh | 60 | 210 | 0 | 3.57 |
| 1978-79 | Pittsburgh | 56 | 180 | 0 | 3.37 |
| 1979-80 | Montreal | 34 | 80 | 0 | 2.51 |
| 1980-81 | Montreal | 25 | 67 | 1 | 3.50 |
| 1981-82 | Montreal | 27 | 68 | 3 | 2.64 |
| 1982-83 | Pittsburgh | 31 | 151 | 1 | 5.31 |
| **Totals** | | 379 | 1257 | 8 | 3.55 |

**HIGHTON, Hector Salisbury**
b. Medicine Hat, Alta., Dec. 10, 1923

| Season | Club | GP | GA | SO | Avg. |
|--------|------|----|----|----|------|
| 1943-44 | Chicago | 24 | 108 | 0 | 4.50 |

**HIMES, Norman**
b. Galt, Ont., Apr. 13, 1903

| Season | Club | GP | GA | SO | Avg. |
|--------|------|----|----|----|------|
| 1928-29 | New York A | 1 | 3 | 0 | 3.00 |

**HODGE, Charles Edward**
b. Lachine, Que., July 28, 1933

| Season | Club | GP | GA | SO | Avg. |
|--------|------|----|----|----|------|
| 1954-55 | Montreal | 14 | 31 | 1 | 2.27 |
| 1957-58 | Montreal | 12 | 31 | 1 | 2.58 |
| 1958-59 | Montreal | 2 | 6 | 0 | 3.00 |
| 1959-60 | Montreal | 1 | 3 | 0 | 3.00 |
| 1960-61 | Montreal | 30 | 76 | 4 | 2.53 |
| 1963-64 | Montreal | 62 | 140 | 8 | 2.26 |
| 1964-65 | Montreal | 52 | 135 | 3 | 2.60 |
| 1965-66 | Montreal | 22 | 56 | 1 | 2.58 |
| 1966-67 | Montreal | 25 | 88 | 3 | 2.56 |
| 1967-68 | Oakland | 56 | 158 | 3 | 2.86 |
| 1968-69 | Oakland | 13 | 48 | 0 | 3.69 |
| 1969-70 | Oakland | 13 | 43 | 0 | 3.48 |
| 1970-71 | Vancouver | 33 | 112 | 0 | 3.41 |
| **Totals** | | 345 | 927 | 24 | 2.70 |

**HOGANSON, Paul Edward**
b. Toronto, Ont., Nov. 12, 1949

| Season | Club | GP | GA | SO | Avg. |
|--------|------|----|----|----|------|
| 1970-71 | Pittsburgh | 2 | 7 | 0 | 7.36 |
| 1973-74 | Los Angeles (WHA) | 26 | 102 | 0 | 4.68 |
| 1974-75 | Baltimore (WHA) | 32 | 122 | 2 | 4.12 |
| 1975-76 | NE-Cin (WHA) | 54 | 177 | 2 | 3.74 |
| 1976-77 | Cin-Ind (WHA) | 28 | 88 | 1 | 4.33 |
| **NHL Totals** | | 2 | 7 | 0 | 7.36 |
| **WHA Totals** | | 140 | 489 | 5 | 4.11 |

**HOGOSTA, Goran**
b. Appelbo, Sweden, Apr. 15, 1954

| Season | Club | GP | GA | SO | Avg. |
|--------|------|----|----|----|------|
| 1977-78 | New York I | 1 | 0 | 0 | 0.00 |
| 1979-80 | Quebec | 21 | 83 | 1 | 4.15 |
| **Totals** | | 22 | 83 | 1 | 4.12 |

**HOLDEN, Mark**
b. Weymouth, Mass., June 12, 1957

| Season | Club | GP | GA | SO | Avg. |
|--------|------|----|----|----|------|
| 1981-82 | Montreal | 1 | 0 | 0 | 0.00 |
| 1982-83 | Montreal | 2 | 6 | 0 | 4.14 |
| **Totals** | | 3 | 6 | 0 | 3.36 |

**HOLLAND, Kenneth Mark**
b. Vernon, B.C., Nov. 10, 1955

| Season | Club | GP | GA | SO | Avg. |
|--------|------|----|----|----|------|
| 1980-81 | Hartford | 1 | 7 | 0 | 7.00 |

**HOLLAND, Robert**
b. Montreal, Que., Sept. 10, 1957

| Season | Club | GP | GA | SO | Avg. |
|--------|------|----|----|----|------|
| 1979-80 | Pittsburgh | 34 | 126 | 1 | 3.83 |
| 1980-81 | Pittsburgh | 10 | 45 | 0 | 5.01 |
| **Totals** | | 44 | 171 | 1 | 4.08 |

**HOLMES, Harold (Hap)**
b. Aurora, Ont., Apr. 15, 1889

| Season | Club | GP | GA | SO | Avg. |
|--------|------|----|----|----|------|
| 1917-18 | Toronto | 16 | 76 | 0 | 4.75 |
| 1918-19 | Toronto | 2 | 9 | 0 | 4.50 |
| 1926-27 | Detroit | 44 | 105 | 6 | 2.39 |
| 1927-28 | Detroit | 44 | 79 | 11 | 1.80 |
| **Totals** | | 106 | 269 | 17 | 2.54 |

**INNESS, Gary George**
b. Toronto, Ont., May 28, 1949

| Season | Club | GP | GA | SO | Avg. |
|--------|------|----|----|----|------|
| 1973-74 | Pittsburgh | 20 | 56 | 0 | 3.26 |
| 1974-75 | Pittsburgh | 57 | 161 | 2 | 3.09 |
| 1975-76 | Pitt-Phil | 25 | 85 | 0 | 3.83 |
| 1976-77 | Philadelphia | 6 | 9 | 0 | 2.57 |
| 1977-78 | Indianapolis (WHA) | 52 | 200 | 0 | 4.21 |
| 1978-79 | Indianapolis (WHA) | 9 | 51 | 0 | 5.02 |
| 1978-79 | Washington | 37 | 130 | 0 | 3.70 |
| 1979-80 | Washington | 14 | 44 | 0 | 3.63 |
| 1980-81 | Washington | 3 | 9 | 0 | 3.00 |
| **NHL Totals** | | 162 | 494 | 2 | 3.40 |
| **WHA Totals** | | 61 | 251 | 0 | 4.35 |

**IRELAND, Randolph**
b. Rosetown, Sask., Apr. 5, 1957

| Season | Club | GP | GA | SO | Avg. |
|--------|------|----|----|----|------|
| 1978-79 | Buffalo | 2 | 3 | 0 | 6.00 |

**IRONS, Robert Richard (Robbie)**
b. Toronto, Ont., Nov. 19, 1946

| Season | Club | GP | GA | SO | Avg. |
|--------|------|----|----|----|------|
| 1968-69 | St Louis | 1 | 0 | 0 | 0.00 |

**IRONSTONE, Joseph**
b. 1897

| Season | Club | GP | GA | SO | Avg. |
|--------|------|----|----|----|------|
| 1927-28 | Toronto | 1 | 0 | 1 | 0.00 |

**JACKSON, Douglas**
b. Winnipeg, Man., Dec. 12, 1924

| Season | Club | GP | GA | SO | Avg. |
|--------|------|----|----|----|------|
| 1947-48 | Chicago | 6 | 42 | 0 | 7.00 |

**JACKSON, Percy**
b. Canmore, Alta., Sept. 21, 1907

| Season | Club | GP | GA | SO | Avg. |
|--------|------|----|----|----|------|
| 1931-32 | Boston | 3 | 7 | 0 | 2.33 |
| 1933-34 | New York A | 1 | 9 | 0 | 9.00 |
| 1934-35 | New York R | 1 | 8 | 0 | 8.00 |
| 1935-36 | Boston | 1 | 1 | 0 | 1.00 |
| **Totals** | | 6 | 25 | 0 | 4.17 |

**JANASZAK, Steven**
b. St. Paul, Minn., Jan. 7, 1957

| Season | Club | GP | GA | SO | Avg. |
|--------|------|----|----|----|------|
| 1979-80 | Minnesota | 1 | 2 | 0 | 2.00 |
| 1981-82 | Colorado | 2 | 13 | 0 | 7.80 |
| **Totals** | | 3 | 15 | 0 | 5.63 |

**JENSEN, Allan Raymond**
b. Hamilton, Ont., Nov. 27, 1958

| Season | Club | GP | GA | SO | Avg. |
|--------|------|----|----|----|------|
| 1980-81 | Detroit | 1 | 7 | 0 | 7.00 |
| 1981-82 | Washington | 26 | 81 | 0 | 3.81 |
| 1982-83 | Washington | 40 | 135 | 1 | 3.44 |
| **Totals** | | 67 | 223 | 1 | 3.63 |

**JOHNSON, Robert Martin (Bob)**
b. Farmington, Mich., Nov. 12, 1948

| Season | Club | GP | GA | SO | Avg. |
|--------|------|----|----|----|------|
| 1972-73 | St Louis | 12 | 26 | 0 | 2.68 |
| 1974-75 | Pittsburgh | 12 | 40 | 0 | 5.04 |
| **Totals** | | 24 | 66 | 0 | 3.74 |

**JOHNSTON, Edward Joseph**
b. Montreal, Que., Nov. 23, 1935

| Season | Club | GP | GA | SO | Avg. |
|--------|------|----|----|----|------|
| 1962-63 | Boston | 50 | 196 | 1 | 4.05 |
| 1963-64 | Boston | 70 | 211 | 6 | 3.01 |
| 1964-65 | Boston | 47 | 163 | 3 | 3.47 |
| 1965-66 | Boston | 33 | 108 | 1 | 3.72 |
| 1966-67 | Boston | 34 | 116 | 0 | 3.70 |
| 1967-68 | Boston | 28 | 73 | 0 | 2.87 |
| 1968-69 | Boston | 24 | 74 | 2 | 3.08 |
| 1969-70 | Boston | 37 | 108 | 3 | 2.98 |
| 1970-71 | Boston | 38 | 96 | 4 | 2.52 |
| 1971-72 | Boston | 38 | 102 | 2 | 2.70 |
| 1972-73 | Boston | 45 | 137 | 5 | 3.27 |
| 1973-74 | Boston | 26 | 78 | 1 | 3.09 |
| 1974-75 | St Louis | 30 | 93 | 2 | 3.10 |
| 1975-76 | St Louis | 38 | 130 | 1 | 3.62 |
| 1976-77 | St Louis | 38 | 108 | 1 | 3.07 |
| 1977-78 | StL-Chi | 16 | 62 | 0 | 4.18 |
| **Totals** | | 592 | 1855 | 32 | 3.25 |

**JUNKIN, Joseph Brian**
b. Belleville, Ont., Sept. 8, 1946

| Season | Club | GP | GA | SO | Avg. |
|--------|------|----|----|----|------|
| 1968-69 | Boston | 1 | 0 | 0 | 0.00 |

**KAARELA, Jari Pekka**
b. Tampere, Finland, Aug. 8, 1958

| Season | Club | GP | GA | SO | Avg. |
|--------|------|----|----|----|------|
| 1980-81 | Colorado | 5 | 22 | 0 | 6.00 |

**KARAKAS, Michael**
b. Aurora, Minn., Dec. 12, 1911

| Season | Club | GP | GA | SO | Avg. |
|--------|------|----|----|----|------|
| 1935-36 | Chicago | 48 | 92 | 9 | 1.91 |
| 1936-37 | Chicago | 48 | 131 | 5 | 2.72 |
| 1937-38 | Chicago | 48 | 139 | 1 | 2.85 |
| 1938-39 | Chicago | 48 | 132 | 5 | 2.75 |
| 1939-40 | Chi-MontM | 22 | 76 | 0 | 3.45 |
| 1943-44 | Chicago | 26 | 79 | 3 | 3.03 |
| 1944-45 | Chicago | 48 | 187 | 4 | 3.89 |
| 1945-46 | Chicago | 48 | 166 | 1 | 3.45 |
| **Totals** | | 336 | 1002 | 28 | 2.98 |

**KEANS, Douglas Frederick**
b. Pembroke, Ont., Jan. 7, 1958

| Season | Club | GP | GA | SO | Avg. |
|--------|------|----|----|----|------|
| 1979-80 | Los Angeles | 10 | 23 | 0 | 2.47 |
| 1980-81 | Los Angeles | 9 | 37 | 0 | 4.89 |
| 1981-82 | Los Angeles | 31 | 103 | 0 | 4.30 |
| 1982-83 | Los Angeles | 6 | 24 | 0 | 4.74 |
| **Totals** | | 56 | 187 | 0 | 4.07 |

**KEENAN, Donald**

| Season | Club | GP | GA | SO | Avg. |
|--------|------|----|----|----|------|
| 1958-59 | Boston | 1 | 4 | 0 | 4.00 |

**KERR, David Alexander**
b. Toronto, Ont., Jan. 11, 1910

| Season | Club | GP | GA | SO | Avg. |
|--------|------|----|----|----|------|
| 1930-31 | Montreal M | 30 | 72 | 1 | 2.40 |
| 1931-32 | New York A | 1 | 6 | 0 | 6.00 |
| 1932-33 | Montreal M | 25 | 57 | 4 | 2.28 |
| 1933-34 | Montreal M | 48 | 122 | 6 | 2.54 |
| 1934-35 | New York R | 37 | 94 | 4 | 2.54 |
| 1935-36 | New York R | 47 | 95 | 8 | 2.02 |
| 1936-37 | New York R | 48 | 106 | 4 | 2.21 |
| 1937-38 | New York R | 48 | 96 | 8 | 2.00 |
| 1938-39 | New York R | 48 | 105 | 6 | 2.19 |
| 1939-40 | New York R | 48 | 77 | 8 | 1.60 |
| 1940-41 | New York R | 48 | 125 | 2 | 2.60 |
| **Totals** | | 428 | 955 | 51 | 2.23 |

**KLYMKIEW, Julian**
b. Winnipeg, Man., July 16, 1933

| Season | Club | GP | GA | SO | Avg. |
|--------|------|----|----|----|------|
| 1958-59 | New York R | 1 | 2 | 0 | 2.00 |

**KURT, Gary David**
b. Kitchener, Ont., Mar. 9, 1947

| Season | Club | GP | GA | SO | Avg. |
|--------|------|----|----|----|------|
| 1971-72 | California | 16 | 60 | 0 | 4.29 |
| 1972-73 | New York (WHA) | 36 | 150 | 0 | 4.78 |
| 1973-74 | New Jersey (WHA) | 20 | 75 | 0 | 4.13 |
| 1974-75 | Phoenix (WHA) | 47 | 156 | 2 | 3.29 |
| 1975-76 | Phoenix (WHA) | 40 | 147 | 1 | 3.72 |
| 1976-77 | Phoenix (WHA) | 33 | 162 | 0 | 5.55 |
| **NHL Totals** | | 16 | 60 | 0 | 4.29 |
| **WHA Totals** | | 176 | 690 | 3 | 4.17 |

**LACROIX, Alfonse**

| Season | Club | GP | GA | SO | Avg. |
|--------|------|----|----|----|------|
| 1925-26 | Montreal | 4 | 15 | 0 | 3.75 |

**LAFERRIERE, Richard Jacques**
b. Hawksbury, Ont., Jan. 3, 1961

| Season | Club | GP | GA | SO | Avg. |
|--------|------|----|----|----|------|
| 1981-82 | Colorado | 1 | 1 | 0 | 3.00 |

| Season | Club | GP | GA | SO | Avg. |
|---|---|---|---|---|---|

**LAROCQUE, Michel Raymond**
b. Hull, Que., Apr. 6, 1952

| Season | Club | GP | GA | SO | Avg. |
|---|---|---|---|---|---|
| 1973-74 | Montreal | 27 | 69 | 0 | 2.89 |
| 1974-75 | Montreal | 25 | 74 | 3 | 3.00 |
| 1975-76 | Montreal | 22 | 50 | 2 | 2.46 |
| 1976-77 | Montreal | 26 | 53 | 4 | 2.09 |
| 1977-78 | Montreal | 30 | 77 | 1 | 2.67 |
| 1978-79 | Montreal | 34 | 94 | 3 | 2.84 |
| 1979-80 | Montreal | 39 | 125 | 3 | 3.32 |
| 1980-81 | Mont-Tor | 36 | 122 | 1 | 3.51 |
| 1981-82 | Toronto | 50 | 207 | 0 | 4.69 |
| 1982-83 | Tor-Phil | 18 | 76 | 0 | 4.77 |
| | **Totals** | 307 | 947 | 17 | 3.28 |

**LASKOSKI, Gary**
b. Ottawa, Ont., June 6, 1959

| Season | Club | GP | GA | SO | Avg. |
|---|---|---|---|---|---|
| 1982-83 | Los Angeles | 46 | 173 | 0 | 4.56 |

**LAXTON, Gordon**
b. Montreal, Que., Mar. 16, 1955

| Season | Club | GP | GA | SO | Avg. |
|---|---|---|---|---|---|
| 1975-76 | Pittsburgh | 8 | 31 | 0 | 4.49 |
| 1976-77 | Pittsburgh | 6 | 26 | 0 | 6.17 |
| 1977-78 | Pittsburgh | 2 | 9 | 0 | 7.40 |
| 1978-79 | Pittsburgh | 1 | 8 | 0 | 8.00 |
| | **Totals** | 17 | 74 | 0 | 5.55 |

**LEGRIS, Claude**
b. Verdun, Que., Nov. 6, 1956

| Season | Club | GP | GA | SO | Avg. |
|---|---|---|---|---|---|
| 1980-81 | Detroit | 3 | 4 | 0 | 3.81 |
| 1981-82 | Detroit | 1 | 0 | 0 | 0.00 |
| | **Totals** | 4 | 4 | 0 | 2.64 |

**LEHMAN, Hugh**
b. Pembroke, Ont., Oct. 27, 1895

| Season | Club | GP | GA | SO | Avg. |
|---|---|---|---|---|---|
| 1926-27 | Chicago | 44 | 116 | 5 | 2.64 |
| 1927-28 | Chicago | 4 | 20 | 1 | 5.00 |
| | **Totals** | 48 | 136 | 6 | 2.83 |

**LEMELIN, Rejean**
b. Sherbrooke, Que., Nov. 19, 1954

| Season | Club | GP | GA | SO | Avg. |
|---|---|---|---|---|---|
| 1978-79 | Atlanta | 18 | 55 | 0 | 3.32 |
| 1979-80 | Atlanta | 3 | 15 | 0 | 6.00 |
| 1980-81 | Calgary | 29 | 88 | 2 | 3.24 |
| 1981-82 | Calgary | 34 | 135 | 0 | 4.34 |
| 1982-83 | Calgary | 39 | 133 | 0 | 3.61 |
| | **Totals** | 123 | 426 | 2 | 3.73 |

**LESSARD, Mario**
b. East Broughton, Que., June 25, 1954

| Season | Club | GP | GA | SO | Avg. |
|---|---|---|---|---|---|
| 1978-79 | Los Angeles | 49 | 148 | 4 | 3.10 |
| 1979-80 | Los Angeles | 50 | 185 | 0 | 3.91 |
| 1980-81 | Los Angeles | 64 | 203 | 2 | 3.25 |
| 1981-82 | Los Angeles | 52 | 213 | 2 | 4.36 |
| 1982-83 | Los Angeles | 19 | 68 | 1 | 4.59 |
| | **Totals** | 234 | 717 | 9 | 3.24 |

**LEVASSEUR, Jean-Louis**
b. Noranda, Que., June 16, 1949

| Season | Club | GP | GA | SO | Avg. |
|---|---|---|---|---|---|
| 1975-76 | Minnesota (WHA) | 4 | 10 | 0 | 3.11 |
| 1976-77 | Minn-Edm (WHA) | 51 | 166 | 2 | 3.40 |
| 1977-78 | NE (WHA) | 27 | 91 | 3 | 3.30 |
| 1978-79 | Quebec (WHA) | 3 | 14 | 0 | 6.00 |
| 1979-80 | Minnesota | 1 | 7 | 0 | 7.00 |
| | **NHL Totals** | 1 | 7 | 0 | 7.00 |
| | **WHA Totals** | 85 | 281 | 5 | 3.43 |

**LINDBERGH, Per-Erik (Pelle)**
b. Stockholm, Sweden, May 24, 1959

| Season | Club | GP | GA | SO | Avg. |
|---|---|---|---|---|---|
| 1981-82 | Philadelphia | 8 | 35 | 0 | 4.38 |
| 1982-83 | Philadelphia | 40 | 116 | 3 | 2.98 |
| | **Totals** | 48 | 151 | 3 | 3.22 |

**LINDSAY, Bert**

| Season | Club | GP | GA | SO | Avg. |
|---|---|---|---|---|---|
| 1918-19 | Toronto | 16 | 83 | 0 | 5.19 |

**LIUT, Michael**
b. Weston, Ont., Jan. 7, 1956

| Season | Club | GP | GA | SO | Avg. |
|---|---|---|---|---|---|
| 1977-78 | Cincinnati (WHA) | 27 | 86 | 0 | 4.25 |
| 1978-79 | Cincinnati (WHA) | 54 | 184 | 3 | 3.47 |
| 1979-80 | St Louis | 64 | 194 | 2 | 3.18 |
| 1980-81 | St Louis | 61 | 199 | 1 | 3.34 |
| 1981-82 | St Louis | 64 | 250 | 2 | 4.06 |
| 1982-83 | St Louis | 68 | 235 | 1 | 3.72 |
| | **NHL Totals** | 257 | 878 | 4 | 3.58 |
| | **WHA Totals** | 81 | 270 | 3 | 3.69 |

**LOCKHART, Howard (Holes)**

| Season | Club | GP | GA | SO | Avg. |
|---|---|---|---|---|---|
| 1919-20 | Tor-Que | 6 | 28 | 0 | 4.67 |
| 1920-21 | Hamilton | 24 | 132 | 1 | 5.50 |
| 1921-22 | Hamilton | 24 | 105 | 0 | 4.38 |
| 1923-24 | Toronto | 1 | 5 | 0 | 5.00 |
| 1924-25 | Boston | 2 | 11 | 0 | 5.50 |
| | **Totals** | 57 | 281 | 1 | 4.93 |

**LOCKETT, Kenneth Richard**
b. Toronto, Ont., Aug. 30, 1947

| Season | Club | GP | GA | SO | Avg. |
|---|---|---|---|---|---|
| 1974-75 | Vancouver | 25 | 48 | 2 | 3.16 |
| 1975-76 | Vancouver | 30 | 83 | 0 | 3.47 |
| | **Totals** | 55 | 131 | 2 | 3.35 |

**LoPRESTI, Peter Jon**
b. Virginia, Minn., May 23, 1954

| Season | Club | GP | GA | SO | Avg. |
|---|---|---|---|---|---|
| 1974-75 | Minnesota | 35 | 137 | 1 | 4.19 |
| 1975-76 | Minnesota | 34 | 123 | 1 | 4.13 |
| 1976-77 | Minnesota | 44 | 156 | 1 | 3.61 |
| 1977-78 | Minnesota | 53 | 216 | 2 | 4.23 |
| 1978-79 | Minnesota | 7 | 28 | 0 | 4.87 |
| 1980-81 | Edmonton | 2 | 8 | 0 | 4.57 |
| | **Totals** | 175 | 668 | 5 | 4.07 |

**LoPRESTI, Samuel**
b. Eveleth, Minn., Jan. 30, 1917

| Season | Club | GP | GA | SO | Avg. |
|---|---|---|---|---|---|
| 1940-41 | Chicago | 27 | 84 | 1 | 3.11 |
| 1941-42 | Chicago | 47 | 152 | 3 | 3.23 |
| | **Totals** | 74 | 236 | 4 | 3.19 |

**LOW, Ronald Albert (Ron)**
b. Birtie, Man., June 21, 1950

| Season | Club | GP | GA | SO | Avg. |
|---|---|---|---|---|---|
| 1972-73 | Toronto | 42 | 152 | 1 | 3.89 |
| 1974-75 | Washington | 48 | 235 | 1 | 5.45 |
| 1975-76 | Washington | 43 | 208 | 0 | 5.45 |
| 1976-77 | Washington | 54 | 188 | 0 | 3.87 |
| 1977-78 | Detroit | 32 | 102 | 1 | 3.37 |
| 1979-80 | Que-Edm | 26 | 88 | 0 | 3.57 |
| 1980-81 | Edmonton | 24 | 93 | 0 | 4.43 |
| 1981-82 | Edmonton | 29 | 100 | 2 | 3.86 |
| 1982-83 | Edm-NJ | 14 | 51 | 0 | 4.30 |
| | **Totals** | 312 | 1217 | 3 | 4.31 |

**LOZINSKI, Larry Peter**
b. Hudson Bay, Sask., Mar. 11, 1958

| Season | Club | GP | GA | SO | Avg. |
|---|---|---|---|---|---|
| 1980-81 | Detroit | 30 | 105 | 0 | 4.32 |

**LUMLEY, Harry (Apple Cheeks)**
b. Owen Sound, Ont., Nov. 11, 1926

| Season | Club | GP | GA | SO | Avg. |
|---|---|---|---|---|---|
| 1943-44 | Det-NYR | 3 | 13 | 0 | 4.33 |
| 1944-45 | Detroit | 37 | 119 | 1 | 3.22 |
| 1945-46 | Detroit | 50 | 159 | 2 | 3.18 |
| 1946-47 | Detroit | 52 | 159 | 3 | 3.05 |
| 1947-48 | Detroit | 60 | 147 | 7 | 2.45 |
| 1948-49 | Detroit | 60 | 145 | 6 | 2.42 |
| 1949-50 | Detroit | 63 | 148 | 7 | 2.35 |
| 1950-51 | Chicago | 64 | 246 | 3 | 3.84 |
| 1951-52 | Chicago | 70 | 241 | 2 | 3.44 |
| 1952-53 | Toronto | 70 | 167 | 10 | 2.38 |
| 1953-54 | Toronto | 69 | 128 | 13 | 1.85 |
| 1954-55 | Toronto | 69 | 134 | 8 | 1.94 |
| 1955-56 | Toronto | 59 | 159 | 3 | 2.69 |
| 1957-58 | Boston | 25 | 71 | 3 | 2.84 |
| 1958-59 | Boston | 11 | 27 | 1 | 2.45 |
| 1959-60 | Boston | 42 | 147 | 2 | 3.50 |
| | **Totals** | 804 | 2210 | 71 | 2.75 |

**MacKENZIE, Shawn**
b. Bedford, N.S., Aug. 22, 1962

| Season | Club | GP | GA | SO | Avg. |
|---|---|---|---|---|---|
| 1982-83 | New Jersey | 6 | 15 | 0 | 6.92 |

**MALARCHUK, Clint**
b. Grande, Alta., May 1, 1961

| Season | Club | GP | GA | SO | Avg. |
|---|---|---|---|---|---|
| 1981-82 | Quebec | 2 | 14 | 0 | 7.00 |
| 1982-83 | Quebec | 15 | 71 | 0 | 4.73 |
| | **Totals** | 17 | 85 | 0 | 5.00 |

**MANIAGO, Cesare**
b. Trail, B.C., Jan. 13, 1939

| Season | Club | GP | GA | SO | Avg. |
|---|---|---|---|---|---|
| 1960-61 | Toronto | 7 | 18 | 0 | 2.57 |
| 1962-63 | Montreal | 14 | 42 | 0 | 3.07 |
| 1965-66 | New York R | 28 | 94 | 2 | 3.50 |
| 1966-67 | New York R | 6 | 14 | 0 | 3.84 |
| 1967-68 | Minnesota | 52 | 133 | 6 | 2.77 |
| 1968-69 | Minnesota | 64 | 198 | 1 | 3.30 |
| 1969-70 | Minnesota | 50 | 163 | 2 | 3.39 |
| 1970-71 | Minnesota | 40 | 107 | 5 | 2.69 |
| 1971-72 | Minnesota | 43 | 112 | 0 | 2.64 |
| 1972-73 | Minnesota | 47 | 132 | 5 | 2.89 |
| 1973-74 | Minnesota | 40 | 138 | 1 | 3.48 |
| 1974-75 | Minnesota | 37 | 149 | 1 | 4.20 |
| 1975-76 | Minnesota | 47 | 151 | 2 | 3.35 |
| 1976-77 | Vancouver | 47 | 151 | 1 | 3.36 |
| 1977-78 | Vancouver | 46 | 172 | 1 | 4.02 |
| | **Totals** | 568 | 1774 | 27 | 3.27 |

**MAROIS, John**

| Season | Club | GP | GA | SO | Avg. |
|---|---|---|---|---|---|
| 1943-44 | Toronto | 1 | 4 | 0 | 4.00 |
| 1953-54 | Chicago | 2 | 11 | 0 | 5.50 |
| | **Totals** | 3 | 15 | 0 | 5.00 |

**MARTIN, Seth**
b. Rossland, B.C., May 4, 1933

| Season | Club | GP | GA | SO | Avg. |
|---|---|---|---|---|---|
| 1967-68 | St Louis | 30 | 67 | 1 | 2.60 |

**MATTSSON, Rainer Markus**
b. Suoneiemi, Finland, July 30, 1957

| Season | Club | GP | GA | SO | Avg. |
|---|---|---|---|---|---|
| 1977-78 | Que-Winn (WHA) | 16 | 60 | 0 | 4.63 |
| 1978-79 | Winnipeg (WHA) | 52 | 181 | 0 | 3.63 |
| 1979-80 | Winnipeg | 21 | 65 | 2 | 3.25 |
| 1980-81 | Winnipeg | 31 | 128 | 1 | 4.50 |
| 1982-83 | Minn-LA | 21 | 71 | 1 | 4.26 |
| | **NHL Totals** | 73 | 264 | 5 | 4.04 |
| | **WHA Totals** | 68 | 241 | 0 | 3.84 |

**MAYER, Gilles**
b. Ottawa, Ont., Aug. 24, 1930

| Season | Club | GP | GA | SO | Avg. |
|---|---|---|---|---|---|
| 1949-50 | Toronto | 1 | 2 | 0 | 2.00 |
| 1953-54 | Toronto | 1 | 3 | 0 | 3.00 |
| 1955-56 | Toronto | 6 | 19 | 0 | 3.17 |
| | **Totals** | 8 | 24 | 0 | 3.00 |

**McAULEY, Kenneth Leslie**
b. Edmonton, Alta., Jan. 9, 1921

| Season | Club | GP | GA | SO | Avg. |
|---|---|---|---|---|---|
| 1943-44 | New York R | 50 | 310 | 0 | 6.20 |
| 1944-45 | New York R | 46 | 227 | 1 | 4.94 |
| | **Totals** | 96 | 537 | 1 | 5.61 |

**McCARTAN, John William (Jack)**
b. St. Paul, Minn., Aug. 5, 1935

| Season | Club | GP | GA | SO | Avg. |
|---|---|---|---|---|---|
| 1959-60 | New York R | 4 | 7 | 0 | 1.75 |
| 1960-61 | New York R | 8 | 36 | 1 | 4.91 |
| 1972-73 | Minnesota (WHA) | 38 | 129 | 1 | 3.58 |
| 1973-74 | Minnesota (WHA) | 2 | 5 | 0 | 7.14 |
| | **NHL Totals** | 12 | 43 | 1 | 3.80 |
| | **WHA Totals** | 40 | 134 | 1 | 3.65 |

**McCOOL, Frank**
b. Calgary, Alta., Oct. 27, 1918

| Season | Club | GP | GA | SO | Avg. |
|---|---|---|---|---|---|
| 1944-45 | Toronto | 50 | 161 | 4 | 3.22 |
| 1945-46 | Toronto | 22 | 81 | 0 | 3.68 |
| | **Totals** | 72 | 242 | 4 | 3.36 |

**McDUFFE, Peter Arnold**
b. Milton, Ont., Feb. 16, 1948

| Season | Club | GP | GA | SO | Avg. |
|---|---|---|---|---|---|
| 1971-72 | St Louis | 10 | 29 | 0 | 3.72 |
| 1972-73 | New York R | 1 | 1 | 0 | 1.00 |

| Season | Club | GP | GA | SO | Avg. |
|---|---|---|---|---|---|
| 1973-74 | New York R | 6 | 18 | 0 | 3.18 |
| 1974-75 | Kansas City | 36 | 148 | 0 | 4.23 |
| 1975-76 | Detroit | 4 | 22 | 0 | 5.50 |
| 1977-78 | Indianapolis (WHA) | 12 | 39 | 0 | 4.34 |
| | **NHL Totals** | 57 | 218 | 0 | 4.08 |
| | **WHA Totals** | 12 | 39 | 0 | 4.34 |

**McGRATTON, Thomas**
b. Brantford, Ont., Oct. 19, 1927

| Season | Club | GP | GA | SO | Avg. |
|---|---|---|---|---|---|
| 1947-48 | Detroit | 1 | 1 | 0 | 1.00 |

**McKENZIE, William Ian**
b. St. Thomas, Ont., Mar. 12, 1949

| Season | Club | GP | GA | SO | Avg. |
|---|---|---|---|---|---|
| 1973-74 | Detroit | 13 | 43 | 1 | 3.53 |
| 1974-75 | Detroit | 13 | 58 | 0 | 4.70 |
| 1975-76 | Kansas City | 22 | 97 | 0 | 5.20 |
| 1976-77 | Colorado | 5 | 8 | 0 | 2.40 |
| 1977-78 | Colorado | 12 | 42 | 0 | 3.85 |
| 1979-80 | Colorado | 26 | 78 | 1 | 3.49 |
| | **Totals** | 91 | 326 | 2 | 4.10 |

**McLACHLAN, Murray**
b. London, Ont., Oct. 20, 1948

| Season | Club | GP | GA | SO | Avg. |
|---|---|---|---|---|---|
| 1970-71 | Toronto | 1 | 4 | 0 | 9.60 |

**McLELLAND, David (Dave)**
b. Penticton, B.C., Nov. 20, 1952

| Season | Club | GP | GA | SO | Avg. |
|---|---|---|---|---|---|
| 1972-73 | Vancouver | 2 | 10 | 0 | 5.00 |

**McLEOD, Donald Martin (Don)**
b. Trail, B.C., Aug. 24, 1946

| Season | Club | GP | GA | SO | Avg. |
|---|---|---|---|---|---|
| 1970-71 | Detroit | 14 | 60 | 0 | 5.15 |
| 1971-72 | Philadelphia | 4 | 14 | 0 | 4.64 |
| 1972-73 | Houston (WHA) | 40 | 143 | 1 | 3.65 |
| 1973-74 | Houston (WHA) | 49 | 127 | 3 | 2.56 |
| 1974-75 | Vancouver (WHA) | 72 | 233 | 1 | 3.34 |
| 1975-76 | Calgary (WHA) | 63 | 206 | 1 | 3.50 |
| 1976-77 | Calgary (WHA) | 66 | 210 | 3 | 3.40 |
| 1977-78 | Que-Edm (WHA) | 40 | 130 | 2 | 3.67 |
| | **NHL Totals** | 18 | 74 | 0 | 5.05 |
| | **WHA Totals** | 330 | 1049 | 11 | 3.33 |

**McLEOD, James Bradley (Jim)**
b. Port Arthur, Ont., Apr. 7, 1937

| Season | Club | GP | GA | SO | Avg. |
|---|---|---|---|---|---|
| 1971-72 | St Louis | 16 | 44 | 0 | 3.00 |
| 1972-73 | Chicago (WHA) | 54 | 166 | 1 | 3.32 |
| 1973-74 | New Jersey (WHA) | 10 | 36 | 0 | 4.18 |
| 1974-75 | Baltimore (WHA) | 16 | 53 | 0 | 4.58 |
| | **NHL Totals** | 16 | 44 | 0 | 3.00 |
| | **WHA Totals** | 80 | 255 | 1 | 3.63 |

**McNAMARA, Gerald**
b. Sturgeon Falls, Ont., Sept. 22, 1934

| Season | Club | GP | GA | SO | Avg. |
|---|---|---|---|---|---|
| 1960-61 | Toronto | 5 | 13 | 0 | 2.60 |
| 1969-70 | Toronto | 1 | 2 | 0 | 6.00 |
| | **Totals** | 6 | 15 | 0 | 2.81 |

**McNEIL, Gerard George**
b. Quebec City, Que., Apr. 17, 1926

| Season | Club | GP | GA | SO | Avg. |
|---|---|---|---|---|---|
| 1947-48 | Montreal | 2 | 7 | 0 | 3.50 |
| 1949-50 | Montreal | 6 | 9 | 1 | 1.50 |
| 1950-51 | Montreal | 70 | 184 | 6 | 2.63 |
| 1951-52 | Montreal | 70 | 164 | 5 | 2.34 |
| 1952-53 | Montreal | 66 | 140 | 10 | 2.12 |
| 1953-54 | Montreal | 53 | 114 | 6 | 2.15 |
| 1956-57 | Montreal | 9 | 32 | 0 | 3.55 |
| | **Totals** | 276 | 650 | 28 | 2.36 |

**McRAE, Gordon Alexander**
b. Sherbrooke, Que., Apr. 12, 1948

| Season | Club | GP | GA | SO | Avg. |
|---|---|---|---|---|---|
| 1972-73 | Toronto | 11 | 39 | 0 | 3.77 |
| 1974-75 | Toronto | 20 | 57 | 0 | 3.22 |
| 1975-76 | Toronto | 20 | 59 | 0 | 3.70 |
| 1976-77 | Toronto | 2 | 9 | 0 | 4.50 |
| 1977-78 | Toronto | 18 | 57 | 1 | 3.29 |
| | **Totals** | 71 | 221 | 1 | 3.49 |

**MELANSON, Roland Joseph**
b. Moncton, N.B., June 28, 1960

| Season | Club | GP | GA | SO | Avg. |
|---|---|---|---|---|---|
| 1980-81 | New York I | 11 | 32 | 0 | 3.10 |
| 1981-82 | New York I | 36 | 114 | 0 | 3.23 |
| 1982-83 | New York I | 44 | 109 | 1 | 2.66 |
| | **Totals** | 91 | 255 | 1 | 2.94 |

**MELOCHE, Gilles**
b. Montreal, Que., July 12, 1950

| Season | Club | GP | GA | SO | Avg. |
|---|---|---|---|---|---|
| 1970-71 | Chicago | 2 | 6 | 0 | 3.00 |
| 1971-72 | California | 56 | 173 | 4 | 3.32 |
| 1972-73 | California | 59 | 235 | 1 | 4.06 |
| 1973-74 | California | 47 | 198 | 1 | 4.24 |
| 1974-75 | California | 47 | 186 | 1 | 4.03 |
| 1975-76 | California | 41 | 140 | 1 | 3.44 |
| 1976-77 | Cleveland | 51 | 171 | 2 | 3.47 |
| 1977-78 | Cleveland | 54 | 195 | 1 | 3.77 |
| 1978-79 | Minnesota | 53 | 173 | 2 | 3.33 |
| 1979-80 | Minnesota | 54 | 160 | 1 | 3.06 |
| 1980-81 | Minnesota | 38 | 120 | 2 | 3.25 |
| 1981-82 | Minnesota | 51 | 175 | 1 | 3.47 |
| 1982-83 | Minnesota | 47 | 160 | 1 | 3.57 |
| | **Totals** | 600 | 2092 | 18 | 3.59 |

**MICALEF, Corrado**
b. Montreal, Que., Apr. 20, 1961

| Season | Club | GP | GA | SO | Avg. |
|---|---|---|---|---|---|
| 1981-82 | Detroit | 18 | 63 | 0 | 4.67 |
| 1982-83 | Detroit | 34 | 106 | 2 | 3.62 |
| | **Totals** | 52 | 169 | 2 | 3.95 |

**MIDDLEBROOK, Lindsay**
b. Collingwood, Ont., Sept. 7, 1955

| Season | Club | GP | GA | SO | Avg. |
|---|---|---|---|---|---|
| 1979-80 | Winnipeg | 10 | 40 | 0 | 4.14 |
| 1980-81 | Winnipeg | 14 | 65 | 0 | 5.97 |
| 1981-82 | Minnesota | 3 | 7 | 0 | 3.00 |
| 1982-83 | NJ-Edm | 10 | 40 | 0 | 5.08 |
| | **Totals** | 37 | 152 | 0 | 4.94 |

**MILLAR, Franklin Allan (Al)**
b. Winnipeg, Man., Sept. 18, 1929

| Season | Club | GP | GA | SO | Avg. |
|---|---|---|---|---|---|
| 1957-58 | Boston | 6 | 25 | 0 | 4.17 |

**MILLEN, Greg**
b. Toronto, Ont., June 25, 1957

| Season | Club | GP | GA | SO | Avg. |
|---|---|---|---|---|---|
| 1978-79 | Pittsburgh | 28 | 86 | 2 | 3.37 |
| 1979-80 | Pittsburgh | 44 | 157 | 2 | 3.64 |
| 1980-81 | Pittsburgh | 63 | 258 | 0 | 4.16 |
| 1981-82 | Hartford | 55 | 229 | 0 | 4.29 |
| 1982-83 | Hartford | 60 | 282 | 1 | 4.81 |
| | **Totals** | 250 | 1012 | 5 | 4.17 |

**MILLER, Joseph**
b. Morrisburg, Ont., Oct. 6, 1900

| Season | Club | GP | GA | SO | Avg. |
|---|---|---|---|---|---|
| 1927-28 | NYA-NYR | 28 | 77 | 5 | 2.75 |
| 1928-29 | Pittsburgh Pi | 44 | 80 | 11 | 1.82 |
| 1929-30 | Pittsburgh Pi | 43 | 179 | 0 | 4.16 |
| 1930-31 | Philadelphia Q | 14 | 50 | 0 | 3.57 |
| | **Totals** | 129 | 386 | 16 | 2.99 |

**MIO, Edward**
b. Windsor, Ont., Jan. 31, 1954

| Season | Club | GP | GA | SO | Avg. |
|---|---|---|---|---|---|
| 1977-78 | Indianapolis (WHA) | 17 | 64 | 0 | 4.27 |
| 1978-79 | Ind-Edm (WHA) | 27 | 84 | 2 | 3.85 |
| 1979-80 | Edmonton | 34 | 120 | 1 | 4.21 |
| 1980-81 | Edmonton | 43 | 155 | 0 | 3.89 |
| 1981-82 | New York R | 25 | 89 | 0 | 3.56 |
| 1982-83 | New York R | 41 | 136 | 2 | 3.45 |
| | **NHL Totals** | 143 | 500 | 3 | 3.77 |
| | **WHA Totals** | 44 | 148 | 2 | 4.02 |

**MITCHELL, Ivan**

| Season | Club | GP | GA | SO | Avg. |
|---|---|---|---|---|---|
| 1919-20 | Toronto | 14 | 68 | 0 | 4.86 |
| 1920-21 | Toronto | 4 | 22 | 0 | 5.50 |
| 1921-22 | Toronto | 2 | 6 | 0 | 3.00 |
| | **Totals** | 20 | 96 | 0 | 4.80 |

**MOFFAT, Michael**
b. Galt, Ont., Feb. 4, 1962

| Season | Club | GP | GA | SO | Avg. |
|---|---|---|---|---|---|
| 1981-82 | Boston | 2 | 6 | 0 | 3.00 |
| 1982-83 | Boston | 13 | 49 | 0 | 4.37 |
| | **Totals** | 15 | 55 | 0 | 4.16 |

**MOOG, Donald Andrew**
b. Penticton, B.C., Feb. 18, 1960

| Season | Club | GP | GA | SO | Avg. |
|---|---|---|---|---|---|
| 1980-81 | Edmonton | 7 | 20 | 0 | 3.83 |
| 1981-82 | Edmonton | 8 | 32 | 0 | 4.81 |
| 1982-83 | Edmonton | 50 | 167 | 1 | 3.54 |
| | **Totals** | 65 | 219 | 1 | 3.71 |

**MOORE, Alfred Ernest (Alfie)**
b. Toronto, Ont.

| Season | Club | GP | GA | SO | Avg. |
|---|---|---|---|---|---|
| 1936-37 | New York A | 18 | 64 | 1 | 3.56 |
| 1938-39 | New York A | 2 | 14 | 0 | 7.00 |
| 1939-40 | Detroit | 1 | 3 | 0 | 3.00 |
| | **Totals** | 21 | 81 | 1 | 3.86 |

**MOORE, Robert David (Robbie)**
b. Sarnia, Ont., May 3, 1954

| Season | Club | GP | GA | SO | Avg. |
|---|---|---|---|---|---|
| 1978-79 | Philadelphia | 5 | 7 | 2 | 1.77 |
| 1982-83 | Washington | 1 | 1 | 0 | 3.00 |
| | **Totals** | 6 | 8 | 0 | 1.87 |

**MORISSETTE, Jean Guy**
b. Causapscal, Que., Dec. 16, 1937

| Season | Club | GP | GA | SO | Avg. |
|---|---|---|---|---|---|
| 1963-64 | Montreal | 1 | 4 | 0 | 6.00 |

**MOWERS, John Thomas**
b. Niagara Falls, Ont., Oct. 29, 1916

| Season | Club | GP | GA | SO | Avg. |
|---|---|---|---|---|---|
| 1940-41 | Detroit | 48 | 102 | 4 | 2.12 |
| 1941-42 | Detroit | 47 | 144 | 5 | 3.06 |
| 1942-43 | Detroit | 50 | 124 | 6 | 2.48 |
| 1946-47 | Detroit | 7 | 29 | 0 | 4.14 |
| | **Totals** | 152 | 399 | 15 | 2.63 |

**MRAZEK, Jerome John**
b. Prince Albert, Sask., Oct. 15, 1951

| Season | Club | GP | GA | SO | Avg. |
|---|---|---|---|---|---|
| 1975-76 | Philadelphia | 1 | 1 | 0 | 10.00 |

**MUMMERY, Harry**

| Season | Club | GP | GA | SO | Avg. |
|---|---|---|---|---|---|
| 1919-20 | Quebec | 2 | 15 | 0 | 7.50 |

**MURPHY, Hal**
b. Montreal, Que., July 6, 1927

| Season | Club | GP | GA | SO | Avg. |
|---|---|---|---|---|---|
| 1952-53 | Montreal | 1 | 4 | 0 | 4.00 |

**MURRAY, Thomas (Mickey)**

| Season | Club | GP | GA | SO | Avg. |
|---|---|---|---|---|---|
| 1929-30 | Montreal | 1 | 4 | 0 | 4.00 |

**MYRE, Louis Phillippe (Phil)**
b. Ste.-Anne-de-Bellevue, Que.,
Nov. 1, 1948

| Season | Club | GP | GA | SO | Avg. |
|---|---|---|---|---|---|
| 1969-70 | Montreal C | 10 | 19 | 0 | 2.15 |
| 1970-71 | Montreal C | 30 | 87 | 1 | 3.11 |
| 1971-72 | Montreal C | 9 | 32 | 0 | 3.63 |
| 1972-73 | Atlanta | 46 | 138 | 2 | 3.03 |
| 1973-74 | Atlanta | 36 | 112 | 0 | 3.33 |
| 1974-75 | Atlanta | 40 | 114 | 5 | 2.85 |
| 1975-76 | Atlanta | 37 | 123 | 1 | 3.47 |
| 1976-77 | Atlanta | 43 | 124 | 3 | 3.07 |
| 1977-78 | Atlanta | 53 | 202 | 1 | 3.86 |
| 1978-79 | St Louis | 39 | 163 | 1 | 4.33 |
| 1979-80 | Philadelphia | 41 | 141 | 0 | 3.57 |
| 1980-81 | Phil-Col | 26 | 94 | 0 | 3.81 |
| 1981-82 | Colorado | 24 | 112 | 0 | 5.35 |
| 1982-83 | Buffalo | 5 | 21 | 0 | 4.20 |
| | **Totals** | 439 | 1482 | 14 | 3.53 |

**NEWTON, Cameron Charles (Cam)**
b. Peterborough, Ont., Feb. 25, 1950

| Season | Club | GP | GA | SO | Avg. |
|---|---|---|---|---|---|
| 1970-71 | Pittsburgh | 5 | 16 | 0 | 3.41 |
| 1972-73 | Pittsburgh | 11 | 35 | 0 | 3.94 |
| 1973-74 | Chicago (WHA) | 45 | 143 | 1 | 3.14 |
| 1974-75 | Chicago (WHA) | 32 | 126 | 0 | 3.97 |
| 1975-76 | Ott-Clev (WHA) | 25 | 83 | 1 | 3.39 |
| | **NHL Totals** | 16 | 51 | 0 | 3.76 |
| | **WHA Totals** | 102 | 352 | 2 | 3.46 |

| Season | Club | GP | GA | SO | Avg. |
|---|---|---|---|---|---|

**NORRIS, Jack Wayne**
b. Saskatoon, Sask., Aug. 5, 1942

| Season | Club | GP | GA | SO | Avg. |
|---|---|---|---|---|---|
| 1964-65 | Boston | 23 | 85 | 1 | 3.70 |
| 1967-68 | Chicago | 7 | 22 | 1 | 3.95 |
| 1968-69 | Chicago | 3 | 10 | 0 | 6.00 |
| 1970-71 | Los Angeles | 25 | 85 | 0 | 3.90 |
| 1972-73 | Alberta (WHA) | 64 | 189 | 1 | 3.06 |
| 1973-74 | Edmonton (WHA) | 53 | 158 | 2 | 3.21 |
| 1974-75 | Phoenix (WHA) | 33 | 107 | 1 | 3.27 |
| 1975-76 | Phoenix (WHA) | 41 | 128 | 1 | 3.18 |
| | **NHL Totals** | 58 | 202 | 2 | 3.89 |
| | **WHA Totals** | 191 | 582 | 5 | 3.16 |

**OLESCHUK, William Stephen**
b. Edmonton, Alta., July 20, 1955

| Season | Club | GP | GA | SO | Avg. |
|---|---|---|---|---|---|
| 1975-76 | Kansas City | 1 | 4 | 0 | 4.00 |
| 1976-77 | Colorado | 2 | 9 | 0 | 5.40 |
| 1978-79 | Colorado | 40 | 136 | 1 | 3.85 |
| 1979-80 | Colorado | 12 | 39 | 0 | 4.20 |
| | **Totals** | 55 | 188 | 1 | 3.98 |

**OLESEVICH, Daniel**
b. Port Colburne, Ont., Aug. 16, 1937

| Season | Club | GP | GA | SO | Avg. |
|---|---|---|---|---|---|
| 1961-62 | New York R | 1 | 2 | 0 | 4.00 |

**OUIMET, Edward John (Ted)**
b. Noranda, Que., July 6, 1947

| Season | Club | GP | GA | SO | Avg. |
|---|---|---|---|---|---|
| 1969-70 | St Louis | 1 | 2 | 0 | 2.00 |

**PAGEAU, Paul**
b. Montreal, Que., Oct. 1, 1959

| Season | Club | GP | GA | SO | Avg. |
|---|---|---|---|---|---|
| 1980-81 | Los Angeles | 1 | 8 | 0 | 8.00 |

**PAILLE, Marcel**
b. Shawinigan Falls, Que., Dec. 8, 1932

| Season | Club | GP | GA | SO | Avg. |
|---|---|---|---|---|---|
| 1957-58 | New York R | 33 | 102 | 1 | 3.10 |
| 1958-59 | New York R | 1 | 4 | 0 | 4.00 |
| 1959-60 | New York R | 17 | 67 | 1 | 3.94 |
| 1960-61 | New York R | 4 | 16 | 0 | 4.00 |
| 1961-62 | New York R | 10 | 28 | 0 | 2.80 |
| 1962-63 | New York R | 3 | 10 | 0 | 3.33 |
| 1964-65 | New York R | 39 | 135 | 0 | 3.58 |
| 1972-73 | Philadelphia (WHA) | 15 | 49 | 0 | 4.81 |
| | **NHL Totals** | 107 | 362 | 2 | 3.42 |
| | **WHA Totals** | 15 | 49 | 0 | 4.81 |

**PALMATEER, Michael**
b. Toronto, Ont., Jan. 13, 1954

| Season | Club | GP | GA | SO | Avg. |
|---|---|---|---|---|---|
| 1976-77 | Toronto | 50 | 154 | 4 | 3.21 |
| 1977-78 | Toronto | 63 | 172 | 5 | 2.74 |
| 1978-79 | Toronto | 58 | 167 | 4 | 2.95 |
| 1979-80 | Toronto | 38 | 125 | 2 | 3.68 |
| 1980-81 | Washington | 49 | 172 | 2 | 3.85 |
| 1981-82 | Washington | 11 | 47 | 0 | 4.83 |
| 1982-83 | Toronto | 53 | 197 | 0 | 3.99 |
| | **Totals** | 322 | 1034 | 17 | 3.39 |

**PARENT, Bernard Marcel (Bernie)**
b. Montreal, Que., Apr. 3, 1945

| Season | Club | GP | GA | SO | Avg. |
|---|---|---|---|---|---|
| 1965-66 | Boston | 39 | 128 | 1 | 3.69 |
| 1966-67 | Boston | 18 | 62 | 0 | 3.64 |
| 1967-68 | Philadelphia | 38 | 93 | 4 | 2.49 |
| 1968-69 | Philadelphia | 58 | 151 | 1 | 2.69 |
| 1969-70 | Philadelphia | 62 | 171 | 3 | 2.79 |
| 1970-71 | Phil-Tor | 48 | 119 | 3 | 2.72 |
| 1971-72 | Toronto | 47 | 116 | 3 | 2.56 |
| 1972-73 | Philadelphia (WHA) | 63 | 220 | 2 | 3.61 |
| 1973-74 | Philadelphia | 73 | 136 | 12 | 1.89 |
| 1974-75 | Philadelphia | 68 | 137 | 12 | 2.03 |
| 1975-76 | Philadelphia | 11 | 24 | 0 | 2.34 |
| 1976-77 | Philadelphia | 61 | 159 | 5 | 2.71 |
| 1977-78 | Philadelphia | 49 | 108 | 7 | 2.22 |
| 1978-79 | Philadelphia | 36 | 89 | 4 | 2.70 |
| | **NHL Totals** | 608 | 1493 | 55 | 2.55 |
| | **WHA Totals** | 63 | 220 | 2 | 3.61 |

**PARENT, Robert John**
b. Windsor, Ont., Feb. 19, 1958

| Season | Club | GP | GA | SO | Avg. |
|---|---|---|---|---|---|
| 1981-82 | Toronto | 2 | 13 | 0 | 6.50 |
| 1982-83 | Toronto | 1 | 2 | 0 | 3.00 |
| | **Totals** | 3 | 15 | 0 | 5.63 |

**PARRO, David**
b. Saskatoon, Sask., Apr. 30, 1957

| Season | Club | GP | GA | SO | Avg. |
|---|---|---|---|---|---|
| 1980-81 | Washington | 18 | 49 | 1 | 3.63 |
| 1981-82 | Washington | 52 | 206 | 1 | 4.20 |
| 1982-83 | Washington | 6 | 19 | 0 | 4.37 |
| | **Totals** | 76 | 274 | 2 | 4.10 |

**PEETERS, Peter**
b. Edmonton, Alta., Aug. 1, 1957

| Season | Club | GP | GA | SO | Avg. |
|---|---|---|---|---|---|
| 1978-79 | Philadelphia | 5 | 16 | 0 | 3.43 |
| 1979-80 | Philadelphia | 40 | 108 | 1 | 2.73 |
| 1980-81 | Philadelphia | 40 | 115 | 2 | 2.96 |
| 1981-82 | Philadelphia | 44 | 160 | 0 | 3.71 |
| 1982-83 | Boston | 62 | 142 | 8 | 2.36 |
| | **Totals** | 191 | 541 | 11 | 2.90 |

**PELLETIER, Marcel**
b. Drummondville, Que., Dec. 6, 1927

| Season | Club | GP | GA | SO | Avg. |
|---|---|---|---|---|---|
| 1950-51 | Chicago | 6 | 29 | 0 | 4.83 |
| 1962-63 | New York R | 2 | 4 | 0 | 2.00 |
| | **Totals** | 8 | 33 | 0 | 4.13 |

**PERREAULT, Robert (Miche)**
b. Trois-Rivières, Que., Jan. 28, 1931

| Season | Club | GP | GA | SO | Avg. |
|---|---|---|---|---|---|
| 1955-56 | Montreal | 6 | 12 | 1 | 2.00 |
| 1958-59 | Detroit | 3 | 9 | 1 | 3.00 |
| 1962-63 | Boston | 22 | 85 | 1 | 3.98 |
| | **Totals** | 31 | 106 | 3 | 3.49 |

**PETTIE, James**
b. Toronto, Ont., Oct. 24, 1953

| Season | Club | GP | GA | SO | Avg. |
|---|---|---|---|---|---|
| 1976-77 | Boston | 1 | 3 | 0 | 3.00 |
| 1977-78 | Boston | 1 | 6 | 0 | 6.00 |
| 1978-79 | Boston | 19 | 62 | 1 | 3.59 |
| | **Totals** | 21 | 71 | 1 | 3.68 |

**PLANTE, Joseph Jacques (Jake the Snake)**
b. Shawinigan Falls, Que., Jan. 17, 1929

| Season | Club | GP | GA | SO | Avg. |
|---|---|---|---|---|---|
| 1952-53 | Montreal | 3 | 4 | 0 | 1.33 |
| 1953-54 | Montreal | 17 | 27 | 5 | 1.59 |
| 1954-55 | Montreal | 52 | 110 | 5 | 2.11 |
| 1955-56 | Montreal | 64 | 119 | 7 | 1.86 |
| 1956-57 | Montreal | 61 | 123 | 9 | 2.02 |
| 1957-58 | Montreal | 57 | 119 | 9 | 2.11 |
| 1958-59 | Montreal | 67 | 144 | 9 | 2.18 |
| 1959-60 | Montreal | 69 | 175 | 3 | 2.54 |
| 1960-61 | Montreal | 40 | 112 | 2 | 2.80 |
| 1961-62 | Montreal | 70 | 166 | 4 | 2.37 |
| 1962-63 | Montreal | 56 | 138 | 5 | 2.49 |
| 1963-64 | New York R | 65 | 220 | 3 | 3.38 |
| 1964-65 | New York R | 33 | 109 | 2 | 3.37 |
| 1968-69 | St Louis | 37 | 70 | 5 | 1.96 |
| 1969-70 | St Louis | 32 | 67 | 5 | 2.19 |
| 1970-71 | Toronto | 40 | 73 | 4 | 1.88 |
| 1971-72 | Toronto | 34 | 86 | 2 | 2.62 |
| 1972-73 | Tor-Bos | 40 | 103 | 3 | 2.81 |
| 1974-75 | Edmonton (WHA) | 40 | 88 | 1 | 3.32 |
| | **NHL Totals** | 837 | 1965 | 82 | 2.37 |
| | **WHA Totals** | 40 | 88 | 1 | 3.32 |

**PLASSE, Michel**
b. Montreal, Que., June 1, 1948

| Season | Club | GP | GA | SO | Avg. |
|---|---|---|---|---|---|
| 1970-71 | St Louis | 1 | 3 | 0 | 3.00 |
| 1972-73 | Montreal | 17 | 40 | 0 | 2.58 |
| 1973-74 | Montreal | 15 | 57 | 0 | 4.08 |
| 1974-75 | KC-Pitt | 44 | 169 | 0 | 4.03 |
| 1975-76 | Pittsburgh | 55 | 178 | 2 | 3.45 |
| 1976-77 | Colorado | 54 | 190 | 0 | 3.82 |
| 1977-78 | Colorado | 25 | 90 | 0 | 3.90 |
| 1978-79 | Colorado | 41 | 152 | 0 | 3.96 |
| 1979-80 | Colorado | 6 | 26 | 0 | 4.77 |
| 1980-81 | Quebec | 33 | 118 | 0 | 3.66 |
| 1981-82 | Quebec | 8 | 35 | 0 | 5.41 |
| | **Totals** | 299 | 1058 | 2 | 3.79 |

**PRONOVOST, Claude**
b. Shawinigan Falls, Que., July 22, 1935

| Season | Club | GP | GA | SO | Avg. |
|---|---|---|---|---|---|
| 1955-56 | Boston | 1 | 0 | 1 | 0.00 |
| 1958-59 | Montreal | 2 | 7 | 0 | 3.50 |
| | **Totals** | 3 | 7 | 1 | 2.33 |

**RAYNER, Claude Earl (Chuck)**
b. Sutherland, Sask., Aug. 11, 1920

| Season | Club | GP | GA | SO | Avg. |
|---|---|---|---|---|---|
| 1940-41 | New York A | 12 | 44 | 0 | 3.66 |
| 1941-42 | Brooklyn | 36 | 129 | 1 | 3.58 |
| 1945-46 | New York R | 41 | 150 | 1 | 3.75 |
| 1946-47 | New York R | 58 | 177 | 5 | 3.05 |
| 1947-48 | New York R | 12 | 42 | 0 | 3.50 |
| 1948-49 | New York R | 58 | 168 | 7 | 2.90 |
| 1949-50 | New York R | 69 | 181 | 6 | 2.62 |
| 1950-51 | New York R | 66 | 187 | 2 | 2.83 |
| 1951-52 | New York R | 53 | 159 | 2 | 3.00 |
| 1952-53 | New York R | 20 | 58 | 1 | 2.90 |
| | **Totals** | 425 | 1295 | 25 | 3.05 |

**REECE, David Barrett**
b. Troy, N.Y., Sept. 13, 1948

| Season | Club | GP | GA | SO | Avg. |
|---|---|---|---|---|---|
| 1975-76 | Boston | 14 | 43 | 2 | 3.32 |

**RESCH, Glenn Allan (Chico)**
b. Moose Jaw, Sask., July 10, 1948

| Season | Club | GP | GA | SO | Avg. |
|---|---|---|---|---|---|
| 1973-74 | New York I | 2 | 6 | 0 | 3.00 |
| 1974-75 | New York I | 25 | 59 | 3 | 2.47 |
| 1975-76 | New York I | 44 | 88 | 7 | 2.07 |
| 1976-77 | New York I | 46 | 103 | 4 | 2.28 |
| 1977-78 | New York I | 45 | 112 | 3 | 2.55 |
| 1978-79 | New York I | 43 | 106 | 2 | 2.50 |
| 1979-80 | New York I | 45 | 132 | 3 | 3.04 |
| 1980-81 | NYI-Col | 40 | 121 | 3 | 3.20 |
| 1981-82 | Colorado | 61 | 230 | 0 | 4.03 |
| 1982-83 | New Jersey | 65 | 242 | 0 | 3.98 |
| | **Totals** | 416 | 1199 | 25 | 3.00 |

**RHEAUME, Herbert**
b. 1925-26 Montreal

| Season | Club | GP | GA | SO | Avg. |
|---|---|---|---|---|---|
| 1925-26 | Montreal | 30 | 92 | 0 | 3.07 |

**RICCI, Nick Joseph**
b. Niagara Falls, Ont., June 3, 1959

| Season | Club | GP | GA | SO | Avg. |
|---|---|---|---|---|---|
| 1979-80 | Pittsburgh | 4 | 14 | 0 | 3.50 |
| 1980-81 | Pittsburgh | 9 | 35 | 0 | 3.89 |
| 1981-82 | Pittsburgh | 3 | 14 | 0 | 3.79 |
| 1982-83 | Pittsburgh | 3 | 16 | 0 | 6.53 |
| | **Totals** | 22 | 79 | 0 | 4.36 |

**RICHARDSON, Terrance Paul**
b. Powell River, B.C., May 7, 1953

| Season | Club | GP | GA | SO | Avg. |
|---|---|---|---|---|---|
| 1973-74 | Detroit | 9 | 28 | 0 | 5.33 |
| 1974-75 | Detroit | 4 | 23 | 0 | 6.83 |
| 1975-76 | Detroit | 1 | 7 | 0 | 7.00 |
| 1976-77 | Detroit | 5 | 18 | 0 | 4.01 |
| 1978-79 | St Louis | 1 | 9 | 0 | 9.00 |
| | **Totals** | 20 | 85 | 0 | 5.63 |

**RIDLEY, Charles Curtis**
b. Minnedosa, Man., Sept. 24, 1951

| Season | Club | GP | GA | SO | Avg. |
|---|---|---|---|---|---|
| 1974-75 | New York R | 2 | 7 | 0 | 5.19 |
| 1975-76 | Vancouver | 9 | 19 | 1 | 2.28 |
| 1976-77 | Vancouver | 37 | 134 | 0 | 3.88 |
| 1977-78 | Vancouver | 40 | 136 | 0 | 4.06 |
| 1979-80 | Van-Tor | 13 | 47 | 0 | 3.98 |
| 1980-81 | Toronto | 3 | 12 | 0 | 5.81 |
| | **Totals** | 104 | 355 | 1 | 3.87 |

**RIGGIN, Dennis Melville**
b. Kincardine, Ont., Apr. 11, 1936

| Season | Club | GP | GA | SO | Avg. |
|---|---|---|---|---|---|
| 1959-60 | Detroit | 9 | 32 | 1 | 3.55 |
| 1962-63 | Detroit | 9 | 22 | 0 | 2.44 |
| | **Totals** | 18 | 54 | 1 | 3.00 |

**RIGGIN, Patrick Michael**
b. Kincardine, Ont., May 26, 1959

| Season | Club | GP | GA | SO | Avg. |
|---|---|---|---|---|---|
| 1978-79 | Birmingham (WHA) | 46 | 158 | 1 | 3.78 |
| 1979-80 | Atlanta | 25 | 73 | 2 | 3.20 |
| 1980-81 | Calgary | 42 | 154 | 0 | 3.83 |
| 1981-82 | Calgary | 52 | 207 | 2 | 4.23 |
| 1982-83 | Washington | 38 | 121 | 0 | 3.36 |
| | **NHL Totals** | 157 | 555 | 4 | 3.75 |
| | **WHA Totals** | 46 | 158 | 1 | 3.78 |

**RING, Robert**

| Season | Club | GP | GA | SO | Avg. |
|---|---|---|---|---|---|
| 1965-66 | Boston | 1 | 4 | 0 | 8.00 |

| Season | Club | GP | GA | SO | Avg. |
|---|---|---|---|---|---|
| **RIVARD, Fernand Joseph** | | | | | |
| b. Grand' Mère, Que., Jan. 18, 1946 | | | | | |
| 1968-69 | Minnesota | 13 | 48 | 0 | 4.38 |
| 1969-70 | Minnesota | 14 | 42 | 1 | 3.15 |
| 1973-74 | Minnesota | 13 | 50 | 1 | 4.28 |
| 1974-75 | Minnesota | 15 | 50 | 0 | 4.24 |
| **Totals** | | 55 | 190 | 2 | 3.98 |
| **ROACH, John Ross** | | | | | |
| b. Fort Perry, Ont., June 23, 1900 | | | | | |
| 1921-22 | Toronto | 22 | 91 | 0 | 4.14 |
| 1922-23 | Toronto | 24 | 86 | 1 | 3.58 |
| 1923-24 | Toronto | 23 | 80 | 1 | 3.48 |
| 1924-25 | Toronto | 30 | 84 | 1 | 2.80 |
| 1925-26 | Toronto | 36 | 117 | 1 | 3.25 |
| 1926-27 | Toronto | 44 | 94 | 4 | 2.14 |
| 1927-28 | Toronto | 43 | 88 | 4 | 2.05 |
| 1928-29 | New York R | 44 | 65 | 13 | 1.48 |
| 1929-30 | New York R | 44 | 143 | 1 | 3.25 |
| 1930-31 | New York R | 44 | 87 | 7 | 1.98 |
| 1931-32 | New York R | 48 | 112 | 9 | 2.33 |
| 1932-33 | Detroit | 48 | 93 | 9 | 1.94 |
| 1933-34 | Detroit | 18 | 47 | 1 | 2.61 |
| 1934-35 | Detroit | 23 | 62 | 4 | 2.70 |
| **Totals** | | 491 | 1249 | 56 | 2.54 |
| **ROBERTS, Maurice (Moe)** | | | | | |
| b. Waterbury, Conn., Dec. 13, 1907 | | | | | |
| 1925-26 | Boston | 1 | 5 | 0 | 5.00 |
| 1931-32 | New York A | 1 | 1 | 0 | 1.00 |
| 1933-34 | New York A | 6 | 25 | 0 | 4.17 |
| 1951-52 | Chicago | 1 | 0 | 0 | 0.00 |
| **Totals** | | 9 | 31 | 0 | 3.72 |
| **ROBERTSON, Earl Cooper** | | | | | |
| b. Bingorgh, Sask., Nov. 24, 1911 | | | | | |
| 1937-38 | New York A | 48 | 111 | 6 | 2.31 |
| 1938-39 | New York A | 46 | 98 | 3 | 2.13 |
| 1939-40 | New York A | 48 | 140 | 6 | 2.92 |
| 1940-41 | New York A | 36 | 142 | 1 | 3.94 |
| 1941-42 | Brooklyn | 12 | 46 | 0 | 3.83 |
| **Totals** | | 190 | 537 | 16 | 2.83 |
| **ROLLINS, Elwin Ira (Al)** | | | | | |
| b. Vanguard, Sask., Oct. 9, 1926 | | | | | |
| 1949-50 | Toronto | 2 | 4 | 1 | 2.00 |
| 1950-51 | Toronto | 40 | 70 | 5 | 1.75 |
| 1951-52 | Toronto | 70 | 154 | 5 | 2.20 |
| 1952-53 | Chicago | 70 | 175 | 6 | 2.50 |
| 1953-54 | Chicago | 66 | 213 | 5 | 3.23 |
| 1954-55 | Chicago | 44 | 150 | 0 | 3.41 |
| 1955-56 | Chicago | 58 | 174 | 3 | 3.00 |
| 1956-57 | Chicago | 70 | 225 | 3 | 3.21 |
| 1959-60 | New York R | 10 | 31 | 0 | 3.10 |
| **Totals** | | 431 | 1221 | 28 | 2.83 |
| **ROMANO, Roberto** | | | | | |
| b. Montreal. Que., Oct. 29, 1962 | | | | | |
| 1982-83 | Pittsburgh | 3 | 18 | 0 | 6.97 |
| **RUPP, Patrick Lloyd** | | | | | |
| b. Detroit, Mich., Aug. 12, 1942 | | | | | |
| 1963-64 | Detroit | 1 | 4 | 0 | 4.00 |
| **RUTHERFORD, James Earl (Jim)** | | | | | |
| b. Beeton, Ont., Feb. 17, 1949 | | | | | |
| 1970-71 | Detroit | 29 | 94 | 1 | 3.76 |
| 1971-72 | Pittsburgh | 40 | 116 | 1 | 3.22 |
| 1972-73 | Pittsburgh | 49 | 129 | 3 | 2.91 |
| 1973-74 | Pitt-Det | 51 | 168 | 0 | 3.53 |
| 1974-75 | Detroit | 59 | 217 | 2 | 3.74 |
| 1975-76 | Detroit | 44 | 158 | 4 | 3.59 |
| 1976-77 | Detroit | 48 | 180 | 0 | 3.94 |
| 1977-78 | Detroit | 43 | 134 | 1 | 3.26 |
| 1978-79 | Detroit | 32 | 103 | 1 | 3.27 |
| 1979-80 | Detroit | 23 | 92 | 1 | 4.16 |
| 1980-81 | Det-Tor-LA | 31 | 135 | 0 | 4.65 |
| 1981-82 | Los Angeles | 7 | 43 | 0 | 6.79 |
| 1982-83 | Detroit | 1 | 7 | 0 | 7.00 |
| **Totals** | | 457 | 1576 | 14 | 3.65 |

| Season | Club | GP | GA | SO | Avg. |
|---|---|---|---|---|---|
| **RUTLEDGE, Wayne Alvin** | | | | | |
| b. Barrie, Ont., Jan. 5, 1942 | | | | | |
| 1967-68 | Los Angeles | 45 | 117 | 2 | 2.87 |
| 1968-69 | Los Angeles | 17 | 56 | 0 | 3.65 |
| 1969-70 | Los Angeles | 20 | 68 | 0 | 4.25 |
| 1972-73 | Houston (WHA) | 37 | 110 | 2 | 2.96 |
| 1973-74 | Houston (WHA) | 25 | 84 | 0 | 3.34 |
| 1974-75 | Houston (WHA) | 35 | 113 | 2 | 3.23 |
| 1975-76 | Houston (WHA) | 25 | 77 | 1 | 3.17 |
| 1976-77 | Houston (WHA) | 42 | 132 | 3 | 3.15 |
| 1977-78 | Houston (WHA) | 12 | 47 | 0 | 4.45 |
| **NHL Totals** | | 82 | 241 | 2 | 3.35 |
| **WHA Totals** | | 176 | 563 | 6 | 3.23 |
| **ST. CROIX, Rick** | | | | | |
| b. Kenora, Ont., Jan. 3, 1955 | | | | | |
| 1977-78 | Philadelphia | 7 | 20 | 0 | 3.04 |
| 1978-79 | Philadelphia | 2 | 6 | 0 | 3.08 |
| 1979-80 | Philadelphia | 1 | 2 | 0 | 2.00 |
| 1980-81 | Philadelphia | 27 | 65 | 2 | 2.49 |
| 1981-82 | Philadelphia | 29 | 112 | 0 | 3.89 |
| 1982-83 | Philadel-Tor | 33 | 112 | 0 | 3.61 |
| **Totals** | | 99 | 317 | 2 | 3.32 |
| **SAUVE, Robert** | | | | | |
| b. Ste. Genevieve, Que., June 17, 1955 | | | | | |
| 1976-77 | Buffalo | 4 | 11 | 0 | 3.59 |
| 1977-78 | Buffalo | 11 | 20 | 0 | 2.50 |
| 1978-79 | Buffalo | 29 | 100 | 0 | 3.73 |
| 1979-80 | Buffalo | 32 | 74 | 4 | 2.36 |
| 1980-81 | Buffalo | 35 | 111 | 2 | 3.17 |
| 1981-82 | Buf-Det | 55 | 200 | 0 | 3.84 |
| 1982-83 | Buffalo | 54 | 179 | 1 | 3.45 |
| **Totals** | | 220 | 695 | 7 | 3.34 |
| **SAWCHUK, Terrance Gordon (Terry)** | | | | | |
| b. Winnipeg, Man., Dec. 28, 1929 | | | | | |
| 1949-50 | Detroit | 7 | 16 | 1 | 2.28 |
| 1950-51 | Detroit | 70 | 139 | 11 | 1.98 |
| 1951-52 | Detroit | 70 | 133 | 12 | 1.90 |
| 1952-53 | Detroit | 63 | 120 | 9 | 1.90 |
| 1953-54 | Detroit | 67 | 129 | 12 | 1.92 |
| 1954-55 | Detroit | 68 | 132 | 12 | 1.94 |
| 1955-56 | Boston | 68 | 181 | 9 | 2.66 |
| 1956-57 | Boston | 34 | 81 | 2 | 2.38 |
| 1957-58 | Detroit | 70 | 207 | 3 | 2.96 |
| 1958-59 | Detroit | 67 | 209 | 5 | 3.12 |
| 1959-60 | Detroit | 58 | 156 | 5 | 2.69 |
| 1960-61 | Detroit | 37 | 113 | 2 | 3.17 |
| 1961-62 | Detroit | 43 | 143 | 5 | 3.32 |
| 1962-63 | Detroit | 48 | 119 | 3 | 2.48 |
| 1963-64 | Detroit | 53 | 138 | 5 | 2.70 |
| 1964-65 | Toronto | 36 | 92 | 1 | 2.56 |
| 1965-66 | Toronto | 26 | 80 | 1 | 3.16 |
| 1966-67 | Toronto | 28 | 66 | 2 | 2.81 |
| 1967-68 | Los Angeles | 36 | 99 | 2 | 3.07 |
| 1968-69 | Detroit | 13 | 28 | 0 | 2.62 |
| 1969-70 | New York R | 7 | 20 | 1 | 2.91 |
| **Totals** | | 959 | 2401 | 103 | 2.50 |
| **SCHAEFER, Joseph** | | | | | |
| b. Long Island City, N.Y., Dec. 21, 1924 | | | | | |
| 1959-60 | New York R | 1 | 5 | 0 | 7.50 |
| 1960-61 | New York R | 1 | 3 | 0 | 3.61 |
| **Totals** | | 2 | 8 | 0 | 5.33 |
| **SEVIGNY, Richard** | | | | | |
| b. Montreal, Que., Apr. 11, 1957 | | | | | |
| 1979-80 | Montreal | 11 | 31 | 0 | 2.94 |
| 1980-81 | Montreal | 33 | 71 | 2 | 2.40 |
| 1981-82 | Montreal | 19 | 53 | 0 | 3.10 |
| 1982-83 | Montreal | 38 | 122 | 1 | 3.44 |
| **Totals** | | 101 | 277 | 3 | 2.99 |
| **SIMMONS, Donald** | | | | | |
| b. Port Colborne, Ont., Sept. 13, 1931 | | | | | |
| 1956-57 | Boston | 26 | 63 | 4 | 2.42 |
| 1957-58 | Boston | 38 | 93 | 5 | 2.49 |

| Season | Club | GP | GA | SO | Avg. |
|---|---|---|---|---|---|
| 1958-59 | Boston | 58 | 184 | 3 | 3.17 |
| 1959-60 | Boston | 28 | 94 | 2 | 3.36 |
| 1960-61 | Boston | 18 | 59 | 1 | 3.28 |
| 1961-62 | Toronto | 9 | 21 | 2 | 2.33 |
| 1962-63 | Toronto | 28 | 70 | 1 | 2.50 |
| 1963-64 | Toronto | 20 | 63 | 3 | 3.15 |
| 1965-66 | New York R | 8 | 37 | 0 | 4.63 |
| 1967-68 | New York R | 5 | 13 | 0 | 2.60 |
| 1968-69 | New York R | 4 | 8 | 0 | 2.33 |
| **Totals** | | 242 | 705 | 21 | 2.92 |
| **SIMMONS, Gary Byrne** | | | | | |
| b. Charlottetown, P.E.I., July 19, 1944 | | | | | |
| 1974-75 | California | 34 | 124 | 2 | 3.67 |
| 1975-76 | California | 40 | 131 | 2 | 3.33 |
| 1976-77 | Clev-LA | 19 | 67 | 1 | 3.72 |
| 1977-78 | Los Angeles | 14 | 44 | 0 | 3.81 |
| **Totals** | | 107 | 366 | 5 | 3.56 |
| **SKIDMORE, Paul** | | | | | |
| b. Smithtown, N.Y., July 22, 1956 | | | | | |
| 1981-82 | St Louis | 2 | 6 | 0 | 3.00 |
| **SKORODENSKY, Warren** | | | | | |
| b. Winnipeg, Man., Mar. 22, 1960 | | | | | |
| 1981-82 | Chicago | 1 | 5 | 0 | 5.00 |
| **SMITH, Allan Robert (Al)** | | | | | |
| b. Toronto, Ont., Nov. 10, 1945 | | | | | |
| 1965-66 | Toronto | 2 | 2 | 0 | 1.94 |
| 1966-67 | Toronto | 1 | 5 | 0 | 5.00 |
| 1968-69 | Toronto | 7 | 16 | 0 | 2.87 |
| 1969-70 | Pittsburgh | 46 | 129 | 2 | 3.03 |
| 1970-71 | Pittsburgh | 46 | 128 | 2 | 3.10 |
| 1971-72 | Detroit | 43 | 135 | 4 | 3.24 |
| 1972-73 | NE (WHA) | 51 | 162 | 3 | 3.17 |
| 1973-74 | NE (WHA) | 55 | 164 | 2 | 3.08 |
| 1974-75 | NE (WHA) | 59 | 202 | 2 | 3.47 |
| 1975-76 | Buffalo | 14 | 43 | 0 | 3.07 |
| 1976-77 | Buffalo | 7 | 19 | 0 | 4.30 |
| 1977-78 | NE (WHA) | 55 | 174 | 2 | 3.22 |
| 1978-79 | NE (WHA) | 40 | 132 | 1 | 3.31 |
| 1979-80 | Hartford | 30 | 107 | 2 | 3.66 |
| 1980-81 | Colorado | 37 | 151 | 0 | 4.75 |
| **NHL Totals** | | 233 | 735 | 10 | 3.46 |
| **WHA Totals** | | 260 | 834 | 10 | 3.25 |
| **SMITH, Gary Edward** | | | | | |
| b. Ottawa, Ont., Feb. 4, 1944 | | | | | |
| 1965-66 | Toronto | 3 | 7 | 0 | 3.55 |
| 1966-67 | Toronto | 2 | 7 | 0 | 3.63 |
| 1967-68 | Oakland | 21 | 60 | 1 | 3.19 |
| 1968-69 | Oakland | 54 | 148 | 4 | 2.96 |
| 1969-70 | Oakland | 65 | 195 | 2 | 3.11 |
| 1970-71 | California | 71 | 256 | 2 | 3.86 |
| 1971-72 | Chicago | 28 | 62 | 5 | 2.41 |
| 1972-73 | Chicago | 23 | 79 | 0 | 3.54 |
| 1973-74 | Vancouver | 66 | 208 | 3 | 3.44 |
| 1974-75 | Vancouver | 72 | 197 | 6 | 3.09 |
| 1975-76 | Vancouver | 51 | 167 | 2 | 3.50 |
| 1976-77 | Minnesota | 36 | 139 | 1 | 3.99 |
| 1977-78 | Wash-Minn | 20 | 77 | 0 | 3.98 |
| 1978-79 | Ind-Winn (WHA) | 22 | 92 | 0 | 4.28 |
| 1979-80 | Winnipeg | 20 | 73 | 0 | 4.08 |
| **NHL Totals** | | 532 | 1675 | 26 | 3.39 |
| **WHA Totals** | | 22 | 92 | 0 | 4.28 |
| **SMITH, Norman** | | | | | |
| b. Toronto, Ont., Mar. 18, 1908 | | | | | |
| 1931-32 | Montreal M | 21 | 68 | 0 | 3.24 |
| 1934-35 | Detroit | 25 | 52 | 2 | 2.09 |
| 1935-36 | Detroit | 48 | 103 | 6 | 2.15 |
| 1936-37 | Detroit | 48 | 102 | 6 | 2.13 |
| 1937-38 | Detroit | 47 | 130 | 3 | 2.77 |
| 1938-39 | Detroit | 4 | 12 | 0 | 3.00 |
| 1943-44 | Detroit | 5 | 15 | 0 | 3.00 |
| 1944-45 | Detroit | 1 | 3 | 0 | 3.00 |
| **Totals** | | 199 | 485 | 17 | 2.44 |

| Season | Club | GP | GA | SO | Avg. |
|---|---|---|---|---|---|

**SMITH, William John (Billy)**
b. Perth, Ont., Dec. 12, 1950

| Season | Club | GP | GA | SO | Avg. |
|---|---|---|---|---|---|
| 1971-72 | Los Angeles | 5 | 23 | 0 | 4.60 |
| 1972-73 | New York I | 37 | 147 | 0 | 4.16 |
| 1973-74 | New York I | 46 | 134 | 0 | 3.07 |
| 1974-75 | New York I | 58 | 156 | 3 | 2.78 |
| 1975-76 | New York I | 39 | 98 | 3 | 2.61 |
| 1976-77 | New York I | 36 | 87 | 2 | 2.50 |
| 1977-78 | New York I | 38 | 95 | 2 | 2.65 |
| 1978-79 | New York I | 40 | 108 | 1 | 2.87 |
| 1979-80 | New York I | 38 | 104 | 2 | 2.95 |
| 1980-81 | New York I | 41 | 129 | 2 | 3.28 |
| 1981-82 | New York I | 46 | 133 | 1 | 2.97 |
| 1982-83 | New York I | 41 | 112 | 1 | 2.87 |
| | **Totals** | **465** | **1326** | **17** | **2.98** |

**SNEDDON, Robert Allan (Bob)**
b. Montreal, Que., May 31, 1944

| Season | Club | GP | GA | SO | Avg. |
|---|---|---|---|---|---|
| 1970-71 | California | 5 | 21 | 0 | 5.60 |

**SOETAERT, Douglas Henry**
b. Edmonton, Alta., Apr. 21, 1955

| Season | Club | GP | GA | SO | Avg. |
|---|---|---|---|---|---|
| 1975-76 | New York R | 8 | 24 | 0 | 5.27 |
| 1976-77 | New York R | 12 | 28 | 1 | 2.95 |
| 1977-78 | New York R | 6 | 20 | 0 | 3.33 |
| 1978-79 | New York R | 17 | 57 | 0 | 3.80 |
| 1979-80 | New York R | 8 | 33 | 0 | 4.55 |
| 1980-81 | New York R | 39 | 152 | 0 | 3.93 |
| 1981-82 | Winnipeg | 39 | 155 | 2 | 4.31 |
| 1982-83 | Winnipeg | 44 | 174 | 0 | 4.12 |
| | **Totals** | **173** | **641** | **3** | **4.03** |

**SPOONER (Red)**

| Season | Club | GP | GA | SO | Avg. |
|---|---|---|---|---|---|
| 1929-30 | Pittsburgh Pi | 1 | 6 | 0 | 6.00 |

**STANIOWSKI, Edward**
b. Moose Jaw, Sask., July 7, 1955

| Season | Club | GP | GA | SO | Avg. |
|---|---|---|---|---|---|
| 1975-76 | St Louis | 11 | 33 | 0 | 3.19 |
| 1976-77 | St Louis | 29 | 108 | 0 | 4.08 |
| 1977-78 | St Louis | 17 | 57 | 0 | 3.86 |
| 1978-79 | St Louis | 39 | 146 | 0 | 3.82 |
| 1979-80 | St Louis | 22 | 80 | 0 | 4.33 |
| 1980-81 | St Louis | 19 | 72 | 0 | 4.28 |
| 1981-82 | Winnipeg | 45 | 174 | 1 | 3.95 |
| 1982-83 | Winnipeg | 17 | 65 | 1 | 4.72 |
| | **Totals** | **199** | **735** | **2** | **4.02** |

**STEFAN, Gregory Steven**
b. Brantford, Ont., Feb. 11, 1961

| Season | Club | GP | GA | SO | Avg. |
|---|---|---|---|---|---|
| 1981-82 | Detroit | 2 | 10 | 0 | 5.00 |
| 1982-83 | Detroit | 35 | 139 | 0 | 4.52 |
| | **Totals** | **37** | **149** | **0** | **4.55** |

**STEIN, Philip J.**
b. Toronto, Ont., Sept. 13, 1913

| Season | Club | GP | GA | SO | Avg. |
|---|---|---|---|---|---|
| 1939-40 | Toronto | 1 | 2 | 0 | 2.00 |

**STEPHENSON, Frederick Wayne**
b. Fort William, Ont., Jan. 29, 1945

| Season | Club | GP | GA | SO | Avg. |
|---|---|---|---|---|---|
| 1971-72 | St Louis | 2 | 9 | 0 | 5.40 |
| 1972-73 | St Louis | 45 | 128 | 1 | 3.03 |
| 1973-74 | St Louis | 40 | 123 | 2 | 3.13 |
| 1974-75 | Philadelphia | 12 | 29 | 1 | 2.72 |
| 1975-76 | Philadelphia | 66 | 164 | 1 | 2.58 |
| 1976-77 | Philadelphia | 21 | 41 | 3 | 2.31 |
| 1977-78 | Philadelphia | 26 | 68 | 3 | 2.75 |
| 1978-79 | Philadelphia | 40 | 122 | 0 | 3.35 |
| 1979-80 | Washington | 56 | 187 | 0 | 3.57 |
| 1980-81 | Washington | 20 | 66 | 1 | 3.92 |
| | **Totals** | **328** | **937** | **14** | **3.06** |

**STEVENSON, Douglas**
b. Regina, Sask., Apr. 6, 1924

| Season | Club | GP | GA | SO | Avg. |
|---|---|---|---|---|---|
| 1944-45 | NYR-Chi | 6 | 27 | 0 | 4.50 |
| 1945-46 | Chicago | 2 | 12 | 0 | 6.00 |
| | **Totals** | **8** | **39** | **0** | **4.88** |

**STEWART, Charles (Doc)**

| Season | Club | GP | GA | SO | Avg. |
|---|---|---|---|---|---|
| 1924-25 | Boston | 21 | 64 | 2 | 3.05 |
| 1925-26 | Boston | 35 | 80 | 6 | 2.29 |
| 1926-27 | Boston | 21 | 49 | 2 | 2.33 |
| | **Totals** | **77** | **193** | **10** | **2.51** |

**STUART, Herbert**

| Season | Club | GP | GA | SO | Avg. |
|---|---|---|---|---|---|
| 1926-27 | Detroit | 3 | 5 | 0 | 1.67 |

**TAUGHER, William**

| Season | Club | GP | GA | SO | Avg. |
|---|---|---|---|---|---|
| 1925-26 | Montreal | 1 | 3 | 0 | 3.00 |

**TAYLOR, Robert Ian**
b. Calgary, Alta., Jan. 24, 1945

| Season | Club | GP | GA | SO | Avg. |
|---|---|---|---|---|---|
| 1971-72 | Philadelphia | 6 | 16 | 0 | 3.00 |
| 1972-73 | Philadelphia | 23 | 78 | 0 | 4.09 |
| 1973-74 | Philadelphia | 8 | 26 | 0 | 4.26 |
| 1974-75 | Philadelphia | 3 | 13 | 0 | 6.50 |
| 1975-76 | Phil-Pitt | 6 | 22 | 0 | 4.15 |
| | **Totals** | **46** | **155** | **0** | **4.10** |

**TENO, Harvey**

| Season | Club | GP | GA | SO | Avg. |
|---|---|---|---|---|---|
| 1938-39 | Detroit | 5 | 15 | 0 | 3.00 |

**THOMAS, Robert Wayne**
b. Ottawa, Ont., Oct. 9, 1947

| Season | Club | GP | GA | SO | Avg. |
|---|---|---|---|---|---|
| 1972-73 | Montreal | 10 | 23 | 1 | 2.37 |
| 1974-75 | Montreal | 42 | 111 | 1 | 2.76 |
| 1975-76 | Toronto | 64 | 196 | 2 | 3.19 |
| 1976-77 | Toronto | 33 | 116 | 1 | 3.86 |
| 1977-78 | New York R | 41 | 141 | 4 | 3.60 |
| 1978-79 | New York R | 31 | 101 | 1 | 3.63 |
| 1979-80 | New York R | 12 | 44 | 0 | 3.95 |
| 1980-81 | New York R | 10 | 34 | 0 | 3.40 |
| | **Totals** | **243** | **766** | **10** | **3.34** |

**THOMPSON, Cecil R. (Tiny)**
b. Sandon, B.C., May 31, 1905

| Season | Club | GP | GA | SO | Avg. |
|---|---|---|---|---|---|
| 1928-29 | Boston | 44 | 52 | 12 | 1.18 |
| 1929-30 | Boston | 44 | 98 | 3 | 2.23 |
| 1930-31 | Boston | 44 | 90 | 3 | 2.05 |
| 1931-32 | Boston | 43 | 104 | 9 | 2.42 |
| 1932-33 | Boston | 48 | 88 | 11 | 1.83 |
| 1933-34 | Boston | 48 | 130 | 5 | 2.71 |
| 1934-35 | Boston | 48 | 112 | 8 | 2.33 |
| 1935-36 | Boston | 48 | 82 | 10 | 1.71 |
| 1936-37 | Boston | 48 | 110 | 6 | 2.29 |
| 1937-38 | Boston | 48 | 89 | 7 | 1.85 |
| 1938-39 | Bos-Det | 44 | 108 | 4 | 2.45 |
| 1939-40 | Detroit | 46 | 120 | 3 | 2.61 |
| | **Totals** | **553** | **1183** | **80** | **2.14** |

**TREMBLAY, Vincent**
b. Quebec City, Que., Oct. 21, 1959

| Season | Club | GP | GA | SO | Avg. |
|---|---|---|---|---|---|
| 1979-80 | Toronto | 10 | 28 | 0 | 5.11 |
| 1980-81 | Toronto | 3 | 16 | 0 | 6.71 |
| 1981-82 | Toronto | 40 | 153 | 1 | 4.52 |
| | **Totals** | **53** | **197** | **1** | **4.72** |

**TUCKER, Edward William**
b. Fort William, Ont., May 7, 1949

| Season | Club | GP | GA | SO | Avg. |
|---|---|---|---|---|---|
| 1973-74 | California | 5 | 10 | 0 | 3.38 |

**TURNER, Joseph**

| Season | Club | GP | GA | SO | Avg. |
|---|---|---|---|---|---|
| 1941-42 | Detroit | 1 | 3 | 0 | 3.00 |

**VACHON, Rogatien (Rogie)**
b. Palmarolle, Que., Sept. 8, 1945

| Season | Club | GP | GA | SO | Avg. |
|---|---|---|---|---|---|
| 1966-67 | Montreal | 19 | 47 | 1 | 2.48 |
| 1967-68 | Montreal | 39 | 92 | 4 | 2.48 |
| 1968-69 | Montreal | 36 | 98 | 2 | 2.87 |
| 1969-70 | Montreal | 64 | 162 | 4 | 2.63 |
| 1970-71 | Montreal | 47 | 118 | 2 | 2.64 |
| 1971-72 | Mont-LA | 29 | 111 | 0 | 4.15 |
| 1972-73 | Los Angeles | 53 | 148 | 4 | 2.85 |
| 1973-74 | Los Angeles | 65 | 175 | 5 | 2.80 |
| 1974-75 | Los Angeles | 54 | 121 | 6 | 2.24 |
| 1975-76 | Los Angeles | 51 | 160 | 5 | 3.14 |
| 1976-77 | Los Angeles | 68 | 184 | 8 | 2.72 |

**STEWART, Charles (Doc)**

| Season | Club | GP | GA | SO | Avg. |
|---|---|---|---|---|---|
| 1977-78 | Los Angeles | 70 | 196 | 4 | 2.86 |
| 1978-79 | Detroit | 50 | 189 | 0 | 3.90 |
| 1979-80 | Detroit | 59 | 209 | 4 | 3.61 |
| 1980-81 | Boston | 53 | 168 | 1 | 3.34 |
| 1981-82 | Boston | 38 | 132 | 1 | 3.66 |
| | **Totals** | **795** | **2310** | **51** | **2.99** |

**VANBIESBROUCK, John**
b. Detroit, Mich., Sept. 4, 1963

| Season | Club | GP | GA | SO | Avg. |
|---|---|---|---|---|---|
| 1981-82 | New York R | 1 | 1 | 0 | 1.00 |

**VEISOR, Michael David**
b. Toronto, Ont., Aug. 25, 1952

| Season | Club | GP | GA | SO | Avg. |
|---|---|---|---|---|---|
| 1973-74 | Chicago | 10 | 20 | 1 | 2.23 |
| 1974-75 | Chicago | 9 | 36 | 0 | 4.70 |
| 1976-77 | Chicago | 3 | 13 | 0 | 4.33 |
| 1977-78 | Chicago | 12 | 31 | 2 | 2.58 |
| 1978-79 | Chicago | 17 | 60 | 0 | 3.53 |
| 1979-80 | Chicago | 11 | 37 | 0 | 3.36 |
| 1980-81 | Hartford | 29 | 118 | 1 | 4.46 |
| 1981-82 | Hartford | 13 | 53 | 0 | 4.54 |
| 1982-83 | Hartford | 23 | 118 | 1 | 5.53 |
| | **Totals** | **127** | **486** | **5** | **4.08** |

**VERNON, Mike**
b. Calgary, Alta., Feb. 24, 1963

| Season | Club | GP | GA | SO | Avg. |
|---|---|---|---|---|---|
| 1982-83 | Calgary | 2 | 11 | 0 | 6.60 |

**VEZINA, Georges**
b. Chicoutimi, Que., Jan., 1887

| Season | Club | GP | GA | SO | Avg. |
|---|---|---|---|---|---|
| 1917-18 | Montreal | 21 | 84 | 1 | 4.00 |
| 1918-19 | Montreal | 18 | 78 | 1 | 4.33 |
| 1919-20 | Montreal | 24 | 113 | 0 | 4.71 |
| 1920-21 | Montreal | 24 | 99 | 1 | 4.13 |
| 1921-22 | Montreal | 24 | 94 | 0 | 3.91 |
| 1922-23 | Montreal | 24 | 62 | 2 | 2.58 |
| 1923-24 | Montreal | 24 | 48 | 3 | 2.00 |
| 1924-25 | Montreal | 30 | 56 | 5 | 1.87 |
| 1925-26 | Montreal | 1 | 1 | 0 | 1.00 |
| | **Totals** | **190** | **635** | **13** | **3.34** |

**VILLEMURE, Gilles**
b. Trois-Rivières, Que., May 30, 1940

| Season | Club | GP | GA | SO | Avg. |
|---|---|---|---|---|---|
| 1963-64 | New York R | 5 | 18 | 0 | 3.60 |
| 1967-68 | New York R | 4 | 8 | 1 | 2.40 |
| 1968-69 | New York R | 4 | 9 | 0 | 2.25 |
| 1970-71 | New York R | 34 | 78 | 4 | 2.29 |
| 1971-72 | New York R | 37 | 74 | 3 | 2.08 |
| 1972-73 | New York R | 34 | 78 | 3 | 2.29 |
| 1973-74 | New York R | 21 | 62 | 0 | 3.53 |
| 1974-75 | New York R | 45 | 130 | 2 | 3.16 |
| 1975-76 | Chicago | 15 | 54 | 0 | 4.29 |
| 1976-77 | Chicago | 6 | 28 | 0 | 5.38 |
| | **Totals** | **205** | **542** | **13** | **2.80** |

**WAKELY, Ernest Alfred Linton (Ernie)**
b. Flin Flon, Man., Nov. 27, 1940

| Season | Club | GP | GA | SO | Avg. |
|---|---|---|---|---|---|
| 1962-63 | Montreal | 1 | 3 | 0 | 3.00 |
| 1968-69 | Montreal | 1 | 4 | 0 | 4.00 |
| 1969-70 | St Louis | 30 | 58 | 4 | 2.11 |
| 1970-71 | St Louis | 51 | 133 | 3 | 2.79 |
| 1971-72 | St Louis | 30 | 92 | 1 | 3.42 |
| 1972-73 | Winnipeg (WHA) | 49 | 152 | 2 | 3.15 |
| 1973-74 | Winnipeg (WHA) | 37 | 123 | 3 | 3.27 |
| 1974-75 | Winn-SD (WHA) | 41 | 131 | 4 | 3.25 |
| 1975-76 | San Diego (WHA) | 67 | 208 | 3 | 3.25 |
| 1976-77 | San Diego (WHA) | 46 | 129 | 3 | 3.09 |
| 1977-78 | Cin-Hou (WHA) | 57 | 192 | 2 | 3.41 |
| 1978-79 | Birmingham (WHA) | 37 | 129 | 0 | 3.76 |
| | **NHL Totals** | **113** | **290** | **8** | **2.79** |
| | **WHA Totals** | **334** | **1064** | **17** | **3.30** |

**WALSH, James Patrick (Flat)**
b. Kingston, Ont., Mar. 23, 1897

| Season | Club | GP | GA | SO | Avg. |
|---|---|---|---|---|---|
| 1926-27 | Montreal M | 1 | 3 | 0 | 3.00 |
| 1928-29 | NYA-MontM | 11 | 9 | 4 | 0.82 |
| 1929-30 | Montreal M | 28 | 71 | 2 | 2.54 |
| 1930-31 | Montreal M | 15 | 34 | 2 | 2.27 |
| 1931-32 | Montreal M | 27 | 71 | 2 | 2.52 |
| 1932-33 | Montreal M | 23 | 62 | 2 | 2.70 |
| | **Totals** | **105** | **250** | **12** | **2.38** |

| Season | Club | GP | GA | SO | Avg. |
|---|---|---|---|---|---|
| **WAMSLEY, Richard** | | | | | |
| b. Simcoe, Ont., May 25, 1959 | | | | | |
| 1980-81 | Montreal | 5 | 8 | 1 | 1.90 |
| 1981-82 | Montreal | 38 | 101 | 2 | 2.75 |
| 1982-83 | Montreal | 46 | 151 | 0 | 3.51 |
| | **Totals** | 89 | 260 | 3 | 3.10 |
| **WATT, James Magnus (Jim)** | | | | | |
| b. Duluth, Minn., May 11, 1950 | | | | | |
| 1973-74 | St Louis | 1 | 2 | 0 | 6.00 |
| **WEEKS, Stephen** | | | | | |
| b. Scarborough, Ont., June 30, 1958 | | | | | |
| 1980-81 | New York R | 1 | 2 | 0 | 2.00 |
| 1981-82 | New York R | 49 | 179 | 1 | 3.77 |
| 1982-83 | New York R | 18 | 68 | 0 | 3.92 |
| | **Totals** | 68 | 249 | 1 | 3.78 |
| **WETZEL, Carl David** | | | | | |
| b. Detroit, Mich., Dec. 12, 1938 | | | | | |
| 1965-65 | Detroit | 1 | 4 | 0 | 8.00 |
| 1967-68 | Minnesota | 5 | 18 | 0 | 4.00 |
| | **Totals** | 6 | 22 | 0 | 4.40 |
| **WILSON, Duncan Shepherd (Dunc)** | | | | | |
| b. Toronto, Ont., Mar. 22, 1948 | | | | | |
| 1969-70 | Philadelphia | 1 | 3 | 0 | 3.00 |
| 1970-71 | Vancouver | 35 | 128 | 0 | 4.28 |
| 1971-72 | Vancouver | 53 | 173 | 1 | 3.61 |
| 1972-73 | Vancouver | 43 | 159 | 1 | 3.94 |
| 1973-74 | Toronto | 24 | 68 | 1 | 2.89 |
| 1974-75 | Tor-NYR | 28 | 99 | 0 | 3.78 |
| 1975-76 | New York R | 20 | 76 | 0 | 4.22 |
| 1976-77 | Pittsburgh | 45 | 129 | 5 | 2.95 |
| 1977-78 | Pittsburgh | 21 | 95 | 0 | 4.83 |
| 1978-79 | Vancouver | 17 | 58 | 0 | 4.17 |
| | **Totals** | 287 | 988 | 8 | 3.99 |

| Season | Club | GP | GA | SO | Avg. |
|---|---|---|---|---|---|
| **WILSON, Ross Ingram (Lefty)** | | | | | |
| b. Toronto, Ont., Oct. 15, 1919 | | | | | |
| 1953-54 | Detroit | 1 | 0 | 0 | 0.00 |
| 1955-56 | Toronto | 1 | 0 | 0 | 0.00 |
| 1957-58 | Boston | 1 | 1 | 0 | 1.20 |
| | **Totals** | 3 | 1 | 0 | 0.67 |
| **WINKLER, Harold Lang** | | | | | |
| b. Gretna, Man., Mar. 20, 1892 | | | | | |
| 1926-27 | NYR-Bos | 31 | 56 | 8 | 1.81 |
| 1927-28 | Boston | 44 | 70 | 15 | 1.59 |
| | **Totals** | 75 | 126 | 23 | 1.68 |
| **WOLFE, Bernard Ronald** | | | | | |
| b. Montreal, Que., Dec. 18, 1951 | | | | | |
| 1975-76 | Washington | 40 | 148 | 0 | 4.16 |
| 1976-77 | Washington | 37 | 114 | 1 | 3.84 |
| 1977-78 | Washington | 25 | 94 | 0 | 4.25 |
| 1978-79 | Washington | 18 | 68 | 0 | 4.73 |
| | **Totals** | 120 | 424 | 1 | 4.17 |
| **WOODS, Alec** | | | | | |
| b. Falkirk, Scotland | | | | | |
| 1936-37 | New York A | 1 | 3 | 0 | 3.00 |
| **WORSLEY, Lorne (Gump)** | | | | | |
| b. Montreal, Que., May 14, 1929 | | | | | |
| 1952-53 | New York R | 50 | 153 | 2 | 3.06 |
| 1954-55 | New York R | 65 | 197 | 4 | 3.03 |
| 1955-56 | New York R | 70 | 203 | 4 | 2.90 |
| 1956-57 | New York R | 68 | 220 | 3 | 3.23 |
| 1957-58 | New York R | 37 | 86 | 4 | 2.32 |
| 1958-59 | New York R | 67 | 205 | 2 | 3.06 |
| 1959-60 | New York R | 39 | 137 | 0 | 3.51 |
| 1960-61 | New York R | 59 | 193 | 1 | 3.29 |
| 1961-62 | New York R | 60 | 174 | 2 | 2.90 |
| 1962-63 | New York R | 67 | 219 | 2 | 3.27 |

| Season | Club | GP | GA | SO | Avg. |
|---|---|---|---|---|---|
| 1963-64 | Montreal | 8 | 22 | 1 | 3.00 |
| 1964-65 | Montreal | 18 | 50 | 1 | 2.78 |
| 1965-66 | Montreal | 51 | 114 | 2 | 2.36 |
| 1966-67 | Montreal | 18 | 47 | 1 | 3.18 |
| 1967-68 | Montreal | 40 | 73 | 6 | 1.98 |
| 1968-69 | Montreal | 30 | 64 | 5 | 2.26 |
| 1969-70 | Mont-Minn | 14 | 34 | 1 | 2.51 |
| 1970-71 | Minnesota | 24 | 57 | 0 | 2.49 |
| 1971-72 | Minnesota | 34 | 68 | 2 | 2.12 |
| 1972-73 | Minnesota | 12 | 30 | 0 | 2.88 |
| 1973-74 | Minnesota | 29 | 86 | 0 | 3.22 |
| | **Totals** | 860 | 2432 | 43 | 2.90 |
| **WORTERS, Roy** | | | | | |
| b. Toronto, Ont., Oct. 19, 1900 | | | | | |
| 1925-26 | Pittsburgh Pi | 35 | 68 | 7 | 1.94 |
| 1926-27 | Pittsburgh Pi | 44 | 108 | 4 | 2.45 |
| 1927-28 | Pittsburgh Pi | 44 | 76 | 11 | 1.73 |
| 1928-29 | New York A | 38 | 46 | 13 | 1.21 |
| 1929-30 | NYA-Mont | 37 | 137 | 2 | 3.70 |
| 1930-31 | New York A | 44 | 74 | 8 | 1.68 |
| 1931-32 | New York A | 40 | 119 | 5 | 2.98 |
| 1932-33 | New York A | 47 | 116 | 5 | 2.47 |
| 1933-34 | New York A | 36 | 77 | 4 | 2.14 |
| 1934-35 | New York A | 48 | 142 | 3 | 2.96 |
| 1935-36 | New York A | 48 | 122 | 3 | 2.54 |
| 1936-37 | New York A | 23 | 69 | 2 | 3.00 |
| | **Totals** | 484 | 1154 | 66 | 2.38 |
| **WORTHY, Christopher (Chris)** | | | | | |
| b. Bristol, England, Oct. 23, 1947 | | | | | |
| 1968-69 | Oakland | 14 | 54 | 0 | 4.12 |
| 1969-70 | Oakland | 1 | 5 | 0 | 5.00 |
| 1970-71 | California | 11 | 39 | 0 | 4.87 |
| 1973-74 | Edmonton (WHA) | 29 | 92 | 1 | 3.80 |
| 1974-75 | Edmonton (WHA) | 28 | 99 | 1 | 3.58 |
| 1975-76 | Edmonton (WHA) | 24 | 98 | 1 | 4.68 |
| | **NHL Totals** | 26 | 98 | 0 | 4.43 |
| | **WHA Totals** | 81 | 289 | 3 | 3.97 |

# NHL COACH DIRECTORY

On your feet all game, pacing back and forth in an area no more than two feet wide. Coast-to-coast road trips. Countless bus rides and practices. And little, if any, job security. That's the lot of the coach in the National Hockey League.

Still, some have thrived on it. Dick Irvin, for example. A member of the Hockey Hall of Fame, he coached for 26 years in the NHL, a record total of 1,437 games. His 690 NHL wins is also a record.

Billy Reay, known for the hat he wore behind the bench, coached for 16 years (1,102 games) with the Chicago Black Hawks and Toronto Maple Leafs and held on to his job despite the fact that he never guided a Stanley cup winner.

Other coaches have not been so fortunate. As the saying goes, "Coaches are hired to be fired," and it's as true in hockey as it is in other major sports. Except for baseball's Billy Martin and the Yankees, hockey differs in that it seems old coaches often resurface with their old teams. Art Ross coached the Boston Bruins four separate times between 1924 and 1945, and Emile Francis took over the coaching reins of the New York Rangers three times in the 1960s and 1970s.

Sid Abel holds the league's "suitcase award," having served as coach in four different cities —Chicago, Detroit, St. Louis (10 games) and Kan-sas City (three games). Coaches who have worked for more extended periods for three franchises include Red Kelly, Scotty Bowman and Roger Neilson.

The following is a list of the coaches who have served in the history of the current NHL franchises:

## NHL COACHES

**Boston**—Art Ross 1924–25 to 1933–34; Frank Patrick 1934–35 to 1935–36; Art Ross 1936–37 to 1938–39; Cooney Weiland 1939–40 to 1940–41; Art Ross 1941–42 to 1944–45; Dit Clapper 1945–46 to 1948–49; George "Buck" Boucher 1949–50; Lynn Patrick 1950–51 to 1954–55; Milt Schmidt 1954–55 to 1960–61; Phil Watson 1961–62; Phil Watson and Milt Schmidt 1962–63; Milt Schmidt 1963–64 to 1965–66; Harry Sinden 1966–67 to 1969–70; Tom Johnson 1970–71 to 1971–72; Tom Johnson and Bep Guidolin 1972–73; Bep Guidolin 1972–73 to 1973–74; Don Cherry 1974–75 to 1978–79; Fred Creighton and Harry Sinden 1979–80; Gerry Cheevers 1980–81 to —.

**Buffalo**—Punch Imlach 1970–71; Punch Imlach and Joe Crozier 1971–72 to 1973–74; Floyd Smith 1974–75 to 1976–77; Marcel Pronovost 1977–78; Marcel Pronovost and Billy Inglis 1978–79; Scott Bowman and Roger Neilson 1979–80; Roger Neilson 1980–81; Jim Roberts and Scott Bowman 1981–82. Scott Bowman 1982–83 to —.

**Calgary**—(Atlanta 1972–73 to 1979–80)—Bernie Geoffrion 1972–73 to 1973–74; Bernie Geoffrion and Fred Creighton 1974–75; Fred Creighton 1974–75 to 1978–79; Al MacNeil 1979–80 to 1982–82. Bob Johnson 1982–83 to —.

*Scotty Bowman can look back on an illustrious career as coach and general manager.*

*The New York Islanders' Al Arbour has reason to cheer: Four straight Stanley Cups.*

**Chicago**—Pete Muldoon 1926–27; Barney Stanley and Hugh Lehman 1927–28; Herb Gardiner 1928–29; Tom Shaughnessy and Bill Tobin 1929–30; Dick Irvin 1930–31; Dick Irvin and Bill Tobin 1931–32; Godfrey Matheson, Emil Iverson and Tommy Gorman 1932–33; Tommy Gorman 1933–34; Clem Loughlin 1934–35 to 1936–37; Bill Stewart 1937–38; Bill Stewart and Paul Thompson 1938–39; Paul Thompson 1939–40 to 1943–44; Paul Thompson and Johnny Gottselig 1944–45; Johnny Gottselig 1945–46 to 1946–47; Johnny Gottselig and Charlie Conacher 1947–48; Charlie Conacher 1948–49 to 1949–50; Ebbie Goodfellow 1950–51 to 1951–52; Sid Abel 1952–53 to 1953–54; Frank Eddolls 1954–55; Dick Irvin 1955–56; Tommy Ivan 1956–57 to 1957–58; Rudy Pilous 1957–58 to 1962–63; Billy Reay, 1963–64 to 1975–76; Billy Reay and Bill White 1976–77; Bob Pulford 1977–78 to 1978–79; Ed Johnston 1979–80; Keith Magnuson 1980–81; Keith Magnuson and Bob Pulford 1981–82. Orval Tessier 1982–83 to —.

**Detroit**—Art Duncan 1926–27; Jack Adams 1927–28 to 1946–47; Tommy Ivan 1947–48 to 1953–54; Jim Skinner 1954–55 to 1957–58; Sid Abel 1957–58 to 1967–68; Bill Gadsby 1968–69 to 1969–70; Sid Abel 1969–70 to 1970–71; Ned Harkness and Doug Barkley 1970–71; Doug Barkley and Johnny Wilson 1971–72; Johnny Wilson 1972–73; Ted Garvin and Alex Delvecchio 1973–74; Alex Delvecchio 1974–75; Doug Barkley and Alex Delvecchio 1975–76; Alex Delvecchio and Larry Wilson 1976–77; Bobby Kromm 1977–78 to 1979–80; Ted Lindsay and Wayne Maxner 1980–81; Wayne Maxner and Billy Dea 1981–82; Nick Polano 1982–83 to —.

**Edmonton**—Glen Sather 1979–80 to —.

**Hartford**—Don Blackburn 1979–80; Don Blackburn and Larry Pleau 1980–81; Larry Pleau 1981–82; Larry Kish, Larry Pleau and John Cunniff 1982–83.

**Los Angeles**—Red Kelly 1967–68 to 1968–69; Hal Laycoe and John Wilson 1969–70; Larry Regan 1970–71; Larry Regan and Fred Glover 1971–72; Bob Pulford 1972–73 to 1976–77; Ron Stewart 1977–78; Bob Berry 1978–79 to 1980–81; Parker MacDonald, Don Perry and Brad Selwood 1981–82; Don Perry 1982–83 to —.

**Minnesota**—Wren Blair 1967–68; John Muckler and Wren Blair, 1968–69; Wren Blair and Charlie Burns 1969–70; Jackie Gordon 1970–71 to 1973–74; Jackie Gordon and Parker MacDonald 1973–74. Jackie Gordon and Charlie Burns 1974–75; Ted Harris 1975–76 to 1976–77; Ted Harris, Andre Beaulieu and Lou Nanne 1977–78; Harry Howell and Glen Sonmor 1978–79; Glen Sonmor 1979–80 to 1981–82; Glen Sonmor and Murray Oliver 1982–83.

**Montreal**—George Kennedy 1917–18 to 1919–20; Leo Dandurand 1920–21 to 1924–25; Cecil Hart 1925–26 to 1931–32; Newsy Lalonde 1932–33 to 1933–34; Newsy Lalonde and Leo Dandurand 1934–35; Sylvio Mantha 1935–36; Cecil Hart 1936–37 to 1937–38; Cecil Hart and Jules Dugal 1938–39; Pit Lepine 1939–40; Dick Irvin 1940–41 to 1954–55; Toe Blake 1955–56 to 1967–68; Claude Ruel 1968–69 to 1969–70; Claude Ruel and Al MacNeil 1970–71; Scotty Bowman 1971–72 to 1978–79; Bernie Geoffrion and Claude Ruel 1979–80; Claude Ruel 1980–81; Bob Berry 1981–82 to —.

**New Jersey Devils** (Kansas City 1974–75 to 1975–76; Colorado 1976–77 to 1981–82)—Bep Guidolin, 1974–75; Bep Guidolin, Sid Abel and Eddie Bush, 1975–76; John Wilson, 1976–77; Pat Kelly, 1977–78; Pat Kelly and Aldo Guidolin, 1978–79; Don Cherry, 1979–80; Bill MacMillan, 1980–81; Bert Marshall and Marshall Johnston, 1981–82; Bill MacMillan, 1982–83 to —.

**New York Islanders**—Phil Goyette and Earl Ingarfield 1972–73; Al Arbour 1973–74 to —.

**New York Rangers**—Lester Patrick 1926–27 to 1938–39; Frank Boucher 1939–40 to 1947–48; Frank Boucher and Lynn Patrick 1948–49; Lynn Patrick 1949–50; Neil Colville 1950–51; Neil Colville and Bill Cook 1951–52; Bill Cook 1952–53; Frank Boucher and Murray Patrick 1953–54; Murray Patrick 1954–55; Phil Watson 1955–56 to 1959–60; Alf Pike 1959–60 to 1960–61; Doug Harvey 1961–62; Murray Patrick and Red Sullivan 1962–63; Red Sullivan 1963–64 to 1964–65; Red Sullivan and Emile Francis 1965–66; Emile Francis 1966–67 to 1967–68; Bernie Geoffrion and Emile Francis 1968–69; Emile Francis 1968–69 to 1972–73. Larry Popein and Emile Francis 1973–74; Emile Francis 1974–75; Ron Stewart and John Ferguson 1975–76; John Ferguson, 1976–77; Jean-Guy Talbot, 1977–78; Fred Shero, 1978–79 to 1979–80; Fred Shero and Craig Patrick, 1980–81; Herb Brooks, 1981–82 to —.

**Philadelphia**—Keith Allen, 1967–68 to 1968–69; Vic Stasiuk, 1969–70 to 1970–71; Fred Shero, 1971–72 to 1977–78; Bob McCammon and Pat Quinn, 1978–79; Pat Quinn, 1979–80 to 1980–81; Pat Quinn and Bob McCammon, 1981–82; Bob McCammon, 1982–83 to —.

**Pittsburgh**—George Sullivan, 1967–68 to 1968–69; Red Kelly, 1969–70 to 1971–72; Red Kelly and Ken Schinkel, 1972–73; Ken Schinkel and Marc Boileau, 1973–74; Marc Boileau, 1974–75; Marc Boileau and Ken Schinkel, 1975–76; Ken Schinkel, 1976–77; John Wilson, 1977–78 to 1979–80; Eddie Johnston, 1980–81 to —.

**Quebec**—Jacques Demers, 1979–80; Maurice Filion and Michel Bergeron, 1980–81; Michel Bergeron, 1981—82 to —.

**St. Louis**—Lynn Patrick and Scotty Bowman, 1967–68; Scotty Bowman 1968–69 to 1969–70; Al Arbour and Scotty Bowman 1970–71; Sid Abel, Bill McCreary and Al Arbour 1971–72; Al Arbour and Jean Guy Talbot 1972–73; Jean Guy Talbot and Lou Angotti 1973–74; Lou Angotti, Lynn Patrick and Garry Young, 1974–75; Garry Young, Lynn Patrick and Leo Boivin, 1975–76; Emile Francis, 1976–77; Leo Boivin and Barclay Plager, 1977–78; Barclay Plager, 1978–79; Barclay Plager and Red Berenson, 1979–80; Red Berenson, 1980–81; Red Berenson and Emile Francis, 1981–82; Emile Francis, 1982–83.

**Toronto**—Conn Smythe 1927–28 to 1929–30; Conn Smythe and Art Duncan 1930–31; Art Duncan and Dick Irvin 1931–32; Dick Irvin 1932–33 to 1939–40; Hap Day 1940–41 to 1949–50; Joe Primeau 1950–51 to 1952–53; King Clancy 1953–54 to 1955–56; Howie Meeker 1956–57; Billy Reay 1957–58 to 1958–59; Punch Imlach 1958–59 to 1968–69; John McLellan 1969–70 to 1972–73; Red Kelly 1973–74 to 1976–77; Roger Neilson, 1977–78 to 1978–79; Floyd Smith, Dick Duff and Punch Imlach, 1979–80; Punch Imlach and Mike Nykoluk, 1980–81; Mike Nykoluk, 1981–82 to —.

**Vancouver**—Hal Laycoe, 1970–71 to 1971–72; Vic Stasiuk, 1972–73; Bill McCreary and Phil Maloney, 1973–74; Phil Maloney, 1974–75 to 1975–76; Phil Maloney and Orland Kurtenbach, 1977–78; Harry Neale, 1978–79 to 1980–81; Harry Neale and Roger Neilson, 1981–82; Roger Neilson, 1982–83 to —.

**Washington**—Jim Anderson, George Sullivan and Milt Schmidt, 1974–75; Milt Schmidt and Tom McVie, 1975–76; Tom McVie 1976–77 to 1977–78; Danny Belisle, 1978–79; Danny Belisle and Gary Green, 1979–80; Gary Green, 1980–81; Gary Green and Bryan Murray, 1981–82; Bryan Murray, 1982–83 to —.

**Winnipeg**—Tom McVie, 1979–80; Tom McVie and Bill Sutherland, 1980–81; Tom Watt, 1981–82 to —.

# GLOSSARY

**Attacking Zone**—Area from an opponent's blue line to goal line.

**Back-Checking**—A forward coming back into his defensive zone to check an opponent off the puck.

**Backhander**—Any shot or pass made with the stick turned around.

**Blue Lines**—Two lines, one at each end of the rink, that are 60 feet from the goal line and define the attacking zone. They are also used to determine offsides. No attacking player may precede the puck over the defending team's blue line.

**Boarding**—To ride or drive an opponent into the dasher boards. Can result in a minor penalty.

**Body-Check**—To use one's body to block an opponent. Legal only when the man hit has the puck or was the last player to have touched it.

**Charging**—Skating three strides or more and crashing into an opponent. Illegal and calls for a minor penalty.

**Checking**—Defending against or guarding an opponent. On a line, a right wing checks the other team's left wing and a left wing checks the opposing right wing. Centers check each other. Checking requires harassing an opposing skater with the aim of making him surrender the puck.

**Crease**—The rectangular area marked off in front of each net. Only a goalie is permitted in the crease and no player may score from there unless he is being pinned in by a defending player.

**Cross-Checking**—To hit an opponent with both hands on the stick and no part of the stick on the ice. Illegal and calls for a penalty.

**Curved Stick**—A stick with a concave rather than flat blade.

**Defending Zone**—The area from a team's goal line to its blue line.

**Deke**—To feint or shift an opponent out of position.

**Delay of Game**—An intentional stoppage in play (i.e., shooting the puck into the stands, pinning a puck against the boards when unchecked, etc.). Illegal and calls for a minor penalty.

**Elbowing**—Hitting an opponent with the elbow. Illegal and calls for a minor penalty.

**Empty-Netter**—A goal scored after the opposition has pulled its goalie for an extra skater.

**Face-Off**—The dropping of the puck between two opposing players to start play. Face-offs follow goals or other stoppages in action and are to hockey what the jump ball is to basketball.

**Fore-Checking**—Checking an opponent in his own zone.

**Freezing the Puck**—Pinning the puck against the boards with a skate or stick in order to force a stoppage in play. Can result in delay of game penalty if no opposing player is on the puck.

**Goal Judge**—Game official who sits in booth directly

*Melees like this one between the Sabres and the Flyers could lead to a range of penalties—major, match, minor, misconduct.*

behind net and signals when a goal has been scored by turning on a red light.

**Hat Trick**—Three (or more) goals by a single player in a game.

**Head-Manning**—Always advancing the puck to a teammate up ice. Never retreating. This is a favorite maneuver of the Edmonton Oilers.

**High-Sticking**—The carrying of the stick above shoulder level. Always illegal and calls for a minor penalty if one player hits another in this way or a face-off if no other infraction occurs.

**Holding**—To use your hands on an opponent or his equipment. Illegal and calls for a minor penalty.

**Hooking**—To impede an opponent with the blade of your stick. Illegal and calls for a minor penalty.

**Icing the Puck**—Shooting the puck from behind the center red line across an opponent's goal line. Usually done to break up an attack and ease pressure. The puck is brought back and a face-off takes place in the defensive zone of the team that iced the puck. No icing is called against a team that is shorthanded because of a penalty.

**Interference**—Body contact with a man not in possession of the puck or who was not the last man to touch the puck. Also called for knocking an opponent's fallen stick out of his reach. Illegal and calls for a minor penalty.

**Kneeing**—Using the knee to check an opponent. Illegal and calls for a minor penalty.

**Linesman**—Secondary official who makes determinations on icing and offsides calls and is empowered to call a minor penalty if a team has too many men on the ice.

**Major Penalty**—A five-minute penalty. (For example, for fighting or spearing.)

**Match Penalty**—Suspension for the balance of the game.

**Minor Penalty**—A two-minute penalty. Most penalties are minors.

**Misconduct Penalty**—A 10-minute penalty against an individual, not a team. A substitute is permitted. Called for various forms of unacceptable behavior or when a player incurs a second major penalty in a game.

**Neutral Zone**—That area between blue lines. The center ice area.

**Offsides**—Called when an attacking player precedes the puck across the opponent's blue line. Illegal and calls for a face-off.

**Offsides Pass**—Called when the puck is passed to a teammate across two or more lines. Illegal and calls for a face-off from point where the pass originated.

**Penalty-Killer**—A player whose job it is to use up time while a teammate is serving a penalty. The best penalty killers are fast skaters who can break up a power play. Once in possession of the puck, the penalty-killer tries to hold onto it and seldom tries to attack. He is content to waste time until his team is at full strength again.

**Playmaker**—Usually a center whose skating and puck-carrying ability enable him to set up or make a play that can lead to a goal.

**Poke Check**—The quick thrust of the stick to take a puck away from an opposing player. Usually done best by defensemen rather than forwards. Legal.

**Power Play**—A manpower advantage resulting from a penalty to the opposing team.

**Puck**—The vulcanized rubber disc used in hockey.

**Red Line**—The line that divides the ice in half.

**Referee**—Head official in the game who has general supervision of play.

**Roughing**—Minor fisticuffs or shoving. Illegal and calls for a minor penalty.

**Shorthanded**—What a team is when it is trying to kill a penalty.

**Slap Shot**—When a player winds and slaps his stick at the puck. Usually a hard but erratic shot.

**Slashing**—To swing stick at an opponent. Illegal and calls for a minor penalty.

**Slot**—The area extending from in front of the net out about 40 feet. Many goals are scored from this area.

**Spearing**—To use the stick as one would a spear. Illegal and calls for a major penalty.

**Stickhandling**—The art of carrying the puck with the stick.

**Sudden-Death Goal**—Any goal scored in overtime of a game. Overtime is only played if a playoff game is tied after three periods.

**Sweep Check**—To swing the stick along the ice to intercept the puck or hamper an opponent. It is legal.

**Tip-In**—A goal scored from just outside the goalie's crease.

**Wash-Out**—Disallowing of a goal by a referee, or disallowing of icing or offsides by a linesman.

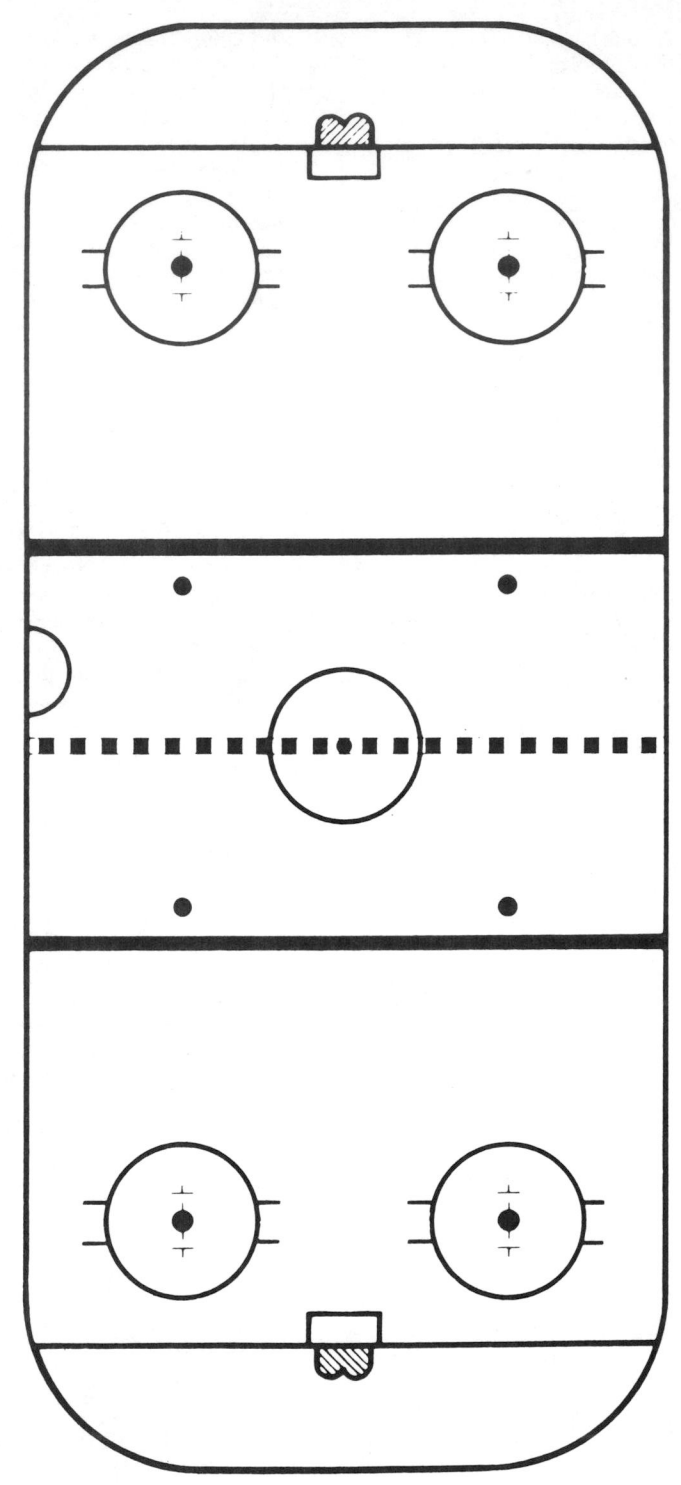

# OFFICIAL NHL RULES

*(Courtesy of the National Hockey League)*

## SECTION ONE — THE RINK

### Rule 1.                    Rink

The game of "Ice Hockey" shall be played on an ice surface known as a "RINK".

(NOTE) *There shall be no markings on the ice except as provided under these rules without the express written permission of the League.*

### Rule 2.                    Dimensions of Rink

(a)    The official size of the rink shall be two hundred feet long and eighty-five feet wide. The corners shall be rounded in the arc of a circle with radius of twenty-eight feet.

The rink shall be surrounded by a wooden or fibreglass wall or fence known as the "boards" which shall extend not less than forty inches and not more than forty-eight inches above the level of the ice surface. The ideal height of the boards above the ice surface shall be forty-two inches. Except for the official markings provided for in these rules the entire playing surface and the boards shall be white in colour except the kick plate at the bottom of the board which shall be light blue or light yellow in colour.

Any variations from any of the foregoing dimensions shall require official authorization by the League.

(b)    The boards shall be constructed in such manner that the surface facing the ice shall be smooth and free of any obstruction or any object that could cause injury to players.

All doors giving access to the playing surface must swing away from the ice surface.

All glass, wire or other types of protective screens and gear used to hold them in position shall be mounted on the boards on the side away from the playing surface.

### Rule 3.                    Goal Posts and Nets

(a)    Ten feet from each end of the rink and in the center of a red line two inches wide, drawn completely across the width of the ice and continued vertically up the side of the boards, regulation goal posts and nets shall be set in such manner as to remain stationary during the progress of a game. The goal posts shall be kept in position by means of metal rods or pipes affixed in the ice or floor and projecting a minimum of eight inches above the ice surface.

Where the length of the playing surface exceeds two hundred feet the goal line and goal posts may be placed not more than fifteen feet from the end of the rink.

(b)    The goal posts shall be of approved design and material, extending vertically four feet above the surface of the ice and set six feet apart measured from the inside of the posts. A cross bar of the same material as the goal posts shall extend from the top of one post to the top of the other.

(NOTE) *For League games the "NHL Official Goal Frame and Net" are approved and adopted. The design and specifications set out in the Plan of Goal printed in this Rule Book are official.*

(c) There shall be attached to each goal frame a net of approved design made of white nylon cord which shall be draped in such a manner as to prevent the puck coming to rest on the outside of it.

A skirt of heavy white nylon fabric or heavy-weight white canvas shall be laced around the "3" base plate of the goal frame in such a way as to protect the net from being cut or broken. This skirt shall not project more than one inch above the base plate.

(NOTE) *The frame of the goal including the small "3" attached to the top crossbar shall be draped with a nylon mesh net so as to completely enclose the back of the frame. The net shall be made of three-ply twisted twine (O.130 inch diameter) or equivalent braided twine of multifilament white nylon with an appropriate tensile strength of 700 pounds. The size of the mesh shall be two and one-half inches (inside measurement) from each knot to each diagonal knot when fully stretched. Knotting shall be made so as to ensure no sliding of the twine. The net shall be laced to the frame with medium white nylon cord no smaller in size than No. 21.*

(d) The goal posts and cross bar shall be painted in red and all other exterior surfaces shall be painted in white.

(e) The red line, two inches wide, between the goal posts on the ice and extended completely across the rink, shall be known as the "GOAL LINE".

(f) The Goal area, enclosed by the goal line and the base of the goal, shall be painted white.

## Rule 4.          Goal Crease

(a) In front of each goal a "GOAL CREASE" area shall be marked by a red line two inches in width.

(b) The goal crease shall be laid out as follows: One foot from the outside of each goal post, lines four feet in length and two inches in width shall be drawn at right angles to the goal line and the points of these lines farthest from the goal line shall be joined by another line, two inches in width.

(c) The goal crease area shall include all the space outlined by the crease lines and extending vertically four feet to the level of the top of the goal frame.

## Rule 5.          Division of Ice Surface

(a) The ice area between the two goals shall be divided into three parts by lines, twelve inches in width, and blue in color, drawn sixty feet out from the goal lines, and extended completely across the rink, parallel with the goal lines, and continued vertically up the side of boards.

(b) That portion of the ice surface in which the goal is situated shall be called the "DEFENDING ZONE" of the team defending that goal; the central portion shall be known as the "NEUTRAL ZONE", and the portion farthest from the defended goal as the "AT-TACKING ZONE".

(c) There shall also be a line, twelve inches in width, and red in color, drawn completely across the rink in center ice, parallel with the goal lines and continued vertically up the side of the boards, known as the "CENTER LINE". This line shall contain at regular

intervals markings of a uniform distinctive design which will easily distinguish it from the two blue lines...the outer edges of which must be continuous.

## Rule 6.          Center Ice Spot and Circle

A circular blue spot, twelve inches in diameter, shall be marked exactly in the center of the rink: and with this spot as a center a circle of fifteen feet radius shall be marked with a blue line two inches in width.

## Rule 7.          Face-off Spots in Neutral Zone

Two red spots two feet in diameter shall be marked on the ice in the Neutral Zone five feet from each blue line. The spots shall be forty-four feet apart and each shall be a uniform distance from the adjacent boards.

## Rule 8.          End Zone Face-off Spots and Circles

(a) In both end zones and on both sides of each goal, red face-off spots and circles shall be marked on the ice. The face-off spots shall be two feet in diameter and extending from each end of the spot and parallel to the boards shall be marked a line six inches in length and two inches wide.

The circles shall be two inches wide with a radius of fifteen feet from the center of the face-off spots. At the outer edge of both sides of each face-off circle and parallel to the goal line shall be marked two red lines, two inches wide and two feet in length and three feet apart.

Parallel to the goal line and equidistant from and on opposite sides of the center of each end face-off spot two red lines six feet in length and three inches in width and six feet apart shall be marked on the ice. Perpendicular from the center of these lines and extending away from the center face-off circle is drawn a line three feet long and three inches wide. (The effect of these lines is to produce a "T" on opposite sides of the center face-off spot.)

(b) The location of the face-offs shall be fixed in the following manner:

Along a line twenty feet from each goal line and parallel to it, mark two points twenty-two feet on both sides of the straight line joining the centers of the two goals. Each such point shall be the center of a face-off spot and circle.

## Rule 9.          Players' Bench

(a) Each rink shall be provided with seats or benches for the use of players of both teams and the accommodations provided including benches and doors shall be uniform for both teams. Such seats or benches shall have accommodation for at least fourteen persons of each team, and shall be placed immediately alongside the ice, in the neutral zone, as near to the center of the rink as possible with doors opening in the Neutral Zone and convenient to the dressing rooms.

Each players' bench should be twenty-four feet in length and when situated in the spectator area they

shall be separated from the spectators by a protective glass of sufficient height so as to afford the necessary protection for the players. The players' benches shall be on the same side of the playing surface opposite the penalty bench and should be separated by a substantial distance.

(NOTE) *Those buildings that were built prior to the introduction of this Rule and in which players' benches were installed on opposite sides of the rink are exempt from this Rule.*

*Where physically possible each Players' Bench shall have two doors opening in the Neutral Zone and all doors opening to the playing surface shall be constructed so that they swing inward.*

(b) None but players in uniform, Manager, Coach and Trainer shall be permitted to occupy the benches so provided.

## Rule 10.                Penalty Bench

(a) Each rink must be provided with benches or seats to be known as the "PENALTY BENCH". These benches or seats must be capable of accommodating a total of ten persons including the Penalty Timekeepers. Separate penalty benches shall be provided for each team and they shall be situated on opposite sides of the Timekeeper's area. The penalty bench(es) must be situated in the Neutral Zone.

(b) On the ice immediately in front of the Penalty Timekeeper's seat there shall be marked in red on the ice a semi-circle of ten feet radius and two inches in width which shall be known as the "REFEREE'S CREASE".

(c) Each "Penalty Bench" shall be protected from the spectator area by means of a glass partition which shall be not less than five feet above the height of the boards.

## Rule 11.           Signal and Timing Devices

(a) Each rink must be provided with a siren, or other suitable sound device, for the use of Timekeepers.

(b) Each rink shall be provided with some form of electrical clock for the purpose of keeping the spectators, players and game officials accurately informed as to all time elements at all stages of the game including the time remaining to be played in any period and the time remaining to be served by at least five penalized players on each team.

Time recording for both game time and penalty time shall show time remaining to be played or served.

(c) Behind each goal electrical lights shall be set up for the use of the Goal Judges. A red light will signify the scoring of a goal. Where automatic lights are available, a green light will signify the end of a period or a game.

(NOTE) *A goal cannot be scored when a green light is showing.*

## Rule 12.                Police Protection

All clubs shall provide adequate police or other protection for all players and officials at all times.

The Referee shall report to the President any failure of this protection observed by him or reported to him with particulars of such failure.

## SECTION TWO — TEAMS

## Rule 13.              Composition of Team

(a) A team shall be composed of six players, who shall be under contract to the club they represent.

(b) Each player and each goalkeeper listed in the line-up of each team shall wear an individual identifying number at least ten inches high on the back of his sweater and, in addition, each player and goalkeeper shall wear his surname in full, in block letters 3" high, across the back of his sweater at shoulder height.

All players of each team shall be dressed uniformly in conformity with approved design and color of their helmets, sweaters, pants, stockings and boots. Any player or goalkeeper not complying with this provision shall not be permitted to participate in the game.

Each Member Club shall design and wear distinctive and contrasting uniforms for their home and road games, no parts of which shall be interchangeable except the pants.

## Rule 14.                Captain of Team

(a) One Captain shall be appointed by each team, and he alone shall have the privilege of discussing with the Referee any questions relating to interpretation of rules which may arise during the progress of a game. He shall wear the letter "C", approximately three inches in height and in contrasting color, in a conspicuous position on the front of his sweater.

(b) The Referee and Official Scorer shall be advised prior to the start of each game, the name of the Captain of the team and the designated substitute.

(c) No goalkeepers shall be entitled to exercise the privilege of Captain.

(d) Only the Captain, when invited to do so by the Referee, shall have the privilege of discussing any point relating to the interpretation of rules. Any Captain or player who comes off the bench and makes any protest or intervention with the Officials for any purpose must be assessed a misconduct penalty in addition to a minor penalty under Rule 42 (b) — Abuse of Officials.

A complaint about a penalty is NOT a matter "relating to the interpretation of the rules" and a minor penalty shall be imposed against any Captain or other player making such a complaint.

(e) No playing Coach or playing Manager shall be permitted to act as Captain.

## Rule 15.                Players in Uniform

(a) At the beginning of each game the Manager or Coach of each team shall list the players and goalkeepers who shall be eligible to play in the game. Not more than eighteen players, exclusive of goalkeepers, shall be permitted.

(b) A list of names and numbers of all eligible players and goalkeepers must be handed to the Referee or Official Scorer before the game, and no change shall be permitted in the list or addition thereto shall be permitted after the commencement of the game.

(c) Each team shall be allowed one goalkeeper on the ice at one time. The goalkeeper may be removed and another "player" substituted. Such substitute shall not be permitted the privileges of the goalkeeper.

(d) Each team shall have on its bench, or on a chair immediately beside the bench, a substitute Goalkeeper who shall at all times be fully dressed and equipped ready to play.

(e) Except when both goalkeepers are incapacitated, no player on the playing roster in that game shall be permitted to wear the equipment of the goalkeeper.

(f) In regular League and Play-off games if both listed goalkeepers are incapacitated, that team shall be entitled to dress and play any available goalkeeper who is eligible. No delay shall be permitted in taking his position in the goal, and he shall be permitted a two-minute warm-up. However, the warm-up is not permitted in the event a goalkeeper is substituted for a penalty shot.

(NOTE) *The two-minute warm-up for a substitute goalkeeper shall be limited to one warm-up per game per goalkeeper.*

(g) The Referee shall report to the President for disciplinary action any delay in making a substitution of goalkeepers.

## Rule 16.       Starting Line-Up

(a) Prior to the start of the game, at the request of the Referee, the Manager or Coach of the visiting team is required to name the starting line-up to the Referee or the Official Scorer. At any time in the game at the request of the Referee, made to the Captain, the visiting team must place a playing line-up on the ice and promptly commence play.

(b) Prior to the start of the game the Manager or Coach of the home team, having been advised by the Official Scorer or the Referee the names of the starting line-up of the visiting team, shall name the starting line-up of the home team which information shall be conveyed by the Official Scorer or the Referee to the Coach of the visiting team.

(c) No change in the starting line-up of either team as given to the Referee or Official Scorer, or in the playing line-up on the ice, shall be made until the game is actually in progress. For an infraction of this rule a bench minor penalty shall be imposed upon the offending team, provided such infraction is called to the attention of the Referee before the second face-off in the first period takes place.

(d) Following the stoppage of play the visiting team shall promptly place a line-up on the ice ready for play and no substitution shall be made from that time until play has been resumed. The home team may then make any desired substitution which does not result in the delay of the game.

If there is any undue delay by either team in changing lines the Referee shall order the offending team or teams to take their positions immediately and not permit a line change.

(NOTE) *When a substitution has been made under the above rule no additional substitution may be made until play commences.*

(e) *The Referee shall give the Visiting Team a reasonable amount of time to make their change after which he shall put up his hand to indicate that no further change shall be made by the Visiting Club. At this point, the Home Team may change immediately. Any attempt by the Visiting Team to make a change after the Referee's signal shall result in the assessment of a bench minor penalty for delay of game.*

## Rule 17.       Equalizing of Teams
### DELETED

## Rule 18.       Change of Players

(a) Players may be changed at any time from the players' bench, provided that the player or players leaving the ice shall always be at the player's bench and out of the play before any change is made.

A goalkeeper may be changed for another player at any time under the conditions set out in this section.

(NOTE 1) *When a goalkeeper leaves his goal area and proceeds to his players' bench for the purpose of substituting another player, the rear Linesman shall be responsible to see that the substitution made is not illegal by reason of the premature departure of the substitute from the bench (before the goalkeeper is within ten feet of the bench). If the substitution is made prematurely, the Linesman shall stop the play immediately by blowing his whistle unless the non-offending team has possession of the puck in which event the stoppage will be delayed until the puck changes hands. There shall be no time penalty to the team making the premature substitution but the resulting face-off will take place on the center "face-off spot".*

(NOTE 2) *The referee shall request that the public address announcer make the following announcement: "Play has been stopped due to premature entry of a player from the players' bench." If in the course of making a substitution the player entering the game plays the puck with his stick, skates or hands or who checks or makes any physical contact with an opposing player while the retiring player is actually on the ice then the infraction of "too many men on the ice" will be called.*

*If in the course of a substitution either the player entering the play or the player retiring is struck by the puck accidentally the play will* not *be stopped and no penalty will be called.*

(b) If by reason of insufficient playing time remaining, or by reason of penalties already imposed, a bench minor penalty is imposed for deliberate illegal substitution (too many men on the ice) which cannot be served in its entirety within the legal playing time, a penalty shot shall be awarded against the offending team.

(c) A player serving a penalty on the penalty bench, who is to be changed after the penalty has been served, must proceed at once by way of the ice and be at his own players' bench before any change can be made.

For any violation of this rule a bench minor penalty shall be imposed.

## Rule 19.       Injured Players

(a) When a player, other than a goalkeeper, is injured or compelled to leave the ice during a game, he may retire

from the game and be replaced by a substitute, but play must continue without the teams leaving the ice.

(b) If a goalkeeper sustains an injury or becomes ill he must be ready to resume play immediately or be replaced by a substitute goalkeeper and NO additional time shall be allowed by the referee for the purpose of enabling the injured or ill goalkeeper to resume his position. (See also Section (d).)

(c) The Referee shall report to the President for disciplinary action any delay in making a goalkeeper substitution.

The substitute goalkeeper shall be subject to the regular rules governing goalkeepers and shall be entitled to the same privileges.

(d) When a substitution for the regular goalkeeper has been made, such regular goalkeeper shall not resume his position until the first stoppage of play thereafter.

(e) If a penalized player has been injured he may proceed to the dressing room without the necessity of taking a seat on the penalty bench. If the injured player receives a minor penalty the penalized team shall immediately put a substitute player without change. If the injured player receives a major penalty the penalized team shall place a substitute player on the penalty bench before the penalty expires and no other replacement for the penalized player shall be permitted to enter the game except from the penalty bench. For violation of this rule a bench minor penalty shall be imposed.

The penalized player who has been injured and been replaced on the penalty bench shall not be eligible to play until his penalty has expired.

(f) When a player is injured so that he cannot continue play or go to his bench, the play shall not be stopped until the injured player's team has secured possession of the puck; if the player's team is in possession of the puck at the time of injury, play shall be stopped immediately, unless his team is in a scoring position.

(NOTE) *In the case where it is obvious that a player has sustained a serious injury the Referee and/or Linesman may stop the play immediately.*

## SECTION THREE — EQUIPMENT

**Rule 20.                    Sticks**

(a) The sticks shall be made of wood or other material approved by the Rules Committee, and must not have any projections. Adhesive tape of any colour may be wrapped around the stick at any place for the purpose of reinforcement or to improve control of the puck. In the case of a goalkeeper's stick, there shall be a knob of white tape or some other protective material approved by the League not less than one-half inch (1/2'') thick at the top of the shaft.

(b) No stick shall exceed fifty-eight inches (58'') in length from heel to the end of the shaft nor more than twelve and one-half inches (12 1/2'') from the heel to the end of the blade.

The blade of the stick shall not be more than three inches in width at any point nor less than two inches. All edges of the blade shall be bevelled. The curvature of the blade of the stick shall be restricted in such a way that the distance of a perpendicular line measured from a straight line drawn from any point at the heel to the end of the blade to the point of maximum curvature shall not exceed one-half inch.

(c) The blade of the goalkeeper's stick shall not exceed three and one-half inches in width at any point except at the heel where it must not exceed four and one-half inches in width; nor shall the goalkeeper's stick exceed fifteen and one-half inches in length from the heel to the end of the blade.

The widened portion of the goalkeeper's stick extending up the shaft from the blade shall not extend more than twenty-six inches from the heel and shall not exceed three and one-half inches in width.

(d) A minor penalty plus a fine of two hundred dollars ($200.00) shall be imposed on any player or goalkeeper who uses a stick not conforming to the provisions of this rule.

(NOTE 1) *When a formal complaint is made by the Captain or designated substitute of a team, against the dimensions of any stick, the Referee shall take the stick to the Timekeeper's bench where the necessary measurement shall be made immediately. The result shall be reported to the Penalty Timekeeper who shall record it on the back of the penalty record.*

*If the complaint is not sustained a bench minor penalty shall be imposed against the complaining Club in addition to a fine of $100.*

(NOTE 2) *A player, who participates in the play while taking a replacement stick to his goalkeeper shall incur a minor penalty under this rule but the automatic fine of two hundred dollars ($200.00) shall not be imposed. If his participation causes a foul resulting in a minor or major penalty the referee shall report the incident to the President for disciplinary action.*

(e) In the event that a player scores on a penalty shot while using an illegal stick the goal shall be disallowed and no further penalty imposed. However, if no goal is scored the player taking the penalty shot shall receive a minor penalty.

(f) A minor penalty plus a ten minute misconduct penalty shall be imposed on any player who refuses to surrender his stick for measurement when requested to do so by the Referee. In addition this player shall be subject to a $200 fine.

**Rule 21.                    Skates**

(a) All hockey skates shall be of a design approved by the Rules Committee. All skates worn by players (but not goalkeepers) and by the Referee and Linesmen shall be equipped with approved safety heel tips.

When the Referee becomes aware that any person is wearing a skate on which the protective heel tip is missing or broken, he shall direct its replacement at the next intermission. If such replacement is not carried out, the Referee shall report the incident to the President for disciplinary action.

(b) The use of speed skates or fancy skates or any skate so designed that it may cause injury is prohibited.

**Rule 22.                    Goalkeeper's Equipment**

(a) With the exception of skates and stick, all the equipment worn by the goalkeeper must be constructed

solely for the purpose of protecting the head or body, and he must not wear any garment or use any contrivance which would give him undue assistance in keeping goal.

(NOTE) *Cages on gloves and abdominal aprons extending down the front of the thighs on the outside of the pants are prohibited. "Cage" shall mean any lacing or webbing or other material in the goalkeeper's glove joining the thumb and index finger which is in excess of the minimum necessary to fill the gap when the goalkeeper's thumb and forefinger in the glove are fully extended and spread and includes any pocket or pouch effect produced by excess lacing or webbing or other material between the thumb and forefinger when fully extended or spread.*

*Protective padding attached to the back or forming part of goalkeeper's gloves shall not exceed eight inches in width nor more than sixteen inches in length at any point.*

(b) The leg guards worn by goalkeepers shall not exceed ten inches in extreme width when on the leg of the player.

(NOTE) *At the commencement of each season and prior to play-offs goalkeepers' leg guards shall be checked by League Staff and any violation of this rule shall be reported to the Club involved and to the President of the League.*

(c) Protective masks of a design approved by the Rules Committee may be worn by goalkeepers.

### Rule 23.                    Protective Equipment

(a) All protective equipment, except gloves, headgear and goalkeepers' leg-guards must be worn under the uniform. For violation of this rule, after warning by the Referee, a minor penalty shall be imposed.

(NOTE) *Players including the goalkeeper violating this rule shall not be permitted to participate in game until such equipment has been corrected or removed.*

(b) All players of both teams shall wear a helmet of design, material and construction approved by the Rules Committee at all times while participating in a game, either on the playing surface or the players' or penalty benches.

Players, who have been under Standard Player's contract to a Member Club of the League, at any time prior to June 1, 1979 may elect for exemption from the operation of this sub-section (b) by execution of an approved Request and Release form and filing it with the League office.

### Rule 24.                    Dangerous Equipment

(a) The use of pads or protectors made of metal, or of any other material likely to cause injury to a player, is prohibited.

(b) A mask or protector of a design approved by the Rules Committee may be worn by a player who has sustained a facial injury.

(NOTE) *All elbow pads which do not have a soft protective outer covering of sponge rubber or similar material at least 1/2 inch thick shall be considered dangerous equipment.*

In the first instance the injured player shall be entitled to wear any protective device prescribed by the Club doctor. If any opposing Club objects to the

device it may record its objection with the President who shall promptly poll the Rules Committee for approval or otherwise.

(c) A glove from which all or part of the palm has been removed or cut to permit the use of the bare hand shall be considered illegal equipment and if any player wears such a glove in play a minor penalty shall be imposed on him.

(NOTE) *The Referee-in-Chief is specifically authorized to make a check of each team's equipment to ensure the compliance with this rule. He shall report his findings to the President for his disciplinary action.*

### Rule 25.                    Puck

(a) The puck shall be made of vulcanized rubber, or other approved material, one inch thick and three inches in diameter and shall weigh between five and a half ounces and six ounces. All pucks used in competition must be approved by the Rules Committee.

(b) The home team shall be responsible for providing an adequate supply of official pucks which shall be kept in a frozen condition. This supply of pucks shall be kept at the penalty bench under the control of one of the regular minor officials or a special attendant.

(NOTE) *As of June 9, 1980, pucks manufactured by the Viceroy Manufacturing Co., the In Glas Co Corporation, and Superior Fabricators Co. have been approved by the Rules Committee.*

(NOTE TO SECTION THREE) *A request for measurement of any equipment covered by this section shall be limited to one request by each Club during the course of any stoppage of play.*

*The Referee may, at his own discretion, measure any equipment used for the first time in the game.*

### SECTION FOUR — PENALTIES

### Rule 26.                    Penalties

Penalties shall be actual playing time and shall be divided into the following classes:

(1) Minor Penalties
(2) Bench Minor Penalties
(3) Major Penalties
(4) Misconduct Penalties
(5) Match Penalties
(6) Penalty Shot.

Where coincident penalties are imposed on players of both teams the penalized players of the visiting team shall take their positions on the penalty bench first in the place designated for visiting players.

(NOTE) *When play is not actually in progress and an offense is committed by any player, the same penalty shall apply as though play were actually in progress.*

### Rule 27.                    Minor Penalties

(a) For a "MINOR PENALTY", any player, other than a goalkeeper, shall be ruled off the ice for two minutes during which time no substitute shall be permitted.

(b) A "BENCH MINOR" penalty involves the removal from the ice of one player of the team against which the penalty is awarded for a period of two minutes. Any player except a goalkeeper of the team may be designated to serve the penalty by the Manager or Coach through the playing Captain and such player shall take his place on the penalty bench promptly and serve the penalty as if it was a minor penalty imposed upon him.

(c) If while a team is "short-handed" by one or more minor or bench minor penalties the opposing team scores a goal, the first of such penalties shall automatically terminate.

(NOTE) *"Short-handed" means that the team must be below the numerical strength of its opponents on the ice at the time the goal is scored. The minor or bench minor penalty which terminates automatically is the one which causes the team scored against to be "short-handed". Thus coincident minor penalties to both teams do NOT cause either side to be "short-handed".*

*This rule shall also apply when a goal is scored on a penalty shot.*

When the minor penalties of two players of the same team terminate at the same time the Captain of that team shall designate to the Referee which of such players will return to the ice first and the Referee will instruct the Penalty Timekeeper accordingly.

When a player receives a major penalty and a minor penalty at the same time the major penalty shall be served first by the penalized player except under Rule 28 (c) in which case the minor penalty will be recorded and served first.

(NOTE) *This applies to the case where BOTH penalties are imposed on the SAME player.*
*See also Note to Rule 33.*

(d) If while a team is short-handed by one penalty (minor or major), co-incident minor penalties of equal duration are imposed against a player of each team, then immediate substitution shall be made for such players.

## Rule 28.    Major Penalties

(a) For the first "MAJOR PENALTY" in any one game, the offender, except the goalkeeper, shall be ruled off the ice for five minutes, during which time no substitute shall be permitted.

An automatic fine of fifty dollars ($50.00) shall also be added when a major penalty is imposed for any foul causing injury to the face or head of an opponent by means of a stick.

(b) For the third major penalty in the same game, to the same player, he shall be ruled off the ice for the balance of the playing time, but a substitute shall be permitted to replace the player so suspended after five minutes shall have elapsed. (Major penalty plus game misconduct penalty with automatic fine of one hundred dollars ($100.00).

(c) When coincident major penalties or coincident penalties of equal duration, including a major penalty, are imposed against players of both teams, the penalized players shall all take their places on the penalty benches and such penalized players shall not leave the penalty bench until the first stoppage of play following the expiry of their respective penalties. Immediate substitutions shall be made for an equal

number of major penalties or *coincident penalties of equal duration including a major penalty to* each team so penalized and the penalties of the players *for* which substitution have been made shall not be taken into account for the purpose of the delayed Rule 33.

Where it is required to determine which of the penalized players shall be designated to serve the delayed penalty under Rule 33 the penalized team shall have the right to make such designation not in conflict with Rule 27.

## Rule 29.    Misconduct Penalties

(a) "MISCONDUCT" penalties to all players except the goalkeeper, involve removal from the game for a period of ten minutes each. A substitute player is permitted to immediately replace a player serving a misconduct penalty. A player whose misconduct penalty has expired shall remain in the penalty box until the next stoppage of play.

When a player receives a minor penalty and a misconduct penalty at the same time, the penalized team shall immediately put a substitute player on the penalty bench and he shall serve the minor penalty without change.

When a player receives a major penalty and a misconduct penalty at the same time, the penalized team shall place a substitute player on the penalty bench before the major penalty expires and no replacement for the penalized player shall be permitted to enter the game except from the penalty bench. Any violation of this provision shall be treated as an illegal substitution under Rule 18 calling for a bench minor penalty.

(b) A misconduct penalty imposed on any player at any time, shall be accompanied with an automatic fine of fifty dollars ($50.00).

(c) A "GAME MISCONDUCT" penalty involves the suspension of a player for the balance of the game but a substitute is permitted to replace immediately the player so removed. A player incurring a game misconduct penalty shall incur an automatic fine of one hundred dollars ($100.00) and the case shall be reported to the President who shall have full power to impose such further penalties by way of suspension or fine on the penalized player or any other player involved in the altercation.

(d) A Game Misconduct penalty shall be imposed on any player or goalkeeper who is the first to intervene in an altercation then in progress. This penalty is in addition to any other penalty incurred in the same incident.

(e) The Referee may impose a "GROSS MISCONDUCT" penalty on any player, Manager, Coach or Trainer who is guilty of gross misconduct of any kind. Any person incurring a "Gross Misconduct" penalty shall be suspended for the balance of the game and shall incur an automatic fine of one hundred dollars ($100) and the case shall be referred to the President of the League for further disciplinary action.

(NOTE) *For all "Game Misconduct" and "Gross Misconduct" penalties regardless of when imposed, a total of ten minutes shall be charged in the records against the offending player.*

(f) In regular League games, any player who incurs a total of three Game Misconduct penalties shall be

suspended automatically for the next League game of his team. For each subsequent Game Misconduct penalty the automatic suspension shall be increased by one game. For each suspension of a player his Club shall be fined one thousand dollars ($1000).

In Play-off games any player who incurs a total of two Game Misconduct penalties shall be suspended automatically for the next Play-off game of his team. For each subsequent Game Misconduct penalty during the Play-offs the automatic suspension shall be increased by one game. For each suspension of a player during Play-offs his Club shall be fined one thousand dollars ($1000).

(NOTE) *Any Game Misconduct penalty for which a player has been assessed an automatic suspension or supplementary discipline in the form of game suspension(s) by the President shall NOT be taken into account when calculating the total number of offences under this subsection.*

*The automatic suspensions incurred under this subsection in respect to League games shall have no effect with respect to violations during Play-off games.*

## Rule 30.            Match Penalties

A "MATCH" penalty involves the suspension of a player for the balance of the game, and the offender shall be ordered to the dressing room immediately. A substitute player is permitted to replace the penalized player after ten minutes playing time has elapsed when the penalty is imposed under Rule 49, and after five minutes actual playing time has elapsed when the penalty is imposed under Rule 44.

(NOTE 1) *Regulations regarding additional penalties and substitutes are specifically covered in individual Rules 44, 49 and 64 any additional penalty shall be served by a player to be designated by the Manager or Coach of the offending team through the playing Captain such player to take his place in the penalty box immediately.*

*For all "MATCH" penalties, regardless of when imposed, or prescribed additional penalties, a total of ten minutes shall be charged in the records against the offending player.*

(NOTE 2) *When coincident match penalties have been imposed under Rule 44, Rule 49 or Rule 64 to a player on both teams Rule 28 (c) covering coincident major penalties will be applicable with respect to player substitution.*

(NOTE 3) *The Referee is required to report all match penalties and the surrounding circumstances to the President of the League immediately following the game in which they occur.*

## Rule 31.            Penalty Shot

(a) Any infraction of the rules which calls for a "Penalty Shot" shall be taken as follows:—

The Referee shall cause to be announced over the public address system the name of the player designated by him or selected by the team entitled to take the shot (as appropriate) and shall then place the puck on the center face-off spot and the player taking the shot will, on the instruction of the Referee, play the puck from there and shall attempt to score on the goalkeeper. The player taking the shot may carry the puck in any part of the Neutral Zone or his own Defending Zone but once the puck has crossed the Attacking Blue Line it must be kept in motion towards the opponent's goal line and once it is shot the play shall be considered complete. No goal can be scored on a rebound of any kind and any time the puck crosses the goal line the shot shall be considered complete.

Only a player designated as a Goalkeeper or Alternate Goalkeeper may defend against the penalty shot.

(b) The Goalkeeper must remain in his crease until the player taking the penalty shot has touched the puck and in the event of violation of this rule or any foul committed by a goalkeeper the Referee shall allow the shot to be taken and if the shot fails he shall permit the penalty shot to be taken over again.

The goalkeeper may attempt to stop the shot in any manner except by throwing his stick or any object, in which case a goal shall be awarded.

(NOTE) *See Rule 80.*

(c) In cases where a penalty shot has been awarded under Rule 50 (c) — deliberately displacing goal post during course of breakaway — under Rule 62 (g) — interference, under Rule 66 (k) — for illegal entry into the game, under Rule 80 (a) — for throwing a stick and under Rule 83 (b) — for fouling from behind, the Referee shall designate the player who has been fouled as the player who shall take the penalty shot.

In cases where a penalty shot has been awarded under Rule 18 (b) — deliberate illegal substitution with insufficient playing time remaining or Rule 50 (d) — deliberately displacing goal post or Rule 53 (c) — falling on the puck in the crease or Rule 57 (d) — picking up the puck from the crease area — the penalty shot shall be taken by a player selected by the Captain of the non-offending team from the players on the ice at the time when the foul was committed. Such selection shall be reported to the Referee and cannot be changed.

If by reason of injury the player designated by the Referee to take the penalty shot is unable to do so within a reasonable time, the shot may be taken by a player selected by the Captain of the non-offending team from the players on the ice when the foul was committed. Such selection shall be reported to the Referee and cannot be changed.

(d) Should the player in respect to whom a penalty shot has been awarded himself commit a foul in connection with the same play or circumstances, either before or after the penalty shot penalty has been awarded, be designated to take the shot he shall first be permitted to do so before being sent to the penalty bench to serve the penalty except when such a penalty is for a game misconduct, gross misconduct or match penalty in which case the penalty shot shall be taken by a player selected by the Captain of the non-offending team from the players on the ice at the time when the foul was committed.

If at the time a penalty shot is awarded the goalkeeper of the penalized team has been removed from the ice to substitute another player the goalkeeper shall be permitted to return to the ice before the penalty shot is taken.

(e) While the penalty shot is being taken, players of both sides shall withdraw to the sides of the rink and beyond the center red line.

(f) If, while the penalty shot is being taken, any player of the opposing team shall have by some action interfered with or distracted the player taking the shot and because of such action the shot should have failed, a second attempt shall be permitted and the Referee shall impose a misconduct penalty on the player so interfering or distracting.

(g) If a goal is scored from a penalty shot the puck shall be faced at center ice in the usual way. If a goal is not scored the puck shall be faced at either of the end face-off spots in the zone in which the penalty shot has been tried.

(h) Should a goal be scored from a penalty shot, a further penalty to the offending player shall not be applied unless the offense for which the penalty shot was awarded was such as to incur a major or match penalty or misconduct penalty, in which case the penalty prescribed for the particular offense, shall be imposed.

If the offense for which the penalty shot was awarded was such as would normally incur a minor penalty, then regardless of whether the penalty shot results in a goal or not, no further minor penalty shall be served.

(i) If the foul upon which the penalty shot is based occurs during actual playing time the penalty shot shall be awarded and taken immediately in the usual manner notwithstanding any delay occasioned by a slow whistle by the Referee to permit the play to be completed which delay results in the expiry of the regular playing time in any period.

The time required for the taking of a penalty shot shall not be included in the regular playing time of any overtime.

## Rule 32.          Goalkeeper's Penalties

(a) A Goalkeeper shall not be sent to the penalty bench for an offense which incurs a minor penalty, but instead the minor penalty shall be served by another member of his team who was on the ice when the offense was committed, said player to be designated by the Manager or Coach of the offending team through the playing Captain and such substitute shall not be changed.

(b) Same as 32 (a) above except change "minor" to "major".

(c) Should a goalkeeper incur three major penalties in one game he shall be ruled off the ice for the balance of the playing time and his place will be taken by a member of his own Club, or by a regular substitute goalkeeper who is available. (Major penalty plus game misconduct penalty and automatic fine of one hundred dollars ($100.00).)

(d) Should a goalkeeper on the ice incur a misconduct penalty this penalty shall be served by another member of his team who was on the ice when the offense was committed, said player to be designated by the Manager or Coach of the offending team through the Captain and, in addition, the goalkeeper shall be fined fifty dollars ($50.00).

(e) Should a goalkeeper incur a game misconduct penalty, his place then will be taken by a member of his own Club, or by a regular substitute goalkeeper who is available, and such player will be allowed the goalkeeper's full equipment. In addition the goalkeeper shall be fined one hundred dollars ($100.00).

(f) Should a goalkeeper incur a match penalty, his place then will be taken by a member of his own Club, or by a substitute goalkeeper who is available, and such player will be allowed the goalkeeper's equipment. However, any additional penalties as specifically called for by the individual rules covering match penalties, will apply, and the offending team shall be penalized accordingly; such additional penalty to be served by another member of the team on the ice at the time the offense was committed, said player to be designated by the Manager or Coach of the offending team through the Captain. (See Rules 44, 49 and 64).

(g) A Goalkeeper incurring a match penalty shall incur an automatic fine of two hundred dollars ($200.00) and the case shall be investigated promptly by the President who shall have full power to impose such further penalty by way of suspension or fine on the penalized goalkeeper or any other player in the altercation.

(h) A minor penalty shall be imposed on a goalkeeper who leaves the immediate vicinity of his crease during an altercation. In addition, he shall be subject to a fine of one hundred dollars ($100.00) and this incident shall be reported to the President for such further disciplinary action as may be required.

(NOTE) *All penalties imposed on goalkeeper regardless of who serves penalty or any substitution, shall be charged in the records against the goalkeeper.*

(i) If a goalkeeper participates in the play in any manner when he is beyond the center red line a minor penalty shall be imposed upon him.

## Rule 33.          Delayed Penalties

(a) If a third player of any team shall be penalized while two players of the same team are serving penalties, the penalty time of the third player shall not commence until the penalty time of one of the two players already penalized shall have elapsed. Nevertheless, the third player penalized must at once proceed to the penalty bench but may be replaced by a substitute until such time as the penalty time of the penalized player shall commence.

(b) When any team shall have three players serving penalties at the same time and because of the delayed penalty rule, a substitute for the third offender is on the ice, none of the three penalized players on the penalty bench may return to the ice until play has stopped. When play has been stopped, the player whose full penalty has expired, may return to the play.

Provided however that the Penalty Timekeeper shall permit the return to the ice in the order of expiry of their penalties, of a player or players when by reason of the expiration of their penalties the penalized team is entitled to have more than four players on the ice.

(c) In the case of delayed penalties, the Referee shall instruct the Penalty Timekeeper that penalized players whose penalties have expired shall only be allowed to return to the ice when there is a stoppage of play.

When the penalties of two players of the same team will expire at the same time the Captain of that team will designate to the Referee which of such players will return to the ice first and the Referee will instruct the Penalty Timekeeper accordingly.

When a major and a minor penalty are imposed at the same time on players of the same team the Penalty Timekeeper shall record the minor as being the first of such penalties.

(NOTE) *This applies to the case where the two penalties are imposed on DIFFERENT players of the same team. See also Note to Rule 27.*

### Rule 34.     Calling of Penalties

(a)  Should an infraction of the rules which would call for a minor, major, misconduct, game misconduct or match penalty be committed by a player of the side in possession of the puck, the Referee shall immediately blow his whistle and give the penalties to the deserving players.

The resulting face-off shall be made at the place where the play was stopped unless the stoppage occurs in the Attacking Zone of the player penalized in which case the face-off shall be made at the nearest face-off spot in the Neutral Zone.

(b)  Should an infraction of the rules which would call for a minor, major, misconduct, game misconduct or match penalty be committed by a player of the team not in possession of the puck, the Referee will blow his whistle and impose the penalty on the offending player upon completion of the play by the team in possession of the puck.

(NOTE) *There shall be no signal given by the Referee for a misconduct or Game Misconduct penalty under this section.*

The resulting face-off shall be made at the place where the play was stopped, unless during the period of a delayed whistle due to a foul by a player of the side NOT in possession, the side in possession ices the puck, shoots the puck so that it goes out of bounds or is unplayable then the face-off following the stoppage shall take place in the Neutral Zone near the Defending Blue Line of the team shooting the puck.

If the penalty or penalties to be imposed are minor penalties and a goal is scored on the play by the non-offending side the minor penalty or penalties shall not be imposed but major and match penalties shall be imposed in the normal manner regardless of whether a goal is scored or not.

(NOTE 1) *"Completion of the play by the team in possession" in this rule means that the puck must have come into the possession and control of an opposing player or has been "frozen." This does not mean a rebound off the goalkeeper, the goal or the boards or any accidental contact with the body or equipment of an opposing player.*

(NOTE 2) *If after the Referee has signalled a penalty but before the whistle has been blown the puck shall enter the goal of the non-offending team as the direct result of the action of a player of that team, the goal shall be allowed and the penalty signalled shall be imposed in the normal manner.*

*If when a team is "short-handed" by reason of one or more minor or bench minor penalties the Referee signals a further minor penalty or penalties against the "short-handed" team and a goal is scored by the non-*

*offending side before the whistle is blown then the goal shall be allowed, the penalty or penalties signalled shall be washed out and the first of the minor penalties already being served shall automatically terminate under Rule 27 (c).*

(c)  Should the same offending player commit other fouls on the same play, either before or after the Referee has blown his whistle, the offending player shall serve such penalties consecutively.

### Rule 34A.     Supplementary Discipline

In addition to the automatic fines and suspensions imposed under these Rules, the President may, at his discretion, investigate any incident that occurs in connection with any Exhibition, League or Play-off game and may assess additional fines and/or suspensions for any offence committed during the course of a game or any aftermath thereof by a player, Trainer Manager, Coach or Club Executive whether or not such offence has been penalized by the Referee.

### Rule 34B.     Suspensions Arising
### from Exhibition Games

Whenever suspensions are imposed as a result of infractions occurring during exhibition games, the President shall exercise his discretion in scheduling the suspensions to ensure that no team shall be short more players in any regular League game than it would have been had the infractions occurred in regular League games.

## SECTION FIVE — OFFICIALS

### Rule 35.     Appointment of Officials

(a)  The President shall appoint a Referee, two Linesmen, Game Timekeeper, Penalty Timekeeper, Official Scorer and two Goal Judges for each game.

(b)  The President shall forward to all clubs a list of Referees, and Off-Ice Officials, all of whom must be treated with proper respect at all times during the season by all players and officials of clubs.

### Rule 36.     Referee

(a)  The REFEREE shall have general supervision of the game, and shall have full control of all game officials and players during the game, including stoppages; and in case of any dispute, his decision shall be final. The Referee shall remain on the ice at the conclusion of each period until all players have proceeded to their dressing rooms.

(b)  All Referees and Linesmen shall be garbed in black trousers and official sweaters.

They shall be equipped with approved whistles and metal tape measures with minimum length of six feet.

(c)  The Referee shall order the teams on the ice at the appointed time for the beginning of a game, and at the commencement of each period. If for any reason there be more than fifteen minutes' delay in the commence-

442  •  THE COMPLETE ENCYCLOPEDIA OF HOCKEY

ment of the game or any undue delay in resuming play after the fifteen minute intervals between periods, the Referee shall state in his report to the President the cause of the delay, and the club or clubs which were at fault.

(d) It shall be his duty to see to it that all players are properly dressed, and that the approved regulation equipment is in use at all times during the game.

(e) The Referee shall, before starting the game, see that the appointed Game Timekeeper, Penalty Timekeeper, Official Scorer and Goal Judges are in their respective places, and satisfy himself that the timing and signalling equipment are in order.

(f) It shall be his duty to impose such penalties as are prescribed by the rules for infractions thereof, and he shall give the final decision in matters of disputed goals. The Referee may consult with the Linesmen or Goal Judge before making his decision.

(g) The Referee shall announce to the Official Scorer or Penalty Timekeeper all goals legally scored as well as penalties, and for what infractions such penalties are imposed.

The Referee shall cause to be announced over the public address system the reason for not allowing a goal every time the goal signal light is turned on in the course of play. This shall be done at the first stoppage of play regardless of any standard signal given by the Referee when the goal signal light was put on in error.

The referee shall report to the Official Scorer the name or number of the goal scorer but he shall *not* give any information or advice with respect to assist.

(NOTE) *The name of the scorer and any player entitled to an assist will be announced on the public address system. In the event that the Referee disallows a goal for any violation of the rules, he shall report the reason for disallowance to the Official Scorer who shall announce the Referee's decision correctly over the public address system.*

*The infraction of the rules for which each penalty has been imposed will be announced correctly, as reported by the Referee, over the public address system. Where players of both teams are penalized on the same play, the penalty to the visiting player will be announced first.*

*Where a penalty is imposed by the Referee which calls for a mandatory or automatic fine, only the time portion of the penalty will be reported by the Referee to the Official scorer and announced on the public address system, and the fine will be collected through the League office.*

(h) The Referee shall see to it that players of opposing teams are separated on the penalty bench to prevent feuding.

(i) He shall not halt the game for any infractions of the rules concerning off-side play at the blue line, or center line or any violation of the "Icing the puck" rule which shall be the function of the Linesman alone, unless the Linesman shall be prevented by some accident from doing so, in which case the duties of the Linesman shall be assumed by the Referee until play is stopped.

(j) Should a Referee accidentally leave the ice or receive an injury which incapacitates him from discharging his duties while play is in progress the game shall be automatically stopped.

(k) If, through misadventure or sickness, the Referee and Linesmen appointed are prevented from appearing, the Managers or Coaches of the two clubs shall agree on a Referee and Linesman. If they are unable to agree, they shall appoint a player from each side who shall act as Referee and Linesman; the player of the home club acting as Referee, and the player of the visiting club as Linesman.

(l) If the regularly appointed officials appear during the progress of the game, they shall at once replace the temporary officials.

(m) Should a Linesman appointed be unable to act at the last minute or through sickness or accident be unable to finish the game, the Referee shall have the power to appoint another, in his stead, if he deems it necessary, or if required to do so by the Manager or Coach of either of the competing teams.

(n) If, owing to illness or accident, the Referee is unable to continue to officiate, one of the Linesmen shall perform such duties as devolved upon the Referee during the balance of the game, the Linesman to be selected by the Referee.

(o) The Referee shall check Club's rosters and all players in uniform before signing reports of the game.

(p) The Referee shall report to the President promptly and in detail the circumstances of any of the following incidents:

(1) When a stick or part thereof is thrown outside the playing area;

(2) Every obscence gesture made by any person involved in the playing or conduct of the game whether as a participant or as an official of either team or of the League, which gesture he has personally observed or which has been brought to his attention by any game official;

(3) When any player, trainer, coach or Club executive becomes involved in an altercation with a spectator.

(4) Every infraction under Rule 77 (c) (slashing).

## Rule 37.                    Linesman

(a) The duty of the LINESMAN is to determine any infractions of the rules concerning off-side play at the blue line, or center line, or any violation of the "Icing the Puck" rule.

He shall stop the play when the puck goes outside the playing area and when it is interfered with by any ineligible person and when it is struck above the height of the shoulder and when the goal post has been displaced from its normal position. He shall stop the play for off-sides occurring on face-offs circles. He shall stop the play when he has observed that a goal has been scored but the referee did not. He shall stop the play when there has been a premature substitution for a goalkeeper under Rule 18 (a) and for injured players under Rule 19 (f) and for a player batting the puck forward to a teammate under Rule 57 (e) and interference by spectators under Rule 63 (a).

(b) He shall face the puck at all times, except at the start of the game, at the beginning of each period and after a goal has been scored.

The Referee may call upon a Linesman to conduct a face-off at any time.

(c) He shall, when requested to do so by the Referee, give his version of any incident that may have taken place during the playing of the game.

(d) He shall not stop the play to impose any penalty except when a major penalty is warranted to a player on the ice when a serious incident has been observed by him but not by the referee and any violation of the Rule 18 (a) & (c) — Change of Players (too many men on the ice) and any violation of Rule 42 (k) (articles thrown on the ice from vicinity of players' or penalty bench) and Rule 42 (l) (interference by Player, Coach, Trainer or Club executive who interferes with game official) and Rule 46 (c) (stick thrown on ice from players' bench) and he shall report such violation to the Referee who shall impose a bench minor penalty against the offending team.

He shall report immediately to the Referee his version of the circumstances with respect to Rule 50 (c) — Delaying the game by deliberately displacing post from its normal position.

He shall report immediately to the Referee his version of any infraction of the rules constituting a major or match foul or Game Misconduct or any conduct calling for a bench minor penalty or misconduct penalty under these rules.

## Rule 38.　　　　　　Goal Judge

(a) There shall be one GOAL JUDGE at each goal. They shall not be members of either club engaged in a game, nor shall they be replaced during its progress, unless after the commencement of the game it becomes apparent that either Goal Judge, on account of partisanship or any other cause, is guilty of giving unjust decisions, when the Referee may appoint another Goal Judge to act in his stead.

(b) Goal Judges shall be stationed behind the goals, during the progress of play, in properly screened cages, so that there can be no interference with their activities; and they shall not change goals during the game.

(c) In the event of a goal being claimed, the Goal Judge of that goal shall decide whether or not the puck has passed between the goal posts and entirely over the goal line, his decision simply being "goal" or "no goal."

## Rule 39.　　　　　　Penalty Timekeeper

(a) The PENALTY TIMEKEEPER shall keep, on the official forms provided, a correct record of all penalties imposed by the officials including the names of the players penalized, the infractions penalized, the duration of each penalty and the time at which each penalty was imposed. He shall report in the Penalty Record each penalty shot awarded, the name of the player taking the shot and the result of the shot.

(b) The Penalty Timekeeper shall check and ensure that the time served by all penalized players is correct. He shall be responsible for the correct posting of penalties on the scoreboard at all times and shall promptly call to the attention of the Referee any discrepancy between the time recorded on the clock and the official correct time and he shall be responsible for making any adjustments ordered by the Referee.

He shall upon request, give a penalized player correct information as to the unexpired time of his penalty.

(NOTE 1) *The infraction of the rules for which each penalty has been imposed will be announced twice over the public address system as reported by the Referee. Where players of both teams are penalized on the same play, the penalty to the visiting player will be announced first.*

(NOTE 2) *Misconduct penalties and co-incident major penalties should not be recorded on the timing device but such penalized players should be alerted and released at the first stoppage of play following the expiration of their penalties.*

(c) Upon the completion of each game, the Penalty Timekeeper shall complete and sign three copies of the Penalty Record to be distributed as quickly as possible to the following persons: —

(1) One copy to the Official Scorer for transmission to the League President;
(2) One copy to the visiting Coach or Manager;
(3) One copy to the home Coach or Manager.

(d) The Referee-in-Chief shall be entitled to inspect, collect and forward to the League headquarters the actual work sheets used by the Penalty Timekeeper in any game.

## Rule 40.　　　　　　Official Scorer

(a) Before the start of the game, the Official Scorer shall obtain from the Manager or Coach of both teams a list of all eligible players and the starting line-up of each team which information shall be made known to the opposing team Manager or Coach before the start of play either personally or through the Referee.

The Official Scorer shall secure the names of the Captain, from the Manager or Coach at the time the line-ups are collected and will indicate those nominated by placing the letter "C" opposite their names on the Referee's Report of Match. All of this information shall be presented to the Referee for his signature at the completion of the game.

(b) The Official Scorer shall keep a record of the goals scored, the scorers, and players to whom assists have been credited, and shall indicate those players on the lists who have actually taken part in the game. He shall also record the time of entry into the game of any substitute goalkeeper. He shall record on the Official Score Sheet a notation where a goal is scored when the goalkeeper has been removed from the ice.

(c) The Official Scorer shall award the points for goals and assists and his decision shall be final. The awards of points for goals and assists shall be announced twice over the public address system and all changes in such awards shall also be announced in the same manner.

No requests for changes in any award of points shall be considered unless they are made at or before the conclusion of actual play in the game by the team Captain.

(d) At the conclusion of the game the Official Scorer shall complete and sign three copies of the Official Score

Sheet for distribution as quickly as possible to the following persons: —

(1) One copy to the League President;

(2) One copy to the visiting Coach or Manager;

(3) One copy to the home Coach or Manager.

(e) The Official Scorer shall also prepare the Official Report of Match for signature by the Referee and forward it to the League President together with the Official Score Sheet and the Penalty Record.

(f) The Official Scorer should be in an elevated position, well away from the Players' Benches, with house telephone communication to the Public Address Announcer.

## Rule 41.    Game Timekeeper

(a) The Game Timekeeper shall record the time of starting and finishing of each period in the game and all playing time during the game.

(b) The Game Timekeeper shall signal the Referee and the competing teams for the start of the game and each succeeding period and the Referee shall start the play promptly in accordance with Rule 81.

To assist in assuring the prompt return to the ice of the teams and the officials the Game Timekeeper shall give a preliminary warning three minutes prior to the resumption of play in each period.

(c) If the rink is not equipped with an automatic gong or bell or siren or, if such device fails to function, the Game Timekeeper shall signal the end of each period by ringing a gong or bell or by blowing a whistle.

(d) He shall cause to be announced on the public address system at the nineteenth minute in each period that there is one minute remaining to be played in the period.

(e) In the event of any dispute regarding time, the matter shall be referred to the Referee for adjustment, and his decision shall be final.

## Rule 41A.    Statistician

(a) There shall be appointed for duty at every game played in the League a Statistician and such assistants or alternates as may be deemed necessary.

(b) The duty of the Statistician(s) is to correctly record on the official League forms supplied all of the data therein provided for concerning the performances of the individual players and the participating teams.

(c) These records shall be compiled and recorded in strict conformity with the instructions printed on the forms supplied and shall be completed as to totals where required and with such accuracy as to ensure that the data supplied is "in balance."

(d) At the conclusion of each game the Statistician shall sign and distribute three copies of the final and correct Statistician's Report to each of the following persons: —

(1) One copy to the League President (through the Official Scorer if possible — otherwise by direct mail);

(2) One copy to the visiting Coach or Manager;

(3) One copy to the home Coach or Manager.

## Rule 42.    Abuse of Officials and other Misconduct

(NOTE) *In the enforcement of this rule the Referee has, in many instances, the option of imposing a "misconduct penalty" or a "bench minor penalty." In principle the Referee is directed to impose a "bench minor penalty" in respect to the violations which occur on or in the immediate vicinity of the players' bench but off the playing surface, and in all cases affecting non-playing personnel or players. A "misconduct penalty" should be imposed for violations which occur on the playing surface or in the penalty bench area and where the penalized player is readily identifiable.*

(a) A misconduct penalty shall be imposed on any player who uses obscene, profane or abusive language to any person or who intentionally knocks or shoots the puck out of the reach of an official who is retrieving it or who deliberately throws any equipment out of the playing area.

(b) A minor penalty shall be assessed to any player who challenges or disputes the rulings of any official during a game. If the player persists in such challenge or dispute he shall be assessed a misconduct penalty and any further dispute will result in a Game Misconduct Penalty being assessed to the offending player.

(c) A misconduct penalty shall be imposed on any player or players who bang the boards with their sticks or other instruments any time.

In the event that the Coach, Trainer, Manager or Club Executive commits an infraction under this Rule a bench minor penalty shall be imposed.

(d) A bench minor penalty shall be imposed on the team of any penalized player who does not proceed directly and immediately to the penalty box and take his place on the penalty bench or to the dressing room when so ordered by the Referee.

Where coincident penalties are imposed on players of both teams the penalized players of the visiting team shall take their positions on the penalty bench first in the place designated for visiting players, or where there is no special designation then on the bench farthest from the gate.

(e) Any player who (following a fight or other altercation in which he has been involved is broken up, and for which he is penalized) fails to proceed directly and immediately to the penalty bench; or who causes any delay by retrieving his equipment (gloves, sticks, etc. shall be delivered to him at the penalty bench by his teammates), shall incur an automatic fine of one hundred dollars ($100.00) in addition to all other penalties or fines incurred.

(f) Any player who persists in continuing or attempting to continue the fight or altercation after he has been ordered by the Referee to stop, or, who resists a Linesman in the discharge of his duties shall, at the discretion of the Referee, incur a Misconduct or a Game Misconduct penalty in addition to any penalties imposed.

(g) A misconduct penalty shall be imposed on any player who, after warning by the Referee, persists in any course of conduct (including threatening or abusive

language or gestures or similar actions) designed to incite an opponent into incurring a penalty.

If, after the assessment of a Misconduct Penalty a player persists in any course of conduct for which he was previously assessed a Misconduct Penalty, he shall be assessed a Game Misconduct Penalty.

(h) In the case of any Club Executive, Manager, Coach or Trainer being guilty of such misconduct, he is to be removed from the bench by order of the Referee, and his case reported to the President for further action.

(i) If any Club Executive, Manager, Coach or Trainer is removed from the bench by order of the Referee, he must not sit near the bench of his club, nor in any way direct or attempt to direct the play of his club.

(j) A bench minor penalty shall be imposed against the offending team if any player, any Club Executive, Manager, Coach or Trainer uses obscene, profane or abusive language or gesture to any person or uses the name of any official coupled with any vociferous remarks.

(k) A bench minor penalty shall be imposed against the offending team if any player, Trainer, Coach, Manager or Club Executive in the vicinity of the players' bench or penalty bench throws anything on the ice during the progress of the game or during stoppage of play.

(NOTE) *The penalty provided under this rule is in addition to any penalty imposed under Rule 46 (c) "Broken Stick."*

(l) A bench minor penalty shall be imposed against the offending team if any player, Trainer, Coach, Manager or Club Executive interferes in any manner with any game official including Referee, Linesmen, Timekeepers or Goal Judges in the performance of their duties.

The Referee may assess further penalties under Rule 67 (Molesting Officials) if he deems them to be warranted.

(m) A misconduct penalty shall be imposed on any player or players who, except for the purpose of taking their positions on the penalty bench, enter or remain in the Referee's Crease while he is reporting to or consulting with any game official including Linesmen, Timekeeper, Penalty Timekeeper, Official Scorer or Announcer.

(n) A minor penalty shall be imposed on any player who is guilty of unsportsmanlike conduct including, but not limited to hair-pulling, biting, grabbing hold of face mask, etc.

## Rule 43.        Adjustment to Clothing and Equipment

(a) Play shall not be stopped nor the game delayed by reason of adjustments to clothing, equipment, shoes, skates or sticks.

For an infringement of this rule, a minor penalty shall be given.

(b) The onus of maintaining clothing and equipment in proper condition shall be upon the player. If adjustments are required, the player shall retire from the ice and play shall continue uninterruptedly with a substitute.

(c) No delay shall be permitted for the repair or adjustment of goalkeeper's equipment. If adjustments are required the goalkeeper will retire from the ice and his

place will be taken by the substitute goalkeeper immediately.

(d) For an infraction of this rule by a goalkeeper, a minor penalty shall be imposed.

## Rule 44.        Attempt to Injure

(a) A match penalty shall be imposed on any player who deliberately attempts to injure an opponent and the circumstances shall be reported to the President for further action. A substitute for the penalized player shall be permitted at the end of the fifth minute.

In addition to the match penalty, the player shall be automatically suspended from further competition until the President has ruled on the issue.

(b) A Game Misconduct penalty shall be imposed on any player who deliberately attempts to injure an Official, Manager, Coach or Trainer in any manner and the circumstances shall be reported to the President for further action.

(NOTE) *The President, upon preliminary investigation indicating the probable imposition of supplementary disciplinary action, may order the immediate suspension of a player who has incurred a match penalty under this rule, pending the final determination of such supplementary disciplinary action.*

## Rule 45.        Board-Checking

(a) A minor or major penalty, at the discretion of the Referee based upon the degree of violence of the impact with the boards, shall be imposed on any player who bodychecks, cross-checks, elbows, charges or trips an opponent in such a manner that causes the opponent to be thrown violently into the boards.

(NOTE) *Any unnecessary contact with a player playing the puck on an obvious "icing" or "off-side" play which results in that player being knocked into the fence is "boarding" and must be penalized as such. In other instances where there is no contact with the fence it should be treated as "charging".*

*"Rolling" an opponent (if he is the puck carrier) along the fence where he is endeavouring to go through too small an opening is not boarding. However, if the opponent is not the puck carrier, then such action should be penalized as boarding, charging, interference or if the arms or stick are employed it should be called holding or hooking.*

(b) When a major penalty is imposed under this Rule for a foul resulting in injury to the face or head of an opponent an automatic fine of fifty dollars ($50) shall be imposed.

## Rule 46.        Broken Stick

(a) A player without a stick may participate in the game. A player whose stick is broken may participate in the game provided he drops the broken portion. A minor penalty shall be imposed for an infraction of this rule.

(NOTE) *A broken stick is one which, in the opinion of the Referee, is unfit for normal play.*

(b) A goalkeeper may continue to play with a broken stick until stoppage of play or until he has been legally provided with a stick.

(c) A player whose stick is broken may not receive a stick thrown on the ice from any part of the rink but must obtain same at his players' bench. A goalkeeper whose stick is broken may not receive a stick thrown on the ice from any part of the rink but may receive a stick from a teammate without proceeding to his players' bench. A minor penalty shall be imposed on the player or goalkeeper receiving a stick illegally under this rule.

(d) A goalkeeper whose stick is broken or illegal may not go to the players' bench for a replacement but must receive his stick from a teammate.

For an infraction of this rule a minor penalty shall be imposed on the goalkeeper.

## Rule 47.     Charging

(a) A minor or major penalty shall be imposed on a player who runs or jumps into or charges an opponent.

(b) When a major penalty is imposed under this rule for a foul, resulting in injury to the face or head of an opponent, an automatic fine of fifty dollars ($50.00) shall be imposed.

(c) A minor or major penalty shall be imposed on a player who charges a goalkeeper while the goalkeeper is within his goal crease.

(NOTE) *If more than two steps or strides are taken it shall be considered a charge.*

*A goalkeeper is NOT "fair game" just because he is outside the goal crease area. A penalty for interference or charging (minor or major) should be called in every case where an opposing player makes unnecessary contact with a goalkeeper.*

*Likewise Referees should be alert to penalize goalkeepers for tripping, slashing or spearing in the vicinity of the goal.*

## Rule 48.     Cross-Checking and Butt-Ending

(a) A minor or major penalty, at the discretion of the Referee, shall be imposed on a player who "cross-checks" an opponent.

(b) A major penalty shall be imposed on any player who "butt-ends" or attempts to "butt-end" an opponent.

(NOTE) *Attempt to "butt-end" shall include all cases where a "butt-end" gesture is made regardless whether body contact is made or not.*

(c) When a major penalty is imposed under this rule an automatic fine of fifty dollars ($50.00) shall also be imposed.

(NOTE) *Cross-check shall mean a check delivered with both hands on the stick and no part of the stick on the ice.*

## Rule 49.     Deliberate Injury of Opponents

(a) A match penalty shall be imposed on a player who deliberately injures an opponent in any manner.

(NOTE) *Any player wearing tape or any other material on his hands who cuts or injures an opponent during an alteration shall receive a match penalty under this rule.*

(b) In addition to the match penalty, the player shall be automatically suspended from further competition until the President has ruled on the issue.

(c) No substitute shall be permitted to take the place of the penalized player until ten minutes actual playing time shall have elapsed, from the time the penalty was imposed.

(d) A Game Misconduct penalty shall be imposed on any player who deliberately injures an Official, Manager, Coach or Trainer in any manner and the circumstances shall be reported to the President for futher action.

## Rule 50.     Delaying the Game

(a) A minor penalty shall be imposed on any player or goalkeeper who delays the game by deliberately shooting or batting the puck with his stick outside the playing area.

(NOTE) *This penalty shall apply also when a player or goalkeeper deliberately bats or shoots the puck with his stick outside the playing area after a stoppage of play.*

(b) A minor penalty shall be imposed on any player or goalkeeper who throws or deliberately bats the puck with his hand or stick outside the playing area.

(c) A minor penalty shall be imposed on any player (including goalkeeper) who delays the game by deliberately displacing a goal post from its normal position. The Referee or Linesmen shall stop play immediately when a goal post has been displaced.

If the goal post is deliberately displaced by a goalkeeper or player during the course of a "break-away" a penalty shot will be awarded to the non-offending team, which shot shall be taken by the player last in possession of the puck.

(NOTE) *A player with a "break-away" is defined as a player in control of the puck with no opposition between him and the opposing goal and with a reasonable scoring opportunity.*

(d) If by reason of insufficient time in the regular playing time or by reason of penalties already imposed the minor penalty awarded to a player for deliberately displacing his own goal post cannot be served in its entirety within the regular playing time of the game or at any time in overtime, a penalty shot shall be awarded against the offending team.

(e) A bench minor penalty shall be imposed upon any team which, after warning by the Referee to its Captain or designated substitute to place the correct number of players on the ice and commence play, fails to comply with the Referee's direction and thereby causes any delay by making additional substitutions, by persisting in having its players off-side, or in any other manner.

## Rule 51.     Elbowing, Kneeing and Head-Butting

(a) A minor or major penalty, at the discretion of the Referee, shall be imposed on any player who uses his elbow or knee in such a manner as to in any way foul an opponent.

(b) When a major penalty is imposed under this rule for a foul resulting in an injury to an opponent an automatic fine of fifty dollars ($50.00) shall also be imposed.

(c) A match penalty shall be imposed on any player who deliberately "head-butts" or attempts to "head-butt"

an opponent during an altercation and the circumstances shall be reported to the President for further action. A substitute shall be permitted at the end of the fifth minute. In the event there is an injury to an opponent resulting from the foul no substitute shall be permitted to take the place of the penalized player until ten minutes actual playing time shall be elapsed.

## Rule 52.                    Face-Offs

(a)  The puck shall be "faced-off" by the Referee or the Linesman dropping the puck on the ice between the sticks of the players "facing-off". Players facing-off will stand squarely facing their opponents' end of the rink approximately one stick length apart with the blade of their sticks on the ice.

When the face-off takes place in any of the end face-off circles the players taking part shall take their position so that they will have one skate on each side and clear of the line running through the face-off spot and with both feet behind him and clear of the line parallel to the goal line. The sticks of both players facing-off shall have the blade on the ice in contact with designated marking.

No other player shall be allowed to enter the face-off circle or come within fifteen feet of the players facing-off the puck, and must stand on side on all face-offs.

If a violation of this sub-section of this rule occurs the Referee or Linesman shall re-face the puck.

(b)  If after warning by the Referee or Linesman either of the players fails to take his proper position for the face-off promptly, the official shall be entitled to face-off the puck notwithstanding such default.

(c)  In the conduct of any face-off anywhere on the playing surface no player facing-off shall make any physical contact with his opponent's body by means of his own body or by his stick except in the course of playing the puck after the face-off has been completed.

For violation of this Rule the Referee shall impose a minor penalty or penalties on the player(s) whose action(s) caused the physical contact.

(NOTE) *"Conduct of any face-off" commences when the Referee designates the place of the face-off and he (or the Linesman) takes up his position to drop the puck.*

(d)  If a player facing-off fails to take his proper position immediately when directed by the Official, the Official may order him replaced for that face-off by any teammate then on the ice.

No substitution of players shall be permitted until the face-off has been completed and play has been resumed except when a penalty is imposed which will affect the on-ice strength of either team.

(e)  A second violation of any of the provisions of subsection (a) hereof by the same team during the same face-off shall be penalized with a minor penalty to the player who commits the second violation of the rule.

(f)  When an infringement of a rule has been committed or a stoppage of play has been caused by any player of the attacking side in the Attacking Zone the ensuing face-off shall be made in the Neutral Zone on the nearest face-off spot.

(NOTE) *This includes stoppage of play caused by player of attacking side shooting the puck on the back of the defending team's net without any intervening action by the defending team.*

(g)  When an infringement of a rule has been committed by players of both sides in the play resulting in the stoppage, the ensuing face-off will be made at the place of such infringement or at the place where play is stopped.

(h)  When stoppage occurs between the end face-off spots and near end of rink the puck shall be faced-off at the end face-off spot, on the side where the stoppage occurs unless otherwise expressly provided by these rules.

(i)  No face-off shall be made within fifteen feet of the goal or sideboards.

(j)  When a goal is illegally scored as a result of a puck being deflected directly from an official anywhere in the defending zone the resulting face-off shall be made at the end face-off spot in the defending zone.

(k)  When the game is stopped for any reason not specifically covered in the official rules, the puck must be faced-off where it was last played.

(l)  The whistle will not be blown by the official to start play. Playing time will commence from the instant the puck is faced-off and will stop when the whistle is blown.

(m)  Following a stoppage of play, should one or both defensemen, who are the point players or any player coming from the bench of the attacking team, enter into the attacking zone beyond the outer edge of the corner face-off circle, the ensuing face-off shall take place at the nearest spot in the neutral zone near the blue line of the defending team.

## Rule 53.                    Falling on Puck

(a)  A minor penalty shall be imposed on a player other than the goalkeeper who deliberately falls on or gathers a puck into his body.

(NOTE) *Any player who drops to his knees to block shots should not be penalized if the puck is shot under them or becomes lodged in their clothing or equipment but any use of the hands to make the puck unplayable should be penalized promptly.*

(b)  A minor penalty shall be imposed on a goalkeeper who (when he is in his own goal crease) deliberately falls on or gathers the puck into his body or who holds or places the puck against any part of the goal in such a manner as to cause a stoppage of play unless he is actually being checked by an opponent.

(NOTE) *Refer to Rule 73 (c) for Rule governing freezing of puck by goalkeeper outside of his crease area.*

(c)  No defending player, except the goalkeeper, will be permitted to fall on the puck or hold the puck or gather a puck into the body or hands when the puck is within the goal crease.

For infringement of this rule, play shall immediately be stopped and a penalty shot shall be ordered against the offending team, but no other penalty shall be given.

(NOTE) *This rule shall be interpreted so that a*

*penalty shot will be awarded only when the puck is in the crease at the instant the offense occurs. However, in cases where the puck is outside the crease, Rule 53 (a) may still apply and a minor penalty may be imposed, even though no penalty shot is awarded.*

## Rule 54.             Fisticuffs

(a) A major or a major and a Game Misconduct penalty, at the discretion of the Referee, shall be imposed on any player who starts fisticuffs.

(b) A minor penalty shall be imposed on a player who, having been struck, shall retaliate with a blow or attempted blow. However, at the discretion of the Referee a major or a double minor penalty or a Game Misconduct penalty may be imposed if such player continues the altercation.

    (NOTE 1) *It is the intent and purpose of this Rule that the Referee shall impose the "Major and Game Misconduct" penalty in all cases when the instigator or retaliator of the fight is the aggressor and is plainly doing so for the purpose of intimidation or punishment.*

    (NOTE 2) *The Referee is provided very wide latitude in the penalties which he may impose under this rule. This is done intentionally to enable him to differentiate between the obvious degrees of responsibility of the participants either for starting the fighting or persisting in continuing the fighting. The discretion provided should be exercised realistically.*

    (NOTE 3) *Referees are directed to employ every means provided by these Rules to stop "brawling" and should use this Rule and Rules 42 (e) and (f) for this purpose.*

(c) A Misconduct or Game Misconduct penalty shall be imposed on any player involved in fisticuffs off the playing surface or with another player who is off the playing surface.

(d) A Game Misconduct penalty, at the discretion of the Referee, shall be imposed on any player or goalkeeper who is the first to intervene in an altercation then in progress except when a match penalty is being imposed in the original altercation. This penalty is in addition to any other penalty incurred in the same incident.

(e) When a fight occurs all players not engaged in the altercation shall move to an area designated by the Referee upon his command.

    Failure to comply with instructions of the Referee will result in a Club fine of one thousand dollars ($1,000) for the first offense, three thousand dollars ($3,000) for the second offense and five thousand dollars ($5,000) for each subsequent offense.

    (NOTE) *In the case of those buildings where the benches are on the same side of the rink the visiting team will proceed to the vicinity of the penalty bench and the home team to the vicinity of its players' bench. In the case where the benches are on opposite sides of the rink each Club will proceed to its own players' bench. However, in the event that the altercation takes place in the neutral zone each Club will proceed to its own defensive zone.*

(f) A Game Misconduct penalty shall be imposed on any player who is assessed a major penalty for fighting following the original altercation.

## Rule 55.             Goals and Assists

    (NOTE) *It is the responsibility of the Official Scorer to award goals and assists, and his decision in this respect is final notwithstanding the report of the Referee or any other game official. Such awards shall be made or withheld strictly in accordance with the provisions of this rule. Therefore, it is essential that the Official Scorer shall be thoroughly familiar with every aspect of this rule, be alert to observe all actions which could affect the making of an award and, above all, the awards must be made or withheld with absolute impartiality.*

    *In case of an obvious error in awarding a goal or an assist which has been announced, it should be corrected promptly but changes should not be made in the official scoring summary after the Referee has signed the Game Report.*

(a) A goal shall be scored when the puck shall have been put between the goal posts by the stick of a player of the attacking side, from in front, and below the cross bar, and entirely across a red line, the width of the diameter of the goal posts drawn on the ice from one goal post to the other.

(b) A goal shall be scored if the puck is put into the goal in any way by a player of the defending side. The player of the attacking side who last played the puck shall be credited with the goal but no assist shall be awarded.

(c) If an attacking player kicks the puck and it is deflected into the net by any player of the defending side except the goalkeeper, the goal shall be allowed. The player who kicked the puck shall be credited with the goal but no assist shall be awarded.

(d) If the puck shall have been deflected into the goal from the shot of an attacking player by striking any part of the person of a player of the same side, a goal shall be allowed. The player who deflected the puck shall be credited with the goal. The goal shall not be allowed if the puck has been kicked, thrown or otherwise deliberately directed into the goal by any means other than a stick.

(e) If a goal is scored as a result of a puck being deflected directly into the net from an official the goal shall not be allowed.

(f) Should a player legally propel a puck into the goal crease of the opponent club and the puck should become loose and available to another player of the attacking side, a goal scored on the play shall be legal.

(g) Any goal scored, other than as covered by the official rules, shall not be allowed.

(h) A "goal" shall be credited in the scoring records to a player who shall have propelled the puck into the opponents' goal. Each "goal" shall count one point in the player's record.

(i) When a player scores a goal an "assist" shall be credited to the player or players taking part in the play immediately preceding the goal, but not more than two assists can be given on any goal. Each "assist" so credited shall count one point in the player's record.

(j) Only one point can be credited to any one player on a goal.

## Rule 56.             Gross Misconduct

Refer to Rule 29 — Misconduct Penalty

## Rule 57. Handling Puck With Hands

(a) If a player, except the goalkeeper, closes his hand on the puck the play shall be stopped and a minor penalty shall be imposed on him. A goalkeeper who holds the puck with his hands for longer than three seconds shall be given a minor penalty.

(b) A goalkeeper must not deliberately hold the puck in any manner which in the opinion of the Referee causes a stoppage of play, nor throw the puck forward towards the opponents' goal, nor deliberately drop the puck into his pads or on to the goal net, nor deliberately pile up snow or obstacles at or near his net, that in the opinion of the Referee would tend to prevent the scoring of a goal.

(NOTE) *The object of this entire rule is to keep the puck in play continuously and any action taken by the goalkeeper which causes an unnecessary stoppage must be penalized without warning.*

(c) The penalty for infringement of this rule by the goalkeeper shall be a minor penalty.

(NOTE) *In the case of puck thrown forward by the goalkeeper being taken by an opponent, the Referee shall allow the resulting play to be completed, and if a goal is scored by the non-offending team, it shall be allowed and no penalty given; but if a goal is not scored, play shall be stopped and a minor penalty shall be imposed against the goalkeeper.*

(d) A minor penalty shall be imposed on a player except the goalkeeper who, while play is in progress, picks up the puck off the ice with his hand.

If a player, except the goalkeeper, while play is in progress, picks up the puck with his hand, from the ice in the goal crease area the play shall be stopped immediately and a penalty shot shall be awarded to the non-offending team.

(e) A player shall be permitted to stop or "bat" a puck in the air with his open hand, or push it along the ice with his hand, and the play shall not be stopped unless in the opinion of the Referee he has deliberately directed the puck to a teammate, in which case the play shall be stopped and the puck faced-off at the spot where the offense occurred.

(NOTE) *The object of this rule is to ensure continuous action and the Referee should NOT stop play unless he is satisfied that the directing of the puck to a teammate was in fact DELIBERATE.*

The puck may not be "batted" with the hand directly into the net at any time, but a goal shall be allowed when the puck has been legally "batted" or is deflected into the goal by a defending player except the goalkeeper.

## Rule 58. High Sticks

(a) The carrying of sticks above the normal height of the shoulder is prohibited, and a minor or major penalty may be imposed on a player violating this Rule, at the discretion of the Referee.

(b) A goal scored from a stick so carried shall not be allowed, except by a player of the defending team.

(c) When a player carries or holds any part of his stick above the height of his shoulder so that injury to the face or head of an opposing player results, the Referee shall have no alternative but to impose a major penalty on the offending player.

When a major penalty is imposed under this rule for a foul resulting in injury to the face or head of an opponent, an automatic fine of fifty dollars ($50.00) shall also be imposed.

(d) Batting the puck above the normal height of the shoulders with the stick is prohibited and when it occurs there shall be a whistle and ensuing face-off at the spot where the offense occured unless:

1. the puck is batted to an opponent in which case the play shall continue.
2. a player of the defending side shall bat the puck into his own goal in which case the goal shall be allowed.

(NOTE) *When player bats the puck to an opponent under sub-section 1 the Referee shall give the "washout" signal immediately. Otherwise he will stop the play.*

(e) When either team is below the numerical strength of its opponent and a player of the team of greater numerical strength causes a stoppage of play by striking the puck with his stick above the height of his shoulder, the resulting face-off shall be made at one of the end face-off spots adjacent to the goal of the team causing the stoppage.

## Rule 59. Holding an Opponent

A minor penalty shall be imposed on a player who holds an opponent with hands or stick or in any other way.

## Rule 60. Hooking

(a) A minor penalty shall be imposed on player who impedes or seeks to impede the progress of an opponent by "hooking" with his stick.

(b) A major penalty shall be imposed on any player who injures an opponent by "hooking".

When a major penalty is imposed under this rule for a foul resulting in injury to the face or head of an opponent, an automatic fine of fifty dollars ($50.00) shall also be imposed.

(NOTE) *When a player is checking another in such a way that there is only stick-to-stick contact such action is NOT either hooking or holding.*

## Rule 61. Icing the Puck

(a) For the purpose of this rule, the center line will divide the ice into halves. Should any player of a team, equal or superior in numerical strength to the opposing team, shoot, bat, or deflect the puck from his own half of the ice, beyond the goal line of the opposing team, play shall be stopped and the puck faced off at the end face-off spot of the offending team, unless on the play the puck shall have entered the net of the opposing team, in which case the goal shall be allowed.

For the purpose of this rule the point of last contact with the puck by the team in possession shall be used to determine whether icing has occurred or not.

(NOTE 1) *If during the period of a delayed whistle due to a foul by a player of the side NOT in possession, the side in possession "ices" the puck then the face-off following the stoppage of play shall take place in the Neutral zone near the Defending Blue Line of the team "icing" the puck.*

(NOTE 2) *When a team is "short-handed" as the result of a penalty and the penalty is about to expire, the decision as to whether there has been an "icing" shall be determined at the instant the penalty expires. The action of the penalized player remaining in the penalty box will not alter the ruling.*

(NOTE 3) *For the purpose of interpretation of this rule "Icing the Puck" is completed the instant the puck is touched first by a defending player (other than the goalkeeper) after it has crossed the Goal Line and if in the action of so touching the puck it is knocked or deflected into the net it is NO goal.*

(NOTE 4) *When the puck is shot and rebounds from the body or stick of an opponent in his own half of the ice so as to cross the goal line of the player shooting it shall not be considered as "icing."*

(NOTE 5) *Notwithstanding the provisions of this section concerning "batting" the puck in respect to the "icing the puck" rule, the provisions of the final paragraph of Rule 57 (e) apply and NO goal can be scored by batting the puck with the hand into the opponent's goal whether intended or not.*

(NOTE 6) *If while the Linesman has signalled a slow whistle for a clean interception under Rule 71 (c), the player intercepting shoots or bats the puck beyond the opponent's goal line in such a manner as to constitute "icing the puck," the Linesman's "slow whistle" shall be considered exhausted the instant the puck crosses the blue line and "icing" shall be called in the usual manner.*

(b)  If a player of the side shooting the puck down the ice who is on-side and eligible to play the puck does so before it is touched by an opposing player, the play shall continue and it shall not be considered a violation of this rule.

(c)  If the puck was so shot by a player of a side below the numerical strength of the opposing team, play shall continue and the face-off shall not take place.

(NOTE) *If the team returns to full strength following a shot by one of its players, play shall continue and the face-off shall not take place.*

(d)  If, however, the puck shall go beyond the goal line in the opposite half of the ice directly from either of the players while facing off, it shall not be considered a violation of the rule.

(e)  If, in the opinion of the Linesman, a player of the opposing team excepting the goalkeeper is able to play the puck before it passes his goal line, but has not done so, the face-off shall not be allowed and play shall continue. If, in the opinion of the Referee, the defending side intentionally abstains from playing the puck promptly when they are in a position to do so, he shall stop the play and order the resulting face-off on the adjacent corner face-off spot nearest the goal of the team at fault.

(NOTE) *The purpose of this section is to enforce continuous action and both Referee and Linesmen should interpret and apply the rule to produce this result.*

(f)  If the puck shall touch any part of a player of the opposing side or his skates or his stick, or if it passes through any part of the goal crease before it shall have reached his goal line, or shall have touched the goalkeeper or his skates or his stick at any time before or after crossing his goal line it shall not be considered as "icing the puck" and play shall continue.

(NOTE) *If the goaltender takes any action to dislodge the puck from back of the nets the icing shall be washed out.*

(g)  If the Linesman shall have erred in calling an "icing the puck" infraction (regardless of whether either team is short-handed) the puck shall be faced on the center ice face-off spot.

**Rule 62.**                           **Interference**

(a)  A minor penalty shall be imposed on a player who interferes with or impedes the progress of an opponent who is not in possession of the puck, or who deliberately knocks a stick out of an opponent's hand or who prevents a player who has dropped his stick or any other piece of equipment from regaining possession of it or who knocks or shoots any abandoned or broken stick or illegal puck or other debris towards an opposing puck carrier in a manner that could cause him to be distracted. (see also Rule 80 (a).)

(NOTE) *The last player to touch the puck — other than a goalkeeper — shall be considered the player in possession. In interpreting this rule the Referee should make sure which of the players is the one creating the interference — Often it is the action and movement of the attacking player which causes the interference since the defending players are entitled to "stand their ground" or "shadow" the attacking players. Players of the side in possession shall not be allowed to "run" deliberate interference for the puck carrier.*

(b)  A minor penalty shall be imposed on any player on the players' bench or on the penalty bench who by means of his stick or his body interferes with the movements of the puck or of any opponent on the ice during the progress of play.

(c)  A minor penalty shall be imposed on a player who, by means of his stick or his body, interferes with or impedes the movements of the goalkeeper by actual physical contact, while he is in his goal crease area unless the puck is already in that area.

(d)  Unless the puck is in the goal crease area, a player of the attacking side may not stand on the goal crease line or in the goal crease or hold his stick in the goal crease area, and if the puck should enter the net while such condition prevails, a goal shall not be allowed, and the puck shall be faced in the neutral zone at face-off spot nearest the attacking zone of the offending team.

A minor penalty shall be imposed on any player of the attacking team who deliberately stands in the goal crease area.

(e)  If a player of the attacking side has been physically interfered with by the action of any defending player so as to cause him to be in the goal crease, and the puck should enter the net while the player so interfered with, is still within the goal crease, the "goal" shall be allowed.

(f)  If when the goalkeeper has been removed from the ice any member of his team (including the goalkeeper) not legally on the ice, including the Manager, Coach or Trainer interferes by means of his body or stick or any other object with the movements of the puck or an opposing player, the Referee shall immediately award a goal to the non-offending team.

(g) When a player, in control of the puck in the opponent's side of the center red line, and having no other opponent to pass than the goalkeeper is interfered with by a stick or any part thereof or any other object thrown or shot by any member of the defending team including the Manager, Coach or Trainer, a penalty shot shall be awarded to the non-offending side.

(NOTE) *The attention of Referees is directed particularly to three types of offensive interference which should be penalized;*

(1) *When the defending team secures possession of the puck in its own end and the other players of that team run interference for the puck carrier by forming a protective screen against forechecker;*

(2) *When a player facing off obstructs his opposite number after the face-off when the opponent is not in possession of the puck;*

(3) *When the puck carrier makes a drop pass and follows through so as to make bodily contact with an opposing player.*

*Defensive interference consists of bodily contact with an opposing player who is not in possession of the puck.*

## Rule 63.     Interference by/with Spectators

(a) In the event of a player being held or interfered with by a spectator, the Referee or Linesman shall blow the whistle and play shall be stopped, unless the team of the player interfered with is in possession of the puck at this time when the play shall be allowed to be completed before blowing the whistle, and the puck shall be faced at the spot where last played at time of stoppage.

(b) Any player who physically interferes with the spectators shall automatically incur a Gross Misconduct penalty and the Referee shall report all such infractions to the President who shall have full power to impose such further penalty as he shall deem appropriate.

(c) In the event that objects are thrown on the ice which interfere with the progress of the game the Referee shall blow the whistle and stop the play, and the puck shall be faced-off at the spot play is stopped.

(NOTE) *The Referee shall report to the President for disciplinary action, all cases in which a player becomes involved in an altercation with a spectator.*

## Rule 64.     Kicking Player

A match penalty shall be imposed on any player who kicks or attempts to kick another player.

In addition to the match penalty, the player shall be automatically suspended from further competition until the President has ruled on the issue.

(NOTE) *Whether or not an injury occurs the Referee may, at his discretion, impose a ten minute time penalty under this rule.*

## Rule 65.     Kicking Puck

Kicking the puck shall be permitted in all zones, but a goal may not be scored by the kick of an attacking player except if an attacking player kicks the puck and it is deflected into the net by any players of the defending side except the goalkeeper.

## Rule 66.     Leaving Players' Bench or Penalty Bench

(a) No player may leave the players' bench or penalty bench at any time during an altercation, or for the purpose of starting an altercation. Substitutions made prior to the altercation shall be permitted provided the players so substituting do not enter the altercation.

(b) For violation of this rule a Double Minor penalty shall be imposed on the player of the team who was first to leave the players' bench or penalty bench during an altercation. If players of both teams leave their respective benches at the same time, the first identifiable player of each team to do so shall incur a Double Minor penalty. A Game Misconduct penalty shall also be imposed on any player who is penalized under this subsection and the Club of a player(s) incurring the Game Misconduct penalty shall incur a fine of one thousand dollars ($1000) for the first such incident, three thousand dollars ($3000) for the second such incident and five thousand dollars ($5000) for the third and each subsequent such incident.

(c) Any player (other than those dealt with under subsection (b) hereof) who leaves his players' bench during an altercation and is assessed any penalty for his actions, shall also incur an automatic Game Misconduct penalty.

(d) A player (other than those dealt with under subsection (b) hereof) who leaves his players' bench during an altercation, shall be subject to an automatic fine of one hundred dollars ($100.00) and the Referee shall report all such infractions to the President who shall have full power to impose such further penalty as he shall deem appropriate.

(NOTE 1) *This automatic fine shall be imposed in addition to the normal penalties imposed for fouls committed by the player after he has left the players' bench.*

(NOTE 2) *For the purpose of determining which player was first to leave his players' bench during altercation the Referee may consult with the Linesmen or Off-Ice Officials.*

(e) In regular League, Exhibition, and Play-off games any player who incurs a penalty under subsection (a) hereof (for leaving the players' bench or penalty bench first) shall be suspended automatically for the next three (3) regular League games of his team. For each subsequent violation by the same player the automatic suspension shall be increased by three (3) games.

Suspensions incurred during regular League play shall carry into the Play-offs.

(f) Except at the end of each period, or on expiration of penalty, no player may at any time leave the penalty bench.

(g) A penalized player who leaves the penalty bench before his penalty has expired, whether play is in progress or not, shall incur an addition minor penalty, after serving his unexpired penalty.

(h) Any penalized player leaving the penalty bench during stoppage of play and during an altercation shall incur a minor penalty plus a Game Misconduct penalty after serving his unexpired time.

(i) If a player leaves the penalty bench before his penalty is fully served, the Penalty Timekeeper shall note the time and signal the Referee who will immediately stop play.

(j) In the case of player returning to the ice before his time has expired through an error of the Penalty Timekeeper, he is not to serve an additional penalty, but must serve his unexpired time.

(k) If a player of an attacking side in possession of the puck shall be in such a position as to have no opposition between him and the opposing goalkeeper, and while in such position he shall be interfered with by a player of the opposing side who shall have illegally entered the game, the Referee shall impose a penalty shot against the side to which the offending player belongs.

(l) If the opposing goalkeeper has been removed and an attacking player in possession of the puck shall have no player of the defending team to pass and a stick or a part thereof or any other object is thrown or shot by an opposing player or the player is fouled from behind thereby being prevented from having a clear shot on an open goal, a goal shall be awarded against the offending team.

If when the opposing goalkeeper has been removed from the ice a player of the side attacking the unattended goal is interfered with by a player who shall have entered the game illegally, the Referee shall immediately award a goal to the non-offending team.

(m) If a Coach or Manager gets on the ice after the start of a period and before that period is ended the Referee shall impose a bench minor penalty against the team and report the incident to the President for disciplinary action.

(n) Any Club Executive or Manager committing the same offense, will be automatically fined two hundred dollars ($200.00).

(o) If a penalized player returns to the ice from the penalty bench before his penalty has expired by his own error or the error of the Penalty Timekeeper, any goal scored by his own team while he is illegally on the ice shall be disallowed, but all penalties imposed on either team shall be served as regular penalties.

(p) If a player shall illegally enter the game from his own players' bench or from the penalty bench, any goal scored by his own team while he is illegally on the ice shall be disallowed, but all penalties imposed against either team shall be served as regular penalties.

(q) A bench minor penalty shall be imposed on a team whose player(s) leave the players' bench for any purpose other than a change of players and when no altercation is in progress.

## Rule 67.    Physical Abuse of Officials

(a) Any player who deliberately strikes an official, deliberately applies physical force in any manner against an official, deliberately makes contact with an official, physically demeans an official or deliberately applies physical force to an official solely for the purpose of getting free of such an official during or immediately following an altercation shall receive a Game Misconduct penalty.

In addition, the following automatic game suspensions shall apply:

Category I
Any player who deliberately strikes an official or who deliberately applies physical force in any manner against an official shall be suspended for 20 games.

Category II
Any player who by his actions physically demeans an official or who deliberately applies physical force to an official solely for the purpose of getting free of such an official during an altercation with another player shall be suspended for three games.

The Referee, immediately after the game in which any such Game Misconduct penalty is imposed, shall after consultation with the linesmen decide the category of the offense. He shall make an oral report to the President and advise of the category of offense.

The player and club involved shall be notified by the League of said decision the morning following the game.

(b) Any Club Executive, Manager, Coach or Trainer who holds or strikes an official, shall be automatically suspended from the game, ordered to the dressing room, and a substantial fine shall be imposed by the President.

## Rule 68.    Obscene or Profane Language or Gestures

(a) Players shall not use obscene gestures on the ice or anywhere in the rink before, during or after the game. For a violation of this rule a game misconduct penalty shall be imposed and the Referee shall report the circumstances to the President of the League for further disciplinary action.

(b) Players shall not use profane language on the ice or anywhere in the rink before, during or after a game. For violation of this Rule, a Misconduct Penalty shall be imposed except when the violation occurs in the vicinity of the players' bench in which case a bench minor penalty shall be imposed.

(NOTE) *It is the responsibility of all game officials and all Club officials to send a confidential report to the President setting out the full details concerning the use of obscene gestures or language by any player, Coach or other official. The President shall take such further disciplinary action as he shall deem appropriate.*

(c) Club Executives, Managers, Coaches and Trainers shall not use obscene or profane language or gestures anywhere in the rink. For violation of this rule a bench minor penalty shall be imposed.

## Rule 69.    Off-Sides

(a) The position of the player's skates and not that of his stick shall be the determining factor in all instances in deciding an "off-side." A player is off-side when both skates are completely over the outer edge of the determining center line or blue line involved in the play.

(NOTE 1) *A player is "on-side" when "either" of his skates are in contact with or on his own side of the line at the instant the puck completely crosses the outer edge of that line regardless of the position of his stick.*

(NOTE 2) *It should be noted that while the position of the player's skates is what determines whether a player is "off-side" nevertheless the question of "off-side" never arises until the puck has completely crossed the outer edge of the line at which time the decision is to be made.*

(b) If in the opinion of the Linesman an intentional off-side play has been made, the puck shall be faced-off at

the end face-off spot in the defending zone of the offending team.

(NOTE 3) *This rule does not apply to a team below the numerical strength of its opponent. In such cases the puck shall be faced-off at the spot from which the pass was made.*

(NOTE 4) *An intentional off-side is one which is made for the purpose of securing a stoppage of play regardless of the reason, or where an off-side play is made under conditions where there is no possibility of completing a legal pass.*

(c) If the Linesmen shall have erred in calling an off-side pass infraction (regardless of whether either team is shorthanded) the puck shall be faced on the center ice face-off spot.

## Rule 70.                          Passes

(a) The puck may be passed by any player to a player of the same side within any one of the three zones into which the ice is divided, but may not be passed forward from a player in one zone to a player of the same side in another zone, except by a player on the defending team, who may make and take forward passes from their own defending zone to the center line without incurring an off-side penalty. This "forward pass" from the Defending Zone must be completed by the pass receiver who is preceded by the puck across the center line, otherwise play shall be stopped and the face-off shall be at the point from which the pass was made.

(NOTE 1) *The position of the puck (not the player's skates) shall be determining factor in deciding from which zone the pass was made.*

(NOTE 2) *Passes may be completed legally at the center red line in exactly the same manner as passes at the attacking blue line.*

(b) Should the puck, having been passed, contact any part of the body, stick or skates of a player of the same side who is legally on-side, the pass shall be considered to have been completed.

(c) The player last touched by the puck shall be deemed to be in possession.

Rebounds off goalkeeper's pads or other equipment shall not be considered as a change of possession or the completion of the play by the team when applying Rule 34 (b).

(d) If a player in the Neutral Zone is preceded into the Attacking Zone by the puck passed from the Neutral Zone he shall be eligible to take possession of the puck anywhere in the Attacking Zone except when the "Icing the Puck" rule applies.

(e) If a player in the same zone from which a pass is made is preceded by the puck into succeeding zones he shall be eligible to take possession of the puck in that zone except where the "Icing the Puck" rule applies.

(f) If an attacking player passes the puck backward toward his own goal from the Attacking Zone, an opponent may play the puck anywhere regardless of whether he (the opponent) was in the same zone at the time the puck was passed or not. (*No "slow whistle"*).

## Rule 71.     Preceding Puck into Attacking Zone

(a) Players of an attacking team must not precede the puck into the Attacking Zone.

(b) For violation of this rule, the play is stopped, and puck shall be faced-off in the Neutral Zone at face-off spot nearest the Attacking Zone of the offending team.

(NOTE) *A player actually controlling the puck who shall cross the line ahead of the puck, shall not be considered "off-side."*

(c) If however, notwithstanding the fact that a member of the attacking team shall have preceded the puck into the Attacking Zone, the puck be cleanly intercepted by a member of the defending team at or near the blue line, and be carried or passed by them into the Neutral Zone the "offside" shall be ignored and play permitted to continue.

(*Officials will carry out this rule by means of the "slow whistle"*).

(d) If a player legally carries or passes the puck back into his own Defending Zone while a player of the opposing team is in such Defending Zone, the "off-side" shall be ignored and play permitted to continue.

(*No "slow whistle"*).

## Rule 72.              Puck Out of Bounds
## or Unplayable

(a) When the puck goes outside the playing area at either end, or either side of the rink or strikes any obstacles above the playing surface other than the boards, glass or wire it shall be faced-off from whence it was shot or deflected, unless otherwise expressly provided in these rules.

(b) When the puck becomes lodged in the netting on the outside of either goal so as to make it unplayable, or if it is frozen between opposing players intentionally or otherwise the Referee shall stop the play and face-off the puck at either of the adjacent face-off spots unless in the opinion of the Referee the stoppage was caused by a player of the attacking team, in which case the resulting face-off shall be conducted in the Neutral Zone.

(NOTE) *This includes stoppage of play caused by player of attacking side shooting the puck on to the back of the defending team's net without any intervening action by the defending team.*

*The defending team and/or the attacking team may play the puck off the net at any time. However, should the puck remain on the net for longer than three seconds, play shall be stopped and the face-off shall take place in the end face-off zone except when the stoppage is caused by the attacking team, then the face-off shall take place on a face-off spot in the neutral zone.*

(c) A minor penalty shall be imposed on a goalkeeper who deliberately drops the puck on the goal netting to cause a stoppage of play.

(d) If the puck comes to rest on top of the boards surrounding the playing area it shall be considered to be in play and may be played legally by hand or stick.

## Rule 73.         Puck Must Be Kept in Motion

(a) The puck must at all times be kept in motion.

(b) Except to carry the puck behind its goal once, a side in possession of the puck in its own defense area shall always advance the puck towards the opposing goal,

except if it shall be prevented from so doing by players of the opposing side.

For the first infraction of this rule play shall be stopped and a face-off shall be made at either end face-off spot adjacent to the goal of the team causing the stoppage and the Referee shall warn the Captain or designated substitute of the offending team of the reason for the face-off. For a second violation by any player of the same team in the same period a minor penalty shall be imposed on the player violating the rule.

(c) A minor penalty shall be imposed on any player including the goalkeeper who holds, freezes or plays the puck with his stick, skates or body in such a manner as to deliberately cause a stoppage of play.

(NOTE) *With regard to a goalkeeper this rule applies outside of his goal crease only.*

(d) A player beyond his defense area shall not pass nor carry the puck backward into his Defense Zone for the purpose of delaying the game except when his team is below the numerical strength of the opponents on the ice.

(e) For an infringement of this rule, the face-off shall be at the nearest end face-off spot in the Defending Zone of the offending team.

## Rule 74.    Puck Out of Sight and Illegal Puck

(a) Should a scramble take place, or a player accidentally fall on the puck, and the puck be out of sight of the Referee, he shall immediately blow his whistle and stop the play. The puck shall then be "faced-off" at the point where the play was stopped, unless otherwise provided for in the rules.

(b) If, at any time while play is in progress a puck other than the one legally in play shall appear on the playing surface, the play shall not be stopped but shall continue with the legal puck until the play then in progress is completed by change of possession.

## Rule 75.    Puck Striking Official

Play shall not be stopped if the puck touches an official anywhere on the rink, regardless of whether a team is short-handed or not.

## Rule 76.    Refusing to Start Play

(a) If, when both teams are on the ice, one team for any reason shall refuse to play when ordered to do so by the Referee, he shall warn the Captain and allow the team so refusing fifteen seconds within which to begin the game or resume play. If at the end of that time the team shall still refuse to play, the Referee shall impose a two-minute penalty on a player of the offending team to be designated by the Manager or Coach of that team, through the playing Captain; and should there be a repetition of the same incident the Referee shall notify the Manager or Coach that he has been fined the sum of two hundred dollars ($200.00). Should the offending team still refuse to play, the Referee shall have no alternative but to declare that the game be forfeited to the non-offending club, and the case shall be reported to the President for further action.

(b) If a team, when ordered to do so by the Referee, through its Club Executive, Manager or Coach, fails to go on the ice, and start play within five minutes, the Club Executive, Manager or Coach shall be fined five hundred dollars ($500.00); the game shall be forfeited, and the case shall be reported to the President for further action.

(NOTE) *The President of the League shall issue instructions pertaining to records, etc., of a forfeited game.*

## Rule 77.    Slashing

(a) A minor or major penalty, at the discretion of the Referee, shall be imposed on any player who impedes or seeks to impede the progress of an opponent by "slashing" with his stick.

(b) A major penalty shall be imposed on any player who injures an opponent by slashing. When a major penalty is imposed under this rule for a foul resulting in injury to the face or head of an opponent, an automatic fine of fifty dollars ($50.00) shall also be imposed.

(NOTE) *Referees should penalize as "slashing" any player who swings his stick at any opposing player (whether in or out of range) without actually striking him or where a player on the pretext of playing the puck makes a wild swing at the puck with the object of intimidating an opponent.*

(c) Any player who swings his stick at another player in the course of any altercation shall be subject to a fine of not less than two hundred dollars ($200.00), with or without suspension, to be imposed by the President.

(NOTE) *The Referee shall impose the normal appropriate penalty provided in the other sections of this rule and shall in addition    report promptly to the President all infractions under this section.*

## Rule 78.    Spearing

(a) A major penalty shall be imposed on a player who spears or attempts to spear an opponent.

(NOTE) *"Attempt to spear" shall include all cases where a spearing gesture is made regardless whether bodily contact is made or not.*

(b) In addition to the major penalty imposed under this rule an automatic fine of fifty dollars $50.00 will also be imposed.

(NOTE 1) *"Spearing" shall mean stabbing an opponent with the point of the stick blade while the stick is being carried with one hand or both hands.*

(NOTE 2) *Spearing may also be treated as a "deliberate attempt to injure" under Rule 44.*

## Rule 79.    Start of Game and Periods

(a) The game shall be commenced at the time scheduled by a "face-off" in the center of the rink and shall be renewed promptly at the conclusion of each intermission in the same manner.

No delay shall be permitted by reason of any ceremony, exhibition, demonstration or presentation unless consented to reasonably in advance by the visiting team.

(b) Home clubs shall have the choice of goals to defend at the start of the game except where both players' benches are on the same side of the rink, in which case the

home club shall start the game defending the goal nearest to its own bench. The teams shall change ends for each succeeding regular or overtime period.

(c) During the pre-game warm-up (which shall not exceed twenty minutes in duration) and before the commencement of play in any period each team shall confine its activity to its own end of the rink so as to leave clear an area thirty feet wide across the center of the Neutral Zone.

(NOTE 1) *The Game Timekeeper shall be responsible for signalling the commencement and termination of the pre-game warm-up and any violation of this rule by the players shall be reported to the President by the Supervisor when in attendance at game.*

(NOTE 2) *Players shall not be permitted to come on the ice during a stoppage in play or at the end of the first and second periods for the purpose of warming-up. The Referee will report any violation of this rule to the President for disciplinary action.*

(d) Fifteen minutes before the time scheduled for the start of the game both teams shall vacate the ice and proceed to their dressing rooms while the ice is being flooded. Both teams shall be signalled by the Game Timekeeper to return to the ice together in time for the scheduled start of the game.

(e) When a team fails to appear on the ice promptly without proper justification a fine shall be assessed against the offending team. The amount of the fine to be decided by the President.

## Rule 80.    Throwing Stick

(a) When any player of the defending side or Manager, Coach or Trainer, deliberately throws or shoots a stick or any part thereof or any other object, at the puck in his Defending Zone, the Referee shall allow the play to be completed and if a goal is not scored a penalty shot shall be awarded to the non-offending side, which shot shall be taken by the player designated by the Referee as the player fouled.

If, however, the goal being unattended and the attacking player having no defending player to pass and having a chance to score on an "open net," a stick or part thereof or any other object, be thrown or shot by any member of the defending team, including the Manager, Coach or Trainer thereby preventing a shot on the "open net" a goal shall be awarded to the attacking side.

(NOTE 1) *If the officials are unable to determine the person against whom the offense was made the offended team through the Captain shall designate the player on the ice at the time the offense was committed who will take the shot.*

(NOTE 2) *For the purpose of this rule, an open net is defined as one from which a goalkeeper has been removed for an additional attacking player.*

(b) A major penalty shall be imposed on any player *on the ice* who throws his stick or any part thereof or any other object in the direction of the puck in any zone, except when such act has been penalized by the assessment of a penalty shot or the award of a goal.

(NOTE) *When a player discards the broken portion of a stick by tossing it to the side of the ice (and not over the boards) in such a way as will not interfere with play or opposing player, no penalty will be imposed for so doing.*

(c) A Misconduct or Game Misconduct penalty, at the discretion of the Referee, shall be imposed on a player who throws his stick or any part thereof outside the playing area. If the offense is committed in protest of an official's decision a minor penalty for unsportsmanlike conduct plus a Game Misconduct penalty shall be assessed to the offending player.

## Rule 81.    Time of Match

(a) The time allowed for a game shall be three twenty-minute periods of actual play with a rest intermission between periods.

Play shall be resumed promptly following each intermission upon the expiry of fifteen minutes from the completion of play in the preceding period. A preliminary warning shall be given by the Game Timekeeper to the officials and to both teams three minutes prior to the resumption of play in each period and the final warning shall be given in sufficient time to enable the teams to resume play promptly.

(NOTE) *For the purpose of keeping the spectators informed as to the time remaining during intermissions the Game Timekeeper will use the electric clock to record length of intermissions.*

(b) The team scoring the greatest number of goals during the three twenty-minute periods shall be the winner, and shall be credited with two points in the League standing.

(c) In the intervals between periods, the ice surface shall be flooded unless mutually agreed to the contrary.

(d) If any unusual delay occurs within five minutes of the end of the first or second periods the Referee may order the next regular intermission to be taken immediately and the balance of the period will be completed on the resumption of play with the teams defending the same goals, after which the teams will change ends and resume play of the ensuing period without delay.

(NOTE) *If a delay takes place with more than five minutes remaining in the first or second period, the Referee will order the next regular intermission to be taken immediately only when requested to do so by the Home Club.*

## Rule 82.    Tied Games

(a) If, at the end of three regular twenty-minute periods the score shall be tied, the game shall be called a "tie" and each team shall be credited with one point in the League standing.

(b) Special conditions for duration and number of periods of play-off games, shall be arranged by the Board of Governors.

## Rule 83.    Tripping

(a) A minor penalty shall be imposed on any player who shall place his stick, knee, foot, arm, hand or elbow in such a manner that it shall cause his opponent to trip or fall.

(NOTE 1) *If in the opinion of the Referee a player is unquestionably hook-checking the puck and obtains possession of it, thereby tripping puck carrier, no penalty shall be imposed.*

(NOTE 2) *Accidental trips occurring simultaneously with or after stoppage of play will not be penalized.*

(b)  When a player, in control of the puck in the opponent's side of the center red line, and having no other opponent to pass than the goalkeeper, is tripped or otherwise fouled from behind thus preventing a reasonable scoring opportunity a penalty shot shall be awarded to the non-offending side. Nevertheless the Referee shall not stop the play until the attacking side has lost possession of the puck to the defending side.

(NOTE) *The intention of this rule is to restore a reasonable scoring opportunity which has been lost by reason of a foul from behind when the foul is committed in the opponent's side of the center red line.*

*By "control of the Puck" is meant the act of propelling the puck with the stick. If while it is being propelled the puck is touched by another player or his equipment or hits the goal or goes free the player shall no longer be considered to be "in control of the puck."*

(c)  If, when the opposing goalkeeper has been removed from the ice, a player in control of the puck is tripped or otherwise fouled with no opposition between him and the opposing goal, thus preventing a reasonable scoring opportunity, the Referee shall immediately stop the play and award a goal to the attacking team.

### Rule 84.           Unnecessary Roughness

At the discretion of the Referee, a minor penalty or double minor penalty may be imposed on any player deemed guilty of unnecessary roughness.

### Rule 85.                 Time-Outs

Each team shall be permitted to take one time-out of thirty seconds duration during the course of regular time or over-time in the case of a play-off game and which must be taken during a normal stoppage of play. Any player designated by the Coach will indicate to the Referee that his team is exercising its option and the Referee will report the time-out to the Game Timekeeper who shall be responsible for signalling the termination of the time-out.

(NOTE) *All players including goalkeepers on the ice at the time of the time-out will be allowed to go to their respective benches. Only one time-out can be taken at a stoppage and no time-out will be allowed after a reasonable amount of time has elapsed during a normal stoppage of play.*

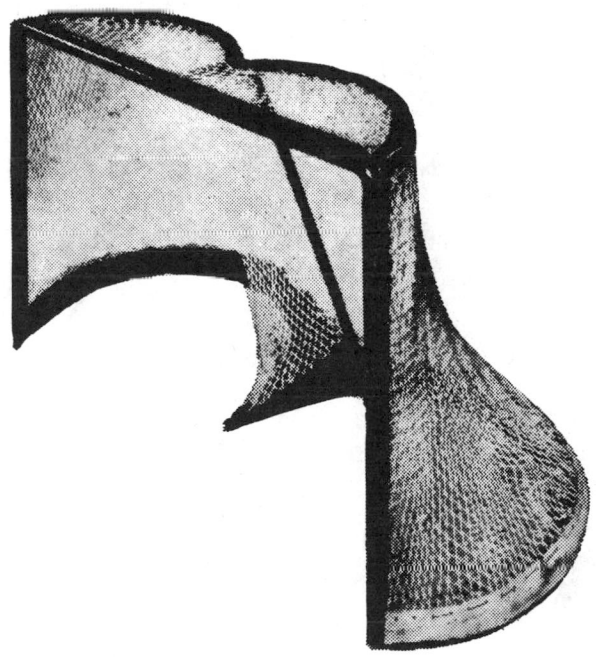

# OFFICIAL SIGNALS

**BOARDING**

Pounding the closed fist of one hand into the open palm of the other hand.

**CHARGING**

Rotating clenched fists around one another in front of chest.

**CROSS-CHECKING**

A forward and backward motion with both fists clenched extending from the chest.

**DELAYED CALLING OF PENALTY**

Referee extends arm and points to penalized player.

**ELBOWING**

Tapping the elbow of the "whistle hand" with the opposite hand.

**HIGH-STICKING**

Holding both fists, clenched, one above the other at the side of the head.

**HOLDING**

Clasping the wrists of "the whistle hand" well in front of the chest.

**HOOKING**

A tugging motion with both arms, as if pulling something toward the stomach.

**ICING**

Linesman's arms folded across the upper chest.

**INTERFERENCE**

Crossed arms stationary in front of chest with fists closed

**KNEEING**

Slapping the knee with palm of hand while keeping both skates on the ice.

**MISCONDUCT**

Place both hands on hips.

**ROUGHING**

A thrusting motion with the arm extending from the side.

**SLASHING**

A chopping motion with the edge of one hand across the opposite forearm.

**SLOW WHISTLE**

Arm in which whistle is not held extended above head. If play returns to neutral zone without stoppage of play arm is drawn down the instant the puck crosses the line.

**SPEARING**

A jabbing motion with both hands thrust out in front of the body.

**TRIPPING**

Strike the right leg with the right hand below the knee keeping both skates on the ice.

**UNSPORTSMAN-LIKE CONDUCT**

Use both hands to form a "T" in front of the chest.

**WASH-OUT**

Both arms swung laterally across the body with palms down.
When used by the Referee it means goal disallowed.

**WASH-OUT**

Both arms swung laterally at shoulder level with palms down. When used by the linesman it means no icing or no off-side.

# INDEX

This index includes all persons, associations, leagues and teams appearing in the encyclopedia with the exception of those whose names appear *only* in the NHL All-Time Player Register and the NHL Coach Directory (Chapter 16); and in any other tabular material. **Boldface numerals** and **color insert** denote references to photo captions.

Johnson, Ernie "Moose," 8, **9,** 256
Johnson, Ivan "Ching," 35, 36, **166,** 174, 256
    career of, 166-67
Johnson, Paul, **300**
Johnson, Thomas Christian, 89, 96, 256
Joliat, Aurel, 11-12, **12,** 17, 34, 35, 38, 42, 256
Juckes, Gordon, 263

**K**
Kansas City Scouts, 121, 128
Karakas, Mike, 41, 45, 47
Keats, Gordon "Duke," 256
Kehoe, Rick, 139
Kelley, Jack, 287
Kelly, Leonard Patrick "Red," 86, 92, 95, 105, 108, **168,** 175, **195,** 215, 256
    All-Star games of, 75, 76, 79, 82, 222, 224
    career of, 167-69
    as coach, 169
Kennedy, George, 9
Kennedy, Theodore, "Ted," 73, 82, 153, 208, 256
    All-Star games of, 221
Kenora Thistles, 195
    famous players with, 254-55, 257-58, 260, 261
Keon, Dave, 92, **93,** 95, 105, 285
Kerr, Dave, 45, 49, **50**
Kilcoursie, Lord, 191
Kilpatrick, General John Reed, 263
Kilrea, Hec, 30-31, 206
Kirby, Chauncey, 191
Kitchener Rangers, 173
Kroc, Ray, 293
Kurtenbach, Orland, **106**

**L**
Labine, Leo, 77
Lach, Elmer, 60, 62, 65, **69,** 79, 207, 248, 256
    All-Star games of, 67, 69, 76
Lacroix, Andre, 287, **289,** 290
Lady Byng Trophy, 18, 23, 31, 39, 41, 43-44, 47, 53, 62, 65, 67, 69, 73, 75-76, 79, 82, 84, 86, 88-89, 92, 95, 99-100, 103, 105, 109, 111-12, 114, 116, 118, 121, 124, 126, 129, 131, 133, 137, 139, 141, 275-76, **276**
Lafleur, Guy, 107, **124,** 125, 128-29, 143, **color insert**
    All-Star games of, 124, 126, 131, 133, 137
Lalonde, Edouard "Newsy," 1, 6-7, 10-12, 17, 35, **36,** 256
Langway, Rod, 144
Laperriere, Jacques, 99, **196**
    All-Star games of, 100, 103, 228-29
Lapointe, Guy, 118, 126
Laprade, Edgar, 65, 73
Larmer, Steve, 144
Larocque, Michel, 131
Larose, Claude, 158, 228
Laviolette, Jean Baptiste "Jack," 256
Laycoe, Hal, 81
Leach, Reggie, 126, 207, 232-33

Leader, G.A. "Al," 263
LeBel, Robert, 263
Leduc, Albert "Battleship," **19**
Lehman, Hughie, 11, 15, 22, 256
Lemaire, Jacques, 128
LeSeur, Percy, 256
Leswick, Tony, 80
Lewis, Herbie, 206, 247
Ley, Rick, 287
Lindsay, R.B. Theodore "Ted," **62,** 69-72, 74, 77-78, 80, 86, **101,** 157-58, **157,** 256
    All-Star games of, 73, 76, 79, 84, 220, 221, 223
    career of, 157-58
Liscombe, Carl, 58
Litzenberger, Ed, 82, 224, 226
Liut, Mike, 139, 233
Lockhart, Thomas F., 263
Loicq, Paul, 263
Los Angeles Kings, 107
Los Angeles Sharks, 287, 289
Loughlin, Clem, 43-44
Lukowich, Morris, 295
Lumley, Harry, 71, 74, 79, **80,** 82, 222-23, 256
Lyle, George, **298**

**M**
McArthur, Dalton, 94
McCartan, Jack, 299
McCarthy, Tom, 8
McClanahan, Rob, **301**
McCool, Frank, 62
McCusker, Red, 15
MacDonald, Kilby, 49
McDonald, Lanny, 131, 215
McDonald, Parker, **97**
McFadden, Jimmy, 69
McGee, Frank, 192, 256, 257
McGiffen, Minnie, 239, 240
McGimsie, William George "Billy," 257
MacGregor, Bruce, 153, 211
MacKay, Duncan "Mickey," 6, 15, **21,** 256
Mackell, Fleming, 79
McKenny, Don, 92, 99
McKenzie, Johnny, 113, 229-30, 285
McLaughlin, Major Frederic, 22, 44, 240, 263
McLean, Hugh, 75
MacLeish, Rick, 119, 121
McMahon, Mike, 207
MacMillan, Bob, 133
McNamara, George, 257
McNeill, Bill, 97, 212
McNeill, Gerry, 73, 79, 80, 90, 208, 222
McVeigh, Rabbit, 238
Mahovlich, Frank, 86, **88,** 167-69, 256
    All-Star games of, 92, 96, 118, 225, 226
Maki, Chico, 212, 229
Malone, Joe, 1, **4,** 7, 8, 12, 17, 62, 215, 256
Maloney, Dan, 122
Maniago, Cesare, 101, 103, 212
Mantha, Sylvio, 256
Maple Leafs, *see* Toronto Maple Leafs

Marotte, Gilles, 150
Marshall, Jack, 256
Martin, Pit, 150
Martin, Richard, 124, 231-32
Masterton, Bill, 109, 228
    Trophy in memory of, 277, **277 top**
Matte, Joe, 8
Maxwell, Fred G. "Steamer," 257
Meeker, Howie, 54, 67, 208
Messier, Mark, 141
Metz, Don, 55
Michigan Stags, 289
Middleton, Rick, 141
Mikita, Stan, **91,** 99, 100, 104, 110, 156-57, 213, 257
    All-Star games of, 95, 96, 103, 105, 109, 230
Miller, Joe, 206
Minnesota Fighting Saints, 287, 290, 292
Minnesota North Stars, 107
    famous players of, 189
Mohns, Doug, 222
Molson, Senator Hartland de Montarville, 263
Montreal Amateur Athletic Association, 191
Montreal Canadiens, 1, 2, 6, 7, 10, 12, 15, 18, 19, 20, 21, 22, 31, 34, 36, 38, 42, 43, 51-53, 55, 58, 61, 62, 64, 65-68, 75, 76-77, 79, 80, 81-88, 92-94, 100-1, 107, 112, 124, 126-29, 193, 195-96, 206-7, 207-8, 210-11, 211-12
    All-Star games with, 219, 222, 223, 224-25, 227
    famous players with, 158-59, 165, 172-73, 178-80, 180-81, 182-83, 185, 188, 189
Montreal Maroons, 17-18, 19, 20, 23, 31, 36, 38, 39, 40, 41, 43, 46, 197, 205-6
    famous players with, 246-61
Montreal Nationals, 1
Montreal Royals, 185
Monreal Shamrocks, 1, **192**
    famous players with, 252, 253-54, 255, 260-61
Montreal Victorias, 249, 252, 254, 260
Monteal Wanderers, 1, 2, 8
    famous players with, 247-53, 254-57
Moore, Alfie, 45
Moore, Dickie, 84, 86, 87, 183, 213, 257
    All-Star games of, 89, 224-25
Moore, Hammy, 173
Moran, Patrick Joseph "Paddy," **194,** 257
Morenz, Howie, 15, 17, 21, 22-23, 31, 32-34, 35, 39, 41, 42, 126, 156, **159,** 256, 257
    career of, 158-59
    as leading scorer, 158
Morris, Bernie, 6, 18
Morrison, Don, 74
Morrison, Doug, 192-93
Morrison, Jim, 88
Morrison, Scotty, 243
Morrow, Ken, 297
Mortson, Gus, 73, 75, 221, 222
Mosdell, Ken, 79, 80, 221

Strachan, Al, 173
Strachan, Thomas, 17
Stuart, Bruce, 261
Stuart, Hod, 261
Sullivan, Red, **73,** 105, 223, 225
Sutherland, Captain James T., 264
Sutherland, Steve, 287
Swedish Olympic team, 300
Sweetland, Sheriff, 191

**T**
Talbot, Jean Guy, 84, 95
Tarasov, Anatoli, V., 264
Tardif, Marc, 290, 293
Taylor, Billy, 55, 69
Taylor, Fred "Cyclone," 1, **2,** 6, 261
Team Canada, **303**
Thomas, Cy, 69
Thompson, Cecil "Tiny," 27, 30-31, 36, 40, **40,** 44, 46-47, 176-77, 261
Thompson, Cliff, 82
Thompson, Errol, 215
Thompson, Paul, 44, 46-47
Thomson, Percy, 8
Toronto Arenas, 7
   famous players with, 245, 257
Toronto Granites, 261
Toronto Maple Leafs, 21, 29-30, 34-35, 36, 37, 39, 41, 44-46, 47, 49-51, 53, 55, 58, 61, 62, 65-68, **68,** 69, 73, 75, 88-90, 92, 94, 95-96, 99, 131, 158, 171, 174, 206-8, 214-17, 287
   All-Star games with, 219, 220, 225-26, 227-28
   famous players with, 163-64, 167-69, 177-78, 186, 246-61
Toronto Marlies, 287
Toronto St. Patricks, 7, 21
   famous players with, 245, 257
Toronto Toros, 287, 292
Torrey, Bill, 130, 148
Tremblay, Gilles, 97, 211
Tremblay, J.C., 114, 285
Trihey, Harry, 261
Trottier, Bryan, 126, 130, 135, 137
   All-Star games of, 131, 133
Turner, Lloyd, 264
Tutt, W. Thayer, 264

**U**
Udvari, Frank, **236,** 241, 262
Ullman, Norman, 99-100, 261
   All-Star games of, 225, 227
Unger, Garry, 230
United States Amateur League, 19
United States Hockey Hall of Fame, *see* Hall of Fame
United States Hockey League, 187
United States Olympic team, **296,** 299, 300

**V**
Vachon, Rogatien, 109
Vadnais, Carol, 170
Vail, Eric, **122,** 124
Valtonen, Jorma, **301**
Vancouver Blazers, 290
Vancouver Millionaires, 6, 8, 11
   famous players with, 254, 256-57, 261
Van Hellemond, Andy, 243, **243**
Van Impe, Ed, 120
Vasko, Elmer "Moose," **90**
Vezina, Georges, 15, 18, 19, 21, 24, 187-88, **187,** 261
   career of, 187-88
   Trophy in memory of, 21, 24, 31, 34, 39, 188, **272**
Vickers, Jack, 128
Vickers, Steve, 118
Villemure, Gilles, 114
Voss, Carl, 40, 264

**W**
Waghorne, Fred, 264
Walker, John Phillip "Jack," 18, 261
Walsh, Martin "Marty," 261
Walton, Mike, 287, **291**
Ward, Jimmy, 206
Warwick, Grant, 54
Washington Capitals, 121
Washington Lions, 166
Watson, Harry, 208, 261
Watson, Jim, 120
Watson, Joe, 120
Watson, Phil, 84
Weiland, Ralph "Cooney," 30, **31,** 165, 261

Wensink, John, **130**
Western Canada Hockey League, *see* Western Hockey League
Western Canadian League, 252-53, 256
Western Hockey League, 11, 18, 19, 39, 183, 287
Westfall, Ed, **102**
Westwick, Harry, 261
Wharram, Ken, 99
   All-Star games of, 105, 227-28
Whitcroft, Fred, 261
Williams, Tiger, 148, 150
Williams, Tommy, 297
Wilson, Cully, 6-7, 10
Wilson, Doug, 141
Wilson, Gordon Allan "Phat," 261
Windsor Bulldogs, 177
Winnipeg Jets, 155, 285-87, 290, 292-93
Winnipeg Senior League, 260
Winnipeg Victorias, 246
Winter Olympics, 297, 299, 300
Wirtz, Arthur M., 264
Wirtz, William, 264
Wiseman, Eddie, 53
World Championships, 297, 300-1
World Hockey Association, 153, 155, 255, 285-95
   beginning of, 116-18
   demise, 135
   final standings; 1972-73, 287; 1973-74, 288; 1974-75, 290; 1975-76, 290; 1976-77, 293; 1977-78, 293
   leading scorers; 1972-73, 287; 1973-74, 288; 1974-75, 290; 1975-76, 292; 1976-77, 293; 1977-78, 294
Worsley, Lorne "Gump," 79, 95, 101, 103, 188-89, **189, 190, 196,** 211, 261-62
   All-Star games of, 109, 229-30
   career of, 188-89
Worters, Roy, 24, **32,** 34, 261

**Y**
Young, Howie, 96, 99

**Z**
Ziegler, John A., Jr., **vi,** 107, 131, **131**